J.GRAHAM

URBAN PLANNING AND DESIGN CRITERIA

URBAN PLANNING AND DESIGN CRITERIA

SECOND EDITION

JOSEPH DE CHIARA
LEE KOPPELMAN

VAN NOSTRAND REINHOLD COMPANY
NEW YORK   CINCINNATI   TORONTO   LONDON   MELBOURNE

Van Nostrand Reinhold Company Regional Offices:
New York Cincinnati Chicago Millbrae Dallas

Van Nostrand Reinhold Company International Offices:
London Toronto Melbourne

Library of Congress Catalog Card Number: 74-16413
ISBN: 0-442-22055-3

Manufactured in the United States of America

Published by Van Nostrand Reinhold Company
450 West 33rd Street, New York, N.Y. 10001

Published simultaneously in Canada by Van Nostrand Reinhold Ltd.

15 14 13 12 11 10 9 8 7 6 5 4 3 2 1

Library of Congress Cataloging in Publication Data

De Chiara, Joseph, 1929—
    Urban planning and design criteria.

    First published in 1969 under title: Planning design
criteria.
    1. Cities and towns—Planning—1945—Hand-
books, manuals, etc. I. Koppelman, Lee, joint author.
II. Title.
NA9031.D4 1974 711 74-16413
ISBN 0-442-22055-3

To
Edith and Connie

FOREWORD

The dynamic growth of contemporary society makes great demands on the evolving field of urban design and planning. Guides, controls and study of this development have matured in the past several decades into an essential and integral element of our methodology of resolving urban problems. However, no single source existed for basic reference material that is needed by the planner and urban designer.

This book gathers into one source vast and important factual references which are necessary to these professionals interested in physical aspects of current urbanization. The need for such a body of technical information has long been felt in this area of broad scope. The detailed information in this publication will assist us greatly to cope with the scale and rationale of the ever-expanding horizons of urban planning. It must be noted, however, that such a book is never complete and the information it contains cannot be all-inclusive or final. Its usefulness rests on its approach in giving the planner, designer and architect the basic pattern of information required to aid in solving the many varied and complex problems of our cities.

Also, the material which is comprehensive in scope, will be highly valuable to all disciplines related to urban planning. This results from the fact that the book, in addition to being a basic reference manual, also offers a wide range of data related to current practices which could be obtained only after extensive research.

This volume may be characterized as being unique literature because it presents maximum useful information with concise graphic explanation. In short, this book will be warmly welcomed by all interested professionals and students who seek to make our environment a more functional and more attractive place to live.

OLINDO GROSSI, Dean
New York Institute of Technology

PREFACE

The first edition, which was entitled *Planning Design Criteria* and published in 1969, was a unique and significant publication. It established for the first time a comprehensive source of reference material dealing with the physical aspects of urban design and city planning. It contained at a single source an extensive amount of essential planning data for practical, day-to-day use. This was accomplished by researching and consolidating a wide range of publications, reports, and other material into its present format. As much as possible, the criteria was presented in graphic form for easier reference.

Over the years, the first edition has become a useful and popular reference source by both professionals and students alike. And just as any extensively used reference source, it requires periodic review and revision to maintain its effectiveness. To meet this need, the second edition has been published. This new edition has almost doubled in size from 380 pages to 640 pages. Much of the existing material has been substantially revised and greatly expanded. Obsolete pages have been eliminated and a great deal of new material has been added. The major new areas included are urban design and environmental planning. Each of the remaining sections have been greatly expanded in size. Overall, more than 300 pages, or over 50 percent of the book, are new or revised pages.

The authors wish to emphasize to the user of this book that the material presented is primarily to give basic or general standards of a particular aspect of the urban scene. This material is not intended to give instructions, formulae, or design patterns that can be automatically followed, nor to supplement detailed engineering studies. These standards are presented to assist in establishing general concepts or directions and to furnish a basis for further analysis and development in the complex planning process.

Primarily, this material is to be used by the urban planner or related professionals to:

1. establish a broad yardstick against which to measure specific proposals;
2. establish preliminary area allocations;
3. assist in establishing programs;
4. clarify conflicting criteria relating to the various areas of activities;

5. provide sufficient basis data to establish preliminary designs and layouts.

Statements and criteria presented in this publication are applicable, generally, to typical conditions and must be modified or even changed to meet specific conditions or requirements.

The material is generally limited to planning principles and practices applicable in the United States which are in use today.

An additional aim of this book is to further the understanding and use of good physical planning principles to create more functional and attractive urban environments.

We would like to take this opportunity to express our appreciation and thanks to the many organizations, agencies, publications, and individuals who have contributed generously to make this publication possible.

January, 1975

**JOSEPH DE CHIARA
LEE KOPPELMAN**

CONTENTS

MASTER PLAN STUDIES AND SPECIAL STUDIES

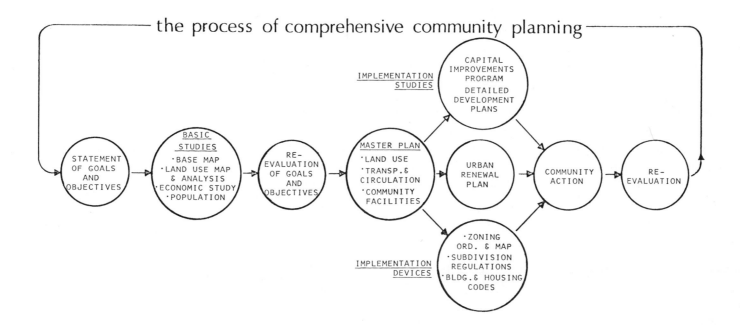

the process of comprehensive community planning

STATEMENT OF GOALS AND OBJECTIVES

BASIC STUDIES
· BASE MAP
· LAND USE MAP & ANALYSIS
· ECONOMIC STUDY
· POPULATION

RE-EVALUATION OF GOALS AND OBJECTIVES

MASTER PLAN
· LAND USE
· TRANSP.& CIRCULATION
· COMMUNITY FACILITIES

IMPLEMENTATION STUDIES

CAPITAL IMPROVEMENTS PROGRAM
DETAILED DEVELOPMENT PLANS

URBAN RENEWAL PLAN

IMPLEMENTATION DEVICES

· ZONING ORD. & MAP
· SUBDIVISION REGULATIONS
· BLDG.& HOUSING CODES

COMMUNITY ACTION

RE-EVALUATION

A planning program has four basic stages: a statement of goals and objectives, basic research, plan preparation, and plan implementation.

The first stage, a general statement of community goals and objectives, allows a planning agency to express the general values and goals of the citizens in regard to future development. Through such a statement, a consensus of future development policy can be formed. Because it indicates broad objectives and how they can be realized, it provides a focus for the formation of plans.

A plan is only as accurate as the basic information it is based on. All pertinent information must be examined and analyzed before any plans can be made. This second step in a planning program is the formation of basic studies, including mapping, and their analysis. The analysis should reveal the community's needs and problems, and examine community objectives.

Once the goals and objectives have been stated and the research accomplished, a plan can be prepared. This plan tries to indicate how private and public action can achieve certain community goals and policies in the next 10 to 20 years. A plan synthesizes the available information and organizes it in various ways to meet specific problems. A plan is not a rigid design for the future; it suggests solutions to specific current problems and to those future problems that can be foreseen. It is a program for action and a guide to future development. For it to be effective, the community must carry it out, not in 20 years, but continuously.

If a plan is viewed as a directive for action, its success depends upon the way it is implemented. One way a plan can be put into operation is by public action. If a community builds its public buildings and its civic developments in accordance with the plan, much can be done to carry out out the proposals of the plan. Private action is also important in effectuating the plan. The plan can mold private development in two ways: by regulations, such as subdivision regulations and zoning ordinances, requiring minimum standards of development; and by influence on private citizens to develop their land in accordance with broad community objectives, benefiting the developers and the whole community.

To be effective, a plan must be revised periodically. Such updating, to make it compatible with changing conditions and an ever-useful document for public and private bodies, is a primary task of the planning agency. Only planning on a day-by-day basis can give a plan any real effect.

BASIC STUDIES AND MAPPING

After planners have determined goals and objectives, they must perform basic research, mapping and analysis to evaluate the community's present environment and its potentials for growth and economic development.

The customary research is described below. In addition to the studies suggested, a certain community may need other special studies to complete the basic research program.

A. Mapping

Any planning in a community requires accurate maps tailored to planning needs.

A base map indicates such existing features as the street system, railroads, rivers, parks or other community facilities.

This map is the foundation for all subsequent maps to be utilized throughout the planning program. As a rule, built-up areas, being more complex, are mapped at larger scales than undeveloped areas.

A map of existing land uses in the community is an important outgrowth of the base map. It shows the current use of each parcel of land, usually divided into such categories as residential commercial, industrial, agricultural, public, semi-public, etc. In addition, it is usually necessary to show the present area of the use. The finished map gives an accurate picture of the existing community and how its land is being utilized.

A slope map showing the topography of the area is studied to analyze land characteristics which influence present and future development. The degree of buildable slope, the existence of sub-soil proper for building and the existence of flood plains are investigated before a land use plan is prepared.

B. Land Use Analysis

The land use map is used to analyze the existing land use pattern for deficiencies. Such a study should determine the quantities and qualities of various land uses and the condition of structures. A land use analysis points out areas of conflict and inefficient development as well as specific areas which are realizing a desirable land use pattern. The land use analysis is also a guide in preparing a land use plan and other important planning elements.

C. Population Studies

A planning program must include research on the present and future population of the community. The plan should also indicate present population trends and development — where population growth may be expected as well as its gross amount. Unless the number and characteristics of the future population are roughly known, it is difficult to determine any realistic plans or proposals

D. Economic Studies

The planning program also needs studies on the community's economic development. Economic studies indicate the way the community makes its living. They analyze industry and its role in the present economy, as well as retail-wholesale trade, agriculture, or any other major producers of economic activity. The economic study also projects the effects of economic trends on the community's future and suggests methods and techniques for achieving a more realistic and balanced economic base.

THE COMMUNITY FACILITIES PLAN

A community facilities plan describes the general location, character, extent and adequacy of all appropriate public facilities, including maps of their present and proposed location and extent.

In developing a community facilities plan, the planning agency must determine community goals and objectives based on the level of municipal services desired. Such a plan should attempt to balance community desires for needed future services. First, an inventory is made of present services and facilities. Then the present level is related to the community goals and the expected needs, to determine the future level and extent of services and facilities.

The following must be determined:

1. The community's future population and its distribution. (This is part of the population study.)

2. The level and types of services the community desires, expressed as local standards and policies for development.

Such local standards for community facilities, when used with a proposed population level and distribution, are a guide in preparing a plan for the placement of schools, the amount and placement of recreational land, the location and extent of public buildings and the need for such environmental health facilities as a sewage system, water supply and a solid waste disposal system.

It is extremely important to integrate the community facilities plan with the land use and transportation plans: the location and arrangement of community investment should implement the land use and transportation plans.

The following outline lists items usually included in a community facilities plan:

1. Open areas
   a. Parks, golf courses, fairgrounds, greenbelts and preserves.
   b. Playground and recreational facilities, including swimming pools and gymnasiums.
   c. Large-scale spectator sport locations.
   d. Rivers and other bodies of water.

2. Educational and Cultural Facilities

   a. Schools. The plan for the school plant shows the type, location and size of present schools to be retained, enlarged or modernized, and new ones to be built. This plan also indicates the area or district and estimated population of each school. Where appropriate, the school plan should show the playground and recreational facilities referred to in the plan for open areas, and other related community and cultural facilities, such as branch libraries and community centers.
   b. Colleges and Universities. These may be shown in relation to the school plan. Both public and private institutions are shown.
   c. Libraries. The plan shows the location of existing and proposed central and branch libraries, possibly in connection with the school plan.
   d. Other educational and cultural facilities. This plan for cultural centers, theaters, museums, zoos, etc., may be part of a general educational and cultural plan in connection with the school plan.

3. Medical Facilities

A plan for medical facilities shows the location, character and capacity of medical centers, hospitals, nursing homes and clinics — those to be retained, those to be altered or enlarged, and those to be built. Where appropriate, this plan may be part of other plans of public facilities, such as those for public buildings and institutions.

4. Religious and Other Institutions

The location of major institutional developments which serve the locality as a whole or which are regional institutions are shown on the land use plan, and may also be shown in the plan for public facilities. Churches, community centers and other local institutions are considered in studies of planning districts and neighborhoods.

5. Public Buildings

A plan for the location and sizes of public buildings shows present facilities to be retained and those to be built. Where a special grouping of public buildings is planned as a civic center or community subcenter, its details may be shown in the studies of planning districts, neighborhoods and community area plans. Public buildings include:
   a. Government buildings, such as the municipal offices, county buildings, post office, state and federal buildings
   b. Public safety buildings and facilities, fire and police stations and control centers, defense control centers and jails
   c. Other public buildings and facilities, such as public markets, civic auditoriums and group-care facilities for children or the aged

6. Environmental Health Facilities

A plan for the location and extent of environmental health facilities aims to deal with present or future problems affecting the physical, mental or social well-being of the community. Because health hazards rarely consider jurisdictional boundaries environmental studies must be on a regional rather than a community basis. These studies should include:
   a. Water supply, including its source, capacity, treatment, storage and distribution
   b. Water pollution control, including the sewage system and waste water treatment methods
   c. Solid waste disposal control by sanitary land fill, incineration or similar methods, and determination of the most appropriate means of collection
   d. Air pollution, including a study of its various sources and means of control
   e. Flood control, including areas subject to inundation, and appropriate development patterns

THE TRANSPORTATION PLAN

A transportation plan is a pattern or alternative patterns of the general location and extent of the community's circulation needs for specific times, as far ahead as it is reasonable to foresee. This again is based upon the goals, objectives and needs of the community. The transportation plan also analyzes the adequacy of existing transportation channels and terminals, their specific requirements and relationships. The purpose is to foresee as accurately as possible all the transportation problems the community faces and to suggest feasible solutions.

A transportation plan is carefully interrelated with the land use plan. A major determinant of how much traffic a particular street will carry is the development and arrangement of the land uses in its vicinity. Conversely, the land use arrangement in an area is determined to a great extent by the traffic patterns. Therefore, integration of the transportation plan and the land use plan is essential.

To prepare a transportation plan, one must study the present transportation pattern in relation to specific objectives for traffic circulation, after discussion and research have clarified basic goals and objectives. Essential to a transportation plan is a system for channeling future traffic: providing transportation arteries with mass transit or highways which will perform the different functions indicated by their specific needs and design.

The transportation plan should also consider any transportation needs for railroads, waterways, harbors and airports.

1. Transit System

The transit plan shows the bus and highspeed transit systems in relation to the employment, shopping, residential and recreational areas they serve; and in relation to time-distance zones of service. The plan indicates express routes and terminal exchange facilities (bus and truck depots, major transfer and connection points). The transit plan should also be related to the major thoroughfare plan and to any railroad system.

2. The Highways

a. Arterial highways are a community's major transportation highways. Their use for primarily inter-city or cross-city traffic depends upon the size of the community. Because they are to carry the most traffic without conflicting with adjacent land uses, they are usually limited-access or controlled-access highways.

b. Collector streets are highways that carry traffic from minor streets to arterial highways. They gather traffic from local streets and distribute it to other local or to major highways.

c. Minor streets are mainly to provide access to individual properties.

By designating each specific street to handle a particular type of traffic, the plan achieves the least interference with the abutting land uses and the greatest efficiency in traffic circulation.

THE LAND USE PLAN

A land use plan is a graphic and written analysis of a desirable and feasible pattern, or alternative patterns. It gives the general location, character, extent and the relationship of future land uses at specified times, as far ahead as it is reasonable to foresee. The analysis is based upon the goals and objectives of the community and upon the necessary research.

The first section contains specific goals and objectives for land use development, based upon the general goals and upon the prior analysis and research. Such goals might indicate a desire for a particular type of residential pattern and might also show the desired amount and types of commercial activity. This section might portray the amount of anticipated industrialization and where in general it could occur.

The next step is to develop local standards for the extent and location of the various types of land uses that will be needed. Local standards set a feasible level of performance and adequacy for each type of land use, both its location and its extent. These may be based on national or state models but should be tailored to the goals and needs of the local community. Such standards might specify the amount of residential land needed for each 1,000 increase in population, the location of schools or the amount and location of commercial property.

The next step is to design a land use plan or plans, showing a feasible pattern or patterns based on the goals and objectives and on the determined local standards.

Such a plan includes at least the following:

1. **Residential**
   Where the size and complexity of a locality require it, residential uses may be subdivided to show:
   a. Low density areas
   b. High density areas
2. **Commercial**
   a. Central business area
   b. Outlying or neighborhood centers
   c. Highway oriented commercial areas
3. **Industry**
   a. Light industry, including warehousing
   b. Heavy industry
4. **Open area, parks and recreation**
   Where appropriate, schools and recreation areas may be combined.
5. **Public and semi-public buildings and institutions**
   a. Educational — schools and colleges
   b. Government buildings
   c. Cultural — libraries, museums and theaters
   d. Public safety buildings — police and fire
   e. Medical — hospital and health centers
   f. Public utility plants and facilities

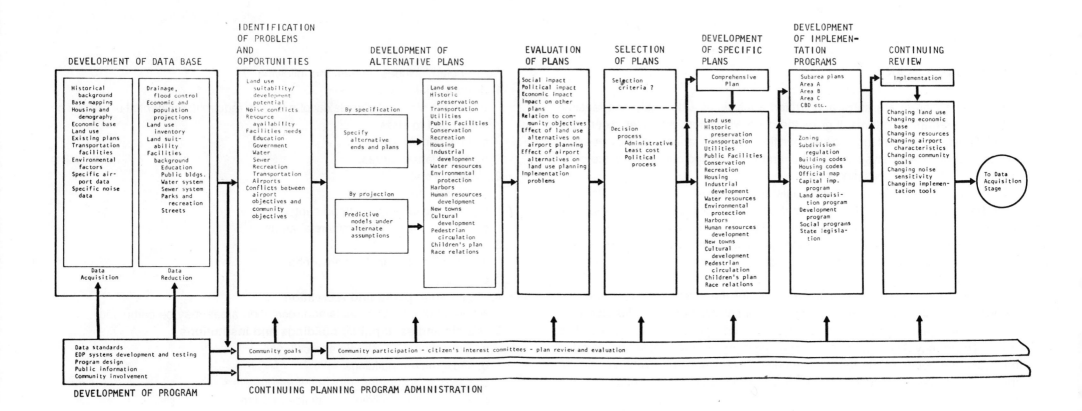

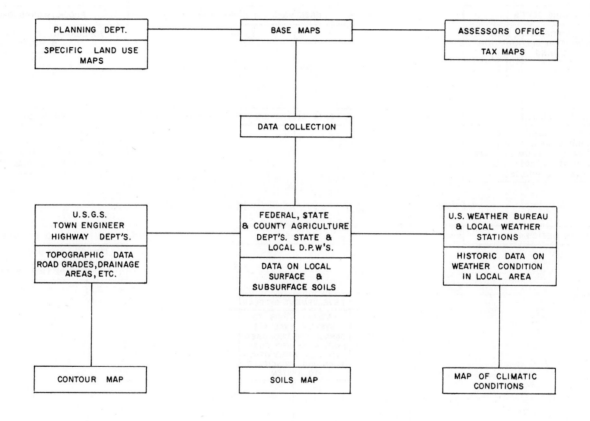

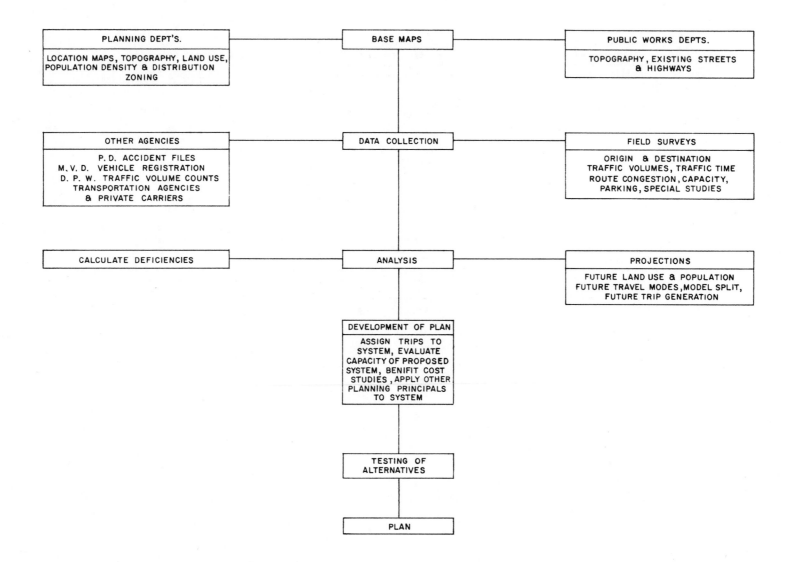

PLANNING DEPT'S.	BASE MAPS	PUBLIC WORKS DEPTS.
LOCATION MAPS, TOPOGRAPHY, LAND USE, POPULATION DENSITY & DISTRIBUTION ZONING		TOPOGRAPHY, EXISTING STREETS & HIGHWAYS

OTHER AGENCIES	DATA COLLECTION	FIELD SURVEYS
P. D. ACCIDENT FILES M. V. D. VEHICLE REGISTRATION D. P. W. TRAFFIC VOLUME COUNTS TRANSPORTATION AGENCIES & PRIVATE CARRIERS		ORIGIN & DESTINATION TRAFFIC VOLUMES, TRAFFIC TIME ROUTE CONGESTION, CAPACITY, PARKING, SPECIAL STUDIES

CALCULATE DEFICIENCIES	ANALYSIS	PROJECTIONS
		FUTURE LAND USE & POPULATION FUTURE TRAVEL MODES, MODEL SPLIT, FUTURE TRIP GENERATION

DEVELOPMENT OF PLAN

ASSIGN TRIPS TO SYSTEM, EVALUATE CAPACITY OF PROPOSED SYSTEM, BENIFIT COST STUDIES, APPLY OTHER PLANNING PRINCIPALS TO SYSTEM

TESTING OF ALTERNATIVES

PLAN

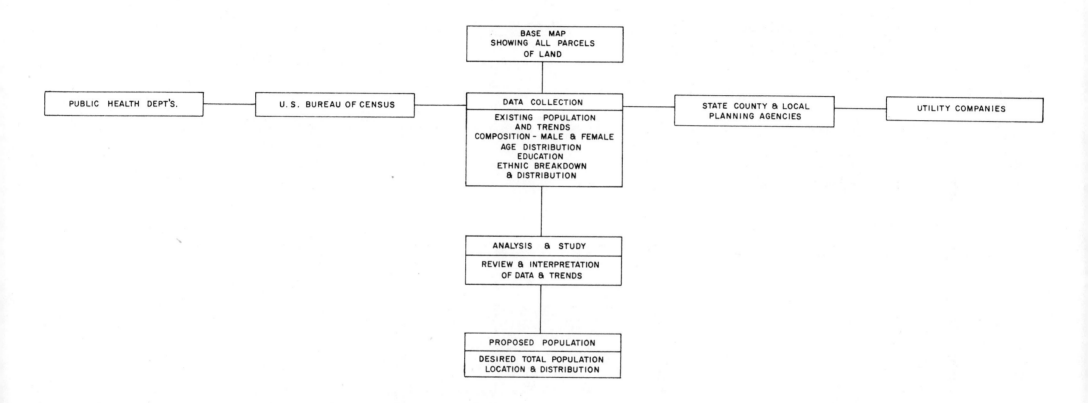

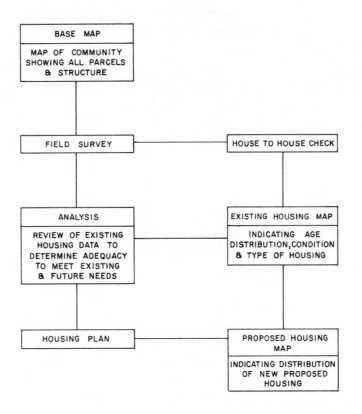

BASE MAP

MAP OF COMMUNITY
SHOWING ALL PARCELS
& STRUCTURE

FIELD SURVEY — HOUSE TO HOUSE CHECK

ANALYSIS

REVIEW OF EXISTING
HOUSING DATA TO
DETERMINE ADEQUACY
TO MEET EXISTING
& FUTURE NEEDS

EXISTING HOUSING MAP

INDICATING AGE
DISTRIBUTION, CONDITION
& TYPE OF HOUSING

HOUSING PLAN

PROPOSED HOUSING
MAP

INDICATING DISTRIBUTION
OF NEW PROPOSED
HOUSING

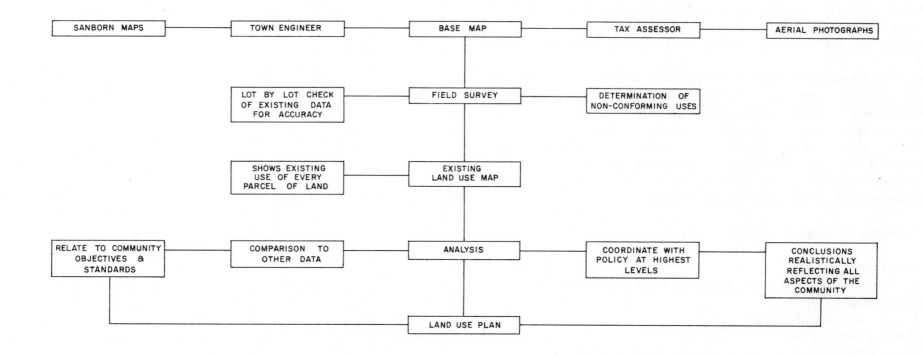

The efficient movement of both people and goods is essential to the economic health of any urban area, particularly a growing one. Comprehensive community planning gives consideration to the interaction of land development and transportation facilities and promotes the most desirable pattern and character of urban growth.

The comprehensive character of the planning process requires that the economic, population, and land use elements be included; that estimates be made of the future demand for all modes of transportation, both public and private, for both persons and goods; that terminal and transfer facilities and traffic control systems be included in the inventories and analyses; and that the entire area within which the forces of development are interrelated, and which is expected to be urbanized within the forecast period, be included. Basic elements for which inventories and analyses are required are as follows:

a. Economic factors affecting development
b. Population
c. Land use
d. Transportation facilities, including those for mass transportation
e. Travel patterns
f. Terminal and transfer facilities
g. Traffic control features
h. Zoning ordinances, subdivision regulations, building codes, etc.
i. Financial resources
j. Social and community-value factors.

The scope of the inventories and the extent to which the various analyses need be carried will, of course, vary depending upon such factors as city size, age, proximity to other centers of population, and growth potential.

A diagram of the overall transportation planning process is shown in Figure 1.

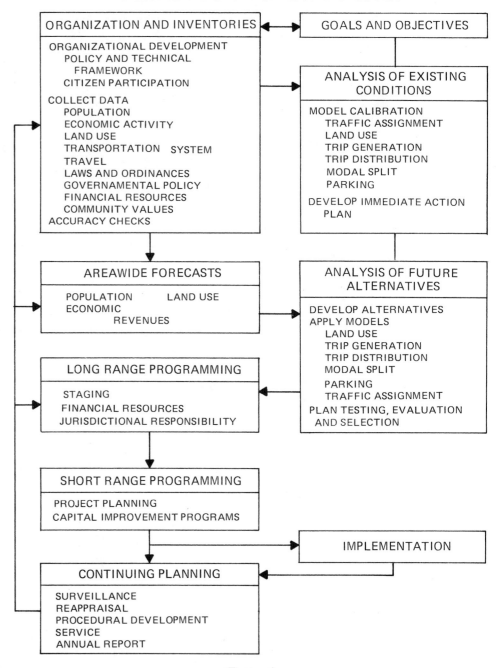

URBAN TRANSPORTATION PLANNING PROCESS

Figure 1.

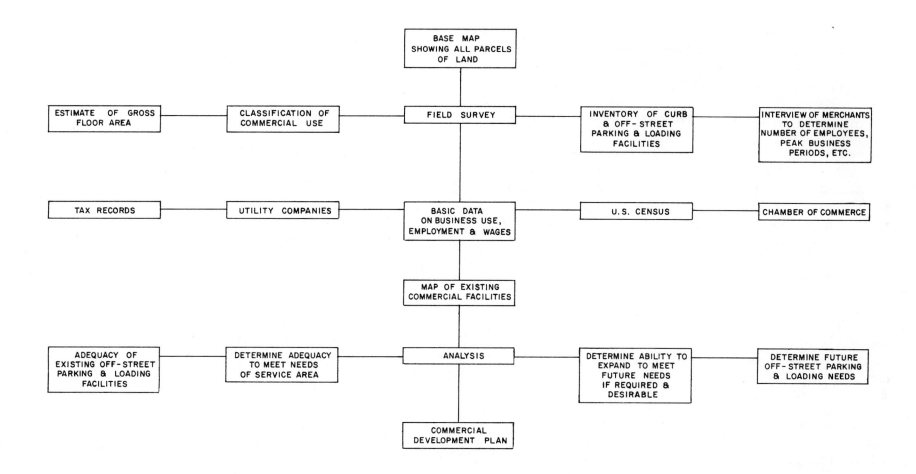

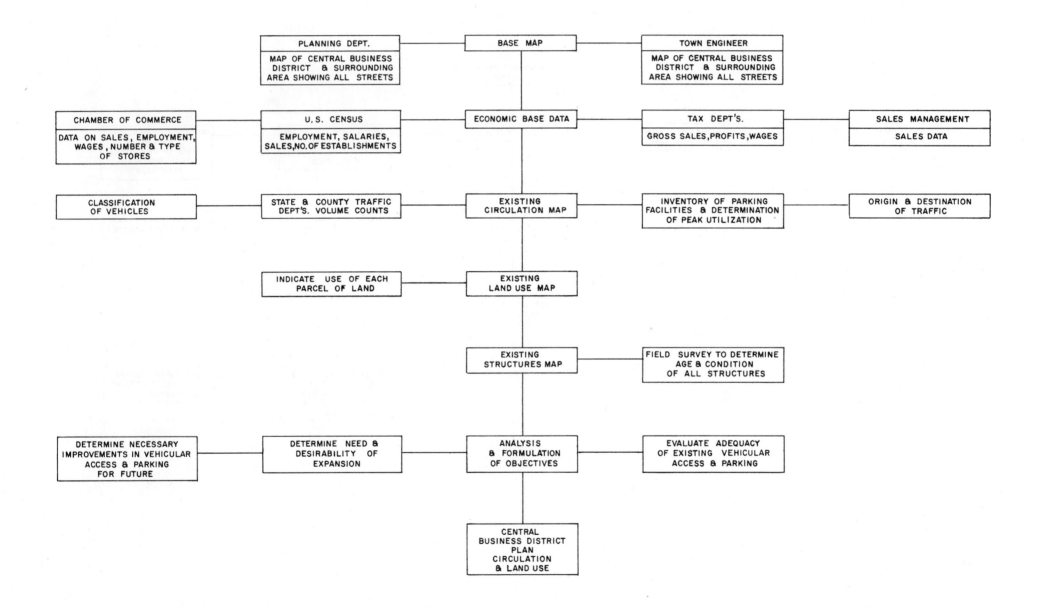

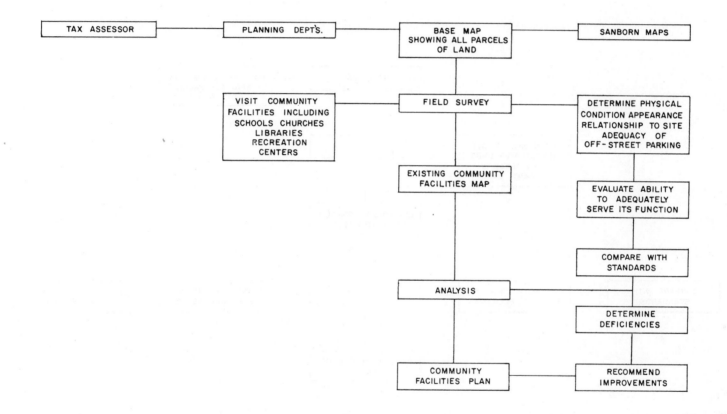

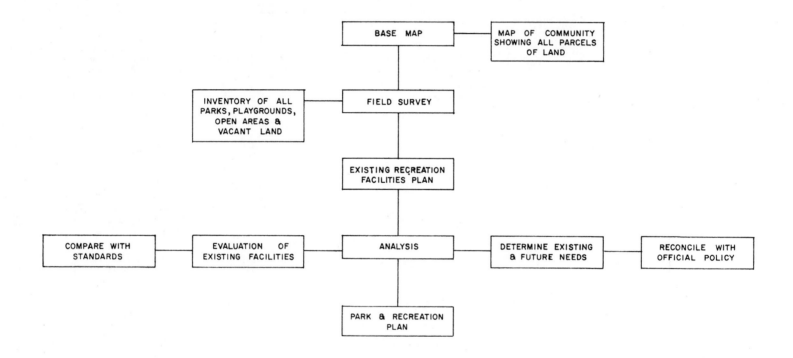

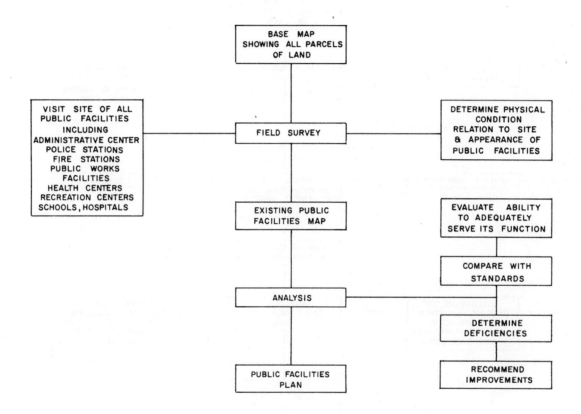

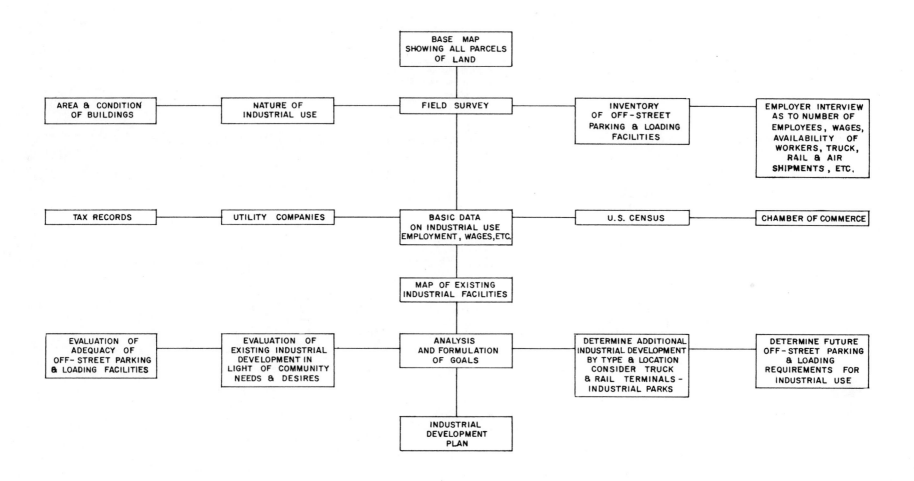

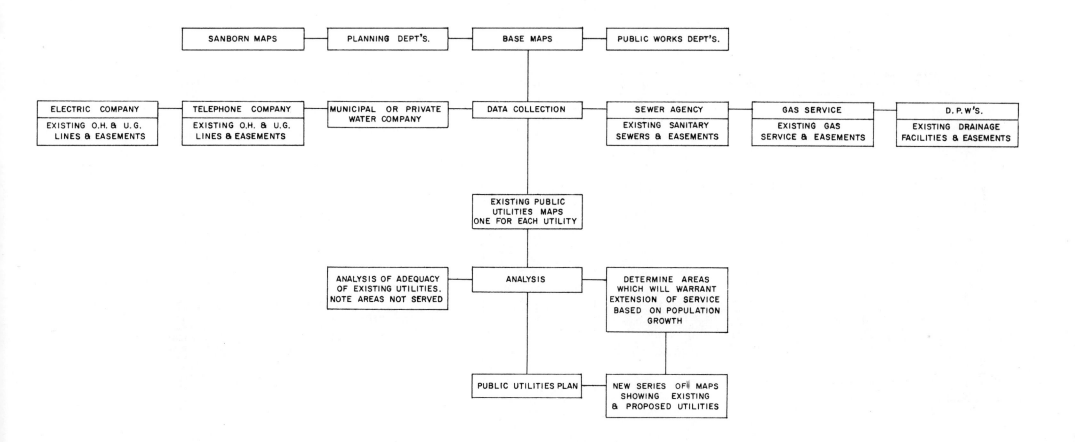

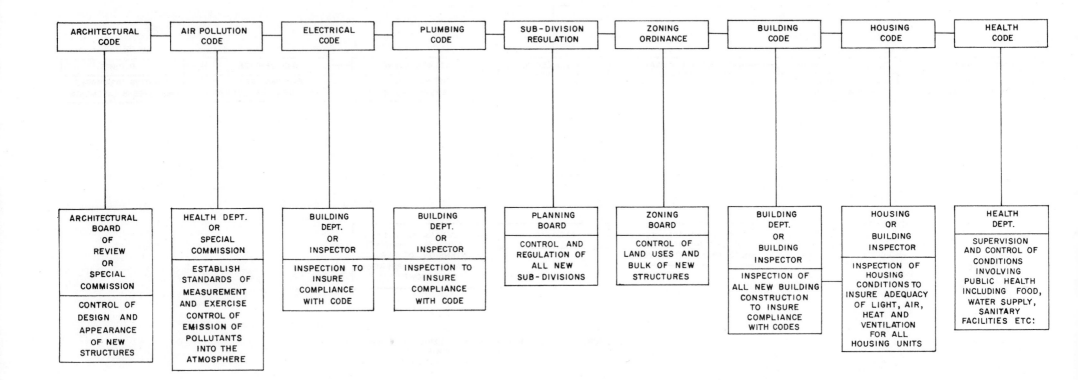

ARCHITECTURAL CODE	AIR POLLUTION CODE	ELECTRICAL CODE	PLUMBING CODE	SUB-DIVISION REGULATION	ZONING ORDINANCE	BUILDING CODE	HOUSING CODE	HEALTH CODE
ARCHITECTURAL BOARD OF REVIEW OR SPECIAL COMMISSION CONTROL OF DESIGN AND APPEARANCE OF NEW STRUCTURES	HEALTH DEPT. OR SPECIAL COMMISSION ESTABLISH STANDARDS OF MEASUREMENT AND EXERCISE CONTROL OF EMISSION OF POLLUTANTS INTO THE ATMOSPHERE	BUILDING DEPT. OR INSPECTOR INSPECTION TO INSURE COMPLIANCE WITH CODE	BUILDING DEPT. OR INSPECTOR INSPECTION TO INSURE COMPLIANCE WITH CODE	PLANNING BOARD CONTROL AND REGULATION OF ALL NEW SUB-DIVISIONS	ZONING BOARD CONTROL OF LAND USES AND BULK OF NEW STRUCTURES	BUILDING DEPT. OR BUILDING INSPECTOR INSPECTION OF ALL NEW BUILDING CONSTRUCTION TO INSURE COMPLIANCE WITH CODES	HOUSING OR BUILDING INSPECTOR INSPECTION OF HOUSING CONDITIONS TO INSURE ADEQUACY OF LIGHT, AIR, HEAT AND VENTILATION FOR ALL HOUSING UNITS	HEALTH DEPT. SUPERVISION AND CONTROL OF CONDITIONS INVOLVING PUBLIC HEALTH INCLUDING FOOD, WATER SUPPLY, SANITARY FACILITIES ETC:

MASTER PLAN PHASES AND ELEMENTS

Planning efforts required for proper development of an airport vary with the size of the area or community which the airport is to serve and with the complexity of the airport for which a master plan is to be established. The phases and elements of study and development which may be included in the master plan effort, whether in toto or in part, are identified below. The extent of their inclusion depends on the size and status of the airport for which the master plan is to be prepared. The magnitude of development of the elements will depend on the size of the community the airport is to serve and on information which may be available from earlier planning efforts, such as State, regional, or metropolitan area airport system plans.

Phase I, Airport Requirements

(1) *Inventory*. The initial step in the preparation of master plans is the collection of all types of data pertaining to the area which the airport is to serve. This includes inventory of existing airport facilities, area planning efforts which may affect the master plan, and historical information related to their development.

(2) *Forecasts of Aviation Demand*. This element of the master plan should provide short, intermediate, and long-range forecasts (approximately 5, 10, and 20 years) of air traffic including based aircraft, aircraft mix, aircraft operations, and enplaned passenger, air cargo, and airport access data. Aviation demand forecasts will be based on social, environmental, economic, and technical factors. It should be kept in mind that 20-year forecasts will be very approximate in nature.

(3) *Demand/Capacity Analysis*. Demand/capacity analysis will provide a basis for determination of facility requirements and feasibility. It should include cost benefit analysis. Demand/capacity analysis should be applied to aircraft opera-

tions versus airfield improvements; to passenger enplanements versus terminal building improvements; to airport access traffic versus access roads and rapid transit facilities; and to other improvements as may be appropriate.

(4) *Facility Requirement Determination*. This element of the airport master plan provides for the establishment of a list of requirements for items such as the length, strength, and number of runways; number of gates; areas of aprons; square footage of terminal buildings and cargo buildings; number of public and employee parking spaces; types of airport access roads and rapid transit facilities; and the overall land area required for the airport. The list of facility requirements should not delve into matters of feasibility, site selection, or design concepts. The list will be used as a basis for making these studies.

(5) *Environmental Study*. Environmental factors should be carefully considered in the development of an airport master plan, both in the site selection process and in the design of the airport. Environmental studies should be made by qualified experts. The results of the studies should be incorporated into the development of the master plan to insure that the airport will be compatible with the environment.

Phase II, Site Selection

Site selection becomes an element of the master plan effort once the need for constructing a new airport has been established. The most important aspect of site selection is the proper evaluation of possible airport locations. In this evaluation the expansion of existing airport sites should also be considered. Evaluation of airport sites should include the study of airspace requirements, environmental factors, community growth, airport access, availability of utilities, land costs, site development costs, and political considerations.

Phase III, Airport Plans

(1) *Airport Layout Plan*. After the airport site has been selected (new or existing) and facility requirements have been established, the master plan process moves on to the development of the airport layout plan. The development of the airport layout plan will establish the configuration of runways, taxiways, and aprons and will set aside areas for the establishment of terminal facilities. The location of air navigation facilities and runway approach zones are also incorporated in the airport layout plan. The airport layout plan provides for the positive dimensioning of airfield facilities.

(2) *Land Use Plan*. The configuration of airfield pavements and approach zones established in the airport layout plan provides the basis for the development of a land use plan for areas on and adjacent to the airport. The land use plan within the airport boundary should set aside areas for establishment of the terminal complex, maintenance facilities, commercial buildings, industrial sites, airport access, buffer zones, recreation sites, and other possible improvements as may be appropriate to the specific airport situation. The land use plan outside the airport boundary will include those areas affected by obstruction clearance criteria and noise exposure factors and should be limited to the suggestion of land uses in those areas. The location of navigation aids should also be shown and considered.

(3) *Terminal Area Plans*. The development of the terminal area plan and plans for components within the terminal area will evolve from the airfield configurations and land use criteria established in the airport layout and land use plans. The degree to which terminal area plans are developed should be limited to concept studies and conceptual drawings. Terminal area plans should provide an overall view of the terminal area and should then provide large scale drawings of important segments within the overall plan. Thus, large scale plans should be provided of terminal building areas, cargo building areas, hangar areas, airport motel sites, commercial and service areas, airport entrance and service roads, and other areas as may be appropriate to the particular airport development.

(4) *Airport Access Plans*. This element of the airport master plan should indicate proposed routings of airport access to central business districts or to points of connection with existing or planned arterial ground transportation systems. Various modes of surface transportation should be considered. The size of access facilities should be based on airport access traffic studies. Since access facilities beyond airport boundaries are normally outside the jurisdiction of airport sponsors, careful coordination will be required with other areawide planning bodies.

Phase IV, Financial Plan

(1) *Schedules of Proposed Development*. Airport master plans are to be developed on the basis of short, intermediate, and long-range aeronautical demand (approximately 5, 10, and 20 years). Therefore, the master plan should indicate stage development of proposed facilities.

(2) *Estimates of Development Costs*. Construction cost estimates of the developments proposed in the airport master plan should be incorporated in the master plan report. These estimates should be related to the proposed schedule of development and should be based on forecast construction costs.

(3) *Economic Feasibility*. Although the primary objective of the airport master plan is to develop a design concept for the entire airport, it is essential to test the economic feasibility of the plan from the standpoints of airport operation and individual facilities and services. Economic feasibility will depend on whether the capital investment required to implement the plan will be able to produce the revenue (which may be supplemented by local subsidies) required to cover annual costs attributable to capital investment plus the annual cost for administration, operation, and maintenance. The terms of economic feasibility should be based on short, intermediate, and long-range forecasts (approximately 5, 10, and 20 years).

(4) *Financing*. After the economic feasibility of the master plan has been established, financing must be obtained for capital improvements proposed in the plan. Financing may be raised from taxes, general obligation bonds, revenue bonds, government assistance, or a combination thereof. The establishment of financing is the final step in the master plan process. Thereafter, the final design and construction of improvements proposed in the plan can be implemented.

Element	Purpose	Type of works and measures
1. Watershed management	Conservation and improvement of the soil, sediment abatement, runoff retardation, forest and grassland maintenance and improvement, water storage, and improvement of water supply.	Soil conservation practices, forest and range management practices, headwaters control structures, debris detention dams, and farm ponds.
2. Flood management	Conservation storage, river regulation, recharging ground water, water supply, development of power, protection of life, reduction of flood damage, and protection of economic developments.	Dams, storage reservoirs, levees, flood walls, channel improvements, floodways, pumping stations, watershed treatment practices, flood-plain zoning. (See 8 below.)
3. Water supply	Provision of water for domestic, industrial, commercial, municipal, and other uses.	Dams, reservoirs, wells, conduits, pumping plants, treatment plants, distribution systems.
4. Navigation	Transportation	Dams, reservoirs, canals, locks, open channel improvements, harbor improvements.
5. Hydroelectric power	Provision of power for economic development and improved farm and living standards.	Dams, reservoirs, penstocks, power plants, transmission lines.
6. Irrigation	Agricultural production	Dams, reservoirs, wells, canals, pumps or pumping plants, weed control and desilting works, distribution systems, drainage facilities, farm land grading, farmsteads.
7. Pollution abatement	Protection of water supplies for municipal, domestic, industrial and agricultural use, and for aquatic life and recreation.	Treatment facilities, private and public. Reservoir storage for augmenting low flows and for water purification, sewage collection systems. Legal control measures.
8. Drainage	Agricultural production and protection of the public health	Ditches, tile drains, levees, pumping stations, soil treatment.
9. Recreational use of water resources	Increased well-being of the people	Reservoirs, lakes, facilities for recreational use, works for pollution control, scenic park and monument reservations, and wilderness areas.
10. Fish and wildlife	Reduction or prevention of fish or wildlife losses due to man's works, enhancement of sports opportunities, provision for expansion in commercial fishing.	Wildlife refuges, fish hatcheries, fish ladders and screens, reservoir storage regulation of stream flows, stocking of streams and reservoirs with fish, pollution control, and land management.
11. Sediment control	Reduction of silt load in streams, protection of reservoirs, improvement of water supply, fostering of fish.	Soil conservation, sound forest practices, proper highway construction, desilting works, channel and revetment works.
12. Salinity control	Abatement or prevention of salt water contamination of agricultural, industrial, and municipal water supplies.	Reservoirs for augmenting low stream flow, barriers.
13. Insect control	Public health. Protection of recreational values. Protection of forests and crops.	Proper design and operation of reservoirs and associated works, drainage and extermination measures.

SOURCE: The Report of the President's Water Resources Policy Commission—1950
A water policy for the American people

THE MAIN ELEMENTS

The main elements in a water resources plan, with their relationship to a comprehensive regional program may be summarized as shown.

In any comprehensive resources development plan these elements must be considered not only in terms of their physical, economic, and social relation one to another, but in terms of their relation to the underlying purposes to be served.

GENERAL PRINCIPLES

1. Each regional plan should be comprehensive and coordinated, covering the conservation, development, and utilization of the natural resources of the region and seeking to meet the needs of agriculture, industry, public health, welfare, and all the other fields in which needs exist that can be satisfied by proper use of the resources of the region.

2. Planning should be approached with the multiple-purpose concept and with the aim of maximum net benefits based on full consideration of alternative plans for meeting existing and anticipated needs. This means that, from the start of planning, full weight must be given to watershed management, municipal and industrial water supply, hydroelectric power, pollution abatement, fish and wildlife, and recreation, as well as to flood control, irrigation, and navigation, to the extent of their importance in the particular region. It should assure joint coordinated action of all interested Federal, State, and local agencies on an effective cooperative basis.

3. Planning should proceed from actual or potential needs to projects and programs in order that basin programs may not become ends in themselves.

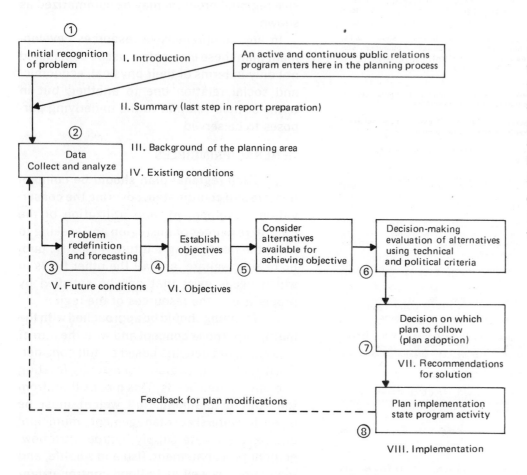

The first step (1) in the planning process is awareness that a problem exists and needs to be solved. The second step (2) is to collect and analyze data relating to the problem. Such analysis makes possible a redefinition of the problem and a forecasting of future situation (3). Problem definition for both the present and future situation helps to suggest objectives (4) that if achieved would serve to solve the problems. Two or more alternatives (5) might be available for solving the problem and achieving objectives. The feasible alternative or alternatives (6) are selected by considering technical, political, social, and other factors. Once this decision has been made a plan for solution of the problems (7) can be adopted. Actual action for carrying out the plan (8) then follows. Effectiveness of the plan is measured during its implementation. These data are fed back into the continuing planning process to guide plan modifications if needed.

Basic planning model. (From Richard O. Toftner, *Developing A State Solid Waste Management Plan,* U.S. Public Health Service Pub. No. 2031, Dept. of HEW, Washington, D.C., 1970.)

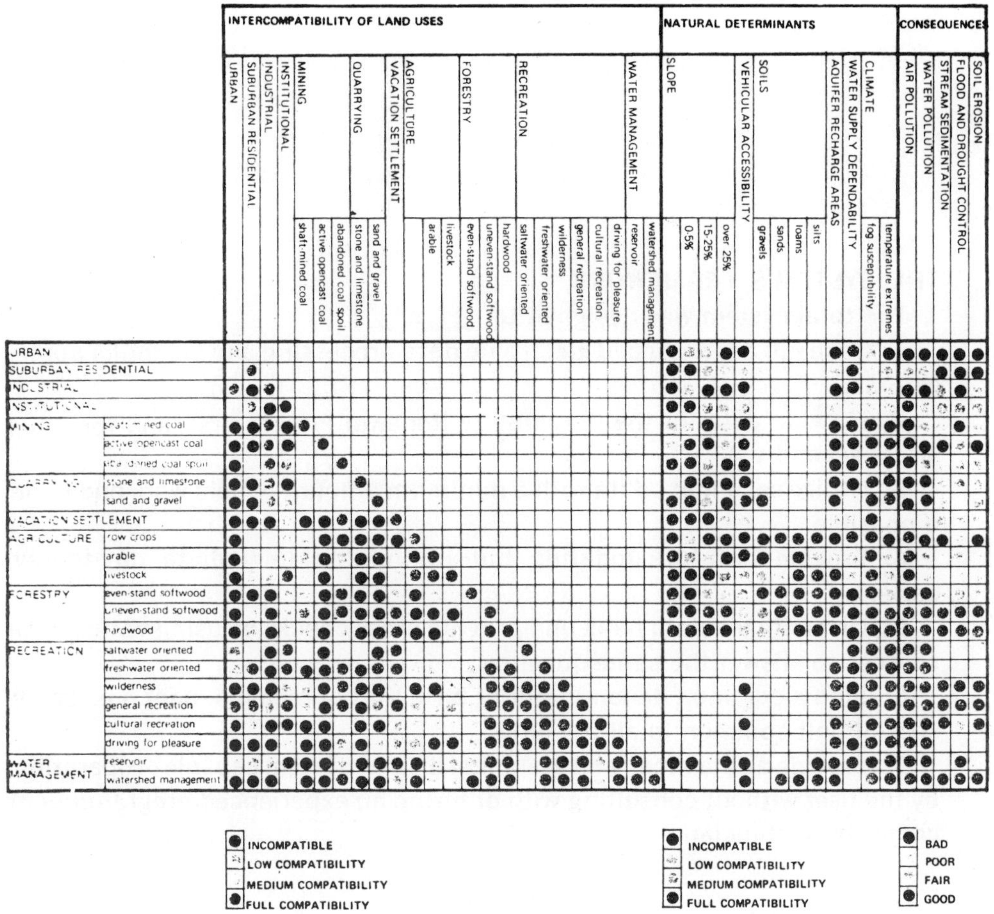

INTERCOMPATIBILITY OF LAND USES | **NATURAL DETERMINANTS** | **CONSEQUENCES**

Row labels (left axis):
- URBAN
- SUBURBAN RESIDENTIAL
- INDUSTRIAL
- INSTITUTIONAL
- MINING — shaft-mined coal
- MINING — active opencast coal
- MINING — abandoned coal spoil
- QUARRYING — stone and limestone
- QUARRYING — sand and gravel
- VACATION SETTLEMENT
- AGRICULTURE — row crops
- AGRICULTURE — arable
- AGRICULTURE — livestock
- FORESTRY — even-stand softwood
- FORESTRY — uneven-stand softwood
- FORESTRY — hardwood
- RECREATION — saltwater oriented
- RECREATION — freshwater oriented
- RECREATION — wilderness
- RECREATION — general recreation
- RECREATION — cultural recreation
- RECREATION — driving for pleasure
- WATER MANAGEMENT — reservoir
- WATER MANAGEMENT — watershed management

Natural determinants column headers:
SLOPE (0-5%, 15-25%, over 25%); SOILS (silts, loams, sands, gravels); AQUIFER RECHARGE AREAS; WATER SUPPLY DEPENDABILITY; CLIMATE (fog susceptibility, temperature extremes); AIR POLLUTION

Consequences column headers:
WATER POLLUTION; STREAM SEDIMENTATION; FLOOD AND DROUGHT CONTROL; SOIL EROSION

Legend (left):
- ● INCOMPATIBLE
- ◪ LOW COMPATIBILITY
- ▢ MEDIUM COMPATIBILITY
- ■ FULL COMPATIBILITY

Legend (center):
- ● INCOMPATIBLE
- ▢ LOW COMPATIBILITY
- ◪ MEDIUM COMPATIBILITY
- ■ FULL COMPATIBILITY

Legend (right):
- ● BAD
- ▢ POOR
- ◪ FAIR
- ■ GOOD

DEGREE OF COMPATIBILITY

Optimum Multiple Land Uses

Studies of intrinsic suitabilities for agriculture, forestry, recreation and urbanization reveal the relative values for each region and for the basin within each of the specified land uses. But we seek not to optimize for single, but for multiple compatible land uses. Towards this end a matrix was developed with all prospective land uses on each coordinate. Each land use was then tested against all others to determine compatibility, incompatibility and two intervening degrees.

From this it was possible to reexamine the single optimum and determine the degree of compatibility with other prospective land uses. Thus, for example, an area that had been shown to have a high potential for forestry would also be compatible with recreation, including wildlife management. Within it there might well be opportunities for limited agriculture — pasture in particular — while the whole area could be managed for water objectives. Yet, in another example, an area that proffered an opportunity for agriculture as dominant land use could also support recreation, some urbanization and limited exploitation of minerals.

Adjacent to the matrix on intercompatibility is another that seeks to identify the resources necessary for prospective land uses — productive soils for agriculture, coal and limestone for mining, flat land and water for urban locations, and so on. The final matrix is devoted to the consequences of the operation of these land uses. Where there is coal mining, there will be acid mine drainage; agriculture is associated with sedimentation, urbanization with sewage, industry with atmospheric pollution. The sum of these, in principle, allows one to consider the intercompatibility of land uses, the natural determinants for their occurrence and the consequences of their operation.

When the results of the matrix are applied, the maximum potential conjunction of coexisting and compatible land uses is revealed. In every case the dominant or codominants are associated with minor compatible land uses.

NOTE: The matrix is applied to the study of the Potomac River Basin.

SOURCE: Design with Nature, Ian L. McHarg,
Doubleday/Natural History Press,
Doubleday & Co. Inc. Garden City, N.Y. 1971.

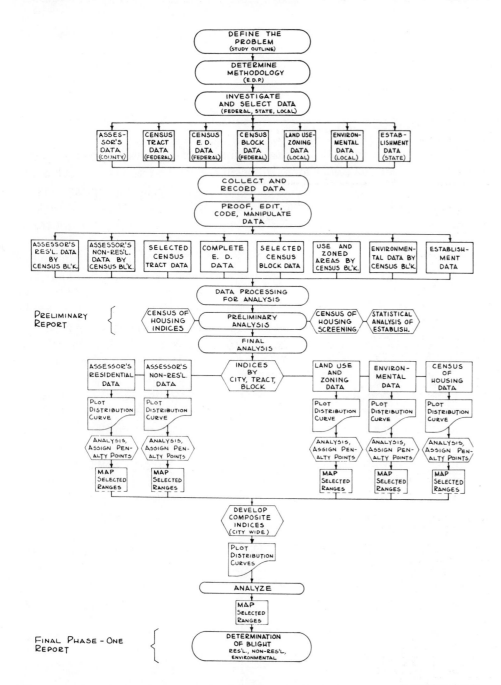

SOURCE: *Urban Renewal Service, Urban Renewal Administration Housing & Home Finance Agency, Wash., D. C.—1962. Spokane C. R. P. Data System Design Using Computer Graphics in Community Renewal*

THE SYSTEM'S FRAMEWORK

The total system was designed to:

1. Take full advantage of electronic data processing and computer applications.

2. Provide data for the Community Renewal Project first, and for other users secondly.

3. Utilize secondary data with a minimum amount of field work and none if possible.

4. Provide for future updating but not on an immediate day-to-day basis.

5. Diversify the data bank and provide cross checks by using varied data sources to answer the same question.

6. Find a common denominator or base unit of measurement, i.e., some spatial unit common to all the data.

7. Provide a data recall and graphical display system capable of operation by the user without consulting with or hiring an experienced programmer or computer technician.

URBAN DESIGN WITHIN
THE COMPREHENSIVE
PLANNING PROCESS

(a) <u>URBAN DESIGN ELEMENT</u>
<u>INTRINSIC IN THE COMPRE-</u>
<u>HENSIVE PLANNING PROCESS</u>

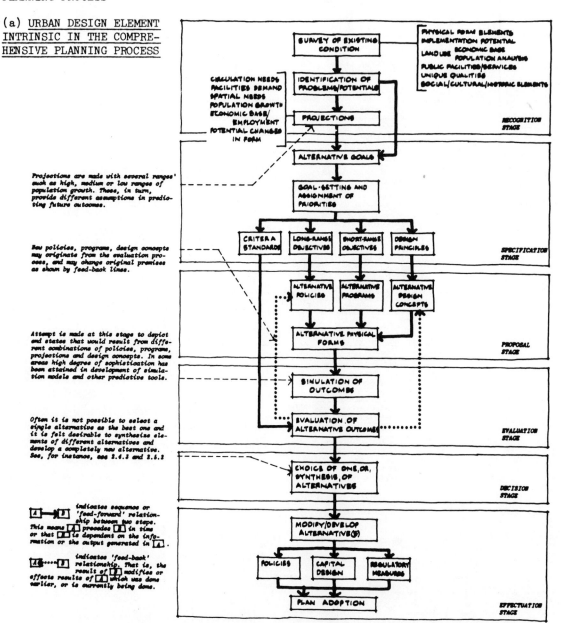

*Projections are made with several ranges
such as high, medium or low ranges of
population growth. These, in turn,
provide different assumptions in predic-
ting future outcomes.*

*New policies, programs, design concepts
may originate from the evaluation process, and may change original premises
as shown by feed-back lines.*

*Attempt is made at this stage to depict
end states that would result from different combinations of policies, programs,
projections and design concepts. In some
areas high degree of sophistication has
been attained in development of simulation models and other predictive tools.*

*Often it is not possible to select a
single alternative as the best one and
it is felt desirable to synthesize elements of different alternatives and
develop a completely new alternative.
See, for instance, see 1.4.3 and 1.5.1*

*indicates sequence or
'feed-forward' relation-
ship between two steps.
This means ▯ precedes ▯ in time
or that ▯ is dependent on the info-
mation or the output generated in ▯.*

*indicates 'feed-back'
relationship. That is, the
result of ▯ modifies or
affects results of ▯ which was done
earlier, or is currently being done.*

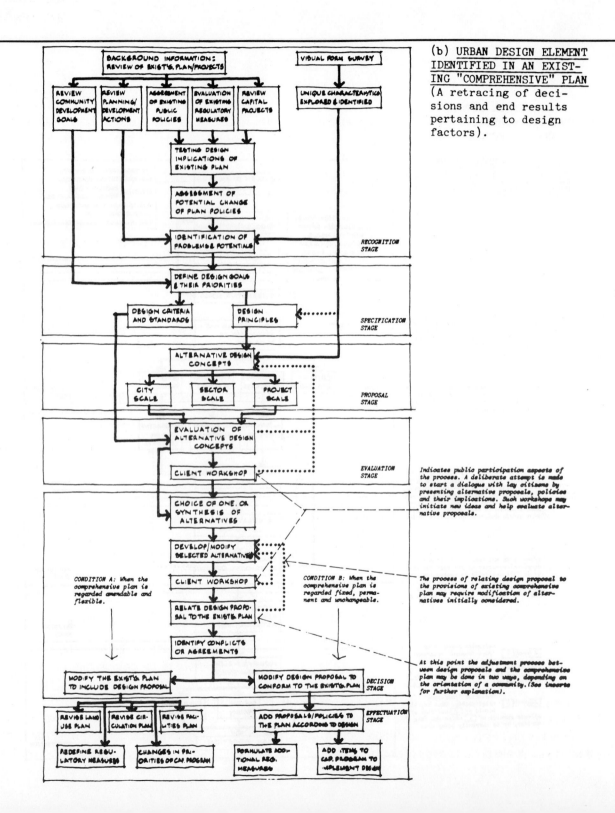

(b) URBAN DESIGN ELEMENT IDENTIFIED IN AN EXIST-ING "COMPREHENSIVE" PLAN (A retracing of decisions and end results pertaining to design factors).

Indicates public participation aspects of the process. A deliberate attempt is made to start a dialogue with lay citizens by presenting alternative proposals, policies and their implications. Such workshops may initiate new ideas and help evaluate alternative proposals.

The process of relating design proposal to the provisions of existing comprehensive plan may require modification of alternatives initially considered.

At this point the adjustment process between design proposals and the comprehensive plan may be done in two ways, depending on the orientation of a community. (See inserts for further explanation).

ARCHITECTURAL SURVEYS

A survey serves a number of purposes indispensable to preservation, publication, and research in the history of architecture, by discovering, studying, and recording historic buildings, structures, and remains. Before attempting to make detailed records in a designated area it is often necessary to take a preliminary inventory, all-inclusive in scope, to locate, identify, evaluate, and index properties architecturally and historically. Only the most basic facts about each structure are recorded during an inventory, but this information is a good basis for selecting the ones deserving more detailed study and extensive recording.

To produce more thorough records, an intensive survey can be made, choosing areas and properties for detailed attention according to criteria discussed below. Measured drawings, photographs, written histories, and technical architectural descriptions are made during an intensive survey:

Once the geographical limits of the area to be surveyed have been determined, the nature of the survey will depend upon whether it is to be broad or specialized as to types, what historic periods are to be included, how intensive the study will be and what kinds of records are to be made. The amount of money or assistance available, as well as the qualifications of the persons taking part, are important in estimating how much work can be done.

Scope of Subjects to be Recorded

This will be determined by the purpose of the survey and the interests of those who will make it. The Historic American Buildings Survey collects information on a wide range of American buildings selected both because of their intrinsic merit and their interest to architects, historians, preservationists and others, and disseminates it for their use. Its purpose is to give a complete résumé of the building art by including all use-types, construction types, and periods. HABS includes workingmen's houses, outbuildings, mills, factories, bridges, and even provisional structures, such as shacks, that so often played an important role in our early history. HABS, as a whole and for individual projects, aims for a balance of subjects as well as the inclusion of all types.

Historic Periods

Good buildings — and important ones — have been erected by every generation in history. In matters of taste there is no style either so elaborate or severe, so "academic" or "spontaneous," that may not be highly regarded by future generations. HABS makes a conscious effort to evaluate periods and styles objectively.

There is a natural interest in an area's earliest buildings and for that reason HABS emphasizes the recording of those periods. These early structures are often the rarest types and are the most likely to be in a poor state of preservation, making it all the more important to consider them for recording. The term "early," of course, is relative; it has a different connotation in Kansas or Oregon than in Massachusetts or Puerto Rico.

Buildings which occupy a significant place in the development of the architecture of a region or of the whole Nation, those which illustrate the distinctive contribution of cultural or ethnic groups, and especially those contributing to the evolution of modern architecture comprise another important category.

As a rule HABS does not record works of living architects or buildings less than 50 years old. Exceptions can be made for highly important structures (as: commercial and industrial examples subject to rapid obsolescence) endangered by radical changes or the threat of demolition, and it is always well to be alert to this possibility. The selection of a terminal date for a given project may depend on the area under consideration, for each has its own principal eras of construction and its own notions about delimiting historical periods.

CRITERIA FOR SELECTING STRUCTURES

Historic District and Area Studies

Sometimes many of the structures in a block or other area form a group which is interesting for its homogeneity, diversity, or because it represents a culture; often an area is legally designated as a historic district to promote its protection and preservation. Structures in such a district deserve to be considered for recording and, in exceptional cases, it may prove desirable to record them all. Even when only part of the structures are to be recorded, it is advantageous to consider the entire area as a unit.

In general, when the structures are more interesting as a group than individually, they should be considered for recording as an area study.

Threat of Destruction or Modification

A significant structure, imminently threatened, demands special attention. If a building is about to be demolished or its character changed by remodeling, it is important to have photographs made, if not drawings. Equal concern should be felt if restoration is contemplated. A record of the structure in its existing state is needed so that after restoration one can know exactly what has been done to it.

In general, recording a building which is carefully maintained is less urgent than recording one threatened by destruction or change.

A single sheet which presents the most basic information about a building.
For some purposes this might suffice.

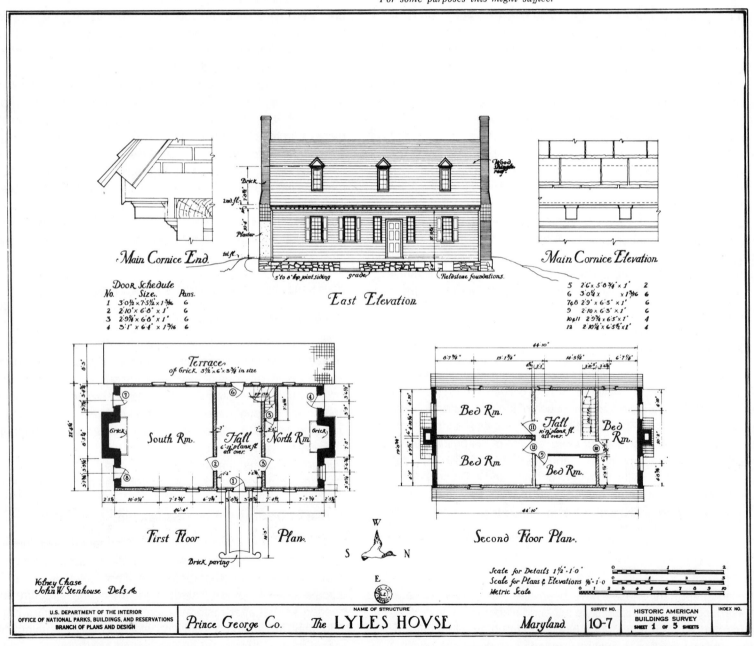

Main Cornice End.

Main Cornice Elevation.

East Elevation.

Door Schedule

No.	Size.	Pans.
1	3'-0½" x 7'-5½" x 1¾"	6
2	2'-10" x 6'-0" x 1"	6
3	2'-9¾" x 6'-6" x 1"	6
4	3'-1" x 6'-4" x 1¾"	6
5	2'-6" x 5'-6¾" x 1"	2
6	3'-0¼" x ... x 1¾"	6
7 & 8	2'-9" x 6'-5" x 1"	6
9	2'-10" x 6'-3" x 1"	6
10 & 11	2'-9¾" x 6'-5" x 1"	4
12	2'-10¼" x 6'-5½" x 1"	4

First Floor Plan.

Terrace of brick 3½" x 6" x 3⅛" in size.

South Rm.   Hall   North Rm.

Brick paving

Second Floor Plan.

Bed Rm.   Hall   Bed Rm.

Bed Rm.   Bed Rm.

Scale for Details 1½"-1'-0"
Scale for Plans & Elevations ⅛"-1'-0"
Metric Scale

Vobrey Chase
John W. Stenhouse Dels A.

U.S. DEPARTMENT OF THE INTERIOR
OFFICE OF NATIONAL PARKS, BUILDINGS, AND RESERVATIONS
BRANCH OF PLANS AND DESIGN

Prince George Co.   NAME OF STRUCTURE   *The* LYLES HOVSE   Maryland.

SURVEY NO.	HISTORIC AMERICAN	INDEX NO.
10-7	BUILDINGS SURVEY	
	SHEET 1 OF 5 SHEETS	

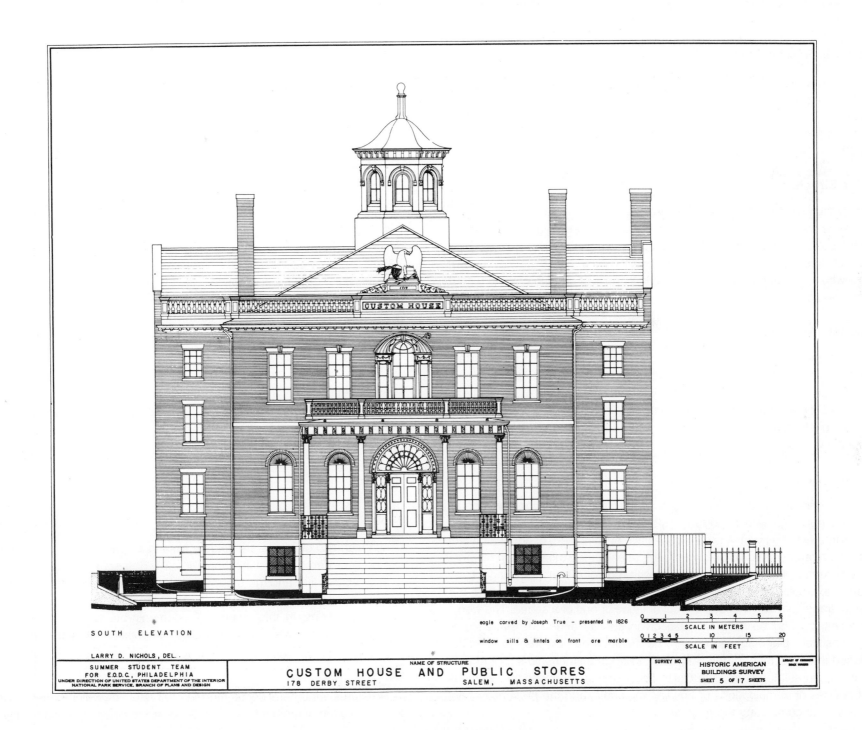

SOUTH ELEVATION

eagle carved by Joseph True – presented in 1826

window sills & lintels on front are marble

SCALE IN METERS

SCALE IN FEET

LARRY D. NICHOLS, DEL.

SUMMER STUDENT TEAM
FOR E.O.D.C., PHILADELPHIA
UNDER DIRECTION OF UNITED STATES DEPARTMENT OF THE INTERIOR
NATIONAL PARK SERVICE, BRANCH OF PLANS AND DESIGN

NAME OF STRUCTURE
CUSTOM HOUSE AND PUBLIC STORES
178 DERBY STREET   SALEM, MASSACHUSETTS

SURVEY NO.

HISTORIC AMERICAN
BUILDINGS SURVEY
SHEET 5 OF 17 SHEETS

LIBRARY OF CONGRESS

Accessibility at Special Times

Access to a building *during* demolition, remodeling, or restoration often makes it possible to find important details exposed, which would not otherwise be observable (as: framing, openings that have been filled, removed features silhouetted on walls). At times just those features which become visible during work are recorded while the opportunity is present.

State of the Structure

Buildings which have remained as they were originally are highly desirable to record because they illustrate exactly a given period. Their value is further enhanced if the setting and auxiliary buildings also remain unchanged. Sometimes a building which has had many additions, especially when their history is known, illustrates a whole sequence of periods and styles, and is of great interest to record for that very reason.

Historical Data Available

The present state of historical knowledge about a given structure is an important factor, since it is preferable to record those about which the most facts are known or are likely to be ascertained. This includes information about the chain of title to the site, names of architect and builder, original plans, specifications, contract agreements, construction vouchers, etc., as well as documentary evidence concerning additions and remodeling.

Historical and Architectural Interest

For the purposes of selection, history and architecture ought to be given equal weight. Some buildings with important historical associations have little or no architectural interest; the reverse is also true. If two buildings are of equal architectural interest, preference should be given to the one with the most known history.

HABS is becoming increasingly concerned with recording major buildings: early or pioneering examples of a building type or style, those illustrating marked, development or transition, and those at the culmination or end of a series. The works of noted architects and builders are also given special attention. Evidence of coherent, consistent planning and design, harmonious proportions, good scale, well designed interiors, refined detailing, and skilled craftsmanship serve to indicate the architectural interest of a structure. This worth is enhanced by ingenious structural devices or combinations of building materials, and the presence of accessory structures completing the ensemble.

Industrial Significance

Increasing interest in the development of technology and awareness of the importance of industry in the evolution of our national culture have served to focus attention on the physical remains of the early industrial age. The new profession of industrial archeology studies and interprets a wide range of such objects, sites, and buildings. It is important to record them as a significant part of our national development.

Civil Engineering

Some historians have long been concerned with structures whose interest is not purely architectural. At present the increasing attention being given by civil engineers to the history of their profession justifies a substantial expansion of recording activity for structures which occupy an important place in that history. Examples which illustrate the application of improved and mechanized techniques of construction, innovations in the use of materials, development of transportation, improvement of health and living standards by means of public works, daring enterprise, and the contributions of noted engineers are important to record.

Fragments

Interesting *parts,* such as frontispieces or fine paneling, that have been separated from the rest of the fabric, may be separately recorded. Similarly, when some rare, important, or beautiful detail is encountered in a building otherwise devoid of interest, the detail should be recorded even though a full record is not made of the rest.

Typicality and Cultural Interest

Although two buildings are seldom alike in all particulars there are some which can be considered especially representative of a series, kind, region, period, culture, or way of life, and therefore valuable. Simple structures such as workmen's houses or slave quarters can be as important to record as more elaborate and fashionable ones, in this respect. To demonstrate typicalness or to illustrate a culture, a structure which is as complete as possible should be selected.

Rarity

Structures which are uncommon in character, or which have uncommon features, are often of great interest and deserve the close attention of anyone making a survey. The same is true of good examples of a kind which was once numerous, but of which only a few remain.

Occasionally, unique buildings are found; they should be given a place in the records.

Assistance to Historians and Preservationists

Research and publication on the history of American architecture are matters of basic concern. The interchange between scholars and historical institutions is widely recognized as mutually beneficial. Scholars make use of material from a collection in their study and writing, bringing it to the attention of a wider public, and often contribute data of considerable value, as well. When making a survey, therefore, it is wise to consider buildings known to be of particular interest to scholars, among others.

The same case can be made for structures of particular interest to preservationists. The recognition given to a building by recording it can be instrumental in saving it from demolition.

To plan a survey in detail one must consider what records will be made of each particular structure. Ideally, each is treated in proportion to its historical importance, although this is not always feasible. Arbitrary limits must sometimes be set.

Measured drawings constitute the highest and most complete type of record; they should be made for the most important buildings, and when restoration is contemplated. They require the services of an architect or experienced draftsman. Precise scale drawings are made, showing the building exactly as it is, in any desired amount of detail. Whenever it is necessary to record floor plans, layouts, dimensions, the exact proportions of a facade or unusual structural information, they are made. Drawings should be accompanied by photographs and documentation.

Photographs are needed even more when no drawings are made; they are used in combination with written information to record all kinds of historic structures. Photographs, both exterior and interior, are the most readily obtainable visual records. They depict general aspects and sepcific details equally well, and can also show the setting. Complex forms and ornamental details can be photographed as readily as simple ones. Photographs should be taken with a view camera on large-size negatives by a professional photographer. Copies of other graphic records and documents constitute valuable additions to the record. Good photographic material is eminently usable for exhibitions and for publication.

History, whether brief or extensive, is *always* important; it forms an essential part of the survey records. The physical history of a structure, its ownership, associated people and events — all should be related accurately, on the basis of documented evidence.

A concisely written architectural description of basic forms, notable features, construction and materials should form part of every record. The more important and unusual a structure is, the more its architectural description should be developed in detail, to supplement the photographs (and measured drawings, if there are any) and to describe features not otherwise clear.

The following illustrative cases show what records HABS made in particular instances, and what factors influenced the choice of records:

HISTORIC DISTRICTS

Historic districts are formally established by a city, State, or nation as units with precise boundaries which are legally defined. Other kinds of areas sometimes have legally defined boundaries and sometimes they do not. In a historic district it is not necessary for all buildings within it to be considered historic. At present there is particular emphasis on recognition of historic districts and their protection; the National Register has shown this unit to be a great new factor in effective preservation in rural areas as well as in urban ones. Among historic districts may be found those which contain a high concentration of historic buildings, industrial complexes, forts, waterfront groupings, and canals with their attendant structures.

Surveys of a historic district (or a comparable area not so designated) may be made for a scholarly purpose (i.e., to study and publish), to fulfill legal requirements (as: to become eligible for grants-in-aid), as a guide to action (preservation or restoration), to record before destruction (as: for flood control), or to gather information needed for prudent management (as: in a park).

HABS makes three types of historic district studies. One is a descriptive analysis of the district as a coherent area, although it may deal with a larger space. Another type is the study of special features (as: the 18th-century buildings, or Shaker community structures), which may or may not be contiguous. The third type of study is the urban planning history which is discussed at length below.

Urban Planning History

A historic district or a whole city may be the subject of analysis and descriptive interpretation; in doing this, data relevant to the origins, historical states, and the existing state are gathered, studied, compared and recorded so as to illustrate the form and character of the district during historical periods, and the changes which occurred over those periods. Major attention is given to recording physical aspects and the events connected with them, but economic and social phenomena are considered essential to an understanding of the physical elements. Studies of this kind are undertaken by persons having broad knowledge of and experience in urban history and culture, often drawing upon the resources of a variety of specialists for matters of detail.

As for area studies in general, projects for urban study are selected with due regard for distinctiveness of character, historical significance, and availability of documentation. Threats of destruction or of sweeping changes increase the urgency of attention. In the larger view, one looks for areas which are representative of their kind and also for those which are unique.

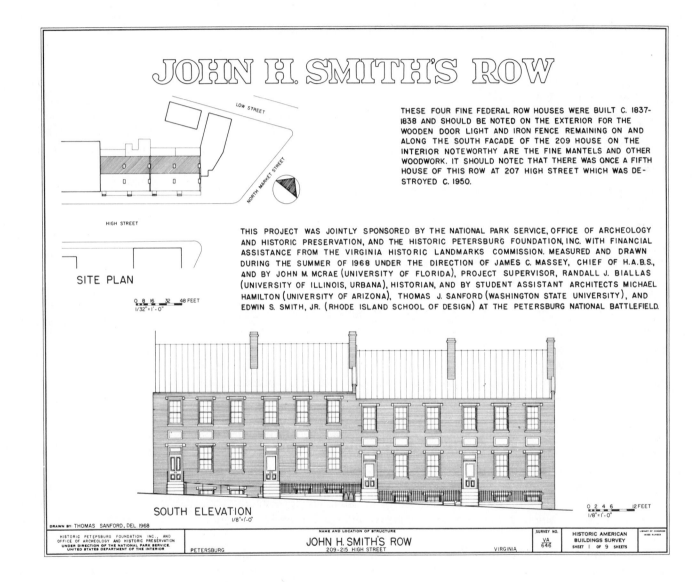

JOHN H. SMITH'S ROW

SITE PLAN

THESE FOUR FINE FEDERAL ROW HOUSES WERE BUILT C. 1837-1838 AND SHOULD BE NOTED ON THE EXTERIOR FOR THE WOODEN DOOR LIGHT AND IRON FENCE REMAINING ON AND ALONG THE SOUTH FACADE OF THE 209 HOUSE ON THE INTERIOR NOTEWORTHY ARE THE FINE MANTELS AND OTHER WOODWORK. IT SHOULD NOTED THAT THERE WAS ONCE A FIFTH HOUSE OF THIS ROW AT 207 HIGH STREET WHICH WAS DESTROYED C. 1950.

THIS PROJECT WAS JOINTLY SPONSORED BY THE NATIONAL PARK SERVICE, OFFICE OF ARCHEOLOGY AND HISTORIC PRESERVATION, AND THE HISTORIC PETERSBURG FOUNDATION, INC. WITH FINANCIAL ASSISTANCE FROM THE VIRGINIA HISTORIC LANDMARKS COMMISSION. MEASURED AND DRAWN DURING THE SUMMER OF 1968 UNDER THE DIRECTION OF JAMES C. MASSEY, CHIEF OF H.A.B.S., AND BY JOHN M. MCRAE (UNIVERSITY OF FLORIDA), PROJECT SUPERVISOR, RANDALL J. BIALLAS (UNIVERSITY OF ILLINOIS, URBANA), HISTORIAN, AND BY STUDENT ASSISTANT ARCHITECTS MICHAEL HAMILTON (UNIVERSITY OF ARIZONA), THOMAS J. SANFORD (WASHINGTON STATE UNIVERSITY), AND EDWIN S. SMITH, JR. (RHODE ISLAND SCHOOL OF DESIGN) AT THE PETERSBURG NATIONAL BATTLEFIELD.

SOUTH ELEVATION
1/8"=1'-0"

DRAWN BY: THOMAS SANFORD, DEL. 1968

HISTORIC PETERSBURG FOUNDATION INC., AND OFFICE OF ARCHEOLOGY AND HISTORIC PRESERVATION UNDER DIRECTION OF THE NATIONAL PARK SERVICE. UNITED STATES DEPARTMENT OF THE INTERIOR

NAME AND LOCATION OF STRUCTURE
JOHN H. SMITH'S ROW
PETERSBURG   209-215 HIGH STREET   VIRGINIA

SURVEY NO.
VA 646

HISTORIC AMERICAN BUILDINGS SURVEY
SHEET 1 OF 9 SHEETS

ELEMENTS OF URBAN DESIGN

PROGRESS DIAGRAMS-
GENERIC DESIGN AND
URBAN DESIGN

a. *Generic Design* (Where an end product may be clearly defined; where the feedback accrues within the realm of the designer himself; where the complications of the public decision-making process are not overtly made part, etc.).

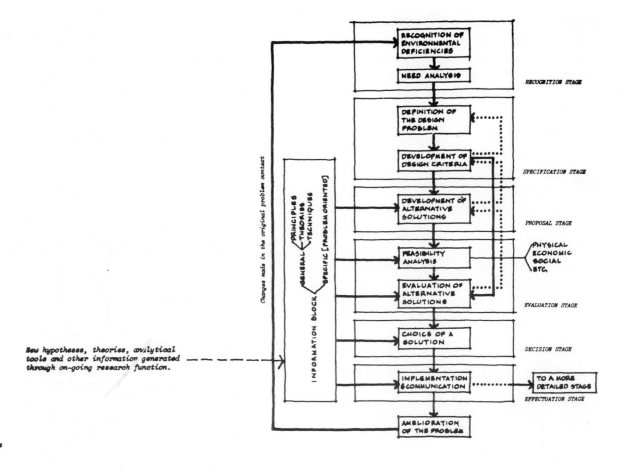

THEORETICAL PROCEDURAL STEPS IN PROCESS SEQUENCE

Recognition Stage: The need for planning and design activity is recognized at this stage. The specific problem areas and their contextual elements are identified and assumptions about the future state of available resources etc. are made.

Specification Stage: Alternative ends are identified and specific ends chosen. These are then specified in terms of goals, objectives, performance criteria and standards.

Proposal Stage: Means for attaining the specified ends are identified. These are often expressed in terms of policies, programs, design concepts, physical plans etc. depending on the scope of a particular problem.

Evaluation Stage: Relative merits of alternative means are evaluated against the criteria specified earlier.

Decision Stage: Choice for a particular alternative is made, or synthesis of different alternatives is made, depending on particular circumstances.

Effectuation Stage: Once a decision on a particular solution is made, it is developed and refined and means for effectuation and staging are formulated. These are expressed in terms of broad strategies and policies, regulatory measures, capital programs and other implementation means.

SOURCE: Urban Design within the Comprehensive Planning Process, M.R. Wolfe and R.D. Shinn, U. of Washington, Seattle, Wash., 1970.

b. *Urban Design* (Where the end product is shaped by clientele response; where varieties of scale are involved, where implementation is shaped by public policies, etc.).

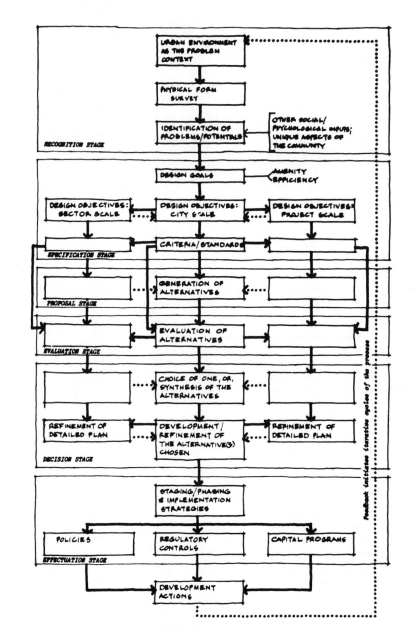

Open space elements by themselves have distinct functions to perform, but it is in a system of open spaces that the structural framework for urban development can be established. A system of open space is created by the fitting together of open spaces in a continuous connected series of open space elements, or in a series of elements disposed in a functional pattern. The characteristic of a system is that each element has a positive relation to the others, and the whole has a form in which each element has a meaningful and functional place.

Single Use Systems

A single use system is based on one type of physical or natural feature, such as stream valley, or on one type of open space development, such as parks.[1] A corridor system made up of streets and highways is a typical urban open space system. A similar system may be developed in a pattern of streets and squares or plazas, where the square serves essentially as the landing, collecting or exchange element in the circulation system.

1. A stream valley system is exampled by that developed at Toronto, Canada, basically a corridor system with some lakefront areas. There a basic single use system is proposed to be expanded into a multi-use system to include water supply, conservation and flood control.

2. Metropolitan Washington is also a basic corridor system using stream valleys and parkway corridors. This is in turn related to the system of urban open spaces in the malls and entourage of large institutional uses.

3. The "Emerald Necklace" greenbelt of Cleveland, Ohio, consists of a continuous park road string joining "beads" of regional reservations, some left in a natural state and some developed for organized recreational uses. The greenbelt system can be found in the Greenbelt communities—Greenbelt, Maryland, Greendale, Wisconsin, and in the regional and new town planning in England.

4. A classic example of a green open space system is Olmstead's system in Boston, Mass., linking park, pond, passageway, and preserve in a varied and vital system.

Multi-Use Systems

Most open systems will be multi-use systems in which utility, green and corridor spaces are combined in a continuous network of open space—building entourage, to streets, to plazas, to parks, to recreational areas, to reservoirs, to flood basins, watersheds, waterways, etc.

In a multi-use system, many of the open elements will in themselves be multi-use open spaces. In large regional systems, this will be characteristic. In new town planning an open space system can be developed as the condition and control of development. In large regional areas, the establishment of an open space system can provide control for urbanization.

1. The Greater Boston open space system is a combination of valleys, park roads and parks and a proposed "green zone." Included are reservoirs and parkways as well as development of river and stream corridors and specific park uses.

2. Regional open space systems can be found in river valley systems, at present too often marked out in separate purpose planning and development. State systems as well need to be developed, combining single program planning such as

recreation, water supply, highways, and river development. These need to be integrated into a complete open space multi-use system.

Functional Characteristics of Systems

The open space system as a structural framework for comprehensive planning and development has a number of design characteristics which identify, establish and organize the system.

A. *Edge:* The edge is the area or line that gives definition to an open space. It is the area where "systems of energy" come together as where water and land meet, or where open space and building development join. The essential function of the edge is to give definition, to establish boundary and form and to join uses. The edge may be the most sensitive part of open space and requires careful treatment. The edge as border is both separator and unifier of open space and development lands. Open space systems may in themselves serve the function of edges in large scale comprehensive planning, for separating various kinds of development, for defining large elements of urban development and giving them form.

B. *Linkage:* The linkage is the open space area that connects the elements of an open space system to provide continuity. A characteristic linkage is that of the corridor space such as a street or highway which connects and gives access to green and utility open spaces. The linkage may be a plaza or other focal point or area which fixes, locates or joins the elements of the open space system. At the regional scale or in the large urban area, waterways and major routes may become the chief kinds of open space linkages.

C. *Penetrants:* The penetrant is the open space area that serves as a break into development such as green wedges and open space areas extending from a linear system. The penetrant serves as a true "breathing space" in urban development, and also helps provide a balancing element of natural landscape with manmade environment. The penetrant can also introduce variety and contrast in development of higher densities.

D. *Focus:* In an open space system, a focus is a place or landmark to give orientation and to organize the sense of direction and distance. In the urban context, this may be a plaza, a square, a monument, the widened area in front of an important building. In the open country, the focus may be a landmark, a special geological feature, a land formation, or even some manmade object. In the forest it may be a clearing, in the desert an oasis.

E. *Continuity:* The fundamental character of a system is that of continuity, with connection and flow elements in series. Natural features such as a river may perform this function. A series of parkways or of connected plazas may provide continuity. One kind of element may merge or connect with another to form a continuous series of open space elements as in the case of the Olmstead open space plan for Boston.

An open space system itself may serve the function of continuity in the urban area, providing the skeletal form, hinging together what otherwise may be disconnected and unrelated development areas. In this sense, the continuity of an open space system can provide a sense of identity and the identification of the urban form.

SOURCE: Where to Build, Technical Bulletin #1, Bureau of Land Management Dept. of the Interior, Washington, D.C. 1968.

[1]This is one of the classifications suggested in Tunnard's and Pushkarev's *Man-Made America: Chaos or Control,* Yale University Press, 1963. Part V, Section III, "The Framework of Open Space Design."

All lands having open space values may be classified according to the nature of the land and the type of open space use: utility spaces, green spaces, corridor spaces. The base of classification for planning is the functional land use of open space, a distinct use in itself and coordinate with other land uses of development.

CLASSIFICATION CODE AND CRITERIA

In any classification system for land uses, a code of classification can be established for open space uses to identify, particularize and assign the open space uses and functions of the land. The classification system given here is based primarily on the functional use of land for open space purposes. It can be applied to categorize the present uses of land for open space purposes, or to assign land for open space purposes in planning an open space system within a comprehensive plan.

The Classification Code

Open space is classified here in three major types: I. Utility Open Spaces; II. Green Open Spaces; and III. Corridor Open Spaces.

Each of these major types is particularized further in a number of subdivisions according to functional uses, which in turn contain a number of specific use types and examples.

Thus the general group of I. Utility Open Spaces, is subdivided into:

A. Resource Lands
B. Urban Utility Spaces
C. Flood Control and Drainage
D. Reserves and Preserves

The subdivision of Resource Lands in turn lists:

1. Forest and Grazing Lands
2. Mining Lands
3. Agricultural Lands
4. Lakes and Rivers for Water Storage and Supply

The classification listing here is comprehensive in character, rather than exhaustive in detail. Within the major groups, subdivisions and sub-items, there can be coded generally all open space uses of land and where necessary still further special examples can be located or placed under the code.

Much land designated for open space purposes will be subject to more than a single use and therefore may be designated IV. Multi-Use Classification, as a major code use area. The subdivisions and sub-items under multi-use classification will be identified according to the designations listed under the other major groups.

Under the multi-use classification may be listed also open spaces used directly in connection with other development but which may be significant in the planning of a comprehensive open space system. For example, a college or university campus, while planned primarily as a building development facility, may contain open space elements or characteristics —athletic fields, etc. so that the campus as a whole can become part of the over-all open space system.

Criteria for Classification

The classifications made here reflect as far as possible the classifications and definitions developed by other agencies such as the Bureau of Outdoor Recreation and State programs involving open space planning and programs. The general criteria to be applied in making classification of land for open space designation include both measurable data and value judgements.

1. *Primary functional use.* Open space should be classified primarily according to its functional use for open space purposes, including both its function as a distinct land use in itself and its relation to other uses.

2. *Relation to development values.* Whether open space values are greater than potential development values and should accordingly be protected against such development, and the degree of protection to be afforded, will be value judgements in classification.

3. *Size of land.* The classification of open spaces can apply to all sizes of open space lands: site, city areas, urban metropolitan areas, regions.

4. *Urban-rural considerations.* Classification can apply to both rural and urban areas, in urban-impacted areas, the urbanized region and the "remote" region.

5. *Intensity of use.* Classification may take into account intensity, frequency or period of use, and these characteristics may be used in making detailed classification within the general code.

6. *Land characteristics.* Classification may take into account such land characteristics as vegetation, soil conditions, geological formation, and previous use treatments.

7. *Other conditions.* Classification may take into account accessibility, ownership (where non-BLM land as well as BLM land may be considered in relation to a comprehensive open space system), activity, historic and other cultural significance and problems of management. These may be considered as modifying aspects or refinements in relation to the primary or general open space functions.

OPEN SPACE CLASSIFICATION

I—*Utility Open Spaces*
  A. Resource Lands
  B. Urban Utility Spaces
  C. Flood Control and Drainage
  D. Reserves and Preserves

II—*Green Open Spaces*
  A. Wilderness Areas
  B. Protected Areas
  C. Natural Park Areas
  D. Urban Park Areas
  E. Recreational Areas
  F. Urban Development Open Spaces

III—*Corridor Open Spaces*
  A. Rights-of-Way
  B. Landing Spaces

IV—*Multi-Use Classification*
  A. Competitive Uses
  B. Complementary Uses
  C. Mixed-use Development and Open Space

I—Utility Open Spaces

This category is based primarily on the productive capacity of land and on its utilization for productive and storage uses.

A. *Resource Lands:* Land and water used for production or extraction of materials.

1. Forest lands
2. Grazing lands
3. Mining lands
4. Agricultural lands
5. Lakes and rivers for water storage and supply

B. *Flood Control and Drainage:* Lands properly unavailable for building unless unusual protective measures are taken; used to protect rural and urban lands alike.

1. Flood Plains and Flood Banks
2. Watersheds and watershed protection areas
3. Drainage ways: Streams, Ditches, Creeks, or other Paths for normal run-off water
4. Erosion Control Areas

C. *Urban Utility Space:* Land areas set aside and used for direct urban needs.

1. Dam sites and reservoirs
2. Land Fills and Waste Disposal areas
3. Sewage Treatment Facilities
4. Borrow Pits

D. *Reserves and Preserves:* Land and water areas set aside and protected for future resource uses.

1. Forests not managed for timber or recreation
2. Areas for Wildlife Refuge, Breeding, Sanctuary
3. Lands reserved for Urban Development

II—Green Open Spaces

This category is based on open spaces where the natural site or condition lends itself most advantageously to use for recreation, parks, building sites, non-extractive uses, and to shape urban development. The use may be limited or intensive, active or passive, large or small.

A. *Primitive or Wilderness Area:* Areas to be left in maximum natural state for scenic, geological and ecological values, for the preservation of vegetation andsanimal life in the natural state. Minimal access; service developed restricted to periphery; no other specific activity for the land.

1. Wilderness Areas designated by Congress, State or other governmental agencies
2. Other Unique Natural Areas

B. *Protected Areas:* Limited access and controlled development required for the protection of special areas of scenic and other natural values.

1. Wildlife Refuges Open to the Public (Example: Arkansas Wild Life Refuge)

2. Scenic Areas, including National Parks and Forests (Example: Bristlecone Pine Area)
3. Areas of Cultural or Historical Interest or Value (Example: Mt. Rushmore National Monument)
4. Coastline and Shore Areas to be Protected from Urban Encroachment (Example: Monterey County, California)

C. *Natural Park Areas:* Areas designated available to the public but maintained in as natural state as possible: often identified by the presence of some natural element unique to the area.

1. National Parks and Forests
2. State Parks
3. Natural Environmental Areas: limited or no man-made facilities
4. Regional Parks: large-scale parks more directly related to urban regional development, ski areas

D. *Urban Park Areas:* Parks more intimately related to local urban metropolitan development as to origin of users as well as to location.

1. Zoos
2. Botanical gardens, aboretum, wooded areas
3. Nature trails, riding areas
4. Special open-air facilities: fairgrounds, aquarenas, amphitheaters, outdoor cultural facilities.
5. Boating, other water facilities

E. *Recreation Areas:* Open spaces developed and assigned for more or less organized outdoor recreational facilities.

1. Recreation Lands: A BLM designation. A tract of land usually several thousand acres in size where recreation is the dominant and primary use. Recreation use may be concentrated in recreation sites or dispersed. Recreation Lands are selected on the basis of unique scenery, geologic, or natural features.
2. Recreation Sites: A BLM designation. Smaller tracts of land, generally less than 500 acres for concentrated recreational use and developed for fairly intensive uses, including camp grounds, picnic sites, scenic, archeological and historic sites.
3. Urban Recreation Areas: varied sized areas relating to local, community-wide or metropolitan area use, including both public and private facilities. These areas include golf courses, play fields, playgrounds, swimming pools, ice rinks, tennis courts, picnic areas, riding and hiking trails, etc.

F. *Urban Development Open Spaces:* Open spaces which shape, control and site urban development.

1. Planned greenbelts and green-wedges
2. Greenways, buffers, separators: creek and other stream routes developed as urban greenways
3. Plazas, malls, concourses, commons, squares
4. Building entourage, setback and open spaces around buildings for planting, etc.

SOURCE: *Where to Build. Technical Bulletin #1 Division of Land Management. Dept. of the Interior, Washington, D.C., 1968.*

III—Corridor Open Spaces

This category includes the open space assigned to the paths and areas of movement or passage. They take into account not only the lines of circulation but also the landing, stopping or interchange spaces which are integrally part of a circulation system.

A. *Rights-of Way Spaces:* Lands specifically designated for specific circulation use.

1. Highways, streets, alleys, drives.
2. Rivers, canals.
3. Railroad, and other rail rapid transit lanes.
4. Utility rights-of-way easements: pipe lines, power lines, irrigation systems.
5. Air lanes designated through zoning and other regulations.

B. *Landing Spaces:* Lands specifically designated for terminal and interchange uses.

1. Parking areas.
2. Airfields, marshalling yards, docks, truck terminal facilities.
3. Interchange areas; cloverleafs, transfer areas, etc.

C. *Scenic and Environmental Corridors:* Lands designated as part of an open space system to preserve scenic views and total environmental character, particularly in connection with highway and other circulation networks.

IV—Multi-Use Classification

A large proportion of open spaces are devoted to more than single uses. A dominant use, such as a water supply reservoir, may control classification assignment (in this case under Utility Open Space) even if other uses may be present, such as allowance for hikers and picnickers and other recreation (Green Space Uses) for the reservoir area. Because of the emphasis on the multi-purpose use of land, the Multi-Use Classification is of great value in the development of an open space system in comprehensive planning.

A. *Multi-Use May be Competitive*

1. Forestry or water supply vs. recreation.
2. Wildlife conservation vs. recreation.
3. Highway corridors vs. park and other open spaces.

B. *Multi-Use May be Complementary*

1. Multi-use for timber, grazing, summer residence, and recreation (Boise District, BLM).
2. Recreation in flood basins and watershed conservation areas.
3. Transportation corridors and green spaces.
4. Hiking Trails along power or pipeline rights-of-way.
5. Bicycle paths along watercourses.
6. Recreation in buffer areas.
7. Recreation and natural conservation.
8. Water supply and recreation.

C. *Multi-Use and Mixture of Uses*

1. Mixture of open space and development: College and other institutional campuses with open space provision and character that can be located in greenbelts and other urban open spaces.
2. Spaces which are not fully accessible to the general public but which are available to a significant portion of the population and could be included in an open system such as private clubs with recreational facilities, commercial amusement and recreation areas, institutional, recreational and garden areas.
3. Other uses which meet the open space definition but have special uses, such as cemeteries, which can be included in an open space system.
4. Compensatory open space as development: open space in relation to density of development such as that which may be "visually borrowed" from adjoining development, or which compensates for lack of space within a development. Compensatory open space comes into play especially in relating building height to land coverage, in greater intensity of building development compensated by additional common open space as in cluster and other planned unit developments.

The continental United States is divided into nine regions for convenience in providing lists of shade trees suitable for areas that have different climates. Overlapping the nine regions are the plant hardiness zones. The regions are shown in Figure 1 and the plant hardiness zones are shown in Figure 2. The regions are based roughly on climate, but within each region, there is a wide range of temperature, rainfall, soil, and other factors. All of these affect plant growth.

To some extent, soil and water requirements of shade trees can be managed but temperature usually is beyond control. Therefore, a knowledge of plant hardiness zones based on average minimum temperatures is important. If there is doubt about the cold hardiness of a tree, information may be obtained from agricultural experiment stations, colleges of agriculture, county agricultural agents, nurserymen, arborists, botanic gardens, and arboretums.

In selecting a shade tree, first check Figures 1 and 2 for the region in which the tree will be planted and the coldest plant hardiness zone in that region. Then check the appropriate regional list for trees that grow in that region.

In the regional lists, the common names of the trees are listed alphabetically for each region under the following headings: Evergreen, broadleaf; Evergreens, needle leaf and scale leaf; Deciduous; Palms; and Leafless.

The lists do not include all the kinds of shade trees that may be grown in a region. More extensive lists usually can be obtained from agricultural experiment stations and departments of horticulture at universities or colleges.

SOURCE: Shade Trees for the Home, U.S. Dept. of Agriculture, Agriculture Handbook #425, Washington, D.C., 1972.

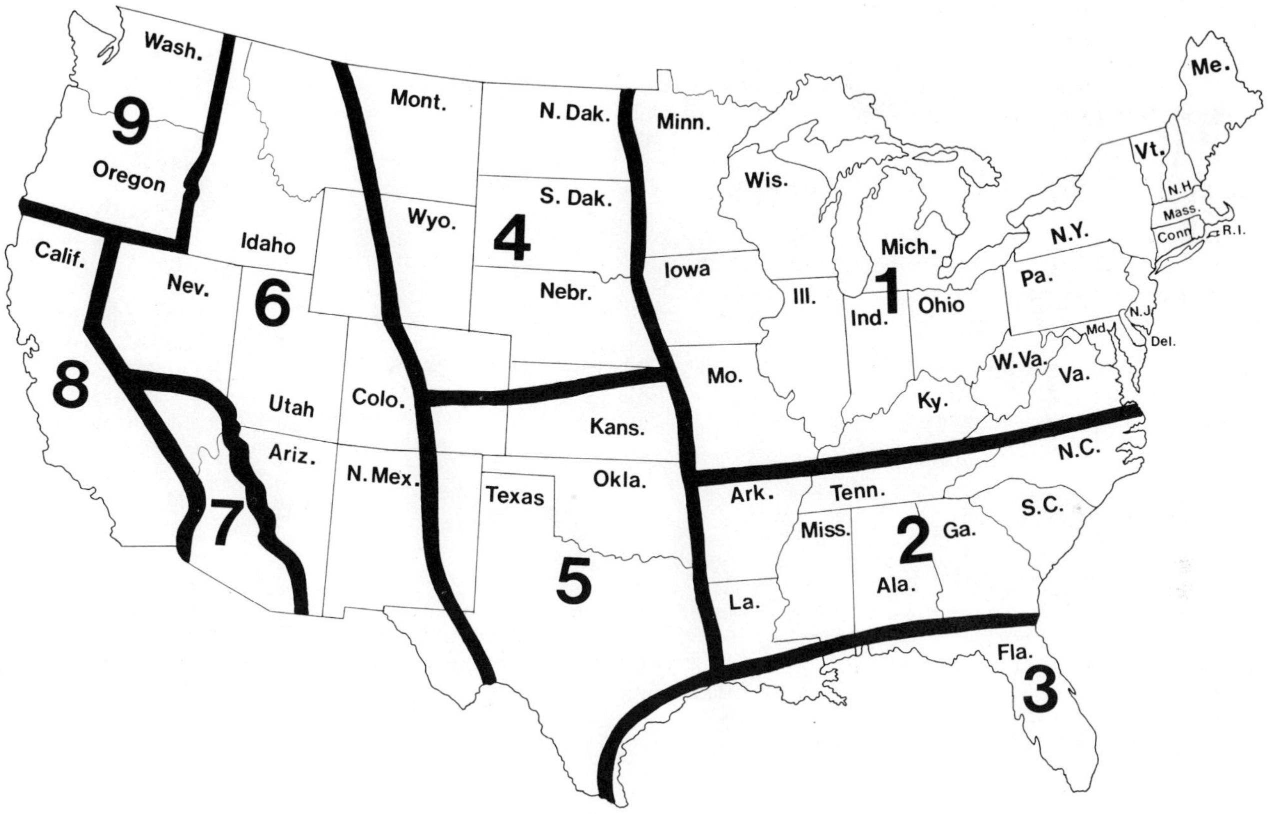

Fig. 1 Regional map.

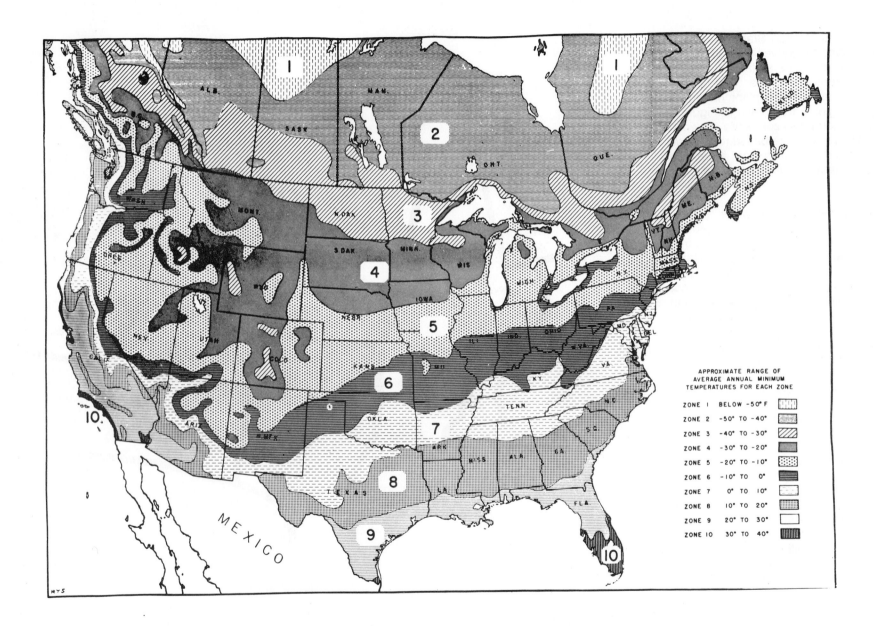

APPROXIMATE RANGE OF
AVERAGE ANNUAL MINIMUM
TEMPERATURES FOR EACH ZONE

ZONE 1   BELOW -50° F
ZONE 2   -50° TO -40°
ZONE 3   -40° TO -30°
ZONE 4   -30° TO -20°
ZONE 5   -20° TO -10°
ZONE 6   -10° TO 0°
ZONE 7   0° TO 10°
ZONE 8   10° TO 20°
ZONE 9   20° TO 30°
ZONE 10   30° TO 40°

Region 1

Evergreens, broadleaf
Holly, American
Magnolia, Southern
Evergreens, needle leaf and scale leaf
Arborvitae, Eastern
Arborvitae, Japanese
Cedar, Deodar
Cedar, Eastern Red
Cedar of Lebanon
Cryptomeria
Fir, White
Hemlock, Canadian
Juniper (See Cedar, Eastern Red)
Lawson False Cypress
Pine, Eastern White
Pine, Red
Spruce, Colorado Blue
Spruce, White
Deciduous
Ash, Green
Ash, White
Aspen, Quaking
Baldcypress
Beech, American
Beech, European
Birch, Cutleaf European
Birch, Paper
Birch, White
Buckeye
Buckeye, Red (See Horse-chestnut, Red)
Catalpa, Northern
Catalpa, Southern
Cork Tree, Amur
Cucumber Tree
Elm, American
Elm, English
Elm, European Field
Elm, Scotch
Ginkgo
Goldenrain Tree
Hackberry, Eastern
Hickory, Bitternut
Hickory, Mockernut
Hickory, Pignut
Hickory, Shagbark
Honeylocust, Thornless

Hornbeam, American
Hornbeam, European
Hornbeam, Hop
Horsechestnut
Horsechestnut, Red
Horsechestnut, Ruby (see Horsechestnut, Red)
Japanese Pagoda Tree
Kalopanax
Katsura
Kentucky Coffeetree
Larch, European
Linden, American
Linden, Littleleaf
Linden, Silver
Locust, Black
London Plane
Magnolia, Cucumber (See Cucumber Tree)
Magnolia, Sweetbay
Maple, Norway
Maple, Red
Maple, Sugar
Maple, Sycamore
Mimosa
Oak, Black
Oak, Bur
Oak, Chestnut
Oak, Northern Red
Oak, Pin
Oak, Scarlet
Oak, Shingle
Oak, Turkey
Oak, White
Oak, Willow
Oak, Yellow
Pear, Bradford
Pignut (See Hickory, Pignut)
Sassafras
Silverbell
Sourgum
Sweetgum
Sycamore
Tamarack
Tulip Poplar
Willow, Weeping
Yellowwood
Zelkova

Region 2

Evergreens, broadleaf
Camphor Tree
Holly, American
Holly, Chinese
Holly, English
Laurelcherry
Magnolia, Southern
Oak, Laurel
Oak, Live
Wax Myrtle
Evergreens, needle leaf and scale leaf
Arborvitae, Eastern
Arborvitae, Oriental
Cedar, Atlas
Cedar, Deodar
Cedar, Eastern Red
Cedar, Incense
Cedar of Lebanon
Cryptomeria
Hemlock, Carolina
Pine, Eastern White
Pine, Loblolly
Pine, Longleaf
Pine, Shortleaf
Pine, Slash
Spruce, Colorado Blue
Spruce, Red
Deciduous
Ash, White
Baldcypress
Beech, American
Beech, European
Birch, Cutleaf European
Buckeye
Catalpa, Northern
Catalpa, Southern
Cherry, Black
Chinaberry
Chinese Tallow Tree
Crape myrtle
Cucumber Tree
Elm, American
Elm, Cedar
Elm, English
Elm, Winged
Ginkgo
Goldenrain Tree
Hackberry, Eastern
Hickory, Bitternut

Hickory, Mockernut
Hickory, Pignut
Hickory, Shagbark
Honeylocust, Thornless
Hornbeam, American
Hornbeam, Hop
Japanese Pagoda Tree
Katsura
Kentucky Coffeetree
Linden, American
Linden, Littleleaf
London Plane
Magnolia, Cucumber (See Cucumber Tree)
Magnolia, Sweetbay
Maple, Norway
Maple, Red
Maple, Silver
Maple, Sycamore
Mimosa
Mulberry, Paper
Oak, Black
Oak, Bur
Oak, Chestnut
Oak, Pin
Oak, Post
Oak, Scarlet
Oak, Southern Red
Oak, Water
Oak, White
Oak, Willow
Pear, Bradford
Pecan
Persimmon
Pignut (See Hickory, Pignut)
Redbud, Eastern
Sassafras
Silverbell
Sourgum
Sourwood
Sweetgum
Sycamore
Tulip Poplar
Umbrella Tree (See Chinaberry)
Yellowwood
Palms
Palmetto, Cabbage

Region 3

Evergreens, broadleaf
African Tuliptree
Bell Flambeau (See African Tuliptree)
Brazilian Pepper
Cajeput
Cocoplum
Fig, Fiddle Leaf
Fig, India Laurel
Fig, Lofty
Geiger Tree
Holly, American
Holly, Chinese
Indian Rubber Tree
Jacaranda
Laurelcherry
Magnolia, Southern
Mahogany, Swamp (See Mahogany, West Indies)
Mahogany, West Indies
Oak, Laurel
Oak, Live
Oxhorn Bucida
Pigeon Plum
Silk Oak
Silver Trumpet
Wax Myrtle
Evergreens, needle leaf and scale leaf
Pine, Longleaf
Pine, Slash
Pine, Spruce
Deciduous
Baldcypress

Bo Tree
Crape Myrtle
Cucumber Tree
Fig, Benjamin
Goldenrain Tree
Linden, American
Magnolia, Cucumber (See Cucumber Tree)
Maple, Red
Mimosa
Mimosa, Lebbek
Oak, Water
Orchid Tree
Pecan
Redbud, Eastern
Royal Poinciana
Sweetgum
Palms
Palm, Coconut
Palm, Cuban Royal
Palm, Fishtail
Palm, Florida Royal
Palm, Manilla
Palm, Mexican Fan (See Palm, Washington)
Palm, Washington
Palmetto, Cabbage
Leafless
Beefwood (S Casuarina)
Beefwood, Horsetail (See Casuarina
Casuarina
Cunningham Beefwood
Scaly Bark Beefwood

Region 4

Evergreens, broadleaf
None
Evergreens, needle leaf and scale leaf
Arborvitae, Eastern
Arborvitae, Oriental
Cedar, Eastern Red
Cedar, Incense
Douglas Fir
Hemlock, Canadian
Juniper (*See* Cedar, Eastern Red)
Juniper, Rocky Mountain
Pine, Austrian
Pine, Ponderosa
Pine, Scotch
Spruce, Colorado Blue
Spruce, White
Deciduous
Ash, Black
Ash, Green
Ash, White
Birch, Cutleaf European
Birch, Paper
Birch, White

Catalpa, Northern
Cherry, Black
Cottonwood, Plains
Elm, American
Elm, Siberian
Hackberry, Eastern
Hackberry, Western
Honeylocust, Thornless
Katsura
Larch, Siberian
Linden, American
Linden, Littleleaf
Maple, Silver
Oak, Bur
Oak, Northern Red
Oak, Pin
Oak, Scarlet
Poplar, Plains (*See* Cottonwood, Plains)
Sugarberry (*See* Hackberry, Western)
Zelkova

Region 5

Evergreens, broadleaf
Oak, Live
Evergreens, needle leaf and scale leaf
Arborvitae, Oriental
Cedar, Atlas
Cedar, Eastern Red
Cryptomeria
Cypress, Arizona
Juniper (*See* Cedar Eastern Red)
Juniper, Rocky Mountain
Pine, Austrian
Pine, Loblolly
Pine, Ponderosa
Spruce, Colorado Blue
Deciduous
Ash, Green
Baldcypress
Beech, European
Buckeye
Catalpa, Northern
Catalpa, Southern
Chinaberry
Desert Willow
Elm, American
Elm, Chinese
Elm, English
Elm, European Field
Elm, Siberian
Goldenrain Tree
Hackberry, Eastern
Hackberry, Western
Honeylocust, Thornless
Huisache

Japanese Pagoda Tree
Katsura
Kentucky Coffeetree
Maple, Silver
Maple, Sycamore
Mesquite
Mulberry, Paper
Mulberry, Russian
Oak, Bur
Oak, Chestnut
Oak, Pin
Oak, Post
Oak, Shumard (*See* Oak Texas)
Oak, Scarlet
Oak, Spanish
Oak, Texas
Oak, Yellow
Pecan
Pistache, Chinese
Redbud, Eastern
Retama
Sassafras
Soapberry, Western
Sugarberry (*See* Hackberry, Western)
Sycamore
Umbrella Tree (*See* Chinaberry)
Zelkova
Palms
Palm, Mexican Fan (*See* Palm, Washington)
Palm, Washington

Region 6

Evergreens, broadleaf
Olive, Common
Olive, Russian
Evergreens, needle leaf and scale leaf
Arborvitae, Giant
Arborvitae, Oriental
Cedar, Atlas
Cedar, Eastern Red
Cedar, Incense
Douglas Fur
Fir, White
Juniper, (*See* Cedar, Eastern Red)
Juniper, Rocky Mountain
Pine, Austrian
Pine, Ponderosa
Spruce, Colorado Blue
Deciduous
Ash, Arizona (*See* Ash, Modesto)
Ash, European
Ash, Green
Ash, Modesto
Beech, European
Buckeye
Buckeye, Red (*See* Horsechestnut, Red)
Catalpa, Northern
Cottonwood, Plains
Elm, American

Elm, Chinese
Elm, European Field
Elm, Siberian
Ginkgo
Goldenrain Tree
Hackberry, Eastern
Honeylocust, Thornless
Horsechestnut
Horsechestnut, Red
Horsechestnut, Ruby (*See* Horsechestnut, Red)
Japanese Pagoda Tree
Katsura
Kentucky Coffeetree
Linden, American
Linden, Littleleaf
London Plane
Maple, Bigleaf
Maple, Norway
Maple, Sugar
Mulberry, Russian
Oak, Bur
Oak, Northern Red
Oak, Pin
Oak, White
Poplar, Plains (*See* Cottonwood, Plains)
Sweetgum
Zelkova

Region 7

Evergreens, broadleaf
Carob
Eucalyptus
Gum *(See* Eucalyptus)
Olive, Common
Olive, Russian
Palo Verde, Blue
Evergreens needle leaf and scale leaf
Cedar, Atlas
Cedar, Deodar
Cedar, Eastern Red
Cypress, Arizona
Cypress, Italian
Douglas Fur
Fir, Silver
Juniper *(See* Cedar, Eastern Red)
Juniper, Rocky Mountain
Pine, Aleppo
Pine, Austrian
Pine, Canary Island
Deciduous
Acacia, Baileys
Ailanthus
Ash, Arizona *(See* Ash, Modesto)
Ash, Green
Ash, Modesto
Baileys Wattle *(See* Acacia, Baileys)
Chinaberry
Cottonwood, Fremont
Cottonwood, Plains

Desert Willow
Elm, Chinese
Elm, Siberian
Ginkgo
Goldenrain Tree
Hackberry, Eastern
Hackberry, Western
Honeylocust, Thornless
Huisache
Linden, Littleleaf
Locust, Black
London Plane
Maple, Silver
Mesquite
Mulberry, Russian
Oak, Pin
Oak, Southern Red
Pecan
Pistache, Chinese
Poplar, Bolleana
Poplar, Carolina
Poplar, Plains *(See* Cottonwood, Plains)
Sugarberry *(See* Hackberry, Western)
Sweetgum
Tree of Heaven *(See* Ailanthus)
Umbrella Tree *(See* Chinaberry)
Wattle, Sydney
Palms
Palm, Canary Date

Region 8

Evergreens, broadleaf
Cajeput
Camphor Tree
Carob
Cherry, Australian Brush
Coral Tree
Eucalyptus
Fig, India Laurel
Fig, Moreton Bay
Gum *(See* Eucalyptus)
Jacaranda
Laurel, California
Laurelcherry
Laurel, Grecian
Magnolia, Southern
Oak, Canyon Live
Oak, Coast Live
Oak, Holly
Oak, Live
Palo Verde, Blue
Tanoak
Evergreens, needle leaf and scale leaf
Arborvitae, Oriental
Cedar, Atlas
Cedar, Deodar
Cedar, Incense
Cedar of Lebanon
Cryptomeria
Cypress, Arizona
Lawson False Cypress
Norfolk Island Pine
Pine, Aleppo
Pine, Canary Island
Spruce, Colorado Blue
Deciduous
Ash, Arizona *(See* Ash, Modesto)
Ash, Modesto
Chinaberry

Chinese Lantern Tree
Cottonwood, Fremont
Desert Willow
Elm, American
Elm, Chinese
Elm, Siberian
Ginkgo
Goldenrain Tree
Hackberry, Eastern
Honeylocust, Thornless
Japanese Pagoda Tree
Locust, Black
London Plane
Maple, Bigleaf
Maple, Norway
Maple, Red
Mimosa
Mulberry, Russian
Oak, Bur
Oak, English
Oak, Northern Red
Oak, Pin
Oak, Scarlet
Oak, Valley
Orchid Tree
Pistache, Chinese
Sweetgum
Tulip Poplar
Umbrella Tree *(See* Chinaberry)
Palms
Palm, Canary Date
Palm, Mexican Fan *(See* Palm, Washington)
Palm, Washington
Leafless
Beefwood *(See* Casuarina)
Beefwood, Horsetail *(See* Casuarina)
Casuarina

Region 9

Evergreens, broadleaf
Holly, English
Madrone
Magnolia, Southern
Tanoak
Evergreens, needle leaf and scale leaf
Arborvitae, Giant
Arborvitae, Oriental
Cedar, Atlas
Cedar, Deodar
Cedar, Incense
Cryptomeria
Lawson False Cypress
Pine, Austrian
Pine, Ponderosa
Spruce, Colorado Blue
Deciduous
Ash, European
Ash, Green
Ash, White
Beech, European
Birch, White
Buckeye, Red *(See* Horsechestnut, Red)
Cork Tree, Amur
Dogwood, Pacific
Elm, American
Elm, Chinese
Elm, English
Elm, Scotch
Elm, Siberian
Ginkgo
Golden Chain Tree
Goldenrain Tree
Honeylocust, Thornless
Hornbeam, American
Horsechestnut

Horsechestnut, Red
Horsechestnut, Ruby *(See* Horsechestnut, Red)
Japanese Pagoda Tree
Kentucky Coffeetree
Linden, American
Linden, Littleleaf
London Plane
Maple, Bigleaf
Maple, Norway
Maple, Red
Maple, Sugar
Mimosa
Oak, Northern Red
Oak, Oregon White
Oak, Pin
Oak, Scarlet
Oak, White
Silverbell
Sourwood
Sweetgum
Tulip Poplar
Yellowwood

SHADE TREES FOR SUBURBAN HOMES

Evergreen:
Canada hemlock
Colorado blue spruce
Eastern white pine
Nikko fir
White fir

In northern part only
Balsam fir
white spruce

Deciduous:
Ame. hornbeam
Amer. mountain-ash
Amer. yellowwood
European beech
Eur. linden
Littleleaf linden
Norway maple
Panicled goldenrain-tree
Pin oak
Scarlet oak
Schwedler maple
Silver linden
Sugar maple
Sweetgum
Tuliptree
Whiteoak

ROADSIDE, BOULEVARD AND AVENUE TREES

Evergreen:
Canada hemlock
Eastern white pine
red pine

Decidious:
Amer. linden
Ame. yellowwood
Black tupelo
Common hackberry
Ginkgo (staminate form)
London planetree
Northern red oak
Norway maple
pin oak
red maple
scarlet oak
silver linden
Schwedler maple
sugar maple
sweetgum
Tuliptree

STREET TREES

Evergreen:
None

Deciduous:
Ailanthus (pistallate form)
Amur corktree
Ginkgo (staminate form)
London planetree
Norway maple
Pin oak
Thornless common honeylocust
Tuliptree

PARK AND GARDEN TREES

Evergreen:
Common Douglas-fir
Oriental spruce
Red pine

Deciduous:
Amur corktree
Bolleana poplar
cutleaf weeping birch
Eastern black walnut
English elm
Golden weeping willow
Japanese pagodatree
Kentucky coffeetree
Paper birch
Rock elm
Scotch elm
Silverpendent linden
Weeping silverpendent linden
White Ash
White oak

TREES WITH AUTUMN COLOR

American hornbeam (orange, scarlet)
American yellowwood (yellow)
Black tupelo (scarlet)
Ginkgo (yellow)
Northern red oak (red)
Norway maple (yellow)
Pin oak (scarlet, dark red)
Red maple (orange, red, scarlet)
scarlet oak (scarlet, dark red)
sugar maple (yellow, orange, scarlet)
Sweetgum (red, scarlet)
tuliptree (yellow)

TREES WITH CONSPICUOUS COLOR

American mountain-ash (white)
American yellowwood (white)
Common horsechestnut (pinkish white)
Japanese pagodatree (yellowish white)
Panicled goldenrain-tree (yellow)
Red maple (red)
Sugar maple (yellowish green)
Tulliptree (greenish yellow)

SOURCE: Trees—Yearbook of Agriculture—1949, U. S. Dept. of Agriculture

■ SOUTHEASTERN REGION

SHADE AND ROADSIDE TREES

Deciduous:
American beech
American elm
American sycamore
Laurel oak
Pecan
Sugarberry
Sweetgum
Water oak
Weeping willow
White oak
Willow oak
Winged elm
Yellow popular

Evergreen:
Live oak
Southern magnolia

STREET TREES

Deciduous:
American elm
American sycamore
Cabbage palmetto
Common crapemyrtle
Laurel oak
Sugar berry
Sweetgum
Water oak
White oak
Willow oak
Winged elm

Evergreen:
Camphor-tree
Live oak
Southern magnolia

PARK AND LAWN TREES

Deciduous:
American beech
American elm
American sycamore
Common crapemyrtel
Eastern redbud
Flowering dogwood
Mimosa
Panicled goldenrain-tree
red maple

Evergreen:
American holly
Southern magnolia

TREES WITH AUTUMN COLOR

Deciduous:
Flowering dogwood
Pin oak
Red maple
Scarlet oak
Sweetgum
Yellow-popular

■ SOUTHERN ROCKY MOUNTAIN REGION

STREET TREES

Deciduous:
Green ash
Lanceleaf poplar
Linden
London Planetree
Narrowleaf poplar
Northern catalpa
Norway maple
Siberian elm
Velvet ash
White Ash

SHADE TREES

Deciduous:
Amer. elm
Boxelder
Plains poplar
red mulberry
white mulberry

TREES WITH CONSPICUOUS FLOWERS

Deciduous:
Black locust
Northern Catalpa

TREES FOR DIFFICULT SITES

Deciduous:
Black locust
Boxelder
Common hackberry
Russian-olive
Siberian elm
Tamarisk
Thornless honeylocust
Tree-of Heaven ailanthus
Velvet ash

TREES WITH AUTUMN COLOR

Deciduous:
Lanceleaf poplar
Lombardy poplar
Narrowleaf poplar
Norway maple
Plains poplar

ROADSIDE TREES

Deciduous:
Black locust
Lombardy poplar

Evergreen:
Arizona cypress
Eucalyptus
Ponderosa Pine

PARK AND GARDEN TREES

Deciduous:
Common hackberry
Russian olive
Tamarisk
Thornless honeylocust
tree of heaven ailanthus

Evergreen:
Aleppo pine
Austrian pine
Colorado pinyon pine
Colorado spruce
Englemann spruce
Rocky mountain juniper
Scotch pine

Evergreen:
Eucalyptus

SOURCE: Trees: Yearbook of Agriculture—1949, U. S. Dept. of Agriculture

SHADE AND PARK TREES

Deciduous:
American Elm
Bur oak
Cottonwood
Green ash
Hackberry
Honeylocust
Russian-olive

Evergreens:
Austrian pine
Eastern redcedar
Ponderosa pine
Rocky mountain cedar

NEBRASKA NORTHWARD:

Deciduous:
Boxelder
Hawthorn
Maples
Willows

Evergreens:
Douglas fir
Scotch pine
Spruce
White fir

NEBRASKA SOUTHWARD:

Deciduous:
Ailanthus
American sycamore
Black locust
Black walnut
Catalpa
Russian mulberry

OKLAHOMA AND TEXAS:

Deciduous:
Chinese elm
Desertwillow
Kentucky coffeetree
soapberry

Evergreen:
Arizona cypress (texas)
Loblolly pine
Shortleaf pine

TREES WITH SNOWY FLOWERS

Black locust
Catalpa
Desertwillow
Hawthorn
Honeylocust

SOURCE: *Trees: Yearbook of Agriculture—1949, U. S. Dept. of Agriculture*

STREET TREES

Deciduous:
American elm
American sycamore
Boxelder
Bur oak
Green ash
Hackberry
Maples
Russian mulberry
Siberian elm

Evergreens:
Austrian pine
Ponderosa pine

TREES WITH SHOWY FOLIAGE IN AUTUMN

Cottonwood (yellow)
Green ash (golden yellow)
Maple (gold and red)
Oak (yellow to red)
Sycamore (clear yellow)

Trees suitable for use on phymatotrichum root rot infected soil:

Deciduous:
Ailanthus
Desertwillow
Hackberry
Mulberry
Soapberry

Evergreens:
Eastern redcedar
Rocky Mountain cedar

■ NORTH PACIFIC COAST AREA

SHADE TREES

American yellowwood

Common hackberry
European linden
pin oak

LAWN TREES

Amer. yellowwood
Atlas-cedar (conifer)
Common hackberry
Eur. Linden
Himalayan pine (conifer)
Oregon white oak
Pacific madrone
Pin oak
Sweet gum, Tuliptree

TREES WITH SHOWY FALL FOLIAGE

Amer. yellowwood
Pin oak
Sweetgum

TREES WITH SHOWY OR FRAGRANT FLOWERS

American yellowwood
Eur. linden
Pacific madrone

a. Acer platanoides — Norway Maple. A wide round-headed, densely foliaged tree. Leaves are five-lobed, quite large, and deep green, turning a golden yellow in the fall. A fine tree for a symmetrical, impenetrable look. Height 40 feet, spread 35 feet.

b. Aesculus hippocastanum — Horse Chestnut. The famous tree which grows on the Champs Elysees. The flowers bloom like white candles in May, coming out with the lovers. A wonderful tree with a handsome, five-fingered leaf, it grows up to 50 feet high with a 30-foot spread.

c. Ailanthus altissima — Chinese Tree of Heaven. The tree that grows in Brooklyn will grow anywhere. It has a fine tropical quality and handsome fruits which hang in clusters. Thin, very often multi-stemmed, finely divided leaves. Height 40 feet, spread 35 feet.

d. Carpinus betulus—European Hornbeam. A fine tree for shearing and pleaching. This was the tree used mostly in Versailles for the high hedges pleached down the allees. A small, elegant leaf and a clean, upright, black-barked trunk. Height 35 feet, spread 25 feet.

e. Fraxinus pennsylvanica lanceolata — Green Ash. A good, all-around, tough, vigorous tree. The bark is most interesting: marked diagonally, and quite black in color. Height 35 feet, spread 30 feet.

f. Ginkgo biloba — Maidenhair Tree. A living fossil which owes its life to the fact that it has been planted for centuries in the temple gardens of China. The females of this species produce evil-smelling fruits, so use only the male. Height 60 feet, spread 35 feet.

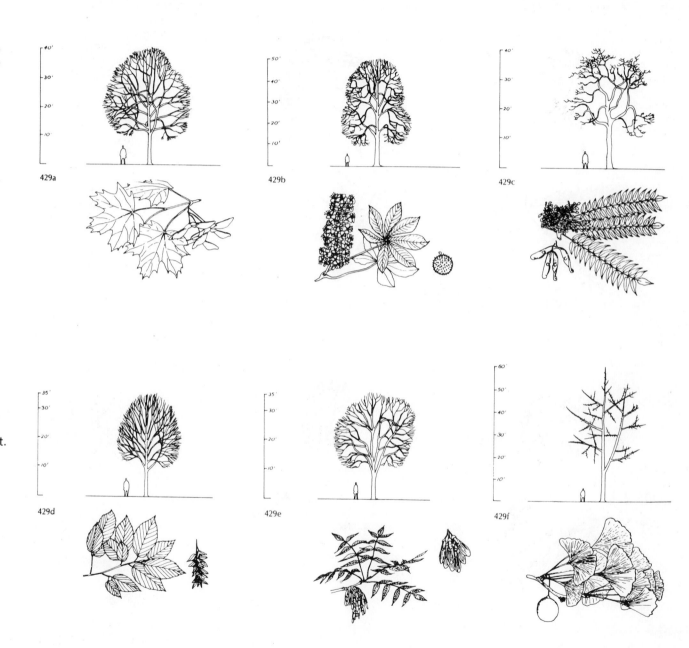

429a

429b

429c

429d

429e

429f

SOURCE: Lawrence Halpirin, Cities, Van Nostrand Reinhold Company, N.Y., 1963.

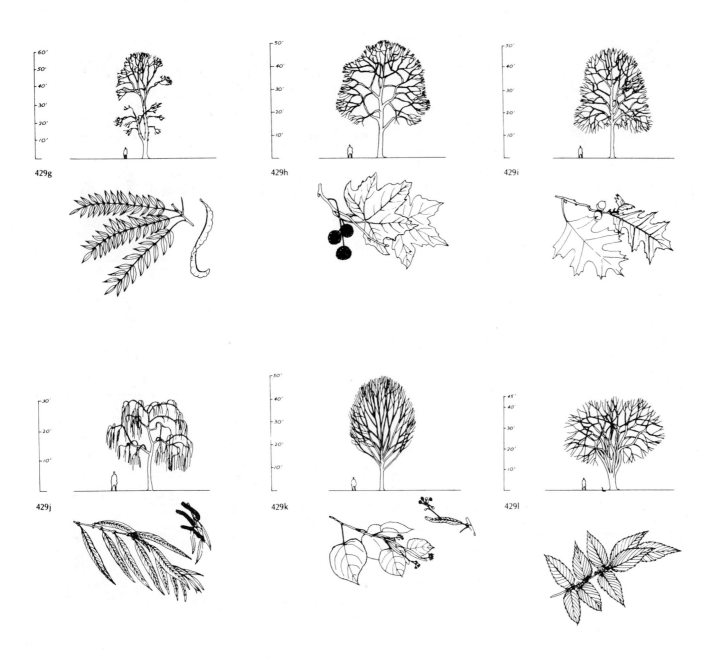

g. Gleditsia triacanthos—Honey Locust. Very high-headed, spreading, umbrella-shaped tree with a beautiful silhouette, deep black bark, and fine textured leaves. Tough and handsome. Height 50 feet, spread 40 feet.

h. Platanus acerifolia — London Plane Tree, Sycamore. The most planted street tree in North America. It can be sheared, pleached, or pollarded with excellent effects, withstands winds and soot admirably. Other excellent sycamores. Platanus orientalis—the Oriental Plane Tree, Platanus racemosa—the California Plane Tree. Height 50 feet, spread 40 feet.

i. Quercus borealis — Red Oak. The best of the Oaks for city conditions, clean, handsome, upright, and all-American. A deeply serrated leaf which turns a brilliant red in the fall. Height 50 feet, spread 40 feet.

j. Salix babylonica — Weeping Willow. Actually a native of China, this willow is not good for a street tree but is wonderful for small parks, playgrounds, backyard gardens. Its long, yellow, whiplike twigs have a fine color when the leaves have fallen. Height 30 feet, spread 30 feet.

k. Tilia cordata — Linden Basswood. The famous "Unter den Linden" tree, an extremely popular street tree in Europe. A beautiful round shape, handsome heart-shaped leaves, and delightful small flowers. The American species, Tilia american (called basswood), makes some of the tastiest honey in the world. Height 50 feet, spread 30 feet.

l. Zelkova serrata — Japanese Zelkova. Very much like the American elm in its shape and leaf, though smaller, and can be used in its place since it is not susceptible to the Dutch elm disease. Height 45 feet, spread 50 feet.

SOURCE: Lawrence Halpirin, Cities, Van Nostrand Reinhold Company, N.Y., 1963.

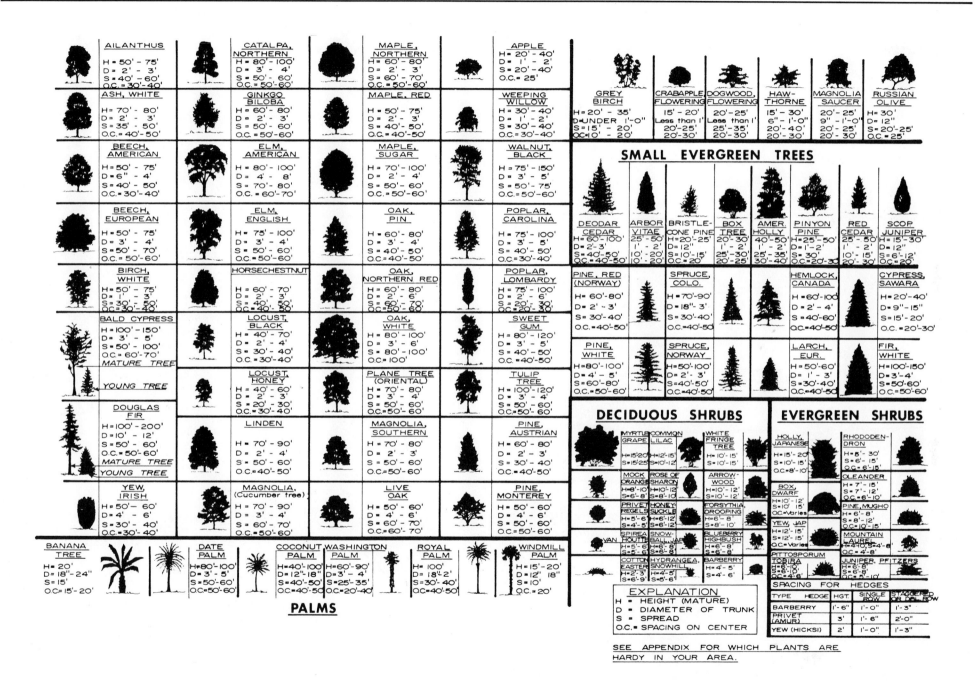

PALMS

SMALL EVERGREEN TREES

DECIDUOUS SHRUBS

EVERGREEN SHRUBS

EXPLANATION
H = HEIGHT (MATURE)
D = DIAMETER OF TRUNK
S = SPREAD
O.C. = SPACING ON CENTER

SEE APPENDIX FOR WHICH PLANTS ARE
HARDY IN YOUR AREA.

TREE LOCATION

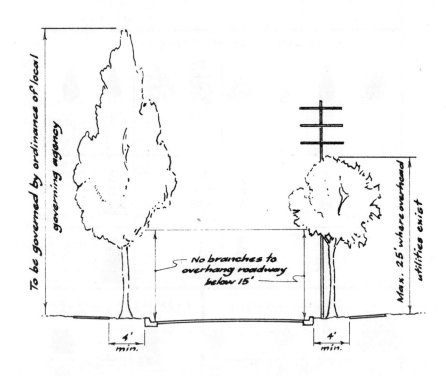

Spacing of trees to depend upon specie and growth characteristics, with min. of 25' apart. All trees within right of way to be planted by permit from governing agency.

STREET NAME SIGN LOCATION

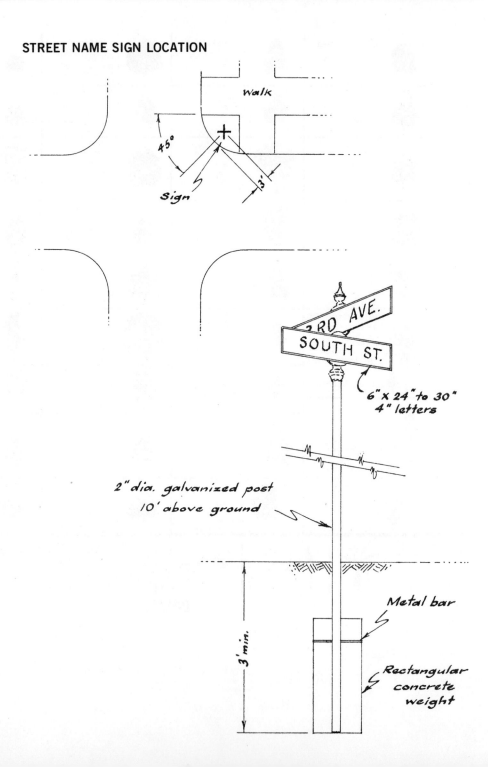

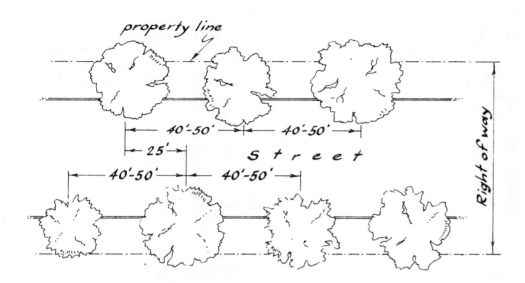

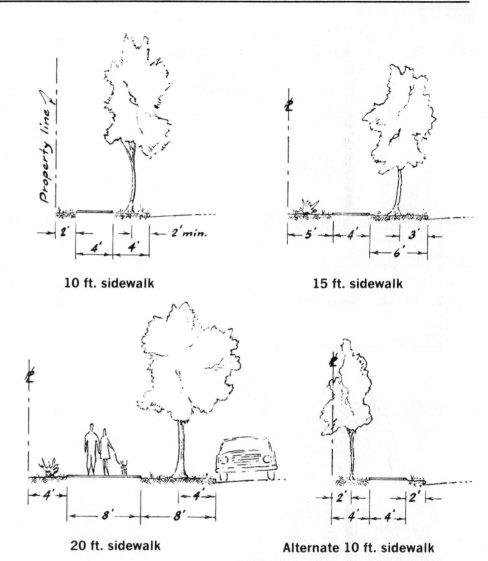

10 ft. sidewalk

15 ft. sidewalk

20 ft. sidewalk

Alternate 10 ft. sidewalk

GENERAL CRITERIA

● Trees should be spaced alternately on each side.

● Trees should be spaced at regular intervals without regard to property lines. This will give the street a well-balanced appearance.

● Trees for an entire block should be planted at the same time.

● Some typical spacing of trees:

Elms, White Oaks	50 ft.
Planet Tree, Soft Maples	45 ft.
Ginkgo, Red Maples	40 ft.

● All trees should be the same kind on a street except to achieve special effects.

There are several advantages of placing trees between sidewalk and property line, which are:

1. House has better screening from street.
2. There is less interference with overhead wires.
3. Tree roots are less likely to be cut with street repairs.
4. Trees usually have better soil.

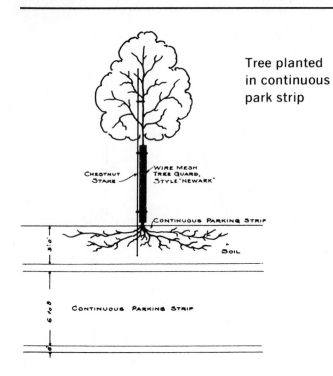

Tree planted
in continuous
park strip

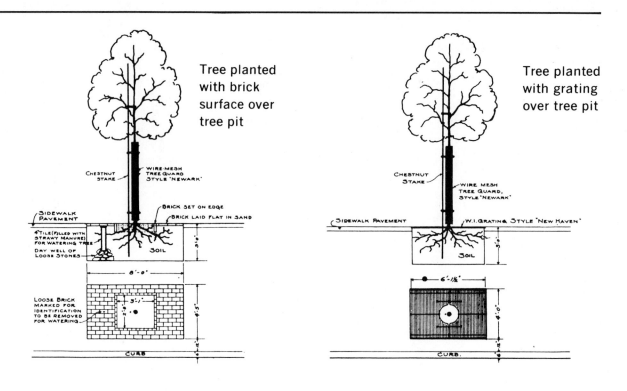

Tree planted
with brick
surface over
tree pit

Tree planted
with grating
over tree pit

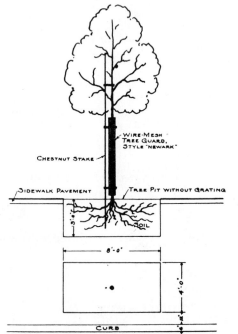

Tree planted
in limited
area

Cross section through small tree planted bare-rooted.

Cross section through small evergreen planted with ball.

SOURCE: A Street Tree System for New York City, Bulletin of NYS College of Forestry at Syracuse University

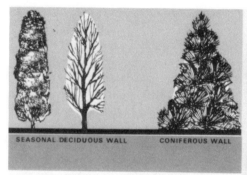

SEASONAL DECIDUOUS WALL   CONIFEROUS WALL

GROUND COVERS FORM FLOORS

The quality and density of the wall depend on the season of the year for a deciduous tree, but remain substantially uniform for a coniferous tree.

Low-growing plants, when used in a mass, form a floor or ground cover.

When used in combination in the landscape, groups of plants form canopies, walls, or floors of vastly varying texture, height, and density.

WALLS   THE INDIVIDUAL'S RELATIONSHIP TO SHRUBS DETERMINES THE BEST HEIGHT FOR A PARTICULAR PLANTING. ANKLE HIGH TO COVER THE GROUND, KNEE HIGH FOR DIRECTION, WAIST HIGH FOR TRAFFIC CONTROL AND PARTIAL ENCLOSURE.

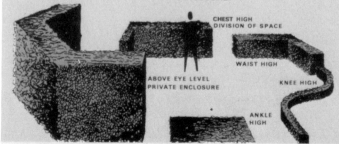

CHEST HIGH DIVISION OF SPACE

WAIST HIGH

ABOVE EYE LEVEL PRIVATE ENCLOSURE

KNEE HIGH

ANKLE HIGH

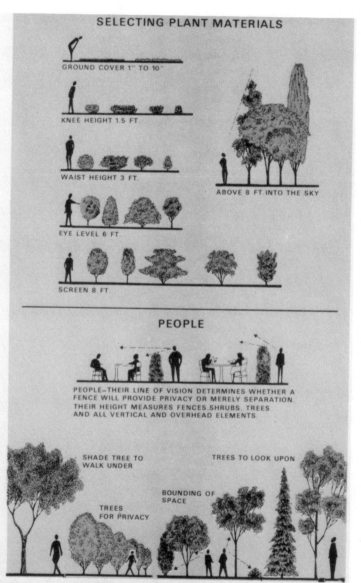

SELECTING PLANT MATERIALS

GROUND COVER 1" TO 10"

KNEE HEIGHT 1.5 FT.

WAIST HEIGHT 3 FT.

EYE LEVEL 6 FT.

SCREEN 8 FT.

ABOVE 8 FT. INTO THE SKY

PEOPLE

PEOPLE—THEIR LINE OF VISION DETERMINES WHETHER A FENCE WILL PROVIDE PRIVACY OR MERELY SEPARATION. THEIR HEIGHT MEASURES FENCES, SHRUBS, TREES AND ALL VERTICAL AND OVERHEAD ELEMENTS.

SHADE TREE TO WALK UNDER

TREES TO LOOK UPON

BOUNDING OF SPACE

TREES FOR PRIVACY

The ultimate height of plants is an important consideration in determining their possible architectural potential.

Type, age, and condition of the plant determine the degree to which an individual plant filters or blocks a view. Spacing, density, volume, height, and width of the planting determines the degree to which a group of plants filter or block a view.

A single plant standing alone may block or interrupt a view. A group of plants, planted in sequence, may form a wall which blocks or screens a view. Plants, because they are alive, are of variable and dynamic density and character—growing and changing daily, seasonally, and yearly. The variability, density, and character of "walls, ceilings, or floors" formed by growing plants is determined by the density, height, volume, and width of the individual plants which make up the architectural element.

Spacing of the individual plants when used in a mass or group determines the opacity, translucency, or transparency of the massed planting.

The inherent character of plants, coupled with their predictability of form and growth-rate, enables environmental designers to select plants according to the density of the walls, canopies, or floors which they will form.

A grouping of a single variety or a grouping of plants having similar form and density may be used to create a uniform screen to filter a view. A grouping of mixed plants with different forms, shapes, densities, and heights, can produce an infinite variety of degrees of view filtration.

The form, texture, color, and density of a plant, as well as the manner in which it is used, determine the ability of a plant or a mass-planting to become an architectural element. Plants may stand alone, may be grouped with others of the same variety, or may be grouped with other varieties, in endless combinations, to form architectural elements.

Since plants have architectural potential, and can be used to create architectural elements, their functions may be categorized as using them for space articulation, for screening, for privacy control, and for progressive realization of an object, activity, or event. A brief description of the functions, reveals that space articulation is "room-making," privacy control is "enclosure," screening is "view blockage," and progressive realization is "enticement or tantalization."

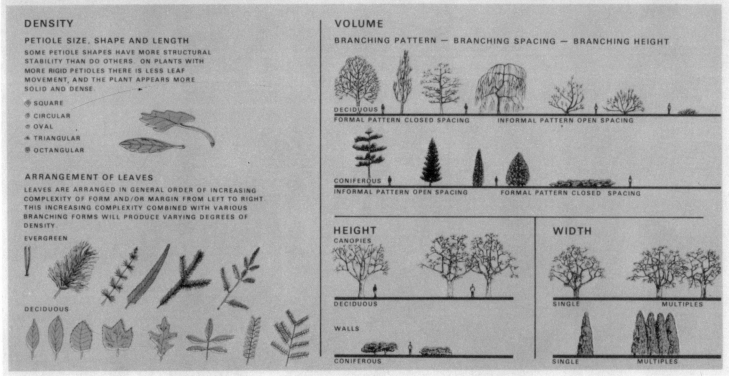

DENSITY

PETIOLE SIZE, SHAPE AND LENGTH
SOME PETIOLE SHAPES HAVE MORE STRUCTURAL STABILITY THAN DO OTHERS. ON PLANTS WITH MORE RIGID PETIOLES THERE IS LESS LEAF MOVEMENT, AND THE PLANT APPEARS MORE SOLID AND DENSE.

⬦ SQUARE
◉ CIRCULAR
⬭ OVAL
▴ TRIANGULAR
⬡ OCTANGULAR

ARRANGEMENT OF LEAVES
LEAVES ARE ARRANGED IN GENERAL ORDER OF INCREASING COMPLEXITY OF FORM AND/OR MARGIN FROM LEFT TO RIGHT. THIS INCREASING COMPLEXITY COMBINED WITH VARIOUS BRANCHING FORMS WILL PRODUCE VARYING DEGREES OF DENSITY.

EVERGREEN

DECIDUOUS

VOLUME

BRANCHING PATTERN — BRANCHING SPACING — BRANCHING HEIGHT

DECIDUOUS
FORMAL PATTERN CLOSED SPACING   INFORMAL PATTERN OPEN SPACING

CONIFEROUS
INFORMAL PATTERN OPEN SPACING   FORMAL PATTERN CLOSED SPACING

HEIGHT
CANOPIES

DECIDUOUS

WALLS

CONIFEROUS

WIDTH

SINGLE   MULTIPLES

SINGLE   MULTIPLES

WALLS REPRESENTATIVE PLANTS INDICATING THE RELATIVE DEGREES OF VISUAL DENSITY. (AT LEAST 6' HIGH)

1. THUJA OCCIDENTALIS
   SHEARED 18" O.C.
2. TSUGA CANADENSIS
   SHEARED 2' O.C.
3. PSEUDOTSUGA TAXIFOLIA
   SHEARED 2' O.C.
4. TAXUS MEDIA HICKSI
   SHEARED 18" O.C.
5. JUNIPERUS CHINENSIS HETZI
   SHEARED 2' O.C.
6. BUXUS SEMPERVIRENS
   SHEARED 9" O.C.
7. PICEA GLAUCA
   SHEARED 2' O.C.
8. PINUS STROBUS
   SHEARED 2' O.C.
9. JUNIPERUS VIRGINIANA
   SHEARED 2' O.C.
10. RHAMNUS CATHARTICA, 'TALLHEDGE'
    SHEARED 1' O.C., SUMMER
11. RIBES ALPINUN
    SHEARED 9" O.C., SUMMER
12. BERBERIS MENTORENSIS
    SHEARED 6" O.C.-DOUBLE ROW, SUMMER
13. EUONYMUS ALATUS
    SHEARED 18" O.C., SUMMER
14. LONICERA TATARICA
    SHEARED 2' O.C., SUMMER
15. LIGUSTRUM AMURENSE
    SHEARED 9" O.C., SUMMER
16. ROSA MULTIFLORA
    SHEARED 6" O.C., SUMMER
17. ULMUS PUMILA
    SHEARED 2' O.C., SUMMER
18. CRATAEGUS CRUSGALLI
    SHEARED 2' O.C., SUMMER
19. PHYSOCARPUS APULIFOLIUS
    SHEARED 9" O.C., SUMMER
20. SYRINGA VULGARIS
    SHEARED 9" O.C., SUMMER

21. VIBURNUM LANTANA
    SHEARED 18" O.C., SUMMER
22. CORNUS MAS
    SHEARED 18" O.C., WINTER
23. BERBERIS KOREANA
    SHEARED 9" O.C., WINTER
24. RHODOTYPOS SCANDENS
    SHEARED 1' O.C., WINTER
25. MALUS SARGENTI
    SHEARED 2' O.C., WINTER
26. COTONEASTER NITIUS
    SHEARED 18" O.C., WINTER
27. QUERCUS IMBRICARIA
    SHEARED 2' O.C., WINTER
28. POPULUS NIGRA ITALICA
    8' O.C. WINTER
29. ELAEAGNUS ANGUSTIFOLIA
    10' O.C., WINTER
30. PHILADELPHIUS VIRGINALIS
    5' O.C., WINTER
31. HIBISCUS SYRIACUS
    6' O.C., WINTER
32. SALIX MATSUDANA TORTUOSA
    8' O.C., WINTER
33. AMELANCHIER CANADENSIS
    10' O.C., WINTER
34. CARPINUS BETULUS
    10' O.C., WINTER
35. BETULA POPULIFOLIA
    15' O.C., WINTER
36. POPULUS TREMULOIDES
    20' O.C., WINTER
37. GLEDITSIA TRIACANTHOS
    25' O.C., WINTER
38. TILIA CORDATA
    30' O.C., WINTER
39. ACER SACCHARUM
    35' O.C., WINTER
40. ULMUS AMERICANA
    40' O.C., WINTER

CEILINGS REPRESENTATIVE PLANTS INDICATING THE RELATIVE DEGREES OF VISUAL DENSITY. (SPACED TO GIVE UNIFORM CEILING DENSITY.)

1. THUJA OCCIDENTALIS
   AMERICAN ARBOR-VITAE
2. JUNIPERUS VIRGINIANA
   EASTERN RED-CEDAR
3. PSEUDOTSUGA TAXIFOLIA
   DOUGLAS-FIR
4. ACER PLATANOIDES
   NORWAY MAPLE, SUMMER
5. LARIX DECIDUA
   EUROPEAN LARCH, SUMMER
6. PICEA PUNGENS
   COLORADO BLUE SPRUCE
7. QUERCUS ALBA
   WHITE OAK, SUMMER
8. CELTIS OCCIDENTALIS
   AMERICAN HACKBERRY, SUMMER
9. ULMUS AMERICANA
   AMERICAN ELM, SUMMER
10. FRAXINUS PENNSYLVANICA LANCEOLATA
    GREEN ASH, SUMMER
11. QUERCUS ALBA
    WHITE OAK, WINTER
12. BETULA POPULIFOLIA
    GREY BIRCH, WINTER
13. MACLURA POMIFERA
    OSAGE-ORANGE, WINTER
14. QUERCUS PALUSTRIS
    PIN OAK, WINTER
15. SORBUS AUCUPARIA
    EUROPEAN MOUNTAIN ASH, WINTER
16. CLADRASTIS LUTEA
    AMERICAN YELLOW-WOOD, WINTER
17. GINKGO BILOBA
    GINKGO, WINTER
18. GLEDITSIA TRIACANTHOS
    COMMON HONEY-LOCUST, WINTER
19. RHUS TYPHINA
    STAGHORN SUMAC, WINTER
20. ROBINIA PSEUDOACACIA
    BLACK LOCUST, WINTER

FLOORS OF EXTERIOR SPACES CREATED BY PLANT MATERIALS RATED BY THEIR ABILITY TO WITHSTAND FOOT TRAFFIC AND THE EASE WITH WHICH THEY ARE ABLE TO BE WALKED UPON.

1. POA PRATENSIS
   KENTUCKY BLUEGRASS
2. THYMUS SERPYLLUM
   THYME
3. ANENARIA VERNA CAESPITOSA
   MOSS SANDWORT
4. ANTHEMIS NOBILIS
   CAMOMILE
5. MATRICARIA TCHIHATCHEWII
   TURFING DAISY

6. CERASTIUM TOMENTOSUM
   SNOW-IN-SUMMER
7. HEDERA HELIX
   ENGLISH IVY
8. AJUGA REPTANS
   BUNGLEWEED
9. COTONEASTER ADPRESSA PRAECOX
   CREEPING COTONEASTER
10. ROSA WICHURAIANA
    MEMORIAL ROSE

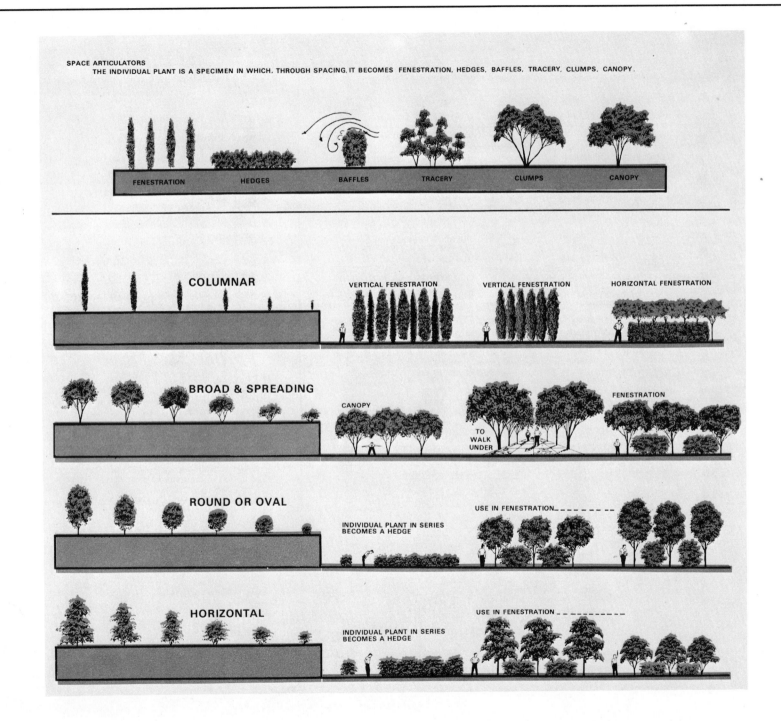

SPACE ARTICULATORS
THE INDIVIDUAL PLANT IS A SPECIMEN IN WHICH, THROUGH SPACING, IT BECOMES FENESTRATION, HEDGES, BAFFLES, TRACERY, CLUMPS, CANOPY.

FENESTRATION   HEDGES   BAFFLES   TRACERY   CLUMPS   CANOPY

COLUMNAR   VERTICAL FENESTRATION   VERTICAL FENESTRATION   HORIZONTAL FENESTRATION

BROAD & SPREADING   CANOPY   TO WALK UNDER   FENESTRATION

ROUND OR OVAL   INDIVIDUAL PLANT IN SERIES BECOMES A HEDGE   USE IN FENESTRATION

HORIZONTAL   INDIVIDUAL PLANT IN SERIES BECOMES A HEDGE   USE IN FENESTRATION

Screening is visually blocking out that which is unsightly with something more harmonious, or at least less offensive. Screening is a means of providing visual control in the landscape through view direction and "negation" of ugliness simply by hiding it. Screening implies isolation, confinement, and concealment of the unwanted, while allowing free access to the remainder of the landscape. Screening has a positive and a negative connotation—positive screening enhances the surroundings, while negative screening blocks ugly surroundings from view.

We are surrounded in our contemporary environment with areas, activities, and objects we would rather not see. We screen or hide these parts of our environment to make them less objectionable and the total environment more acceptable. Typical areas in our contemporary environment commonly screened are: junk yards, service areas and facilities, construction activities, storage areas, parking lots, industrial facilities, electrical transformer yards, power facilities of all types, athletic fields and areas, roadways and driveways, outdoor air-conditioning units, cemeteries, and activities unrelated to the surroundings.

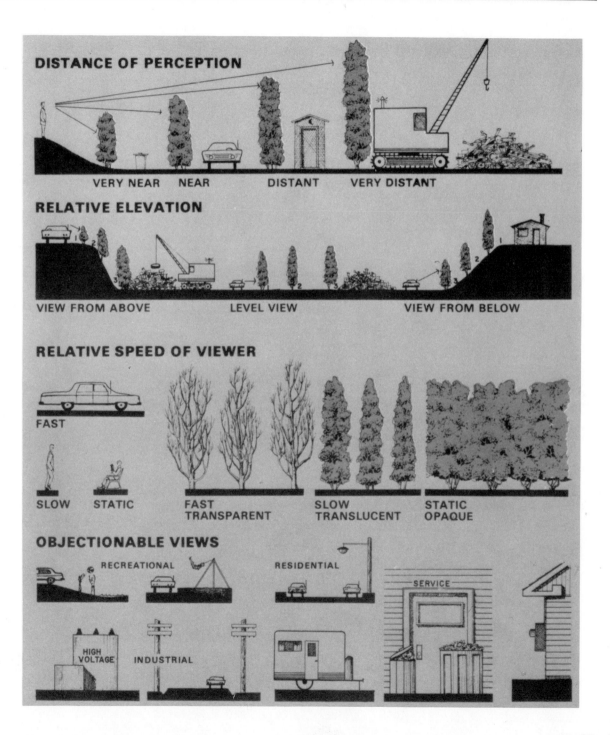

DISTANCE OF PERCEPTION

VERY NEAR   NEAR   DISTANT   VERY DISTANT

RELATIVE ELEVATION

VIEW FROM ABOVE   LEVEL VIEW   VIEW FROM BELOW

RELATIVE SPEED OF VIEWER

FAST

SLOW   STATIC   FAST TRANSPARENT   SLOW TRANSLUCENT   STATIC OPAQUE

OBJECTIONABLE VIEWS

RECREATIONAL   RESIDENTIAL   SERVICE

HIGH VOLTAGE   INDUSTRIAL

PRIVACY CONTROL

It is necessary to differentiate between privacy control and screening. Screening allows free access through the landscape while inhibiting certain views. Privacy control secludes a particular area from its surroundings. Planting for screening is concealing unsightly views, so that the remainder of the landscape may be opened up to unassailed human view.

Planting for privacy control is secluding an area from its surrounding for special use. The same design concepts may be used either for privacy control or screening. The difference depends upon point-of-view and intent of either the viewer or the user.

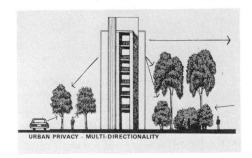

URBAN PRIVACY - MULTI-DIRECTIONALITY

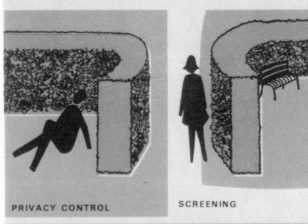

PRIVACY CONTROL   SCREENING

PRIVACY CONTROL PLANTING   SCREEN PLANTING

JUNK

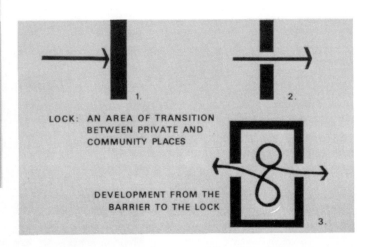

LOCK: AN AREA OF TRANSITION BETWEEN PRIVATE AND COMMUNITY PLACES

DEVELOPMENT FROM THE BARRIER TO THE LOCK

WATER EROSION

Water is the most common soil eroding agent. It erodes by the impact of raindrops on bare soil, thereby displacing the soil and causing it to mix with the water and to be carried away (splash erosion). As water runs off from saturated soils, it carries loose soil particles with it. Once surface soil is removed and held in suspension by moving water, it acts as a scouring agent, loosening and removing more soil.

Run-off erosion is classified four ways: sheet erosion, rill erosion, gully erosion, and slip erosion. Sheet erosion is the removal of the entire soil layer from an exposed site at once. As erosion continues on an exposed site, softer areas in the surface wash away faster, and small rills, or troughs, carrying water and soil downslope, are formed. As more water and soil flow down the rills, they jam together, become deeper and form gullies, which become deep and expansive if not controlled. Slip erosion is the release of water-saturated, unstable types of soil on steep slopes, sliding downslope as a mass.

Plants can be used to control and prevent water-caused soil erosion in at least three ways. Leaves and branches form canopies or blankets interrupting raindrops, thus reducing splash erosion. Roots form fibrous masses within the soil, holding it in place. Leaves and other dead parts of plants on the soil surface increase the organic material in the soil, loosening it and increasing its water rate absorption.

Splash erosion is controlled at different levels. Rain is first intercepted and held momentarily at a canopy level. Large trees are most effective for this purpose. However, raindrops intercepted at high canopy level regain some force unless they are intercepted again before reaching the soil. The second level at which they are intercepted is at the understory trees or large shrub level. Below either of these two levels, raindrops are intercepted by grasses, ferns, and low shrubs at ground level. The denser the foliage, the more efficient it will be in preventing splash erosion. Deciduous plants are more effective than conifers in preventing splash erosion, because of the spread of their leaf patterns. This is true only when they are in leaf.

Run-off erosion is best controlled by plants having shallow, fibrous roots, which spread throughout the soil. Their secondary roots and root hairs intercept and hold the soil in place. These root systems tend to loosen the soil and add organic matter, which increases the soil's permeability. The plant stems or stalks, particularly grasses, also control run-off by interferring with and intercepting the water as it flows across the ground.

Plants are more effective and attractive than most other paving and slope erosion control devices; therefore, they should be used when grading and changing the natural landforms.

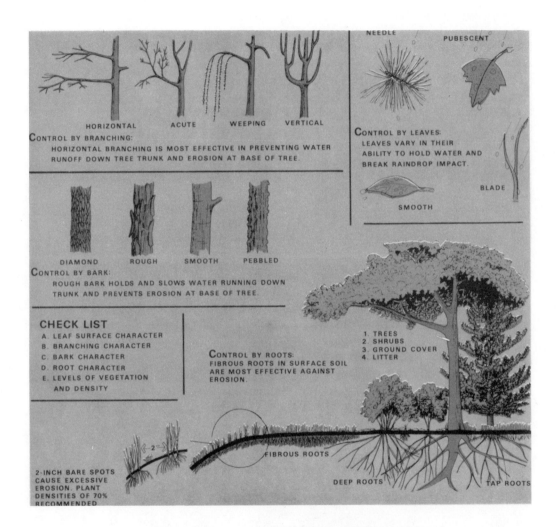

Plants Control Wind

Basically, plants control wind by obstruction, guidance, deflection, and filtration. The differentiation is not only one of the degree of effectiveness of plants, but of the techniques of placing plants. A number of references are available which refer to the ways in which plants control wind and their effectiveness in doing so. However, it must be remembered that plants as natural elements are not always absolutely predictable in their size, shape, and growth rate, and consequently in their absolute effectiveness.

Obstruction with trees, as with all other barriers, reduces windspeed by increasing the resistance to windflow. Coniferous and deciduous trees and shrubs used individually or in combination affect air movement.

Plants may be used in conjunction with landforms and architectural materials to alter the airflow over the landscape, and around or through buildings.

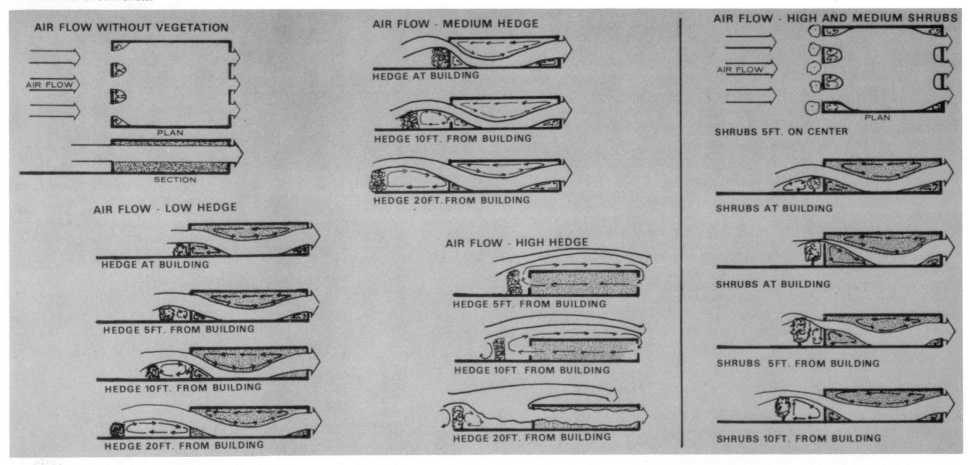

AIR FLOW WITHOUT VEGETATION

PLAN

SECTION

AIR FLOW - LOW HEDGE

HEDGE AT BUILDING

HEDGE 5FT. FROM BUILDING

HEDGE 10FT. FROM BUILDING

HEDGE 20FT. FROM BUILDING

AIR FLOW - MEDIUM HEDGE

HEDGE AT BUILDING

HEDGE 10FT. FROM BUILDING

HEDGE 20FT. FROM BUILDING

AIR FLOW - HIGH HEDGE

HEDGE 5FT. FROM BUILDING

HEDGE 10FT. FROM BUILDING

HEDGE 20FT. FROM BUILDING

AIR FLOW - HIGH AND MEDIUM SHRUBS

PLAN

SHRUBS 5FT. ON CENTER

SHRUBS AT BUILDING

SHRUBS AT BUILDING

SHRUBS 5FT. FROM BUILDING

SHRUBS 10FT. FROM BUILDING

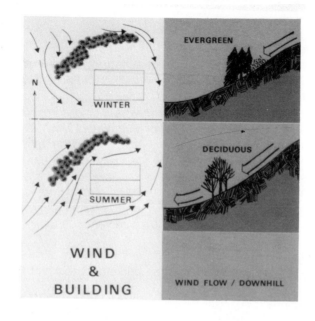

WIND
&
BUILDING

WIND FLOW / DOWNHILL

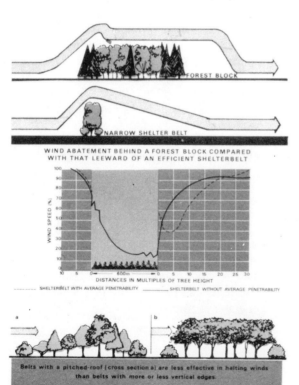

WIND ABATEMENT BEHIND A FOREST BLOCK COMPARED
WITH THAT LEEWARD OF AN EFFICIENT SHELTERBELT

DISTANCES IN MULTIPLES OF TREE HEIGHT

········· SHELTERBELT WITH AVERAGE PENETRABILITY ———— SHELTERBELT WITHOUT AVERAGE PENETRABILITY

Belts with a pitched-roof (cross section a) are less effective in halting winds
than belts with more or less vertical edges.

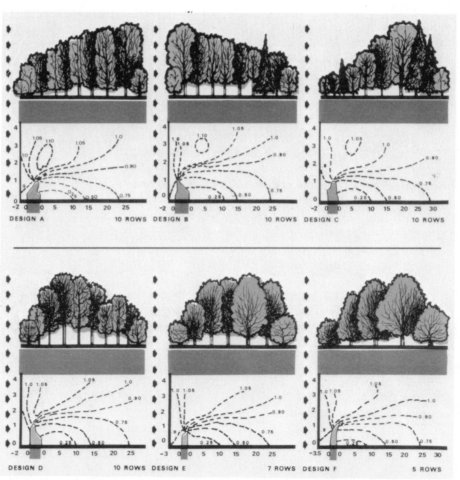

Following are descriptions of common lawn grasses and ground cover plants, including statements on how they grow, where they grow best, their requirements, and how to establish them.

GRASSES

Annual Bluegrass

Annual bluegrass (Poa annua) has little value as permanent turf because it dies suddenly when high temperatures occur in June, July, or August. It is used chiefly to overseed warm-season turf grasses during the winter months. Only small amounts of seed are available. It normally begins growth in late summer or early fall from seed produced earlier in the same year. It will often grow throughout the winter.

Annual bluegrass requires a cool, moist soil of low acidity and good fertility. It will survive under close mowing and shade. It produces large quantities of seed heads even when mowed as low as ¼ inch. It is a pest in many highly specialized turf areas, particularly golf courses.

Bahiagrass

Bahiagrass (Paspalum notatum) is a low-growing perennial that spreads by short, heavy runners. It grows best in the southern Coastal Plains region. It is established by seeding.

Common bahia, which has extremely coarse-textured leaves, is recommended for forage only. Paraguay and Pensacola, strains having finer-textured leaves than common bahia, are useful on large areas such as airfields, where good cover is more important than turf quality. These strains produce a dense, rather coarse and uneven turf, and are difficult to mow with an ordinary reel-type mower.

Bermudagrass

Many varieties or strains of bermudagrass (Cynodon dactylon) are sold. Each variety generally has a specialized use. Common bermuda, a coarse-textured grass, is the only variety for which seed is available. Other varieties are established vegetatively.

SOURCE: *Better Lawns* Home & Garden Bulletin No. 51, U.S. Dept. of Agriculture.

Bermudagrass is commonly grown in the southern part of the United States. Common seeded bermudagrass is not suited to the northern part of the United States, but vegetative plantings of cold-tolerant selections have survived as far north as Chicago and New York.

Varieties of bermudagrass used in lawns in the southern part of the United States include Tiflawn, Tufcote, Midway, Everglades No. 1, Ormond, Sunturf, Texturf 10, and Texturf 1F. Tiflawn is finer in texture than common bermudagrass, and it is deep green. It has outstanding disease-resistant qualities. Tiflawn is a vigorous grower and will form a heavy mat unless it is mowed closely and often. The texture of Everglades No. 1 is finer than that of Tiflawn, and the green is darker. This grass tends to grow prostrate. Ormond is coarser in texture and grows more upright than Everglades No. 1. Of the three varieties, Everglades No. 1 requires the least maintenance.

Varieties of bermudagrass that are used in high-quality lawns receiving maximum maintenance, and in golf course putting greens and fairways, include Tifgreen, Tiffine, Tifway, Bayshore, and Tifdwarf. These varieties are medium green. They are fine in texture.

A variety of bermudagrass called U–3 has been grown successfully in the vicinity of Philadelphia, Pa., Norfolk, Nebr., Cleveland, Ohio, and St. Louis, Mo. It is most widely used in the so-called "crabgrass belt," a roughly triangular region cornered on Philadelphia, St. Louis, and Richmond, Va. U–3 has finer blades than common bermudagrass. It resists disease and insect damage, and holds its color later into the fall when properly fertilized. It grows well in hot, humid weather.

Bermudagrass grows vigorously, spreading by aboveground runners and underground rootstalks. It often becomes a serious pest in flower beds and other cultivated areas. once established in those places it is difficult to eradicate.

Bermudagrass will not thrive under conditions of shade, poor drainage, high acidity, or low fertility. It requires frequent heavy applications of nitrogen in readily available form. Although drought resistant, it requires moderate amounts of water during dry periods. It must be clipped closely in order to form a dense turf.

Blue Gramagrass

Blue gramagrass (Bouteloua gracilis) is a low-growing, perennial grass that is adapted to a wide range of soil conditions throughout the Great Plains region. It is highly drought resistant. Its use as a turf grass is limited to cool, dry places where little or no irrigation water is available.

Blue gramagrass is a bunch-type grass that can be established easily from seed. Unless watered, it becomes semidormant and turns brown during severe drought periods. Seed produced in a given area should be used for plantings in that area only.

Buffalograss

Buffalograss *(Buchloe dactyloides)* is a stoloniferous perenial grass that is used commonly in sunny lawns of prairie homes in the Great Plains region. It is highly drought resistant. The grass is fined leaved and dense during the growing season. It turns from grayish green to the color of straw when growth stops in the fall. It grows best in welldrained, fairly heavy soils. Buffalograss can be established by sodding or seeding.

Canada Bluegrass

Canada bluegrass *(Poa compressa)* forms a thin, poor-quality, open turf. It can be used in seed mixtures on playgrounds, athletic fields, or similar areas.

Canada bluegrass will grow in sandy or gravelly soils of low fertility. It will not grow well in soils having high acidity or poor drainage. It will not withstand clipping below 1½ inches. It is extremely tough and resists wear.

Carpetgrass

Carpetgrass *(Axonopus compressus)* is a rapidly spreading stoloniferous perennial grass that produces a dense, compact turf under mowing, but is quite coarse textured. It can be established quickly by seeding or by sprigging or sodding. Seeding is the cheapest method.

Carpetgrass grows best in moist, sandy-loam soils or those that have a relatively high-moisture content throughout the year. It does not grow well in dry soils or in regions that remain dry during part of the growing season. It will thrive under limited fertilization in poor soils, but is extremely sensitive to lack of iron. It resists disease and insect damage, but does not tolerate salt water spray. It will withstand trampling and heavy wear.

Carpetgrass produces tall seed heads that are difficult to mow and make the lawn look rough or rugged. Mowing frequently with a rotary mower to a height of 1 inch is recommended.

Centipedegrass

Centipedegrass *(Eremochloa ephiruroides)* spreads rapidly by short creeping stems that form new plants at each node. It forms a dense, vigorous turf that is highly resistant to weed invasion. It is usually established vegetatively; some seed is available.

Centipedegrass is considered the best low-maintenance lawn grass in the southern part of the United States. It requires less mowing, less watering, and less fertilizing than other southern lawn grasses. It is seldom damaged by disease or insects, but may be severely damaged by salt water spray. It is sensitive to the lack of iron. An annual application of a complete fertilizer will improve the quality of centipedegrass lawns. Although it is drought resistant, centipedegrass should be watered during dry periods.

Centipedegrass should not be planted in farm lawns; it may escape into pastures and destroy their grazing value.

Colonial Bentgrass

Colonial bentgrass *(Agrostis tenuis)* is a fine-textured, tufted-type grass with few creeping stems and rhizomes. It forms a dense turf when heavily seeded and closely mowed.

Colonial bentgrass is used chiefly in high-quality lawns and putting greens. It is more expensive to maintain than ordinary lawn grasses. It is popular in the New England States, Washington, and Oregon.

Colonial bentgrass requires fertile soil and frequent fertilizer applications. It must be watered during dry periods. It is susceptible to a wide variety of diseases. It must be mowed closely; when cut about ¾ inch it becomes fluffy and forms an undesirable spongy mat.

Several strains of colonial bentgrass are sold. Highland is the hardiest variety. It is bluish green. It grows moderately fast. Another variety, Astoria, is bright green. It is not as drought resistant or as aggressive as Highland. Although Astoria requires more care than Highland, it produces a better-quality lawn if properly managed. Other colonial bentgrasses suitable for lawns include New Zealand browntop and some strains of German bentgrass.

REGIONS OF GRASS ADAPTATIONS

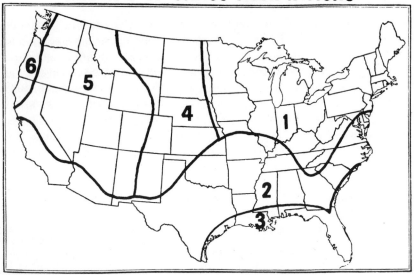

U.S. DEPARTMENT OF AGRICULTURE

Climatic regions of the U.S. in which the following grasses are suitable for lawns: Region 1. Common Kentucky bluegrass, Merion Kentucky bluegrass, red fescue, and Colonial bentgrass. Tall fescue, bermudagrass, and zoysiagrass in southern portion of the region. Region 2. Bermudagrass and zoysiagrass. Centipedegrass, carpetgrass, and St. Augustinegrass in southern portion of the region with tall fescue and Kentucky bluegrass in some northern areas. Region 3. St. Augustinegrass, bermudagrass, zoysiagrass, carpetgrass, and bahiagrass. Region 4. Nonirrigated areas: Crested wheatgrass, buffalograss, and blue gramagrass. Irrigated areas: Kentucky bluegrass and red fescue. Region 5. Nonirrigated areas: Crested wheatgrass. Irrigated areas: Kentucky bluegrass and red fescue. Region 6. Colonial bentgrass and Kentucky bluegrass.

Creeping Bentgrass

Creeping bentgrass *(Agrostis palustris)* is not often used in home lawns, but it is used extensively in golf course putting greens throughout the United States. It has profuse creeping stems that produce roots and stems at every node, and it develops a dense sod. It must be mowed closely (3/16 to 3/8 inch), brushed regularly, and topdressed periodically to prevent formation of an undesirable mat or thatch.

Creeping bentgrass requires soils having high fertility, low acidity, good drainage, and high water-holding capacity. A regular program of fertilization, watering, and disease control must be followed to maintain good-quality turf.

Varieties available include Seaside, which is established by seeding and is used in golf greens along the west coast; Penncross, a seeded type that is available for specialized turf areas; and several strains that have been selected from established greens and are established vegetatively — Arlington, Collins, Cohansey, Washington, Congressional, Toronto, Norbeck, Pennlu, and Old Orchard.

Crested Wheatgrass

Crested wheatgrass *(Agropyron cristatum)* is a perennial bunchgrass. It thrives in most soils in the central and northern Great Plains and Intermountain regions. It is recommended in dry, cool areas of those regions where irrigation water is not available. It is established by seeding.

Crested wheatgrass will withstand long, dry periods and heavy wear if not cut too closely. It makes most of its growth in the spring and fall; it becomes semidormant and turns brown in the hot summer months.

Japanese Lawngrass

Japanese lawngrass *(Zoysia japonica)* is a low-growing perennial that spreads by aboveground runners and shallow rootstocks. It forms a dense turf that resists weed invasion and disease and insect damage.

Japanese lawngrass grows best in the region south of a line drawn from Philadelphia, Pa., westward to San Francisco, Calif. It will survive in the region north of that line but its use there, except in some localities, is impracticable because of the short summer growing season. The grass turns the color of straw when the first killing frost occurs in the fall and it remains off-color until warm spring weather.

Common Japanese lawngrass is coarse in texture. It is somewhat undesirable for home lawn use but is excellent for large areas such as airfields and playgrounds. Meyer zoysia, a selection of common Japanese lawngrass, is more desirable than Japanese lawngrass for home lawns. It is more vigorous, retains its color later in the fall, and regains it earlier in the spring. Meyer zoysia sod is available from a number of nurseries. There is no seed.

Although Japanese lawngrass will survive in soils of low fertility, it makes best growth when given liberal applications of complete fertilizers having a high nitrogen content. It is relatively drought tolerant in the humid regions. It is highly resistant to wear and will withstand close clipping.

Japanese lawngrass may be established by sprig planting the stems, by spot sodding, or by seeding. Three to four growing seasons are generally required to get complete coverage.

Emerald zoysia is a hybrid between Japanese lawngrass and mascarene grass that has proven superior to Meyer zoysia in the southern part of the United States. The grass is fine leafed, dense growing and dark green in color.

Kentucky Bluegrass

Kentucky bluegrass *(Poa pratensis)* is a hardy, long-lived, sodforming grass that spreads by underground rootstocks. It is one of the most widely used lawn grasses in the United States. It is the basic lawn grass in cool, humid regions and in cool, dry regions where adequate irrigation water is available. It is propagated entirely by seed.

Common Kentucky bluegrass will not withstand poor drainage or high acidity. It grows best in heavy, well-drained soils of good fertility that are neutral or nearly neutral in reaction. In soils of low fertility, liberal applications of nitrogen, phosphorus, and potash are needed. Bluegrass is highly drought resistant; it has the ability to go into a semidormant condition during hot summer months.

Common Kentucky bluegrass may be injured if mowed shorter than 1½ inches. It will not tolerate heavy shade. Because it becomes established slowly, common

Kentucky bluegrass is often planted with faster-growing grasses that provide cover and prevent weed invasion while the bluegrass is becoming established.

Merion

Merion Kentucky bluegrass has proved superior to common Kentucky bluegrass in many regions of the United States. It can be clipped more closely, and is less susceptible to leafspot disease than common Kentucky bluegrass, although it is susceptible to rust. Merion Kentucky bluegrass also appears to be more heat and drought tolerant, more vigorous, and more resistant to weed invasion than common Kentucky bluegrass. For best growth, it requires greater fertility and more maintenance than common Kentucky bluegrass. It responds well to high applications of nitrogen.

Among other varieties of Kentucky bluegrass found commercially are: Newport, Park, Delta, Pennstar, Windsor, Prato, and Fylking.

Kikuyugrass

Kikuyugrass *(Pennisetum clandestinum)* is a perennial grass that spreads by coarse underground rootstocks. It produces a coarse-textured spongy or matted turf that is 3 to 5 inches thick and difficult to mow at lawn height. Its use has been confined to localities in coastal California, where it is now considered a pest and is being eradicated. It is not recommended for lawn use.

Manilagrass

Manilagrass *(Zoysia matrella)* is closely related to Japanese lawngrass and has many similar characteristics. It is stoloniferous, and forms a dense carpetlike turf that resists weeds, wear, disease, and insect damage. Manilagrass is adapted to the southern part of the United States.

Manilagrass is sensitive to highly acid soils. It responds well to liberal applications of nitrogenous fertilizer. It turns brown when the first killing occurs and remains dormant until spring. It is established by sprigging or spot sodding.

Mascarenegrass

Mascarenegrass *(Zoysia tenuifolia)* is a low-growing stoloniferous grass that is adapted to very few locations in the United States. Its growth requirements with respect to moisture, nutrients, and soil are about the same as those for manilagrass, but it is not as winter hardy as manilagrass or Japanese lawngrass. It becomes sodbound and humps up as it grows older, which encourages weed invasion. Limited amounts of mascarenegrass sod are available in Florida and California.

Meadow Fescue

Meadow fescue *(Festuca elatior)* is a hardy, short-lived perennial that is used primarily for pasture and hay. It does not form a solid sod. It grows best in heavy, moist soils, and will withstand extremely wet soils. An excellent seed producer, it is often found in poor-quality lawn seed mixtures.

Orchardgrass

Orchardgrass *(Dactylis glomerata)* is a tall-growing, perennial bunch grass that forms coarse-textured tufts but never a solid turf. It does not grow well in soils having high acidity or poor drainage, but it resists drought and tolerates shade. It can withstand low fertility. Seed is abundant, and it is sometimes used in poor-quality lawn seed mixtures.

Red Fescue and Chewings Fescue

Red fescue *(Festuca rubra)* and Chewings fescue *(F. rubra var. commutata)* rate next to Kentucky bluegrass as the most popular lawn grasses in the cool humid regions of the United States. Red fescue spreads slowly by underground rootstocks. Chewings fescue is a bunch-type grower. Both are established by seeding.

Both fescues are used extensively in lawn seed mixtures. They grow well in shaded areas, and they tolerate high acidity. They require good drainage but will grow in poor, droughty soils.

Red fescue and Chewings fescue are fine textured. They have bristlelike leaves that stand upright. When seeded heavily they form a dense sod that resists wear. They heal slowly when injured by insects, disease, or other means. Mowing consistently below 1½ inches can cause severe damage. The grasses grow slowly.

Improved strains of red fescue on the market include Pennlawn, Illahee, and Rainier. No improved strains of Chewings fescue are on the market.

Redtop

Under lawn conditions, redtop *(Agrostis alba)* is a short-lived perennial. It seldom lives more than two seasons when closely mowed. It is commonly used in lawn seed mixtures in the northern temperate regions of the United States to provide quick cover while more permanent grasses are developing. It is often seeded alone in temporary lawns. In the southern part of the United States it is used for winter overseeding of bermudagrass to provide year-round green color.

Heavy seeding helps overcome redtop's tendency to develop a coarse open-type turf. Redtop tolerates a wide range of soil and climatic conditions, including temperature extremes. It grows in soils that are highly acid and poorly drained. It resists drought and has a low fertility requirement.

Rescuegrass

Rescuegrass *(Bromus catharticus)* is a short-lived perennial bunch grass that grows best in fertile soils in humid regions where the winters are mild. It is sometimes used in the southern part of the United States as a winter grass in large bermudagrass plantings, such as golf course fairways.

Rough Bluegrass

Rough bluegrass *(Poa trivialis)*, also known as roughstalk bluegrass, is a shade-tolerant perennial that is useful in lawns only in the extreme northern part of the United States. It is established by seeding. It is seriously injured by hot, dry weather. It has leaves of the same texture as Kentucky bluegrass. The stems and leaves lie flat, giving the turf a glassy appearance. Rough stalk meadowgrass is lighter green than Kentucky bluegrass. It spreads by short aboveground runners.

Roughstalk meadowgrass has a shallow root system, and will not withstand heavy wear. It should be used in shady areas where the traffic is not heavy.

Ryegrass

Italian or annual ryegrass *(Lolium multiflorum)* and perennial ryegrass *(Lolium perenne)* are propagated entirely by seed that is produced in the Pacific Northwest, or imported. Much of the ryegrass used for lawns in the United States is a mixture of annual, perennial, and intermediate types.

Many commercial lawn seed mixtures contain too much ryegrass; the ryegrass competes with the permanent grass seedlings for moisture and nutrients. On sloping areas, it is sometimes advisable to include a small amount of ryegrass in the lawn seed mixture to help prevent soil erosion. The use of perennial ryegrass in lawn seed mixtures often results in ragged-appearing lawns that are difficult to mow. Coarse clumps of ryegrass may persist in the lawn for several years.

In the southern part of the United States annual or common ryegrass is used for winter overseeding of bermudagrass in lawns, and on golf greens and tees.

St. Augustinegrass

St. Augustinegrass *(Stenotaphrum secundatum)* is the No. 1 shade grass of the southernmost States. It is a creeping perennial; it spreads by long runners that produce short, leafy branches. It can be grown successfully south of Augusta, Ga., and Birmingham, Ala., and westward to the coastal regions of Texas. It is established vegetatively. Seed is not available.

St. Augustinegrass will withstand salt water spray. It grows best in moist soils of good fertility. It produces good turf in the muck soils of Florida. Liberal applications of high-nitrogen fertilizers are necessary, especially in sandy soils.

St. Augustinegrass can be seriously damaged by chinch bugs, and it is susceptible to armyworm damage and several turf diseases.

Tall Fescue

Tall fescue *(Festuca arundinacea)* is a tall-growing perennial bunch grass that has coarse, dense basal leaves and a strong, fibrous root system. It is also used for pasture. It is established by seeding.

Because of their wear-resistant qualities, two improved strains of tall fescue, Kentucky 31 fescue and Alta fescue, are used often on play areas, athletic fields, airfields, service yards, and other areas where a heavy, tough turf is needed rather than a fine-textured turf.

Tall fescue will grow in wet or dry, acid or alkaline soils, but it grows best in well-drained, fertile soils. It will withstand a moderate amount of shade.

Timothy

Timothy *(Phleum pratense)* is a coarse perennial bunch grass that grows best in the northern humid regions of the United States where its main use is hay for livestock. It has no use as a lawn grass, but it is often found in poor-quality lawn seed mixtures. It is sometimes suitable in nonuse areas to provide cover.

Weeping Lovegrass

Weeping lovegrass *(Eragrostis curvula)* is a vigorous perennial bunch grass that grows best in the southern Great Plains region. It is an excellent erosion-control plant on nonuse areas but is not good for home lawns because it will not withstand frequent close mowing. It grows in any type of soil but grows best in sandy loams.

Velvet Bentgrass

Velvet bentgrass *(Agrostis canina),* the finest textured of the bentgrasses, is used mainly in high-quality lawns and putting greens in the New England States and the Pacific Northwest. It forms an extremely dense turf from creeping stems. It can be established by seeding or by vegetative planting.

Velvet bentgrass is adapted to a wide range of soil conditions but makes its best growth on well-drained, fertile soils having low acidity. It is not as aggressive as creeping bentgrass and is slow to recover from all types of injury. It requires close mowing, regular brushing, and periodic topdressing. A regular program of fertilizing, watering, and disease control is necessary to maintain high-quality turf.

GROUND COVER PLANTS

Vines and other low-growing plants can often be planted on areas where it is difficult to establish or maintain satisfactory grass cover. Such areas include heavily shaded places, steep banks, rough and rocky areas, terraces, and drainage ditches.

Dichondra

Dichondra (*Dichondra repens, D. Carolinensis*) is a perennial that forms a low, dense mat under favorable conditions. It can be established by seeding or by vegetative planting. Dichondra is native to the Coastal Plain States from Virginia to Texas, but it is not considered a desirable lawn plant except in central and southern California.

Dichondra is closely related to the milkweed and the morning-glory. Its leaves are pale green, and kidney shaped. It grows best in heavy soils. The plant does not require a high fertility level, but it requires large amounts of water. It will grow in partial shade, but is stemmy and undesirable and will crowd out all other vegetation, including bermudagrass.

English Ivy

English ivy (*Hedera lelix*) is a hardy trailing evergreen vine that thrives in shaded areas but will grow in direct sunlight. It develops a very dense mat that should be pruned occasionally. English ivy is particularly useful on steep banks or around the base of trees.

Japanese Snakebeard (Mondo)

Japanese snakebeard (*Ophiopogon japonica*), or Lilyturf, is a bunch-growing member of the lily family. It grows 8 to 12 inches high, and bears purple to white flowers. It is used in the southern part of the United States under trees in poor soils. It is propagated vegetatively, and should be set close together because it spreads slowly.

Japanese Spurge

Japanese spurge (*Pachysandra terminalis*), or Pachysandra, is a low-growing evergreen plant that spreads by suckers. The plants are about 8 inches high. They have dense wedge-shaped leaves and bear inconspicuous greenish-white flowers. They are established by division or by cuttings. Plants should be set 1 foot apart.

Japanese spurge is used in the Eastern United States from New England to Georgia. It is particularly recommended in Virginia, North Carolina, South Carolina, Kentucky, and Tennessee.

Lippia

Lippia (*Lippia canescens*) is used as a substitute for grass throughout the Southwest, particularly in Arizona. Lippia leaves are dark green. They are oblong, and seldom more than 1 inch long. Lippia will not survive temperatures below freezing, and may be injured by temperatures somewhat higher than freezing. It is also susceptible to nematode damage. Lippia has been known to crowd out bermudagrass when mowed regularly. It is established by vegetative planting.

Partridge Berry

Partridge berry (*Mitchella repens*) is a low-growing creeping evergreen that is native to the Southeastern United States. It grows well in shaded areas having moist, fertile soils. Its leaves are small, glossy, and round. It produces pinkish-white flowers in the spring; these are followed by scarlet fruit in the fall and winter.

Partridge berry is established by cuttings from vegetative material that can be found along streambanks and in wooded areas in the southeastern part of the country.

Periwinkle, Common

Common periwinkle (*Vinca minor*), or myrtle, is a hardy low-growing evergreen that spreads by creeping stems. It has small, dark-green, glossy leaves. It develops violet blue flowers.

Common periwinkle will form a dense mat that shades out weeds and grasses. It grows best in moist soils that are high in organic matter. It is partial to dense shade, but it will grow satisfactorily under dry conditions in direct sunlight. Periwinkle is established by cuttings and can be planted any time when the soil is not frozen.

White Clover

White clover (*Trifolium repens*) is regarded by some as a desirable ground cover plant in lawns. It is regarded by others as a pest.

Grass growing in proximity to white clover may be benefited by the nitrogen-fixing ability of the nodules on the clover roots. The plant often grows in patches of varying size, giving the lawn an uneven appearance. Some persons object to the white flower the plants form, and to the fact that it attracts bees. Another disadvantage is that white clover disappears during hot, dry weather. Contrary to claims made, white clover will not compete successfully with crabgrass.

CEMENT CONCRETE CURBS

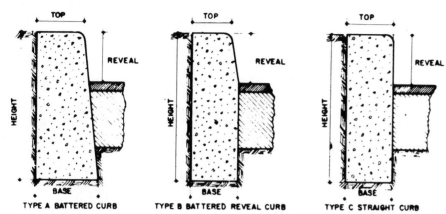

TYPE A BATTERED CURB   TYPE B BATTERED REVEAL CURB   TYPE C STRAIGHT CURB

CEMENT CONCRETE VALLEY GUTTER

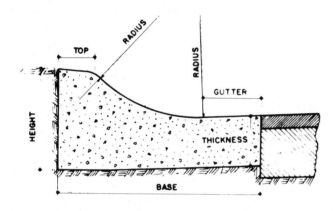

CEMENT CONCRETE ROLLED CURB AND GUTTER

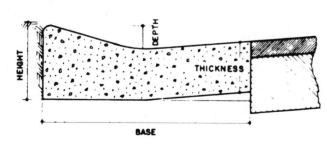

SOURCE: Federal Housing Administration, Data Sheets, 100, 200, 250, 300, 500, 600

CEMENT CONCRETE CURBS AND GUTTERS

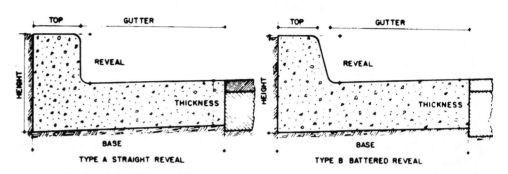

TYPE A STRAIGHT REVEAL   TYPE B BATTERED REVEAL

BITUMINOUS CURB AND GUTTER
COLD LAID BITUMINOUS CONCRETE (PLANT MIXED)

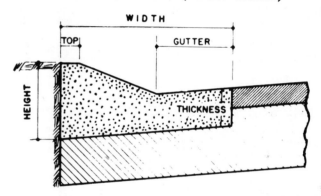

STONE CURB
GRANITE, MEDINA SANDSTONE OR BLUESTONE

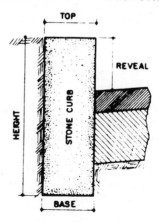

FLAGSTONE PAVING

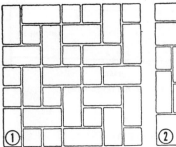

① RECTANGULAR (Limited Sizes)

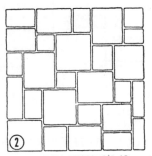

② RANDOM RECTANGULAR

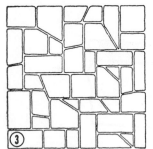

③ RANDOM SEMI-IRREGULAR

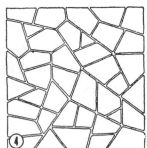

④ RANDOM IRREGULAR (Fitted)

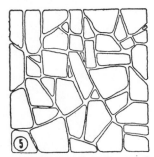

⑤ RANDOM IRREGULAR (Not Fitted)

The paving of walks and terraces with flagstones furnishes a desirable transition from the manmade geometrical formality of the building to the freedom and naturalness of the lawn and garden. Bluestone, limestone, stratified natural stones from the vicinity, cast stone and slate are commonly used materials. For terraces, it is important that the stones have level surfaces and that they be laid on concrete if furniture is to be used —see *Detail A* on following *Data Sheet*. The method shown in *Detail C* on the following *Data Sheet* may eventually result in tipping and movement of the stones out of level.

GARDEN WALKS

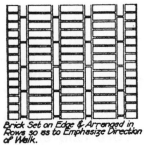

Brick Set on Edge & Arranged in Rows so as to Emphasize Direction of Walk.

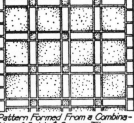

Pattern Formed From a Combination of Brick & Square Tile.

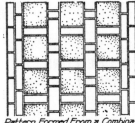

Pattern Formed From a Combination of Brick & Square Tile.

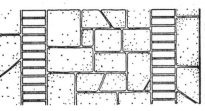

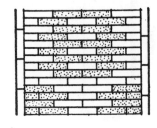

Basket-Weave Pattern of Brick & Small Inserts of Broken Brick or Small Square Tile.

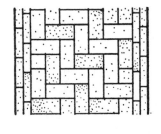

Basket-Weave Pattern Frequently Used in Spanish Gardens.

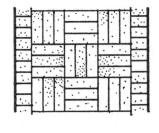

Basket-Weave Pattern of Brick Laid Flat & Diagonally.

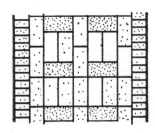

A great variety of patterns & color schemes are possible in the combination of brick & stone.

Wide Flagstone Walk or Terrace Pavement with Border of Brick.

BRICK PATTERNS FOR WALKS

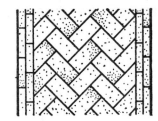

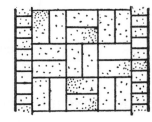

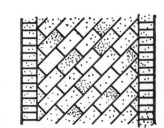

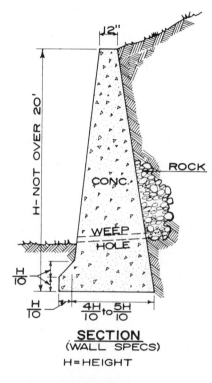

12"

H-NOT OVER 20'

ROCK

CONC.

WEEP
HOLE

H
10

H
10

4H   5H
10 to 10

SECTION
(WALL SPECS)

H=HEIGHT

CONCRETE

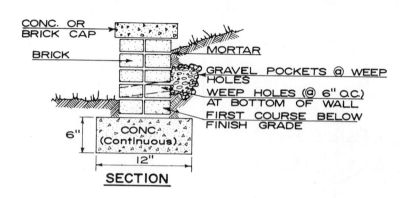

CONC. OR
BRICK CAP

BRICK

MORTAR

GRAVEL POCKETS @ WEEP
HOLES

WEEP HOLES (@ 6" O.C.)
AT BOTTOM OF WALL

FIRST COURSE BELOW
FINISH GRADE

6"

CONC.
(Continuous)

12"

SECTION

BRICK

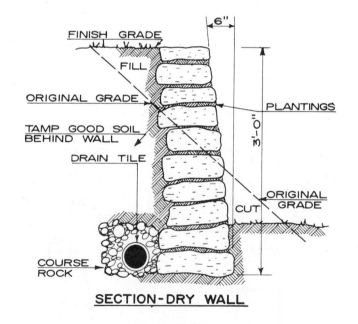

FINISH GRADE

6"

FILL

ORIGINAL GRADE

PLANTINGS

TAMP GOOD SOIL
BEHIND WALL

3'-0"

DRAIN TILE

ORIGINAL
GRADE

CUT

COURSE
ROCK

SECTION-DRY WALL

STONE

ASHLAR   RUBBLE

TYPES OF STONEWORK

SOURCE: Landscape Development, Dept. of the Interior, Littleton, Colorado.

Wood pole lines

Steel tower lines

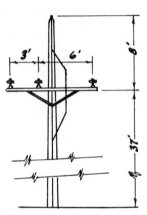

Average span 300'

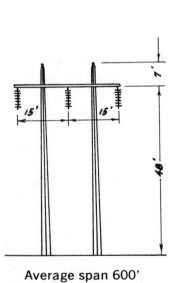

Average span 600'

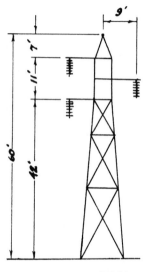

Average span 700'

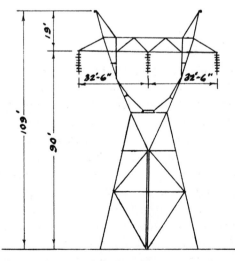

Average span 900'

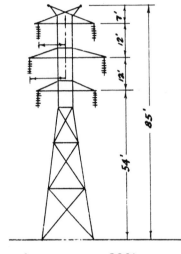

Average span 800'

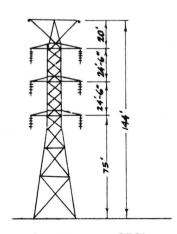

Average span 850'

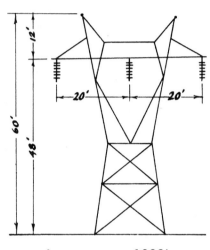

Average span 1000'

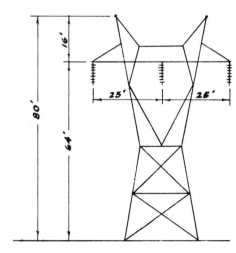

Average span 1000'

LIGHTING POLE SPACING

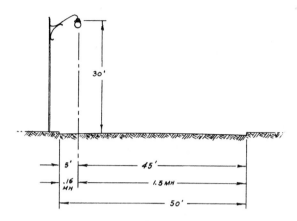

Staggered longitudinal spacing

Typical layout of luminaires

SOURCE: American Standard Practice for Roadway Lighting, American Standards Association, New York, New York, 1963.

HYDRANT SPACING

The choice of hydrants for public service is based on the same consider-ations as the choice of hydrants for private fire service. One point in which private and public practice may differ is that public hydrants are generally equipped with a gate valve between the hydrant and the main so as to make repairs to the hydrant possible without shutting down the street main.

In general, hydrants should be placed with consideration to their possible use. Hose lines more than 400 or 500 ft long result in delay and undue pressure losses in hose lines. Therefore, hydrants should be distributed not more than 300 or 400 ft from the buildings to be protected. Where it is the fire department practice to use hose lines direct from hydrants, to prevent undue friction losses, lines must be kept shorter than in the case of lines from pumpers, and hydrants must be spaced about 100 ft closer together.

A rough rule to follow is to place one hydrant near each street intersec-tion and to set intermediate hydrants where the distance between intersec-tions exceeds 350 to 400 ft.

A street lighting pole is the assembly of a shaft and bracket or equipment used for supporting a street lighting luminaire and other appurtenances. Because of the divided opinion concerning the value of the psychological effect of white-way street lighting, there are, in general, two types of street light poles available for use: the upright pole and the pendant pole. The upright pole acts as a strut supporting and luminaire while the pendant pole has single or double brackets which support the luminaire. Various types and heights of upright and pendant poles are available for most any condition. However, the trend is towards taller, streamlined units with supporting brackets of the type and length necessary to place the luminaires over the area of the roadway to be lighted. Practical limitations of present-day mechanical equipment used in lamp replacement and maintenance work has for the present, standardized the pendant pole heights generally within the range of 25 to 35 ft. Such heights must be coordinated with the proper lamp type, pole spacing, mounting height ratio and transverse location.

While the primary function of the street lighting brackets or mast arm is to position the luminaire where it will render the most effective nighttime service, adequate strength and pleasing daytime appearance are important factors. The brackets and mast arms are available in steel, aluminum or concrete. Both single and twin-unit brackets for mounting the luminaire are available for the requirements of the installation. Twin brackets are sometimes used on the center esplanades for parkway and freeway lighting on wide divided streets, while single brackets remain the standard for the majority of the installations. Common bracket sizes vary from 4 ft to 16 ft in nominal length and are of horizontal or upsweep design to suit the individual luminaire requirements. On some upsweep brackets, it is necessary to use one and sometimes two sway braces. With the introduction of fluorescent street lighting there are indications that the bracket and luminaire are becoming an integral unit.

With the varying amounts of upsweep encountered in the different bracket styles, no set rules for the attachment of the luminaire to the bracket can be established. However, a cardinal point to be considered during assembly is to have the axis of the luminaire perpendicular to the surface to be lighted except where the type of illumination pattern desired is achieved through varying the axis angle.

The engineer will find that the planning of street light systems is enhanced by the wide selection of poles and brackets available which makes it relatively easy to design an installation of functional beauty to best serve the needs of the community.

SOURCE: American Standard Practice for Roadway Lighting, American Standards Association, New York, New York, 1963.

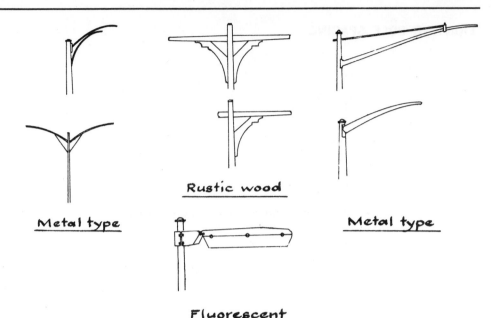

Rustic wood

Metal type

Fluorescent

Metal type

Type Pole	Description	Advantages	Disadvantages
Aluminum	made from aluminum alloy	resistant to corrosion little maintenance light weight relative easy installation lower cost	less durable and rugged low tensile strength for hanging pendants
steel	made with alloy steels	highly durable and rugged high tensile strength for hanging pendants	needs painting against corrosion relatively heavy
concrete, pre-stressed	made by a centrifugal machine process of pre-stressed, reinforced concrete with marble or crushed granite aggregate	little or no maintenance no corrosion highly durable and rugged	relatively heavy, requires heavy equipment for installation difficult to attach signs or other appurtenances
wood	made from hewn western red cedar, turned cedar, or pine	rustic character little or no initial maintenance	must be fully creosoted or pentachloro-phenol treated for proper wear solid post does not permit interior wiring or other equipment

OVERHEAD CONSTRUCTION-SERVICE POLES

Line Poles—Standard   In a large majority of light locations, the ordinary standard line poles can be used for the support of the street lighting luminaire. Usually these poles also carry crossarms, supporting distribution feeders, municipal wires, and telephone conductors. Although interference is frequently experienced, street lighting luminaires can ordinarily be installed properly, provided the proper mast arm or bracket is used. Care must be taken to provide proper mounting height and to place the luminaire so as to avoid tree interference.

Nonline Poles   Nonline poles to support street lighting luminaires will be installed in streets wherever necessary. Such poles will be required when distribution circuits are run on line poles in alleys or along the rear of lot lines. In some cases the street light supply wires are run from the line poles to each nonline pole supporting a street lighting luminaire, thereby eliminating wires running parallel to the streets. This enhances the appearance of the street lighting system. (See Fig. 1)

Shaved Poles for Better Appearance   Where appearance is considered especially important, choice of pole may be limited to:

1. Specially selected straight poles.
2. Certain species of wood with superior decay resistance without preservative treatment.
3. Special preservative treatment such as napherate (green-salt), water-borne preservatives, or general spirit soluble agents, these treatments to provide cleanliness and/or ready adherence of paint.

Shaving may be specified for neat appearance. Poles are classified by butt and top diameter. Class of pole is determined by the load to be carried.

In the interest of economy, wood poles are in general use in many of our smaller cities in lieu of more expensive poles made of concrete, steel, or aluminum.

Some companies have found it economical to return their old line poles to the pole yard where they rotary shave the pole, leaving only the hard wood center. This gives a usable pole for very little cost.

Available Pole Space   Many street lighting installations do not require additional investment for new poles. If the existing service poles have proper spacing, they may be used to support the street lighting luminaires.

Pole space can be conserved by straddling the secondary wires with a mast arm installation.

Typical Situations   Brackets or mast arms used to support the luminaires should have sufficient rise so the luminaire is suspended properly over the street for the best lighting.

Local Rules and Practices   Local rules and safety practices of utility companies sometimes prohibit the installation of street light brackets and luminaires on service poles be-cause of the hazard to maintenance personnel. In some states there are regulations prohibiting the installation of street lights on poles carrying high-voltage distribution feeders. Local and state regulations concerning this matter should be investigated. If necessary, separate poles may be installed for the street lights.

UNDERGROUND CONSTRUCTION

The Upright Ornamental   The old type upright ornamental street lighting poles became obsolete in the late 1930's and are consequently not recommended for modern lighting. With the old type upright poles, much of the light was lost, inasmuch as it was not directed to the street surfaces.

Modern Poles for Underground Construction—General Requirements

Mounting Height   The mounting height of luminaires will depend on the lamp size and type of luminaires that are being used. The Illuminating Engineering Society's standards for mounting heights should be rigidly followed. Mounting heights must be higher with the modern-type luminaires. It is considered permissible with lamp sizes varying from 2,500 to 6,000 lumens to use a mounting height of 25 feet. With the use of 10,000 lumens or more, mounting heights of 30 to 35 feet are desirable. Lower mounting heights are permissible on streets where the brightness contrast is relatively low and reflectance from surrounding surfaces is not too objectionable.

Mechanical Strength   Present-day manufacturers of non-wood poles for street lighting have designed them to withstand wind velocities up to 101 miles per hour. Manufacturers should be consulted where unusual circumstances arise. Street lighting engineers and architects, when designing modern lighting systems, are giving increased consideration to aesthetics. In the design of modern street lighting systems the 11-gauge and 7-gauge tubular standards are commonly used.

Acceptable Aesthetic Design   There are in existence many custom-built street light pole installations, where the poles have been designed to blend with the structures upon which they are supported. Ornamental street lighting poles have been designed to support streamlined luminaires.

The modern trend is toward the use of plain, functional units.

Special Pole Requirements for Underground Construction

Sub-Bases for Bolt-Down Posts   In the installation of bases for bolt-down ornamental poles, consideration must be given to the type of pole. Figure 3 is an illustration of a typical base. Consideration must also be given to the type of soil. Sandy soils require a heavier base than heavy soils. Supports for 11-gauge steel pole standards may have a base depth of around 5½ feet, while 3-gauge steel poles may have a base depth of up to 7 feet. Suitable grounding must be provided as required by code specifications. Conduit with a 90-degree bend is ordinarily provided as an inlet for the street light cables.

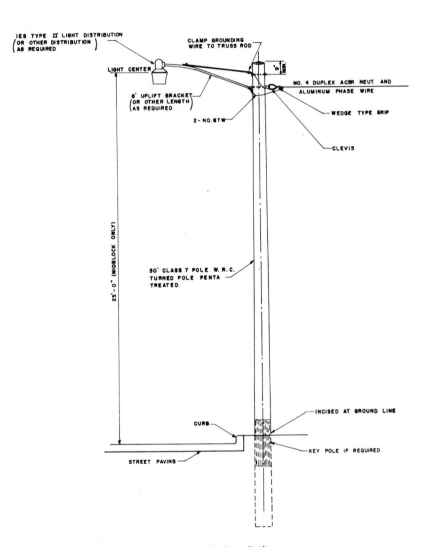

IES TYPE II LIGHT DISTRIBUTION
(OR OTHER DISTRIBUTION
AS REQUIRED)

LIGHT CENTER

CLAMP GROUNDING
WIRE TO TRUSS ROD

"D" MIN.

NO. 4 DUPLEX ACSR NEUT. AND
ALUMINUM PHASE WIRE

8' UPLIFT BRACKET
(OR OTHER LENGTH
AS REQUIRED)

WEDGE TYPE GRIP

2- NO. 8TW

CLEVIS

25'-0" (MIDBLOCK ONLY)

30' CLASS 7 POLE W.R.C.
TURNED POLE PENTA
TREATED

INCISED AT GROUND LINE

CURB

KEY POLE IF REQUIRED

STREET PAVING

Non-line pole installation.

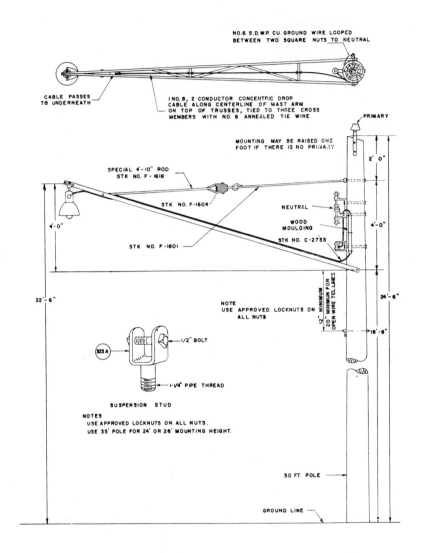

NO.6 S.D.W.P. CU. GROUND WIRE LOOPED
BETWEEN TWO SQUARE NUTS TO NEUTRAL

CABLE PASSES
TO UNDERNEATH

NO. 8, 2 CONDUCTOR CONCENTRIC DROP
CABLE ALONG CENTERLINE OF MAST ARM
ON TOP OF TRUSSES, TIED TO THREE CROSS
MEMBERS WITH NO. 8 ANNEALED TIE WIRE.

PRIMARY

MOUNTING MAY BE RAISED ONE
FOOT IF THERE IS NO PRIMARY

SPECIAL 4'-10" ROD
STK NO. F-1618

STK NO. F-1604

NEUTRAL

WOOD
MOULDING

STK NO. F-1601

STK NO. C-2733

4'-0"

2'- 0"

4'- 0"

22'- 6"

NOTE
USE APPROVED LOCKNUTS ON
ALL NUTS

12" MINIMUM
20" MINIMUM FOR
OPEN WIRE TELLURES

24'- 6"

18'- 6"

323 A

1/2" BOLT

1-1/4" PIPE THREAD

SUSPENSION STUD

NOTES
USE APPROVED LOCKNUTS ON ALL NUTS.
USE 35' POLE FOR 24' OR 26' MOUNTING HEIGHT.

30 FT. POLE

GROUND LINE

**Mast arm construction. Standard 14-foot trussweld mast arm on 30-foot pole, rigid
mounting of fixture, 4-foot upsweep mounting, for multiple service only.**

Available Poles for Underground Construction Areas

Steel

Design.   Steel poles have been, for years, very popular and widely accepted for all types of lighting applications. Steel poles have the advantage of strength, rigidity, and durability.

Some ornamental installations have involved the use of intricately designed standards. The more popular modern steel poles are tubular in shape and of simple design.

Modern street lighting systems utilize a considerable number of davit-type poles. Davit-type poles are available with tilts ranging from 5 to 25 degrees. Tilt depends on the width of the street and illumination intensity required.

Construction.   Steel poles are manufactured with either circular or octagonal cross sections. The present trend in design and construction of poles is toward larger diameters. This trend is due largely to longer brackets and heavier luminaires. The poles used should be in accordance with EEI and NEMA standards.

Installation.   Steel street light poles are usually bolted to a concrete base.

Aluminum

Design.   Some aluminum poles manufactured correspond in general appearance to the popular steel designs, while others represent an entirely new structural concept. The brushed satin finish exterior surface of aluminum poles is pleasing to the eye. Streamlining of brackets is often employed to harmonize their appearance with the gracefully tapered pole.

Construction.   Aluminum appears to offer certain advantages. With bolted-type bases, installation labor costs are reduced because the poles are lighter in weight than steel or concrete poles. Tests show that these poles, with suitable attention to design to allow for the particular characteristics of the alloy, can be as strong as their steel counterparts. Some designs may be even more resistant to denting than other commonly used metal poles. Aluminum alloys most usually employed combine strength with resistance to corrosion, even in salty atmospheres. It appears that where severe corrosion is encountered, aluminum poles may retain their strength for a longer period of time than steel.

Concrete

Design.   Several companies manufacture concrete street light poles. The design is usually octagonal or round.

Construction.   Concrete poles, which have wide acceptance, are fabricated by centrifugal machine processes with pre-stressed, reinforced concrete. They are rigid, strong, and durable, but have the disadvantage of relatively great weight. Concrete poles are pleasing in appearance and are corrosion-resistant to most atmospheric conditions. The combination of pre-stressed steel reinforcement and spun pressure-dense concrete produces a pole of great durability. The use of high-tensile steel plus pre-stressing makes possible some reduction of weight and of the cross sectional area over previous designs.

Installation.   Where soil conditions permit, concrete poles are usually installed with integral butts, eliminating the need for separate bases. Where facilities are available for handling and a number can be installed at once, this feature makes for a very real saving in installation cost.

Wood

Line Poles.   Wood line poles, when used as supports for lighting, should be selected with due care, for aesthetic reasons. For the ultimate in appearance and convenience of installation, the poles should be turned, shaped, and sanded.

Special Requirements

Auxiliary Bracing for Long Mast Arm Types   All manufacturers produce mast arms in lengths varying from eight to 20 feet. Bracket arms for ornamental lighting poles and wood poles are designed with varying configurations in lengths up to ten feet. Brackets should be capable of supporting without failure a 250-pound vertical load and a 50-pound side force as applied at the luminaire end. Figure 4 has set examples of bracing, required for the longer arms.

Straight Brackets

Available Types and Sizes   Straight and right-angle, bend-type brackets extend to eight feet (see Fig. 5) and are constructed of galvanized steel or aluminum. The brackets are designed for metal, concrete, and wood pole mountings. Braces attached to both sides of the poles, or to the center only, support the brackets from either below or above, depending upon the manufacturer's design. This design provides strength and rigidity.

Typical Application   The straight bracket is used more often where no interference with distribution circuits exists. Figure 5 shows this type of bracket.

Upsweep Brackets

Advantages   To gain mounting height, upsweep brackets of aluminum or galvanized steel can be obtained with overhangs from four to 12 feet. These brackets are usually designed with pole plates welded in position, thus simplifying the installation. Brackets are manufactured with tilts ranging from 5 to 25 degrees.

Upsweep brackets are commonly used on line poles. The advantage of using the upsweep bracket is that pole space is kept available for other than street light equipment; thus, Code standard mounting heights may be maintained even though available mounting space may be lower than required if straight or right-angle brackets were employed.

Typical Types and Sizes   The various types and lengths of upsweep brackets are shown in Fig. 4. They vary in size from 4 to 8 feet. The longer type requires braces to give adequate strength.

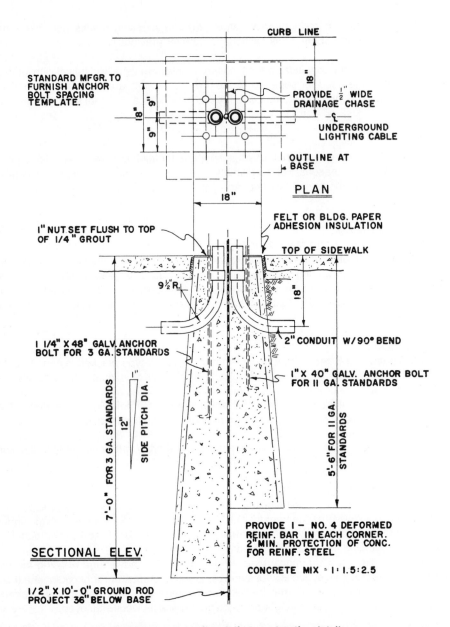

STANDARD MFGR. TO FURNISH ANCHOR BOLT SPACING TEMPLATE.

CURB LINE

18"

PROVIDE 1/2" WIDE DRAINAGE CHASE

UNDERGROUND LIGHTING CABLE

OUTLINE AT BASE

18" 9" 9"

9"

18"

PLAN

1" NUT SET FLUSH TO TOP OF 1/4" GROUT

FELT OR BLDG. PAPER ADHESION INSULATION

TOP OF SIDEWALK

9½ R.

18"

1 1/4" X 48" GALV. ANCHOR BOLT FOR 3 GA. STANDARDS

2" CONDUIT W/90° BEND

1" X 40" GALV. ANCHOR BOLT FOR 11 GA. STANDARDS

7'-0" FOR 3 GA. STANDARDS

12"

SIDE PITCH DIA.

5'-6" FOR 11 GA. STANDARDS

SECTIONAL ELEV.

PROVIDE 1 – NO. 4 DEFORMED REINF. BAR IN EACH CORNER. 2" MIN. PROTECTION OF CONC. FOR REINF. STEEL

CONCRETE MIX = 1:1.5:2.5

1/2" X 10'-0" GROUND ROD PROJECT 36" BELOW BASE

Street lighting pole foundation construction details.

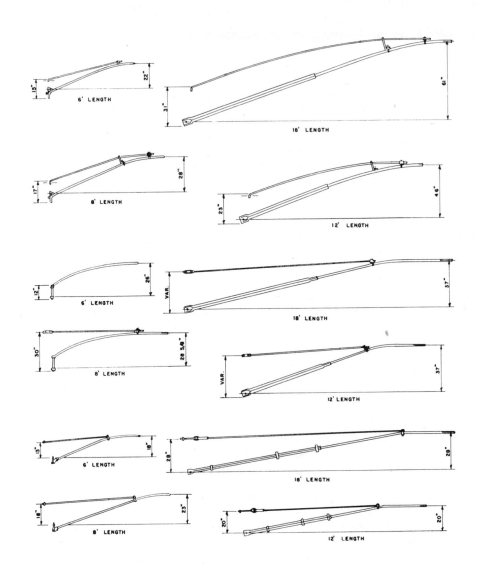

6' LENGTH 15" 22"

8' LENGTH 17" 28"

6' LENGTH 12" 26"

8' LENGTH 30" 28 5/8"

6' LENGTH 13" 18"

8' LENGTH 18" 23"

18' LENGTH 3" 61"

12' LENGTH 23" 46"

18' LENGTH VAR. 37"

12' LENGTH VAR. 37"

18' LENGTH 28" 28"

12' LENGTH 20" 20"

Typical brackets in common use—uplift-type mast arm.

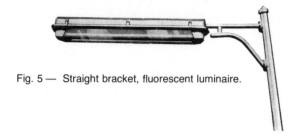

Fig. 5 — Straight bracket, fluorescent luminaire.

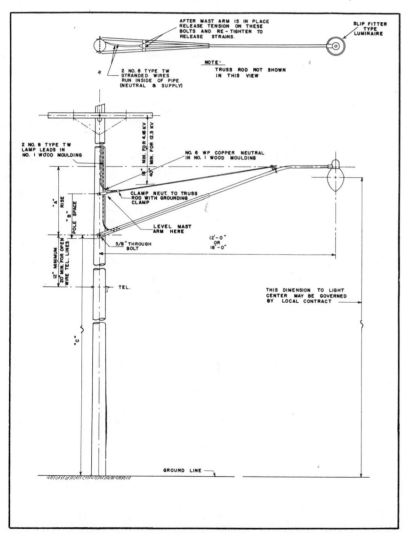

Fig. 6 — Typical upsweep bracket. Detail for installation of rigid fixture mounting on upsweep mast arm, 12-foot and 18-foot arms.

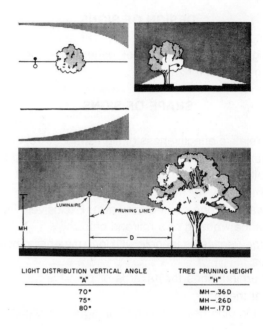

Fig. 1 — Tree trimming guide to street lighting.

LIGHT DISTRIBUTION VERTICAL ANGLE "A"	TREE PRUNING HEIGHT "H"
70°	MH−.36D
75°	MH−.26D
80°	MH−.17D

TREE TRIMMING

Low-hanging branches and trees that are too close to street lamps throw shadows on the street and may seriously impair the effectiveness of the lighting result. In many cases, trees have been allowed to grow up and completely surround the lamp, thus nullifying its purpose and wasting the taxpayers' money. Proper pruning of trees not only can restore the illumination to its original efficacy, but it will not detract from the appearance of the street, nor do any damage to the trees themselves.

The first requirement is that municipal and utility personnel recognize that a problem exists; the second is to assign the responsibility for appropriate action. The municipal authority, which pays for street lighting, has prime interest in the kind of street lighting that is provided, hence it would seem that it should take the initiative and arrange for a tree trimming program. Because of its special knowledge, the utility is in a position to furnish information such as that contained in the American Standard Practice which calls for removal only of those offending branches which fall below the cone of maximum candlepower. Midway between luminaires, for example, the trim line is lower, and the branches in this area which need not be trimmed may actually provide a desirable screening effect, reducing glare by night and enhancing the daytime appearance of the street. See Fig. 1.

DESIGN OF SIGNS

Uniformity in design includes shape, color, dimensions, symbols, wording, lettering, and illumination or reflectorization.

SHAPE OF SIGNS

In a study of the relative effectiveness of sign shape, size, color, and message, *shape* and *color* were found to be the most significant in producing recognition.

The use of the following shapes is specified in the MUTCD:

1. *Octagon:* Exclusively for the STOP sign.

2. *Equilateral triangle* (one point downward): Exclusively for the YIELD sign.

3. *Round:* Advance warning of a railroad crossing.

4. *Pennant shape* (isosceles triangle with long dimension horizontal): Warning of no-passing zones.

5. *Diamond:* Warning signs for hazards or possible hazards existing on the roadway or adjacent thereto.

6. *Rectangle* (long dimension vertical): All regulatory signs *except* STOP and YIELD signs.

7. *Rectangle* (long dimension horizontal): All guide signs, with the exception of certain route markers and recreational area guide signs.

8. *Pentagon* (point up): All school advance warning and school crossing signs.

9. *Trapezoid:* Recreational guide signs.

10. *Special shapes* may be used for special purposes, such as the *crossbuck* for railroad crossings, and the various *shield* shapes for state and interstate route markings.

SIGN COLORS

In the MUTCD the following colors are specified for use:

1. *Red:* The background color for STOP signs, DO NOT ENTER messages, and WRONG WAY signs; the legend color for parking prohibition signs, route markers, and YIELD signs.

2. *Black:* The background color for ONE-WAY signs, weigh station signs, and night speed limit signs; the legend color on white, yellow, and orange backgrounds.

3. *White:* The background color for route markers, guide signs, fallout shelter directional signs, and regulatory signs (exept for STOP signs); the legend color on brown, green, blue, black, and red backgrounds.

4. *Orange:* Only as a background for construction and maintenance signs.

5. *Yellow:* The background color for warning signs, except for construction, maintenance, and school areas.

6. *Brown:* The background color for recreational, scenic, or cultural guide signs.

7. *Blue:* The background color for motorist service guide or informational signs.

8. *Green:* The background color for guide signs, other than those using brown, white, or blue, and for mileposts; the legend color for permissive parking regulation signs.

Four other colors *(purple, light blue, coral,* and *strong yellow-green)* were identified as useful for highway purposes, but were reserved for future needs.

Source: Manual on Uniform Traffic Control Devices, *U.S. Dept. of Transportation, Federal Highway Adm., 1971.*

Typical route markings at intersections (for one direction of travel only)

Height and lateral location of signs—typical installations.

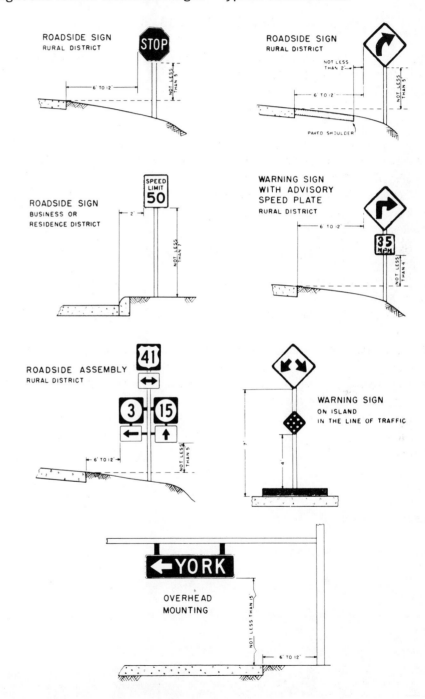

SOURCE: Manual on Uniform Traffic Control Devices, U. S. Dept. of Commerce, Wash., D. C.—1961

PHYSICAL AND CLIMATIC CHARACTERISTICS

Normal Monthly Maximum Temperature—Selected Cities

[In Fahrenheit degrees. Airport data unless otherwise noted. Based on standard 30-year period, 1931 to 1960]

State and Station	Jan.	Feb.	Mar.	Apr.	May	June	July	Aug.	Sept.	Oct.	Nov.	Dec.	Annual avg.
Ala — Mobile	62.3	64.7	70.3	77.5	85.9	91.4	92.0	91.2	87.4	80.3	69.6	63.9	78.0
Alaska — Juneau	30.1	32.1	36.5	45.4	53.6	60.8	62.7	61.5	55.2	46.5	39.2	32.7	46.4
Ariz — Phoenix	64.0	68.1	75.0	83.9	92.9	101.6	104.6	101.6	98.2	86.7	73.7	66.1	84.7
Ark — Little Rock	50.6	54.6	62.7	73.5	81.5	89.7	92.7	92.4	86.3	76.0	61.3	52.1	72.8
Calif — Los Angeles	63.8	63.7	65.0	66.9	68.7	71.1	75.9	75.4	75.8	73.0	71.0	66.5	69.7
Sacramento	53.2	58.6	64.8	71.4	78.2	86.5	93.4	91.9	88.2	77.6	64.2	54.6	73.6
San Francisco [1]	55.8	58.6	60.7	61.9	63.4	65.0	64.3	64.9	68.9	68.3	63.7	57.5	62.8
Colo — Denver	42.1	44.6	49.9	60.5	70.5	82.0	88.4	86.8	79.0	66.6	51.7	45.2	63.9
Conn — Hartford	34.7	36.0	45.3	59.6	72.0	80.5	85.0	82.7	74.7	64.8	50.9	37.6	60.3
Del — Wilmington	41.3	42.4	50.5	62.5	73.4	81.8	86.2	84.2	77.9	67.3	55.1	43.5	63.8
D.C — Washington	44.3	46.1	53.8	65.8	75.5	83.4	87.0	85.0	78.6	68.3	56.5	45.6	65.8
Fla — Jacksonville	66.8	68.5	73.3	79.6	86.4	90.5	92.0	91.4	87.6	80.2	72.2	66.7	79.6
Miami	75.8	77.0	79.8	82.6	85.4	88.0	88.8	89.7	88.0	84.7	80.2	77.1	83.1
Ga — Atlanta	52.0	53.7	60.3	70.1	78.9	85.7	87.0	86.6	81.8	72.4	60.9	52.4	70.2
Hawaii — Honolulu	79.1	78.8	79.2	80.2	81.8	83.8	84.9	85.2	84.2	82.0	79.2		81.9
Idaho — Boise	36.1	42.4	51.5	62.3	71.9	80.5	91.4	88.7	78.8	65.3	48.4	39.4	63.1
Ill — Chicago	33.0	34.7	43.5	57.4	69.1	79.5	84.1	82.4	74.8	63.4	47.1	35.7	58.7
Peoria	33.7	36.6	46.7	61.2	72.3	82.3	87.0	85.1	77.8	66.5	48.6	36.8	61.2
Ind — Indianapolis	37.1	39.4	48.1	61.2	72.0	81.8	86.0	84.7	78.0	66.8	50.0	39.0	62.0
Iowa — Des Moines	28.5	32.2	42.9	59.4	71.4	81.3	87.3	84.7	76.9	65.7	46.5	33.5	59.2
Kans — Wichita	41.6	47.0	55.9	68.2	77.1	87.7	92.4	92.8	83.7	71.7	55.1	44.9	68.2
Ky — Louisville	43.5	45.6	53.8	66.4	76.2	85.0	88.5	87.3	81.3	69.6	54.4	44.7	66.4
La — New Orleans	64.4	66.7	71.2	77.7	84.4	89.6	90.6	90.7	87.2	80.3	70.3	65.3	78.2
Maine — Portland	31.8	33.5	40.7	52.5	64.2	73.1	79.5	78.4	70.2	59.8	47.6	35.3	55.6
Md — Baltimore	44.2	45.5	53.6	65.8	75.9	83.5	87.2	85.0	78.6	68.4	56.5	45.7	65.8
Mass — Boston	36.8	37.4	44.6	55.7	67.5	76.5	81.9	80.0	73.4	62.7	51.9	40.1	59.0
Mich — Detroit	33.0	33.9	42.3	56.4	68.6	79.1	83.9	81.9	74.2	62.8	47.1	35.7	58.2
Sault Ste. Marie	23.1	24.0	31.7	46.4	59.9	69.9	75.6	74.0	64.4	54.5	39.6	27.3	49.2
Minn — Duluth	17.9	21.4	31.1	47.1	60.6	70.3	77.1	74.6	64.7	54.5	35.1	22.3	48.1
Minneapolis-St. Paul	22.4	26.3	37.2	55.7	69.1	78.1	83.9	81.3	72.2	60.6	40.5	27.4	54.6
Miss — Jackson	58.3	61.6	68.6	77.2	85.2	91.2	92.9	93.1	88.3	79.6	67.5	59.9	77.0
Mo — Kansas City	39.9	44.8	52.6	65.6	75.1	85.2	91.9	90.3	82.7	71.6	54.5	43.7	66.5
St. Louis	40.2	44.0	52.8	65.9	75.1	85.1	89.2	87.3	81.3	70.1	53.7	43.0	65.6
Mont — Great Falls	31.6	34.0	41.1	55.2	65.7	72.9	84.7	81.8	71.2	59.3	44.2	35.8	56.5
Nebr — Omaha	31.7	36.0	46.4	62.4	73.9	83.8	89.7	86.9	78.5	67.5	48.9	37.2	61.9
Nev — Reno	44.6	49.8	57.3	65.4	71.5	80.3	89.4	88.3	81.2	69.0	55.7	47.3	66.7
N.H — Concord	31.7	33.5	41.7	55.9	69.3	77.7	82.8	80.6	72.4	61.7	47.9	35.1	57.5
N.J — Atlantic City	42.9	43.3	49.7	60.3	71.0	79.2	83.8	82.2	76.0	66.5	55.5	45.1	63.0
N.Mex — Albuquerque	46.4	52.2	58.8	69.1	78.3	88.6	91.2	88.0	82.3	70.7	56.1	48.3	69.2
N.Y — Albany	31.0	32.5	41.9	56.7	69.5	77.9	81.4	79.0	71.4	60.1	46.5	34.5	57.7
Buffalo	30.8	31.0	38.6	52.9	65.5	75.1	80.1	78.6	71.5	60.1	46.5	34.3	55.4
New York [1]	39.5	40.3	47.8	59.6	71.4	79.8	85.3	83.3	76.8	66.3	53.7	42.1	62.2
N.C — Charlotte	51.4	53.7	60.0	71.0	79.4	87.6	88.8	87.8	81.9	72.8	60.7	51.3	70.5
Raleigh	51.9	54.0	61.3	71.8	79.4	86.3	88.1	87.1	82.0	72.8	62.2	52.3	70.6
N.Dak — Bismarck	19.6	23.3	35.1	54.9	68.2	76.5	85.7	83.7	72.6	59.4	38.6	26.9	53.7
Ohio — Cincinnati [1]	41.3	43.4	52.0	64.4	74.9	83.8	87.5	86.4	80.3	68.9	53.2	42.6	64.9
Cleveland	35.4	36.1	43.9	57.3	68.9	78.3	82.4	80.8	74.5	63.4	48.8	37.0	58.9
Columbus	37.8	39.5	48.4	62.2	73.5	82.9	86.6	85.0	77.6	65.8	50.6	39.6	62.5
Okla — Oklahoma City	45.9	51.3	59.5	70.6	78.1	87.4	92.8	93.5	84.7	73.9	58.8	49.2	70.5
Oreg — Portland	43.7	48.8	54.2	61.7	67.5	71.8	78.6	77.9	73.7	63.2	51.7	46.5	61.6
Pa — Philadelphia	40.3	41.8	50.3	62.6	73.4	81.6	85.9	83.7	77.2	66.5	54.0	42.3	63.3
Pittsburgh	36.5	37.6	46.1	60.0	71.4	79.9	83.3	81.9	75.5	63.7	49.5	38.1	60.3
R.I — Providence	37.3	38.3	45.3	56.6	67.7	76.1	81.4	80.0	73.1	63.4	52.2	40.4	59.3
S.C — Columbia	58.2	60.5	66.5	76.3	84.7	91.5	92.5	91.2	86.1	77.4	66.7	58.2	75.8
S.Dak — Sioux Falls	25.1	29.1	39.4	57.0	70.1	79.4	86.0	83.3	73.5	61.9	42.5	30.3	56.5
Tenn — Memphis	50.6	53.9	61.4	72.1	80.1	88.3	91.1	90.7	85.6	75.7	61.5	52.5	72.0
Nashville	48.8	51.4	59.4	70.8	79.8	88.4	90.7	89.9	84.5	73.7	59.1	50.3	70.6
Tex — Dallas	55.8	59.5	67.0	75.4	82.7	90.9	94.5	95.0	88.3	78.8	65.7	58.0	76.0
El Paso	56.3	62.4	69.4	78.2	86.9	95.4	94.9	93.0	87.5	78.8	66.3	57.5	77.2
Houston	63.6	65.5	71.7	78.0	85.7	91.1	92.1	92.8	89.1	82.3	71.1	65.4	79.0
Utah — Salt Lake City	36.8	42.0	52.0	63.4	74.0	83.7	94.1	90.8	80.3	65.2	47.5	39.0	64.1
Vt — Burlington	25.4	27.1	36.3	52.4	66.4	77.1	81.9	79.6	70.6	58.6	43.4	30.2	54.1
Va — Norfolk	50.2	51.0	57.2	68.0	77.3	84.9	87.9	86.2	80.9	70.9	61.0	51.8	68.9
Richmond	48.3	50.6	59.1	70.4	79.3	86.8	89.4	86.5	81.8	70.6	59.9	49.8	69.4
Wash — Seattle-Tacoma	43.6	47.0	51.3	58.2	65.6	69.9	75.6	74.6	69.3	60.3	49.6	45.9	59.2
Spokane	31.4	37.4	47.0	58.6	69.3	74.5	85.6	83.0	74.7	60.1	42.9	39.3	58.4
W.Va — Charleston	45.2	46.9	54.5	66.3	76.7	83.2	85.6	84.3	79.5	69.3	55.3	45.6	66.0
Wis — Milwaukee	28.3	30.2	38.8	53.1	63.9	73.9	78.9	77.7	70.7	60.1	44.1	32.0	54.3
Wyo — Cheyenne	37.2	39.4	44.1	55.5	65.1	76.5	85.2	82.8	74.2	62.7	47.2	41.6	59.3
P.R — San Juan	81.3	81.8	83.1	84.0	85.8	87.1	87.1	87.8	87.8	87.1	85.0	82.7	85.1

[1] City office data.

Source: U.S. National Oceanic and Atmospheric Administration, *Local Climatological Data.* Monthly with annual summary.

PERIOD 1899-1938

SOURCE: Climate and Man Yearbook of Agriculture—1941 Dept. of Agriculture

NORMAL MONTHLY MINIMUM TEMPERATURE—SELECTED CITIES

[In Fahrenheit degrees. Airport data unless otherwise noted. Based on standard 30-year period, 1931 to 1960]

STATE AND STATION		Jan.	Feb.	Mar.	Apr.	May	June	July	Aug.	Sept.	Oct.	Nov.	Dec.	Annual avg.
Ala.	Mobile	43.7	45.7	50.3	57.6	65.3	71.5	73.1	73.0	68.3	59.5	48.2	44.3	58.4
Alaska.	Juneau	20.0	21.4	24.3	30.5	37.6	43.7	47.8	46.6	42.5	36.7	29.4	24.0	33.7
Ariz.	Phoenix	35.3	38.9	42.9	50.4	57.1	65.5	75.0	73.4	67.3	54.6	42.4	37.0	53.3
Ark.	Little Rock	30.5	34.1	40.9	51.2	59.5	68.0	71.1	70.1	62.2	50.2	37.6	31.7	50.6
Calif.	Los Angeles	45.0	46.7	48.9	51.9	55.2	58.5	62.3	62.8	61.1	56.8	51.0	47.3	54.0
	Sacramento	37.2	39.8	42.0	45.3	49.7	54.4	57.4	56.3	55.0	49.4	41.6	38.1	47.2
	San Francisco [1]	45.5	47.3	48.6	49.5	51.3	53.1	53.3	53.9	55.1	54.4	51.0	47.4	50.9
Colo.	Denver	14.8	18.3	22.8	32.3	41.8	51.0	57.4	56.2	47.0	36.2	23.6	18.0	35.0
Conn.	Hartford	17.3	18.2	26.7	37.3	47.7	56.9	61.8	59.7	51.8	41.2	31.6	20.2	39.2
Del.	Wilmington	25.5	25.2	32.0	41.6	52.0	61.0	65.8	64.3	57.3	45.9	35.7	26.7	44.4
D.C.	Washington	29.5	29.4	35.8	45.6	56.0	64.9	69.3	67.9	60.7	49.6	38.9	30.5	48.2
Fla.	Jacksonville	45.0	46.5	51.1	57.8	65.1	71.1	73.2	73.2	71.1	61.8	51.2	45.5	59.4
	Miami	57.9	58.8	61.1	65.8	69.7	73.5	74.7	74.9	74.6	70.9	64.6	59.1	67.1
Ga.	Atlanta	37.3	38.4	42.5	50.2	59.2	67.5	70.7	69.8	64.3	52.4	41.5	37.1	52.6
Hawaii.	Honolulu	65.8	66.0	66.4	68.1	70.0	72.0	73.0	73.8	73.2	72.1	69.7	67.9	69.8
Idaho.	Boise	22.1	26.5	31.9	37.4	44.5	51.1	59.0	55.5	46.6	37.9	28.7	25.0	38.9
Ill.	Chicago	19.0	20.6	29.0	40.5	50.9	61.5	67.1	65.9	57.4	46.7	32.6	22.5	42.8
	Peoria	17.6	20.1	28.4	40.3	50.7	61.1	65.0	63.5	55.0	44.1	30.7	21.3	41.5
Ind.	Indianapolis	21.0	22.8	29.7	40.3	50.7	60.4	64.3	62.7	54.9	44.0	31.8	23.2	42.2
Iowa.	Des Moines	11.3	14.6	24.6	38.0	49.8	60.7	65.2	63.4	53.8	42.6	27.6	17.0	39.1
Kans.	Wichita	22.3	25.6	33.0	45.2	54.9	65.2	69.4	68.8	58.9	48.0	33.7	26.6	46.0
Ky.	Louisville	26.5	26.0	32.8	43.1	52.6	61.8	66.6	65.1	57.7	46.2	34.9	27.8	45.1
La.	New Orleans	44.8	47.5	51.6	58.1	64.4	70.5	72.6	73.0	69.3	60.5	49.6	45.5	59.0
Maine.	Portland	11.7	12.1	22.0	32.4	41.7	51.1	56.7	55.2	47.2	37.4	28.6	16.3	34.4
Md.	Baltimore	25.3	25.8	32.5	42.6	52.8	61.4	66.4	65.0	57.6	45.6	34.4	25.9	44.6
Mass.	Boston	23.0	23.1	30.7	40.0	50.1	59.2	65.4	63.3	57.1	47.2	37.8	26.5	43.6
Mich.	Detroit	20.7	20.4	27.3	38.8	49.4	60.3	64.8	63.6	56.0	44.7	33.7	24.1	42.0
	Sault Ste. Marie	8.4	7.4	15.8	29.6	39.3	48.0	53.5	54.0	47.1	38.1	26.9	14.4	31.9
Minn.	Duluth	-0.6	0.1	11.4	26.9	37.7	47.3	53.9	52.9	43.7	34.6	19.5	5.7	27.8
	Minneapolis-St. Paul	2.3	5.0	17.6	32.8	45.4	55.5	60.7	58.6	48.5	37.2	21.8	8.7	32.8
Miss.	Jackson	37.4	39.4	44.4	52.5	60.9	68.4	71.7	70.9	64.7	54.4	43.4	38.9	53.9
Mo.	Kansas City	23.4	26.7	34.0	45.8	56.0	66.5	71.0	69.2	59.9	48.7	34.6	27.9	47.0
	St. Louis	23.5	25.3	32.4	43.8	53.3	63.1	66.9	66.3	57.6	46.6	34.5	26.5	45.0
Mont.	Great Falls	12.5	13.6	20.2	31.9	40.2	46.9	54.1	51.8	43.5	35.6	24.4	18.8	32.8
Nebr.	Omaha	12.9	17.0	27.3	40.9	52.1	62.4	67.3	65.5	55.3	43.8	28.8	19.1	41.0
Nev.	Reno	16.2	21.4	25.6	30.5	36.3	39.8	45.9	42.7	36.4	29.4	20.8	16.4	30.1
N.H.	Concord	10.6	11.8	21.7	21.7	41.6	51.3	56.4	54.1	46.2	35.6	27.2	14.8	33.6
N.J.	Atlantic City	26.6	26.1	32.4	41.7	51.5	60.7	66.4	65.1	58.4	47.8	37.9	28.1	45.2
N. Mex.	Albuquerque	23.5	27.5	32.7	42.2	51.9	61.1	65.8	64.3	57.6	45.3	31.1	25.6	44.1
N.Y.	Albany	14.4	14.8	24.0	35.7	46.3	55.8	60.5	58.5	50.3	39.8	30.6	18.5	37.4
	Buffalo	18.2	17.2	24.4	34.0	44.1	54.5	59.4	58.1	51.2	41.4	31.7	21.1	37.9
	New York [1]	26.9	26.4	33.2	43.1	53.4	62.5	68.2	66.8	60.1	50.3	40.3	29.7	46.7
N.C.	Charlotte	34.0	34.7	41.0	49.6	58.6	66.6	69.5	69.5	63.3	52.2	40.1	34.1	51.1
	Raleigh	31.3	31.9	37.8	46.8	55.7	63.9	67.6	66.7	60.4	48.2	37.7	31.4	48.3
N. Dak.	Bismarck	0.1	3.7	17.3	32.1	43.6	52.4	57.7	54.8	44.7	34.0	19.1	8.6	30.7
Ohio.	Cincinnati [1]	26.1	26.7	33.3	43.9	53.5	63.0	66.3	64.9	57.6	46.8	36.0	27.9	45.5
	Cleveland	21.3	20.8	26.3	36.7	47.0	57.2	61.3	60.0	53.8	43.4	33.7	24.0	40.5
	Columbus	22.0	22.7	29.3	39.4	49.4	58.6	62.9	61.4	54.2	42.5	31.8	23.4	41.5
Okla.	Oklahoma City	28.1	31.2	37.5	49.1	58.6	68.5	72.2	72.0	62.9	51.8	38.0	31.4	50.1
Oreg.	Portland	33.0	35.1	37.9	41.8	47.2	52.2	55.7	55.2	50.7	45.1	38.4	36.1	44.0
Pa.	Philadelphia	24.3	24.6	31.6	41.4	51.8	60.4	65.2	63.5	56.2	44.9	34.5	25.5	43.7
	Pittsburgh	21.2	20.7	27.4	37.9	48.1	56.9	60.9	59.6	52.8	42.4	32.0	23.2	40.3
R.I.	Providence	21.0	21.1	28.6	37.7	47.2	56.3	62.7	60.9	53.3	42.9	33.8	23.5	40.8
S.C.	Columbia	35.6	36.3	42.3	50.8	59.6	67.9	70.7	69.7	64.5	52.0	40.7	34.5	52.1
S. Dak.	Sioux Falls	5.2	9.0	20.8	34.7	46.5	56.8	62.5	60.3	50.0	38.6	22.7	11.9	34.9
Tenn.	Memphis	32.4	34.3	40.7	50.7	60.4	68.6	71.5	70.3	62.1	50.5	38.7	32.5	51.1
	Nashville	30.9	32.5	38.7	48.4	57.4	66.3	69.6	68.4	61.1	49.3	37.9	32.4	49.4
Tex.	Dallas	36.0	39.4	45.2	54.6	63.1	71.7	75.3	75.0	67.4	56.8	44.1	38.1	55.6
	El Paso	29.5	35.7	40.3	48.5	56.9	66.5	68.9	67.7	61.4	50.0	36.1	30.7	49.4
	Houston	43.6	46.0	50.8	59.0	66.2	72.0	73.8	73.6	69.3	60.4	50.5	45.9	59.3
Utah.	Salt Lake City	17.5	22.9	28.8	36.4	43.8	51.0	59.6	58.2	48.5	38.2	25.9	21.2	37.7
Vt.	Burlington	6.9	7.6	17.0	30.0	41.2	51.2	56.0	53.8	46.1	36.6	27.1	12.8	32.2
Va.	Norfolk	32.2	32.2	38.7	47.9	57.7	66.3	69.6	68.8	64.3	53.1	41.8	33.1	50.5
	Richmond	29.0	29.2	36.3	45.8	54.6	63.4	66.7	65.4	58.6	46.7	37.1	29.5	46.9
Wash.	Seattle-Tacoma	33.0	34.5	36.2	40.1	45.3	49.7	54.1	53.6	50.5	44.4	38.1	35.7	42.9
	Spokane	19.2	22.5	29.1	35.9	43.1	49.3	55.4	52.9	47.0	38.0	28.5	24.2	37.1
W.Va.	Charleston	27.9	28.0	34.3	44.3	52.8	60.8	64.2	63.3	56.8	45.3	35.2	28.6	45.1
Wis.	Milwaukee	12.8	14.6	23.2	34.1	42.9	52.6	58.4	57.5	49.9	39.9	27.5	17.1	35.9
Wyo.	Cheyenne	13.6	15.2	20.7	29.6	40.6	49.5	54.8	52.6	43.0	32.2	21.2	17.4	32.5
P.R.	San Juan	67.4	67.0	67.5	69.2	71.5	72.9	73.7	74.0	73.2	72.8	71.4	69.6	70.9

[1] City office data.

Source: U.S. National Oceanic and Atmospheric Administration, *Local Climatological Data.* Monthly with annual summary.

PERIOD 1899-1938

SOURCE: Climate and Man Yearbook of Agriculture—1941 Dept. of Agriculture

AVERAGE PERCENTAGE OF POSSIBLE SUNSHINE—SELECTED CITIES

[Airport data, for period of record through 1971, except as noted]

STATE AND STATION	Length of record (yrs.)	Jan.	Feb.	Mar.	Apr.	May	June	July	Aug.	Sept.	Oct.	Nov.	Dec.	Annual
Ala. — Mobile [1]	48	49	51	57	65	69	67	61	63	64	72	62	48	61
Alaska — Juneau	26	33	31	37	39	38	35	30	30	24	19	23	20	31
Ariz. — Phoenix	76	78	80	83	88	93	94	84	85	89	88	84	77	86
Ark. — Little Rock	29	46	53	56	60	67	72	70	71	67	69	56	47	62
Calif. — Los Angeles [2]	31	71	72	73	69	66	65	82	83	79	73	74	71	73
Sacramento	23	45	61	71	80	86	92	98	96	94	86	65	46	79
San Francisco [2]	35	56	63	69	73	72	72	66	66	73	71	63	54	67
Colo. — Denver	22	72	71	71	67	64	70	71	72	75	74	66	68	70
Conn. — Hartford	17	57	56	57	56	58	59	61	64	60	58	45	49	58
Del. — Wilmington [1]	25	50	54	57	57	59	64	63	61	60	60	54	51	58
D.C. — Washington	23	49	51	56	56	58	65	62	63	63	60	50	48	57
Fla. — Jacksonville	21	58	61	66	71	70	61	60	58	52	55	61	56	61
Miami [2][3]	22	68	74	74	72	68	62	62	63	58	59	66	65	66
Ga. — Atlanta	37	48	52	57	65	69	67	62	66	64	67	60	50	61
Hawaii — Honolulu	19	63	65	69	69	71	73	77	77	75	67	61	60	69
Idaho — Boise	32	42	52	62	68	71	75	89	86	82	68	46	40	68
Ill. — Chicago	29	44	47	51	53	61	67	69	68	64	61	41	40	57
Peoria	28	46	50	52	56	60	66	69	69	66	64	46	41	58
Ind. — Indianapolis	29	41	51	52	56	62	68	70	72	68	65	43	40	59
Iowa — Des Moines	21	51	55	56	56	60	67	71	70	65	63	51	45	60
Kans. — Wichita	18	58	59	61	62	63	68	73	73	68	67	62	57	65
Ky. — Louisville	24	41	46	51	56	63	67	66	69	67	63	47	41	58
La. — New Orleans [2][4]	46	49	51	57	65	69	67	61	63	64	72	62	48	61
Maine — Portland	31	55	59	58	57	57	61	65	65	62	58	46	54	59
Md. — Baltimore	21	52	55	55	55	58	64	66	63	62	59	51	49	58
Mass. — Boston	36	53	57	58	56	58	63	65	66	64	61	51	54	60
Mich. — Detroit [5]	32	32	43	49	52	59	65	70	65	61	56	35	32	54
Sault Ste. Marie	30	34	45	54	53	55	58	63	59	45	42	23	27	47
Minn. — Duluth	21	50	56	59	55	55	59	67	63	52	49	34	40	55
Minneapolis-St. Paul	33	50	57	54	56	58	62	70	67	61	57	39	40	58
Miss. — Jackson	7	46	56	61	60	66	70	63	61	63	64	55	43	60
Mo. — Kansas City	38	53	56	58	60	63	68	76	73	68	67	57	50	64
St. Louis	12	52	51	54	57	63	68	70	67	66	63	50	43	59
Mont. — Great Falls	29	51	59	68	63	64	65	81	78	67	61	46	47	64
Nebr. — Omaha	36	54	55	55	59	62	67	76	71	67	67	53	48	62
Nev. — Reno	29	65	69	74	79	79	83	92	93	91	82	70	62	80
N.H. — Concord	30	51	54	52	52	54	58	62	60	55	54	41	48	54
N.J. — Atlantic City	11	53	49	54	52	55	61	58	62	60	57	51	44	55
N. Mex. — Albuquerque	32	73	74	74	77	80	83	76	76	81	80	78	71	77
N.Y. — Albany	33	46	51	53	53	55	60	64	62	57	54	37	40	54
Buffalo	28	33	40	47	52	59	67	69	67	61	54	30	29	53
New York [2]	95	51	55	57	59	62	65	65	64	63	61	52	50	59
N.C. — Charlotte	21	56	59	64	69	70	71	69	71	68	69	63	60	66
Raleigh	17	56	59	65	63	60	61	62	61	62	62	64	58	61
N. Dak. — Bismark	32	55	56	60	59	63	63	77	74	65	60	45	48	62
Ohio — Cincinnati [2]	56	42	45	51	56	61	68	69	67	67	60	45	39	54
Cleveland	30	31	37	45	53	60	66	69	67	65	60	55	31	52
Columbus	20	38	42	46	53	60	64	66	67	65	59	40	32	55
Okla. — Oklahoma City	19	58	61	64	62	65	73	76	78	72	68	62	58	67
Oreg. — Portland	22	23	36	41	48	53	50	69	63	58	40	29	20	47
Pa. — Philadelphia	29	50	53	57	56	58	64	62	62	61	60	53	51	58
Pittsburgh	19	37	39	47	50	55	61	63	63	63	58	41	32	52
R.I. — Providence	18	57	56	57	56	58	59	59	59	59	59	49	54	57
S.C. — Columbia	18	58	60	65	67	67	65	64	66	65	65	65	62	64
S. Dak. — Sioux Falls [1]	27	54	59	55	60	63	67	77	74	67	65	52	48	63
Tenn. — Memphis	21	48	53	57	63	70	73	73	76	72	72	59	50	65
Nashville	30	40	47	52	59	63	68	65	66	64	64	51	41	58
Tex. — Dallas	31	51	53	58	57	61	73	77	76	70	66	62	55	65
El Paso	29	78	82	84	87	89	89	79	81	82	84	83	77	83
Houston [6]	7	47	56	57	54	62	72	74	70	66	73	60	50	62
Utah — Salt Lake City	34	47	54	64	67	73	78	83	82	83	74	54	44	69
Vt. — Burlington	28	42	48	54	51	57	62	66	63	56	50	31	34	53
Va. — Norfolk	18	57	58	63	66	67	68	65	65	65	60	61	58	63
Richmond	21	51	54	59	62	65	67	65	64	64	59	55	51	60
Wash. — Seattle-Tacoma	6	19	46	49	49	56	54	66	66	57	37	27	15	48
Spokane	24	25	41	54	60	63	66	81	78	70	51	29	20	57
W. Va. — Charleston [1]	69	31	36	42	49	56	60	62	60	60	54	37	29	48
Wis. — Milwaukee	31	44	46	51	54	59	64	71	68	61	57	41	39	56
Wyo. — Cheyenne	36	62	64	64	60	58	65	69	67	69	69	61	59	64
P.R. — San Jaun	16	65	68	74	69	60	58	66	68	63	63	61	58	64

[1] Data not available; figures are for a nearby station. [2] City office data.
[3] Record through 1964. [4] Record through 1963. [5] Record through 1966. [6] Record through 1969.

Source: U.S. National Oceanic and Atmospheric Administration, *Local Climatological Data*, Monthly with annual summary.

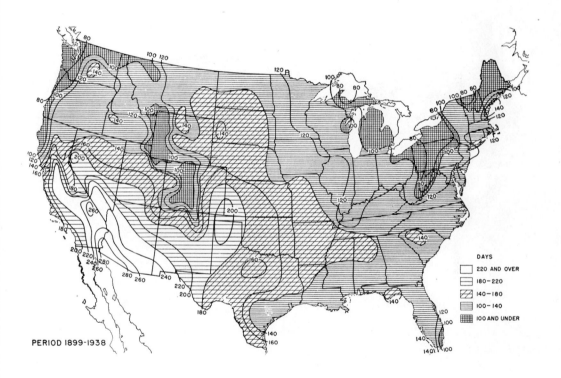

PERIOD 1899-1938

DAYS
- 220 AND OVER
- 180–220
- 140–180
- 100–140
- 100 AND UNDER

SOURCE: Climate and Man Yearbook of Agriculture—1941 Dept. of Agriculture

PRECIPITATION

Precipitation in the United States averages 30 inches a year, with a variation of from under 10 to more than 80 inches. The Great Plains receives from 20 to 30 inches. The Great Plains to the Rocky Mountains, from 15 to 20 inches; and in the lowlands of the Intermountain Region, from 10 to 15 inches. In Nevada, southeastern California, and southwestern Arizona, the precipitation is under 10 inches a year, the least in the nation. On the West Coast, precipitation is the highest in the United States, averaging more than 80 inches in places.

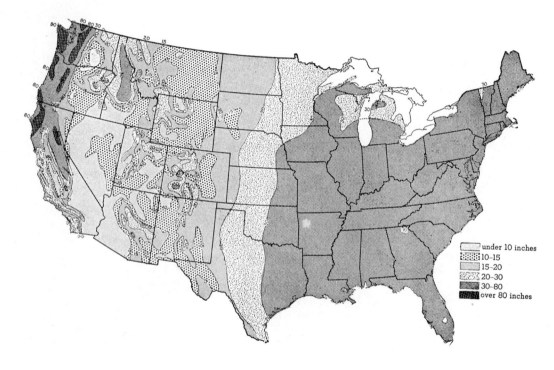

under 10 inches
10-15
15-20
20-30
30-80
over 80 inches

SOURCE: A Water Policy for the American People. Vol. 1, The Report of the President's Water Resources Policy Commission—1950

NORMAL MONTHLY AND ANNUAL PRECIPITATION—SELECTED CITIES

[In inches. Airport data unless otherwise noted. Based on standard 30-year period, 1931 to 1960. T denotes trace. See *Historical Statistics, Colonial Times to 1957*, series J 136–265, for related data]

STATE AND STATION		Jan.	Feb.	Mar.	Apr.	May	June	July	Aug.	Sept.	Oct.	Nov.	Dec.	Annual
Ala___	Mobile_____	4.64	4.59	7.23	6.36	4.88	6.23	9.67	6.44	6.25	3.03	3.35	5.46	68.13
Alaska_	Juneau_____	4.00	3.06	3.27	2.87	3.24	3.39	4.49	5.02	6.67	8.33	6.06	4.22	54.62
Ariz___	Phoenix_____	0.73	0.85	0.66	0.32	0.13	0.09	0.77	1.12	0.73	0.46	0.49	0.85	7.20
Ark___	Little Rock___	5.22	4.33	4.81	4.93	5.28	3.61	3.34	2.82	3.23	2.88	4.12	4.09	48.66
Calif__	Los Angeles___	2.66	2.88	1.79	1.05	0.13	0.05	0.01	0.02	0.17	0.39	1.09	2.39	12.63
	Sacramento___	3.18	2.99	2.36	1.40	0.59	0.10	T	0.02	0.19	0.77	1.45	3.24	16.29
	San Francisco_	4.01	3.48	2.69	1.30	0.48	0.11	0.01	0.02	0.19	0.74	1.57	4.09	18.69
Colo__	Denver_____	0.55	0.69	1.21	2.11	2.70	1.44	1.53	1.28	1.13	1.01	0.69	0.47	14.81
Conn__	Hartford_____	3.58	2.94	3.80	3.73	3.41	3.70	3.61	4.01	3.65	3.18	3.84	3.47	42.92
Del___	Wilmington___	3.40	2.95	4.02	3.33	3.53	4.07	4.25	5.59	3.95	2.91	3.53	3.03	44.56
D.C.__	Washington___	3.03	2.47	3.21	3.15	4.14	3.21	4.15	4.90	3.83	3.07	2.84	2.78	40.78
Fla___	Jacksonville__	2.45	2.91	3.49	3.55	3.47	6.33	7.68	6.85	7.56	5.16	1.69	2.22	53.36
	Miami_____	2.03	1.87	2.27	3.88	6.44	7.37	6.75	6.97	9.47	8.21	2.83	1.67	59.76
Ga___	Atlanta_____	4.44	4.51	5.37	4.47	3.16	3.83	4.72	3.60	3.26	2.44	2.96	4.38	47.14
Hawaii	Honolulu_____	3.76	3.30	2.89	1.31	0.99	0.33	0.44	0.89	0.99	1.84	2.16	2.99	21.89
Idaho_	Boise_____	1.32	1.33	1.32	1.16	1.29	0.89	0.21	0.16	0.39	0.84	1.20	1.32	11.43
Ill____	Chicago_____	1.86	1.60	2.74	3.04	3.73	4.07	3.37	3.16	2.73	2.78	2.20	1.90	33.18
	Peoria_____	1.88	1.71	2.85	3.97	4.27	4.08	3.54	2.88	3.05	2.53	2.14	1.94	34.84
Ind___	Indianapolis__	3.05	2.28	3.41	3.74	3.99	4.62	3.50	3.03	3.24	2.62	3.09	2.68	39.25
Iowa__	Des Moines___	1.30	1.10	2.09	2.53	4.07	4.71	3.06	3.67	2.88	2.06	1.76	1.14	30.37
Kans__	Wichita_____	0.81	0.92	1.64	2.30	3.97	4.21	3.64	2.87	3.22	2.40	1.49	0.94	28.41
Ky____	Louisville____	4.10	3.29	4.59	3.82	3.90	3.99	3.36	2.97	2.63	2.25	3.20	3.22	41.32
La____	New Orleans__	3.84	3.99	5.34	4.55	4.38	4.43	6.72	5.34	5.03	2.84	3.34	4.10	53.90
Maine_	Portland_____	4.37	3.80	4.34	3.73	3.41	3.18	2.86	2.42	3.52	3.20	4.17	3.85	42.85
Md____	Baltimore____	3.43	2.89	3.82	3.60	3.98	3.29	4.22	5.19	3.33	3.18	3.13	2.99	43.05
Mass__	Boston_____	3.94	3.32	4.22	3.77	3.34	3.48	2.88	3.66	3.46	3.14	3.93	3.63	42.77
Mich__	Detroit_____	2.05	2.08	2.42	3.00	3.53	2.83	2.82	2.86	2.44	2.63	2.21	2.08	30.95
	Sault Ste. Marie_	2.07	1.50	1.81	2.16	2.77	3.30	2.48	2.89	3.81	2.82	3.33	2.28	31.22
Minn__	Duluth_____	1.15	0.96	1.62	2.36	3.29	4.27	3.54	3.81	2.86	2.17	1.78	1.16	28.97
	Minneapolis-St. Paul_	0.70	0.78	1.53	1.85	3.19	4.00	3.27	3.18	2.43	1.59	1.40	0.86	24.78
Miss__	Jackson_____	5.18	4.96	5.74	4.91	4.38	3.79	4.76	3.33	2.53	2.04	3.90	5.30	50.82
Mo____	Kansas City___	1.41	1.24	2.49	3.56	4.40	4.57	3.19	3.77	3.25	2.86	1.80	1.53	34.07
	St. Louis_____	1.98	2.04	3.08	3.71	3.73	4.29	3.30	3.02	2.76	2.86	2.57	1.97	35.31
Mont__	Great Falls____	0.61	0.74	0.92	0.98	2.10	2.90	1.28	1.26	1.20	0.73	0.75	0.60	14.07
Nebr__	Omaha_____	0.82	0.95	1.45	2.56	3.48	4.53	3.37	3.98	2.63	1.73	1.26	0.80	27.56
Nev___	Reno_____	1.19	1.02	0.68	0.54	0.52	0.37	0.27	0.17	0.23	0.51	0.57	1.08	7.15
N.H.__	Concord_____	3.23	2.48	3.26	3.31	3.17	3.60	3.41	2.96	3.75	2.66	3.72	3.25	38.80
N.J.__	Atlantic City__	3.56	3.13	3.91	3.41	3.51	2.83	3.72	4.90	3.31	3.20	3.66	3.22	42.36
N. Mex.	Albuquerque__	0.41	0.38	0.48	0.47	0.75	0.57	1.20	1.33	0.95	0.75	0.38	0.46	8.13
N.Y.__	Albany_____	2.47	2.20	2.72	2.77	3.47	3.25	3.49	3.07	3.58	2.77	2.70	2.59	35.08
	Buffalo_____	2.84	2.72	3.24	3.01	2.95	2.54	2.57	3.05	3.13	3.00	3.60	3.00	35.65
	New York [1]__	3.31	2.84	4.01	3.43	3.67	3.31	3.70	4.44	3.87	3.14	3.39	3.26	42.37
N.C.__	Charlotte_____	3.53	3.55	4.39	3.49	3.11	3.61	4.88	4.22	3.49	2.96	2.53	3.62	43.38
	Raleigh_____	3.22	3.23	3.35	3.52	3.52	3.70	5.49	5.20	3.85	2.71	2.77	3.02	43.58
N. Dak.	Bismarck_____	0.44	0.43	0.78	1.22	1.97	3.40	2.19	1.73	1.19	0.85	0.59	0.36	15.15
Ohio__	Cincinnati [1]__	3.67	2.80	3.89	3.63	3.80	4.18	3.59	3.28	2.71	2.24	2.95	2.77	39.51
	Cleveland_____	2.67	2.33	3.13	3.41	3.52	3.43	3.31	3.28	2.90	2.42	2.61	2.34	35.35
	Columbus_____	3.16	2.31	3.16	3.49	4.00	4.16	3.93	2.86	2.65	2.11	2.50	2.34	36.67
Okla__	Oklahoma City_	1.31	1.37	1.97	3.12	5.19	4.47	2.37	2.52	3.02	2.51	1.56	1.41	30.82
Oreg__	Portland_____	5.37	4.22	3.83	2.09	1.99	1.67	0.41	0.65	1.63	3.61	5.33	6.38	37.18
Pa____	Philadelphia___	3.32	2.80	3.80	3.40	3.74	4.05	4.16	4.63	3.46	2.78	3.40	2.94	42.48
	Pittsburgh____	2.97	2.19	3.32	3.08	3.91	3.78	3.88	3.31	2.54	2.52	2.24	2.40	36.14
R.I.__	Providence____	3.81	3.10	4.14	3.75	3.35	2.76	2.91	3.96	3.52	3.10	4.11	3.62	42.13
S.C.__	Columbia_____	3.02	3.74	4.26	4.01	3.54	3.85	6.09	5.74	4.31	2.38	2.36	3.52	46.82
S. Dak.	Sioux Falls____	0.62	0.93	1.54	2.31	3.38	4.35	2.84	3.59	2.61	1.25	1.00	0.74	25.16
Tenn__	Memphis_____	6.07	4.69	5.07	4.63	4.23	3.68	3.54	2.97	2.82	2.72	4.38	4.93	49.73
	Nashville_____	5.49	4.51	5.19	3.74	3.72	3.25	3.72	2.86	2.87	2.32	3.28	4.19	45.15
Tex___	Dallas_____	2.32	2.55	2.85	4.00	4.83	3.24	1.94	1.93	2.82	2.70	2.70	2.67	34.55
	El Paso_____	0.46	0.41	0.35	0.29	0.40	0.69	1.29	1.19	1.14	0.85	0.33	0.49	7.89
	Houston_____	3.78	3.44	2.67	3.24	4.32	3.69	4.29	4.27	4.26	3.77	3.86	4.36	45.95
Utah__	Salt Lake City__	1.35	1.18	1.56	1.76	1.40	0.98	0.58	0.87	0.53	1.15	1.30	1.24	13.90
Vt____	Burlington____	1.95	1.79	2.11	2.63	2.99	3.49	3.85	3.37	3.31	2.97	2.62	2.13	33.21
Va____	Norfolk_____	3.33	3.21	3.45	3.16	3.36	3.61	5.92	5.97	4.22	2.92	3.05	2.74	44.94
	Richmond_____	3.46	2.90	3.42	3.15	3.72	3.75	5.61	5.54	3.65	3.00	3.04	2.97	44.21
Wash__	Seattle-Tacoma_	5.73	4.24	3.79	2.40	1.73	1.58	0.81	0.95	2.05	4.02	5.35	6.29	38.94
	Spokane_____	2.44	1.86	1.50	0.91	1.21	1.49	0.38	0.41	0.75	1.57	2.24	2.43	17.19
W.Va._	Charleston____	4.32	3.53	4.34	3.68	3.71	3.69	5.67	3.95	2.92	2.58	2.79	3.25	44.42
Wis___	Milwaukee____	1.83	1.40	2.31	2.53	3.16	3.64	2.95	3.06	2.72	2.10	2.18	1.63	29.51
Wyo___	Cheyenne_____	0.52	0.56	1.21	1.88	2.52	2.11	1.82	1.44	1.10	0.83	0.62	0.45	15.06
P.R.__	San Juan_____	4.70	2.90	2.20	3.72	7.12	5.66	6.25	7.13	6.76	5.83	6.49	5.45	64.21

[1] City office data.

Source: U.S. National Oceanic and Atmospheric Administration, *Local Climatological Data*. Monthly with annual summary.

Average Total Snow and Ice Pellets—Selected Cities

[In inches. Airport data, except as noted. For period of record through 1971. T denotes trace]

STATE AND STATION	Length of record (yrs.)	Jan.	Feb.	Mar.	Apr.	May	June	July	Aug.	Sept.	Oct.	Nov.	Dec.	Annual
Ala. — Mobile	30	0.1	0.1	0.1	-	-	-	-	-	-	-	T	0.1	0.4
Alaska — Juneau	28	23.0	20.9	19.2	5.1	0.1	T	-	-	T	1.2	11.6	23.6	104.7
Ariz. — Phoenix	34	T	T	-	T	-	-	-	-	-	-	-	T	T
Ark. — Little Rock	29	2.4	1.4	0.6	T	-	-	-	-	-	-	0.2	1.1	5.7
Calif. — Los Angeles	36	T	T	-	-	-	-	-	-	-	-	-	T	T
Sacramento	23	T	T	T	-	-	-	-	-	-	-	-	T	T
San Francisco	44	T	T	T	-	-	-	-	-	-	-	-	T	T
Colo. — Denver	37	8.2	8.1	12.7	9.0	1.5	T	-	-	2.0	3.7	7.2	5.7	58.1
Conn. — Hartford	17	11.5	13.3	13.9	1.8	T	-	-	-	-	T	2.0	13.9	56.4
Del. — Wilmington	24	6.0	5.7	4.2	0.1	T	-	-	-	-	T	1.2	4.5	21.7
D.C. — Washington	28	5.1	5.2	2.7	T	T	-	-	-	-	T	0.8	4.1	17.7
Fla. — Jacksonville	29	T	0.1	T	-	-	-	-	-	-	-	-	T	0.1
Miami	28	-	-	-	-	-	-	-	-	-	-	-	-	-
Ga. — Atlanta	37	0.8	0.5	0.3	-	-	-	-	-	-	-	T	0.2	1.8
Hawaii — Honolulu	25	-	-	-	-	-	-	-	-	-	-	-	-	-
Idaho — Boise	32	7.8	3.9	1.9	0.8	0.1	T	T	-	-	0.2	1.5	5.4	21.6
Ill. — Chicago	29	9.7	8.0	7.7	1.1	T	-	-	-	-	0.3	2.5	9.7	38.9
Peoria	28	5.5	4.6	4.9	0.6	T	-	-	-	-	0.1	1.7	5.4	22.8
Ind. — Indianapolis	40	4.9	5.1	3.8	0.4	T	-	-	-	-	T	2.1	4.3	20.5
Iowa — Des Moines	32	8.4	6.7	7.6	1.2	T	-	-	-	T	0.1	2.2	6.0	32.1
Kans. — Wichita	18	3.7	3.9	3.5	0.1	-	-	-	-	-	T	0.6	3.2	15.0
Ky. — Louisville	24	5.5	4.9	4.1	0.1	-	-	-	-	-	T	1.4	2.5	18.6
La. — New Orleans	24	T	0.1	T	-	-	-	-	-	-	-	-	-	0.2
Maine — Portland	31	18.4	21.0	14.1	3.0	0.3	-	-	-	T	0.3	3.1	15.2	75.4
Md. — Baltimore	21	5.7	6.3	5.5	0.1	T	-	-	-	-	T	1.3	5.1	24.0
Mass. — Boston	36	12.4	12.1	8.4	0.7	T	-	-	-	-	T	1.3	8.1	43.0
Mich. — Detroit	36	8.0	7.7	5.5	1.2	T	-	-	-	-	T	2.6	6.7	31.7
Sault Ste. Marie	30	24.6	17.9	14.4	4.5	0.7	T	-	T	0.2	2.2	14.8	26.0	105.3
Minn. — Duluth	28	16.6	12.0	13.6	7.2	1.0	T	-	T	T	1.3	10.1	16.2	78.0
Minneapolis-St. Paul	33	8.5	8.3	10.6	2.3	0.2	-	-	-	0.1	0.3	5.9	8.7	44.9
Miss. — Jackson	8	0.2	0.5	0.7	T	-	-	-	-	-	-	T	-	1.4
Mo. — Kansas City	38	5.6	4.0	4.0	0.7	T	-	-	-	-	T	1.0	4.5	19.8
St. Louis	35	4.2	3.9	4.6	0.3	T	-	-	-	-	T	1.1	3.0	17.1
Mont. — Great Falls	34	9.7	9.0	9.6	6.4	1.4	0.5	T	-	1.3	2.5	7.5	8.3	56.2
Nebr. — Omaha	36	8.0	7.5	7.2	0.8	0.1	-	-	-	T	0.3	2.2	5.9	32.0
Nev. — Reno	29	6.6	4.9	5.2	1.5	1.1	T	-	-	T	0.4	1.7	5.0	26.4
N.H. — Concord	30	16.9	15.8	11.5	1.9	0.2	-	-	-	-	0.1	4.0	13.7	64.1
N.J. — Atlantic City	27	5.2	5.2	3.5	0.3	-	-	-	-	-	T	0.5	2.7	17.4
N. Mex. — Albuquerque	32	1.9	1.8	1.7	0.3	T	-	-	-	-	T	1.2	2.8	9.7
N.Y. — Albany	25	15.3	15.2	12.8	2.3	0.1	-	-	-	-	0.1	3.8	16.2	65.8
Buffalo	28	22.3	17.8	12.1	2.6	0.2	-	-	-	T	0.2	12.6	20.2	88.0
New York [1]	103	7.7	8.6	5.4	1.0	T	-	-	-	-	-	1.0	6.1	29.8
N.C. — Charlotte	32	2.3	1.5	1.2	T	-	-	-	-	-	-	0.1	0.6	5.7
Raleigh	27	2.9	2.0	1.4	T	-	-	-	-	-	-	0.1	1.0	7.4
N. Dak. — Bismarck	32	7.2	6.2	7.8	4.1	1.2	T	-	-	0.3	1.2	4.9	6.0	38.9
Ohio — Cincinnati [1]	56	5.2	4.3	3.5	0.5	T	-	-	-	-	0.1	1.5	4.0	19.1
Cleveland	30	10.1	10.6	10.5	2.1	T	-	-	-	T	0.6	5.6	10.4	49.9
Columbus	24	7.3	6.2	5.4	0.6	T	-	-	-	T	0.1	3.0	6.1	28.7
Okla. — Oklahoma City	32	2.9	2.4	2.0	T	-	-	-	-	-	T	0.3	1.6	9.2
Oreg. — Portland	31	4.9	0.9	0.7	T	T	-	-	-	-	T	0.3	1.6	8.4
Pa. — Philadelphia	29	5.7	6.1	4.1	0.3	T	-	-	-	-	T	0.8	4.6	21.6
Pittsburgh	19	11.0	10.6	10.4	1.6	0.3	-	-	-	-	0.2	4.2	9.0	47.3
R.I. — Providence	18	10.0	10.2	10.6	0.7	-	-	-	-	-	0.1	0.5	8.7	40.8
S.C. — Columbia	24	0.4	0.3	0.2	-	-	-	-	-	-	-	T	0.4	1.3
S. Dak. — Sioux Falls	26	6.1	10.1	10.7	1.8	T	-	-	-	T	0.4	3.9	7.9	40.9
Tenn. — Memphis	21	2.2	1.4	1.5	T	-	-	-	-	-	-	T	1.2	6.3
Nashville	30	3.8	2.9	2.0	0.1	-	-	-	-	-	T	0.7	2.2	11.7
Tex. — Dallas	31	1.2	0.4	0.2	-	-	-	-	-	-	-	T	0.2	2.0
El Paso	32	1.3	0.8	0.4	T	-	-	-	-	-	-	0.9	1.0	4.4
Houston	37	0.2	0.2	T	-	-	-	-	-	-	-	-	T	0.4
Utah — Salt Lake City	43	13.2	9.7	9.3	4.1	0.5	T	-	-	0.1	1.0	6.0	11.8	55.7
Vt. — Burlington	28	17.6	17.8	12.0	2.6	0.3	-	-	-	T	6.8	6.3	19.2	76.5
Va. — Norfolk	23	3.3	1.9	0.8	0.1	-	-	-	-	-	T	-	1.4	7.5
Richmond	34	5.6	3.3	3.2	0.2	-	-	-	-	-	T	0.5	2.2	15.0
Wash. — Seattle-Tacoma	27	7.4	1.9	2.0	T	-	-	-	-	-	0.1	1.1	3.2	15.7
Spokane	24	19.0	7.3	5.1	0.5	0.2	T	-	-	-	0.5	5.3	16.4	54.3
W. Va. — Charleston	24	8.5	7.8	4.4	0.3	T	-	-	-	-	0.2	2.9	5.1	29.2
Wis. — Milwaukee	31	12.8	7.9	9.6	1.1	T	-	-	-	-	T	2.6	9.5	43.5
Wyo. — Cheyenne	36	5.9	6.0	11.4	9.5	3.6	0.4	-	-	0.8	3.5	5.8	5.0	51.9
P.R. — San Juan	17	-	-	-	-	-	-	-	-	-	-	-	-	-

- Represents zero. [1] City office data.

Source: U.S. National Oceanic and Atmospheric Administration, *Local Climatological Data.* Monthly with annual summary.

PERIOD 1899-1938

SOURCE: Climate and Man Yearbook of Agriculture—1941 Dept. of Agriculture

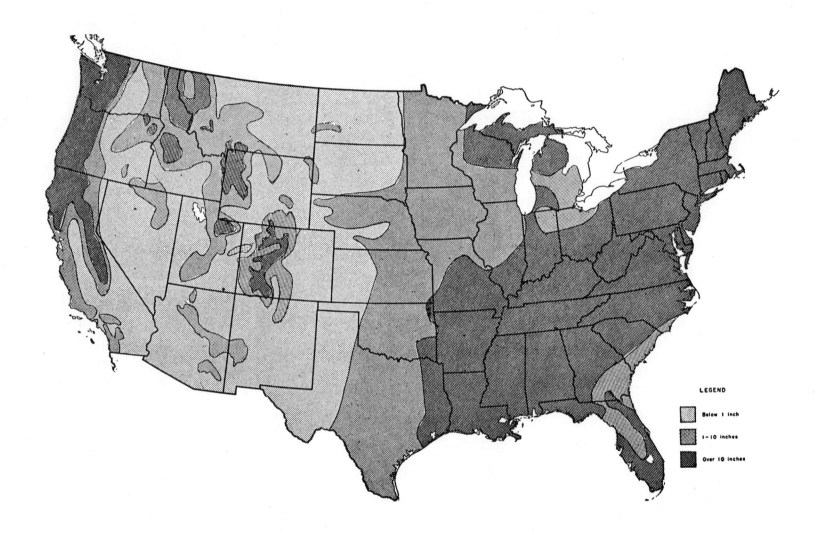

LEGEND

Below 1 inch

1-10 inches

Over 10 inches

SOURCE: The Report of the President's Water Resources Policy Commission—1950
A water policy for the American people

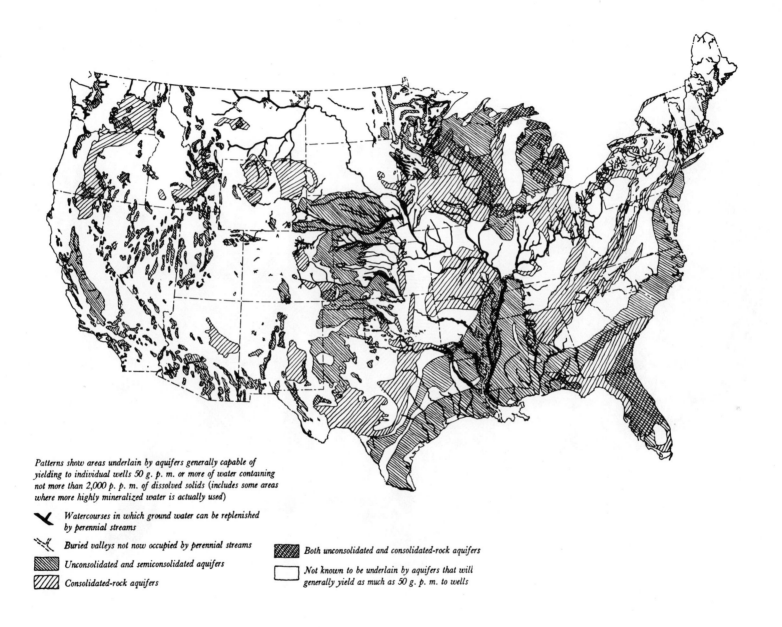

Patterns show areas underlain by aquifers generally capable of
yielding to individual wells 50 g. p. m. or more of water containing
not more than 2,000 p. p. m. of dissolved solids (includes some areas
where more highly mineralized water is actually used)

Watercourses in which ground water can be replenished
by perennial streams

Buried valleys not now occupied by perennial streams

Unconsolidated and semiconsolidated aquifers

Consolidated-rock aquifers

Both unconsolidated and consolidated-rock aquifers

Not known to be underlain by aquifers that will
generally yield as much as 50 g. p. m. to wells

SOURCE: Yearbook of Agriculture U. S. Dept. of Agriculture 1955

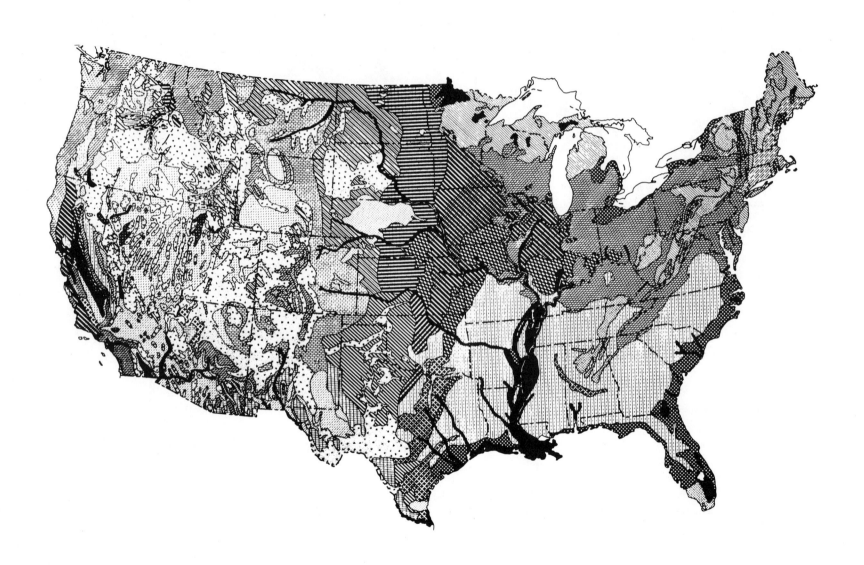

ZONAL

Great groups of soils with well-developed soil characteristics, reflecting the dominating influence of climate and vegetation. (As shown on the map, many small areas of intrazonal and azonal soils are included.)

PODZOL SOILS

 Light-colored leached soils of cool, humid forested regions.

BROWN PODZOLIC SOILS

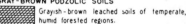 Brown leached soils of cool-temperate, humid forested regions.

GRAY-BROWN PODZOLIC SOILS

 Grayish-brown leached soils of temperate, humid forested regions.

RED AND YELLOW PODZOLIC SOILS

 Red or yellow leached soils of warm-temperate, humid forested regions.

PRAIRIE SOILS

 Very dark brown soils of cool and temperate, relatively humid grasslands.

REDDISH PRAIRIE SOILS

 Dark reddish-brown soils of warm-temperate, relatively humid grasslands.

CHERNOZEM SOILS

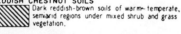 Dark-brown to nearly black soils of cool and temperate, subhumid grasslands.

CHESTNUT SOILS

Dark-brown soils of cool and temperate, subhumid to semiarid grasslands.

REDDISH CHESTNUT SOILS

Dark reddish-brown soils of warm-temperate, semiarid regions under mixed shrub and grass vegetation.

BROWN SOILS

Brown soils of cool and temperate, semiarid grasslands.

REDDISH BROWN SOILS

Reddish-brown soils of warm-temperate to hot, semiarid to arid regions, under mixed shrub and grass vegetation.

NONCALCIC BROWN SOILS

Brown or light reddish-brown soils of warm-temperate, wet-dry, semiarid regions, under mixed forest, shrub, and grass vegetation.

SIEROZEM OR GRAY DESERT SOILS

Gray soils of cool to temperate, arid regions, under shrub and grass vegetation.

RED DESERT SOILS

Light reddish-brown soils of warm-temperate to hot, arid regions, under shrub vegetation.

INTRAZONAL

Great groups of soils with more or less well-developed soil characteristics reflecting the dominating influence of some local factor of relief, parent material, or age over the normal effect of climate and vegetation. (Many areas of these soils are included with zonal groups on the map.)

PLANOSOLS

 Soils with strongly leached surface horizons over claypans on nearly flat land in cool to warm, humid to subhumid regions, under grass or forest vegetation.

RENDZINA SOILS

 Dark grayish-brown to black soils developed from soft limy materials in cool to warm, humid to subhumid regions, mostly under grass vegetation.

SOLONCHAK (1) AND SOLONETZ (2) SOILS

 (1) Light-colored soils with high concentration of soluble salts, in subhumid to arid regions, under salt-loving plants.

(2) Dark-colored soils with hard prismatic subsoils, usually strongly alkaline, in subhumid or semiarid regions under grass or shrub vegetation.

WIESENBÖDEN (1); GROUND WATER PODZOL (2), AND HALF-BOG SOILS (3)

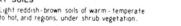 (1) Dark-brown to black soils developed with poor drainage under grasses in humid and subhumid regions.

(2) Gray sandy soils with brown cemented sandy subsoils developed under forests from nearly level imperfectly drained sand in humid regions.

(3) Poorly drained, shallow, dark peaty or mucky soils underlain by gray mineral soil, in humid regions, under swamp-forests.

BOG SOILS

 Poorly drained dark peat or muck soils underlain by peat, mostly in humid regions, under swamp or marsh types of vegetation.

The areas of each great soil group shown on the map include areas of other groups too small to be shown separately. Especially are there small areas of the azonal and intrazonal groups included in the areas of zonal groups.

AZONAL

Soils without well-developed soil characteristics. (Many areas of these soils are included with other groups on the map.)

LITHOSOLS AND SHALLOW SOILS
(ARID-SUBHUMID)

(HUMID)

 Shallow soils consisting largely of an imperfectly weathered mass of rock fragments, largely but not exclusively on steep slopes.

SANDS (DRY)

Very sandy soils.

ALLUVIAL SOILS

Soils developing from recently deposited alluvium that have had little or no modification by processes of soil formation.

SOURCE: Roy L. Donahue. Soils: An Introduction to Soils and Plant Growth. © *1965, 2nd Ed.*
(After map, "Soil Associations of the United States," published in Soils and Men, Yearbook of Agriculture for 1938)
General pattern of Great Soil Groups
Courtesy Division of Soil Survey, Bureau of Plant Industry, U. S. D. A.

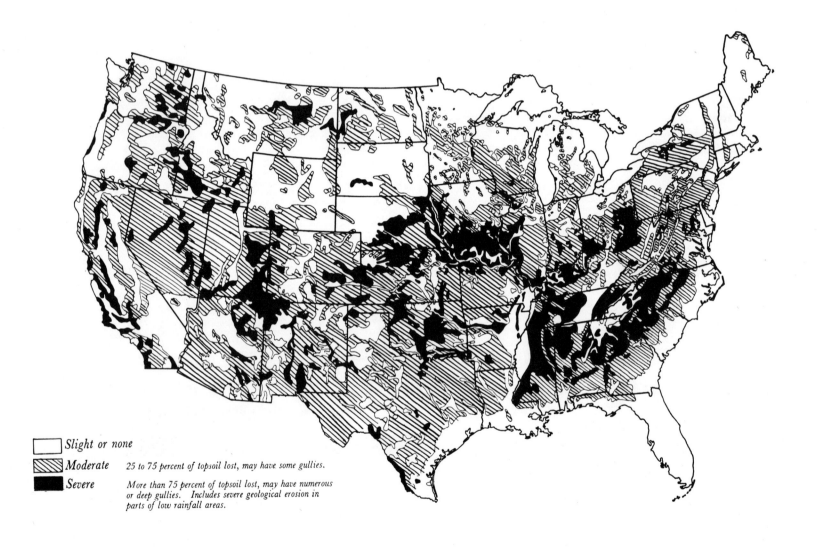

Slight or none

Moderate   *25 to 75 percent of topsoil lost, may have some gullies.*

Severe   *More than 75 percent of topsoil lost, may have numerous or deep gullies. Includes severe geological erosion in parts of low rainfall areas.*

SOURCE: The Report of the President's Water Resources Policy Commission—1950
A Water Policy for the American People

SOME COMMON TOPOGRAPHIC POSITIONS:

Area 1 is a flood plain. It is subject to flooding during heavy storms.

Area 2 is an alluvial fan. The soil has been forming over the years as a result of water eroding material from the watershed above and depositing it near the mouth of the waterway. An alluvial fan can be hard hit by flash floods after heavy rains unless an adequate water-disposal system has been provided to control the runoff from the watershed above.

Area 3 is an upland waterway where water flowing from the higher surrounding land will concentrate. Natural waterways should not be used unless an adequate ditch or diversion terrace has been constructed to divert water from the site.

Area 4 is a low depressed area where water accumulates from higher surrounding areas. These soils remain wet and spongy for long periods.

Area 5 is a steep hillside. Many soils on steep slopes are shallow to rock. Some are subject to severe slippage. On all slopes, one must be careful of soil movement through gravity or by water erosion. Yet some steep hillsides can be used safely as building sites. The problem can be solved by studying the soils and avoiding the bad ones.

Area 6 is a deep, well-drained soil found on ridgetops and gently sloping hillsides. Generally these areas have the smallest water-management problems. They are the best building sites, other things being equal.

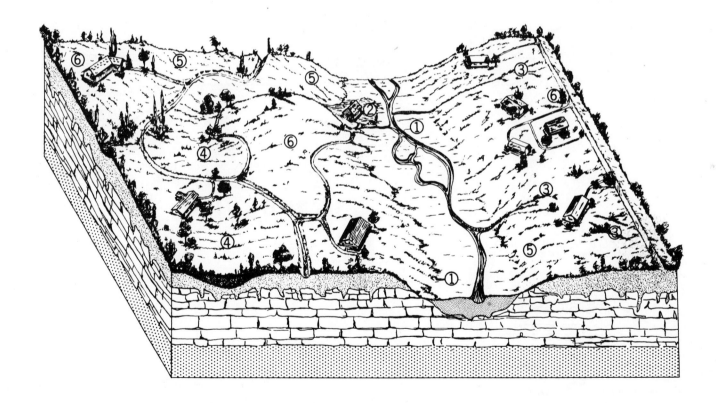

Source: Know the Soil You Build On. *Soil Conservation Service, U.S. Dept. of Agriculture, Washington, D.C. 1967.*

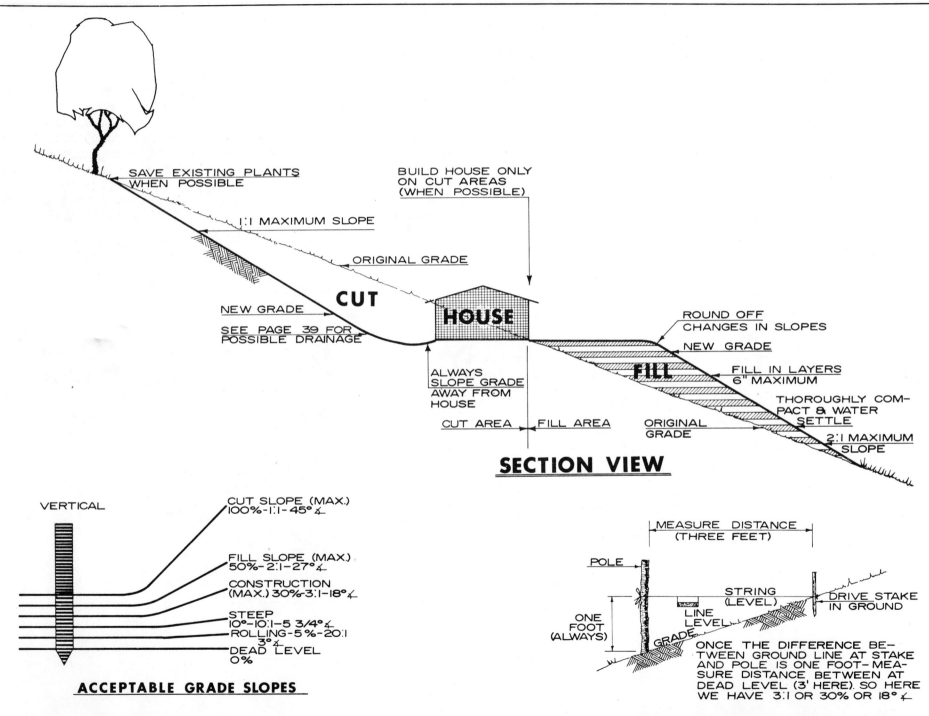

SAVE EXISTING PLANTS WHEN POSSIBLE

BUILD HOUSE ONLY ON CUT AREAS (WHEN POSSIBLE)

1:1 MAXIMUM SLOPE

ORIGINAL GRADE

CUT

HOUSE

NEW GRADE

SEE PAGE 39 FOR POSSIBLE DRAINAGE

ALWAYS SLOPE GRADE AWAY FROM HOUSE

CUT AREA   FILL AREA

ROUND OFF CHANGES IN SLOPES

NEW GRADE

FILL

FILL IN LAYERS 6" MAXIMUM

THOROUGHLY COMPACT & WATER SETTLE

ORIGINAL GRADE

2:1 MAXIMUM SLOPE

SECTION VIEW

VERTICAL

CUT SLOPE (MAX.) 100%-1:1-45°∠

FILL SLOPE (MAX.) 50%-2:1-27°∠

CONSTRUCTION (MAX.) 30%-3:1-18°∠

STEEP 10°-10:1-5 3/4°∠

ROLLING-5%-20:1 3°∠

DEAD LEVEL 0%

ACCEPTABLE GRADE SLOPES

MEASURE DISTANCE (THREE FEET)

POLE

STRING (LEVEL)

LINE LEVEL

DRIVE STAKE IN GROUND

ONE FOOT (ALWAYS)

GRADE

ONCE THE DIFFERENCE BETWEEN GROUND LINE AT STAKE AND POLE IS ONE FOOT-MEASURE DISTANCE BETWEEN AT DEAD LEVEL (3' HERE). SO HERE WE HAVE 3:1 OR 30% OR 18°∠

HOW TO DETERMINE SLOPE

SOURCE: Landscape Development, Dept. of the Interior, Littleton, Colorado.

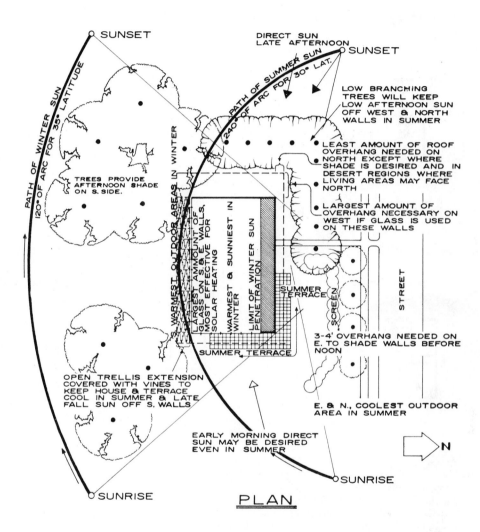

SUNSET

DIRECT SUN
LATE AFTERNOON

SUNSET

LOW BRANCHING
TREES WILL KEEP
LOW AFTERNOON SUN
OFF WEST & NORTH
WALLS IN SUMMER

LEAST AMOUNT OF ROOF
OVERHANG NEEDED ON
NORTH EXCEPT WHERE
SHADE IS DESIRED AND IN
DESERT REGIONS WHERE
LIVING AREAS MAY FACE
NORTH

LARGEST AMOUNT OF
OVERHANG NECESSARY ON
WEST IF GLASS IS USED
ON THESE WALLS

PATH OF WINTER SUN
120° OF ARC FOR 35° LATITUDE

PATH OF SUMMER SUN
240° OF ARC FOR 30° LAT.

TREES PROVIDE
AFTERNOON SHADE
ON S. SIDE.

WARMEST OUTDOOR AREAS IN WINTER

LARGEST AMMOUNT OF
GLASS ON S. & E. WALLS,
MOST EFFECTIVE FOR
SOLAR HEATING

WARMEST & SUNNIEST IN
WINTER

LIMIT OF WINTER SUN
PENETRATION

SUMMER
TERRACE

SCREEN

STREET

3-4' OVERHANG NEEDED ON
E. TO SHADE WALLS BEFORE
NOON

SUMMER TERRACE

OPEN TRELLIS EXTENSION
COVERED WITH VINES TO
KEEP HOUSE & TERRACE
COOL IN SUMMER & LATE
FALL SUN OFF S. WALLS

E. & N., COOLEST OUTDOOR
AREA IN SUMMER

EARLY MORNING DIRECT
SUN MAY BE DESIRED
EVEN IN SUMMER

N

SUNRISE

SUNRISE

PLAN

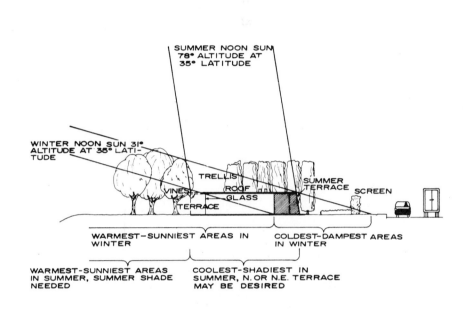

SUMMER NOON SUN
78° ALTITUDE AT
35° LATITUDE

WINTER NOON SUN 31°
ALTITUDE AT 35° LATI-
TUDE

TRELLIS

ROOF

VINES

SUMMER
TERRACE

GLASS

SCREEN

TERRACE

WARMEST-SUNNIEST AREAS IN
WINTER

COLDEST-DAMPEST AREAS
IN WINTER

WARMEST-SUNNIEST AREAS
IN SUMMER, SUMMER SHADE
NEEDED

COOLEST-SHADIEST IN
SUMMER, N. OR N.E. TERRACE
MAY BE DESIRED

ELEVATION

SOURCE: *Landscape Development, Dept. of the Interior, Littleton, Colorado.*

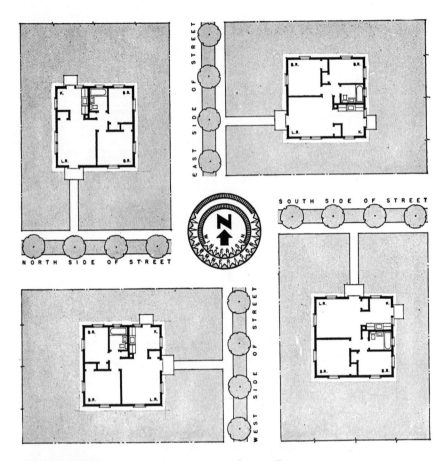

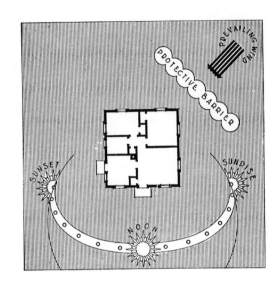

IN THE NORTH houses are usually built with a compact plan for economy and comfort in winter weather. Living rooms should be located to receive as much sunlight as possible. Protection should be provided against cold prevailing winter winds. This protective barrier, among others, may be buildings, trees or glazed storm sash.

ORIENTATION of a house is an important factor affecting its livability. This planning principle concerns the relationship of rooms to sunlight, prevailing winds and view. The living room should be bright, cheerful, have plenty of sunlight and the best view from its windows if possible. Morning sunlight generally is desirable in the dining space and the kitchen should be located to avoid the heat of afternoon sun. Bedrooms should have sunlight some time during the day. Geographical location has a bearing on orientation as well as the plan. Any compact plan can be correctly orientated by rotating the plan or reversing it, when necessary, as shown by the above use of the basic two-bedroom plan for sites on different sides of the street. The only change in plan required is the relocation of the entrance door and living room windows.

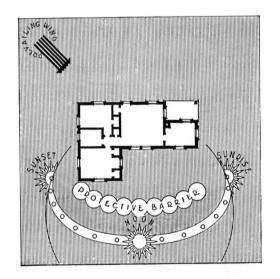

IN THE SOUTH cross ventilation of rooms is more important for livability than a compact plan. Houses should be designed and located to take advantage of the prevailing summer winds common to their locality. Desirable protection from the sun may be obtained through the use of trees, window blinds, awnings, or other means.

SOURCE: Principles of Planning Small Houses, Technical Bulletin #4, Federal Housing Administration.

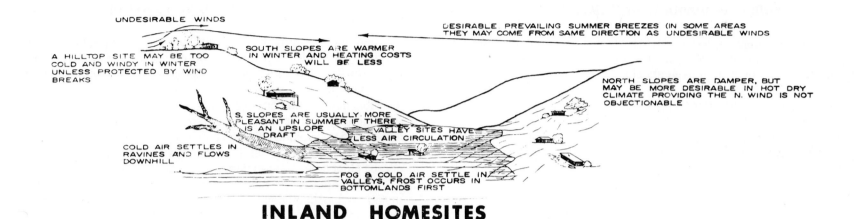

UNDESIRABLE WINDS

DESIRABLE PREVAILING SUMMER BREEZES (IN SOME AREAS THEY MAY COME FROM SAME DIRECTION AS UNDESIRABLE WINDS

SOUTH SLOPES ARE WARMER IN WINTER AND HEATING COSTS WILL BE LESS

A HILLTOP SITE MAY BE TOO COLD AND WINDY IN WINTER UNLESS PROTECTED BY WIND BREAKS

NORTH SLOPES ARE DAMPER, BUT MAY BE MORE DESIRABLE IN HOT DRY CLIMATE PROVIDING THE N. WIND IS NOT OBJECTIONABLE

S. SLOPES ARE USUALLY MORE PLEASANT IN SUMMER IF THERE IS AN UPSLOPE DRAFT

VALLEY SITES HAVE LESS AIR CIRCULATION

COLD AIR SETTLES IN RAVINES AND FLOWS DOWNHILL

FOG & COLD AIR SETTLE IN VALLEYS, FROST OCCURS IN BOTTOMLANDS FIRST

INLAND HOMESITES

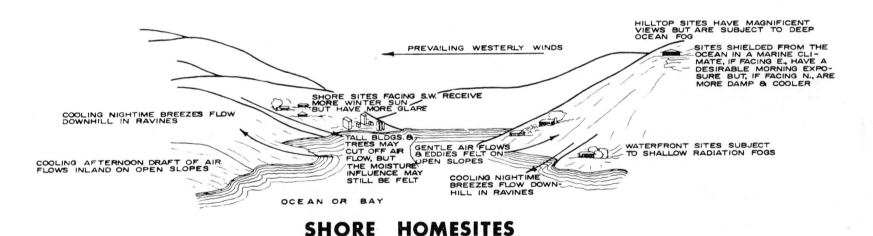

HILLTOP SITES HAVE MAGNIFICENT VIEWS BUT ARE SUBJECT TO DEEP OCEAN FOG

PREVAILING WESTERLY WINDS

SITES SHIELDED FROM THE OCEAN IN A MARINE CLIMATE, IF FACING E., HAVE A DESIRABLE MORNING EXPOSURE BUT, IF FACING N., ARE MORE DAMP & COOLER

SHORE SITES FACING S.W. RECEIVE MORE WINTER SUN BUT HAVE MORE GLARE

COOLING NIGHTIME BREEZES FLOW DOWNHILL IN RAVINES

TALL BLDGS. & TREES MAY CUT OFF AIR FLOW, BUT THE MOISTURE INFLUENCE MAY STILL BE FELT

GENTLE AIR FLOWS & EDDIES FELT ON OPEN SLOPES

WATERFRONT SITES SUBJECT TO SHALLOW RADIATION FOGS

COOLING AFTERNOON DRAFT OF AIR FLOWS INLAND ON OPEN SLOPES

COOLING NIGHTIME BREEZES FLOW DOWNHILL IN RAVINES

OCEAN OR BAY

SHORE HOMESITES

SOURCE: Landscape Development, Dept. of the Interior, Littleton, Colorado.

SURFACE-DRAINAGE SYSTEMS

The basic surface-drainage systems are the parallel, the random, and the cross-slope or diversion system. The system to be used will depend upon the requirements of the site. The system used should:

1. Fit the farming system.

2. Cause water to flow readily from land to ditch without harmful erosion or deposition of silt.

3. Have adequate capacity to carry the flow.

4. Be designed for construction and maintenance with appropriate equipment locally available.

THE RANDOM SYSTEM

Where the topography is irregular, but so flat or gently sloping as to have wet depressions scattered over the area as shown in Figure 2, a random system is used. The field ditches should be so located that they will transect as many depressions as feasible along a course through the lowest part of the field toward an available outlet. The course should be selected so as to provide the least interference with farming operations and a minimum of deep earth cuts. Cuts over three feet should be avoided although these sometimes are necessary to reach an outlet and leave a farmable field. Field ditches should ordinarily not be shallower than one-half foot deep or deeper than one foot where they are to be crossed frequently by farming equipment. Side slopes for handling farm equipment should be determined from local guides. Ditches should extend completely through depressions, as shown in Figure 2, to assure complete drainage. Land grading, smoothing or bedding will usually be necessary on the less permeable soils to assure complete surface water removal.

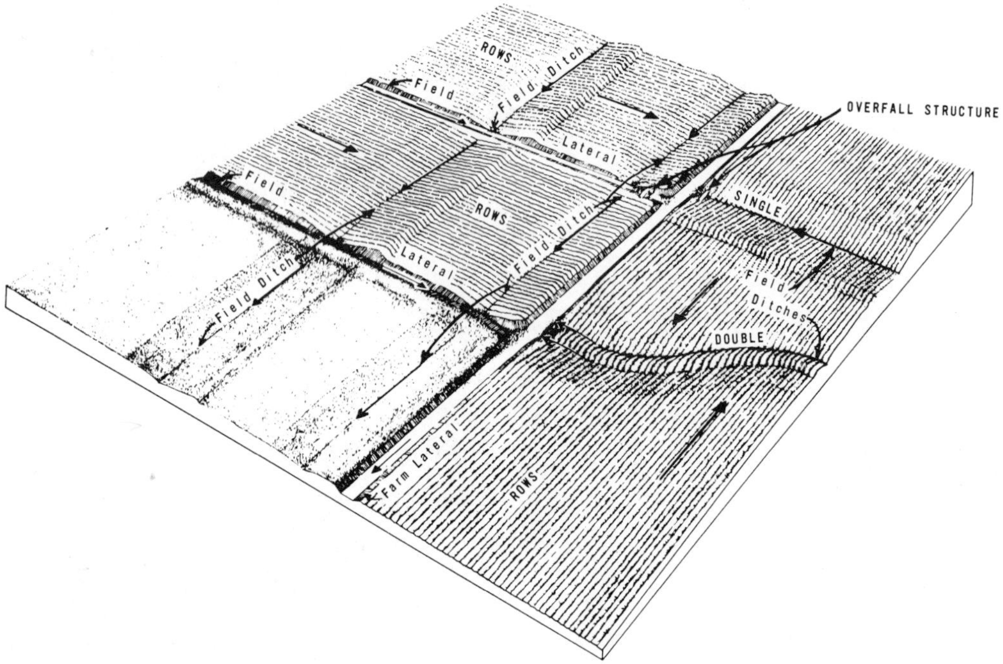

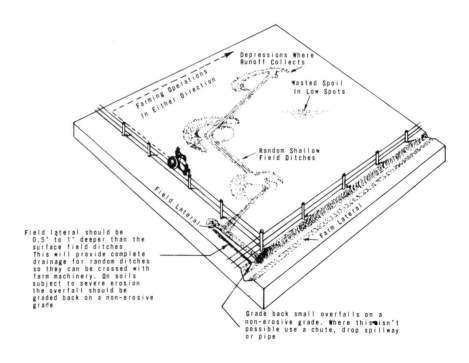

Figure 2   *Random system.*

Figure 1   Typical layout — individual farm drainage system. (Where the ground surface is undulating, ditches and drains will meander.)

Source: Drainage of Agricultural Land, *Soil Conservation Service, U.S. Dept. of Agriculture, Water Information Center, Inc., Port Washington, N.Y.*

THE PARALLEL SYSTEM

Where topography is flat and regular, and a random system is impractical or inadequate, field ditches should be established in a parallel but not necessarily equidistant pattern as shown in Figures 1 and 3. Orientation of field ditches will depend upon direction of land slope; location of diversions, cross-slope ditches and mains and laterals of the disposal system; and access of the established lands to farming equipment. Usually, field ditches should run parallel to each other across a field to discharge into field laterals bordering the field. Laterals and mains should be deeper than the field ditches to provide free outfall. Surfaces of lands should be graded and smoothed for uninterrupted flow along crop rows or over the land surfaces, when rows are not maintained.

When soils are permeable and the field ditches will dry out in about the same time as the adjoining land surface, crop rows may be run across the field ditches so that they collect and carry the row water directly to field laterals.

When crop rows are establiuhed parallel to field ditches, row ditches must be planned to drain rows through depressions and to reduce row lengths. Such ditches are temporary installations and are cut by hand shovel or plow during the course of farming operations.

THE CROSS-SLOPE SYSTEM (DIVERSION SYSTEM)

Use the cross-slope system (a) to drain sloping land that may be wet because of slowly permeable soil (b) to prevent the accumulation of water from higher land, and (c) to prevent the concentration of water in shallow pockets within the field. This system consists of one or more diversions, terraces, or field ditches built across the slope. As water flows downhill—either in the furrows between rows on cultivated land, or as sheet flow on hay land and permanent grassland it is intercepted and carried off (Figure 4).

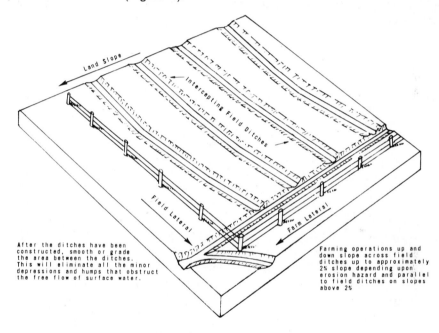

After the ditches have been constructed, smooth or grade the area between the ditches. This will eliminate all the minor depressions and humps that obstruct the free flow of surface water.

Farming operations up and down slope across field ditches up to approximately 2% slope depending upon erosion hazard and parallel to field ditches on slopes above 2%

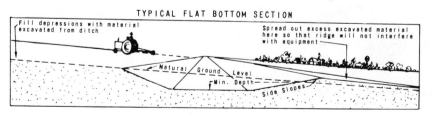

TYPICAL FLAT BOTTOM SECTION

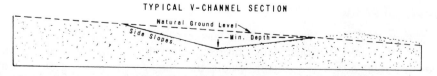

TYPICAL V-CHANNEL SECTION

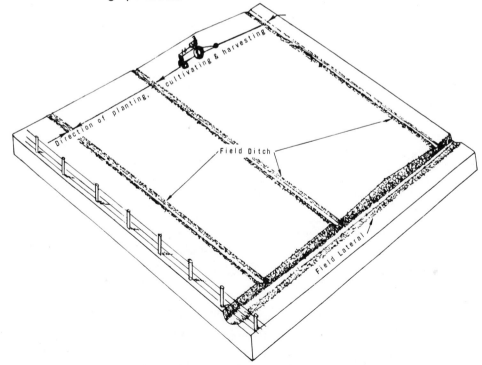

Figure 3   Parallel system
(Illustrates field layout suited to growing a variety of row crops, including cotton, corn, soybeans, sugarcane, grain sorghum, etc.)

Figure 4   Cross slope system on slight to moderate slopes

KINDS OF PONDS

An embankment pond is made by building an embankment or dam across a stream or watercourse. These ponds are usually built where stream valleys are depressed enough to permit storing 6 feet or more of water. The land slopes range from gentle to steep.

An excavated pond is made by digging a pit or dugout in nearly level areas. Because their capacity is obtained almost entirely by digging, excavated ponds are used where only a small supply of water is needed. Some ponds are built in gentle to moderately sloping areas and their capacity is obtained both by excavating and by building a dam.

Embankment ponds

Suitability of a pond site depends on the capacity of the soils in the reservoir area to hold water. The soils should contain a layer of material that is impervious and thick enough to prevent excessive seepage. Clays and silty clays are excellent for this purpose; sandy clays are usually satisfactory. Coarse-textured sands and sand-gravel mixtures are highly pervious and therefore usually unsuitable. The absence of a layer of impervious material over part of the ponded area does not necessarily mean that you must abandon the proposed site. You can treat these parts of the area by one of several methods, but any of these methods can be expensive.

Some limestone areas are especially hazardous as pond sites. There may be crevices, sinks, or channels in the limestone below the soil mantle that are not visible from the surface. These may empty the pond in a short time. In addition many soils in these areas are granular. Since the granules do not break down readily in water, the soils remain highly permeable. Without extensive investigations and laboratory tests, it is difficult to recognize all the factors that may make a limestone site undesirable. The best clue to the suitability of a site in one of these areas is the degree of success others have had with farm ponds in the immediate vicinity.

Make soil borings at intervals over the area to be covered with water unless you know that the soils are sufficiently impervious and that leakage will not be a problem. Three or four per acre may be enough if the soils are uniform. More may be required if there are significant differences.

Excavated Ponds

Excavated ponds are the simplest to build in relatively flat terrain. Because their capacity is obtained almost solely by excavation, their practical size is limited. They are best suited to locations where the demand for water is small. Since excavated ponds can be built to expose a minimum water surface area is proportion to their volume, they are advantageous in areas where evaporation losses are high and water is scarce. The ease with which they can be constructed, their compactness, their relative safety from flood-flow damage, and their low maintenance requirements make them popular in many sections of the country.

There are two kinds of excavated ponds. One is fed by surface runoff and the other is fed by groundwater aquifers, usually layers of sand and gravel. Some ponds may be fed from both of these sources.

The general location of an excavated pond depends largely on the purpose or purposes for which the water is to be used. The specific location more often than not is influenced by topography.

Excavated ponds fed by surface runoff may be located in almost any kind of topography. They are, however, most satisfactory and most commonly used in areas of comparatively flat but well-drained terrain. A pond may be located in a broad natural drainageway or to one side of a drainageway if the runoff can be diverted into the pond. The low point of a natural depression is often a good location. After the pond is filled, excess runoff escapes through regular drainageways.

Excavated ponds fed by ground-water aquifers can be located only in areas of flat or nearly flat topography. If possible, they should be located where the permanent water table is within a few feet of the surface.

 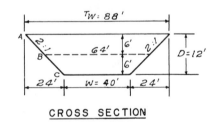

CROSS SECTION

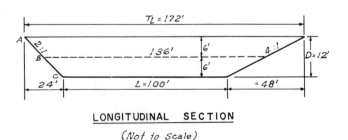

LONGITUDINAL SECTION

(Not to Scale)

Typical sections of an excavated pond. Note fenced desilting area above pond.

Source: Ponds, *Soil Conservation Service, U.S. Dept. of Agriculture, Washington, D.C., 1971.*

General — Dams may be classified into a number of different categories, depending upon the purpose of the classification. For the purposes of this manual, it is convenient to consider three broad classifications according to: Use, hydraulic design, or materials comprising the structure.

Classification According to Use — Dams may be classified according to the broad function which they are to serve, such as storage, diversion, or detention. Refinements of classification can also be made by considering specific functions involved.

Storage dams are constructed to impound water in periods of surplus supply for use in periods of deficient supply. These periods may be seasonal, annual, or longer. Many small dams impound the spring runoff for use in the summer dry season. Storage dams may be further classified according to the purpose of the storage, such as water supply, recreation, fish and wildlife, hydroelectric power generation, irrigation, etc. The specific purpose or purposes which are to be served by a storage dam often have an influence in the design of the structure, and may establish criteria such as the amount of reservoir fluctuation which may be expected and the amount of reservoir seepage which may be permitted.

Diversion dams are ordinarily constructed to provide head for carrying water into ditches, canals, or other conveyance systems to the place of use. They are used for irrigation developments, for diversion from a live stream to an off-channel-location storage reservoir, for municipal and industrial uses, or for any combination of the above.

Detention dams are constructed to retard flood runoff and minimize the effect of sudden floods. Detention dams fall into two main types. In one type, the water is temporarily stored, and released through an outlet structure at a rate which will not exceed the carrying capacity of the channel downstream. In the other type, the water is held as long as possible and allowed to seep into pervious banks or gravel strata in the foundation. The latter type is sometimes called a water-spreading dam or dike because its main purpose is to recharge the underground water supply. Detention dams are also constructed to trap sediment. These often are called debris dams.

Although this is not as common on small projects as on large developments, often dams are constructed to serve more than one purpose. Where multiple purposes are involved, a reservoir allocation is usually made to each of the separate uses. A common multipurpose project involving small dams combines storage, flood control, and recreational uses.

Classification by Hydraulic Design — Dams may also be classified as overflow or nonoverflow dams.

Overflow dams are designed to carry discharge over their crests. They must be made of materials which will not be eroded by such discharges. Concrete, masonry, steel, and wood are required excepting for overflow structures only a few feet high.

Nonoverflow dams are those which are not designed to be overtopped. This type of design extends the choice of materials to include earthfill and rockfill dams.

Often the two types are combined to form a composite structure consisting of, for example, an overflow concrete gravity dam with dikes of earthfill construction.

Classification by Materials — The most common classification used for purposes of discussion of design procedures is based upon the materials comprising the structure. This classification also usually recognizes the basic type of design such as, for example, concrete *gravity* dam or concrete *arch* dam.

This text is limited in scope to consideration of the more common type of small dams which are constructed under present day conditions, namely, *earthfill, rockfill,* and *concrete gravity.* Other types of dams, including concrete arch, concrete buttress, and timber dams, are discussed briefly.

Earthfill — Earthfill dams are the most common type of dam, principally because their construction involves utilization of materials in the natural state requiring a minimum of processing. Moreover, the foundation requirements for earthfill dams are less stringent than for other types. It is likely that earthfill dams will continue to be more prevalent than other types for storage purposes, partly because the number of sites favorable for concrete structures is decreasing as a result of extensive water storage development, particularly in arid and semiarid regions where the conservation of water for irrigation is a fundamental necessity.

Although the earthfill classification includes several types, the development of modern excavating, hauling, and compacting equipment for earth materials has made the rolled-fill type so economical as to virtually replace the semihydraulic- and hydraulic-fill types of earthfill dams. This is especially true for the construction of small structures where the relatively small amount of material to be handled precludes the establishment of the large plant required for efficient hydraulic operations. For this reason, only the rolled-fill type of earthfill dam is treated in this text. Earthfill dams of the rolled-fill type are further classified as "homogeneous," "zoned," or 'diaphragm."

H. G. ARTHUR, Director of Design and Construction, Bureau of Reclamation.

Source: Design of Small Dams, *Bureau of Reclamation, U.S. Dept. of the Interior, Washington, D.C., 1973.*

Earthfill dams require supplementary structures to serve as spillways. The principal disadvantage of an earthfill dam is that it will be damaged or even may be destroyed under the erosive action of water flowing over it if sufficient spillway capacity is not provided. It is also subject to serious damage or even failure due to burrowing of animals unless special precautions are taken. Unless the site is offstream, provision must be made for diversion of the stream during construction through the damsite by means of a conduit, or around the damsite by means of a tunnel. Otherwise, special provisions, including the use of heavy rock sections, must be incorporated in the design to permit overflowing of the embankment during construction. This latter type of diversion should be attempted only by those experienced in this field.

Rockfill — The rockfill dam uses rock of all sizes to provide stability and an impervious membrane to provide watertightness. The membrane may be an upstream facing of impervious soil, a concrete slab, asphaltic concrete paving, steel plates, or another similar device; or it may be an interior thin core of impervious soil.

Like the earth embankments, the rockfill dam is subject to damage or destruction by the overflow of water and so must be provided with a spillway of adequate capacity to prevent overtopping of the dam. An exception is the extremely low diversion dam where the rockfill facing is designed specifically to withstand overflows. Rockfill dams require foundations which will not be subject to settlement of magnitudes sufficient to rupture the watertight membrane. The only suitable foundations, therefore, are rock or compact sand and gravel.

The rockfill type is adapted to remote locations where the supply of good rock is ample, where suitable soil for an earthfill dam is not available, and where the construction of a concrete dam would be too costly.

Concrete Gravity — The concrete gravity dam is adapted to sites where there is a reasonably sound rock foundation, although low structures may be founded on alluvial foundations if adequate cutoffs are provided. It is well adapted for use as an overflow spillway crest and, because of this advantage, it is often used for the spillway feature of earthfill and rockfill dams or as the overflow section of a diversion dam.

In the early 1900's, some gravity dams were constructed of stone. However, the amount of hand labor required in this operation has been responsible for the exclusive use of concrete in modern gravity dam construction.

Gravity dams may be either straight or curved in plan. The curved plan may offer some advantage in both cost and safety. Also, occasionally the upstream curvature will locate that part of the dam on higher bedrock foundation.

Concrete Arch. A concrete arch dam is adaptable to sites where the ratio of width between abutments to height is not great and where the foundation at the abutments is solid rock capable of resisting arch thrust. Because the design of an arch dam is quite specialized, a detailed discussion of this type of design is not included in this text.

Concrete Buttress. Buttress dams comprise flat deck and multiple arch structures. They require about 60 percent less concrete than solid gravity dams, but the increased formwork and reinforcement steel required usually offset the savings in concrete. A number of buttress dams were built in the 1930's when the ratio of labor cost to materials cost was comparatively low. This type of construction usually is not competitive with other types of dams when labor costs are high.

The design of buttress dams is based on the knowledge and judgment that comes only from specialized experience in that field. Because of this fact and because of the limited application for the construction of buttress dams under present day conditions, the design of this type of structure is not included in this text.

Other Types. Dams of other types than those mentioned above have been built, but in most cases they meet some unusual local requirement or are of an experimental nature. In a few instances, structural steel has been used both for the deck and for the supporting framework of dams. Prior to 1920, a number of timber dams were constructed, particularly in the Northwest. The amount of labor involved in the timber dam, coupled with the short life of the structure, makes this type of structure uneconomical for modern construction.

GENERAL

Dikes are embankments constructed of earth or other suitable materials to protect land against overflow or flooding from streams, lakes, and tidal influences, and also to protect flat land from diffused surface waters. Dikes are generally used for the following purposes:

1. To protect bottom lands along one or both banks of a stream or channel from overflow caused by high stages or backwater from the outlet.

2. To provide additional out-of-bank capacity for floodways.

3. To provide floodways across bottom lands for conveyance of upland runoff to streams.

4. To protect the shores of lakes, desilting basins and impoundments against wave action and inundation during high water stages.

5. To protect coastal areas of oceans, bays, and estuaries against overflow from diurnal and wind storm tides.

6. To protect lands in areas of high rainfall and flat topography from diffused surface waters.

Dikes are intended to protect land against overflows of intermittent occurrence and short duration and not against continuous impoundment as in the case of dams. When restricting flood flows along streams, dikes tend to increase water surface elevation, velocities, and maximum discharges within the confined stream reaches and also increase the rate of flood wave travel downstream.

Dikes complicate drainage of the lands they protect. Facilities for runoff from protected areas must be provided at all stages of flow unless adequate storage is available. Ordinarily, discharge through dikes is obtained by gravity flow through conduits equipped with automatic flap or tide gates. Such gates prevent reverse flow into protected areas when stages on the water side of dikes are higher than on the land side. When prolonged flood stages prevent gravity outflow, the runoff from protected areas must be accumulated and stored temporarily in low areas behind the dikes; be removed continuously by pumps; or disposed of by a combination of these two methods.

CLASSIFICATION OF DIKES

The requirements for construction of dikes are governed by site conditions and design criteria. The design requirements are determined by value of crops and property and the hazard to life within the area to be protected. Dikes are classified as shown in Table 1 in accordance with these factors.

Reference is made to Engineering Standard for Dike, Code 356, SCS National Engineering Handbook, Section 2.

TABLE 1   Dike Classification

Class	Conditions	Design and Construction Requirements
I	1. Possible loss of life should failure occur. 2. High value land and improvements to be protected. 3. Complex site conditions. 4. The head of water against the dike in excess of 12 feet above normal ground, excluding sloughs, old channels and other low areas.	1. Design height equal to design water depth plus freeboard or wave height allowance of 2 feet or more. 2. Design water depth measured or computed for the greater of the record floor or the 100 year frequency flood. When loss of life or high value property damage are not a primary consideration, the greater of the 50 year frequency flood or the desired level of protection. 3. Cross section design according to site exposure to wave action and soil stability analysis. 4. Stable mineral soil required in foundation and embankment. 5. Construction according to site conditions and criteria for earth embankments. Refer to SCS National Engineering Handbook, Section 20.
II	1. Agricultural lands of medium to high capability with primary improvements in farmsteads and other valuable facilities. 2. The head of water against the dike less than 12 feet above normal ground excluding sloughs, old channels and other low areas.	1. Design water heights exceeding 4 feet to be based on a 25 year frequency or greater flood. When this degree of protection is not economically or physically feasible a flood frequency less than 25 years may be used if fuse plug sections or other suitable relief measures are included in the design.

2. Stable mineral soils required in the embankment. Organic soils permissible only as surface covering not in excess of 1 foot.

3. Cross section design based on design water sheight and the method of construction.

4. Construction with material compacted by equipment travel or dumped and shaped.

III 1. Agricultural lands of relatively low capability with improvements of low value.

2. The head of water against the dike not more than 6 feet for mineral soils or 4 feet for organic soils excluding sloughs, old channels and low areas.

1. Design based on SCS State Standards considering the site conditions.

2. Construction with materials available and suitable for use.

INVESTIGATIONS FOR DIKES

The intensity of investigations for dikes depends upon the class of dike required and a careful evaluation and consideration of the site conditions present. The following is a discussion of investigations needed for dike location, determination of high water levels, foundation materials and embankment materials.

Dike location

After the classification of the dike is determined, the initial step in investigation and design is establishment of a tentative location. This involves consideration of:

1. The land use and improvements, both existing and proposed, within the area to be protected. This data may be used in evaluating economic feasibility.

2. Anticipated flood stages.

3. The manner in which drainage of the protected area will be provided.

4. Rights-of-way involved.

5. Physical problems to be encountered, especially soil conditions relating to foundation and fill for the embankment and access for construction and maintenance.

The following should be considered in the final dike location:

1. Construction on soils that provide the most favorable foundation conditions and the best embankment materials. The location of Class III dikes will generally be parallel with units of the drainage system.

2. The shortest, most feasible and economical route consistent with protecting the largest usable area.

3. Avoidance of hazards, such as sloughs, sharp eroding bends in watercourses, and direct exposure to significant reaches of open water.

4. Utilization of natural protection against waves, such as permanent stands of trees, reeds or brush. Trees and brush should not be allowed to grow on the dike, however.

5. Bordering public roads or property lines for purposes of access and easements.

6. Coordination with units of the drainage system of the protected areas.

7. Use of natural storage basins within the protected areas to reduce pumping requirements and gate sizes.

8. The effect, if any, on existing dikes and adjacent lands which will result from the dike construction.

LAND USE

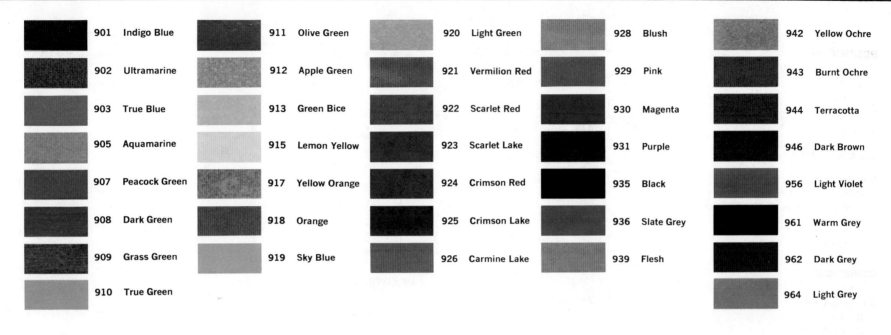

901 Indigo Blue	911 Olive Green	920 Light Green	928 Blush	942 Yellow Ochre
902 Ultramarine	912 Apple Green	921 Vermilion Red	929 Pink	943 Burnt Ochre
903 True Blue	913 Green Bice	922 Scarlet Red	930 Magenta	944 Terracotta
905 Aquamarine	915 Lemon Yellow	923 Scarlet Lake	931 Purple	946 Dark Brown
907 Peacock Green	917 Yellow Orange	924 Crimson Red	935 Black	956 Light Violet
908 Dark Green	918 Orange	925 Crimson Lake	936 Slate Grey	961 Warm Grey
909 Grass Green	919 Sky Blue	926 Carmine Lake	939 Flesh	962 Dark Grey
910 True Green				964 Light Grey

RESIDENTIAL — Prismacolor

Single-family	SF	☐	915 Lemon Yellow
2-family	2F	☐	939 Flesh (or 942)
3— and 4—family	34F	☐	917 Yellow Orange
Boarding and rooming houses	BH	☐	943 Burnt Ochre
Multiple dwelling (over 4-family)	APT	☐	946 Dark Brown
Tourists and trailer courts	T	☐	930 Magenta
Hotel	H	☐	931 Purple

BUSINESS & COMMERCIAL

Local (neighborhood) business	LB	☐	929 Pink
Offices and banks	OB	☐	921 Vermilion Red
General business	GB	☐	923 Scarlet Lake
Intensive business, theatres, recreation	IB	☐	925 Crimson Lake

INDUSTRIAL

Light industry	LM	☐	964 Light Gray
Railroads and public utilities	PM	☐	962 Dark Gray
Heavy industry	HM	☐	935 Black

PUBLIC — Prismacolor

Parks	P	☐	910 True Green
Public schools	P	☐	909 Grass Green
Public buildings	P	☐	903 Dark Green

QUASI-PUBLIC

Quasi-public open uses	QP	☐	903 True Blue (or 904)
Churches	QP	☐	902 Ultramarine
Quasi-public buildings & institutions	QP	☐	901 Indigo Blue
Cemeteries	QP	☐	905 Aquamarine

AGRICULTURAL

Crop land	AC	☐	912 Apple Green
Livestock land	AL	☐	911 Olive Green

MINING

	E	☐	No color

VACANT LAND

	V	☐	No color

Colors and numbers refer to PRISMACOLOR PENCILS as manufactured by EAGLE PENCIL CO. Because of production complexities, colors as shown are approximate; for precise color and variations consult manufacturer's color chart.

SOURCE: Mapping for Planning Publication No. 101 Public Administration Service, Chicago, Ill.

RESIDENTIAL   **Prismacolor**

Single Family   ☐ 915 Lemon Yellow

Two Families   ☐ 942 Yellow Ochre

3 and 4 Families   ☐ 943 Burnt Ochre

5 or More Families   ☐ 946 Dark Brown

Noninstitutional Group Housing   ☐ 918 Orange
  (Farm Labor Camps, Rooming and
  Boarding Houses, Fraternity, Sorority,
  etc.)

Trailer Park   ☐ 946 (Hatched)

COMMERCIAL

Shopping Center: [C] 925 Crimson Lake
  R Regional
  C Community
  N Neighborhood

Self-generative, Auto-oriented   ☐ 929 Pink
  (Including "Strip Commercial")

Other Retail Commercial   ☐ 922 Scarlet Red
  (Including Major Business, Streets, CBDs,
  Small Clusters, Individual Stores)

Offices, Banks and Clinics   ☐ 928 Blush
  (Outside Shopping Districts)

PUBLIC BUILDINGS   **Prismacolor**

Schools   [7-9] 919 Sky Blue

  N K-6 7-9
  10-12 JC
  C Grade Level
  P Private
     (plus name)

Public Buildings and offices   [CC] 902 Ultramarine
  CC Civic Center

Quasi-Public Buildings   [H] 901 Indigo Blue
  C Church
  H Hospitals

INDUSTRIAL

Nonmanufacturing — Extractive   ☐ 964 Warm Grey-Very Light

Nonmanufacturing   ☐ 936 Slate Grey
  (Warehouses, Wholesale, Heavy
  Commerical)

Manufacturing   [3] 961 Warm Grey
  1-5 Nuisance Value

Transportation   ☐ 956 Light Violet

Utilities   ☐ 931 Purple

FOR COLOR REFER TO PRISMACOLOR PENCILS COLOR CHART ON PAGE 115

SOURCE: Land Use Inventory Manual County of Santa Clara Planning Dept. San Jose, Calif—1964

OPEN SPACE

RECREATION

Prismacolor

Local Parks, Playgrounds and Playfields
(Serving a Neighborhood or District)
    N Neighborhood Park
    D District Park
    P Playground
    F Playfield

   [D] 913 Green Bice

Urban or Metropolitan Area Parks
(Serving a Community or
Metropolitan Area)

   [ ] 910 True Green

Private Open Space
    G Golf
    R Commercial Recreation

   [R] 912 Apple Green

CEMETERY

   [C] 912 Apple Green

AGRICULTURE

Agriculture: Orchard   [ ] 911 Olive Green

Agriculture: Nonorchard, Intensive
Cultivated   [ ] 907 Peacock Green

Grazing, Range Land   [ ] 920 Light Green

Agriculture: Livestock, Dairy Miscellaneous
Animal   [ ] 907 (Hatched)

NONURBAN

Forest and Brush   [ ] 908 Dark Green

Lakes, Reservoirs and Bay   [ ] 905 Aquamarine

Creeks and Channels   [ ] 905 (Solid Line)

Water Conservation and Flood control   [ ] 905 (Hatched)

Marshlands   [ ] 920 Light Green

VACANT URBAN

A SIMPLIFIED SET OF LAND USE CATEGORIES

In communities with simpler or less intensive patterns of development or in suburban, peripheral, or rural areas a less detailed system of land use categories is often adequate. The following suggested list follows the principles discussed above and is essentially a combination of similar uses into more general classifications.

RESIDENTIAL

Prismacolor

Single-family	**SF**	[ ]	915 Lemon Yellow
Intensive residential (combining 2–family—2F, 3– and 4–family—34F, and boarding houses)	**BH**	[ ]	943 Burnt Ochre
Multiple dwelling	**APT**	[ ]	946 Dark Brown
Hotel (including tourist and trailer courts — T)	**HT**	[ ]	931 Purple

BUSINESS AND COMMERCIAL

Local (neighborhood) business	**LB**	[ ]	929 Pink
General business (including offices and banks — OB, and intensive business — IB)	**GB**	[ ]	923 Scarlet Lake

INDUSTRIAL

Light industry (including public utilities — PM)	**LM**	[ ]	964 Light Gray
Heavy industry	**HM**	[ ]	935 Black

PUBLIC AND QUASI-PUBLIC

Parks	**P**	[ ]	910 True Green
Schools and public buildings	**P**	[ ]	909 Grass Green
Quasi-public open uses	**QP**	[ ]	903 True Blue
Churches and institutional bldgs.	**QP**	[ ]	901 Indigo Blue
Cemeteries	**QP**	[ ]	905 Aquamarine

AGRICULTURAL

All types — AC, AL	**AA**	[ ]	912 Apple Green

VACANT LAND

	V	[ ]	No color

FOR COLOR REFER TO PRISMACOLOR PENCILS COLOR CHART ON PAGE 115

SOURCE: Land Use Inventory Manual County of Santa Clara Planning Dept. San Jose, Calif—1964

SOURCE: Mapping for Planning Publication No. 101 Public Administration Service, Chicago, Ill.

AGE OF BUILDINGS

For presenting data in mapped form describing the age of structures the following scale will be found to be generally applicable. Where special conditions extent and subdivisions may be varied.

COLOR LEGEND FOR AGE OF BUILDINGS

Building Age Category		Prismacolor
Under 5 years	☐	915 Lemon Yellow
Over 5 to 15 years	☐	918 Orange
Over 15 to 25 years	☐	926 Carmine Lake
Over 25 to 35 years	☐	931 Purple
Over 35 years	☐	901 Indigo Blue

SQUARE FEET OF LOT AREA PER FAMILY

A map indicating the square feet of lot area per family gives a general indication of the density of population as it defines various areas and, in indicating in general the prevailing lot sizes per family, provides a basic study for zoning. The standards and color scale are suggestions only as the prevailing patterns of lot sizes vary from one community to another. It should be noted that a color not in the ascending color scale (pink) is used to indicate types of residential land uses (boarding and rooming houses) which are difficult to measure but where a relatively high density is probable.

COLOR LEGEND — LOT AREA PER FAMILY

Number Square Feet Per Family		Prismacolor
0 — 1,000 Sq. Ft.	☐	935 Black
1,000 — 2,000 Sq. Ft.	☐	946 Dark Brown
2,000 — 3,500 Sq. Ft.	☐	944 Terracotta
3,500 — 5,000 Sq. Ft.	☐	921 Vermilion Red
5,000 — 6,500 Sq. Ft.	☐	918 Orange
6,500 — 8,000 Sq. Ft.	☐	942 Yellow Ochre
8,000 — 12,000 Sq. Ft.	☐	917 Yellow Orange
12,000 — Over Sq. Ft.	☐	915 Lemon Yellow
Occupied by rooming and boarding houses	☐	929 Pink

SOURCE: *Mapping for Planning Publication No. 101 Public Administration Service, Chicago, Ill.*

TAX DELINQUENCY OF REAL PROPERTY

Knowledge of the length of time real property has been tax delinquent is often an important factor in planning for community development. The following scale, while generally applicable, may require some adjustment to meet local conditions where the effects of existing statutes of limitations or the powers of the governmental agency to foreclose and take title have direct relationship to the length of time the property can remain tax delinquent.

COLOR LEGEND FOR TAX DELINQUENCY OF REAL PROPERTY

Time Delinquent		Prismacolor
Over 0 to 2 years	☐	915 Lemon Yellow
Over 2 to 5 years	☐	939 Flesh
Over 5 to 10 years	☐	943 Burnt Ochre
Over 10 to 15 years	☐	946 Dark Brown

COLOR LEGEND FOR LAND VALUES

Values		Prismacolor
$ 0.00 — 0.04	☐	915 Lemon Yellow
0.05 — 0.08	☐	917 Yellow Orange
0.09 — 0.16	☐	942 Yellow Ochre
0.17 — 0.25	☐	912 Apple Green
0.26 — 0.55	☐	911 Olive Green
0.56 — 1.00	☐	909 Grass Green
1.01 — 2.00	☐	908 Dark Green
2.01 — 4.00	☐	901 Indigo Blue
4.01 — 8.00	☐	931 Purple
8.00 — Over	☐	924 Crimson Red
Not Assessed	☐	964 Light Gray

FOR COLOR REFER TO PRISMACOLOR PENCILS COLOR CHART ON PAGE 115

1. GENERAL STRUCTURE

The standard system for coding land use activity is comprised of 9 one-digit categories (2 of which have been assigned to "manufacturing"), 67 two-digit categories, 294 three-digit categories, and 772 four-digit categories. The categories at the four-digit level identify land use activity in the greatest detail, and as the system is aggregated to the three-, two-, and one digit levels the categories become more generalized. The structure of this classification system, therefore, permits an agency to select the level of detail considered most appropriate for analysis and presentation of its data.

THE CATEGORIES AT THE TWO-DIGIT LEVEL OF GENERALIZATION ARE

Code	Category	Code	Category
1	Residential.	7	Cultural, entertainment, and recreational.
2 and 3	Manufacturing.		
4	Transportation, communication, and utilities.	8	Resource production and extraction.
5	Trade.	9	Undeveloped land and water areas.
6	Services.		

THE CATEGORIES AT THE TWO-DIGIT LEVEL OF GENERALIZATION ARE:

Code	Category	Code	Category
1	Residential.	11	Household units.
		12	Group quarters.
		13	Residential hotels.
		14	Mobile home parks or courts.
		15	Transient lodgings.
		19	Other residential.[1]
2	Manufacturing.	21	Food and kindred products—manufacturing.
		22	Textile mill products—manufacturing.
		23	Apparel and other finished products made from fabrics, leather, and similar materials—manufacturing.
		24	Lumber and wood products (except furniture)—manufacturing.
		25	Furniture and fixtures—manufacturing.
		26	Paper and allied products—manufacturing.
		27	Printing, publishing, and allied industries.
		28	Chemicals and allied products—manufacturing.
		29	Petroleum refining and related industries.
3	Manufacturing (continued).	31	Rubber and miscellaneous plastic products—manufacturing.
		32	Stone, clay, and glass products—manufacturing.
		33	Primary metal industries.
		34	Fabricated metal products—manufacturing.
		35	Professional, scientific, and controlling instruments; photographic and optical goods; watches and clocks—manufacturing.
		39	Miscellaneous manufacturing, NEC.

Code	Category	Code	Category
4	Transportation, communication, and utilities.	41	Railroad, rapid rail transit, and street railway transportation.
		42	Motor vehicle transportation.
		43	Aircraft transportation.
		44	Marine craft transportation.
		45	Highway and street right-of-way.
		46	Automobile parking.
		47	Communication.
		48	Utilities.
		49	Other transportation, communication, and utilities, NEC.
5	Trade.	51	Wholesale trade.
		52	Retail trade—building materials, hardware, and farm equipment.
		53	Retail trade—general merchandise.
		54	Retail trade—food.
		55	Retail trade—automotive, marine craft, aircraft, and accessories.
		56	Retail trade—apparel and accessories.
		57	Retail trade—furniture, home furnishings, and equipment.
		58	Retail trade—eating and drinking.
		59	Other retail trade, NEC.
6	Services.	61	Finance, insurance, and real estate services.
		62	Personal services.
		63	Business services.
		64	Repair services.
		65	Professional services.
		66	Contract construction services.
		67	Governmental services.
		68	Educational services.
		69	Miscellaneous services.
7	Cultural, entertainment, and recreational.	71	Cultural activities and nature exhibitions.
		72	Public assembly.
		73	Amusements.
		74	Recreational activities.
		75	Resorts and group camps.
		76	Parks
		79	Other cultural, entertainment, and recreational, NEC.
8	Resource production and extraction.	81	Agriculture.
		82	Agricultural related activities.
		83	Forestry activities and related services.
		84	Fishing activities and related services.
		85	Mining activities and related services.
		89	Other resource production and extraction, NEC.
9	Undeveloped land and water areas.	91	Undeveloped and unused land area (excluding noncommercial forest development).
		92	Noncommercial forest development.
		93	Water areas.
		94	Vacant floor area.
		95	Under construction.
		99	Other undeveloped land and water areas, NEC.

SOURCE: Standard Land USE Coding Manual Urban Renewal Administration, HHFA Bureau of Public Roads, Dept of Commerce Washington, D. C.

2. Purpose and Use of the Auxiliary Codes

There are certain land use activities that are generally found separated from, but are functionally and organizationally linked to other activities. For example:

a. A warehouse operated by a retail concern primarily for its own use and not for public storage;

b. A parking area operated by a manufacturing concern for use by its own employees and not for public parking;

c. An office performing management functions as part of a mining concern which has mines in several States.

These are all important space uses in themselves. However, they are also significant in their relationship to the parent activity they serve.

To provide a link between certain significant auxiliary functions and the parent activities they serve, a series of one-digit "Auxiliary" categories are provided. These should be used with the standard system for coding land use activity. The auxiliary categories are as follows:

Code	Auxiliary categories	Code	Auxiliary categories
0	Not an auxiliary.	5	Automobile parking.[5]
1	Central or administrative office.[4]	6	Motor vehicle garage (maintenance and/or storage of vehicles).
2	Sales office.	7	Steam and power plant.
3	Research and development.	8–9	(Open codes).[6]
4	Warehousing and storage.		

[4] Central or administrative offices are those offices engaged in general administrative, supervisory, purchasing, accounting, or other management functions.

[5] A minimum of 5,000 square feet or approximately 17 parking spaces is necessary before the area can be identified as auxiliary parking area.

[6] Planning agencies desiring to distinguish additional types of auxiliary categories other than those defined (e.g., recreational activities that are subsidiary to or serving another activity) should use open codes 8 and 9.

Codes 1 through 7 should be used when one of the listed activities can be determined to be subsidiary to or serving another activity. For example, if a research and development laboratory of a manufacturer of pharmaceutical preparations is located down the street from the actual manufacturing plant itself, the laboratory would be considered as an auxiliary and would be coded as follows:

Basic activity code	Auxiliary code	Combined activity code
(Pharmaceutical preparations—manufacturing)	(Research and development)	
2834	3	2834–3

An automobile parking area over 5,000 square feet which is an adjunct to an activity, e.g., a grocery store, and which is not used for other purposes in the same sense as a public parking area would be coded as follows:

Basic activity code	Auxiliary code	Combined activity code
(Groceries—retail)	(Automobile parking)	
5410	5	5410–5

The sales office of a manufacturing concern that is separately located from the actual factory, whether it be next door in a separate building, across the street, on the other side of the town, or in another city, is considered as serving the manufacturing process. Similarly, the permanent office of a construction company is considered as serving the construction activity. Therefore, these office activities would be coded as follows:

Basic activity code	Auxiliary code	Combined activity code
(Farm machinery and equipment—manufacturing)	(Sales office)	
3422	2	3422–2
(Building construction—general contractor services)	(Central or administrative office)	
6611	1	6611–1

With respect to wholesaling activity (code 51), those wholesalers without stock (i.e., they do not have a definite storage area set aside to maintain a volume of stock on hand) are also considered to be auxiliary, and they are identified by one of the auxiliary codes, accordingly. For example:

Basic activity code	Auxiliary code	Combined activity code
(Fruits and vegetables, fresh—wholesale)	(With stock)	
5147	0	5147–0
(Fruits and vegetables, fresh—wholesale)	(Sales office, without stock)	
5147	2	5147–2

On the other hand, an independent research, development, and testing laboratory would not be considered as an auxiliary activity, and it would be coded under its respective activity category, code 6391. Parking is coded in a similar way if it is public parking or parking serving more than one concern, such as the parking area of a shopping center. The following examples illustrate this:

Basic activity code	Auxiliary code	Combined activity code
(Research, development, and testing services)	(Not an auxiliary)	
6391	0	6391–0
(Automobile parking)	(Not an auxiliary)	
4600	0	4600–0

The preceding discussion and illustrations of the use of the auxiliary codes are centered primarily on the problem of preserving the linkage between related activities while at the same time identifying important land uses. It is recognized that for some planning studies, such as open space or recreation planning, the two open codes (8 and 9) may not provide sufficient categories for identifying recreational or open space uses which are a part of some larger activity. If it is found necessary or desirable to identify such related uses, a new and separate series of auxiliary codes should be developed to accommodate the needs of the special study, thereby preserving the original auxiliary codes for comparability over a period of time and between cities.

SOURCE: *Standard Land Use Coding Manual Urban Renewal Administration, HHFA Bureau of Public Roads, Dept of Commerce Washington, d. c.*

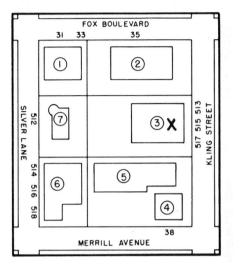

Block Plan

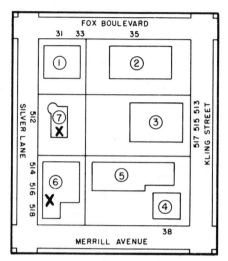

Parcel Schematic

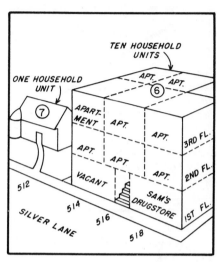

Block Plan

Parcel Schematic

				FIELD OPERATION						OFFICE OPERATION				
Street No.	Street Name	Building No.	Floor	Description of Activity	Auxiliary?	Activity Ownership	Residential Structure Type	No. of Household Units		Activity Code	Auxiliary Code	Ownership Code	Structure Code	No. of Household Units
1	2	3	4	5	6	7	8	9		5'	6'	7'	8'	9'
513	KLING ST.	3	1	HOME FURNITURE CO. (RETAIL)	—	PRIVATE	—	—		5711	0	20	—	—
515	KLING ST.	3	1	NICK'S BAKERY (WITH OVENS IN REAR)	—	PRIVATE	—	—		5461	0	20	—	—
517	KLING ST.	3	2	BIG TOWN REAL ESTATE CO. (REAL ESTATE AGENTS & BROKERS-OFFICES)	—	PRIVATE	—	—		6152	0	20	—	—
517	KLING ST.	3	2	PHYSICIAN'S OFFICE	—	PRIVATE	—	—		6511	0	20	—	—
517	KLING ST.	3	2	JONES CHEMICAL CORP (SALES OFF. OF AGRICULTURAL FERTILIZER MFG.)	X	PRIVATE	—	—		2870	2	20	—	—
517	KLING ST.	3	2	AJAX CONSTRUCTION CO. (GENERAL OFFICES – HOME BUILDERS)	X	PRIVATE	—	—		6611	1	20	—	—
517	KLING ST.	3	2	LAW FIRM (OFFICES)	—	PRIVATE	—	—		6520	0	20	—	—
517	KLING ST.	3	3	HAPPY INSURANCE CO. (REGIONAL OFFICE OF COMPANY)	X	PRIVATE	—	—		6141	1	20	—	—
517	KLING ST.	3	4	RDT LABORATORIES (DEVELOPMENT LABORATORIES FOR RDT INDUSTRIES – RADIO TRANSMITTING EQUIPMENT MFG.)	X	PRIVATE	—	—		3436	3	20	—	—
513 – 517	KLING ST.	—	—	PARKING FOR VISITORS & EMPLOYEES IN THE REAR (20 SPACES)	—	PRIVATE	—	—		4600	0	20	—	—

Example of Land Use Entries on a Field Listing Form

				FIELD OPERATION						OFFICE OPERATION				
Street No.	Street Name	Building No.	Floor	Description of Activity	Auxiliary?	Activity Ownership	Residential Structure Type	No. of Household Units		Activity Code	Auxiliary Code	Ownership Code	Structure Code	No. of Household Units
1	2	3	4	5	6	7	8	9		5'	6'	7'	8'	9'
518	SILVER LANE	6	1	SAM'S DRUG STORE	—	PRIVATE	—	—		5910	0	20	—	—
516	SILVER LANE	6	2 & 3	HOUSEHOLD UNITS	—	PRIVATE	WALK-UP APART.	10		1100	0	20	31	10
514	SILVER LANE	6	1	VACANT FLOOR AREA	—	—	—	—		9400	0	—	—	—
512	SILVER LANE	7	1	HOUSEHOLD UNITS	—	PRIVATE	SINGLE UNIT – DETACHED	1		1100	0	20	11	01

Example of Land Use Entries on a Field Listing Form

SOURCE: Standard Land Use Coding Manual Urban Renewal Administration, HHFA Bureau of Public Roads, Dept. of Commerce Washington, D. C.

HUMAN ACTIVITIES

LAND USE CATEGORY	SLUCM[1] CODE	Intensive Conversation	Casual Conversation	Telephone Use	Sleeping	Eating	Reading	Meditation	Writing	Studying	Seminar, Group Discussion	Classroom, Lecture	Individual Creative Activity	Live Theater	Watching Films	Watching Television	Listening to Music	Ceremony, Tradition	Public Events, Assemblies	Spectator Sports	Public Mass Recreation	Physical Recreation	Outdoor Activities	Urban Outdoor Activities	Extended Child Care	Driving	Shopping	Technical Manual Work	Skilled Manual Work	Manual Work	Equipment Operation	Noise-Sensitive Equipment
Residential - Single Family, Duplex	11x[2]	M	M	M	H	H	M	M	M	M	M	L	H	L	L	H	M	H	L	L	L	M	M	H	H	L	L	L	M	M	L	L
Residential - Mobile Homes	14	M	M	M	H	H	M	M	M	M	M	L	H	L	L	H	M	H	L	L	L	M	L	H	H	L	L	L	M	M	L	L
Residential - Multiple Family, Dormitories, etc.	11x, 12, 13, 19	M	M	M	H	H	M	M	M	M	M	L	H	L	L	H	M	H	L	L	L	M	L	H	H	L	L	L	M	M	L	L
Transient Lodging	15	L	M	M	H	H	M	M	L	M	M	M	L	L	L	H	M	L	L	L	L	L	M	M	L	L	L	L	L	L	L	L
School classrooms, Libraries, Churches	68, 7111	H	M	M	L	L	H	M	H	H	H	H	H	L	L	M	M	H	H	L	L	M	L	H	H	L	L	L	M	M	L	L
Hospitals, Nursing Homes	651	M	M	M	H	H	M	M	L	L	M	L	M	M	L	M	M	L	L	L	L	M	L	M	H	L	L	H	M	M	L	M
Auditoriums, Concert Halls, Music Shells	721	L	M	L	L	L	L	L	L	L	L	H	L	L	M	L	H	L	H	H	H	H	L	L	L	L	L	L	L	L	L	H
Sports Arenas, Outdoor Spectator Sports	722	L	M	L	L	L	L	L	L	L	L	L	H	L	L	L	L	H	H	H	L	L	L	L	L	L	L	L	L	L	L	H
Playgrounds, Neighborhood Parks	761, 762	L	M	L	L	M	M	L	L	M	L	M	L	L	L	L	M	L	L	M	L	M	M	M	H	H	L	L	L	L	L	L
Golf Courses, Riding Stables, Water Rec., Cemeteries	741x, 743x, 744	L	M	L	L	L	L	M	L	L	L	L	L	M	L	L	L	L	L	L	L	H	M	H	L	L	L	L	L	L	L	L
Office Buildings, Personal, Business and Professional	61, 62, 63, 69, 65[3]	M	M	M	L	L	L	L	M	L	H	M	M	L	L	L	L	L	L	L	M	L	L	L	L	L	L	L	L	L	L	M
Commercial - Retail, Movie Theaters, Restaurants	53, 54, 56, 57, 59	M	M	L	L	H	L	L	L	L	L	L	L	L	H	L	L	L	L	L	L	L	L	L	L	L	H	L	L	M	L	L
Commercial - Wholesale, Some Retail, Ind., Mfg., Util.	51, 52, 64, 2, 3, 4	L	L	L	L	L	L	L	L	L	L	L	L	L	L	L	L	L	L	L	L	L	L	L	L	L	M	L	H	H	H	M
Manufacturing, Communications (Noise Sensitive)	35, 47	L	L	L	L	L	L	L	L	L	L	L	L	L	L	L	L	L	L	L	L	L	L	L	L	L	L	L	H	H	H	M
Livestock Farming, Animal Breeding	815, 816, 817	L	L	L	L	L	L	L	L	L	L	L	L	L	L	L	L	L	L	L	L	L	L	L	L	L	L	L	L	H	H	L
Agriculture (except Livestock), Mining, Fishing	81, 82, 83, 84, 85, 91, 93	L	L	L	L	L	L	L	L	L	L	L	L	L	L	L	L	L	L	L	L	L	L	L	L	L	L	L	L	H	H	L
Public Right-of-Way	45	L	L	L	L	L	L	L	L	L	L	L	L	L	L	L	L	L	L	L	L	M	M	L	H	L	L	L	L	L	H	L
Extensive Natural Recreation Areas	91, 92, 93, 99, 7491, 75	L	L	L	H	H	L	M	L	L	L	L	L	L	L	L	L	L	L	L	L	L	H	M	L	H	L	L	L	L	L	L

H: Activity critical to normal function of land use.

M: Activity important to normal function of land use.

L: Activity of secondary importance - land use generally able to function satisfactorily if activity cannot be performed.

[1] Standard Land Use Coding Manual.

[2] "x" represents a SLUCM category narrower or broader than, but generally inclusive of, the category described.

[3] Except hospitals.

[4] Matrix is intended as a guide to assist local planners in establishing a similar table for their particular community and land use classification system.

For each prospective land use there will be certain factors of greatest importance and these can be selected. Moreover, there will be a ranking of importance and so the factors can be arranged in a hierarchy. In addition, in certain cases some factors will be conducive to specific land uses while others are restrictive. In the selection of areas intrinsically suitable for conservation, the factors selected were: features of historic value, high quality forests and marshes, bay beaches, streams, water-associated wildlife habitats, intertidal wildlife habitats, unique geological and physiographic features, scenic land and water features and scarce ecological associations. As an example of conductive and restrictive factors, selection of the most suitable areas for residential land use would include attractive surroundings, and so scenic land features, locations near water and the presence of historic sites and buildings will be positive factors, while excessive slopes, poor drainage and susceptibility to flooding will be negative factors.

The application of this concept can be seen in the adjacent charts. Over thirty factors were considered. Those considered were subdivided in the categories of climate, geology, physiography, hydrology, soils, vegetation, wildlife habitats and land use. Within each of these categories data were collected on factors of importance to all prospective land use. For the original sources—climate, geology, etc., the factors of greatest importance were selected. In the general subject of climate the matter of air pollution was deemed important as was tidal inundation from hurricanes. Within the category of geology features of unique scientfic value were identified and the major surface rock types were classed for compressive strength. Following the identification of the most important factors, each one was evaluated in a gradient of five values. For instance, serpentine and diabase constitute class one foundation conditions while marsh and swamp occupy the lowest rank on the scale. All factors were so evaluated. The relevance of the factors considered to specific land uses was next indicated. Further, the direction of the value system was shown. A gray dot indicates rank order from left to right. A black dot indicates the reverse order. Moreover the importance of the factor must also be evaluated. Factors of highest importance are shown with full black and gray dots; lower values decrease in color and tonal intensity.

ECOLOGICAL FACTOR	RANKING CRITERIA	PHENOMENA RANK I	II	III	IV	V	VALUE FOR LAND USE C P A R I
CLIMATE							
AIR POLLUTION	INCIDENCE MAX ► MIN	High	Medium	Low		Lowest	● ● ● ●
TIDAL INUNDATION	INCIDENCE MAX ► MIN	Highest Recorded	Highest Projected			Above Flood-Line	● ● ●
GEOLOGY							
FEATURES OF UNIQUE, SCIENTIFIC AND EDUCATIONAL VALUE	SCARCITY MAX ► MIN	1 Ancient Lakebeds 2 Drainage Outlets	1 Terminal Moraine 2 Limit of Glaciation 3 Boulder Trail	Serpentine Hill	Palisades Outlier	1 Beach 2 Buried Valleys 3 Clay Pits 4 Gravel Pits	● ●
FOUNDATION CONDITIONS	COMPRESSIVE STRENGTH MAX ► MIN	1 Serpentine 2 Diabase	Shale	Cretaceous Sediments	Filled Marsh	Marsh and Swamp	● ●
PHYSIOGRAPHY							
FEATURES OF UNIQUE, SCIENTIFIC AND EDUCATIONAL VALUE	SCARCITY MAX ► MIN	Hummocks and kettleholes within the Terminal Moraine	Palisades Outlier	Moraine Scarps and lakes along the Bay Shore	Breaks in Serpentine Ridge		● ●
LAND FEATURES OF SCENIC VALUE	DISTINCTIVE MOST ► LEAST	Serpentine Ridge and Promontories	Beach	1 Escarpments 2 Enclosed Valleys	1 Berms 2 Promontories 3 Hummocks	Undifferentiated	● ● ● ●
WATER FEATURES OF SCENIC VALUE	DISTINCTIVE MOST ► LEAST	Bay	Lake	1 Pond 2 Streams	Marsh	1 The Narrows 2 Kill Van Kull 3 Arthur Kill	● ● ●
RIPARIAN LANDS OF WATER FEATURES	VULNERABILITY MOST ► LEAST	Marsh	1 Stream 2 Ponds	Lake	Bay	1 The Narrows 2 Kill Van Kull 3 Arthur Kill	● ● ●
BEACHES ALONG THE BAY	VULNERABILITY MOST ► LEAST	Moraine Scarps	Coves	Sand Beach			● ● ● ●
SURFACE DRAINAGE	PROPORTION OF SURFACE WATER TO LAND AREA MOST ► LEAST	Marsh and swamp	Areas of constricted drainage	Dense stream/swale network	Intermediate stream/swale network	Sparse stream/swale network	● ● ● ●
SLOPE	GRADIENT HIGH ► LOW	Over 25%	25–10%	10–5%	5–2½%	2½–0%	● ● ●
HYDROLOGY							
MARINE Commercial Craft	NAVIGABLE CHANNELS DEEPEST ► SHALLOWEST	The Narrows	Kill Van Kull	Arthur Kill	Fresh Kill	Raritan Bay	● ●
Pleasure Craft	FREE EXPANSE OF WATER LARGEST ► SMALLEST	Raritan Bay	Fresh Kill	The Narrows	Arthur Kill	Kill Van Kull	● ● ●
FRESH WATER Active recreation (swimming, paddling, model-boat sailing, etc.)	EXPANSE OF WATER LARGEST ► SMALLEST	Silver Lake	1 Clove Lake 2 Grassmere Lake 3 Ohrbach Lake 4 Arbutus Lake 5 Wolfes Pond	Other ponds	Streams		● ● ●
Stream-side recreation (fishing, trails, etc.)	SCENIC MOST ► LEAST	Nonurbanized perennial streams	Nonurbanized intermittent streams	Semiurbanized streams	Urbanized streams		● ●
WATERSHEDS FOR STREAM QUALITY PROTECTION	SCENIC STREAMS MOST ► LEAST	Nonurbanized perennial streams	Nonurbanized intermittent streams	Semiurbanized streams	Urbanized streams		● ● ● ●
AQUIFERS	YIELD HIGHEST ► LOWEST	Buried valleys		Cretaceous Sediments		Crystalline rocks	● ●
AQUIFER RECHARGE ZONES	IMPORTANT AQUIFERS MOST ► LEAST	Buried valleys		Cretaceous Sediments		Crystalline rocks	● ●

C CONSERVATION. P PASSIVE RECREATION. A ACTIVE RECREATION. R RESIDENTIAL DEVELOPMENT. I COMMERCIAL & INDUSTRIAL DEVELOPMENT

ECOLOGICAL FACTOR	RANKING CRITERIA	PHENOMENA RANK I	II	III	IV	V	VALUE FOR LAND USE C P A R I
PEDOLOGY							
SOIL DRAINAGE	PERMEABILITY AS INDICATED BY THE HEIGHT OF WATER TABLE MOST ► LEAST	Excellent-good	Good-fair	Fair-poor	Poor	Nil	● ● ● ●
FOUNDATION CONDITIONS	COMPRESSIVE STRENGTH AND STABILITY MOST ► LEAST	Gravelly to stony, sandy loams	Gravelly sand or silt loams	Gravelly sandy to fine sandy loam	1 Sandy loam 2 Gravel 3 Beach sands	1 Alluvium 2 Swamp Muck 3 Tidal marshlands 4 Made land	● ● ● ●
EROSION	SUSCEPTIBILITY MOST ► LEAST	Steep slopes over 10%	Any slope on gravelly sandy to fine sandy loam	Moderate slopes (2%-10%) on gravelly sand or silt loams 1 2 Gravelly to stony sandy loams	Slopes (0-2½%) on gravelly sand or silt loams	Other soils	● ● ● ●
VEGETATION							
EXISTING FOREST	QUALITY BEST ► POOREST	Excellent	Good	Poor	Disturbed	None	● ● ● ●
FOREST TYPE	SCARCITY MOST ► LEAST	1 Lowland 2 Upland dry	Marsh	Upland	Upland moist	Absence	● ● ●
EXISTING MARSHES	QUALITY BEST ► POOREST	Good	Fair		Poor (filled)	None	● ● ●
WILDLIFE							
EXISTING HABITATS	SCARCITY MOST ► LEAST	Intertidal	Water-related	Field and forest	Urban	Marine	● ● ●
INTERTIDAL SPECIES	ENVIRONMENTAL QUALITY BASED ON INTENSITY OF SHORE ACTIVITY LEAST ► MOST ACTIVITY	1	2	3	4	5	● ● ●
WATER-ASSOCIATED SPECIES	ENVIRONMENTAL QUALITY BASED ON THE DEGREE OF URBANIZATION NON URBANIZED ► FULLY URBANIZED	1	2	3	4	5	● ● ●
FIELD AND FOREST SPECIES	FOREST QUALITY BEST ► POOREST	1	2	3			● ● ●
URBAN-RELATED SPECIES	PRESENCE OF TREES ABUNDANT ► ABSENT	1				3	●
LAND USE							
FEATURES OF UNIQUE, EDUCATIONAL, AND HISTORICAL VALUE	IMPORTANCE MOST ► LEAST	Richmond Town	1 Amboy Road 2 Tottenville Conference	Area with abundance of landmarks	Area with sparseness of landmarks	Area with absence of landmarks	● ● ●
FEATURES OF SCENIC VALUE	DISTINCTIVE MOST ► LEAST	The Verazzano Bridge	Ocean Liner Channel	Manhattan Ferry	1 The Goethals Bridge 2 The Outerbridge crossing 3 The Bayonne Bridge	Absence	● ● ● ●
EXISTING AND POTENTIAL RECREATION RESOURCES	AVAILABILITY MOST ► LEAST	1 Existing public open space 2 Existing Institutions	Potential nonurbanized recreation areas	Potential urbanized recreation areas	Vacant land (with low recreation potential)	Urbanized areas	● ● ●

C CONSERVATION. P PASSIVE RECREATION. A ACTIVE RECREATION. R RESIDENTIAL DEVELOPMENT; I COMMERCIAL & INDUSTRIAL DEVELOPMENT

SOURCE: Design with Nature, *Ian. C. McHarg, Doubleday Natural History Press, Doubleday & Co. Inc., Garden City, N.Y., 1971.*

Author's Note: The data shown in the charts was for a study of Staten Island, NYC.

Environmental conditions differ greatly, not only between regions, but often because of minor differences in elevation or location. Each environmental factor—topography, geology, soil, hydrology, vegetation, wildlife, climate, and visual and spatial form—has various responses to, or capacity for, a particular use or development. Thus, the ability to predict or control the impact of a particular use on the environment will require detailed information on the composition of the environment with respect to those factors. The development of knowledge about the tolerance of particular environments to various uses at an early stage is essential, both to meaningful planning for land uses in a particular area and to the development of appropriate operating rules and controls for permitted uses.

Classification of the public lands to provide for different degrees of environmental quality would provide guidance for controlling the location of activities, so as to minimize their impacts. This approach—a systematic classification and inventory of important environmental considerations on each area of public lands as part of the agencies' land use decisionmaking—will give assurance that environmental effects will be taken into account in public land decisions.

We propose that the system of environmental quality classification be based on desirable levels of quality to be maintained in each area for the major components of the environment, such as water, air, esthetics or scenery, and composition of the ecosystem. This should be done in close cooperation with the states, and where the states or local governments have developed satisfactory classifications, as, for example, in connection with water quality standards, these would be incorporated in the public land classifications.

EXAMPLE
POSSIBLE CLASSIFICATION SYSTEM FOR ENVIRONMENTAL MANAGEMENT

Environmental Category	Quality Related to Purpose	Environmental Attributes to be Monitored and Managed WATER	Management Actions
W-1	Fishery, and other components of the biotic system.	High level of dissolved oxygen. Exacting tolerances for temperature, trace minerals, pH, toxic chemicals, nutrients, . . . Low silt and organic matter.	Prohibit land grading, landfills, vegetative clearing, burning, mining, except where environmental review and impact studies prove that stringent measures can keep changes to environmental atttributes within tolerances.
W-2	Domestic water supply, swimming, industrial uses requiring high quality water.	High to moderate levels of dissolved oxygen. Moderate temperature fluctuation. Limits on trace minerals, pH, toxic chemicals and nutrients over a range of tolerances related to resource uses.	Permit moderate disturbances (prohibited above), but only upon determination of each developments' distrubance factors and contribution to the stream or lake's budget for sediment, etc.
W-3	Irrigated agriculture, industrial cooling water.	Control of dissolved salts and toxic materials	Strict controls on activities that disturb soils and lead to leaching of salts or flow of acidic or otherwise toxic materials from public lands.

BIOSYSTEM MAINTENANCE

B-1	Perpetuation of full natural biosystem—for recreation, education, scientific study.	Minimum of man induced changes in species composition, biomass, food chains, habitat conditions, predator-prey relationships, and population dynamics.	Perpetuate natural ecosystem processes or manage to compensate. Logging, mining, and construction, etc. normally excluded.
B-2	Limited modification of biosystem to produce specific goods or services (native range management, selective cutting in mixed hardwoods).	Minor changes in plant and animal species composition. Minor changes in habitat for preferred species. Some alterations of wildlife populations.	Alter natural system only when environmental review and impact studies allow full prediction and control over specific changes. Mitigative and corrective measures to be specified in resource management plans for timber, recreation, etc.
B-3	Major modification to maximize output of a particular product or use (single species managment for commercial timber production; primary management for elk).	Large scale vegetative type conversions. Major change of habitat for preferred species.	Intensive uses or developments normally permitted if environmental review and impact studies indicate biosystem losses are offset by value of goods and services.

SOURCE: Environmental Quality–1973 Council of Environmental Quality, Wash., D.C.

QUALITY OF EXPERIENCE

E-1 Visual and esthetic environments as related to recreational, residential, and travel purposes.

High capacity for direct and detailed sensory involvement. Naturaldominance of form, scale, and proportion. High constraint, vividness, image creation, and unity.

Avoid disturbance of natural pattern. Prohibit intrusions of logging, mining, intensive recreation, roads, power lines, etc., except insofar as environmental design studies indicate that intentional display of resource management is consistent with scenic management objectives.

E-2 Cultural, historical, and informational values for recreational and educational purposes.

Unique, archetypal, rare, or transitory artifacts or locations relative to the environmental context.

Preservation or restoration. Prohibit competing land uses. Protect from overuse by recreationists and collectors.

E-3 Personal and social experiences free from crowding, development, and noise.

High capacity for isolation and interaction with national environment. Minimum intrusion of manmade structures and facilities and man-induced changes. Low artificial noise levels (vehicles, aircraft, radios).

Limit number of recreation visitors through rationing of physical design. Prohibit or minimize noise producing intrusions. Prohibit development of structures except where design studies show minimum disturbance.

E-4 Natural biological and physical features.

Unique or dramatic landforms or features (not necessarily of biological importance). High capacity for orientation (as with landmarks). Rare or especially archetypal geologic formations.

Modify resource management practices to enhance such features. Prohibit or restrict extractive or product-oriented uses except as they may be shown to complement feature-oriented uses.

AIR QUALITY

A-1 Human health protection (respiration; sight; skin).

A-2 Natural biosystem protection (carbon dioxide-oxygen exchange balance; foliage burn).

A-3 Materials protection (corrosion; etching; stain).

A-4 Esthetics protection (haze; ordors).

Hold levels and combinations of oxides of sulfur and carbon, hydrocarbons, photochemical oxidents, and particle (solid) matter to tolerances required to support each purpose of air quality maintenance on both a 24 hour and annual basis. Maintain natural background levels of particle matter in ambient air in rural areas to the extent possible. Specific conditions to be maintained depend on different meteorological conditions, climate (wet, dry) topography, and latitude-longitude.

Control use of internal combustion engines on public land areas to hold hydrocarbon and particle matter below necessary levels. Control dust generated by mining and logging, and by recreational vehicles and logging and ore trucks traveling on unpaved land. Control stack emissions from on and offsite pulp and paper mills, concentrate mills, organic fueled power generating plants, and other industrial plants to hold particle matter and gaseous pollutants to necessary levels. Burning of logging waste and controlled burning of forest and rangelands for management purposes to be regulated daily and seasonally to meet necessary air quality requirements.

POPULATION

MATHEMATICAL PROJECTIONS

1. The simplest mathematical procedure is to compute the average numerical population change per decade in the past, and then to project this numerical increase into the future. This is called an "arithmetical projection," and it should produce the same result as a straight-line graphic projection on plain coordinate paper.

To illustrate, from 1900 to 1950 the population of California increased an average of 1,823,000 per decade; assuming the same numerical increase, the population, which was 10,586,000 in 1950, would be 12,409,000 in 1960, and 14,232,000 in 1970.

2. Another simple method is to compute the average rate of population change for the area per decade in the past, and then project this average rate, or percent change, into the future. This is called a "geometric projection," and corresponds to a graphic projection on semi-logarithmic paper.

For example, the average rate of increase per decade of the population of California during 1900—50 was approximately 49 percent. Projecting this average rate gives a population of 15,773,000 in 1960, and 23,502,000 in 1970.

3. A more refined procedure is to plot the curve of past population growth on a semi-logarithmic scale and then to develop by the method of least squares an exponential equation that best fits the past curve. From this equation the size of the population in future years can readily be compute

4. Another technique is to fit some other mathematical curve, such as the "logistic" curve, to the curve of past population growth of the area, and then to determine the size of the future population therefrom.

The logistic curve is based on a "law of growth in a limited area" propounded and mathematically developed by P. F. Verhulst in 1838. It is shaped like an elongated and flattened letter S.

The logistic curve implies a constantly decreasing rate of increase per amount of population per unit of time after the initial increment of increase. Its validity for area subject to net in-migration that might accelerate for a time the rate of increase relative to the size of the population, is questionable.

The advantage of graphic or mathematical projections is that they are the easiest to make. They generally are better suited to areas which have had

SOURCE: Van Beuren Stanbery, Better Population
Forecasting for Areas and Communities,
U.S. Dept of Commerce, Wash. D. C.

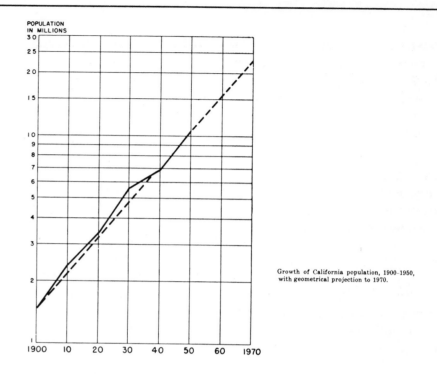

Growth of California population, 1900–1950, with geometrical projection to 1970.

relatively constant changes per decade in the size of their populations, and for which no marked changes from past trends appear likely, than for areas subject to rapid or erratic fluctuations in population. Obviously, they should be more dependable for short-term projections of 5 to 10 years, than for longer projections.

The weakness of such projections is that they are founded on the assumption that the factors and conditions which produced population growth or decline in the area in the past will continue unchanged and will have the same effects in the future, or that they are derived from an assumed curve of population growth. In view of the changes that have recently taken place in fertility, mortality, and migration trends, projections of this kind are becoming less reliable.

As indicated before, graphic and mathematical projections are useful, however, as rough checks on those obtained by other methods. In the absence of other data and analyses, an arithmetical projection might be used as a probable minimum forecast, and a geometrical projection as a maximum figure.

PROJECTIONS OF NET MIGRATION AND OF NATURAL INCREASE

Population forecasts are frequently obtained by making separate but related projections of net migration and of natural increase and adding the figures. Because migration affects the number of births and deaths in an area, projections of net migration are made before those for natural increase.

MIGRATION PROJECTIONS

Logically founded projections of net migration can be developed from study of net migration in the area in the past and the conditions causing people to more into or out of it.

The direction and approximate volume and composition of net migration into or out of the area during recent decades are first determined.

Changes that have occurred, or appear likely to occur, in the conditions and relationships affecting migration in the area are considered. Finally, the probable effects of such changes on net migration during the forecast period are reviewed and appraised.

With these analyses and appraisals, it is usually possible to develop reasonable high and low projections for net migration. At least, they provide some indication whether net migration during the next decade may be expected to be about the same as, or larger or smaller than, that of the preceding decade.

NATURAL INCREASE PROJECTIONS

Projections of natural increase are made by a variety of techniques. Some of them produce approximate figures while others give more precise results. Principal factors to be considered are the racial, sex, and age composition of the area population, and its future birth and death rates.

The most precise, but also the most laborious, procedure is the "cohort-survival" technique. Briefly, this is as follows:

The survivors of the resident population of each sex on the forecast date are first computed for each 5-year or 10-year age group from age-specific mortality tables and trends.

The total net migration projected for the area to the forecast date is then distributed by sex and by age, and added to, or subtracted from, the figures for the surviving residents in the corresponding age groups. It should be noted that the sex and age characteristics of the migrant population are usually quite different from those of the resident populations of the areas from which they move or in which they settle. The sex and age distribution of net migrations into or out of the particular area or its State during recent decades therefore should be carefully analyzed and used as guides in estimating the sex and age distribution of the projected net migration.

Birth rates by age of mother during the forecast period are then projected or assumed. The expected number of births is then obtained by multiplying the assumed age-specific birth rates by the average number of women in each 5-year age group within the child-bearing ages during the forecast period. This average figure is usually obtained by adding the number of women at the beginning and end of the forecast period in each 5-year age group, and dividing by two. The survivors of those births on the forecast date are then computed by using death rates of young children. As the number of male births usually exceeds the number of female births in the ratio of about 105 or 106 to 100, this should be taken into account in precise calculations.

The cohort-survival procedure does not directly measure natural increase itself. Instead, the population projection is obtained by adding the survivors of the resident population, the expected net migration, and the survivors of babies born to former residents and to newcomers during the period. If the net migration is outward, the estimate of births is reduced because of the smaller average number of women in the child bearing ages. Since most of the migrants are between ages 20 45 years, when they move, net out-migration tends to reduce the crude birth rate also. Further refinements, such as allowances for births to in-migrant women who die during the period, are sometimes included in the calculations.

This is being relied on more and more for population projections. For most areas and communities, it should yield better forecasts than other methods, particularly for projections not exceeding two decades.

This method takes into account the size of the area's population at the beginning of the forecast period, and the effects of a population of that size on future births, deaths, and migration. Other methods do not provide as accurate measures of the effects of changes in the size of the population from decade to decade.

SOURCE: Van Beuren Stanbery, Better Population Forecasting for Areas and Communities. U.S. Dept of Commerce, Wash. D. C.

PROJECTIONS BASED ON RELATIONSHIPS OF POPULATION GROWTH IN AN AREA TO GROWTH IN OTHER AREAS

Population growth in an area or community is usually more closely related to, or affected by, economic and population changes in the economic region or State in which it lies. Future population changes in those larger areas may have an important influence on growth or decline in the smaller area. Hence, past relationships between population growth in an area or community and that of its economic region or State are valuable guides for projection of the local population. If logically-founded population projections for the Nation, State or economic region are available, projections for the area or community can be derived directly therefrom.

STATISTICAL PROJECTIONS BASED ON RELATIVE RATES OF PAST GROWTH

Statistical projections of the relationships of population growth in a particular area to growth in other areas can be made in various ways. The simplest procedure is to compute the percentages that the population of the particular area represented of the population of its economic region, its State, and the Nation in past census years, and plot them on graph paper. The line or curve of these percentages can then be projected to the forecast date by techniques similar to those for projections of population growth curves described for mathematical methods.

Applying the projected percentages to population projection figures for the Nation, the State, or the economic region will produce numerical projections of the population of the area for applicable forecast dates. If projections for the larger areas are not available, or are considered unreliable, the forecaster can make his own projections for them.

Purely statistical projections made by this method should be used with caution. Former relationships between population growth in the area under consideration and that in other areas may suddenly change. Moreover, the economic and social forces that cause births and migration to increase, or decline, nationally exert differing effects at different times on particular areas. Some areas have shown fairly consistent trends between their population growth and that of their region, State, or the Nation. Others have shown divergent or erratic relationships to population changes in the larger areas. For these, this method appears less valid than for areas exhibiting more consistent trends. A recent evaluation of this method finds it of limited value for forecasting the populations of isolated cities.

SOURCE: Van Beuren Stanbery, Better Population Forecasting for Areas and Communities, U.S. Dept of Commerce, Wash. D. C.

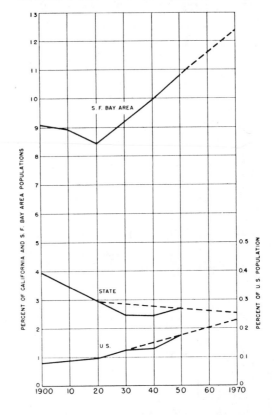

Santa Clara county population as a percent of population of San Francisco Bay area, of California, and of the United States, 1900-1950, with illustrative projections to 1970.

On the other hand, these procedures have several advantages over method I. The factors affecting population growth in the area or community may be more clearly visualized and appraised with a knowledge of its past relationships to growth in its economic region, State, and the Nation than if these relationships have not been studied. It may be easier to foresee and evaluate the effects of new conditions that may change past relationships than it would be to appraise the prospects for future growth in the area irrespective of the rate of growth in other areas. Population projections for the Nation and for States have generally been closer to the mark than those for smaller areas or communities. By trying in their projections with those for the larger area, the range for error may be lessened.

Projections made by this method are also valuable as guides and checks in establishing projections developed by other procedures.

ESTIMATED AND PROJECTED POPULATION, BY AGE AND SEX: 1950 TO 2000

[In thousands. As of July 1. Includes Armed Forces abroad. Projections are consistent with the April 1, 1970 census. These projections were prepared using the "cohort-component" technique and assume a slight improvement in mortality, an annual net immigration of 400,000, and a completed cohort fertility rate (i.e., the average number of births per 1,000 women upon completion of childbearing) that will move gradually toward the following levels: Series C—2,800; Series D—2,500; Series E—2,100; Series F—1,800. See p. 1 for derivation of estimates and projections]

YEAR, SERIES, AND SEX	Total, all ages	Under 5 years	5-9 years	10-14 years	15-19 years	20-24 years	25-29 years	30-34 years	35-39 years	40-44 years	45-54 years	55-64 years	65-74 years	75 years and over	Median age
TOTAL															
1950	152,271	16,410	13,375	11,213	10,675	11,680	12,362	11,674	11,347	10,290	17,453	13,396	8,493	3,904	30.2
1960	180,671	20,337	18,812	16,923	13,455	11,124	10,939	11,979	12,542	11,680	20,573	15,627	11,055	5,624	29.4
1970	204,879	17,167	19,888	20,800	19,301	17,192	13,687	11,570	11,174	11,982	23,287	18,651	12,482	7,695	28.0
1972	208,837	17,242	18,702	20,804	20,101	18,219	15,045	12,308	11,125	11,648	23,591	19,104	12,845	8,104	28.1
Percent of total:															
1950	100.0	10.8	8.8	7.4	7.0	7.7	8.1	7.7	7.5	6.8	11.5	8.8	5.6	2.6	(X)
1960	100.0	11.3	10.4	9.4	7.4	6.2	6.1	6.6	6.9	6.5	11.4	8.6	6.1	3.1	(X)
1970	100.0	8.4	9.7	10.2	9.4	8.4	6.7	5.6	5.5	5.8	11.4	9.1	6.1	3.8	(X)
1972	100.0	8.3	9.0	10.0	9.6	8.7	7.2	5.9	5.3	5.6	11.3	9.1	6.2	3.9	(X)
Projections:															
1975—C	215,872	18,710	17,318	20,062	20,943	19,404	17,312	13,802	11,604	11,117	23,563	19,867	13,549	8,621	28.3
D	215,324	18,162													28.4
E	213,925	16,763													28.6
F	213,378	16,216													28.7
1980—C	230,955	23,449	18,847	17,497	20,221	21,067	19,544	17,418	13,822	11,548	22,406	21,083	14,680	9,371	28.7
D	228,676	21,716	18,301												29.0
E	224,132	18,566	16,907												29.6
F	221,848	16,827	16,353												29.8
1990—C	266,238	27,149	26,893	23,745	19,194	17,823	20,501	21,290	19,615	17,287	24,617	20,357	16,769	10,999	29.5
D	258,692	24,368	24,396	22,021	18,650										30.4
E	246,639	20,531	20,704	18,885	17,262										31.8
F	239,084	17,752	18,201	17,154	16,719										32.7
2000—C	300,406	28,458	26,879	27,440	27,209	24,038	19,510	18,110	20,580	21,102	35,730	22,508	16,291	12,551	29.1
D	285,969	24,545	23,858	24,670	24,724	22,327	18,972								31.1
E	264,435	19,152	19,694	20,849	21,048	19,216	17,599								34.0
F	250,686	15,802	16,814	18,083	18,556	17,499	17,062								35.8
MALE															
1950	75,849	8,362	6,811	5,707	5,381	5,794	6,071	5,733	5,585	5,121	8,715	6,714	4,091	1,766	29.8
1960	89,319	10,336	9,566	8,602	6,809	5,563	5,425	5,902	6,140	5,733	10,139	7,560	5,134	2,411	28.5
1970	100,264	8,752	10,134	10,595	9,802	8,649	6,796	5,708	5,484	5,838	11,236	8,817	5,454	2,996	26.6
1972	102,051	8,803	9,526	10,600	10,226	9,178	7,482	6,080	5,456	5,686	11,355	8,990	5,584	3,087	26.8
Projections:															
1975—C	105,372	9,564	8,823	10,218	10,652	9,806	8,661	6,829	5,704	5,426	11,327	9,293	5,875	3,195	27.1
D	105,092	9,284													27.2
E	104,377	8,569													27.4
F	104,097	8,289													27.5
1980—C	112,726	11,983	9,627	8,910	10,284	10,666	9,831	8,690	6,819	5,649	10,781	9,776	6,329	3,381	27.5
D	111,562	11,098	9,348												27.8
E	109,240	9,488	8,636												28.4
F	108,073	8,599	8,358												28.7
1990—C	130,388	13,876	13,737	12,122	9,786	9,021	10,335	10,705	9,814	8,564	11,922	9,424	7,135	3,946	28.2
D	126,533	12,455	12,461	11,241	9,509										29.2
E	120,376	10,494	10,575	9,640	8,800										30.6
F	116,516	9,073	9,296	8,756	8,524										31.5
2000—C	147,804	14,548	13,732	14,012	13,875	12,210	9,866	9,107	10,326	10,544	17,558	10,523	6,965	4,538	27.8
D	140,433	12,547	12,188	12,597	12,608	11,339	9,592								29.7
E	129,439	9,790	10,060	10,645	10,732	9,755	8,895								32.7
F	122,423	8,078	8,589	9,232	9,461	8,881	8,622								34.6
FEMALE															
1950	76,422	8,048	6,564	5,506	5,294	5,886	6,291	5,942	5,762	5,169	8,738	6,682	4,402	2,139	30.5
1960	91,352	10,001	9,246	8,322	6,646	5,561	5,514	6,077	6,402	5,947	10,434	8,068	5,921	3,213	30.3
1970	104,615	8,415	9,754	10,205	9,499	8,543	6,891	5,862	5,690	6,143	12,051	9,834	7,028	4,699	29.3
1972	106,786	8,439	9,176	10,204	9,876	9,041	7,564	6,228	5,670	5,962	12,236	10,113	7,261	5,017	29.4
Projections:															
1975—C	110,500	9,146	8,495	9,844	10,291	9,598	8,351	6,973	5,899	5,691	12,237	10,574	7,674	5,426	29.6
D	110,232	8,878													29.6
E	109,548	8,194													29.8
F	109,281	7,927													29.9
1980—C	118,229	11,465	9,220	8,587	9,937	10,401	9,714	8,728	7,004	5,899	11,625	11,307	8,352	5,991	29.9
D	117,115	10,619	8,953												30.2
E	114,893	9,078	8,271												30.8
F	113,776	8,228	8,005												31.2
1990—C	135,849	13,273	13,156	11,623	9,407	8,801	10,155	10,585	9,801	8,723	12,695	10,934	9,635	7,052	30.7
D	132,159	11,913	11,935	10,780	9,141										31.6
E	126,253	10,037	10,130	9,245	8,462										33.0
F	122,568	8,679	8,905	8,398	8,196										33.8
2000—C	152,602	13,910	13,147	13,428	13,333	11,828	9,645	9,003	10,254	10,558	18,172	11,986	9,325	8,013	30.6
D	145,536	11,997	11,669	12,073	12,116	10,988	9,380								32.5
E	134,991	9,331	9,633	10,204	10,316	9,461	8,704								35.4
F	128,264	7,724	8,225	8,851	9,095	8,618	8,440								37.0

X Not applicable.

Source: U.S. Bureau of the Census, *Current Population Reports*, series P-25, Nos. 311, 483, and 493.

UNITED STATES POPULATION—PROJECTIONS TO 2000

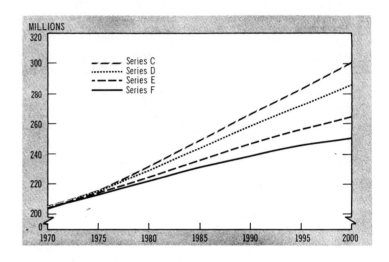

MILLIONS

- Series C
- Series D
- Series E
- Series F

HOUSEHOLDS, BY NUMBER OF PERSONS: 1950 TO 1972

Number in thousands.

SIZE OF HOUSEHOLD	1950 [1]	1955	1960	1965	1967	1968	1969	1970	1971	1972
Total	43,468	47,788	52,610	57,251	58,845	60,446	61,806	62,874	64,374	66,676
1 person	4,737	5,212	6,871	8,603	9,139	9,743	10,333	10,692	11,375	12,189
2 persons	12,529	13,612	14,616	16,067	16,659	17,272	17,916	18,129	18,774	19,482
3 persons	9,808	9,725	9,941	10,230	10,334	10,513	10,698	10,903	11,002	11,542
4 persons	7,729	9,052	9,277	9,239	9,496	9,565	9,714	9,935	9,996	10,679
5 persons	4,357	5,291	6,064	6,293	6,235	6,281	6,345	6,532	6,599	6,431
6 persons	2,196	2,568	2,976	3,316	3,468	3,605	3,534	3,505	3,414	3,374
7 or more persons	2,113	2,328	2,865	3,503	3,527	3,467	3,266	3,178	3,214	2,979
Percent of total	100.0	100.0	100.0	100.0	100.0	100.0	100.0	100.0	100.0	100.0
1 person	10.9	10.9	13.1	15.0	15.5	16.1	16.7	17.0	17.7	18.3
2 persons	28.8	28.5	27.8	28.1	28.3	28.6	29.0	28.8	29.2	29.2
3 persons	22.6	20.4	18.9	17.9	17.6	17.4	17.3	17.3	17.1	17.3
4 persons	17.8	18.9	17.6	16.1	16.1	15.8	15.7	15.8	15.5	16.0
5 persons	10.0	11.1	11.5	11.0	10.6	10.4	10.3	10.4	10.3	9.6
6 persons	5.1	5.4	5.7	5.8	5.9	6.0	5.7	5.6	5.3	5.1
7 or more persons	4.9	4.9	5.4	6.1	6.0	5.7	5.3	5.1	5.0	4.5

[1] Covers related persons only; therefore, not strictly comparable with later years.

FAMILIES, BY CHARACTERISTICS: 1972

Number in thousands. As of March. Based on Current Population Survey; includes members of the Armed Forces living off post or with their families on post, but excludes all other members of the Armed Forces;

	ALL FAMILIES		MALE HEAD — Married, wife present		MALE HEAD — Other marital status		FEMALE HEAD		FAMILIES OF NEGRO AND OTHER RACES	
CHARACTERISTIC	Number	Percent	Number	Percent	Number	Percent	Number	Percent	Number	Percent
All families	53,296	100.0	45,752	100.0	1,353	100.0	6,191	100.0	5,655	100.0
White	47,641	89.4	42,039	91.9	1,113	82.3	4,489	72.5	(X)	(X)
Negro and other	5,655	10.6	3,713	8.1	239	17.7	1,702	27.5	5,655	100.0
Size of family:										
2 persons	18,862	35.4	15,446	33.8	759	56.1	2,656	42.9	1,625	28.7
3 persons	11,305	21.2	9,378	20.5	317	23.4	1,610	26.0	1,187	21.0
4 persons	10,524	19.7	9,500	20.8	152	11.2	872	14.1	1,020	18.0
5 persons	6,362	11.9	5,805	12.7	74	5.5	483	7.8	632	11.2
6 persons	3,325	6.2	3,033	6.6	13	1.0	278	4.5	494	8.7
7 or more persons	2,919	5.5	2,590	5.7	37	2.7	292	4.7	696	12.3
Own children under age 18:										
None	23,851	44.8	20,270	44.3	987	72.9	2,594	41.9	2,132	37.7
1	10,050	18.9	8,556	18.7	171	12.6	1,323	21.4	1,097	19.4
2	9,388	17.6	8,218	18.0	111	8.2	1,059	17.1	926	16.4
3	5,411	10.2	4,730	10.3	47	3.5	634	10.2	608	10.8
4 or more	4,597	8.6	3,979	8.7	37	2.7	581	9.4	892	15.8
Own children under age 6:										
None	39,654	74.4	33,554	73.3	1,283	94.8	4,817	77.8	3,930	69.5
1	8,690	16.3	7,786	17.0	56	4.1	847	13.7	1,023	18.1
2	4,021	7.5	3,605	7.9	12	0.9	404	6.5	498	8.8
3 or more	930	1.7	807	1.8	1	0.1	122	2.0	203	3.6

X Not applicable.

BIRTHS AND BIRTH RATES: 1950 TO 1971

In thousands, except as indicated. Prior to 1960, excludes Alaska and Hawaii. For 1950 and 1955, births adjusted for underregistration; thereafter, registered births.

ITEM	1950	1955	1960	1965	1967	1968	1969	1970 (prel.)	1971 (prel.)
Live births	3,632	4,104	4,258	3,760	3,521	3,502	3,571	3,718	3,559
Percent urban [1]	60.6	61.0	62.3	54.5	54.6	54.0	(NA)	(NA)	(NA)
White	3,108	3,488	3,601	3,124	2,923	2,912	2,939	3,078	2,943
Negro and other	524	617	657	636	598	589	632	640	616
Percent of total	14.4	15.0	15.4	16.9	17.0	16.8	17.7	17.2	17.3
Male	1,863	2,103	2,180	1,927	1,803	1,796	1,829	1,907	1,826
Female	1,768	2,001	2,078	1,833	1,718	1,705	1,742	1,811	1,733
Males per 100 females	105.4	105.1	104.9	105.1	105.0	105.3	105.0	105.3	105.4
Birth rate per 1,000 population	24.1	25.0	23.7	19.4	17.8	17.5	17.7	18.2	17.3
White	23.0	23.8	22.7	18.3	16.8	16.6	16.6	15.5	(NA)
Negro and other	33.3	34.7	32.1	27.6	25.0	24.2	25.4	25.2	(NA)
Male	24.9	25.8	24.7	20.3	18.7	18.4	18.6	19.1	(NA)
Female	23.3	23.9	22.8	18.6	17.0	16.7	16.8	17.3	(NA)
Plural births per 1,000 live births	20.9	21.1	20.4	20.1	19.7	20.1	(NA)	(NA)	(NA)

NA Not available. [1] Based on registered births. For definition of urban, see text, p. 2; beginning 1965, cities and other urban places of 2,500 to 10,000 ceased to be classified as "urban" by source.

DEATHS AND DEATH RATES: 1920 TO 1971

Prior to 1960, excludes Alaska and Hawaii. Excludes fetal deaths. Population enumerated as of April 1 for 1940, 1950, 1960, and 1970, and estimated as of July 1 for all other years.

ITEM	1920	1930	1940	1950	1960	1965	1967	1968	1969	1970 [1]	1971 [1]
DEATHS											
Total ——1,000	1,118	1,327	1,417	1,452	1,712	1,828	1,851	1,930	1,922	1,921	1,921
Percent urban [2]	(NA)	(NA)	(NA)	64.6	65.9	56.4	56.4	56.3	55.9	(NA)	(NA)
White ——1,000	991	1,137	1,231	1,276	1,505	1,605	1,627	1,690	1,684	1,681	1,684
Negro and other ——1,000	127	190	186	176	207	223	224	241	238	240	236
Male ——1,000	586	727	791	828	976	1,035	1,046	1,087	1,081	1,079	1,076
Female ——1,000	532	601	626	625	736	793	805	843	841	842	845
DEATH RATES [3]											
Total	13.0	11.3	10.8	9.6	9.5	9.4	9.4	9.7	9.5	9.4	9.3
White	12.6	10.8	10.4	9.5	9.5	9.4	9.4	9.6	9.5	9.4	9.3
Negro and other	17.7	16.3	13.8	11.2	10.1	9.6	9.4	9.9	9.6	9.5	9.1
Male	13.4	12.3	12.0	11.1	11.0	10.9	10.8	11.1	11.0	10.8	10.7
Female	12.6	10.4	9.5	8.2	8.1	8.0	8.0	8.2	8.1	8.0	8.0
Age:											
Under 1 year	92.3	69.0	54.9	33.0	27.0	24.1	22.3	22.3	21.5	20.4	18.6
1–4 years	9.9	5.6	2.9	1.4	1.1	0.9	0.9	0.9	0.9	0.8	0.8
5–14 years	2.6	1.7	1.0	0.6	0.5	0.4	0.4	0.4	0.4	0.4	0.4
15–24 years	4.9	3.3	2.0	1.3	1.1	1.1	1.2	1.2	1.3	1.3	1.3
25–34 years	6.8	4.7	3.1	1.8	1.5	1.5	1.5	1.6	1.6	1.6	1.6
35–44 years	8.1	6.8	5.2	3.6	3.0	3.1	3.1	3.2	3.2	3.1	3.1
45–54 years	12.2	12.2	10.6	8.5	7.6	7.4	7.3	7.5	7.3	7.2	7.0
55–64 years	23.6	24.0	[4] 22.2	[4] 19.0	17.4	16.7	17.2	16.8	16.6	16.6	16.1
65–74 years	52.5	51.4	[4] 48.4	[4] 41.0	38.2	37.9	37.5	38.5	37.4	36.7	35.8
75–84 years	118.9	112.7	112.0	93.3	87.5	81.9	79.0	80.8	79.0	77.7	77.4
85 years and over	248.3	228.0	235.7	202.0	198.6	202.0	194.2	196.1	190.8	178.7	175.5

NA Not available. [1] Preliminary. Based on a 10-percent sample of deaths. [2] For definition of urban, see text, p. 2. [3] Per 1,000 population of specified groups. [4] Based on enumerated population adjusted for age bias in population other than white at ages 55–69 years.

Source: U.S. National Center for Health Statistics, *Vital Statistics of the United States*, annual, and unpublished data.

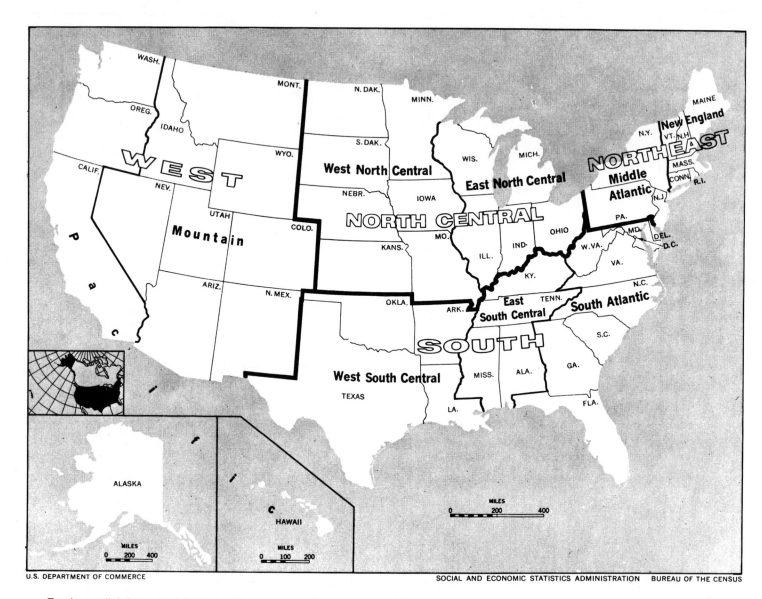

U.S. DEPARTMENT OF COMMERCE

SOCIAL AND ECONOMIC STATISTICS ADMINISTRATION   BUREAU OF THE CENSUS

Regions, divisions, and States.—The geographic groupings of States by regions and divisions are the groupings used by the Bureau of the Census. Under this arrangement, the United States is first divided into four regions. The regions are divided, in turn, into a total of nine geographic divisions, each of which is composed of a specific group of contiguous States.

POPULATION, RANK, PERCENT CHANGE, AND DENSITY—STATES AND PUERTO RICO: 1920 TO 1970

As of Census date: Jan. 1, 1920; Apr. 1 thereafter; except as noted. Insofar as possible, population shown is that of present area of State. Minus sign (—) denotes decrease.

STATE OR OTHER AREA	POPULATION (1,000)						RANK					
	1920	1930	1940	1950	1960	1970	1920	1930	1940	1950	1960	1970
United States	**106,022**	**123,203**	**132,165**	**151,326**	**179,323**	**[2]203,212**	(X)	(X)	(X)	(X)	(X)	(X)
Regions:												
Northeast	29,662	34,427	35,977	39,478	44,678	49,041	(X)	(X)	(X)	(X)	(X)	(X)
North Central	34,020	38,594	40,143	44,461	51,619	56,572	(X)	(X)	(X)	(X)	(X)	(X)
South	33,126	37,858	41,666	47,197	54,973	62,795	(X)	(X)	(X)	(X)	(X)	(X)
West	9,214	12,324	14,379	20,190	28,053	34,804	(X)	(X)	(X)	(X)	(X)	(X)
New England	**7,401**	**8,166**	**8,437**	**9,314**	**10,509**	**11,842**	(X)	(X)	(X)	(X)	(X)	(X)
Maine	768	797	847	914	969	992	35	35	35	35	36	38
New Hampshire	443	465	492	533	607	738	41	41	44	44	45	41
Vermont	352	360	359	378	390	444	44	46	46	46	47	48
Massachusetts	3,852	4,250	4,317	4,691	5,149	5,689	6	8	8	9	9	10
Rhode Island	604	687	713	792	859	947	38	37	36	36	39	39
Connecticut	1,381	1,607	1,709	2,007	2,535	3,032	29	29	31	28	25	24
Middle Atlantic	**22,261**	**26,261**	**27,539**	**30,164**	**34,168**	**37,199**	(X)	(X)	(X)	(X)	(X)	(X)
New York	10,385	12,588	13,479	14,830	16,782	18,237	1	1	1	1	1	2
New Jersey	3,156	4,041	4,160	4,835	6,067	7,168	10	9	9	8	8	8
Pennsylvania	8,720	9,631	9,900	10,498	11,319	11,794	2	2	2	3	3	3
East North Central	**21,476**	**25,297**	**26,626**	**30,399**	**36,225**	**40,252**	(X)	(X)	(X)	(X)	(X)	(X)
Ohio	5,759	6,647	6,908	7,947	9,706	10,652	4	4	4	5	5	6
Indiana	2,930	3,239	3,428	3,934	4,662	5,194	11	11	12	12	11	11
Illinois	6,485	7,631	7,897	8,712	10,081	11,114	3	3	3	4	4	5
Michigan	3,668	4,842	5,256	6,372	7,823	8,875	7	7	7	7	7	7
Wisconsin	2,632	2,939	3,138	3,435	3,952	4,418	13	13	13	14	15	16
West North Central	**12,544**	**13,297**	**13,517**	**14,061**	**15,394**	**16,319**	(X)	(X)	(X)	(X)	(X)	(X)
Minnesota	2,387	2,564	2,792	2,982	3,414	3,805	17	18	18	18	18	19
Iowa	2,404	2,471	2,538	2,621	2,758	2,824	16	19	20	22	24	25
Missouri	3,404	3,629	3,785	3,955	4,320	4,677	9	10	10	11	13	13
North Dakota	647	681	642	620	632	618	36	38	38	41	44	45
South Dakota	637	693	643	653	681	666	37	36	37	40	40	44
Nebraska	1,296	1,378	1,316	1,326	1,411	1,483	31	32	32	33	34	35
Kansas	1,769	1,881	1,801	1,905	2,179	2,247	24	24	29	31	28	28
South Atlantic	**13,990**	**15,794**	**17,823**	**21,182**	**25,972**	**30,671**	(X)	(X)	(X)	(X)	(X)	(X)
Delaware	223	238	267	318	446	548	47	47	47	47	46	46
Maryland	1,450	1,632	1,821	2,343	3,101	3,922	28	28	28	24	21	18
D.C.	438	487	663	802	764	757	(X)	(X)	(X)	(X)	(X)	(X)
Virginia	2,309	2,422	2,678	3,319	3,967	4,648	20	20	19	15	14	14
West Virginia	1,464	1,729	1,902	2,006	1,860	1,744	27	27	25	29	30	34
North Carolina	2,559	3,170	3,572	4,062	4,556	5,082	14	12	11	10	12	12
South Carolina	1,684	1,739	1,900	2,117	2,383	2,591	26	26	26	27	26	26
Georgia	2,896	2,909	3,124	3,445	3,943	4,590	12	14	14	13	16	15
Florida	968	1,468	1,897	2,771	4,952	6,789	32	31	27	20	10	9
East South Central	**8,893**	**9,887**	**10,778**	**11,477**	**12,050**	**12,803**	(X)	(X)	(X)	(X)	(X)	(X)
Kentucky	2,417	2,615	2,846	2,945	3,038	3,219	15	17	16	19	22	23
Tennessee	2,338	2,617	2,916	3,292	3,567	3,924	19	16	15	16	17	17
Alabama	2,348	2,646	2,833	3,062	3,267	3,444	18	15	17	17	19	21
Mississippi	1,791	2,010	2,184	2,179	2,178	2,217	23	23	23	26	29	29
West South Central	**10,242**	**12,177**	**13,065**	**14,538**	**16,951**	**19,321**	(X)	(X)	(X)	(X)	(X)	(X)
Arkansas	1,752	1,854	1,949	1,910	1,786	1,923	25	25	24	30	31	32
Louisiana	1,799	2,102	2,364	2,684	3,257	3,641	22	22	21	21	20	20
Oklahoma	2,028	2,396	2,336	2,233	2,328	2,559	21	21	22	25	27	27
Texas	4,663	5,825	6,415	7,711	9,580	11,197	5	5	6	6	6	4
Mountain	**3,336**	**3,702**	**4,150**	**5,075**	**6,855**	**8,282**	(X)	(X)	(X)	(X)	(X)	(X)
Montana	549	538	559	591	675	694	39	39	39	42	41	43
Idaho	432	445	525	589	667	713	42	42	42	43	42	42
Wyoming	194	226	251	291	330	332	48	48	48	48	48	49
Colorado	940	1,036	1,123	1,325	1,754	2,207	33	33	33	34	33	30
New Mexico	360	423	532	681	951	1,016	43	44	41	39	37	37
Arizona	334	436	499	750	1,302	1,771	45	43	43	37	35	33
Utah	449	508	550	689	891	1,059	40	40	40	38	38	36
Nevada	77	91	110	160	285	489	49	49	49	49	49	47
Pacific	**5,878**	**8,622**	**10,229**	**15,115**	**21,198**	**26,523**	(X)	(X)	(X)	(X)	(X)	(X)
Washington	1,357	1,563	1,736	2,379	2,853	3,409	30	30	30	23	23	22
Oregon	783	954	1,090	1,521	1,769	2,091	34	34	34	32	32	31
California	3,427	5,677	6,907	10,586	15,717	19,953	8	6	5	2	2	1
Alaska	55	[3]59	[3]73	129	226	300	50	50	50	50	50	50
Hawaii	256	368	423	500	633	769	46	45	45	45	43	40
Puerto Rico	1,300	1,544	1,869	2,211	2,350	2,712	(X)	(X)	(X)	(X)	(X)	(X)

X Not applicable. Z Less than 0.05 percent. [1] For United States, population of United States has been divided by total land area. For each State and Puerto Rico, population at given census has been divided by land area as then constituted. [2] See footnote 1, table 1. [3] 1930 as of Oct. 1, 1929; 1940 as of Oct. 1, 1939.

PERCENT CHANGE					POPULATION PER SQUARE MILE [1]						STATE OR OTHER AREA
1920–1930	1930–1940	1940–1950	1950–1960	1960–1970	1920	1930	1940	1950	1960	1970	
16.2	**7.3**	**14.5**	**18.5**	**13.3**	**29.9**	**34.7**	**37.2**	**42.6**	**50.6**	**57.5**	**United States.**
											Regions:
16.1	4.5	9.7	13.2	9.8	183.1	210.3	219.8	241.2	273.4	300.4	Northeast.
13.4	4.0	10.8	16.1	9.6	45.0	51.1	53.1	58.8	68.6	75.2	North Central.
14.3	10.1	13.3	16.5	14.2	37.7	43.0	47.4	53.7	62.8	71.9	South.
33.7	16.7	40.4	38.9	24.1	5.3	7.0	8.2	11.5	16.0	19.9	West.
10.3	**3.3**	**10.4**	**12.8**	**12.7**	**119.4**	**129.2**	**133.5**	**147.5**	**166.8**	**188.1**	**New England.**
3.8	6.2	7.9	6.1	2.4	25.7	25.7	27.3	29.4	31.3	32.1	Maine.
5.0	5.6	8.5	13.8	21.5	49.1	51.6	54.5	59.1	67.2	81.7	New Hampshire.
2.0	—0.1	5.2	3.2	14.0	38.6	38.8	38.7	40.7	42.0	47.9	Vermont.
10.3	1.6	8.7	9.8	10.5	479.2	537.4	545.9	596.2	657.3	727.0	Massachusetts.
13.7	3.8	11.0	8.5	10.1	566.4	649.8	674.2	748.5	819.3	902.5	Rhode Island.
16.4	6.4	17.4	26.3	19.6	286.4	328.0	348.9	409.7	520.6	623.6	Connecticut.
18.0	**4.9**	**9.5**	**13.3**	**8.9**	**222.6**	**261.3**	**274.0**	**300.1**	**340.2**	**370.8**	**Middle Atlantic.**
21.2	7.1	10.0	13.2	8.7	217.9	262.6	281.2	309.3	350.6	381.3	New York.
28.1	2.9	16.2	25.5	18.2	420.0	537.3	553.1	642.8	805.5	953.1	New Jersey.
10.5	2.8	6.0	7.8	4.2	194.5	213.8	219.8	233.1	251.4	262.3	Pennsylvania.
17.8	**5.3**	**14.2**	**19.2**	**11.1**	**87.5**	**103.2**	**108.7**	**124.1**	**148.2**	**164.9**	**East North Central.**
15.4	3.9	15.0	22.1	9.7	141.4	161.6	168.0	193.8	236.6	260.0	Ohio.
10.5	5.8	14.8	18.5	11.4	81.3	89.4	94.7	108.7	128.8	143.9	Indiana.
17.7	3.5	10.3	15.7	10.2	115.7	136.4	141.2	155.8	180.4	199.4	Illinois.
32.0	8.5	21.2	22.8	13.4	63.8	84.9	92.2	111.7	137.7	156.2	Michigan.
11.7	6.8	9.5	15.1	11.8	47.6	53.7	57.3	62.8	72.6	81.1	Wisconsin.
6.0	**1.7**	**4.0**	**9.5**	**6.0**	**24.6**	**26.0**	**26.5**	**27.5**	**30.3**	**32.1**	**West North Central.**
7.4	8.9	6.8	14.5	11.5	29.5	32.0	34.9	37.3	43.1	48.0	Minnesota.
2.8	2.7	3.3	5.2	2.4	43.2	44.1	45.3	46.8	49.2	50.5	Iowa.
6.6	4.3	4.5	9.2	8.3	49.5	52.4	54.6	57.1	62.6	67.8	Missouri.
5.3	—5.7	—3.5	2.1	—2.3	9.2	9.7	9.2	8.8	9.1	8.9	North Dakota.
8.8	—7.2	1.5	4.3	—2.2	8.3	9.1	8.4	8.5	9.0	8.8	South Dakota.
6.3	—4.5	0.7	6.5	5.1	16.9	18.0	17.2	17.3	18.4	19.4	Nebraska.
6.3	—4.3	5.8	14.3	3.1	21.6	22.9	21.9	23.2	26.6	27.5	Kansas.
12.9	**12.9**	**18.8**	**22.6**	**18.1**	**52.0**	**58.8**	**66.4**	**79.0**	**97.1**	**114.9**	**South Atlantic.**
6.9	11.8	19.4	40.3	22.8	113.5	120.5	134.7	160.8	225.2	276.5	Delaware.
12.5	11.6	28.6	32.3	26.5	145.8	165.0	184.2	237.1	313.5	396.6	Maryland.
11.3	36.2	21.0	—4.8	—1.0	7,293	7,982	10,870	13,151	12,442	12,402	D.C.
4.9	10.6	23.9	19.5	17.2	57.4	60.7	67.1	83.2	99.6	116.9	Virginia.
18.1	10.0	5.4	—7.2	—6.2	60.9	71.8	79.0	83.3	77.2	72.5	West Virginia.
23.9	12.7	13.7	12.2	11.5	52.5	64.5	72.7	82.7	93.2	104.1	North Carolina.
3.3	9.3	11.4	12.5	8.7	55.2	56.8	62.1	69.9	78.7	85.7	South Carolina.
0.4	7.4	10.3	14.5	16.4	49.3	49.7	53.4	58.9	67.8	79.0	Georgia.
51.6	29.2	46.1	78.7	37.1	17.7	27.1	35.0	51.1	91.5	125.5	Florida.
11.2	**9.0**	**6.5**	**5.0**	**6.3**	**49.5**	**54.8**	**59.7**	**63.8**	**67.2**	**71.5**	**East South Central.**
8.2	8.8	3.5	3.2	5.9	60.1	65.2	70.9	73.9	76.2	81.2	Kentucky.
11.9	11.4	12.9	8.4	10.0	56.1	62.4	69.5	78.8	86.2	94.9	Tennessee.
12.7	7.1	8.1	6.7	5.4	45.8	51.8	55.5	59.9	64.2	67.9	Alabama.
12.2	8.7	—0.2	(Z)	1.8	38.6	42.4	46.1	46.1	46.0	46.9	Mississippi.
18.9	**7.3**	**11.3**	**16.6**	**14.0**	**23.8**	**28.3**	**30.3**	**33.8**	**39.5**	**45.2**	**West South Central.**
5.8	5.1	—2.0	—6.5	7.7	33.4	35.2	37.0	36.3	34.2	37.0	Arkansas.
16.9	12.5	13.5	21.4	11.8	39.6	46.5	52.3	59.4	72.2	81.0	Louisiana.
18.1	—2.5	—4.4	4.3	9.9	29.2	34.6	33.7	32.4	33.8	37.2	Oklahoma.
24.9	10.1	20.2	24.2	16.9	17.8	22.1	24.3	29.3	36.4	42.7	Texas.
11.0	**12.1**	**22.3**	**35.1**	**20.8**	**3.9**	**4.3**	**4.8**	**5.9**	**8.0**	**9.7**	**Mountain.**
—2.1	4.1	5.6	14.2	2.9	3.8	3.7	3.8	4.1	4.6	4.8	Montana.
3.0	17.9	12.1	13.3	6.8	5.2	5.4	6.3	7.1	8.1	8.6	Idaho.
16.0	11.2	15.9	13.6	0.7	2.0	2.3	2.6	3.0	3.4	3.4	Wyoming.
10.2	8.4	18.0	32.4	25.8	9.1	10.0	10.8	12.8	16.9	21.3	Colorado.
17.5	25.6	28.1	39.6	6.8	2.9	3.5	4.4	5.6	7.8	8.4	New Mexico.
30.3	14.6	50.1	73.7	36.0	2.9	3.8	4.4	6.6	11.5	15.6	Arizona.
13.0	8.4	25.2	29.3	18.9	5.5	6.2	6.7	8.4	10.8	12.9	Utah.
17.6	21.1	45.2	78.2	71.3	0.7	0.8	1.0	1.5	2.6	4.4	Nevada.
46.7	**18.7**	**47.8**	**40.2**	**25.1**	**6.6**	**9.6**	**11.4**	**16.8**	**23.8**	**29.7**	**Pacific.**
15.2	11.1	37.0	19.9	19.5	20.3	23.3	25.9	35.6	42.8	51.2	Washington.
21.8	14.2	39.6	16.3	18.2	8.2	9.9	11.3	15.8	18.4	21.7	Oregon.
65.7	21.7	53.3	48.5	27.0	22.0	36.2	44.1	67.5	100.4	127.6	California.
7.7	22.3	77.4	75.8	32.8	0.1	[2]0.1	[2]0.1	0.2	0.4	0.5	Alaska.
43.9	14.8	18.2	26.6	21.5	39.9	57.5	66.0	78.0	98.5	119.6	Hawaii.
18.8	21.1	18.3	6.3	15.4	379.7	451.0	546.1	645.8	686.4	792.8	Puerto Rico.

Source: U.S. Bureau of the Census, *U.S. Census of Population: 1970*, vol. I, part A.

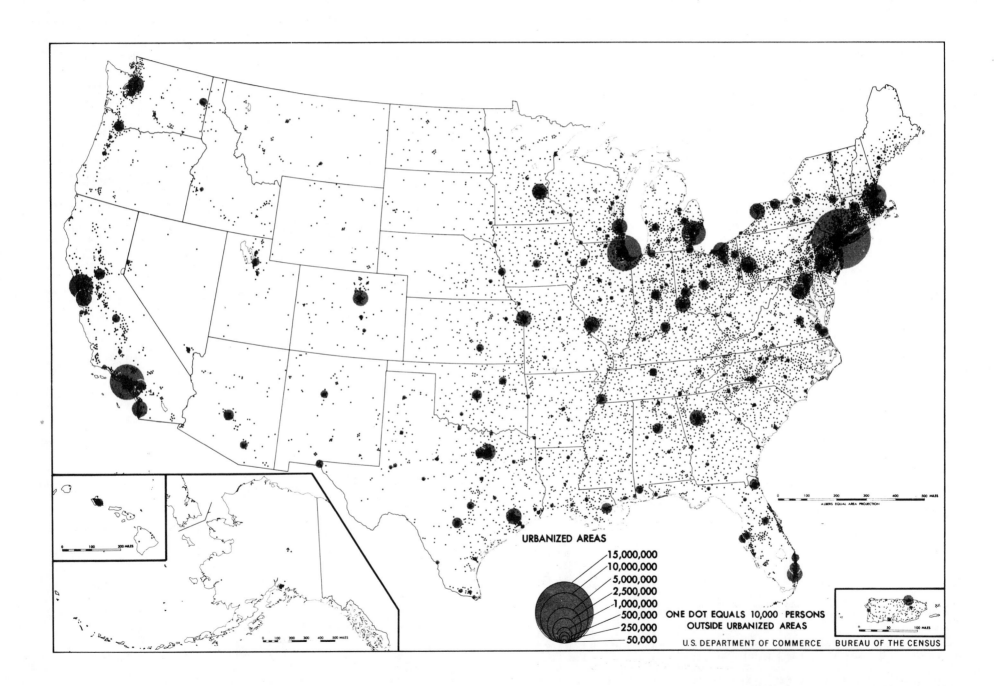

URBANIZED AREAS

15,000,000
10,000,000
5,000,000
2,500,000
1,000,000
500,000
250,000
50,000

ONE DOT EQUALS 10,000 PERSONS
OUTSIDE URBANIZED AREAS

U.S. DEPARTMENT OF COMMERCE

ALBERS EQUAL AREA PROJECTION

BUREAU OF THE CENSUS

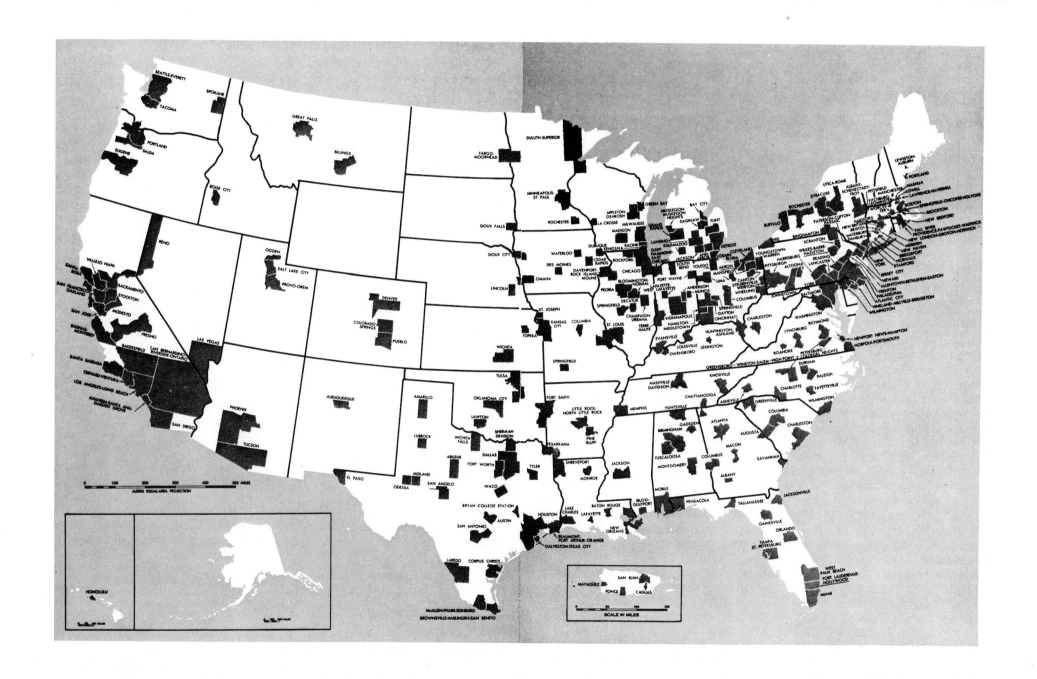

Standard Metropolitan Statistical Areas

For many types of analysis, the entire area in and around a city, in which the activities form an integrated economic and social system, needs to be considered as a unit.

The Bureau of the Census, in 1910, introduced *Metropolitan Districts* to its system of area classification. This marked the first use by the Bureau of a unit for reporting data for large cities and their environs. Originally defined for every city of over 200,000 population, *Metropolitan Districts* were extended, by 1940, to cover each incorporated city of 50,000 or more inhabitants and included adjacent and contiguous minor civil divisions or incorporated places having a population density of 150 persons per square mile or more. A major limitation to the *Metropolitan District* concept from the standpoint of statistical presentation was the fact that not many data beyond those available from the census of population and housing were compiled or available for minor civil divisions. Also, prior to 1950, other area classifications, defined in different ways and designed for special purposes, were developed, e.g., industrial areas of the census of manufactures and labor market areas of the Bureau of Employment Security (now Manpower Administration).

The *Standard Metropolitan Area* (SMA) concept of 1950 was developed by the Federal Committee on Standard Metropolitan Areas, composed of representatives of interested Federal agencies, including the Bureau of the Census, and sponsored by the Bureau of the Budget (now Office of Management and Budget) so that a wider variety of statistical data might be presented on a uniform basis. The SMA consisted of one or more contiguous counties containing at least one city of 50,000 inhabitants or more. Additional counties had to meet certain criteria of metropolitan character and social and economic integration with the central city in order to be classified within an SMA. The SMA differed from the old *Metropolitan District* in that it was not based primarily upon density criteria.

The name, SMA, was changed to Standard Metropolitan Statistical Area (SMSA) in 1959 to reflect the nature and purpose of the areas. The SMSA classification provides a distinction between metropolitan and nonmetropolitan areas by type of residence, supplementing the older rural-urban, farm-nonfarm distinctions. Further, SMSA's take into account places of industrial concentration (labor demand) and of population concentration (labor supply). The SMSA has been used extensively by numerous government agencies as a standard area for data gathering, analysis, and publication of statistics.

Since the release of the *County and City Data Book, 1967,* new SMSA's have been established and the definitions of several have been changed. Every city of 50,000 inhabitants or more plus twin cities with 50,000 or more according to the 1970 Census of Population will eventually be included in an SMSA. As of February 1971, there were 243 SMSA's in the United States.

The definition of an individual SMSA involves two considerations: First, a city or cities of specified population to constitute the central city and to identify the county in which it is located as the central county; and second, economic and social relationships with contiguous counties which are metropolitan in character, so that the periphery of the specific metropolitan area may be determined.[1] SMSA's may cross State lines.

Population Criteria. The criteria for population relate to a city or cities of specified size according to the 1970 Census of Population.

1. Each standard metropolitan statistical area must include at least:

a. One city with 50,000 inhabitants or more, or

b. Two cities having contiguous boundaries and constituting, for general economic and social purposes, a single community with a combined population at least 50,000, the smaller of which must have a population of at least 15,000.

2. If two or more adjacent counties each have a city of 50,000 inhabitants or more (or twin cities under 1b above) and the cities are within 20 miles of each other (city limits to city limits), they are to be included in the same area unless there is definite evidence that the two cities are not economically and socially integrated.

Criteria of Metropolitan Character

The criteria of metropolitan character relate primarily to the attributes of the county as a place of work or as a home for a concentration of nonagricultural workers. Specifically, these criteria are:

3. At least 75 percent of the labor force of the county must be in the nonagricultural labor force.[2]

4. In addition to criterion 3, the county must meet at least one of the following conditions:

a. It must have 50 percent or more of its population living in contiguous minor civil divisions[3] with a density of at least 150 persons per square mile in an unbroken chain of minor civil divisions with such density radiating from a central city in the area.

b. The number of nonagricultural workers employed in the county must equal at least 10 percent of the number of nonagricultural workers employed in the county containing the largest city in the area, or be the place of employment of 10,000 nonagricultural workers.

c. The nonagricultural labor force living in the county must equal at least 10 percent of the number in the nonagricultural labor force living in the county containing the largest city in the area, or be the place of residence of a nonagricultural labor force of 10,000.

[1]Central cities are those appearing in the standard metropolitan statistical area title. A contiguous county either adjoins the county or counties containing the largest city in the area or adjoins an intermediate county integrated with the central county. There is no limit to the number of tiers of outlying metropolitan counties so long as all other criteria are met.

[2]Nonagricultural labor force is defined as those employed in nonagricultural occupations, those experienced unemployed whose last occupation was a nonagricultural occupation, members of the Armed Forces, and new workers.

[3]A contiguous minor civil division either adjoins a central city in a standard metropolitan statistical area or adjoins an intermediate minor civil division of qualifying population density. There is no limit to the number of tiers of contiguous minor civil divisions so long as the minimum density requirement is met in each tier.

ing the largest city in the area, or be the place of residence of a nonagricultural labor force of 10,000.

5. In New England, the city and town are administratively more important than the county, and data are compiled locally for such minor civil divisions. Here, towns and cities are the units used in defining standard metropolitan statistical areas. In New England, because smaller units are used and more restricted areas result, a population density criterion of at least 100 persons per square mile is used as the measure of metropolitan character.

Criteria of Integration

The criteria of integration relate primarily to the extent of economic and social communication between the outlying counties and central county.

6. A county is regarded as integrated with the county or counties containing the central cities of the area if either of the following criteria is met:

a. Fifteen percent of the workers living in the county work in the county or counties containing central cities of the area, or

b. Twenty-five percent of those working in the county live in the county or counties containing central cities of the area.

Criteria for Titles

The criteria for titles relate primarily to the size and number of central cities.

7. The complete title of an SMSA identifies the central city or cities and the State or States in which the SMSA is located:

a. The name of the standard metropolitan statistical area is that of the largest city.

b. The addition of up to two city names may be made in the area title, on the basis and in the order of the following criteria:

(1) The additional city or cities have at least 250,000 inhabitants.

(2) The additional city or cities have a population of one-third or more of that of the largest city and a minimum population of 25,000 except that both city names are used in those instances where cities qualify under criterion 1b.

c. In addition to city names, the area titles contain the name of the State or States in which the area is located.

Standard Consolidated Areas

In view of the special importance of the metropolitan complexes around New York and Chicago, the Nation's largest cities, several contiguous SMSA's and additional counties that do not appear to meet the formal integration criteria but do have strong interrelationships of other kinds have been combined into the New York, N.Y.–Northeastern New Jersey and Chicago, Ill.–Northwestern Indiana Standard Consolidated Areas (SCA's), respectively.

State Economic Areas and Economic Subregions

State economic areas (SEA's) are relatively homogeneous subdivisions of States. They consist of single counties or groups of counties which have similar economic and social characteristics. The boundaries of these areas have been drawn in such a way that each State is subdivided into relatively few parts, with each part having certain significant characteristics which distinguish it from adjoining areas.

The State economic areas have been designed for use in tabulating and publishing census data of various types and for other purposes.

The combination of counties into State economic areas has been made for the entire country and, in the process, the larger standard metropolitan statistical areas (those in 1960 with a central city of 50,000 or more and a total population of 100,000 or more) have been recognized as metropolitan State economic areas. When a standard metropolitan statistical area is located in two or more States, each State part becomes a metropolitan State economic area. In New England this correspondence does not exist because State economic areas are composed of counties, whereas standard metropolitan statistical areas are composed of towns. Here a county with more than half its population in one or more standard metropolitan statistical areas is classified as a metropolitan State economic area if the county or combination of counties containing the standard metropolitan statistical area or areas has 100,000 inhabitants or more.

Economic subregions represent combinations of State economic areas. The 510 State economic areas are consolidated into a set of 121 subregions which cut across State lines but which, as intended, preserve to a great extent the homogeneous character of the State economic areas. No changes were made in the boundaries of the 119 economic subregions of 1950 in conterminous United States.

Counties

The primary divisions of States are, in general, termed counties. In Louisiana, these divisions are known as parishes. There are no counties in Alaska; in their place, data are shown for statistical equivalents of counties, designated as census divisions.

Urbanized Areas

The major objective of the Census Bureau in delineating urbanized areas is to provide a better separation of urban and rural population in the vicinity of the larger cities. An urbanized area consists of a central city, or cities, and surrounding closely settled territory. The specific criteria for the delineation of an urbanized area are as follows:

1. a. A central city of 50,000 inhabitants or more in 1960, in a special census conducted by the Census Bureau since 1960, or in the 1970 census; or

b. Twin cities, i.e., cities with contiguous boundaries and constituting, for general social and economic purposes, a single community with a combined population of at least 50,000 and with the smaller of the twin cities having a population of at least 15,000.

2. Surrounding closely settled territory, including the following (but excluding the rural portions of extended cities; see "extended cities," below):

a. Incorporated places of 2,500 inhabitants or more.

b. Incorporated places with fewer than 2,500 inhabitants, provided that each has a closely settled area of 100 housing units or more.

c. Small parcels of land normally less than one square mile in area having a population density of 1,000 inhabitants or more per square mile. The areas of large nonresidential tracts devoted to such urban land uses as railroad yards, airports, factories, parks, golf courses, and cemeteries are excluded in computing the population density.

d. Other similar small areas in unincorporated territory with lower population density provided that they serve
- to eliminate enclaves, or
- to close indentations in the urbanized areas of one mile or less across the open end, or
- to link outlying enumeration districts of qualifying density that are not more than 1½ miles from the main body of the urbanized area.

The 1970 criteria are essentially the same as those used in 1960 with two exceptions. The extended city concept is new for 1970 (see below). Secondly, in 1960, towns in the New England States, townships in New Jersey and Pennsylvania, and counties elsewhere, which were classified as urban in accordance with specific criteria, were included in the contiguous urbanized areas. In 1970, only those portions of towns and townships in these States that met the rules followed in defining urbanized areas elsewhere in the United States are included.

All persons residing in an urbanized area are classified as urban. The urbanized area population is sometimes divided into those in the "central city (or cities)" and those in the remainder of the area or the "urban fringe." The "central city" category consists of the population of the cities named in the title of the urbanized area. The title is limited to three names and normally lists the largest city first and the other qualifying cities in size order; this order is in many cases based on 1960 population because most names were fixed before the 1970 counts were available. For the other cities to be listed in the title, they must have (a) 250,000 inhabitants or more or (b) at least one-third the population of the largest city and a population of 25,000 or more (except in the case of the small twin cities).

There is generally one urbanized area in each standard metropolitan statistical area. Sometimes, however, there are two because there exists another qualifying city with 50,000 inhabitants or more whose surrounding urban fringe is separated from the urban fringe of the larger central city or cities. (The Chicago metropolitan area has three urbanized areas.) In other cases, a single urbanized area covers portions of two or more standard metropolitan statistical areas. One metropolitan area (New London-Groton-Norwich, Conn.) has no urbanized area.

A map of urbanized areas appears on p. 141.

Cities

The designation "city," in general, refers to a political subdivision of a State within a defined area over which a municipal corporation has been established to provide local government functions and facilities. "Cities" as used refers to those places which are incorporated as cities, boroughs, towns, and villages with the exception that towns are not recognized as incorporated places in the New England States, New York, and Wisconsin, and boroughs are not recognized in Alaska. The towns in these States are minor civil divisions similar to the townships in some States and are not necessarily thickly settled centers of population such as the cities, boroughs, towns, and villages in other States.

Extended Cities

Over the 1960–1970 decade there was an increasing trend toward the extension of city boundaries to include territory essentially rural in character. Examples are city-county consolidations such as the creation of the city of Chesapeake, Va., from South Norfolk city and Norfolk County and the extension of Oklahoma City, Okla., into five counties. The classification of all the inhabitants of such cities as urban would include in the urban population persons whose environment is primarily rural in character. In order to separate these people from those residing in the closely settled portions of such cities, the Bureau of the Census examined patterns of population density and classified a portion or portions of each such city as rural. An extended city contains one or more areas, each of at least 5 square miles in extent and with a population density of less than 100 persons per square mile according to the 1970 census. The area or areas constitute at least 25 percent of the land area of the legal city or total 25 square miles or more.

These cities—designated as extended cities—thus consist of an urban part and a rural part. When an extended city is a central city of an urbanized area or a standard metropolitan area only the urban part is considered as the central city.

Places

Two types of places are recognized in the census reports—incorporated places and unincorporated places, as defined below.

Incorporated Places

These are political units incorporated as cities, boroughs, towns, and villages with the following exceptions: (a) boroughs in Alaska, (b) towns in the New England States, New York, and Wisconsin, and (c) townships in New Jersey and Pennsylvania. Boroughs in Alaska are treated as county subdivisions and may include one or more incorporated places. The towns in New England, New York, and Wisconsin are minor civil divisions and are not necessarily thickly settled population centers. The townships in New Jersey and Pennsylvania, although incorporated in one legal sense of the word in that some possess powers and functions similar to those of incorporated places, are not regarded by the Census Bureau as incorporated.

In Hawaii, there are no incorporated places in the sense of functioning local governmental units. The State, however, has recognized places and established boundaries for them. Such places are treated as incorporated in the 1970 census.

Unincorporated Places

As in the 1950 and 1960 censuses, the Census Bureau, for 1970, delineated boundaries for closely settled population centers without corporate limits. Each place so delineated possesses a definite nucleus of residences and has its boundaries drawn to include, if feasible, all the surrounding closely settled area. Within urbanized areas, unincorporated places were shown only if they had 5,000 inhabitants or more and there was an expression of local interest in their recognition.

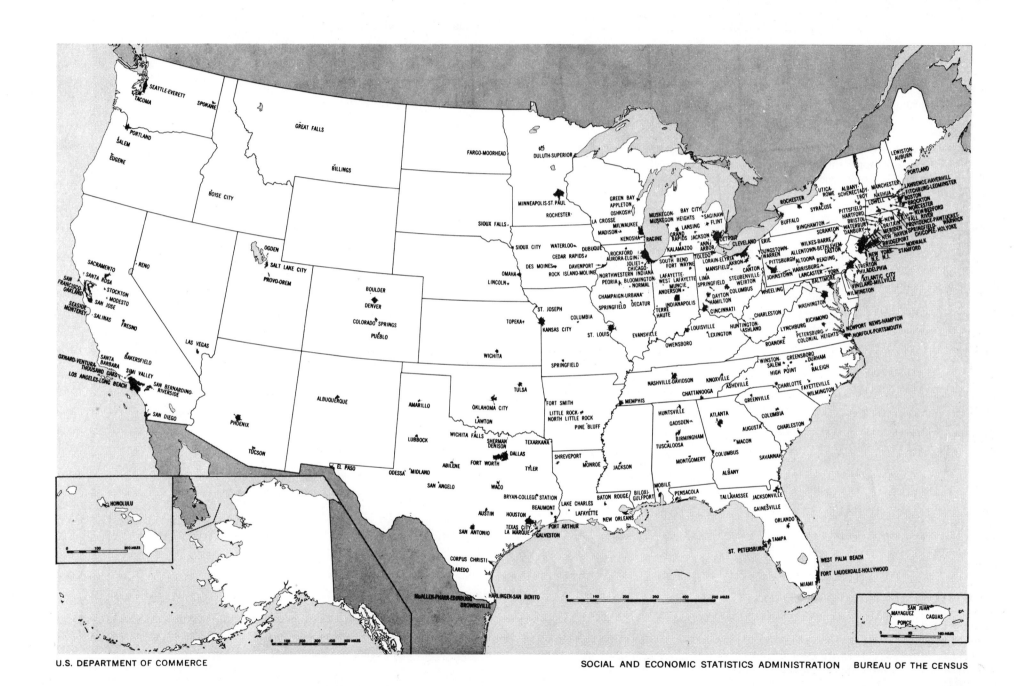

U.S. DEPARTMENT OF COMMERCE

SOCIAL AND ECONOMIC STATISTICS ADMINISTRATION   BUREAU OF THE CENSUS

OTHER AREAS

The Bureau of the Census also collects and compiles statistics for other geographic entities. Some of these are described below.

Congressional Districts

Congressional district boundaries are determined by State legislative bodies. Within recent years, however, the Federal Courts have intervened in defining the boundaries of districts in a number of States either because of a failure to take redistricting action on the part of the legislative bodies or because action taken was deemed unsatisfactory on legal grounds.

Central Business Districts and Major Retail Centers

The primary objective of delineating "central business districts" (CBD's) was to provide a basis for comparing changes in business activity in the central business district with those in the remainder of the metropolitan area or of the central city. The delineation was accomplished by the Bureau of the Census with the cooperation of local census tract committees representing a variety of local interests.

Since there were no generally accepted rules for determining what a CBD area should comprise, the Census Bureau, in defining the CBD, described it as an area of very high land valuation, an area characterized by a high concentration of retail businesses, offices, theaters, hotels, and "service" businesses, and an area of high traffic flow; and required that the CBD ordinarily should be defined to follow existing tract lines, i.e., to consist of one or more whole census tracts (see below).

CBD's have been delineated in each city of 100,000 inhabitants or more in an SMSA (according to the census of population or a subsequent special census).

Major retail centers (MRC's) were defined by the Bureau of the Census as those concentrations of retail stores (located inside the standard metropolitan statistical areas in which the CBD cities are located but outside of the CBD's themselves) having at least $5 million in retail sales and at least 10 retail establishments, one of which is classified as a department store. MRC's include not only the planned shopping center but also the older string street and neighborhood developments which meet the above criteria.

Data on establishments, sales or receipts, and payroll for retail trade, hotels, and theaters for the CBD's and MRC's of each of selected large cities are shown in *U.S. Census of Business: 1967, Vol. III, Major Retail Centers.*

City Blocks

According to Bureau of the Census usage, a city block is usually a well-defined rectangular piece of land bounded by streets or roads. It may, however, be irregular in shape or bounded by railroad tracks, streams, or other features. 1970 housing census data by blocks are available for 236 urbanized areas and for 42 other types of areas (e.g., smaller cities, counties, etc.) where local authorities contracted with the Bureau of the Census to collect, process, and publish the date on a block basis. These data and identifying maps are presented in *U.S. Census of Housing: 1970, Vol. III, Block Statistics,* Series HC (3).

Census County Divisions

For purposes of presenting census statistics, counties in 21 States have been subdivided by the Bureau of the Census into statistical areas called "census county divisions" (CCD's). These divisions are used instead of the election precincts, townships, or other minor civil divisions (MCD's, see below) for which census statistics were previously reported because the boundaries of such MCD's changed frequently, were indefinite or imaginary, or were not well known by many of the inhabitants.

CCD's were established first in the State of Washington for use in the 1950 census. Between 1950 and 1970 they were established in 20 additional States, of which 10 are in the West—Arizona, California, Colorado, Hawaii, Idaho, Montana, New Mexico, Oregon, Utah, and Wyoming; nine in the South—Alabama, Delaware, Florida, Georgia, Kentucky, Oklahoma, South Carolina, Tennessee, and Texas; and one in the North—North Dakota.

CCD boundaries normally follow physical features such as roads, highways, trails, railroads, power lines, streams, and ridges. Larger incorporated places are recognized as separate divisions, even though their boundaries may change as the result of annexations. Cities with 10,000 inhabitants or more generally are separate divisions. In addition, some incorporated places with as few as 2,500 inhabitants may be separate divisions. An unincorporated enclave within a city is included in the same CCD as the city.

In areas with census tracts (see above) the usual practice is that each CCD is a census tract or group of tracts, or the combination of two CCD's represents one census tract.

The boundaries of CCD's were reviewed with officials in each county and various State agencies and were approved by the governors (or their representatives) of the States. Maps showing CCD boundaries and population data for these county subdivisions in each State are provided in *U.S. Census of Population: 1970,* Vol. I, *Characteristics of the Population,* Part A, "Number of Inhabitants."

Census Tracts

Census tracts are small areas into which large cities and their adjacent areas have been divided for statistical purposes. Tract boundaries were established cooperatively in each standard metropolitan statistical area (SMSA) by a local committee and the Bureau of the Census and were generally designed to achieve some uniformity of population characteristics, economic status, and living conditions. The average tract has about 4,000 residents. Tract boundaries were established with the intention of being maintained over a long time so that comparisons may be made from census to census.

For a further discussion of census tract data and their uses, see Bureau of the Census, *Census Tract Manual.*

Minor Civil Divisions

These component parts of counties have been used traditionally for the presentation of statistics. They represent political or administrative subdivisions of the States and may be townships, precincts, districts, independent municipalities, etc. In a number of States, however, these areas are unsatisfactory as a basis for compiling local statistics, because they have lost their original significance, are too small, have frequent boundary changes, or have indefinite boundaries. For those States, the Bureau of the Census, therefore, has defined statistical areas designated as census county divisions (see above).

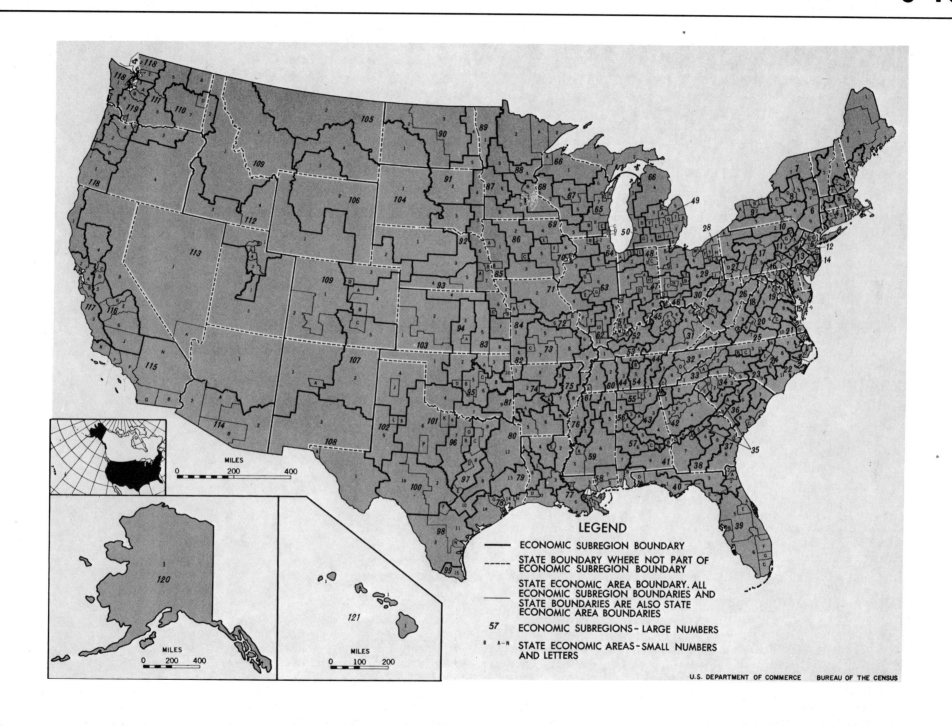

LEGEND

ECONOMIC SUBREGION BOUNDARY

STATE BOUNDARY WHERE NOT PART OF ECONOMIC SUBREGION BOUNDARY

STATE ECONOMIC AREA BOUNDARY. ALL ECONOMIC SUBREGION BOUNDARIES AND STATE BOUNDARIES ARE ALSO STATE ECONOMIC AREA BOUNDARIES

57   ECONOMIC SUBREGIONS – LARGE NUMBERS

8 A–N   STATE ECONOMIC AREAS – SMALL NUMBERS AND LETTERS

U.S. DEPARTMENT OF COMMERCE   BUREAU OF THE CENSUS

HOUSING

1 Young couple marries. Their living needs are basic. The five areas used might possibly be contained in one room.

2 Upon the arrival of the first blessed event the areas would have to be expanded. The need for storage is increased, and eventually an additional sleeping area is necessary.

3 The second blessed event requires increased storage and a general increase of the five major areas.

4 The third blessed event requires additional sleeping area with all facilities, plus an additional separate bathing and washing area.

5 At this point the family and house should remain stable, with an increase in living-recreation areas.

6 About this time the first child leaves home, decreasing needs in the house and reducing the family to four persons.

7 The second child leaves, and the house area needed decreases.

8 The third child leaves, bringing the family back to its original state: two persons. The only area that might remain stable is the storage area, for items accumulated are seldom lost or reduced to any great extent.

9 The family may eventually be reduced to one, so that needs are less than at the beginning.

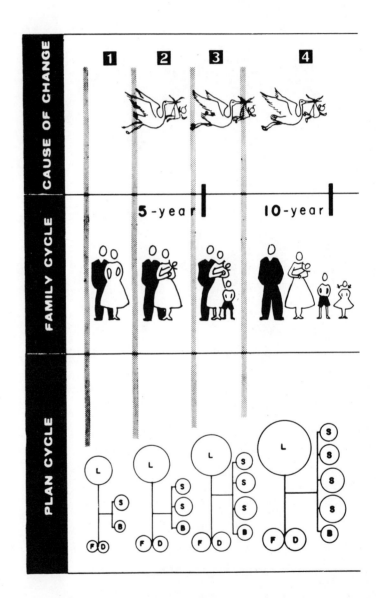

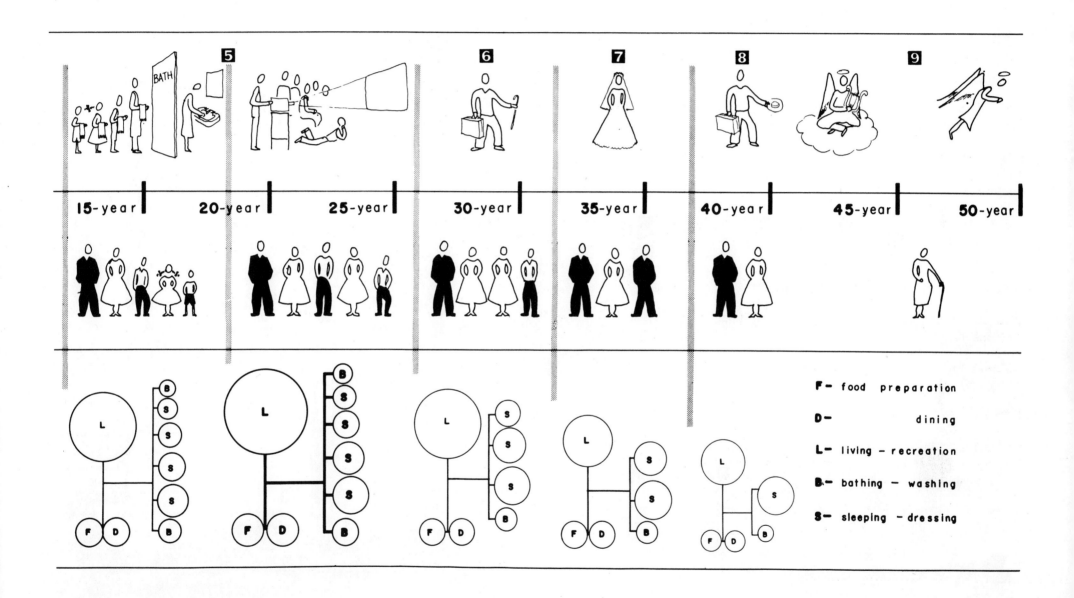

5		6	7	8	9
15-year	20-year	25-year	30-year	35-year	40-year	45-year	50-year

F— food preparation

D— dining

L— living – recreation

B— bathing – washing

S— sleeping – dressing

SOURCE: An investigation of the Small House. Pratt Institute School of Architecture

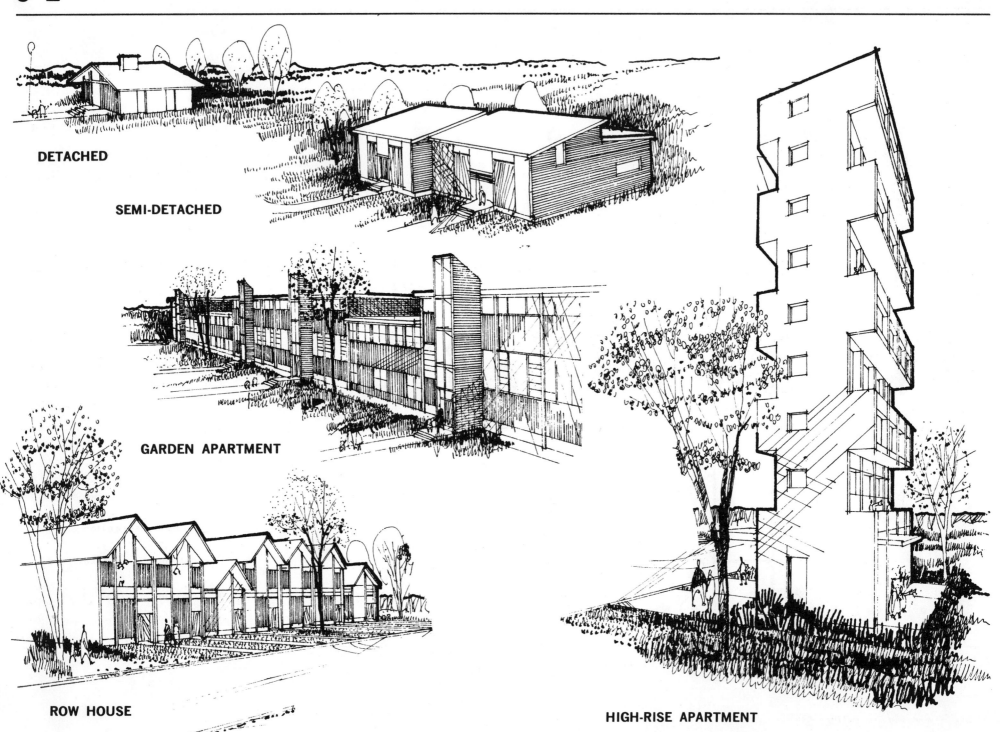

DETACHED

SEMI-DETACHED

GARDEN APARTMENT

ROW HOUSE

HIGH-RISE APARTMENT

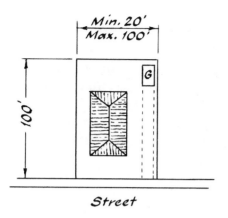

DETACHED HOUSE—One or Two-Family

Probably the most popular type of housing in the U. S. completely independent of any other structure. Garage is located within main building or in separate structure. Generally owner-occupied.

Type of construction includes a wide range, most common are frame and brick veneer. Older houses generally are 2 stories while newer houses are one story.

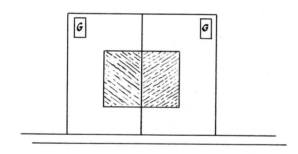

SEMI-ATTACHED (Semi-Detached) One or Two-Family

Utilizes a common wall between houses for economy. Has similar characteristics of detached house except it is usually located on a smaller lot. Separate and independent entrances are maintained. This type of dwelling is usually 2 stories high.

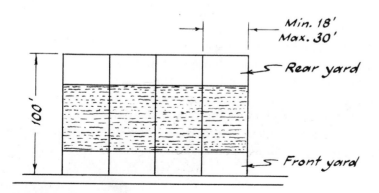

ROW HOUSES (Town Houses)

This type of housing can also be either one-family or two-family. Common walls are used on both sides of the structure for economy. The shape tends to be narrow and deep to maximumize the number of units in a row. Recently in urban areas, the town house has emerged as a popular type of dwelling. This town house is usually one-family and owner-occupied.

The height is most frequently 2 story and construction is brick or brick veneer.

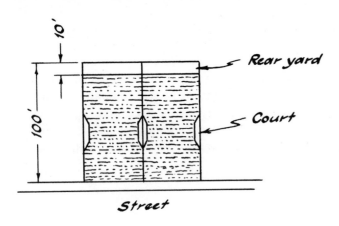

TENEMENT HOUSE

Mostly built during the latter part of the 19th century and early part of the 20th century. Common in most cities. Characterized by high percentage of lot coverage, inadequate light and air, bathroom facilities, and obsolete room layout. Generally of frame and masonry construction. Maximum height 5 or 6 stories often located in older parts of the community.

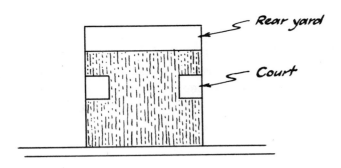

APARTMENT HOUSE (Low Rise)

Common type of multiple dwelling. It is provided with adequate light and air. Construction is usually non-fireproof with brick exterior.

Height is often 5-8 stories; building is provided with an elevator. Lot coverage is moderate. (50%—70%)

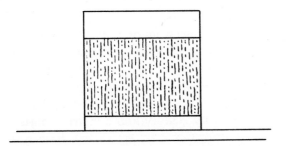

APARTMENT HOUSE (High Rise)

Type of construction necessitated by high land costs in built-up urban areas. Range in height from 6 to 40 stories.

Construction is fireproof with steel frame or poured concrete.

Lot coverage generally less than low-rise apartment house.

Most of these structures are relatively new and are provided with good room layouts, light and air, and several elevators.

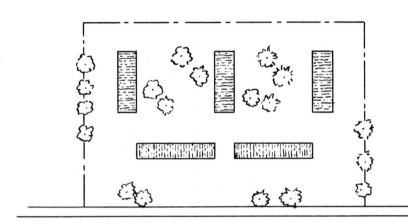

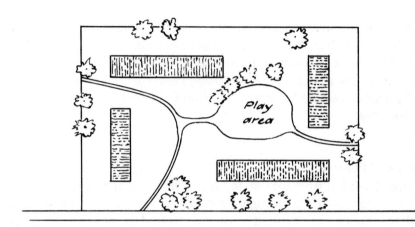

GARDEN APARTMENTS

Most common type of rental housing in suburban or moderately built-up areas; built on a large plot of land under one ownership and provided with some community facilities.

Type of construction is usually frame or brick veneer.

Height of buildings are 1 or 2 stories.

Lot coverage is generally less than apartment houses. Landscaping and open space is moderate.

Garden apartments are usually rental-occupied. In recent years there has been an increase in cooperative and condominium ownership.

PROJECT

A project involves more than one building on a large site, usually a superblock. The type of housing can be either low or high-rise. The site is characterized by low land coverage (20–40%) and provision of basic community facilities, such as play areas and sitting areas. Construction is dependent upon height of building. Because of low lot coverage, the project often has extensive landscaping and open areas.

The project usually is under one ownership and the dwelling units are rented. In recent years there has been an increase in cooperative and condominium ownership.

The tenement house is characteristic of most slum areas in urban centers such as New York City. Although most were built during the second half of the 19th century, a substantial percentage still exist today.

The typical floor plan progressed through several stages of development, generally defined as type A) "Railroad" Plan B) "Dumbbell" Plan, and C) the "New-Law" plan.

"RAILROAD" PLAN

This was built full from lot line to lot line and covered 90% of the entire lot. All the interior rooms, ranging from 8 to 12 rooms, had no light or ventilation. Privies were located in the rear yard. Height of building were 6 and 7 stories high.

"DUMBBELL" PLAN

The buildings were similar to the Railroad Plan except that side courts were introduced providing some additional light and air. Additional toilet facilities were introduced on each floor, in the public hall.

"NEW-LAW" PLAN

The typical lot was increased to 50 ft. width and the lot coverage reduced to approximately 70%. Larger courts permitted some light and air in all rooms. Toilet facilities were included in each apartment. Rooms were still small and the units poorly laid out.

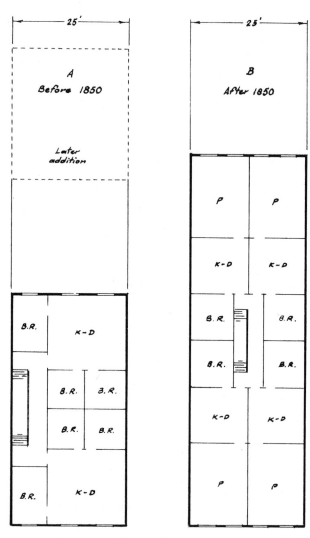

RAILROAD

Lot size—25' x 100'
Lot coverage—90%
Height of building—6 7 stories
Apts. per floor—4

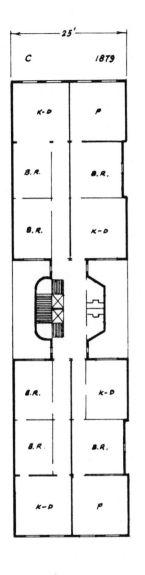

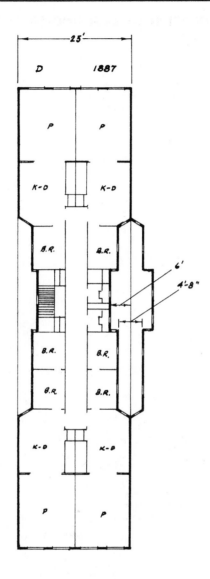

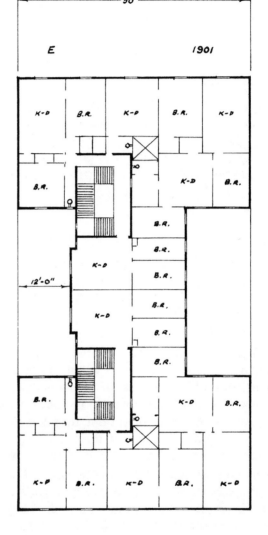

DUMBBELL

MODIFIED DUMBBELL

NEW LAW

Lot size—25' x 100'
Lot coverage—90%
Height of building—5 6 stories
Apts. per floor—4

Lot size—50' x 100'
Lot coverage—70%
Height of building—5 6 stories
Apts. per floor—7 8

GENERAL CONSIDERATIONS

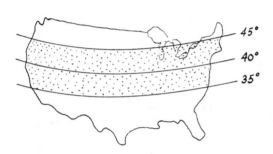

Although the study of orientation is a comprehensive and detailed science, the knowledge and use of a few basic rules will mean comfort and economy for the home owner, and a better house for the developer. The latitude belt between 35° and 45° across our country includes many of the most populated areas. This set of solar conditions thus has a wide application. Below this latitude belt, in most locations, the capturing of summer breezes and protection from intense sun heat is the main consideration. Above the latitude belt shown, the protection from cold winter winds and using the warming rays of the sun in winter is the prime objective. Using the solar conditions of the 35° to 45° belt, except as noted, it is well to remember that the information here becomes more general and less exact as the distance increases from its midpoint of 40°.

LOCATION OF BUILDING ON LOT

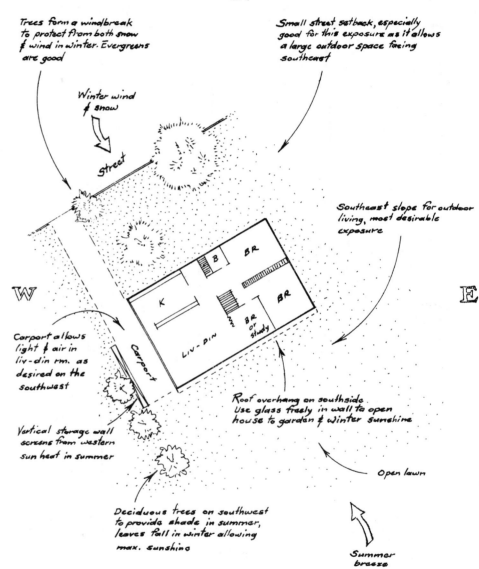

Trees form a windbreak to protect from both snow & wind in winter. Evergreens are good

Small street setback, especially good for this exposure as it allows a large outdoor space facing southeast

Winter wind & snow

Southeast slope for outdoor living, most desirable exposure

Carport allows light & air in liv-din rm. as desired on the southwest

Vertical storage wall screens from western sun heat in summer

Roof overhang on southside. Use glass freely in wall to open house to garden & winter sunshine

Open lawn

Deciduous trees on southwest to provide shade in summer, leaves fall in winter allowing max. sunshine

Summer breeze

SOURCE: House and Site United. Housing and Home Finance Agency, Wash. D. C. 1952

ORIENTING HOUSE AND LOT

● The sun has an extended arc and is high overhead at noon in summer. It has a much reduced arc and is low in the sky at noon in winter. A house needs protection from this overhead summer sun, but in winter the object is to capture all the sunshine possible.

● The direction a slope faces is important for solar orientation. Although other factors may outweigh this one in using land and placing the house, always consider the compass directions.

A south slope is very desirable.

Select an east slope in preference to a west slope.

Don't pick a north slope if you can help it.

A southeast slope is the best of all.

Don't put a house in a valley bottom, keep it up on the slope.

● Use a roof overhang on the south side of a house. An overhang on any other side may serve another purpose, but it is a protection against summer sun only when facing a generally south exposure.

● Use something upright on the west side, such as planting or garage to protect house against summer afternoon sun-heat.

● Screen the northwest direction to protect against cold winter wind. Some ways of doing this are the use of evergreen trees, high ground to the north, the garage, or perhaps the house next door. In summer let the south breeze get at the house.

● In the South, below 35° latitude, use an open type house to catch the summer breeze. Maximum outdoor living can be practiced for a major part of the year. Wide, overhead cover should be freely used to protect both enclosed and open areas of the house from intense summer heat.

● Large glass windows are really suitable only on the south side. Reduce the size of windows on the north side. Unprotected west windows are the worst of all, because of hot summer sun.

● A few feet below ground, the temperature is cool in summer and warm in winter. Don't sell short the basement, especially if you have a slope, one side can then be located at grade level. It then becomes a comfortable and desirable ground floor. In some sections of the South, however, such as the Gulf Coast, the living areas of the house must often be raised well above the ground, due to dampness and insects at ground level.

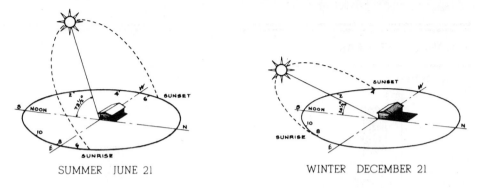

SUMMER JUNE 21   WINTER DECEMBER 21

POSITION OF SUN AT NOON FOR 40° N. LATITUDE

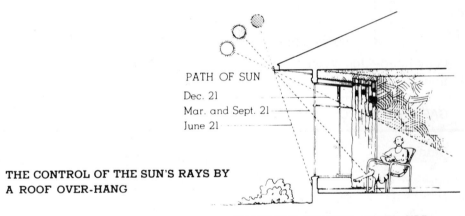

PATH OF SUN
Dec. 21
Mar. and Sept. 21
June 21

THE CONTROL OF THE SUN'S RAYS BY A ROOF OVER-HANG

SHADE LINE AT NOON—SOUTH SIDE

● Warm air is lighter than cold air and will rise. Provide for cool air to come into the house near the ground and allow warm air to escape high in rooms, or in the attic.

SOURCE: House and Site United. Housing and Home Finance Agency, Wash. D. C. 1952

(Plans are diagrammatic and not to scale)

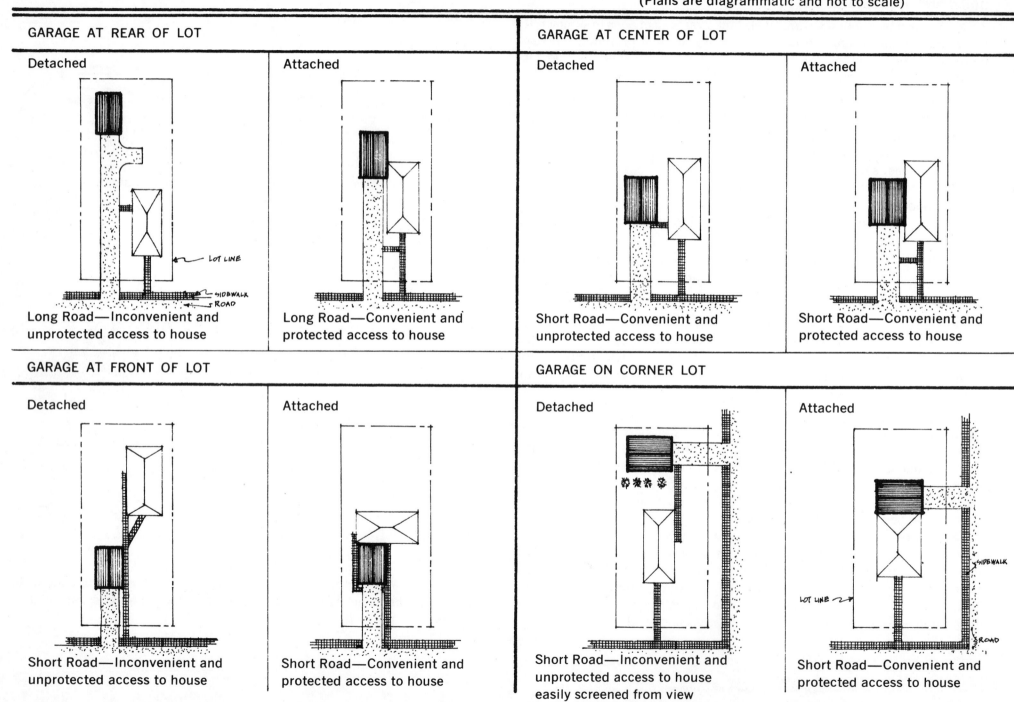

GARAGE AT REAR OF LOT

Detached

Long Road—Inconvenient and unprotected access to house

Attached

Long Road—Convenient and protected access to house

GARAGE AT CENTER OF LOT

Detached

Short Road—Convenient and unprotected access to house

Attached

Short Road—Convenient and protected access to house

GARAGE AT FRONT OF LOT

Detached

Short Road—Inconvenient and unprotected access to house

Attached

Short Road—Convenient and protected access to house

GARAGE ON CORNER LOT

Detached

Short Road—Inconvenient and unprotected access to house easily screened from view

Attached

Short Road—Convenient and protected access to house

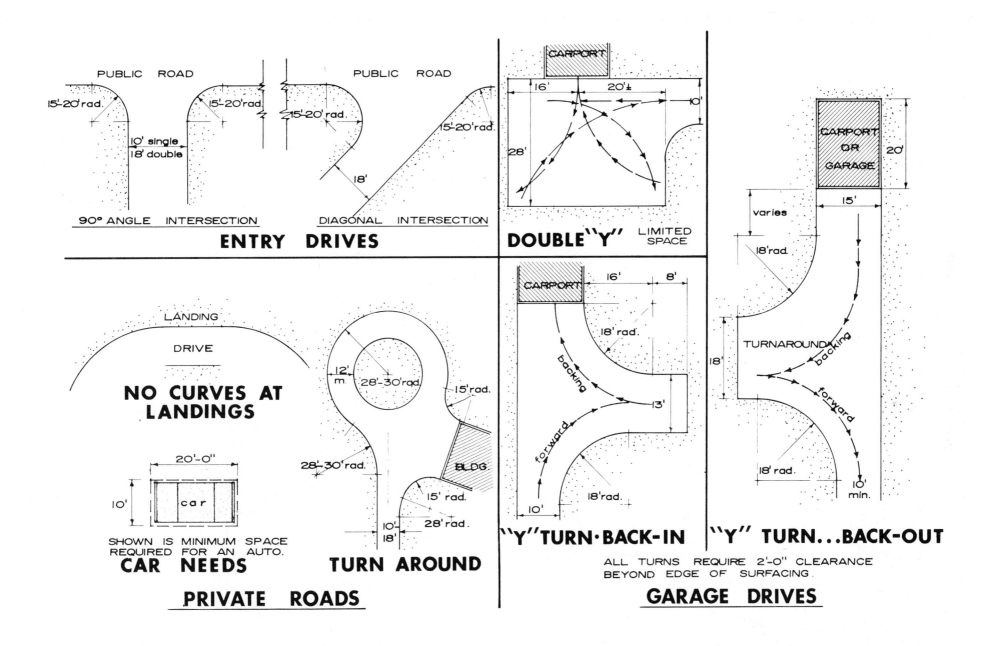

PUBLIC ROAD

15'-20'rad.

15'-20'rad.

10' single
18' double

90° ANGLE INTERSECTION

PUBLIC ROAD

15'-20'rad.

15'-20'rad.

18'

DIAGONAL INTERSECTION

ENTRY DRIVES

CARPORT

16' 20'± 10'

28'

DOUBLE "Y" LIMITED SPACE

CARPORT OR GARAGE

20'

15'

varies

18'rad.

LANDING

DRIVE

NO CURVES AT LANDINGS

20'-0"

10' car

SHOWN IS MINIMUM SPACE
REQUIRED FOR AN AUTO.

CAR NEEDS

12' min.

28'-30'rad.

15'rad.

28'-30'rad.

BLDG

15'rad.

10'
18'

28'rad.

TURN AROUND

PRIVATE ROADS

CARPORT

16' 8'

18'rad.

backing

13'

forward

10' 18'rad.

"Y" TURN·BACK-IN

TURNAROUND

backing

18'

forward

18'rad.

10' min.

"Y" TURN...BACK-OUT

ALL TURNS REQUIRE 2'-0" CLEARANCE
BEYOND EDGE OF SURFACING.

GARAGE DRIVES

SOURCE: Landscape Development, Dept. of the Interior, Littleton, Colorado.

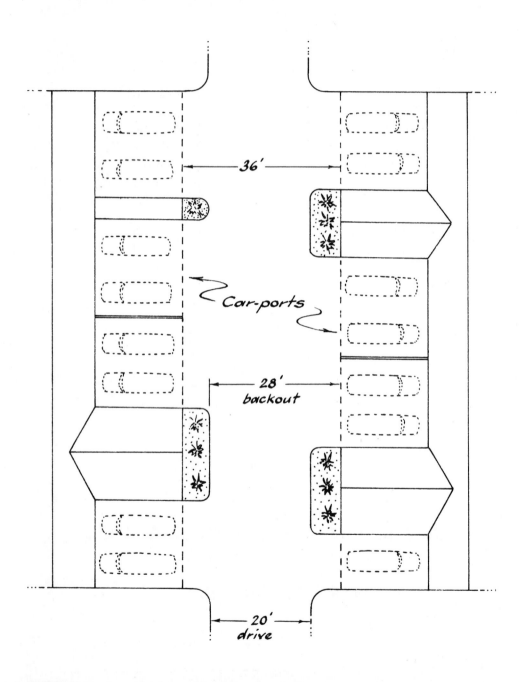

GENERAL

Driveways shall be provided on the site where necessary for convenient access to the living units, garage compounds, parking areas, service entrances of buildings, collection of refuse and all other necessary services. Driveways shall enter public streets at safe locations.

DRIVEWAY CIRCULATION

Driveways shall be planned for convenient circulation suitable for traffic needs and safety. Culs-de-sac shall be provided with adequate paved vehicular turning space, usually a turning circle of at least 80 feet in diameter, except for short straight service driveways with light traffic.

DRIVEWAYS WIDTHS

Driveways shall have two traffic lanes for their entire length, usually 18 feet in addition to any parking space, except that a single lane may be used for short straight service driveways where two-way traffic is not anticipate

Garages, carports and parking bays shall be set back at least 8 feet from the nearest edge of any moving traffic lane to the extent necessary to provide sight lines for safe entry into the traffic way.

SOURCE: Minimum Property Requirements, FHA, Dept. of Housing and Urban Development, Washington, D. C.

Wall or window (2)

Note:

Dimension measured from center to center of window

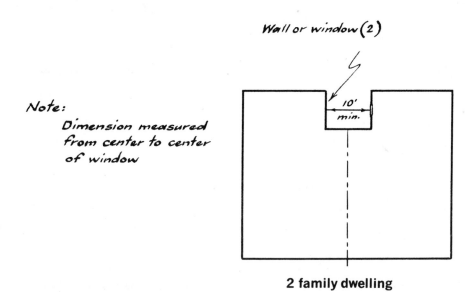

10' min.

2 family dwelling

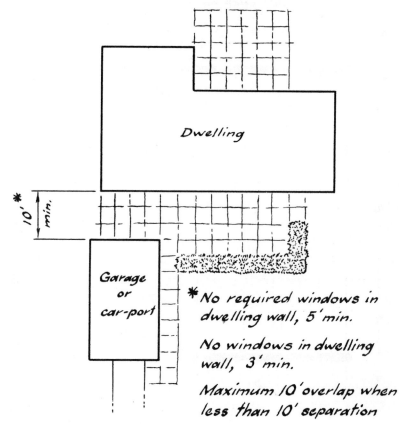

10' min.

Dwelling

Garage or car-port

* No required windows in dwelling wall, 5' min.

No windows in dwelling wall, 3' min.

Maximum 10' overlap when less than 10' separation

Distance between buildings

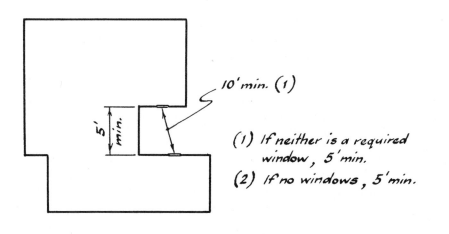

10' min. (1)

5' min.

(1) If neither is a required window, 5' min.

(2) If no windows, 5' min.

Outer courts

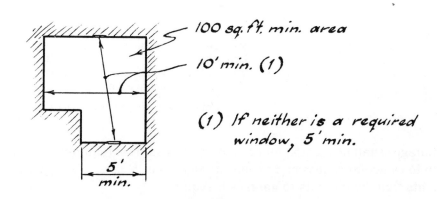

100 sq. ft. min. area

10' min. (1)

5' min.

(1) If neither is a required window, 5' min.

Inner courts

SOURCE: Minimum Property Requirements, FHA, Dept. of Housing and Urban Development, Washington, D. C.

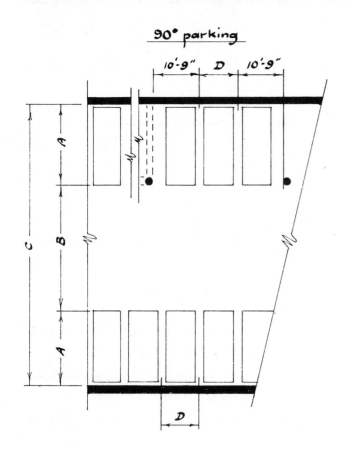

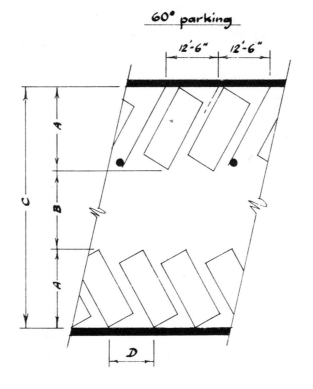

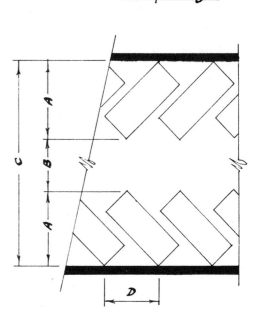

| | | Dimensions | | | |
| Space | Tenant parking | | | Attendant parking | | |
	45°	60°	90°	45°	60°	90°
Stall depth perpendicular to aisle (A)	17'-6"	19'-0"	18'-0"	17'2"	18'-10"	18'0"
Aisle width .... (B)	12'-8"	18'-0"	29'-0"	12'-8"	17'-4"	22'-0"
Unit parking depth .... (C)	47'-8"	56'-0"	65'-0"	47'-0"	55'-0"	58'-0"
Stall width parallel to aisle .... (D)	12'-8"	10'-6"	9'-0"	11'-4"	9'-3"	8'-0"

Note: Where 45° and 60° parking is necessary, one way traffic should be planned.

Garages shall be located for convenient access. This requirement applies
both to vehicular access and to pedestrian access. Means of easy access by
tenants from living units to garages is required.

SOURCE: Minimum Property Requirements, FHA, Dept. of Housing and Urban Development, Wash., D. C.

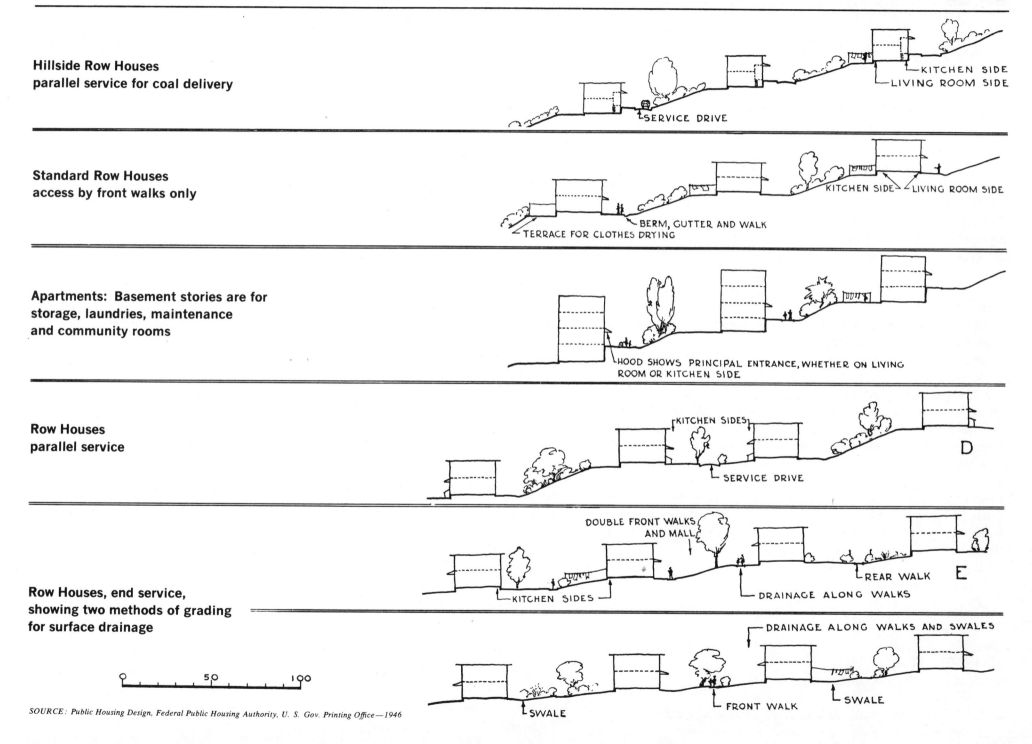

Hillside Row Houses
parallel service for coal delivery

KITCHEN SIDE
LIVING ROOM SIDE
SERVICE DRIVE

Standard Row Houses
access by front walks only

KITCHEN SIDE
LIVING ROOM SIDE
BERM, GUTTER AND WALK
TERRACE FOR CLOTHES DRYING

Apartments: Basement stories are for storage, laundries, maintenance and community rooms

HOOD SHOWS PRINCIPAL ENTRANCE, WHETHER ON LIVING ROOM OR KITCHEN SIDE

Row Houses
parallel service

KITCHEN SIDES
SERVICE DRIVE
D

Row Houses, end service,
showing two methods of grading for surface drainage

DOUBLE FRONT WALKS AND MALL
REAR WALK
E
KITCHEN SIDES
DRAINAGE ALONG WALKS

DRAINAGE ALONG WALKS AND SWALES
FRONT WALK
SWALE
SWALE

50   100

SOURCE: *Public Housing Design, Federal Public Housing Authority, U. S. Gov. Printing Office—1946*

The following table gives desirable limits for slopes on different types of areas. Deviations may be warranted by especially favorable conditions, such as porous soils, mild climates, or light rainfall; also if local experience indicates that other gradients are satisfactory.

Failure to provide positive pitch away from buildings and to give open areas adequate slopes has necessitated costly regrading and reconstruction work on numerous projects. The trouble has been due in part to inaccurate construction, but incomplete or poorly conceived plans have been a contributing cause.

Of two basic design methods, one provides for drainage mainly across grassed areas, generally through "swales", until the water reaches streets, drives, or storm sewer inlets. This scheme, requiring the flow of water from walks onto lawns, is not altogether effective when slopes are inadequate and finished grading is not accurately executed, or if the turf is above the walk level. Swale drainage occasionally is carried under walks by small culverts (six- to eight-inch pipes or boxes). These are slight hazards and frequently become stopped. The other method employs walks to a considerable extent as drainage channels. This scheme has met some objection; nevertheless, it generally is more economical and practical than the use of swales, and it has been used far more widely. Moreover, when walks have been given proper cross and longitudinal slopes, with sewer inlets provided at points of concentrated storm water flow, there has been no serious inconvenience or complications.

DESIRABLE SLOPES

	Percent Slope	
	Maximum	Minimum
Streets, service drives and parking areas ..	8.00	[1]0.50
Collector and approach walks	[2]10.00	0.50
Entrance walks	[3]4.00	1.00
Ramps	15.00	....
Paved play and sitting areas	2.00	0.50
Paved laundry yards	5.00	0.50
Paved gutters	....	0.50
Project lawn areas	[4]25.00	1.00
Tenant yards	10.00	1.00
Grassed playgrounds	4.00	0.50
Swales	[5]10.00	[6]1.00
Grassed banks	4 to 1 slope	
Planted banks	2 to 1 slope	
	(3 to 1 preferable)	

[1] 0.75% for dished section.
[2] Less where icy conditions may occur frequently.
[3] Slopes up to 10% or more are satisfactory provided walks are long enough to employ a curved profile, so that a slope not exceeding 4% can be used adjoining the building platform. See also preceding note.
[4] Steepest grade recommended for power mower.
[5] Less for drainage areas of more than approximately ½ acre.
[6] 2.00% preferable in all cases, particularly so where swales cross walks.

SOURCE: Public Housing Design, National Housing Agency, Federal Public Housing Agency—1946

The row house has long been advocated for rental housing for urban families with children as a good compromise between the desirability of a detached single-family house and the economic necessity of multifamily units. It is decidedly preferable from the viewpoint of the tenants because of greater livability. The results of surveys in both public and private housing indicate that families want to have direct access to the house, an individual yard or garden, and a place for small children to play close to the house where they can be easily supervised. These are features which the row house can provide.

From the management point of view, row house projects can be designed for maximum tenant maintenance of land area. They can also be designed for either individual heating installations or a central heating plant. Individual heating installations, though of higher operating cost to the tenant, result in lower maintenance cost to the management.

PRIVATE GARDEN

Privacy is an important factor in row house design. All house types show, therefore, a 2-foot extension of the party walls beyond the face of the building on either side. Sitting-out terraces on the garden side are separated by wing-walls, 6 feet long and 6 feet high. These wing-walls do not have to be of masonry material, although preferably they should be of a permanent rather than of a temporary nature.

PUBLIC ACCESS

Another arrangement which insures more privacy is the concentration of services from the front. The problem of refuse collection is solved by means of a masonry enclosure, 3 feet wide, 4 feet high, and 10 feet long for two living units. Access doors to the enclosure are from the side facing the building, away from street view. A flower box built into the top of the enclosure makes the appearance pleasing and attractive to the passer-by. A hose-bib connection facilitates cleaning and reduces odors to a minimum.

An entry-space for each living unit presents another privacy feature and is absolutely necessary for service-from-the-front planning. The conventional direct entrance from the street into the living room reduces privacy and is the cause of annoyance to many housewives.

THE 20-FOOT ROW HOUSE

Plan Type A has a gross floor area of 1,000 square feet. Living-dining areas are combined into one room, 12- by 19-feet. This room should face

SOURCE: Technical Bulletin, HHFA, May June — 1950

THE 20FT. ROW HOUSE

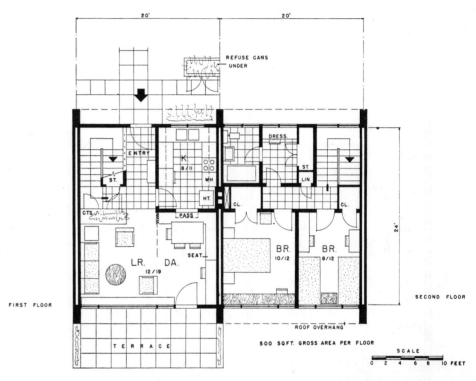

south. The dining area has direct communication with the kitchen by means of a pass, and can be screened off from the living area with a curtain, bookshelves, a permanent plywood screen, or other media. A large coat closet, 2 feet by 6 feet 6 inches, separates the stairhall from the living room. Its height can be held to 6 feet if an effect of greater spaciousness for the whole living area is desired. The space under the stairs is used for storage.

In addition to accommodating standard equipment, the kitchen provides space for a heater, water heater, and washing machine. If individual heat is planned, duct work is reduced to a minimum. If central heat is provided, the kitchen will gain 3 more feet of counter and cabinet space. On the second floor are two bedrooms, the bathroom (tub on opposite side from the window), and a small dressing alcove with a storage closet. Bedroom window sills are high so that furniture can be placed under them. All plumbing is concentrated in one wall. One flue services the heater and hot water heater. Hot water lines are short. The outdoor terrace, linking garden to living room, can be used in complete privacy.

163

THE 25FT. ROW HOUSE

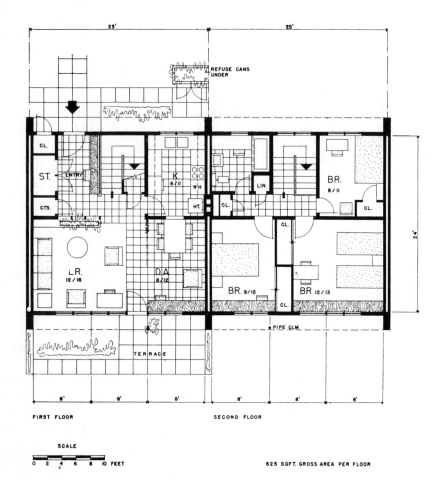

FIRST FLOOR   SECOND FLOOR

SCALE
0 2 4 6 8 10 FEET

625 SQ.FT. GROSS AREA PER FLOOR

THE 30FT. ROW HOUSE

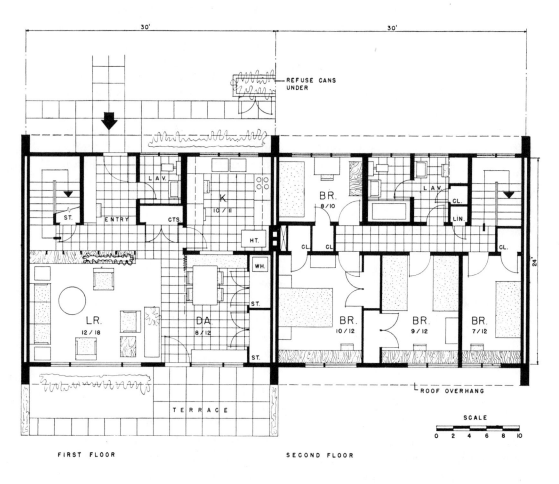

FIRST FLOOR   SECOND FLOOR

SCALE
0 2 4 6 8 10

750 SQ.FT. GROSS AREA PER FLOOR

The 25-Foot Row House

Plan Type A has a gross floor area of 1,250 square feet. Living and dining are combined into one spacious room facing the garden side and should have south orientation. Two of the three bedrooms on the second floor will then have south orientation, also. Storage closets are ample and include a large storage space off the entry, as well as a smaller one accessible from the outside, for tools and deliveries. Mechanical installations are similar to those of the 20-foot row house.

The 30-Foot Row House

Plan Type A has a gross floor area of 1,500 square feet. The basic arrangement of rooms is similar to the preceding row house types, except for the addition of a first-floor lavatory off the entry. Three of the four bedrooms upstairs face the same direction as the living-dining combination downstairs. This direction should be generally south.

SOURCE: Technical Bulletin, HHFA May July—1950

THE MINIMUM PLAN

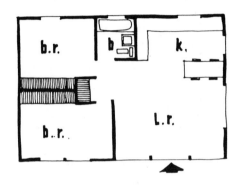

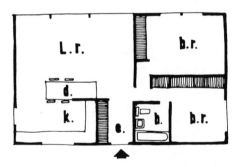

THE SIMPLE AND OFFSET RECTANGLE

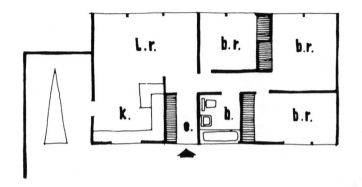

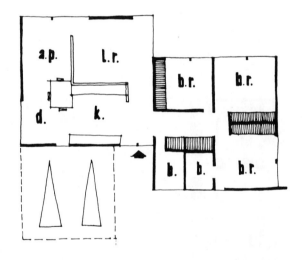

The most common plan developed by the tract builder has been the simple one-story rectangle. The box shape, with a minimum of exterior walls and concentrated plumbing, was easy and cheap to build and was readily sold in a period of extreme housing shortage. Today, however, the minimum two bedroom plan is inadequate for all but a few families.

SOURCE: D. Q. Jones and F. Emmons, Builder's Homes for Better Living, Reinhold Publishing Corp., N. Y.

The original rectangular plan may be expended by the simple addition of a third bedroom into one of the layouts most popular with builders.

A further modification is the offset rectangle plan which reduces circulation space, provides a possible garden terrace in the rear of the house, and allows for greater interest on the street elevation. The addition of a family, or all-purpose, room gives greater flexibility and use to the living area, while the second bath off the master bedroom adds an essential requirement in a house of this size.

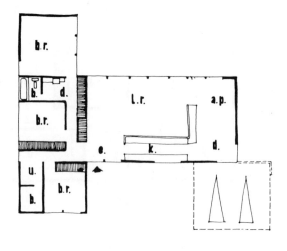

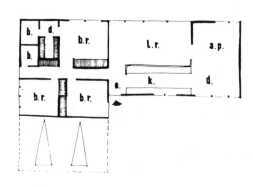

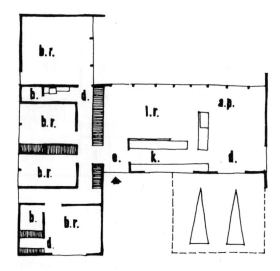

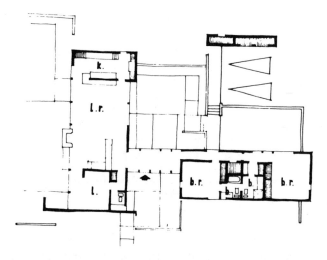

These plans are adaptations of the offset rectangle plan. They allow greater flexibility of layout, good separation of living and sleeping areas, and compact circulation. Interesting street elevations are possible with many variations. From a structural standpoint they may be a little more costly to build because of greater exterior wall area and irregular roof framing plan.

One additional advantage in a plan type such as the "T" or "L", where the sleeping and living areas are separate sections, is that a four bedroom sleeping unit can easily be substituted for the three bedroom unit previously shown. This allows a builder to combine one or more standardized living units with either three or four bedroom sleeping units as required.

SOURCE: D. Q. Jones and F. Emmons, Builder's Homes for Better Living, Reinhold Publishing Corp., N. Y.

THE "H" AND "U" PLANS

THE UTILITY CORE PLAN

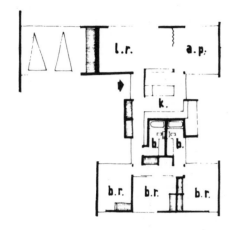

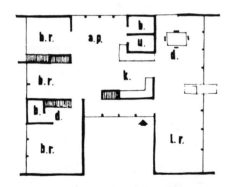

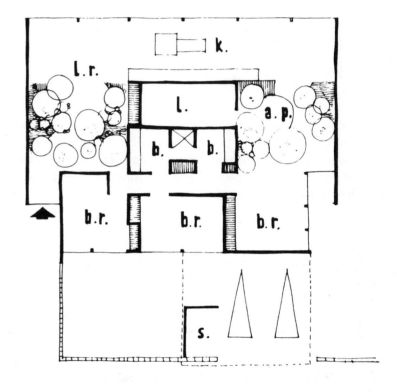

The "H" and "U" type plans divide living and sleeping units into separate sections. This layout is especially applicable to a utility core concept in which the kitchen becomes part of the connecting link. Excellent separation of activities is achieved, and useful patios are afforded shelter and privacy. In addition, each room can receive cross ventilation. The chief disadvantage of these types is in the long perimeter walls (almost fifty percent more than the same space in a simple rectangle), resulting in higher construction cost as well as increased expense of heating and air conditioning.

The rectangular utility core plan has several advantages. The house may be almost square and very compact, with a good concentration of utilities. In addition, the core acts as a buffer between the sleeping and living zones. The problems of this plan include the difficulty of properly relating the kitchen, garage and main entrances, and the excessive circulation space that is often required. This can be helped by opening up the exterior walls and actually using the lot as circulation and access in areas of mild climate.

SOURCE: D. Q. Jones and F. Emmons, Builder's Homes for Better Living, Reinhold Publishing Corp., N. Y.

THE IN-LINE PLAN

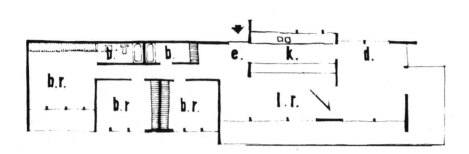

The in-line plan is an excellent solution for many unusual site conditions. On a narrow lot it allows access to side patios and outdoor areas; on steep hillsides it allows the maximum economy of construction and land usage. It can have good circulation (at the expense of a long corridor) and the same good orientation for all the rooms.

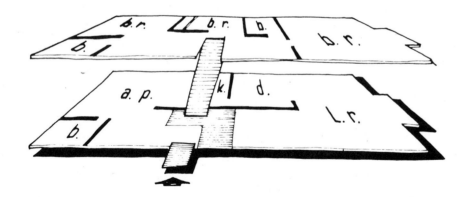

The plan may be adapted to a two-story house, where it helps to concentrate circulation and utilities, while retaining the advantage of providing the best orientation for both floors.

THE SPLIT LEVEL PLAN

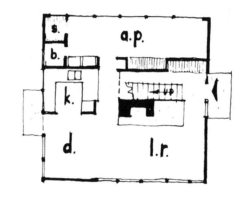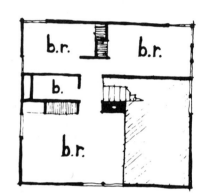

The split-level plan produces a maximum of total interior area for a house of small over-all size, and its separate levels can give greater privacy and interest in each area. It is very adaptable to sloping lots, and helps to solve the problems of deep foundations in northern climates. However, it may require a somewhat complicated framing system, and is difficult to relate to outdoor areas without special terracing or grading.

This pen drawing illustrates a modern adaptation of the salt box. Note the overhang on the second floor.

This drawing illustrates an adaptation of an early American Colonial L-shaped plan using a steep gambrel roof.

Salt-box Colonial

Roof	Long slope on one side of the gable; no overhang. Dormers on the long sloping side. May have gambrel fronted roof. Long slope toward the direction of winter winds.
Walls	Siding or shakes—little ornamentations. Double-hung windows and doors, symmetrical in appearance; shutters.
Height	1½ or 2 stories.
Chimney	Large, centrally located in plan.
Plan	Compact, rectangular.

Early American Colonial

Roof	Steep gable, wood shingles.
Walls	Siding, stained; small doublehung or casement windows, symmetrical; second floor overhangs; drops used.
Height	2½ stories.
Chimney	Large centrally located in plan.
Plan	Compact, rectangular.

SOURCE: Architectural Drafting, George K. Stegman and Harry J. Stegman, American Technical Society, Chicago, Ill., 1966.

This modern adaptation of the New England Colonial was designed with a breezeway and garage.

The Cape Cod colonial may be enhanced by adding shutters and side lights on either side of the door and yet still retain an authentic colonial appearance.

New England Colonial

Roof	Gable medium pitch, no overhang. Gambrel, no overhang on gable or eaves.
Walls	Siding, shingles, brick.
	Double-hung windows and doors placed symmetrically; shutters. Only entrance ornamented.
Height	1, 1½, 2, and 2½ stories.
Chimney	Large, centrally located in plan.
Plan	Square or rectangular, additions can be made.

Cape Cod Colonial

Roof	Medium pitch gable. Small overhang on cornice.
Walls	Siding, painted. Double-hung windows —symmetrically placed.
Height	1½ stories.
Chimney	Large, centrally located in plan.
Plan	Compact, rectangular—wings may be added

SOURCE: Architectural Drafting, *George K. Stegman and Harry J. Stegman, American Technical Society, Chicago, Ill., 1966.*

This modern Dutch Colonial is built on a sloping site and is designed with sufficient overhang to provide a comfortable porch.

This modern example of the Southern Colonial uses an off-center entrance yet still maintains the dignity of the style.

Southern Colonial

Roof	Hip, gable, or flat. Slate or metal.
Walls	Brick, stucco. Large double-hung windows and doors (symmetrical). Ornamentation of wood. Elaborate entrance, using turned or paneled posts.
Height	2 stories.
Chimney	At each end projecting from or flush with gable end or short sides.
Plan	Limited flexibility (not advisable for small lot).

Dutch Colonial

Roof	Steep gable, gambrel, flush gable and eaves, or flush gable and flared eaves.
Walls	Brick, stone, wide siding, long shingles or combination. Double-hung windows and doors symmetrically placed.
Height	1½ to 2½ stories.
Chimney	Flush or projected on gable ends.
Plan	Rectangular, may have additions.

   The true Dutch Colonial was typified by a steep gable roof. On some houses the coping on the gable walls extended several inches above the roof and the chimneys were flush with these walls. The Dutch builders were probably acquainted with the gambrel roof through the English and Flemish colonists. The gambrel roof was adopted during the 18th Century. A combination of the wide gambrel with the flared overhang was apparently developed by the Flemish but credited to the Dutch. The gambrel type roof, however, is synonymous with "Dutch Colonial."

SOURCE: Architectural Drafting, *George K. Stegman and Harry J. Stegman, American Technical Society, Chicago, Ill., 1966.*

Many ranch-style houses are planned around a patio, court, or breezeway.

Frequently the contemporary ranchtype house has a rectangular floor plan and a wide overhang.

Ranch House

Roof	Gable—slightly pitched, flat or shed. Wide overhangs, roof lower over garage and breezeway.
Walls	Wood or masonry or combinations of materials. Large windows. Entrance without ornamentation.
Height	1 story.
Chimney	Large, centrally located or projecting.
Plan	Low, rambling for urban area. Open planning. Built-in furniture.

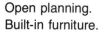

In many "ranches" a porch-like projection is added by extending the roof beyond the normal overhang.

The ranch-type house may assume many plan shapes and may be designed to fit problem lots. The casual appearance of its design gives a feeling of openness.

SOURCE Architectural Drafting, *George K. Stegman and Harry J. Stegman, American Technical Society, Chicago, Ill., 1966.*

A split level designed for a sloping site uses mid-levels to the best advantage.

The contemporary house fits the needs of the owner. It combines new methods of construction, new materials, and aesthetic principles into a functional whole.

Split Level

Roof	Flat, shed, or low or medium pitched gable. Irregular roof lines.
Walls	Masonry, wood, or combination. Windows may be large, and/or regular types.
Height	Part 1 story, part 2 story.
Plan	Compact, economical, space-saving. Fits problem lots, sloping sites.

Contemporary

Roof	Flat or low pitched, gable and shed.

SOURCE: Architectural Drafting, *George K. Stegman and Harry J. Stegman, American Technical Society, Chicago, Ill., 1966.*

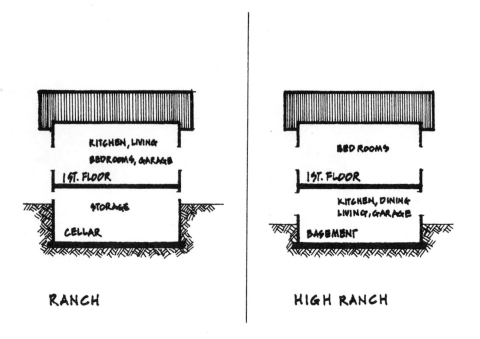

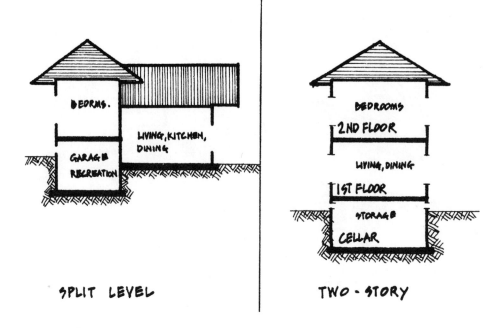

RANCH

The Ranch-type house is the traditional one-story house. All activities, cooking, dining, living and sleeping are on one level close to the ground. The house may or may not have a cellar, which is generally used for storage or minor activities. Older houses had high pitched roofs for expansion. The newer houses have low pitched roofs without provisions for expansion. This is the simplest type of construction.

HIGH RANCH

The High Ranch is similar to a ranch except that the main level is raised out of the ground allowing light and air into the basement. This lower level is then utilized as additional living space. One of the kitchen-dining-living areas can be located there, or the space can be used for additional bedrooms. The major advantage of this type of house over the traditional ranch is the utilization of the lower level for living purposes rather than storage or incidental use.

SPLIT-LEVEL

The split-level house separates the living activities into three levels. The kitchen-dining-living is the main level close to the ground. The sleeping level is located ½ level above the main level. The garage-recreation room-utility level is ½ level below the main level. The main advantage is the partial separation of activities and greater privacy. Disadvantages are the up and down stair movement and more complicated construction.

TWO-STORY

The two-story house is characteristic of most older houses. The lower level contains the kitchen-dining-living areas. The upper floor contains the sleeping areas. This type of house most often has a cellar for storage. The main advantage is the complete separation of living and sleeping activities for maximum privacy. The major disadvantage is the up and down stair movement. Construction is more complicated than the ranch type house. Also, there is less lot coverage than the other types.

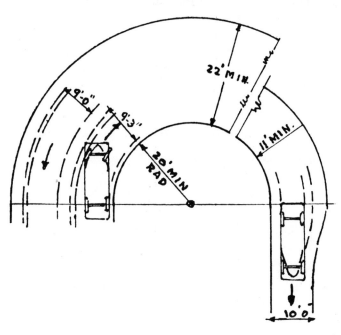

180° turns

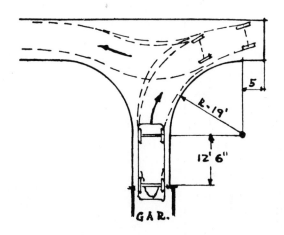

Tee turn out of garage

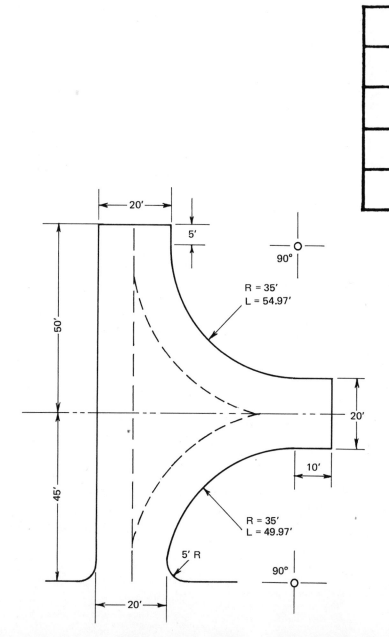

Garage compound

SOURCE: Eugene Henry Klaber, Housing Design, Reinhold Publishing Corp.—1954

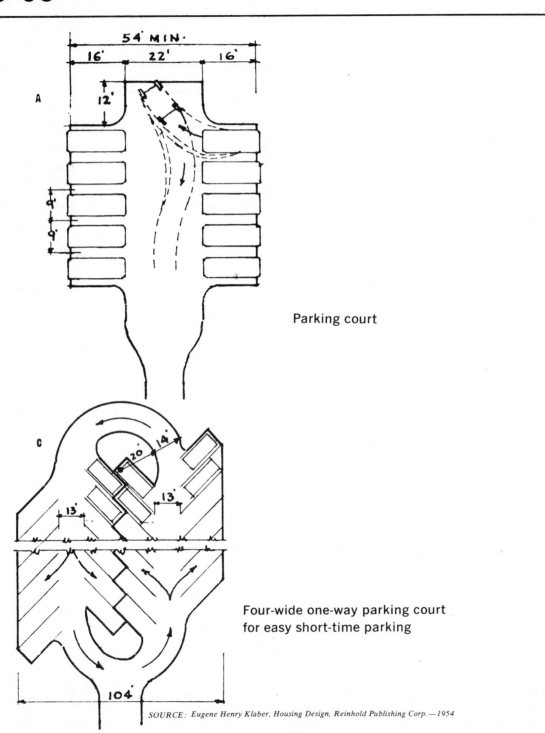

Parking court

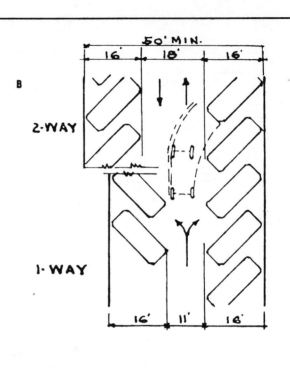

Diagonal

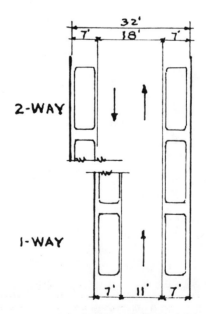

Four-wide one-way parking court
for easy short-time parking

Street parking at curb

SOURCE: *Eugene Henry Klaber, Housing Design, Reinhold Publishing Corp.* —1954

Housing Units—Selected Characteristics, by States: 1970

STATE	ALL YEAR-ROUND HOUSING UNITS Total (1,000)	Median[1] number of rooms	OCCUPIED HOUSING UNITS Total (1,000)	Percent—With all plumbing facilities[2] Total	Percent—1.01 or more persons per room	Owner occupied	Occupied by minority races	Median[1] value, owner occupied	Median[1] monthly rent, renter occupied	AVAILABLE HOUSING UNITS Homeowner vacancy rate[3]	Rental vacancy rate[4]
U.S.	67,657	5.0	63,450	94.0	7.0	62.9	11.0	$17,000	$89	1.2	6.6
N.E.	3,844	5.2	3,645	96.0	5.8	60.9	3.5	20,700	88	0.8	5.0
Maine	337	5.2	303	87.7	5.7	70.1	0.5	12,800	69	1.4	7.2
N.H.	247	5.2	225	94.6	6.0	68.2	0.5	16,400	79	1.3	6.6
Vt.	149	5.5	132	94.1	5.7	69.1	0.4	16,400	76	1.4	6.6
Mass.	1,836	5.2	1,760	96.7	5.8	57.5	3.5	20,600	89	0.7	4.7
R.I.	306	5.1	292	97.2	5.8	57.9	2.9	18,200	65	0.7	5.8
Conn.	968	5.2	933	97.5	6.0	62.5	5.8	25,500	105	0.7	4.2
M.A.	12,331	5.1	11,837	96.8	6.3	56.6	10.7	18,900	93	0.8	3.5
N.Y.	6,152	4.7	5,914	97.2	7.3	47.3	12.3	22,500	95	0.7	2.9
N.J.	2,303	5.2	2,218	97.7	5.9	60.9	10.3	23,400	111	0.7	3.3
Pa.	3,876	5.6	3,705	95.6	5.1	68.8	8.3	13,600	73	0.8	5.0
E.N.C.	13,108	5.1	12,383	95.7	6.9	67.5	9.3	17,500	93	1.0	6.7
Ohio	3,447	5.3	3,289	95.5	6.0	67.7	8.9	17,600	83	0.9	6.2
Ind.	1,712	5.0	1,609	94.5	7.3	71.7	6.3	13,800	82	1.3	8.3
Ill.	3,693	4.9	3,502	95.9	7.4	59.4	12.0	19,800	107	1.0	6.5
Mich.	2,842	5.2	2,653	96.8	7.3	74.4	11.0	17,500	93	1.1	7.8
Wis.	1,414	5.2	1,329	94.5	6.7	69.1	3.0	17,300	91	0.9	4.7
W.N.C.	5,559	5.0	5,154	93.5	6.4	69.3	4.4	14,500	79	1.2	8.2
Minn.	1,219	5.1	1,154	93.5	6.8	71.5	1.6	18,000	101	0.8	5.8
Iowa	955	5.3	896	93.9	5.4	71.7	1.2	13,900	77	1.1	7.5
Mo.	1,664	4.8	1,521	92.3	7.0	67.2	9.3	14,400	74	1.4	9.8
N. Dak.	200	5.0	182	89.9	7.9	68.4	1.9	13,000	77	1.4	8.0
S. Dak.	222	5.1	201	90.0	7.2	69.6	3.3	11,400	69	1.4	8.1
Nebr.	512	5.1	474	95.6	5.9	66.4	2.9	12,400	77	1.4	7.7
Kans.	787	5.1	727	95.8	5.6	69.1	4.7	12,100	75	1.5	9.3
S.A.	10,142	5.0	9,438	90.0	6.8	63.5	18.0	15,100	81	1.4	7.5
Del.	175	5.7	165	95.5	4.8	68.0	13.1	17,100	89	1.2	6.6
Md.	1,235	5.5	1,175	95.9	5.9	58.8	16.2	18,700	110	1.0	5.0
D.C.	278	3.9	263	97.9	11.9	28.2	63.7	21,300	110	1.2	5.3
Va.	1,484	5.2	1,391	87.9	5.2	62.0	16.3	17,100	92	1.2	5.7
W. Va.	592	5.1	547	83.7	5.6	68.9	4.1	11,300	52	1.2	7.5
N.C.	1,618	5.0	1,510	85.6	6.5	65.4	19.3	12,800	59	1.2	7.0
S.C.	805	5.1	734	82.6	7.1	66.1	25.4	13,000	50	1.7	9.2
Ga.	1,466	5.0	1,369	87.7	7.3	61.1	22.3	14,600	65	1.4	7.5
Fla.	2,489	4.7	2,285	95.1	7.9	68.6	12.5	15,000	92	1.8	10.7
E.S.C.	4,169	5.0	3,868	83.0	6.9	66.7	17.3	12,200	56	1.2	8.3
Ky.	1,060	4.9	984	81.1	6.5	66.9	7.1	12,600	63	1.1	8.6
Tenn.	1,297	5.0	1,213	86.4	6.7	66.7	13.9	12,500	62	1.2	7.7
Ala.	1,115	5.0	1,034	84.3	6.7	66.7	22.5	12,200	48	1.2	8.6
Miss.	697	4.9	637	77.3	7.9	66.3	31.1	11,200	46	1.3	8.6
W.S.C.	6,565	4.8	5,952	91.8	9.0	65.3	14.6	12,000	68	1.8	10.7
Ark.	673	4.7	615	83.2	6.8	66.7	15.6	10,500	53	1.5	8.3
La.	1,146	4.8	1,052	89.4	11.3	63.1	26.6	14,600	62	1.4	9.8
Okla.	938	4.9	851	94.0	6.2	69.2	9.3	11,100	64	1.8	11.9
Tex.	3,808	4.8	3,432	93.5	9.4	64.7	12.1	12,000	76	1.9	11.1
Mt.	2,718	4.8	2,518	95.5	8.8	65.5	4.4	16,300	86	1.4	7.7
Mont.	240	4.6	217	93.4	8.5	65.7	3.0	14,000	71	1.3	9.8
Idaho	238	4.8	219	93.6	8.6	70.1	1.4	14,100	70	1.2	7.9
Wyo.	114	4.7	105	95.8	8.1	66.4	2.1	15,300	72	1.5	8.5
Colo.	742	4.9	691	96.4	6.4	63.4	3.8	17,300	97	1.2	6.6
N. Mex.	322	4.7	289	91.1	11.3	66.4	7.2	13,000	72	2.7	10.2
Ariz.	578	4.6	539	95.3	10.4	65.3	6.8	16,300	90	1.1	7.9
Utah	312	5.0	298	97.9	10.2	69.3	2.1	16,800	80	0.7	5.6
Nev.	172	4.6	160	97.3	8.4	58.5	6.6	22,400	123	1.9	6.6
Pac.	9,220	4.7	8,653	97.9	7.5	57.1	9.6	21,900	110	1.3	6.3
Wash.	1,204	4.9	1,106	97.4	5.2	66.8	3.9	18,500	94	1.6	10.8
Oreg.	735	5.0	692	97.0	5.3	66.1	2.3	15,400	86	1.1	7.3
Calif.	6,977	4.7	6,574	98.3	7.7	54.9	9.8	23,100	113	1.3	5.7
Alaska	88	4.1	79	86.2	12.2	50.3	15.4	22,700	171	1.4	6.9
Hawaii	216	4.6	203	94.7	18.6	46.9	58.4	35,100	120	1.3	4.5

[1] For definition of median, see preface. [2] Includes hot and cold piped water, as well as a flush toilet and bathtub or a shower inside the structure for exclusive use of the people in the unit.
[3] Base is total of units occupied by owners and available vacant units for sale.
[4] Base is total of units occupied by renters and available vacant units for rent.

Source: U.S. Bureau of the Census, *U.S. Census of Housing, 1970*, vol. I.

Housing Units—Summary of Characteristics: 1960 and 1970

In thousands, except percent.

ITEM	1960	1970	ITEM	1960	1970
All housing units	58,326	68,679	Occupied units, total—Continued: Renter-occupied units	20,227	23,565
Vacant, seasonal, and migratory	1,742	1,022	With monthly rent of—[4] Less than $40	2,277	1,864
All year-round units	56,584	67,657	$40–$59	3,999	2,925
Urban	40,764	50,143	$60–$79	4,906	4,098
Rural	17,562	18,536	$80–$99	3,490	3,301
Units in one unit structures[1][2]	44,525	46,791	$100–$119	1,693	2,520
Percent of total	76.4	69.1	$120–$149	973	3,024
Units in 2–4 unit structures[2]	7,552	9,007	$150 or more	571	3,274
Units in 5-or-more unit structures[2]	6,238	9,829	Median monthly rent........dol.	71	89
Units lacking some or all plumbing facilities[2]	7,699	4,672	Units with—[2]		
Percent of total	13.2	6.9	1–2 rooms	4,409	3,764
Year structure built:[2]			3–4 rooms	19,425	21,701
1965 or later	(X)	8,874	5 rooms	14,323	16,874
1960–1964	(X)	8,082	6-or-more rooms	20,161	25,318
1950–1959	16,046	14,499	Median number of rooms	4.9	5.0
1940–1949	8,640	8,786	Persons per unit........median	3.0	2.7
1939 or earlier	33,632	27,458	Units with—[5]		
Percent units built prior to 1940	57.7	40.6	Telephone........percent	78.5	81.6
Occupied units, total	53,024	63,450	Air conditioning........percent	12.4	35.8
With Negro head of household	(NA)	6,180	Home food freezer........percent	18.4	28.2
Percent of total occupied	(NA)	9.7	One or more automobiles.percent	78.4	82.5
Owner-occupied units	32,797	39,885	Vacancy rate:		
With value of—[3]			Homeowner units	1.6	1.2
Less than $5,000	3,182	1,934	Rental units	6.7	6.6
$5,000–$9,999	6,747	4,966			
$10,000–$14,999	7,632	6,403			
$15,000–$19,999	4,723	6,435			
$20,000–$24,999	1,900	4,674			
$25,000–$34,999	1,227	4,436			
$35,000 or more	762	3,041			
Median value........dol.	11,900	17,000			

NA Not available. X Not applicable. [1] Excludes mobile homes or trailers. [2] Based on a complete-count basis, but tabulated on a 20-percent sample basis. [3] Limited to one-family homes on less than 10 acres and no business on property. [4] Excludes one-family homes on 10 acres or more. [5] Occupied housing units.

Source: U.S. Bureau of the Census, *U.S. Census of Housing: 1960*, vol. I, and *1970*, vol. I.

COOPERATIVE (CO-OPERATIVE)

"Cooperative" as it is applied to housing means: co-operative (joint operation) of a housing development by those who live in it. All of the property of a cooperative housing development is owned by a corporation. The corporation's "Articles of Incorporation" and "By-Laws" are specially designed so the corporation can be owned and operated by its members (stockholders). A member of a cooperative does not directly own his dwelling unit; he owns a membership certificate or stock in the corporation which carries with it the exclusive right to occupy a dwelling unit and to participate in the operation of the corporation directly as an elected Board member or indirectly as a voter. The law gives a corporation virtually the same rights and imposes the same responsibilities on it as a human being. The law permits only the elected Board to officially act for the corporation. The purpose of a board is to eliminate one-man decisions in corporations. The board is kept small in number (usually 5 or 7) so the membership can elect its most reasonable and talented people to make decisions.

A cooperative is a unique form of homeownership in that the cooperative corporation holds title to the dwelling units and directly assumes the mortgage, tax and other obligations necessary to finance and operate the development, thereby, relieving the members from any direct liability for those items. Each member signs a three year occupancy agreement with the cooperative corporation. The agreement automatically renews itself at the end of the three year period if the member is not in violation of the rules adopted by the board of directors or given notice to leave. Members support the cooperative mortgagor corporation through their occupancy agreements, which eliminates the necessity for each member to be an individual mortgagor under a mortgage contract. Each member pays his proportionate share of a budget that contains an estimate by the board of directors of the annual cost to operate the corporation. If the budget is overestimated each member is entitled to his proportionate share of what is called a "patronage refund." Each member is entitled to his proportionate share of the real estate taxes and mortgage interest paid by the corporation for use on his personal income tax statement. If all of the assets of the cooperative corporation are sold the members in occupancy at that time are entitled to their proportionate share of the amount remaining after all obligations have been paid. If a member decides to leave the cooperative his membership certificate or stock can be sold in accordance with a transfer value and rules set forth in the by-laws.

SOURCE: HUD, FHA Comparison of Cooperative and Condominium Housing, 1972.

CONDOMINIUM

Condominium ownership is created by a special real estate law that permits individual dwelling unit estates to be established within a total and larger property estate. The individual estates are technically established by use of vertical and horizontal planes (surfaces) which are usually identified: vertically, as the walls (not room partitions) of the unit and, horizontally, as the floors and ceilings of the unit. The exact location of the building structure on the property and the exact location of the unit within the structure are described in the plat (location map) and in the architectural plans. Each is also described in legal language in a master deed (sometimes called a declaration or plan of apartment ownership). After all of the individual unit estates have been described within the total property estate, all of what remains, such as the land and structural parts of the buildings, becomes a common estate to be owned jointly by the owners of the individual estates.

When the master deed is recorded it extends the condominium laws of the state in which the condominium is located to the property. It also establishes an association which provides for the use and the maintenance of the common estate to be governed by a board of directors or "board of managers" elected from among the owners of the individual estates. The internal government is controlled by the by-laws which are recorded with the master deed. The by-laws can usually be changed by a vote of the majority of individual owners but changes in the master deed normally require consent of 100% of the owners. A board governs the common estate in much the same manner as a cooperative governs the property within the single estate it owns. The fundamental difference is that a cooperative corporation owns everything and a condominium association owns nothing. Condominium owners own their individual estate and an undivided interest in the common estate.

Condominium owners may also own a membership certificate in a "non-profit/non-equity" cooperative corporation or homeowners' association that holds title to recreation areas that are shared by a number of separate condominium developments. The equity under such circumstances is built up in the individual condominium unit and not in the recreation property.

Initial sales and resales of the dwelling units in a condominium that was approved as a project by HUD prior to construction can be sold for cash or financed under unsubsidized Section 234(c) or subsidized Section 235(i) of the National Housing Act with a VA Guaranteed Loan or with a Federal National Mortgage Association (FNMA) conventional loan. Standard conventional loans are also permitted.

GENERALIZED TERMS AND DEFINITIONS

COOPERATIVE

The articles of incorporation and by-laws of a cooperative corporation—Must be approved by the corporation commission of the state in which it is incorporated before it can legally do business. The by-laws spell out how the members relate to the corporation and how the governing board of directors will be elected or removed by a majority vote of the membership.

Membership Certificate—A certificate (like stock) showing evidence of ownership in a cooperative corporation. Rights under the certificate are usually governed by personal property laws.

Occupancy agreement—A contract between each member and the corporation that spells out the rights and obligations of the member to the corporation and the corporation to the member. It basically gives the member an exclusive right to occupy a unit, participate in the government of the corporation, receive tax benefits and equity increases in return for financial and personal support of the corporation. The occupancy agreement together with the membership certificate is the basis of cooperative ownership.

Subscription agreement—A document used to sell a membership in a cooperative.

Proportionate share—A percentage developed by dividing the valuation placed on a dwelling unit by the total valuation of the project at the time the cooperative corporation takes title to the property. The percentage attaches to each unit and determines the share of the annual budget to be borne by the member living in the unit, his share of the annual amount paid by the cooperative for real estate tax and mortgage interest for his personal tax report and his share of the proceeds, if any, when the project is sold.

CONDOMINIUM

Fee simple interest (fee)—Ownership of a unit with unrestricted right of disposal.

Common or undivided interest—Joint ownership with other fee owners of all land and areas within the structures that are not described as units. The interest is defined by a percentage of a total area but not actually cut into parts.

Convey—To transfer title from one person to another.

Deed—A document used to transfer a fee simple interest in the unit together with an undivided interest in the common estate.

Title—Evidence of a right of ownership such as a Deed.

Plat and plans—Drawings used by surveyors and architects to show the exact location of utilities, streets, the buildings and units within the buildings in relationship to the boundary lines of the total property.

Converting a property to a condominium regime—The act of recording the master deed, together with plat and plans, in a local courthouse to show evidence that the property has been converted from traditional real estate law to condominium law.

Unit value ratio—A percentage developed by dividing the appraised value of a unit by the total value of all units. The percentage attaches to the dwelling unit and determines the percentage of value of the common estate coupled to that unit, the percentage of votes the owner of the unit has in the government of the common estate and the percentage of operating costs of the common area he must bear.

COMPARISON OF SIMILAR TERMS

	Cooperatives	Condominium
Mortgagor	The cooperative corporation	Each individual owner that borrowed money to purchase the unit
Mortgagee	The lending institution	Same
Monthly Charge	Proportionate share of all costs including mortgage	Percentage of common estate costs. Any mortgage payments on the individually owned unit are paid separately as are those assessed on the individual unit.
Real Estate Taxes	Assessed on the property of the cooperative corporation	Assessed on the individual unit
Voting	Each member has one vote.	Each owner has the number of votes representing the percentage of value of his unit to the total of all units.
Mortgage Term	Cooperative corporation usually has 40 years—member is not a mortgagor.	Owner usually has 30 years—condominium is not a mortgagor.
Closing or Settlement costs	Costs in additon to the price of the corporate property including mortgage service charge, title search, insurance and transfer of ownership charges paid when the cooperative first purchases the property. Only a small transfer fee is charged to transfer future membership in the cooperative.	Costs in addition to the price of a unit and its undivided interest in the common estate including mortgage service charge, title search, insurance and transfer of ownership charges paid each time the unit is resold or refinanced.
Equity	Increase in the value of a membership certificate over and above the initial or "downpayment" resulting from member's monthly contribution toward payment of the corporate mortgage.	Increase in value of ownership interest in the unit as the owner pays off his mortgage and from market value appreciation.
Escrow Funds	Subscription or downpayments required to be held unused until the viable cooperative is assured. Transfer of membership funds are sometimes escrowed until the transfer is complete.	Subscription or downpayments required to be held unused until the condominium regime is recorded on the property and titles are conveyed to each buyer. Escrows are usually used in each resale situation. The deed is held in escrow until all conditions of the sale (including any prepayments) have been met.

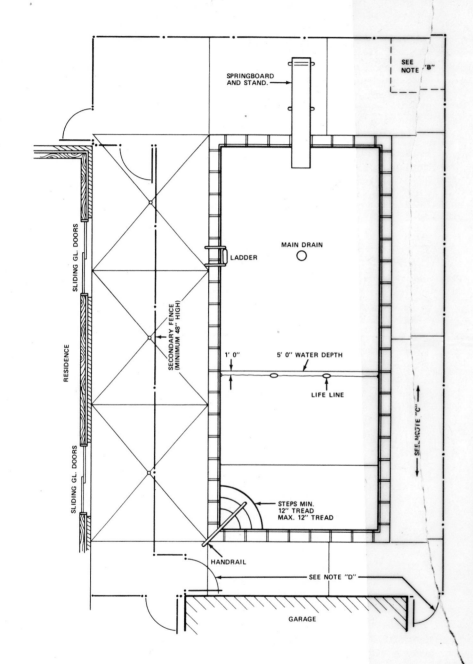

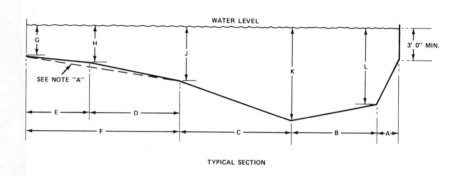

TYPICAL SECTION

SIZE	A	B	C	D	E	F	G	H	J	K	L	Length of Springboard	Overhang	Height of Diving Board Stand
12 x 28	1' 6"	7' 0"	7' 0"	6' 6"	6' 0"		2' 6"	3' 0"	4' 6"	6' 6"	5' 0"	0	0	None
12 x 30	1' 6"	7' 0"	9' 0"	6' 6"	6' 0"		2' 6"	3' 0"	4' 6"	6' 6"	5' 0"	0	0	None
12 x 32	1' 6"	7' 0"	9' 0"	8' 6"	6' 0"		3' 0"	3' 6"	5' 0"	7' 6"	6' 0"	8' 0"	1' 6"	Deck Level
15 x 30	1' 6"	7' 0"	8' 6"	7' 0"	6' 0"		3' 0"	3' 6"	5' 0"	7' 6"	6' 0"	8' 0"	1' 6"	Deck Level
15 x 32	1' 6"	7' 0"	9' 0"	8' 6"	6' 0"		3' 0"	3' 6"	5' 0"	7' 6"	6' 0"	8' 0"	1' 6"	Deck Level
15 x 35	2' 0"	8' 0"	10' 6"	8' 6"	6' 0"		3' 0"	3' 6"	5' 0"	8' 6"	7' 0"	10' 0"	2' 0"	Deck Level to 12"
16 x 35	2' 0"	8' 0"	10' 6"	8' 6"	6' 0"		3' 0"	3' 6"	5' 0"	8' 6"	7' 0"	10' 0"	2' 0"	Deck Level to 12"
16 x 40	2' 0"	8' 0"	10' 6"	13' 6"	6' 0"		3' 0"	3' 6"	5' 0"	8' 6"	7' 0"	10' 0"	2' 6"	12" to 18"
18 x 38	2' 0"	8' 0"	12' 6"	9' 6"	6' 0"		3' 0"	3' 6"	5' 0"	8' 6"	7' 0"	10' 0"	3' 0"	12" to 18"
18 x 40	3' 0"	9' 0"	11' 6"	.	.	16' 6"	3' 0"	See Note A	5' 0"	9' 0"	7' 6"	12' 0"	3' 0"	12" to 39"
20 x 40	3' 0"	9' 0"	11' 6"	.	.	16' 6"	3' 0"	See Note A	5' 0"	9' 0"	7' 6"	12' 0"	3' 0"	12" to 39"

NOTE "A"   FLOOR TO SLOPE FROM 3' 0" DEEP TO A UNIFORM SLOPE TO THE 5' 0" DEPTH.

NOTE "B"   PROVIDE APPROX. 30 SQ. FT. OF FLOOR SPACE FOR FILTRATION EQUIPMENT (PREFERABLY INSIDE BUILDING).

NOTE "C"   SLOPE WALKS AWAY FROM POOL AT 1/4" PER 1' 0". PROVIDE DRAINS AS REQUIRED.

NOTE "D"   PROVIDE SELF-CLOSING, SELF-LATCHING GATES. CAPABLE OF BEING LOCKED.

SOURCE: A Design Guide for Home Safety, U.S. Dept. of Housing and Urban Development, Washington, D.C., 1972.

AREAS	MINIMUM	MAXIMUM	PREFERRED
1. Entrance Courts - Baby Parking	750 Sq. Ft.	1500 Sq. Ft.	1000 Sq. FT.
2. Childrens Center Play Area			
With three playrooms	4500 Sq. Ft.	5000 Sq. Ft.	5000 Sq. Ft.
With four playrooms	6000 Sq. Ft.	6500 Sq. Ft.	6500 Sq. Ft.
3. Landscape Storage Yard			1000 Sq. Ft.

BENCHES			
1. Distance from Windows	15 Feet		25 Feet
2. Quantity	One Unit per 3-5 D.U.		

BUILDING LOCATIONS - NOTE: Consult Design Department for variances in S:A projects

1. Setback from Project Property Line	10 Feet	NOTE: Allow 3" leeway beyond minimum setbacks from project property lines if setbacks are legally required.
2. Between Building Corners:	50 Feet	
3. Between Building Walls:		
One-story Building	50 Feet	
Add 5 Ft. for each additional story		

MAIN ENTRANCE LOCATIONS

(Perimeter building - from Project Property Line)	10 Feet	100 Feet	50 Feet
NOTE: See also Zoning Ordinance			

DRAIN BASINS - SILL COCKS - STREET WASHERS - PROJECT FIRE HYDRANTS

1. Distance, D.Bs from trees	10 Feet	-	-
2. Distance, D.Bs from benches	5 Feet	-	10 Feet
3. Distance, Sill Cocks to farthest planting	100 Feet	300 Feet	200 Feet
4. Distance, Street Washers in large lawn areas	-	-	200 Feet
5. From Fire Hydrants to Benches, cars, etc.	15 Feet	-	-

GRADES			
1. Lawns	1%	1 ft.Vertical to 3 ft. horizontal	2%
2. All open paved areas	1%	3%	2%
3. Roads and Fire Lanes	1%	5%	2%
Roads - Access	1%	10%	2%
4. Walks - Yard	1%	4%	2%
Walks - Building Entrances	1%	8%	2%
5. Ramps - Treads (min. tread 2 ft. 6 in.)	1%	10%	5%
6. Benches	1%	3%	2%

STEPPED RAMPS	MINIMUM	MAXIMUM	PREFERRED
1. Risers	5 In.	7½ In.	6 In.
2. Length of treads			5 Ft.

ROADWAYS - WIDTHS			
1. Access to buildings	10 Ft.	20 Ft.	15 Ft.
2. Fire lanes	12 Ft.	20 Ft.	15 Ft.
3. Rounded corners	R=15 Ft.	(Consult NYCHA)	

SHRUBS			
1. Distance from buildings			None
2. Spacing (distance between centers of plants)	Equal to first numeral of plant height, i.e., 3'-4' shrub = 3' O.C. Narrow upright plants should be spaced closer.		

SHRUBS AND TREES			
1. Distance from steam lines and drain basins	10.ft.		
2. Distance from other underground utilities	5 ft.		

TREES			
1. Change in grade - cut		6 In.	
Change in grade - fill		3 Ft. (In tree wells)	
2. In paved areas - (size of tree)		4 In. to 5 In. Caliper	
3. Proposed trees			
Major trees - space between (in rows)	20 Ft.	50 Ft.	25-30 Ft.
4. Spacing from benches and fences	4½ Ft.		

WALKS			
1. Service-widths to meter & tank rooms	2½ Ft.		2½ Ft.
2. Yard - widths	Conc. 8 Ft. Asph. 10 Ft.	18 Ft.	10 Ft.
3. Main entrance - widths	10 Ft.		15 Ft.
4. Rounded or cut corners			(R=6 Ft.)
5. Laundry and perambulator room walks			6 Ft.
6. Distance from buildings	10 Ft.		
7. Bumper strips			5 Ft.- 6 In.

STREET TREE PLANTING

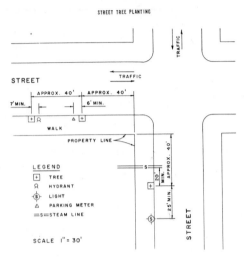

LEGEND

- ⊞ TREE
- Ω HYDRANT
- Ⓢ LIGHT
- △ PARKING METER
- =S= STEAM LINE

SCALE 1"= 30'

STREET TREES SHOULD NOT BE PLANTED IN FRONT OF ENTRANCES TO BUILDINGS OR PLAYGROUNDS.
WHERE SIDEWALKS ARE AS NARROW AS 10', THE TREE PIT SHALL BE 4'x6'x3' IN PLACE OF THE STANDARD 5'x5'x3' DEEP.
WHERE TREE PITS ARE 4'x6'x3' DEEP THE TREES SHALL HAVE 2 STAKES PLACED PARALLEL TO CURB.
WHERE TREE PITS ARE 5'x5'x3' DEEP, TREES SHALL HAVE 3 STAKES.
LOCATE TREES 2' TO 3' FROM GAS OR OIL BOXES.

SOURCE: Memo to Architects, New York City Housing Authority–1970.

Roads and Parking Facilities

All roads in mobile home developments should provide for convenient vehicular circulation. Pavements should be of adequate width to accommodate anticipated parking and traffic loads.

The proper design of street intersections is an important safety consideration. Within 100 feet of intersections, streets should be, approximately, at right angles. Street intersections should be at least 150 feet apart, and the intersection of more than two streets at one point should be avoided.

Street grades should not be excessive, especially at intersections. It is suggested that grades be less than 8 percent whenever possible; however, short runs of up to 12 percent can be used if necessary. All streets should be provided with a smooth, hard, and dense surface that is properly drained and durable under normal use and weather conditions.

Offstreet parking, in the form of parking bays or individual parking spaces on each lot, should be provided to reduce traffic hazards and improve the appearance of the mobile home development. Each mobile home lot should be designed to provide offstreet parking for two automobiles. Parking may be in tandem.

Walkways

All mobile home developments should be provided with walkways where pedestrian traffic is expected to be concentrated, such as around recreation, management, or service areas, and where pedestrian and vehicular traffic might interfere with each other. It is recommended that these common walks be at least 3½ feet wide.

Walks also should be provided on each individual lot to connect with a common walk, street, or other paved surface. Such walks should be at least 2 feet wide.

Mobile Home Lots

It is recommended that a single-unit mobile home stand, which is the foundation provided for the mobile home, occupy a maximum area of not more than one-third of the respective lot area. The accumulated floor area of the mobile home and its accessory structures should not exceed two-thirds of the total area of the lot. Each lot should contain at least 2800 square feet. For the doublewide units, it is also recommended that the mobile home stand occupy a maximum area of not more than one-third of the total lot area. For such a unit the minimum lot area should contain 4,500 square feet.

These lot requirements are recommended to ensure adequate clearances between the mobile homes and other structures while easily accommodating the units of various sizes and their appurtenances. Other advantages of these lot requirements are that they facilitate later changes, such as carports or other ac-

SOURCE: Environmental Health Guide for Mobile Home Communities, Mobile Home Manufacturers Association, 1973.

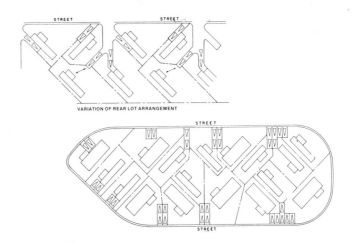

Figure 4. Typical Mobile Home Modules and Arrangements

cessory structures to mobile homes, and they also provide protection against premature obsolescence of the mobile home development.

Since it is generally agreed that small lots contribute to overcrowding and create an undesirable appearance, especially when used to accommodate the larger mobile homes, a practical program to eliminate undersized lots should be developed by the local governmental agency that has the authority. The program should be agreeable to all organizations concerned, including mobile home development operators and owners, the local health authority, and other involved groups. Once adopted, such a program should be enforced to assure that all mobile home lots not meeting established minimum space requirements will be eliminated.

The lots within any mobile home development should not all be of the same size and shape if mobile homes of different sizes are to be accommodated and if effective use is to be made of the available space. All mobile homes and their accessory structures should be set back a minimum of 10 feet from paved streets.

Recreation Areas

Mobile home developments that accommodate 25 or more mobile homes should be provided with at least one easily accessible recreation area. If the community is to be designed to serve a cross section of age groups it is recommended that separate areas be provided in order to serve the needs of each such group. Recreational separation will help provide much better play control areas and increase individual safety. Recreational areas for teenagers' use should be given special consideration in developing them for their especially active needs.

For safety reasons, recreation areas always should be located where they are free of traffic hazards.

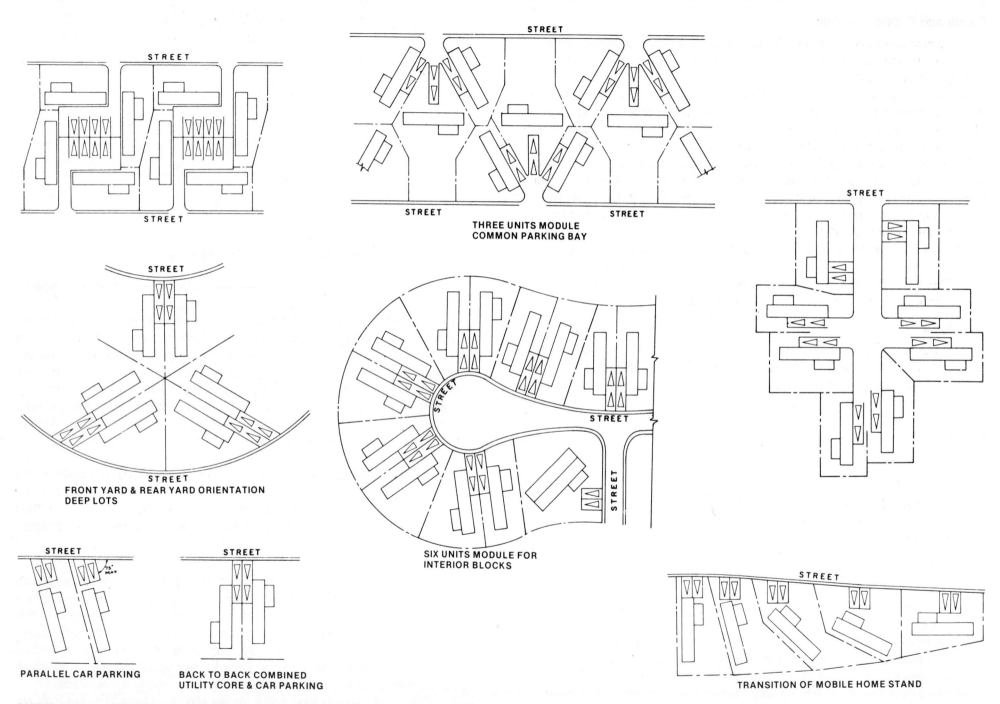

STREET

STREET

STREET

STREET

**THREE UNITS MODULE
COMMON PARKING BAY**

STREET

STREET

**FRONT YARD & REAR YARD ORIENTATION
DEEP LOTS**

STREET

STREET

STREET

**SIX UNITS MODULE FOR
INTERIOR BLOCKS**

STREET

STREET

STREET

PARALLEL CAR PARKING

**BACK TO BACK COMBINED
UTILITY CORE & CAR PARKING**

STREET

TRANSITION OF MOBILE HOME STAND

SOURCE: Environmental Health Guide for Mobile Home Communities, Mobile Homes Manufacturers Association, 1973.

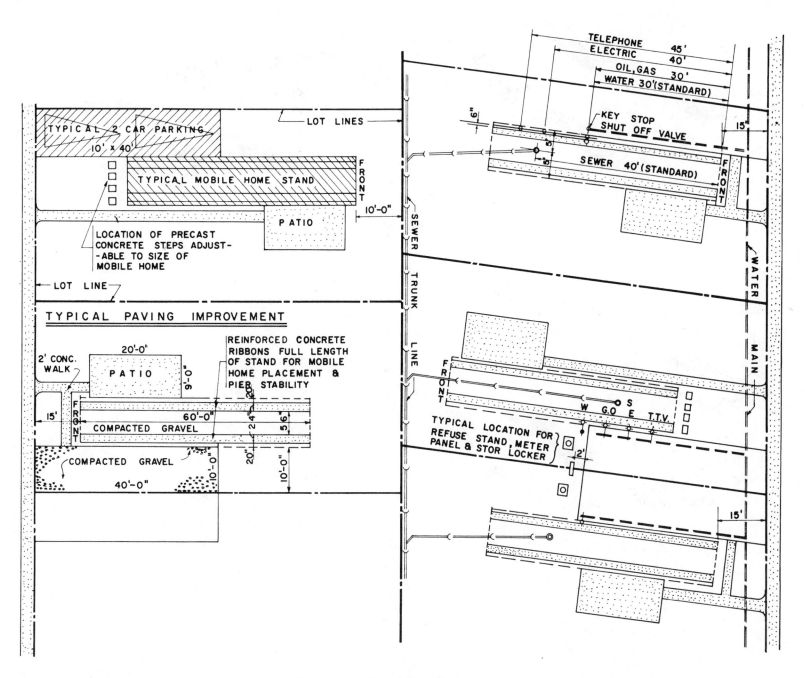

TYPICAL 2 CAR PARKING
10' x 40'

TYPICAL MOBILE HOME STAND

FRONT

PATIO

LOT LINES

LOCATION OF PRECAST
CONCRETE STEPS ADJUST-
-ABLE TO SIZE OF
MOBILE HOME

LOT LINE

10'-0"

TELEPHONE
ELECTRIC   45'
                40'
OIL, GAS 30'
WATER 30'(STANDARD)

6"

KEY STOP
SHUT OFF VALVE

15'

SEWER 40'(STANDARD)

FRONT

SEWER TRUNK LINE

WATER MAIN

TYPICAL PAVING IMPROVEMENT

2' CONC.
WALK

20'-0"
PATIO

6'-0"

REINFORCED CONCRETE
RIBBONS FULL LENGTH
OF STAND FOR MOBILE
HOME PLACEMENT &
PIER STABILITY

15'

FRONT

60'-0"
COMPACTED GRAVEL

24"   56"

20'

10'-0"

COMPACTED GRAVEL

40'-0"

10'-0"

FRONT

W G.O E T.T.V.
S

TYPICAL LOCATION FOR
REFUSE STAND, METER
PANEL & STOR LOCKER

2'

15'

Service Connections and Paving Requirements

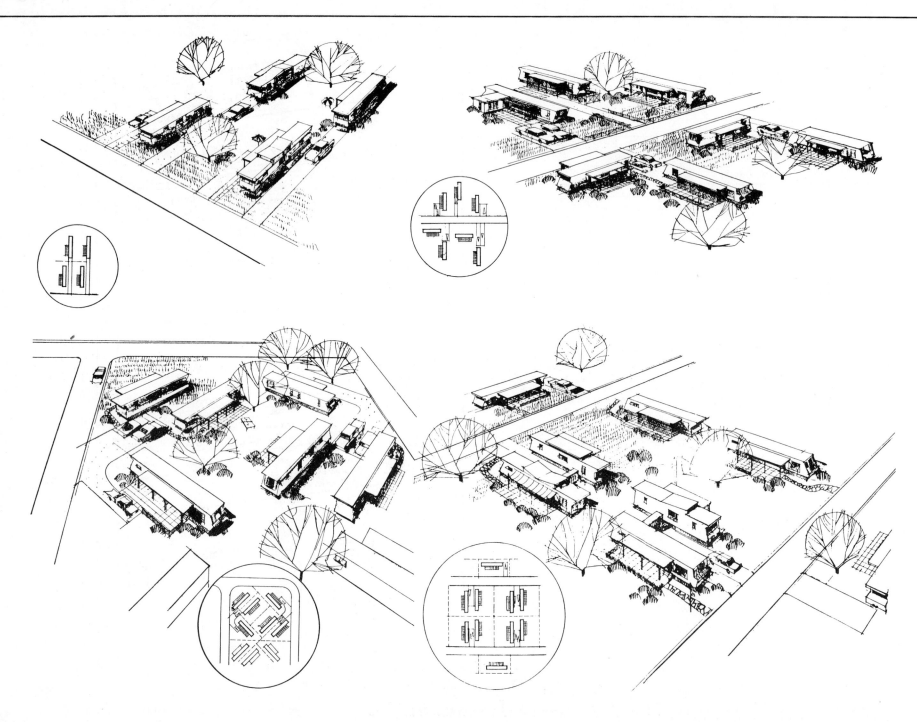

SOURCE: Mobile Homes Manufacturers Association, Park Division

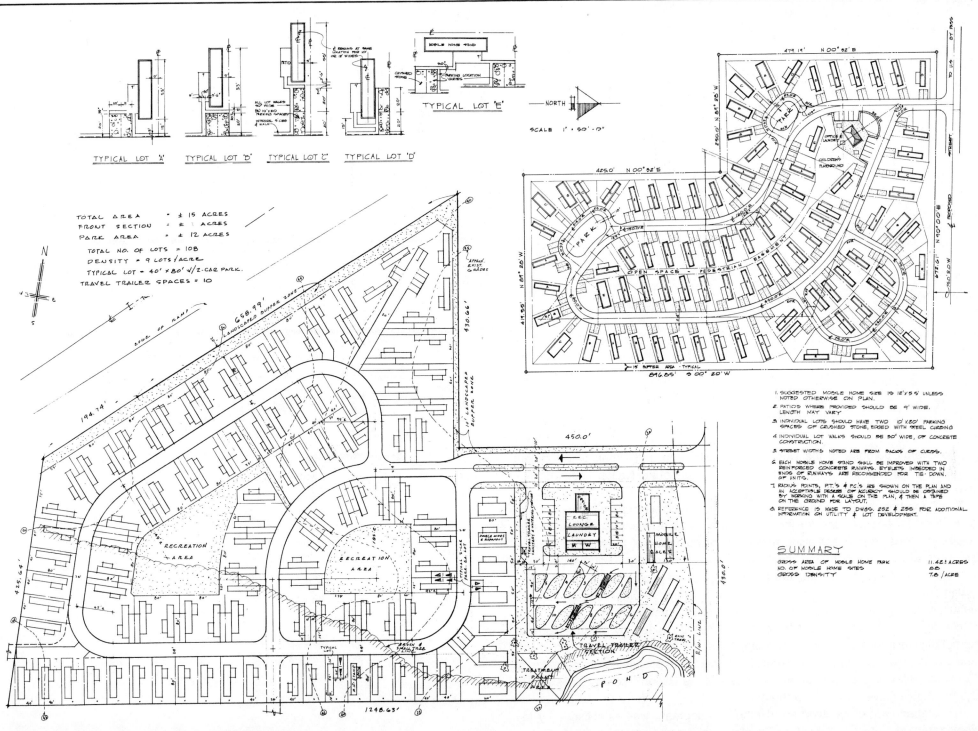

TYPICAL LOT 'A' TYPICAL LOT 'B' TYPICAL LOT 'C' TYPICAL LOT 'D'

TYPICAL LOT 'E'

NORTH

SCALE 1" = 50'-0"

MOBILE HOME STAND

TOTAL AREA = ± 15 ACRES
FRONT SECTION = ± ACRES
PARK AREA = ± 12 ACRES

TOTAL NO. OF LOTS = 108
DENSITY = 9 LOTS/ACRE
TYPICAL LOT = 40' X 80' W/2-CAR PARK.
TRAVEL TRAILER SPACES = 10

1. SUGGESTED MOBILE HOME SIZE IS 12' X 55' UNLESS NOTED OTHERWISE ON PLAN.
2. PATIOS WHERE PROVIDED SHOULD BE 9' WIDE. LENGTH MAY VARY.
3. INDIVIDUAL LOTS SHOULD HAVE TWO 10' X 20' PARKING SPACES OF CRUSHED STONE, EDGED WITH STEEL CURBING.
4. INDIVIDUAL LOT WALKS SHOULD BE 30" WIDE, OF CONCRETE CONSTRUCTION.
5. STREET WIDTHS NOTED ARE FROM BACKS OF CURBS.
6. EACH MOBILE HOME STAND SHALL BE IMPROVED WITH TWO REINFORCED CONCRETE RUNWAYS. EYELETS IMBEDDED IN ENDS OF RUNWAYS ARE RECOMMENDED FOR TIE-DOWN OF UNITS.
7. RADIUS POINTS, P.T.'S & PC'S ARE SHOWN ON THE PLAN AND AN ACCEPTABLE DEGREE OF ACCURACY SHOULD BE OBTAINED BY WORKING WITH A SCALE ON THE PLAN, & THEN A TAPE ON THE GROUND FOR LAYOUT.
8. REFERENCE IS MADE TO DWGS. 252 & 255 FOR ADDITIONAL INFORMATION ON UTILITY & LOT DEVELOPMENT.

SUMMARY

GROSS AREA OF MOBILE HOME PARK	11.42± ACRES
NO. OF MOBILE HOME SITES	88
GROSS DENSITY	7.8 /ACRE

SOURCE: Mobile Homes Manufacturers Association, Land Development Division

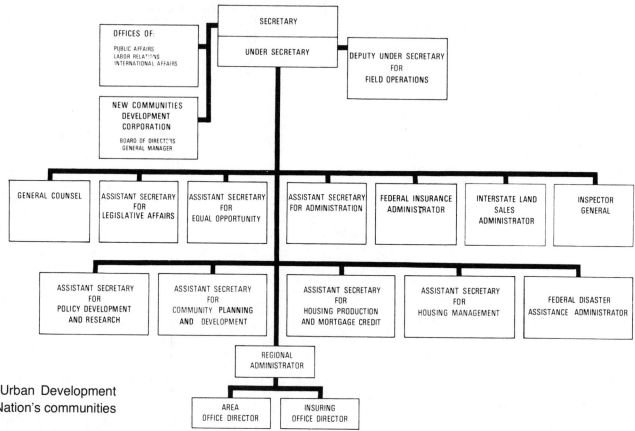

The overall purpose of the Department of Housing and Urban Development (HUD) is to assist in providing for sound development of the Nation's communities and metropolitan areas.

The Department was created to administer the principal programs which provide assistance for housing and for the development of the Nation's communities; to assist the President in achieving maximum coordination of the various Federal activities which have a major effect upon urban community, suburban, or metropolitan development; to encourage the solution of problems of housing and urban development through State, county, town, village, or other local and private action, including promotion of interstate, regional, and metropolitan cooperation; to encourage the maximum contributions that may be made by vigorous private homebuilding and mortgage lending industries to housing, urban development, and the national economy; and to provide for full and appropriate consideration, at the national level, of the needs and interests of the Nation's communities and of the people who live and work in them.

The Department of Housing and Urban Development was established by the Department of Housing and Urban Development Act of September 9, 1965.

SOURCE: U.S. Government Manual *General Services Adm. Washington, D.C.*

APHA Appraisal Method. The American Public Health Association appraisal method for measuring the quality of housing was developed by the Committee on the Hygiene of Housing between 1944 and 1950. This method attempts to eliminate or minimize individual opinion so as to arrive at a numerical value of the quality of housing that may be compared with results in other cities and may be reproduced in the same city by different evaluators using the same system. It is also of value to measure the quality of housing in a selected area, say at 5-year intervals, to evaluate the effects of an enforcement program or lack of an enforcement program. The appraisal method measures the quality of the dwellings and dwelling units as well as the environment in which they are located.

The items included in the APHA dwelling appraisal, Tables 2 and 3, are grouped under "Facilities," "Maintenance," and "Occupancy." Additional information obtained includes rent, income of family, number of lodgers, race, type of structure, number of dwelling units, and commercial or business use. The environmental survey reflects the proximity and effects of industry, heavy traffic, recreational facilities, schools, churches, business and shopping centers, smoke, noise, dust, and other factors that determine the suitability of an area for residential use.

The rating of housing quality is based on a penalty scoring system, shown in Table 2. A theoretical maximum penalty score is 600. The practical maximum is 300; the median is around 75. A score of zero would indicate all standards are met. An interpretation of the dwelling and environmental scores is shown in Table 5. It is apparent therefore that according to this scoring system, either the sum of dwelling and environmental scores or a dwelling or environmental score of 200 or greater would classify the housing as unfit.

Application of the APHA appraisal method requires trained personnel and experienced supervision. The survey staff should be divorced from other routine work so as to concentrate on the job at hand and produce information that can be put to use before it becomes out-of-date. In practice, it is found desirable to select a limited area or areas for pilot study. The information thus obtained can be used as a basis for determining need for extension of the survey, need for new or revised minimum housing standards, extent of the housing problem, development of coordination between existing official and voluntary agencies, the part private enterprise and public works can play, public information needs, and so forth.

Census Data. Much valuable information is collected in the U.S. Census of Population and Housing. Information summarized in the 1970 Census includes number of dwelling (housing) units; the population per owner- and renter-occupied unit; the number vacant; the number of dwelling units with private bath, including hot and cold piped water as well as flush toilet and bathtub or shower, and the number lacking some or all these facilities; the number of dwelling units occupied by whites and Negroes; the number of dwelling units having 1.00 or fewer persons per room, the number with 1.01 to 1.50, and the number with 1.51 or more; the monthly rental; and the value or sale price of owner-occupied one-family homes. Other statistics on selected population characteristics for areas with 2,500 or more inhabitants and for counties are available. This information can be used as additional criteria to supplement reasons for specific program planning. Plotting the data on maps or overlays will show concentrations sometimes not discernible by other means.

The accuracy of census data for measuring housing quality has been questioned and hence should be checked, particularly if it is to be used for appraisal or redevelopment purposes. It is nevertheless a good tool in the absence of a better one.

Development needs for residential areas bear a more substantial relationship to open space needs than any other type of generalized land use—mainly since it is presently such a large percentage of developed land in urban areas. Residential needs are directly related to density. The general standards recommended by the Committee on the Hygiene of Housing of the American Public Health Association are shown in Table I.

For residential areas as a whole it must be remembered to add in what is needed for schools, neighborhood shopping, streets, recreation, open space, etc. when using this type of standard. This is not to say that higher or lower densities are not acceptable. Many cities have examples at both extremes.

This trend is toward greater amounts of usable open space through more sensitive arrangements of dwelling units on the land, whether in 1-story single-family structures or in high density towers. The old standards are continued in the newer designs only in the matter of total densities. Cluster development and new towns illustrate this trend of planning large areas at one time—in planned unit developments.

TABLE 1 Residential Densities Recommended by The American Public Health Association

One- and Two-Family	DU's Per Net Acre	
Dwelling Unit Type	Desirable	Maximum
1-family detached	5	7
1-family semi-detached *or* 2-family detached	10	12
1-family attached (row) *or* 2-family semi-detached	16	19
Multi-Family		
2-story	25	30
3-story	40	45
6-story	65	75
9-story	75	85
13-story	85	95

TABLE 2 Appraisal Items and Maximum Standard Penalty Scores (APHA)

Item	Maximum Score	Item	Maximum Score
A. Facilities		17. Rooms lacking window*	30
		18. Rooms lacking closet	8
Structure:		19. Rooms of substandard area	10
1. Main access	6	20. Combined room facilities‡	
2. Water supply* (source)	25		
3. Sewer connection*	25	*B. Maintenance*	
4. Daylight obstruction	20	21. Toilet condition index	12
5. Stairs and fire escapes	30	22. Deterioration index* (structure, unit)§	50
6. Public hall lighting	18		
		23. Infestation index (structure, unit)§	15
Unit:		24. Sanitary index (structure, unit)§	30
7. Location in structure	8		
8. Kitchen facilities	24	25. Basement condition index	13
9. Toilet* (location, type, sharing)†	45	*C. Occupancy*	
10. Bath* (location, type, sharing)†	20	26. Room crowding: persons per room*	30
11. Water supply* (location and type)	15	27. Room crowding: persons per sleeping room*	25
12. Washing facilities	8		
13. Dual egress*	30	28. Area crowding: sleeping area per person*	30
14. Electric lighting*	15		
15. Central heating	3	29. Area crowding: nonsleeping area per person	25
16. Rooms lacking installed heat*	20	30. Doubling of basic families	10

Source: *An Appraisal Method for Measuring the Quality of Housing,* Part II, "Appraisal of Dwelling Conditions," American Public Health Association, Washington, D.C., 1946.

Note: 1. Maximum theoretical total dwelling score is 600, broken down as:

Facilities 360   Maintenance 120   Occupancy 120

2. Housing total = dwelling total + environmental total.

* Condition constituting a basic deficiency.

† Item score is total of subscores for location, type, and sharing of toilet or bath facilities.

‡ Item score is total of scores for items 16-19 inclusive. This duplicate score is not included in the total for a dwelling but is recorded for analysis.

§ Item score is total of subscores for structure and unit.

SOURCE: Environmental Engineering and Sanitation, *2nd Edition, Joseph Solvato, Wiley-Interscience, John-Wiley & Sons, Inc., New York, 1972.*

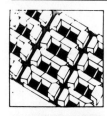

a. private open space on grade adjacent to dwelling unit;
common open space reduced to access.

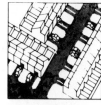

a. individual parking on grade adjacent to dwelling unit.

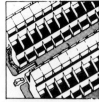

b. private open space on/in building structure, adjacent to dwelling unit;
common open space reduced to access.

b. common parking on grade, adjacent to and shared by groups of dwelling units.

c. private open space on grade or on/in building structure, adjacent to dwelling unit;
common open space shared by groups of dwelling units.

c. common parking on grade, integrated with common open space, adjacent/near to and shared by groups of dwelling units.

d. private open space on grade or on/in building structure, adjacent to dwelling unit;
common open space, integrated with parking shared by groups of dwelling units.

d. common parking on grade, near to and shared by groups of dwelling units.

e. common open space shared by groups of dwelling units.

e. common parking in building structure below housing, shared by groups/all dwelling units.

f. common open space integrated with parking, shared by groups of dwelling units.

f. common parking on grade, separate from and shared by all dwelling units.

g. common open space shared by all dwelling units.

g. common parking in separate building structure, shared by all dwelling units.

BASIC DEFICIENCIES OF DWELLINGS (APHA)

Item*	Condition Constituting a Basic Deficiency†
A. Facilities	
2.	Source of water supply specifically disapproved by local health department.
3.	Means of sewage disposal specifically disapproved by local health department.
9.	Toilet shared with other dwelling unit, outside structure or of disapproved type (flush hopper or nonstandard privy).
10.	Installed bath lacking, shared with other dwelling unit or outside structure.
11.	Water supply outside dwelling unit.
13.	Dual egress from unit lacking.
14.	No electric lighting installed in unit.
16.	Three-fourths or more of rooms in unit lacking installed heater.‡
17.	Outside window lacking in any room of unit.‡
B. Maintenance	
22.	Deterioration of class 2 or 3 (penalty score, by composite index, of 15 points or over).
C. Occupancy	
26.	Room crowding: over 1.5 persons/room.
27.	Room crowding: number of occupants equals or exceeds 2 times the number of sleeping rooms plus 2.
28.	Area crowding: less than 40 ft² of sleeping area/person.

Note: Some authorities include as a basic deficiency unvented gas space heater, unvented gas hot-water heater, open gas burner for heating, lack of hot and cold running water.

*Numbers refer to items in Table 11-2, "Appraisal Items and Maximum Standard Penalty Scores."

†Of the 13 defects that can be designated basic deficiencies, 11 are so classified when the item penalty score equals or exceeds 10 points. Bath (item 10) becomes a basic deficiency at 8 points for reasons involving comparability to the U.S. Housing Census; deterioration (item 22) at 15 points for reasons internal to that item.

‡The criterion of basic deficiency for this item is adjusted for number of rooms in the unit.

HOUSING QUALITY SCORES (APHA)

Factor	A—Good	B—Acceptable	C—Borderline	D—Substandard	E—Unfit
Dwelling score	0 to 29	30 to 59	60 to 89	90 to 119	120 or greater
Environmental score	0 to 19	20 to 39	40 to 59	60 to 79	80 or greater
Sum of dwelling and environmental scores	0 to 49	50 to 99	100 to 149	150 to 199	200 or greater

SOURCE: Environmental Engineering and Sanitation. 2nd Edition. Joseph Solvato. Wiley-Interscience. John Wiley & Sons Inc., New York, 1972.

ENVIRONMENTAL SURVEY—STANDARD PENALTY SCORES (APHA)

Item	Maximum* Penalty Score
A. Land crowding	
1. Coverage by structures—70% or more of block area covered.	24
2. Residential building density—ratio of residential floor area to total = 4 or more.	20
3. Population density—gross residential floor area per person 150 ft² or less.	10
4. Residential yard areas—less than 20 ft wide and 625 ft² in 70% of residences.	16
B. Nonresidential land areas	
5. Areal incidence of nonresidential land use—50% or more nonresidential.	13
6. Linear incidence of nonresidential land use—50% or more nonresidential.	13
7. Specific nonresidential nuisances and hazards—noise and vibration, objectionable odors, fire or explosion, vermin, rodents, insects, smoke or dust, night glare, dilapidated structure, insanitary lot.	30
8. Hazards to morals and the public peace—poolrooms, gambling places, bars, prostitution, liquor stores, nightclubs.	10
9. Smoke incidence—industries, docks, railroad yards, soft-coal use.	6
C. Hazards and nuisances from transportation system	
10. Street traffic—type of traffic, dwelling setback, width of streets.	20
11. Railroads or switchyards—amount of noise, vibration, smoke, trains.	24
12. Airports or airlines—location of dwelling with respect to runways and approaches.	20
D. Hazards and nuisances from natural causes	
13. Surface flooding—rivers, streams, tide, groundwater, drainage annual or more.	20
14. Swamps or marshes—within 1000 yd, malarial mosquitoes.	24
15. Topography—pits, rock outcrops, steep slopes, slides.	16
E. Inadequate utilities and sanitation	
16. Sanitary sewerage system—available (within 300 ft), adequate.	24
17. Public water supply—available, adequate pressure and quantity.	20
18. Streets and walks—grade, pavement, curbs, grass, sidewalks.	10
F. Inadequate basic community facilities	
19. Elementary public schools—beyond ⅔ mi, 3 or more dangerous crossings.	10
20. Public playgrounds—less than 0.75 acres/1000 persons.	8
21. Public playfields—less than 1.25 acres/1000 persons.	4
22. Other public parks—less than 1.00 acres/1000 persons.	8
23. Public transportation—beyond ⅔ mi, less than 2 buses/hr.	12
24. Food stores—dairy, vegetable, meat, grocery, bread, more than ⅓ mi.	6

Source: An Appraisal Method for Measuring the Quality of Housing, Part III, "Appraisal of Neighborhood Environment," American Public Health Association, Washington, D.C., 1950.

*Maximum environment total = 368.

SUB-DIVISION AND LAND DEVELOPMENT

PROCEDURE FOR PLANNING BOARD APPROVAL OF SUBDIVISIONS
(IN LIEU OF GOVERNING BODY APPROVAL)

ALTERNATE "A"

IN ACCORDANCE WITH THE LOCAL SUBDIVISION ORDINANCE
PROVIDED SUCH ORDINANCE ESTABLISHES RULES, REGULATIONS AND STANDARDS FOR PLAT APPROVAL

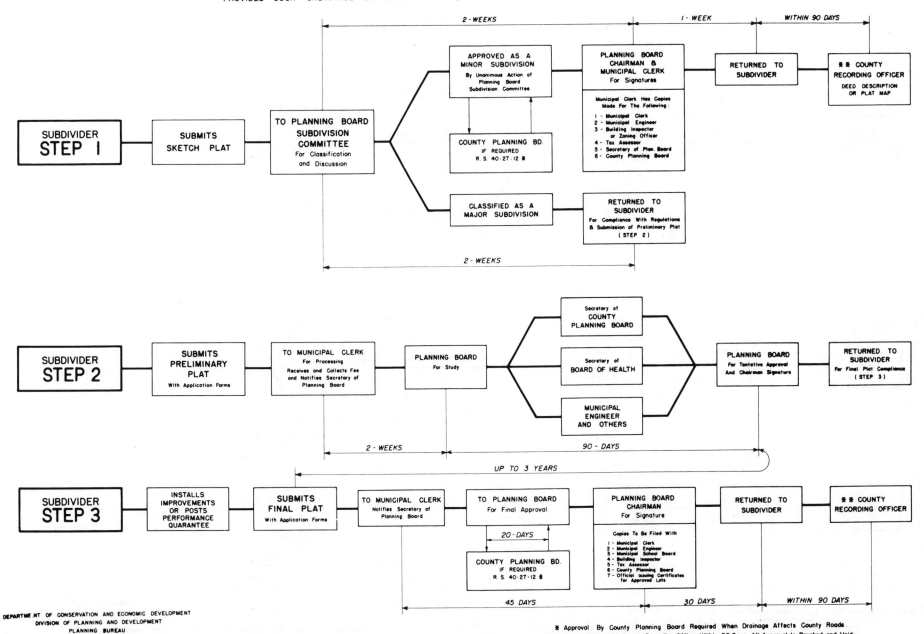

DEPARTMENT OF CONSERVATION AND ECONOMIC DEVELOPMENT
DIVISION OF PLANNING AND DEVELOPMENT
PLANNING BUREAU
SEPTEMBER 1959

※ Approval By County Planning Board Required When Drainage Affects County Roads.
※※ If Not Filed With County Recording Officer Within 90 Days, All Approval Is Revoked and Void.

PROCEDURE FOR <u>GOVERNING BODY APPROVAL</u> OF SUBDIVISIONS
AFTER FAVORABLE REFERRAL BY THE PLANNING BOARD
IN ACCORDANCE WITH THE LOCAL SUBDIVISION ORDINANCE
PROVIDED SUCH ORDINANCE ESTABLISHES RULES, REGULATIONS AND STANDARDS FOR PLAT APPROVAL

<u>ALTERNATE "B"</u>

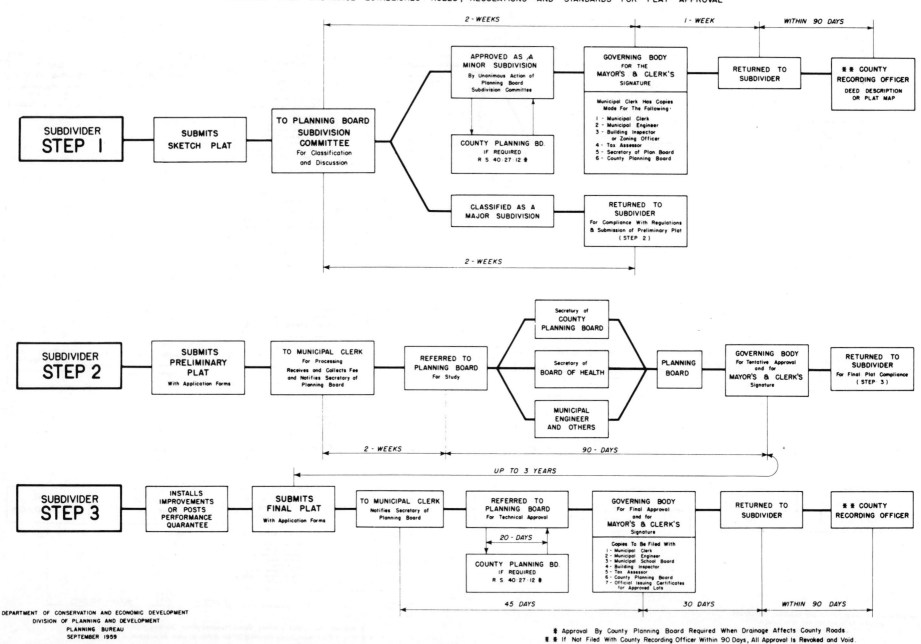

DEPARTMENT OF CONSERVATION AND ECONOMIC DEVELOPMENT
DIVISION OF PLANNING AND DEVELOPMENT
PLANNING BUREAU
SEPTEMBER 1959

✶ Approval By County Planning Board Required When Drainage Affects County Roads.
✶✶ If Not Filed With County Recording Officer Within 90 Days, All Approval Is Revoked and Void.

COMPUTING CHART

TO FIND THE TOTAL COST OF AN IMPROVED LOT
(RAW LAND AND STREET IMPROVEMENTS)

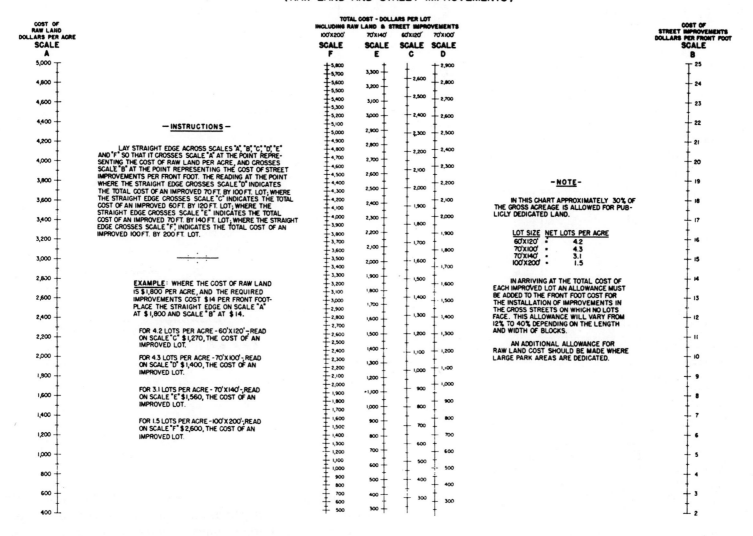

COST OF
RAW LAND
DOLLARS PER ACRE
SCALE A

TOTAL COST - DOLLARS PER LOT
INCLUDING RAW LAND & STREET IMPROVEMENTS
100'X200' — **SCALE F**
70'X140' — **SCALE E**
60'X120' — **SCALE C**
70'X100' — **SCALE D**

COST OF
STREET IMPROVEMENTS
DOLLARS PER FRONT FOOT
SCALE B

— INSTRUCTIONS —

LAY STRAIGHT EDGE ACROSS SCALES "A", "B", "C", "D", "E" AND "F" SO THAT IT CROSSES SCALE "A" AT THE POINT REPRESENTING THE COST OF RAW LAND PER ACRE, AND CROSSES SCALE "B" AT THE POINT REPRESENTING THE COST OF STREET IMPROVEMENTS PER FRONT FOOT. THE READING AT THE POINT WHERE THE STRAIGHT EDGE CROSSES SCALE "D" INDICATES THE TOTAL COST OF AN IMPROVED 70 FT. BY 100 FT. LOT; WHERE THE STRAIGHT EDGE CROSSES SCALE "C" INDICATES THE TOTAL COST OF AN IMPROVED 60 FT. BY 120 FT. LOT; WHERE THE STRAIGHT EDGE CROSSES SCALE "E" INDICATES THE TOTAL COST OF AN IMPROVED 70 FT. BY 140 FT. LOT; WHERE THE STRAIGHT EDGE CROSSES SCALE "F" INDICATES THE TOTAL COST OF AN IMPROVED 100 FT. BY 200 FT. LOT.

EXAMPLE: WHERE THE COST OF RAW LAND IS $1,800 PER ACRE, AND THE REQUIRED IMPROVEMENTS COST $14 PER FRONT FOOT - PLACE THE STRAIGHT EDGE ON SCALE "A" AT $1,800 AND SCALE "B" AT $14.

FOR 4.2 LOTS PER ACRE - 60'X120' - READ ON SCALE "C" $1,270, THE COST OF AN IMPROVED LOT.

FOR 4.3 LOTS PER ACRE - 70'X100' - READ ON SCALE "D" $1,400, THE COST OF AN IMPROVED LOT.

FOR 3.1 LOTS PER ACRE - 70'X140' - READ ON SCALE "E" $1,560, THE COST OF AN IMPROVED LOT.

FOR 1.5 LOTS PER ACRE - 100'X200' - READ ON SCALE "F" $2,600, THE COST OF AN IMPROVED LOT.

— NOTE —

IN THIS CHART APPROXIMATELY 30% OF THE GROSS ACREAGE IS ALLOWED FOR PUBLICLY DEDICATED LAND.

LOT SIZE	NET LOTS PER ACRE
60'X120'	4.2
70'X100'	4.3
70'X140'	3.1
100'X200'	1.5

IN ARRIVING AT THE TOTAL COST OF EACH IMPROVED LOT AN ALLOWANCE MUST BE ADDED TO THE FRONT FOOT COST FOR THE INSTALLATION OF IMPROVEMENTS IN THE CROSS STREETS ON WHICH NO LOTS FACE. THIS ALLOWANCE WILL VARY FROM 12% TO 40% DEPENDING ON THE LENGTH AND WIDTH OF BLOCKS.

AN ADDITIONAL ALLOWANCE FOR RAW LAND COST SHOULD BE MADE WHERE LARGE PARK AREAS ARE DEDICATED.

SOURCE: Federal Housing Administration, Washington, D. C.

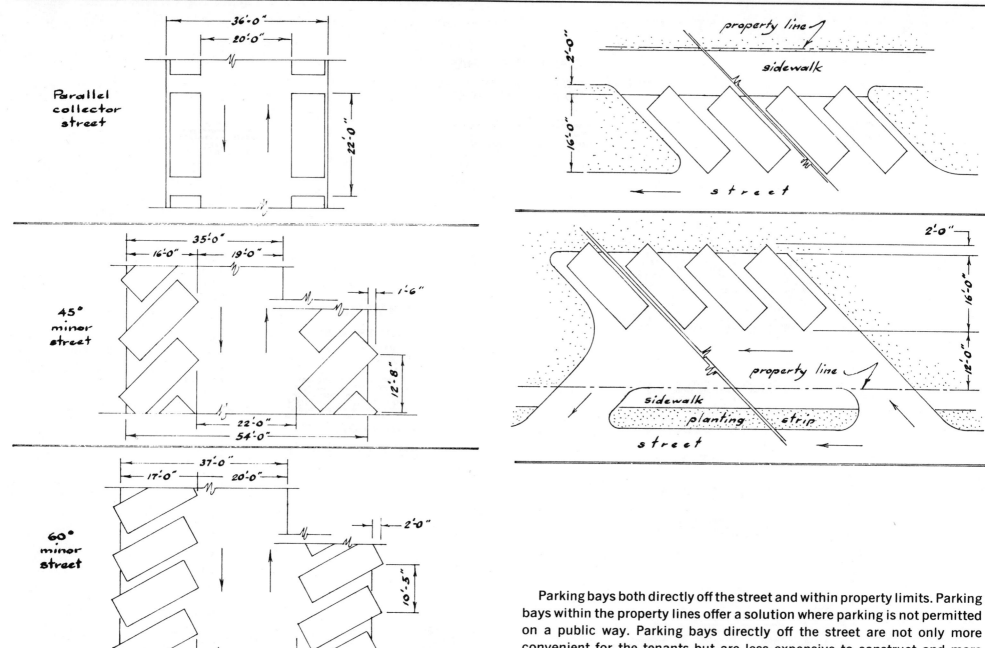

Parallel collector street

36'-0"
20'-0"
22'-0"

45° minor street

35'-0"
16'-0" 19'-0"
1'-6"
12'-8"
22'-0"
54'-0"

60° minor street

37'-0"
17'-0" 20'-0"
2'-0"
10'-5"
22'-0"
56'-0"

property line
sidewalk
2'-0"
16'-0"
street

2'-0"
16'-0"
12'-0"
property line
sidewalk
planting strip
street

Parking bays both directly off the street and within property limits. Parking bays within the property lines offer a solution where parking is not permitted on a public way. Parking bays directly off the street are not only more convenient for the tenants but are less expensive to construct and more economical to maintain. These should be used, however, only on minor streets. The illustrations are for streets with two-way traffic.

SOURCE: *Minimum Property Standards, for 1 and 2-Family Houses, FHA, Dept, of Housing and Urban Development, Washington, D. C.*

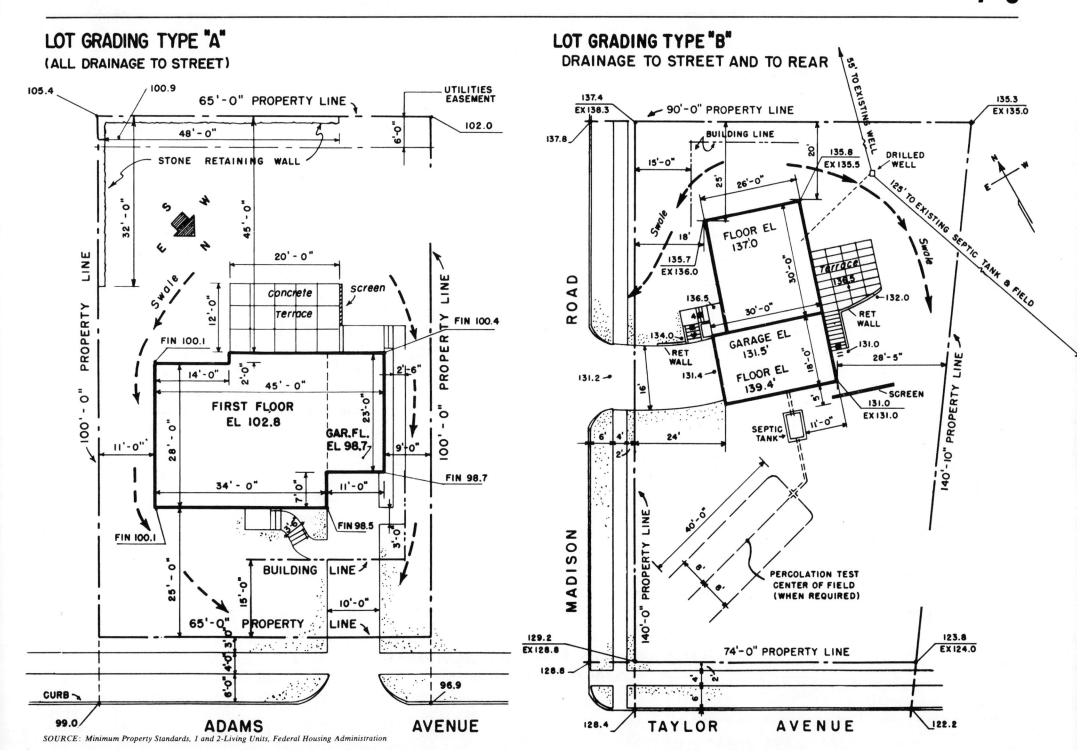

LOT GRADING TYPE "A"
(ALL DRAINAGE TO STREET)

LOT GRADING TYPE "B"
DRAINAGE TO STREET AND TO REAR

SOURCE: Minimum Property Standards, 1 and 2-Living Units, Federal Housing Administration

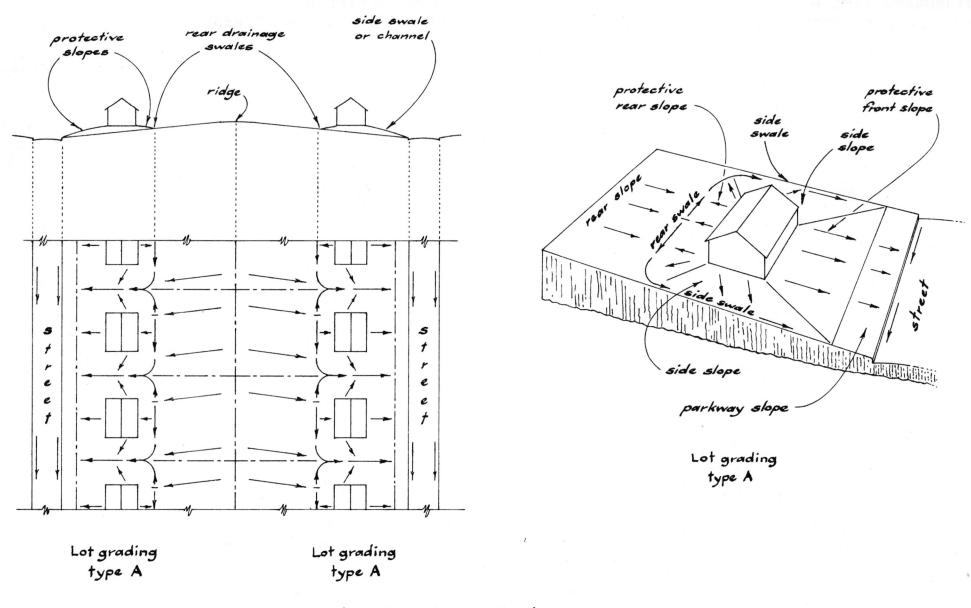

protective slopes

rear drainage swales

side swale or channel

ridge

street

street

Lot grading type A

Lot grading type A

protective rear slope

side swale

side slope

protective front slope

rear slope

rear swale

side swale

street

side slope

parkway slope

Lot grading type A

Lot grading type A, all drainage to street ridge along rear lot lines

SOURCE: *Minimum Property Requirements, Federal Housing Administration, Washington, D. C.*

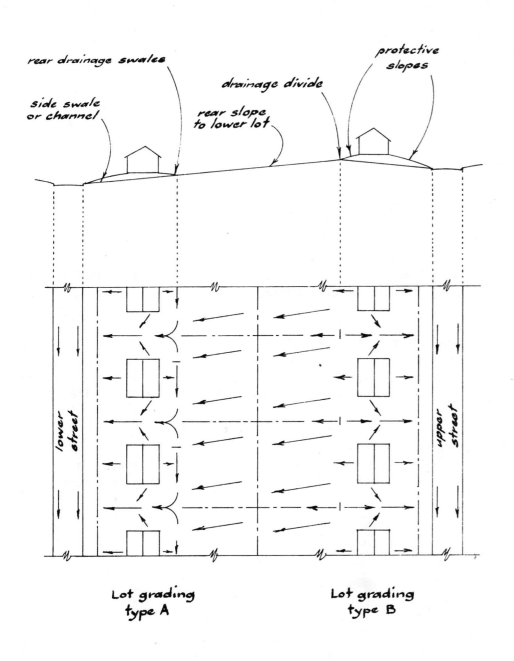

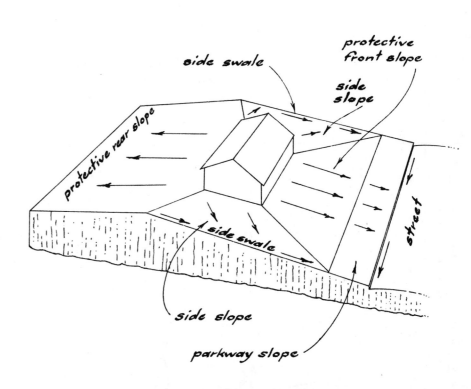

Lot grading type B, drainage both to street and to rear lot line

Lot grading type A

Lot grading type B

SOURCE: *Minimum Property Requirements, Federal Housing Administration, Washington, D. C.*

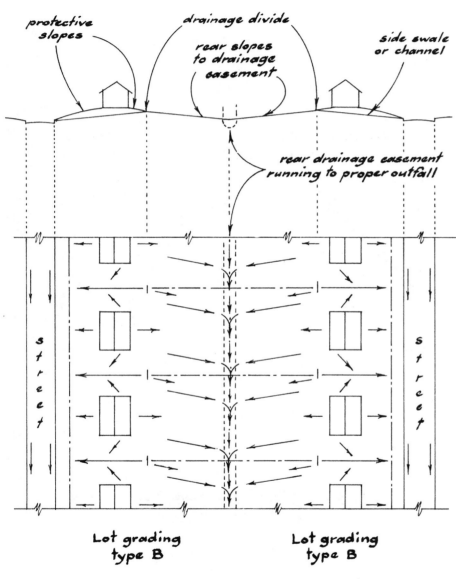

protective slopes

drainage divide

rear slopes to drainage easement

side swale or channel

rear drainage easement running to proper outfall

s t r e e t

s t r e e t

Lot grading type B

Lot grading type B

Valley along rear lot lines

BLOCK GRADING TYPES

Grading Type A—(see plate 6–7)

This method is the simplest of all the methods. It provides for a ridge (high point) along the rear lot lines, then each lot is sloped down directly to the street, independent of other lots.

Grading Type B—(see plate 6–8)

This method provides for drainage to a valley (low point) along rear lot lines. The front portion is drained towards the street. The drainage along the rear lot lines will require an easement to properly handle the runoff.

Grading Type C—(see plate 6–10)

This method is similar to type B except that the drainage runs to side swales or channels. From the side of the house the water flows back to the rear lot line.

SOURCE: Minimum Property Requirements, Federal Housing Administration, Washington, D. C.

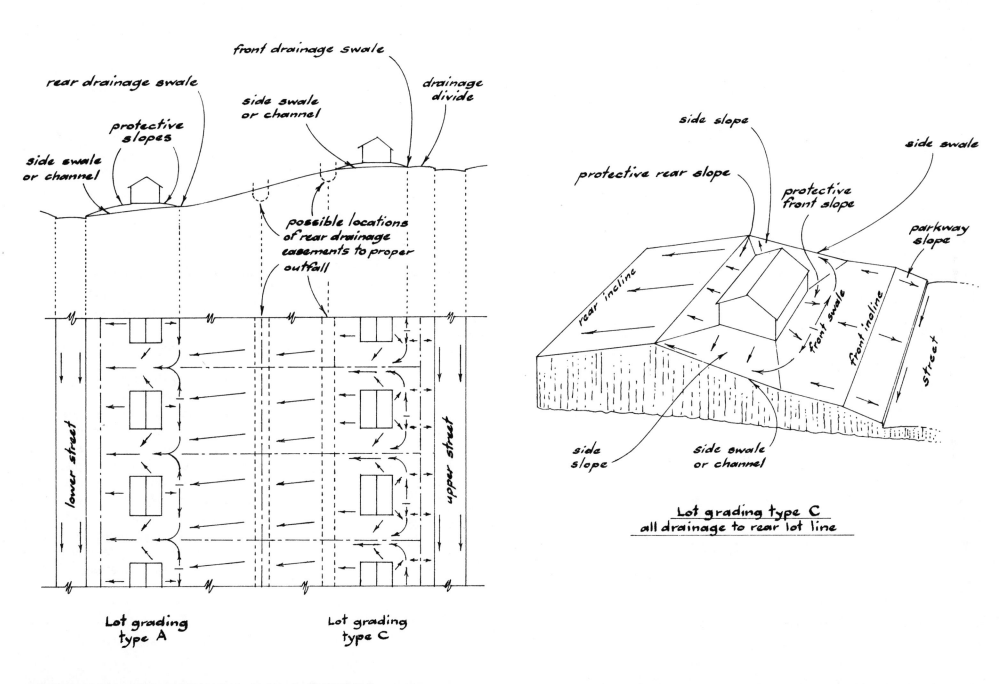

rear drainage swale

front drainage swale

side swale or channel

drainage divide

protective slopes

side swale or channel

possible locations of rear drainage easements to proper outfall

lower street

upper street

Lot grading type A

Lot grading type C

side slope

protective rear slope

protective front slope

side swale

parkway slope

rear incline

front swale

front incline

street

side slope

side swale or channel

Lot grading type C
all drainage to rear lot line

SOURCE: *Minimum Property Requirements, Federal Housing Administration, Washington, D. C.*

TYPES OF STREETS

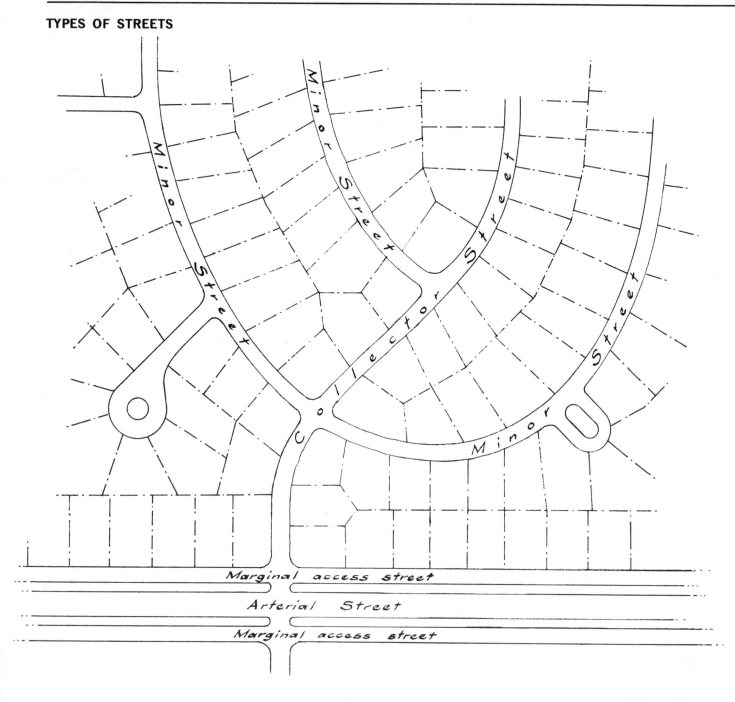

The term **"street"** means a way for vehicular traffic, whether designated as a street, highway, thoroughfare, parkway, throughway, road, avenue, boulevard, lane, place, or however otherwise designated:

1. Arterial streets and highways are those which are used primarily for fast or heavy traffic. Right-of-way width 80–120 feet.

2. Collector streets are those which carry traffic from minor streets to the major system of arterial streets and highways, including the principal entrance streets of a residential development and streets for circulation within such a development. Right-of-way width 60–80 feet.

3. Minor streets are those which are used primarily for access to the abutting properties. Right-of-way width 50–60 feet.

4. Marginal access streets are minor streets which are parallel to and adjacent to arterial streets and highways; and which provide access to abutting properties and protection from through traffic. Right-of-way width 40 feet.

5. Alleys are minor ways which are used primarily for vehicular service access to the back or the side of properties otherwise abutting on a street.

SOURCE: *Control of Land Sub-Division, NYS Dept. of Commerce, Albany, N. Y.*

Nomenclature adopted by the Association of State Highway Officials

TYPICAL

The pattern of streets and lots set out by the land subdivider provides the framework for groups of houses. Many interesting and individual street arrangements can be devised by considering the shape and contours of the land and by properly routing traffic.

The grid street plan is a handicap to effective house grouping and can only be obtained by occasional set-backs and the use of planting to conceal the monotony of the plan. On the other hand the street plan of the subdivision should be simple and straightforward; it should arise out of a reasonable and economical use of the space with an eye for the appearance and architectural effects of the buildings to be placed there.

Curved streets have a pleasant and natural effect, particularly when they are justified by topographical conditions. But excessive use of curved streets on flat land may be both dangerous and uneconomical unless done with careful planning.

The dead-end or cul-de-sac street provides the most complete privacy and traffic separation. The closure of the street clearly distinguishes an individual group of houses, and by limiting the number of houses to be served it is possible to use a street of economical dimensions and light construction. (The turning circle of a dead-end street should be not less than 80 feet in outside diameter. Also, in order to provide manoeuvring space for fire-fighting equipment and other emergencies there should be a space not less than 100 feet in diameter clear of trees and other permanent obstructions. A pedestrian lane from one turning circle to the next may provide additional egress; under normal circumstances this can be closed to vehicular traffic.)

The loop street provides the privacy, safety and economy of a dead-end street without the difficulties of turning; traffic circulates easily to and from a collector street. The loop street in various proportions and shapes provides interesting opportunities for the grouping of houses, particularly if some park space can be introduced.

The need to provide off-street parking suggests a number of interesting opportunities for small house groups served by parking bays. Houses grouped around a quadrangle or motor court can have a very pleasant character and are economical in the use of public street space.

In setting out a pattern of residential streets a T intersection of streets is safer than a cross intersection because traffic on one street is brought to a halt. The special hazard of the grid plan is the multiplication of cross intersections.

SOURCE: Principles of Small House Grouping, Central Mortgage and Housing Corporation, Ottawa, Canada

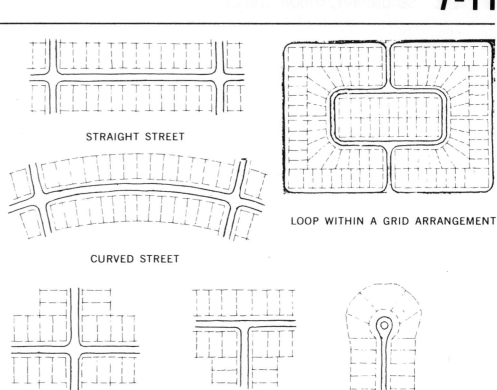

STRAIGHT STREET

CURVED STREET

LOOP WITHIN A GRID ARRANGEMENT

CROSS INTERSECTION TEE INTERSECTION  CUL DE SAC

INTERSECTIONS

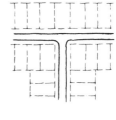

LOOP

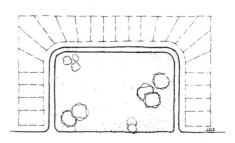

LOOP WITH GREEN

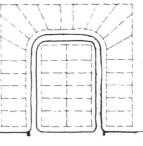

SIX LOT ARRANGEMENT 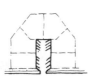 MOTOR COURT PARKING BAY

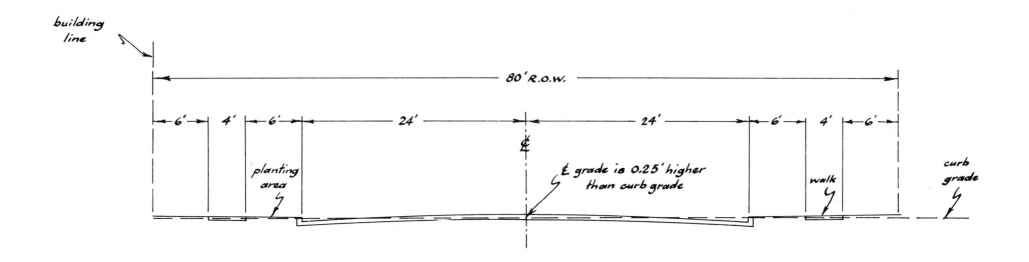

Secondary street
(residential)

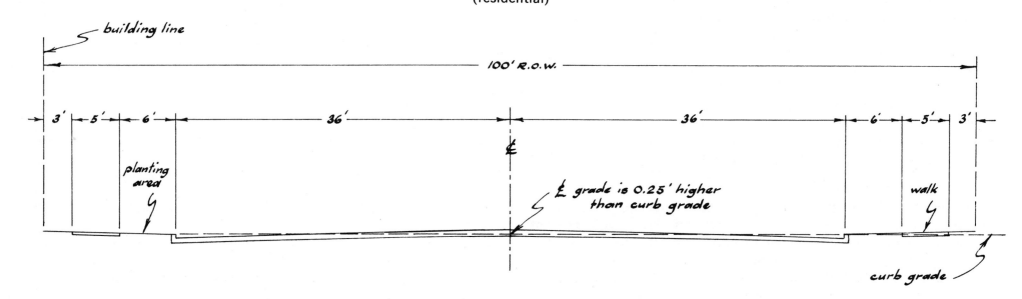

Major street

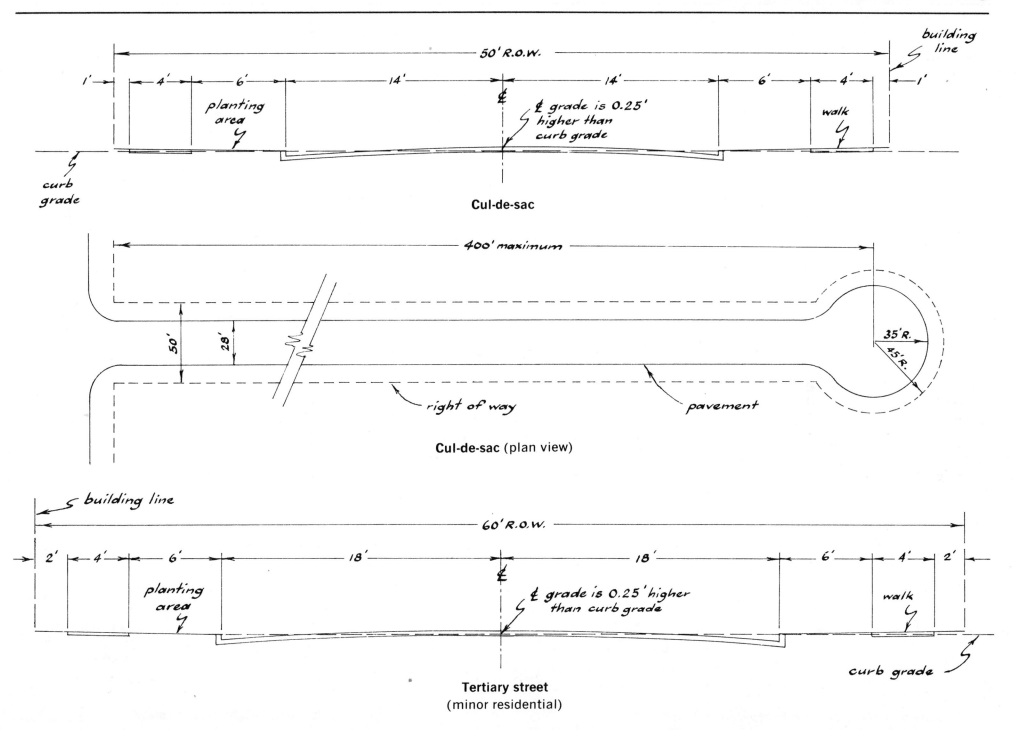

Cul-de-sac

Cul-de-sac (plan view)

Tertiary street
(minor residential)

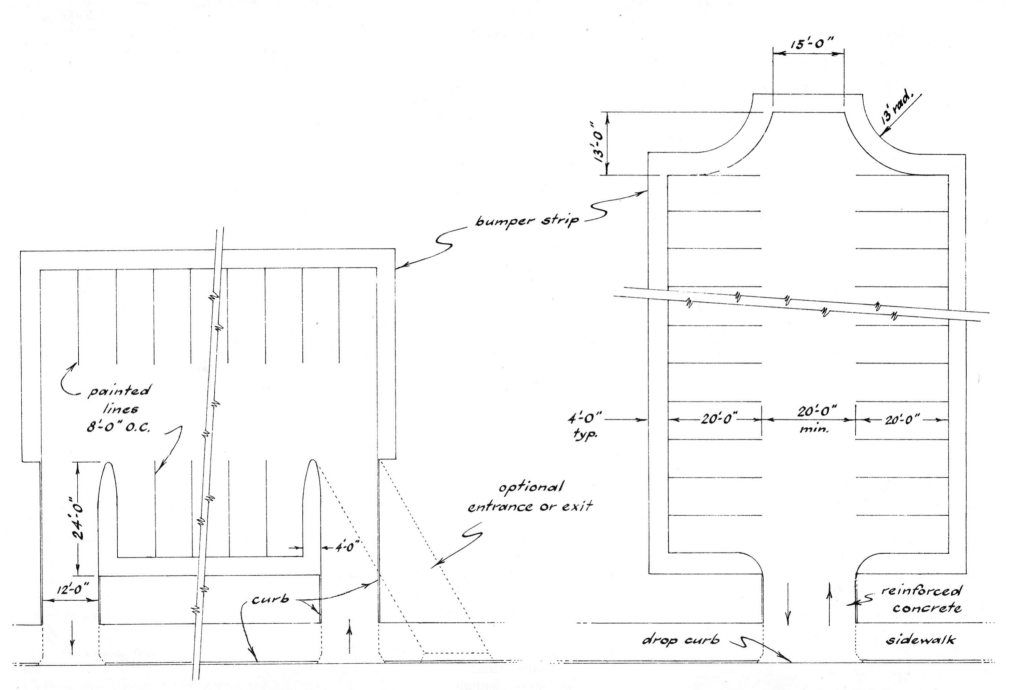

Parking parallel to street with separate entrance and exit

SOURCE: NYC Housing Authority. Memo to Architects—1952

Parking—right angle to street

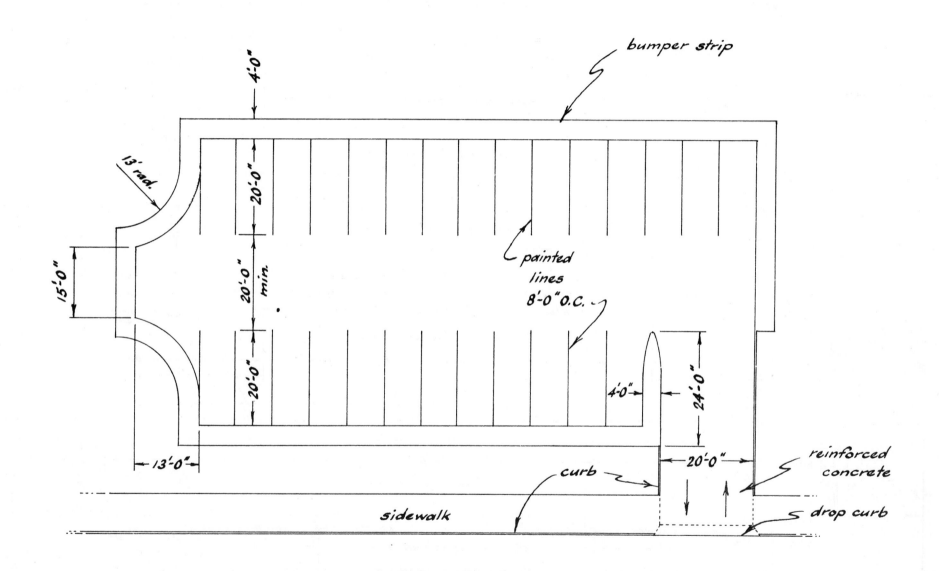

Parking parallel to street with combined entrance and exit

SOURCE: Memo to Architects, NYC Housing Authority—1952

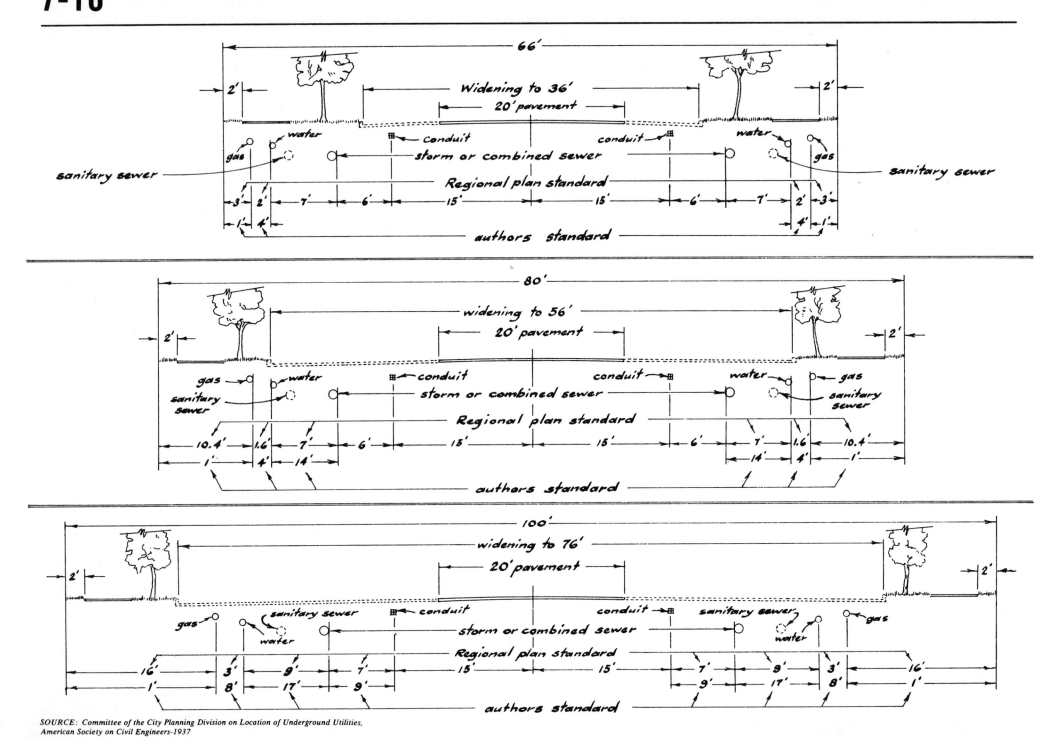

SOURCE: *Committee of the City Planning Division on Location of Underground Utilities,*
American Society on Civil Engineers-1937

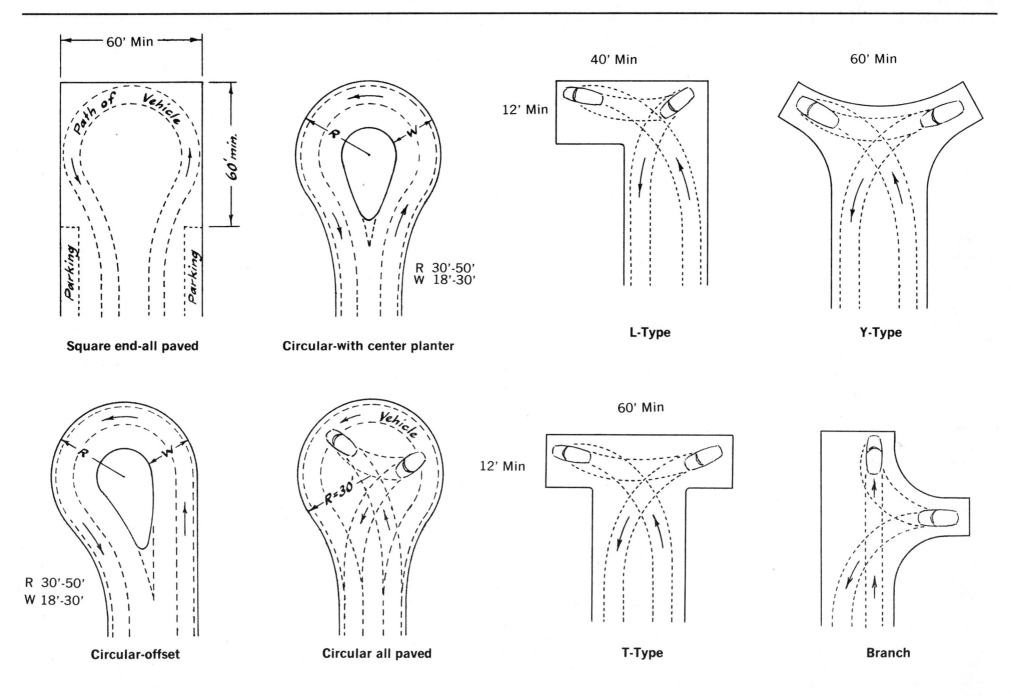

Square end-all paved

Circular-with center planter

R 30'-50'
W 18'-30'

L-Type

Y-Type

Circular-offset

R 30'-50'
W 18'-30'

Circular all paved

R=30'

T-Type

Branch

note - Dimensions Indicated are for Passenger Cars Only, for Trucks and Other Vehicles, Sizes Must be Increased Accordingly.

STREET AND AVENUE SYSTEM

One of the simplest systems employed in naming streets is to give the name "street" to streets running generally east-west and the name "avenue" to streets running generally north-south or vice-versa. Such a system could be applied whether streets are given name designations or number designations. The assignment of the word "street" to streets running in one direction and the word "avenue" to streets running in the opposite direction has the advantage of limiting the address search to either north-south or east-west streets.

Whether streets are given name designations or number designations is of not too much concern. It is quickly apparent that streets given number designations such as First Ave. Second Ave. etc., are easier to locate than streets named after birds, trees, states, etc. As a general rule, however, a city would not give number designations to both north-south and east-west streets. Number designation for streets running in one direction and same designation for streets running in the opposite direction is commonplace. The system becomes more workable when the streets and avenues are named in such a way that the name of the street informs one of its approximate location in relation to other streets and in relation to the base lines. For example, if north-south public ways were designated as "avenues" and named after states and the furthermost avenues in the western edge of the city were given names of states which began with the letter "A" (Arizona, Arkansas, etc.) progressing down the alphabet to the letters "X" and "Y" "Z" on the eastern edge of the city, then "Arkansas Ave." would indicate that the street ran north-south and that it was in the far western part of the city.

A disadvantage of the street and avenue naming system is that it is too general to enable streets to be located easily and quickly in large cities. The use of alphabetical street naming order does not readily lend itself to change.

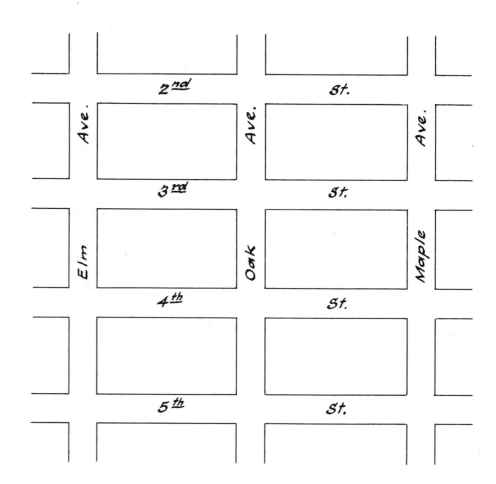

SOURCE: *A Guide to Street Naming and Property Numbering, Southern Association of State Planning and Development Agencies-1952*

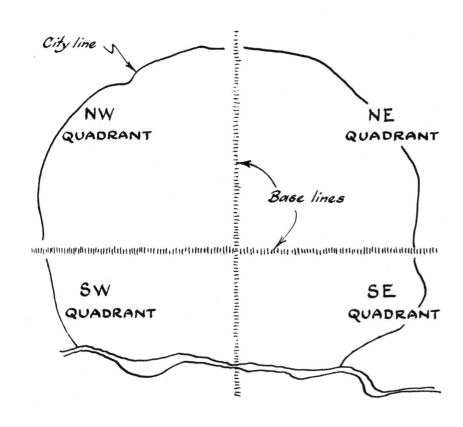

QUADRANT SYSTEM

Basic to most street naming systems is the use of two **base lines**—running generally east-west and the other running generally north-south—which divide the city into four quadrants. The base lines are actually the extension of the intersecting lines which form the point of reference. By incorporating directional letters as part of the street name, any street is easily located as far as the quadrant in which it lies. For example, it is observed that Elm St. lies to the north, and to the east of the base lines.

SOURCE: *A Guide to Street Naming and Property Numbering, Southern Association of State Planning and Development Agencies-1952*

It is therefore in the northeast quadrant, and the correct name of the street would be Elm N. E. Also streets running generally in one direction, say, east-west, could be given the suffix "street" and streets running generally in the opposite direction would be known as "avenues". An address of "339 Elm Ave. N. E." would inform one that the house faces a public way running north-south, located in the northeast quadrant and approximately ⅓ of a block beyond the third block north of the base line.

The specific purpose of a uniform and orderly street system is to enable one to find a street (and a street number) as quickly and easily as possible. When a system is to be adopted, it should be as simple as possible, and should allow for systematic expansion of the system as the community grows. A system which is not flexible and does not make allowances for future growth is hardly worth the effort, since within a comparatively short time the addition of new streets will create anew the confusion which the reform was supposed to correct.

The coordinate of Lyman St. Numbering System was developed by Richard R. Lyman, a civil engineer, some 23 years ago. Mr. Lyman was appointed to serve on a committee established to devise a method of numbering streets in a city so that it would be possible for a traveler to find an address in a city without the aid of a map. In this guide the system developed by Mr. Lyman is called the coordinate system because any address is a coordinate of two values—some value or distance along one base line and some distance along the other base line.

The coordinate system is similar to other street naming systems which utilize two base lines, or reference lines which run approximately at right angles to each other. These base lines form the division lines between north, south, east and west. Under the coordinate system, streets are given numbers instead of names and the numbers are in fact street names.

The illustration shows how streets are numbered (or named) by hundreds—100 for each block away from the two axes. Streets parallel to the north of the base line labeled E. W. are given the designation "north" as part of the street number; streets parallel to and south of the E. W. base line are given the designation "south". In a similar manner "east" and "west" designations are given streets parallel to the N. S. base line. It will be observed that the E. W. base line runs along the center line of the street numbered "O East" and "O West" and likewise, the N. S. base line runs along the center line of the street numbered "O North" and O South".

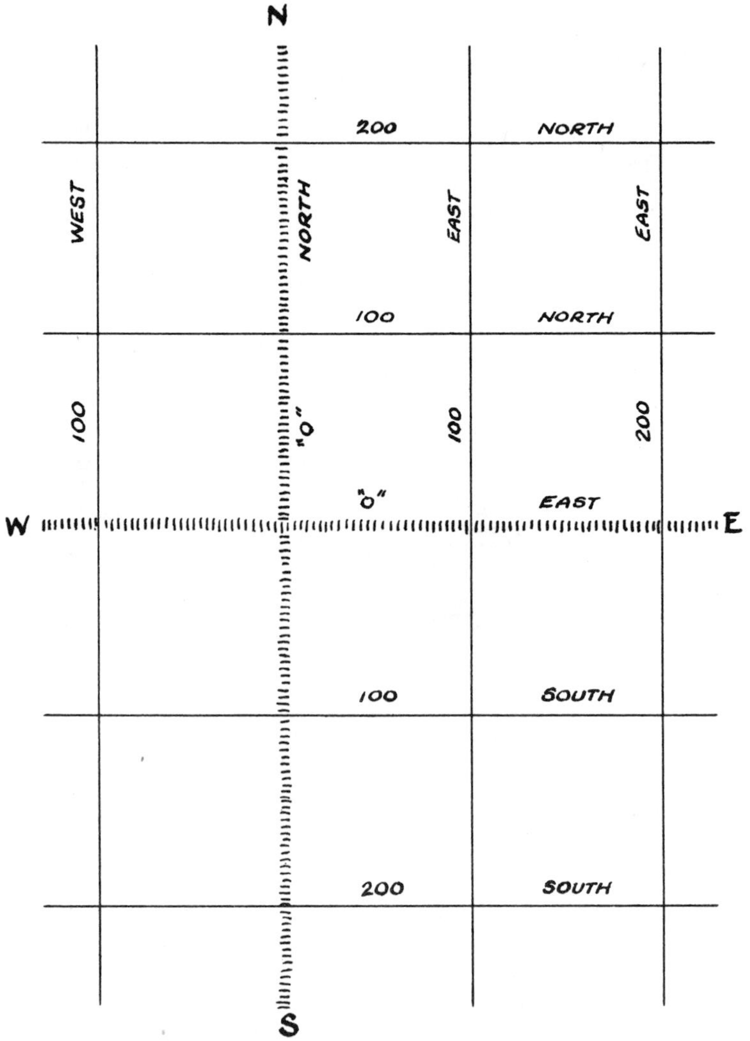

SOURCE: *A Guide to Street Naming and Property Numbering, Southern Association of State Planning and Development Agencies-1952*

After streets have been named systematically a plan must be worked out for numbering property which   buts the streets. Systematic property numbering is of questionable value unless the property numbering plan is integrated with street naming.

BASE LINES AND GRID LINES

Fundamental to a property numbering system is the establishment of a point of reference to which all property is related. This point of reference is usually established near the center of the city, and may be thought of as the intersection of two imaginary lines. from such a point outward in four directions—north, south, east and west—property is numbered as it relates to the reference point. The reference point is, of course, identical with the intersection of the base lines established for street naming.

It is axiomatic that every property numbering system is based upon some point of reference. Without such reference point property numbers could have no sequence or order. Parallel to these base lines, "grid lines", or "correction lines" are established to divide property into blocks for numbering purposes. The grid lines indicate the division between block number changes where property numbers change from one hundred to the next higher hundred. The residents of most American cities are accustomed to a gridiron street pattern with parallel streets more or less equal distance apart. Such a street pattern easily lends itself to establishment of block number changes at street intersections and most people have long accustomed themselves to such a system.

PROPERTY NUMBERING INTERVALS

The property or front footage along the street is given a number rather than a particular structure. This principle is in recognition of the fact that there is no good way of knowing how many structures will eventually be built on vacant land within blocks, and that any numbering scheme which attempted to number structures consecutively leaves no flexibility to accommodate change.

SOURCE: *A Guide to Street Naming and Property Numbering, Southern Association of State Planning and Development Agencies-1952*

By assigning a property number to an interval of front footage along the street a system is established whereby change and growth are conveniently handled. This number interval may be selected to fit the particular need. In central business districts where lots are customarily smaller, a small interval may be needed; low density residential areas may more suitably be assigned numbers according to a greater interval. An interval of 20 feet, maybe 50 feet, may fit the requirements for a particular residential area; business areas and very dense residential areas may require a smaller interval, say, ten or fifteen feet. As a general rule, it is wise to select a property numbering interval of short length, say, ten feet for business areas and perhaps 20 to 25 feet for other areas. Haphazard changes in the interval length should be avoided since a particular house number on one street should correspond in location to a house similarly situated on a parallel street on the other side of the city.

ASSIGNMENT OF HOUSE NUMBERS

Once the numbering interval has been selected assignment of numbers to existing structures can be made by measuring the number of intervals from the grid line nearest the base line and actually assigning to each building the number of the interval in which the front entrance falls.

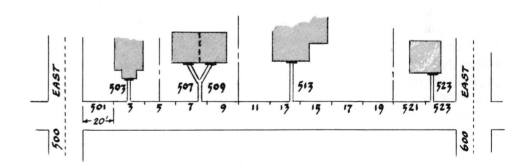

Measurements are made from grid line nearest the base line. Numbers are assigned to FRONT ENTRANCE.

Houses front on arterial street—access from marginal access street

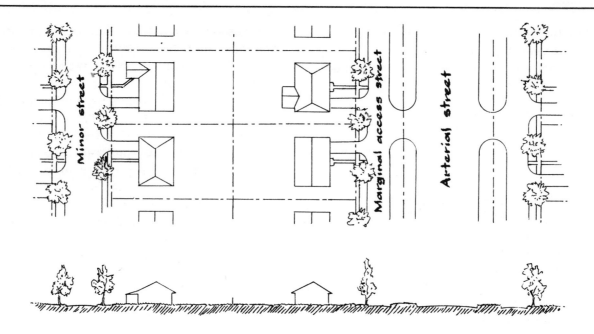

When houses must front on an arterial street, a marginal access street should be provided for these houses. This will eliminate any conflict between through and local circulation.

Houses front on minor street—access from minor street only

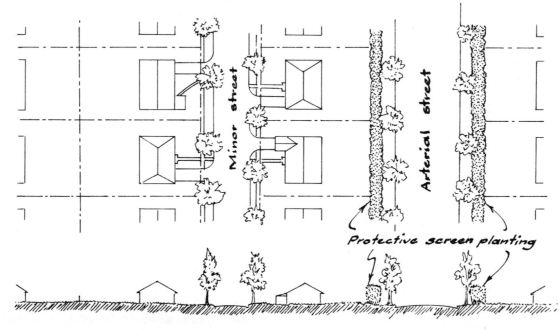

Houses should always front on a minor street. If the subdivision is properly designed, there will be a minimum of traffic on the minor street providing a maximum of privacy and safety.

SOURCE: Land Subdivision Regulations, Housing and Home Finance Agency, Washington, D. C.

DRIVEWAY LOCATIONS

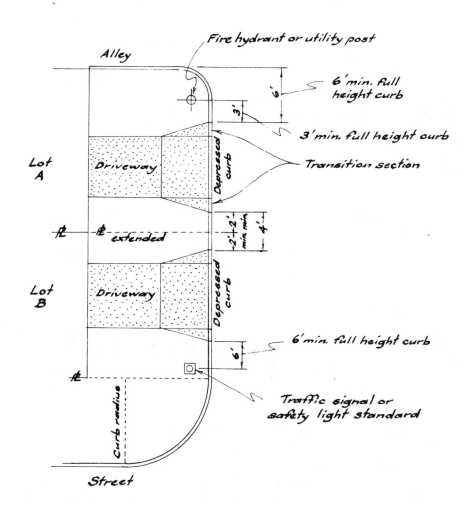

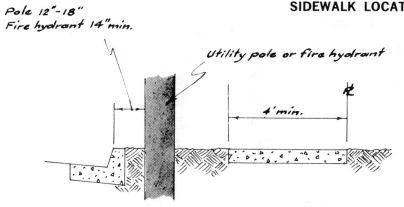

SIDEWALK LOCATIONS

Sidewalk adjacent to property line

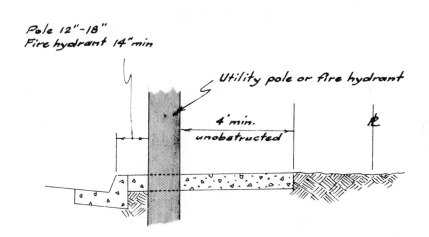

Sidewalk contiguous with curbing

Note: Other sidewalk dimensions, details, & specifications per standards of municipality in control.

SOURCE: Street and Urban Road Maintenance, Research Foundation, American Public Works Association

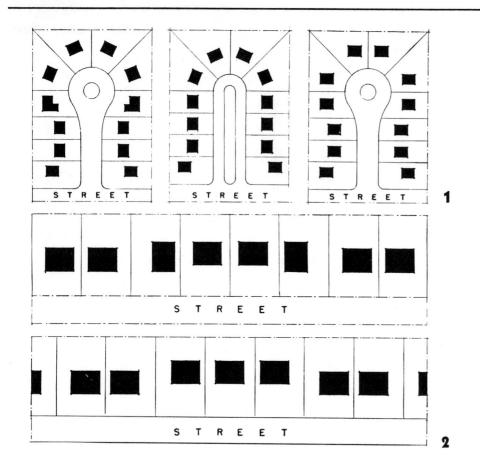

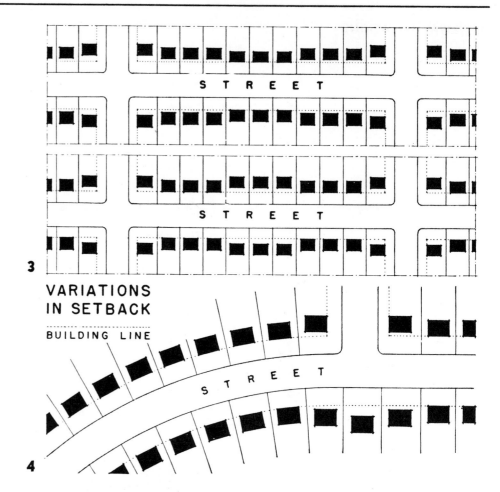

VARIATIONS IN SETBACK

BUILDING LINE

1. The location of houses on culs-de-sac should result in a well-arranged group of dwellings with an appearance of spaciousness. Especial care is required to avoid an unpleasant angular relationship of individual houses to those on either side. Congested appearance is avoided if not more than five houses front on the turnaround.

2. Variations in grouping of houses to further avoid monotony can be obtained by varying the widths of side yards. Where all houses on the street are located in the center of each lot, there is a monotonous regularity in spacing even though the exteriors are varied in design. Variations in the widths of side yards should be so arranged that an appearance of openness results through the increased space between groups of dwellings. Setback and side-yard variations should be considered in relation to the design of individual houses.

SOURCE: Principles of Planning Small Houses, Technical Bulletin #4 Federal Housing Administration

3. When streets are straight and all houses are set back equidistant from the street line, a monotonous street appearance usually results. This can be avoided by varying the setback of the houses from the street. The setback should apply to groups of houses and the variation from the required building line should seldom exceed ten feet—less than ten feet usually being desirable. Variation in the location of houses to preserve existing trees or other natural features of the site also will avoid monotony in street appearance.

4. When streets are decidedly curved, monotony resulting from locating houses equidistant from the street line is generally overcome due to the changing vista of houses built to a curving setback line. However, slight variations in setback of house groups may also be desirable.

The general practice of subdividing land for suburban expansion was based on the widely accepted urban gridiron pattern—streets at right angles, each block two lots deep, sometimes with an alley through the middle of the block, sometimes without.

This pattern is the easiest one for division of land for sale but not always the most efficient one for use, since the proportion of street area to lot area may be too high in relation to land use demands. Furthermore, this pattern may not be related to open space characteristics of an area—each parcel or land holding may be wholly or arbitrarily divided into a grid pattern without relation to other parcels (subdivision leap frogging) or without relation to natural ground form and grade.

Change in the straight gridiron pattern began to be evident in the 1930's, especially with the introduction of the curvilinear street, larger blocks and some public open space reservation. The Federal Housing Administration has had a large share in these changes in its requirements, published guides and standards for subdivisions, and advisory consultive service for review and revision of proposed subdivisions. (See Fig. 2)

The average lot size in subdivisions has steadily increased. Today ¼ acre is typical in many subdivisions. Two-thirds of all the vacant land in the New York region is zoned for half-acre lots or larger.

The densities are rather low and there is a good deal of open space—space that is not built upon—as illustrated by the accompanying table.

The kind of subdivision of relatively low density represents a good deal of open space—yard space and the associated street space make up a predominant part of the land use with only 5 to 25% given over to building use. The open space is divided into small pieces, and limited to immediate family use.

Air views or plans of subdivisions like these show the even spread of houses across the land. Each house is in the middle of the lot, a little more yard in back than in front. Each yard is probably much like the other, and the natural land form, as well as the tree, may have been bulldozed away. What remains is hundreds of little parcels all exactly alike, each with a house which differs little from its neighbor—the "straight vanilla" subdivision.

Cluster Development

A cluster development is one in which a number of dwelling units are grouped, leaving some land undivided for common use. It may mean grouping the same number of units allowed in a given subdivision or zoned area on smaller than usual or minimum lot, with the remainder of land available as a common area—the density remains the same, but some larger pieces of land, hopefully with some

SOURCE: *Where Not to Build*, Technical Bulletin 1 Bureau of Land Management Dept. of the Interior *Washington, D.C.,* *1968.*

interesting natural features such as a creek or wooded hillside, left undivided and uninvaded and open for common use. Cluster development will be found increasingly in use and may become the dominant pattern of residential development.

Common open space is the key element. This may be a recreation core or a park-like natural area.

Development costs are lower since there are fewer for developing and less linear feet of utilities for dwelling. Sewerage is cheaper and there is less runoff with cluster since there is less paving and more ground surface to absorb water. Cluster can also concentrate building where drainage can best be handled, leaving natural water courses and the drainage network in its natural state.

The open space element in cluster development in its best use is part of a general open space system, rather than a series or collection of isolated areas. The open spaces of the cluster pattern are far more effective and should be planned to connect with public open spaces such as parks and schools and with open space arrangements of other developments or subdivisions.

A key question is the ownership and management of the open space areas in cluster development. The common open space is primarily for the people of the development and while it may benefit the community at large, it should not be used as a substitute or alternative to other public spaces needed for parks, schools, and other civic facilities or improvements.

The cluster common area may be deeded to the public, or (as is considered best by some) owned cooperatively by the homeowner through a Homeowners Association, or maintained through the formation of a special district.

Comparative Residential Subdivisions

Lot Size	Net Density	Net Coverage	Place
5,000 sq. ft.	about 8 families/acre	about 30%	Lakewood-Long Beach, Calif.
7,500 sq. ft.	about 6 families/acre	about 17%	Port Charlotte, Fla.
10,000 sq. ft.	about 4 families/acre	about 12%	West Hartford, Conn.
20,000 sq. ft.	about 2 families/acre	about 8%	Fairfield, Conn.

Tunnard, Christopher, and Pushkarev, Boris. *Man-Made America*. (Yale University Press, New Haven, 1963) pp. 90–91.

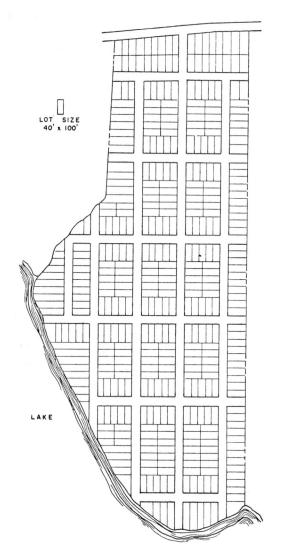

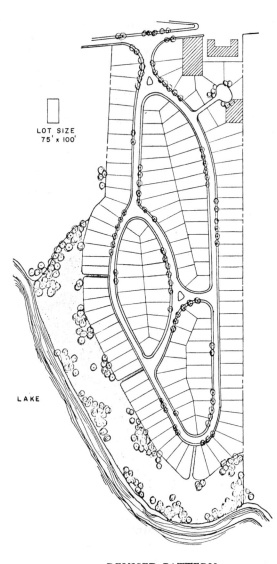

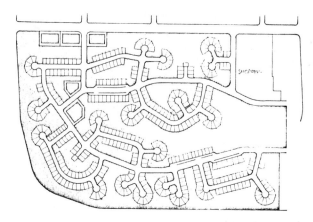

CLUSTER SUBDIVISION

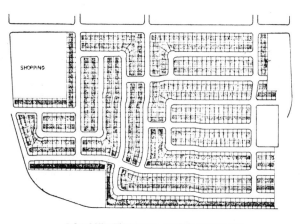

CONVENTIONAL SUBDIVISION

TYPICAL SUBDIVISION PATTERN

For this type of subdivision plan is marked by excessive amounts of street construction, lots blocking the shoreline, and no open space.

REVISED PATTERN

This revised plan, though of fewer building lots, provides amenities of better building lots, and preservation of the shoreline in community open space.

Alternative For Subdividing

Comparison of a Conventional Subdivision and a Cluster Subdivision

32	Acres in streets	24
22,500	Linear feet of street	16,055
29	Percent of site in streets	19
80	Acres in building sites	41
590	Dwelling units	604
0	Acres of usable open space	51

Excerpted from "The Common Green" brochure, limited edition published by Santa Clara County Planning Department, 1961.

PLANNED UNIT DEVELOPMENT

The planned unit development is slightly different than cluster, although the basic principle is similar. Both seek a more flexible approach to permit development of large areas as a whole. Cluster usually is limited to residential development, permitting a higher density if the resulting open space is legally permanently open. The advantages of cluster are also characteristic of planned unit development. A further advantage comes from a design freedom which is not possible under single lot–single building consideration.

Planned unit development is a broader concept than cluster. It may apply to commercial and industrial as well as residential development areas. In some cases a mixture of uses—one or more residential types of residence plus commercial—is allowed. A major difference between planned unit development and cluster is that the specific condition under which the development will be allowed are general in nature for planned unit development, and frequently not applied until actual plans are proposed. In this case, much is left to the discretion of the administrator, the review board, or other controlling authority.

Administrative discretion seems to be one of the larger problems of planned unit development. The real probelm is recognition of and a framework for relating planned development and comprehensive planning.

The planned unit development has three major characteristics:

1. Planned unit developments usually involve areas and undertakings of large scale, ranging from campus type developments planned as a whole to new towns.

2. They usually involve a mixture of uses and types. The single use or type falls more into the class of the more usual subdivision.

3. They usually involve stage-by-stage development over a relatively long period of time during which buildings, arrangements and uses may have to be replanned to meet the changes of requirements, technology, financing, or even concepts.

In the planning of the planned unit development, great emphasis can be given to the structuring of the plan in meaningful open spaces—roads, parks, and the other open spaces that make up an open space system—rather than on the rigid detailing of building development—in order to leave room for flexibility and change in building development, to provide different "mixtures" and to provide a basic control in stage by stage development.

THE MIX

Traditionally, the city, large and small, was a place of mixture. It brought together a wide variety of people and activities in a relatively limited space. People came to the city to be part of this mixture.

The desire to reduce congestion, the need to escape adverse effects of an unplanned and uncontrolled environment and the expansive growth of the urban areas were among the forces that led to a general separation of uses in zoning and otherwise. Segregation seemed to be in order in all respects.

Today there is a search for a freedom to mix and this is reflected to some degree in planning. The uniformity of suburban development has been under attack and there are an increasing number of examples of mixing of types and uses, especially in large scale development, the mixture of single family, town house and high rise apartment house; the provision of shipping, institutional and other non-residential uses in residential development. The planned unit development is an attempt to find a flexible means of re-introducing diversity and mixture in newer urban growth.

LAND USE INTENSITY (LUI) REQUIREMENTS

This section is concerned with the definitions and calculations required to satisfy the LUI requirements.

a. LUI According to Occupant Categories. The normal LUI is the intensity to be approximated in the average project. The lower part of the allowable range might be used for projects in rural areas. The upper part of the range should be used in some urban areas or where property must be acquired and land costs are high. In setting the LUI, consideration should be given not only to the current program but also to future programs and the relationship of the LUI chosen to the total available land for housing. The normal LUI and the acceptable ranges for all occupant categories are shown in Table 1.

b. Calculation. Page 226 shows the format and the chart to be used in making these calculations. Table 1 presents the same data in tabular form from LUI 3.0 to 4.5. While the chart is accurate to one decimal place for LUI and two places for FAR if greater accuracy is desired, interpolations can be made in Table 1 or substitutions made in the following formulas:

$$LUI + \frac{1.903 + \log FAR}{.301}$$

$$\log FAR + .301 \; LUI - 1.903$$

For instance if

$$FAR + 0.273,$$

then:

$$LUI + \frac{1.903 + 9.436 - 10.000}{.301} = 4.45$$

c. Project Boundaries. In establishing boundaries for computation of LUI numbers, the following criteria shall be observed.

1. Along Existing Streets. The boundary line shall follow the centerline of existing streets abutting the project. If a main thoroughfare (nonresidential street), serving not only the housing project but also other areas, is hazardous or noisy, the project boundary may be offset not more than 20 feet from the right-of-way. Any perimeter drainage should be included within this buffer zone if possible.

2. Along New Streets. The boundary shall follow the centerline of those new perimeter streets required to serve the housing project. However, the entire right-of-way shall be included within the contract limit line and in any computations made for land acquisition.

3. Along Undefined Boundaries. Where the boundaries of the site are not defined by roads or other boundaries, natural or man-made, the boundary shall be established at a distance of 40 feet from the backs or fronts of the housing units and 20 feet from the sides, or 20 feet from the backs or fronts of living units facing usable open spaces having reasonable expectancy of remaining open permanently.

d. Exclusions. Open areas should be so integrated with the project that it will be difficult to dedicate them to use for which they were not intended. Therefore, areas of a size and shape that make them suitable as a site for future housing, or for other buildings, shall not be included within the boundaries of the project. However, space may be included for carports and small laundry buildings, provided that the buildings are indicated on the site plans.

TABLE 1 LAND USE INTENSITY (LUI) RATIOS

LUI Land-Use Intensity	FAR Floor Area Ratio	OSR Open Space Ratio	LSR Livability Space Ratio	RSR Recreation Space Ratio
3.0	.100	8.0	6.5	.25
3.1	.107	7.4	5.8	.24
3.2	.115	6.9	5.2	.23
3.3	.123	6.4	4.7	.23
3.4	.132	5.9	4.2	.22
3.5	.141	5.5	3.8	.21
3.6	.152	5.1	3.5	.20
3.7	.162	4.8	3.3	.20
3.8	.174	4.4	3.0	.19
3.9	.187	4.2	2.8	.19
4.0	.200	3.8	2.6	.18
4.1	.214	3.6	2.4	.18
4.2	.230	3.3	.22	.17
4.3	.246	3.0	2.0	.16
4.4	.264	2.8	1.8	.16
4.5	.283	2.6	1.7	.15

"**1. Unusable Land.** Land not beneficial to residential use due to location or character such as swamps, drainage ditches, ravines, dense woods, and swales, and utility strips when their presence renders land unusable for residential use.

"**2. Nonresidential Land.** Land used for such purposes as maintenance buildings, fire stations and community use facilities such as swimming pools, baseball diamonds, tennis courts, or other developed sports areas. Boundaries for these facilities shall be established at exterior wall or fence faces or at the surfaced limits of parking or storage areas.

"**3. Residential Land Area.** Area within project boundaries, excluding unusable land and nonresidential land.

"**4. Floor Area.** The sum of area for residential use on the several floors of a living unit measured from the faces of the exterior walls; the floor area includes halls, lobbies, stairways, and elevator shafts, interior storage areas, and the basement or lowest story to extent used for residential purposes. The floor area does not include relatively open exterior balconies, any terraces, patios, atriums, porches, or balconies which are not covered; any garages or carports or any area used for mechanical equipment.

"**6. Building Area.** Consists of the floor area at ground level of all buildings occupying space within the residential land area. Included are any enclosed storage facilities, enclosed trash/garbage storage areas, garages, carports, whether partially or entirely open, covered porches, breezeways, et cetera. In making computations, consideration should be given to the total ground area covered by enclosed building space. Areas are measured from the faces of the exterior line of omitted walls at the mean-grade level of each building. Fenced or otherwise enclosed patios are excluded from the computations as are all roof overhangs.

"**9. Car Movement Area.** One-half of abutting streets plus on-site streets and roads, aprons, and drives to individual garages or carports where drives are too short for additional car storage.

"**10. Open Car Storage Area.** Parking courts and drives to individual garages and carports where drives are large enough for additional car storage. Excludes area of garages and carports included in computing Building Area and areas not surfaced for vehicular traffic, such as islands.

"**13. Recreation Space.** Livability space countable as recreation space. Open green area may be counted as recreation space if the space has minimum area of 10,000 square feet with an average dimension of not less than 100 feet and no dimension less than 50 feet. In those cases where project boundaries must be described artificially, and where perpetuity exists adjacent to these boundaries, areas with a maximum depth of 100 feet, beginning at a point 20 feet away from any residential wall containing windows on the ground floor, or beginning at the face of any windowless wall may be included in the calculation of the recreation space. However, such recreation space outside of the project boundary is not considered within the project LUI computation.

"**16. Number of Car Spaces.** Including garages, carports, and driveways to individual garages or carports capable of parking one or two cars (normally 1.5 parking spaces per living unit will be provided, but this does not preclude a greater number where costs, criteria, or siting permit)."

Housing Types and Open Areas

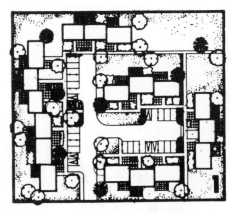

1 18 1-STORY TOWNHOUSES

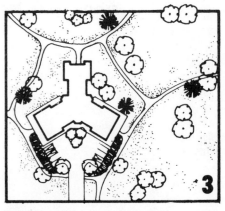

2 18 2-STORY TOWNHOUSES

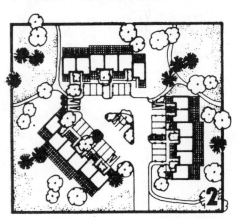

3 1 18-UNIT MULTI

	1	**2**	**3**
UNITS	18	18	18
LA	104,000	104,000	104,000
BA	24,390	14,208	11,750
FA	20,790	23,332	25,530
FAR	0.20	0.22	0.25
OS	79,610	89,792	92,250
OSR	3.8	3.8	3.6
LUI	4.0	4.0	4.3

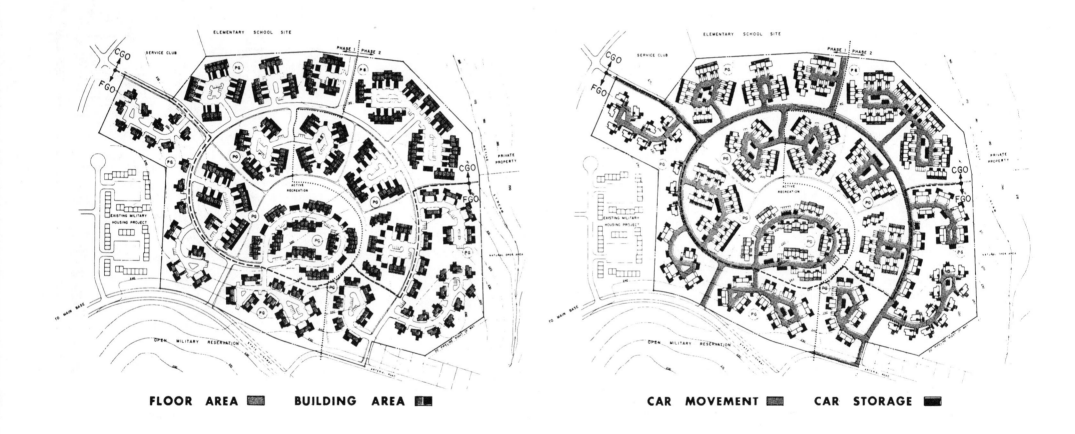

FLOOR AREA ▓ **BUILDING AREA** ▮▮

CAR MOVEMENT ▓ **CAR STORAGE** ▬

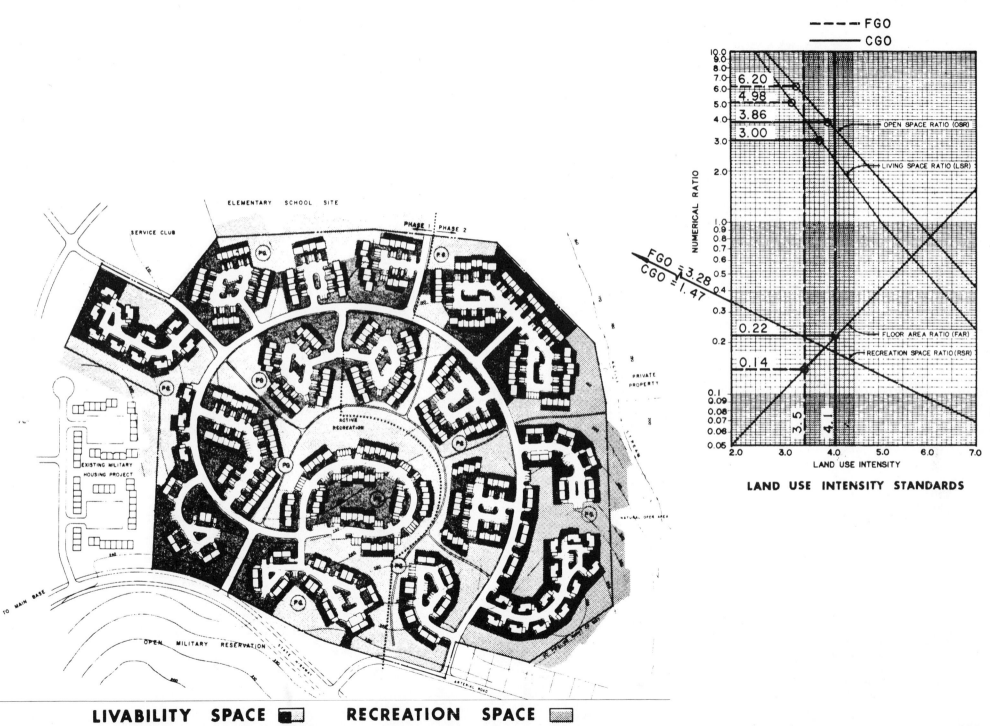

FGO
CGO

6.20
4.98
3.86
3.00

OPEN SPACE RATIO (OSR)

LIVING SPACE RATIO (LSR)

FGO = 3.28
CGO = 1.47

NUMERICAL RATIO

0.22
0.14

FLOOR AREA RATIO (FAR)

RECREATION SPACE RATIO (RSR)

3.5   4.1

LAND USE INTENSITY

LAND USE INTENSITY STANDARDS

ELEMENTARY SCHOOL SITE

SERVICE CLUB

PHASE 1   PHASE 2

EXISTING MILITARY
HOUSING PROJECT

ACTIVE
RECREATION

PRIVATE
PROPERTY

NATURAL OPEN AREA

TO MAIN BASE

OPEN MILITARY RESERVATION

STATE HIGHWAY

ARTERIAL ROAD

LIVABILITY SPACE ■   **RECREATION SPACE** ▨

Form for Land Use Intensity Computations

Chart for Land Use Intensity Computations

LAND USE INTENSITY COMPUTATIONS

Installation_____ FY_____ Occupant Category_____

A. PROJECT COMPOSITION:

HOUSE TYPE	NUMBER	FOLIO TYPE	FLOOR AREA TOTAL GROSS SQ. FT.
2 BR	_____	_____	_____
2 BR	_____	_____	_____
3 BR	_____	_____	_____
3 BR	_____	_____	_____
3 BR	_____	_____	_____
3 BR	_____	_____	_____
4 BR	_____	_____	_____
4 BR	_____	_____	_____
Total	_____		_____

B. RATIOS

(Taken from curves for Land Use Intensity Standards.)

	REQUIRED FOR COMPUTED LUI	ACTUAL FOR PROJECT
Land-use Intensity (LUI)	xxxxxx°	LUI _____
Floor Area Ratio (FAR)	Maximum FAR _____	FAR _____
Open Space Ratio (OSR)	Minimum OSR _____	OSR _____
Livability Space Ratio (LSR)	Minimum LSR _____	LSR _____
Recreation Space Ratio (RSR)	Minimum RSR _____	RSR _____
Car Ratio (CR)	Minimum CR _____	CR _____

C. COMPUTATION OF LUI AND RATIOS

(See Explanatory Notes)

ITEM	AREAS (SQ. FT.) AND RATIOS
1. Unusable Land	_____
2. Non-residential Land	_____
3. Residential Land Area (LA)	_____
4. Floor Area (FA)	_____
5. Floor Area Ratio (FAR) FA ÷ LA	_____
6. Building Area (BA)	_____
7. Open space (OS) LA − BA	_____
8. Open Space Ratio (OSR) OS ÷ FA	_____
9. Car Movement Area	_____
10. Open Car Storage Area	_____
11. Livability Space (LS) OS − (9 + 10)	_____
12. Livability Space Ratio (LSR) LS ÷ FA	_____
13. Recreation Space (RS)	_____
14. Recreation Space Ratio (RSR) RS ÷ FA	_____
15. Number of Living Units	_____
16. Number of Car Spaces	_____
17. Car Ratio (CR) 16 ÷ 15	_____

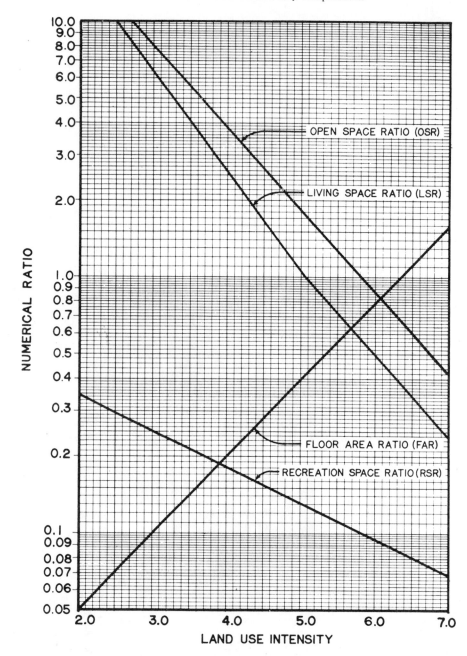

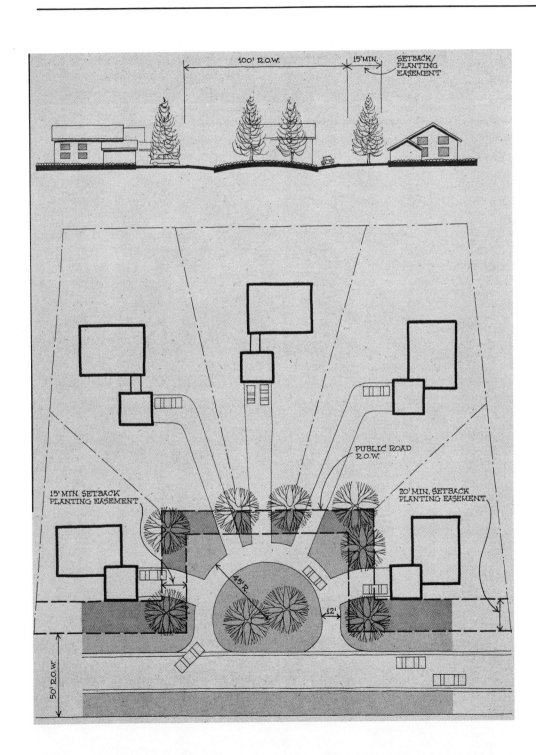

The new town is Gananda, and it is being built on almost 10,000 acres outside of Rochester, N.Y. Its single-family clusters, shown here and on the next two pages, range in density from just under three per acre to five per acre. And when these clusters are combined with duplex, fourplex and townhouse clusters, the result is a project with an astonishing amount of open land.

The cluster layout shown here creates a density of 2.75 units per acre and is used mostly for houses priced from $50,000 up. Instead of a conventional cul-de-sac, a small, one-way loop takes traffic off the collector road; long driveways, acceptable in houses of this price range, lead from the loop to the houses.

In place of the usual planting strip between street and sidewalks (there are no sidewalks), there is a 15′ planting easement abutting the public right of way. This takes the landscaping out of the way of piled-up snow and also adds to the privacy of the houses. Maintenance of the planting areas, including the island inside the loop, is handled by a homeowners' association.

SOURCE: House & Home. *Oct. 1973.*

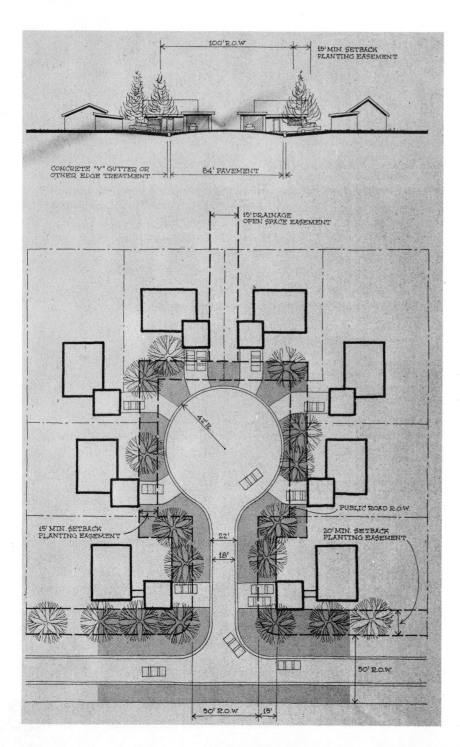

The density of this type of cluster in Gananda is about 3.8 units per acre, and there are marked changes from the cluster shown on the previous page.

The cul-de-sac must now serve eight driveways, not five, so a longer road and a conventional turnaround are used. There is no island in the turnaround—a concession to snowplowing and also a means of keeping the paved area relatively small. Note that the diameter of the circle is only 84'—smaller than many municipalities will allow, but ample for fire trucks and moving vans.

The increased impervious cover now makes it necessary to put a drainage easement at the rear of the cluster where it can lead into the common area. However, the volume of storm water should be much less than if the eight houses fronted on a collector street in the usual manner.

The cul-de-sac itself is a public right of way, so all road maintenance will be done by the municipality. The 15' planting easement, maintained by the homeowners' association, remains.

SOURCE: House & Home. Oct. 1973.

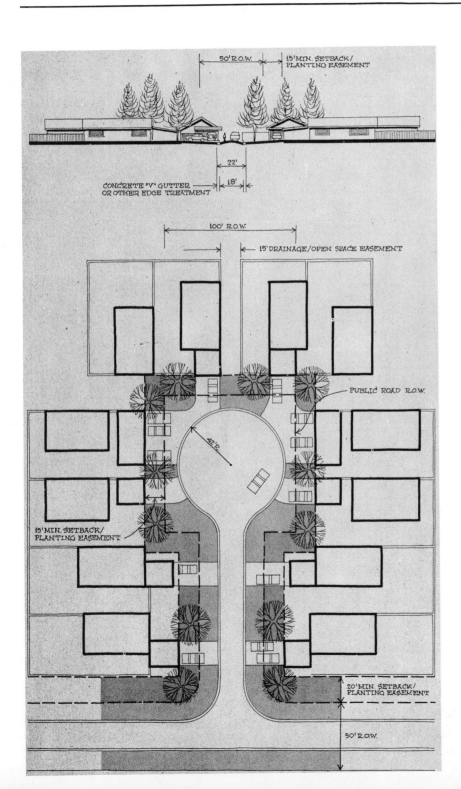

50' R.O.W.

15'MIN. SETBACK/
PLANTING EASEMENT

22'

18'

CONCRETE "V" GUTTER
OR OTHER EDGE TREATMENT

100' R.O.W.

15'DRAINAGE/OPEN SPACE EASEMENT

PUBLIC ROAD R.O.W.

42'R

15'MIN. SETBACK/
PLANTING EASEMENT

20'MIN. SETBACK/
PLANTING EASEMENT

50' R.O.W.

Patio houses represent the highest single-family density in Gananda; typically, 12 of them around a cul-de-sac like this one produce a density of 5½ units per acre. The lots are small—about 4,500 sq ft. But they are completely enclosed by a 6'-high wall, so every square foot is usable. And there is more privacy than most houses could get on a half-acre lot.

One of the biggest problems in most patio-house projects is the forbidding streetscape produced by lines of patio walls. In the cluster layout the width of the turnaround lessens this problem. And in the overall plan of Gananda, patio clusters are interspersed with other types so there is no heavy concentration of walled areas.

SOURCE: House & Home. *Oct. 1973.*

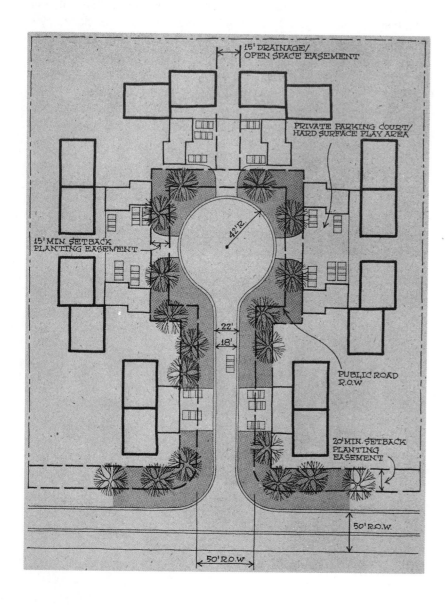

15' DRAINAGE/ OPEN SPACE EASEMENT

PRIVATE PARKING COURT/ HARD SURFACE PLAY AREA

42'R.

15' MIN. SETBACK PLANTING EASEMENT

22'

18'

PUBLIC ROAD R.O.W.

20' MIN. SETBACK PLANTING EASEMENT

50' R.O.W.

50' R.O.W.

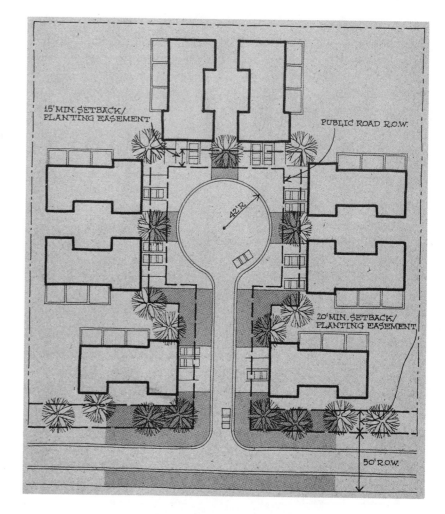

15' MIN. SETBACK/ PLANTING EASEMENT

PUBLIC ROAD R.O.W.

42'R.

20' MIN. SETBACK/ PLANTING EASEMENT

50' R.O.W.

The two clusters shown here are not for single-family houses, but for duplexes and fourplexes. They are included because they demonstrate the versatility of the cluster, and because they are basic elements of Gananda's planning which combines relatively high overall density with a heavy proportion of single-family units.

The duplexes, at the left, create a density of 4.2 units per acre, and are sold on fee-simple lots. The fourplexes, at the right, have a density of nine per acre, and are sold as condominiums.

Not shown, but also part of the project, are townhouse clusters on the same type of culs-de-sac and with densities roughly the same as the fourplex clusters.

SOURCE: House & Home. Oct. 1973.

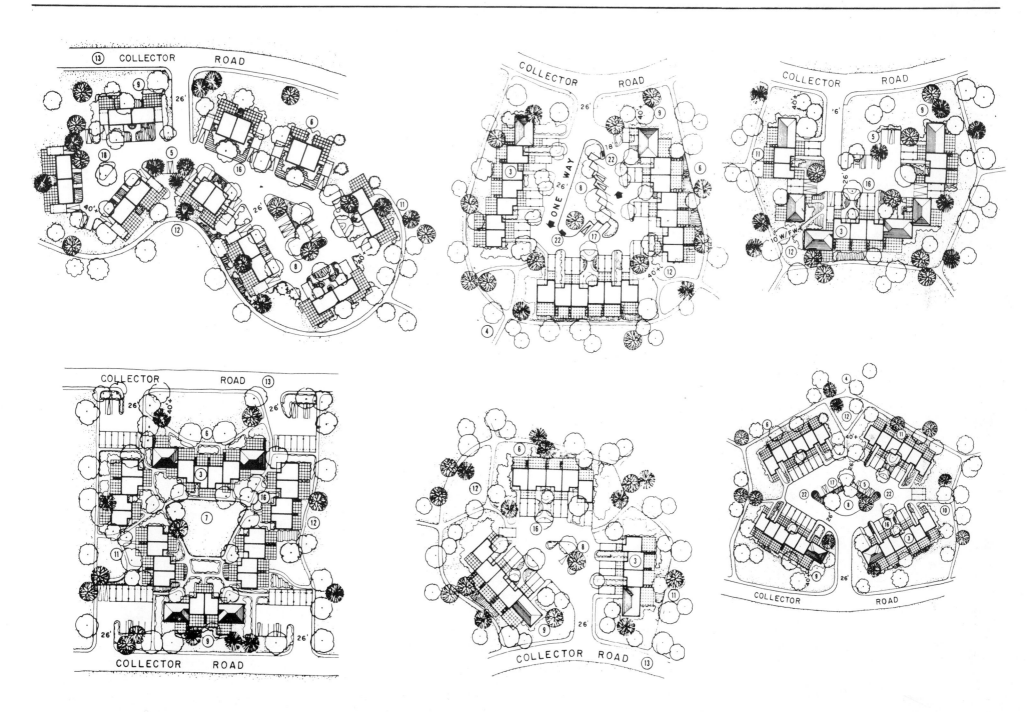

SOURCE: *Design Manual—Family Housing, Dept. of the Navy, Naval Facilities Engineering Command, Washington, D.C. 1971.*

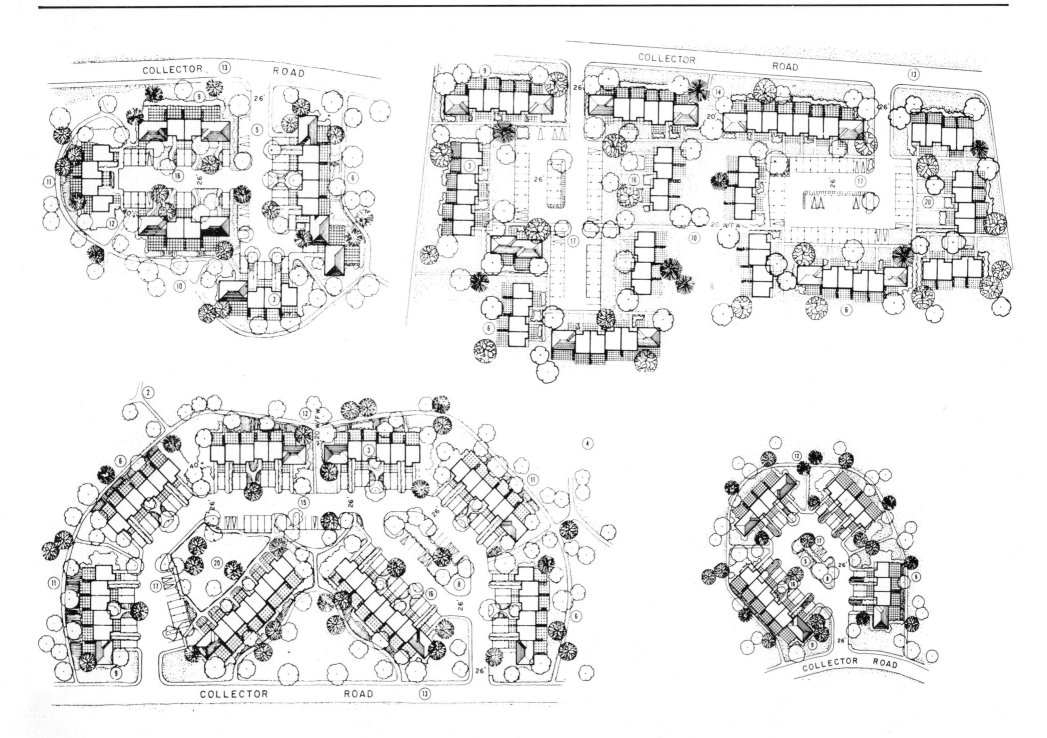

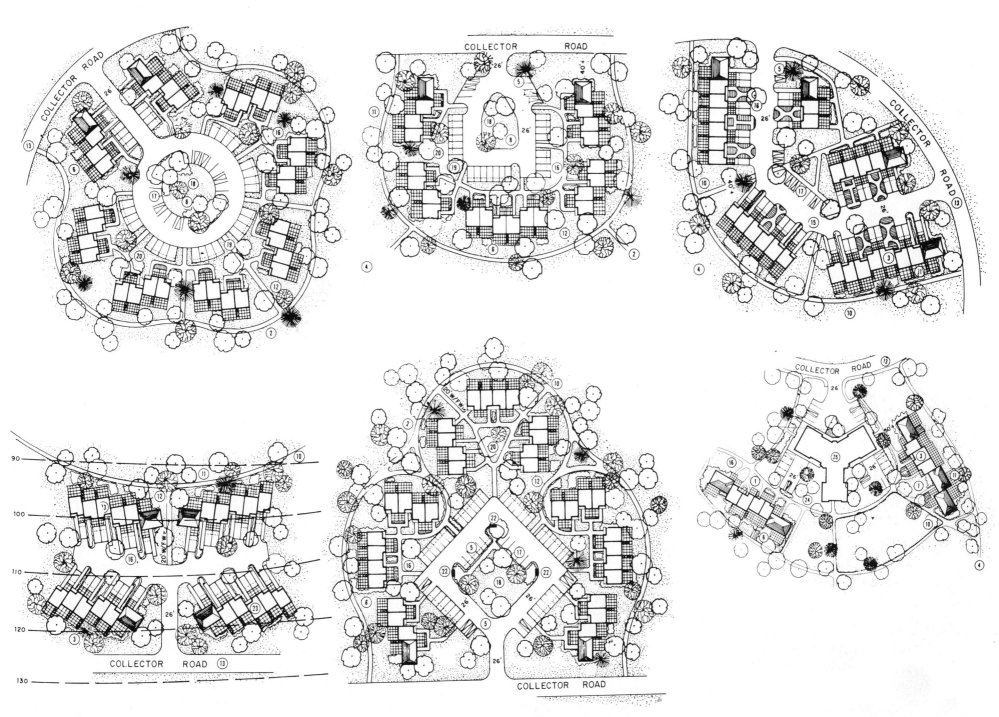

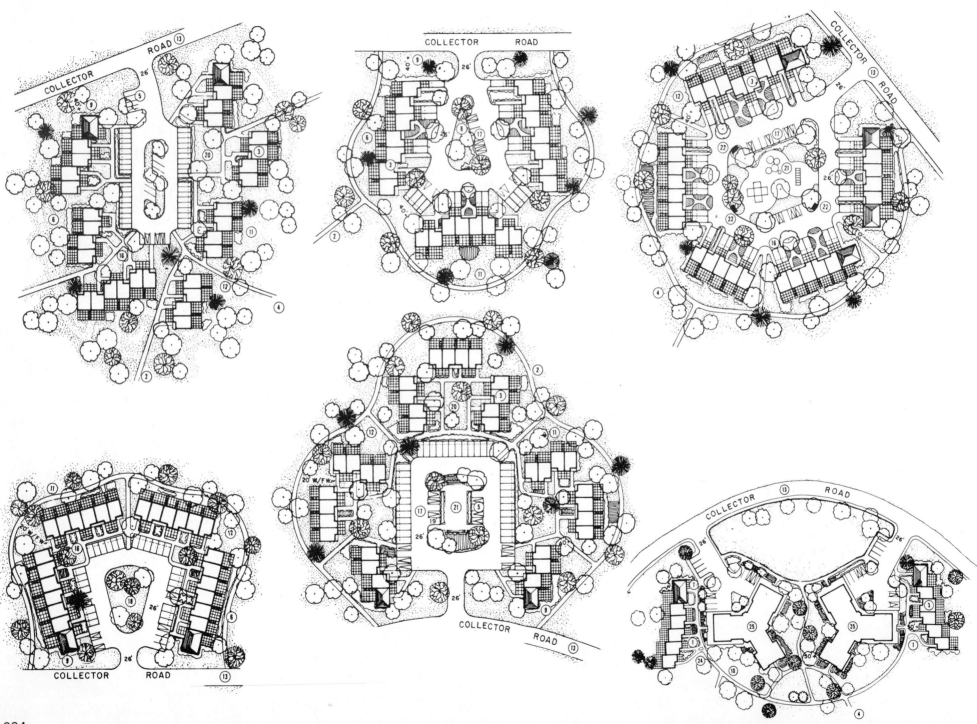

VEHICULAR CIRCULATION

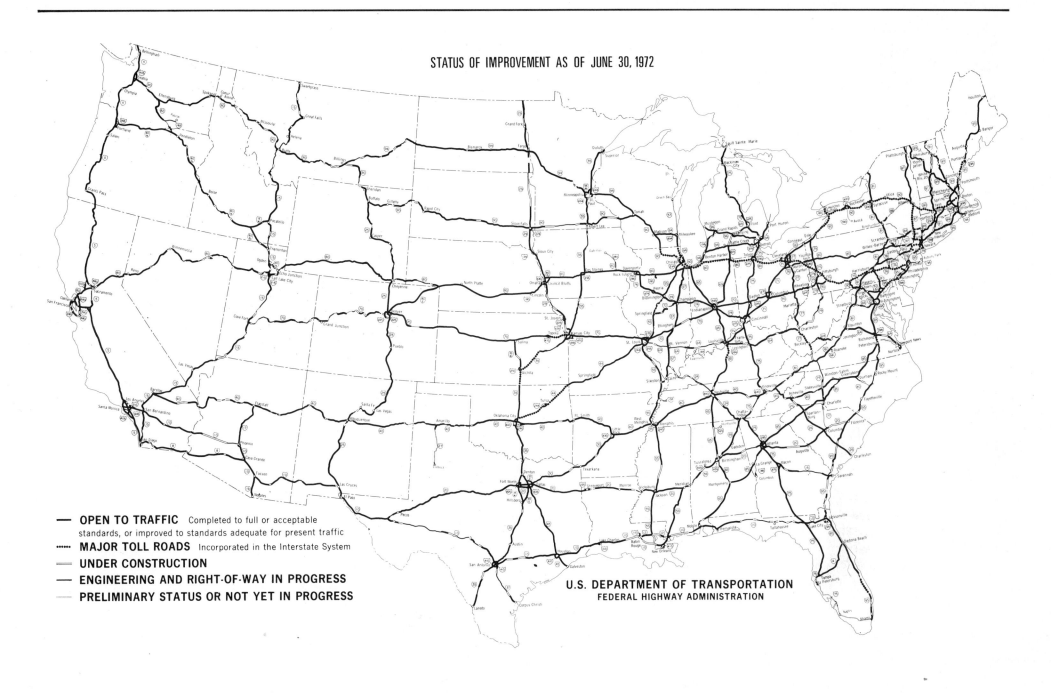

STATUS OF IMPROVEMENT AS OF JUNE 30, 1972

OPEN TO TRAFFIC Completed to full or acceptable standards, or improved to standards adequate for present traffic

MAJOR TOLL ROADS Incorporated in the Interstate System

UNDER CONSTRUCTION

ENGINEERING AND RIGHT-OF-WAY IN PROGRESS

PRELIMINARY STATUS OR NOT YET IN PROGRESS

U.S. DEPARTMENT OF TRANSPORTATION
FEDERAL HIGHWAY ADMINISTRATION

HIGHWAY CLASSIFICATION

Highway systems are grouped into a number of different classifications for administrative, planning, and design purposes. The Federal Aid financing system, state-county-city's administrative systems, and commercial-industrial-residential-recreational systems are examples of the variety of highway classifications.

In the most basic classification system for design work, highways and streets are grouped into: (1) interstate, primary (excluding interstate), secondary, and tertiary road classes in rural areas, and (2) expressway, arterial, collector, and local road classes in urban areas. These classifications usually carry with them a set of suggested minimum design standards which are in keeping with the importance of the system and are governed by the specific transportation services the system is to perform. The principal consideration for designating roads into systems are the travel desires of the public, land-access requirements based on existing and future land use, and continuity of the system. Four basic purposes of urban street systems have been suggested:

1. Expressway system (including freeways and parkways)—providing for expeditious movement of large volumes of through traffic between areas and across the city, and not intended to provide land-access service.

2. Major arterial system—providing for the through traffic movement between areas and across the city, and direct access to abutting property; subject to necessary control of entrances, exists, and curb use.

3. Collect or street system—providing for traffic movement between major arterials and local streets, and direct access to abutting property.

4. Local street system—providing for direct access to abutting land, and for local traffic movements.

These basic purposes of city street systems are similar to those of rural interstate, primary, secondary, and tertiary highways, respectively, so far as the various degrees of accommodation of through traffic and land access is concerned. However, regional as well as national highway transportation requirements must be met by rural highways. The Tables compare the overall criteria of urban street and rural highway classifications.

The principles and elements of geometric design for both urban and rural facilities are generally the same. However, to meet urban and rural traffic demands, design details are often varied because speeds, traffic composition, lengths and purposes of trips, etc., are not the same.

SOURCE: Standards for Street Facilities and Services, Procedure Manual 7A, National Committee on Urban Transportation, Public Administration Service, Chicago, 1958, p. 11.

URBAN STREET CLASSIFICATION CRITERIA

Element	System			
	Expressway	Major Arterial	Collector	Local
Service function:				
Movement	primary	primary	equal	secondary
Access	none	secondary	equal	primary
Principal trip length	over 3 miles	over 1 mile	under 1 mile	under ½ mile
Use by transit	express	regular	regular	none, except C.B.D.
Linkage:				
Land uses	major generators & C.B.D.	secondary generators & C.B.D.	local areas	individual sites
Rural highways	interstate & state primary	state primary & secondary	county roads	none
Spacing	1-3 miles	1 mile	½ mile	.....
Percentage of system	0-8	20-35		65-80

RURAL ROAD CLASSIFICATION CRITERIA*

Element	System			
	Interstate	Primary	Secondary	Tertiary
Service function:				
Movement	primary	primary	equal	secondary
Access	controlled	secondary	equal	primary
Linkage to:				
Geographic	major cities	smaller cities	smaller cities & regions	farm-to-market
Urban streets	expressways	expressways & major arterials	major arterials & collectors	collectors & local
Percentage of system	2	17	10	71

*Includes surfaced roads only.

Type of Facility	Function and Design Features	Spacing	Widths		Desirable Maximum Grades	Speed	Other Features
			R.O.W.	Pavement			
Freeways	Provide regional and metropolitan continuity and unity. Limited access; no grade crossings; no traffic stops.	Variable; related to regional pattern of population and industrial centers	200–300'	Varies; 12' per lane; 8–10' shoulders both sides of each roadway; 8'–60' median strip.	3%	60 mph	Depressed, at grade, or elevated. Preferably depressed, through urban areas. Require intensive landscaping, service roads, or adequate rear lot building set-back lines (75') where service roads are not provided.
Expressways	Provide metropolitan and city continuity and unity. Limited access; some channelized grade crossings and signals at major intersections. Parking prohibited.	Variable; generally radial or circumferential	200–250'	Varies 12' per lane; 8-10' shoulders; 8-30' median strip.	4%	50 mph	Generally at grade. Requires landscaping and service roads or adequate rear lot building set-back lines (75') where service roads are not provided.
Major Roads (Major Arterials)	Provide unity throughout contiguous urban area. Usually form boundaries for neighborhoods. Minor access control; channelized intersections; parking generally prohibited.	1½ to 2 miles	120–150'	84' maximum for 4 lanes, parking and median strip.	4%	35–45 mph	Require 5' wide detached sidewalks in urban areas, planting strips (5'–10' wide or more) and adequate building set-back lines (30') for buildings fronting on street; 60' for buildings backing on street.
Secondary Roads (Minor Arterials)	Main feeder streets. Signals where needed; stop signs on side streets. Occasionally form boundaries for neighborhoods.	¾ to 1 mile	80'	60'	5%	35–40 mph	Require 5' wide detached sidewalks, planting strips between sidewalks and curb 5' to 10' or more, and adequate building set-back lines (30').
Collector Streets	Main interior streets. Stop signs on side streets.	¼ to ½ mile	64'	44' (2–12' traffic lanes; 2–10' parking lanes)	5%	30 mph	Require at least 4' wide detached sidewalks; vertical curbs; planting strips are desirable; building set-back lines 30' from right of way.
Local Streets	Local service streets. Non-conducive to through traffic.	at blocks	50'	36' where street parking is permitted.	6%	25 mph	Sidewalks at least 4' in width for densities greater than 1 d.u./acre, and curbs and gutters.
Cul-de-sac	Street open at only one end, with provision for a turn-around at the other.	only wherever practical	50' (90' dia. turn-around)	30'–36' (75' turn-around)	5%		Should not have a length greater than 500 feet.

SOURCE: George Nez, Standards for New Urban Development–The Denver Background, Reprinted by Permission of Urban Land, Vol. 20, No. 5, Urban Land Institute, 1200 18th Street, N.W., Washington, D.C.

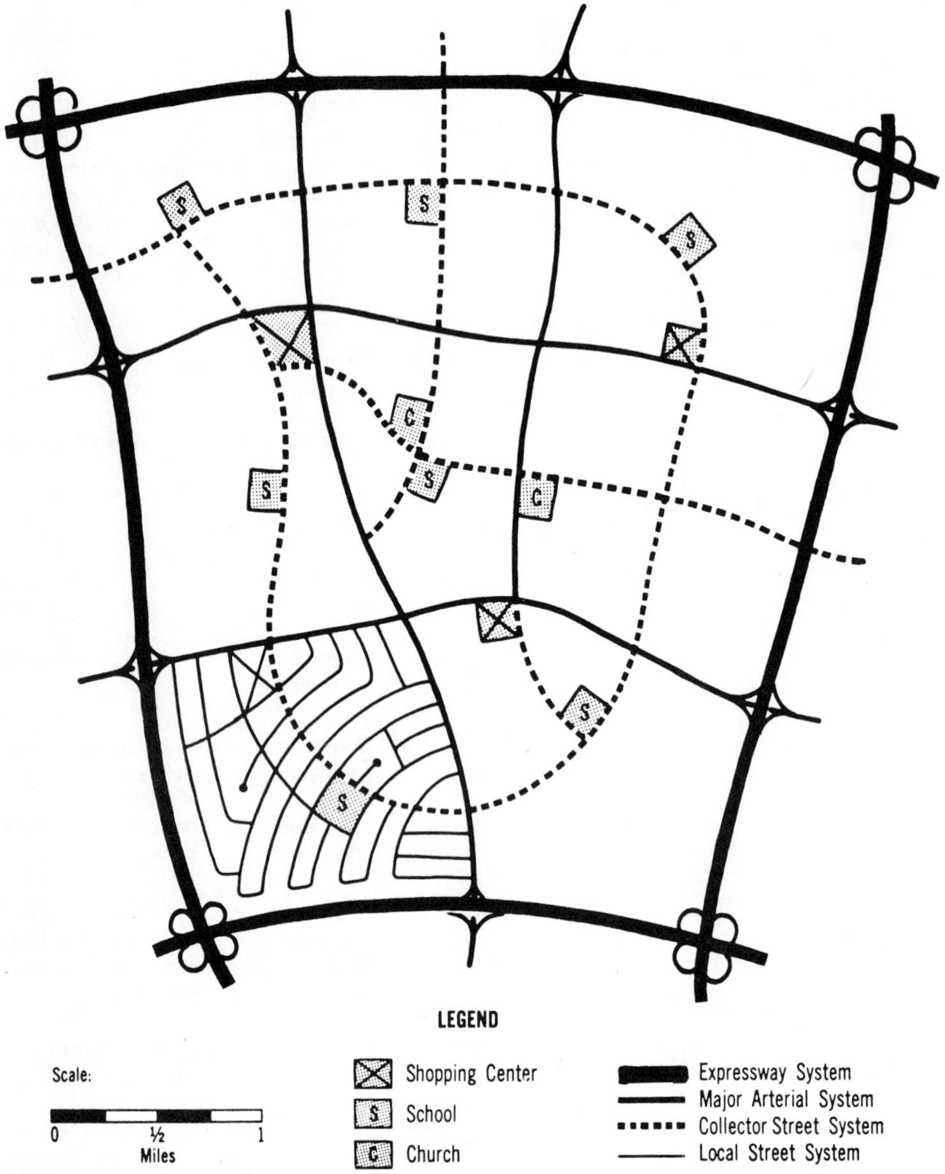
S
S
S
S
S
S
S
C
C
LEGEND
Scale:
0
½
1
Miles
Shopping Center
School
Church
Expressway System
Major Arterial System
Collector Street System
Local Street System

SUMMARY OF STREET CLASSIFICATION CRITERIA

Element	System: Expressway	Major Arterial	Collector	Local
Service Function				
movement	primary	primary	equal	secondary
access	none	secondary	equal	primary
principal trip length	over 3 miles	over 1 mile	under 1 mile	under 1/2 mile
use by transit	express	regular	regular	none, except C.B.D.
Linkage				
Land Uses	major generators & C.B.D.	secondary generators & C.B.D.	local areas	individual sites
Rural Highways	interstate & state primary	state primary & secondary	county roads	none
Spacing	1-3 miles	1 mile	1/2 mile	----
Percentage of System	0 - 8		20 - 35	65 - 80

SOURCE: Standards for Street Facilities and Services, Procedure Manual 7A, National Committee on Urban Transportation, Public Administration Service, Chicago, Ill. 1958.

TRAFFIC DESIGN ELEMENTS

Traffic element	Explanation and nation-wide percentage or factor
Average daily traffic: ADT	Average 24-hour volume for a given year; total for both directions of travel, unless otherwise specified. Directional or one-way ADT is an average 24-hour volume in one direction of travel only.
Current traffic	ADT composed of existing trips, including attracted traffic, that would use the improvement if opened to traffic today (current year specified.)
Future traffic	ADT that would use a highway in the future (future year specified). Future traffic may be obtained by adding generated traffic, normal traffic growth, and development traffic to current traffic, or by multiplying current traffic by the traffic projection factor.
Traffic projection factor	Future traffic divided by current traffic. General range, 1.5 to 2.5 for 20-year period.
Design hour volume: DHV	Future hourly volume for use in design (two-way unless otherwise specified), usually the 30th highest hourly volume of the design year (30HV) or equivalent, the approximate value of which can be obtained by the application of the following percentages to future traffic (ADT). The design hour volume, when expressed in terms of all types of vehicles, should be accompanied by factor T, the percentage of trucks during peak hours. Or, the design hour volume may be broken down to the number of passenger vehicles and the number of trucks.
Relation between DHV and ADT: K	DHV expressed as a percentage of ADT, both two-way; normal range 12 to 18. Or, DHV expressed as a percentage of ADT, both one-way; normal range, 16 to 24.
Directional distribution: D	One-way volume in predominant direction of travel expressed as a percentage of two-way DHV. General range, 50 to 80. Average, 67.
Composition of traffic: T	Trucks (exclusive of light delivery trucks) expressed as a percentage of DHV. Average 10 to 12.

DESIGN HOUR VOLUMES
TYPICAL TRAFFIC-FLOW DIAGRAMS

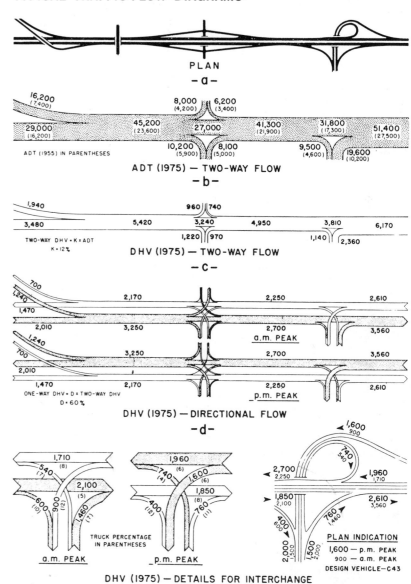

SOURCE: *A Policy on Geometric Design of Rural Highways, American Association of State Highway Officials, Washington, D.C., 1954. A Policy of Arterial Highways in Urban Areas, American Association of State Highway Officials, Washington, D.C., 1960.*

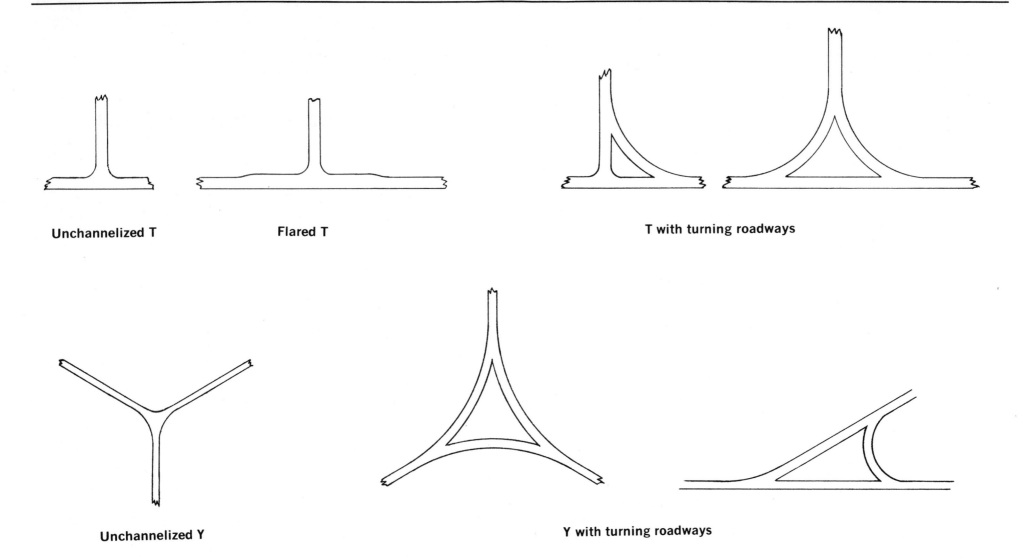

Unchannelized T **Flared T** **T with turning roadways**

Unchannelized Y **Y with turning roadways**

3 leg intersections

At-Grade Intersections. Most highways intersect at grade. At-grade intersections should provide for anticipated turning and crossing movements. Many factors enter into the choice of type of intersection, but the principal controls are the design hour volume of traffic, the character of traffic (both through and turning), and the design speed.

Basic types of at-grade intersections are T or Y (three-leg), four-leg, and rotary. In a particular case the type is determined primarily by the number of intersection legs, the physical controls of topography, the traffic pattern (traffic fluctuation), and the desired type of operation.

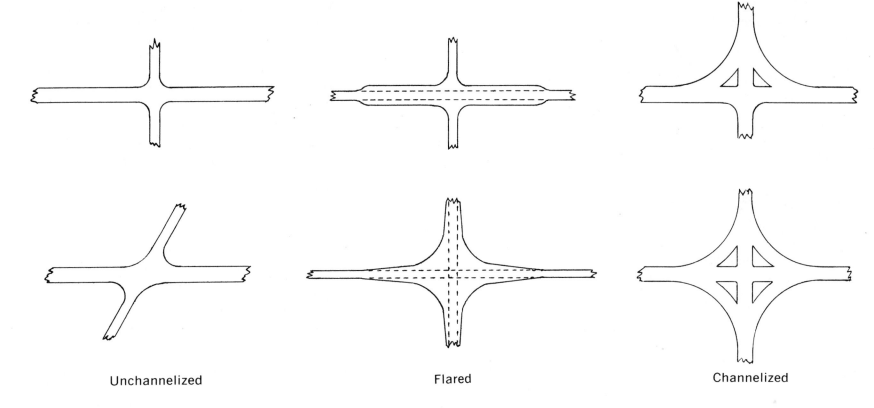

Unchannelized   Flared   Channelized

4 leg intersections

Three-leg (T or Y) and four-leg intersections may be plain flared, or channelized. A *flared* intersection is one in which the number of traffic lanes or the pavement width exceeds the number of lanes or the width of the normal section of highway. A *rotary* intersection is one in which all traffic merges into, and emerges from, a one-way road around a central island. It is a form of channelized intersection.

Rotaries are not regularly included in newly designed roads, but they are still used where the amount of turning traffic approaches or exceeds the through volume, and where more than four intersection legs would otherwise produce complex arrangement or difficult operation. The use of rotaries should be restricted to design hour volumes (total entering the intersection from all legs) of 3000 vehicles or less. Rotaries are generally considered undesirable from an operational standpoint because of the high number of weaving movements which must be made in a relatively short distance.

Multileg intersection

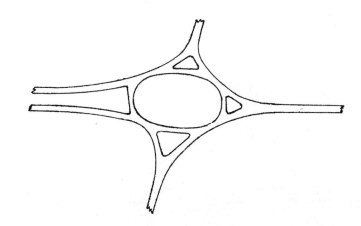

Rotary intersection

243

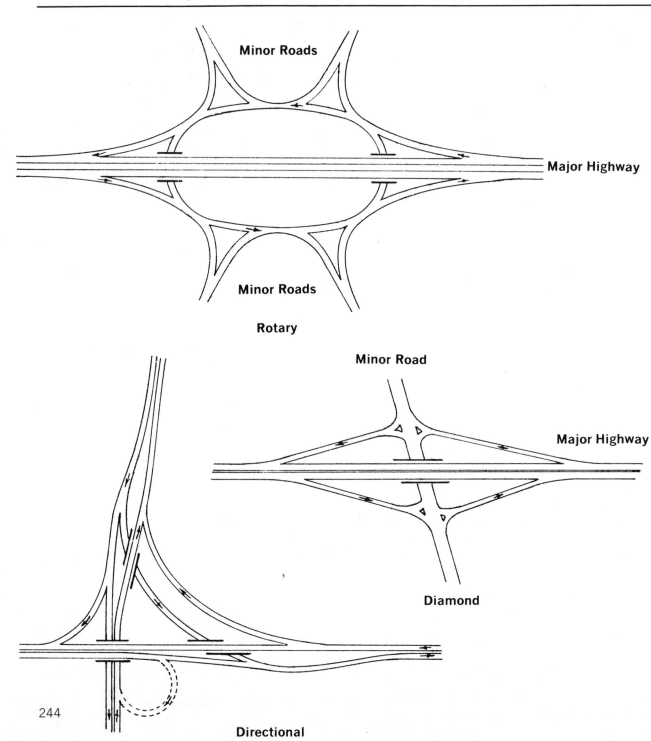

Minor Roads

Major Highway

Minor Roads

Rotary

Minor Road

Major Highway

Diamond

Directional

Interchanges

The volume of traffic that can pass through an intersection can approach or equal the sum of the open-road capacities of two intersecting highways if the roadways are placed at different levels, thus enabling through traffic on both highways to flow without interruption. With connecting roadways for the turning movements, and adequate facilities for turning vehicles to slow down or speed up clear of through-traffic lanes, all traffic can proceed through the insection with little or no interference.

The type of grade separation, or interchange type, and its design, is influenced by many factors, but those of greatest importance are: design hour volumes, character of traffic, design speed, topography, available right-of-way, and cost.

There are several basic interchange forms, or patterns of ramps, for turning movements at a grade separation. Their application to a particular site is determined by the number of intersection legs, the expected volumes of through and turning movements, and the physical controls of topography.

Three-leg interchanges have the overall geometric form of a T (or trumpet). These are shown in general form as items (a) and (b) of Figure 00.

The most common four-leg interchange is the *cloverleaf*. The cloverleaf shown in Figure 3-10(d) has a full complement of ramps, with a separate one-way ramp for each turning movement. Direct left turns are not possible. Drivers desiring to turn left are required to travel beyond the point of through-road intersection, and to turn right through about 270 degrees, before gaining the desired direction. This is an undesirable feature of the cloverleaf design.

The term *partial cloverleaf* designates those layouts with less than a full complement of ramps. In the partial cloverleaf shown in Figure 00 ramps are shown in two quadrants. All movements are provided for, but left turns at grade are required on the minor road.

The *diamond* type of interchange, Figure 00, has four one-way ramps. It is especially adaptable to major-minor highway intersections with limited right-of-way. However, left turns from and into the minor road must be executed at grade on minor roads.

Directional interchanges are those having ramps which tend to follow the natural direction of traffic movement. [See Figure 00 for one example.] One or more of the left turn movements is handled by a direct, or nearly direct, connection between major cross roadways.

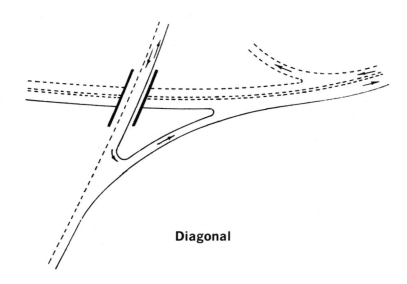

Diagonal

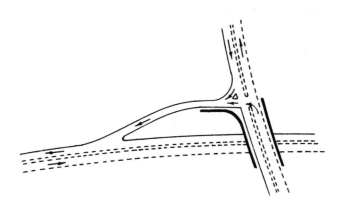

Parallel

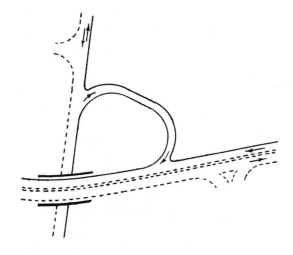

Loop

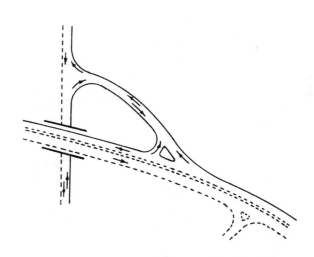

Cloverleaf: two-way

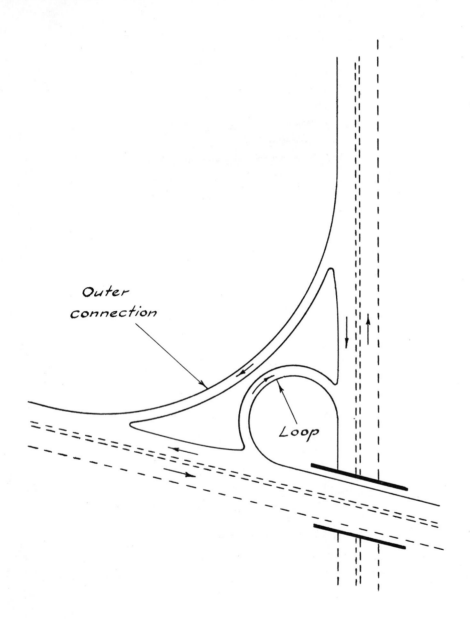

Cloverleaf: one-way

Outer connection

Loop

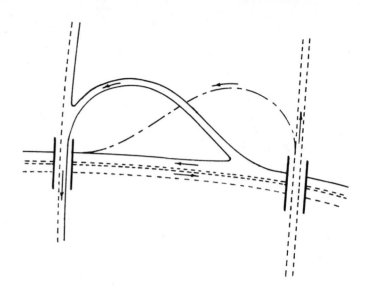

Semidirect connection

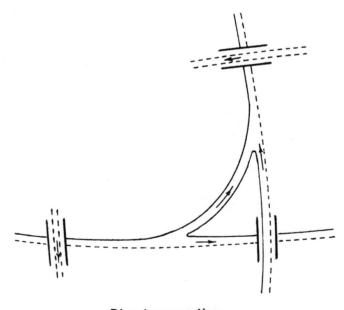

Direct connection

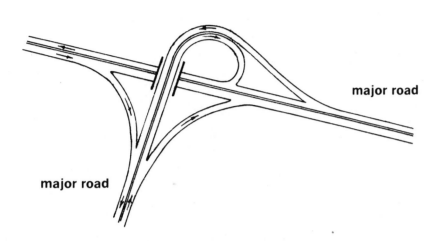

T or trumpet

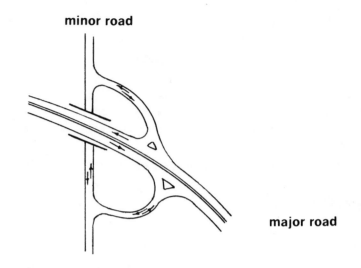

Partial cloverleaf
(ramps in two quadrants)

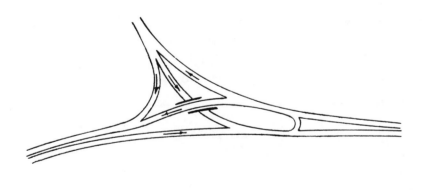

Y

all legs equal

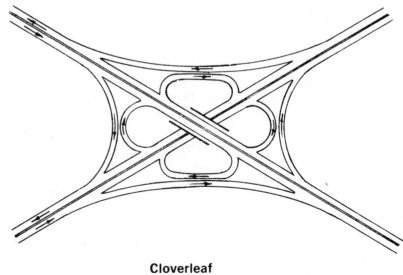

Cloverleaf
two major highways

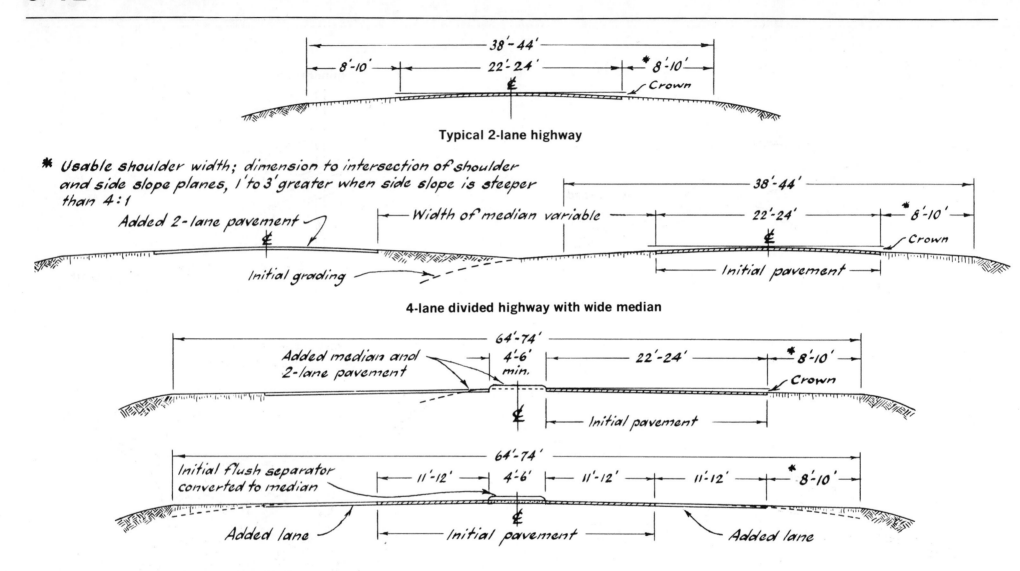

Typical 2-lane highway

4-lane divided highway with wide median

4-lane divided highway with narrow median

SOURCE: *A Policy on Geometric Design of Rural Highways, American Association of State Highway Officials, Washington, D.C., 1954.*

* Usable shoulder width; dimension to intersection of shoulder and side slope planes, 1' to 3' greater when side slope is steeper than 4:1

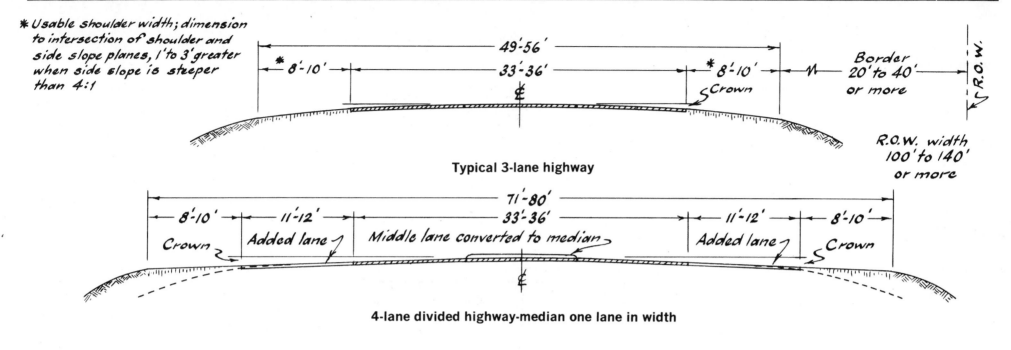

Typical 3-lane highway

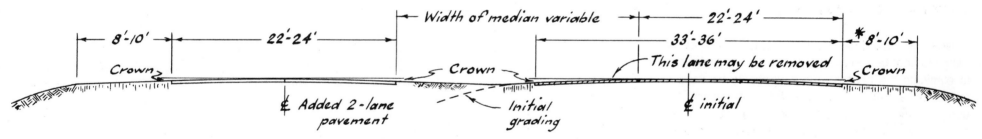

4-lane divided highway-median one lane in width

4-lane divided highway with wide median

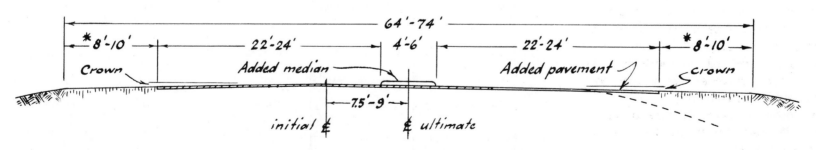

4-lane divided highway with narrow median

SOURCE: A Policy on Geometric Design of Rural Highways, American Association of State Highway Officials, Washington, D.C., 1954.

COMMON GUARDRAIL TYPES

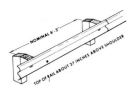

The W-section beam type guardrail is the most common type of roadside barrier in use today. Experience with the 6 ft. 3 in. post spacing indicates a need for a short piece of rail (about 1 ft.) at nonsplice post connections to reduce the possibility of shear failure of the rail element at the post.

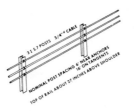

The three-strand cable weak post design illustrated was developed and tested by the State of New York. The application of this type rail must be limited to areas where rather large lateral deflections can be tolerated.

The box beam weak post design illustrated was developed and tested by the State of New York. The shorter post spacings are used where deflection may be a problem.

Examples of guardrails that have proven satisfactory in in-service performance.

EFFECTIVE DESIGN AND APPLICATION

When a hazardous roadside feature or appurtenance cannot be removed, relocated, or redesignated to eliminate the hazard, guardrail should be used to redirect an errant vehicle away from the hazard. The use of guardrails should be considered early in the design process when the potential exists for altering the design to eliminate guardrail need. Supervisory construction and maintenance personnel should be familiar with the principles of guardrail application so that final field adjustment of each installation can be made based on operational experience. Information on field adjustment and operational experience should be made available to the designers to broaden their knowledge of guardrail application.

Considerable research and study of new concepts in design and material use and guardrail application and warrants are now under way.

SYSTEM	CABLE	"W" Beam (Steel Weak Post)	BOX BEAM		BLOCKED-OUT "W" BM (WOOD POST)	BLOCKED-OUT "W" BEAM (STEEL POST)
DEFLECTION	12 ft.	8 ft	4 ft	2 ft	2 ft	4 ft
POST SPACING	16' - 0"	12' - 6" Nominal	6' - 0"	4' - 0"	6' - 3"	6' - 3"
POST	S3x5.7	S3x5.7			8x8" Douglas Fir	W6x8.5
BEAM	Three 3/4" Dia Steel Cables	Steel "W" Section	6x6x0. 180" Steel Tube		Steel "W" Section	Steel "W" Section
OFFSET BRACKETS			L5x3-1/2x1/4" Steel Angle 4-1/2" Lg		8x8x14" Douglas Fir Bloc	W6x8.5
MOUNTING	5/16" Dia Steel Hook Bolts	5/16" Dia Steel Bolt	3/8" Dia Steel Bolt (beam to angle)		3/8" Carriage Bolts	5/8" Dia Steel Bolt
FOOTING	1/4" Steel Plate Welded to Post	1/4" Steel Plate Welded to post	1/4" Steel Plate Welded to Post		None	None
DEVELOPED BY	New York	New York	New York		California	
REMARKS	Revised 1971	Revised 1971	Increase height of rail from 30 to 35 in. on the outside of superelevated curve. Revised 1971		Southern yellow pine is acceptable alternate to Douglas fir.	

SOURCE: A Handbook of Highway Safety Design and Operating Practices, *U.S. Dept of Transportation, Federal Highway Dept. — 1973, Washington, D.C.*

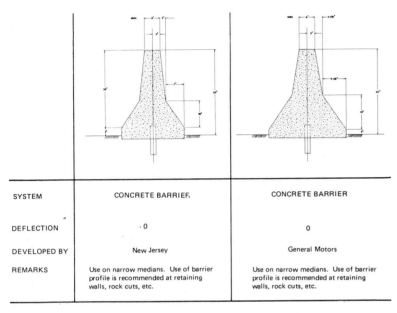

SYSTEM	CONCRETE BARRIER	CONCRETE BARRIER
DEFLECTION	0	0
DEVELOPED BY	New Jersey	General Motors
REMARKS	Use on narrow medians. Use of barrier profile is recommended at retaining walls, rock cuts, etc.	Use on narrow medians. Use of barrier profile is recommended at retaining walls, rock cuts, etc.

SYSTEM	MBI CABLE	MB2 "W" BEAM	MB3 BOX BEAM	MB4W BLOCKED-OUT "W" BEAM (Wood Post)	MB4S BLOCKED-OUT "W" BEAM (Steel Post)
	11 ft	7 ft	4 ft	2 ft	4 ft
POST SPACING	8' - 0''	12' - 6'' Nominal	6' - 0''	6' - 3''	6' - 3''
POST	H2-1/4x4.1	S3x5.7	S3x5.7	8x8'' Douglas Fir	W6x8.5
BEAM	Two 3/4'' Dia Steel Cables	Two Steel "W" Sections	8x6x1/4'' Steel Tube	Two Steel "W" Sections Two C6x8.2 Steel Sections (rub rails)	Two Steel "W" Sections
OFFSET BRACKETS				Two 8x8x14'' Douglas Fir Blocks	Two W6x8.5
MOUNTINGS	1/2'' Dia Steel "U" Bolts	5/16'' Dia Bolts	Steel Paddles	5/8'' Carriage Bolts	5/8'' Dia Steel Bolts
FOOTINGS	Details Vary With Application	1/4'' Steel Plate Welded to Post	1/4'' Steel Plate Welded to Post	None	None
DEVELOPED BY	California	New York	New York	California	
REMARKS	Use on flat medians or on saw-tooth sections with slope flatter than 3:1 or with step less than 6 inches in height.	For saw-tooth medians use two guardrail installations. Revised 1971	Use on flat medians or on saw-tooth sections with slope flatter than 3:1 or with step less than 6 inches in height. Revised 1971	Stagger beam heights when the saw-tooth step is over 6 inches high and/or the median slope is 3:1 or steeper. Southern yellow pine is acceptable alternate for Douglas fir. A "W" beam centered at 10 inches above grade is an acceptable alternate rub rail.	This system has been tested at 67 mph, 16 deg MB4S is considered operational based on test experience of G4S and considerable field experience.

MEDIAN BARRIER TYPES

Examples of median barriers that have proved satisfactory in in-service performance.

Median barriers are used mainly to prevent vehicles from crossing the median and causing head-on collisions. Although median barriers generally decrease accident severity, the number of accidents may increase. For this reason median barriers should only be installed where they are clearly justified.

Desirable median barrier performance characteristics are:

1. Containment. The vehicle must not get beyond the barrier. If a barrier is required, the consequences of penetration are presumably more serious than perhaps a sudden stop at the barrier.

2. Minimized injury potential. To reduce the inherent hazards of barrier collision, the vehicle must be redirected or decelerated at the lowest rate possible without exceeding allowable barrier deflection. The barrier must not rebound the vehicle across the highway and create a hazard to following or adjacent traffic.

3. Designed for both economic installation and maintenance.

4. Attractive appearance.

Median barriers are generally not considered warranted when median width exceeds 40 feet except on the basis of adverse accident experience.

SOURCE: A Handbook of Highway Safety Design and Operating Practices, U.S. Dept of Transportation, Federal Highway Dept. — 1973, Washington, D.C.

PASSENGER CAPACITIES PER LANE OR TRACK

	Facility	Vehicles per Lane[1] per Hour	Effective Capacity at Various Passengers per Vehicle			
			1.25	1.50	1.75	2.00
Private Automobile	City Street, Design FlowRate	600	750	900	1,050	1,200
	City Street, Capacity	800	1,000	1,200	1,400	1,600
	Freeway, Deisgn FlowRate	1,500	1,875	2,250	2,625	3,000
	Freeway, Capacity	2,000	2,500	3,000	3,500	4,000

	Facility	Vehicles per Lane[1] per Hour	Headway (min.)	Effective Passenger Capacity for Various Loading Ratios			
				75%	100%	125%	150%
Transit Bus (50 seats)	City Street	60	1.00	2,250	3,000	3,750	4,500
	City Street	90	0.67	3,375	4,500	5,625	6,750
	City Street or Freeway	120**	0.50	4,500	6,000	7,500	9,000
	Freeway	180**	0.33	6,750	9,000	11,250	13,500
	Freeway	240**	0.25	9,000	12,000	15,000	18,000

	Type of Train	Trains per Track per Hour[1]	Headway (min.)	Effective Passenger Capacity Passengers per Car			
				100	120	150	180
Rail Rapid Transit Train		20	3.00	12,000	14,400	18,000	21,600
	6-Car Train	30	2.00	18,000	21,600	27,000	32,400
		40	1.50	24,000	28,800	36,000	43,200
		20	3.00	20,000	24,000	30,000	36,000
	10-Car Train	30	2.00	30,000	36,000	45,000	54,000
		40	1.50	40,000	48,000	60,000	72,000

*This table provides the elements necessary to determine the number of persons that may be accommodated per facility. Example of the number of persons carried in the peak direction on representative facilities are: 8-lane freeway — 7500 to 16,000 persons per hour. 2-track rail rapid transit with 6 car trains — 12,000 to 43,000 persons per hour.

This table considers capacity only. A more complete comparison must consider demand and level of service which reflect convenience, flexibility of use, comfort, and many other factors.

**Capacity would be limited by design of bus turn outs and type of operation.

Roadway Continuity

■ These cross sections for a roadway with a narrow median illustrate the desirability of providing continuity of design for varying conditons.

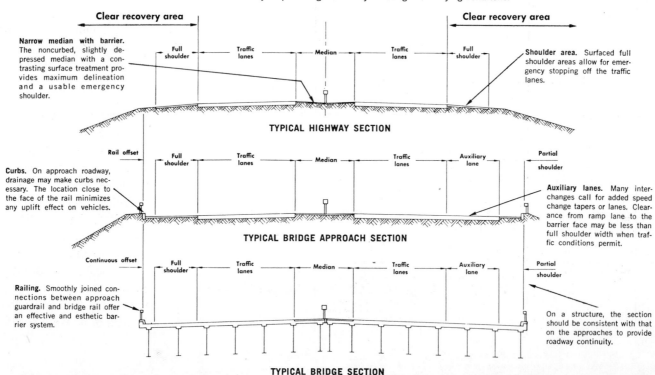

Narrow median with barrier. The noncurbed, slightly depressed median with a contrasting surface treatment provides maximum delineation and a usable emergency shoulder.

Shoulder area. Surfaced full shoulder areas allow for emergency stopping off the traffic lanes.

TYPICAL HIGHWAY SECTION

Curbs. On approach roadway, drainage may make curbs necessary. The location close to the face of the rail minimizes any uplift effect on vehicles.

Auxiliary lanes. Many interchanges call for added speed change tapers or lanes. Clearance from ramp lane to the barrier face may be less than full shoulder width when traffic conditions permit.

TYPICAL BRIDGE APPROACH SECTION

Railing. Smoothly joined connections between approach guardrail and bridge rail offer an effective and esthetic barrier system.

On a structure, the section should be consistent with that on the approaches to provide roadway continuity.

TYPICAL BRIDGE SECTION

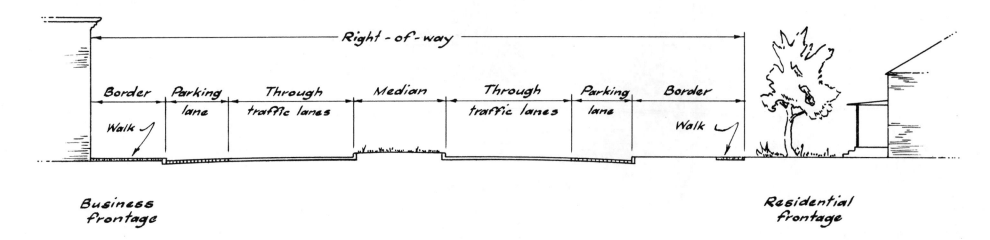

Divided, with parking lanes

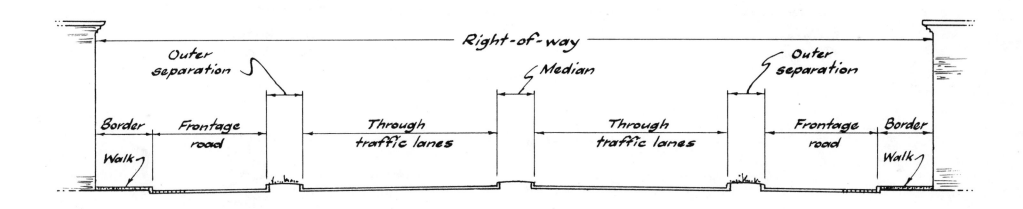

Divided, with separated parking and service lanes

SOURCE: A Policy of Arterial Highways in Urban Areas, American Association of State Highway Officials, Washington, D.C., 1960.

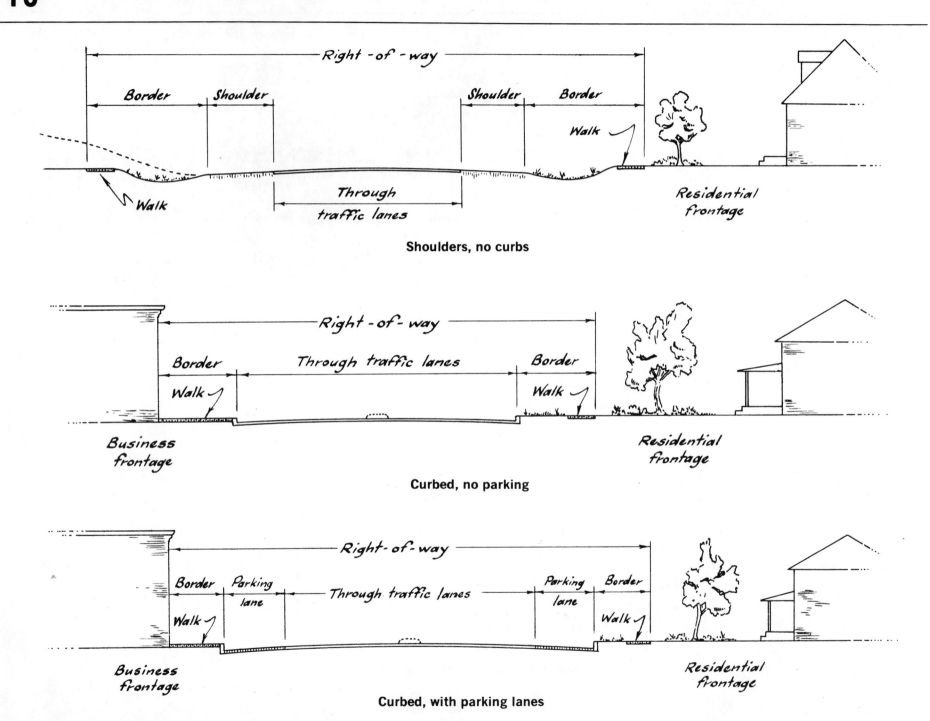

Shoulders, no curbs

Curbed, no parking

Curbed, with parking lanes

SOURCE: *A Policy of Arterial Highways in Urban Areas, American Association of State Highway Officials, Washington, D.C., 1960.*

TYPES OF PARKING FACILITIES

On-Street Facilities: On-street, or curb, parking can be divided into three classes:

1. Unrestricted Curb Parking
2. Restricted Curb Parking
   a. Police Controlled (through enforcing restrictions posted on signs)
   b. Meter Controlled

On-street parking is convenient only for the parker fortunate enough to find space reasonably near his destination. It is inconvenient, and to a degree unsafe, for the majority of motorists in moving cars.

In areas of concentrated land use, such as city central business districts, disadvantages far outweigh any advantages claimed for on-street parking.

Off-Street Parking Facilities: Two basic types of off-street parking facilities are:

1. Surface Lots
2. Multi-Floor Structures
   a. Ramp garages
   b. Mechanical parking devices

Off-street facilities, considered in terms of ownership and operation, develop other classifications:

1. Privately owned and operated
2. Publicly owned, privately operated
3. Publicly owned and operated

All types of off-street facilities have been operated successfully. No one type can be labeled the best. The success of each depends on local conditions, siting, operations, and other circumstances.

Angle parking accommodates more vehicles per unit of curb space than parallel parking. This advantage increases as widths of the angle increase, until at ninety degrees nearly two and one-half times as many spaces are possible. But as the angle increases, so do requirements of roadway width used for parking and additional width needed for maneuvering into and out of spaces.

Ninety-degree parking at the curb is rarely permissible and only under special conditions, as in wide market-district streets where small trucks back to the curb for the sale or delivery of produce. Usually sixty degrees is the maximum practicable, and the forty-five-degree stalls generally give best results. Steeper angles require more maneuvering space, while flatter angles use nearly as much curb space as parallel parking.

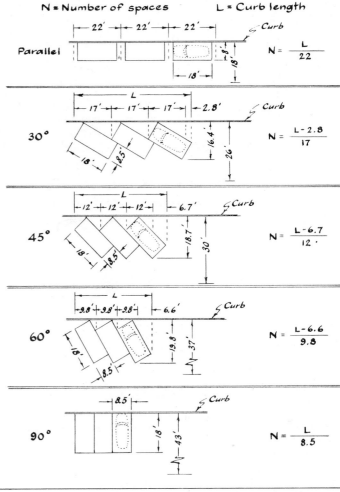

Street Space Used for Various Parking Positions*

Stall width	Position at curb	Width of street used when parked	Street width needed for parking plus maneuvering	Length of curb per car	Cars parked per 100 feet
7 feet	Parallel	7 feet	17 feet	22 feet	4.5
8 feet	45	18.4 feet	30.4 feet	11.3 feet	8.2
	60	19.6 feet	38.6 feet	9.2 feet	9.5
	90	18.0 feet	46.0 feet	8.0 feet	12.5
8 feet 6 in.	45	18.7 feet	29.7 feet	12.0 feet	7.8
	60	19.8 feet	37.8 feet	9.8 feet	9.5
	90	18.0 feet	43.0 feet	8.5 feet	11.5
9 feet	45	19.1 feet	30.1 feet	12.7 feet	7.37
	60	20.0 feet	37.0 feet	10.4 feet	9.0
	90	18.0 feet	41.0 feet	9.0 feet	11.1

* Based on stall widths as shown, including lines   Car length   18 feet
     No overhang of curb   width   6 feet 6 inches
                                    wheel base   10 feet 6 inches
                                    overall turning diameter 23 feet 3 inches

SOURCE: Solving Parking Problems, Bureau of Planning New York State Dept. of Commerce, Albany, N. Y.

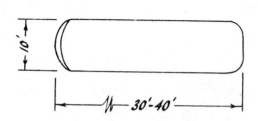

Typical bus dimensions.........
For smaller buses - use lower dimensions
For larger buses - use higher dimensions

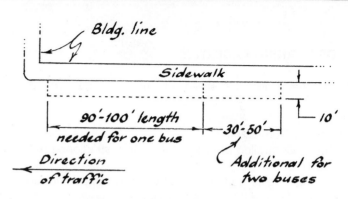

Near-side bus stop

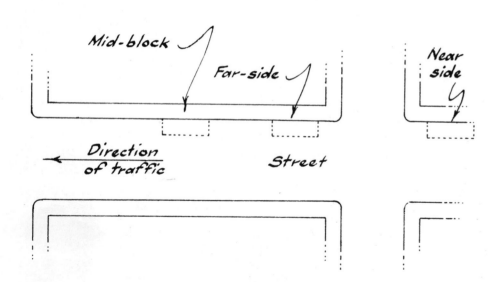

Mid-block

Far-side

Near side

Direction of traffic

Street

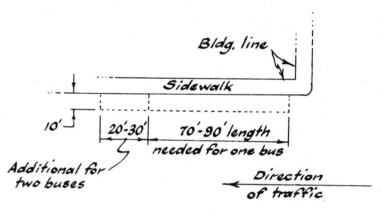

Far-side bus stop

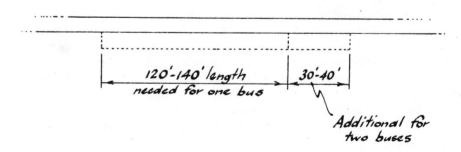

Mid-block

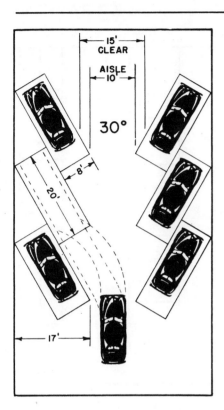

30-DEGREE ANGLE

gives you easy parking but takes a lot of space.

Cars per 100 lineal feet of double bay . . . 12

Area required per car in double bay . . . 425 sq. ft.

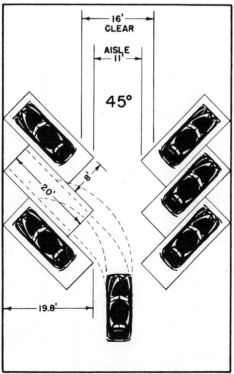

45-DEGREE ANGLE

gives you easy parking also but will park more cars.

Cars per 100 lineal feet of double bay . . . 16

Area required per car in double bay . . . 388 sq. ft.

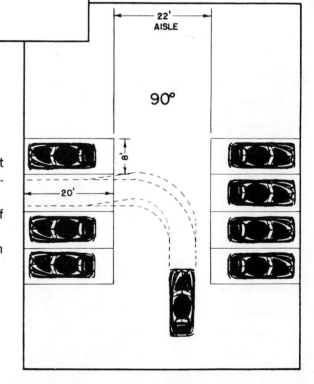

60-DEGREE ANGLE

is most popular method. Parks a lot of cars with easy access.

Cars per 100 lineal feet of double bay . . . 20

Area required per car in double bay . . . 330 sq. ft.

90-DEGREE ANGLE

Handles the most cars but difficult for some drivers. Permits two-way traffic flow.

Cars per 100 lineal feet of double bay . . . 25

Area required per car in double bay . . . 268 sq. ft.

SOURCE: Solving Parking Problems, Bureau of Planning, Department of Commerce, State of N. Y.

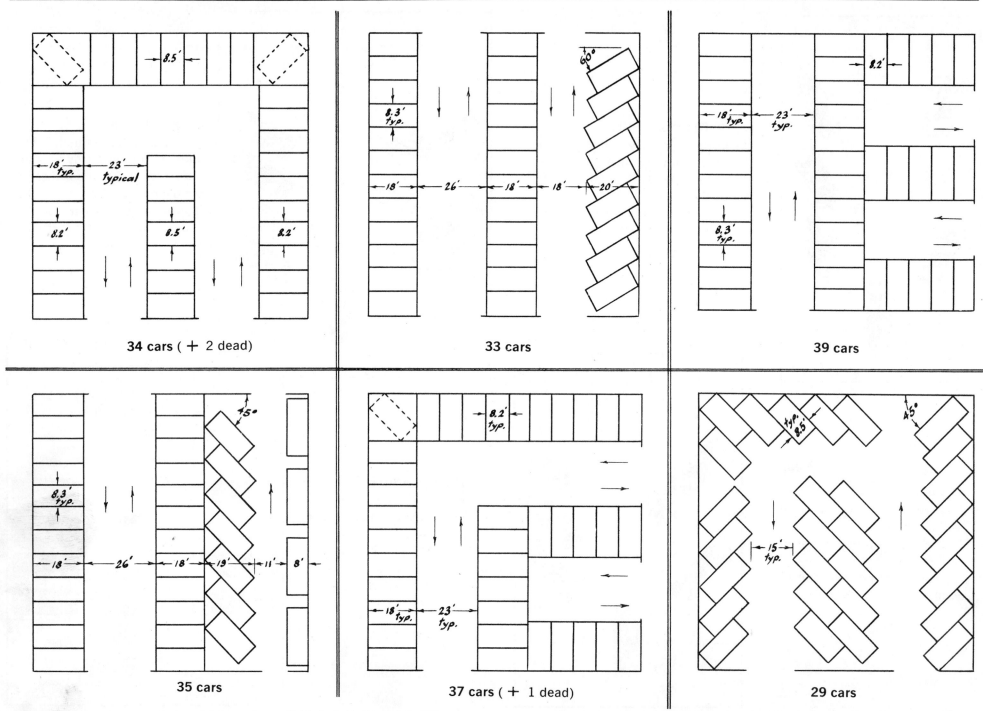

34 cars (+ 2 dead)

33 cars

39 cars

35 cars

37 cars (+ 1 dead)

29 cars

SOURCE: Parking Guide for Cities, U.S. Dept. of Commerce, Bureau of Public Roads, Washington, D.C., 1956.

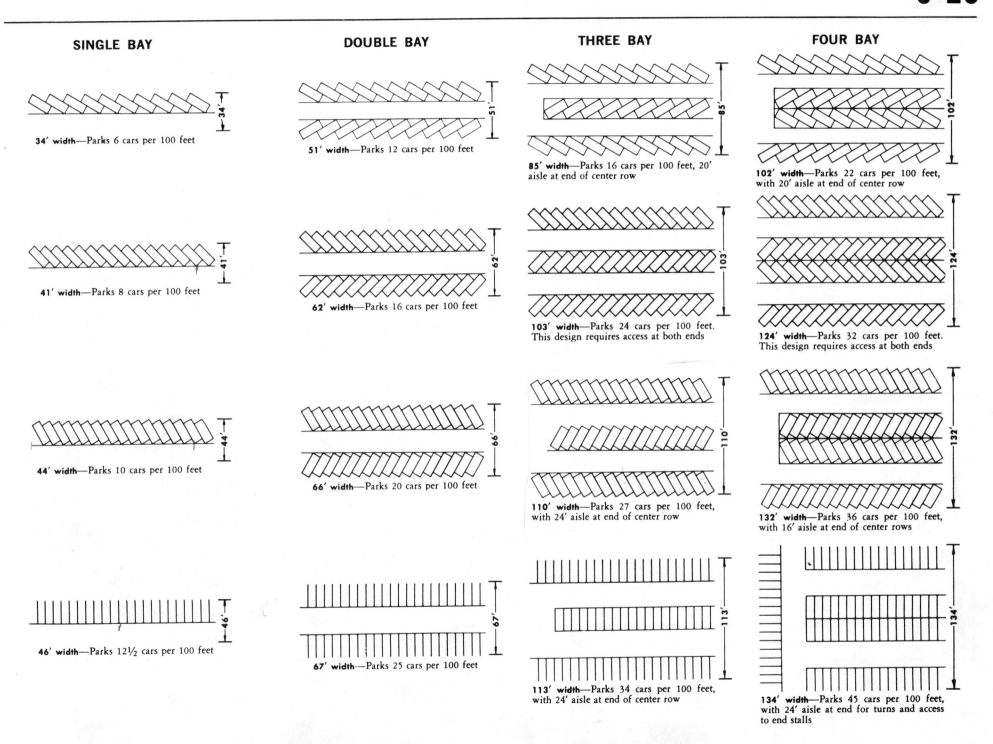

SINGLE BAY

34′ width—Parks 6 cars per 100 feet

41′ width—Parks 8 cars per 100 feet

44′ width—Parks 10 cars per 100 feet

46′ width—Parks 12½ cars per 100 feet

DOUBLE BAY

51′ width—Parks 12 cars per 100 feet

62′ width—Parks 16 cars per 100 feet

66′ width—Parks 20 cars per 100 feet

67′ width—Parks 25 cars per 100 feet

THREE BAY

85′ width—Parks 16 cars per 100 feet, 20′ aisle at end of center row

103′ width—Parks 24 cars per 100 feet. This design requires access at both ends

110′ width—Parks 27 cars per 100 feet, with 24′ aisle at end of center row

113′ width—Parks 34 cars per 100 feet, with 24′ aisle at end of center row

FOUR BAY

102′ width—Parks 22 cars per 100 feet, with 20′ aisle at end of center row

124′ width—Parks 32 cars per 100 feet. This design requires access at both ends

132′ width—Parks 36 cars per 100 feet, with 16′ aisle at end of center rows

134′ width—Parks 45 cars per 100 feet, with 24′ aisle at end for turns and access to end stalls

Major Divisions		Name	Value as Foundation When Not Subject to Frost Action	Value as Base Directly Under Wearing Surface	Potential Frost Action	Compressibility and Expansion	Drainage Characteristics	Compaction Equipment	Unit Dry Weight Lb. Per Cu. Ft.
COARSE GRAINED SOILS	GRAVEL AND GRAVELLY SOILS	Gravel or sandy gravel, well-graded	Excellent	Good	None to very slight	Almost none	Excellent	Crawler type tractor, rubber tired equipment, steel wheeled roller	125-140
		Gravel or sandy gravel, poorly-graded	Good to excellent	Poor to fair	None to very slight	Almost none	Excellent	Crawler type tractor, rubber tired equipment, steel wheeled roller	120-130
		Gravel or sandy gravel, uniformly graded	Good	Good	None to very slight	Almost none	Excellent	Crawler type tractor, rubber tired equipment	115-125
		Silty gravel or silty sandy gravel	Good to excellent	Fair to good	Slight to medium	Very slight	Fair to poor	Rubber tired equipment, sheepsfoot roller, close control of moisture	130-145
		Clayey gravel or clayey sandy gravel	Good	Poor	Slight to medium	Slight	Poor to practically impervious	Rubber tired equipment, sheepsfoot roller	120-140
	SAND AND SANDY SOILS	Sand or gravelly sand, well-graded	Good	Poor	None to very slight	Almost none	Excellent	Crawler type tractor, rubber tired equipment	110-130
		Sand or gravelly sand, poorly-graded	Fair to good	Poor to not suitable	None to very slight	Almost none	Excellent	Crawler type tractor, rubber tired equipment	105-120
		Sand or gravelly sand, uniformly graded	Fair to good	Not suitable	None to very slight	Almost none	Excellent	Crawler type tractor, rubber tired equipment	100-115
		Silty sand or silty gravelly sand	Good	Poor	Slight to high	Very slight	Fair to poor	Rubber tired equipment, sheepsfoot roller; close control of moisture	120-135
		Clayey sand or clayey gravelly sand	Fair to good	Not suitable	Slight to high	Slight to medium	Poor to practically impervious	Rubber tired equipment, sheepsfoot roller	105-130
FINE GRAINED SOILS	LOW COMPRESSIBILITY LL < 50	Silts, sandy silts, gravelly silts, or diatomaceous soils	Fair to poor	Not suitable	Medium to very high	Slight to medium	Fair to poor	Rubber tired equipment, sheepsfoot roller; close control of moisture	100-125
		Lean clays, sandy clays, or gravelly clays	Fair to poor	Not suitable	Medium to high	Medium	Practically impervious	Rubber tired equipment, sheepsfoot roller	100-125
		Organic silts or lean organic clays	Poor	Not suitable	Medium to high	Medium to high	Poor	Rubber tired equipment, sheepsfoot roller	90-105
	HIGH COMPRESSIBILITY LL > 50	Micaceous clays or diatomaceous soils	Poor	Not suitable	Medium to very high	High	Fair to poor	Rubber tired equipment, sheepsfoot roller	80-100
		Fat clays	Poor to very poor	Not suitable	Medium	High	Practically impervious	Rubber tired equipment, sheepsfoot roller	90-110
		Fat organic clays	Poor to very poor	Not suitable	Medium	High	Practically impervious	Rubber tired equipment, sheepsfoot roller	80-105
PEAT AND OTHER FIBROUS ORGANIC SOILS		Peat, humus, and other	Not suitable	Not suitable	Slight	Very high	Fair to poor	Compaction not practical	—

SOURCE: Adapted from U.S. Army Corps of Engineers, Engineering Manual, Part XII, Chapter B, Appendix "A".

The subject of highway capacity not only concerns itself with the ultimate carrying ability of various facilities, but also with the relative service characteristics of facilities operating at some fraction of their capacity volume. Thus, a study of highway capacity is at once a quantitative and a qualitative study, which permits evaluation of both the adequacy and the quality of vehicle service being provided by the facility under study.

The *Highway Capacity Manual*[1] is the most complete and authoritative source on capacity and, like the original edition,[2] is largely based on empirical data rather than theoretical development.

Capacity analyses are necessary inputs to many traffic engineering evaluations:

1. Deficiencies in the existing highway system may be evaluated by comparing measured volumes to the capacity of existing facilities.
2. Proposed changes in the existing street system, such as changes in geometrics, signalization, parking regulations, converting to one-way operation, turn restrictions, etc., must all be evaluated for their effect on capacity.
3. The design of new facilities must always be based upon capacity analyses coupled with projected demands.
4. The comparison of the relative effectiveness of alternate modes of transportation in serving a particular demand is often partially based on capacity analyses.

DEFINITIONS

Capacity Terms

The original Capacity Manual utilized three capacity terms: *basic capacity, possible capacity,* and *practical capacity.*

Basic capacity was the maximum number of passenger cars that could pass a given point on a lane or roadway under ideal traffic and roadway conditions in one hour.

Possible capacity was similarly defined for prevailing roadway and traffic conditions.

Practical capacity referred to the maximum number of passenger cars that could pass a point in one hour without causing unreasonable delay, hazard, or restriction.

The new Manual replaces these with the terms *capacity* and *level of service.*

Capacity is defined as the maximum number of vehicles that can pass over a given section of a lane or roadway, in one direction (or in both directions for a two-lane or three-lane highway), during a given time period (one hour unless otherwise specified), under prevailing roadway and traffic conditions. The current term of *capacity* is synonymous with the earlier term of *possible capacity*. As previously, it is the volume of traffic that cannot be exceeded in actuality without changing one or more of the conditions that prevail. Roadway conditions refer to the physical features of the roadway, which do not change unless some construction or reconstruction is performed. Traffic conditions refer to the characteristics of traffic using the roadway, which may change hourly.

The former *basic capacity* has been replaced with the term *capacity under ideal conditions*. Ideal prevailing roadway and traffic conditions are characterized by:

1. Uninterrupted flow, free from side interferences of vehicles and pedestrians
2. Passenger cars only in the traffic stream
3. Twelve-foot traffic lanes, with adequate shoulders and no lateral obstructions within 6 feet of the edge of pavement
4. For rural highways, horizontal and vertical alignment satisfactory for average highway speeds of 70 miles per hour or greater, and no restricted(less than 1,500 feet) passing sight distances on two-lane and three-lane highways

The concept of *level of service* has replaced *practical capacity*. Level of service is associated with different operating conditions that occur on a facility when it accommodates

various traffic volumes. It is a qualitative measure of the effect of a number of factors which include:

1. Speed and travel time
2. Traffic interruptions
3. Freedom to maneuver
4. Driver comfort and convenience
5. Safety
6. Vehicle operating costs

The concept of level of service is carried throughout the new Manual, and it is applied to all highway elements. Six levels of service have been established, designated by the letters A through F, providing for best to worst service in terms of driver satisfaction. For a given highway facility, different levels of service will be selected to provide for appropriate operating characteristics on the various components of the facility. However, these operating conditions should be in harmony with each other; that is, they should be of approximately equal acceptability to average drivers. Different highway elements and types of facilities include: intersection, ramp, weaving section, ramp terminal, speed-change lane, freeway, uncontrolled-access multi-lane highway, two-lane or three-lane highway, arterial street, downtown street, etc. There is an important distinction between capacity and level of service, and it should be clearly understood. A given lane or roadway may provide a wide range of levels of service (depending essentially on speed and volume), but the lane or roadway has only one capacity. In practice, any given highway, or component thereof, may operate at a wide range of levels of service,depending upon the time of day, day of week, and period of the year.

Service volume is the maximum number of vehicles that can pass over a given section of a lane or roadway, in one direction on multi-lane highways (or in both directions on a two- or three-lane highway), during a specified time period, while operating conditions are maintained corresponding to the selected or specified level of service. In the absence of a time modifier, service volume is an hourly volume.

Roadway Terms

Control of Access

Full control of access: The authority to control access is exercised to give preference to through traffic, by providing access connections with selected public roads only, and by prohibiting crossings at grade or direct private driveway connections.

Partial control of access: The authority to control access is exercised to give preference to through traffic to a degree that, in addition to access connections with selected public roads, there may be some crossings at grade and some private driveway connections.

Uncontrolled access: The authority having jurisdiction over a highway, street, or road does not limit the number of point of ingress or egress, except through the exercise of control over the placement and the geometrics of connections as necessary for the safety of the traveling public.

Functional Types

Arterial highway: A highway primarily for through traffic, usually on a continuous route, not having access control.

Expressway: A divided arterial highway for through traffic, with full orpartial control of access, and generally with grade separations at major intersections.

Freeway: An expressway with full control of access.

Parkway: An arterial highway for noncommercial traffic with full or partial control of access.

Traffic Engineering: Theory and Practice Louis J. Pignataro, Prentice-Hall, Inc., Englewood Cliffs, N.J. 1973

Major street or major highway: An arterial highway with intersections at grade and direct access to abutting property, and on which geometric design and traffic control measures are used to expedite the safe movement of through traffic.

Through street or **through highway:** Every highway, or portion thereof, at the entrance to which vehicular traffic from intersecting highways is required by law to stop or yield before entering or crossing.

Local street or **local road:** A street or road primarily for access to residence, business, or other abutting property.

Frontage road: A road contiguous to, and generally parallelling, an expressway, freeway, parkway, or through street. It is designed so as to intercept, collect, and distribute traffic desiring to cross, enter, or leave such a highway and to furnish access to property that otherwise would be isolated as a result of the controlled-access feature. It is sometimes called a *service road.*

Terrain

Level terrain: Any combination of gradients, length of grade, or horizontal or vertical alignment that permits trucks to maintain speeds that are equal to, or approach the speeds of, passenger cars.

Rolling terrain: Any combination of gradients, length of grade, or horizontal or vertical alinement that causes trucks to reduce their speeds substantially below that of passenger cars on some sections of the highway, but which does not involve a sustained crawl speed by trucks for any substantial distance.

Mountainous terrain: Any combination of gradients, length of grade, or horizontal or vertical alinement that will cause trucks to operate at crawl speed for considerable distances or at frequent intervals.

Sustained grade: A continuous highway grade of appreciable length and consistent or nearly consistent gradient.

Traffic Operations Terms

Peak-hour traffic: The highest number of vehicles found to be passing over a section of a lane or a roadway during 60 consecutive minutes. This term may be applied to a daily peak hour or a yearly peak hour.

Rate of flow: The hourly representation of the number of vehicles that pass over a given section of a lane or a roadway for some period less than one hour. It is obtained by expanding the number of vehicles to an hourly rate, but multiplying the number of vehicles during a specified time period by the ratio of 60 minutes to the number of minutes during which the flow occurred.

Interrupted flow: A condition in which a vehicle traversing a section of a lane or a roadway is required to stop by a cause outside the traffic stream, such as signs or signals at an intersection or a junction. Stoppage of vehicles by causes internal to the traffic stream does not constitute interrupted flow.

Uninterrupted flow: A condition in which a vehicle traversing a section of a lane or a roadway is not required to stop by any cause external to the traffic stream, although vehicles may be stopped by causes internal to the traffic stream.

Peak hour factor: A ratio of the volume occurring during the peak hour to the maximum rate of flow during a given time period within the peak hour. It is a measure of peaking characteristics, whose maximum attainable value is unity. The term must be qualified by a specified short period within the hour; this is usually 5 or 6 minutes for freeway operation, and 15 minutes for intersection operation.

Traffic Engineering: Theory and Practice Louis J. Pignataro, Prentice-Hall, Inc., Englewood Cliffs, N.J. 1973

Land Use and Development Terms

Central Business District (CBD): That portion of a municipality in which the dominant land use is for intense business activity. This district is characterized by large numbers of pedestrians, commercial vehicle loadings of goods and people, a heavy demand for parking space, and high parking turnover.

Fringe area: That portion of a municipality immediately outside the CBD in which there is a wide range in type of business activity. It generally includes small businesses, light industry, warehousing, automobile service activities, and intermediate strip development, as well as some concentrated residential areas. This area is characterized by moderate pedestrian traffic and a lower parking turnover than is found in the CBD, but it may include large parking areas serving the CBD.

Outlying business district: That portion of a municipality, or an area within the influence of a municipality, normally separated geographically by some distance from the CBD and its fringe area, in which the principal land use is for business activity. This district is characterized by relatively high parking demand and turnover and moderate pedestrian traffic.

Residential area: That portion of a municipality, or an area within the influence of a municipality, in which the dominant land use is residential development, but where small business areas may be included. This area is characterized by few pedestrians and a low parking turnover.

STREAM CHARACTERISTICS

Stream characteristics of a roadway is a measure of its ability to accommodate traffic. Although this ability depends to a large extent on the physical features of the roadway, there are other factors not directly related to roadway features which are of major importance in determining the capacity of any roadway. Many of these factors relate to variations in the traffic demand and the interaction of vehicles in the traffic stream. An understanding of stream characteristics is basic to achieving a thorough insight into capacity analysis techniques.

Spacing and Headway Characteristics

Spacing is defined as the interval in distance from head to head of successive vehicles, and *headway* as the interval in time between individual vehicles measured from head to head as they pass a given point. These two measures describe the longitudinal arrangement of vehicles in a traffic stream.

The relationship between spacing and headway is dependent on speed, with:

$$\text{Headway (second)} = \frac{\text{spacing (feet)}}{\text{speed (feet per second)}} \tag{1}$$

The relationship between average spacing and density is as follows:

$$\text{Density (vehicles per mile)} = \frac{5,280 \text{ (feet per mile)}}{\text{average spacing (feet per vehicle)}} \tag{2}$$

The relationship between average headway and volume may be expressed as follows:

$$\text{Volume (vehicles per hour)} = \frac{3,600 \text{ (second per hour)}}{\text{average headway (second per vehicle)}} \tag{3}$$

Spacing as a Measure of Capacity.

Few drivers, if any, operate their vehicles in identically the same manner, or react in the same manner when exposed to similar conditions. It is impossible, therefore, to predict the effect of various roadway and traffic conditions on an individual driver. It has been found, however, that the combined effect on traffic as a whole can be predicted with reasonable accuracy.

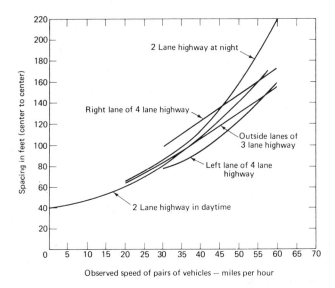

Fig 1. Minimum spacings allowed by the average driver when trailing another vehicle, at various speeds (*Source: J. Baerwald (Ed.), Traffic Engineering Handbook, 3rd Ed., I.T.E., Wash., D.C., 1965*)

All drivers do not maintain the same spacing to the vehicle ahead when traveling at a given speed. Figure 1 shows the minimum distance-spacings allowed by the average driver at different speeds for several conditions. Similar curves for other conditions may also be presented, but the curves in Figure 1 are sufficient to show that the average driver increases the distance-spacing between vehicles as his speed increases, and that the spacing is also influenced by the characteristics of the highway.

Using the data shown in Figure 1, it is possible to determine the maximum number of passenger cars, one behind the other, that can pass a point in one hour at any given speed, if this given speed is maintained by all vehicles. The following relationship could be used to compute the maximum volume of the traffic lane at the given speed:

Volume (vehicles per hour)
$$= \frac{5,280 \text{ (feet per mile)} \times \text{speed (miles per hour)}}{\text{spacing (feet per vehicle)}} \qquad (4)$$

If volume is plotted against speed using the above relationship, it will be found that the highest volume of a traffic lane is approximately 2,000 passenger vehicles per hour, when vehicles travel at about 30 miles per hour. This is the maximum capacity of a traffic lane operating under conditions of uninterrupted flow. Any traffic variable, or any roadway condition that prevents vehicles from moving safely at a speed of 30 miles per hour, lowers the capacity of the traffic lane.

A traffic lane can attain maximum capacity only if the following conditions exist:

1. There must be at least two lanes for the exclusive use of traffic traveling in one direction.
2. There must be no differentials in speeds of vehicles. All vehicles must travel at approximately the same speed.
3. There must be practically no commercial vehicles.

Traffic Engineering: Theory and Practice Louis J. Pignataro, Prentice-Hall, Inc., Englewood Cliffs, N.J. 1973

4. The widths of traffic lanes, shoulders, and clearances to vertical obstructions beyond the edge of the traffic lane must be adequate.
5. There must be no merging, weaving, or turning movements.
6. There must be no parking, loading, unloading, or stopping of vehicles.
7. There must be no restrictive sight distances, grades, improperly superelevated curves, signalized intersections, or interference by pedestrians.

Under actual operating conditions, if the above requirements are satisfied, it is possible to attain the following basic capacities for the different types of highways, assuming the capacity of a traffic lane is 2,000 vehicles per hour.

1. *Two-lane, two-way highways:* On two-lane roads, with few opposing vehicles, traffic can fill one lane by immediately passing into gaps that form. This single lane might reach the capacity of 2,000 vehicles per hour. However, as passing is restricted by vehicles from the opposite direction, the spaces that develop in the lane cannot be filled by passing maneuvers. Instead, breaks form in the traffic stream in each direction. Capacity in one direction, then, is affected by volume in the opposite direction. It has been established that the ideal capacity of a two-lane road in both directions is 2,000 vehicles per hour, regardless of the distribution between lanes.
2. *Three-lane, two-way highways:* The center lane of a three-lane road serves vehicles performing passing maneuvers in either direction. Vehicles can, therefore, completely fill the outside lanes by utilizing the center lane for passing. Thus, the ideal capacity of a three-lane, two-way road is 4,000 vehicles per hour total in both directions. The ideal capacity is limited to 2,000 vehicles for one direction.
3. *Multi-lane highways:* Multi-lane roads can be designed to meet all the conditions listed above. Therefore, the ideal capacity for a multi-lane highway is 2,000 vehicles per hour per lane, regardless of the number of lanes.

   On two- and three-lane roads, two lanes for the exclusive use of traffic traveling in the one direction are not available. The character of operation is therefore entirely different on these roads from that on multi-lane highways, since vehicles performing passing maneuvers are forced to use a traffic lane that is provided for vehicles traveling in the opposite direction. Consequently, the ideal capacities of two- and three-lane roads are much lower than for multi-lane roads.

Headway Distribution. If all the vehicles using a highway were equally spaced, determination of maximum volumes or levels of congestion would be fairly simple. However, vehicles tend to form groups or "platoons," even at low volumes. Individual headways show a wide degree of variation, with many vehicles queuing at short headways and others separated by large time gaps.

Figures 3.29 and 3.30 of the Capacity Manual show headway distributions for vehicles traveling in the same direction on typical two- and four-lane rural highways for various volumes with uninterrupted flow. Under nearly all volume conditions, these curves show that approximately two-thirds of all vehicles are spaced at, or less than, the average headway between vehicles.

On multi-lane facilities, some drivers will accept smaller headways than others, and these tend to gravitate to the median lane. Thus, volumes for median freeway lanes on many facilities have consistently carried volumes of 2,200 vehicles per hour. However, drivers accepting larger headways tend to remain in the right-hand lane, and capacity for this lane may be lower than 2,000 passenger cars per hour. Therefore, the indicated maximum capacity of 2,000 passenger cars per hour is reasonable when one takes into account the headway variation from lane to lane.

Further description of vehicular spacing characteristics can be made in mathematical terms. Under certain circumstances, vehicle spacing at a point will follow a random distribution. Such a distribution can be described mathematically by the *Poisson distribution.* Complete discussions of the application of the Poisson distribution to vehicular spacing characteristics are available.

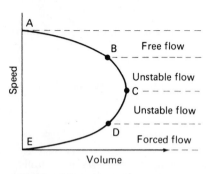

Fig. 2. Speed vs. Volume

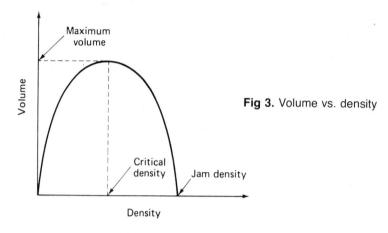

Fig 3. Volume vs. density

Relationships of Speed, Volume, and Density

Principles of physics, dynamics, hydraulics, and the laws of various sciences are being applied to the theory of movement of traffic with varying degrees of success. Analytical models of traffic flow are extremely useful, even though they have not, as yet, been developed to completely describe the complex interrelationships affecting the traffic stream. These models permit a more thorough approach to operational problems and can lead to the application of optimizing techniques for the control of traffic.

Speed-Volume Relationships. The basic speed-volume relationship for uninterrupted flow is that as volume increases, the space-mean-speed of traffic decreases until the critical density is reached. Thereafter both volume and speed decrease. The general form of this relationship is shown in Figure 2. The *AB* portion of the relationship is normally classified as the *free flow* condition, the *BCD* portion as the *unstable* flow condition (with volume at point *C* representing critical density), and the *DE* portion as the *forced* or *breakdown flow* condition. Numerous studies have confirmed the characteristic shape of the speed-volume relationship, and have indicated that the zone of free flow is essentially a linear relationship.

An extensive study to establish speed-volume relationships on many urban signalized streets (interrupted flow) in Chicago revealed that speed remained essentially constant when volume did not exceed about 70 per cent of capacity. Thereafter, speed decreased almost to less than 5 miles per hour, linearly, as volume approached capacity.[25] Somewhat similar results were obtained in another study.

Speed-Density Relationships. The speed-density relationship for uninterrupted flow is similar to the speed-volume relationship in that in the upper range, speed decreases with increasing volume and density. Density, however, continues to increase past the point of critical density, whereas volume decreases. Early studies found a linear relationship between average density and space-mean-speed. More recent studies have mathematically fitted best curves to observed data, resulting in exponential curves and bell-shaped curves. A statistical analysis of these various speed-density relationships was undertaken, and the linear relationship exhibited excellent correlation.

The speed-density relationship for interrupted flow is very similar to that under uninterrupted flow conditions, and most of the studies found a linear relationship.

Volume-Density Relationships. The basic volume-density relationship for both uninterrupted and interrupted flow conditions is that as density increases from zero (when there are no vehicles), volume increases to the point of critical density. Thereafter volume decreases as density continues to increase to a maximum value, known as *jam density* (when all vehicles are stopped). The general form of this relationship is shown in Figure 3. Numerous studies have confirmed the characteristic shape of the volume-density relationship. A study measured stopped vehicle spacings to determine the jam density. Jam density was found to be 210 vehicles per lane-mile.

CAPACITY AND LEVEL OF SERVICE

Capacity for Uninterrupted Flow Conditions

Under ideal roadway and traffic conditions, the fundamental capacities for uninterrupted flow conditions for different types of highways are shown in Table 1. Justification for the use of these values is essentially based on the reasoning outlined under Spacing as a Measure of Capacity.

Capacity for Interrupted Flow Conditions

Unlike uninterrupted flow, it is not feasible to define fundamental capacities under ideal conditions because of the large number of variables involved. In general, the following two basic limitations can be established.

1. Rarely does a traffic lane on an urban arterial carry volumes at a rate greater than 2,000 passenger cars per hour of green signal, even with ideal signal progression.
2. A line of vehicles, all of which are stopped by an interruption, will rarely move away from the interruption at a rate greater than 1,500 passenger cars per hour per lane. This is based on an average departure headway of 2.4 seconds.

Levels of Service

This concept is best defined in terms of units of measure familiar to drivers using the given highway. For uninterrupted flow on freeways, rural highways, and some suburban highways, operating speeds are used to define the levels. On urban arterials, where interrupted flow exists and the degree of delay varies widely, average overall travel speed is a better measure. On downtown streets, approximate speed measures are used. At individual intersections, it is not possible to use speeds as a measure. Instead, the degree of loading is used, that is, the percentage of green signal phases fully utilized by moving traffic.

A second factor used to evaluate level of service is either the ratio of demand volume to capacity, or the ratio of service volume to capacity. Demand volume is used instead of service volume when the level of service is evaluated for an existing facility.

Traffic Engineering: Theory and Practice Louis J. Pignataro, Prentice-Hall, Inc., Englewood Cliffs, N.J. 1973

TABLE 1. Capacity Under Ideal Conditions

Type of Facility	Capacity (pcph)
Two-lane, two-way roadways	2,000, total both directions
Three-lane, two-way roadways	4,000, total both directions
Multi-lane roadways	2,000, each lane, average

The following criteria have been established for determining capacity and level of service relationships:

1. Volume and capacity are expressed in *numbers of passenger cars per hour* for subsections of each section of roadway.
2. Level of service, strictly defined, applies to a section of roadway of significant length.
3. Analysis of volume and speed is made for each point or subsection of the highway having relatively uniform conditions. The weighted operating speed, or average overall travel speed, is then determined for the entire section, and a corresponding level of service is identified.
4. Variables used to measure capacity include roadway type, geometrics, average highway speed, traffic composition, and time variations in volume. For level of service, additional elements include speed and volume-to-capacity ratios.
5. Values of speed and volume-to-capacity ratio which define levels of service are established for each of the following types of facilities:
   a. Freeways and other expressways
   b. Other multi-lane highways
   c. Two- and three-lane highways
   d. Urban arterial streets
   e. Downtown streets

Related levels of service are established for different point elements, including intersections, ramp junctions, and weaving sections.

Attempts have been made to model the level of service concept.

OPERATING CONDITIONS FOR LEVELS OF SERVICE

Parameters for Measuring Levels of Service. The six levels of service each represent a range, the extreme of which is defined by the upper volume limit and the lower speed limit. Traffic-operational freedom on a highway is considered equal to or greater than Level of Service A, B, C, D, or E as the case may be, when two conditions are met. For largely uninterrupted flow, these conditions are:

1. Operating speeds or average overall speeds are equal to or greater than a standard value for the level considered.
2. The ratio of the demand volume or service volume to the capacity of any subsection does not exceed a standard value for that level.

Levels of Service: Definitions. The six levels of service are generally described as follows for simple uninterrupted flows. More specific descriptions for each highway element, including interrupted as well as uninterrupted flow, are presented later appropriate headings.

Level of Service A: This is a condition of free flow, accompanied by low volumes and high speeds. Traffic density will be low, with uninterrupted flow speeds controlled by driver desires, speed limits, and physical roadway conditions. There is little or no restriction in maneuverability due to the presence of other vehicles, and drivers can maintain their desired speeds with little or no delay.

Traffic Engineering: Theory and Practice Louis J. Pignataro, Prentice-Hall, Inc. Englewood Cliffs, N.J. 1973

Level of Service B: This occurs in the zone of stable flow, with operating speeds beginning to be restricted somewhat by traffic conditions. Drivers still have reasonable freedom to select their speed and lane of operation. Reductions in speed are not unreasonable, with a low probability of traffic flow being restricted. The lower limit (lowest speed, highest volume) of this level of service has been used in the design of rural highways.

Level of Service C: This is still in the zone of stable flow, but speeds and maneuverability are more closely controlled by the higher volumes. Most of the drivers are restricted in their freedom to select their own speed, change lanes, or pass. A relatively satisfactory operating speed is still obtained, with service volumes suitable for urban design practice.

Level of Service D: This level of service approaches unstable flow, with tolerable operating speeds being maintained, though considerably affected by changes in operating conditions. Fluctuations in volume and temporary restrictions to flow may cause substantial drops in operating speeds. Drivers have little freedom to maneuver, and comfort and convenience are low. These conditions can be tolerated, however, for short periods of time.

Level of Service E: This cannot be described by speed alone, but represents operations at lower operating speeds, typically, but not always, in the neighborhood of 30 miles per hour, with volumes at or near the capacity of the highway. Flow is unstable, and there may be stoppages of momentary duration. This level of service is associated with operation of a facility at capacity flows.

Level of Service F: This describes a forced-flow operation at low speeds, where volumes are below capacity. In the extreme, both speed and volume can drop to zero. These conditions usually result from queues of vehicles backing up from a restriction downstream. The section under study will be serving as a storage area during parts or all of the peak hour. Speeds are reduced substantially and stoppages may occur for short or long periods of time because of the downstream congestion.

FACTORS AFFECTING CAPACITY AND SERVICE VOLUMES

It is seldom that traffic and roadway conditions are ideal, and therefore fundamental capacities must be decreased to take into consideration the many factors that adversely affect traffic flow. Service volumes are affected in a similar way.

The various factors affecting capacity and service volumes are divided into two categories: roadway factors and traffic factors.

Roadway Factors

Lane Width. Twelve-foot lanes are considered ideal for heavy volumes of mixed traffic, and a lane of narrower width will restrict capacity.

Lateral Clearance. Objects closer than 6 feet from the edge of the pavement reduce the effective width of the roadway. The magnitude of the effect depends upon the closeness of the objects to the pavement and their frequency. Adjustments for lane width and lateral clearance are combined into one correction factor which is applied to the capacity under ideal conditions.

Shoulders. Adequate shoulders must be provided as a refuge for stopped vehicles if capacities are to be maintained on the through lanes.

Auxiliary Lanes. These include parking lanes, speed-change lanes, turning and storage lanes, weaving lanes, and truck-climbing lanes. Each of these lanes provides additional pavement width to accommodate special uses, helping to maintain the capacity of the through roadway.

Surface Conditions. Poor pavement surface conditions may influence the attainment of high speed, thereby affecting the better levels of service, but capacity may be very little affected.

Alinement. Poor alinement prevents the attainment of high speed, thereby affecting the better levels of service. It also affects capacity on two- and three-lane roads when passing sight distance is restricted to less than 1,500 feet.

Grades. Grades affect service volumes and capacity in three ways:

1. Vehicle braking distance is less on upgrades and greater on downgrades than on level grades. This permits shorter spacings between vehicles that are climbing grades, and requires longer spacings between vehicles going downgrades, in order to maintain a safe headway.

2. The presence 9f a grade generally causes a restriction in the sight distance, thereby affecting the percentage of highway on which passing maneuvers can be performed safely. This would only apply to two- and three-lane highways.

3. Commercial vehicles, with their normal loads, travel at slower speeds on upgrades than on level grades, especially if the grade is long and steep. This is also true to some extent with passenger cars. Most passenger cars, however, can negotiate long 6 and 7 per cent grades at speeds above 30 miles per hour. The effect that grades up to 7 per cent have on capacity as related to the performance of passenger cars is therefore generally negligible. Capacity may be little influenced until speeds of heavy vehicles are reduced to about 30 miles per hour, but service volumes for specific levels of service are significantly affected.

Providing climbing lanes can greatly reduce the adverse effect of grades by almost entirely removing the influence of commercial vehicles. This is as true for multi-lane highways as it is for two-lane highways.

Traffic Factors

Highways which have identical roadway factors may have different capacities depending upon the composition, habits, and desires of the traffic using them, and the controls which must be exercised over that traffic.

These considerations are taken into account by means of traffic factors.

Trucks. Commercial vehicles (vehicles with dual tires on one or more axles) under all conditions take up more space than passenger cars, and their presence is taken into consideration by determining the "passenger car equivalent" which represents the number of passenger cars that each truck is equivalent to under specific conditions.

If E = passenger car equivalent, and P_T = percentage of trucks, a service volume in passenger cars can be converted to mixed traffic through multiplication by the truck adjustment factor, $100/(100 - P_T + E_T P_T)$. Similarly, a volume of mixed traffic can be converted to equivalent passenger cars through multiplication by the reciprocal of the truck adjustment factor.

Buses. Intercity buses have better performance characteristics than do trucks, and one bus is assumed to be equivalent to 1.6 passenger cars for a wide variety of level and rolling conditions on multi-lane highways and streets. Local transit buses operating on city streets affect capacity in quite a different manner, and special procedures and charts have been developed to determine their influence.

Lane Distribution. The distribution of total traffic volume among the various lanes of a multi-lane facility varies with the lane location and with changes in volume. Even though the lane adjacent to the shoulder carries a smaller volume than the other lanes, no special correction is made because the fundamental capacity is stated as an average of 2,000 passenger cars per hour per lane, regardless of distribution.

Variations of Traffic Flow. Traffic volume variations within the peak hour can seriously affect flow conditions. Capacity analyses are based on traffic volume over a full hour, since capacity is defined in terms of vehicles per hour. However, the rate of traffic flow for intervals of less than one hour can substantially exceed the peak-hour rate. Therefore, it is necessary to provide excess capacity over the full hour to accommodate the peak intervals of flow, because when demand exceeds capacity, congestion will extend over a much longer time than just for the duration of the peak interval. For such purposes, a period of 5 to 15 minutes is employed for peak intervals. The relationship between the peak interval and the peak-hour volume is expressed by a peak-hour factor as follows:

For intersections:

$$\text{Peak-hour factor} = \frac{\text{peak-hour volume}}{4(\text{15-minutes peak volume})}$$

For freeways:

$$\text{Peak-hour factor} = \frac{\text{peak-hour volume}}{12(\text{5- minutes peak volume})}$$

The maximum value of the peak-hour factor in unity.

Traffic Interruptions. Any feature or device installed on a street or highway which requires some or all traffic to stop will reduce that highway's ability to carry traffic. Once stopped, traffic can depart at a rate of about 1,500 passenger cars per hour per lane, based on an average headway of 2.4 seconds. Since uninterrupted flow may reach 2,000 passenger cars per hour per lane, any stops imposed on heavy uninterrupted flows are likely to cause back-up of traffic.

Typical interruptions include at-grade intersections, toll gates, drawbridges, and railroad grade crossings. As long as rates of flow are below 1,500 passenger cars per hour per lane, probably only level of service will be affected in the latter three cases; but at higher volumes, queuing will develop. At-grade intersections cause significant restrictions to flow, and special procedures have been developed to analyze them.

Traffic Engineering: Theory and Practice Louis J. Pignataro, Prentice-Hall, Inc., Englewood Cliffs, N.J. 1973

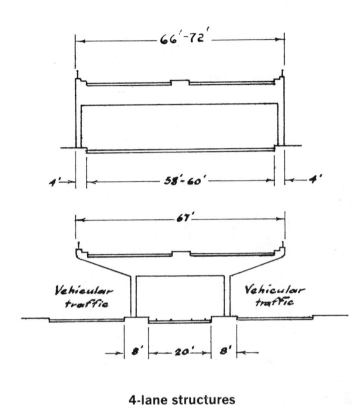

4-lane structures

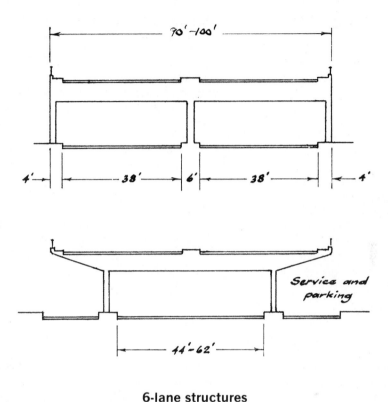

6-lane structures

ADVANTAGES

1. Elevated construction does not generally affect the existing street system.

2. Elevated construction usually requires less right-of-way than a depressed highway.

3. An elevated highway can be easily drained and does not require extensive relocation of existing utilities.

4. An elevated highway generally is less costly than an on-grade or depressed highway in built-up urban areas.

DISADVANTAGES

1. Elevated highways may affect light, air, or view of adjacent development.

2. Elevated highway ramps are upgrade for traffic entering and downgrade for traffic leaving the highway. This is contrary to traffic deceleration and acceleration requirements.

3. An elevated highway can easily become a visual obstacle if not properly related to the surrounding urban environment.

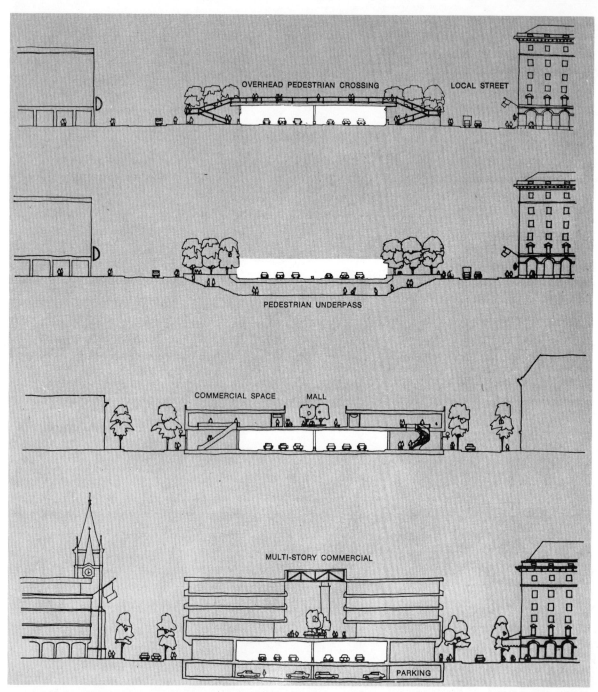

OVERHEAD PEDESTRIAN CROSSING   LOCAL STREET

PEDESTRIAN UNDERPASS

COMMERCIAL SPACE   MALL

MULTI-STORY COMMERCIAL

PARKING

SOURCE: *The Freeway in the City, Urban Advisors to the Federal Highway Administrators, Dept. of Transportation, Washington, D.C. 1968.*

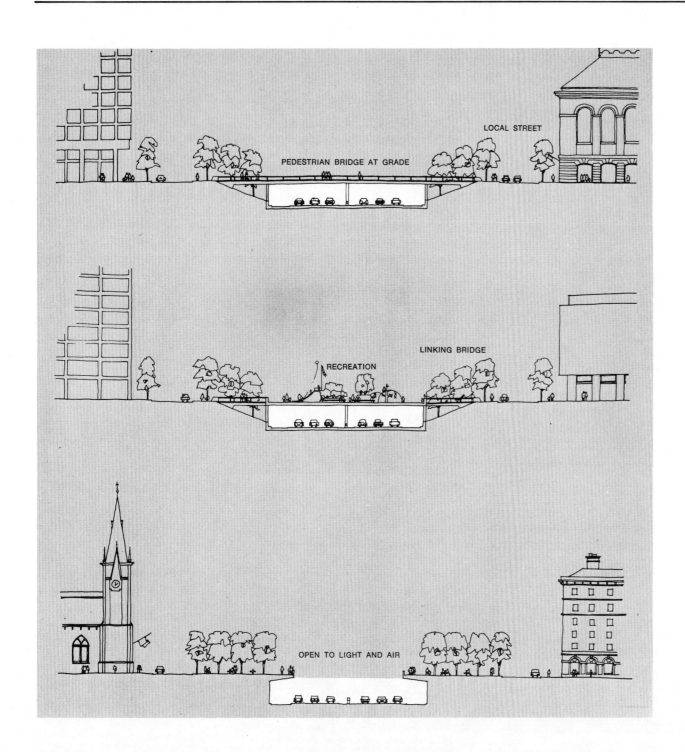

PEDESTRIAN BRIDGE AT GRADE

LOCAL STREET

LINKING BRIDGE

RECREATION

OPEN TO LIGHT AND AIR

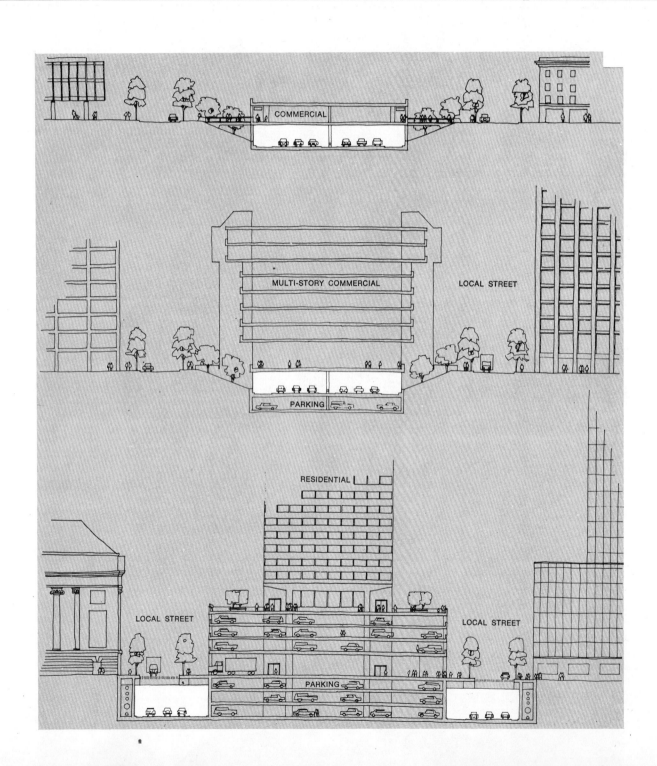

COMMERCIAL

MULTI-STORY COMMERCIAL   LOCAL STREET

PARKING

RESIDENTIAL

LOCAL STREET   LOCAL STREET

PARKING

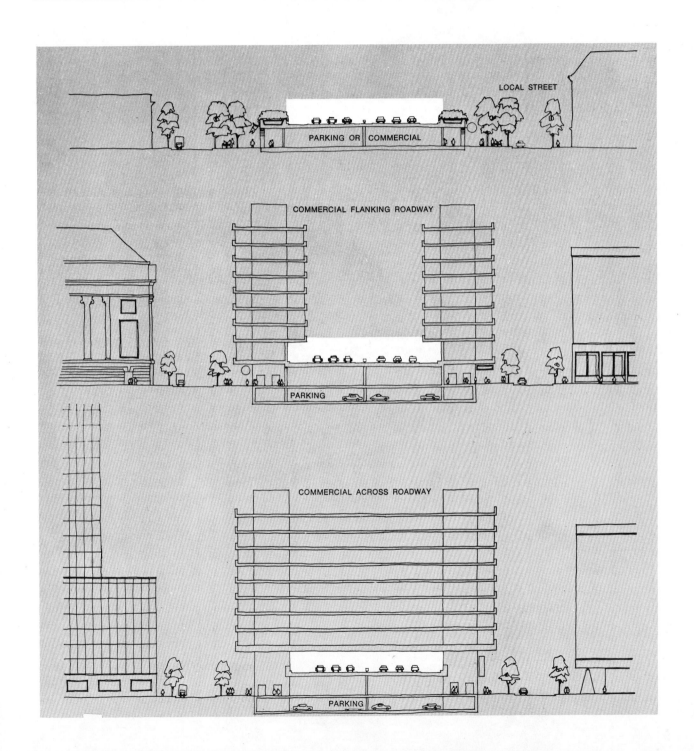

LOCAL STREET

PARKING OR COMMERCIAL

COMMERCIAL FLANKING ROADWAY

PARKING

COMMERCIAL ACROSS ROADWAY

PARKING

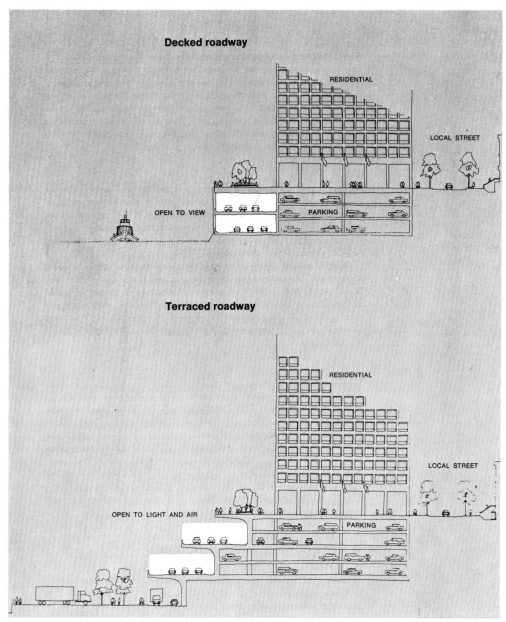

Decked roadway

RESIDENTIAL

LOCAL STREET

OPEN TO VIEW

PARKING

Terraced roadway

RESIDENTIAL

LOCAL STREET

OPEN TO LIGHT AND AIR

PARKING

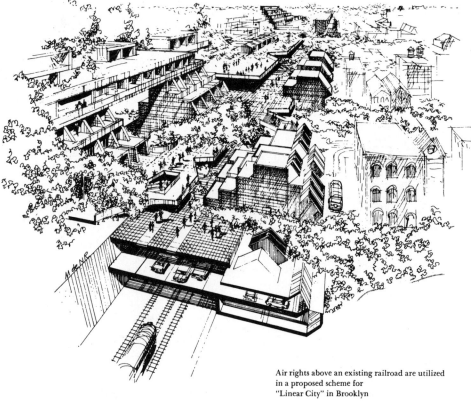

Air rights above an existing railroad are utilized in a proposed scheme for "Linear City" in Brooklyn

SOURCE: The Freeway in the City, Urban Advisors to the Federal Highway Administrators, Dept. of Transportation, Washington, D.C., 1968.

ROADS

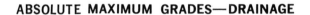

The minimum grade for good ditch drainage is 0.50%. 1% is preferable and 0.25% is the absolute minimum.

STREETS

The minimum grade for good gutter drainage is 0.30%. With great care in construction an absolute minimum of 0.10% may be used.

MAXIMUM DITCH GRADES—DRAINAGE

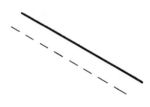

1% to 3%—sodded ditches
2% to 5%—ditch checks,
sod or paved ditch of concrete,
bitum. or rubble.

Silty soils will erode on grades over 1%. Most soils will erode on grades over 2%.

ABSOLUTE MAXIMUM GRADES—DRAINAGE

The steepest grades on existing paved highways or streets in the U. S. A. are 9% to 12% for highways and 30% to 32% for urban streets.

The average commercial vehicle can ascend a continuous 17% grade in low gear; use only for ramps, access, driveways.

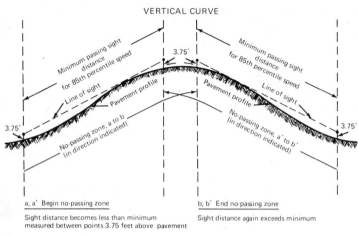

VERTICAL CURVE

a, a' Begin no-passing zone

Sight distance becomes less than minimum
measured between points 3.75 feet above pavement

b, b' End no-passing zone

Sight distance again exceeds minimum

Note: No-passing zones in opposite directions may or may not overlap,
depending on alignment.

HORIZONTAL CURVE

a, a' Begin no-passing zone

Sight distance, measured along
center line (or right-hand lane line
on three lane road) becomes less
than minimum

b, b' End no-passing zone

Sight distance again exceeds
minimum

Note: No-passing zones in opposite directions may or may not overlap,
depending on alignment.

***Method of locating and determining the limits of no-passing zones at vertical
and horizontal curves.***

MINIMUM VERTICAL AND HORIZONTAL SIGHT DISTANCES

	DESIGNED PASSING—PROVIDE AS OFTEN AS PRACTICABLE				NON-PASSING
	2 lane highway		3 lane highway		provide at all points on all
speed	desirable	absolute	desirable	absolute	highways
30 mph	600'	500'			200'
40	1100	900			275
50	1600	1400	1100'	900'	350
60	2300	2100	1500	1300	475
70	3200	2900	2000	1800	600
80					750
90					950
100					1200

SOURCE: Manual on Uniform Traffic Control Devices, U.S. Dept. of Commerce, Washington, D.C., 1971.

Population, vehicles, and vehicular travel in the United States, 1930-1960

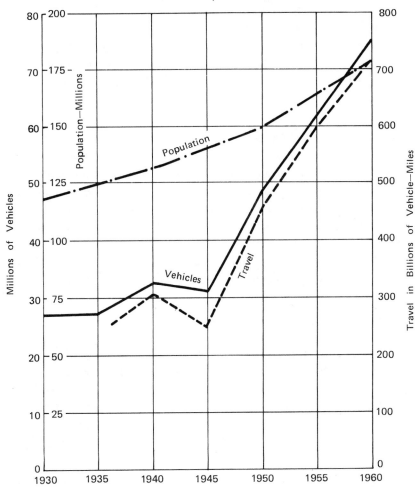

Population, vehicles, and vehicular travel in the United States, 1930-1960.

SOURCE: U.S. Bureau of Public Roads and U.S. Bureau of the Census. No travel data prior to 1936.

SOURCE: Statistical Abstracts of the U.S.–1967, U.S. Dept. of Commerce, Washington, D.C.

MOTOR-VEHICLE REGISTRATIONS, 1950 TO 1971, AND DRIVERS LICENSES, 1970, BY STATES

[In thousands, except as indicated. Motor-vehicle registrations include publicly owned vehicles; for uniformity, figures have been adjusted to a calendar-year basis as registration years in States differ; figures represent net numbers where possible, excluding re-registrations and nonresident registrations]

STATE	AUTOMOBILES, TRUCKS, AND BUSES				1971			Motor-cycles (incl. official),[1] 1971	DRIVERS LICENSES, 1970	Percent	
	1950	1960	1965	1970	Total	Private and commercial			Total[2]	Male drivers	Drivers under 25 years
						Auto-mobiles (incl. taxicabs)	Trucks and buses				
U.S.[3]	49,300	73,869	90,358	108,407	112,922	92,255	18,977	3,343.9	111,543	56.8	(NA)
Ala	686	1,282	1,663	1,966	2,093	1,650	413	51.9	1,740	57.2	(NA)
Alaska	(NA)	81	109	139	151	100	45	9.6	141	53.9	22.6
Ariz	271	624	825	1,093	1,185	885	277	42.9	1,124	55.7	27.2
Ark	477	708	914	1,043	1,075	747	314	23.8	1,058	56.7	21.0
Calif	4,620	7,799	9,989	11,901	12,324	10,160	1,978	614.6	11,646	55.0	20.9
Colo	564	924	1,158	1,442	1,548	1,170	351	57.0	1,379	60.7	29.9
Conn	716	1,107	1,415	1,733	1,791	1,619	149	43.0	1,724	53.6	21.5
Del	108	192	244	312	317	261	50	6.0	327	54.4	22.0
D.C	195	206	236	257	260	232	17	4.0	339	61.1	18.2
Fla	985	2,367	3,037	4,120	4,534	3,899	572	122.0	3,994	56.4	(NA)
Ga	898	1,512	1,990	2,584	2,753	2,188	530	66.0	2,710	57.3	(NA)
Hawaii	138	231	310	405	426	372	47	10.0	501	60.3	25.5
Idaho	272	375	434	474	509	351	145	32.0	484	58.9	(NA)
Ill	2,651	3,776	4,437	5,238	5,383	4,646	680	134.2	5,752	56.6	22.2
Ind	1,435	2,046	2,427	2,815	2,903	2,333	543	88.9	2,699	54.5	23.5
Iowa	1,072	1,325	1,549	1,790	1,842	1,417	392	79.1	1,678	56.0	23.0
Kans	853	1,163	1,369	1,548	1,599	1,149	425	74.5	1,453	53.3	24.5
Ky	784	1,198	1,500	1,763	1,860	1,440	396	29.6	1,609	58.5	21.6
La	707	1,177	1,442	1,742	1,832	1,426	382	34.0	1,782	57.3	(NA)
Maine	276	374	424	515	537	430	100	12.7	513	56.0	20.7
Md	685	1,155	1,481	1,872	2,003	1,724	257	34.8	2,054	56.9	23.8
Mass	1,280	1,803	2,104	2,575	2,700	2,421	245	52.7	2,988	54.4	21.5
Mich	2,433	3,306	3,991	4,569	4,740	4,029	641	194.0	5,127	57.1	23.1
Minn	1,169	1,592	1,890	2,207	2,293	1,808	454	89.2	2,310	57.1	23.1
Miss	484	723	921	1,117	1,176	864	294	20.4	1,237	58.9	22.5
Mo	1,261	1,720	2,085	2,408	2,498	1,944	530	67.8	2,569	54.9	23.2
Mont	265	373	429	485	511	326	175	30.0	409	55.3	22.4
Nebr	569	734	849	974	1,033	743	274	38.5	934	54.7	(NA)
Nev	77	175	266	355	373	275	85	19.3	337	55.8	20.6
N.H	172	267	331	362	375	312	56	12.7	427	55.7	21.8
N.J	1,579	2,401	2,980	3,586	3,737	3,337	334	57.4	4,029	55.9	19.3
N. Mex	238	426	525	637	661	460	186	27.4	577	55.6	(NA)
N.Y	3,735	5,067	5,939	6,718	6,891	6,130	659	77.7	8,056	58.4	18.9
N.C	1,056	1,720	2,156	2,826	3,002	2,345	577	60.4	2,743	55.5	25.5
N. Dak	276	345	396	428	444	276	159	13.3	331	56.2	25.3
Ohio	2,795	4,087	4,935	5,975	6,043	5,328	657	152.1	6,105	60.4	19.7
Okla	831	1,184	1,438	1,713	1,789	1,261	501	71.2	1,621	54.1	23.3
Oreg	689	919	1,119	1,369	1,432	1,156	245	69.8	1,304	59.6	16.2
Pa	3,010	4,287	4,968	5,819	6,011	5,195	751	147.4	6,213	59.0	21.7
R.I	251	341	406	488	509	449	54	13.2	504	56.6	(NA)
S.C	579	879	1,094	1,360	1,383	1,114	245	19.1	1,409	57.9	16.8
S. Dak	290	354	398	426	442	298	133	13.9	411	55.2	26.2
Tenn	858	1,307	1,655	2,050	2,136	1,696	407	57.7	2,078	55.7	22.9
Tex	2,968	4,457	5,610	6,693	6,984	5,308	1,567	186.2	6,380	56.4	(NA)
Utah	247	417	525	626	711	509	188	37.8	615	55.8	(NA)
Vt	121	152	175	229	237	193	40	9.0	253	56.5	(NA)
Va	918	1,426	1,800	2,263	2,410	1,992	369	41.0	2,345	57.0	22.6
Wash	924	1,377	1,659	2,102	2,163	1,643	476	74.7	1,920	55.2	22.9
W. Va	482	601	696	860	826	619	193	47.0	913	59.4	26.8
Wis	1,201	1,600	1,839	2,188	2,230	1,864	333	60.1	2,460	57.2	24.2
Wyo	145	207	225	247	257	163	88	12.5	229	58.1	29.6

NA Not available.
[1] Excludes vehicles owned by military services.
[2] Estimated from data reported by States for current and previous years; allowance has been made for deaths, emigration, or revocation by some States.
[3] Incomplete data for some States.

Source: U.S. Federal Highway Administration, *Highway Statistics*, annual; *Drivers Licenses*, annual; and unpublished data.

BIKEWAYS

The term "Bikeway" is used to define all facilities that explicitly provide for bicycle travel. Bikeways, then, can be anything from fully grade-separated facilities to simple signed streets. The following three classes of bikeway are defined:

Class I: A completely separated right-of-way designated for the exclusive use of bicycles. Crossflows by pedestrians and motorists are minimized.

Class II: A restricted right-of-way designated for the exclusive or semi-exclusive use of bicycles. Through-travel by motor vehicles or pedestrians is not allowed, however vehicle parking may be allowed. Cross-flows by motorists, for example to gain access to driveways or parking facilities, is allowed; pedestrian cross-flows, for example to gain access to parking facilities or associated land use, is allowed.

Class III: A shared right-of-way designated as such by signs placed on vertical posts or stencilled on the pavement. Any bikeway which shares its through-traffic right-of-way with either or both moving (not parking) motor vehicles and pedestrians is considered a Class III bikeway.

Class I bikeways typically may be found in parks, recreation areas, rural areas, and new developments where the routes are so laid out as to be completely separate from both roadways and pedestrian paths. In existing built-up urban areas provision of Class I bikeways might be infeasible when considered in light of the available right-of-way, the associated land use, and cost. In such cases it is appropriate to consider feasibility in terms of a set of Class II bikeway alternatives. Class III bikeways, as often found in this country, achieve only symbolic separation of the travel modes; as such they may be feasible only under the most ideal situations.

Several characteristics of the bikeway must be specified if it is to be rationally designed. These include the design speed of the facility, the space required by the bicycle and cyclist, minimum widths and clearances, grade, radius of curvature, bikeway surface, and drainage. In the following portions of this section each of these characteristics shall be discussed and, where appropriate, design recommendations shall be given.

BIKEWAY DESIGN SPEED

The speed that a cyclist travels is dependent upon several factors which include the type of bicycle and gearing, grade, surface, the direction and magnitude of the wind, air resistance, and the physical condition of the bicyclist. Although bike riders have been clocked at speeds in excess of 30 mph, most persons ride at less than half this rate.

For bikeway design purposes a speed of 10 mph is a conservative value to use in setting criteria for minimum widths and radii of curvature on level bikeways.

BIKEWAY WIDTH AND CLEARANCES

The width required for a bikeway is one of the primary considerations in bikeway design. Since the cost and feasibility of providing the bikeway varies with its width, it is necessary to determine minimum specifications subject to the space required for the cyclist, allowance for lateral movement between cyclists, allowance for lateral clearance to obstructions, and allowance for clearance to other hazards.

SOURCE: Bikeway Planning Criteria & Guidelines, University of California, 1972.

Virtually all countries in which bikeways are provided specify suggested minimum specifications. Most of these are identical to or slightly vary from specifications used in German bikeway design.

Owing to the wide acceptance of the German standards it is suggested that at the present they be used to set *minimums* for the widths of Class I and Class II bikeways in the United States. However, it is recommended that more liberal standards based upon a "comfortable" maneuvering allowance, be employed wherever the available space and costs allow.

GERMAN SPECIFICATIONS

The width requirements and horizontal and vertical clearances for a single-lane bikeway are shown schematically in Fig. 1. Minimum width consists of a 1.96

foot lateral cyclist space and a 0.66 foot maneuvering allowance on each side of the cyclist. Minimum recommended horizontal clearance to obstructions is 0.25 meters (0.82 feet). Curbing on a bikeway in excess of two inches in height is considered a vertical obstruction.

A vertical clearance allowance to overhead obstruction of 0.8 feet is recommended. In terms of the static vertical space requirement (7.4 feet), overhead obstructions should be no less than 8.2 feet from the surface of the bikeway.

Minimum width recommendations for multiple lane bikeways, are shown in Fig. 2. These minimums for multiple lane bikeways are based on provision of a maneuvering allowance *only* between pairs of cyclists; no maneuvering allowance is provided between the cyclist and the edge of the bikeway as in the one-lane case.

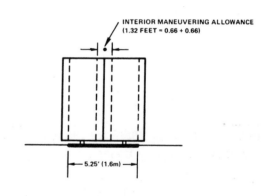

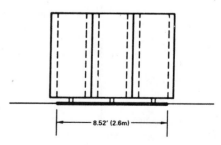

Figure 1. Single Lane Bikeway: Minimum Effective Width, Horizontal and Vertical Clearance to Static Obstructions. (Based on German Specification)

Figure 2. Minimum Effective Width for Two and Three Lane Bikeways Based on German Specifications (Clearances not Shown)

SOURCE: Bikeway Planning Criteria & Guidelines, University of California, 1972.

In terms of the minimum desirable number of lanes, a single lane on a Class I bikeway is not particularly effective since it doesn't allow passing without leaving the bikeway. As a recommended minimum on Class I bikeways, two lanes should thus be provided to allow a passing lane capability.

On Class II bikeways the minimum number of lanes that should be provided depends upon where on the street the bikeway is incorporated.

In Class II bikeways additional clearance should be allowed for "dynamic" obstructions. The most obvious example of this is when the bikeway is located adjacent to a parking lane. Since opening doors constitute a dynamic hazard to cyclists, an additional clearance for the car door should be allowed if adequate clearance is not provided in the parking lane and high parking density and turnover exist. Similarly the proximity of the bikeway to traffic lanes (and the speed, volume and mix of passing traffic) may require additional clearance if barriers are not provided and if the traffic lane is not wide enough to provide the necessary spatial separation.

GRADE

Cyclist characteristics (age, weight, conditioning, oxygen uptake, etc.), bicycle characteristics (gear ratios, type of cycle, tires, weight, etc.), wind velocity, air resistance, and road surface are major determinants of maximum acceptable bikeway grades and the length such grades should be in effect.

Source (1) recommends a 4-5% grade for one-speed cycles with a 9-10% maximum on "short" runs.

VOLUME CRITERIA FOR SEPARATED BIKEWAYS

Internationally, separated bikeways (Class I, II) have generally been recommended where:

1. Significant regular bicycle traffic exists, and/or
2. Significant future bicycle traffic is forecast, and/or
3. Significant motor vehicle traffic is present on the roadway.

TABLE 1 Minimum Effective Width for Class I and Class II Bikeways as a Function of Number of Bikeway Lanes

Number of Lanes (One Way)	MINIMUM EFFECTIVE WIDTH (FT)	
	German Specifications	Modified German Specifications Based upon a Comfortable Maneuvering Allowance at a 10 mph Design Speed
1	3. 3 (1m)	3. 3
2	5. 3 (1. 6m)	6. 4
3	8. 5 (2. 6m)	10. 9
4	11. 8 (3. 6m)	15. 3

SOURCE: Bikeway Planning Criteria & Guidelines, University of California, 1972.

DESIGN OF TURNING ROADWAY

Design Vehicles—A design vehicle is a selected motor vehicle of a designated type, the weight, dimensions and operating characteristics of which are used to establish highway design controls to accomodate vehicles of that type. The dimensions and minimum turning path of a design vehicle is a design control that affects principally the radius and width of pavement in intersection areas.

DESIGN VEHICLES & MINIMUM TURNING PATHS

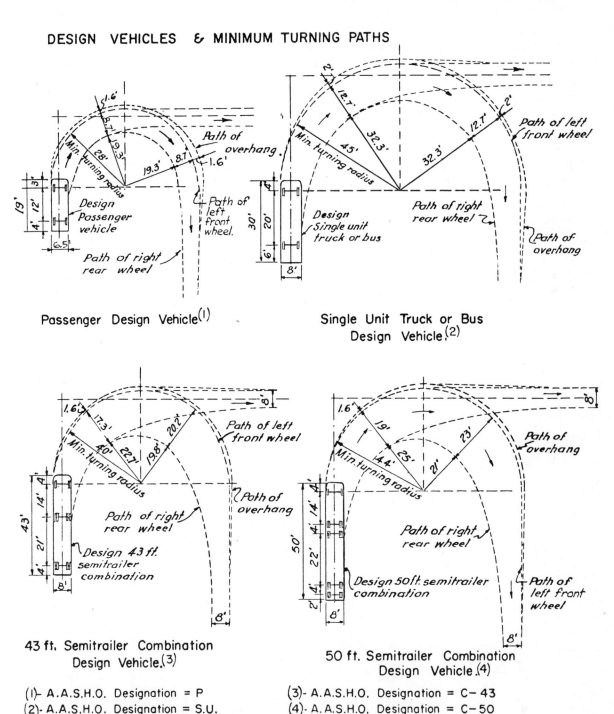

Passenger Design Vehicle[1]

Single Unit Truck or Bus Design Vehicle[2]

43 ft. Semitrailer Combination Design Vehicle[3]

50 ft. Semitrailer Combination Design Vehicle[4]

(1)- A.A.S.H.O. Designation = P
(2)- A.A.S.H.O. Designation = S.U.
(3)- A.A.S.H.O. Designation = C-43
(4)- A.A.S.H.O. Designation = C-50

AIR AND RAIL TRANSPORTATION

NATIONAL SYSTEM OF AIRPORTS

The National System of Airports consists of those public, civil, and joint use (military/civil) airport facilities within the United States and its territories considered necessary to provide a system of airports adequate to anticipate and meet the needs of civil aeronautics. By law, these airports are identified periodically in the FAA's National Airport System Plan (NASP) which was formerly the National Airport Plan (NAP).

New Classification. The new national airport classification system is based on the concept that all airports in the system have a functional role—this role being reasonably discernible by what the landing facility currently does or is projected into the future as having a need to accommodate in terms of its level of public service (enplaning passengers) and its level of aeronautical operational density (aircraft operations). The new classification system will reflect both the current level of service provided by the airports and projected demand for development purposes rather than merely the type of users. Categories of airports under the new classification system can be developed further to provide additional information on facility requirements of the total airport. Included could be such features as the terminal area, runway, separation criteria, geometric considerations, approaches, landing aids, etc., all based on a specific system requirement for airports in that category. Anticipated uses of the classification system are:

1. The identification of present system facilities and future system requirements;

2. Evaluations of both present and future needs from a national system planning point of view; and

3. Guidance for minimum design and safety standards for each of the airport subsystems.

SYSTEM DESCRIPTION

The new national airport classification system consists of three distinct subsystems of airports, differentiated by level of public service, that is, the number of enplaning passengers that are, or planned to be, accommodated by the airports.

Each subsystem is further classified into three levels of aeronautical operational density (aircraft operations) for planning purposes. This is shown in Figure 1. The following paragraphs discuss each of the major subsystems.

a. The Primary System

1. This system identifies airports with the highest level of public service within the national system. Therefore, it is considered important to the national air transportation system. This system consists of three subcategories representing various levels of aeronautical operational density primarily identified with air carrier served airports. The operational density levels are relevant to the runway capacity requirements of the airport.

2. Airports included in this category will, in most cases, be located in the largest of our metropolitan areas. The system will serve high to medium flows of intercity and international aeronautical needs, with airport facilities capable of handling the largest and most sophisticated aircraft in the air carrier and general aviation fleets.

3. The ideal airport configuration for each subcategory will normally be typified by a parallel runway system (with the exception of STOL operations and exclusion of crosswind runways) with adequate separation to permit simultaneous operations under IFR weather conditions and a terminal with a capacity for high-density passenger flow.

4. Each of the airports in the Primary System will have a requirement for an airport traffic control tower and an instrument approach procedure. In addition, for STOL service there will be a requirement for offset approaches to permit either use of separate airspace in terminal areas of conventional airports or avoidance of obstructions and populated areas at city-center locations.

b. Secondary System

1. The Secondary System identifies the next highest level of public service airports in the national system. It consists of those airports defined as having a secondary public service role and is also divided into three operational density subcategories.

AERONAUTICAL ACTIVITY LEVELS FOR
FUNCTIONAL ROLE AIRPORT CLASSIFICATION SYSTEM

Airport Category	(NASP Codes)	Public Service Level (Annual Enplaned Passengers)	Aeronautical Operational Density (Annual Aircraft Operations)
Primary System		More than 1,000,000	
High Density	(P1)		More than 350,000
Medium Density	(P2)		250,000 to 350,000
Low Density	(P3)		Less than 250,000
Secondary System		50,000 to 1,000,000	
High Density	(S1)		More than 250,000
Medium Density	(S2)		100,000 to 250,000
Low Density	(S3)		Less than 100,000
Feeder System		Less than 50,000	
High Density	(F1)		More than 100,000
Medium Density	(F2)		20,000 to 100,000
Low Density	(F3)		Less than 20,000

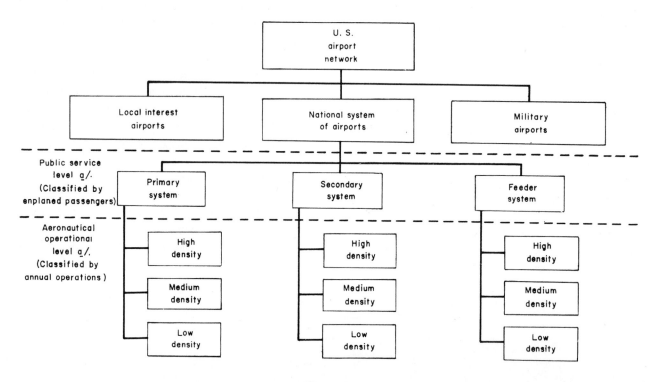

Figure 1

2. The role of airports in this subsystem will dictate a configuration characterized by at least a single full-length runway (excluding crosswind runways), as opposed to parallel runways at the Primary System airports. Where additional capacity is needed, the capacity may be provided for with a short runway of sufficient length to meet that need. Thus, airports in the Secondary System may in some cases have a requirement for a short runway as a reliever to the principal runway.

3. The airports in this category are typified by a medium to low density passenger flow and terminal facility requirements, with a runway length based on a critical length of haul that may vary from short to long range.

4. Usually the airports serving general aviation only in this category function principally as relievers to the airports used by air carriers in the larger communities. Aeronautical demand in some of these cases might be typified by a justification for service by large business transports or business jets; however, based on today's experience the percentages may relatively be very low.

5. The airport activity levels of the Secondary System will, in most cases, justify an airport traffic control tower and landing aids under currently applicable criteria.

c. Feeder System

1. The Feeder System category identifies the lowest public service level for airports within the national system. Airport facility requirements are less than for airports in the first two systems due to the smaller amounts of activity to be accommodated. Although of lower level of activity, the bulk of the air carrier served airports are in this system category. These airports exhibit differences principally in the size of the passenger terminals and runway lengths.

2. Airport configuration for this category will be typified by a single runway (excluding crosswind runways) with associated taxiways and a low density passenger terminal. A large proportion of airports in this category will have need for electronic landing aids, with only the high and medium aeronautical operational density subcategories having a requirement for a control tower.

3. Critical aircraft types for the air carrier served airports will usually be twin jets for the DC-9, B-737 type operated over short stage lengths. Exceptions to this may be required where, because of airline routings, longer stage lengths are necessary.

4. At "smaller" communities, general aviation activity demands on the airport may far surpass those imposed by air carrier service. However, the design configuration of the airport, where served by air carrier, is usually based on the air carrier used aircraft because of its greater facility requirements.

5. The airports exclusively serving general aviation within the Feeder System are typified by a low-density, single-runway airport similar in configuration to the "general utility category." They can accommodate about 95 percent of the general aviation fleet up to 12,500 pounds gross weight.

CLASSIFICATION CRITERIA

a. The aeronautical activity levels selected for the classification categories are fairly definitive of the size of airports presently or required in the system, particularly for long-range planning purposes. Adjustments to these limits may be made in the future, and possibly additional categories added, following further analyses on the effect of an airport's role on facility requirements.

b. Aeronautical activity levels in terms of enplaning passengers and total aircraft operations are considered most representative of intercity transportation demand and are types of activity for which statistics are normally collected and forecast. This was, in part, the basis for the selection of aeronautical activity levels to differentiate the airport classification categories discussed herein. The activity levels selected for differentiating the categories are presented in Fig. 1.

Figure 1 summarizes land use recommendations related to NEF contours or zones.

It has been modified from previous versions to reflect the four noise compatibility zones as used in Department of Housing and Urban Development Circular 1390.2. These four compatibility zones are defined by noise levels and by departmental procedures required in HUD Circular 1390.2. As used here, the definitions relate to suitability for construction, as used in HUD's "Noise Assessment Guidelines.

Different considerations are involved in determining sensitivities for differing land uses and activities. Most major land uses actually involve a variety of different human activities having differing noise sensitivities. Noise level limits for satisfactory speech communication across a conference table are different than those for satisfactory telephone usage. Noise level limits for desk tasks not involving speech communication are considerably higher than the limits that would allow successful voice communication in a classroom. And, as a further example, an industrial plant may encompass work areas having widely different noise sensitivities—ranging from rather stringent requirements in conference rooms and executive offices to more moderate requirements in drafting offices or typing areas, to manufacturing areas where noise from machinery or operations creates a noise environment in which even very high level noise intrusions would not be noticed.

The noise sensitivity code used in the table provides a gross ranking of the land use in terms of noise sensitivity, with the number 1 indicating the land uses most sensitive to noise and 5 the land use least sensitive. The approximate relationship between the noise sensitivity code rating and the NEF level at which new construction or development *is not* desirable is given below:

Noise Sensitivity Code	Approximate Noise Exposure Forecast Value Where New Construction or Development is Not Desirable
1	30
2	35
3	40
4	45
5	50-55

Figure 1

LAND USE CATEGORY	SLUCM[1] CODE	NSC[2]	LAND USE INTERPRETATION FOR NEF VALUE
Residential - Single Family, Duplex, Mobile Homes	11x[3]	1	
Residential - Multiple Family, Dormitories, etc.	11x, 12, 13, 19	1	
Transient Lodging	15	2	
School classrooms, Libraries, Cnurches	68 7111	1	
Hospitals, Nursing Homes	651	1	
Auditoriums, Concert Halls, Music Shells	721	1	
Sports Arenas, Outdoor Spectator Sports	722	1	
Playgrounds, Neighborhood Parks	761, 762	1	
Golf Courses, Riding Stables, Water Rec., Cemeteries	741x, 743x, 744	2	
Office Buildings, Personal, Business and Professional	61, 62, 63, 69, 65[4]	3	
Commercial - Retail, Movie Theaters, Restaurants	53, 54, 56, 57, 59	3	
Commercial - Wholesale, Some Retail, Ind., Mfg., Util.	51, 52, 64, 2, 3, 4	4	
Manufacturing, Communications (Noise Sensitive)	35, 47	2	
Livestock Farming, Animal Breeding	815, 816, 817	3	
Agriculture (except Livestock), Mining, Fishing	81, 82, 83, 84, 85, 91, 93	5	
Public Right-of-Way	45	5	
Extensive Natural Recreation Areas	91, 92, 93, 99, 7491, 75	3	

(NEF value scale across top: 10, 20, 30, 40, 50)

Clearly Acceptable   Normally Acceptable   Normally Unacceptable   Clearly Unacceptable

Clearly acceptable: The noise exposure is such that the activities associated with the land use may be carried out with essentially no interference from aircraft noise. (Residential areas: both indoor and outdoor noise environments are pleasant.)

Normally acceptable: The noise exposure is great enough to be of some concern, but common building constructions will make the indoor environment acceptable, even for sleeping quarters. (Residential areas: the outdoor environment will be reasonably pleasant for recreation and play.)

Normally unacceptable: The noise exposure is significantly more severe so that unusual and costly building constructions are necessary to ensure adequate performance of activities. (Residential areas: barriers must be erected between the site and prominent noise sources to make the outdoor environment tolerable.)

Clearly unacceptable: The noise exposure at the site is so severe that construction costs to make the indoor environment acceptable for performance of activities would be prohibitive. (Residential areas: the outdoor environment would be intolerable for normal residential use.)

[1] Standard Land Use Coding Manual.

[2] Noise Sensitivity Code (see page 53).

[3] x represents SLUCM category broader or narrower than, but generally inclusive of, the category described.

[4] Excluding hospitals.

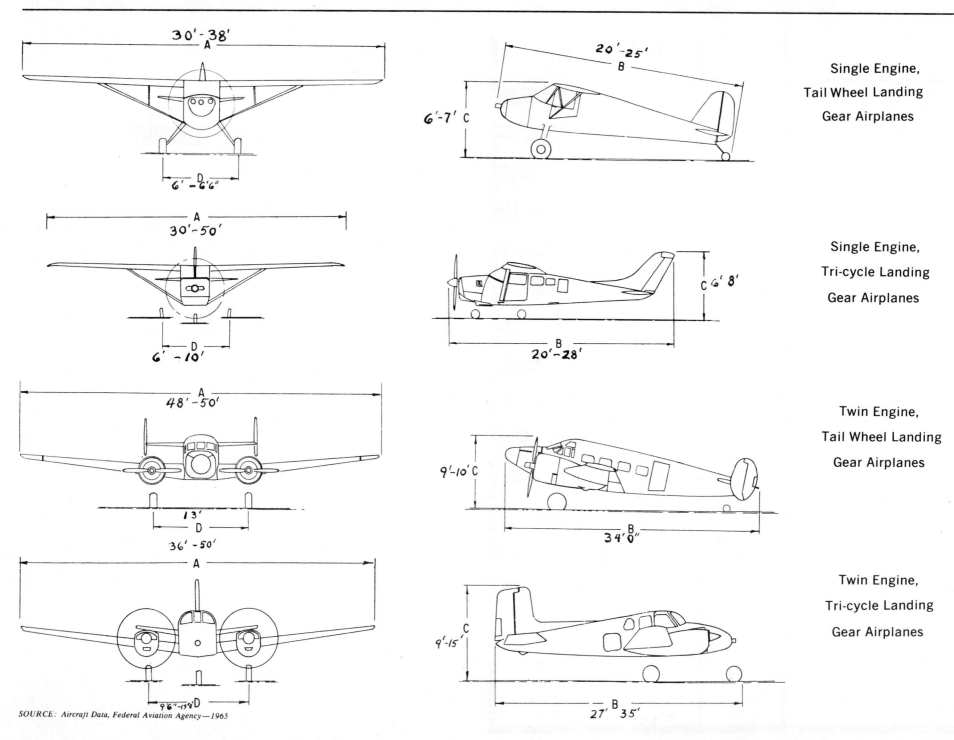

Single Engine,
Tail Wheel Landing
Gear Airplanes

Single Engine,
Tri-cycle Landing
Gear Airplanes

Twin Engine,
Tail Wheel Landing
Gear Airplanes

Twin Engine,
Tri-cycle Landing
Gear Airplanes

SOURCE: Aircraft Data, Federal Aviation Agency—1965

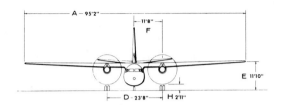
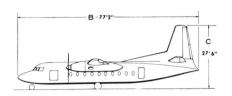

Fairchild F-27, F-27B

Rolls Royce Dart 511 Engine

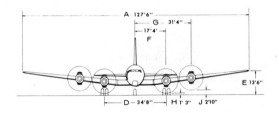
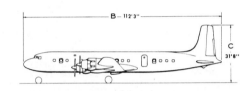

Douglas DC 7C

Wright R3350 Engine

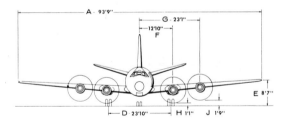
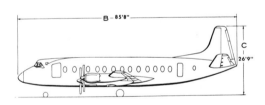

Vickers Viscount—V810

Rolls Royce Dart 525 Engine

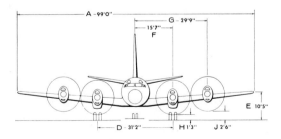
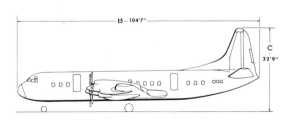

Lockheed 188C

Allison 501—D13 Engine

SOURCE: Aircraft Data, Federal Aviation Agency–1965.

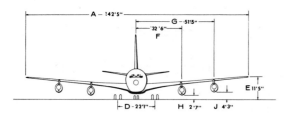

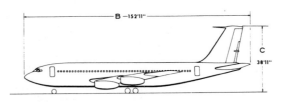

Boeing 707—400

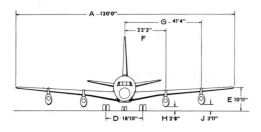

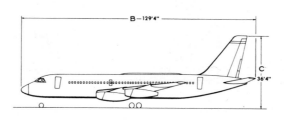

Convair 880
General Electric 805—3 Engine

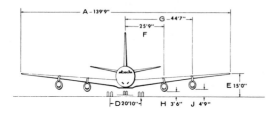

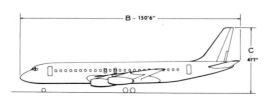

Douglas DC 8
JT3C6 Engine

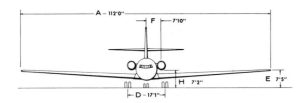

Carvelle SE 210
Rolls Royce Avon 522 Engine

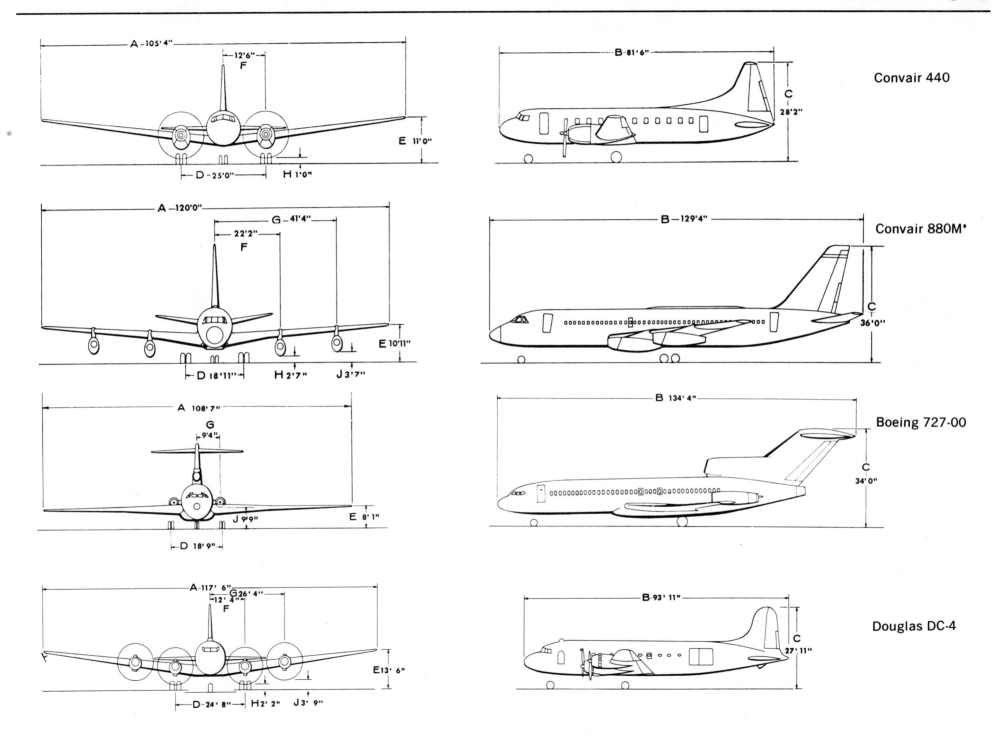

A –105'4"
12'6"
F
B –81'6"
C
28'2"
E 11'0"
D – 25'0"
H 1'0"
Convair 440

A –120'0"
G – 41'4"
22'2"
F
B – 129'4"
C
36'0"
E 10'11"
D 18'11"
H 2'7"
J 3'7"
Convair 880M'

A 108'7"
G
9'4"
B 134'4"
C
34'0"
J 9'9"
E 8'1"
D 18'9"
Boeing 727-00

A –117' 6"
G 26' 4"
12' 4"
F
B 93' 11"
C
27'11"
E 13' 6"
D – 24' 8"
H 2' 2"
J 3' 9"
Douglas DC-4

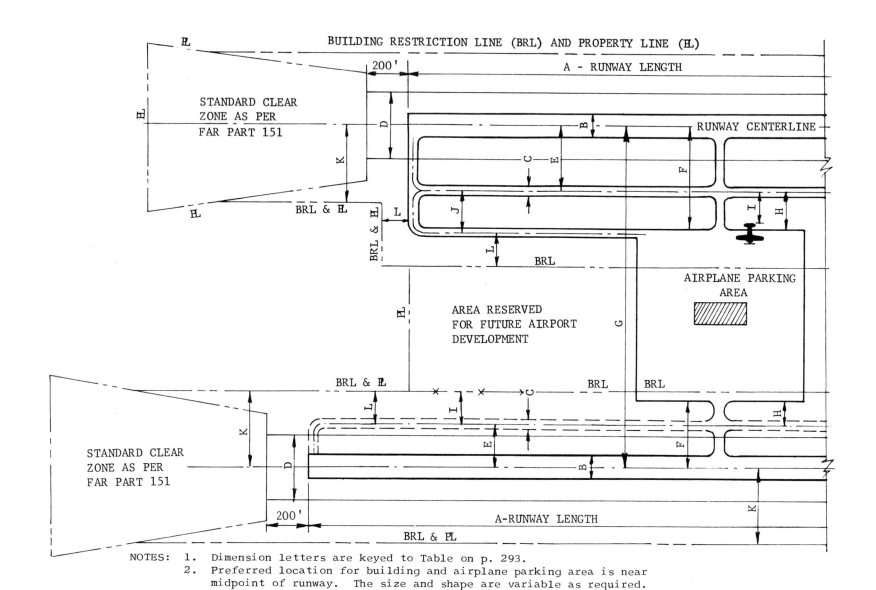

BUILDING RESTRICTION LINE (BRL) AND PROPERTY LINE (PL)

STANDARD CLEAR ZONE AS PER FAR PART 151

AREA RESERVED FOR FUTURE AIRPORT DEVELOPMENT

AIRPLANE PARKING AREA

RUNWAY CENTERLINE

A - RUNWAY LENGTH

STANDARD CLEAR ZONE AS PER FAR PART 151

A-RUNWAY LENGTH

BRL & PL

NOTES: 1. Dimension letters are keyed to Table on p. 293.
        2. Preferred location for building and airplane parking area is near
            midpoint of runway. The size and shape are variable as required.

Item	DIM[1]	Non-Precision Runway		General Transport	Precision Runway for Basic or General Transport
		Basic Transport			
		A[2]	B		
Runway Length	A		4	As required by critical airplane	As required by critical airplane
Width-Runway	B	75'	100'	100'	150'
Taxiway	C	40'[3]	40'[3]	40'[3]	40'[3]
Runway Safety Area	D	150'	300'	300'	500'
Runway Centerline to					
Taxiway Centerline	E	200'	200'	300'	400'
Airplane Parking Area	F	275'	300'	475'	650'
Parallel Runway	G	As per Current FAA Criteria			
Taxiway Centerline to					
Airplane Parking Area	H	75'	100'	175'	250'
Fixed or Movable Obstacle	I	50'	75'	100'	200'
Parallel Taxiway	J	150'	150'	200'	300'
Building Restriction Line to					
Runway Centerline	K	250'	300'	350'	750'
Taxiway Centerline	L	50'	75'	100'	200'

[1]Letters are keyed to those shown as dimensions on p. 292.
[2]Basic Transport Column A is to be used only at those low activity sites where an existing utility runway, having no anticipated need for an instrument approach procedure of any kind, is extended for business jets. For all other basic transport airports use Column B.
[3]Make straight taxiway sections 50 feet when airplanes with a wheel tread over 25 feet will use the airport. A width of 60 feet will be required for airplanes with tread over 35 feet.
Runway Length. Recommended runway lengths for basic transport and general transport airplanes are based on performance curves developed from FAA approved flight manuals in accordance with the provisions of FAR Parts 25 and 91.

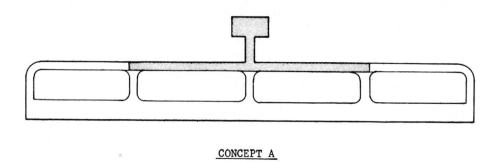

CONCEPT A

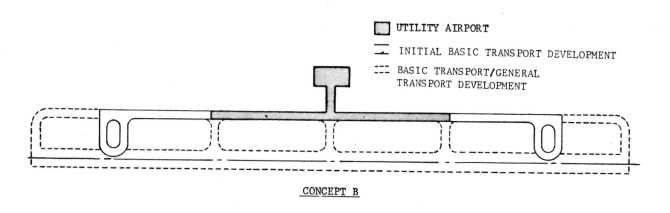

CONCEPT B

Figure 4

ALTERNATE SCHEME FOR EXPANSION OF EXISTING GENERAL UTILITY AIRPORT

Alternatives. Alternate methods, which may be employed when it is desired to have an airport "grow" from a utility type to a basic transport or general transport airport, as shown in Figure 4.

1. Concept A allows the original utility airport runway to be utilized as a taxiway with a new runway built at the proper separation from the taxiway.

2. In Concept B the extension is added to the utility airport runway as an initial development. In the ultimate development, the original runway becomes the taxiway with a new runway construction at the proper separation from the taxiway.

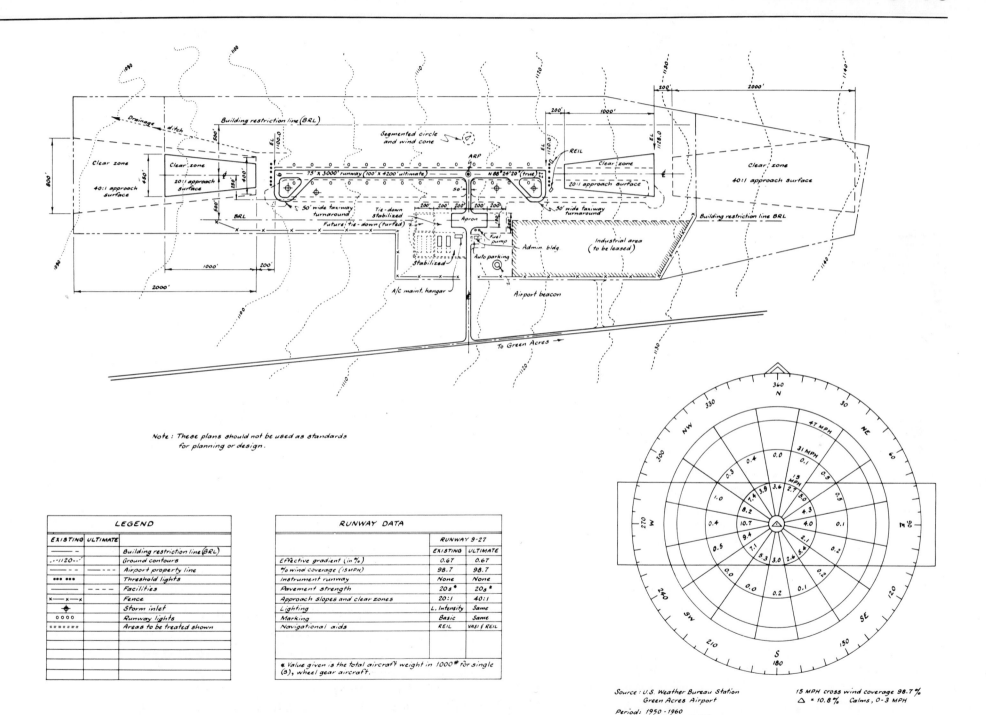

Note : These plans should not be used as standards for planning or design.

LEGEND

EXISTING	ULTIMATE	
————	————	Building restriction line (BRL)
..-1120-..	..-1120-..	Ground contours
— — — —	— — — —	Airport property line
••• •••		Threshold lights
– – – –		Facilities
x — x — x		Fence
✛		Storm inlet
0000		Runway lights
======		Areas to be treated shown

RUNWAY DATA

	RUNWAY 9-27	
	EXISTING	ULTIMATE
Effective gradient (in %)	0.67	0.67
% wind coverage (15 MPH)	98.7	98.7
Instrument runway	None	None
Pavement strength	20s *	20s *
Approach slopes and clear zones	20:1	40:1
Lighting	L. Intensity	Same
Marking	Basic	Same
Navigational aids	REIL	VASI & REIL

* Value given is the total aircraft weight in 1000# for single (S), wheel gear aircraft.

Source : U.S. Weather Bureau Station
Green Acres Airport
Period: 1950 - 1960
(All weather winds)

15 MPH cross wind coverage 98.7 %
△ = 10.8 % Calms, 0 - 3 MPH

WIND ROSE

SOURCE: Preparation of Airport Layout Plans, Federal Aviation Agency–1965.

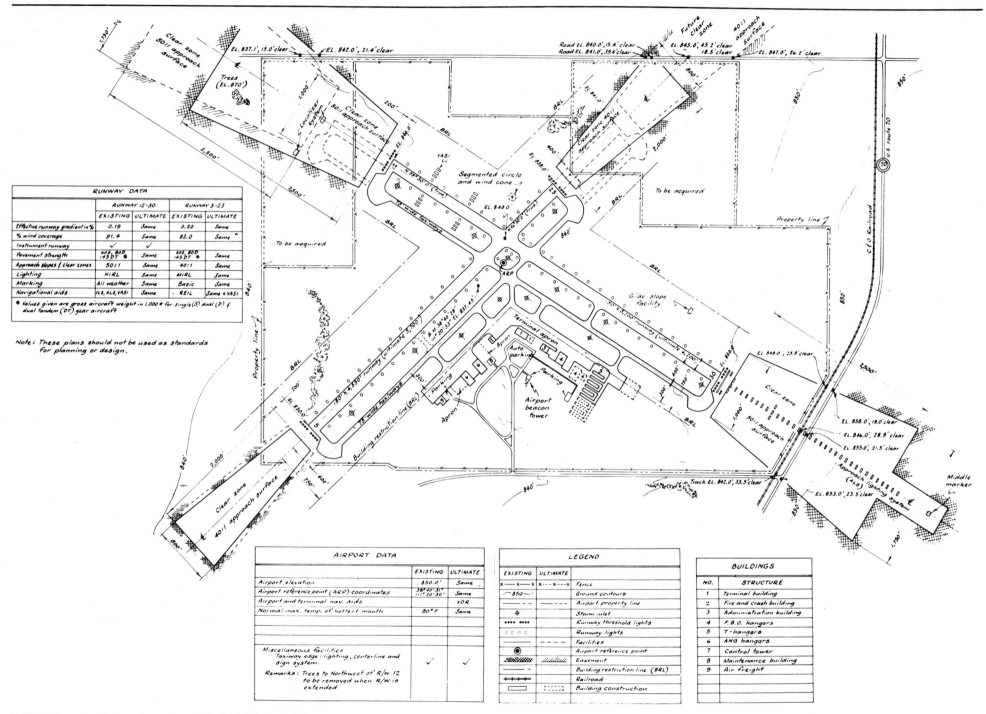

RUNWAY DATA

	RUNWAY 12-30		RUNWAY 5-23	
	EXISTING	ULTIMATE	EXISTING	ULTIMATE
Effective runway gradient in %	0.19	Same	0.20	Same
% wind coverage	91.4	Same	83.0	Same
Instrument runway	✓		✓	
Pavement strength	60S, 80D 145 DT *	Same	60S, 80D 145 DT *	Same
Approach slopes & clear zones	50:1	Same	40:1	Same
Lighting	HIRL	Same	MIRL	Same
Marking	All weather	Same	Basic	Same
Navigational aids	ILS, ALS, VASI	Same	REIL	Same + VASI

* Values given are gross aircraft weight in 1,000 # for single (S) dual (D) & dual tandem (DT) gear aircraft

Note: These plans should not be used as standards for planning or design.

AIRPORT DATA

	EXISTING	ULTIMATE
Airport elevation	850.0'	Same
Airport reference point (ARP) coordinates	38°40'31" 111°20'30"	Same
Airport and terminal nav. aids		VOR
Normal max. temp. of hottest month	80°F	Same
Miscellaneous facilities Taxiway edge lighting, centerline and sign system.	✓	✓
Remarks: Trees to Northwest of R/w 12 to be removed when R/w is extended		

LEGEND

EXISTING	ULTIMATE	
x — x — x	x --- x --- x	Fence
—850—	—	Ground contours
	—	Airport property line
⊕		Storm inlet
•••• ••••		Runway threshold lights
o o o o		Runway lights
	— — —	Facilities
⊚		Airport reference point
▨▨▨▨	|||||||	Easement
—	-	Building restriction line (BRL)
＋＋＋＋		Railroad
▭	⠿⠿⠿	Building construction

BUILDINGS

NO.	STRUCTURE
1	Terminal building
2	Fire and crash building
3	Administration building
4	F.B.O. hangars
5	T-hangars
6	ANG hangars
7	Control tower
8	Maintenance building
9	Air freight

SOURCE: Preparation of Airport Layout Plans, Federal Aviation Agency–1965.

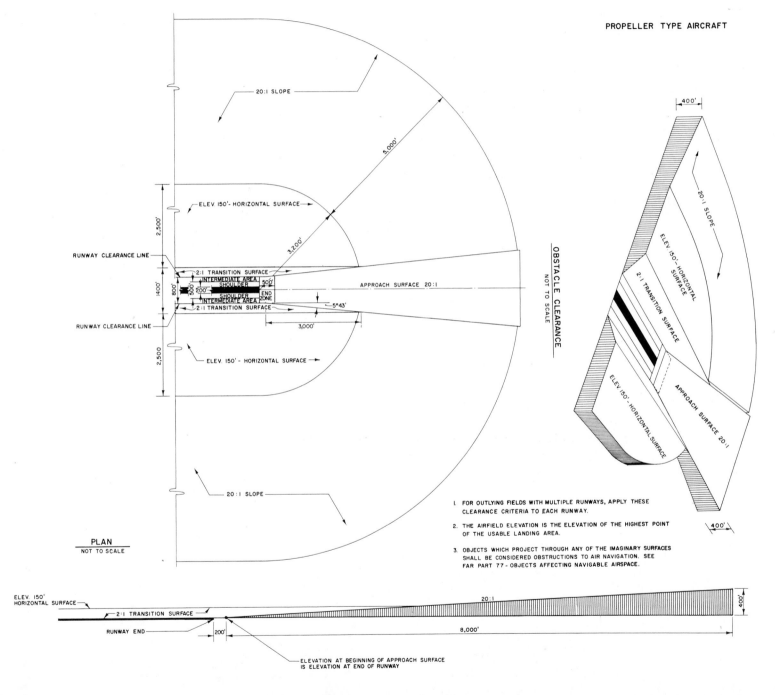

PROPELLER TYPE AIRCRAFT

20:1 SLOPE

5,000'

ELEV. 150'- HORIZONTAL SURFACE

3,200'

RUNWAY CLEARANCE LINE

2:1 TRANSITION SURFACE

INTERMEDIATE AREA
SHOULDER
500'
APPROACH SURFACE 20:1
SHOULDER
END ZONE
INTERMEDIATE AREA

2:1 TRANSITION SURFACE

5°43'

RUNWAY CLEARANCE LINE

3,000'

ELEV. 150' - HORIZONTAL SURFACE

OBSTACLE CLEARANCE
NOT TO SCALE

20:1 SLOPE

2,500'

1,400'

800'

500'

200'

2,500'

PLAN
NOT TO SCALE

400'

ELEV. 150'- HORIZONTAL SURFACE

20:1 SLOPE

2:1 TRANSITION SURFACE

APPROACH SURFACE 20:1

ELEV. 150'- HORIZONTAL SURFACE

400'

1. FOR OUTLYING FIELDS WITH MULTIPLE RUNWAYS, APPLY THESE
CLEARANCE CRITERIA TO EACH RUNWAY.

2. THE AIRFIELD ELEVATION IS THE ELEVATION OF THE HIGHEST POINT
OF THE USABLE LANDING AREA.

3. OBJECTS WHICH PROJECT THROUGH ANY OF THE IMAGINARY SURFACES
SHALL BE CONSIDERED OBSTRUCTIONS TO AIR NAVIGATION. SEE
FAR PART 77 - OBJECTS AFFECTING NAVIGABLE AIRSPACE.

ELEV. 150'
HORIZONTAL SURFACE

20:1

400'

2:1 TRANSITION SURFACE

RUNWAY END

200'

8,000'

ELEVATION AT BEGINNING OF APPROACH SURFACE
IS ELEVATION AT END OF RUNWAY

SECTIONAL ELEVATION ON CENTERLINE OF RUNWAY
NOT TO SCALE

297

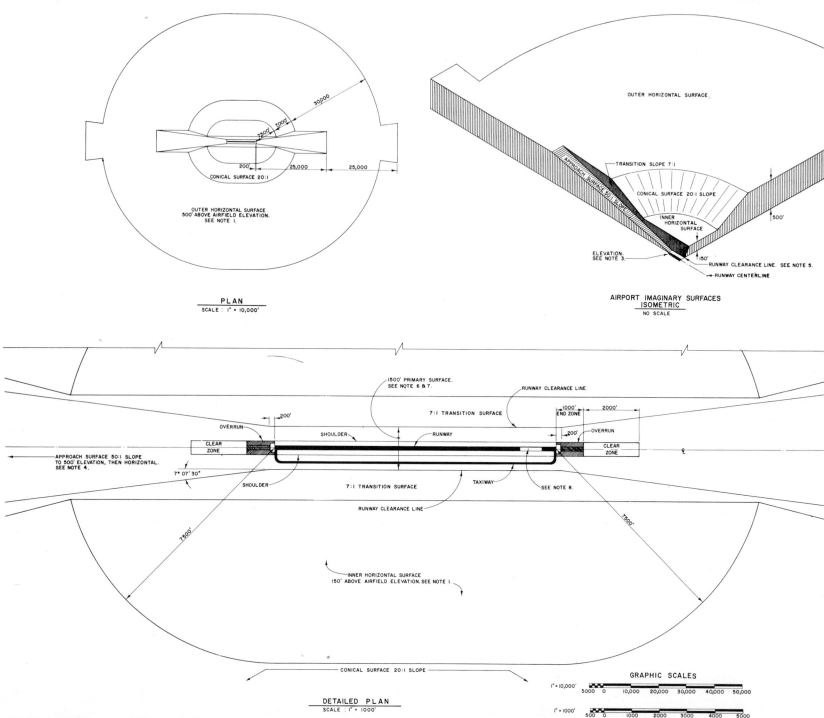

PLAN
SCALE : 1" = 10,000'

AIRPORT IMAGINARY SURFACES
ISOMETRIC
NO SCALE

In the PLAN diagram:
- 30,000
- 7000
- 7500'
- OUTER HORIZONTAL SURFACE 500' ABOVE AIRFIELD ELEVATION. SEE NOTE 1.
- 200'
- 25,000
- 25,000
- CONICAL SURFACE 20:1

In the ISOMETRIC diagram:
- OUTER HORIZONTAL SURFACE
- TRANSITION SLOPE 7:1
- APPROACH SURFACE 50:1 SLOPE
- CONICAL SURFACE 20:1 SLOPE
- INNER HORIZONTAL SURFACE
- 500'
- ELEVATION. SEE NOTE 3.
- 150'
- RUNWAY CLEARANCE LINE. SEE NOTE 5.
- RUNWAY CENTERLINE

In the DETAILED PLAN:
- 1500' PRIMARY SURFACE. SEE NOTE 6 & 7.
- RUNWAY CLEARANCE LINE
- 7:1 TRANSITION SURFACE
- 1000' END ZONE
- 2000'
- 200'
- OVERRUN
- 200'
- OVERRUN
- SHOULDER
- RUNWAY
- CLEAR ZONE
- CLEAR ZONE
- APPROACH SURFACE 50:1 SLOPE TO 500' ELEVATION, THEN HORIZONTAL. SEE NOTE 4.
- 7° 07' 30"
- SHOULDER
- 7:1 TRANSITION SURFACE
- TAXIWAY
- SEE NOTE 8.
- RUNWAY CLEARANCE LINE
- 7500'
- 7500'
- INNER HORIZONTAL SURFACE 150' ABOVE AIRFIELD ELEVATION. SEE NOTE 1.
- CONICAL SURFACE 20:1 SLOPE

DETAILED PLAN
SCALE : 1" = 1000'

GRAPHIC SCALES

1" = 10,000'
5000 0 10,000 20,000 30,000 40,000 50,000

1" = 1000'
500 0 1000 2000 3000 4000 5000

SOURCE: Naval Facilities Engineering Command Dept of the Navy, Wash., D.C.

1. The inner horizontal surface is at an elevation of 150 feet above the established airfield elevation; the outer horizontal surface is at 500 feet.

2. The airfield elevation is the elevation of the highest point of the usable landing area.

3. The elevation of the point of beginning of the approach slope is the same as the elevation of the end of the runway.

4. At fields which accommodate propeller aircraft, the approach surface slope shall be 20:1.

5. The runway clearance line defines the lateral limit of the primary surface and is 750 feet on each side of the runway centerline.

6. The primary surface is a surface longitudinally centered on the runway and extending 200 feet beyond the runway ends.

7. The elevation of any point on the longitudinal profile of a primary surface, including extensions, coincides with the elevation of the centerline of the runway, or extension, as appropriate.

8. For airfields with multiple runways, apply these clearance criteria to each runway.

9. The approach surfaces terminate 200 feet beyond the runway ends.

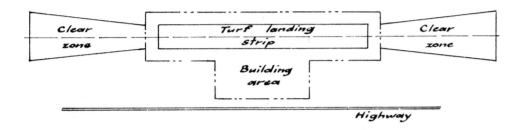

Approximate min. land areas required for small

airports at specified elevations

Elevation of site in feet	Landing strip [1] dimensions in feet			Acreage required [2]	
	Width	Length		Min.	Max.
		Min.	Max.		
Sea level	250	1800	3400	27	43
1000	250	1900	3600	28	45
2000	250	2100	3900	30	48
3000	250	2200	4100	31	51
4000	250	2300	4400	32	53
5000	250	2400	4600	33	55

[1] Landing strip lengths are shown to the nearest 100′ after correcting sea level lengths for elevation.

[2] Based on min. rectangular parcals of land as shown on above sketch. In addition, adequate property interests should be acquired in the 16 acres contained in the clear zones.

SOURCE: *Small Airports, Federal Aviation Agency*

Future airport requirements should be carefully considered when acquiring land. It is desirable that the area obtained be adequate for development to the size required for the foreseeable future. Where boundaries of present ownership make it necessary to acquire more land than is actually required for the initial development, the portion not needed immediately for the full airport development may be put to other revenue-producing uses until it is needed.

Specific land requirements cannot be given because of the variable conditions that may be encountered, but the accompanying table may be used to estimate the minimum amount of property that will be required. The indicated acreages are based on landing-strip lengths corrected only for elevation, minimum building area, and clear-zone requirements.

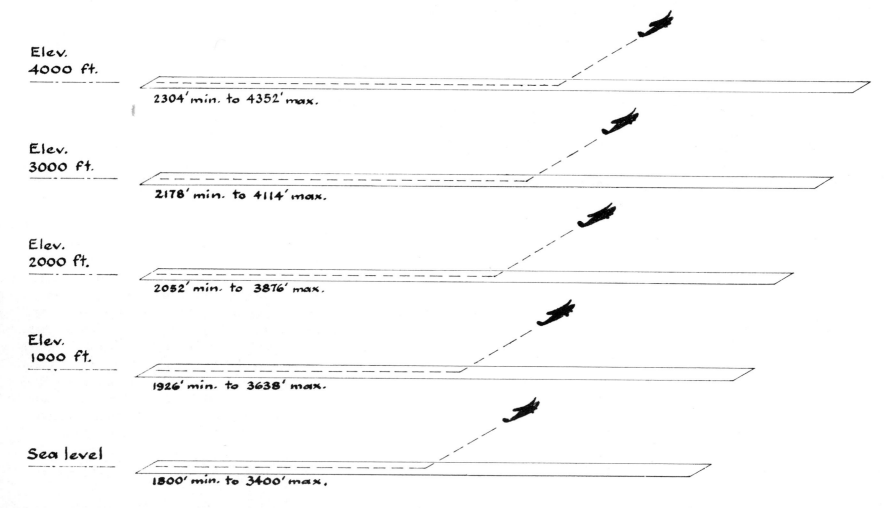

Elev.
4000 ft.
2304' min. to 4352' max.

Elev.
3000 ft.
2178' min. to 4114' max.

Elev.
2000 ft.
2052' min. to 3876' max.

Elev.
1000 ft.
1926' min. to 3638' max.

Sea level
1800' min. to 3400' max.

Small, or secondary, airports are generally designed for personal flying, whether it be for business or pleasure.

The popular kinds of aircraft in use at these airports range from small single-engine trainers of low horsepower to light twin-eigine-type aircraft. In between are the three- and four-passenger single-engine aircraft of medium horsepower. These vary widely in size and performance, affecting the required length of the landing strip. Obviously, a small single-engine aircraft of 1,200 pounds gross weight requires a shorter landing strip than does a multi-engine aircraft of much greater gross weight. For the aircraft that will use secondary airports, landing strips having lengths of 1,800 feet to 3,200 feet at sea level are adequate. If the landing strips are properly designed, these airports will accommodate aircraft having gross weights up to 12,500 pounds.

A major factor affecting the size of the airport is the elevation of the site above sea level. The above illustrates the effect of elevation on the distance required for an aircraft to gain sufficient speed to become airborne. To compensate for this effect, the basic sea-level length should be increased 7 percent for each 1,000 feet that the airport is above sea level.

SOURCE: Small Airports, Federal Aviation Agency

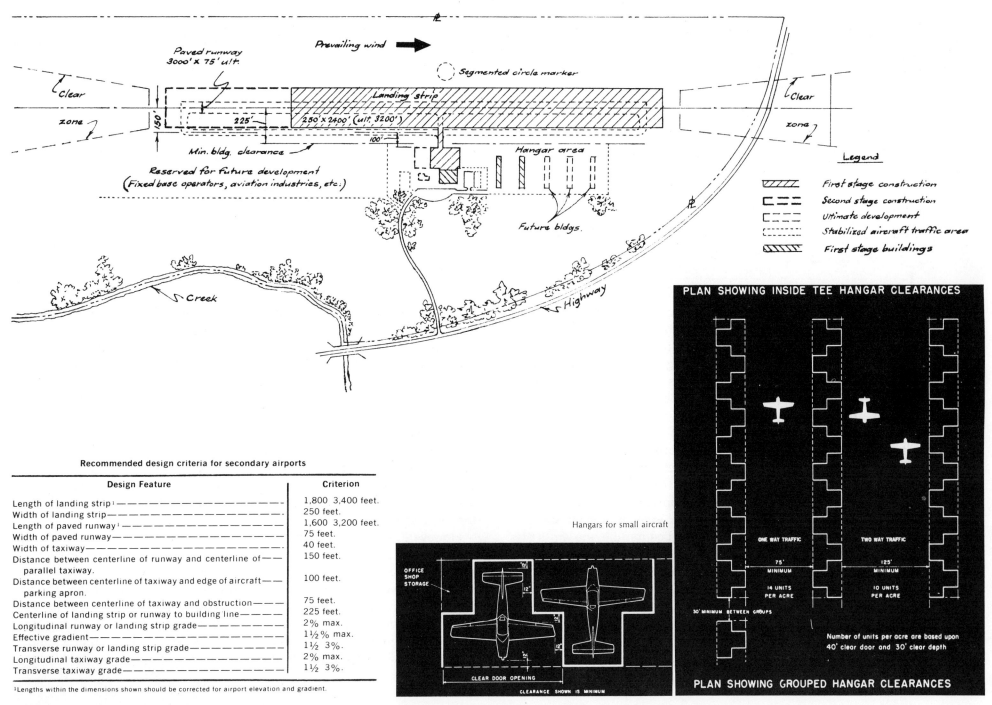

Paved runway
3000' x 75' ult.

Prevailing wind →

Segmented circle marker

Clear zone

Landing strip

50'

225'

250' x 2400' (ult. 3200')

Min. bldg. clearance

100'

Hangar area

Reserved for future development
(Fixed base operators, aviation industries, etc.)

Future bldgs.

Clear zone

Creek

Highway

Legend

First stage construction

Second stage construction

Ultimate development

Stabilized aircraft traffic area

First stage buildings

Recommended design criteria for secondary airports

Design Feature	Criterion
Length of landing strip[1]	1,800 3,400 feet.
Width of landing strip	250 feet.
Length of paved runway[1]	1,600 3,200 feet.
Width of paved runway	75 feet.
Width of taxiway	40 feet.
Distance between centerline of runway and centerline of parallel taxiway.	150 feet.
Distance between centerline of taxiway and edge of aircraft parking apron.	100 feet.
Distance between centerline of taxiway and obstruction	75 feet.
Centerline of landing strip or runway to building line	225 feet.
Longitudinal runway or landing strip grade	2% max.
Effective gradient	1½% max.
Transverse runway or landing strip grade	1½ 3%.
Longitudinal taxiway grade	2% max.
Transverse taxiway grade	1½ 3%.

[1]Lengths within the dimensions shown should be corrected for airport elevation and gradient.

SOURCE: *Small Airports, Federal Aviation Agency*

Hangars for small aircraft

PLAN SHOWING INSIDE TEE HANGAR CLEARANCES

ONE WAY TRAFFIC

TWO WAY TRAFFIC

75' MINIMUM

125' MINIMUM

14 UNITS PER ACRE

10 UNITS PER ACRE

30' MINIMUM BETWEEN GROUPS

OFFICE SHOP STORAGE

12"

12"

CLEAR DOOR OPENING

CLEARANCE SHOWN IS MINIMUM

Number of units per acre are based upon
40' clear door and 30' clear depth

PLAN SHOWING GROUPED HANGAR CLEARANCES

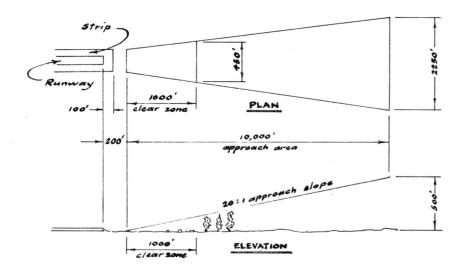

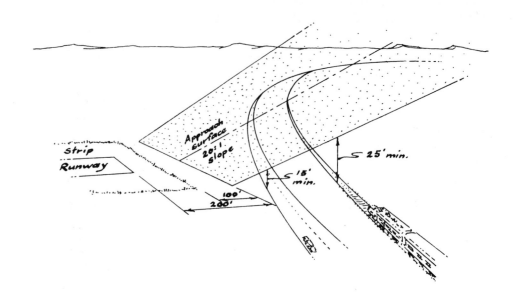

Obstructions to flight in the local area is an important factor that should be considered in choosing a site. They consist of fences, trees, pole lines, buildings, and other natural or manmade objects in the area immediately adjacent to the airport. In some instances, the ground itself may slope upward from the end of the landing strip to such an extent that it constitutes an obstruction to aircraft operation. If obstructions exist around a site on which an airport is to be built, their removal is imperative, though it may involve considerable expense and litigation.

Aircraft when taking off or landing gain or lose altitude very slowly compared to their forward speed. Because of this characteristic, they need space at the ends of the landing strips, known as "approach areas," over which they may safely gain or lose altitude. An approach area begins at a point 200 feet from the end of the runway and extends a distance of 10,000 feet. Being symmetrical about the extended centerline, the width of the approach area increases with distance from the end of the landing strip. An approach area should be free of obstructions that exceed a height of 1 foot above the end of the landing strip for each 20 feet of distance from the end of the strip.

At small airports, the most critical portion of the approach area is the first 1,000 feet. This area, known as the "clear zone," is the innermost portion of the approach area. Its configuration and dimensions are shown in figure 2. The purchase of land in this zone is recommended. If this cannot be done, sufficient control over the land should be acquired to allow for the removal of existing obstructions and to control the future use of the land and any construction thereon which would interfere with operations at the airport.

The FAA does not regard the clear zone as an "overrun area" or "landing strip extension." Therefore, it is not necessary to grade the area, but obstructions must be removed. Naturally, a level area is preferable, but it is not required. Fences, ditches, and other minor obstacles are permitted. In the same vein, roads and railroads are not objectionable in clear zones providing they comply with the recognized clearance standard (see fig. 3). Clearance does not ordinarily present a problem in the approach area beyond the clear zone.

However, certain clearance restrictions exist for railroads and highways located anywhere in the approach area. At least the minimum clearances as shown in figure 3 are required. The "critical clearance" is the vertical distance between the 20:1 approach surface and the edge of the highway pavement, or the railroad rail nearest the end of the landing strip. This clearance should not be less than 15 feet over highways, or 25 feet over railroads. Regardless of topography, in no case should the end of a landing strip be closer than 100 feet to the nearest edge of a highway or railroad.

SOURCE: Small Airports, Federal Aviation Agency

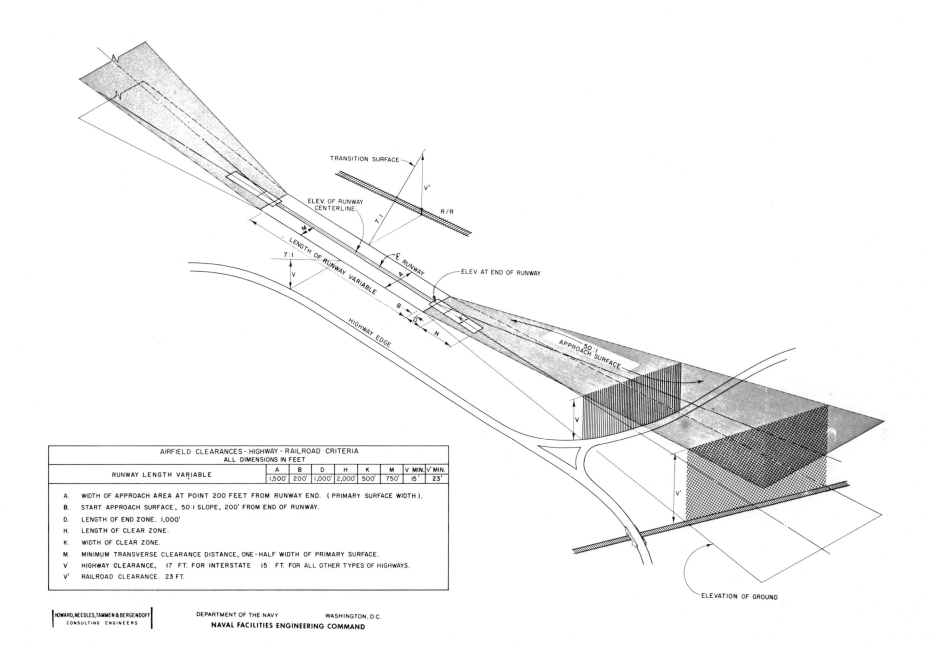

TRANSITION SURFACE

V'

ELEV. OF RUNWAY CENTERLINE

R/R

7:1

LENGTH OF RUNWAY VARIABLE

Ȼ RUNWAY

A

ELEV. AT END OF RUNWAY

7:1

V

B

D

H

HIGHWAY EDGE

50:1 APPROACH SURFACE

V

V'

V'

ELEVATION OF GROUND

AIRFIELD CLEARANCES - HIGHWAY - RAILROAD CRITERIA ALL DIMENSIONS IN FEET								
	A	B	D	H	K	M	V MIN.	V' MIN.
RUNWAY LENGTH VARIABLE	1,500'	200'	1,000'	2,000'	500'	750'	15'	23'

A.   WIDTH OF APPROACH AREA AT POINT 200 FEET FROM RUNWAY END. (PRIMARY SURFACE WIDTH).

B.   START APPROACH SURFACE, 50:1 SLOPE, 200' FROM END OF RUNWAY.

D.   LENGTH OF END ZONE. 1,000'

H.   LENGTH OF CLEAR ZONE.

K.   WIDTH OF CLEAR ZONE.

M.   MINIMUM TRANSVERSE CLEARANCE DISTANCE, ONE-HALF WIDTH OF PRIMARY SURFACE.

V   HIGHWAY CLEARANCE, 17 FT. FOR INTERSTATE   15 FT. FOR ALL OTHER TYPES OF HIGHWAYS.

V'   RAILROAD CLEARANCE. 23 FT.

| HOWARD, NEEDLES, TAMMEN & BERGENDOFF CONSULTING ENGINEERS | DEPARTMENT OF THE NAVY   WASHINGTON, D.C. **NAVAL FACILITIES ENGINEERING COMMAND** |

GENERAL. Classification of heliports/helistops is provided to indicate the major differences between kinds of installations for helicopter operations. The differences lie mainly in use, types of helicopters served, and the nature of supporting facilities included on the heliport. Classification is helpful in planning and zoning for heliports and serves to relate the operational factors involved to land use considerations.

a. Use. A heliport/helistop is either a privately operated exclusive use facility, on which the operator has control over the type and number of helicopters which may use it, or it is a publicly owned and operated facility open to any helicopter operator.

b. Size. A heliport/helistop may be any size down to the minimum recommended in this chapter and defined in Chapter 9. The size refers to the dimensions of the landing and takeoff area.

c. Helicopter Types. Helicopter types refer to those in the normal category as defined in FAR Part 27 or those in the transport category as defined in FAR Part 29.

    1. Normal category helicopters are machines 6,000 pounds or less maximum gross weight operated principally in private, business, charter, or commercial flying other than air carrier operations.

    2. Transport category helicopters are single-engine or multi-engine machines of unlimited weight operated in scheduled or nonscheduled passenger service.

d. Supporting Facilities. These refer to passenger and/or cargo facilities, helicopter parking, fueling, and maintenance provisions on the heliport. A helistop has none of these facilities except that it may be a pickup and discharge point for passengers or cargo.

HELIPORT CLASSIFICATION. Heliports are classified in accordance with uses, as follows:

    Class I—Private

    Class II—Public (Small)
    Class III—Public (Large)

1. Private Heliport (Class I). The landing and takeoff area dimensions are selected by the owner and are based on the overall length of the helicopter. Minimum length of the area should be at least 1.5 times the overall length of the helicopter and the width equal to the length. For example, if the largest helicopter to be served has an overall length of 60 feet, the minimum dimensions would be 90 feet by 90 feet (Figure 8).

2. Small Public Heliport (Class II). The landing and takeoff area dimensions should be sufficient to accommodate any of the various models of helicopters in the normal category, the airworthiness requirements of which are defined in FAR Part 27 (formerly CAR 6). These heliports should have a minimum landing and takeoff area length of 2.0 times the overall length of the helicopter and a width of 1.5 times the overall helicopter length (Figure 9).

3. Large Public Heliport (Class III). The landing and takeoff area dimensions should be sufficient to accommodate any model helicopter in the normal and transport categories, the airworthiness requirements of which are defined in FAR Parts 27 and 29 (formerly CARs 6 and 7). These heliports should have a minimum landing and takeoff area length of 2.0 times the overall length of the helicopter and a width of 1.5 times the overall helicopter length (Figure 10).

They are further subclassified in accordance with their available support facilities, as follows:

    Subclass A—Minimum support facilities—no buildings, maintenance or fueling (a helistop).

    Subclass B—Limited support facilities—no maintenance or fueling.

    Subclass C—Complete support facilities.

Note: Any heliport may be either privately or publicly owned or operated. Whether it is private or public does not affect its subclassification.

SOURCE: Heliport Design Guide Federal Aviation Agency-1959

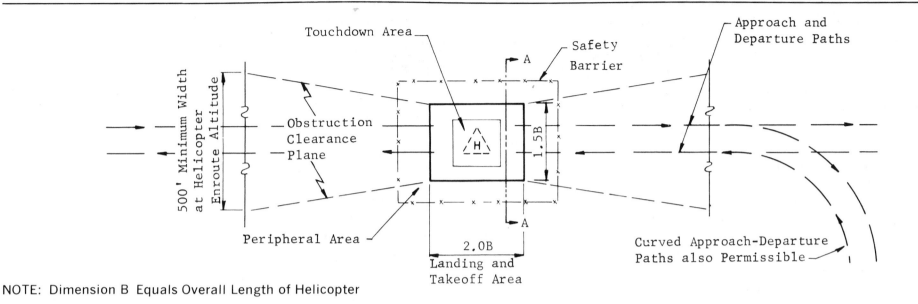

NOTE: Dimension B Equals Overall Length of Helicopter

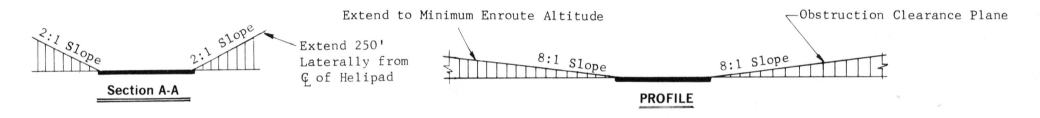

HELIPORT LAYOUT. The size, shape, and appurtenances of heliports are determined by a variety of interrelated factors—principally the nature of the site available, size and performance of the helicopter, and the buildings or other objects in the surrounding area. Although heliports may be square, rectangular, or circular, an irregular-shaped site may be equally functional. Minimum operational safety requirements will not vary from one design to another.

    a. Landing and Takeoff Area. Since landing and takeoff areas should provide sufficient space for the helicopter to maneuver, size depends to a large extent on the overall length of the helicopter, i.e., the tip to tip dimension of the rotor system. These dimensions vary considerably according to the type of helicopter.

Heliports at Elevations Less Than 1,000 Feet Above Sea Level. Minimum recommended landing and takeoff area dimensions shown above are applicable to all heliports 1,000 feet above sea level or less.

Heliports at Elevations More Than 1,000 Feet Above Sea Level. For elevations of more than 1,000 feet above sea level, it is recommended that consideration be given to increasing the length of the landing and takeoff area or diameter (if circular) by 15 percent per 1,000 feet of sea level elevation above 1,000 feet or that part thereof, in order to prevent drastic off-loading of non-supercharged helicopters. For example, on a heliport 3,000 feet above sea level, the minimum length would be increased by 30 percent.

SOURCE: Heliport Design Guide, Federal Aviation Agency–1959.

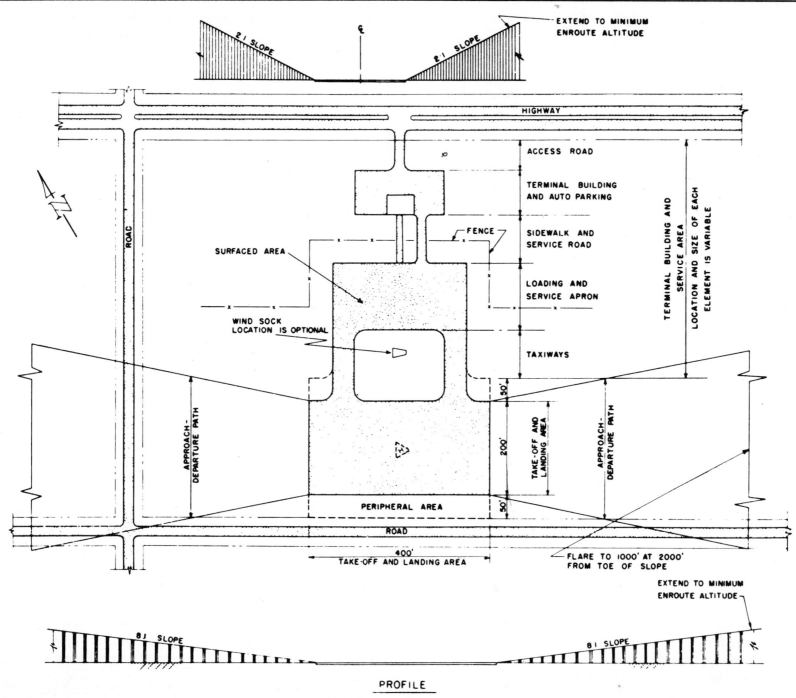

SOURCE: *Heliport Design Guide, Federal Aviation Agency—1959*

Perspective View of
Approach-Departure Path

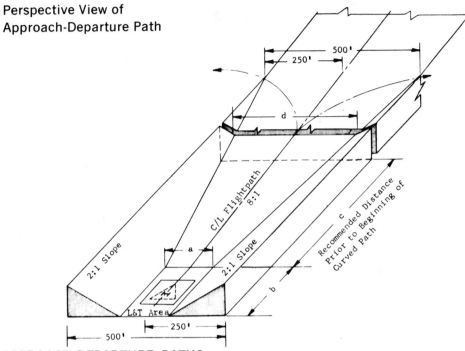

Minimum Angles Between Approach-Departure Paths

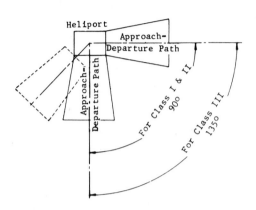

APPROACH-DEPARTURE PATHS

a. General. Approach-departure paths are selected to provide the most advantageous lines of flight to and from the landing and takeoff area. These paths are considered as beginning at the edge of the landing and takeoff area and usually are aligned as directly as possible into the prevailing winds. It is generally necessary to have at least two paths which should be separated by an arc of at least 90 degrees for Class I and Class II heliports and 135 degrees for Class III heliports . Curved paths are quite practical and are necessary in many cases to provide a suitable route. Emergency landing areas must be available along all approach-departure paths for all heliports except those heliports serving multiengine helicopters able to continue flight and meet certain climb performance on one engine.

b. Approach-Departure Clearance Surfaces. Obstruction clearance planes in the direction of the approach-departure paths extend outward and upward from the edge of the landing and takeoff area to the enroute altitude at an angle of eight feet horizontally to one foot vertically (8:1). The width of the sloping plane surface coincides with the dimension of the landing and takeoff area at the heliport boundary and flares uniformly to a width of 500 feet at the enroute altitude. The planes are symmetrical about the center-lines of the approach-departure paths.

SOURCE: Heliport Design Guide, Federal Aviation Agency–1959.

Heliport Class	FAR Category Helicopter	a	b	c	d	Minimum Angle Between Approach-Departure Paths
I Private	FAR Part 27, 29 (CAR 6 & 7)	1.5	1.5	300'	200'	90°
II Small Public	FAR Part 27 (CAR 6)	1.5	2.0	300'	300'	90°
III Large Public	FAR Part 27, 29 (CAR 6 & 7	* 1.5	* 2.0	400'	300'	135°

Dimensions a and b:
(1) are expressed as multiples of overall helicopter length.
(2) may be increased or decreased upon evaluation of the site by FAA.

*For scheduled airline operations, other factors, related to a specific site would need to be considered.

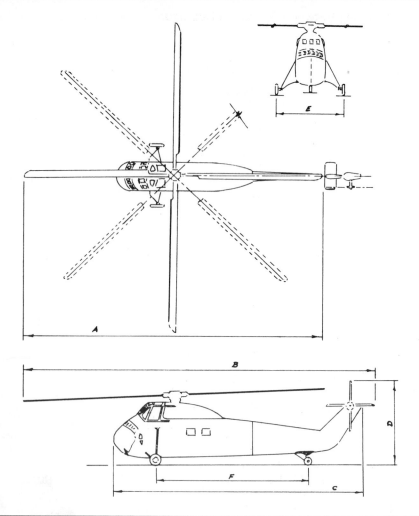

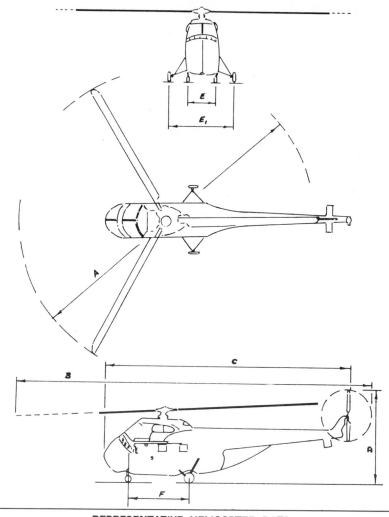

REPRESENTATIVE HELICOPTER DATA										
Company	Model Designation	A Rotor Diam.	B Length O.A.	C Length Fuselage	D Height	E Tread Forward	E₁ Tread Aft	F Wheel Base	Max. Gr. Wt. (1000 Lbs.)	No. of Engs.
Doman	LZ5-2	48'-0"	62'-11"	38'-0"	16'-1"	7'-6"		7'-9"	5.2	1
Kaman	K-600	47'-0"	*47'-0"	25'-2"	15'-7"	6'-11"	8'-4"	8'-2"	7.5	1
Omega	SB-12	39'-0"	47'-5"	38'-6"	13'-0"	3'-9"	11'-9"	10'-0"	4.35	2
Sikorsky	S-55A	53'-0"	62'-3"	42'-2"	15'-3"	4'-8"	11'-0"	10'-6"	7.5	1
Republic	Alouette SE 3130	33'-6"	40'-10"	31'-10"	9'-0"	6'-10"	—	10'-0"	3.3	1
Republic	DJINN SO 1221	36'-0"	29'-3"	17'-3"	8'-6"	6'-2"	—	9'-0"	1.7	1

*No tail rotor

SOURCE: Heliport Design Guide, FAA—1959

REPRESENTATIVE HELICOPTER DATA									
Company	Model Designation	A Rotor Diam.	B Length O.A.	C Length Fuselage	D Height	E Tread	F Wheel Base	Max. Gr. Wt. (1000 Lbs.)	No. of Engs.
Bell	47-J	37'-2"	43'-5"	32'-5"	9'-4"	7'-6"	9'-7" Skids	2.8	1
Bell	47G-2	35'-2"	41'-5"	30'-5"	9'-5"	7'-6"	10'-1" Skids	2.5	1
Bell	204	44'-0"	53'-0"	42'-8"	11'-3"	8'-4"	10'-10" Skids	7.2	1
Cessna	CH-1	35'-0"	42'-8"	32'-1"	11'-8"	8'-4"	Skids	3.0	1
Hiller	12-C	35'-0"	40'-6"	29'-5"	9'-9"	7'-8"	Skids	2.5	1
Sikorsky	S-56	72'-0"	82'-10"	64'-11"	21'-6"	19'-9"	36'-11"	31.0	2
Sikorsky	S-58	56'-0"	65'-10"	47'-2"	15'-11"	12'0"	28'-3"	13.0	1
Sikorsky	S-62	53'-0"	62'-3"	44'-7"	16'-0"	11'-0"	17'-10"	7.5	1
(Possible Future Helicopter)		100'-0"	120'-0"	80'-0"	25'-0"	25'-0"	50'-0"	50.0	3 Or More

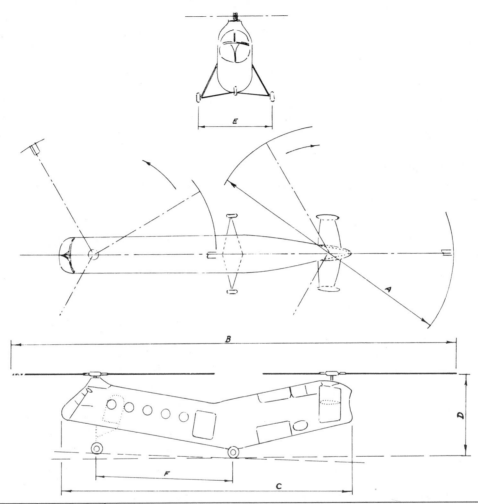

		REPRESENTATIVE HELICOPTER DATA							
Company	Model Designation	A Rotor Diam.	B Length O.A.	C Length Fuselage	D Height	E Tread	F Wheel Base	Max. Gr. Wt. (1000 Lbs.)	No. of Engs.
Vertol	42/44	44'-0"	86'-4"	52'-6"	15'-5"	14'-4"	24'-6"	15.0	1
Vertol	107	48'-4"	81'-8"	44'-7"	16'-10"	13'-11"	24'-9"	16.65	2
Vertol	YHC-1B	59'-0"	97'-6"	50'-0"	18'-4"	10'-4"	21'-0"	33.0	2
Kaman/Forey	Rotodyne	104'-0"	*104'-0"	64'-6"	25'-0"	28'-0"	21'-0"	60.0	2**

*No tail rotor
**Plus 4 tip jets

SOURCE: Heliport Design Guide, FAA—1959

309

STOL PORTS

a. The criteria outlines the basic physical, technical, (short take-off and landing) factors which should be considered in planning and establishing metropolitan STOL ports. The information is based on STOL aircraft performance and research studies conducted by both industry and Government.

b. The criteria provided are advisory in nature and do not establish requirements except where Federal funds are used for the development of a STOL port. Further, the specific recommendations presented are for the average or usual situation and may not be appropriate in every case. To assist in the interpretation of the criteria, it is recommended that technical advice be obtained from appropriate industry representatives and FAA technical personnel. Through consultations, the community can be assured of professional assistance in developing a STOL port that is safe, efficient, and compatible with its environment.

BACKGROUND

a. The term STOL has been widely used without having an official definition beyond Short Take Off and Landing. The FAA has recognized the necessity for a definition, but believes the definition should cover the STOL transportation system rather than the aircraft alone.

b. As is apparent, a STOL port will also accommodate VTOL (Vertical Take Off and Landing) aircraft.

POTENTIAL ROLE

The greatest potential of STOL aircraft is in the role of short-haul transportation (up to 500 miles). The use of STOL for city-center to city-center and intracity air passenger traffic would serve two prime purposes—provide better service to the passenger, and relieve airspace and ground congestion at larger airports. Most of our large and medium hub airports are becoming congested, in regard to both available airspace and to passenger facilities. In some cases, surface accessibility is in shorter supply than air accessibility. If the trend continues as forecast, the problem will worsen. In view of this, when developing a metropolitan STOL system, it is important to recommend site locations which are accessible to users and compatible with airspace use. Such a system should provide relief for large and medium hub airports and benefit both long and short-haul passengers.

SOURCE: Planning and Design criteria for Metropolitan STOL Ports, Department of Transportation, FAA-1970.

RUNWAY ORIENTATION

One of the primary factors influencing runway orientation is wind. Ideally, the runway should be aligned with the prevailing winds. It is recognized that the limited number of STOL port sites will minimize the opportunity for the runway to have optimum wind coverage. On the other hand, it is also recognized that the availability of a crosswind runway on a metropolitan STOL port will be rare. Accordingly, the designer should attempt to obtain maximum wind coverage. The minimum desirable wind coverage is 95 percent based on the total hours of available weather observations. In other words, the objective is to attain more than 95 percent usability (preferably 98 percent). The allowable crosswind component will be determined by the crosswind capabilities of the most critical aircraft expected to operate at the STOL port.

TERMINOLOGY

The following are definitions of terms as they are used herein:

a. *Approach/Departure Surface.* An imaginary plane extending outward and upward from the ends of the primary surface at a slope of 15 feet horizontally to 1-foot vertically (15:1).

b. *Metropolitan Area.* An area intended to denote a built-up or urban area, and not a Standard Metropolitan Statistical Area (SMSA).

c. *Metropolitan STOL Port.* An airport designed to accommodate STOL aircraft and located in or near major activity centers of a metropolitan area.

d. *Primary Surface.* An imaginary plane centered on the runway. Its width is 300 feet. Its length coincides with the length of the runway safety area.

e. *Runway Safety Area.* An area symmetrically located about the runway which is constructed to support (without major damage) aircraft which might inadvertently traverse it. Its width extends 50 feet beyond each runway edge. Its length extends 100 feet beyond each runway end.

f. *STOL Runways.* A runway specifically designated and marked for STOL aircraft operations.

g. *Transitional Surface.* An imaginary surface adjacent to each side of the primary surface and a portion of the approach surfaces. It extends outward and upward at a slope of 4-feet horizontally to 1-foot vertically (4:1).

h. *STOL Aircraft.* An aircraft which has the capability of operating from a STOL runway in accordance with applicable airworthiness and operational regulations.

i. *VTOL Aircraft.* An aircraft which has the capability of vertical takeoff and landing. These aircraft include, but are not limited to, helicopters.

GENERAL

During the process of developing these design criteria, certain assumptions had to be made because of the lack of commitment of large STOL aircraft to civil production. Therefore, these standards represent considered judgment of what constitutes a practical set of criteria considering available data, safety, noise, environment, and economics. It is apparent that the shorter the runway the easier it will be to locate a STOL port site, and the greater will be its compatibility with the local environment. On the other hand, the criteria cannot be so restrictive that aircraft manufacturers will be unable to produce a vehicle which can operate safely and economically from the STOL port.

DESIGN CRITERIA

The following criteria have been developed based on STOL aircraft, bidirectional runway operations, and a precision instrument approach. See Figures 1 and 2 for illustration of specific dimensions.

RUNWAY LENGTH DETERMINATION

A discussion of takeoff and landing runway lengths is needed to establish a common understanding of the terms used. This is particularly necessary for the case of the elevated STOL port, where reference to FAR field length cannot be considered in the same context as the conventional airport.

Design Criteria[1] for Metropolitan Stol Ports

Deisgn Item	Recommended Criteria	Comment
a. Runway Length at Sea Level and 90 F	1,500 feet to 1,800 feet	Correction for elevation and temperature to be made on the basis of individual aircraft performance.
b. Runway Width	100 feet	Widening may be desirable if wind coverage is less than 95%.
c. Runway Safety Area Width	200 feet	Widening may be desirable if wind coverage is less than 95%. If elevated a 300-foot width is recommonded for the structure.
d. Runway Safety Area Length	1,700 feet to 2,000 feet	If elevated, the structure would be within this range.
e. Taxiway Width	60 feet	Based on expected configuration of second generation aircraft.
f. Runway c_L[2] to Taxiway c_L	200 feet	Based on expected configuration of second generation aircraft.
g. Runway c_L to Edge of Parked Aircraft	250 feet	Based on expected configuration of second generation aircraft.
h. Runway c_L to Building Line	300 feet	Height controlled by transitional surface.
i. Taxiway c_L to Fixed Obstacle	100 feet	Based on second generation aircraft.
j. Runway c_L to Holding Line	150 feet	Based on second generation aircraft. See paragraphs 15 and 16.
k. Separation Between Parallel Runways		
l. Protection Surfaces:		
1. Primary Surface Length	Runway length plus 100 feet on each end.	
2. Primary Surface Width	300 feet	Based on the use of microwave instrument approach equipment.
3. Approach/Departure Surface Length	10,000 feet	
4. Approach/Departure Surface Slope	15:1	
5. Approach/Departure Surface Width at:		Approach/departure surface is 765 feet wide at 1,500 feet from beginning.
Beginning	300 feet	
10,000 feet	3,400 feet	
6. Transitional Surface Slope	4:1	
7. Transitional Surface Maximum Height	100 feet	
m. Clear Zone:		
1. Length	750 feet	
2. Inter Width	300 feet	Begins at end of primary surface
3. Outer Width	532 feet	
n. Pavement Strength	150,000 pounds gross weight on dual tandem gear.	Based on second generation aircraft.

[1] The criteria are subject to change as further experience is gained.
[2] c_L Centerline

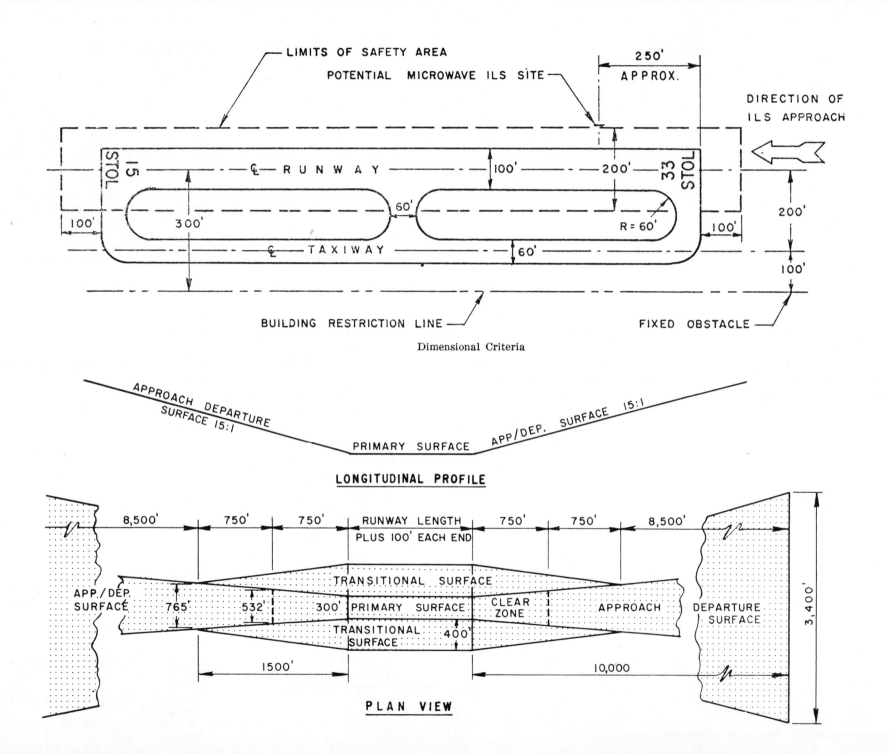

Dimensional Criteria

LONGITUDINAL PROFILE

PLAN VIEW

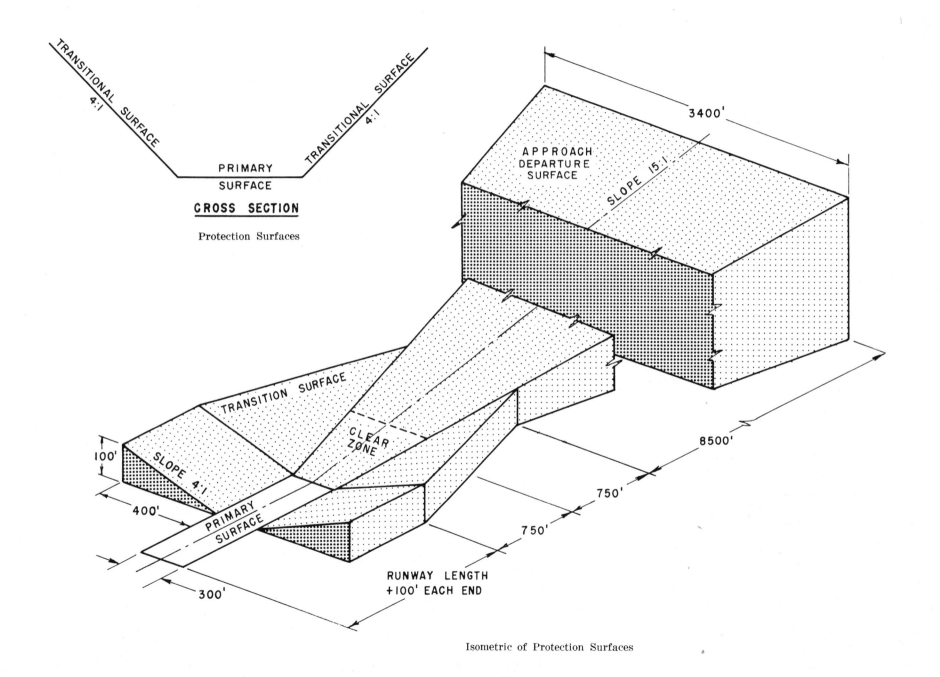

CROSS SECTION

Protection Surfaces

Isometric of Protection Surfaces

313

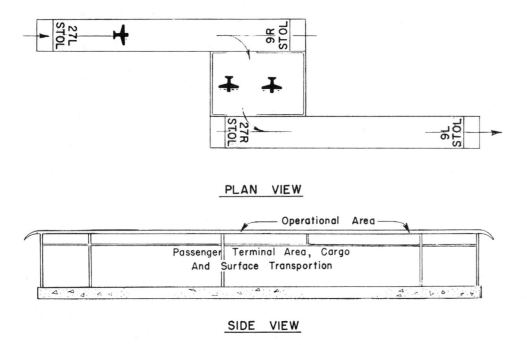

PLAN VIEW

SIDE VIEW

Figure 1

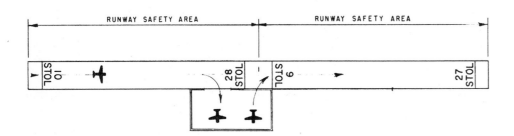

Figure 2

POTENTIAL CONFIGURATIONS

In many metropolitan areas, siting of a STOL port may necessitate an elevated structure. At such sites, the designer should strive to achieve vertical loading and unloading of passengers and cargo; i.e., from one level to another. Such a design will allow an operational area that is virtually free of fixed obstacles. Each STOL port should be designed with due consideration of local conditions, particularly the configuration of the land available and surrounding land uses. Figure 1 shows one possible layout of the staggered runway concept. One runway is used primarily for landing and the other for takeoff. This configuration allows a considerable reduction in the total operational area by eliminating parallel taxiways. Also, the flow of traffic is optimized, since no aircraft backout or turning around is involved. Figure 2 shows the tandem runway concept. Again, one runway is used for landing and the other for takeoff, but not simultaneously. Spacing must be provided for taxiing past parked aircraft and aircraft backout for turning around. The figures are intended to illustrate the new approach which must be taken in the planning and design of STOL ports; they are not intended to require a parallel runway configuration.

THE WATER-OPERATING AREA

Most natural water areas will provide, without modification, the required dimensions necessary for seaplane operations. Where the available water area is limited, the minimum water-operating area must consist of one water lane for landings and take-offs and a taxi channel. A turning basin will be necessary in cases where turning must be confined to a restricted area because of water depth requirements or for the segregation of other water surface-craft activities. In some cases anchorage areas may be necessary.

RECOMMENDED MINIMUM STANDARDS FOR WATER LANDING AREAS

Minimum length in feet (Sea level)	Minimum width in feet	Minimum depth in feet	Turning basin in feet-diameter	Remarks
2.500	200	3	None	Minimum for limited small float plane operation. Approaches should be 20:1 or flatter for a distance of at least 2 miles.
3,500	300	4	None	Minimum for limited commercial operation. Approaches should be 40:1 or flatter for a distance of at least 2 miles.
5,000	500	10	1,000	Minimum for extensive commercial operation. Approaches should be 40:1 or flatter for a distance of at least 2 miles.
10,000	700	15	2,000	Unlimited. Approaches should be 50:1 or flatter for a distance of at least 2 miles.

The lengths indicated above for glassy water, no wind, sea level conditions at standard temperature of 59° Fahrenheit.

The lengths shown will be increased at the rate of 7 percent for each 1,000 feet of elevation above sea level. This corrected length shall be further increased at the rate of one-half of 1 percent for each degree that the mean temperature of the hottest month of the year, averaged over a period of years, exceeds the standard temperature.

See figure 5 which contains a chart entitled "Effect of Elevation and Temperature on Water-Lane Lengths."

SOURCE: Seaplane Facilities, Civil Aeronautics Administration, U. S. Dept. of Commerce, Wash., D. C.—1950

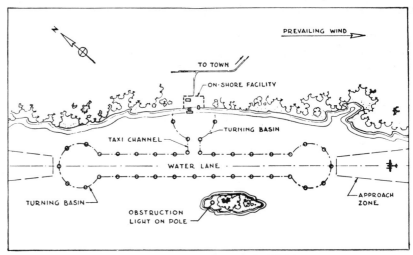

GENERAL OPERATING AREA

APPROACH ZONES

For seaplane operations the ideal approach zone is one which permits unobstructed approaches over water at a ratio of 40 : 1 or flatter, with ample clearance on either side of the approach zone center line. The width of the zone should increase from the ends of the water lanes so that at a distance of one mile from the end of the water lane, the zone is approximately the width of the water lane plus 1,000 feet.

Under favorable temperature conditions a water-borne aircraft will leave the water and fly level for approximately four (4) seconds and a distance of about 400 feet before starting to climb. The rate of climb after this four-second period is about 20 : 1. This ratio allows for a very limited margin of safety and requires maximum aircraft and engine performance at full load. Where commercial operations are anticipated, it is recommended that the approach angle should be 40 : 1 or flatter.

The approach zones should be over water, wherever possible, thereby permitting a reasonably safe landing in the event of power failure during initial climb or landing approach. Furthermore, for obvious safety reasons, climbs and approaches should not be made over populated areas, beaches and similar shore developments. Apart from the all-important safety factors involved, such maneuvers can create ill will and antagonism on the part of local inhabitants and boating interests. Where a suitable water area exists and the shore and surrounding development prohibits straight-away approach zones, it may be possible to establish operations in which an over-water climbing turn or let-down procedure is used.

TYPICAL LAYOUT OF ON-SHORE AND SHORE-LINE DEVELOPMENT

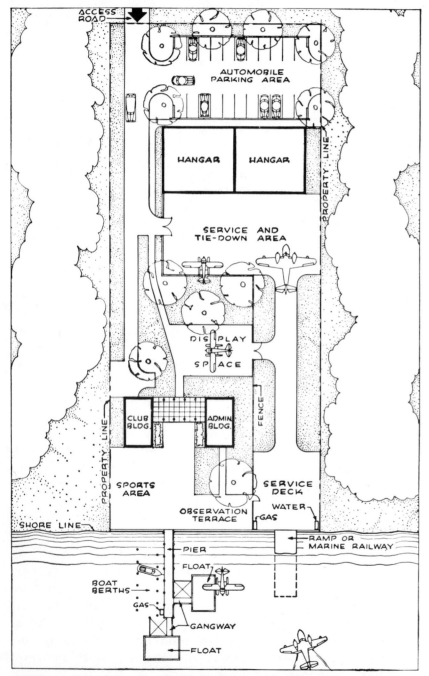

SOURCE: *Seaplane Facilities, Civil Aeronautics Administration, U. S. Dept. of Commerce, Wash., D. C.—1950*

No site for the on-shore development should be given serious consideration until it is known that adequate room is available for all of the space-taking elements required. Determination of size will require a knowledge of: (1) How many planes will need hangars or tie-down space; (2) how many car parking spaces will be necessary; (3) how many patrons will use the facility; (4) whether a small office will suffice or whether an administration building with facilities for eating, refreshments, and other nonaviation activities is required; (5) how much outdoor common space, such as for lawns, walks, terrace, etc., is needed. Answers to numbers 1 and 2 can be fairly accurately measured while 3, 4, and 5 will depend upon local conditions varying from a very simple installation, in remote recreation areas, to large installations in metropolitan areas. Minimum unit requirements are as follows:

MINIMUM UNIT REQUIREMENTS FOR A SINGLE ON-SHORE FACILITY

Item	Facility	Area in Square Feet
1 plane	Hangar or tie-down space	3,000
1 car	Parking space	250
Office	Small building	80
Common outdoor space	Walks, lawn, or open space	20 percent of above total

To compute the number of square feet for a given facility, multiples of the above criteria may be used. For example, a facility basing 15 aircraft in the water and 6 on land would need a maximum of 21 car-parking spaces (one for each plane) during maximum use period, plus one for each employee; i.e., approximately 25 cars or 6,250 square feet of area. Hangar or tie-down space for 6 planes would occupy 18,000 square feet. One small office building with food counter would require another 400 square feet. Finally, the common outdoor use space would occupy about 4,930 square feet (this figure representing 20 percent of the sum of the other areas). Accordingly, the total area would amount to about 29,580 square feet or about seven-tenths of an acre.

In addition to being adequate in size, the shore facility should be located reasonably close to the water-operating area to eliminate long taxiing operations.

The availability of utilities such as electricity, water, telephone and sewage should be investigated. The basic installation may not require all utilities, but water and sanitary facilities of some sort should be provided for at all locations. In remote rural areas, established water lines and sewerage facilities will be out of the question. If such is the case, well water and chemical toilet units are feasible. State or local sanitary codes must be respected when it is planned to install water and sanitary facilities of this nature.

The most desirable sites have a moderately sloping shore-line and a water depth suitable to permit aircraft taxiing operations as close to the shore-line as possible. Excessive fluctuations in water level are not desirable since this condition requires expensive shore-line installations. Care should be taken to determine whether the water level off-shore will permit aircraft operations when the water level is low.

In all cases, the area for a seaplane facility should be sufficient in extent to form a complete unit without any interior private holdings and with good boundary alignment for complete land utilization and protection. It may also be desirable in some cases to secure a liberal set-back from the highway in order to protect the project and adjacent property from noise and glare and to provide room for widening any highway paralleling the property line. If sufficient land is available, a greenbelt all around the project will enhance the desirability of a seaplane facility in a neighborhood area.

In the simplest case, the internal airport access would comprise a means of transporting passengers from the shore to the airport. Thus, it is assumed in Figure 1 that the entire passenger check-in and unloading facilities will be located on the offshore site. The access link must provide enough capacity to carry peak-hour traffic between shore and offshore airport.

In Figure 1, a more complex situation arises; it is assumed that a terminal may be located onshore and passengers are transported to the offshore site for airplane boarding. The onshore terminal complex would contain parking facilities, passenger check-in and waiting rooms, airline offices, baggage handling facilities, and other related airport facilities which need not be located offshore.

The basic differences in facility requirements will include:

- The area for the onshore terminal
- The potentially different transportation linkup area on shore
- The parking area requirements onshore, if private automobiles are excluded from the offshore site
- The potential difference in size and cost of the ground-transportation link

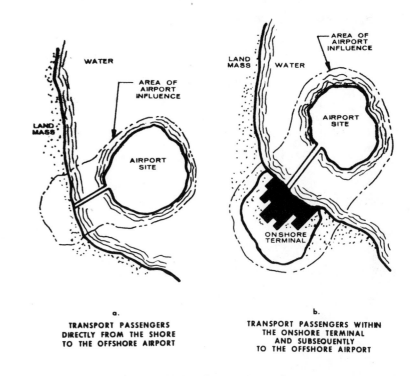

a.
TRANSPORT PASSENGERS DIRECTLY FROM THE SHORE TO THE OFFSHORE AIRPORT

b.
TRANSPORT PASSENGERS WITHIN THE ONSHORE TERMINAL AND SUBSEQUENTLY TO THE OFFSHORE AIRPORT

Figure 1   Offshore airport internal access.

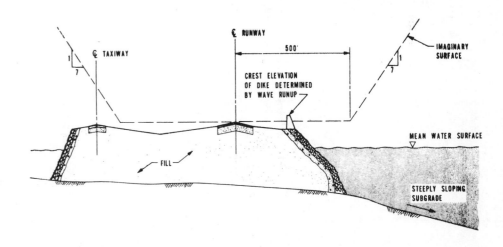

Figure 2   Lateral obstruction clearance — offshore fill airport.

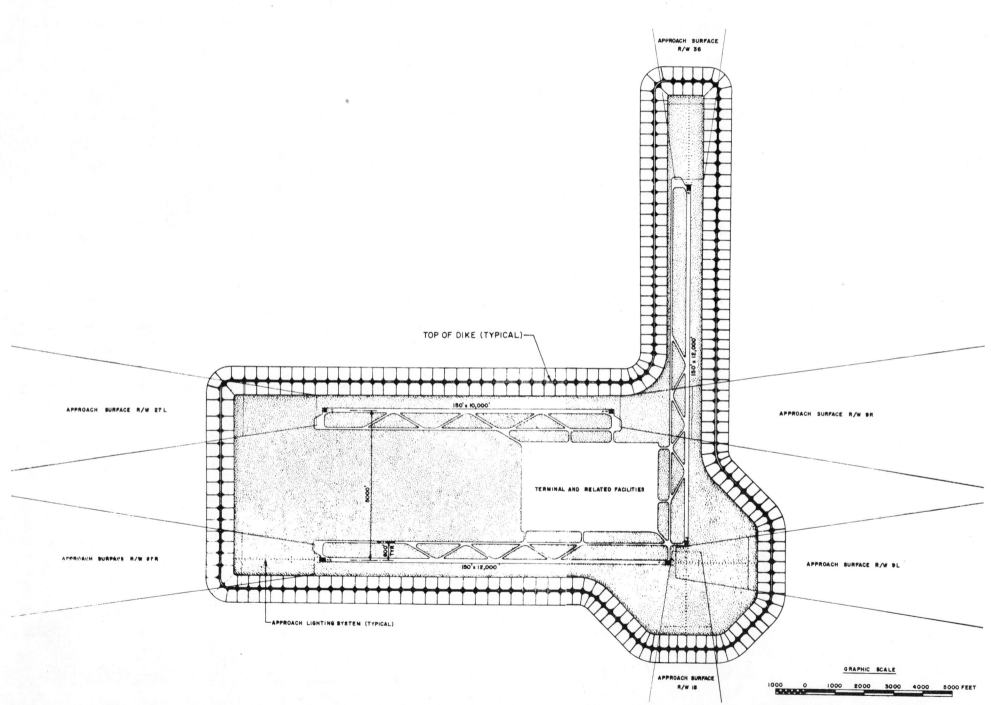

APPROACH SURFACE R/W 36

TOP OF DIKE (TYPICAL)

150' x 12,000'

APPROACH SURFACE R/W 27 L

150' x 10,000'

APPROACH SURFACE R/W 9R

TERMINAL AND RELATED FACILITIES

APPROACH SURFACE R/W 27R

150' x 12,000'

APPROACH SURFACE R/W 9L

APPROACH LIGHTING SYSTEM (TYPICAL)

APPROACH SURFACE R/W 18

GRAPHIC SCALE

1000   0   1000   2000   3000   4000   5000 FEET

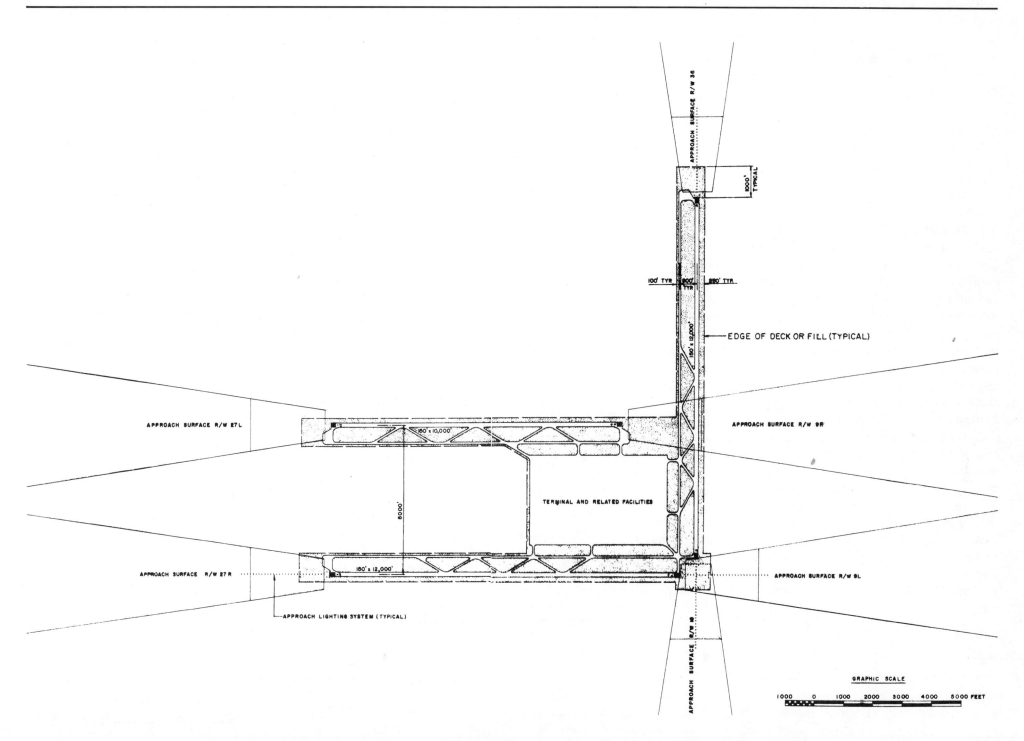

APPROACH SURFACE R/W 36

1000' TYPICAL

100' TYR | 200' TYR | 250' TYR

150' x 12,000'

EDGE OF DECK OR FILL (TYPICAL)

APPROACH SURFACE R/W 27 L

150' x 10,000'

APPROACH SURFACE R/W 9R

TERMINAL AND RELATED FACILITIES

5000'

APPROACH SURFACE R/W 27 R

150' x 12,000'

APPROACH SURFACE R/W 9L

APPROACH LIGHTING SYSTEM (TYPICAL)

APPROACH SURFACE R/W 18

GRAPHIC SCALE

1000 0 1000 2000 3000 4000 5000 FEET

OFFSHORE AIRPORTS AND RELATED CONSTRUCTION

General Considerations

For purposes of classification, offshore airport construction is considered in four basic categories based on the type of structure involved. These are:

- Fill
- Dike and polder
- Pile or caisson
- Floating

1. Fill Concept This is the conventional method used for many years to reclaim land in relatively shallow fringe-water areas. This structure normally consists of a general fill constructed to a sufficient elevation to prevent wave overtopping under normal conditions. The general fill is contained and protected from erosion by various types of marine structures such as sheet piling, armor stone, concrete seawalls and breakwaters. Examination of a number of existing fringe-water airports clearly points out the consistent use of the fill approach for reclaiming large land areas for initial and expansion requirements. Reasons for this are related to economics and the lack of any urgent need to do otherwise. Although the fill concept is expected to remain the primary construction method for many years to come, the urgency now exists to evaluate the other construction concepts to meet particular site peculiar requirements.

2. Dike and Polder Concept The polder concept involves the reclamation of low-lying land from the water by enclosing the area to be reclaimed with an impervious dike and then dewatering the enclosed area. This method of reclamation has been practiced for many years in the Netherlands. Dike and polder construction in the Netherlands has involved a continuous struggle to hold land that has been reclaimed. Many catastrophic failures of dikes have occurred.

When the land to be reclaimed is relatively impervious to percolation of water and not subject to heavy wave action, the dike and polder method is both practical and economical. However, of the four concepts considered, the potential for a spectacular failure of the entire system is greatest with the dike and polder concept.

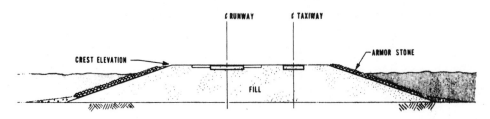

Figure 3 Fill concept — section.

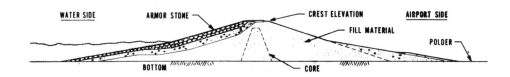

Figure 4 Dike and polder concept — dike section.

An important variation of the dike and polder concept applicable to shallow water, is the dike enclosure of a fill area with the fill area at an elevation only slightly above the mean water surface. In this case, the dike acts to exclude waves, tsunamis, tidal surge or other phenomena resulting in abnormally high water. This modified concept may represent, for some locations, an optimum combination of the dike and polder and the fill concepts.

3. Pile or Caisson Concept

This involves a platform-like structure having a deck supported on the marine foundation by piles or caissons. In this concept, the deck would be placed at a sufficiently high elevation so that normal wave action would pass below the deck without overtopping. The substructure could be supported by either end bearing or friction piles or a combination of both. Construction of this type is exemplified by the "Texas Towers" built along the east coast of the U.S. and, more recently, by the offshore platforms developed for the petroleum industry. Foundation conditions play an important role in determining the suitability of this construction concept.

4. Floating Concept

The design of a floating offshore airport will require the solution of some interesting and unique problems. Among these are the assurance of flotation, methods of mooring, and systems to minimize the effects of wave motion.

There are no floating structures in existence today, in the context of modern airport requirements, that furnish a precedence for the problems to be encountered in this concept, particularly if the airport were to be constructed in the open sea.

5. Raft Concept

The raft concept of floating airport design envisions constructing a number of hollow floating rectangles, towing them to an assembly site and fastening them together to form the complete floating structure.

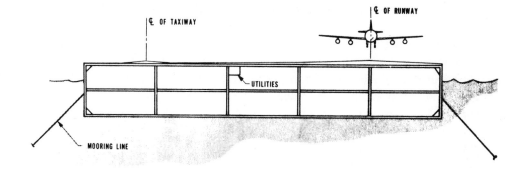

Figure 6 Pile concept — section.

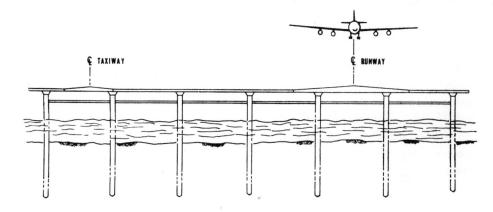

Figure 7 Floating concept — section.

PHYSICAL CHARACTERISTICS

The effects of urban transportation facilities upon their immediately adjacent environment often represent land-use impacts of critical importance. The physical characteristics of alternative transportation forms, in terms of vehicles, rights-of-way, and terminals, can generally give us a good picture of what these local impacts are likely to be. A number of basic physical features, however, are either open to technological modification or flexible from a design standpoint. These include such characteristics as noise, air pollution, visual or aesthetic effects of right-of-way, and visual effects of terminal area development.

Because such features are either undetermined or open to improvement within specific urban environments, and where specific technologies are under consideration, they have not been included in this general evaluation. Instead, four broad characteristics of right-of-way and terminal location and development are roughly sketched, as applied to each of the 24 basic transportation forms. The ratings shown in Tables 1 and 2 are probably the most subjective, and the most open to modification in specific situations, of any of the evaluations presented in this section.

The need for a *continuous right-of-way* can sometimes lead to substantial environmental problems, particularly where high-speed, direct route transportation forms are involved. Disruption of existing land-use patterns, heightened by an inability to follow "natural" or "least resistance" paths, are the main potential difficulties, and these are generally associated with rapid rail (high speed), automobile (freeway), automatic continuous motion vehicle (high speed), small automatically controlled vehicle (high speed), dual transport system, dual travelway bus, and dual travelway auto. Of course, many of these problems can be relieved through the use of underground or elevated facilities, as in the case of rapid rail (low speed, subway), monorail (existing and improved), and pneumatic tube (low speed).

Table 1 CURRENT TRANSPORT TECHNOLOGIES: PHYSICAL CHARACTERISTICS

Transportation Type or Form		Performance Characteristics	Physical Characteristics			
			Continuous Right-of-Way	Flexible Route Location	Integration with Other Modes	Integration with Adjacent Land-Use
Walking		Speed: 2-3 MPH Capacity: N/A	2	3	3	3
Pedestrian Assister		Speed: 1-5 MPH Capacity: 7,200 Pass./Hour	3	3	3	3
Vertical Motion Device		Speed: 1-2 MPH Capacity: 7,200 Pass./Hour	3	3	3	3
Two-Wheel Vehicle		Speed: 10-25 MPH Capacity: N/A	2	3	3	3
Monorail		Speed: 10-35 MPH Capacity: 5,000-16,000 Pass./Hour	3	3	2	3
Express Bus		Speed: 25-40 MPH Capacity: 8,000-30,000 Pass./Hour	2	2	2	2
Rail	Low Speed	Speed: 20-40 MPH Capacity: 10,000-40,000 Pass./Hour	3	2	2	3
	High Speed	Speed: 80-100 MPH Capacity: N/A	1	1	2	2
Watercraft		Speed: 15-35 MPH Capacity: N/A	3	1	1	1
Rotary Wing Aircraft		Speed: 45-70 MPH Capacity: N/A	3	3	1	1
Fixed Wing Aircraft		Speed: 100-600 MPH Capacity: N/A	3	3	1	1
Street Transit		Speed: 10-50 MPH Capacity: 300-8,000 Pass./Hour	2	3	3	2
Automobile		Speed: 10-60 MPH Capacity: 300-1,000 Pass./Hour	1	2	2	1

1 – Substantial Environmental Problems
2 – Significant Environmental Problems
3 – Limited Environmental Problems

SOURCE: Guidelines for New Systems of Urban Transportation, *Vol. 1: Urban Needs and Potentials. Barton-Aschman Associates, 1968 HUD, Washington, D.C.*

Opportunities for *flexible route location* are also important in helping to coordinate new transportation facilities with existing urban development. The principal factors involved here are the maneuverability of transit vehicles in terms of size and operating speed, so that patterns of development may be followed and complemented. Again, transportation forms operating at high speeds are most likely to generate environmental problems as to route inflexibility. These include the forms mentioned above, with the addition of pneumatic tube (low and high speed) and watercraft (existing and improved). Single vehicles which are operated independently (buses or autos) tend to result in more easily located routes and rights-of-way.

Integration with other modes of transportation, either through occupying the same right-of-way or through modal interchange at common terminals, can also be an important characteristic of transportation alternatives. Three of the future transport technologies in Table 2—dual transport system, dual travelway bus, and dual travelway auto—are especially important in this respect, because they could essentially operate as two combined modes. They would utilize two different right-of-way systems, with no time loss in switching between them. High-speed transportation forms would appear to offer the least in integration potential, both because of the need for direct or straight rights-of-way, and because of relatively distant station or terminal spacing. Opportunities for integration would be relatively fewer. These technologies include automatic continuous motion vehicle (high speed), small automatically controlled vehicle (high speed), and pneumatic tube (high speed).

Finally, opportunities for *integration with adjacent land-use* can often be vital factors in achieving maximum coordination between transportation and land-use systems. Some of the important considerations here are the possible use of air rights for terminal area developments, for instance, beneath elevated monorails or over underground rail subways or pneumatic tubes; the right-of-way width required, one reason automobile freeways are usually so poorly integrated; the need for vehicle storage areas at terminals, possibly preempting land which could be put to more productive use; and the size and speed of transit vehicles, with smaller, slower vehicles affording more opportunities for right-of-way integration as part of single buildings, woven through a group of buildings, or as part of a landscaped setting.

TABLE 2
FUTURE TRANSPORT TECHNOLOGIES: PHYSICAL CHARACTERISTICS

Transportation Type or Form			Performance Characteristics	Physical Characteristics			
				Continuous Right-of-Way	Flexible Route Location	Integration with Other Modes	Integration with Adjacent Land-Use
Pedestrian Conveyor			Speed: 1-12 MPH Capacity: 4,500-7,200 Pass./Hour	3	3	3	3
Elevator			Speed: 2-20 MPH Capacity: 500-700 Pass./Hour	3	3	3	3
Automatic Continuous Motion Vehicle	Low Speed		Speed: 12-30 MPH Capacity: 5,400-6,800 Pass./Hour	3	3	3	3
	High Speed		Speed: 50-120 MPH Capacity: 55,000 Pass./Hour	1	1	1	2
Automatically Controlled Vehicle	Small Vehicle	Low Speed	Speed: 30-60 MPH Capacity: 5,000-18,000 Pass./Hour	2	2	2	3
		High Speed	Speed: 150-200 MPH Capacity: N/A	1	1	1	2
	Large Vehicle		Speed: 20-45 MPH Capacity: 4,000-35,000 Pass./Hour	2	2	2	2
Pneumatic Tube	Low Speed		Speed: 30-80 MPH	3	1	2	3
	High Speed		Speed: Over 100 MPH	2	1	1	3
Monorail			Speed: 35-90 MPH Capacity: 15,000-20,000 Pass./Hour	3	2	2	3
Low-Speed Guideway Vehicle			Speed: 13-20 MPH Capacity: 1,800-10,000 Pass./Hour	3	3	3	3
Dual Transport System	Manual Control		Speed: 10-20 MPH Capacity: 300-1,500 Pass./Hour	2	3	2	2
	Automatic Control		Speed: 50-90 MPH Capacity: 10,000-60,000 Pass./Hour	1	1	2	2
Dual Travelway	Bus	Regular Road	Speed: 10-60 MPH Capacity: 2,000-8,000 Pass./Hour	2	3	2	2
		Special Roadway	Speed: 30-70 MPH Capacity: 10,000-40,000 Pass./Hour	1	2	2	2
	Auto	Regular Road	Speed: 10-60 MPH Capacity: 400-1,500 Pass./Hour	2	3	2	2
		Special Guideway	Speed: 50-90 MPH Capacity: 5,000-24,000 Pass./Hour	1	1	2	1
Small Manually Controlled Vehicle			Speed: 12-20 MPH Capacity: 600-2,000 Pass./Hour	3	3	2	2
Water Vehicle			Speed: 40-80 MPH Capacity: N/A	3	1	1	1
Vertical/Short Take-off and Landing Aircraft			Speed: 100-400 MPH Capacity: N/A	3	3	1	1

1 - Substantial Environmental Problems
2 - Significant Environmental Problems
3 - Limited Environmental Problems

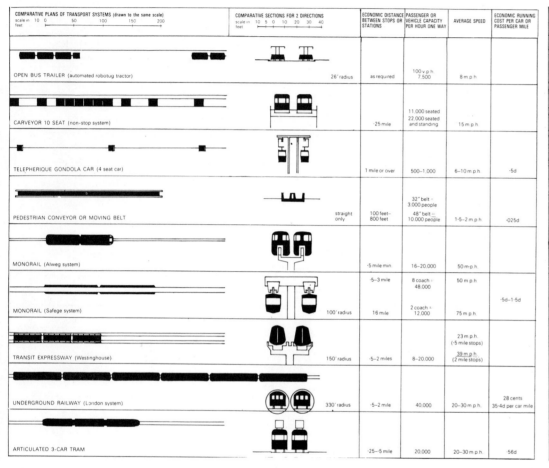

COMPARATIVE PLANS OF TRANSPORT SYSTEMS (drawn to the same scale) scale in feet	COMPARATIVE SECTIONS FOR 2 DIRECTIONS	ECONOMIC DISTANCE BETWEEN STOPS OR STATIONS	PASSENGER OR VEHICLE CAPACITY PER HOUR ONE WAY	AVERAGE SPEED	ECONOMIC RUNNING COST PER CAR OR PASSENGER MILE
OPEN BUS TRAILER (automated robotug tractor)	26' radius	as required	100 v.p.h. 7,500	8 m.p.h.	
CARVEYOR 10 SEAT (non-stop system)		.25 mile	11,000 seated 22,000 seated and standing	15 m.p.h.	
TELEPHERIQUE GONDOLA CAR (4 seat car)		1 mile or over	500-1,000	6-10 m.p.h.	.5d
PEDESTRIAN CONVEYOR OR MOVING BELT	straight only	100 feet- 800 feet	32" belt 3,000 people 48" belt 10,000 people	1.5-2 m.p.h.	.025d
MONORAIL (Alweg system)		.5 mile min.	16-20,000	50 m.p.h.	
MONORAIL (Safege system)	100 radius	.5-3 mile 16 mile	8 coach 48,000 2 coach 12,000	50 m.p.h. 75 m.p.h.	.5d-1.5d
TRANSIT EXPRESSWAY (Westinghouse)	150' radius	.5-2 miles	8-20,000	23 m.p.h. (.5 mile stops) 39 m.p.h. (2 mile stops)	
UNDERGROUND RAILWAY (London system)	330' radius	.5-2 mile	40,000	20-30 m.p.h.	28 cents 35-4d per car mile
ARTICULATED 3-CAR TRAM		.25-.5 mile	20,000	20-30 m.p.h.	.56d

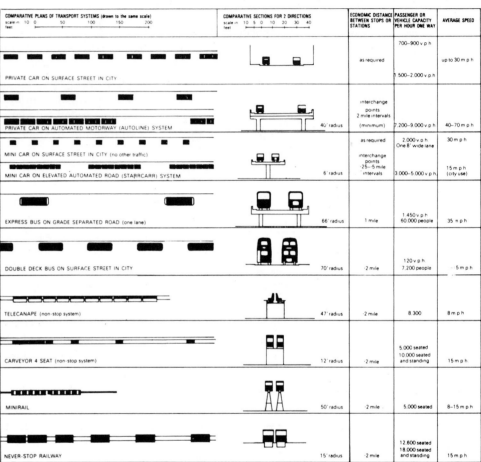

COMPARATIVE PLANS OF TRANSPORT SYSTEMS (drawn to the same scale) scale in feet	COMPARATIVE SECTIONS FOR 2 DIRECTIONS	ECONOMIC DISTANCE BETWEEN STOPS OR STATIONS	PASSENGER OR VEHICLE CAPACITY PER HOUR ONE WAY	AVERAGE SPEED
PRIVATE CAR ON SURFACE STREET IN CITY		as required	700-900 v.p.h 1,500-2,000 v.p.h.	up to 30 m.p.h
PRIVATE CAR ON AUTOMATED MOTORWAY (AUTOLINE) SYSTEM	40' radius	interchange points 2 mile intervals (minimum)	7,200-9,000 v.p.h	40-70 m.p.h
MINI CAR ON SURFACE STREET IN CITY (no other traffic)		as required	2,000 v.p.h One 8' wide lane	30 m.p.h
MINI CAR ON ELEVATED AUTOMATED ROAD (STARRCARR) SYSTEM	6' radius	interchange points .25-.5 mile intervals	3,000-5,000 v.p.h	15 m.p.h (city use)
EXPRESS BUS ON GRADE SEPARATED ROAD (one lane)	66' radius	1 mile	1,450 v.p.h 60,000 people	35 m.p.h
DOUBLE DECK BUS ON SURFACE STREET IN CITY	70' radius	.2 mile	120 v.p.h 7,200 people	.5 m.p.h
TELECANAPE (non-stop system)	47' radius	.2 mile	8,300	8 m.p.h
CARVEYOR 4 SEAT (non-stop system)	12' radius	.2 mile	5,000 seated 10,000 seated and standing	15 m.p.h
MINIRAIL	50' radius	.2 mile	5,000 seated	8-15 m.p.h
NEVER-STOP RAILWAY	15' radius	.2 mile	12,600 seated 18,000 seated and standing	15 m.p.h

SOURCE: Brian Richards, New Movements in Cities, Reinhold Publishing Corp., New York, 1966.

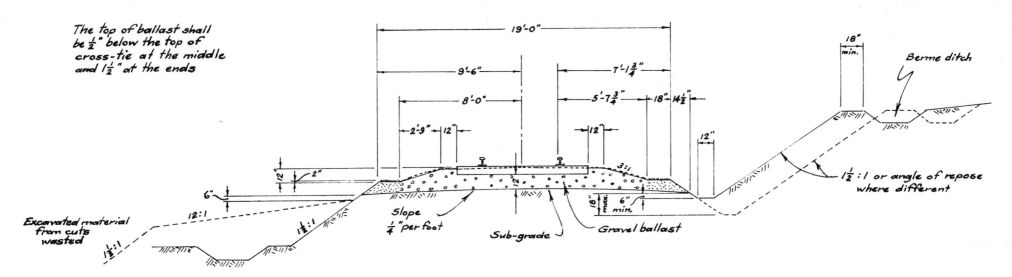

Single main track on tangent

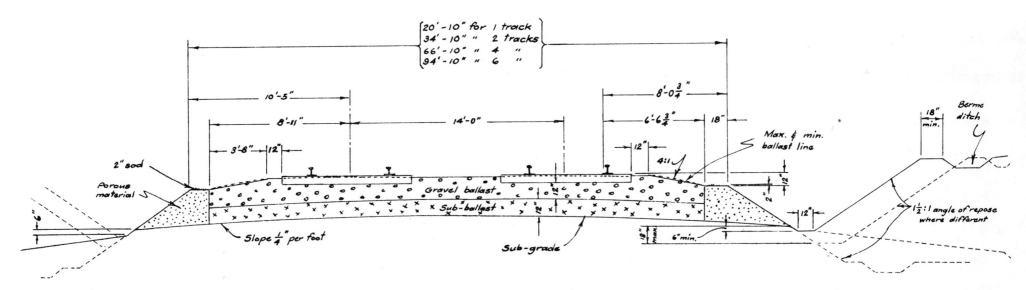

Double main track on tangent

SOURCE: Adopted from Railway Engineering and Maintenance, Cyclopedia–1922.

EDUCATIONAL FACILITIES

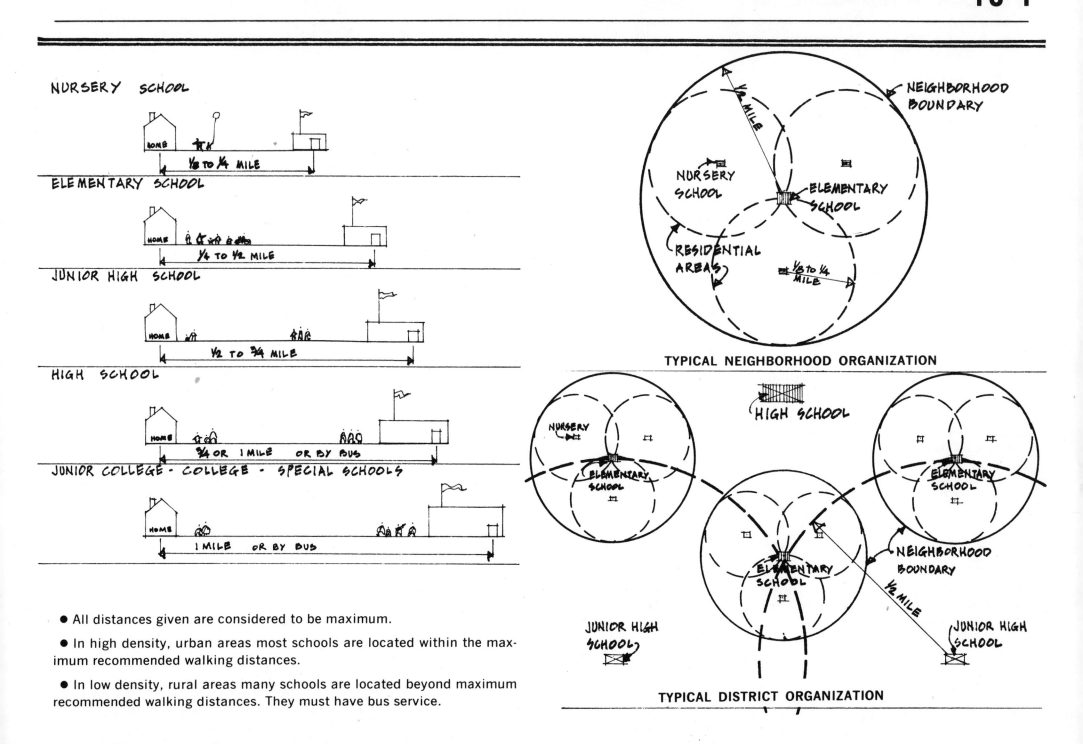

NURSERY SCHOOL

HOME — ⅛ TO ¼ MILE

ELEMENTARY SCHOOL

HOME — ¼ TO ½ MILE

JUNIOR HIGH SCHOOL

HOME — ½ TO ¾ MILE

HIGH SCHOOL

HOME — ¾ OR 1 MILE OR BY BUS

JUNIOR COLLEGE · COLLEGE · SPECIAL SCHOOLS

HOME — 1 MILE OR BY BUS

NEIGHBORHOOD BOUNDARY

NURSERY SCHOOL

ELEMENTARY SCHOOL

RESIDENTIAL AREAS

½ MILE

⅛ TO ¼ MILE

TYPICAL NEIGHBORHOOD ORGANIZATION

HIGH SCHOOL

NURSERY

ELEMENTARY SCHOOL

ELEMENTARY SCHOOL

ELEMENTARY SCHOOL

NEIGHBORHOOD BOUNDARY

½ MILE

JUNIOR HIGH SCHOOL

JUNIOR HIGH SCHOOL

TYPICAL DISTRICT ORGANIZATION

- All distances given are considered to be maximum.
- In high density, urban areas most schools are located within the maximum recommended walking distances.
- In low density, rural areas many schools are located beyond maximum recommended walking distances. They must have bus service.

Assumed Family Size	3.5 persons	Area Required	4 classes—4000 SF
			6 classes—6000 SF
			8 classes—8000 SF
Assumed Population Characteristics	60 children of Nursery School age per 1000 persons or 275–300 families		
		Accessory Facilities	Playlot or children's play area with equipment. Play area should be completely fenced in from other activities
Number of Children of Nursery School Age Per Family	.20 children		
		Radius of Area Served	1–2 blocks—desirable
Age of Children Served	2½ to 5 years old		⅛ mile—maximum
Size of Nursery School	Minimum—4 classes (60 children)		
	Average—6 classes (90 children)	Design Features	Nursery School should be accessible by footpath from dwelling units without crossing any streets. If street must be crossed it should be minor street
	Maximum—8 classes (120 children)		
Population Served	4 classes—1000 persons 275–300 families		
	6 classes—1500 persons 425–450 families	General Location	Near an Elementary School or Community Center
	8 classes—2000 persons 550–600 families	Accessory Parking	1 space for each 2 classes

These figures will vary for most areas. They are based on a full cross-section of the population. Population figures should be checked for local age distribution and birth trends for any specific location.

Assumed Family Size — 3.5 persons

Assumed Population Characteristics — 175 children of Elementary School age per 1000 persons or 275–300 families

Number of Children of Elementary School Age Per Family — .54 children

Age of Children Served — 5 thru 11 years

Size of Elementary School —
Minimum—250 pupils
Average—800 pupils
Maximum—1200 pupils

Size of Typical Class — 30–32 pupils

Population Served —
Minimum school—1500 persons
Average school—5000 persons
Maximum school—7000 persons

Area Required —
Minimum school—7–8 acres
Average school—12–14 acres
Maximum school—16–18 acres

Accessory Facilities —
Playground completely equipped for a wide range of activities
Playground area should be completely screened from street

Radius of Area Served —
¼ miles—desirable
½ mile—maximum

Design Features — Elementary School should be accessible by foot-path from dwelling units without crossing any streets. If street must be crossed it should be a minor street

General Location — Near center of residential area, near or adjacent to other community facilities

Accessory Parking — One space per class plus 3 spaces

These figures will vary for most areas. They are based on a full cross-section of the population. Population figures should be checked for local age distribution and birth trends for any specific location.

Assumed Family Size	3.5 persons	Area Required	Minimum school—18–20 acres
			Average school—24–26 acres
Assumed Population Characteristics	75 children of Junior High School age per 1000 persons 275–300 families		Maximum school—30–32 acres
Number of Children of Jr. High School Age Per Family	.22 children	Accessory Facilities	Playfield completely equipped for a wide range of game activities
Age of Children Served	12 to 14 years	Radius of Area Served	½ mile—desirable
			¾ miles—maximum
Size of Junior High School	Minimum school—800 pupils		
	Average school—1200 pupils		
	Maximum school—1600 pupils	Design Features	School should be away from major arterial streets; pedestrian walkways from other areas should be provided
Size of Typical Class	30–32 pupils		
Population Served	Minimum school—10,000 persons 2,750–3,000 families		
	Average school—16,000 persons 4,500–5,000 families	General Location	Located near concentration of dwelling units or near center of residential area
	Maximum school—20,000 persons 5,800–6,000 families	Accessory Parking	One space per classroom plus six spaces

These figures will vary for most areas. They are based on a full cross-section of the population. Population figures should be checked for local age distribution and birth trends for any specific location.

Assumed Family Size	3.5 persons	Area Required	Minimum—32–34 acres
			Average—40–42 acres
Assumed Population Characteristics	75 children of High School age per 1000 persons or 275 to 300 families		Maximum—48–50 acres
Number of Children of High School Age Per Family	.22 children	Accessory Facilities	Playfield completely equipped for a wide range of game activities
Age of Children Served	15–18 years	Radius of Area Served	¾ mile—desirable
			1 mile—maximum
Size of High School	Minimum—1000 pupils		
	Average—1800 pupils	Design Features	School should be located adjacent to a park area.
	Maximum—2600 pupils		School should be adequately screened from noise or objectionable uses
Size of Typical Class	30–35 pupils		
Population Served	Minimum—14,000 persons	General Location	School should be centrally located for easy access.
	3,800–4,000 families		Proximity to other community facilities is advantageous
	Average—24,000 persons		
	6,800–7,000 families		
	Maximum—34,000 persons		
	9,800–10,000 families	Accessory Parking	1 space per classroom plus 16 spaces

These figures will vary for most areas. They are based on a full cross-section of the population. Population figures should be checked for local age distribution and birth trends for any specific location.

DIMENSIONS FOR GAME AREAS[1]

Type of game	Elementary	Upper grades	High school	Area size (square feet)
1	2	3	4	5
Basketball	40' x 60'	42' x 74'	50' x 84'	5,000
Volleyball	25' x 50'	25' x 50'	30' x 60'	2,800
Badminton			20' x 44'	1,800
Paddle tennis			20' x 44'	1,800
Deck tennis			18' x 40'	1,800
Tennis		36' x 78'	36' x 78'	7,200
Ice hockey			85' x 200'	17,000
Field hockey			180' x 300'	54,000
Horseshoes		10' x 40'	10' x 50'	1,000
Shuffleboard			6' x 52'	648
Lawn bowling			14' x 110'	7,800
Tetherball	10' circle	12' circle	12' circle	
Croquet	38' x 60'	38' x 60'	38' x 60'	2,275
Handball	18' x 26'	18' x 26'	20' x 34'	1,280
Baseball			350' x 350'	122,500
Archery		50' x 150'	50' x 300'	20,000
Softball (12" ball)[2]	150' x 150'	200' x 200'	250' x 250'	62,500
Football—with 440-yard track—220-yard straightaway			300' x 600'	180,000
Touch football		120' x 300'	160' x 360'	68,400
6-Man football			120' x 300'	49,000
Soccer			165' x 300'	57,600

[1] Athletic Institute, Inc. *Planning Facilities for Health, Physical Education, and Recreation.*
The Institute, 209 South State St., Chicago 4, Ill. 1956. p. 26.
[2] Dimensions vary with size of ball used.

SIZES OF PLAYGROUND APPARATUS

In the following table are given the dimensions and approximate use areas of several types of apparatus frequently installed on children's playgrounds. Since the types of equipment made by the various manufacturers differ somewhat the dimensions and areas given are merely suggested. Furthermore, it is not likely that all of the apparatus listed will be found on a single playground. It is desirable to provide the safety zones around all apparatus, especially that which is movable.

Type of Apparatus	Length of Apparatus	Height of Apparatus	Space Required
Circular traveling rings	10' dia.	12'	25' dia.
Gang slide	16'	8'	20'x45'
Giant stride		12'	32' dia
Horizontal bar	6'	8' upright	12'x20'
Horizontal ladder	16'	7'-6"	8'x24'
Merry-go-round	10' dia.		30' dia.
Sand box on table	6'x10' to 10'x20'		12'x16' to 16'x30'
Slide	16'	8'	12'x30'
Slide-spiral	35'	18'	25'x35'
Swings—set of 3	15' at top	12'	30'x35'
Swings—set of 6	30' at top	12'	30'x50'
Teeters—set of 4	12' to 15'	2'-6"	20'x20'
Traveling rings—set of 6	40' at top	14'	20'x60'

The Jungles Gymn and other outdoor gymnasium outfits are manufactured in several sizes and combinations which occupy widely different areas. It is advisable to have all such equipment placed at least 15' from the nearest fences, building or other apparatus.

The wading pool may be any desired size or shape altho it is usually rectangular or circular. The circular pools generally have a diameter of from 40' to 75'.

The platform for dancing may be in any desired dimension. An average size would be 20'x30' to 30'x40'. According to a number of authorities from 40 to 50 square feet per child is the amount of space which should be provided for apparatus play.

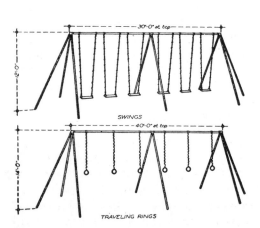

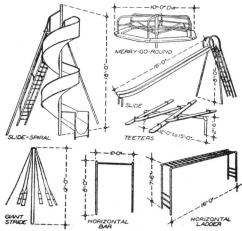

SIZES OF PLAYGROUND EQUIPMENT

SOURCE: School Sites—Selection, Development, and Utilization. U. S. Dept. of Health, Education, and Welfare, Office of Education

The Park-school concept of combining education and recreation facilities on a single site, has great merit. This combination makes possible a wider variety of opportunities on less acreage and at a lower cost than do separate installations. This approach is discussed here as it applies to areas at the neighborhood, community, and citywide levels.

Separately-located recreation areas are also treated since there may be certain circumstances under which the park-school may not be possible. It must be emphasized, however, that the combined approach is highly recommended.

NEIGHBORHOOD AREAS AND FACILITIES

Playlot. A playlot is a small recreation area designed for the safe play of pre-school children.

Location: As an independent unit, the playlot is most frequently utilized in large housing projects or in other densely-populated urban areas with high concentrations of preschool-age children. More often, it is incorporated as a vital feature of a larger recreation area. If a community is able to operate a neighborhood playground within one-quarter mile of every home, playlots should be located at the playground sites. A location near a playground entrance, close to rest rooms, and away from active game areas is desirable.

Size: The space devoted to a playlot depends upon the total open space available for development on a particular site. It may vary from 2,500 to 10,000 square feet.

General Features: The playlot should be enclosed with a low fence or solid plant materials in order to assist mothers or guardians in safeguarding their children. Careful thought should be given to placement of benches, with and without shade, for ease of supervision and comfort for parents and guardians. A drinking fountain with a step for tots will serve both children and adults.

Play equipment geared to the preschool child should combine attractive traditional play apparatus with creative, imaginative equipment. Such proven favorites as chair, bucket, and glidertype swings, six-foot slides, and a small merry-go-round can be used safely. Hours of imaginative play will be enjoyed with such features as a simulated train, boat, airplane, and playhouse, and Fiberglas or concrete animals. A small climbing structure should be included as well as facilities for sand play.

NEIGHBORHOOD PARK-SCHOOL (ELEMENTARY)

The neighborhood park-school is the primary unit in planning for physical education, recreation, and health education. This is a combination of an elementary school, neighborhood park, and playground. It is planned in such a manner that all areas and facilities are used to meet the educational and recreational needs of the people living in a neighborhood. It is essential that areas and facilities be cooperatively planned for the dual purpose of instruction and recreation, and that the school and community recreation programs be coordinated for maximum use of these areas and facilities by the entire neighborhood.

Location: The neighborhood park-school should service an area with a maximum radius of one-half mile and a population of approximately 8,000 people. Any deviation in the population density (larger or smaller communities) may alter the service radius and/or acreage required for this installation.

Size: The minimum area recommended for a neighborhood park-school is 20 acres.

General Features: It is suggested that this area be developed as follows:

School building	2.0
Parking	1.0
Playlot and apparatus	1.0
Hard-surface game courts and multiple-use area	2.5
Turf field-games area	5.5
Park area, including space for drama and quiet activities	5.5
Buffer zones and circulation	2.0
Recreation service building	.2
Corner for senior citizens	.3
Total	20.0

The school building should be at the edge of the area to provide for maximum development and utilization of the site, and playground equipment should be located far enough from the building to keep noise from interfering with class instruction.

A sepaate building containing the recreation leader's headquarters and public rest-room facilities should be provided in close proximity to hard-surface and game areas.

Hard-surface areas should be contiguous to provide a larger area for recreational, recess, physical education, and intramural activities. The field area should be large enough for baseball and softball diamonds to accommodate all age levels, for various field games, and for special events. Paths and walks between areas should be placed so as to avoid traffic over lawns, and the arrangement of facilities and landscaping should make for ease of supervision.

NEIGHBORHOOD PLAYGROUND

Designed primarily to serve children under 14 years of age, the neighborhood playground should have additional features to interest teen-agers and adults. The trend in recent years is for the neighborhood playground to become increasingly the center of activity for the wide variety of needs expressed by all residents. The more diversified interests of today's recreation consumer challenge the facility planner to provide for a broader program, with more attention devoted to multiple use by different age groups.

SOURCE: *Planning Areas and Facilities for Health, Physical Education and Recreation,* The Athletic Institute and American Association for Health, Physical Education, and Recreation Revised, 1966.

Modern planning for outdoor recreation at the neighborhood level places heavy emphasis on combining elementary-school needs with those of the community. This type of joint development is treated in the immediately preceding section on the neighborhood park-school.

Where elementary-school facilities are unavailable or inadequate, or joint development is impossible, a separate playground will be needed in each neighborhood.

Location: The neighborhood playground serves the recreation needs of the same population served by the neighborhood elementary school. Its maximum use radius will seldom exceed one-half mile, with most of the attendance originating within a quarter-mile distance. It should be located close to the center of the area to be served and away from heavily-traveled streets and other barriers to easy and safe access.

Size: In order to have the desired features, the neighborhood playground would normally require a minimum of eight acres. The particular facilities required will depend on the nature of the neighborhood, with space being allocated according to needs.

General Features: It is recommended that this area be developed as follows:

	Acres
Turf area for softball, touch football, soccer, speedball, and other field games	3.00
Hard-surface area for court games, such as netball, basketball, volleyball, and handball	.50
Open space for informal play	.50
Corner for senior citizens	.30
Space for quiet games, storytelling, and crafts	.20
Playlot	.20
Children's outdoor theater	.15
Apparatus area for elementary-age children	.25
Service building for rest rooms, storage, and equipment issue, or a small clubhouse with some indoor activity space	.15
Circulation, landscaping, and buffer zones	2.00
Undesignated space	.75
Total	8.00

Depending upon the relationship of the site to school and other recreation facilities in the neighborhood, optional features such as a recreation building, a park, tennis courts, or a swimming pool might be located at the neighborhood playground. If climatic conditions warrant, a spray or wading pool should be provided. The following space for optional features should be added to the standards listed above:

	Acres
Recreation building	.2
Park area (if there is no neighborhood park)	2.0
Swimming pool	.5
Tennis courts	.4
Total	3.1

The addition of optional features may require provision for off-street parking.

Equipment: The following types of equipment are recommended:

Several pieces of equipment designed as simulated stagecoaches, fire engines, boats, locomotives, etc.

Physical-fitness or obstacle-course features, such as a scaling wall, cargo net climber, etc.

Balance beam

Climbing structure, not to exceed 9' high

Horizontal ladder, not to exceed 7' high

Three horizontal bars with fixed heights, of rust-resistant metal

Straight slide 8' high or spiral slide 10' high

Six or more conventional swings, with low protective barriers

Pipe equipment formed into shapes

Sculptured forms

Merry-go-round, safety-type

The various apparatus groupings should be separated by plantings or attractive medium-height fencing.

NEIGHBORHOOD PARK

The neighborhood park is land set aside primarily for passive recreation. Ideally, it gives the impression of being rural, sylvan, or natural in its character. It emphasizes horticultural features, with spacious turf areas bordered by trees, shrubs, and sometimes floral arrangements. It is essential in densely-populated areas, but not required where there is ample yard space attached to individual home sites.

Location: A park should be provided for each neighborhood. In many neighborhoods, it will be incorporated in the park-school site or neighborhood playground. A separate location is required if this combination is not feasible.

Size: A separately-located neighborhood park normally requires three to five acres. As a measure of expediency, however, an isolated area as small as one or two acres may be used. Sometimes the neighborhood park function can be satisfactorily included as a portion of a community or citywide park.

General Features: The neighborhood park plays an important role in setting standards for community aesthetics. Therefore, it should include open lawn areas, plantings, and walks. Sculptured forms, pools, and fountains should also be considered for ornamentation. Creative planning will utilize contouring, contrasting surfaces, masonry, and other modern techniques to provide both eye appeal and utility.

COMMUNITY AREAS AND FACILITIES

Community Park-School (Junior High)

The community park-school (junior high), a joint development of school and community, provides an economical and practical approach to a communitywide facility for educational, cultural, social, and recreational programs. This educational and recreational center generally refers to the combination of a junior high school and a community park.

SOURCE: *Planning Areas and Facilities for Health, Physical Education and Recreation,* The Athletic Institute and American Association for Health, Physical Education, and Recreation Revised, 1966.

Location: It is suggested that this facility provide service for an area with a radius of ½ to 1½ miles. Such an area will normally contain 20,000 to 30,000 people, but population density may modify the size of the area served.

Size: Based upon current formulas for establishing junior-highschool and community-park sites, a minimum area of 35 acres is desirable.

General Features: It is suggested that the area be developed as follows:

	Acres
Buildings (school and community recreation)	5.00
Turf field-games area	8.00
Hard-surface games court and multiple-use area	2.75
Tennis courts	1.00
Football field with 440-yard track (220-yard straightaway)	4.00
Baseball field with hooded backstop	3.00
Playlot and apparatus	1.00
Park and natural areas	5.00
Parking	1.25
Buffer zones and circulation	4.00
Total	35.00

The following may be included as standard or optional features:

Swimming pool (usually related to the building)
Nature study trails and/or center
Day-camping center

There are many optional features which may be included in the community park-school. The inclusion of these is dependent upon the section of the country, available space, topography, community needs, climate, socio-economic composition of the community, and other variables. The following may be included as optional features:

Archery range	Hard-surface area for dancing
Band shell	Horseshoe pits
Boccie courts	Ice-skating or roller-skating rink
Botanical garden	Lake for boating
Croquet courts	Lawn-bowling greens
Golf-driving range	Lighted courts and fields
Golf-putting course	Shuffleboard courts

In designing the community park-school, planners should consider the proper placement of apparatus and areas which serve multiple use, and also bear in mind appropriate safety features in the development of each area or facility.

COMMUNITY PARK-SCHOOL (SENIOR HIGH)

A community park-school (senior high) is planned to provide facilities for youth and adults to meet a wide range of educational and recreational needs and interests on a single site. It generally refers to a combination of a high school and a community park.

It is essential that coordination and cooperation be exercised by school and municipal authorities to insure the maximum development and use of all facilities for instruction and recreation, both during and after school hours.

Location: It is suggested that the population density of the area as well as the total population of the community determine the scope and size of the area to be served by this facility. For example, the higher the population density, the smaller the service radius.

Size: Based on current formulas, a minimum area of 50 acres is suggested.

The site size should be based upon program needs, which will include: the physical education instructional program; school-supervised games, sports, and athletics; and school and community recreation activities during out-of-school hours.

General Features: It is suggested that the area be developed as follows:

	Acres
Buildings (including a gymnasium and an aquatics center)	6.00
Turf field-games area for instruction, intramurals, interscholastic athletics practice, and recreation use	8.00
Hard-surface games court and multiple-use area	3.00
Tennis courts	1.50
Apparatus area for instructional use (optional)	.12
Recreation area	5.00
Hard-surface area (for shuffleboard and outdoor bowling)	
Turf area (for horseshoes and croquet)	
Turf area (for golf and archery)	
Football field with bleachers and 440-yard track (220-yard straightaway)	6.00
Baseball field	3.50
Playlot and apparatus	.50
Park and natural areas	5.00
Recreation building with senior-citizen center	.50
Parking and driver-education range	6.00
Buffer zones and circulation	5.00
Total	50.12

For other features which may be incorporated into this facility, see the sections devoted to the community park-school (junior high) and the citywide or district park.

An adequate number of each kind of facility should be provided to permit full participation by the largest group that will be using the facility at any given time.

The total community park-school area should be landscaped to create a park-like setting which enhances and does not interfere with the instructional and recreational areas.

SOURCE: *Planning Areas and Facilities for Health, Physical Education and Recreation,* The Athletic Institute and American Association for Health, Physical Education, and Recreation Revised, 1966.

COMMUNITY PARK AND PLAYFIELD

The community park and playfield is designed to provide a variety of active and passive recreational services for all age groups of a community served by a large junior high school (20,000 to 30,000 residents). Primary requisites are outdoor fields for organized sports, indoor space for various activities, special facilities, and horticultural development.

Location: It is highly desirable that this facility be incorporated into the complex of a community park-school (junior high). Where this is not feasible, the community park and playfield should be located within ½ to 1½ miles of residents in its service area, depending upon population density and ease of access.

Size: A separate community park and playfield requires an area of 15 to 20 acres. At least two-thirds of the area should be developed for active recreation purposes.

General Features: The following should be provided:

Fields for baseball, football, field hockey, soccer, and softball

Courts for tennis, basketball, boccie, volleyball, handball, horseshoes, shuffleboard, paddle tennis, and other games

Recreation building containing an auditorium, a gymnasium, and special-use rooms for crafts, dramatics, and social activities

Quiet recreation area

Hard-surface area for dodgeball and kickball

May include a neighborhood playground. (See features under Neighborhood Playground)

CITYWIDE OR DISTRICT PARK

The citywide or district park serves a district of a larger city, or a total community of a smaller city. This facility should serve a population of from 50,000 to 100,000. It is designed to provide a wide variety of activities.

Location: This facility should be incorporated with a high school as a park-school development. Where this is not feasible, consideration should be given to placing the park as close as possible to the center of the population to be served. The land available will be a determining factor in site selection. While the service area will vary according to population density, a normal use radius is two to four miles.

Size: The citywide or district park may have from 50 to 100 acres.

General Features: Depending upon available acreage, topography, and natural features, the citywide or district park will contain a large number of different components. These would include, but not be limited to, the following:

A number of fields for baseball, football, soccer, and softball

Tennis center

Winter sports facilities

Day-camp center

Picnic areas (group and family)

Bicycling paths or tracks

Swimming pool

Lake for water sports

Pitch-and-putt golf course

Recreation building

Nature-centered trails

Skating rinks (ice and roller)

Playlot and apparatus

Parking areas

Outdoor theater

The above facilities should be separated by large turf and landscaped areas. Natural areas and perimeter buffers should be provided.

SOURCE: Planning Areas and Facilities for Health, Physical Education and Recreation, The Athletic Institute and American Association for Health, Physical Education, and Recreation Revised, 1966.

One of the great planning advantages of the education park is its potential to provide visual stress to the importance of the school in the community, as well as to provide for shared open space. The diagram shows how this advantage can be achieved by either *cluster* or *linear* development. Under the "scattered" concept of school location, i.e., the neighborhood school, school facilities are dispersed throughout a community with no interrelationship among schools and with inefficient use of the land.

A total of 65 acres is required for nine scattered-site schools. Utilizing the compact *cluster* plan, the same nine schools are brought together on a common site, sharing facilities and land, and giving a strong focus to the school in the community. With this model, the convenience of the neighborhood school is preserved to a high degree and only 55 acres are required.

In the *linear* concept, the schools are connected by a strip containing 55 acres. Again, the schools are given high visibility and prominence, they share space, and they are strung along a community, or perhaps between two communities, leading to the possibility of joint housing or commercial development. The linear concept could be best applied along a significant transportation corridor.

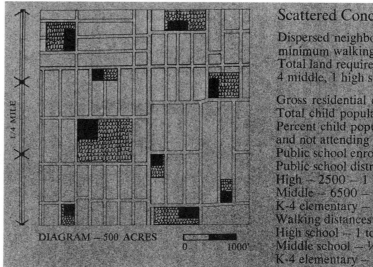

DIAGRAM — 500 ACRES
0   1000'

Scattered Concept

Dispersed neighborhood schools with minimum walking distances.
Total land required for 4 elementary, 4 middle, 1 high school : 65 acres

Gross residential density — 20 families/a
Total child population — 20,000 persons
Percent child population not of school ag and not attending public school — 30%
Public school enrollment — 13,000
Public school distribution
High — 2500 — 1 high school
Middle — 6500 — 4 middle schools
K-4 elementary — 4000 — 4 K-4 schools
Walking distances — (Phila. standards)
High school — 1 to 2 miles
Middle school — ½ to 1½ miles
K-4 elementary — ⅜ to ½ mile

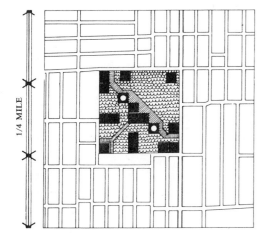

Compact Cluster Concept

The same schools clustered on single site.
Sharing of common functions.
Total land required — 55 acres.
Walking distance standards maintained.

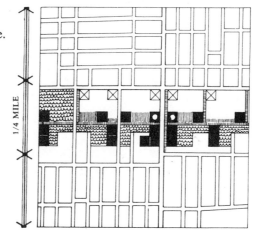

0   1000'

Linear Concept

Grouping of individual sites along linear strip permitting the sharing of common and more specialized functions; integration of park and other community facilities.
Total land required — 55 acres.

EACH DIAGRAM — 500 ACRES

SOURCE: *Report on the Education Park,* Corde Corp., Wilton, Conn., 1967.

YEARS OF SCHOOL COMPLETED, BY RACE AND SEX: 1960 TO 1972

Persons 25 years old and over. 1960 data as of April 1, based on 25-percent sample; 1970–72 data as of March, based on Current Population Survey;

YEAR, RACE, AND SEX	Persons 25 years old and over (1,000)	Elementary school 0-4 years	5-7 years	8 years	High school 1-3 years	4 years	College 1-3 years	4 years or more	Median school years completed
1960, all races	99,438	8.3	13.8	17.5	19.2	24.6	8.8	7.7	10.6
White	89,581	6.7	12.8	18.1	19.3	25.8	9.3	8.1	10.9
Male	43,259	7.4	13.7	18.4	18.9	22.2	9.1	10.3	10.7
Female	46,322	6.0	11.9	17.8	19.6	29.2	9.5	6.0	11.2
Negro	9,054	23.8	24.2	12.9	19.0	12.9	4.1	3.1	8.2
Male	4,240	28.3	23.9	12.3	17.3	11.3	4.1	2.8	7.7
Female	4,814	19.8	24.5	13.4	20.5	14.3	4.1	3.3	8.6
1970, all races	109,310	5.3	9.1	13.4	17.1	34.0	10.2	11.0	12.2
White	98,112	4.2	8.3	13.6	16.5	35.2	10.7	11.6	12.2
Male	46,606	4.5	8.8	13.9	15.6	30.9	11.3	15.0	12.2
Female	51,506	3.9	7.8	13.4	17.3	39.0	10.1	8.6	12.2
Negro	10,089	15.1	16.7	11.2	23.3	23.4	5.9	4.5	9.9
Male	4,619	18.6	16.0	11.1	21.9	22.2	5.7	4.6	9.6
Female	5,470	12.1	17.3	11.3	24.5	24.4	6.0	4.4	10.2
1972, all races	111,133	4.6	8.3	11.9	17.0	35.2	10.9	12.0	12.2
White	99,543	3.7	7.4	12.2	16.3	36.4	11.4	12.6	12.3
Male	47,133	3.9	7.8	12.4	15.6	32.2	12.0	16.2	12.3
Female	52,410	3.4	7.1	12.0	17.0	40.2	10.9	9.4	12.3
Negro	10,403	12.8	17.0	9.6	24.0	24.9	6.5	5.1	10.5
Male	4,635	15.6	17.4	9.6	21.8	23.8	6.4	5.5	10.1
Female	5,768	10.6	16.7	9.7	25.8	25.8	6.6	4.8	10.4

Source: U.S. Bureau of the Census, *U.S. Census of Population: 1960*, vol. I and *Current Population Reports*, series P-20.

SCHOOL ENROLLMENT, BY TYPE OF SCHOOL: 1930 TO 1970

[In thousands. Prior to 1960, excludes Alaska and Hawaii. Beginning 1964, data as of fall of preceding year]

ITEM	1930	1940	1950	1960	1964	1966	1970
Total	29,652	29,751	31,319	45,228	51,191	54,306	58,766
Kindergarten[1]	786	661	1,175	2,293	2,555	2,493	2,821
Public[1]	723	595	1,034	1,923	2,132	2,262	2,601
Nonpublic[1]	54	57	[2]133	[2]354	[2]404	212	[3]200
Grades 1-8[4]	22,953	20,466	21,032	30,119	32,147	33,266	34,290
Public[1]	20,555	18,237	18,353	25,679	27,172	28,315	29,996
Nonpublic[1]	2,255	2,096	[3]2,575	[3]4,286	4,796	4,763	[3]4,100
Residential schools for exceptional children[5]	[6]124	56	[7]49	[8]59	75	[3]85	[3]87
Federal schools for Indians	19	17	20	25	29	32	34
Federal schools on Federal installations	(NA)	(NA)	(NA)	19	28	29	[3]33
Grades 9-12 and postgraduate[4]	4,812	7,130	6,453	9,600	12,255	13,021	14,518
Public high schools[1]	4,399	6,601	5,725	8,485	10,883	11,597	13,022
Nonpublic high schools[1]	341	458	[3]672	[3]1,035	1,287	1,329	[3]1,400
Residential schools for exceptional children[5]	[6]4	10	[7]10	[8]24	31	[3]35	[3]37
Federal schools for Indians	8	7	8	12	13	14	12
Federal schools on Federal installations	(NA)	(NA)	(NA)	1	2	[3]3	[3]3
Higher education[1]	1,101	1,494	2,659	3,216	4,234	5,526	7,136
Publicly controlled	533	797	1,355	1,832	2,633	3,624	5,112
Privately controlled	568	698	1,304	1,384	1,601	1,902	2,024

NA Not available.
[1] Excludes subcollegiate departments of institutions of higher education, residential schools for exceptional children, and Federal schools, except that, for kindergarten, available data are included in the totals.
[2] Source: U.S. Bureau of the Census, *Current Population Reports*, series P–20.
[3] Estimated.   [4] Includes subcollegiate departments of institutions of higher education, not shown separately.
[5] Schools for the blind, deaf, mentally deficient, epileptic, and delinquent.
[6] 1927 data.   [7] 1946 data.   [8] Estimate based on 1958 survey.

Source: U.S. Office of Education, *Biennial Survey of Education in the United States*, chapter on Statistical Summary of Education; *Digest of Educational Statistics*, annual; and unpublished data.

SCHOOL ENROLLMENT, BY SEX AND BY LEVEL: 1950 TO 1990

[In thousands, except percent. As of fall of year. Prior to 1960, excludes Alaska and Hawaii. Civilian noninstitutional population 5 to 34 years old. Elementary includes kindergarten and grades 1–8; high school, grades 9–12 and postgraduates; and colleges, 1–4 year colleges and graduate and professional schools. Series shown represent projections based on different combinations of assumptions about population and enrollment rates. For basis of population projections, see headnote, table 3. Enrollment Series 1 and 2 are both based on the assumption that age-specific enrollment rates will continue to increase. Series 1 assumes a relatively rapid increase in the rates following the experience of 1950–52 to 1969–70; the projected rates are adjusted to tie in with the estimates for 1970. Series 2 assumes a more moderate increase based on an average of the projected rates in Series 1 and rates in 1970. More detailed methodology is given in source]

YEAR AND SERIES	TOTAL Total enrolled	Elementary school	High school	College	MALE Total enrolled	Elementary school	High school	College	FEMALE Total enrolled	Elementary school	High school	College
ESTIMATES												
1950	30,276	21,406	6,656	2,214	15,859	11,000	3,344	1,515	14,417	10,406	3,312	699
1960	46,259	32,441	10,249	3,570	24,234	16,711	5,184	2,339	22,025	15,730	5,065	1,231
1970	58,804	36,676	14,715	7,413	30,590	18,767	7,422	4,401	28,216	17,909	7,294	3,013
1972	58,416	34,934	15,169	8,313	30,464	17,930	7,681	4,853	27,953	17,005	7,488	3,460
Percent increase:												
1950–60	52.8	51.6	54.0	61.2	52.8	51.9	55.0	54.4	52.8	51.2	52.9	76.1
1960–70	27.1	13.1	43.6	107.6	26.2	12.3	43.2	88.2	28.1	13.9	44.0	144.8
PROJECTIONS												
Series C–1:												
1975	58,730	32,915	16,114	9,700	30,857	16,865	8,159	5,833	27,873	16,051	7,956	3,867
1980	61,147	34,565	15,133	11,449	32,264	17,698	7,670	6,896	28,884	16,867	7,463	4,554
1985	68,403	42,026	14,523	11,854	35,969	21,515	7,139	7,315	32,434	20,511	7,207	4,716
1990	78,681	47,960	18,037	12,684	41,184	24,572	9,094	7,517	37,497	23,387	8,943	5,167
Series C–2:												
1975	57,917	32,832	15,939	9,147	30,422	16,823	8,071	5,528	27,495	16,008	7,867	3,619
1980	59,471	34,374	14,814	10,284	31,364	17,603	7,514	6,247	28,107	16,771	7,300	4,037
1985	66,042	41,719	14,117	10,207	34,703	21,362	7,122	6,219	31,339	20,356	6,995	3,988
1990	75,614	47,560	17,462	10,592	39,551	24,373	8,820	6,358	36,063	23,187	8,643	4,233
Series E–1:												
1975	58,709	32,895	16,114	9,700	30,846	16,854	8,159	5,833	27,863	16,040	7,956	3,867
1980	59,417	32,835	15,133	11,449	31,385	16,819	7,670	6,896	28,032	16,015	7,463	4,554
1985	62,300	36,075	14,372	11,854	32,868	18,486	7,243	7,139	29,433	17,589	7,128	4,716
1990	66,878	38,378	16,035	12,465	35,166	19,673	8,091	7,402	31,712	18,705	7,943	5,063
Series E–2:												
1975	57,897	32,811	15,939	9,147	30,412	16,813	8,071	5,528	27,484	15,998	7,867	3,619
1980	57,763	32,665	14,814	10,284	30,497	16,736	7,514	6,247	27,266	15,930	7,300	4,037
1985	59,997	35,824	13,966	10,207	31,630	18,361	7,050	6,219	28,367	17,463	6,916	3,988
1990	63,959	38,064	15,498	10,397	33,607	19,516	7,836	6,255	30,351	18,547	7,662	4,142

Source: U.S. Bureau of the Census, *Current Population Reports*, series P–20, and series P–25, No. 473.

NEIGHBORHOOD AND COMMUNITY FACILITIES

NEIGHBORHOOD COMMUNITY FACILITIES AS A WHOLE

GROUPING

The facilities should, if possible, be grouped together in the direction of the major traffic flow from the development area to the outside, accessible by direct pedestrian and automobile routes. Such grouping will encourage the use of all facilities.

The existence of a physical center of the neighborhood stimulates the growth of community relationships and the acceptance of community responsibilities by the residents.

As most community facilities require comparatively flat land, topography will, to some extent, govern their grouping and location. Special situations may occur in which such grouping will not be advisable, especially where existing facilities must be taken into account.

Within the group, the various community facilities should be physically separated from each other to prevent conflict of circulation. It is especially important that pedestrian access to the school be separate from all vehicular access to other facilities.

TOTAL LAND REQUIREMENTS

For many neighborhood planning purposes, it is desirable to know community facility land requirements as a whole. Therefore, is a summation of these requirements. It should be noted that this table combines recommended and assumed areas; the values given are therefore not to be considered mandatory standards.

USE OF EXISTING FACILITIES

Before final decisions are made in regard to the provision of neighborhood community facilities, the area should be examined for available existing facilities. Special care must be taken to check the capacity as well as the location of such facilities. There may be city-wide or district facilities that can also be used by the neighborhood and that will in reality be so used if they provide good service and are readily accessible.

The possibility of using these facilities should be investigated if any of them exist within acceptable distance from the development.

LAND AREA OF ALL NEIGHBORHOOD COMMUNITY FACILITIES

Component Uses and Aggregate Area, by Type of Development and Population of Neighborhood [a]

TYPE OF DEVELOPMENT	NEIGHBORHOOD POPULATION				
	1,000 persons 275 families	2,000 persons 550 families	3,000 persons 825 families	4,000 persons 1,100 families	5,000 persons 1,375 families
ONE- OR TWO-FAMILY DEVELOPMENT [b]					
Area in Component Uses					
1) Acres in school site..............	1.20	1.20	1.50	1.80	2.20
2) Acres in playground.............	2.75	3.25	4.00	5.00	6.00
3) Acres in park..................	1.50	2.00	2.50	3.00	3.50
4) Acres in shopping center........	.80	1.20	2.20	2.60	3.00
5) Acres in general community facilities [c].................	.38	.76	1.20	1.50	1.90
Aggregate Area					
6) Acres: total...................	6.63	8.41	11.40	13.90	16.60
7) Acres per 1,000 persons.........	6.63	4.20	3.80	3.47	3.32
8) Square feet per family..........	1,050	670	600	550	530
MULTI-FAMILY DEVELOPMENT [d]					
Area in Component Uses					
1) Acres in school site..............	1.20	1.20	1.50	1.80	2.20
2) Acres in playground.............	2.75	3.25	4.00	5.00	6.00
3) Acres in park..................	2.00	3.00	4.00	5.00	6.00
4) Acres in shopping center........	.80	1.20	2.20	2.60	3.00
5) Acres in general community facilities [c].................	.38	.76	1.20	1.50	1.90
Aggregate Area					
6) Acres: total...................	7.13	9.41	12.90	15.90	19.10
7) Acres per 1,000 persons.........	7.13	4.70	4.30	3.97	3.82
8) Square feet per family..........	1,130	745	680	630	610

a This table combines the recommended or assumed values
b With private lot area of less than ¼ acre per family (for private lots of ¼ acre or more, park area may be omitted).
c Allowance for indoor social and cultural facilities (church, assembly hall, etc.) or separate health center, nursery school, etc.
d Or other development predominantly without private yards.

SOURCE: *Planning the Neighborhood by the American Public Health Association, Committee on the Hygiene of Housing, Public Administration Service, Chicago, Ill. 1960*

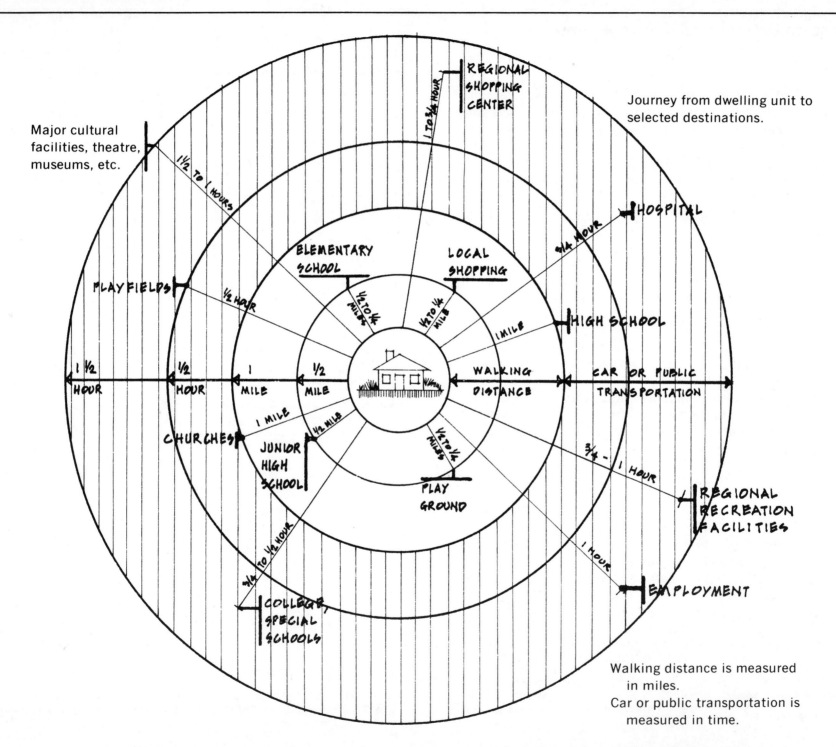

Journey from dwelling unit to selected destinations.

Major cultural facilities, theatre, museums, etc.

REGIONAL SHOPPING CENTER

1 TO 3/4 HOUR

1/2 TO 1 HOURS

HOSPITAL

3/4 HOUR

ELEMENTARY SCHOOL

LOCAL SHOPPING

PLAYFIELDS

1/2 HOUR

1/4 TO 1/4 MILES

1/4 TO 1/4 MILE

1 MILE

HIGH SCHOOL

1 1/2 HOUR

1/2 HOUR

1 MILE

1/2 MILE

WALKING DISTANCE

CAR OR PUBLIC TRANSPORTATION

1 MILE

1/2 MILE

1/4 TO 1/4 MILES

CHURCHES

JUNIOR HIGH SCHOOL

PLAY GROUND

3/4 - 1 HOUR

REGIONAL RECREATION FACILITIES

3/4 TO 1/2 HOUR

1 HOUR

EMPLOYMENT

COLLEGE, SPECIAL SCHOOLS

Walking distance is measured in miles.
Car or public transportation is measured in time.

General

Playlots should be provided for preschool children up to 6 years of age primarily in conjunction with multifamily (townhouse and apartment) developments and, in single-family neighborhoods remote from elementary schools. They are a necessary element of such developments to complement common open-space areas. Playlots may include (1) an enclosed area for play equipment and such special facilities as a sand area and a spray pool; (2) an open, turfed area for active play; and (3) a shaded area for quiet activities.

Location of Playlots

Playlots should be included as an integral part of the housing area design, and are desirably located within 300 to 400 ft of each living unit served. A playlot should be accessible without crossing any street, and the walkways thereto should have an easy gradient for pushing strollers and carriages. Playlots may be included in playgrounds close to housing areas to serve the preschool age group in the adjoining neighborhood.

Size of Playlots

The enclosed area for play equipment and special facilities should be based on a minimum of 70 sq ft per child, which is equivalent to 21 sq ft per family on the average basis of 0.3 preschool child per family. A minimum enclosed area of approximately 2,000 sq ft will serve some 30 preschool children (about 100 families). Such a size will accommodate only a limited selection of play equipment. To accommodate a full range of equipment and special facilities, including a spray pool, the minimum enclosed area should be about 4,000 sq ft, which would serve up to 50 preschool children (about 165 families). Additional space is required to accommodate the elements of the playlot outside of the enclosed area, as listed in the next paragraph. A turfed area at least 40 ft square should be provided for active games.

Playlot Activity Spaces and Elements

A playlot should comprise the following basic activity spaces and elements:
1. An enclosed area with play equipment and special facilities including
   a. Play equipment such as climbers, slides, swing sets, playwalls and playhouses, and play sculpture
   b. A sand area
   c. A spray pool
2. An open, turfed area for running and active play
3. A shaded area for quiet activities
4. Miscellaneous elements, including benches for supervising parents; walks and other paved areas wide enough for strollers, carriages, tricycles, wagons, etc.; play space dividers (fences, walks, trees, shrubs), a step-up drinking fountain, trash containers, and landscape planting.

Layout of Playlots

The specific layout and shape of each playlot will be governed by the existing site conditions and the facilities to be provided. General principles of layout, are described as follows:
1. The intensively used part of the playlot with play equipment and special facilities should be surrounded by a low enclosure with supplemental planting, and provided with one entrance-exit. This design will discourage intrusion by animals or older children, provide adequate and safe control over the children, and prevent the area from becoming a thoroughfare. Adequate drainage should be provided.

2. Equipment should be selected and arranged with adequate surrounding space in small, natural play groups. Traffic flow should be planned to encourage movement throughout the playlot in a safe, orderly manner. This traffic flow may be facilitated with walks, plantings, low walls and benches.
3. Equipment which enables large numbers of children to play without taking turns (climbers, play sculpture) should be located near the entrance, yet positioned so that it will not cause congestion. With such an arrangement, children will tend to move more slowly to equipment that limits participation and requires turns (swings, slides), thereby modifying the load factor and reducing conflicts.
4. Sand areas, play walls, playhouses, and play sculpture should be located away from such pieces of equipment as swings and slides for safety and to promote a creative atmosphere for the child's world of make believe. Artificial or natural shade is desirable over the sedentary play pieces, where children will play on hot days without immediate supervision. Play sculpture may be placed in the sand area to enhance its value by providing a greater variety of play opportunities. A portion of the area should be maintained free of equipment for general sand play that is not in conflict with traffic flow.
5. Swings or other moving equipment should be located near the outside of the equipment area, and should be sufficiently separated by walls or fences to discourage children from walking into them while they are moving. Swings should be oriented toward the best view and away from the sun. Sliding equipment should preferably face north away from the summer sun. Equipment with metal surfaces should be located in available shade.
6. Spray pools should be centrally located, and step-up drinking fountains strategically placed for convenience and economy in relation to water supply and waste disposal lines.
7. The open, turfed area for running and active play, and the shaded area for such quiet activities as reading and storytelling, should be closely related to the enclosed equipment area and serve as buffer space around it.
8. Nonmovable benches should be conveniently located to assure good visibility and protection of the children at play. Durable trash containers should be provided and conveniently located to maintain a neat, orderly appearance.

Playground Characteristics

1. The playground is the chief center of outdoor play for kindergarten and school age children from 5 to 12 years of age. It also offers some opportunities for recreation for young people and adults.
2. The playground at every elementary school should be of sufficient size and design, and properly maintained to serve both the elementary educational program and the recreational needs of all age groups in the neighborhood. Since education and recreation programs complement each other in many ways, unnecessary duplication of essential outdoor recreational facilities should be avoided. Only where this joint function is not feasible should a separate playground be developed.
3. A playground may include (a) a playlot for preschool children, (b) an enclosed playground equipment area for elementary school children, (c) an open, turfed area for active games, (d) shaded areas for quiet activities, (e) a paved, multipurpose area, (f) an area for field games, and (g) circulation and buffer space.

Location of Playground

A playground is an integral part of a complete elementary school development. School playgrounds and other playgrounds should be readily accessible from and conveniently related to the housing area served. A playground should be within ¼ to ½ mile of every family housing unit.

Size and Number of Playgrounds

Recommended size of a playground is a minimum of 6 to 8 acres, which would serve approximately 1,000 to 1,500 families. The smallest playground that will accommodate essential activity spaces is about 3 acres, serving approximately 250 families (about 110 elementary school children). This minimum area should be increased at the rate of 0.2 to 0.4 acres for each additional 50 families. More than one playground should be provided where (1) a complete school playground is not feasible, (2) the population to be served exceeds 1,500 families, or (3) the distance from the housing units is too great.

Playground Activity Spaces and Elements

A playground should contain the following basic activity spaces and elements:

1. A playlot, as described in the preceding section, with equipment and surfacing as recommended.
2. An enclosed playground equipment area with supplemental planting for elementary school children, and with equipment as recommended.
3. An open, turfed area for informal active games for elementary school children.
4. Shaded areas for quiet activities such as reading, storytelling, quiet games, handicrafts, picnicking and horseshoe pitching for both children and adults.
5. A paved and well-lighted multipurpose area large enough for (a) activities such as roller skating, dancing, hopscotch, four square, and captain ball, and (b) games requiring specific courts, such as basketball, volleyball, tennis, handball, badminton, paddle tennis, and shuffleboard.
6. An area for field games, preferably well-lighted, (including softball, junior baseball, touch or flag football, soccer, track and field activities, and other games), which will also serve for informal play of field sports and kite flying, and be used occasionally for pageants, field days, and other community activities.
7. Miscellaneous elements such as public shelter, storage space, toilet facilities, drinking fountains, walks, benches, trash containers, and buffer zones with planting.

Layout of Playgounds

The layout of a playground will vary according to size of available area, its topography, and the specific activities desired. It should fit the site with maximum preservation of the existing terrain and such natural site features as large shade trees, interesting ground forms, rock outcrops and streams. These features should be integrated into the layout to the maximum extent feasible for appropriate activity spaces, as natural divisions of various use areas, and for landscape interest. Grading should be kept to a minimum consistent with activity needs, adequate drainage and erosion control. General principles of layout, are described as follows:

1. The playlot and the playground equipment area should be located adjacent to the school and to each other.
2. An open, turfed area for informal active play should be located close to the playlot and the playground equipment area for convenient use by all elementary school children.
3. Areas for quiet activities for children and adults should be somewhat removed from active play spaces and should be close to tree-shaded areas and other natural features of the site.
4. The paved multipurpose area should be set off from other areas by planting and so located near the school gymnasium that it may be used for physical education without disturbing other school classes. All posts or net supports required on the courts should be constructed with sleeves and caps which will permit removal of the posts and their supports.
5. The area for field games should be located on fairly level, well-drained land with finished grades not in excess of 2.5 percent; a minimum grade of 1 percent is acceptable on pervious soils having good percolation for proper drainage.
6. In general, the area of a playground may be divided as follows: (a) Approximately half of the area should be parklike, including the open, turfed areas for active play, the shaded areas for quiet activities, and the miscellaneous elements as described in 7 below; (b) the other half of the area should include ¾ to 1 acre for the playlot, playground equipment area, and the paved, multipurpose area, and 1¾ acres (for softball) to 4 acres (for baseball) for the field games area.
7. The playground site should be fully developed with landscape planting for activity control and traffic control, and for attractiveness. This site also should have accessible public shelter, storage for maintenance and recreation equipment, toilet facilities, drinking fountains, walks wide enough for strollers and carriages, bicycle paths, benches for adults and children, and trash containers.

General Equipment Selection Factors

The following general factors should be considered in selecting equipment for playlots and playgrounds.

Developmental and Recreational Values. All equipment should contribute to the healthy growth and recreational enjoyment of the child, so that he learns to coordinate, cooperate, compete, create, enjoy, and acquire confidence. Play equipment should:

1. Develop strength, agility, coordination, balance, and courage.
2. Stimulate the child to learn social skills of sharing and playing with others, and to compete in a spirit of fair play.
3. Encourage each child to be creative and have play experiences which are meaningful to him.
4. Permit the child to have fun and a sense of complete enjoyment.
5. Assist the child in making the transition from playlot to playground.

Child Preference and Capacity. Play equipment, to be selected with due regard to the child's changing preference, maturity, and capacity, should:

1. Be scaled and proportioned to meet the child's physical and emotional capacities at different age levels.
2. Permit the child to do some things alone without direct adult supervision or assistance.
3. Provide a wide variety of play opportunities to accommodate changing interests of the child.
4. Free the child's imagination.
5. Meet a variety of interests, abilities, and aptitudes.

Safety of Participants. All play equipment should be designed and built for safety of the participants, and:

1. Be free of all sharp protruding surfaces caused by welds, rivets, bolts, or joints.
2. Have sufficient structural strength to withstand the expected loads.
3. Be designed to discourage incorrect use and to minimize accidents; examples are seats that discourage children from standing in swings, slides that require children to sit down before sliding, and steps or ladders that discourage more than one participant at a time.
4. Have hand or safety rails on all steps and ladders, and nonskid treads on all steps.
5. Be installed in accordance with the specific directions of the manufacturer.
6. Be placed over suitable surfaces that will reduce the danger of injury or abrasions in the event a child falls from the climbing, moving or sliding equipment. (A safe landing surface should be provided at the end of a slide chute.)

Durability of Equipment. Equipment that is durable should be selected. It should be made of materials which are of sufficient strength and quality to withstand normal play wear. Wood should be used only where metal or plastics have serious disadvantages. All metal parts should be galvanized or manufactured of corrosion-resistant metals. All movable bearings should be of an oilless type. Equipment should be designed as vandal-resistant as possible (for example, wire-reinforced seats for swings).

Equipment with Eye Appeal. All play equipment should be designed and selected for function, for visual appeal to stimulate the child's imagination, with pleasing proportions and with colors in harmonious contrast to each other and the surroundings. Play equipment may have a central theme, to reflect historical significance of the area, a storybook land, a nautical motif or a space flight motif. The theme may be carried out by constructing retaining or separation walls to resemble a corral, ship, or airplane, and by appropriate design of such elements as paving, benches, and trash cans.

Ease of Maintenance. Equipment should be selected which requires a minimum of maintenance. Purchased equipment should be products of established manufacturers who can provide a standard parts list. Equipment parts which are subject to wear should be replaceable. Color should be impregnated into the material, if feasible, to avoid repainting. Sand areas should be surrounded by a retaining wall and be maintained regularly to remove foreign objects and loosen the sand as a suitable play medium.

Supervision. Equipment should be selected that requires a minimum of direct supervision.

Basic Play Equipment

General. Play equipment may include swings, slides, and merry-go-rounds, various types of climbers; balancing equipment such as balance beams, conduit, leaping posts, and boxes; hanging equipment such as parallel bars, horizontal bars, and ladders: play walls and playhouses; and a variety of play sculpture forms. Different types of play equipment should be provided for preschool children and for elementary school children to meet the developmental and recreational needs of the two age groups.

Playlot Equipment for Preschool Children. The following table indicates types, quantities, and minimum play space requirements for various types of equipment totaling about 2,800 sq ft; this area, plus additional space for circulation and play space dividers, will accommodate a full range of playlot equipment serving a neighborhood containing approximately 50 preschool children (about 165 families).

Equipment	Number of pieces	Play space requirements, ft
Climber	1	10 x 25
Junior swing set (4 swings)	1	16 x 32
Play sculpture	1	10 x 10
Play wall or playhouse	1	15 x 15
Sand area	1	15 x 15
Slide	1	10 x 25
Spray pool (including deck)	1	36 x 36

Smaller playlots may be developed to serve a neighborhood containing some 30 children (about 100 families), using a limited selection of equipment with play space requirements totaling about 1,200 sq ft; this area, plus additional space for circulation and play space dividers, should consider the following desirable priorities: (1) a sand area; (2) a climbing device such as a climber, a play wall or a piece of play sculpture; (3) a slide, and (4) a swing set. Where several playlots are provided, the equipment selections should be complementary, rather than all being the same type. For example, one playlot may include play walls or a playhouse, while another playlot may provide a piece of play sculpture. Also, such a costly but popular item as a spray pool may be justified in only one out of every two or three playlots provided.

Playground Equipment for Elementary School Children. The following table indicates types, quantities, and minimum play space requirements totaling about 6,600 sq ft; this area, plus additional space for circulation, miscellaneous elements, and buffer zones, will accommodate a full range of playground equipment serving approximately 50 children at one time.

Equipment	Number of pieces	Play space requirements, ft
Balance beam	1	15 x 30
Climbers	3	21 x 50
Climbing poles	3	10 x 20
Horizontal bars	3	15 x 30
Horizontal ladder	1	15 x 30
Merry-go-round	1	40 x 40
Parallel bars	1	15 x 30
Senior swing set (6 swings)	1	30 x 45
Slide	1	12 x 35

Surfacing

General. Selection of suitable surfacing materials for each type of play area and for circulation paths or walks, roads, and parking areas, should be based on the following considerations:

1. *Function*. The surface should suit the purpose and the specific function of the area (such as surfaces for court games or field games, and surfaces under play equipment). The surface should also be considered from the basis of whether the area is multipurpose or single-purpose, and for seasonal or year-round usage.

2. *Economy*. The factors of economy are the initial cost, replacement cost, and maintenance cost. Often an initially more expensive surfacing is the least expensive in the long run because of reduced maintenance.

3. *Durability*. The durability of the surface should be evaluated in light of its resistance to the general wear caused by the participants, and resistance to extended periods of outdoor weathering such as sunlight, rain, freezing, sand, and dust.

4. *Cleanliness*. The surface should be clean and attractive to participants, it should not attract or harbor insects or rodents, and it should not track into adjacent buildings or cause discoloration to children's clothing.

5. *Maintenance*. Maintenance must be evaluated not only in light of the cost, but also of the time when the facility is not available for use due to repair or upkeep.

6. *Safety*. The safety of the participants is a primary consideration in selecting a play surface and should not be compromised for the sake of economy.

7. *Appearance*. A surface which has an attractive appearance and harmonizes with its surroundings is very desirable. Surfacing materials should encourage optimum use and enjoyment by all participants, and channel the activities in an orderly manner by providing visual contrasts.

Evaluation of Surfacing Materials

1. *Turf*. This material is generally considered to be the best surface for many of the recreation activities carried on at playlots and playgrounds. Although turf is not feasible for play areas having heavy participant use, most park and recreation authorities recommend using turf wherever practicable. Underground irrigation sprinkler systems with rubber top valves should be specified in areas with inadequate seasonal rainfall to maintain a turf cover. Major reasons for using turf are that it is relatively soft, providing greater safety than other surfaces, and it has a pleasing, restful appearance with great appeal to participants. A turf surface is especially suitable for open and informal play areas for younger children, and the large field game areas for sports and general recreation use.

2. *Bituminous Concrete*. This flexible paving material is the most generally used material for paving play areas. The designer should note that various asphalt grades and mixes are available, as well as color-coatings to improve appearance and maintenance. A suitable mix and careful grade control should be used to obtain a smooth, even surface, economical construction, and little or no maintenance. Bituminous concrete pavement is especially useful for paved, multipurpose areas, for tennis, basketball, and volleyball courts, roller skating and ice skating rinks, and for walks, roads, and parking areas.

3. *Portland Cement Concrete*. This rigid paving material is the most favored type of surface for use in specialized areas where permanence is desired, and to provide uniformity, maximum durability, and little or no maintenance. A Portland cement concrete surface is especially useful for court games requiring a true, even surface, such as tennis and handball, for shuffleboard courts, roller skating and ice skating rinks, and for walks, curbs, roads, and parking areas.[1]

4. *Synthetic Materials*. Synthetic materials that have a cushioning effect are being used by some school, park and recreation departments, primarily for safety, under play equipment. Several companies have developed successful resilient materials which provide excellent safety surfaces; these have been more expensive than the other materials discussed.

5. *Miscellaneous Materials*. Materials used for specific areas include sand, sawdust, tanbark, or wood chips around and under play equipment, earth on baseball diamond infields, and brick, flagstone, or tile on walks and terraces.

[1]NOTE: Portland cement concrete and bituminous concrete surfaces are generally considered for many of the same uses. Selection of either one should include appropriateness for the purpose intended, the initial cost, and long-term cost, at each location.

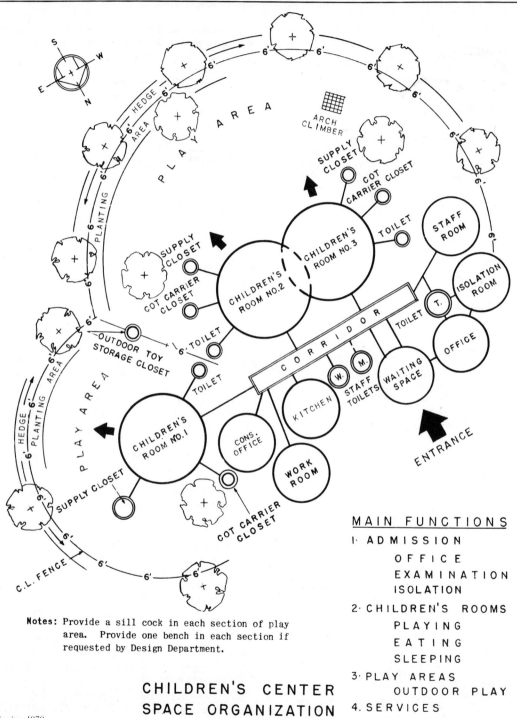

Notes: Provide a sill cock in each section of play area. Provide one bench in each section if requested by Design Department.

CHILDREN'S CENTER
SPACE ORGANIZATION

MAIN FUNCTIONS

1. ADMISSION
   OFFICE
   EXAMINATION
   ISOLATION
2. CHILDREN'S ROOMS
   PLAYING
   EATING
   SLEEPING
3. PLAY AREAS
   OUTDOOR PLAY
4. SERVICES

SOURCE: Memo to Architects, N.Y.C. Housing Authority, 1970.

GENERAL SITE REQUIREMENTS

☐ Easily Accessible
☐ Preferably on main thoroughfare
☐ Located in a subshopping area
☐ Located near a neighborhood center. Ease of parking is advantageous, but not so important as to justify an otherwise undesirable location. A park—often suggested—usually has little to recommend it
☐ A minimum of 20 years expansion of service & community growth should be possible

TYPES AND CHARACTERISTICS

Type	Area Served	Population Served	Miscellaneous
CENTRAL or MAIN	Whole City or Municipality	No Limit & Varies	Should be within a block or two of main business & shopping area & convenient to main traffic & transportation arteries.
BRANCH	1 to 1½ miles	Minimum Is from 25,000 to 55,000 People	Should be easily accessible. These requirement are for cities of 100,000 people or more.
SUB-BRANCH	Detached Areas & Smaller Cities	Varies	Frequently not open every day or housed in a library-owned building. Can be in community buildings or schools or rented quarters.

THE MINIMUM BOOK STOCK OF ANY LIBRARY, AS AN INDEPENDENT UNIT, SHOULD BE 6,000 VOLUMES REGARDLESS OF POPULATION SERVED.

POPULATION OF LIBRARY AREA		Volumes	Up to
Minimum	Maximum	per Capita	Volumes
6,000	10,000	3.0	25,000
10,000	35,000	2.5	70,000
35,000	100,000	2.0	175,000
100,000	200,000	1.75	300,000
200,000	1,000,000	1.5	1,000,000
Over 1,000,000		1.0	

TABLE 1   Experience Formulas for Library Size and Costs

Population size	Book stock — volumes per capita	No. of seats per 1,000 population	Circulation — volumes per capita	Total sq ft per capita	Desirable, first floor, sq ft per capita
Under 10,000	3½-5	10	10	0.7-0.8	0.5-0.7
10,000-35,000	2¾-3	5	9.5	0.6-0.65	0.4-0.45
35,000-100,000	2½-2¾	3	9	0.5-0.6	0.25-0.3
100,000-200,000	1¾-2	2	8	0.4-0.5	0.15-0.2
200,000-500,000	1¼-1½	1¼	7	0.35-0.4	0.1-0.125
500,000 and up	1-1¼	1	6.5	0.3	0.06-0.08

SOURCE: Joseph L. Wheeler and Herbert Goldhor, Practical Administration of Public Libraries (New York: Harper and Row, 1962) p. 554.

TABLE 2   Guidelines for Determining Minimum Space Requirements

Population served	Shelving Space*			Reader space, sq ft	Staff work space, sq ft	Estimated additional space needed, sq ft‡	Total floor space, sq ft
	Size of book collection, volumes	Linear feet of shelving†	Amount of floor space, sq ft				
Under 2,499	10,000	1,300	1,000	Min. 400 for 13 seats, at 30 sq ft per reader space	300	300	2,000
2,500-4,999	10,000, plus 3 per capita for pop. over 3,500	1,300. Add 1 ft of shelving for every 8 vols. over 10,000	1,000. Add 1 sq ft for every 10 vols. over 10,000	Min. 500 for 16 seats. Add 5 seats per 1,000 over 3,500 pop. served, at 30 sq ft per reader space	300	700	2,500, or 0.7 sq ft per capita, whichever is greater
5,000-9,999	15,000, plus 2 per capita for pop. over 5,000	1,875. Add 1 ft of shelving for every 8 vols. over 15,000	1,500. Add 1 sq ft for every 10 vols. over 15,000	Min. 700 for 23 seats. Add 4 seats per 1,000 over 5,000 pop. served, at 30 sq ft per reader space	500. Add 150 sq ft for each full-time staff member over 3	1,000	3,500, or 0.7 sq ft per capita, whichever is greater
10,000-24,999	20,000, plus 2 per capita for pop. over 10,000	2,500. Add 1 ft of shelving for every 8 vols. over 20,000	2,000. Add 1 sq ft for every 10 vols. over 20,000	Min. 1,200 for 40 seats. Add 4 seats per 1,000 over 10,000 pop. served, at 30 sq ft per reader space	1,000. Add 150 sq ft for each full-time staff member over 7	1,800	7,000, or 0.7 sq ft per capita, whichever is greater
25,000-49,999	50,000, plus 2. per capita for pop. over 25,000	6,300 Add 1 ft of shelving for every 8 vols. over 50,000	5,000. Add 1 sq ft for every 10 vols. over 50,000	Min. 2,250 for 75 seats. Add 3 seats per 1,000 over 25,000 pop. served, at 30 sq ft per reader space	1,500. Add 150 sq ft for each full-time staff member over 13	5,250	15,000, or 0.6 sq ft per capita, whichever is greater

SOURCE: American Library Association, Subcommittee on Standards for Small Libraries, Public Library Association, Interim Standards for Small Public Libraries: Guidelines Toward Achieving the Goals of Public Library Service (Chicago: The Association, 1962), p. 15. This brief 16-page report is based on standards set forth in ALA's, Public Library Service; A Guide to Evaluation with Minimum Standards. It is intended to provide interim standards for libraries serving populations of less than 50,000 until these libraries can meet the standards of ALA's Public Library Service.
*Libraries in systems need only to provide shelving for basic collection plus number of books on loan from resource center at any one time.
† A standard library shelf equals 3 lin ft.
‡ Space for circulation desk, heating and cooling equipment, multipurpose room, stairways, supplies, toilets, etc., as required by community needs and the program of library services.

CHURCH SERVING ONE NEIGHBORHOOD ONLY

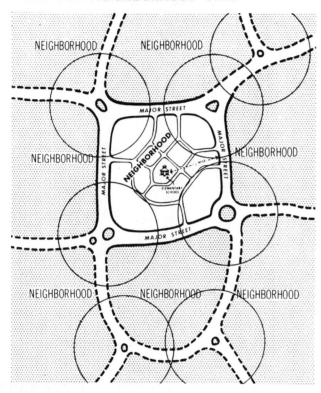

MEMBERSHIP STANDARDS

C. A. Perry estimated that a population of 5,000 persons could probably support three churches of about 1,500 persons each. The Conference on Church Extension suggested one Protestant church for each 1,500 to 2,500 persons. It should be noted that on the national basis about 60 per cent of the population may be expected to affiliate with a local church. In the western region this percentage is considerably lower. Thus, on the average, a population of 1,500 might be expected to produce a church of 900 constituents, disregarding the churching of some people outside of the neighborhood, and internal heterogeneity of the population which may cut the degree of affiliation to one specific church.

Many urban churchmen believe that a church of about 500 members is the optimum size of a neighborhood institution, while a downtown church, to support a diversified staff and program, may need 1,500 or 2,000 or even more.

AREA-REQUIREMENTS

There is no common uniform agreement as to the adequate size of a church site. Certainly the size of the site will depend upon the size of the church which is being projected, and the scope of the program. If an outdoor recreational program is desired, that will increase the size appreciably. If a parochial school is to be included, this will mean another appreciable increase in site needs. In most cases, landscaping and off-street parking should be provided for.

SOURCE: Robert C. Hoover & Everett L. Perry, Church and City Planning, Bureau of Research and Survey, National Council of the Churches of Christ in the U. S. A.

LOCATION OF CHURCHES SERVING MORE THAN ONE NEIGHBORHOOD

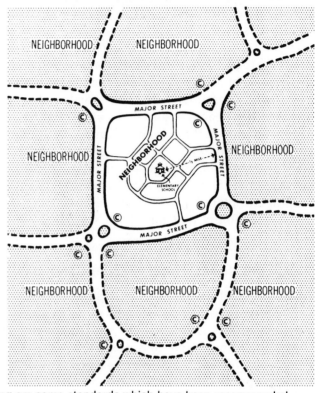

1 The following are some standards which have been recommended.

Source	Acres Recommended for Church Site
1. Conference on Church Extension Standards based on:[a] (below)	
0–400 membership	1 acre
400–800 membership	2 acres
800–1,200 membership	3 acres
1,200 or more members	4 acres
2. Presbyterian Board of Missions[b]	3 acres (on the average)
3. Urban Land Institute[c]	3–5 acres (Preferably near a shopping center)
4. Van Osdal[d]	5–6 acres (for a 600 seat church with 150 parking spaces)
	8 acres (For a Catholic church with a parochial school)

[a] Sanderson, Ross W., condensed report, conference on church extension, 1953, N.Y. National Council of Churches.
[b] Perry, Everett L., Selections of a Church Site, The City Church, September, 1953.
[c] Urban Land Institute, Community Builders Handbook, 1954, p. 89.
[d] Van Osdal, N. K., Jr. "The Church and the Planned Community," The City Church, May, 1952.

ILLUSTRATIVE NEED CALCULATION

Calculating general hospital bed needs is a basic tool in matching area-wide resources to needs.

The following contain an illustrative calculation of bed need for a hypothetical planning region with a target-year population of about 250,000. The example makes use of assumed figures which in actual practice would be obtained from health departments, hospitals, and related medical facilities. While an attempt has been made to use realistic figures in the illustration, one should not assume that the need figures derived in the example will apply to any actual planning region with a quarter-million population.

The example illustrates one method of calculating need. For didactic purposes it carries out the calculations in considerable detail. In working out bed needs for an actual planning region, more or less detail can be used depending on the availability and quality of statistics pertaining to the particular area.

STEP I—CALCULATING TOTAL PROJECTED PATIENT DAYS

The initial step in projecting the number of short-term, general hospital beds needed in the target year is a calculation of the expected total annual number of patient days. This is equal to the sum of projected patient days for each of the population's age and sex groupings. The number of projected patient days for each age and sex group may be derived by substituting the appropriate data in the following equation.

Projected population in thousands for the target year	$\times$ Current patient days per thousand population	= Projected patient days in the target year

The figures on population and use rate are given in the example. In actual practice, these statistics would have to be obtained from local sources.

Calculating Total Projected Patient Days

	Projected population in thousands for target year		Present patient days per thousand population		Projected patient days in target year	Totals
A. Under 15	41.9	$\times$	315. 1	=	13,203	
B. 15–24	16.2	$\times$	745. 8	=	12,082	
C. 25–44	32.7	$\times$	698. 7	=	22,847	
D. 45–64	23.8	$\times$	1,366. 7	=	32,527	
E. 65–74	5.6	$\times$	1,920. 4	=	10,754	
F. +	2.5	$\times$	1,945. 1	=	4,863	
G. Total projected patient days for males				=		96,276
Females:						
H. Under 15	40.9	$\times$	274. 2	=	11,215	
I. 15–24	18.7	$\times$	1,029. 6	=	19,254	
J. 25–44	36.5	$\times$	1,125. 4	=	41,077	
K. 45–64	24.7	$\times$	1.022. 2	=	25,248	
L. 65–74	6.3	$\times$	1,504. 9	=	9,481	
M. 75+	3.2	$\times$	1,924. 1	=	6,157	
N. Total projected patient days for females				=		112,432
O. Total projected patient days (line G+line N)				=		208,708

STEP II—CALCULATING PROJECTED PATIENT DAYS FOR MAJOR CLINICAL SERVICES

The number of projected patient days for medical and surgical, pediatric, and obstetrical patients can now be calculated. Projected obstetrical and pediatric days are calculated individually from known data and subtracted from total projected patient days (line "O", Step I) to obtain the projected number of patient days from medical and surgical cases.

1. Calculating Projected Obstetrical Patient Days

Projected obstetrical patient days	= Average length of stay per delivery	$\times$ Projected number of deliveries

A. Projected number of females 15–44, in thousands (Step I, line I+line J.) = 55.2

B. Current deliveries per 1,000 females 15–44 (Obtained from Health Departmnts or calculated from other available data.) .... = 95.6

C. Projected annual number of deliveries (Step II, line A × line B.) .... = 5,277.0

D. Current number of hospital days per delivery (Data obtained either from Health Departments, or directly from hospitals. Use figures pertaining to local facilities only.) .... = 4.5

E. Projected obstetrical patient days (Step II, line C × line D.) .... = 23,747.0

2. Calculating Projected Pediatric Patient Days

Projected pediatric patient days	=	Projected patient days for males under 15 (Step I, line A)	+	Projected patient days for females under 15 (Step I, line H)

F. Projected pediatric patient days = 13,203 + 11,215 .... = 24.418

3. Calculating Projected Medical and Surgical Patient Days

Projected medical and surgical patient days	=	Total projected patient days (Step I, line O)	−	Sum of Projected obstetrical and pediatric patient days (Step II, line E plus line F)

G. Projected medical and surgical patient days = 208,708 − 48,165 .... = 160,543

SOURCE: Procedures for Areawide Health Facility Planning, U. S. Dept. of Health, Education and Welfare, Public Health Service Publication No. 930-B-3—1963

STEP III—CALCULATING PROJECTED AVERAGE DAILY CENSUS

The following equation can be used to calculate projected average daily census:

Projected average daily census	=	Projected patient days	=	Number of days in year

	Projected patient days (see step II)	Days in year	Average daily census
A. Projected medical and surgical average daily census	160,543 ÷	365 =	439.8
B. Projected pediatric average daily census	24,418 ÷	365 =	66.9
C. Projected obstetrical average daily census	23,747 ÷	365 =	65.1

STEP IV—CALCULATING PROJECTED BED NEED

Assume that the planning agency has recommended the following occupancy goal:

	Present occupancy
Medical and surgical beds	85
Pediatric beds	75
Obstetrical beds	75

The equation below will then yield the number of beds needed.

Projected bed need	=	Average daily census ÷	Occupancy goal

	Projected average daily census (see step III)	Occupancy goal	Number of beds needed
A. Medical and surgical	439.8 ÷	.85 =	517
B. Pediatric	66.9 ÷	.75 =	89
C. Obstetrical	65.1 ÷	.75 =	87
D. Total short-term, general beds needed in the planning region		=	693

The need for long-term beds should be calculated on the basis of the size of the population that will be 65 years of age or older in the target year and on an occupancy goal of 95 percent or higher.

The same basic equation used for calculating short-term, acute bed need may be employed to determine the number of long-term beds required. The occupancy goal chosen for long-term beds, however, should be 95 percent or higher, and the number of patient days projected for the target year should be determined on the basis of the population 65 years of age and older.

Because of the prolonged length of stay associated with chronic illness, long-term facilities, unlike general hospitals, are not characterized by wide day-to-day fluctuations in occupancy. As a result, average occupancy in nursing homes and other long-term facilities is usually rather high. In addition, the need for long-term facilities is particularly related to the older segments of the population, since the vast preponderance of chronic illness occurs in the older age groups.

Wide variations occur from State to State and within States with respect to the proportion of the total population presented by the aged. Therefore, figures used in calculating the projected number of long-term patient days should be based solely on population data relating to the aged population in the particular planning region.

STEP V—CALCULATING BASIC LONG-TERM BED NEEDS

The ratio of persons receiving care in existing long-term facilities to the population 65 years of age and older should be determined as an initial step in calculating long-term bed needs. The magnitude of the present institutional population can usually be found in health department and / or welfare department statistics.

To continue the example, assume that appropriate data have shown that the present patient population of long-term care facilities represents 5 percent of the 65-and-over age group. While the calculation shown below is based on the continuation of present patterns of service, planning officials should recognize that possible changes in the financing of care may bring about substantial changes in the demand for long-term beds.

1. Determining the Long-Term Average Daily Census

	Projected population 65 and over (see step I)	Long-term patients ÷ population 65 and over	Average daily census
A. Long-term average daily census .... =	17,600	× 0.05	= 880

2. Determining the Number of Long-Term Beds Needed

	Long-term average daily census	Desirable occupancy rate	Long-term beds needed
B. Long-term beds needed .... =	880	÷ 0.95	= 926

SOURCE: *Planning Areas and Facilities for Health, Physical Education and Recreation, The Athletic Institute and American Association for Health, Physical Education, and Recreation, Revised–1966.*

The Grading Schedule is a means of classifying municipalities with reference to their fire defenses and physical conditions. From a study of pertinent conditions and performance records extending over many years, certain standards have been developed; these are set forth in the Schedule, and the various features of fire defense in the municipality under consideration are compared with them. For each deviation from these standards, deficiency points are assigned, the number depending upon the importance of the item and the degree of deviation. The natural and structural features that increase the general hazard, and the lack or inadequacy of laws or of their enforcement for the control of unsatisfactory conditions, are graded in the same way. The total number of deficiency points charged against the municipality determines its relative classification. The word "municipality" is used in a broad sense to include cities, towns, villages, or other municipal organizations.

The Table shows the various features considered, as well as the relative value and maximum number of deficiency points allocated to each.

RELATIVE GRADING OF MUNICIPALITIES IN FIRE DEFENSES AND PHYSICAL CONDITIONS

Points of Deficiency	Relative Class of Municipality
0– 500	First
501–1,000	Second
1,001–1,500	Third
1,501–2,000	Fourth
2,501–2,500	Fifth
2,501–3,000	Sixth
3,001–3,500	Seventh
3,501–4,000	Eighth
4,001–4,500	Ninth#
More than 4,500	Tenth*

A ninth-class municipality is one (a) receiving 4001 to 4500 points of deficiency, or (b) receiving less than 4001 points but having no recognized wather supply.

* A tenth-class municipality is one (a) receiving more than 4500 points of deficiency, or (b) without a recognized water supply and having a fire department grading tenth-class, or (c) with a water supply and no fire department, or (d) with no fire protection.

RELATIVE VALUES AND MAXIMUM DEFICIENCY POINTS

Feature	Per Cent	Points
Water Supply	34	1,700
Fire Department	30	1,500
Fire Alarm	11	550
Fire Prevention	7	350
Building Department	4	200
Structural Conditions	14	700
	100	5,000

SOURCE: *Standard Schedule for Grading Cities and Towns of the U. S., National Board of Fire Underwriters*—1956 New York, Chicago, San Francisco.

Fire stations are major capital improvements and will be in use for many years. Therefore, their locations should be selected with care so as to result in the best fire protection possible, considering both life hazard and value of buildings and contents.

Many points should be considered when choosing the location so that the company or companies to be housed in the new station will provide good coverage of the area to be protected and quick response to alarms of fire or other emergency calls.

The type of area to be protected, that is, business, industrial, warehouse, institutional, residential, or a combination of them, is an important factor

Stations should be near extensive industrial or business districts and near districts where there is a high life hazard, even though this often appears to be out of line with a plan of uniform distribution.

Sufficient stations should be provided so that no point in a high value district will be more than 1 mile travel distance from an engine company or 1¼ miles travel distance from a ladder company except that for districts requiring a fire flow of 9000 gpm or more, these distances should be ¾ mile and 1 mile respectively, and in districts requiring a fire flow less than 4500 gpm these distances may be 1½ miles and 2 miles respectively. Distribution should also provide for ready concentration of companies to multiple alarm fires in any high value district, and in areas where the life hazard is severe, without stripping other sections of protection in case of a second fire.

The majority of building fires occur in and around the older portions of most cities where congestion is greater, values higher, and buildings lack those structural features essential to protect life and to restrict the spread of fire. Therefore there should be no general elimination of stations or companies, nor wider spacing in these portions of most cities. Exceptions are where a station is in an area no longer of high value, is so situated that company runs are all in one direction, or the effective response has been reduced by limited access highways or other construction; in these instances, relocation would be desirable.

In average residential districts, response distances may be increased up to 2 miles for engine companies and 3 miles for ladder companies or companies providing adequate ladder service. However, for closely built residential districts requiring more than 2000 gpm fire flow or having buildings 3 or more stories in height, including tenement houses, apartments, or hotels, the distances should be reduced to 1½ and 2 miles respectively. Where the life hazard is above normal, it may be necessary to further reduce these distances to 1 and 1¼ miles, respectively.

Topographical features of a city also affect station location and the total number required. A city divided into two or more portions by rivers, bluffs, mountains, and similar natural barriers, with few means for companies to respond from one portion to another, requires additional stations to provide proper protection. The same is true when there are man-made barriers, such as railroad tracks, limited access highways, and canals; the possibility of delay in response because of railroad crossings at grade, drawbridges, and heavy traffic must be considered. A hillside location is not satisfactory, nor is one at the bottom of the hill when many responses must be made up grade. Where heavily traveled streets enter into the problem, a station may be located on a parallel street or a cross street with the traffic lights at nearby intersections arranged for control from the station in order to permit response across or onto the heavily traveled street; locating a station directly on such a street is ordinarily not desirable. One-way streets pose another problem which may be handled by traffic lights controlled from the station.

Remote sections of a city, separated from the major portion by intervening municipalities, will generally require at least one station, unless the area is very small.

When stations are to be built in outlying areas, it should be remembered that a location too close to the city limits reduces the response area, thereby decreasing efficiency. However, when locating an outlying station and the possibility of the city annexing additional territory exists, the total area requiring protection in the future should be considered.

Many cities have been faced with the problem of providing protection in newly annexed areas. When an area to be annexed is large and well populated, it is possible that at least one additional company and station will be needed to provide proper protection for this area alone. Plans for protecting such areas should be made well in advance of the date of annexation.

A site at an intersection is good as it permits response in more than two directions. Stations should be set well back from the curb line, especially where the street is narrow. The lot should be of ample size so as to provide parking facilities for the men, and adequate space for holding company drills.

Proposed locations of fire stations may be submitted to the office of the local insurance inspection board or to the American Insurance Association (formerly the National Board of Fire Underwriters) for comment. Such requests should be directed to the organization which made the last municipal fire protection survey in the municipality concerned.

SOURCE: *Special Interest Bulletin No. 176, National Board of Fire Underwriters—1963*

GENERAL REQUIREMENTS

Where it is necessary to develop an entirely new water supply system for a suburban area, the "Standard Schedule for Grading Cities and Towns of the United States With Reference to Their Fire Defenses and Physical Conditions" (1) should be used as a guide in providing adequate fire protection.

The required fire flow for the principal business district in the average municipality is obtained by the use of the formula:

$$G = 1,020\sqrt{P}\ (1 - 0.01\sqrt{P}),$$

where G is the required fire flow in gallons per minute and P is the population in thousands. The flow may be increased or decreased in accordance with structural conditions and degree of congestion. In many new suburban areas, the fire flow indicated by the formula will be reduced because there are a number of small scattered business districts instead of a single large one. Where buildings, such as super-markets, have excessive area, the fire flow indicated by the formula (or perhaps even more) will be needed because of the large amount of combustible material that may be under one roof. Where suburbs contain industrial, institutional, or other sections that require fire flows in excess of that necessary for the principal business district, the highest required fire flow should govern the design. Fire flows of 1,000 gpm should be available for 4 hr, the duration increasing with larger fire flows up to a maximum of 10 hr for 2,500 gpm or more.

REQUIRED FIRE FLOW

Population	Required Fire flow for Average City gpm	mgd	Duration, hours	Population	Required Fire flow for Average City gpm	mgd	Duration, hours
1,000	1,000	1.44	4	22,000	4,500	6.48	10
1,500	1,250	1.80	5	27,000	5,000	7.20	10
2,000	1,500	2.16	6	33,000	5,500	7.92	10
3,000	1,750	2.52	7	40,000	6,000	8.64	10
4,000	2,000	2.88	8	55,000	7,000	10.08	10
5,000	2,250	3.24	9	75,000	8,000	11.52	10
6,000	2,500	3.60	10	95,000	9,000	12.96	10
10,000	3,000	4.32	10	120,000	10,000	14.40	10
13,000	3,500	5.04	10	150,000	11,000	15.84	10
17,000	4,000	5.76	10	200,000	12,000	17.28	10

Over 200,000 population, 12,000 gpm, with 2,000 to 8,000 gpm additional for a second fire, for a 10-hour duration.

SOURCE: *Standard Schedule for Grading Cities and Towns of the U. S., National Board of Fire Underwriters—1956 New York, Chicago, San Francisco*

The required fire flow for residential districts consisting of small-area, one-family dwellings one or two stories in height varies from 500 to 2,000 gpm for 2—4 hr, depending on the degree of exposure between buildings.

In order to provide an adequate supply, the system should be capable of delivering the maximum fire flow required for the specified duration with consumption at the maximum daily rate. To meet this requirement the capacity of the supply works can be made equal to the maximum daily consumption rate and sufficient storage can be provided on the distribution system to deliver the required fire flow.

RESERVE CAPACITY

It is obvious that some reserve capacity should be available in the supply works. Those dependent on pumps should be capable of delivering the required fire flow for the specified time during a 5-day period with consumption at the maximum daily rate and any two pumps out of service.

SOURCE: *Kenneth J. Carl, Engr., Fire Protection, Journal American Water Works Association, Vol. 47, No. 10—1955*

LAND AREA PER FAMILY FOR NEIGHBORHOODS OF VARIOUS SIZES
Basic Allowance, in Square Feet, by Type of Dwelling and Population of Neighborhood [a]

DWELLING TYPE	NEIGHBORHOOD POPULATION				
	1,000 persons 275 families	2,000 persons 550 families	3,000 persons 825 families	4,000 persons 1,100 families	5,000 persons 1,375 families
	Square Feet per Family				
ONE- OR TWO-FAMILY DWELLINGS					
1-family detached	9,060	8,600	8,520	8,460	8,440
1-family semidetached *or* 2-family detached	6,460	6,000	5,920	5,860	5,840
1-family attached (row) *or* 2-family semidetached	4,360	3,900	3,820	3,760	3,740
MULTI-FAMILY DWELLINGS					
2-story	3,425	2,960	2,885	2,825	2,795
3-story	2,825	2,360	2,285	2,225	2,195
6-story	2,210	1,745	1,670	1,610	1,580
9-story	2,095	1,630	1,555	1,495	1,465
13-story	2,030	1,565	1,490	1,430	1,400

[a] Calculated, with street allowances added.

LAND AREA PER FAMILY FOR NEIGHBORHOOD OF 5,000 PERSONS (1,375 FAMILIES) [a]
Illustrative Calculation of Basic Allowances, in Square Feet, by Type of Dwelling [b]

DWELLING TYPE	LAND AREA IN SQUARE FEET PER FAMILY AND PER CENT OF TOTAL									
	Net Residential		Streets Serving Dwellings [d]		Community Facilities		Streets Serving Com. Fac.		TOTAL	
ONE- OR TWO-FAMILY DWELLINGS										
1-family detached	6,000	71%	1,800	22%	530	6%	110	1%	8,440	100%
1-family semidetached *or* 2-family detached	4,000	68	1,200	21	530	9	110	2	5,840	100
1-family attached (row) *or* 2-family semidetached	2,400	64	700	19	530	14	110	3	3,740	100
MULTI-FAMILY DWELLINGS										
2-story	1,465	53	600	21	610	22	120	4	2,795	100
3-story	985	45	480	21	610	28	120	6	2,195	100
6-story	570	36	280	18	610	39	120	7	1,580	100
9-story	515	35	220	15	610	42	120	8	1,465	100
13-story	450	32	220	15	610	44	120	9	1,400	100

[a] Assumed: average family size 3.6 persons.
[b] Organization of this and later tables by dwelling types does not imply that a neighborhood should consist of one dwelling type alone
[d] Will vary locally with volume of traffic, street widths, parking scheme, etc.
Allowance is approximately 20 per cent of area of community facilities.

SOURCE: Planning the Neighborhood, by the American Public Health Association, Committee on the Hygiene of Housing, Public Administration Service, Chicago, Ill. 1960

NEIGHBORHOOD DENSITY: PERSONS PER ACRE [a]
Basic Allowance, by Type of Dwelling and Population of Neighborhood

DWELLING TYPE	NEIGHBORHOOD POPULATION				
	1,000 persons 275 families	2,000 persons 550 families	3,000 persons 825 families	4,000 persons 1,100 families	5,000 persons 1,375 families
	Persons per Acre				
ONE- OR TWO-FAMILY DWELLINGS					
1-family detached	17	18	18	18	19
1-family semidetached *or* 2-family detached	24	26	27	27	27
1-family attached (row) *or* 2-family semidetached	36	40	41	42	42
MULTI-FAMILY DWELLINGS					
2-story	46	53	54	56	56
3-story	56	66	69	71	72
6-story	71	90	94	98	99
9-story	75	96	101	105	107
13-story	77	100	105	110	112

[a] Calculated, assuming average family size of 3.6 persons.

NEIGHBORHOOD DENSITY: FAMILIES PER ACRE
Basic Allowance, by Type of Dwelling and Population of Neighborhood

DWELLING TYPE	NEIGHBORHOOD POPULATION				
	1,000 persons 275 families	2,000 persons 550 families	3,000 persons 825 families	4,000 persons 1,100 families	5,000 persons 1,375 families
	Families per Acre				
ONE OR TWO-FAMILY DWELLINGS					
1-family detached	4.8	5.1	5.1	5.1	5.2
1-family semidetached *or* 2-family detached	6.8	7.3	7.4	7.4	7.5
1-family attached (row) *or* 2-family semidetached	10.0	11.2	11.4	11.6	11.7
MULTI-FAMILY DWELLINGS					
2-story	12.7	14.7	15.1	15.5	15.6
3-story	15.5	18.5	19.1	19.6	19.9
6-story	19.7	25.0	26.1	27.1	27.6
9-story	20.8	26.8	28.0	29.2	29.8
13-story	21.5	27.8	29.2	30.5	31.2

USE OF DENSITIES IN DESIGN AND LEGAL CONTROL

The fact that neighborhood density figures are based on a combination of all neighborhood land makes them a valuable tool in planning and housing. They are used early in the planning process to set the broad limits of total population in relation to the size of the site. They provide a method for expressing total land and population ratios for the purpose of preliminary cost estimates. They make it possible to calculate the various possible combinations of dwelling types desired to make up a neighborhood.

Neighborhood densities, in addition to their use in planning individual neighborhoods, offer a tool for the city in setting over-all patterns for population density. By control of over-all densities through zoning, master plans, etc., the local government can and should keep all densities within the limits necessary to health and amenity, and should establish a density pattern to obtain the most efficient population distribution, not only from the point of view of the neighborhood but of the city as a whole. The adequacy of city-wide utility systems, transit, education, recreation and other municipal services is affected by the density pattern, which, if unplanned, may cause serious spot over-loading.

PARKS AND RECREATION

PURPOSE, FUNCTIONS, AND OBJECTIVES

County and regional parks and preserves are recreation areas that serve the residents of more than one municipality, and whose size, location, and characteristics make it desirable that their development and operation be undertaken by regional cooperative agencies.

With some exceptions, the preserves generally consist of extensive land areas with relatively little development for recreation. Conservancy areas, wildlife refuges, and flood-control areas fall in this category and are often made accessible for recreation use. County and regional parks are land areas which are usually more intensively developed for recreation purposes and which supplement the facilities and activities furnished by the urban parks and recreation areas.

Many municipalities have difficulty in providing land areas to satisfy the recreation demands of their population. Regional studies should be made to determine existing facilities, future demand, and potential for acquisition and development of new facilities to meet present and future needs. To undertake these studies and to administer park areas that are formed to serve the population of more than one governmental unit, it is desirable that regional cooperative agencies be established.

The following are examples of different types of agencies: counties, such as Essex County, New Jersey, and Westchester County, New York; special-purpose authorities, such as the Huron-Clinton Metropolitan Authority and the Cleveland Metropolitan Park District; regional agencies, such as the East Bay Regional Park District in California; state agencies, such as the Huntington Beach State Park in California and the Jones Beach State Park in New York; or interstate agencies, such as the Palisades Interstate Park Commission in New Jersey and New York. Although the greatest number of park visitors will be from the population centers nearest the county or regional park, the increasing mobility of the population as a whole will permit people from greater distances to use regional facilities.

CRITERIA FOR COUNTY AND REGIONAL PARKS

Certain criteria can be established for the size, location, and types of county park facilities required to meet present and future needs. At the present time, adequate lands are still available and their cost must be evaluated in terms of their present and future value to the welfare of the people. For example, a recreation program appropriate for a regional or county park might require 1,000 acres, with a minimum of 400 to 500 acres recommended.

Although suitable acreage of this size may appear to be difficult to secure, a careful analysis may sometimes reveal land areas designated as submarginal which can be developed for recreation.

TYPES OF ACTIVITIES IN COUNTY AND REGIONAL PARKS

The activities for which facilities are usually developed in county and regional parks fall into the four general classifications described below.

- **Passive Recreation**—This includes driving for pleasure, picnicking, sightseeing, outdoor events, walking for pleasure, and nature walks.
- **Water**—This includes fishing, boating of all types, water skiing, swimming, underwater recreation, and surfing.
- **Active Programs**—This includes games and sports, horseback riding, and bicycling.
- **Primitive**—This includes camping and hiking.

PARKWAYS

The original concept of parkways as landscaped pleasure drives connecting major park areas is still valid. The basic idea of incorporating a passenger car roadway and a pleasure way for leisurely travel and enjoyment of the scenery is still a predominant characteristic of parkways. In the United States, there are several outstanding examples of such parkways in existence.

With the creation of extensive regional parks outside of the immediate metropolitan area, it will be necessary to construct traffic arteries to facilitate travel from the urban area to these parks. The planning and construction of new roads in accordance with parkway standards, or the expansion and improvement of existing roads by acquisition of scenic easements, should be given every consideration in planning for regional park facilities. An outstanding example of such a parkway is the Palisades Interstate Parkway, leading from the George Washington Bridge in New York City to the Bear Mountain-Harriman State Park, approximately 40 miles north of the City in New York State. This limited-access, landscaped parkway provides a pleasurable approach to this vast recreational area serving the metropolitan population of New York City.

During the past 30 years, a new parkway concept has evolved whose right-of-way incorporates sufficient land areas to constitute, in effect, an elongated park. When this concept is used, consideration should be given to the acquisiton of a sufficiently wide right-of-way to provide for equestrian, pedestrian, and cycling paths, and also extended areas for appropriate recreation activities to serve local requirements. These might include picnic areas, rest areas, scenic vistas, and service areas.

The parkway right-of-way, held in fee simple, can be expanded by the acquisition of scenic easements for varying distances parallel to the parkway. These are especially desirable to preserve scenic vistas and to prevent aesthetic blight by prohibiting the erection of billboards and other obtrusive structures. Average right-of-way widths vary from 200 to 1,000 feet, with scenic easements extending varying distances depending on the types of peripheral development.

It is generally desirable that parkways should be designed to provide for divided roadways with landscaped center malls. To keep the pavement width to a minimum, consideration should be given to the use of low curbs and grass shoulders. The design should provide for a flowing horizontal and vertical alignment and the development or preservation of vistas and offscapes.

When designing parkways, it is essential that the distinction between parkways and other major highways such as freeways, throughways, and expressways, be constantly kept in mind.

SOURCE: *Planning Areas and Facilities for Health, Physical Education and Recreation.* The Athletic Institute and American Association for Health, Physical Education, and Recreation Revised, 1966.

STATE PARKS

State parks are relatively spacious areas of scenic or wilderness character, which may also contain historic, archaeological, ecological, geological, or other scientific values. They are preserved as nearly as possible in their original or natural condition, and appropriate types of recreation are permitted where they will not destroy or impair the features and values to be preserved. Commercial exploitation of resources is usually prohibited.

The historic, scientific, inspirational, and wilderness values of state parks are usually of sufficient significance to attract visitors from all sections of the state, and perhaps outside the state. Population pressures have forced many states to reevaluate their criteria in establishing state parks. The time is approaching when any large acreage reasonably close to centers of population must be considered.

State parks vary in size from a relatively few acres preserving a historic building or archaeological site to large wilderness areas containing many thousands of acres. Today, some state parks are intensively developed from a recreation standpoint and provide camping, picnicking, hiking, fishing, horseback riding, golf, winter sports, and all types of water sports. Group camps, resident camps, and nature centers are also included in some states.

STATE FORESTS

State forests are areas established and managed primarily for timber production, watershed protection, and wildlife management. However, with the increasing pressure for additional areas for recreation, this is becoming an increasingly important use where it is compatible with the primary purpose for which the forest was established.

NATIONAL PARKS

Beginning with the creation of Yellowstone National Park in 1872, the United States has established a system of national parks, monuments, historic sites, and other types of areas which include the most inspiring of the nation's scenery as well as sites distinguished for their historic importance or scientific interest. National parks are large land areas, essentially of primitive or wilderness character, which contain scenery or natural wonders so outstanding in quality that they have been designated and set aside by the Federal Government to be preserved unimpaired for the benefit, enjoyment, and inspiration of the people.

Since outstanding natural scenery is where you find it, national parks are located without regard for the relationship they may have to population concentrations. However, with improvements in transportation facilities, many national parks once

considered remote are experiencing tremendous increases in visitation and distance is becoming a less-important factor each year.

Recreation activities in national parks are generally those which can be provided with the least impairment of natural features. They may include any or all of the following: sightseeing, camping, picnicking, hiking, fishing, horseback riding, boating, swimming, natural study, and most types of winter sports.

NATIONAL FORESTS

National forests are federal lands administered under a multiple-use policy for outdoor recreation, timber, range, watershed, and fish and wildlife purposes. They encompass very large acreages although not always in a single block. They may include within their boundaries large areas set aside as primitive wilderness areas where all development is excluded except for trails and primitive camping.

To meet ever-increasing demands, the U.S. Forest Service has, in recent years, greatly accelerated its program for promoting recreational facilities in the national forests, including a tremendous expansion in camp grounds and picnic areas. In addition to fostering hunting, fishing, hiking, horseback riding, water sports, and other outdoor activities, the Forest Service also issues permits to private interests for the construction of lodges with adjoining cabins and extensive winter sports areas.

NATIONAL RECREATION AREAS

National recreation areas are spacious areas developed, managed, and conserved to provide broad public recreation opportunities. National seashores and national waterways also fall into this general category in that broad recreation oppotunities are permitted. In general, this type of area is selected on the basis of providing nonurban recreational opportunities accessible to large numbers of people. Therefore, geographical distribution of these areas and their relationship to concentrations of people are paramount considerations. Exceptions are made, however, especially in the case of large artificial water impondments, where the recreation potential is such as to warrant national status. Many of these large reservoirs are in relatively remote and inaccessible areas.

No specific criteria have been established for national recreation areas, and general policies concerning their management and operation are still being formulated. In general, they should contain a minimum of 20,000 acres. Recreation activities include all those listed under national parks and, in addition, can include hunting, areas for individual and team sports, swimming pools, resident camps and education centers, and, in some cases, golf courses.

SOURCE: *Planning Areas and Facilities for Health, Physical Education and Recreation*, The Athletic Institute and American Association for Health, Physical Education, and Recreation Revised, 1966.

A. Standards for Recreational Activities

Type of Recreational Activity	Space Requirements for Activity Per Population	Ideal Size of Space Required for Activity	Recreational Area Wherein Activity May Be Located
Active Recreation			
1. Children's Play Area (with equipment)	0.5 acre/1,000 pop.	1 acre	Playgrounds-Neighborhood Parks Community Parks, School Paygrounds
2. Field Play Areas for Young Children	1.5 acres/1,000 pop.	3 acres	Playgrounds-Neighborhood Parks Community Parks
3. Older Children-Adult Field Sports Activities	1.5 acres/1,000 pop.	15 acres	Playfield-Community Park District Park
4. Tennis-Outdoor Basketball Other Court Sports	1.0 acres/5,000 pop.	2 acres	Playfield-Community Park
5. Swimming	1 outdoor pool/25,000	Competition size plus wading pool 2 acres	Playfield-Community Park
6. Major Boating Activities	100 acres/50,000	100 acres and over	District Park-Regional Park or Reservation
7. Hiking-Camping-Horseback Riding-Nature Study	10 acres/1,000 pop.	500–1,000 acres	Large District Park-Regional Park
8. Golfing	1–18 hole course per 50,000 pop.	120 acres	Community Park-District Park
Passive Recreation			
1. Picnicking	4 acres/1,000 pop.	varies	All parks
2. Passive Water Sports Fishing-Rowing-Canoeing	1 Lake or Lagoon per 25,000 pop.	20 acre water area	Community Park Special Regional Reservations
3. Zoos, Arboretums, Botanical Gardens	1 acre/1,000 pop.	100 acres	Large District Park or Special Facility
Other			
1. Parking at Recreational Areas	1 acre/1,000 pop.	varies	Playfields, Community, District & Regional Parks
2. Indoor Recreation Centers	1 acre/10,000 pop.	1–2 acres	Community Parks
3. Outdoor Theaters, Band Shells	1 acre/25,000 pop.	5 acres	District Parks

B. Standards for Recreation Areas

Type of Area	Acres Per 1000 Population	Size of Site		Radius of Area Served
		Ideal	Minimum	
Playgrounds	1.5	4 acres	2 acres	0.5 miles
Neighborhood Parks	2.0	10	5	0.5
Playfields	1.5	15	10	1.5
Community Parks	3.5	100	40	2.0
District Parks	2.0	200	100	3.0
Regional Parks and Reservations	15.0	500–1,000	varies	10.0

SOURCE: George Nez, Standards for New Urban Development—The Denver Background, Reprinted by Permission of Urban Land, Vol. 20, No. 5, Urban Land Institute, 1200 18th Street, N.W., Washington, D.C.

The term "park" is frequently used generically and applied to many different kinds of areas. Most of the States use a number of classifications based upon considerations such as character, use, custom, and statutory requirements. These vary from State to State, and more than 60 classifications are currently in use. And there are extensive public areas reserved for purposes other than recreation which also offer recreation opportunities in addition to the use for which they were primarily intended.

NATIONAL

Established areas administered by agencies of the Federal Government, and potential areas of national significance, have been classified in accordance with the following definitions:

National Parks.—Spacious land areas essentially of primitive or wilderness character which contain scenery and natural wonders so outstanding in quality that their preservation intact has been provided for by their having been designated and set aside by the Federal Government to be preserved unimpaired for the benefit, enjoyment, and inspiration of the people.

National Monuments.—Nationally significant landmarks, structures, objects, or areas of scientific or prehistoric interest so designated by the Federal Government for preservation and public use.

National Recreation Areas.—Spacious areas selected, developed, managed, and conserved to provide broad public recreation opportunities which can best be provided by the Federal Government or where there is a Federal responsiblity to conserve and develop recreation opportunities.

National Seashores.—Natural coastal areas set aside for the preservation and public recreation use of their nationally significant scenic, scientific, historic, or recreation values, or a combination of such values. (The term "national lakeshores" has been used recently to designate similar types of proposed areas on the Great Lakes, and "national rivers" has been suggested in proposals to preserve free-flowing streams.)

National Parkways.—Federally owned elongated parks featuring roads designated for pleasure travel, and embracing scenic, recreational, or historic features of national significance. Access from adjoining properties is limited and commercial traffic is not permitted. National parkways have sufficient merit and character to make them a national attraction and not merely a means of travel from one region to another. National parkways can be established only by acts of Congress.

National Historic Sites.—Historic sites, buildings, or objects so designated in recognition of their national significance.

National Memorials.—Structures or areas designated to commemorate ideas, events, or personages of national significance.

National Battlefields.—Battlefields of national significance preserved in part, or in entirety, for the inspiration and benefit of the people.

National Wildlife Refuges.—Areas administered by the Bureau of Sport Fisheries and Wildlife, designated for the protection and propagation of game animals, birds, and fish, within which certain outdoor recreation facilities and activities are permitted as long as they do not interfere with the primary purposes of the refuges.

National Forests.—Federal lands administered by the Forest Service, U.S. Department of Agriculture, under a multiple-use policy for outdoor recreation, range, timber, watershed, and wildlife and fish purposes.

STATE AND LOCAL

In formulating recommendations to establish potential State, local, quasi-public, and private areas, they should be classified in accordance with the definitions that follow. These

SOURCE: Parks—U.S. Dept. of Parks, Washington, D.C.

are based on definitions adopted by the Board of Directors of the National Conference on State Parks.

Parks.—Relatively spacious areas of outstanding scenic and wilderness character, oftentimes containing also significant historical, archeological, ecological, geological, and other scientific values, preserved as nearly as possible in their original or natural condition and providing opportunity for appropriate types of recreation where such will not destroy or impair the features and values to be preserved. Commercial exploitation of resources is usually prohibited.

Monuments and Historic Sites.—Areas, usually limited in size, established primarily to preserve objects of historic and scientific interest, and places commemorating important persons or historic events. The facilities usually provided are those required for the safety and comfort of the visiting public, such as access, parking, water sanitation, interpretive devices and sometimes facilities for picnicking and other recreation facilities.

Recreation Areas.—Areas selected and developed primarily to provide nonurban outdoor recreation opportunities to meet other than purely local needs but having the best available scenic quality. Hunting and some other recreation activities usually associated with parks may be permitted. Commercial exploitation of resources is usually prohibited.

Waysides.—Relatively small areas along highways selected for their scenic or historical significance and providing opportunity for the traveler to relax, enjoy a scenic view, read a historical marker, or have a picnic lunch.

In addition to the preceding definitions adopted by the National Conference on State Parks, other types of areas are defined as follows:

Wilderness.—Areas to preserve primeval environment and devoted primarily to such wilderness types of educational and recreational uses as are consistent with the maintenance of the natural character of the area.

Nature Preserves.—Areas, often limited in size, established for the purpose of preserving distinctive natural communities of plants and animals for their scientific and esthetic interest.

Beaches.—Areas with frontage on the oceans, lakes, and streams designed primarily to provide swimming, boating, fishing, and other waterfront activities. Other coastal areas acquired primarily for the scenic and scientific values are included in the classification "parks."

Parkways.—Elongated or "ribbon" parks featuring a motor road for noncommercial traffic, connecting parks, monuments, beaches, and recreation areas or otherwise affording an opportunity for pleasant and safe driving. Access and roadside developments are controlled. As an adjunct to the motor road, appropriate facilities such as turnouts, picnic areas, and other recreation developments are frequently provided where space permits.

Scenic Roads.—Generally, rural highways, existing or proposed, located in areas having such highly scenic or cultural values that their further development for emphasis on safe and pleasant recreation motoring is justified, including facilities for interpretation of cultural features, for picnicking and camping and development of other recreation potentialities for the roadside.

Trials.—Extended and usually continuous strips of land or water established independently of other routes of travel and dedicated, through ownership or easement, to recreational travel, including hiking, bicycling, horseback riding, or canoeing.

Free-Flowing Streams.—Streams or portions of streams that are still unmodified by the works of man or that, in spite of such modification, retain natural scenic qualities and recreation opportunities. There must be provision for adequate protection against undesirable streamside developments, and for the preservation through public control of the existing character and quality of the adjacent landscape.

Forests.—Areas established and managed primarily for timber production and watershed protection. Recreation is an increasingly important use.

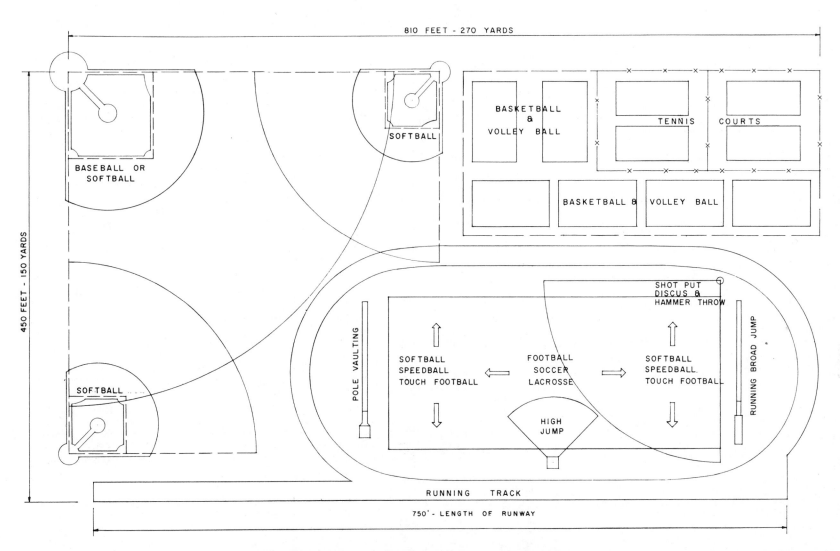

810 FEET - 270 YARDS

450 FEET - 150 YARDS

BASEBALL OR
SOFTBALL

SOFTBALL

SOFTBALL

BASKETBALL
&
VOLLEY BALL

TENNIS COURTS

BASKETBALL & VOLLEY BALL

SHOT PUT
DISCUS &
HAMMER THROW

POLE VAULTING

SOFTBALL
SPEEDBALL
TOUCH FOOTBALL

FOOTBALL
SOCCER
LACROSSE

SOFTBALL
SPEEDBALL
TOUCH FOOTBALL

RUNNING BROAD JUMP

HIGH
JUMP

RUNNING TRACK

750' - LENGTH OF RUNWAY

SUGGESTED LAYOUT FOR ATHLETIC FIELD

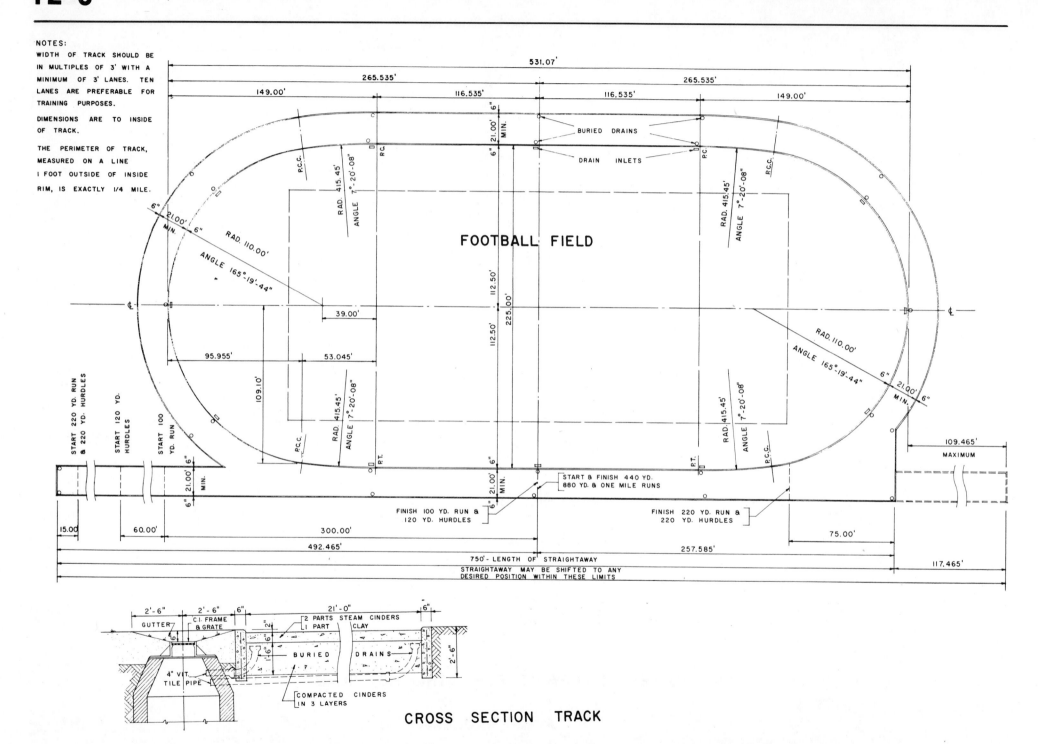

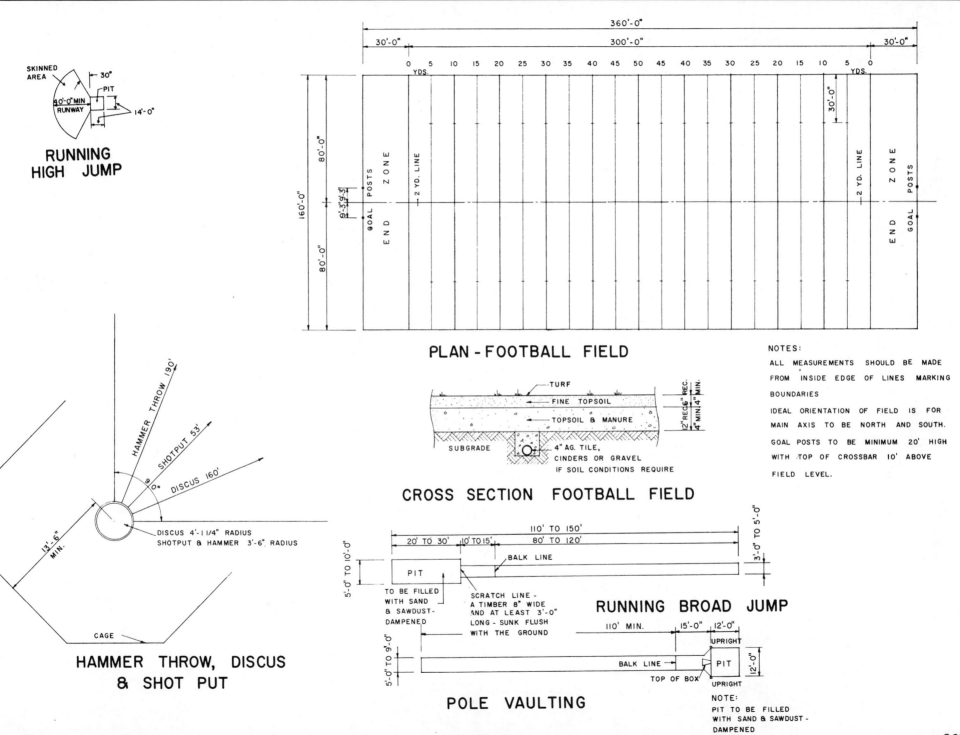

RUNNING HIGH JUMP

PLAN - FOOTBALL FIELD

CROSS SECTION FOOTBALL FIELD

HAMMER THROW, DISCUS & SHOT PUT

RUNNING BROAD JUMP

POLE VAULTING

NOTES:

ALL MEASUREMENTS SHOULD BE MADE FROM INSIDE EDGE OF LINES MARKING BOUNDARIES

IDEAL ORIENTATION OF FIELD IS FOR MAIN AXIS TO BE NORTH AND SOUTH.

GOAL POSTS TO BE MINIMUM 20' HIGH WITH TOP OF CROSSBAR 10' ABOVE FIELD LEVEL.

NOTE:
PIT TO BE FILLED WITH SAND & SAWDUST - DAMPENED

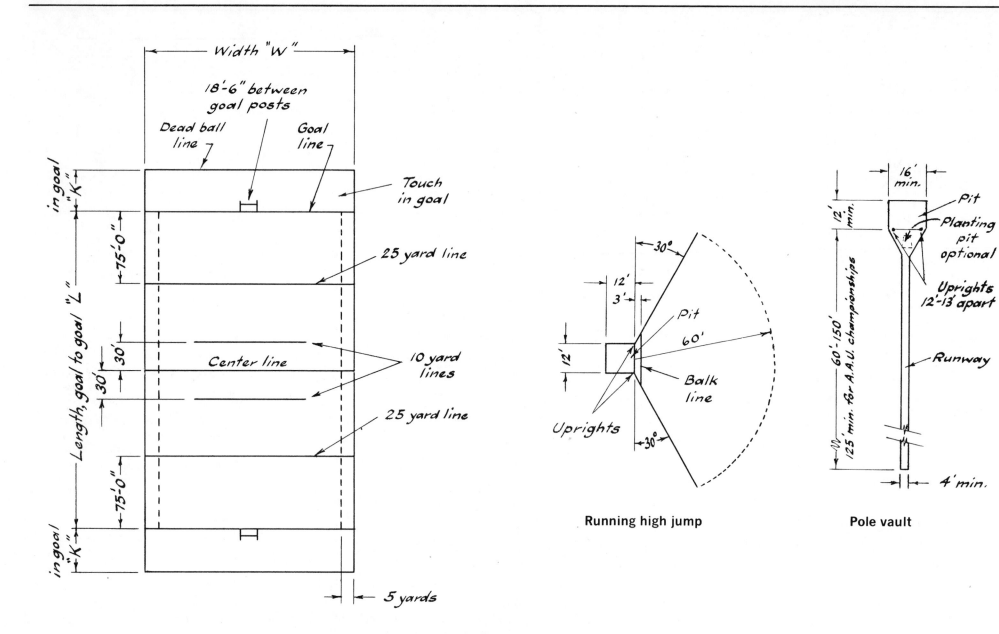

Rugby football (R.F.U.)

Running high jump

Pole vault

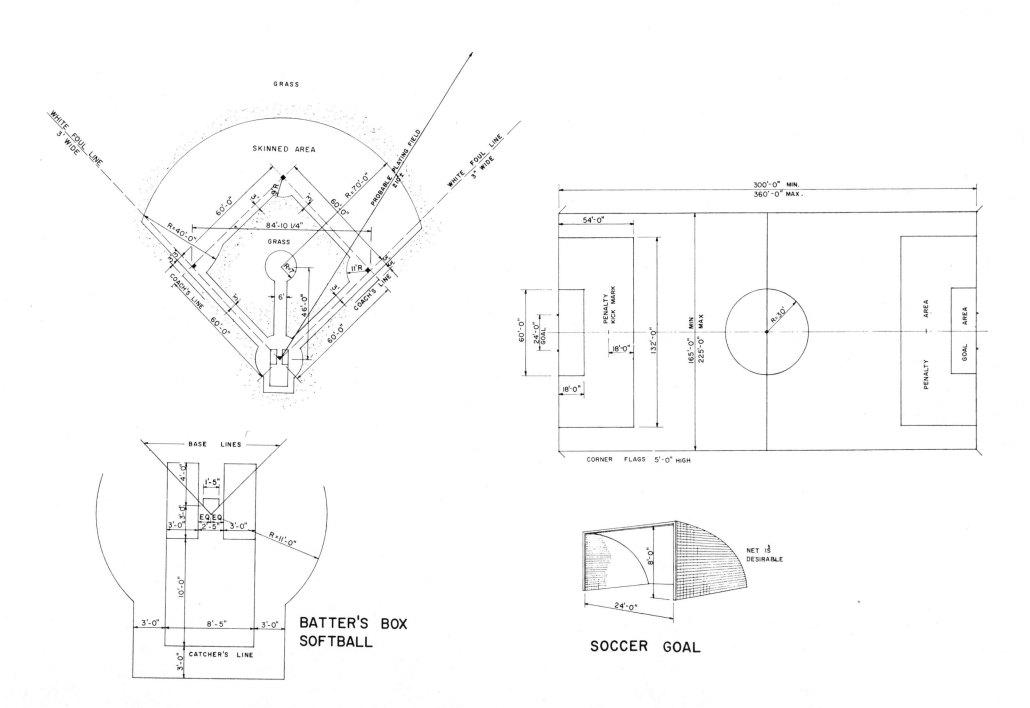

GRASS

SKINNED AREA

WHITE FOUL LINE
3" WIDE

WHITE FOUL LINE
3" WIDE

PROBABLE PLAYING FIELD
210'±

GRASS

R=40'-0"

60'-0"

R=70'-0"

60'-0"

84'-10 1/4"

9'R

R=7'

11'R

6'

46'-0"

COACH'S LINE 60'-0"

COACH'S LINE

60'-0"

BASE LINES

4'-0"

1'-5"

3'-0" 3'-0"

EQ EQ
2'-5"

3'-0"

R=11'-0"

10'-0"

3'-0"   8'-5"   3'-0"

CATCHER'S LINE

3'-0"

**BATTER'S BOX
SOFTBALL**

300'-0" MIN.
360'-0" MAX.

54'-0"

60'-0"

24'-0"
GOAL

PENALTY KICK MARK

18'-0"

132'-0"

165'-0" MIN
225'-0" MAX

R=30'

PENALTY   AREA

GOAL AREA

18'-0"

CORNER FLAGS 5'-0" HIGH

8'-0"

NET IS
DESIRABLE

24'-0"

SOCCER GOAL

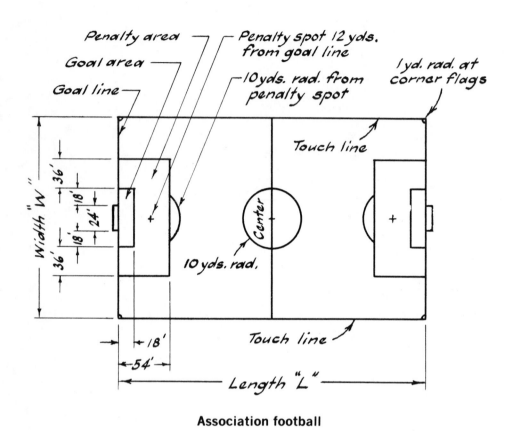

Association football

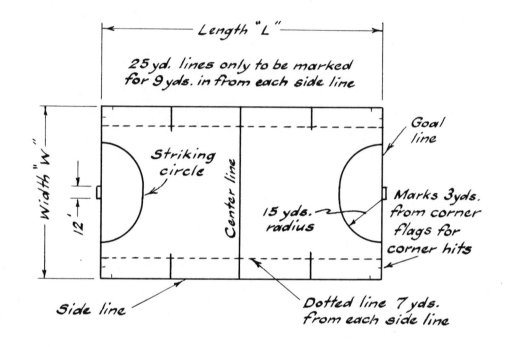

Hockey

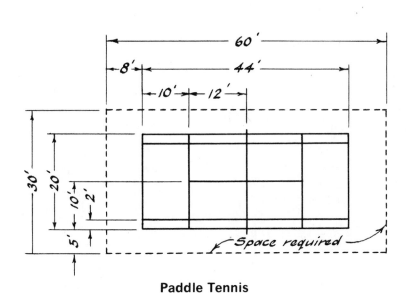

Paddle Tennis

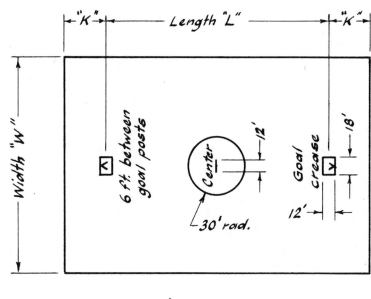

Lacrosse

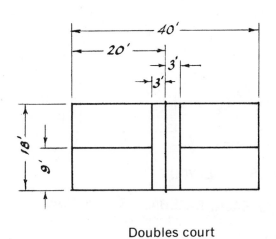

Doubles court

Deck Tennis

Lacrosse	provide	generally
(Box or Field)	one per 20,000 persons	located in community park

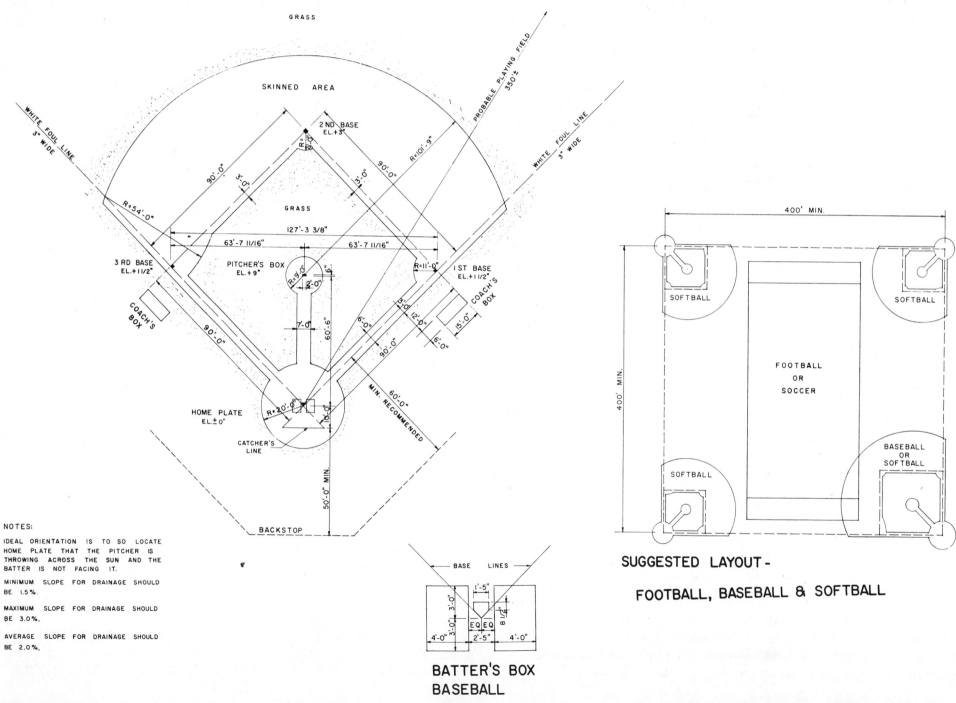

GRASS

PROBABLE PLAYING FIELD 350'±

SKINNED AREA

WHITE FOUL LINE 3" WIDE

WHITE FOUL LINE 3" WIDE

2ND BASE EL.+3"

R="9'-0"

90'-0"

3'-0"

3'-0"

90'-0"

R=10'-9"

GRASS

R=54'-0"

127'-3 3/8"

63'-7 11/16"   63'-7 11/16"

3RD BASE EL.+11/2"

PITCHER'S BOX EL.+9"

R=11'-0"

1ST BASE EL.+11/2"

R=9'-0"

2'-0"

COACH'S BOX

COACH'S BOX

90'-0"

7'-0"

60'-6"

5'-0"

6'-0"

12'-0"

15'-0"

90'-0"

6'-0"

MIN. RECOMMENDED

60'-0"

R=20'-0"

10'-0"

HOME PLATE EL.±0"

CATCHER'S LINE

50'-0" MIN.

BACKSTOP

SUGGESTED LAYOUT -

FOOTBALL, BASEBALL & SOFTBALL

400' MIN.

400' MIN.

SOFTBALL

SOFTBALL

FOOTBALL OR SOCCER

SOFTBALL

BASEBALL OR SOFTBALL

NOTES:

IDEAL ORIENTATION IS TO SO LOCATE HOME PLATE THAT THE PITCHER IS THROWING ACROSS THE SUN AND THE BATTER IS NOT FACING IT.

MINIMUM SLOPE FOR DRAINAGE SHOULD BE 1.5%.

MAXIMUM SLOPE FOR DRAINAGE SHOULD BE 3.0%.

AVERAGE SLOPE FOR DRAINAGE SHOULD BE 2.0%.

BASE   LINES

1'-5"

3'-0"

8 1/2"

EQ EQ

4'-0"   2'-5"   4'-0"

BATTER'S BOX
BASEBALL

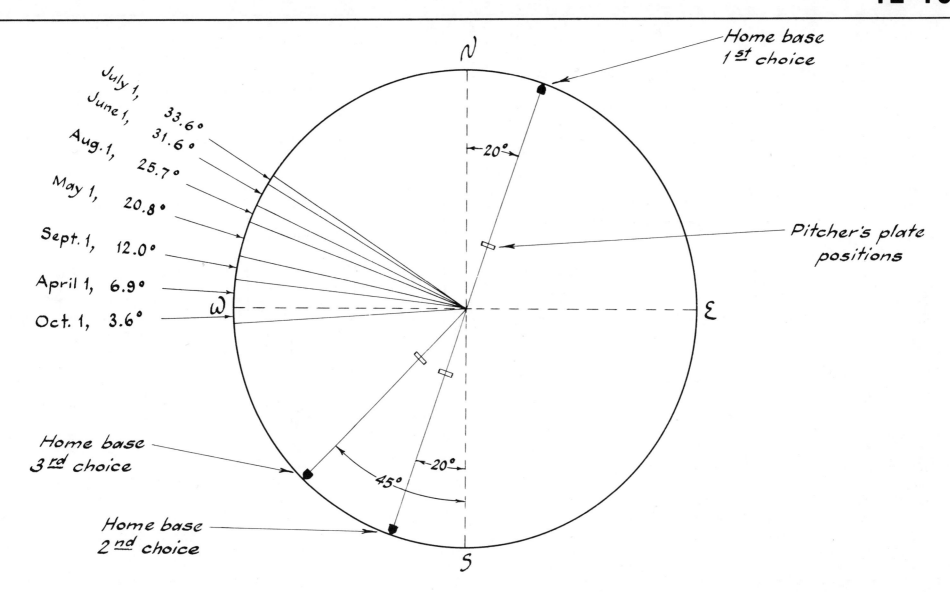

ORIENTATION

To ensure minimum nuisance from the sun when sighting balls in mid-air it is desirable that the principal line of play of any game should be away from the direction of the setting sun.

So far as team games are concerned the advantage of good orientation should always be weighed against the effects of surface gradients where, for economic or other reasons, these have to be accepted of greater severity than is normally advisable. Quite apart from the effect on the run of the ball the physical strain of play increases in proportion to the gradient. It is therefore recommended that where the surface gradient exceeds 1 in 40, the main direction of play should be transverse to the inclination irrespective of the demands of good orientation.

Where high buildings, trees or surrounding hills effectively screen the sun at low altitude, some latitude in the interpretation of orientation requirements is permissible, particularly if a more satisfactory layout results.

373

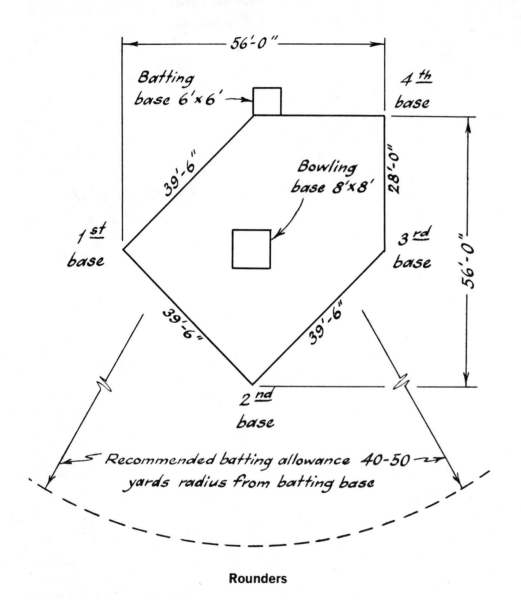

Rounders

Batting base 6'x6'

56'-0"

4th base

Bowling base 8'x8'

39'-6"

28'-0"

1st base

3rd base

56'-0"

39'-6"

39'-6"

2nd base

Recommended batting allowance 40-50 yards radius from batting base

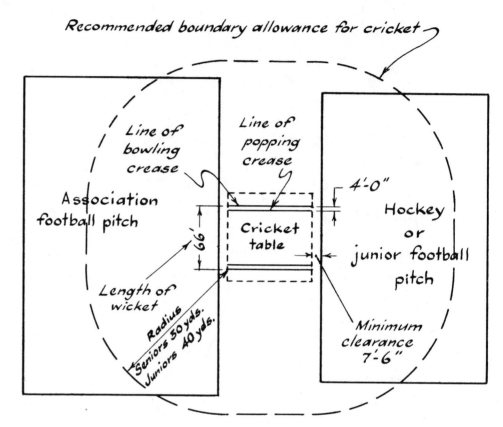

Cricket

Recommended boundary allowance for cricket

Association football pitch

Line of bowling crease

Line of popping crease

4'-0"

Cricket table

Hockey or junior football pitch

66'

Length of wicket

Radius Seniors 50 yds. Juniors 40 yds.

Minimum clearance 7'-6"

SHUFFLEBOARD COURTS

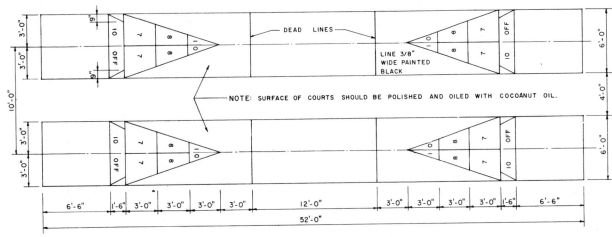

NOTE:
DIMENSIONS OF LINES ARE FROM CENTER TO CENTER, EXCEPT FOR BORDER LINES WHICH ARE TO OUTSIDE OF COURT.

DEAD LINES

LINE 3/8" WIDE PAINTED BLACK

NOTE: SURFACE OF COURTS SHOULD BE POLISHED AND OILED WITH COCOANUT OIL.

6'-6" 1'-6" 3'-0" 3'-0" 3'-0" 3'-0" 12'-0" 3'-0" 3'-0" 3'-0" 3'-0" 1'-6" 6'-6"

52'-0"

PLAN OF TWO COURTS

GRADE 3 1/2" RUBBED CONCRETE 4 x 4 x #6 W.M.

6" CINDER FILL IF SOIL CONDITIONS REQUIRE

SECTION

HANDBALL COURTS

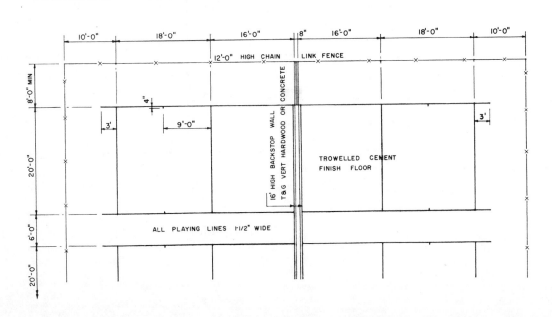

10'-0" 18'-0" 16'-0" 8" 16'-0" 18'-0" 10'-0"

12'-0" HIGH CHAIN LINK FENCE

4"

3' 9'-0" 3'

TROWELLED CEMENT FINISH FLOOR

16' HIGH BACKSTOP WALL T&G VERT HARDWOOD OR CONCRETE

ALL PLAYING LINES 1-1/2" WIDE

BADMINTON COURTS

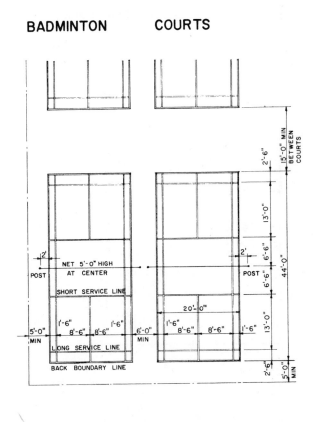

15'-0" MIN BETWEEN COURTS

2'-6"

13'-0"

6'-6"

6'-6"

44'-0"

13'-0"

2'-6"

5'-0" MIN

NET 5'-0" HIGH AT CENTER

SHORT SERVICE LINE

LONG SERVICE LINE

BACK BOUNDARY LINE

POST POST

2' 2'

20'-0"

5'-0" MIN 1'-6" 8'-6" 8'-6" 1'-6" 6'-0" MIN 1'-6" 8'-6" 8'-6" 1'-6"

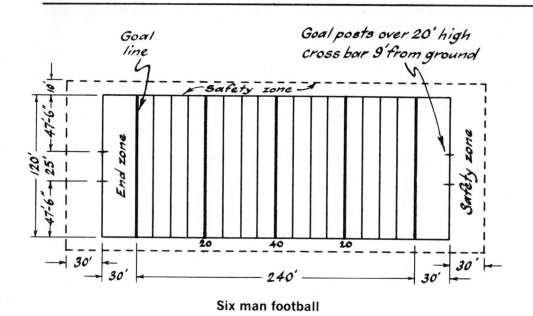

Six man football

Shuffle board

Field hockey—women

Doubles court—may be lined for singles only

Badminton

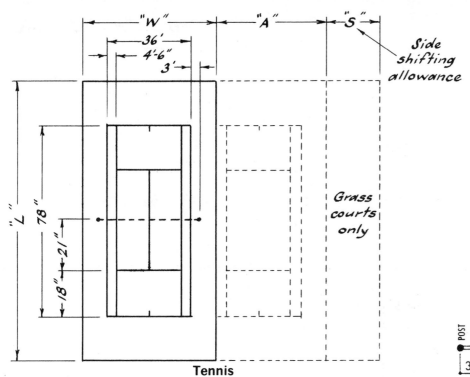

Tennis

Double

Single

For economy of construction and convenience of use and maintenance, tennis courts should be grouped together as a block. It is preferable for courts to be sited side by side rather than end on. The former arrangement is not only better for the players but is not so costly as less surfacing and intermediate stop netting are required. Odd shaped areas between the courts and the boundary should, if possible, be avoided as they increase the difficulties of maintenance and seldom serve any useful purpose.

Where levelling is necessary, due allowance must be made for banks or retaining walls.

A shelter with front open and provided with seats is desirable.

Type of Court	Overall Length "L"	Overall width of first court "W"	Additional width for each further court "A"	Side shifting allowance (grass courts only) "S"
	Feet	Feet	Feet	Feet
HARD				
Tournament	120–130	60–65	48–50½	—
Public Schools	114	56	46	—
High School	114	56	46	—
GRASS				
Tournament	120	60	48	24
Public Schools	110	56	46	23
High School	110	56	46	23

Tennis Courts one location per 5,000 persons usually combined with some other facility

377

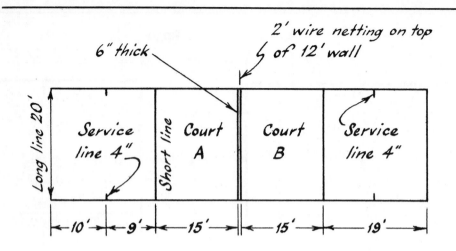

Handball

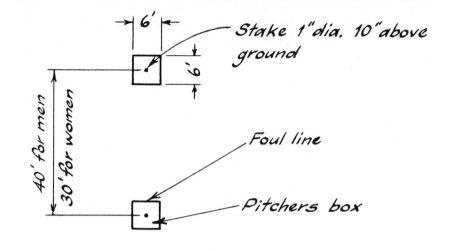

Horseshoe Pit

Dimensions are 100' x 50' and the marginal clearance should not be less than 5' all round. Where sited side by side the margin between pitches should be increased to 10'.

Netball

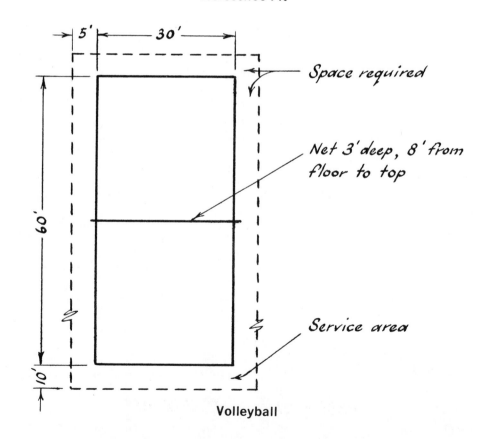

Volleyball

BASKETBALL COURT

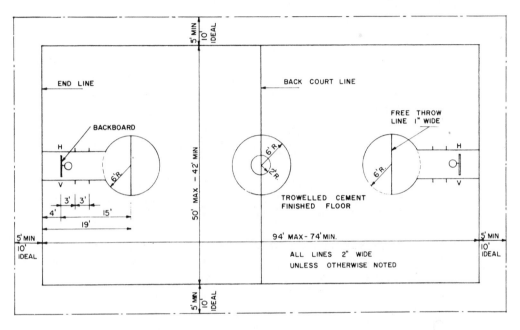

ALL LINES 2" WIDE
UNLESS OTHERWISE NOTED

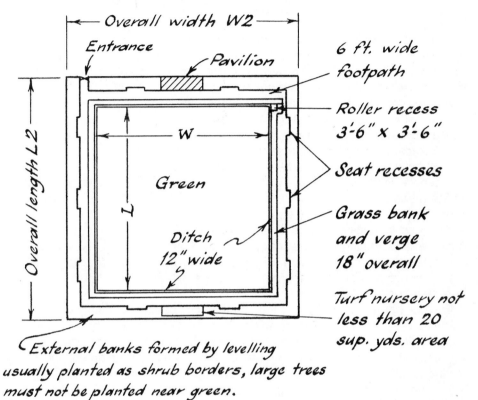

Flat rink Bowling Green

RECOMMENDED DIMENSIONS

Rinks	Green width "W"		Green length "L"	Overall width "W2"		Overall length "L2"
	Ft.	ins.	Feet	Ft.	ins.	Feet
2	52	6	126	86	6	160
3	73	6	126	107	6	160
4	94	6	126	128	6	160
5	115	6	126	149	6	160
6	126	0	126	160	0	160

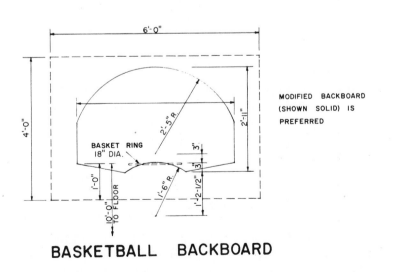

MODIFIED BACKBOARD
(SHOWN SOLID) IS
PREFERRED

BASKETBALL BACKBOARD

GOLF COURSES

The design, construction, operation, and maintenance of golf courses is too vast a subject to be covered in detail in this publication. The information herein is presented to introduce the reader to the basic requirements for the successful development of golf-course facilities.

Existing topography, vegetation, soil conditions, water courses, and property outline will dictate the amount of land required for a golf course. The following space requirements generally apply:

- Standard 18-hole golf course — 120 to 160 acres
- Standard 9-hole golf course — 70 to 90 acres
- 9-hole par-3 golf course — 45 to 60 acres (including one or two par-4 holes)

These areas are normally sufficient to include a practice putting green, a practice driving range, the clubhouse area, and parking facilities.

The practice putting green should be equal in size to the largest putting surface on the course. Putting surfaces may vary in size from 3,000 to 15,000 square feet.

Where possible, fairways should be oriented in a north-south direction. Fairways with a line of play into the northwest are especially bad and should be avoided wherever possible.

The clubhouse is the control center for the golf course. Its primary function is to serve as the place where golfers register daily and pay fees for the use of the golf facilities. It is necessary that the clubhouse be located as near as possible to the 1st and 10th tees, the 9th and 18th greens, the practice putting green, and the tee for the practice driving range. The size of the clubhouse and the services it provides may vary with local conditions and intensity of use. The services may include various combinations of the following:

- Locker rooms
- Shower rooms
- Toilet facilities
- Dining room or snack bar
- Lounge
- Manager's office
- Pro shop (where golf merchandise may be purchased)
- Caddy-cart storage room
- Heating unit
- Maintenance storage room

Careful attention should be given to the location of the pro shop so that maximum supervision can be given all clubhouse and course activities.

In order to insure the maximum orderly use of the course, a "starter" must be provided to verify the golfers' registration on the course and to advise them when to tee-off. A shelter separate from the clubhouse is often provided for the starter. If such provision is made, it must necessarily be located immediately adjacent to the 1st and 10th tees.

PAR-3 GOLF COURSE

The par-3 course, or the 'cut-down' of the regulation golf course is in every respect similar to the regulation layout. Where land is at a premium, the par-3 course can provide all of the advantages of a regulation course.

Total yardages for the 9-hole course range from just under 300 yards to nearly 400 yards. An 18-hole course can vary from 600 to 2700 yards. A short course of par-3 is designed so that no hole exceeds a maximum of 200 yards; however, a number of short courses feature a few par-4 holes and occasionally a par-5.

The constriction of land has probably been one of the most significant factors in the development of the par-3 course. With the advent of increased traffic and expanded suburban areas, prime acreage for golf course is at a premium, and 160 acres is a great deal of land to allocate to an 18-hole golf course. The par-3 course is not a substitute for the longer regulation golf course, but in those areas where the availability of land, limitation of water, and the expense of maintenance dictate a limited golf facility, the par-3 course fills a need.

Acreage

The 50 to 60 acres required for a well-planned, 18-hole par-3 course, compared to the 130-acre tract required for a regulation course, make an appreciable difference. In many cases where no golf courses could ever be considered, a 9-hole par-3 on 5 acres can be accomplished.

SOURCE: Planning Areas and Facilities for Health, Physical Education and Recreation, Athletic Institute & American Ass. for Health, Physical Education, and Recreation, 1966.

Facility	Standard	Facility	Standard
9 hole golf course	One 9 hole course for each 25,000 people. Each golf course has 75 acres that include:	18 hole golf course	One 18 hole course for each 50,000 people. Each golf course has 150 acres that include:
	a. fairways, roughs, greens, and tees, 43 acres. **b.** clubhouse, .25 acre. **c.** parking area and service roads, 1.75 acres. **d.** natural area, 20 acres. **e.** landscape area, 10 acres.		**a.** fairways, roughs, greens, and tees, 86 acres. **b.** clubhouse, .50 acre. **c.** parking area and service roads, 3.5 acres. **d.** natural area, 40 acres. **e.** landscape area, 20 acres.
Sacramento County Planning Commission	One 9 hole of public course for each community of 25,000 people or less. Minimum of 50 acres.		One 18 hole course for each 60,000 people. Minimum of 125 acres.
National Golf Foundation, Inc.	An 80 acre golf course located in a gently rolling area with some trees is preferable. Minimum of 50 acres.		160 acres for a good course. Minimum of 110 acres.
	Can accommodate 350 persons per day.		Can accommodate 500 to 550 persons per day.
			18 holes of golf for every 20,000 people. Each additional 18 hole course requires about 30,000 people. A course should not be located over 20 miles from a population center.
			The land area needed per course ranges from 160 to 200 acres depending upon topography and shape of land. A rule of thumb is: 10 acres per golf hole for average courses. A small course may get by with 5 acres per hole.
			One 18 hole course for every 50,000 people. Ideal size of course is 120 acres. Golf course may be located within a community or district park.

There are two general types of golf courses in use today—9-hole and 18-hole, the 18 hole course is the standard layout, the nine hole course is a short course with the fairways and greens smaller than those of a regulation course but similar in every other way.

The average length of an 18-hole course is 6500 yards while a 9-hole course is less than half of this length.

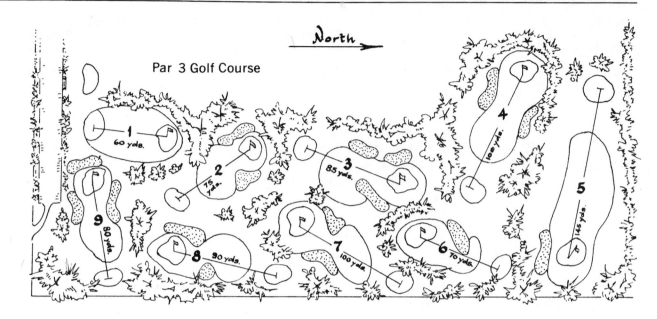

North

Par 3 Golf Course

Nine-hole, par 3 course designed for maximum land use at minimum cost. Grassy bunkers and hollows can be substituted for sand traps indicated on plan to further cut cost of construction and maintenance as well as to speed up play for greater traffic capacity. Designed for 15 acre area.

SOURCE: Golf Operators Handbook, edited by Ben Chlevin, National Golf Foundation, Inc.,—1956, p. 86

	Minimum area required	Maximum area required	No. of parking spaces	Population served	Service radius	Average length
9-hole course	60 acres	80 acres	100 cars	1 hole per 3000 persons or 27,000 persons	½–¾ hour by car or public transportation	Approx. 2250 yards
18-hole course	120 acres	160 acres	200 cars	1 hole per 1500 persons or 25,000 persons	1 hour max. by car or public transportation	6500 yards

ROQUE COURT

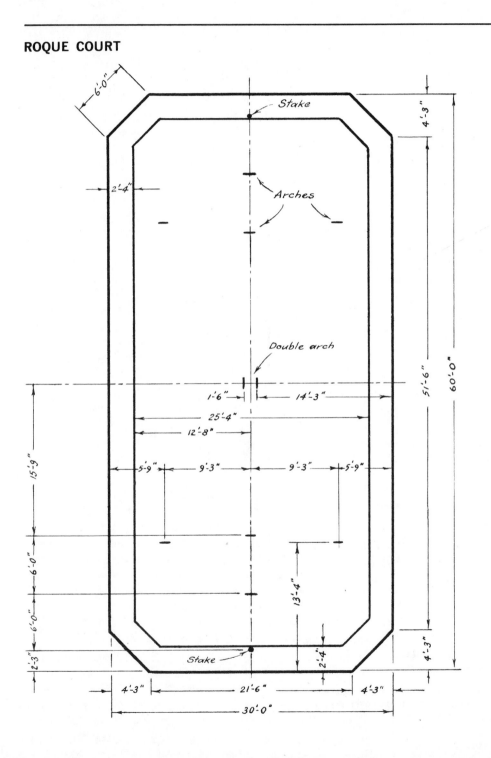

Stake
Arches
Double arch
6'-0"
4'-3"
2'-4"
51'-6"
60'-0"
1'-6"
14'-3"
25'-4"
12'-8"
5'-9"
9'-3"
9'-3"
5'-9"
15'-9"
6'-0"
6'-0"
13'-4"
2'-3"
2'-4"
4'-3"
4'-3"
21'-6"
4'-3"
30'-0"
Stake

CROQUET COURT

Stake
2'-6"
8'-0"
7'-0"
15'-0"
Boundary line
Playing line
Wickets or arches
60'-0"
30'-0"
2'-6"
Stake
5'-9"
9'-3"
15'-0"
30'-0"

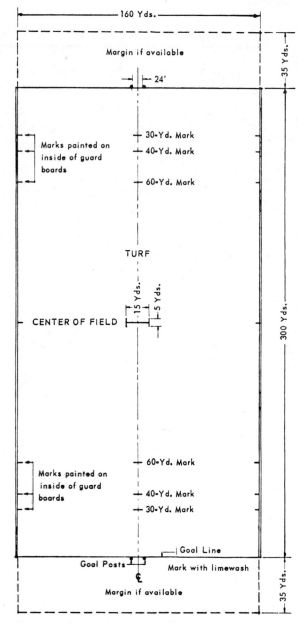

160 Yds.

Margin if available

24'

35 Yds.

Marks painted on inside of guard boards

30-Yd. Mark
40-Yd. Mark

60-Yd. Mark

TURF

300 Yds.

15 Yds.
5 Yds.

CENTER OF FIELD

Marks painted on inside of guard boards

60-Yd. Mark

40-Yd. Mark

30-Yd. Mark

Goal Line
Goal Posts
Mark with limewash

Margin if available

35 Yds.

PLAN

NOTE: Field to be smooth and covered with good heavy turf.

Minimum surface slope is 1.5%

POLO GOAL POST ELEVATION

12'' X 18'' Flag

2' - 0''

8''

1½'' X 4' Flag Pole

Upper 8' of post to be painted white

8' - 0''

10' Minimum

Lower 4' to be painted a dark color

4' - 0''

25 LB. Weight on inside

1' - 6'   24' - 0'' Face to face

Wood members to be pressure treated with paintable oil-borne preservative.

NOTE: Hollow goal post may be made of cane basket-ware or other light material and covered with felt and painted canvas.

POLO GUARD BOARD ELEVATION

3''   1''

1''

Field side painted white

Back painted green

10''

3''

14''

1' - 11''

2'' X 3'' Stakes 5' - 0'' O.C.

SOURCE: Office of Engineers, U.S. Army.

OUTDOOR SHOOTING AREAS

Rifle Range

The advisability of constructing an outdoor rifle range on a school, college, or recreation site will depend on several factors: (1) the terrain and location of the parcels of land; (2) the availability of nearby outdoor ranges owned by sportsmen's clubs, military organizations, and other groups which might be used for instruction and recreational shooting; and (3) the location of indoor ranges.

If an outdoor range is developed, the target area should be protected, preferably by natural embankments. If the land is level, adequate banks of soil can be constructed that will reinforce the other types of backstops used. It is always desirable to have a good-size area with plenty of unused space back of the target. A 50-foot range is sufficient for most instructional and recreational programs, since the .22-caliber rifle will be used in most instances.

In considering a range, it would be advisable to consult the National Rifle Association and, if possible, have the site inspected by a member of the NRA staff. Detailed information on specifications can be obtained from the National Rifle Association, 1600 Rhode Island Avenue, N.W., Washington, D.C.

Shotgun-Shooting Area

Shotgun shooting and games like skeet are becoming increasingly popular. There may not be adequate facilities for trap and skeet in nearby gun clubs, police ranges, and military establishments. In such circumstances, an open area can be used for skeet by utilizing hand traps.

If the adjacent property, such as open fields, woods, or swamps, is not being used during the time of shooting, skeet can be conducted safely under the supervision of a qualified instructor. The National Rifle Association has detailed information on shotgun shooting and facilities.

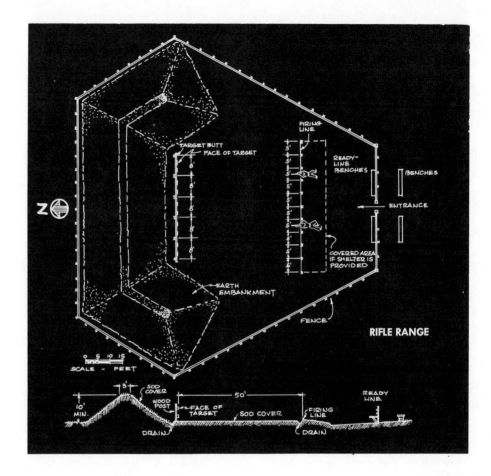

RIFLE RANGE

SOURCE: Planning Areas and Facilities for Health, Physical Education & Recreation.

SOURCE: Campsites and Facilities, Boy Scouts of America, New Brunswick, N.J. 1964.

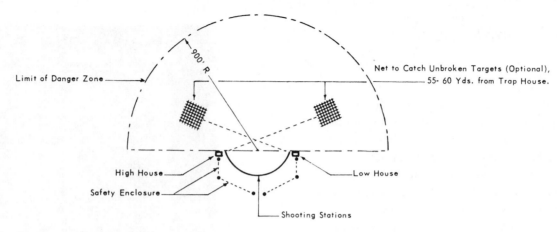

SAFETY & SALVAGE PRECAUTIONS

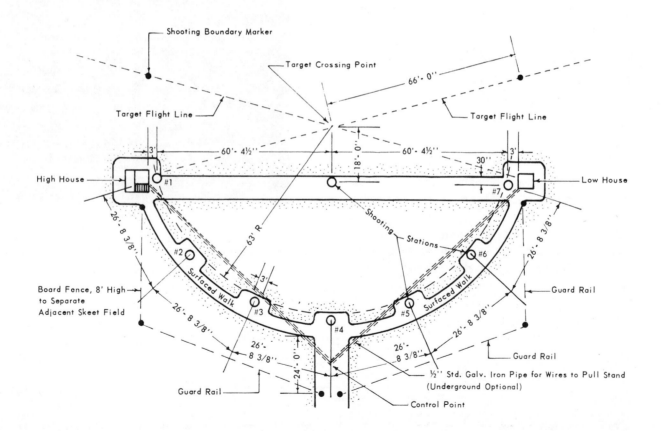

SOURCE: Office of Engineers, U.S. Army.

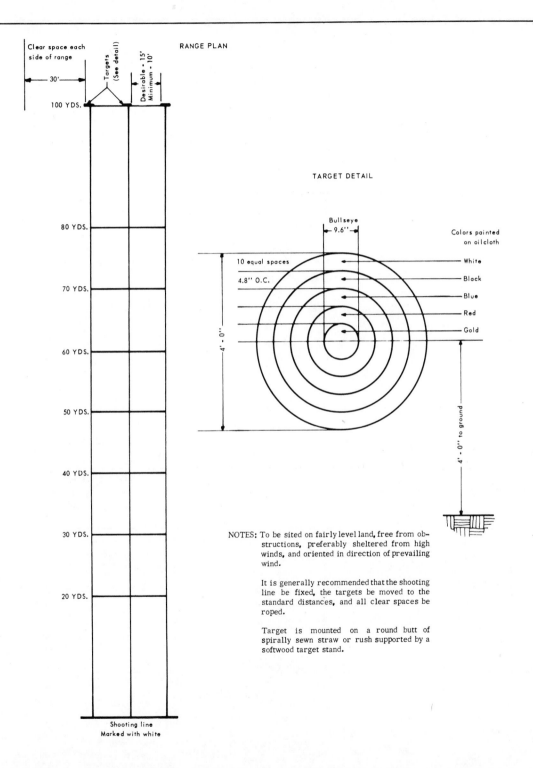

RANGE PLAN

Clear space each side of range

30'

Targets (See detail)

Desirable - 15'
Minimum - 10'

100 YDS.

80 YDS.

70 YDS.

60 YDS.

50 YDS.

40 YDS.

30 YDS.

20 YDS.

Shooting line
Marked with white

TARGET DETAIL

Bullseye

9.6''

Colors painted on oilcloth

10 equal spaces

4.8'' O.C.

White
Black
Blue
Red
Gold

4' - 0''

4' - 0'' to ground

NOTES: To be sited on fairly level land, free from obstructions, preferably sheltered from high winds, and oriented in direction of prevailing wind.

It is generally recommended that the shooting line be fixed, the targets be moved to the standard distances, and all clear spaces be roped.

Target is mounted on a round butt of spirally sewn straw or rush supported by a softwood target stand.

SOURCE: Office of Engineers, U.S. Army.

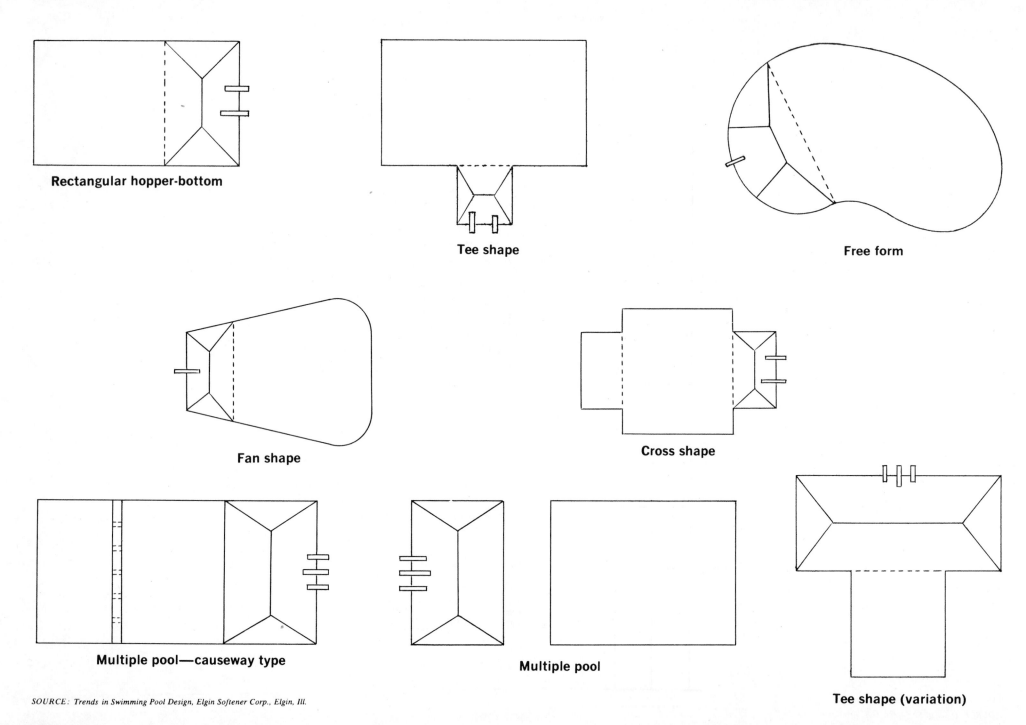

Rectangular hopper-bottom

Tee shape

Free form

Fan shape

Cross shape

Multiple pool—causeway type

Multiple pool

Tee shape (variation)

SOURCE: Trends in Swimming Pool Design, Elgin Softener Corp., Elgin, Ill.

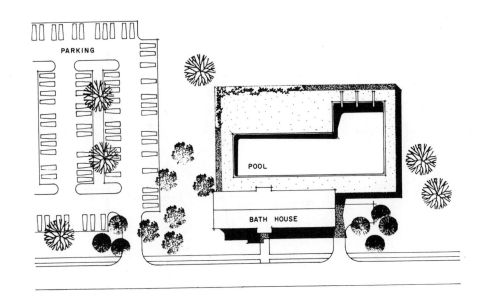

PARKING

POOL

BATH HOUSE

TYPICAL SITE PLAN
SCALE 1"= 50'

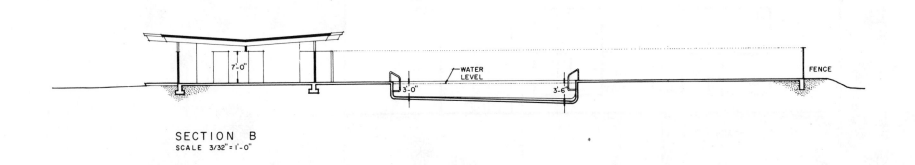

FENCE · 3 METER BOARD · WATER LEVEL · 12'-0" · 5'-0" · 3'-0"

SECTION A
SCALE 3/32"= 1'-0"

7'-0" · WATER LEVEL · 3'-0" · 3'-6" · FENCE

SECTION B
SCALE 3/32"= 1'-0"

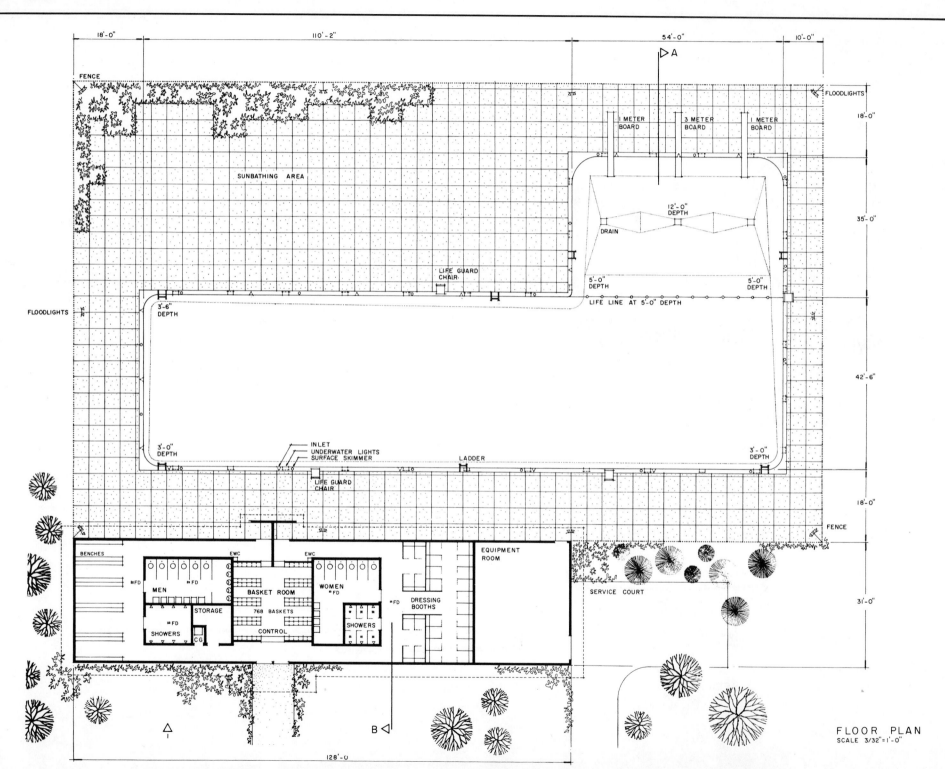

FLOOR PLAN
SCALE 3/32"=1'-0"

4-WALL HANDBALL COURT

SQUASH COURT

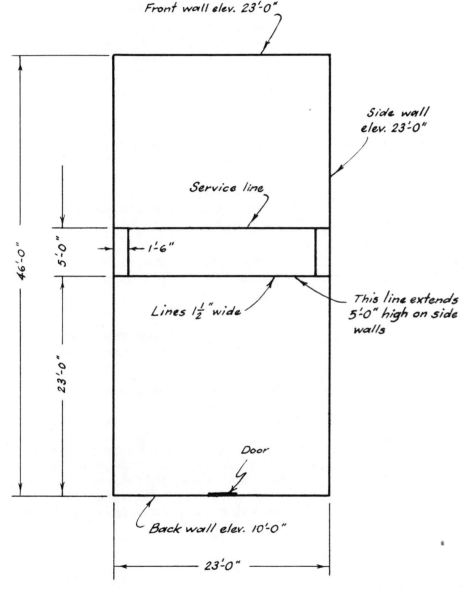

Front wall elev. 23'-0"

Side wall elev. 23'-0"

Service line

1'-6"

46'-0"

5'-0"

Lines 1½" wide

This line extends 5'-0" high on side walls

23'-0"

Door

Back wall elev. 10'-0"

23'-0"

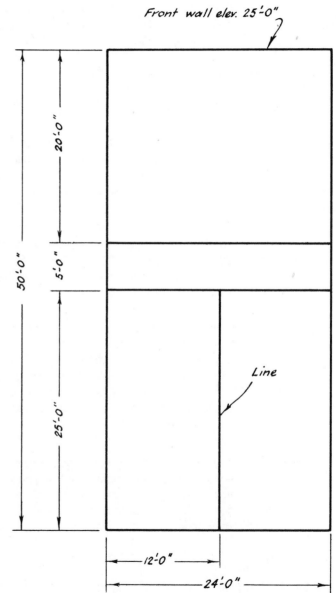

Front wall elev. 25'-0"

20'-0"

50'-0"

5'-0"

25'-0"

Line

12'-0"

24'-0"

Facility	Standard
shoreline—ocean, lake, reservoir, or stream	25 effective feet of shoreline for each 1000 population, accommodates 150 persons per day, and 50 persons at one time. 25 effective feet include: **a.** 5000 sq. ft. for sunbathing. **b.** 2500 sq. ft. for buffer and picnic area. **c.** 1000 sq. ft. for water area for swimming. An effective foot consists of one lineal foot of shore with 100 footwide band of water suitable for swimming; 200 foot-wide strip of beach for sunbathing; 100 foot-wide buffer zone for utilities and picnicking.
beach	A shoreline swimming unit should have a length of 600 ft. and a width of 665 ft. (565 ft. of width is land and 100 ft. is water). Maximum shoreline length should not exceed 3600 ft. A minimum unit of 9.2 acres (1.4 acres of water and 7.8 acres of land) has a 200 foot wide beach or play area and a 100 foot wide buffer zone for installation of utilities, tables, etc. The balance, 265 ft., accommodates 300 cars at a time. Minimum facilities are a change house, and sanitary facilities. At any one time an optimum capacity of 1200 persons may use the minimum shoreline facility. A turnover rate of 3 is expected. This allows 3600 persons to use the area on an average summer Sunday or 461.5 user days per.

Facility	Standard
beach, rural area	3 supporting areas for each acre of beach. The acre of beach accommodates 185 swimmers, over 12 years old, at any given time. This provides 200 sq. ft. of beach per swimmer. With an average daily turnover of 3, the acre of beach and its 3 supporting acres accommodate 555 swimmers per day.
beach, urban area	4 supporting acres for each acre of beach. The acre of beach accommodates 370 swimmers at a time. This provides 100 sq. ft. of beach per swimmer. With an average daily turnover rate of 3, the beach area accommodates 1110 swimmers per day.
beaches	150 sq. ft. of water for each swimmer in the water. 300 sq. ft. of land for each swimmer not in the water.
beach	100 to 200 sq. ft. of swimmable water per swimmer. 50 to 100 sq. ft. of beach per swimmer. Between 15% to 30% of swimmers are in the water at one time.
beach	Most of the time there are more persons on the beach sunning than in the water. Since the amount of usable water space per person ranges from 50 to 100 sq. ft. the available site will determine the capacity of a particular bathing beach.

Facility	Standard	Facility	Standard
major boating activities	100 acres for every 50,000 population. Ideal size of 100 acres and over. May be located within a district park, regional park or reservation.	motor boat area	It takes 20 acres of water to support one power boat. 13 boats in the water would require 260 surface acres of open water to support a ramp.
row boating and canoeing	1 lake or lagoon for every 25,000 people. Ideal size of 20 acres of water area. May be located in a community park or special regional reservations.	boat access unit	1 boat access unit capable of launching one boat at one time, serving 125 trailered boats or storage facilities berthing, mooring and the like for 100 non-trailered boats. 75 boats will operate from one access unit on the season's peak day and 50 boats on an optimum day.
trip canoeing	Average number of canoes a day is 6, with 2 men per canoe. Average daily trip distance is 15 miles. Streams must have an average flow of 100 cubic feet a second in order to be generally suitable for canoeing.		Service radius of 25 miles for day-use boaters; 75 to 175 miles for weekend-users; 135 to 250 miles for vacation boaters.
canoe area	Estimating 2 persons per canoe per ½ mile of stream. Larger streams could probably handle one canoe per ¼ mile of stream.	boating	1 ramp on 1-½ acres for every 125 boat owners if boaters average 8 trips a year. 21,000 sq. ft. of parking space per ramp, assuming a parking lot capacity equal to maximum ramp capacity.
water skiing area	One ski boat requires 40 acres of water, therefore, 13 ski boats would require 520 acres of water to support one ski boat ramp.	boat ramp	A boat ramp occupies one acre of ground space and can accommodate launching and retrieving of about 40 boats per day per launching lane. 60 cars with boat trailers can be parked in area.
boating	¼ acre of water for every 1000 persons. Boating area located in a county park that allows 12 acres for every 1000 population.		Ramps generally service 160 surface acres of water available for boating. Each ramp has at least one 75-foot vehicular turn-around.

Size and Scope

The size and scope of a marina will vary, depending on the requirements of the area involved. It is suggested that knowledgeable and experienced personnel be engaged to conduct a study of the number, types, and sizes of existing boats in the area, the number and size of existing berthing facilities, and the condition of such existing facilities. The survey should also include the potential population growth in the community and surrounding area to determine the future boat ownership. An accurate and comprehensive evaluation of such a study is the first step in planning a marina.

The data in the foregoing study will determine the next important consideration in laying out a marina: that of choosing the correct number of slips of each size that will be required. In most marinas, boats of many sizes will be served and efficient planning will foresee the necessary number of slips to accommodate boats under 18 feet long, those from 18 to 24 feet long, those from 25 to 36 feet long, and so on. The determination of the number and size of slips should be based on the needs of the community to be served.

Site Selection

Factors that will influence the final choice of a site are: foundation material in both the land and the water area; tidal ranges (to determine types and detail of construction); possible wave hazards; prevailing winds; icing conditions during the winter; water depth (dredging is possible but quite expensive); and highways and transportation systems near the proposed site. Without this basic information, consideration of a site could well be wasted time and effort.

Regulatory Considerations

After the site has been chosen and the type of marina determined, the planners must meet any legal requirements. A consultation with the district engineer is not only desirable but, in most cases, required. Local zoning, planning, construction, health, fire, and public-works ordinances must be satisfied before making large capital investments.

Factors to be Considered in Planning

The location, community needs, and proposed use should determine which of several types of marinas will be planned. The boating industry generally makes a distinction between the fresh-water marina and the salt-water marina. The operator of a salt-water marina must deal with the nagging problems of erosion, rust, and exposure more than the operator of a fresh-water marina, so compensation must be made for this in the initial planning. The planner must also solve the tide problem in designing the piers, slips, and ramps in a salt-water marina. Another distinction between salt-water and fresh-water marinas is that the salt-water marina must generally accommodate more of the large yachts and cruisers that are capable of seagoing trips.

Some marina operators prefer to serve the small-boat owner because the initial investment in the facility is much less, as are operating costs and general maintenance. On the other hand, some marina operators concentrate on the larger craft on the basis that there is more margin of profit in servicing the more expensive boats. A great many marina operators serve both small and large-boat owners and allocate space for each type of boat. In planning a marina, there are basic inclusions that must be figured in the way of equipment and facilities. Beyond these, there are extras which can be added.

The docks and piers of a marina can be constructed of wood, steel, or aluminum. They can be of the fixed, anchored type or the more popular floating type. If wood is used, it becomes subject to damage from a number of causes, such as rot, termites or other insects, or marine organisms. Preservatives are commercially available to treat these conditions, and care should be taken to treat those areas most vulnerable, such as where wood rests on wood, where wood rests on cement or on the ground, on the end grain, and in joints, cracks, or crevices. Most metal will give more satisfactory service if protected with proper finishes. Base coats of metallic oxide or aluminum paints will effectively guard against corrosion or oxidation. The fixed, anchored dock will have piles driven to a solid footing and the length of these piles will depend on the depth of water and penetration.

Most marinas have floating docks because these are more attractive and adapt more easily to expansions, changes, and rearrangement for varying boat sizes. To adequately support floating struc-

tures, a variety of materials and methods may be employed. Those most commonly used are: 55-gallon drums; wooden box floats; plastic foam (effective in salt water because it resists rust and corrosion); precast concrete floats; and wooden logs. In any design of floatation material, it is well to apply a safety factor that will give some reserve buoyancy. For stability, long, thin, wide shapes are preferable to short, narrow, high shapes.

Slips are the mooring spaces for boats and extend out from either side of the dock or pier. Each boat has its own allotted slip that must be easily accessible to the owner. Boat slips are the main revenue-producing facility at a marina, and rentals depend upon the size of the boat. Each slip must be equipped to secure the boat at both the bow and the stern. Many marinas offer catwalks on either side of the slip to facilitate the loading and unloading of passengers and cargo. Since many boats remain in their slip for days without being used, the marina operator may consider offering covered slips to boat owners. The coverings can be of wood, canvas, or aluminum and will vary in size with the boat being accommodated.

A launching ramp at a marina is a service facility that is in great demand by boating enthusiasts who prefer to keep their boats at home on boat trailers. The launching service becomes a source of extra revenue for the marina operator. The ramp may be of either the floating design or a permanent structure. The floating design has the advantage of being adaptable to tidewater locations by virtue of hinge plates that enable the far half of the ramp to rise and fall with the water-level variations while the near end is anchored to the shore and is held in place by piles. The permanent launching ramps are particularly suited to municipal waterfronts. This kind of ramp should be an extension of good access roadways and be near parking facilities for automobiles and trailers. Permanent launching ramps can be constructed of concrete, precast concrete, asphalt, cinders, or gravel. Determination of the material to be used should be based on such variables as soil conditions, climate, erosion, currents and waterfront conditions, availability of materials, and costs.

In the development of launching ramps, it is often desirable to cut back into a bank away from the shoreline to form the gradual slope of the ramp. To hold the earth embankment in place on each side of the ramp, small bulkheads can be constructed. In some cases, the bulkheads should extend into the water some distance in order to protect the underwater section of the ramp from erosion by currents and wave action. Bulkheads can be constructed of wood, concrete, or corrugated metal. Each of these materials has its advantage, depending upon soil and bottom conditions, tidal variations, seasonal changes in weather, and the possibility of floods and other abnormal conditions.

At marina locations that are bulkheaded and where space is limited, the launching of smaller boats can be handled by either a monorail and trolley hoist, or a launching derrick. With these arrangements, the boats are lifted directly from the trailer, placed in position over the water, and lowered. Many of the larger and more expensive marinas have a hoist over each slip to keep the boats out of the water when not in use. These can be operated either by hand or electrically.

At coastal and larger lake marinas, the planners must include provision for a breakwater to lessen the destructive sea waves and resulting beach erosion, and also to facilitate refueling and other normal dockside activities. The breakwater may be of the standard heavy stone-wall design or possibly the new "wave traps" of floating structures of fabric and plastic. In either case, breakwater engineering is skilled and precise work that requires consultation with professionals.

Another basic inclusion in a marina is some sort of structure to house administrative offices, the sales room for new motors and accessories, the repair shop, and perhaps a refreshment area. The extent of this building will depend on the needs of the marina as it serves its customers, and the lengths to which the owner-management of the marina wishes to go to provide more than basic services.

Parking space fo cars and trailers must not be underestimated in the planning of a marina. Too often, drivers who are inexperienced at hauling trailers can cause monumental tie-ups and delays if parking space is less than the demand warrants.

The above inclusions are considered prerequisites for a successful marina operation. Beyond these, the planners of a marina can include numerous extras to enhance the service and beauty of their facilities. These extras include: private lockers; electricity for boats afloat or ashore; toilets and showers; restaurant services; overnight hotel accommodations; complete gas, oil, diesel-fuel, and boat-supply service; and complete year-round, onshore sheltered storage.

Because marinas vary so greatly in their design, function, location, and capacity, it is virtually impossible to arrive at standard conclusions and judgments concerning a model marina.

SOURCE: Planning Areas and Facilities for Health, Physical Education and Recreation.

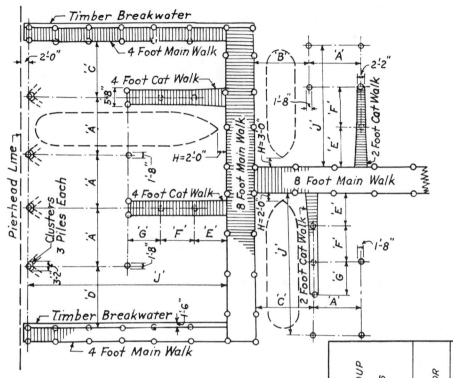

TYPICAL PLEASURE BOAT BASIN

DIMENSION DIAGRAM

FOR

SLIPS AND CAT WALKS

PLATE NO. 2

NOTE: Use this diagram in conjunction with Table I to determine widths of slips, lengths of cat walks and locations for stern anchor piles. Fixed dimensions shown are considered as sufficient for construction purposes.

TABLE 1

DIMENSIONS FOR SLIPS AND CATWALKS

NOTE: Use this tabulation in conjunction with Plate No. 2 to obtain widths of slips, lengths of Catwalks and locations of stern anchor piles. This Tabulation is based upon the use of Traveler Irons.

LENGTH GROUP FOR YACHTS	BEAM TO BE PROVIDED FOR	MIN. CLEARANCE FOR BEAM	MIN. CLEAR WIDTH OF SLIP	ALLOWANCE FOR HALF ANCHOR PILE	ALLOWANCE FOR HALF OF CATWALK	GROSS SLIP WIDTH TYPE "A"	GROSS SLIP WIDTH TYPE "B"	GROSS SLIP WIDTH TYPE "C"	GROSS SLIP WIDTH TYPE "D"	USABLE WIDTH OF CATWALK	1ST CATWALK SPAN LENGTH "E"	2ND CATWALK SPAN LENGTH "F"	3RD CATWALK SPAN LENGTH "G"	TOTAL LENGTH OF CATWALK	DISTANCE "J" TO ANCHOR PILE
20' to 25'	7'-6"	3'-0"	10'-6"	10"	1'-1"	12'-5"	12'-2"	12'-5"	—	2'-0"	10'-0"	8'-0"	—	18'-0"	28'-0"
	8'-6"	3'-0"	11'-6"	10"	1'-1"	13'-5"	13'-2"	13'-5"	—	2'-0"	10'-0"	8'-0"	—	18'-0"	28'-0"
25' to 30'	7'-6"	3'-0"	10'-6"	10"	1'-1"	12'-5"	12'-2"	12'-5"	—	2'-0"	10'-0"	10'-0"	—	20'-0"	33'-0"
	9'-6"	3'-0"	12'-6"	10"	1'-1"	14'-5"	14'-2"	14'-5"	—	2'-0"	10'-0"	10'-0"	—	20'-0"	33'-0"
30' to 35'	8'-6"	3'-0"	11'-6"	10"	1'-1"	13'-5"	13'-2"	13'-5"	—	2'-0"	12'-0"	10'-0"	—	22'-0"	38'-0"
	11'-6"	3'-0"	14'-6"	10"	1'-1"	16'-5"	16'-2"	16'-5"	—	2'-0"	12'-0"	10'-0"	—	22'-0"	38'-0"
35' to 40'	9'-6"	3'-6"	13'-0"	10"	1'-1"	14'-11"	14'-8"	14'-11"	—	2'-0"	12'-0"	12'-0"	—	24'-0"	42'-0"
	12'-0"	3'-6"	15'-6"	10"	1'-1"	17'-5"	17'-2"	17'-5"	—	2'-0"	12'-0"	12'-0"	—	24'-0"	42'-0"
40' to 45'	9'-6"	4'-0"	13'-6"	10"	1'-1"	15'-5"	15'-2"	15'-5"	—	2'-0"	14'-0"	12'-0"	—	26'-0"	47'-0"
	12'-6"	4'-0"	16'-6"	10"	1'-1"	18'-5"	18'-2"	18'-5"	—	2'-0"	14'-0"	12'-0"	—	26'-0"	47'-0"
45' to 50'	10'-6"	4'-0"	14'-6"	10"	1'-1"	16'-5"	16'-2"	16'-5"	—	2'-0"	9'-0"	9'-0"	10'-0"	28'-0"	52'-0"
	13'-6"	4'-0"	17'-6"	10"	1'-1"	19'-5"	19'-2"	19'-5"	—	2'-0"	9'-0"	9'-0"	10'-0'	28'-0"	52'-0"
50' to 60'	11'-6"	5'-0"	16'-6"	1'-7"	1'-1"	19'-2"	18'-11"	18'-5"	—	2'-0"	11'-0"	11'-0"	12'-0"	34'-0"	61'-0"
	14'-6"	5'-0"	19'-6"	1'-7"	1'-1"	22'-2"	21'-11"	21'-5"	—	2'-0"	11'-0"	11'-0"	12'-0"	34'-0"	61'-0"
60' to 70'	12'-6"	5'-0"	17'-6"	1'-7"	2'-10"	21'-11"	19'-11"	21'-2"	—	4'-0"	11'-0"	11'-0"	12'-0"	34'-0"	72'-0"
	14'-6"	5'-0"	19'-6"	1'-7"	2'-10"	23'-11"	21'-11"	23'-2"	—	4'-0"	11'-0"	11'-0"	12'-0"	34'-0"	72'-0"
	16'-0"	5'-0"	21'-0"	1'-7"	2'-10"	25'-5"	23'-5"	24'-8"	—	4'-0"	11'-0"	11'-0"	12'-0"	34'-0"	72'-0"
70' to 80'	13'-0"	5'-0"	18'-0"	1'-7"	2'-10"	22'-5"	20'-5"	21'-8"	—	4'-0"	11'-0"	11'-0"	12'-0"	34'-0"	82'-0"
	16'-6"	5'-0"	21'-6"	1'-7"	2'-10"	25'-11"	24'-11"	26'-2"	24'-7"	4'-0"	11'-0"	11'-0"	12'-0"	34'-0"	82'-0"

SOURCE: Marinas, The National Association of Engine and Boat Manufacturers, Inc., New York, NY—1947

Facility	Standard	Facility	Standard
neighborhood pool	One pool for each 3200 people. Pool with 1800 sq. ft. of water surface serves 150 persons at a time.	pool	A minimum pool unit is one acre. It has space for a pool 75 ft. by 36 ft. or 2700 sq. ft. Facilities include bath house, filters, safety and sanitary equipment, and parking space fo 90 autos.
community pool	One pool for each 25,000 people. Pool with 4500 sq. ft. of water surface serves 150 persons at a time.		The pool provides space for 203 persons at one time with a turnover rate of 3; daily capacity would be 609 persons.
pool	Minimum of 27 sq. ft. of water surface for each swimmer with a ratio of 2 square feet of deck area per square foot of water area.	pool	A minimum of 27 sq. ft. of water per swimmer for recreational swimming; 45 sq. ft. per person for teaching purposes.
	Total number of pools should serve between 3 to 5% of the total population at one time.	anchored fishing boats	4 to 7 boats per acre of water area.
pool	20 sq. ft. of pool and deck area for each 10,000 people in major metropolitan areas.	trolling fishery boats	2 to 4 boats per acre of water area.
pool	15 sq. ft. of water surface for each bather; 30 sq. ft. of water surface for each swimmer. A bather is a person who does not go into water over 5 feet in depth.	power and sail boats	3 acres of water area per boat.
		fishing	Minimum of 3 surface acres per lake. Lake should be located within an hour's drive or approximately 50 miles of a city of 20,000 persons or the equivalent in smaller communities, and should be within 5 to 10 miles of a good highway with an all-weather road to property.
	Deck area should always equal or exceed square footage of water area since not more than ¼ of the swimmers will be in the water at any one time.		
	For cities under 30,000 in population, the maximum daily attendance expected at pools is 5% to 10% of total population.	boat fishing	A fishing boat requires 8 acres of water. 13 fishing boats require 104 acres of water to support one boat ramp.
pool	8000 to 5250 sq. ft. of water surface per pool. There should be from 2 to 3-½ times more paved deck surface than water.		

Facility	Standard	Facility	Standard
hiking for one day or less	Well defined and maintained tread up to 10 ft. wide, grades not to exceed 5% average with a maximum of 15%. Minimum parking for 25 autos at any access point. On short, scenic, well known trails this might be extended to 100 auto parking spaces.	riding and hiking trails	Trails should be located to offer hikers or riders as many interesting vistas or views as possible. Interpretive signs should be used. On extended trails rest stops should be about every 3-5 miles and overnight stops, about every 10-20 miles. In heavily used areas, overnight stops may be equipped with tables, fireplaces, and pit toilets. The trail should be planned with numerous access points and interconnecting links. Average sustained grades of trails should not exceed 8%; sections of 4% or less, at least 500 ft. in length, should be used every mile if practical.
hiking for extended trips	Well defined trail with average grades of 5% and none to exceed 15%. Overnight hiking trails should be provided at intervals of about 5 hours hiking time. Minimum size of 3 to 5 acres.		Width of trails vary, depending upon use as shown below: **a.** hiking trails will be as narrow as possible to permit single file use, with widened areas every 200 to 500 yds. where terrain permits. **b.** riding trails where no pack stock is used can be a little wider than a hiking trail with more frequent passing areas. **c.** a pack trail needs 8 ft. of clearing although the tread will be considerably narrower. **d.** an interpretive foot path will be about 4 ft. wide for medium use and 6-8 ft. wide for very heavy use. **e.** multiple use trails will be designed for widest expected use.
hiking trail	Minimum of 10 acres provide a 3 mile trail, and a 1-½ mile trail.		
designated horse trail	Generally, riding trails are ten feet in width over a distance of 20 miles, and encompass 24 acres of land. It will require two camping sites of five acres, 15 to 20 miles apart. One horse per mile is trail capacity. People use a horse trail in groups of four or five. Since a trail of 20 miles will take about 3.3 hours to ride, a turnover of 2 is considered a reasonable capacity to produce 132 users per optimum day.	nature trail	50 people per mile of trail. Trails are 1 to 2 miles long. With a turnover rate of 8, there are 400 people per mile of trail per day.
		nature trail	A nature trail is estimated as 10 feet wide and two miles in length. The trail occupies an area of 2.4 acres.

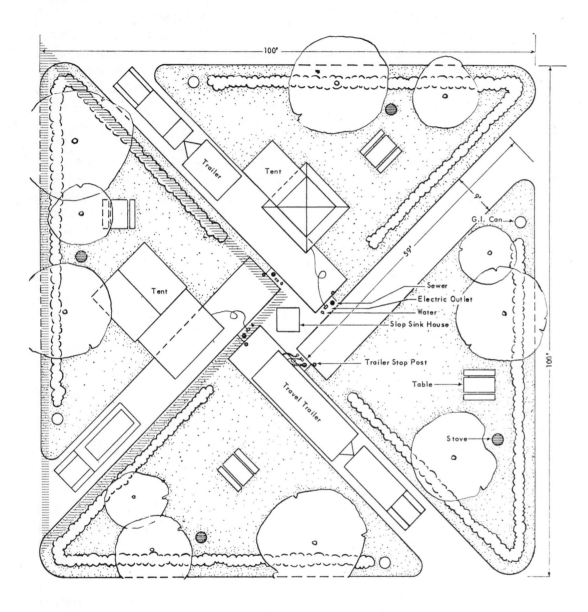

Designed with full utility connections (water, electricity, sewer) at low per-site cost, the 'shamrock' type of campground affords each family camping group approximately 2400 square feet of camping area including parking spur.

It was designed to serve both recreation vehicle campers and tent campers with a small slop sink house for the tenters to dispose of waste water.

Note that each site is situated so as to face outward on the perimeter roads, and each site is isolated from the others and the road by plant screening. Utilities coming to one central point serve four sites at less cost per site than would be the case where sites are arranged side by side.

Twelve campsites, with necessary access roads, per acre could be developed under this 'shamrock' arrangement.

SOURCE: National Park Service, U.S. Department of the Interior.

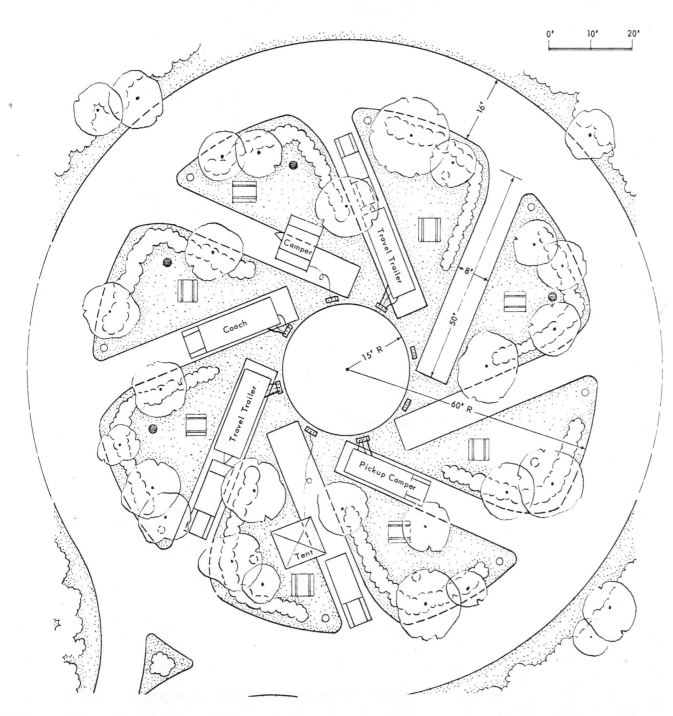

Designed primarily as a "destination" type of campground, this one would serve eight family camping groups with full utility connections (water, sewer, electricity) provided for recreation vehicles from one point. Each site offers an area of approximately 1850 square feet which includes the parking spur, a ⅛th portion of the center island, and a ½ portion of the circumferential road fronting each site.

Both tent and recreation vehicle campers could be accommodated and, with the addition of a toilet building in the circle, the entire 'daisy' could serve as a short term group camp for tent or trailer groups of 32 or more people.

Utilities radiate outward from the circle to the rear of each of the eight sites.

SOURCE: Contributed by Ira B. Lykes, National Park Service, U.S. Department of the Interior.

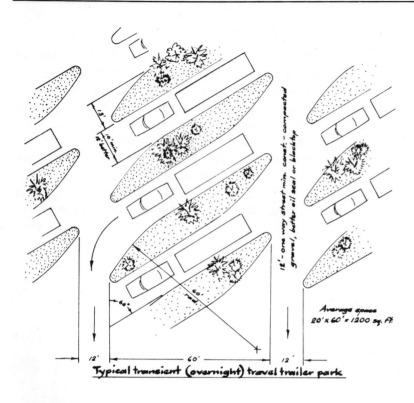

Typical transient (overnight) travel trailer park

Average space
20' x 60' = 1200 sq. ft.

12' - one way street min. const. - compacted gravel, kistre oil seal or blacktop

Typical resort (destination) travel trailer park

Redwood edging

Black top — Com. gravel

Streets - compacted gravel, oil sealed or blacktop paving

22' min. - 2 way street no car parking

Barbecue

Sewer
Elec.
Water
Trailer

Patio - conc. or flagstone 8' x 10'

22' min.

50'

Average space - 30' x 50' = 1500 sq. ft.

A typical mountain resort travel trailer park

Parking
Lodge
Toilets & Showers
PLAYGROUND
Central travel trailer sanitary station
Central travel trailer water station
Toilets & Showers

RECOMMENDED FACILITIES

For Overnight Parks

1. Absolute Minimum: Central travel trailer sanitary & water stations & toilets.
2. Fair: Individual electrical outlets, central travel trailer sanitary & water stations, and toilets.
3. Good: Individual electrical outlets, central travel trailer sanitary & water stations, toilets and showers.
4. Better: Individual electrical & water outlets, several individual sewer connections, one or more central travel trailer sanitary station, toilets, showers and coin-operated laundry.
5. Best: Individual electrical water & sewer connections, toilets & showers, coin-operated laundry and picnic tables.

For Destination Parks

1. Absolute Minimum: Back-in parking, individual electrical outlets, central travel trailer sanitary & water stations, and toilets & showers.
2. Fair: Back-in parking, individual electrical & water connections, central travel trailer sanitary station, toilets & showers.
3. Good: Drive-through parking, individual electrical & water connections, central travel trailer sanitary station, toilets, showers, coin-operated laundry, and picnic tables.
4. Better: Drive-through parking, individual electrical & water connections, central travel trailer sanitary station, toilets, showers, coin-operated laundry, picnic tables and grocery.
5. Best: Drive-through parking, individual electrical, water & sewer connections, toilets, showers, coin-operated laundry, picnic tables, grocery. Also barbecue, bottled gas, travel trailer parts for sale, plus bait & other fishing and sport accessories. Recreation building and swimming pool may be on a "pay as you go" basis.

SOURCE: Environmental Health Practice in Recreational Areas, Public Health Service, U.S. Dept. of Health, Education, and Welfare, Washington, D.C.

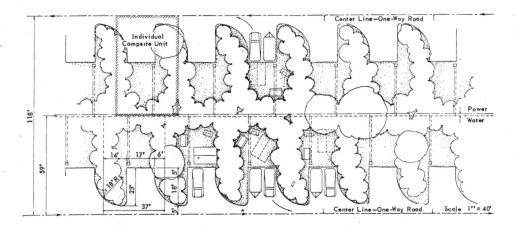

TRAILER CAMPSITE UNIT A

Area per unit—2,183 square feet including half of roadway. Approximate road surface per unit including spur—80 square yards. Campsites per acre—approximately 20.

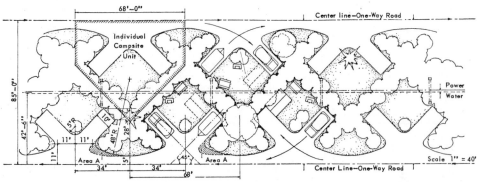

TRAILER CAMPSITE UNIT C

Area per unit—2,890 square feet including half of roadway. Approximate road surface per unit including spur—130 square yards. Campsites per acre—approximately 15.

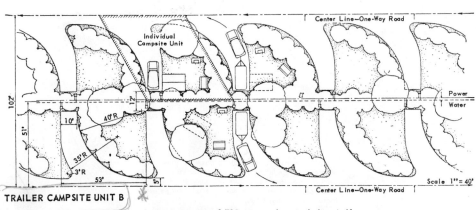

TRAILER CAMPSITE UNIT B

Area per unit—2,703 square feet including half of roadway. Approximate road surface per unit including spur—106 square yards. Campsites per acre approximately 16.

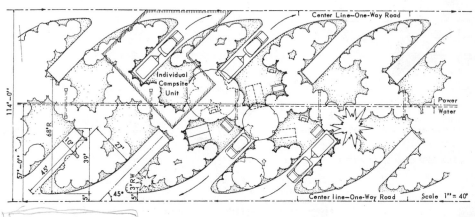

TRAILER CAMPSITE UNIT D

Area per unit—2,076 square feet including half of roadway. Approximate road surface per unit including spur—118 square yards. Campsites per acre—approximately 14.

SOURCE: National Park Service, U.S. Department of the Interior.

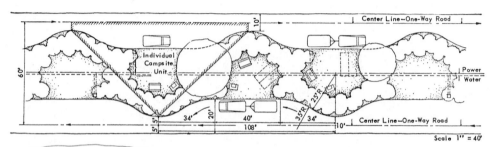

TRAILER CAMPSITE UNIT E

Area per unit—3,240 square feet, including half of roadway. Approximate road surface per unit including bypass—130 square yards. Campsites per area—approximately 14.

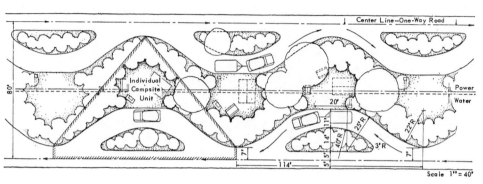

TRAILER CAMPSITE UNIT G

Area per unit—4,560 feet, including half of roadway. Approximate road surface per unit including bypass—183 square yards. Campsites per acre—approximately 10.

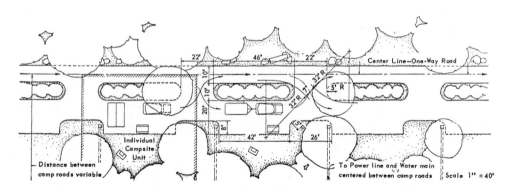

TRAILER CAMPSITE UNIT F

Area per unit, assuming depth of 60 feet—4,080 square feet including half of roadway. Approximate road surface per unit including bypass—190 square yards. Campsites per acre—approximately 11.

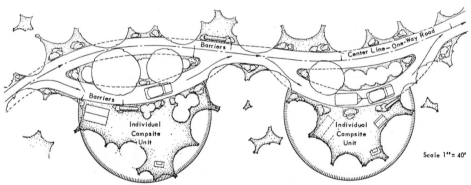

TRAILER CAMPSITE UNIT H

Statistics of campsite units such as these are indeterminate, because space allocation, road surface area per unit, and the number of campsites per acre are governed entirely by natural factors individual to site.

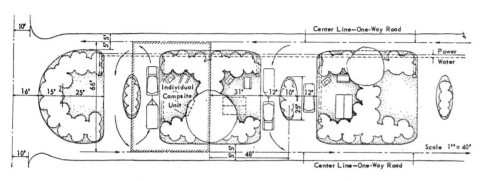

TRAILER CAMPSITE UNIT I

Area per unit—3,168 square feet including half of roadway. Approximate road surface per unit including link—160 square yards. Campsites per acre—approximately 14.

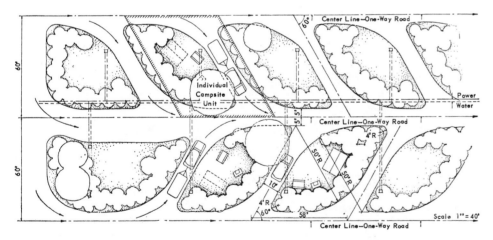

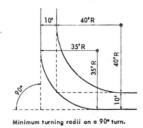

TRAILER CAMPSITE UNIT J

Area per unit—3,480 square feet including half of roadway. Approximate road surface per unit including link—163 square yards. Campsites per acre—approximately 12.

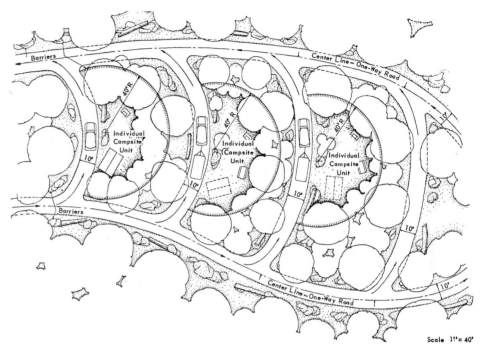

TRAILER CAMPSITE UNIT K

Because campsite units of this type conform to no prescribed pattern, statistical data cannot be compiled.

TURNS FOR CAR AND TRAILER ON A ONE-WAY ROAD

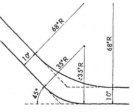

Minimum turning radii on a 90° turn.　　Minimum turning radii on a 60° turn.　　Minimum turning radii on a 45° turn.

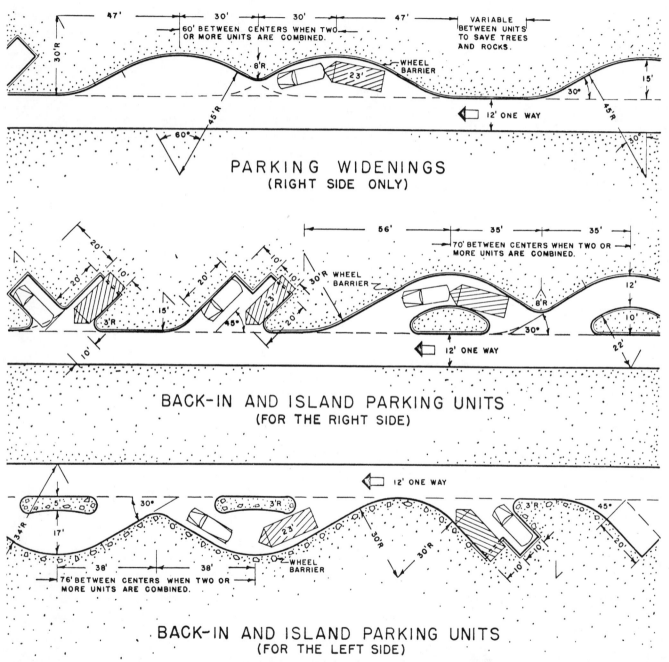

PARKING WIDENINGS
(RIGHT SIDE ONLY)

BACK-IN AND ISLAND PARKING UNITS
(FOR THE RIGHT SIDE)

BACK-IN AND ISLAND PARKING UNITS
(FOR THE LEFT SIDE)

These parking spaces show different ways of providing for trailers in campgrounds. No utility connections are suggested. In planning parking spaces for trailers it should be remembered that the doors to most are located on the right side. Back-in spaces long enough for both car and trailer are not recommended because the difficulty of parking increases as the backing distance increases. The pull-through parking spaces illustrated by the hypothetical trailer court, less the utility connections, are also satisfactory for campgrounds. The size of the parking spaces for campgrounds is sufficient to park a 23-foot-long trailer plus a 20-foot-long towing vehicle.

SOURCE: National Park Service.

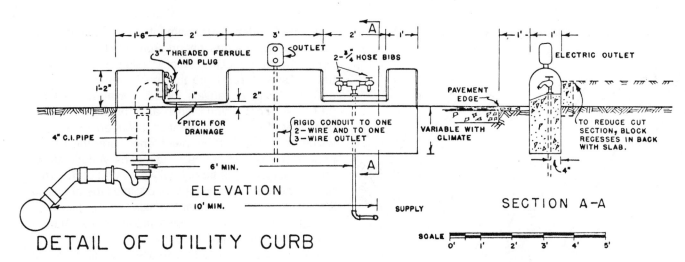

DETAIL OF UTILITY CURB

ELEVATION

SECTION A-A

SCALE
0' 1' 2' 3' 4' 5'

These drawings illustrate two methods of protecting the utility connections from damage by careless drivers, and reducing damage by vandalism.

In the Utility Curb the connections are embedded in the curb itself. In the other drawing the connections are embedded in concrete collars and further protected by a curb at the edge of the parking space.

A 45 degree sewer connection, rather than the 90 degree connection shown, might make it easier to attach the sewer line from the trailer.

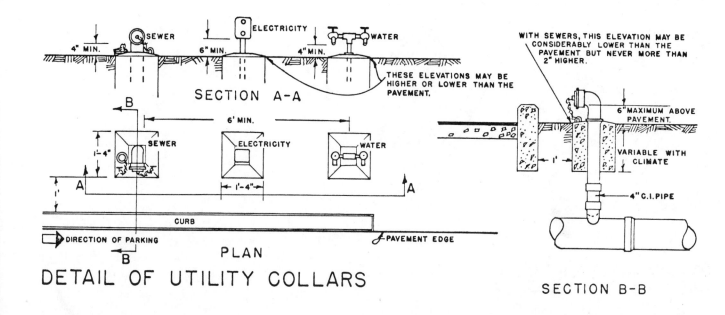

DETAIL OF UTILITY COLLARS

SECTION A-A

PLAN

SECTION B-B

SOURCE: National Park Service.

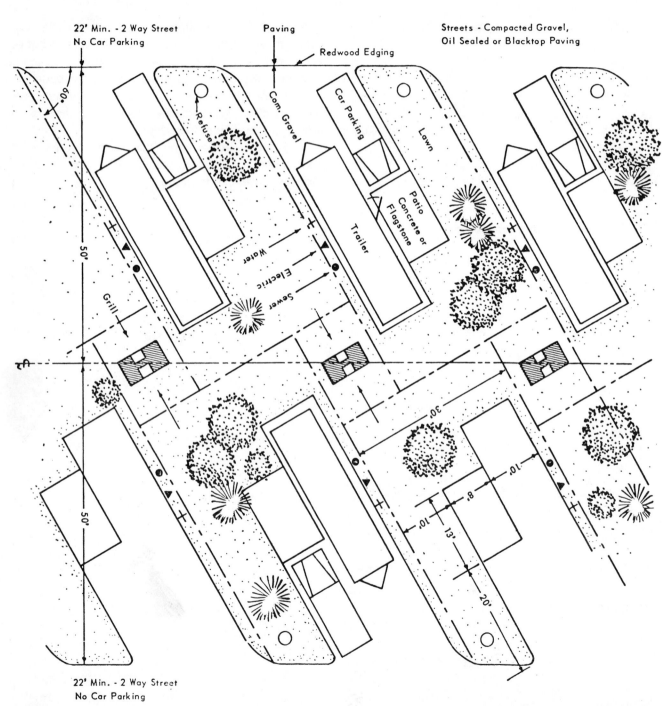

A nearly ideal arrangement for accommodating travel trailers at a destination area, this layout was designed by the Park Division of Mobile Homes Manufacturers Association. Note that each trailer site is fully equipped with essentials including water, electricity, and sewer connections; each also has its own refuse container. Note the separation between trailer sites which can be effectively heightened, and the site enhanced by planting of trees and shrubs. A patio of concrete or flagstone is thoughtfully provided at the trailer door. If desired a picnic table and some type of grill can also be provided at or near the patio, or the grill can be placed in the back as shown providing two back to back trailer sites with outdoor cooking facilities.

It should be noted that these sites may also be used for tent camping if desired. The trailer parking space need not be paved but should be firm and as nearly level as possible.

SOURCE: Mobile Homes Manufacturers Assn.

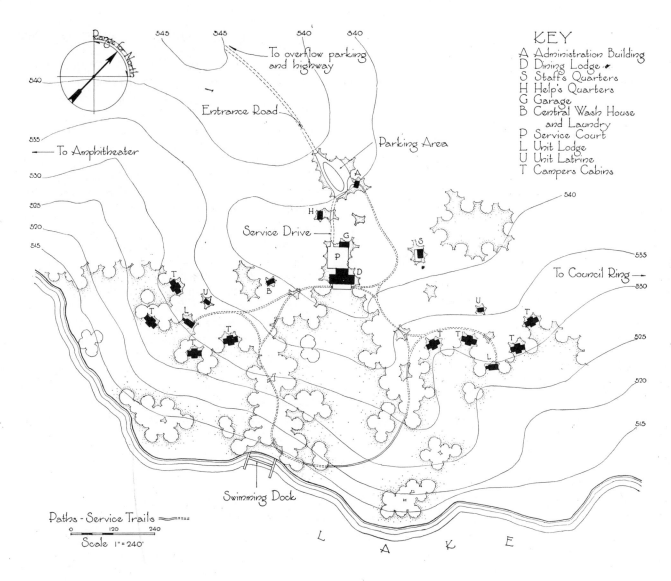

A MEDIUM-SIZED ORGANIZED CAMP ON A LAKE-FRONT SITE

KEY
A Administration Building
D Dining Lodge
S Staff's Quarters
H Help's Quarters
G Garage
B Central Wash House
    and Laundry
P Service Court
L Unit Lodge
U Unit Latrine
T Campers Cabins

The camp lay-out pictured above assumes a lake-front site and a capacity range, of from 48 to 64 campers, which are the extremes hereinbefore specified for a medium-sized camp. The plan divides the campers into two units, each unit supplied with a lodge and a latrine. The sleeping cabins indicated are of the "saddlebag" type recommended in camps for very small children—a counselor's room and entrance porch flanked by two four-cot campers' rooms. Thus each unit accommodates 32 campers and from four to eight counselors.

For older children or adults eight four-bed tents or cabins in each unit are a preferable arrangement. Better still than two such units are three units of four or five four-cot tents or cabins, with a leader's cabin, lodge, and latrine to serve each unit.

In camps of this capacity, dining lodge, central washhouse, and separate quarters for the director and central staff and for help are probably essential; administration building and garage are less important. In the absence of a building that is specifically an infirmary, a cabin can serve when illness descends on the camp. Nature study and craft work in a camp of this size can be outdoor pursuits mainly. In inclement weather the unit lodges can harbor these activities.

SOURCE: Park and Recreation Structures, Part III: Overnight and Organized Camp Facilities, *Albert H. Good, U.S. Dept. of the Interior National Park Service, 1938.*

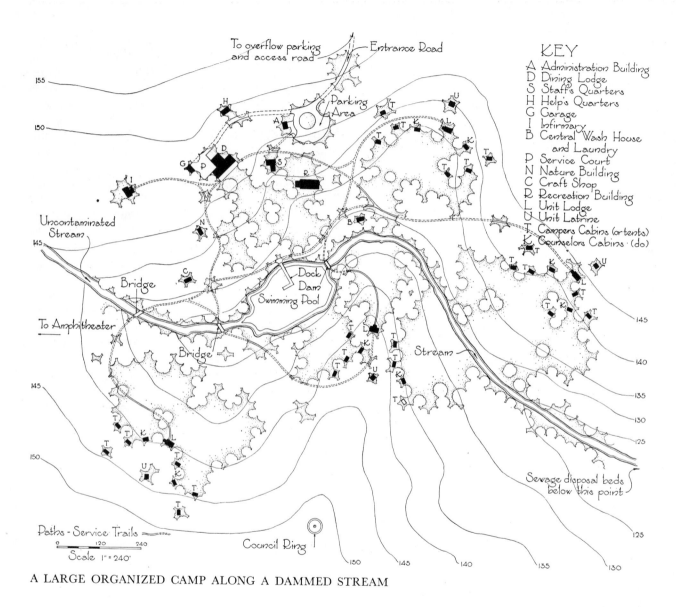

KEY
A Administration Building
D Dining Lodge
S Staff's Quarters
H Help's Quarters
G Garage
I Infirmary
B Central Wash House
   and Laundry
P Service Court
N Nature Building
C Craft Shop
R Recreation Building
L Unit Lodge
U Unit Latrine
T Campers Cabins (or tents)
K Counselors Cabins (do)

Paths - Service Trails
Scale 1" = 240'

A LARGE ORGANIZED CAMP ALONG A DAMMED STREAM

Up to this point the camp plans shown have been premised on lake frontage—always conducive to an outward-looking plotting of buildings. When lake frontage is lacking, a camp plan that faces in upon itself naturally evolves. By damming an uncontaminated stream, something in the nature of a millpond or miniature lake can be created. A naturalized swimming pool, the modern version of the "swimmin' hole" can be scenically very attractive in a quiet way. The distribution of camp buildings so that they face the pool is logical. The structures may be located on one side of the stream only, but, if the pond is small, utilizing both sides of the stream makes for a more intimate lay-out.

As arbitrarily detailed above, this 72- to 96- capacity camp is formed of four 24-camper units, each comprising six four-cot campers' cabins. The lay-out might be varied to range from three to six units of other capacities if recommended maximum camp population were not exceeded. Probably the central recreation building among all the structures here shown is least important to the successful operation of most camps.

The primary requirements for a camp on terrain of this character are an unpolluted stream and a carefully installed system of sanitation that insures discharge from the sewage disposal beds serving the camp well downstream from the site.

SOURCE: Park and Recreation Structures, Part III: Overnight and Organized Camp Facilities, *Albert H. Good, U.S. Dept. of the Interior National Park Service, 1938.*

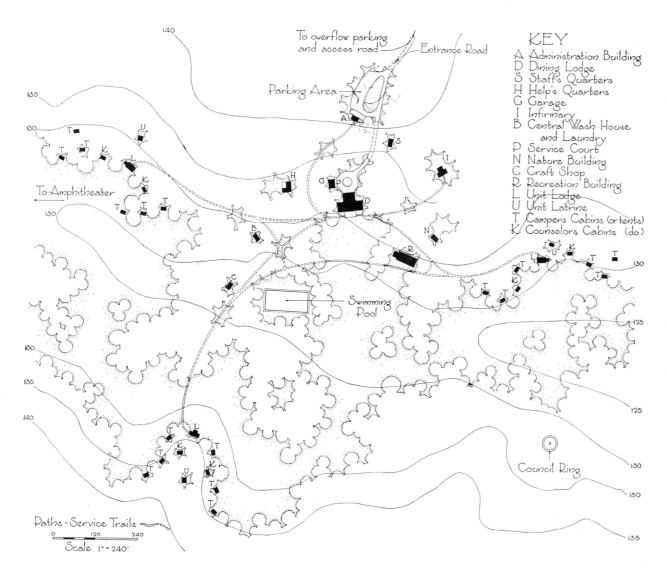

KEY

A Administration Building
D Dining Lodge
S Staff's Quarters
H Help's Quarters
G Garage
I Infirmary
B Central Wash House
   and Laundry
P Service Court
N Nature Building
C Craft Shop
R Recreation Building
L Unit Lodge
U Unit Latrine
T Campers Cabins (or tents)
K Counselors Cabins (do)

Paths - Service Trails

Scale 1" = 240'

A LARGE ORGANIZED CAMP WITH FORMAL SWIMMING POOL

When lake frontage is lacking, the formal swimming pool is the alternative of the naturalized lake of the preceding lay-out. In fact, with no uncontaminated stream nearby, the formal pool supplied with water pumped from a well or piped from a distance is the forced substitute. It induces a layout that looks inward, with the swimming pool often located centrally in the campsite.

The lay-out above shows three units outlying from the administrative group. Each includes six four-cot cabins, two counselors' cabins, a lodge, and a latrine. This makes a 72-capacity camp, but within the 72- to 96-population range of the large camp, other combinations of units of several capacities are naturally many.

A central recreation building has more purpose in a camp without lake frontage than in one which benefits from the many activities offered by a recreational lake. A restricted field of outdoor activities justifies, indeed forces, the substitution of other recreational pursuits for those that are denied.

In a well-conducted camp dependent on a constructed pool for swimming, the swimmers will be required to take shower baths before entering the pool. Therefore, the central washhouse to be most convenient will be located near the pool.

SOURCE: Park and Recreation Structures, Part III: Overnight and Organized Camp Facilities, *Albert H. Good, U.S. Dept. of the Interior National Park Service, 1938.*

In the camp area a tent or shelter is almost always used and the camp stove is the generally acceptable cooking unit. The automobile must be parked very close to the camp unit because it is continuously in use as the family larder to which access must be procured before and after each of the three daily meals. A separate general parking area removed from the camp units is not a practicable solution to the problem.

The solving of the design for the camp unit is more of a problem than the picnic area unit involving only the table and fireplace.

The camp unit may be occupied by the automobile alone, or by an automobile with a trailer. The trailer presents a problem which is different from the problem when only the automobile is used.

The two sketches "A" and "B" indicate two of the methods for developing the camp unit in connection with the trailer. The more practical method of providing space for the automobile and trailer is that of developing a loop, as shown in sketch "B." This loop, when meeting the requirements of a single camp unit, may be a one-way narrow drive, or only of sufficient width to provide for the automobile and trailer, or where the loop meets the requirements of two or more camp units the roadway should be "two-way."

It may be desirable in some locations, where a loop is not practicable, to use a spur in which to back the automobile and trailer, as shown in sketch "A." There may be other camp units in which it is desirable to provide for one or more families in a single parking space adjacent to the camp unit, as shown in sketch "C."

The sketches marked "D" to "O", inclusive, show the possibilities for the arrangement of the camp unit in order to provide for the automobile, tent, camp stove (and where desired, campfire) and the picnic table. In some areas, a warming-fire may not be required, and therefore only a camp stove is used, as shown in sketches "F", "H", "J", and "N."

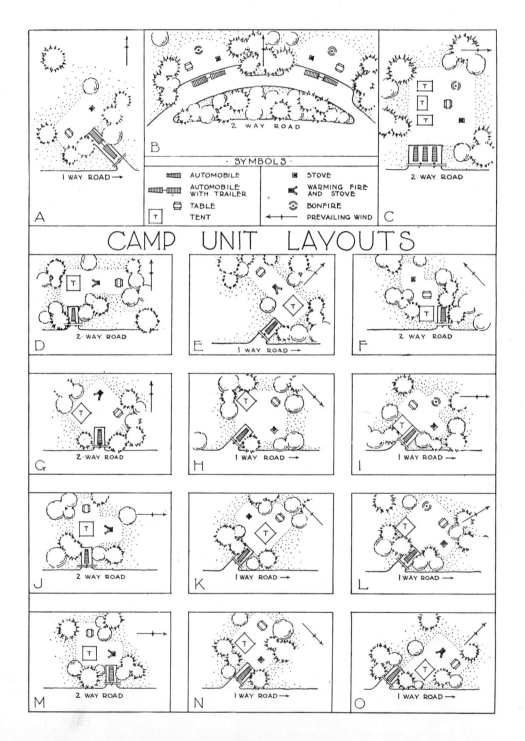

CAMP UNIT LAYOUTS

SOURCE: Camp Stoves and Fireplaces, *Forest Service, U.S. Dept. of Agriculture.*

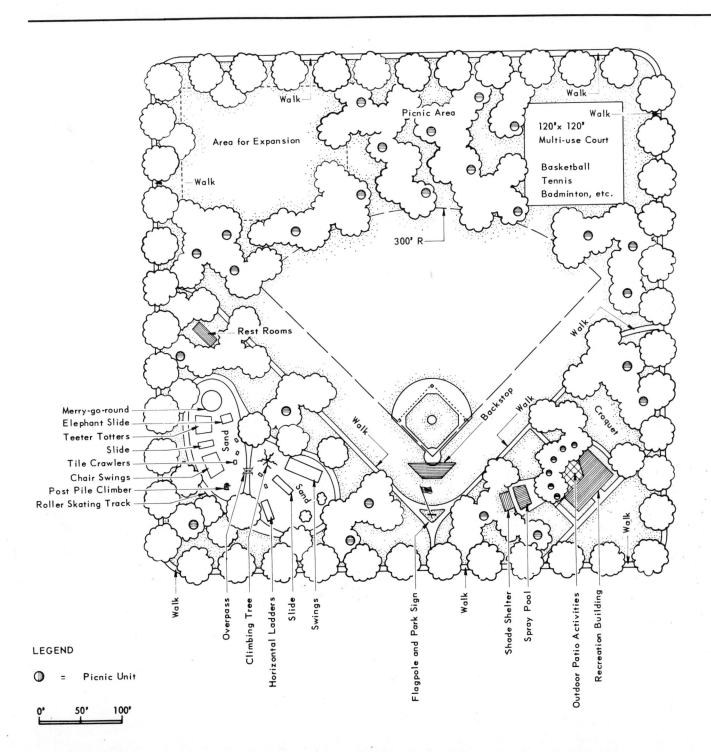

Walk
Picnic Area
Walk
Walk
Area for Expansion
Walk
120' x 120'
Multi-use Court

Basketball
Tennis
Badminton, etc.

300' R

Rest Rooms

Merry-go-round
Elephant Slide
Teeter Totters
Slide
Tile Crawlers
Chair Swings
Post Pile Climber
Roller Skating Track

Sand

Sand

Walk

Backstop

Walk

Walk

Croquet

Walk

Walk
Overpass
Climbing Tree
Horizontal Ladders
Slide
Swings
Flagpole and Park Sign
Walk
Shade Shelter
Spray Pool
Outdoor Patio Activities
Recreation Building

LEGEND

◍ = Picnic Unit

0'   50'   100'

The U.S. Department of Agriculture, Soil Conservation Service provides this Sample Park Plan No. 1 of Pioneer Park, Kern County Public Works Department, California.

Screening with trees and shrubs gives this multi-purpose urban recreation area a much desired natural setting without interfering with the many play activities provided.

SOURCE: U.S. Dept. of Agriculture, Soil Conservation Service.

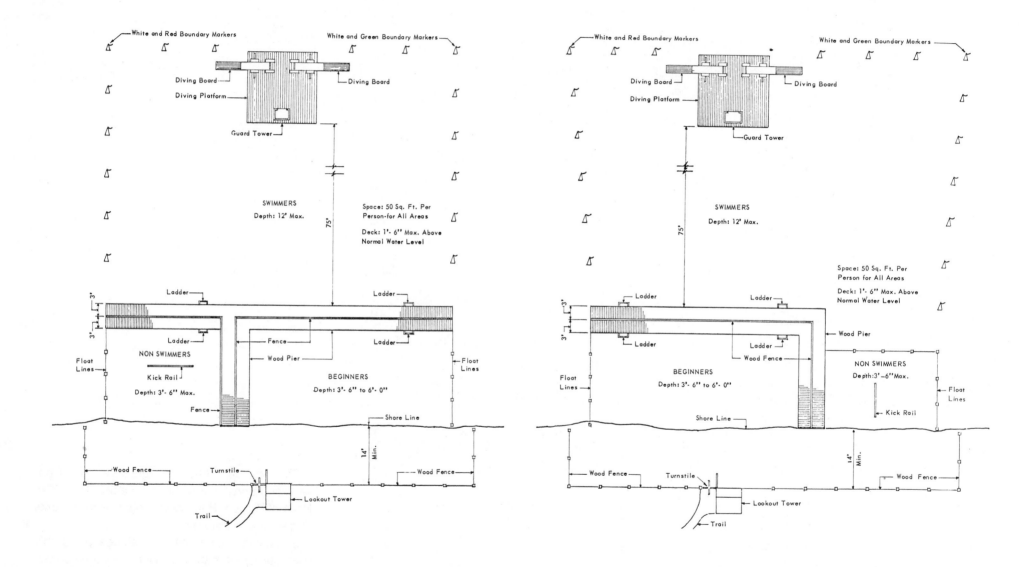

SOURCE: Boy Scouts of America

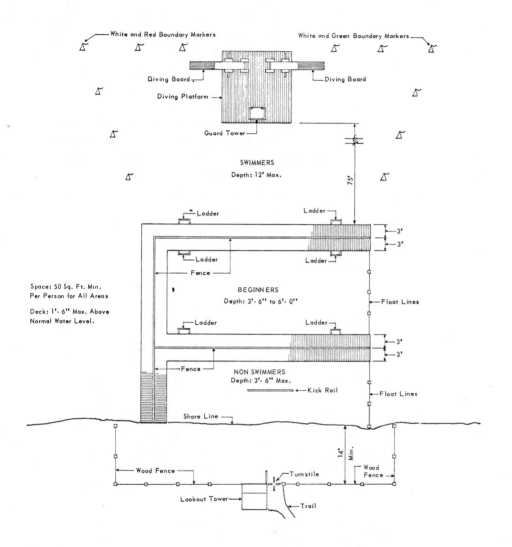

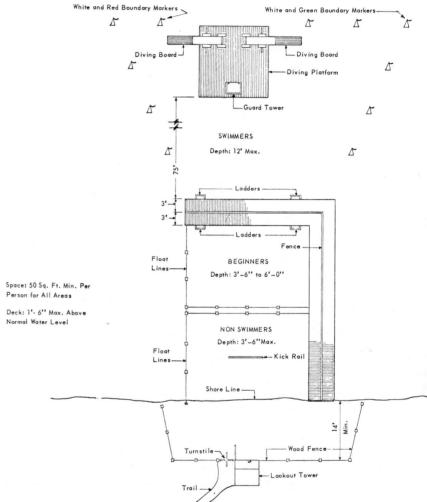

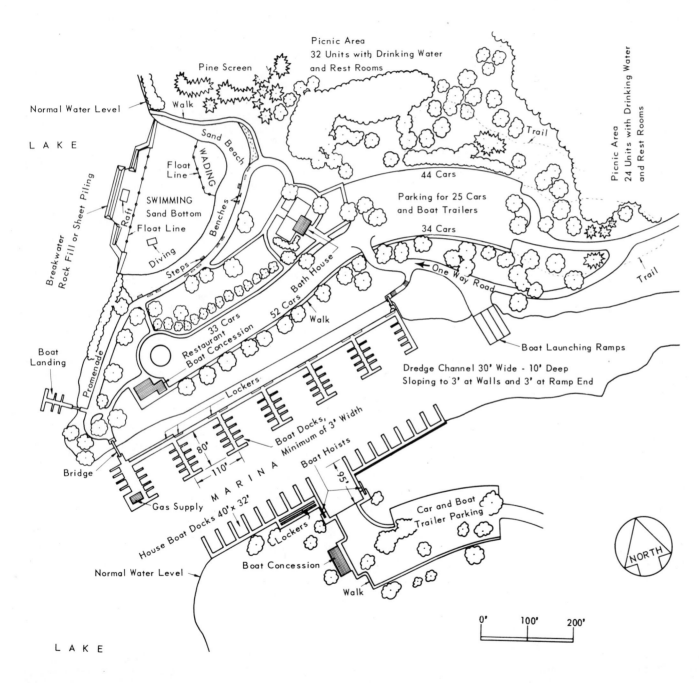

Picnic Area
32 Units with Drinking Water
and Rest Rooms

Pine Screen

Walk

Normal Water Level

Trail

L A K E

Float
Line

Sand Beach

WADING

Picnic Area
24 Units with Drinking Water
and Rest Rooms

SWIMMING
Sand Bottom

44 Cars

Float Line

Parking for 25 Cars
and Boat Trailers

Raft

Breakwater
Rock Fill or Sheet Piling

Benches

Diving

34 Cars

Steps

One Way Road

Trail

33 Cars

Restaurant
Boat Concession

52 Cars

Bath House

Walk

Boat Launching Ramps

Boat
Landing

Promenade

Lockers

Dredge Channel 30' Wide - 10' Deep
Sloping to 3' at Walls and 3' at Ramp End

Bridge

80'

110'

Boat Docks,
Minimum of 3' Width

Boat Hoists

95'

M A R I N A

Gas Supply

House Boat Docks 40' x 32'

Lockers

Car and Boat
Trailer Parking

Boat Concession

Normal Water Level

Walk

NORTH

L A K E

0'   100'   200'

A well arranged layout on a peninsula; the center of boating activity is on the southside of the peninsula keeping it away from the break-water-protected swimming area. The boat hoist launching area is across the embayment from the docks relieving the peninsula of much of the congestion which would occur at the boat docks. A 45-foot wide launching ramp is provided on the north side with easy access one-way road serving it, and with parking space for cars with boat trailers apart from the 85-car parking area which serves both the beach and the marina.

Sample Park Plan No. 3, Buckhorn Lake State Park, Kentucky Department of Parks.

SOURCE: U.S. Dept. of Agriculture, Soil Conservation Service.

ICE-SKATING RINKS

Ice-skating facilities are feeling the impact of modern technology in more and more communities each year, with artifically-frozen ice replacing naturally-frozen skating areas. With this change, people are finding a new pleasure in out-of-doors recreation on the ice. Artificial rinks provide smooth ice in moderate weather, a combination especially desirable for older skaters. No longer is it necessary to brave the bitter cold to enjoy good ice for skating. With the advent of mechanical freezing, the skating season has been extended from a 20- to 60-day average season to a 140-day season, depending on climatic conditions.

This does not mean that natural-ice rinks have gone out of style, but it does mean artificial rinks are replacing natural rinks as central or regional facilities. Natural-ice rinks are continuing to serve as a supplemental neighborhood facility in many communities. Skaters have not become completely disenchanted with a natural-ice facility, and a considerable number prefer the rugged pleasure of an old-fashioned skating experience.

Artificial-Ice Rinks

The function of an artificial-ice rink will determine many of its characteristics, such as size, cover, seating, and service rooms. If it is planned to include hockey as an activity of the rink, the size should be 85' x 185' or 200'. A general-purpose rink is usually an outdoor rink of 85' x 185' surrounded by dasher boards and with warming-house facilities for large numbers of skaters. It is generally agreed that the area per skater should be 30 square feet. Thus, the safe capacity of a general-purpose rink of the size mentioned would be 524 skaters. There are many variations of the general pattern to accommodate individual needs and limitations.

Natural-Ice Rinks

Preseason Preparations. If the rink is to be laid on the ground, sufficient moisture will be needed to provide ground frost. Water the area if a dry condition prevails. If a temporary dike is needed, it should be made in the fall so that settling can take place. If the rink is to be made on a concrete surface such as a tennis court, all drains should be sealed. Hoses, hydrants, nozzles, and scraping and snow-removal equipment should all be checked out prior to rink-building time. Ponds, streams, and lakes should be considered as possible ice-skating sites and necessary safety precautions taken in regard to ice thickness.

Sport Adaptations. Ice rinks may have a sport function as well as providing a recreation service. Figure skating requires nothing more than a smooth unobstructed ice surface. In some parts of the country, curling is a popular ice sport.

If ice hockey is to a part of the rink's activity schedule, goals will be needed and dasher boards will have to be installed to enclose an area as near 85' x 185' as possible. Dasher boards are heavily reinforced to stand the shock of players being pushed against them. They stand 4' high and come in lengths of 8' or 10'. The dasher-board enclosure should have round corners since square corners are found to be dangerous. A kick board 6" or 8" wide is fastened at the base of the dasher boards and is replaced as often as necessary. Dasher boards will reflect sunlight and cause melting of the ice. For this reason, they should be painted a dark color. Because it is difficult to follow the puck if the dasher boards are too dark, a shade of gray is recommended. If the hockey rink is indoors, the dasher boards can be painted a light color without causing a melting problem. If night hockey is anticipated, adequate lighting to insure seeing the fast-moving puck is essential for safety reasons.

Colored hockey lines on an outdoor rink create a melting problem on sunny days. This can be reduced by using vegetable dye in a water solution. The Ice Skating Institute of America has published a detailed technical paper on marking ice-hockey rinks and has developed a routing head for cutting lines in the ice.

Racing may be made a part of the natural-ice rink program by laying out a track of 4, 6, 8, or more laps to the mile. The track boundaries can be designated by drilling holes and inserting flags on short staffs. Many communities hold annual racing derbies for general participation. In some instances, skating clubs develop and the competition intensifies. As the quality of competition improves, so must the quality of the facility. Such refinements are explained in manuals of the Amateur Skating Union, an affiliate of the Amateur Athletic Union.

Warming Houses. Consideration should be given to the use of existing park buildings for warming houses in conjunction with skating rinks. Portable buildings may be used as warming houses as well as for other seasonal purposes.
Ice Skating Rink. 25 sq. ft. per person actually skating. Between 3 to 5 hard surfaced tennis courts can be flooded and used for ice skating.

SOURCE: *Planning Areas and Facilities for Health, Physical Education, and Recreation.* The Athletic Institute and American Association for Health, Physical Education, and Recreation Revised, 1966.

SKI COURSES

Skiing is an activity which has become exceedingly popular in the past few years, and it is, indeed, a fine outdoor sport. If climatic conditions are suitable and desirable topographic features available, a school or a park and recreation department should look into the possibility of developing the facilities needed to foster this sport.

The provision of skiing in a school or public recreation system should be approached from an instructional standpoint, the theory being to give participants some basic instruction in the sport so they can enjoy it as a leisure-time activity in the resort areas that have more ideal facilities. If the park system contains ideal skiing hills with plenty of room, regular ski courses may be developed. Some of the basic facilities required for the instructional type of ski development are: proper topographical features; a headquarters building to be used for rental of equipment, a refectory, etc.; a ski tow; and slopes which may be used for instructional purposes for the various types of classes.

Normally, the series of classes is broken into three units: beginners, advanced, and expert. It is the opinion of ski instructors that the beginners' ski class, in relation to recreational skiing, is by far the most important.

Basic instruction in skiing may be conducted in classes not exceeding 25 to 30 beginners. For this group, a gentle and short slope with a relatively large flat run-out area is desirable. This permits a beginner to have complete control of himself and allows him to gain confidence in the use of his skis. In the advanced group, classes are much smaller, and in the expert group, instruction becomes almost individual. In each "promotion", hills become longer and a little steeper.

Beginners' Classes—The following criteria are recommended for the selection of facilities for beginners' classes:

- Flat-top hill area, 50 sq. ft. per skier, 25 skiers per class
- Slope about 75' to 100' long, drop in grade of 15', or 4:1 slope
- Starting line at top of slope, 100' wide
- Run-out at bottom of slope should be flat or uphill
- Slope should face east or northeast
- Instructional area should be free of stones, woods, etc.
- Protective cover, such as trees or brush, around the area is desirable

Advanced Classes—The following criteria are suggested for the selection of facilities for advanced classes:

- Top of hill about same as for beginners
- Slope is most important; should be about 3:1, and 100' to 150' long
- Width of hill or slope should be minimum of 150' because of speed and space required for turning movements
- Classes may use only a portion of slope in instructional processes

Expert Classes—The following criteria are recommended for the selection of facilities for expert classes:

- These classes can use same hill as advanced classes, longer and steeper hill desirable
- Should be enough downhill length to permit a minimum of three turning movements—for example, 250' on a 3 to 1 slope
- Greater width required than that of slope for advanced classes
  Skiing is so popular that many ski centers utilize artificial snow-making equipment when weather conditions threaten to halt the program.

COASTING HILLS

Often a community has a hill, or hills, suitable for coasting, which become meccas for children with sleds, toboggans, and other coasting devices after every snowfall. In the absence of a natural coasting hill, some park and public works departments have built a coasting hill. These hills are usually located in a park safely guarded from the hazards of street traffic.

In developing local coasting areas, care should be taken to incorporate adequate safety features. Plenty of room should be provided between sled runs, and up traffic should be isolated from the down traffic. The area should be as free as possible from hazards, such as nearby trees, grills, benches, or other park paraphernalia.

Communities that develop an extensive response to coasting or skiing may want to counter adverse weather with the use of artificial-snow equipment, or improve the activity with a ski lift. Most resort areas have such equipment and know its capacities and limitations.

SOURCE: *Planning Areas and Facilities for Health, Physical Education and Recreation.* The Athletic Institute and American Association for Health, Physical Education, and Recreation Revised, 1966.

ski areas	The average skier demands 8000 vertical feet of skiing per day. This is four trips on a slope with a 2000 foot vertical drop or 16 trips on a 500 foot slope. The range of skier demands depends upon degree of skill possessed. An average expert skier wants 12,000 vertical feet of skiing per day; an average beginner wants 5600 vertical feet. Vacation-oriented ski areas are characterized by relatively remote location, luxury facilities, variety of terrain, relatively dependable snowfall, and a season that usually has 80 to 85 skiing days. These areas are generally found on larger mountains and include a multi-lift complex and spacious base lodge.	ski slopes	Standards for beginner classes include: (a) flat-top hill area, 50 sq. ft. for each skier, 25 skiers per class; (b) slope about 75 ft. to 100 ft. long, drop in grade of 15 ft.

The average skier demands 8000 vertical feet of skiing per day. This is four trips on a slope with a 2000 foot vertical drop or 16 trips on a 500 foot slope. The range of skier demands depends upon degree of skill possessed. An average expert skier wants 12,000 vertical feet of skiing per day; an average beginner wants 5600 vertical feet. Vacation-oriented ski areas are characterized by relatively remote location, luxury facilities, variety of terrain, relatively dependable snowfall, and a season that usually has 80 to 85 skiing days. These areas are generally found on larger mountains and include a multi-lift complex and spacious base lodge.

Vacation-oriented ski areas are characterized by relatively remote location, luxury facilities, variety of terrain, relatively dependable snowfall, and a season that usually has 80 to 85 skiing days. These areas are generally found on larger mountains and include a multi-lift complex and spacious base lodge.

Weekend-oriented ski areas are characterized by somewhat limited ski terrain, relative ease of access, and a minimum of supporting facilities. Areas are located in snow belts and are found between population centers and vacation-oriented areas.

Areas oriented to day skiers are located within an hour's drive of a major population center. They have extremely limited terrain.

Ski slopes are measured in terms of vertical descent and overall length. Novice slopes vary from 0% to 20% grade, intermediate slopes from 20% to 35%, and expert class slopes from 35% on up. It is not necessary that all portions of a slope stay within these standards. The minimum width of a slope should be no less than 100 to 250 feet.

ski slopes

Standards for beginner classes include: (a) flat-top hill area, 50 sq. ft. for each skier, 25 skiers per class; (b) slope about 75 ft. to 100 ft. long, drop in grade of 15 ft.

Standards for advanced skier classes include: (a) top of hill about same as for beginners; (b) slope should be about 3 to 1, and 100 ft. to 150 ft. long; (c) width of slope should be minimum of 150.

Standards for expert skier classes include: (a) same hill as advanced classes, however, longer and steeper hill is desirable; (b) should be enough downhill length to permit a minimum of three turning movements—for example, 250 ft. on a 3 to 1 slope; (c) greater width required than that of slope for advanced classes.

Athletic Institute.

ski slope

Minimum size of 100 acres with north facing slopes protected by trees in order to cut winds and allow snow to accumulate. Annual snowfall of 60 inches or more, or capacity for making an equivalent in artificial snow.

ski slope

1 acre of ski slope for each 20–30 skiers. Parking of 1 acre for each 10 acres of ski slope to accommodate 75 autos.

snow play

1 acre of slope for each 60 snow players. 1 acre of parking area. 5 acres of snow play slope to accommodate 75 autos.

SOURCE: National Recreation and Park Association, Bulletin no. 36.

The problem of getting to the ski runs and upper slopes has to a great extent been solved by engineering. Ski lifts in eight basic types are: Aerial Tramway, Gondola Chair Lift (double), T. Bar, Disc Type Trainer Lift, and Rope Tow. Selection is dictated by the following criteria: capacity, cost, terrain, climatic conditions, operation and maintenance, ski removal, prestige and competition, and safety.

A continuous operation utilizing chair or traction type can accommodate in excess of 900 skiers per hour. Selection of the above is dictated by the number of runs and variety of other facilities.

Terrain will also govern the selection of tows. Rope tows require even, concave ground, while traction types are best utilized with continuously rising ground with minimum cross-slopes. Chair lifts are the most flexible, but great care should be taken not to position the ropes too far above the ground. In many areas there are code limitations which must be a investigated before any commitments are made. The United States Forest Services and the American Standard Safety Code for Aerial Passenger Tramways should be used as a guide.

Gondolas and Aerial Tramways can be constructed completely independent of existing terrain, but it must be borne in mind that smooth operation may be seriously hampered if too many supports are needed.

Choice of an exposed or enclosed type of lift may be determined by the climate of the run area. Where high winds and low temperatures prevail, these types are still acceptable under severe conditions since they allow for maximum passenger protection. In any case, open chairs in high winds are risky.

Traction types require continual maintenance and limit the runs to the area adjacent to the lift, since no traffic is possible with traction equipment. But removal of skis is never necessary as it is with gondolas or tramways. Gondolas, incidentally, should never be considered for slopes less than 6,000 feet.

Lift Classification and Description

1. Aerial Tramway. The "ultimate" in aerial passenger transportation. This type is prevalent in Europe and incorporates an enclosed carrier or carriers reciprocating between terminals or stations. Carriers are generally supported by stationary cables and propelled by a haulage cable whose direction may be reversed. Carriers are permanently attached to haul ropes; loading and discharge are static.

2. Gondola Lift. The "latest" in ski area transport. Again, enclosed carriers of varying capacity circulate between terminals travelling on parallel cables. The hauling rope is in continuous circulation and only loaded or returning carriers are on the line. Carriers detach for static loading and discharge.

3. Chair Lift. The "standard" in United States ski areas. Open single or double chair units are generally attached permanently to a continuously circulating cable which suspends and transports the passenger above ground. Skiers are loaded and discharged while the lift continues at constant speed; foot passengers are loaded and unloaded static or at reduced speed.

4. Traction-type Lifts. The original concept in ski lifts and encompassing any device wherein the skier is propelled up-slope by being pulled or pushed.

　　a. T-Bar. A traction type using a single cable and propelling two persons side-by-side using a T-shaped bar to push the skier from behind. T units are attached to the cable by either "spring-boxes" using a flexible reeled cable or telescoping rigid tubes.

　　b. J-Bar. Same as T-Bar but using a J-shaped bar for a single skier.

　　c. Disc Lifts. A traction type employing a tube or flexible cable with a disc attached and placed between the legs of a skier to propel him up-slope.

　　d. Trainer or Nursery Lifts. A unit generally of the traction type, slow moving and intended for novice skiers.

　　e. Rope Tow. A traction type wherein a skier is pulled up slope by grasping with his hands or other means a continuously circulating rope.

　　f. Convertible T-Bar-Chair Lifts. A combination offering high winter capacity of the traction type and moderate summer capacity as a chair.

The Public Space for the lodge: the lobby, meeting rooms, recreation rooms, and administrative facilities are very much similar to those described in the Management chapter. However, materials for construction must be impervious to water and heavy ski shoes. A good maintenance program can double the life of a ski resort.

LIFT COMPARISON CHART

LIFT TYPE	Reasonable Capacity Per Hour Each Way (1—see below)	Usual Rope Speed Ft./Min. (2)	Reasonable Length of Line (3)	Maximum Graduate of Slope (4)	Usual Passengers per Carrier (5)	Relative Safety (6)	Lift Life Expectancy in Years	Suitable for Year Around Usage (11)	Number of Operating Personnel (12)
Aerial Tramway	450	1,500	10,000	75°	8–80	100	25	Yes	4
Gondola	500	500	10,000	40°	2–6	90	15	Yes	5
Chair Lift (Double)	1,000	500	8,500	40°	1 or 2	90	15	Yes	3
T-Bar	1,000	500	5,000	40°	2	90	15	No	2
Convertible T-Bar Chair Lift	1,000 / 350	500 / 300	5,000	40°	2	90	15	Yes	2
Disc Type	750	700	5,000	40°	1	80	10	No	2
Trainer Lift (Traction)	600	350	2,000	30°	1 or 2	90	15	No	1
Rope Tow	1,000	1,000	1,000	25°	—	70	5	No	1

(1) Limited by codes in some areas.
(2) Vary with design, types, codes, etc.
(3) Guide only, greater lengths possible all types.
(4) Regulated by local codes & design types.
(5) Attendant in car required after 6.

(6) Reflects authors opinion only.
(7) Variable depending upon operating practice—no allowance here for management, maintenance or ticket sales personnel.

SOURCE: Resort Hotels, E. Abroben, Van Nostrand Reinhold, 1965. The description and chart were compiled for Ski Business by Charles Dwyer of Colorado.

AMPHITHEATERS

The "cultural reawakening" that has been sweeping the country during the past few years has resulted in a demand for suitable facilities, both indoor and outdoor, for operas, plays, band and orchestral concerts, pageants, festivals, holiday programs, and civic celebrations. When performed outdoors, such activities usually require a stage or band shell with adjoining amphitheater capable of accommodating large numbers of spectators.

Selection of the proper site for an outdoor theater is of primary importance. It should have good acoustical properties and be located in a quiet place away from the noise of traffic or of groups at play. A natural bowl or depression on a hillside with a slope of 10 to 20 degrees, preferably bordered by slopes or densely-wooded areas, provides a fine location.

At some theaters, people sit on the turf of the slope comprising the amphitheater. At others, permanent seats are installed. Terraces with a turf surface are not recommended because they are too difficult to maintain. Sufficient level space should be provided at the rear of the seating area for the circulation of spectators, and aisles should be wide enough to facilitate the seating of large numbers in a short period of time. Public comfort stations and refreshment facilities are usually provided near the entrance to the amphitheater. Provision for the nearby parking of automobiles is essential, but parking areas must be located where noises and car lights do not disturb the theater.

The dimensions of the stage are determined by the proposed uses, but rarely should a stage be less than 50 feet in width or 30 feet in depth. The rear of the stage may be a wall or high hedge, or even a planting of trees, and the wings may be formed by natural plant materials. However, the band shell, or music shell, is more satisfactory for projecting voices and sounds free from echoes and interference to the people in the audience. A vertical rear wall with inclined ceiling is not only the simplest and most economical to construct, but affords excellent acoustical qualities.

The band shell usually contains dressing rooms, toilets, storage space, and rooms for the control of amplifying and lighting equipment, although sometimes these facilities are provided in separate structures near the back of the stage. An orchestra pit is generally located between the auditorium and the stage.

PICNIC AREAS

Picnicking use varies from a single-family picnic to a large group picnic involving several thousand people. Accommodations range within these two extremes and require careful planning to ensure proper control and maintenance.

SOURCE: *Planning Areas and Facilities for Health, Physical Education and Recreation*, The Athletic Institute and American Association for Health, Physical Education, and Recreation Revised, 1966.

In large parks providing picnic groves and fireplaces accommodating an appreciable number of people, a large-size open shelter with a fireplace in one end is highly desirable to give shelter in case of sudden rainstorms. Shelters are built in varying sizes from 20' x 30', accommodating approximately 60 persons seated at picnic tables, to 30' x 50', which will accommodate about 150 people. It has also been found desirable in some areas to provide electrical service for night-picnic use.

In congested city areas where it is anticipated that picnic groups will be large, the development of a picnic area that is served by a portable type of table is highly desirable because these tables can be moved around, making it possible to distribute wear on the grass surfaces. If space is available, it may even be possible to close off certain sections of the picnic area for a season or two to allow the replenishment of the grass.

The areas where heavy concentrations will take place, such as near the picnic shelter, toilets, and drinking fountains, should be hard-surfaced. These sections, then, should have tables for large groups, and preferably, should be located near the parking area. The area for smaller gatherings and play equipment should be located beyond the facilities for large picnic groups. The groupings of picnic facilities, such as tables, easily-accessible trash receptacles, and fire grates, should be designed to take advantage of the topographical features, trees, fine views, and other similar factors that make an outing a pleasurable experience.

Tables of various kinds of material are available. In congested or metropolitan areas where picnic grounds are subject to continuous vandalism and destruction, and where there is not much supervision, picnic tables that will withstand abuses from the general public should be provided. Normally, this will require a table in a fixed location and with a hard-surface area under it.

In the more native or natural areas away from heavy populations, such as county or state parks, heavy rustic types of wooden picnic tables and facilities may be more desirable because of their appearance and the fact that they blend with the natural surroundings. Usually, these types of areas are not as heavily used, are not so susceptible to vandalism, and have more space available for the distribution of picnic uses so that the surfaces of these areas do not become worn out, as is frequently true of city parks.

Other features that may be incorporated in picnic areas are a council ring, barbecue pit, and picnic shelter. There seems to be a general trend toward people bringing their own cooking utensils, and it has also been the experience over past years that a small picnic grate for charcoal use is highly satisfactory and more economical to construct. A large fireplace made of stone or other similar material is subject to vandalism and deterioration due to weather conditions.

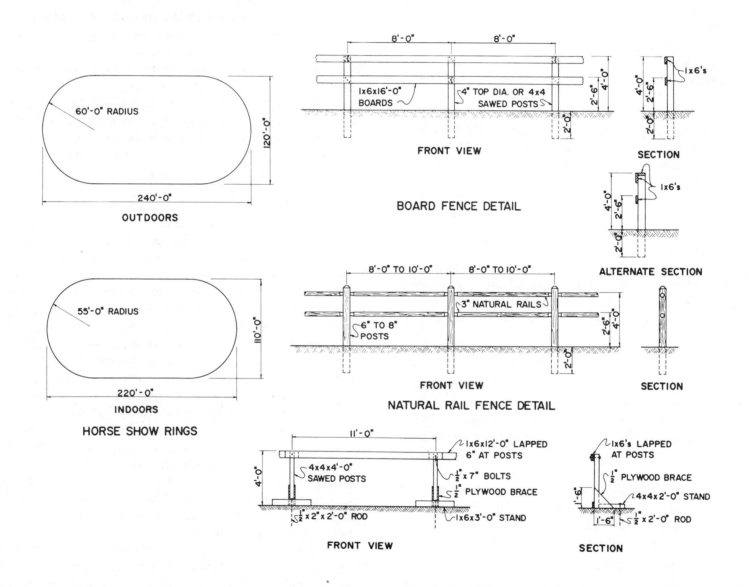

8'-0"   8'-0"

1x6x16'-0"
BOARDS

4" TOP DIA. OR 4x4
SAWED POSTS

2'-6"   4'-0"   2'-0"

FRONT VIEW

1x6's

4'-0"   2'-6"   2'-0"

SECTION

1x6's

4'-0"   2'-6"   2'-0"

ALTERNATE SECTION

BOARD FENCE DETAIL

60'-0" RADIUS

120'-0"

240'-0"

OUTDOORS

8'-0" TO 10'-0"   8'-0" TO 10'-0"

3" NATURAL RAILS

6" TO 8"
POSTS

2'-6"   4'-0"   2'-0"

FRONT VIEW   SECTION

NATURAL RAIL FENCE DETAIL

55'-0" RADIUS

110'-0"

220'-0"

INDOORS

HORSE SHOW RINGS

11'-0"

1x6x12'-0" LAPPED
6" AT POSTS

4x4x4'-0"
SAWED POSTS

½" x 7" BOLTS

½" PLYWOOD BRACE

4'-0"

½" x 2" x 2'-0" ROD

1x6x3'-0" STAND

FRONT VIEW

1x6's LAPPED
AT POSTS

½" PLYWOOD BRACE

4x4x2'-0" STAND

1'-6"   1'-6"

½" x 2'-0" ROD

SECTION

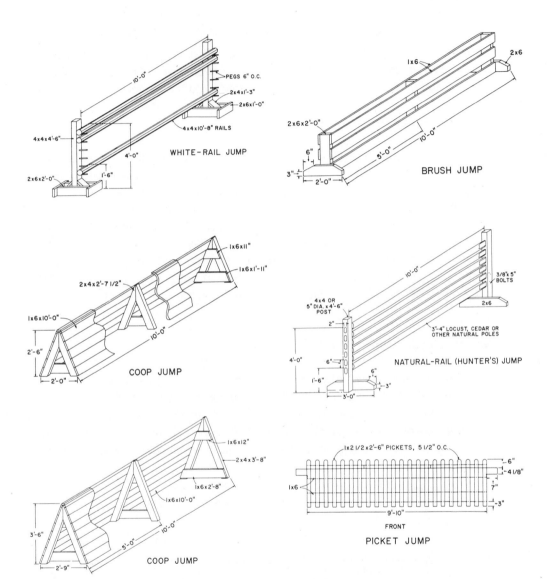

WHITE-RAIL JUMP

BRUSH JUMP

COOP JUMP

NATURAL-RAIL (HUNTER'S) JUMP

COOP JUMP

PICKET JUMP

BRIDLE PATHS

Horseback riding is popular with all age groups, but is generally restricted to the larger park areas because of space requirements. Riding trails are usually a minimum of 10′ in width to permit riders going in opposite directions to pass in safety. Except in very steep hillside terrain, very little is required in the way of construction. Clearing, a small amount of leveling, removal of large rocks and boulders, and trimming or removal of low-hanging tree limbs constitute the major items. Most small streams can be forded, but an occasional bridge may be required as well as cross drainage on steep gradients. No special surfacing is required except that a gravel base may be needed in wet or boggy areas that cannot be avoided. Tanbark, cinders, and other materials are also used frequently on heavily used trails and in areas of concentrated use around hitching racks and in riding rings.

Stables and adjoining facilities, such as feed racks, holding corrals, riding rings, and hitching racks, should be located a minimum of 500′ from the nearest public-use area because of the fly-and-odor problem. The size of these facilities will, of course, depend on the number of horses being used in the operation. However, the stable will ordinarily contain a limited number of horse stalls, a feed-storage room, a tack room, a small office, and toilet facilities for men and women. A fenced enclosure, commonly called a holding corral or paddock, into which the horses can be turned at the end of the day is required. A surfaced riding ring, sometimes encircled with a rail fence, is frequently provided for training novices in the fundamentals of riding.

SOURCE: *Planning Areas and Facilities for Health, Physical Education, and Recreation. The Athletic Institute and American Association for Health, Physical Education and Recreation, revised 1966.*

BICYCLE PATHS

Cycling is becoming an increasingly popular form of recreation for all age groups, especially since the development of geared bicycles, which makes it possible to cycle over moderately rolling terrain without too much effort. In the larger community, citywide, district and regional parks, consideration should be given to providing separate bicycle paths. In addition to making possible a pleasant experience, these paths also serve to separate bicycle riders from vehicle and pedestrian traffic.

Bicycle paths can meander through wooded areas, skirt the edges of open areas, and may, in many instances, parallel existing roadways or walks where it is possible to provide a suitable median or buffer strip. The paths do not need to be highly engineered and can generally follow closely the existing ground surfaces so as to reduce grading to a minimum. Paths should be a minimum of 6' in width, hard surfaced, and, on cut or fill sections, provided with a minimum shoulder of 12". Bicycle stands should be provided adjacent to buildings or other points of interest or activity.

In larger parks, and especially those somewhat distant from urban areas, rental facilities are not only desirable, but also provide a source of income for the concessionaire or park operating authority. Facilities need be no more than a large stand to which cycles not in use can be securely chained or locked.

GARDENS

Gardens of various kinds serve a definite leisure-time function in a park system. They should be developed to provide for visual, cultural, and educational equipment.

Formal Gardens

Formal gardens are designed to create certain accent points and to play up certain features. They are laid out in a symmetrical or asymmetrical manner. A formal garden may be composed entirely of one type of plant (such as roses), may consist of various types of assorted plant materials, or may be made up of a series of individual gardens comprised of single types of plant units. Features such as a water fountain and statuary can be incorporated into the design.

Informal Gardens

Informal gardens should have long, sweeping lawn areas to serve as a setting for plants and flower beds. Plants may include large specimen trees, flowering trees, shrubs, and vines. The flower borders can be of varied plants.

All the plants should be of interest to the average homeowner and should be useful in helping him select plants for his own yard. Attempts should be made to keep abreast of the latest introductions and to display those types of plants which are hardy to the particular region in which the garden is located. This aspect of planting for the homeowner should be stressed in both formal and informal gardens, and occasional demonstrations of plant cultural practices should be provided.

Naturalistic and Native Gardens

Naturalistic and native, or wildflower, gardens are established in a wilderness location where the plants native to the region can be assembled in one area so they are easily accessible to the citizens. This may require an area of varied topography—lowlands, highlands, and prairies—and also an area that has varied soil conditions—all the way from alkaline to acid—to accommodate the various types of plants.

SOURCE: *Planning Areas and Facilities for Health, Physical Education and Recreation*. The Athletic Institute and American Association for Health, Physical Education, and Recreation Revised, 1966.

RECOMMENDED SURFACINGS FOR RECREATION AREAS, RELATED TO DENSITY

Kind of area	Low and moderate density areas (Singles, twins, row houses, and flats)	High density areas (apartments)
General recreation area ..	Turf, natural soil	Bituminous concrete and sandclay, natural soil.
Special play areas: Child service play yards Game courts	80% turf, 20% concrete .... Bituminous concrete, portland cement concrete, sand-clay, turf.	80% turf, 20% concrete. Bituminous concrete, portland cement concrete, sand-clay, cork asphalt.
Under playground apparatus	Lightloam, sand, tanbark, sawdust, shavings, turf.	Light loam, sand, tanbark, sawdust, shavings.
Crafts and story-telling	Any hard surfacing or turf	Any hard surface or turf.
Outdoor parties, dances, roller skating, etc.	Any smooth, hard surfacing	Any smooth, hard surfacing.
Local play areas: For small children	Principally turf or natural earth, and smooth hard paving.	Principally a smooth hard paving and some turf or natural earth.
For all age groups	Turf, bituminous concrete, portland cement, concrete.	Bituminous concrete, cork asphalt, portland cement concrete.
Sitting areas	Bituminous concrete, portland cement concrete, brick, precast concrete slabs, flagstones.	

SOURCE: Adapted from Public Housing Design, National Housing Agency, Federal Public Housing Agency—1946

ADVANTAGES AND DISADVANTAGES OF VARIOUS SURFACINGS FOR RECREATION AREAS

Surfacing Type	Advantages	Disadvantages
Turf	Soft surface, ideal for many play purposes. Low first cost.	Cannot be used in wet weather. Difficult to maintain.
Natural soil	Low first cost. Soft surface	Muddy in wet weather, dusty in dry weather.
Gravel	Low first cost. Pleasing appearance	Child throw it about to such extent that it is unsuitable for any use as surfacing in housing developmens.
Sand-clay and clay-gravel	Low cost when suitable material available. Reasonably soft surface.	Difficult to get properly proportioned mixture.
Brick (on sand cushion) ..	Attractive appearance	Initial cost relatively high.
Stone paving blocks (on sand cushion or natural soil).	Low cost when salvaged from old pavements. Satisfactory appearance. Durability.	Surface too rough for play use.
Precast concrete slabs (on sand or natural soil).	Year-round utility. Satisfactory appearance.	Maintenance cost relatively high.
Flagstones (on sand or natural soil).	Year-round utility. Pleasing appearance. Durability.	
Bituminous concrete.	Good surface for most play purposes when properly specified and laid. Not so hard on feet as portland cement concrete. Year round utility.	Rough and abrasive unless properly specified and constructed. (Competent inspection essential for good workmanship.) Hot for bare feet. May become soft. Unattractive in large areas.
Cork asphalt.	Resiliency. Excellent surface for many play purposes. Year-round utility. Satisfactory appearance.	Comparatively high cost. (Competent inspection essential to good workmanship). Softens in very hot weather.
Portland cement concrete	Year-round utility. Minimum maintenance expense. Good surface for wheel toys, roller skating and some court games.	Lacks resiliency. Initial cost relatively high. Large areas require expansion joints. Whiteness and glare of large areas unattractive.

COMMERCIAL DEVELOPMENT

COMMERCIAL FACILITIES

    A. Shopping Centers**

	Neighborhood Center*	Community Center*	Regional Center*
1. Major function	Sale of convenience goods and personal services	Some functions of the Neighborhood Center plus sale of shopping goods (wearing apparel, appliances, etc.)	Some functions of Community Center plus sale of general merchandise, apparel, furniture, etc.
2. Leading tenants	Super market and drugstore	Variety store and small dept. store	One or more large, major dept. stores
3. Location	Intersection of collector streets a/c secondary roads	Intersections of major roads and/or expressways	Intersections of expressways and/or freeways
4. Radius of service area	½ mile	2 miles	4 miles
5. Min. population to support center	4,000	35,000	150,000
6. Site area (gross land area)	4-8 acres	10–30 acres	40–100 acres and over
7. Desirable maximum size of center as percentage of total area served	1.25% (1 acre/1,000 pop.)	1.00% (0.75 acres/1,000 pop.)	0.50% (0.67 acres/1,000 pop.)
8. Ranges of Gross Floor Area	30,000–75,000 sq. ft.	100,000–250,000 sq. ft.	400,000–1,000,000 sq. ft.
9. Number of stores and shops	5–20	15–40	40–80
10. Parking requirements***	Parking ratio: 4 to 1 (Parking area is four times gross floor area of building; 400 sq. ft. per parking space) 200–600 spaces	1,000–3,000 spaces	4,000 spaces and over

* "A group of commerical establishments, planned, developed, owened, and managed as a unit, with off-street parking provided on the property (in direct ratio to the building area), and related in size (gross floor area) and type of shops to the trade area that the unit serves—generally in an outlying or suburban territory." Definition of the Community Builders Council, ULI.

** The Community Builders Council, ULI offers the following indicators for types and sizes in Shopping Centers (see Community Builders Handbook, Executive Edition, 1960, page 217).

	Neighborhood	Community	Regional
Average Gross Leasable Area	50,000 sq. ft.	150,000 sq. ft.	400,000 sq. ft.
Ranges in GLA	30,000–100,000 sq. ft.	100,000–300,000 sq. ft.	300,000 to over 1,000,000 sq. ft.
Usual Minimum Site Area	4 acres	10 acres	30 acres
Minimum Support	7,500 to 40,000 people	40,000 to 150,000 people	100,000 or more people

*** The CBC recommends a parking ratio of 3 sq. ft. of parking area to 1 square foot of gross floor area be used for planning calculations only. For operations the parking index is more realistic (see Community Builders Handbook, Executive Edition, 1960, pages 300–305).

SOURCE: George Nez, Standards for New Urban Development—The Denver Background,
Reprinted by Permission of Urban Land, Vol 20, No 5 Urban Land Institute, 1200 18th Street, N. W., Wash. D. C.

Four density classifications have been selected for the first variable. These are:

a. Less than 1 d.u. per gross acre (average: 0.5 d.u./acre)
b. Between 1 and 2.9 d.u. per gross acre (average: 2.0 d.u./acre)
c. Between 3.0 and 4.9 d.u. per gross acre (average: 3.5 d.u./acre)
d. Between 5 and 15 d.u. per gross acre (average: 8.0 d.u./acre)

Three distance classifications have been selected for the second variable:

a. **FRINGE DEVELOPMENT:** development that is contiguous to, and an extension of, an established urban area.

b. **SEMI-INDEPENDENT DEVELOPMENT:** non-contiguous development some distance from an urban area, but able to be served with public utilities through major extensions of utilities available in central city.

c. **INDEPENDENT DEVELOPMENT:** Outlying development with own public utilities and some economic base, but within the regional pattern of a large central city.

EFFECTS OF DISTANCE AND DENSITY ON CHARACTERISTICS OF SHOPPING CENTERS

I. DISTANCE FROM A LARGE URBAN AREA	NEIGHBORHOOD SHOPPING CENTER	COMMUNITY SHOPPING CENTER	DISTRICT OR SUB-REGIONAL SHOPPING CENTERS
1. Fringe Development	Characteristics and space requirements unaffected.	Not required for poulations of less than 20,000 unless distance from existing centers is sufficient (over 1½ miles) to warrant the construction of a new community center in anticipation of continuing fringe growth.	Not normally required.
2. Semi-Independent Outlying Development	Characteristics and space requirements unaffected.	Center required capable of serving at least 35,000 persons with service radius of 1½–2 miles. Second center considered when population exceeds 40,000.	District center should be considered if total population potential for the area surrounding the development exceeds 101,000. Second center considered for population of 200,000 or over.
3. Independent Outlying Development	Characteristics and space requirements unaffected.	Center required in practically every case. Standard requirements apply.	Shopping centers, district-wide sub-regional, should be considered for developments with population potential of over 50,000.
II. VARYING DENSITY			
1. Less than 1 d.u. per acre	Larger than standard centers: greater service radius, more parking spaces required.	Standard size and space requirements; smaller percentage of total area; greater service radius (3–4 miles).	Not required.
2. 1-2.9 d.u. per acre	Considerably larger than standard centers, but to lesser degree than the case above.	Standard size and space requirements; greater service radius (2–3 miles).	Marginal conditions for establishment of district center; dependent upon adjacent land uses.
3. 3-4.9 d.u. per acre	Standard requirements.	Standard requirements.	Standard requirements.
4. 5-15 d.u. per acre	Larger than standard center (4–5 percent of total area); less than standard parking requirements. In this density neighborhood shopping centers generally display characteristics of community shopping centers.	Function of community centers served by the larger neighborhood shopping centers.	District centers larger than the standard center: serves populations of 200,000–3,00,000, with radius of 2–3 miles. Standard parking requirements.

Retail Element	General Character	Source of Customers	Store Types	Parking	Traffic	Goods Sold
1. Central Business District A. Inner Core B. Inner Belt C. Outer belt	Inner core and belt solidly commercial. The business and recreational heart of metropolitan economy. Residents fill in back streets. Typically, residential areas are blighted.	Come from all parts of city and tributary area. Sites are most accessible to most consumers. Intra-city transportation converges in this element.	Largest in floor space and volume. Multi-story department store is symbolic. Home of leading specialty shops. Outer belt activity less intense. These stores do smaller volume per unit.	Totally inadquate in inner core and belt. Trend to provide public lots and commerical parking lots to supplement limited curb parking in inner belt and outer belt.	Extremely heavy, congested during peak periods.	Shopping and specialty goods emphasis. Area is center of apparel, home furnishings, other department store lines. Service and other commerical activities found in belts.
2. Main Business Thoroughfares ("String streets")	Mixed zone or retail and light industrial enterprises and working class homes. Featured by long series of miscellaneous stores.	Basically trade is transient, consisting of commuters, suburbanites, and inter-city automotive traffic. Some patronage also from neighorhood residents.	Concentration of larger food stores, automobile dealers, and supply houses, service and convenience goods stores.	Usually dependent on curb parking. Inadequate during most periods.	Streets are main traffic arteries. Usually heavy, but particularly so during commuting peaks.	Essentially business streets. Stores are widely spaced over length of artery.
3. Secondary Commercial Subdistricts (unplanned) A. Neighborhood B. Community or District S. Suburban or Outer	More residential than first two elements. Owner occupied residences increase with distance from general business districts. The sub-districts tend to appear, island-like, along string streets.	Come basically from A, B, or C trade areas. The districts developed as city grew at focal points of intra-city transportation. Dependent on traffic brought by public carriers.	Unplanned competition featuring convenience and shopping goods. "B" and "C" tend to be miniatures of central business districts.	Mostly curb, plus some off-street parking provided by individual merchants.	Since stores typically clustered at key intersections and transfer points of public carriers, this traffic is heavy.	Convenience goods featured in "A". Increasing shopping goods emphasis in "B" and "C".

Retail Element	General Character	Source of Customers	Store Types	Parking	Traffic	Goods Sold

3a. Controlled Secondary Sub Centers
  a. Neighborhood
  b. Community or District
  c. Suburban or Outer
	Waste area and marginal stores at a minimum. Found near more prosperous residential areas. Unified architecturally. Most built after World War II. New, fresh appearance compared to 3.	Greater dependence on automotive traffic. Parking provided so customers drawn from greater distances than in case of unplanned centers. generally found in suburban districts.	Balanced collection of supplementary stores possessing aesthetic appeal. Centers stress convenience and service, not price appeals.	Provided on a cooperative basis within the center. Parking and other facilities related in size to surrounding trade area.	Parking for private automobiles key consideration. Even so, peak periods automotive traffic heavy.	Attempt made to present an integrated retail organism to customers coming from a, b, or c distances: a stresses convenience goods; b and c feature shopping and specialty merchandise.

4. Neighborhood Business Streets	Residential with commercial usage distinctly secondary.	Neighborhood is primary source. Most customers come from within walking or five minute driving distance.	Usually rows of convenience goods outlets found in center of neighborhood community.	Mostly curb. Due to convenience goods nature of most items sold, parking turnover is rapid.	Heavy during peak hours. Otherwise not a handicap to trade.	Emphasis on food and drugs. Grocery store—drug combination frequent. Service stores common.
5. Small Clusters and Scattered Individual Stores	More thinly populated residential areas. Neighborhoods served tend to be middle class.	Come from homes not within easy reach of larger elements in structure. Many walk to stores.	Smallest outlets in structure. Many are marginal. This classification dominated by food and general stores.	Curb and small lot parking usually adequate.	Usually not a problem. The lack of traffic congestion, plus the availability of parking, represents an appeal of this element to customers beyond their normal range.	Usually supplementary and not directly competitive.
6. Controlled Regional Shopping Centers	Overall unity obvious at a glance. Landscaped frequently. Off-street parking. Harmonious effect is objective. May be equipped to serve as area's civic and cultural center.	Draw from families within 30 minute driving range. Customers typically come from a number of suburban communities. Pull varies with effectiveness of central business district retailers and competing centers.	Attempt made to duplicate shopping facilities of central business district with minimum of overlapping. "One stop shopping in the suburbs."	Usually best facilities in metropolitan area. Adequate for all but occasional peak periods.	Problem usually under control as a result of co-ordinated planning.	One or two department store branches and satellite stores offer widest range of merchandise and services outside central business district.

SOURCE: Eugene J. Kelley, *Shopping Centers*, The ENO Foundation for Highway Traffic Control, Saugatuck, Conn.—1956

LOCATION AND ACCESS

Location—From the standpoint of location, a shopping center must be unassailable. It should be impractical for another project, similar in type and size, to be introduced and compete successfully with your center because of its better location, greater convenience, better merchandising and improved services.

The Council mentions several maxims about location: "Be sure that your site is located near a well-populated residential area or one that is growing so rapidly that it gives promise of soon being able to support the size shopping center you contemplate building." "The side of the street on which the center is located can spell profit or loss. The right-hand side of an outbound route is preferable where shopping is done largely by the going-home commuter. Where shopping is done by the housewife, as is the case with most neighborhood centers, the center should be city-ward of the tributary population."

There is no rule of thumb for locating shopping centers. Walking distance is no criterion, particularly in suburban locations. But in urban areas where high density, multi-family housing is part of the general development plan, walking distance plus transportation, and the type and relation to commercial area outside the project are important factors to consider.

In new residential subdivisions, where a shopping center can be justified, it should be located so that the site is on the main thoroughfare offering access to the subdivision. The interior streets of the subdivision should be planned to lead to the center from the directly tributary area.

In new large-scale residential developments such as a satellite community or new town on several thousand acres of land, the shopping center location should be selected and the area determined while the general development plan is in its preliminary planning stage. In these cases, site selection becomes part of the overall master planning procedure. The developer and his planners have the opportunity of choosing the most advantageous shopping center site in accordance with the principles of site selection, thus creating a nearly ideal shopping center location.

Access—should be easy and convenient. It should be possible to turn off the highway directly into the site. Easy access means free-flowing traffic to reach the site. Left turns require specially constructed lanes for turning movement. Right turns on a heavy traffic way require deceleration lanes for easy entrance and exit. If cars moving into or out of a center create traffic bottlenecks, community resentment arises. Congestion at entrances or back-ups on a major traffic route can be fatal. Redesigning traffic flow at the entrances to a center requires cooperation with the traffic engineers and local highway departments. If the access road system cannot carry the additional traffic and turning movements generated by the center, the cost of improvements must be investigated. This step includes whether costs will be borne by the highway construction authorities, by the developer, or shared—and in what proportion.

Adequate access may add to the traffic load, but it must not add to the traffic problem. Because of heavy night shopping habits, shopping center peak hour traffic flow does not usually coincide with ordinary rush-hour traffic. Even for small centers, major customer traffic from outside the immediate neighborhood must not filter through nearby residential streets, creating nuisances and irritations for the local residents and neighbors.

Entrances into and out of a center must be well separated from a major street intersection (at least 100 to 150 feet from the corner). At neighborhood centers it is possible for access to be on only one side of the site. In other words, the site may front on one important access street only. As mentioned earlier, locations directly on major expressways carrying high-speed traffic are desirable but adequate provision must be made for safe and convenient access into and out of the parking areas without interfering with the travelled way.

A site accessible *only from a ramp* at a cloverleaf grade separation for two intersecting highways does not offer easy access. Because the grade separation treatment is complicated and confusing to drivers, psychological resistance can be created or persons not familiar with the access roadways may take a wrong turn. Highway authorities should recognize that the shopping center is in the category of a public service facility and should cooperate through the erection of directional signs.

A location at the intersection of two heavily travelled expressways produces a strong location for a center—when access from each of the expressways can be worked out. Ideal access to a regional shopping center at a major highway interchange requires sufficient simplicity to make ingress and egress easy for even the first time shopper. However, proper site planning, signing, and the fact that repeat shoppers will soon develop their own ingress and egress patterns, may keep a relatively poor access situation from being a fatal deterrent to the location.

Members of the Council make other observations about access: "Entrances to and exits from the parking areas too close to a major intersection can create a traffic congestion problem."

It is good for the location to be accessible from a major highway. "The ability to see the center from a controlled access freeway is important from the advertising value derived from the site's unobstructed visibility."

If there is a choice available, the site for a regional center should be selected where it has access from a radial highway leading to the city and from a circumferential highway that taps the urbanized residential periphery of the metropolitan area.

SHAPE

A site all in one piece is preferred. A site divided by a traffic way interrupts the continuity for shopping, impedes the flow of pedestrians, complicates customer car movement within the site, and contradicts the basic principle of unity for the shopping facility. Once a site is unified, never dedicate any streets within the center.

A regularly shaped property without acute angles, odd projections or indentations is best for efficient layout even though faults in the shape can be corrected by adjustments and ingenuity. But without extensive frontage, the center cannot enjoy the advantages of being viewed from access thoroughfares.

Site depths cannot be specified with any meaning. Site depths of perhaps 400 feet or more distinguish shopping center developments from the old standard strip commercial areas which were usually zoned only 100 or 150 feet in depth. James B. Douglas points out: "Any site depth is only a generalization. You must know the type of center to be built and the total acreage involved. The standard strip commercial areas of the past are no longer proper design for commercial developments. Requirements for parking, access, and circulation in shopping centers require much greater depth than required by the out-of-date strip developments."

SOURCE: Community Builders Handbook, Anniversary Edition 1968 Urban Land Institute, Washington, D.C.

Any awkward, very irregular shape to the property (even though the total site area is sufficient) should be avoided because portions of the site may be unusable or, if used, result in excessive walking distances, poor parking arrangements, or expensive solutions. Occasionally, an irregular site can result in an ingenious solution, though this is the exception.

SIZE

The area necessary for the type of center is important. There must be sufficient site area for the initial development indicated by the trade area analysis with room for expansion and for buffer strips where needed. See footnote[33] for a rule of thumb to gauge site adequacy in a preliminary way. The site needs at least the minimum acreage set up by the preliminary estimates from the market analysis.

Where there is strong possibility for growth within the trade area, the size of the site should provide for the initial development plus space for growth. In suburban locations, the initial price of the land normally will be low enough to permit acquisition of sufficient site area to avoid later expense for double-decking the parking area or for a parking structure. Allowing enough space to grow is a safeguard for the future, particularly for a neighborhood center in a mushrooming suburb. Frequently, a successful center has been built without reserving extra land for future growth—for increased parking and for additional sales area. For example, Highland Park Shopping Village, that prototype of shopping centers, to remedy the original limitation on its site area as its trade area and the prestige of its retail outlets grew, had to resort to the expensive solution of building an underground garage for additional parking spaces and first floor shops.

A site too large for the immediate development contemplated has the advantage of having land in reserve for expansion and strengthening of the center later. Interim uses can be introduced, a garden shop, for example. Any unneeded commercial land can be developed for uses compatible with the shopping center, such as apartments, motel, medical clinic, or suburban office building.

However, no more retail space should be constructed than is needed for the original development. But, as the Council points out, where a shopping center experiences a full measure of success by meeting its potential sales volume through its ability to draw the ultimate in purchasing power from its trade area, then some one will inevitably try to tap this success by building competition nearby—if land is available and the zoning situation will allow the additional use. The possibility that open land zoned for residential uses across the street from a shopping center may be changed to permit additional business use is always present.

TOPOGRAPHY AND PHYSICAL CHARACTERISTICS

Topography of the site is another important factor. A steeply sloping site may require excessive filling or cutting for the parking areas. Even if the cuts and fills can be balanced, the earth moving operation adds to costs in site preparation. If the land cost is low, this extra site preparation work sometimes can be absorbed into the overall economics of the construction.

If the slope across the site corresponds to grades on surrounding roads, then an opportunity for a two-level arrangement of buildings and parking may exist. However, a two-level merchandising scheme poses planning and leasing complications and requires skillful solutions. The chances for taking advantage of sloping site conditions are greater in large projects than in small neighborhood centers. Stores in a neighborhood center are more easily arranged in a one-level layout. In a large regional center there is opportunity for taking advantage of sloping site conditions by introducing vertical circulation for customers within the larger tenant spaces and for obtaining pedestrian access directly into the store areas from different parking levels.

UTILITIES

Availability of utilities at or near the site is a positive factor in site selection. Long runs to reach utility connections are a development cost to be avoided. Off-site development costs usually can be adjusted with the municipality and customarily with the private utility company. To minimize time-consuming negotiations with officials, make sure the site is at least within easy reach of required water supply and sewage disposal facilities.

No precise policy for a shopping center's off-site improvements has been established even though in some cities a policy is evolving for residential development.

THE BUILDING PATTERN

There are typical patterns for shopping center buildings, each susceptible to variations to suit the particular characteristics of the site. Essentially, patterns are the strip, the "L," the "U," the cluster. (The mall is a pedestrian circulation pattern. A "mall center" is a term used to convey the fact that the building pattern includes a pedestrian shopping concourse, either enclosed or open air.)

There has been a steady evolution of shopping center design from its original

SOURCE: Community Builders Handbook, *Anniversary Edition 1968 Urban Land Institute, Washington, D.C.*

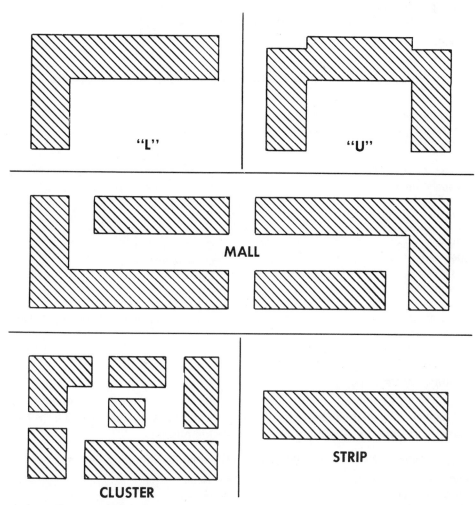

Basic Shopping Center Patterns

The strip—a line of stores tied together by a canopy over the pedestrian walk extending along entrance front to stores. Economical for small centers. Excessive walking distances and difficult merchandising results from excessive length for a strip center.

The ''L''—basically a strip with one end turned. Adaptable to corner locations.

The ''U''—basically a strip with both ends turned in same direction.

The mall—essentially a pedestrian way offering frontage for two facing strips. The mall may also take other shapes, an ''L'' for example.

The cluster—a group of retail buildings separated by short pedestrian malls or courts.

concept as a strip, with parking, through the L-shape, the U-shape, the mall, the cluster, and then the adaptation of these two latter forms to enclosure and air-conditioning. Furthermore, there has been the innovation of ''stacking'' or double-level arrangement of the retail facilities. This treatment is a solution called for by site design to answer problems of extremes in walking distances otherwise imposed by a large, single-level regional center, by the steepness of topography, by the shape of a particular parcel of land or by a relatively small but high value parcel of ground.

There has been a strong tendency toward the enclosure of the mall or the cluster, and the enclosure and air-conditioning of a sidewalk in front of a strip neighborhood center. The added cost of enclosure and air-conditioning often can be partially offset by reduced costs in store front construction and simplification of store air-conditioning. For most climates, the extra construction cost is more than offset by the added volume resulting from the greater customer appeal and from the fact that under adverse weather conditions shopping in this type of center becomes an attractive thing to do rather than something to be avoided except in extreme necessity.

The strip is basically a straight line of stores tied together by a canopy over the pedestrian walk extending along the entrance fronts to the stores. Normally, the strip is set back from the access street with most of the parking placed between the street and the building.

The strip is best adapted to the neighborhood center. An interesting and successful variation of the strip exists when the two major units—usually a market and drugstore—are placed at either end of the strip and are perhaps 12 feet forward from the intermediate line of stores. The sidewalk in front of the intermediate stores connecting with side entrances of the market and the drugstore can be enclosed and air-conditioned. A strip is generally the cheapest structure to build. It is the easiest to adapt to most site conditions. As the center grows, a strip can be elongated. [1]

The ''L'' is basically a strip with one end turned; **the ''U''** is a strip with both ends turned in the same direction. In most cases the intent of the ''L'' or ''U'' is to reduce the length of an otherwise over-long strip. The ''L'' shape is adaptable for site conditions at two important intersecting roads. The ''L'' can be turned in either direction for site orientation. Another use of the ''L'' or ''U'' is to make maximum use of sites close to being square, wherein a strip development would under-utilize the capacity of the site and provide redundant parking. In general, the ''L'' is suitable

---

[1]Care must be taken to avoid lengthening the strip beyond a distance that people walk comfortably. About 400 feet is usual, though there are examples of successful strip centers of 750 feet and longer. Chain stores like strips. Apparently people are willing to walk farther in a shopping center than they are downtown. Also, developers find with ample parking in the center people will drive back and forth within the center to the sections of the center in which they wish to shop.

SOURCE: Community Builders Handbook, *Anniversary Edition 1968 Urban Land Institute, Washington, D.C.*

for large neighborhood and smaller community centers: the "U" for larger community centers.

The mall is essentially a pedestrian way offering frontage for two facing strips. The mall becomes a pedestrian street for back and forth shopping movement. It has become the most generally accepted pattern for the regional center and can also be applied to community-size centers. The mall itself may become "L" shaped, as, for example, at Gulfgate Shopping Center in Houston and at North Park in Dallas. It may even become a "T". The mall has particularly come into its own for the regional center as more and more regional centers have been keyed to multiple department stores. The mall is particularly well adapted for enclosure and air-conditioning.

The cluster is a group of buildings separated by pedestrian malls or courts and generally grouped around a single key tenant. The cluster is most often found in the regional center geared to a single department store. If neither expansion nor the addition of a second department store is intended, then the cluster is probably the best type of development for a one-department store regional center.

An early and highly successful example of the cluster is Northland in Detroit. A more recent example is Century Plaza Center in Los Angeles. The cluster type favors the core key tenant from the standpoint of pedestrian flow. The cluster plan thus has considerable appeal for those department stores that develop centers in which their own unit is the key tenant. The disadvantage to the smaller tenant is in his being exposed to only one-fourth or one-third of the key tenant's traffic, whereas the key tenant is exposed on all sides to any pedestrian flow generated by the smaller units.

Regardless of the building pattern, strip, "L," "U," mall, or cluster — there are basic design principles that the experienced developer and architect understand but the inexperienced overlook. For example, a mall if it is too wide, is expensive and discourages back and forth movement for impulse buying. If a mall is too narrow, it becomes crowded, hard to keep clean, and difficult to use for promotional activities. Forty to 50 feet is the right width for most mall situations. Often a mall can be widened at one or two spots for a court treatment both for design purposes and for permitting promotional activities.

Other common design errors in any building pattern include provision of uniform widths and/or depths for all types of stores, difficulties in servicing smaller stores without interfering with pedestrian or auto traffic, and "dead" spaces that are both difficult to lease and difficult for pedestrian access. Multiple corners, setbacks, odd angles, and the like should be avoided particularly. They often appear attractive from the standpoint of the designing architect since seemingly they lend individuality and character to the project, but they also add substantially to capital costs and tend to decrease rather than increase impulse buying.

Neighborhood Centers

A list of tenants most frequently found in neighborhood centers as extracted from *The Dollars and Cents of Shopping Centers: 1966* is offered for use as guides.

Tenants Most Frequently Found in Neighborhood Shopping Centers

Food and Food Service
Supermarket
Restaurant

General Merchandise
Variety Store

Clothing and Shoes
Ladies' Wear
Family Shoe
Other Retail
Hardware
Drugs (with fountains)
Services
Beauty Shop
Barber Shop
Cleaners and Dyers
Coin Laundries

Offices
Medical and Dental

Other Tenants Might Be
Florist
Service Grocery or Delicatessen
Radio, TV, Music, and Records
Gifts, Stationery, and Books
Infants and Children's Wear
Candy and Nuts
Lingerie and Hosiery
Liquor
Jewelry
Men's Wear
Sporting Goods and Camera Supplies

Community Centers

Community centers, being an "in-between" type of center, offer a greater array of tenant classifications than do neighborhood centers. Again, an extract from *The Dollars and Cents of Shopping Centers: 1966* is offered.

Tenants Most Frequently Found in Community Shopping Centers

Food and Food Service
Supermarket
Restaurant
General Merchandise
Junior Department Store
Variety Store
Clothing and Shoes
Ladies' Wear
Children's Wear
Men's Wear
Family Shoe

Other Retail*
Hardware
Drugs
Jewelry
Cards and Gifts
Services
Beauty Shop
Barber Shop
Cleaners and Dyers
Financial and Offices
Bank
Medical and Dental Offices

(*Plus all those tenants found in Neighborhood Centers)

SOURCE: Community Builders Handbook, *Anniversary Edition 1968 Urban Land Institute, Washington, D.C.*

Through the entire site planning procedure the architect must remain aware of the architectural expression of the center toward surrounding streets, toward the parking lots and toward pedestrian areas. Site planning must also be directed toward gaining impressive vistas, a well-composed silhouette and well-proportioned spaces between the structures.

Although the schematics on these pages attempt to illustrate the procedure of site planning, they do not aim to give precise information as to the size of each land usage category but rather to illustrate, in a general way, the size of the main planning elements in relation to each other and to show to what degree the planner can adapt a project to the size of the site.

ASSUMPTIONS FOR 3 SCHEMATICS

The schematics are based on the assumption of a regional center with a gross building area (BA) of about 600,000 square feet, of which 500,000 square feet are rental area (RA). Of this rental area a department store occupies 200,000 square feet. The Transportation Area (TA) is shown to be approximately three times the rental area. (Transportation area is understood to be that portion of the site which is necessary for parking, internal traffic roads, bus stations, pick-up stations, taxi stands.) The pedestrian area (SP) is assumed to be slightly less than the rental area on the ground. It consists of malls, courts, sidewalks along the parking side of the stores, and walkways in the parking area. The buffer areas (BUA) surround the parking area.

Case A shows the site needed if all structures are one-story high, without basement, and if all parking is on one level. (SA = BA + SP + TA + BUA). For such an arrangement, a site of approximately 66 acres is necessary.

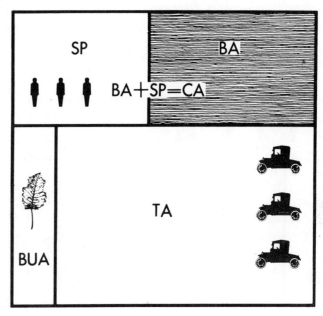

SA = BA + SP + TA + BUA
  BA = Building Area
  SP = Space between Structures
  BA + SP = CA (Shopping Core Area)
  TA = Transportation Area
  BUA = Buffer Area
TA consists of PA (Parking Area)
          MA (Traffic Movement Area)
          PT (Public Transportation Area)
Assumptions: CA is 1,100,000 sq. ft.
          TA is RA × 3 (RA is Rental Area)
            or 1,500,000 sq. ft.*
          BUA is 250,000 sq. ft.
          SA (Site Area) is 2,850,000 sq. ft.
            or approximately 66 acres.

*Alternate method for figuring TA:
  500,000 sq. ft. (RA) × 7 cars per 1,000 sq. ft. =
  3500 cars × 400 sq. ft. per car = 1,400,000 sq. ft.

SOURCE: Shopping Towns USA, Victor Gruen and Larry Smith, Reinhold Publishing Corp., New York 1965

Case B shows an arrangement in which the department store consists of basement, first floor and second floor. All other stores have basements and first floors. It is assumed that the largest portion of the service area is taken up by service roads. The building arrangement described above has been used in many shopping centers (Northland, Eastland, etc.). For such a building arrangement a site of approximately 55 acres is necessary. (SA = BAG + SP + TA + BUA).

Case C assumes again that one-level parking will prevail but that merchandising generally will be on three levels (similar to Southdale.) Thus all stores would utilize basement, first floor and second floor, while the department store would be arranged on four levels, having a third floor. In this arrangement 48 acres are needed. (SA = BAG + SPG + TA + BUA).

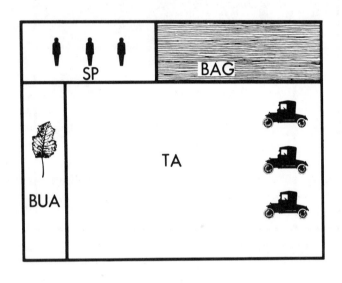

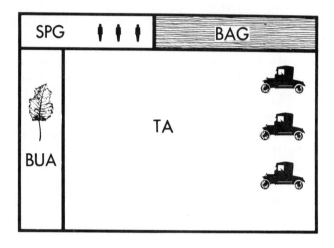

SA = BAG (Building Ground Area) + SP +TA + BUA

    Assumptions: BAG = Department Store + Other Rental + Non-rental Area

                             3   2

On the basis of previous assumption, this results in 66,000 sq. ft. + 200,000 sq. ft. + 50,000 sq. ft. or

                   316,000 sq. ft.

SP	=	270,000 sq. ft.
TA	=	1,500,000 sq. ft.
BUA	=	250,000 sq. ft.
SA	=	2,336,000 sq. ft.

            or approximately 55 acres.

SA = BAC + SPG + TA + BUA

    Assumptions: BGA = Department Store + Other Rental Area

                             4   3

        + Non-rental Area on Ground Level

On the basis of the earlier assumptions, this is expressed in figures as follows:

BAG = 50,000 + 100,000 + 33,000 sq. ft.

            or   183,000 sq. ft.

SPG	=	150,000 sq. ft.
TA	=	1,500,000 sq. ft.
BUA	=	250,000 sq. ft.
SA	=	2,083,000 sq. ft.

           or approximately 48 acres.

SOURCE: Shopping Towns USA, Victor Gruen and Larry Smith, Reinhold Publishing Corp., New York

A row of stores along the highway.

■   SHOPS

├─┤   PARKING

Case Study A. The center is comprised of a row of stores, 2,000 feet along the highway. The shopper parks at the curb in front of a store, walks into the store, transacts his business, walks out again, is likely to enter his car and drive off. In this case pedestrian traffic of the second type, shopping traffic, is limited.

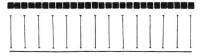

Stores moved back from the highway permit parking in front.

Case Study B. The 2,000-foot-long row of stores is moved back from the highway sufficiently to permit parking in front. Sidewalks, or even covered walkways, encourage foot traffic along the store fronts. This is obviously vastly superior to the first case, as the driver may be converted into a pedestrian some distance away from the entrance door to a specific store, and thus a certain amount of shopping traffic will be created. However, this shopping traffic will still be limited. A distance of 2,000 feet between the extreme ends of the store strip is not conducive to inter-shopping. Having made one purchase the shopper will in many cases return to the car and drive to the store that is next on his list. Besides the disadvantage of the distance between retail units, the sidewalk, which immediately adjoins a parking lot which in turn immediately adjoins a highway, does not represent an attractive walking environment. Even if two powerful magnets, let us say a department store and a junior department store, were to be located at the extreme ends of the 2,000-foot-long shopping strip, the amount of foot traffic generated in the area between them which would require passing intervening stores, would be limited and only a few merchants would benefit.

SOURCE: Shopping Towns USA, Victor Gruen and Larry Smith, Reinhold Publishing Corp., New York

The strip is divided into two rows of stores, opposite each other, along a pedestrian mall with parking on each side. A magnet is placed at each end.

Case Study C. The 2,000-foot store-strip is divided into two halves, creating two 1,000-foot-long strips arranged opposite each other along a pedestrian mall with parking on each side. In this case shopping traffic will be much greater for several reasons:

1. A highly desirable pedestrian area shielded from the noise, smells, confusion and dangers of automobile traffic is created.

2. The two main magnets will be only 1,000 feet apart if placed at extreme ends; therefore the likelihood of interchanging shopping traffic will be much greater and stores located between the two magnets will profit from participation in that traffic.

If, on the other hand, only one main magnet exists and that is located on an extreme end of the mall, then shopping traffic will be reduced because of lack of interchange. Stores furthest removed from the magnet will participate only to a very slight degree in the traffic generated by the main magnet.

Mall center with only one magnet.

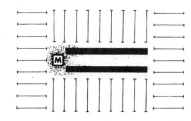

Case Study D. This is a mall arrangement as in Case Study C, but because there is only one main magnet, it is moved to a center position on one side of the mall. Shopping traffic will be improved if compared with Case Study C.

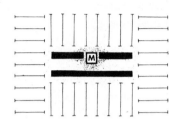

Mall center with magnet centrally placed.

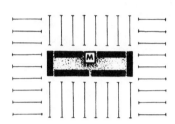

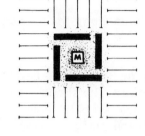

The cluster type arrangement.

■ SHOPS

├─── PARKING

Ⓜ MAGNET

FOOT TRAFFIC

Case Study E. The major tenant is placed in the center of a cluster arrangement. Nearly all stores thus become neighbors of the most powerful shopping-traffic puller. In contrast to previously discussed cases where all retail units were exposed to parking traffic and shopping traffic, this arrangement exposes the main tenant to shopping traffic only. Because of the superior pulling power of a major department store, this results in no detriment to its business but offers the opportunity of guiding shopping traffic from parking areas along the frontage of other stores toward the center of the cluster.

SOURCE: Shopping Towns USA, Victor Gruen and Larry Smith, Reinhold Publishing Corp., New York

Case Study F. This case exemplifies what we will call the introverted center. All store fronts are turned toward the inside of the building cluster. The structures turn their backs to the parking areas and the surrounding roads. Shopping centers following planning principles of this type diminish or completely exclude the possibility of entering individual stores from the parking lot. Shopping traffic is, by plan, funneled through a limited number of entrance arcades into pedestrian areas. Thus density of shopping traffic may be markedly increased and the opportunity to plan its direction and flow increased.

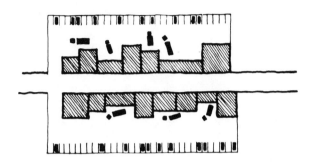

Figure 1

Figure 1 shows a shopping center which relies for accessibility on existing public roads but which provides parking spaces behind the stores. The delivery of goods also takes place there. This arrangement—left over from the old strip development—creates a split personality for the center. The representative storefronts face the public road, but the customer enters at a rear door, very often the same one through which merchandise is carried in and garbage carried out.

Figures 2 and 3 show centers which also rely for accessibility on the public roads but where parking is arranged in front of the stores. In this manner, it is possible to bring about a separation between the customer's traffic and delivery and service traffic (which takes place at the rear of the stores). Storefronts and signs can then be logically arranged facing the parking area, where the customer can see them from the public road as well as from the parking lot.

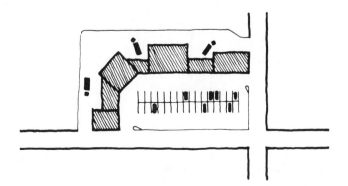

Figure 2

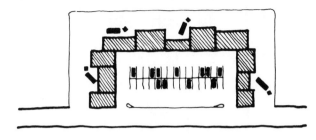

Figure 3

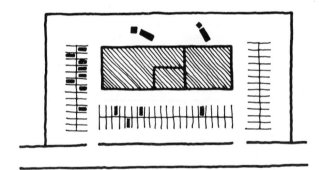

Figure 4

Figure 4 still relies on the public roads for accessibility but surrounds a block of stores on three sides with parking facilities and reserves the rear for goods delivery and services. This type of arrangement exists in many cases in Europe where the rentable area is then usually utilized by a supermarket in combination with a variety store and a few smaller stores or services.

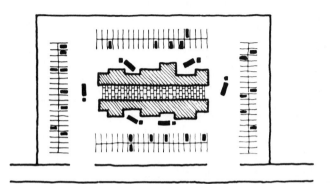

Figure 5

Figure 5 is the first one which introduces a separate area for pedestrians in the form of a pedestrian mall. This prototype can either exist by attaching itself to a public road or by introducing its own circulatory road system which is then connected to the public road network.

Figure 3-6

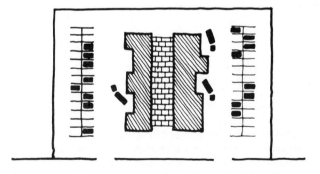

Figure 6

Figure 6 is just a variation of the theme. Both arrangements have the disadvantage that the delivery traffic is not separated from customer traffic and that the customer is given the choice of entering the store either from the parking area or through the pedestrian mall. We refer to this type as "extroverted centers" and they are often plagued by the fact that the pedestrian mall lacks "animation."

SOURCE: Centers for Urban Environment, Victor Gruen, Van Nostrand Reinhold, 1973.

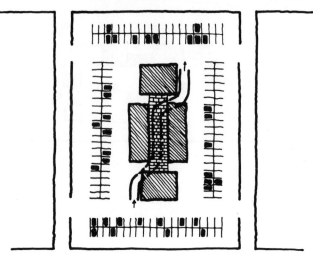

Figure 8

Figure 8 shows the same arrangement as 7 but enhanced by the introduction of a basement into which an underground delivery road (represented by the broken line) is incorporated. This prototype effects a separation between customers' traffic and delivery and service traffic.

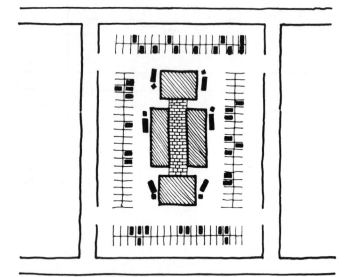

Figure 7

Figure 7 represents a regional center with two major magnets. Access to parking is accomplished by its own circulatory road which is then connected at two or three points to major public roads. The prototype suffers from the fact that there is no separation between the delivery traffic and the customers' traffic. Centers of this type are executed either as "extroverted centers" (with show windows, signs, and entrances to the stores directed to both the parking area and the pedestrian mall) or as "introverted centers." In the latter case, all show windows, entrances, and signs are directed toward the mall, which can be reached only through arcades from the parking area. Thus, pedestrian movement is concentrated in the mall, which then becomes truly animated. The duplication of expenditures for show windows, doors, and signs is avoided. A superior pedestrian environment is created.

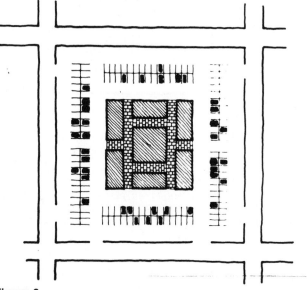

Figure 9

Figure 9 shows a similar arrangement for a shopping center when only one major department store is available. Here

also, a basement with delivery roads should exist in order to avoid the conflicts and the wastage of land which always occurs when deliveries are made on the surface."

Types shown in Figures 5 to 9 can be executed as "open centers" or as "enclosed climatized centers."

The number of basic prototypes is enlarged when it comes to the introduction of more than one magnet (department store).

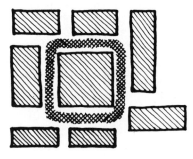

Figure 10

Figure 10 indicates the main pedestrian flow pattern in the case of one department store (this illustrates schematically the arrangement exemplified by Northland Center near Detroit).

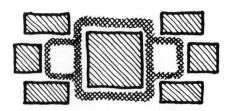

Figure 11

Figure 11 is a variation of the theme as exemplified by the Old Orchard Center near Chicago.

SOURCE: Centers for Urban Environment, Victor Gruen, Van Nostrand Reinhold, 1973.

Figures 12 to 15 illustrate typical arrangements when three department stores are introduced. In each case, the intensity of pedestrian movement would tend to flow from one of the main magnets to the others, as indicated. We find that in prototypes 12 and 13 a balance of intensity of the pedestrian flow can be achieved, which benefits the tenants' stores because it is equally distributed between the magnets. In those two cases, the distances which the pedestrian has to walk from a central point are kept reasonably short. (Figure 13 shows schematically the approach exemplified by Randhurst Center near Chicago.)

The prototype shown in Figure 14, which places one of the department stores in the middle of a very long mall, tends to bring about a concentration of pedestrian traffic in the center of the mall and therefore establishes an imbalance, giving the centrally located department store and the adjoining stores a greater exposure to pedestrian traffic than the two department stores on the extreme ends. The danger that the mall becomes too long and that, because of being arranged in one straight line, it does not provide any variety and surprise for the customer, is also a disadvantage.

Figure 12

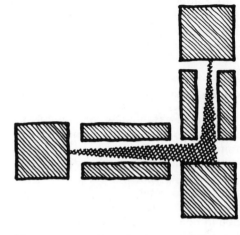

Figure 15

Figure 14

The prototype in Figure 15, representing an L-shaped mall, also creates an uneven distribution of the pedestrian flow and therefore unequal opportunities for the three department stores and the adjoining tenant stores. If the three department stores are of approximately equal size and quality, the exposure to pedestrian traffic will tend to be the strongest at the location in the corner of the "L."

Preferable is a T-shaped arrangement (Figure 12), which could easily be adopted for four magnets by enlarging the T-shaped mall to a cross mall.

Figure 16

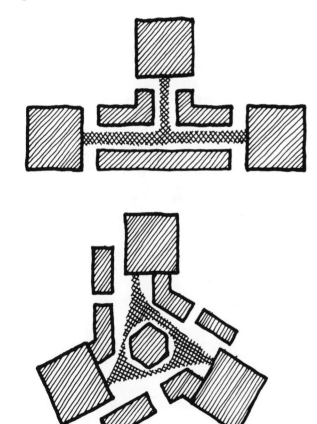

Finally, Figures 16 and 17 show two approaches to the center with two magnets. Figure 16 represents the simplest and most often used solution. Figure 17 is a variation as it was utilized, for example, in Southdale, near Minneapolis, where the mall is considerably widened to a court and the large stores are arranged in diagonal positions. Thus space for additional tenant stores is gained on both ends of the pedestrian area through the considerable width of the court, and opportunities for the placement of kiosks and for the holding of public events are created.

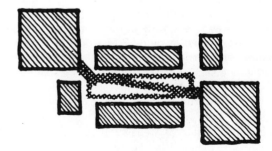

Figure 17

Figure 13

SOURCE: *Centers for Urban Environment,* Victor Gruen, Van Nostrand Reinhold, 1973.

The space for parking customers' cars is a basic requirement in shopping center site planning and development. The layout of the parking space must assist in making the center serve its prime function—that of an attractive and profitable market place. In providing the indispensable parking, the only questions are how much area to provide and how best to arrange the car spaces. The parking spaces so provided are an essential auxiliary to the commercial use and not a commercial use in itself.

1. How Much Parking

From the site area standpoint, parking takes up more area than all other physical features of the shopping center combined. The parking for each project must be given careful consideration.

The number of parking spaces needed for a shopping center depends upon factors affecting the parking demand. These are:

Size and type of center
Composition of the tenancy
Location in relation to customer traffic from public transportation
Character and income level of the trade area
Amount of walk-in trade generated from nearby areas
Local parking habits; rate of turnover in the parking spaces; peak loads encountered
Size and shape of the property
Cost of the land and maintenance costs.

By taking the above factors into consideration, the parking area can be gauged in relation to the need. See the recommended standard that follows.

Two terms are used to describe parking in its relationship to the shopping center structure: the parking ratio and the parking index.

(a) Parking Ratio

Parking ratio is a relationship between the **area** devoted to parking and the **area** devoted to building. This ratio is best expressed in terms of gross floor area.

For **planning purposes** and for **estimating adequacy** of site area, the parking ratio is a useful way to estimate parking area requirements in preliminary site planning.

The ratio, stated as being 2 to 1 or 3 to 1, for example, allows for a preliminary measurement of the site's parking capacity including allocations for the car stalls, the moving aisles, access drives, planting spaces, pedestrian walkways—the appurtenances of parking.

In estimating the site's parking capacity by the ratio method, it is best to allow 400 square feet of area per car. This allowance includes access drives, storage spaces, and incidental areas such as landscape plots and unusable corners.

(The recommended standard of 5.5 spaces per 1,000 sq. ft. of GLA is equivalent to a parking ratio of 2.2 sq. ft. of parking area for one sq. ft. of gross leasable area. In other words, a 2.2 to 1 ratio is more appropriate than a 3 to 1 ratio if the ratio formula is to be used in a zoning ordinance.)

SOURCE: By Permission From "The Community Builders Handbook" Prepared by the Executive Group of the Community Builders Council of Urban Land Institute, Edited by J. Ross McKeever, Copyright 1968, Urban Land Institute, 1200 18th Street, Wash. D. C. 20036 526 PP& 20.

(b) Parking Index

The relationship between the number of car parking spaces and the retail space furnishes the index for parking need.

The area in retail selling space varies according to the tenant type; the display of goods; the method of selling; the number, size, and variety of items, etc. For this reason, selling space as a unit against which to make comparisons is too variable for reliable computation. But the gross leasable area, i. e., the total gross floor area within buildings which is occupied exclusively by individual tenants and upon which the tenants pay rent, is measurable. Each tenant's gross leasable area is described in the lease document. Gross leasable area (abbreviated GLA) becomes, then, a known factor for measuring parking spaces in relationship to retail area for statistical analyses.

The type of tenancy has much to do with the number of parking spaces needed—for example a supermarket requires more spaces than does a furniture store. Ordinarily there is overlap and turnover of space from one tenant's use to another.

The parking index is the number of car parking spaces per 1,000 square feet of gross leasable area.

As a unit to indicate the number of parking spaces needed in relation to tenant occupancy, the parking index has the advantage of not requiring adjustments or explanations to show the assignments made for area per car, arrangement of the spaces, provision for car circulation, size and shape of the site, etc.

(c) Recommended Standard

The Community Builders Council in 1949[1] formulated the parking ratio as a basis for parking in relation to shopping center planning. Since then, the number of on-site parking spaces needed to accommodate retail customers and other users of a center's facilities has been a problem with several answers. Shopping center owners have often held one point of view, tenants another, and public officials have had local zoning ordinances incorporate requirements for off-street parking that have proved unrealistic or excessive in actual practice.

For a long time, shopping center owners, lenders, and tenants have been striving to arrive at scientifically determined guidelines that would establish valid yardsticks based on experience at shopping centers serving the public.[2] Accordingly, Urban Land Institute conducted a survey of conditions existing in shopping centers. The summary of these findings[3] follows:

1. In operational practice and hence for development planning purposes, where there is virtually no walk-in trade nor public transit usage, the provision of 5.5 car parking spaces per thousand square feet of gross leasable area is adequate as a standard to meet the demand for parking space at shopping centers. This standard accommodates the need for parking spaces at shopping centers for all but the ten highest hours of demand during an entire year. These ten highest hours occur during the three peak days of the year. It is uneconomic to provide parking space for such limited peak demands.

1. *Shopping Centers, An Analysis.* Technical Bulletin 11 (out-of-print), Urban Land Institute.
2. One step toward this yardstick was the formulation of the parking index as the measurement for number of spaces created rather than an area as an evidence for adequacy.
3. See *Parking Requirements for Shopping Centers.* Technical Bulletin 53, Urban Land Institute.

2. Office space usage up to 20% of the gross leasable area can be added to the center's complex without a noticeable increase in the peak parking demand.

3. Where there is a significant volume of walk-in customers or arrivals by means of public transit, or where there are other mitigating circumstances such as a limited trading area of unusual arrays of tenant classifications that have unusually low parking requirements, then the parking space provision cited above can be reduced proportionately.

4. As found in zoning ordinances at present, most of the regulations for shopping center parking call for a substantially greater amount of parking spaces than are found to be necessary in actual practice.

The findings lead to the following general conclusions: off-street parking needs have been overestimated by shopping center developers, lenders, and tenants; similarly, off-street parking requirements being asked for are excessive in many zoning ordinances.

Accordingly, for shopping centers of all sizes it is recommended that a standard of 5.5 parking spaces per thousand square feet of gross leasable area be established generally.[1]

In determining area for parking purposes, 400 square feet should be allotted for each car. This figure includes space assignable to moving lanes, access drives, pedestrian walks, drive-up windows, and grocery loading areas, as well as landscaped areas to be incorporated in the site layout as a part of the circulation and parking for the center.

It is impractical to design the parking provision for the peak load—the Saturday before Christmas, for example. At other times the parking area will have a deserted look. Barren parking lots react on people unfavorably. In addition, an excessive parking space allocation cannot be justified by the economics involved. Variations in shopping hours, types of tenancy and rates of turnover help level peak parking demands.

Parking space demand at a shopping center is tempered by the fact that a shopper buys in several stores while parking his car only once—"one stop shopping," while at a single detached store the parking services only a single transaction. This shopping characteristic differentiates parking space requirements for shopping centers from parking provisions at free-standing, commercial enterprises—a difference not accounted for in most zoning ordinances which set parking for business on a single unit relationship. A large furniture store is an example of a tenant with low parking requirements; a supermarket generates the greatest need for parking space at any location.

Since the area required by a parking space varies with a parking lot's layout, the Community Builders Council uses the parking index, or number of car spaces provided per 1,000 square feet of gross leasable area, rather than the parking ratio which relates the area of the parking space to the building area.

1 The basic study (*op. cit.*) shows that this standard would satisfy the parking requirements for all shopping periods during a year with the possible exception of ten peak hours or less than one-half of one percent of the total shopping hours during a year. The standard includes parking spaces for employees and incorporates a reserve allocation enabling free traffic movement within the parking area. The calculations assumed 400 square feet per parking space.

SOURCE: By Permission From "The Community Builders Handbook" Prepared by the Executive Group of the Community Builders Council of Urban Land Institute, Edited by J. Ross McKeever, Copyright 1968, Urban Land Institute, 1200 18th Street, Wash. D.C. 20036 526 PP & 20.

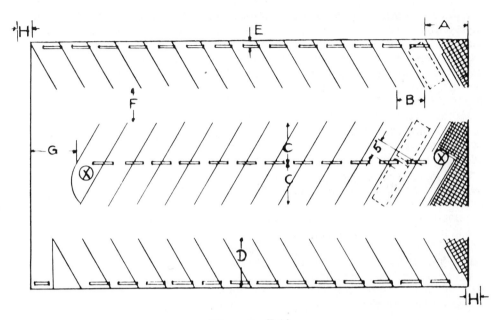

Dimension Table

Dimensions when parking at any of these angles

		45°	50°	55°	60°	90°
Offset	A	18′	15′8″	13′4″	11′	1′6″
Car Space	B	12′	11′4″	10′8″	10′	8′7″
Stall Depth	C	16′	16′8″	17′4″	18′	18′6″
Stall Depth	D	18′	18′4″	18′8″	19′	19′
Overhang	E	2′	2′1″	2′2″	2′3″	2′9″
Driveway	F	13′	14′6″	16′	17′6″	25′
Turnaround	G	17′	16′	15′	14′	14′
Extra	H	6′	5′	4′	3′	0

Parking Lot Layout (Diagram)

The schematic drawing above illustrates 60-degree diagonal parking within an area approximately 100′ × 150′. The table shows the dimensions for 45, 55, 60, and 90-degree parking which are the most used patterns.

To determine the number of cars that can be parked in each of the four banks:

1. Deduct the area lost in parking the first car. (Dimension "A" in the above sketch)

2. Then divide the car space, (dimension "B") into the total length of each bank of cars, plus the extra factor "H", if there is any extra space.

The shaded space may be used for planting. Dotted lines illustrate two large cars in parking position with alternate wheels against block—bumpers separated. Light standards are represented by "X".

Source: BUILDINGS, The Magazine of Building Management.

LOCATION AND SIZE

Tributary Area. The small neighborhood type of shopping center should be considered as a local convenience and service facility which must depend largely for its success on supplying the everyday needs of a limited residential population within a relatively small surrounding tributary trading area. It is only rarely that the small center will draw a substantial amount of trade from other areas. It should be borne in mind that unless there is a strong trend toward population growth within the trade area, not every small center is a potential community center.

Experience has shown that neighborhood convenience centers need a *minimum* of 1,000 families within the immediate tributary area in order to have a fair chance of success. With this population, a minimum center of 8–12 shops with a minimum site area of 4 acres can usually be supported under average conditions. A supermarket or drug store will be the main tenant and average gross floor area of the center will be 40,000 square feet, though the range may be over this figure for average size.

Support of the center must be gauged in terms of the average buying power of the families in the primary trade area; a low to medium income group may require up to twice this number of families. With a supermarket as major tenant it will draw easily from a distance of one and a half miles.

Competition. The second factor to consider is the location of a shopping center with relation to both the existing and probable future competition which may be expected from other business districts. Well located shopping centers may, on the average, be found at intervals of ½ to 1 mile, depending upon the type of development in terms of families per acre or square mile and the range of income groups to be served.

It is not advisable to generalize too broadly in determining the tributary area of any given center, as local factors will be determining. The point should be made, however, that one strong center with its own tributary area is always better than two weak ones with substantially overlapping areas. Where there is existing competition or potentially favorable locations for shopping centers within distances substantially less than those mentioned, the developer should consider his own project with extreme care.

Access Streets. The third factor from the location standpoint is the relation of the street system to the contemplated shopping center. Best locations will normally be found on major streets and preferably at or near the intersections of main or secondary thoroughfares. The specific location should also be situated so that it is easily accessible from its tributary area, both by pedestrian and vehicular traffic. Centers which have been located off the main traffic routes with access to them only over minor residential streets have seldom proved successful. If possible, choose a site where the street system within the tributary shopping area feeds more or less directionally toward the shopping center area. If a new area is being developed, the access street system can, of course, be designed with this element in mind.

Topography. The fourth factor is topography. A shopping center site ordinarily should be relatively level with grades not exceeding 2½ to 3 percent—flatter if possible. Greater grades create a resistance to local shoppers as well as to passing street traffic. Grades at store fronts of not over 1 to 1¼ percent are ideal in that they provide adequate drainage and permit store floors to slope without grade breaks at frequent intervals. A sloping site may be adapted by using split-level construction in the building.

Many authorities advocate that a small center be located on the "going home" side of the street. This will usually depend on the type and size of the center, local shopping habits, relation to the expected tributary area served, and the availability of adequate site area.

Utilities. Availability of utilities at or close to the site is a positive factor in off-site improvements. Long runs to reach available utility connections should be avoided. On-site improvements are items installed at the developer's expense as part of his overall building construction costs. Besides the utilities these include the roadways for interior circulation on the property, parking areas, outside lighting, and landscaping.

PLANNING THE SITE

Store Types. The initial site for a small center should generally not contain less than four to five acres. Site depths of 400 feet are desirable in order to provide both off-street parking and store service. This depth is, of course, not always obtainable where sites are in areas already subdivided. The developer should not overlook the possibility of expanding his center at some future time, and, if possible, he should reserve additional land for this purpose which can be put to some temporary commercial use in the interim period. Initial construction might contemplate approximately 10 stores in the following order:

1. Supermarket.
2. Drug Store—with some eating facilities.
3. Cleaner and Dyer Shop, which could be combined with a laundry agency.
4. Beauty Parlor.
5. Filling Station.
6. Bakery (this might depend on provision by grocery).
7. Shoe Repair.
8. Laundry Agency (possibly in rear of another store).
9. Variety Shop.
10. Barber Shop.

Variations from this basic list, of course, will occur, depending upon the individual case. For instance, in an area of small apartments, a restaurant might be desirable among the first ten tenants. The drug store and supermarket form the basis for any center, however, and no center can be considered complete without them.

Store Grouping. The grouping of stores in a small center does not assume the importance which is involved in the larger center. However, the location of the drug store and supermarket will tend to anchor the group. The drug store should usually have the prime location, preferably the corner store, if the development is at the intersection of two streets. The other end of the group should normally be occupied by the supermarket. The smaller shops located between have the benefit of the pedestrian traffic generated between the two. If the center grows, the relocation of one or more tenants will probably become desirable.

SOURCE: Home Builders Manual for Land Development, *2nd Edition*, National Association of Home Builders, Washington, D.C.

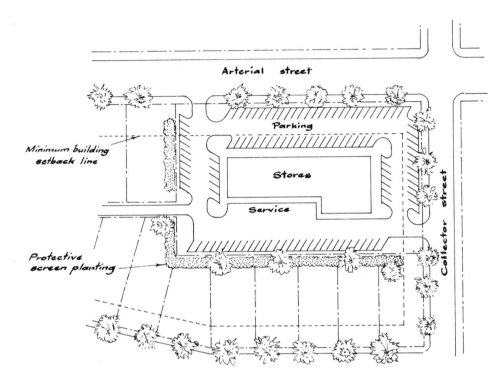

The location of the neighborhood shopping center is generally located on the arterial street at the intersection of a collector street. Adequate parking in relationship to number of stores must be provided. The houses adjacent to the shopping center must be properly protected with planting or fences.

Crude Standards for Estimating Space Requirements of Neighborhood and Community Shopping Centers

Selected Neighborhood Populaion Sizes in Residential Communities of 30-50,000	Acres of Combined Community-Neighborhood Shopping Area Per 1,000 Population at Various Parking Ratios		
	2:1	3:1	4:1
5,000	0.7	0.9	1.1
2,500	0.8	1.0	1.3
1,000	1.1	1.5	1.8

(A parking ratio is the amount of square feet of parking space for every square foot of ground area covered by store buildings.)

Commercial land uses are usually broken down into three general types for purposes of estimating space needs—the central business district, the outlying shopping center, the neighborhood or highway service centers. Estimates are based on population figures and business activity—that is, the market, actual or projected. The chief measurement of use in relation to open space is in reference to parking and parking ratios.

In most widespread current use are standards which relate to suburban or neighborhood commercial space, most often used in connection with new development.

SOURCE: Land Subdivision Regulations, Housing and Home Finance Agency, Washington, D. C.

SOURCE: Where not to Build Technical Bulletin #1 Bureau of Land Management Dept. of the Interior, Wash., D.C. 1968.

PARKING NEEDS

A fair percentage of the patronage of any local center comes from the walk-in trade, yet the provision of adequate and well placed parking space is quite as important as in the large regional center. Even where walk-in trade is as high as 60 percent, a ratio of at least two square feet of parking space to one square foot of store area is needed with few exceptions, such as in areas where the use of the automobile for local shopping is less convenient than the short walk involved. For the normal single-family development, however, at least two-thirds to three-fourths of the shopping center's site must be devoted to parking.

PARKING SPACE

In the past, the standard for parking areas was 2 or 3 square feet to each square foot of store. A more accurate standard is 6 to 10 parking spaces to each 1,000 square feet of store area. Some parking layouts are very wasteful. It's the actual number of parking spaces that count. For years there was considerable argument as to whether front or rear parking was better. Today opinion has settled for parking on all sides, but not farther than 350 feet away from the stores.

While the area ratio of 2:1, 3:1, etc., has become a familiar method of defining the amount of parking space in relation to store area, the measurement is not particularly accurate nor adaptable to comparisons among centers. Owners are apt to consider a site of three acres, with one acre of store area, as providing a two to one parking ratio. Actually, part of the remaining two acres is occupied by sidewalk, service areas, driveway aprons, and landscaping. In other instances, an irregular site such as a triangle or one with an odd width or depth will make it impossible to utilize the space efficiently. The changing dimensions of new car models is also a factor in figuring parking ratio.

In order to arrive at a more reliable measure of space requirements, the ULI has developed studies which show that an efficiently planned site should provide for approximately 6.7 car spaces on a two to one ratio, and 10 car spaces on a three to one ratio. (See Figure 1.)

As an example, on an area of 8.6 acres the following allocations of space can be made: 2.3 acres for shops, 4.6 acres for parking, and 1.7 acres for pedestrian walks, service, and planting. Allotting at least 300 square feet of area for each car space, including aisles and approaches, this plan provides for 6.7 car spaces to 1,000 square feet of first-floor store area. This is approximately a parking ratio of two-to-one.

A three-to-one parking ratio allows 10 cars to 1,000 feet of store area. As the space devoted to pedestrians and service will not increase proportionately, this item may be reduced to about 16 per cent of the total site area. The following table shows relationships applying in each case:

Parking ratios.

	Ratio of 2-to-1	Parking	Ratio of 3-to-1	Parking
Area of center	375,000 sq. ft.	100%	475,000 sq. ft.	100%
Area of parking	200,000 " "	53.3	300,000 " "	63.2
Area of stores (1st floor)	100,000 " "	26.7	100,000 " "	21.0
Area for pedestrians, service, and planting.	75,000 " "	20.0	75,000 " "	15.8
	Per 1,000 sq. ft. of store—6.7 cars		Per 1,000 sq. ft. of store—10.0 cars	

LOCATION OF PARKING

Opinions differ as to the proper location of parking space in relation to the stores served. If a predominant walk-in trade is expected, the stores should be nearer the highway, the front parking area providing space for two rows of cars.

Drive-in customers want to park close to the store to which they are going. Parking for 85 percent of the time when stores are open can be provided conveniently by two to four rows of car spaces, located between the street line and the sidewalk. This spacing will require 60 to 65 feet for one double row of parking with central aisle for two-way circulation or 120 to 130 feet for two double rows.

Any greater dimensions are wasteful of space and lesser dimensions increase the difficulty of parking. Easy movement is the important consideration in parking layout. Parking depth and the covered walk dimensions determine minimum setbacks from the street for store buildings. A double row of cars on one or both ends of the store building is advisable where drug stores or supermarkets are the end units.

A minimum width for rear service and employees' parking area should be 40 feet plus a 4–5 foot sidewalk, providing for one tier of cars adjacent to the rear property line of the site. A better arrangement is a minimum of 65–70 feet which will permit the near service area to be used for employee parking.

Arguments against in-front parking are that the stores stand too far back to be seen, and that, except for peak hours, the center looks deserted, which, from a sales psychology standpoint, is bad.

Experienced operators of shopping centers who have had opportunity to check the theorists, agree that some parking on all sides of a center is desirable; that the farthest space should not be more than 350 feet from the stores, and that the spaces must be distributed for convenience to stores having the largest number of customers during peak periods.

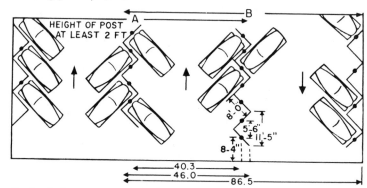

Two herringbone patterns are shown--in each case by only quite limited sections. In the A plan, cars are all parked in the same direction, and cars move in the same direction in each aisle. If the aisle entered is full, the driver must leave the lot and circle the block. If the B plan had been used, the same driver could have turned within the lot and returned down the next aisle, where cars are parked in the opposite direction. (From PARKING MANUAL, American Automobile Association)

Figure 1 Parking area layout. Herringbone pattern—45 degrees. Self Parking—270 sq. ft. per car.

SOURCE: Home Builders Manual for Land Development. *2nd Edition. National Association of Home Builders, Washington, D.C.*

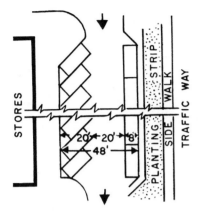

Parking in Restricted Widths

45 degree stalls – width	8'-0"	9'-0"
No. of cars per 100 ft. of curb	9	8
Parallel stalls	20'-0"	20'-0"
No. cars per 100 ft. of curb	5	5
No. of cars per acre excluding approaches	126	117

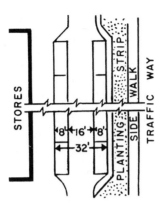

Parking in Narrow Widths

Parallel stalls – width	20'-0"
No. of cars per 100 ft. of curb	5
No. of cars per acre excluding approaches	136

Note: Parallel parking space is seldom used as efficiently as is diagonal or right-angle parking with proper marking.

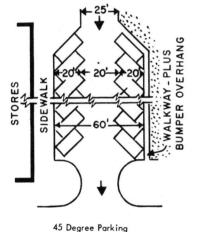

45 Degree Parking

Width of car stalls	8'-0"	9'-0"
No. of cars per 100 ft. of curb	9	8
Curb occupied per car	11'-4"	12'-9"
No. of cars per acre excluding approaches	130	116

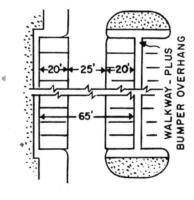

90 Degree – Right Angle Parking

Width of car stalls	8'-0"	9'-0"
No. of cars per 100 ft. of curb	12	11
Curb occupied per car	8'-0"	9'-0"
No. of cars per acre excluding approaches	168	148

Note: Many developers feel the walkway between cars may be omitted.

Figure 2 Diagrams of parking area layout for shopping centers.

DIVISION OF PARKING STALLS AND BAYS

Increasing width of the modern automobile and wide doors on certain models have affected the design of parking areas. Several years ago stalls 8 ft. wide were satisfactory; today, however, a 9 ft. width is usual with 9½ feet preferable.

The angle at which cars are parked influences car spacing to some extent. Cars parked at a sharp diagonal will allow for door clearance which the 90-degree head-on parking does not permit.

Head-in or 90 degree parking is preferred over angle parking wherever space permits. With perpendicular parking, two-way movement is possible through the parking lanes. This makes for greatly increased convenience and flexibility. Where space must be reduced below a 60 foot width of bay, one-way movement and diagonal parking is necessary.

Two rows of head-on parking require a minimum width of 60 feet. This plan gains flexibility in that the cars can move in and out from both directions. (See Figure 2.)

Two rows of diagonal parking can be accommodated in 50 to 55 feet, although 60 feet is preferable. The advantage is that less maneuvering is needed to get into the car space. The disadvantage is that traffic must move in one direction only, with exits and entrances separated.

Parking bays directly off busy access streets requiring cars to back into traffic lanes are a serious traffic hazard and are not recommended for any shopping center, no matter how tight the site area may be.

Because they prevent making changes in the parking pattern, permanent concrete curbs or walks within the parking space have not often proved practical. After a few months use, however, such concrete space markers usually prove desirable, except for regions where snow removal is a winter long problem.

Painted lines two inches wide or low metal buttons held by fasteners placed in the black top paving are considered satisfactory space markers, and allow for changes in the parking pattern if any rearrangement is necessary.

SOURCE: Home Builders Manual for Land Development, *2nd Edition 1958 National Association of Home Builders, Washington, D.C.*

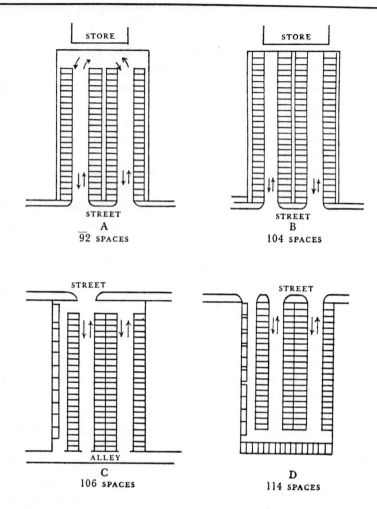

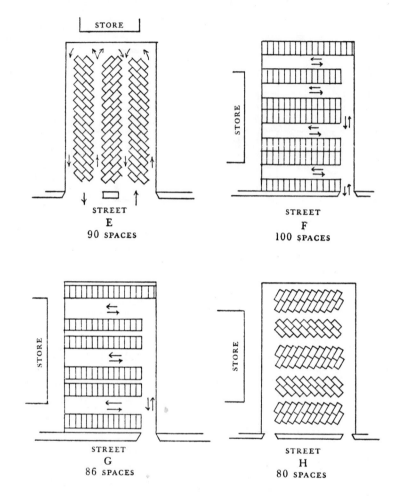

The illustrations above show eight possible ways of laying out an area 140 feet by 225 feet, under various controlling conditions.

Plan A. The 140-foot width permits two ninety-degree units of sixty-one feet each with three six-foot pedestrian paths, and provides ninety-two spaces.

Plan B uses a similar layout to provide 104 spaces, but omission of the transverse aisle prevents passage from one unit to the other.

Plan C. By omitting the pedestrian walks, space is gained for ten parallel stalls, possible only because of availability of an alley for exit.

Plan D. Without benefit of an alley this provides 114 spaces and still has a transverse aisle for easier circulation and to permit use of the parallel stalls.

Plan E. This offers the easier parking afforded by angle stalls, and has one-way circulation, but provides only ninety stalls. This could be served by a single entrance-exit.

Plan F. By using the ninety-degree pattern this provides 100 stalls and needs only one entrance-exit. This pattern might be improved by placing the main travel aisle in the center, with parking aisle branching to each side.

Plan G. This uses a pattern similar to that in F, but sacrifices one row or fourteen stalls to provide pedestrian walkways.

Plan H. This provides fewer spaces than for G but affords the easier parking of angle stalls.

It cannot be assumed that the layout which provides the largest number of spaces is thereby the best, even for a commercial lot operated by attendants. A lot provided by a store to attract customers usually sacrifices some capacity to give convenience and comfort. Where meters are to be used, or where screening or landscaping is desired, space must be allowed, and so on.

SOURCE: Parking, *The End Foundation for Highway Traffic Control, Saugatuck, Conn, 1957.*

Interfloor Ramp Systems

A number of interfloor ramp system concepts exist to travel the approximately ten-foot difference in floor levels. Some concepts have been used successfully since the first garages of the 1920's, and others have evolved recently. Many make use of sloping floor driving and parking aisles, for the entire interfloor movement, while some systems provide separate and exclusive ramps. The ramp may be straight, curved or circular, or a combination of them, and the choice will be based upon the shape of the site and the size of the garage. Interfloor ramp systems are classified as follows:

• *Single straight ramp, with two-way traffic* (Figure 1). All up and down travel takes place on a series of sloping parallel planes, one above the other and wide enough for cars to pass in opposite directions. In a continuous up or down trip, the normal floor driving aisles are used to travel between the beginning and ending of each sloping ramp. The ramp width is usually 20 to 24 feet, with widenings at the ends for turning movements.

• *Two parallel straight ramps, each with one-way traffic* (Figure 2). The ramps provide one-way travel, an advantage in an active traffic situation.

The separation of the ramps may be advantageous in the basic layout of the building, especially when planning the street access points. Each ramp is usually 11 to 12 feet wide.

• *Sloping floor ramp (continuous ramp) with two-way traffic* (Figure 3). A garage of this type consists almost entirely of a single continuous "rectangular spiral" ramp, the slope being four to six percent, about one-half the slope of straight and circular ramps. The relatively flat slope permits comfortable parking on both sides of the driving aisle "ramps" and does not require the use of additional building or site area to be used for interfloor travel. This economy, together with proven customer acceptance, makes it an extremely popular design solution.

• *Double sloping floor ramp, for one-way traffic* (Figure 4). For longer sites, it is possible to achieve one-way traffic aisles with parking along the aisle on every level. In effect, two sloping floor garage units are laid out end to end, and in the level center section, where the two units meet, traffic can change over from up to down and vice versa. This permits complete flexibility in the desired parking angle, limited only by the available lot width.

• *Staggered (split level) floor ramps* (Figure 5). Split level floor construction requires the length of the ramp travel to be about one-half the usual interfloor distance. This was one of the most common designs for many years. Split-level floors can overlap as much as five to six feet at the "split," which increases space efficiency, and makes a narrow site workable. As with straight ramp systems, ramps can be wide for two-way travel or narrow for two sets of one-way travel, but the latter is much more common.

• *Circular-spiral ramps.* The most common spiral ramp design provides for a one-way, single lane ramp from floor to floor. Such a ramp provides for travel without interference except for the small portion of the spiral which is relatively level as the driving path is carried across the typical parking floor. Circular ramps are most often located in the corners of rectangular structures to minimize the loss of floor space, or they are attached to the normal rectangular structure where additional site area is available. The single lane spiral has an inside curb radius of approximately 30 feet and an outside curb radius of 41 to 44 feet, depending on vehicle overhang provisions to clear vertical obstructions beyond the curb. Circular spiral ramps are used only on occasion for larger garages because of the site area that is taken from the typical parking floor.

• *Combination ramps.* High capacity parking structures, and other special conditions, may be served best with an express ramp in one direction of travel—usually for exiting travel—and this can lead to the use of one ramp for entering, rising travel and another for exiting, descending travel. Many combinations of the above six methods can be created to satisfy individual requirements.

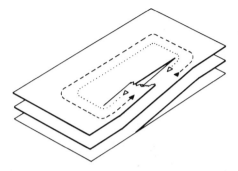

FIGURE 1 — Two-way Straight Ramp

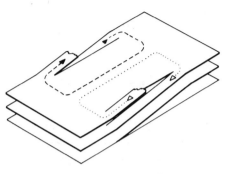

FIGURE 2 — Parallel Straight Ramp

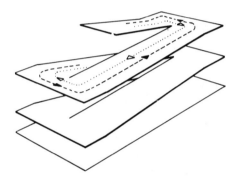

FIGURE 3 — Sloping Floor

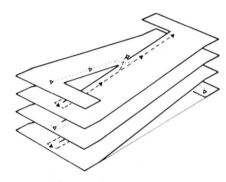

FIGURE 4 — Double Sloping Floor Ramp

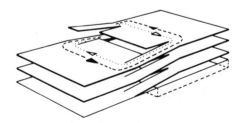

FIGURE 5 — Staggered Floor

SOURCE: Technical Report on Steel Framed Parking Structures, *United State Steel Corp., 1973.*

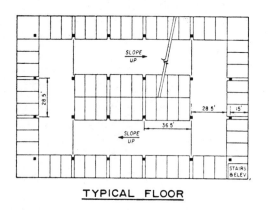

TYPICAL FLOOR

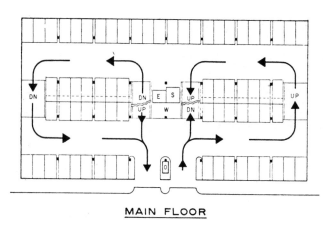

MAIN FLOOR

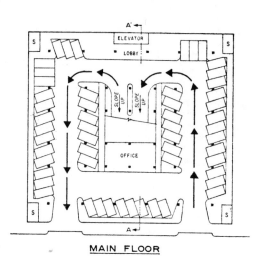

MAIN FLOOR

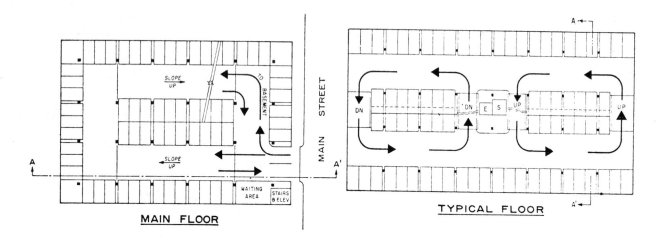

MAIN FLOOR

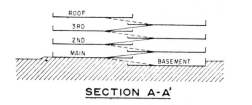

TYPICAL FLOOR

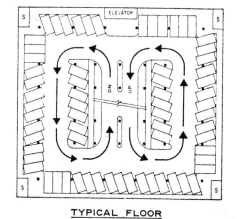

TYPICAL FLOOR

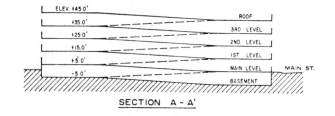

SECTION A-A'

FIGURE 6 — Functional plan for sloping-floor garage.

SECTION A-A'

FIGURE 7 — Functional plan for staggered-floor garage.

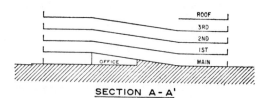

SECTION A-A'

FIGURE 8 — Functional plan for straight-ramp garage.

The following *design requirements* for service stations, entrances and exits were recommended:

a. Not more than two driveways from one property to any one highway should be permittéd.

b. The maximum width of any one driveway should be forty to fifty feet, with the following exception: that exits to one-way roadways should not exceed thirty to thirty-five feet.

These dimensions to be measured parallel to the highway centerline at curb or shoulder line.

c. The angle of any driveway should not be less than forty-five degrees.

d. Driveway return radii should not exceed forty feet.

e. Pump islands should be no closer than fifteen feet to the right of way line.

f. Any two driveways connecting with a single highway should be separated by an island area. The side of the island next to and parallel to the highway should be located at the curb or ditch line. The island should extend to the right of way line and should have a minimum length of ten to twenty feet at the right of way line.

g. An island area adjacent to the property line extended measuring five feet parallel to the roadway at the curb or ditch line, should be reserved, in case the adjacent property owners request driveways.

h. All islands within the right of way should be delineated by curbs, posts, guard rails, or planting.

i. The following conditions should apply to corner islands:

1. No driveway should encroach upon curb or pavement radii at intersections.

2. No driveway should cross reserved corner sight distance areas.

3. Minimum distances from side road right of way line to edge of driveways should be thirty feet on the major road, and fifteen feet for urban conditions. This is to apply if no conflict with preceding conditions exist.

j. The permissible grade of driveways should be specified, and the need for approval of drainage provisions should be spelled out.

k. Parking, loading or servicing of vehicles should not be permitted on the right of way.

To illustrate the application of these recommendations to typical service station layouts, sketches showing various conditions are shown.

Setback Requirements: Roadside business buildings situated close to the pavement cause innumerable difficulties:

a. Conceal vehicles about to enter the highway.

b. Complicate entrances and exits.

c. Make arrangements for parking space complicated and less attractive and usable.

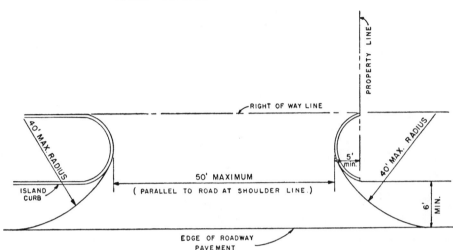

A TYPICAL ENTRANCE SHOWING
RADII CONNECTION WITH PAVEMENT.

SOURCE: "Report of the Subcommittee on Roadside Control of the Committee on Traffic of the American Association of State Highway Officials."

TYPICAL ENTRANCE
RURAL SERVICE STATION
(PARALLEL PUMP ISLANDS)

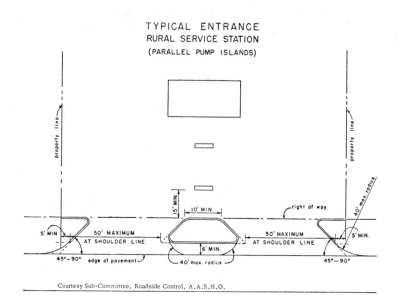

Courtesy Sub-Committee, Roadside Control, A.A.S.H.O.

TYPICAL ENTRANCE
RURAL SERVICE STATION
(WITH RESERVED SIGHT DISTANCE AREA)

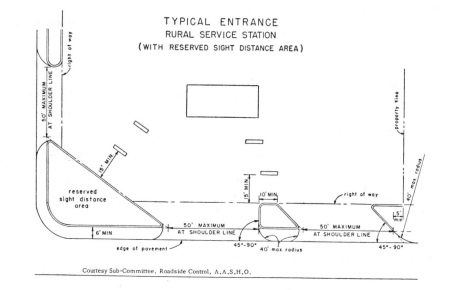

Courtesy Sub-Committee, Roadside Control, A.A.S.H.O.

TYPICAL ENTRANCE
RURAL SERVICE STATION
(WITHOUT RESERVED SIGHT DISTANCE AREA)

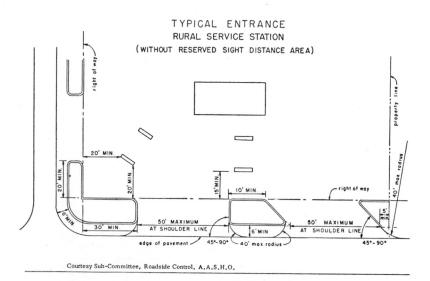

Courtesy Sub-Committee, Roadside Control, A.A.S.H.O.

TYPICAL ENTRANCE
URBAN SERVICE STATION

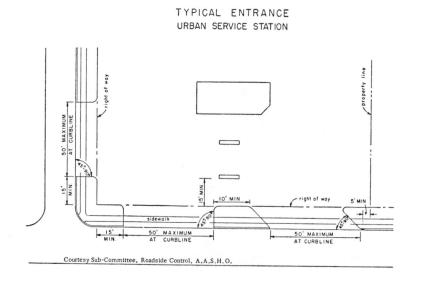

Courtesy Sub-Committee, Roadside Control, A.A.S.H.O.

DRIVE-IN BANKING: DRIVE-IN APPROACHES

Traffic congestion has become an ever increasing problem in many cities. Rather than lose customers banks have adopted drive-in facilities, shown on the next page. These accommodations are best placed when located off a main traffic artery away from crowded business areas. Besides the drive-in feature there should also be adequate parking facilities as the bank will also offer regular in-door banking service as not all types of transactions can be handled at drive-in windows. Drive-in stations, when possible, should be incorporated in the in-door tellers' area so that drive-in tellers may work at the inside counter when drive-in activity is light.

Drive-in facilities have proven highly successful when properly placed, handling 250 and more transactions per day. Important considerations in placement are: (1) proper and adequate approach to the drive-in window; (2) driveway in front of the stations should be straight and parallel to the station; and (3) driveway entrances and exits should be clearly marked. Traffic signals have been used to regulate traffic flow, especially if there are several windows.

The schematics below show only tellers' windows in relation to several possible approaches. Except for several of the island stations, which are obviously isolated, the tellers' windows shown are part of a bank building. All dimensions given are minimum.

DRIVE-IN APPROACHES

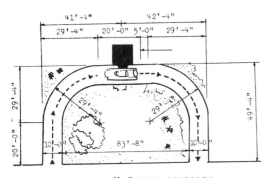

MID-BLOCK "U" TYPE APPROACH

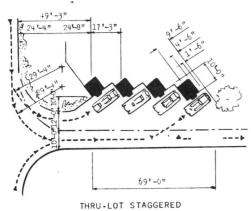

THRU-LOT STAGGERED

CURVED APPROACH THRU CORNER

Note: Streets and sidewalks not shown but must be considered. Curb cut radius 15' min. to 20' desirable. Pitch of driveway 1/8" min. to 1'-0". See Ramsey & Sleeper, Architectural Graphic Standards.

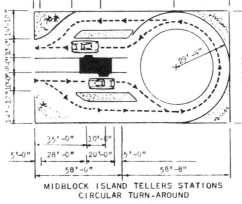

MIDBLOCK ISLAND TELLERS STATIONS
CIRCULAR TURN-AROUND

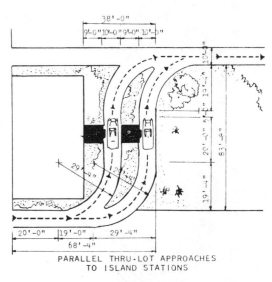

PARALLEL THRU-LOT APPROACHES
TO ISLAND STATIONS

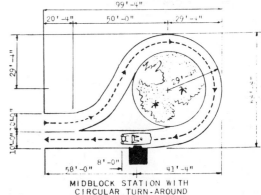

MIDBLOCK STATION WITH
CIRCULAR TURN-AROUND

SOURCE: Mosler Safe Co.

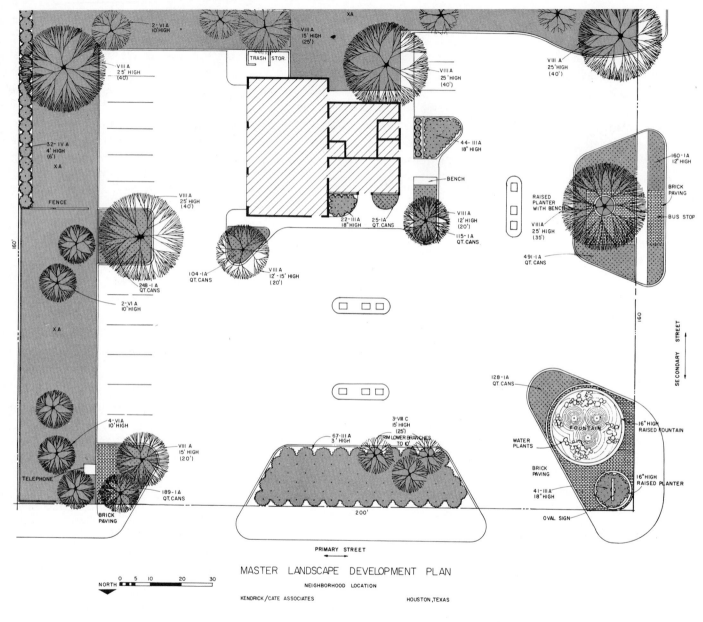

NEIGHBORHOOD LOCATION

1. Company owned.
2. Three bay
3. Side entrance
4. Brick
5. 200' x 160'
6. Secondary street leads to subdivision.
7. Primary street feeder route to town.
8. High traffic on primary street.
9. Traffic peaks during morning and evening rush.
10. Traffic light on corner.

MASTER LANDSCAPE DEVELOPMENT PLAN

NEIGHBORHOOD LOCATION

KENDRICK/CATE ASSOCIATES   HOUSTON, TEXAS

SOURCE: Landscaping for Profit. Edited by William J. Cronin, Jr., Exxon Company, USA.

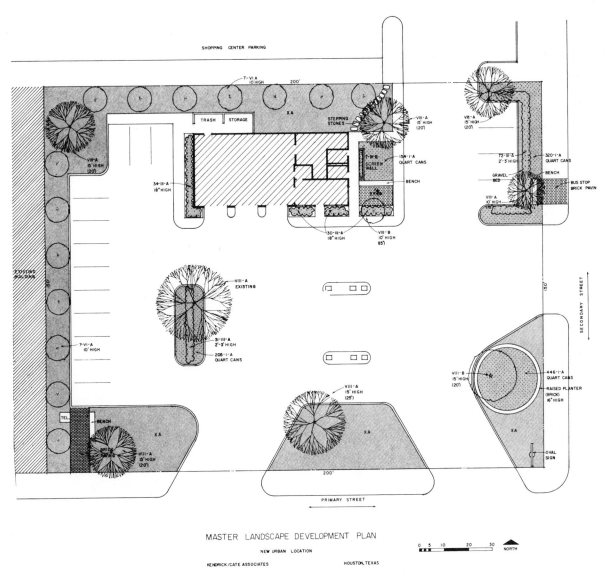

MASTER LANDSCAPE DEVELOPMENT PLAN

NEW URBAN LOCATION

KENDRICK/CATE ASSOCIATES   HOUSTON, TEXAS

0 5 10   20   30   NORTH

URBAN LOCATION

1. Company owned
2. Two bay, contemporary design
3. Field Stone.
4. Business district 200' x 150'
5. Large shopping center and parking lot to the rear.
6. Neighbor on the West, three story office building extending to the sidewalk.
7. Considerable foot traffic to and from shopping center.
8. Purchase agreement specifies opening to parking lot.

SOURCE: Landscaping for Profit. *Edited by William J. Cronin, Jr., Exxon Company, USA.*

INDUSTRIAL DEVELOPMENT

1. Basic Relationships:
   (a) Working Force as a percent of total population.   35–40%
   (b) Workers in industrial areas as percentage of total Working Force.   30–35%
   (c) Workers in Heavy Industry as percentage of workers in industrial areas.   60–70%
   (d) Workers in Light Industry as percentage of workers in industrial areas.   30–40%
   (e) Workers in basic industry (manufacture of goods for export from area) as percentage of theoretical community size.   10%

2. Worker-Area Ratios:

Average Number of Workers Per Gross Acre of Industrial Land

	Heavy Industry	Light Industry	Industrial Park
Present Ratios	8	28	18
Expected Future Ratios	6	22	16

3. Land Requirement of Industry:
   (a) Total Gross Land requirement for all Industry.   12 acres/1,000 popluation
   (b) Land requirements for Light Industry.   2 acres/1,000 population
   (c) Land requirements for Heavy Industry.   10 acres/1,000 population
   (d) Land requirements for pre-planned industrial complex (Industrial Park):*

Minimum	320 acres
Ideal	640 acres

   (e) Requirements for industrial land reserve:

   reserve land for minimum of 50 years future growth

4. General Requirements for Industrial Location:
   (a) Fast, easy and convenient access to good tratransportation facilities including rail, highway and air.
   (b) Reasonable location with respect to labor supply, raw materials source and markets.
   (c) An adequate amount of suitable land, free from foundation and drainage problems with a sufficient reserve for future growth.
   (d) An adequate and reliable supply of utilities: water, waste disposal, power and fuel.
   (e) Protection from encroachment of residential or other land uses.
   (f) Location so as to minimize obnoxious external effects on neighboring non-industrial land uses.

SOURCE: George Nez, Standards for New Urban Development—The Denver Background,
Reprinted by Permission of Urban Land, Vol 20, No 5 Urban Land Institute, 1200 18th Street, N. W., Wash., D. C.

PURPOSE OF THE CLASSIFICATION

The Standard Industrial Classification was developed for use in the classification of establishments by type of activity in which engaged; for purposes of facilitating the collection, tabulation, presentation, and analysis of data relating to establishments; and for promoting uniformity and comparability in the presentation of statistical data collected by various agencies of the United States Government, State agencies, trade associations, and private research organizations.

SCOPE OF THE CLASSIFICATION

The Classification is intended to cover the entire field of economic activities: agriculture, forestry, and fisheries; mining; construction; manufacturing; transportation, communication, electric, gas, and sanitary services; wholesale and retail trade; finance, insurance, and real estate; services; and government.

PRINCIPLES OF THE CLASSIFICATION

The Classification was prepared by the Technical Committee on Standard Industrial Classification.

In preparing the Classification, the Technical Committee was guided by the following general principles:

1. The Classification should conform to the existing structure of American industry.

2. The reporting units to be classified are establishments, rather than legal entities or companies.

3. Each establishment is to be classified according to its major activity.

4. To be recognized as an industry, each group of establishments must have significance from the standpoint of the number of persons employed, volume of business, and other important economic features, such as the number of establishments.

BASIS OF ESTABLISHMENT CLASSIFICATION-CODE ASSIGNMENT

Each establishment is assigned an industry code on the basis of its major activity, which is determined by the product or group of products produced or handled, or services rendered. Ideally, the principal product or service should be determined by reference to "value added." In practice, however, it is rarely possible to obtain this information for individual products or services, and it becomes necessary to adopt some other criteria which may be expected to give approximately the same results. It is recommended, therefore, that, as far as possible, the following characteristics be used for each of the major economic sections:

Economic Section	Characteristics
Agriculture, forestry, and fisheries (except agricultural services)	Value of production
Mining	Value of production
Construction	Value of work done
Manufacturing	Value of production
Wholesale and retail trade	Value of sales
Finance, insurance, and real estate	Value of receipts
Services (including agricultural services)	Value of receipts
Transportation, communication, electric, gas, and sanitary services	Value of receipts
Government	Function

Occasionally, in cases of mixed business, the above characteristics cannot be determined or estimated for each product or service, and less frequently a classification based upon the recommended characteristic will not represent adequately the process or activity of the establishment. In such cases, if employment information is available, the major activity should be determined by the activity in which the greatest number of employees worked.

SOURCE: The Standard Industrial Classification, Executive Office of the President, Bureau of the Budget

STRUCTURE OF CLASSIFICATION

The structure of the Classification makes it possible to classify establishments by industry on a two-digit, a three-digit, or a four-digit basis, according to the degree of detail in information which may be needed. It permits an agency to select the level of detail considered most appropriate for presentation of its data. Also, it permits an agency to use additional subdivisions in adopting this Classification for its own use, while still retaining comparability with the classifications used by other agencies. Furthermore, comparability with the Classification may be maintained on a two-digit basis by combining groups or industries within a Major Group; similarly, comparability may be maintained on a three-digit basis by combining industries within a three-digit group.

DEFINITION OF ESTABLISHMENT

The Standard Industrial Classification distinguishes two broad classes of establishments: (1) "operating establishments" or economic units which produce goods or services; and (2) central administrative office and auxiliary units which manage or provide services for other establishments of the same company.

Operating Establishments.—An "operating establishment" is an economic unit which produces goods or services—for example, a farm, a mine, a factory, a store. In most instances, the establishment is at a single physical location; and it is engaged in only one, or predominantly one, type of economic activity for which an industry code is applicable.

Where a single physical location encompasses two or more distinct and separate economic activities for which different industrial classification codes seem applicable, such activities should be treated as separate establishments and classified in separate industries, provided it is determined that: (1) such activities are not ordinarily associated with one another at common physical locations; (2) no one industry description in the Standard Industrial Classification includes such combined activities; (3) the employment in each such economic activity is significant; and (4) reports can be prepared on the number of employees, their wages and salaries, and other establishment type data. An establishment is not necessarily identical with the business concern or firm, which may consist of one or more establishments. Also, it is to be distinguished from organizational subunits, departments, or divisions within an establishment. Supplemental interpretations of the definition of an establishment are included in the industry descriptions of the Standard Industrial Classification.

Central Offices and Auxiliary Units.—A central administrative office is an establishment primarily engaged in management and general administrative functions performed centrally for other establishments of the same company.

An auxiliary unit is an establishment primarily engaged in performing supporting services for other establishments of the same company rather than for the general public or for other business firms.

Activities of the type performed at separate central administrative office and auxiliary establishments are, in fact, normally carried on as an integral part of individual operating establishments. Hence, this type of activity is only partially measured by the statistics on separately reported central administrative office and auxiliary establishments.

  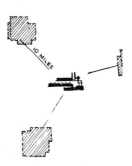

Three locations: peripheral, central and rural locations

A peripheral location outside city limits is characteristic, especially where transportation is paramount, but it must be within the urban distribution area. This means:

Containment within central express and pickup districts where rates are lowest. (In Chicago this zone extends 18 mi. beyond the city.) A powerful district may itself cause extension of low rates.

Containment within the local switching district of at least one railroad, and preferably in a terminal district so freight rates will not exceed adjoining metropolitan areas, especially in handling less-than-carload lots, which are highly important to small plants, and service may be better. In a big city where there is a terminal railroad its line may be preferable to a trunk line as a site because it will save some 24 hours on each interchange.

Situation on a good highway close enough to town so less-than-truckload quantities can be organized.

Lower land costs for today's one-story spread-out plants favor the peripheral location.

Labor must likewise be available, at distances that require no excessive travel time.

A central location may be preferable for the class of industry that may be called market- or contact-dominated. Example, a type of medium-sized plant whose salesmen have to keep running back and forth from the plant to clients' purchasing offices and would not easily be talked into moving to a suburban location.

Atop high land prices the city center usually offers difficulties of assembly short of condemnation under the federal redevelopment title; atop that, difficulties are increasingly imposed through requirements of off-street parking and loading.

Rural locations are still more exceptional. Plants that need to be close to raw materials, low-cost electric power or bodies of water may locate in rural areas.

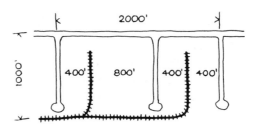

Interlaced, railway and auto transportation systems avoid crossings. Rail lead can be located off center to give any variation in depth of lots which may be desired by prospect.

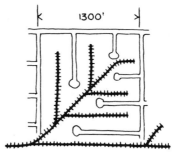

Diagonal rail lead interlaced with roads offers greater choice of lot shapes and sizes than in system illustrated (above). Diagonal system has further advantage of requiring less space for track to become parallel to buildings.

Minimum size for a profitable operation is not less than 80 acres; the maximum depends on the size of the individual plants, with 150 acres the preferred top limit where plants average 50,000 sq. ft., but more land where plants are bigger.

Size of lots depends on plant sizes, land coverage (anywhere from 30% to 60% as a maximum, the latter more typical) and distance from street to railroad siding (at least 200' and seldom over 500'). Lot sizes and shapes are more easily varied where railroads come in at the diagonal.

Expansion can be handled by requiring each tenant to rent a certain amount of expansion land (few tenants foresee their need) or options may be given, say for two years, on adjacent lots.

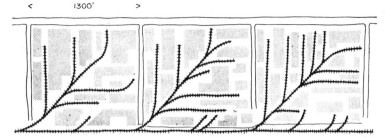

Rail-dominated district, such as early Clearing Industrial District (p. 114), has large plants, high densities, frequently uses more than one spur track per plant and makes relatively little provision for trucking as part of industrial process.

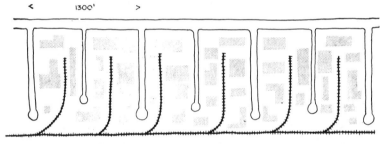

Balanced transportation is provided in practically all new districts. Plants in general cover less area and use both trucks and railway cars. Flow is not always from railway to truck but may be reversed or mixed.

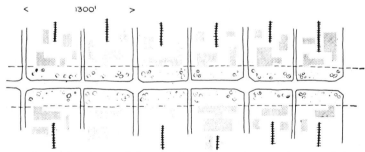

Auto-dominated district has some industries, such as research laboratories, which could very well get along without railroad. Employees' parking is the dominant factor, although trucks and railways are necessary for some of the industries in an "Industrial Park."

A basic problem of the district is to avoid rail and road interference. Ideally, the rail leads and the dead-end access streets come in from the main lines at opposite sides like interlacing fingers, avoiding crossings (middle sketch). In a diagonal scheme the rails lie in a tree pattern diagonal to the lot, and access streets are fed in from around the periphery, again interlacing without crossings.

The typical block may have rails coming in at a diagonal to the buildings (see uppermost of the three sketches). The $\frac{1}{4}$-mi. square block served by a diagonal railroad lead with branches is particularly suitable to districts where rail traffic is to be dominant. Within this $\frac{1}{4}$-mi. block it is possible to get an almost infinite variety of side-track layouts and shapes and sizes of lots.

An alternate is a series of blocks with railroad spurs coming in at right angles between the access roads, the way an alley runs up the middle of an ordinary city block (middle sketch).

This type of plan leads to an orderly looking community but it is neither so flexible nor so economic in its use of land in relation to the railraod as the diagonal type.

Water is no longer important except in unusual cases; truck transportation is universal, and virtually all districts also use rails. Opinions vary as to the relative advantage of having a district served by one railroad or two, since a single line may be expected to do more to promote the district but two lines may compete giving more attentive service.

SOURCE: Reprinted from the Architectural Forum, April—1954. Copyright by Urban America, Inc.

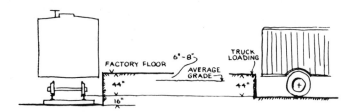

Depressed tracks and loading area bring floors of vehicles level with factory floor. It costs less usually to lay plant floor on grade and excavate tracks and trucks than to raise floor. In most districts railway leads and side tracks are depressed throughout entire district. In early districts only truck-loading areas were below grade. Some recent districts have entire street systems about 3' below grade.

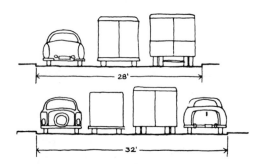

Paving width should be 28' or 32' wide. Paving 30' wide has been extensively used but is wider than needed for three vehicles, not wide enough for four. Major streets are now being laid out with 40' paving needed for four lanes if traffic is to be kept moving while cars are parking on one side of street.

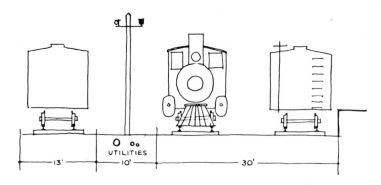

Utility strip alongside railway lead and side tracks is preferred to utilities in parking area on either side of street. When usual setback from street was 15' to 25', utilities generally came in from street side, but with today's 75' to 100' setbacks it is more economical to come in from rear.

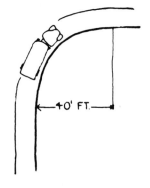

Corners must be designed to take trucks. If radius is too short, truck will have to use second lane to make turn. Throughout Southwest where combinations of tractor, semi-trailer and four-wheel trailer are used, it is desirable to use still longer radius.

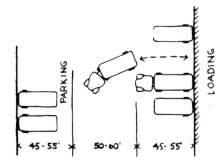

Plenty of truck space is needed for loading, parking and maneuvering. It is better to overdesign than skimp on space as time costs more than space. Warehousing is becoming increasingly important to industrial districts. Half the Clearing District's current construction is for warehouses. Photo shows truck terminals.

SOURCE: Reprinted From The Architectural Forum, April—1954. Copyright By Urban America, Inc.

Offstreet Truck-loading Docks or Berths

Figure 1 shows suggested layouts for docking facilities for tractor-trailer combinations, as listed in the table below.

For general use, the stalls, doors, etc. should be at least twelve feet wide, and overhead clearance fourteen feet. Dock heights vary from forty-four inches for smaller trucks to forty-eight to fifty inches for heavy-duty units, and ramps or jacks often are used to adjust differences in levels of truck beds and dock height.

The dock area needed for each stall depends upon the capacity of the units being served, the height to which tiers may be stacked upon the dock, the elevator or other service available for clearing the dock, and the frequency of arrival of trucks (i.e., the tonnage per dock per day).

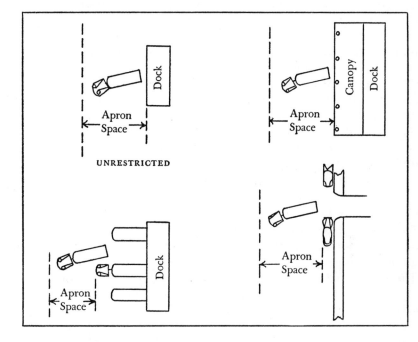

Figure 1 Loading dock layout.

SOURCE: Parking. The End Foundation for Highway Traffic Control, Saugatuck, Conn., 1957.

1. NOISE

A "decibel" is a unit of measurement of the intensity of sound (the sound pressure level).

A "sound level meter" is an instrument standardized by the American Standards Association, which is used for measurement of the intensity of sound and is calibrated in decibels.

An "octave band" is one of a series of eight bands which cover the normal range of frequencies included in sound measurements. Such octave bands serve to define the sound in term of its pitch components.

An "octave band analyzer" is an instrument used in conjunction with a sound level meter to measure sound in each of eight octave bands.

An "impact noise analyzer" is an instrument used in conjunction with the sound level meter to measure the peak intensities of short duration sounds

METHOD OF MEASUREMENT

For the purpose of measuring the intensity or frequency of sound, the sound level meter, the octave band analyzer, and the impact noise analyzer shall be employed.

The "C" network and the "slow" meter response of the sound level meter shall be used. Sounds of short duration, as from forge hammers, punch presses, and metal shears, which cannot be measured accurately with the sound level meter, shall be measured with the impact noise analyzer as manufactured by the General Radio Company, or its equivalent, in order to determine the peak value of the impact.

MAXIMUM PERMITTED DECIBEL LEVELS

The sound pressure level resulting from any activity, whether open or enclosed, shall not exceed, at any point on or beyond any lot line, the maximum permitted decibel levels for the octave band as set forth in the following table.

MAXIMUM PERMITTED SOUND PRESSURE LEVEL
(in decibels)

Octave band (cycles per second)	
20 to 75	79
75 to 150	74
150 to 300	66
300 to 600	59
600 to 1,200	53
1,200 to 2,400	47
2,400 to 4,800	41
Above 4,800	39

SOURCE: Adapted from New York City Zoning Ordinance—1961

2. VIBRATION

"Steady state vibrations" are earth-borne oscillations that are continuous. Discrete pulses that occur more frequently than 100 times per minute shall be considered to be steady state vibrations.

"Impact vibrations" are earth-borne oscillations occurring in discrete pulses at or less than 100 pulses per minute.

A "frequency" is the number of oscillations per second of a vibration.

A "three-component measuring system" is a device for recording the intensity of any vibration in three mutually perpendicular directions.

MAXIMUM PERMITTED STEADY STATE VIBRATION DISPLACEMENT

No activity shall cause or create a steady state vibration at any point on any lot line, with a displacement in excess of the permitted steady state vibration displacement for the frequencies as set forth in the following table.

MAXIMUM PERMITTED IMPACT VIBRATION DISPLACEMENT

No activity shall cause or create an impact vibration, at any point on any lot line, with a displacement in excess of the permitted impact vibration displacement for the frequencies as set forth in the following table.

MAXIMUM PERMITTED STEADY STATE VIBRATION DISPLACEMENT
(in inches)

Frequency (cycles per second)	
10 and below	.0008
10–20	.0005
20–30	.0003
30–40	.0002
40–50	.0001
50–60	.0001
60 and over	.0001

MAXIMUM PERMITTED IMPACT VIBRATION DISPLACEMENT
(in inches)

Frequency (cycles per second)	M1
10 and below	.0016
10–20	.0010
20–30	.0006
30–40	.0004
40–50	.0002
50–60	.0002
60 and over	.0002

3. SMOKE, DUST, AND OTHER PARTICULATE MATTER

"Particulate matter" is any finely divided liquid or solid matter capable of being air- or gas-borne.

"Dust" is solid particulate matter capable of being air- or gas-borne.

"Process weight" is the total weight of all materials used in any process which discharges dust into the atmosphere. Such materials shall include solid fuels, but not liquid or gaseous fuels or combustion air.

"Combustion for indirect heating" is the burning of fuel in equipment, such as steam boilers, water or air heaters, stills, or brew kettles, where there is no contact between the products of combustion and the materials being heated.

"Standard Smoke Chart numbers" are the numbers on the Standard Smoke Chart indicating graduations of light-obscuring capacity of smoke.

"Smoke" is any visible emission into the open air from any source, except emissions of an uncontaminated water vapor.

A "smoke unit" is a measure of the quantity of smoke being discharged and is the number obtained by multiplying the smoke density in a Standard Smoke Chart number by the time of emission in minutes. For example, the emission of Standard Smoke Chart number 1 for one minute equals one smoke unit.

MAXIMUM PERMITTED EMISSION OF SMOKE

The density of emission of smoke during normal operations shall not exceed Standard Smoke Chart number 2, and the quantity of smoke shall not exceed a maximum of 10 smoke units per hour per stack.

MAXIMUM PERMITTED EMISSION OF DUST

a. RELATED TO COMBUSTION FOR INDIRECT HEATING

The emission into the atmosphere of dust related to combustion for indirect heating from any source shall not exceed the maximum number of pounds of dust per million British thermal units heat input per hour as set forth herein:

The maximum permitted emission shall be 0.50 pounds per minimum-size plants producing a heat input of 10 million or less British thermal units per hour and 0.15 for maximum-size plants producing a heat input of 10,000 million or more British thermal units per hour. All intermediate values shall be determined from a straight line plotted on log graph paper.

b. RELATED TO PROCESSES

The emission into the atmosphere of process dust or other particulate matter which is unrelated to combustion for indirect heating or incineration shall not exceed 0.50 pounds per hour for 100 pounds of process weight or 50 pounds per hour for 100,000 pounds of process weight. All intermediate values shall be determined from a straight line plotted on log graph paper.

4. ODOROUS MATTER

The emission of odorous matter in such quantities as to be readily detectable at any point along lot lines or to produce a public nuisance or hazard beyond lot lines is prohibited.

5. TOXIC OR NOXIOUS MATTER

"Toxic or noxious matter" is any solid, liquid, or gaseous matter, including but not limited to gases, vapors, dusts, fumes, and mists, containing properties which by chemical means are:

a. Inherently harmful and likely to destroy life or impair health, or

b. Capable of causing injury to the well-being of persons or damage to property.

REGULATION OF TOXIC OR NOXIOUS MATTER

The emission of such matter shall be so controlled that no concentration at or beyond lot lines shall be detrimental to or endanger the public health, safety, comfort, and other aspects of the general welfare, or cause damage or injury to property.

6. RADIATION HAZARDS

"Fireproof containers" shall include steel or concrete containers and shall not include lead or other low-melting metals or alloys, unless the lead or low-melting metal or alloys are completely encased in steel.

MAXIMUM PERMITTED QUANTITIES OF UNSEALED RADIOACTIVE MATERIAL

Unsealed radioactive materials shall not be manufactured, utilized, or stored (unless such materials are stored in a fireproof container at or below ground level) in excess of one million times the quantities set forth in Column 1 of the table in Section 38-2 of the Industrial Code Rule No. 38, relating to Radiation Protection of the New York State Department of Labor.

SOURCE: ADAPTED FROM New York City Zoning Ordinance—1961

MAXIMUM PERMITTED QUANTITIES OF FISSIONABLE MATERIALS

No one of the following fissionable materials shall be assembled at any one point, place, or work area on a zoning lot in a quantity equal to or in excess of the amount set forth herein:

Material	Quantity
Uranium-233	200 grams
Plutonium-239	200 grams
Uranium-235	350 grams

7. FIRE AND EXPLOSIVE HAZARDS

"Slow burning" materials are materials which will not ignite or actively support combustion during an exposure for 5 minutes to a temperature of 1,200°F. and which, therefore, do not constitute an active fuel.

MODERATE BURNING

"Moderate burning" materials are materials which in themselves burn moderately and may contain small quantities of a higher grade of combustibility.

FREE BURNING

"Free burning" materials are materials constituting an active fuel.

INTENSE BURNING

"Intense burning" materials are materials which by virtue of low ignition temperature, high rate of burning, and large heat evolution burn with great intensity.

FLAMMABLE OR EXPLOSIVE

"Flammable or explosive" materials are materials which produce flammable or explosive vapors or gases under ordinary weather temperature including liquids with an open cup flash point of less than 100°F.

The "open cup flash point" is the temperature at which a liquid sample produces sufficient vapor to flash but not ignite when in contact with a flame in a Tagliabue open cup tester.

ORIGINAL SEALED CONTAINERS

"Original sealed containers" are containers with a capacity of not more than 55 gallons.

CLASSIFICATIONS

Materials are divided into four classifications or ratings based on the degree of fire and explosive hazard. The rating of liquids is established by specified open cup flash points.

a. Class I includes slow burning to moderate burning materials. This shall include all liquids with an open cup flash point of 182°F. or more.

b. Class II includes free burning to intense burning materials. This shall include all liquids with an open cup flash point between 100°F. and 182°F.

c. Class III includes materials which produce flammable or explosive vapors or gases under ordinary weather temperature. This shall include all liquids with an open cup flash point of less than 100°F.

d. Class IV includes materials which decompose by detonation, including but not limited to all primary explosives.

REGULATIONS APPLYING TO CLASS I MATERIALS OR PRODUCTS

Class I materials or products may be stored, manufactured, or utilized in manufacturing processes or other production.

REGULATIONS APPLYING TO CLASS II AND CLASS III MATERIALS OR PRODUCTS

Class II materials or products may be stored, manufactured, or utilized in manufacturing processes or other production only in accordance with the following provisions:

1. Such storage, manufacture or utilization shall be carried on only within buildings or other structures which are completely enclosed by incombustible exterior walls;

2. Such buildings or other structures shall either be set back at least 40 feet from any lot lines, or in lieu thereof, all such buildings shall be protected throughout by an automatic fire extinguishing system.

8. HUMIDITY, HEAT, OR GLARE

Any activity producing excessive humidity in the form of steam or moist air, or producing intense heat or glare, shall be carried out within an enclosure and in such a manner as not to be perceptible at or beyond any lot line.

SUBDIVISION

Size and location requirements of individual industries vary widely. The areas of the Park, should be subdivided into parcels averaging ten acres each. This size parcel permits initial construction of 200-foot by 200-foot buildings, covering about ten percent of the area (40,000 square feet) with allowance for ultimate expansion of two to three times the initial construction. Depending on the specific needs of industries desiring to locate here, the parcels may be further subdivided or combined. Such modifications, if executed with care, will not adversely affect the overall master plan. A minimum parcel size of not less than two acres should be established.

The following site standards have been established and must be adhered to by all industries locating in the Industrial Park.

- Minimum land-to-building ratio of 4:1.
- Minimum building setback of 50 feet from main roads. Such setback areas must be appropriately landscaped.
- Minimum side lot setback of 50 feet. Such side lot areas may be devoted to paved parking.
- A 200-foot buffer strip is required by zoning regulations and must be maintained. It serves to protect the character of the park.
- All parking must be to the rear or side of buildings.
- All parking lots must be paved.
- No truck loading docks or doors are permitted on the front of buildings. Such docks or doors shall be located at sides or rears of buildings. This requirement also applies to rail siding facilities.

The following provisions relative to types of industry and architecture must be met.

- Plans of all proposed buildings must be submitted for approval prior to the start of construction.
- Building exteriors on all four sides shall be constructed of materials considered first class exterior finishes. In the case of expansion walls only, concrete blocks will be allowed as the finish of the exterior wall. Stucco is not considered a first class finish.
- All buildings must have a sprinkler system for fire protection.
- Outside storage must be appropriately screened on all sides.

CRITERIA FOR SIDETRACK SERVICE

The standards presented below relative to track layout, clearances, grade crossings and grade crossing protection, are based on requirements of the New Haven Railroad and the standards for highway grade crossings are based on the Commonwealth of Massachusetts requirements. These standards are as follows:

- No. 10 connections off the main track.
- No. 8 connections off switching tracks.
- Minimum track centers—13 feet.
- Maximum curvature—19 degrees (i.e. minimum radius—300 feet).
- Maximum grade—1.5 percent.

The railroad has in certain instances relaxed its requirements for curvature and grade. This should be discussed in detail prior to entering into any agreements.

INTERIOR ROADS

To insure smooth flow of traffic and easy access to individual plants by truck and trailers, minimum interior roads should have 100-foot right-of-way and 40-foot pavements. Any turn-arounds should have a minimum 60-foot radius.

COMMERCIAL SERVICES

Dependent upon size of the park, commercial facilities may be provided to serve the employees and visitors. Such facilities may include a branch bank, restaurant, stores of various types, small office building, and a motel.

UTILITIES

Adequate provisions for present and future requirements of water supply, sanitary sewers, storm sewers, electric and gas lines must be provided.

SOURCE: ARA Casebook No. 12, Area Redevelopment Agency, U. S. Dept of Commerce—1965

PHYSICAL PLANNING

Coordination in the Preparation of the Airport Layout Plan

If the airport is considered a suitable location for an airport industrial park, the industrial park's location and land requirements should be taken into account during the preparation of the airport layout plan.

Economy of layout and operations requires that the airport industrial park be one contiguous area. In order to achieve this contiguity, careful study of the other airport land requirements must be made. It is advisable to free the maximum amount of land for industrial development consistent with retaining full expansion capability for essential airport uses such as aircraft movement areas, passenger and freight terminals, aircraft parking aprons, navigation aids, automobile parking areas, and aircraft maintenance areas.

Location on the Airport

The land available for development for an airport industrial park should be located so as to take full advantage of its airport situation.

A location which often is a good choice for the industrial park is on the side of the runway opposite the terminal. This is particularly true at airports used by air carriers, where diversion of industrial traffic from the terminal traffic boulevard is advisable. Also, in this area, airport supporting services are not competing for land to use for activities such as terminal auto parking and commercial concessions. (See Fig. 2.)

A location in the vicinity of the general aviation area has the advantage of being close to the area where the aircraft will be stored and maintained. This location keeps ground taxi time at a minimum. (See Fig. 3.)

Taxiway Access

The taxiway system connecting the aircraft movement areas with the individual units of the industrial park should be decided upon in the early stages of planning. The access routes are a determining factor in the development pattern. Proper planning of these traffic lanes will conserve land valuable for other uses—uses more productive of revenue. Determination must be made at an early stage of the proportion of the tract to be served by taxiways to the aircraft movement area of the airport. The airport owner reserves the right to establish a user charge for the privilege of access through these taxiways to the common use landing area.

Opinion is divided as to the necessity of providing taxiway access to each lot because of the relatively large amount of land this requires. In most cases a compromise can be reached by providing access to those lots closest to the aircraft movement areas. A 50-ft service taxiway within a 150-ft right of way is generally sufficient for business aircraft. To minimize conflict with the street system, it is recommended that the taxiway right-of-way be located at the rear of the lots served and that the blocks be long and narrow to reduce the number of intersections between streets and taxiways. (See Fig. 2)

Two interesting variations for providing access to the aircraft movement areas are:

1. A taxiway provided to those lots directly abutting the aircraft movement areas. (See Fig. 4)

2. A taxiway into an aircraft parking apron which is surrounded by industrial lots. (See Fig. 5.)

In projects where no taxiway into the airport industrial park is provided, reasonable accessibility can be had by locating the industrial area in close proximity to the general aviation apron. (See Fig. 1.)

Railroad Access

If a rail service is available to the site, a 20-ft right-of-way is sufficient for a single track spur. Determination should be made in advance of the proportion of the lots to receive rail service. The rail service right-of-way should be located on the opposite end of the lots from the vehicular right-of-way.

Contact with the railroad serving the area should be made to assure construction that will meet the railroad's standards. In most cases, cost of the railroad spur will have to be paid for by the management of the industrial park, but there are instances when the railroad has paid the cost of the spur track. Usually, if the railroad spur is paid for by the railroad, title to the right-of-way will have to be passed to the railroad.

Street System

The widths of the right-of-way and the pavement depend on the anticipated traffic demand. Excessive pavement width, in addition to its high cost, has the tendency to encourage on-street parking which creates traffic problems. Minimum pavement widths and strict enforcement of on-street parking prohibitions are recommended.

Curbs and gutters rather than drainage ditches are recommended in order to keep the right-of-way width to a minimum; these will facilitate drainage of the site and also assure a cleaner, more attractive site.

Airport industrial parks surveyed show considerable variation in the widths of pavements and rights of way selected. With enforcement of on-street parking prohibitions and the use of curbs and gutters, the right-of-way should be a minimum of 40 ft for a 24-ft (2-lane) pavement. These dimensions are sufficient for secondary streets. Additional lanes are required in larger developments to add capacity to meet peak hour demands. For larger developments, on streets which will have a substantial number of industrial installations, a 60-ft right-of-way is recommended so that two additional lanes of traffic can be added when the demand warrants.

For primary feeder streets, a minimum of 48 ft of pavement within a 60-ft right-of-way is recommended.

Street intersections should have a curb radius of at least 40 ft to accommodate tractor-trailer vehicles.

It is recommended that the number of entrances into the industrial park be as few as possible to discourage use of the circulation system by traffic which is not directly related to the park. The entrances should be from a public thoroughfare with at least equivalent capacity and be separate from the airport entrance road in order to avoid traffic mix with those vehicles serving or visiting the airport.

Off-Street Parking and Loading

Off-Street Parking This should be provided for all vehicles which come into the airport industrial park. Parking spaces should be provided for employees, visitors, company vehicles and all trucks.

Employee Parking In airport industrial parks virtually all employees drive to work. Consideration should be given to overlapping requirements of successive shifts. Provision should be made for one parking space for every 1.3 employees on the combined shifts. Allowance of 300 square feet should be made for maneuvering and parking each vehicle.

Visitor Parking Parking space for visitors should be provided at the rate of one parking space for every 15 employees on the main shift.

Company Vehicles Provision of one parking space for each company vehicle is recommended.

Truck Loading Docks Loading docks should accommodate truck trailers and local pickup trucks. To accommodate truck trailers, berths should be 14 ft wide by 60 feet deep with an additional depth of 60 ft for maneuvering. For local pickup trucks, berths 10 ft wide by 20 ft deep are sufficient with a 20-ft additional depth for maneuvering. Loading docks should not be located on the street side of the building.

Entrance Driveways Entrance driveways for truck access should be offset from the truck parking ramp to prevent trucks from backing from the street into a loading dock. Curb radii of 25 ft minimum are recommended for truck access drives. Driveways for automobiles should have minimum curb radii of 15 ft.

SOURCE: *Planning the Airport Industrial Park, Federal Aviation Administration, Department of Transportaion, Washington, D.C., 1965.*

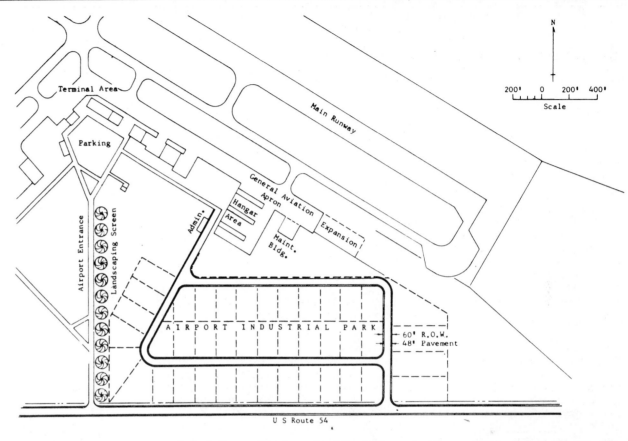

Fig. 1 Industrial park without taxiway access located adjacent to the general aviation area.

Building Setbacks

The airport industrial parks surveyed indicate a variety of setback standards which are generally related to the size of the lots in the particular developments. Aesthetic considerations are significant and no single set of standards will be applicable to all airport industrial parks. The main goal is to retain a feeling of open space in the development. In addition, setbacks may be related to the topography, rougher terrain generally requiring greater setbacks to minimize the amount of site work to the developer and to neighboring tenants. On most airports, the land developed for industry will be relatively flat, which would permit setbacks to be the minimum required for aesthetic considerations, free movement of fire apparatus around structures and meeting the requirements of local ordinances.

A 30-ft front setback from the property line, using the street rights-of-way previously discussed, will allow approximately 36 to 48 ft from the edge of the street pavement. This should be sufficient in projects where the smallest lots are ½ acre or less.

Side and rear setbacks of at least 25 ft are recommended for fire safety separation, aircraft clearance and architectural harmony.

A further measure that is recommended for assuring the parklike quality of the development is to limit the amount of each site permitted to be occupied by structures. Site coverage of 60 percent should be a maximum although 50 percent is preferable.

Site Layout

An airport industrial park should be at least 50 acres to justify the management effort required for planning, promotion, and continuing operation.

Block dimensions are determined in part by the depths established for groups of lots. Within the block it is then possible to adjust lot widths to suit the needs of individual tenants.

A variety of block sizes based on lot depths of 150 ft up to 500 ft allows for inclusion in the project of sites varying from about ⅓ of an acre to 10 acres. Minimum lot width should be about 100 ft in order to provide buildable sites for small industries.

It is recommended that blocks be as long as practicable to reduce the costs incurred in the construction of cross streets. Within the industrial park, there is little need for lot-to-lot circulation because most traffic is to and from destinations outside the industrial park.

Stage construction usually is a necessity because of flexibility and cost considerations. Sections that are opened for development should be improved so that lots offered for lease or sale are developed lots rather than raw land. Streets and utilities should be provided ready for use at the sites.

Utilities

Utilities that are essential are water, sanitary sewer system, electric power, gas distribution, fire hydrants and storm sewers adequate for drainage on and off site. Utilities are provided by the sponsor through his own resources, or by arrangement with the local utility companies, so that the tenant is only required to connect his installation to existing systems.

Utility easements may be provided in the rights-of-way reserved for streets or rail spurs. Underground utilities may be provided in aircraft taxiway rights-of-way.

Park Center

Reservation of an area for a park center should be made in larger projects. This center would include the offices of the park management and maintenance functions. Facilities for the common use of park tenants could be offered, such as restaurant, banking facilities, small shops for sale of sundries and, possibly, motel facilities for the accommodation of overnight guests. Other commercial services and personal conveniences could be provided at the discretion of the park management in the park center.

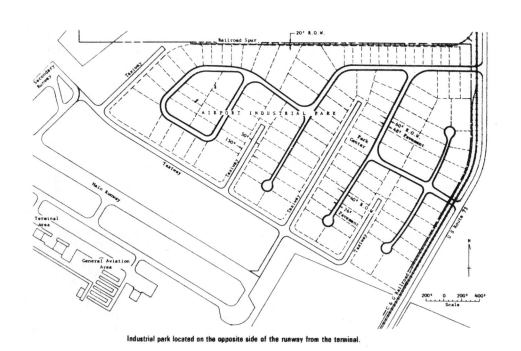

Industrial park located on the opposite side of the runway from the terminal.

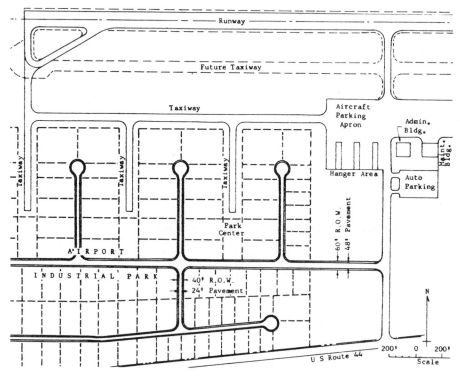

Industrial park located in the vicinity of the general aviation area.

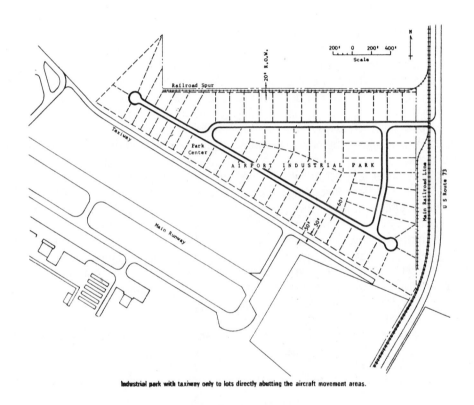

Industrial park with taxiway only to lots directly abutting the aircraft movement areas.

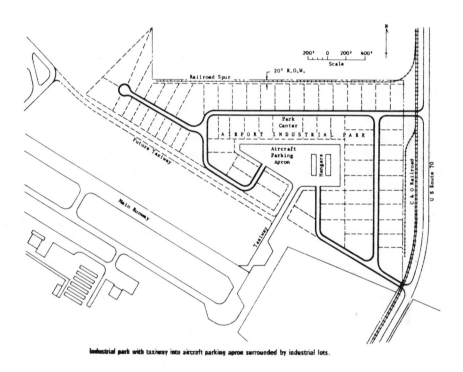

Industrial park with taxiway into aircraft parking apron surrounded by industrial lots.

PLANNING A PORT

The decision to build a port, and its location, generally will be determined by factors having to do with (1) its need and economic justification, (2) prospective volume of seaborne commerce, and (3) availability of inland communications by both land and water. These considerations must precede the technical studies and planning of the port and are briefly follows:

1. The need for a port may arise in a number of ways:

a. A naval base or a military terminal may be needed to supply inland army or air bases.

b. A seaport may be needed to serve a nearby inland city which has grown to the extent of requiring an outlet for its foreign commerce. The development of a port is usually, but not always, associated with the growth of the city of which it is a part.

c. The need for a privately owned commercial port will arise when it is required as a shipping terminal for the commodity or product which is being developed and for which shipping facilities are either not available or not economical to use. In recent years the development of sources of raw materials such as iron ore, bauxite, oil, and copper, in places such as Canada, South America, Africa, and the Far East, has resulted in the construction of new commercial ports in many parts of the world.

d. Generally, the building of a municipal port requires the expenditure of a large sum of money which in many cases will have to be raised by bond issues or by borrowing from banks, unless it is government-subsidized. Therefore, the project to be economically feasible will have to show an income above its operating costs, sufficient to cover the fixed charges. A privately owned commercial port does not require the same economic justification because it is usually secondary to the main project. For instance, once it has been decided to develop iron ore in a certain location where transportation by ore carrier is required, a shipping terminal is a necessity, and the only question that arises would be its most desirable and economical location within a relatively limited area.

2. Before embarking upon the construction of a municipal port, extensive surveys and studies will have to be made to determine the initial and future commerce anticipated from the tributary area where the freight rates will be less than to competing ports. Privately owned commercial ports, on the other hand, generally have their tonnages fairly well established over the life of the project, and the port can be designed to meet these requirements.

3. The availability of inland communications has an important bearing on the location of a port. Unless the tributary area is served with good highways, railroads, and waterways leading to inland cities, or the terrain and conditions are favorable for the development or enlargement of these arteries of communication, a port will not flourish. There are many excellent natural harbor locations which from an engineering standpoint would be ideal for the construction of a port, but which are poorly situated with respect to inland communications. A glance at the great harbors of the world will show that these are served by extensive arteries of communication.

Assuming that the above studies have been made and the general location of the harbor has been established, as well as its principal use and the type and tonnage of traffic to be handled, the next step, which in some cases will have been initiated during the above studies, will be to make preliminary studies and layouts of the port in preparation for making a complete site investigation to gather all the information which will be needed in making the final design of the port.

Information for this preliminary planning can usually be obtained from the following sources: the U.S. Department of Commerce through the United States Coast and Geodetic Survey, the Navy Department through the Hydrographic Office, and the United States Corps of Engineers, who have surveyed a great many of our navigable waters. Charts or information can be obtained from the U.S. Government Printing Office, Washington 25, D.C., or from the nearest U.S. District Engineer's Office. These charts are very valuable in the initial planning of the harbor as they give information on the depth of water, the general character of the bottom, and the range of tides. Meteorological data covering winds, temperature, and rainfall are published by the U.S. Weather Bureau, Washington 25, D.C. If there is no U.S. Weather Bureau near the site, this information may possibly be obtained from the nearest airport. The tremendous increase in air traffic in all parts of the world during recent years has opened up a new source of information on weather conditions. Tide and current tables are published by the U.S. Department of Commerce, Coast and Geodetic Survey, and can be obtained from the U.S. Government Printing Office, Washington 25, D.C.

If the port is to be located in some part of the country or world where none of the above information is available, it will be necessary to make a preliminary site reconnaissance. For the preliminary survey, aerial contour mapping may be a quick and convenient way of obtaining topography. Aerial photographs will be useful, especially in examining the coast and adjacent shore for suitable locations of the port, if this has not been already fixed by other strategic reasons. Aerial photography will often show up shoals, reefs, mouths of rivers, and other important details along the shore. Soundings can be taken quite quickly with a fathometer, giving a general picture of the depths of water, even though they may not be accurately located and referenced to fixed monuments and base lines. The depth and presence of rock, as well as the depth of over-burden, can be determined.

SOURCE: Design & Construction of Ports & Marine Structures, Alonzo Def. Quinn, McGraw-Hill Book Co., 1961.

With the general requirements of the port having been established and preliminary site information obtained, the next step will be to make preliminary studies of harbor and port layouts, which will usually be supplemented with approximate cost estimates based on certain assumptions which will have to be verified when making the site investigation. This preliminary planning will include the following:

Determining Best Location of Harbor. Unless the site is fixed by specific requirements of the port, several locations of the harbor will have to be studied, to determine the most protected location involving the least amount of dredging and with the most favorable bottom conditions as well as a shore area suitable for the development of the terminal facilities.

It may be impossible to fulfill all of the above conditions, as one or more may predominate to the exclusion of others. For instance, the shore terrain, both as to condition of ground and elevation or because of the location of a river, may make it mandatory to locate the harbor at a specific location. Also, existing communication facilities or their future construction may control the location, as it may be impossible because of impassable terrain to bring in a railroad or highway connection at a point where the water conditions may be most favorable for the location of the harbor. Since all ports, unless they are only marine transfer stations, must be fed by land or inland waterway communications, it follows that their terminus will have a major bearing on the location of the port. The adjacent shore may be low and swampy, requiring expensive foundations for terminal facilities. However, if the harbor or channel requires dredging, and the material is sand, it may be spoiled in the port area to make land at little additional cost. On the other hand the adjacent shore may be precipitous and high above the water, making it virtually impossible to find sufficient area for the onshore facilities, except for bulk material terminals, which utilize conveyors and pipelines for loading and unloading the ships, and where the terminal storage and other facilities may be located some distance inland from the harbor. Also, rocky cliffs along the shore may be excavated to provide rock for the construction of breakwaters and the area on shore thus formed may be used for the terminal facilities. Generally, the level of the port area onshore should be at or a little above the level of the docks. In a great many areas, where the range of tide is only 2 to 3 ft, the ideal level for the adjacent land would be 15 to 20 ft above low water. In areas where higher tides or tidal waves may occur, the adjacent land should be well above these levels. Rivers with large variations in river stage—some places as much as 50 ft—will need to have high ground above maximum flood stage for the location of the terminal facilities.

The depth of water, other things being equal, will be a major factor in the location of the port. A deep-water bay is, of course, ideal, but where the port must be located along the exposed coast, a study of the hydrographic charts will generally indicate areas where the water is deep close to shore and other areas where the required harbor depth would not be reached for several thousand feet offshore. The latter might require a prohibitive amount of dredging. However, the deep-water location may find the water a short distance offshore so deep that the construction

SOURCE: Design & Construction of Ports & Marine Structures. Alonzo Def. Quinn. McGraw-Hill Book Co, 1961.

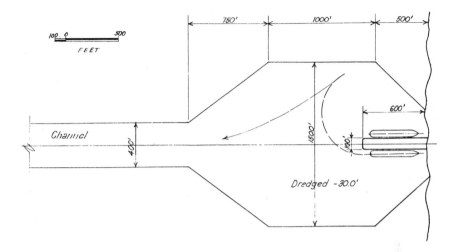

Fig. 1 A typical layout for a very small artificial harbor.

of protective breakwaters may be of prohibitive cost. In cases where bulk materials are to be shipped, the only solution may be an offshore anchorage with submarine pipeline, if liquids are to be handled, or a lightly constructed trestle or ropeway may be used to transport bulk solids such as bauxite, iron ore, and salt.

Bottom conditions are of utmost importance. The underwater excavation of rock is very expensive, and this should be avoided if at all possible, except in special cases where it may be combined with the construction of the dock.

However, the bottom may consist of a very deep bed of soft material, such as mud, silt, or clay, which, although it can be removed easily with suction dredges, would make the construction of breakwaters and docks very expensive, if not prohibitive, because of poor foundation conditions.

Size and Shape of Harbor and Turning Basin. The number and size of ships using a harbor will determine its size to a large extent, but existing site conditions will also have an important influence. Generally speaking, unless the harbor is a natural one, its size will be kept as small as will permit safe and reasonably comfortable operations to take place. The use of tugs to assist the maneuvering of the ships in docking may also influence the size of the harbor. The minimum harbor area is the space required for the docks plus the turning basin in front of them, and in some layouts, where the ship is turned by warping it around the end of the pier or turning dolphin, the harbor may be further restricted in area. For instance, a harbor with a single pier and turning basin and a long approach channel from the open sea, as shown in Fig. 1, requires the minimum amount of space and can accommodate two 500-ft ships. This artificial harbor is formed by dredging a channel through shallow water, protected by offshore reefs and islands, and enlarging the inshore end to provide the minimum area of harbor which will accommodate the shipping requirements specified for the project. In leaving its berth the ship must

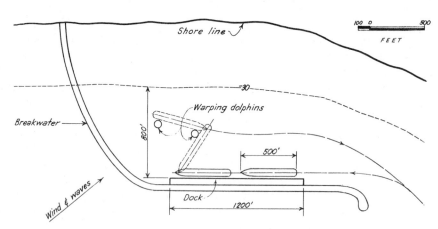

Fig. 2 An artificial harbor restricted in area because of deep water.

warp itself around the end of the pier so as not to have to back out through the long approach channel.

Figure 2 shows a second type of restricted harbor area. Here, the prevailing wind and waves are in one direction, and quiet water is obtained in the harbor by a curved breakwater parallel and connecting to the shore at one end. Because of the rapid increase in depth of water offshore, it is necessary to restrict the width of the harbor and to use a breakwater pier or quay type of construction accommodating two 600-ft vessels with turning dolphins.

One type of the less restricted harbor is long and narrow with an entrance at one end and an opening for leaving at the opposite end, as shown in Fig. 3. Berthing accommodations are for three 600-ft and one 400-ft ship along a 2,500-ft wharf.

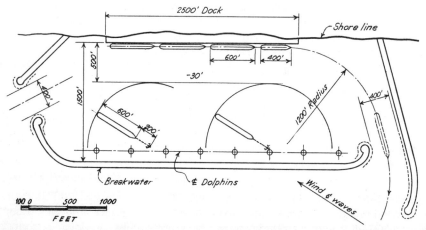

Fig. 3 An artificial harbor of medium size with separate openings for entering and leaving.

The 1,500-ft width of harbor is adequate for anchoring two vessels awaiting their turn to dock.

Another less restricted harbor is the more or less square type of harbor, protected with two breakwater arms, with one opening, several docks, and a large turning basin having an area sufficient to inscribe a turning circle with a radius equal to twice the length of the largest ship. This is the smallest radius a ship can comfortably turn on, under continuous headway, without the help of a tug. Figure 4 shows such a harbor. However, there is still little space to anchor vessels awaiting their turn to dock or to take refuge from storms, without interfering with traffic to and from the docks. The minimum size turning basin is one with a radius equal to the length of the ship, but this requires careful maneuvering of the ship to make the turn.

Figure 5 is one of the finest natural harbor locations in the Western Hemisphere, where ocean-going vessels can seek refuge in time of storm. Only recently has it been developed as a shipping terminal, and there is ample room for additional docks, their locations being more or less controlled by the condition of the bay bottom and the terrain on shore. The bay is approximately 6 miles in width and 6 miles long, and it is protected at its entrance by several islands, which are far enough apart to provide deep-water channel approaches, yet geographically so situated as to provide almost complete protection to the bay. The waves within the bay seldom exceed 3 ft in height, and these are generated by the wind blowing across the exposed surface of the water. It must be kept in mind that if a natural harbor is too large, it may permit the generation of local waves within the harbor, which will make berthing difficult, if not impossible, without breakwater protection or the formation of an inner harbor to protect the docks. For comfortable berthing the wave height should not exceed 2 ft, and winds should not exceed 10 to 15 miles per hour, although wave heights up to 4 ft have been allowed where bulk cargo is being handled and where the wind direction is such as to hold the ship off the dock. In general, winds and current are more bothersome in docking a vessel, when light, than are the relatively small harbor waves, and may necessitate the use of a tug.

Figure 6 shows an artificial harbor large enough to provide berthing space for 14 ocean-going vessels and a number of smaller coastal vessels, a turning basin, and additional space for the shallower draft vessels to anchor for protection from storms or to await their turn in docking. The area of the harbor covers about 1½ square miles. The relatively shallow water permits the construction of breakwater protection, which provides an area for anchoring coastal vessels and, supplemented by dredging a limited area within the harbor, enables the port to be used by ocean-going vessels as well. It is important to keep in mind that these large ships can usually ride out a storm which would normally require the smaller coastal vessels to seek shelter, and, therefore, it is not so important to provide a deep-water anchorage for them within the harbor, as for the smaller vessels.

The above are typical examples of harbor layouts, but each harbor must be studied in light of existing conditions and specific requirements for that particular project.

SOURCE: Design & Construction of Ports & Marine Structures. Alonzo Def. Quinn. McGraw-Hill Book Co., 1961.

Type, Location, and Height of Breakwaters. Breakwaters are required for the protection of artificial and semi-natural harbors. Their location and extent will depend upon the direction of the maximum waves, the configuration of the shore line, and the minimum size of harbor required for the anticipated traffic in the port. They may consist of two "arms" out from the shore, plus a single breakwater, more or less parallel to the shore, thereby providing two openings to the harbor, as shown in Fig. 3, or one opening when connected to one of the arms, usually resulting in a curved alignment, as indicated in Fig. 2; or the harbor may be protected with a single arm out from shore; or it may be protected by two arms converging near their outshore ends and overlapping to form a protected entrance to the harbor, such as shown in Fig. 4. The selection of the most suitable arrangement will depend principally upon the direction of the maximum waves, and its effectiveness in quieting the harbor may be checked by model tests.

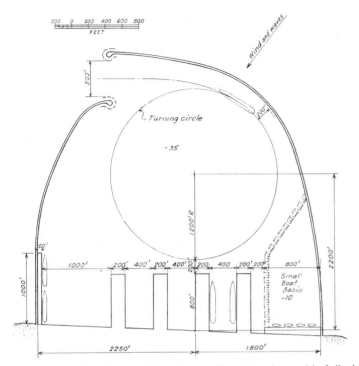

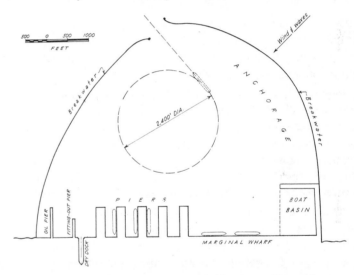

Fig. 6 A typical layout for a very large artificial harbor with anchorage area.

The Pier or wharf provides the meeting place and the transshipment platform at which cargo and passengers are exchanged between land and water transportation carriers. In the field of ocean transportation, a pier or wharf is, at one and the same time, a terminal point for rail, highway, pipeline, and inland waterway carriers, and a terminal point for ocean ships. Upon the proper design and workable layout of piers and wharves, depends in a large measure the degree of efficiency in the handling of cargo, directly effecting the all important turn-around time and resultant expenses of ships in ports. Great stress is currently being placed upon all factors affecting the turn-around time of ships with primary emphasis on the han-

Fig. 4 A typical layout for a medium-size artificial harbor with full-size turning basin.

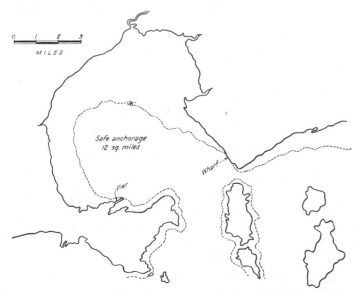

Fig. 5 A natural harbor with a very large anchorage area.

SOURCE: Design & Construction of Ports & Marine Structures. Alonzo Def. Quinn. McGraw-Hill Book Co. 1961.

dling of cargo to and from the berthing facility (the pier or wharf) and the ship's hold.

PHYSICAL TYPES AND USE CLASSIFICATIONS

There are two basic ship berthing facilities (other than the specialized facilities for tanker vessels), namely, the so-called finger pier and the marginal wharf (or quay). From a construction point of view, there are three general types of piers —the open type, the solid-fill type, and a combination of open and solid. Wharves (other than solid-fill quays) are normally open-type structures, often described as marginal wharves.

A pier is a structure extending outward at an angle from the shore into navigable waters normally permitting the berthing of vessels on both sides along its entire length.

A wharf is a structure extending parallel with the shore line, connected to the shore at more than one point (usually with a continuous connection), and providing, in most cases, berthing at the outshore face of the structure only.

A number of piers and/or wharves physically grouped together and operated as a unit, usually with upland storage warehouses and open storage space, often fenced-in, is sometimes referred to as a marine terminal, although the term is often applied to a single pier or wharf.

Piers and wharves are generally separately provided for the following classifications of cargo:

1. *General Cargo*—The conventional break-bulk (loose package) facility provided with a transit shed or sheds for the preassembly of outbound cargo and the orderly disposition of inbound cargo via rail, highway, and inland waterway carriers to interior points. Aprons, representing the paved surface of the pier or wharf-substructure between the face of the transit shed and the water face or edge of the pier or wharf, are provided for "landing" the cargo alongside the vessel. Banana cargoes are often handled at conventional general cargo terminals as the specialized shoreside gantry crane/conveyor equipment or the portable sideport conveyor equipment for banana cargoes can be relocated or removed for the handling of a general cargo vessel and its cargo. General cargo can also be handled at grain berths when the grain facilities are so arranged that storage silos or bins are inshore from the berthing facility apron and only the grain conveyor galleries are located upon the apron. In certain cases (where location permits), general cargo facilities are utilized interchangeably for bulk petroleum and other liquid transshipment purposes, through pipelines carried beneath the surface of the pier or wharf. Breakbulk general cargo facilities are also being utilized for containerized general cargo including so-called van (highway trailer size) containers, the latter where apron widths and vehicle approaches to and over the berth apron are adequate.

2. *Grain*—Usually equipped with shipside enclosed galleries and conveyors to carry the grain to and from storage bins, so arranged as to permit discharge by gravity through chutes to the ship's hold. In the discharge of grain from a vessel, pneumatic suckers and vertical conveyors known as a "marine legs" are used. Terminal facilities include car and truck unloading and weighing facilities.

3. *Ore and Coal Terminals*—Usually equipped with "Hulett" unloaders, unloading bridges and unloading towers and often conveyor belts to transfer the material from the unloader inshore to rail cars or stockpiles. In the ship loading operation, railroad cars are usually handled by a mechanical dumping device which inverts the car and dumps the material into a hopper. The material then flows by gravity through chutes into the hold of the vessel. Ground storage or stockpiles for these materials are often provided in the vicinity of the terminal where land is available.

4. *Oil Terminals*—Usually consisting of berthing facilities, pipelines to the shore, and shoreside tank storage facilities (tank farms). Special piers for petroleum products usually consist of mooring and bresting dolphins connected by narrow trestles which support the pipelines. The mooring, bresting, and impact forces of the ship are absorbed by the dolphins instead of the whole pier structure. The pier is provided with a loading deck which supports the pipe valves and the hose handling derricks. Generally, tankers and oil barges are equipped with adequate pumping equipment to discharge their own cargoes. The handling of petroleum and highly inflammable liquids requires that oil terminals be located at considerable distances from other commercial terminals and usually on the seaward side. Petroleum plants are subject to state and local regulations due to fire and explosive hazards.

5. *Container Terminals (so-called)*—Until recently, other than certain specialized terminals for both roll-on roll-off and lift-on lift-off of railroad cars, most in-port handling of "containers" (up to and including the van size), off and on ocean vessels was performed at established general cargo facilities, either with shore-based or ship-mounted cranes. Recently, however, major specialized terminals have been designed and constructed in connection with the ocean transportation of containers.

SOURCE: Port Design and Construction, *American Association of Port Authorities, Washington, D.C., 1964.*

It is now proposed to offer and to discuss very briefly some general cargo terminal design criteria concerning principal characteristics. Such criteria relate to general cargo public marine terminals generally, without regard to trade route requirements or specialized steamship services. Also, indicated below are averages of certain critical dimensions and transit shed areas per berth, based upon this listing:

1. BERTH LENGTHS

Wharves & Piers	613 ft.
Wharves only	606 ft.
Piers only	604 ft.

2. APRON WIDTH*

	No R.R. Tracks	1 R.R. Track	2 R.R. Tracks
Wharves & Piers	21 ft.	26.25 ft.	39.42 ft.
Wharves only	31 ft.	35 ft.	42.05 ft.
Piers only	16 ft.	25 ft.	33.5 ft.

*Includes number with gantry crane installations.

3. CLEAR PILING HEIGHT—TRANSIT SHEDS ....20 ft.
(EXCLUDING SHEDS WITH ARCHED ROOF CONSTRUCTION)

4. GROSS TRANSIT SHED SPACE—per berth

Wharves & Piers	84,520 sq. ft.
Wharves only	85,675 sq. ft
Piers only	83,222 sq. ft.

Of the above, the two most controversial "dimensions" are the width of the berth apron, and the total square footage (area) of transit shed space provided for each ship's berth.

The width of the berth apron is, of course, directly affected by the number of railroad tracks placed upon the apron as well as by any requirement for apron gantry cranes. But even without the provision of such trackage, the opinions of port operators and designers are at considerable variance.

The area of transit shed space provided per ship's berth at public general cargo terminals is largely a function of two factors, 1) the size of the port in which the facility is located, and 2)—and undoubtedly a reflection of the previous factor—the kind of trade engaged in by the vessels using the facility. At the larger ports serving a major metropolitan area as a part of its hinterland, the resultant demands of commerce and trade will generate shipload movements and frequent sailings, requiring greatly increased transit shed space per berth. Consequently, with the larger vessels in today's merchant marine, the allowances of shed space has trended upward as high as 120,000 square feet per berth at certain major ports. Conversely, the inevitable pattern of general cargo movement in small ports is small lots and infrequent traffic. As a result, the general pattern at smaller ports has been the provision of shed space in the amounts of from 35,000 to 50,000 square feet per berth, although most recent construction in such ports indicates this allowance is increasing sharply.

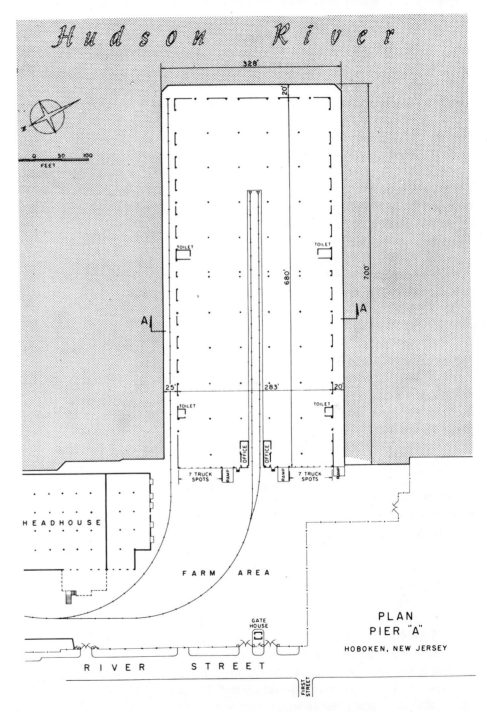

SOURCE: Port Design and Construction. *American Association of Port Authorities, Washington, D.C., 1964.*

Suggested Principal Dimensioning for General Cargo Public Marine Terminal Facilities

(Based upon requirements for C-4 class vessels)

1. DESIGN DEPTHS OF BERTHS—36 ft. below mean low water. Based upon draft loaded of 32'9½" of the C4-S-A4 "large cargo" class vessel, with allowance for lower low tides and two feet bottom clearance. Later design of this class, the C4-S-1A "Mariner" draws only 31'6" loaded, although this vessel is larger dimensionally and in bale cubic. It is considered unlikely that conventional general cargo vessels of either larger size or draft will be developed, certainly not as a class.

2. BERTH LENGTH—Unit—600 ft. equivalents.

3. PIER LENGTH—Optimum 700 ft. overall—based upon the 572'-0" length of the latest C4 class vessel with maximum allowance for proper ship mooring. Two berths in line—1200 ft. overall. No specific allowance for lighter or barge berthing.

4. MARGINAL WHARF LENGTH—Overall

    a. One berth—700 ft.

    b. Multiple berths—number of berths times 600 ft.

    c. Add additional length required for approach structure for wharf apron railroad tracks, if any.

5. APRON WIDTH—Piers & Wharves

    a. Basic width—30 ft.

    b. No additional width allowance for one apron railroad track; add 8'6" for two apron tracks; add 22'0" for three apron tracks.

    c. For half portal apron gantry crane add 5 ft. to above widths; for full portal crane add 10 ft.

    d. *Example:* Minimum total width for apron with two railroad tracks and full portal gantry crane—48'6".

        Note: At 13½ ft. center to center spacing of railroad tracks, a minimum width of 10 ft. clear for truck or fire lane is provided under conditions of all tracks occupied and holding cars of maximum width.

6. WHARF WIDTH—Overall platform or deck. Includes apron, shed and rear platform widths, truck (and rail) loading space and feeder roadway. Based upon 30 ft. apron and 165 ft wide shed—290 ft. overall. Increase as required by wider apron and shed.

7. PIER WIDTH—Finger, single transit shed. Width of berthing aprons plus width of transit shed (as determined below).

        Note: No consideration is here given to any requirement for arbitrary increase in pier width to provide lay berth at face of pier.

8. TRANSIT SHED—Area and dimensions.

    a. *Area*—optimum of 90,000 sq. ft. per berth (exclusive of areas for interior railroad track wells or interior surface tracks). Includes 40% allowance for aisles and other non-storage areas. Based upon bale cubic (760,000) of the C4-class vessel and 12 ft. piling height.

    b. *Size* for pier, finger, single shed.

        (1) *Length*—length of pier minus provision for apron on face (outshore end) of pier (minimum 20 ft. for lay berth, 30 ft. for working berth).

        (2) *Width*—as determined by requirement to provide 90,000 sq. ft. of gross shed space per berth (exclusive of interior track areas), divided by shed length.

    c. *Size*—for wharf.

        (1) *Length*—550 ft.—provides covered space opposite entire length of maximum size vessel. Provides space for end access roadway to apron and shed floor.

        (2) Width—165 ft. (minimum).

9. PLATFORM WIDTH, rear of wharf shed—20 ft. Should be covered with a full width canopy.

10. CLEAR SHED PILING HEIGHT—20 ft. (underside of roof framing).

11. WALL COLUMNS, longitudinal spacing—20/22 ft. minimum bay.

12. INTERIOR COLUMNS, both directions—minimum 40 ft; 60 ft. to 70 ft. is good practice.

13. DOOR OPENINGS—In each alternate bay, on both sides of shed. Minimum opening 18 ft. wide, 15 ft. high on both apron and platform sides.

14. DOUBLE PIERS—Berth and shed dimensions established per foregoing. Distance between edges of rear platforms (depressed well for railroad tracks and truck loading spots)—commercial optimum 132 ft., Army requirement 142 ft.

15. PIER OR WHARF ELEVATION—At an ordinary general cargo ship berth, the surface of the pier or wharf should be at least 6 feet above the highwater level at spring tides.

16. PIER SLIPS—The width of a slip, i.e., the clear distance between piers, depends upon the lengths of piers, the beam of ships normally using the piers, and whether lighters and tugboats are required. If two adjacent piers are each long enough to accommodate only one ship on a side and there is no lighterage of barging anticipated, the width of the slip need only be equal to the combined beam of the vessels in addition to the space necessary for the maneuvering of the tugboats. Assuming the beam of the vessels to be 70 feet and a length of 100 feet for tugboats, the minimum width of the slip between piers should be about 300 ft. Additional width must be allowed for the handling of larger ships, freight or bunkering lighters and, if the piers are long enough to permit docking ships end to end, space must be allowed between vessels tied up at the outer end of the slip to permit a ship to be moved into or out of the berths at the inner end of the slip.

On the following pages are a tabulation of recent marine terminal developments, giving their principal dimensions and features, and a number of photographs showing the physical layout of some modern terminals as well as interior views of certain of the transit sheds.

SOURCE: Port Design and Construction, *American Association of Port Authorities, Washington, D.C., 1964.*

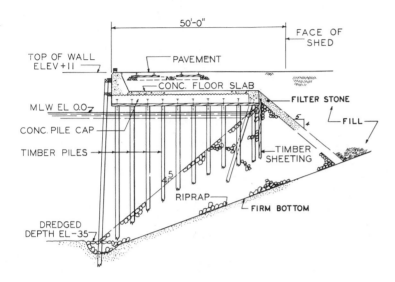

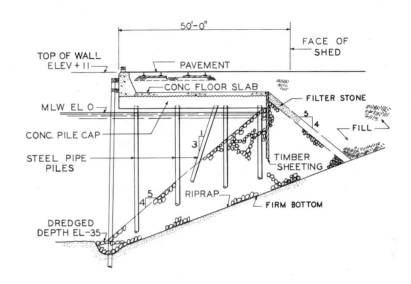

Open-type wharf construction. Concrete relieving platform on timber piles.

Open-type wharf construction. Concrete relieving platform on steel pipe piles.

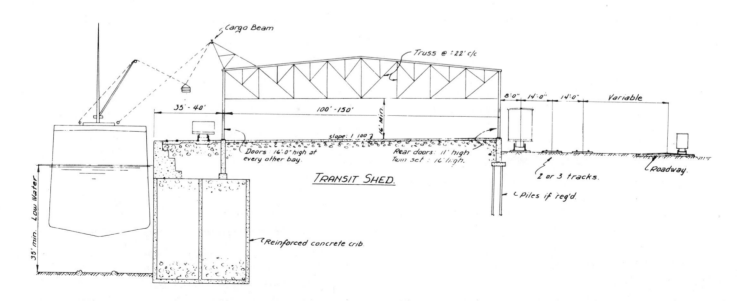

Wharf with transit shed—solid fill-type wharf construction. Typical cross-section.

SOURCE: Port Design and Construction. American Association of Port Authorities, Washington, D.C., 1964.

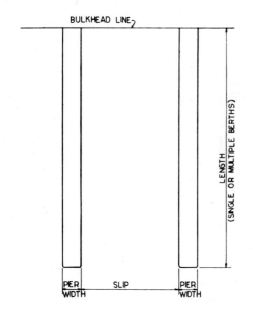

RIGHT ANGLE PIER

ACUTE ANGLE PIER

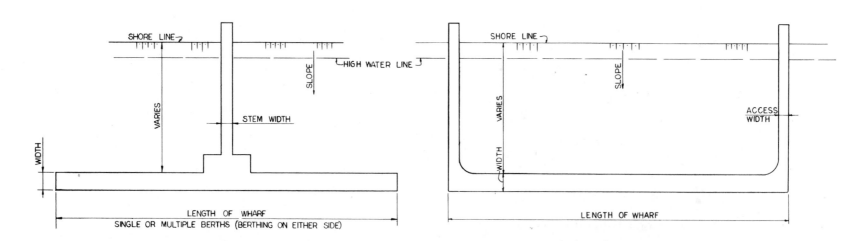

T-TYPE MARGINAL WHARF

U-TYPE MARGINAL WHARF

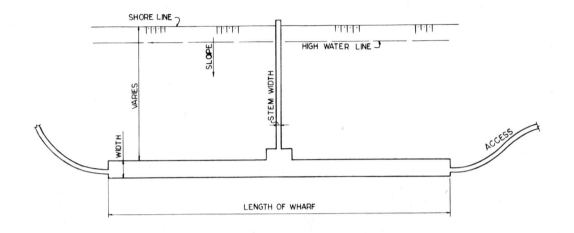

MARGINAL WHARF
PARALLEL TO BANK

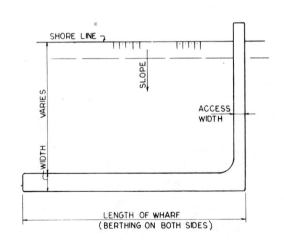

L-TYPE MARGINAL WHARF

NOTE: THIS DEFINITIVE DRAWING IS FOR REFERENCE AND PLANNING PURPOSES ONLY.

TYPICAL PIER CONSTRUCTION

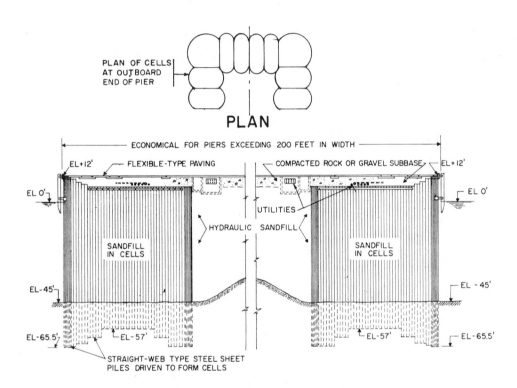

PLAN OF CELLS AT OUTBOARD END OF PIER

PLAN

ECONOMICAL FOR PIERS EXCEEDING 200 FEET IN WIDTH

EL+12'
FLEXIBLE-TYPE PAVING
COMPACTED ROCK OR GRAVEL SUBBASE
EL+12'

EL 0'
EL 0'

UTILITIES

HYDRAULIC SANDFILL

SANDFILL IN CELLS
SANDFILL IN CELLS

EL-45'
EL -45'

EL-65.5'
EL-57'
EL-57'
EL-65.5'

STRAIGHT-WEB TYPE STEEL SHEET PILES DRIVEN TO FORM CELLS

TRANSVERSE SECTION
SOLID PIER - CELLULAR CONSTRUCTION

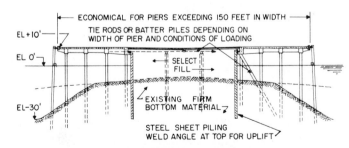

ECONOMICAL FOR PIERS EXCEEDING 150 FEET IN WIDTH

EL+10'
TIE RODS OR BATTER PILES DEPENDING ON WIDTH OF PIER AND CONDITIONS OF LOADING

EL 0'

SELECT FILL

EXISTING FIRM BOTTOM MATERIAL

EL-30'

STEEL SHEET PILING WELD ANGLE AT TOP FOR UPLIFT

TRANSVERSE SECTION
COMBINATION PIER- OPEN MARGIN AND FILLED CENTER

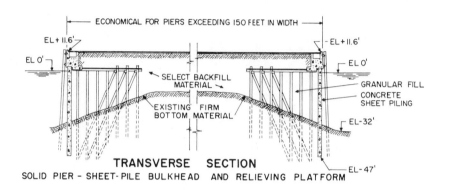

ECONOMICAL FOR PIERS EXCEEDING 150 FEET IN WIDTH

EL+11.6'
EL+11.6'

EL 0'
EL 0'

SELECT BACKFILL MATERIAL
GRANULAR FILL
CONCRETE SHEET PILING

EXISTING FIRM BOTTOM MATERIAL

EL-32'

EL-47'

TRANSVERSE SECTION
SOLID PIER - SHEET-PILE BULKHEAD AND RELIEVING PLATFORM

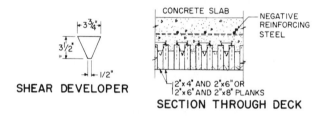

$3\frac{3}{4}$"

$3\frac{1}{2}$"

1/2"

SHEAR DEVELOPER

CONCRETE SLAB
NEGATIVE REINFORCING STEEL

2"x 4" AND 2"x 6" OR 2"x 6" AND 2"x 8" PLANKS

SECTION THROUGH DECK

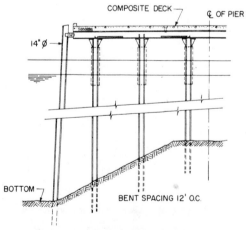

COMPOSITE DECK
ℂ OF PIER

14" ∅

BOTTOM

BENT SPACING 12' O.C.

HALF TRANSVERSE SECTION
STEEL FRAME - COMPOSITE DECK

TYPICAL OPEN PIER CONSTRUCTION

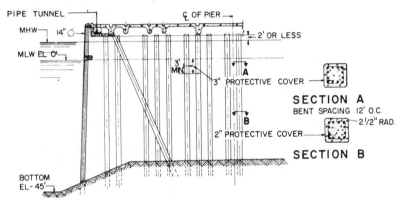

HALF TRANSVERSE SECTION
CONCRETE PIER - PRECAST PILES

SECTION A
BENT SPACING 12' O.C.

SECTION B

PIPE TUNNEL

MHW   14" ⌀

MLW EL 0'

2' OR LESS

3' MIN.

3" PROTECTIVE COVER

2" PROTECTIVE COVER

2½" RAD.

BOTTOM EL- 45'

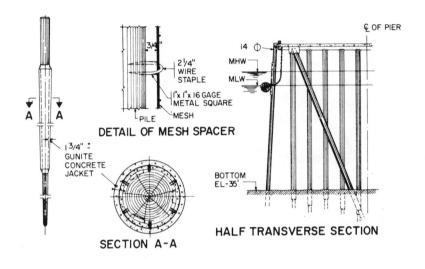

DETAIL OF MESH SPACER

¾"

2¼" WIRE STAPLE

1"x 1"x 16 GAGE METAL SQUARE MESH

PILE

A   A

1¾" ± GUNITE CONCRETE JACKET

SECTION A-A

HALF TRANSVERSE SECTION

14 ⌀

MHW

MLW

BOTTOM EL-35'

& OF PIER

PIER - COMPOSITE CONSTRUCTION

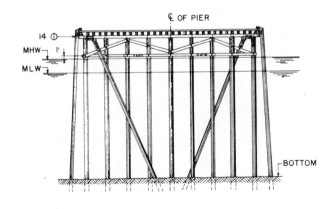

PIER - TIMBER CONSTRUCTION

& OF PIER

14 ⌀

MHW

MLW

1"

BOTTOM

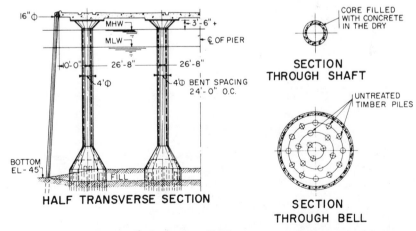

HALF TRANSVERSE SECTION

16" ⌀

MHW

MLW

3'-6" +

& OF PIER

10'-0"

26'-8"

26'-8"

4' ⌀

4' ⌀ BENT SPACING 24'-0" O.C.

BOTTOM EL- 45'

FILL

SECTION THROUGH SHAFT

CORE FILLED WITH CONCRETE IN THE DRY

SECTION THROUGH BELL

UNTREATED TIMBER PILES

CONCRETE PIER - PRECAST CYLINDERS AND BELLS

SOURCE: Dept. of the Navy, Washington, D.C.

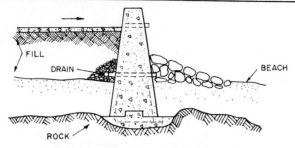

VERTICAL-FACE SEAWALL

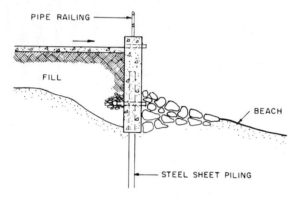

VERTICAL-FACE SEAWALL

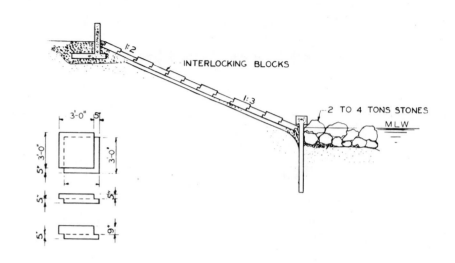

INTERLOCKING CONCRETE BLOCK REVETMENT

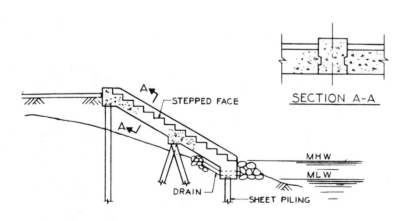

STEPPED FACE SEAWALL

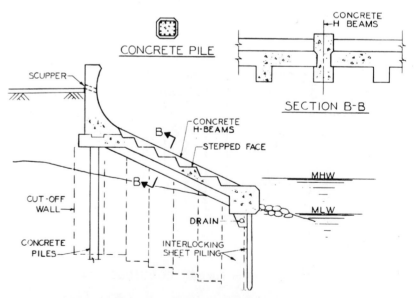

CONCRETE COMBINATION STEPPED AND CURVED-FACE SEAWALL

SOURCE: Dept. of the Navy, Washington, D.C.

ANGLES AND RADII TO BE
DETERMINED BY SITE CONDITIONS

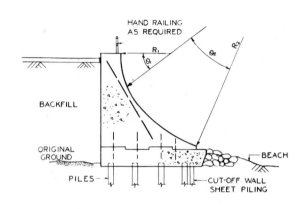

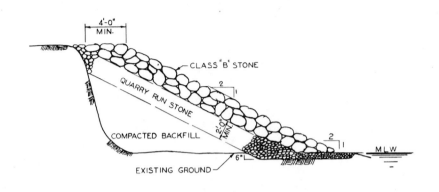

CURVED FACE SEAWALL

REVETMENT

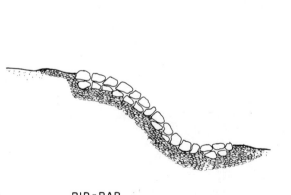

RIP-RAP

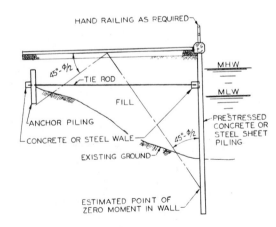

WHERE ∅ = ANGLE OF INTERNAL FRICTION

ANCHORED BULKHEAD

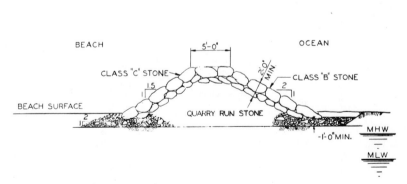

RUBBLE MOUND SEAWALL

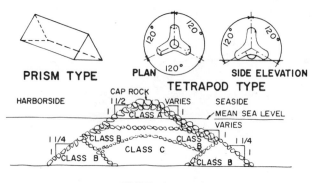

PRISM TYPE

PLAN

SIDE ELEVATION

TETRAPOD TYPE

TYPE A

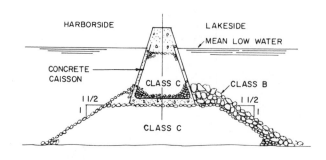

TYPE B

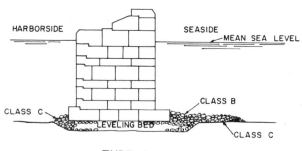

TYPE C

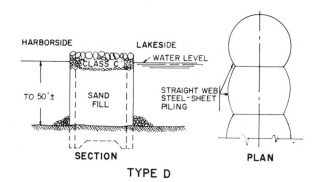

TYPE D

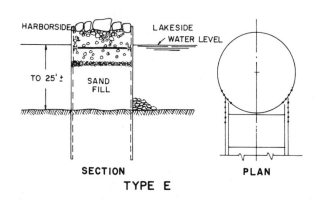

SECTION

PLAN

TYPE E

TYPE F

SOURCE: Dept. of the Navy, Washington, D.C.

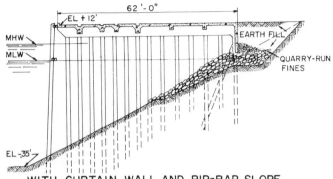

WITH CURTAIN WALL AND RIP-RAP SLOPE

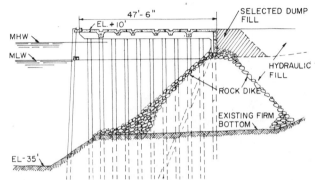

WITH CURTAIN WALL AND ROCK DIKE

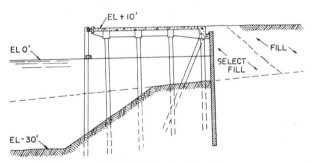

WITHOUT RELIEVING PLATFORM

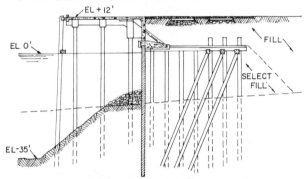

WITH RELIEVING PLATFORM

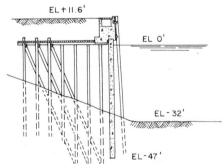

WITH SHEET-PILE BULKHEAD AND
RELIEVING PLATFORM

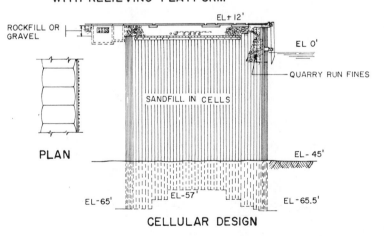

PLAN

CELLULAR DESIGN

NOTE: THIS DEFINITIVE DRAWING IS FOR REFERENCE AND PLANNING PURPOSES ONLY.

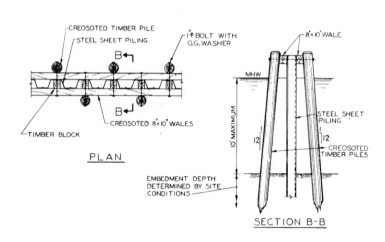

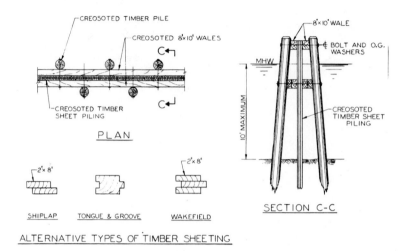

PLAN

SECTION B-B

STEEL SHEET PILE GROIN

ALTERNATIVE TYPES OF TIMBER SHEETING

SHIPLAP   TONGUE & GROOVE   WAKEFIELD

SECTION C-C

TIMBER GROIN

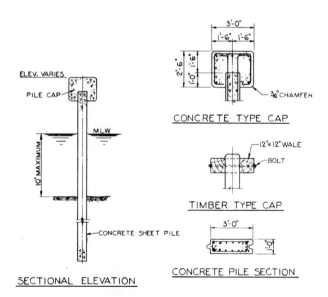

SECTIONAL ELEVATION

CONCRETE TYPE CAP

TIMBER TYPE CAP

CONCRETE PILE SECTION

PRESTRESSED CONCRETE SHEET PILE GROIN

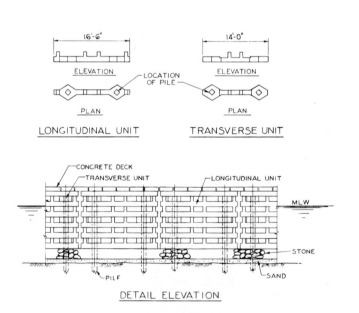

ELEVATION   ELEVATION

LOCATION OF PILE

PLAN   PLAN

LONGITUDINAL UNIT   TRANSVERSE UNIT

DETAIL ELEVATION

PRECAST CONCRETE CRIB
PERMEABLE GROIN (SYDNEY M. WOOD DESIGN)

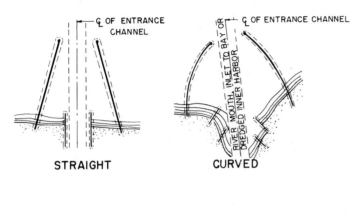

STRAIGHT   CURVED

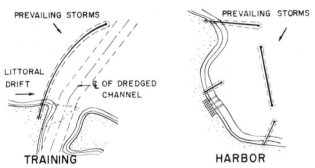

TRAINING   HARBOR

JETTY ALIGNMENT

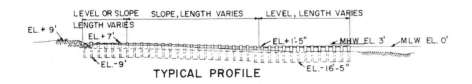

TYPICAL PROFILE

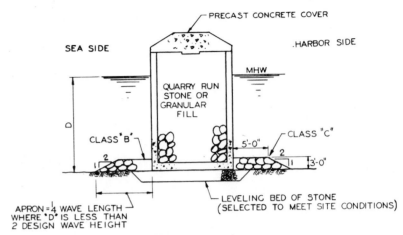

CROSS SECTION

PRECAST CONCRETE JETTY

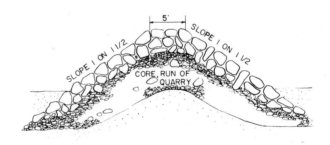

CROSS SECTION

RUBBLE MOUND JETTY OR GROIN

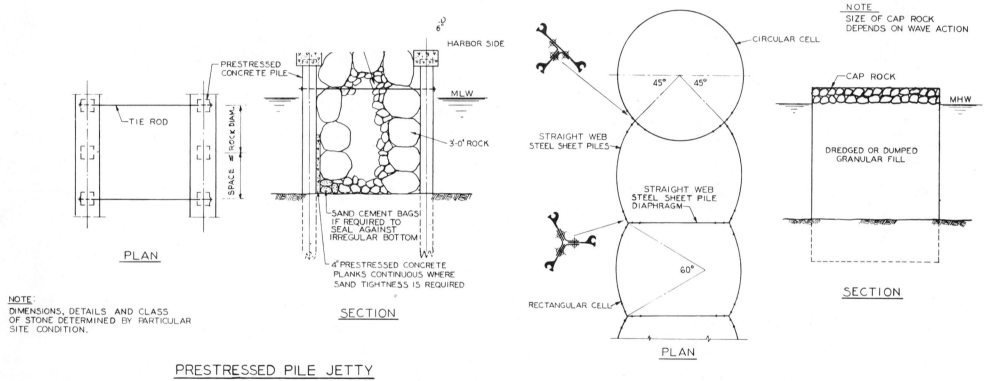

PLAN

NOTE:
DIMENSIONS, DETAILS AND CLASS OF STONE DETERMINED BY PARTICULAR SITE CONDITION.

PRESTRESSED CONCRETE PILE

TIE ROD

SPACE ≤ ROCK DIAM.

HARBOR SIDE

MLW

3'-0" ROCK

SAND CEMENT BAGS IF REQUIRED TO SEAL AGAINST IRREGULAR BOTTOM

4" PRESTRESSED CONCRETE PLANKS CONTINUOUS WHERE SAND TIGHTNESS IS REQUIRED

SECTION

PRESTRESSED PILE JETTY

CIRCULAR CELL

STRAIGHT WEB STEEL SHEET PILES

STRAIGHT WEB STEEL SHEET PILE DIAPHRAGM

RECTANGULAR CELL

45° 45°

60°

PLAN

CELLULAR JETTY

NOTE
SIZE OF CAP ROCK DEPENDS ON WAVE ACTION

CAP ROCK

MHW

DREDGED OR DUMPED GRANULAR FILL

SECTION

NEIGHBORHOOD UNIT AND
NEW TOWN CONCEPTS

Three different descriptions of land use patterns have been devised to describe resulting spatial organization of urban areas. Eech theory sets forth certain general tendencies of arrangement which allegedly will prevail unless modified by topographical or other disturbing influences. These descriptions indicate that urban land uses are distributed within concentric zones, sectors, or multiple nuclei. A condensed description of each theory follows. 6

Concentric zone. The most influential advocate of the concentric zone theory was Ernest W. Burgess, whose theory was cited by Fisher and Fisher and others writing in the area of community organization. Burgess assumed that the modern American city would take the form of five concentric urban zones. In outline, the zones are:

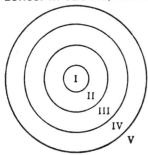

Concentric Zone Description
(Supposedly applicable to all cities.)
Zones
I. The Central Business District.

II. Zone in Transition.

III. Zone of Independent Workingmen's Homes.

IV. Zone of Better Residences.

V. The Commuters' Zone.

[a] Adapted from E. W. Burgess, "Urban Areas," Chicago: An Experiment in Social Science Research, ed. by T. V. Smith and L. D. White (Chicago: University of Chicago Press, 1929), p. 115.

Sector: This theory holds that residential land uses tend to be arranged in sectors or wedges radiating from the center of a city. While each community has a different pattern, rent areas tend to conform to a pattern of sectors rather than to concentric circles.

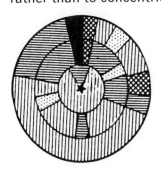

Sector Description
(Arrangement of sectors differs from city to city.)
Theoretical Pattern of Monthly Rent Distribution

less than $10

$10-$19.99

$20-$29.99

$30-$49.99

$50 and over

[b] Theoretical pattern of rent distribution in Indianapolis. From The Structure and Growth of Residential Neighborhoods in American Cities (Washington, D. C.: Federal Housing Adm), p. 77.

SOURCE: Eugene J. Kelley Shopping Centers, The ENO Foundation for Highway Traffic Control, Saugatuck, Conn.—1956

Multiple Nuclei. Harris and Ullman combine the concentric zone and sector theories to explain the arrangement of land uses.

In many cities the land use pattern is built not around a single center but around several discrete nuclei. In some cities these nuclei have existed from the very origins of the city; in others they have developed as the growth of the city stimulated migration and specialization. . . . The initial nucleus of the city stimulated may be the retail district in a central place city, the port or rail facilities in a breakoff city, or the factory, mine, or beach in a specialized function city.

The rise of separate nuclei and differentiated districts reflects a combination of the following four factors:

1. Certain activities require specialized facilities.

2. Certain like activities group together because they profit from cohesion.

3. Certain unlike activities are detrimental to each other.

4. Certain activities are unable to afford the rents of the most desirable sites.

The number of nuclei which result from historical development and the operation of localization forces vary greatly from city to city. The larger the city, the more numerous and specialized are the nuclei.

Multiple-Nuclei Description
(Arrangement of nuclei differs from city to city.)

District
1. Central Business District.
2. Wholesale Light Manufacturing.
3. Low-Class Residential.
4. Medium-Class Residential.
5. High-Class Residential.
6. Heavy Manufacturing.
7. Outlying Business District.
8. Residential Suburb.
9. Industrial Suburb.

[c] From C. D. Harris and E. L. Ullman, "The Nature of Cities," The Annals of the American Academy of Political and Social Science, Vol. 242 (November 1945), p. 13.

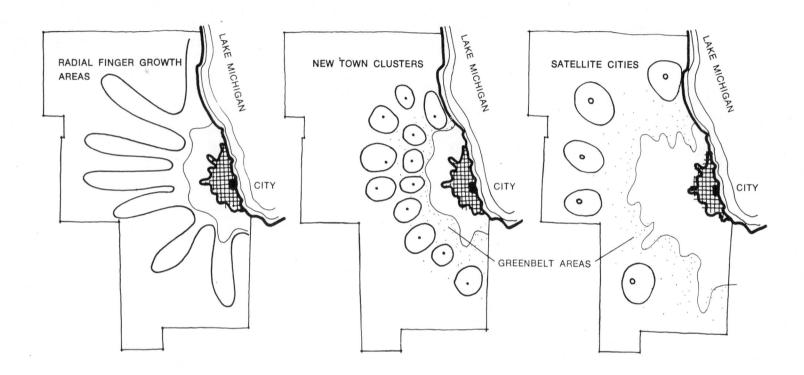

In the FINGER plan concept of regional development, a main mover would be mass transit. The probable result would be growth in narrow bands or corridors along commuter transit routes. Expressways would move circumferentially and radially between the fingers.

The CLUSTER concept promotes the growth of balanced "new town" clusters. Their populations would range from 10,000 to 100,000 persons and each cluster would be served by an interconnected system of expressways and major highways

aligned between clusters, providing easy multi-directional travel in all parts of the region. Supplementary mass transit systems would generally connect cluster centers with each other and with the center city.

The SATELLITE plan of development envisions major self-sufficient satellite cities of 500,000 to 1,000,000 population. Each would embrace its own commercial and cultural center or centers and would be defined and surrounded by extensive green belts of agricultural, flood plain, or other open space land. Expressways would loop between and interconnect satellites and the regional core. Rapid transit would link all centers to each other and to the core.

SOURCE: The Freeway in the City, *The Urban Advisors to the Federal Highway Administrator, Dept of Transportation, 1968.*

NEW TOWN CONCEPTS

The expansion of central cities, and the distressing character of urban fringe development, began to stimulate new thinking as some of these problems became apparent in the Victorian industrial centers in England. The original proposals for new towns were, to be sure, romantic in conception. A population of the right "mix" was to be isolated in the green countryside in a complete environment—farm, residence, factory, stores, schools, churches, and recreation. There were trial attempts at establishing such new towns and some were successful— Letchworth, and Welwyn, Ebeneezer Howard's garden cities, are delightful even today.

The first reactions to the new town concept in the United States took the physical form of residential suburbs. That is, the distinguishing physical elements of green space, lower densities, vehicular separations and a more or less nostalgic country air were appropriated for residential development on the urban fringe. Several of these pioneering developments of the twenties and thirties have been extremely successful. The greenbelt towns—Greenbelt, Maryland; Greenhills, Ohio; and Greendale, Wisconsin—are still today very fine residential developments.

Other attempts in planning of complete new communities have been made, such as Park Forest, Illinois, where the new town would provide not only suburban residential living but a full complex of urban facilities and activities for work, play and institutions as well as dwellings. In England and other places in Europe, this concept has been carried far in the development of new cities with industrial base and sensitive development of commercial and recreational spaces.

In this country the new town concept is again emerging as a way to meet urban growth, among other things to make the best use of land. It is estimated that our present rate of urbanization at 30 acres per hundred people would take 10.5 million acres to provide for 35 million people—that 350 towns at 100,000 inhabitants each would consume only 3.5 million acres based on examples of new towns of low density with abundant open space, and would use only 10 acres for a hundred people.

A recent example is Reston, in Fairfax County, Virginia, a new residential city of 75,000 people. It is a true cluster plan with houses concentrated in seven villages of about 10,000 people each. There are golf courses and lakes. The first section of 25,000 units in three town-house clusters has just been completed. The significance of this project is two-fold. It does provide for a mix of people—different family sizes, different age groups, different incomes—in different physical settings. Further, it is located in open countryside, 20 minutes from Washington, D.C. Significance lies in the fact that there is a projected "Plan for the year 2,000" for Washington, which proposes that the inevitable growth of the region be accomplished through the establishment of satellite cities, rather than by uncontrolled urban sprawl. The pattern is exemplified in Reston and other similar developments in the area, such as Columbia, Maryland, planned for ultimate population of 110,000.

Reston has a total of 6,810 acres of which 1500 are to be in common lakes, parks, common greens, etc. It will provide for all types of units, the First Village planned for 143 detached houses, 227 town houses and a tower containing 61 units, and the village center at the end of a lake is planned with an apartment tower and shops. Ultimately it is hoped that light industry, research parks and cultural facilities will be part of the fairly complete city.

The plan is based on a cluster system of seven villages with intervening woods and meadows left open. There will be five golf courses and two lakes for boating and fishing. The plan carefully respects the natural drainage network.

There are currently perhaps more than 100 new town developments, many in the western states, few in the sense of complete cities, most representing large scale residential communities but they follow the principles of planned unit development and the cluster idea.

There are two fundamental open space concepts in the new town idea:

1. *They include the greenbelt principle, that is the use of green space (which may also serve multiple open space use) to define and control development. In this sense they usually provide for a green belt system around the town and around or between its component parts.*

2. *They provide for a maximum of open space for common use which at the same time compensates in open space for compact building development.*

It may be expected that new town concepts will be increasingly applied in the western states, perhaps with an initial emphasis on the metropolitan and urban area but also in the most undeveloped areas in connection with new mining and other development.

OPEN SPACE ELEMENT IN DEVELOPMENT

Open space has a functional use in itself, as a land resource, as a land use for recreation, as a corridor space for transportation. It also has a functional use in development, while serving these functions, in providing for a system of control in building development patterns. The open space elements of development can become the key to better or poorer planning of urban and suburban growth.

In building development, the way open space elements are used or deployed determines the character and quality of the development and are the key factors in the efficient use of land in development.

It is the use of the open space elements that such development patterns as cluster, planned unit development, and new towns have shown the ways to build more desirable communities, with greater economy in development, and with general acceptance by the market, by people who live in them, by the builders who build them, and by the officials who have to pass on them.

It is, therefore, of great importance that a full understanding of these open space elements in development be acquired for the assignment and allocation of land uses, as a guide to the disposal of land for development.

SEPARATORS AND BUFFERS—Separators and buffers are open space lands which are used to separate incompatible elements or one type of land use from another,

1. for practical reasons of controlling such conditions as noise, fumes or haphazard traffic access;

2. for aesthetic reasons of identifying and defining areas.

They may be in the form of planned areas of open space in themselves, whether for single or multiple use (separators) or as open space *edges* (buffers). While they serve to separate, they at the same time can also be unifying elements in providing continuity of open space systems, using golf courses, lakes, streams, parks and other open space uses in the systems.

SOURCE: Where Not to Build, *Technical Bulletin #1, Bureau of Land Management, U.S. Dept. of the Interior, Washington, D.C., 1968.*

The size of separators and buffers will depend on the particular function they serve in a particular situation. Size will depend also on whether the element is used narrowly as buffer or whether it is also used for multi-purpose open space such as recreation and park use as well.

There are a number of types of separators and buffers.

1. *Greenbelts*. These are in general continuous green open space to define development areas at large scale. They are generally considered open country or natural areas, to limit the area of planned development, but at large scale especially are best used for multi-purposes. They may accordingly provide for major trunk intercity highways, parks and recreation and utility open spaces including farming and forests. They may also be considered as locations for secondary open space use such as educational and other institutional campuses.

2. *Green ways*. These are green space penetrants, fingers, or wedges, that may follow drainage ways or other natural forms, usually best used in linking up with other elements of an open space system.

3. *Corridor separators*. In some cases, an expressway system can be used as a separator or means of definition of a development. In such cases, the right-of-way should be sufficiently large to provide green space use for separation and buffering.

4. *Strip buffers*. These can be used to separate residence from highways and other traffic arteries, around commercial developments, parking lots. Size would depend on whether the buffer is planted or not. There is probably a minimum width of 30–50 feet for a densely planted buffer.

5. *Area buffers*. These may be used to protect one use from another adverse use such as residential from noise or fumes or nuisance, or to protect edges of water reservoirs.

CENTER PIECES—The center piece open space is that which is generally enclosed by development as a central focus of space for gathering and assembly or mixture of people and activities. Its functions are to give a sense of place and orientation as well as provide breathing space within development. It is a place to be, a place to see, to pause, to meet, to rest.

The center piece may be of any scale and any intensity of use from a small common green area of ¼ acre to a major park or a body of water. One of the trends in development today is the use or creation of lakes around which development can be planned as in the case of Reston, Virginia. Some secondary open spaces, such as a college campus, may be used and an even more familiar example is the use of a school or neighborhood park as a center open space. The general types are:

1. *Squares, plazas or malls*. These are traditional open space centerpieces long used in urban development at both large and small, intimate scale.

2. *Courts and patios*. These are familiar in residential development and are again becoming in common use in residential planning.

3. *Campuses*. These, whether at smaller scale of local schools or larger scale

for institutions in the hundreds of acres, provide open space character to serve centerpiece functions.

4. *Parks and other national areas*. Such open green space areas are frequently used as development center pieces: ranging from golf courses, lakes, recreation facilities either in single or multiple use. Landmarks or special identifying natural forms may sometimes be a strategic point for location of a centerpiece open space.

While the centerpiece is enclosed by development, it need not be isolated as an open space. Squares, plazas and other center pieces will be connected with the total open space system in the street system, and greenways can also be used to tie in the center piece open space as a part of the over-all open space system. Certain developments in themselves with strong open space elements, such as large shopping centers with huge parking areas take on the function of center pieces.

DISTRIBUTORS—The distributor open spaces are chiefly the channels for movement but they also include the open spaces used to link up elements of an open space system, as in the case of creeks or other water ways, landscaped streets such as boulevards, and simple green strips. They are essentially the linear open space elements of an open space system. They link the different uses and various center pieces. They may be combined with buffers or separators as indicated or they may serve purely as distributors in themselves.

Distributors may also be the means to combine surface and multi-level uses in development and circulation. Overpasses, underpass and other structures to meet grade and multi-level purposes are involved in this use.

Distribution can serve more than one use, for circulation and for green space purposes. They include:

1. *Streets, highways and roads,* giving access through the landing spaces and the system of distribution both to development and open spaces.

2. *Waterways*, creeks and rivers and other water channels which link up elements of the open space.

3. *Other distributor greenways*, such as trails, paths, and green space linear ties between other open space elements.

THE OVERALL PATTERN—URBAN, SUBURBAN, EXURBAN, COUNTRYSIDE, AND THE MIX

The application of the open space concept must come in daily detailed decisions. This is the level at which all concepts are proved or disproved. The intent of the concept is very wide in scope. It is primarily to use open space as a positive functional use, to provide space and facilities to meet the open space needs of people; it is also a means to define and control building development in planning.

It would be of value then to take into consideration the overall pattern in which open space is not only allocated for specific open space uses but is also used to organize, plan, and direct development of other use.

The overall patterns can only be generalized as types to give a sense of the overall scheme that may be developed. Certain it is that no one overall pattern will be used everywhere—different stages of development and different locations will influence strongly the kind of pattern that may develop even though older ideas and ideas from elsewhere will affect the local development. Of more importance is the fact of large metropolitan expansion and regional urbanization with development reaching far distances in relation to city centers. Because consideration must be given to regions and huge areas of large scale development, the matter of the over-all pattern is of significance as a guide to the more immediate and local decision.

The overall patterns can be generalized as follows:

1. *Dispersion*. This is a relatively low density pattern of spread based mainly on individual land holdings, in effect a continuation of the pattern that has been followed greatly up to now. It seems to be most easily followed in flat country. Frank Lloyd Wright's Broadacre city of the 1930's exemplifies this pattern. The open space characteristics are tied in mostly with individual holdings and the open space system is in a widely dispersed pattern of small areas. This follows a familiar pattern of uninterrupted suburban spread in all directions.

2. *Radial Pattern*. This retains a strong dominant central or core city with development outwards along radials which would be separated by open space wedges of the countryside as a basic open space system. Development would be essentially linear with suburban development interspersed along the radiating fingers.

3. *The Galaxy*. In this pattern, development would be bunched in relatively small units, each with an internal peak and each separated from the others by open space or development of very low density. Urban and suburban concentration would make up the units and possibly a kind of exurban development might be found in the areas between. The open space system would consist of a series of connected open space areas among and between the development area units.

4. *The Ring*. In this pattern a central area left open or at very low density would be surrounded by a ring of high densities or special activities like a wheel or doughnut. The San Francisco Bay area might be taken as an example and in Holland, for example, a national policy suggests the development of a series of cities surrounding open agricultural land. The open space system in this pattern would depend on some major open space area as the hole of the doughnut.

In all these patterns, the nature of the open space system would be the controlling factor and provide the controlling characteristic. While there may be some concern over different patterns, it would seem that the first of these, uncontrolled dispersion and spread will continue unless some positive point of view is developed in urban-growth, both in government and out. The new town approach is of major concern now, being pursued in practice by growing use of the cluster and planned unit development. What is also needed is positive policy for regional development and a positive open space policy based on the concept of open space as a control and structure for the development pattern can help establish the way in which urban growth can be met as it makes further demands on land.

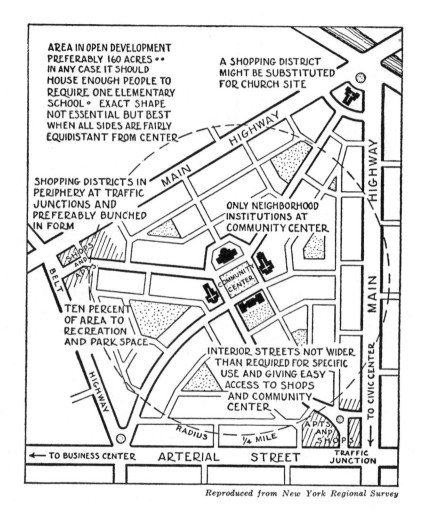

Reproduced from New York Regional Survey

In a preliminary study in 1926 and in a report published by the Committee on the Regional Plan of New York and Its Environs in 1929, Perry enunciated his Neighborhood Theory. Its six basic principles were:

1. Major arterials and through traffic routes should not pass through residential neighborhoods. Instead, these streets should provide the boundaries of the neighborhood.

2. Interior street patterns should be designed and constructed through use of cul-de-sacs, curved layout and light duty surfacing so as to encourage a quiet, safe, low volume traffic movement and preservation of the residential atmosphere.

3. The population of the neighborhood should be that which is necessary to support its elementary school. (When Perry formulated his theory, this population was estimated at about 5,000 persons; current elementary school size standards probably would lower the figure to 3,000-4,000 persons.)

4. The neighborhood focal point should be the elementary school centrally located on a common or green, along with other institutions that have service areas coincident with the neighborhood boundaries.

5. The neighborhood would occupy an approximately 160 acres with a density of 10 families per acre. The shape would be such that no child would walk more than one-half mile to school.

6. The unit would be served by shopping facilities, churches, a library, and a community center located near the elementary school.

SOURCE: New York Regional Survey of New York and its Environs—1929

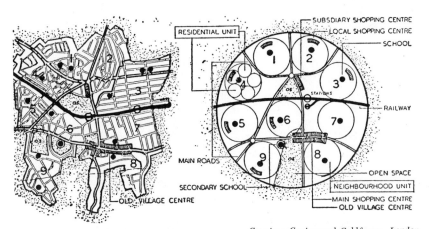

Courtesy Carter and Goldfinger, London

KEY

SECONDARY SCHOOL
SENIOR "
JUNIOR "
INFANT "
SHOPPING CENTRE
TRAFFIC ROADS
RAILWAY
RAILWAY STATIONS
OPEN SPACES

Population Per Unit

1	4500	5	3000
2	4500	6	2500
3	6500	7	3000
4	4000	8	1600
	9	5500	

THE COUNTY OF LONDON PLAN

The neighborhood unit was the primary planning unit in the development of this city plan. The sketch on the right is the diagrammatic organization of neighborhood units; the sketch on the left shows the application of this general scheme to a specific district of the city.

SOURCE: Gallion and Eisner, *The Urban Pattern,* copyright 1963, D. Van Nostrand Co. Inc., Princeton, N.J.

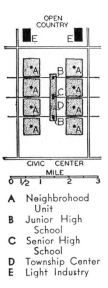

A Neighborhood Unit
B Junior High School
C Senior High School
D Township Center
E Light Industry

A NEIGHBORHOOD UNIT BY JOSÉ SERT

This diagram illustrates an organization of neighborhood units suggested by José Sert. While some authorities have stated that the maximum walking distance from home to the elementary school should be one-half mile, this diagram indicates a maximum distance of about one-quarter mile, which is the standard accepted by a number of communities. In contrast to a population density of 20–25 persons assumed as a desirable average in many communities, Sert assumes a density of two or three times this number, which may account for the shorter walking distances he proposes from homes to the several schools in his scheme.

The elementary school occupies a central position in the neighborhood unit, and a group of these units—six to eight in number—constitute a "township" with a population of between 56,000 and 80,000 people. A junior high school serves four neighborhoods; a senior high school serves the eight units; these facilities are situated within a "township center" surrounded by a "greenbelt." The neighborhood unit includes the elementary school, pre-school play-lots, playground, church, shopping center, library, and emergency clinic. The "township center" includes the junior and senior high schools, community auditorium and meeting rooms, concert hall, theaters, main shopping center, recreation and administrative center.

Traffic ways by-pass the neighborhood units and connect them with the "civic center," which includes the regional facilities for administration, education, hotels, trade and recreation, and transportation stations on one side, and on the other side are the locations for light industrial plants. All these elements are separated from each other by "greenbelts," and the open countryside is accessible to all the people.

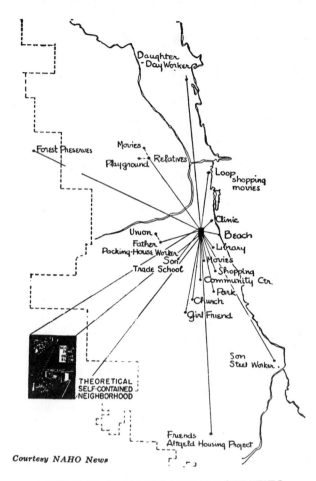

Courtesy NAHO News

A TYPICAL FAMILY'S DAILY ACTIVITIES

The distribution of a family's daily activities in Chicago is interestingly portrayed in this map and illustrates two salient facts:

1. The advantages which might well accrue to the family by the assembly of neighborhood facilities within convenient distance from the home: shopping, school, recreation, community center, movies, library, church, clinic, etc. Such a physical organization of neighborhood facilities would not fulfil the social requirements of all the families living in the neighborhood, but their convenient presence would avoid the necessity to travel inordinate distances for many who are not so inclined.

2. The necessity for adequate transportation—circulation—about the urban framework, to relieve the time and strain now imposed upon the urban dweller in his daily travel to and from his work, his friends, and the less frequent, though not less necessary, cultural facilities a city makes available.

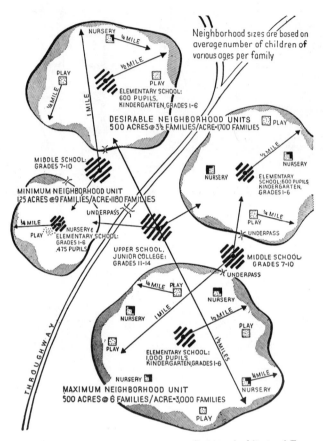

Courtesy Architectural Forum

The physical organization of neighborhood units and community groups, integrated with the transportation system of the city, is intended to accomplish these objectives and thereby remove the necessity for the range of travel currently imposed and illustrated in this map.

THE NEIGHBORHOOD UNIT

The organization of neighborhood elements suggested by N.L. Engelhardt, Jr. A more complete diagram of neighborhood units grouped in relation to the various levels of school facilities. It will be noted that a radius of one-half mile is adopted as the maximum walking distance to the elementary school but playgrounds and nursery schools for small children are proposed with a radius of one-quarter mile walking distance for the families in the neighborhood.

SOURCE: Gallion and Eisner, *The Urban Pattern,* copyright 1963, D. Van Nostrand Co. Inc., Princeton, N.J.

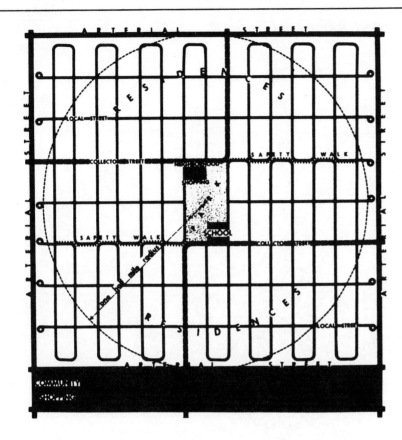

THE NEIGHBORHOOD UNIT—CLARENCE STEIN

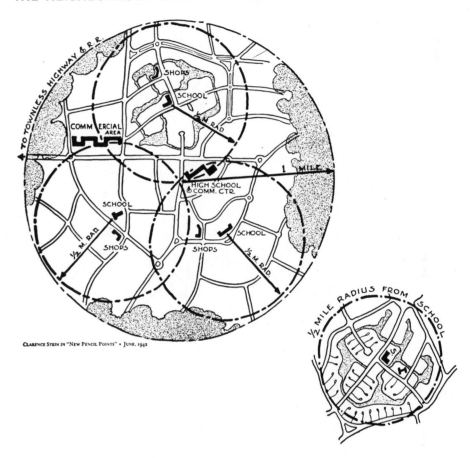

CLARENCE STEIN IN "NEW PENCIL POINTS" • JUNE, 1942

A sound area for living with:

1. Adequate school and parks within a half mile walk

2. Major streets around rather than through the neighborhood

3. Separate residential and non-residential districts

4. Population large enough to support an elementary school, usually 5,000 to 10,000 people

5. Some neighborhood stores and services

The elementary school is the center of the unit and within a one-half mile radius of all residents in the neighborhood. A small shopping center for daily needs is located near the school. Most residential streets are suggested as cul-de-sac or "dead-end" roads to eliminate through traffic, and park space flows through the neighborhood in a manner reminiscent of the Radburn plan.

The grouping of three neighborhood units served by a high school and one or two major commercial centers, the radius for walking distance to these facilities being one mile.

SOURCE: Reproduced from Comprehensive Planning for The Whittier Neighborhood, courtesy of Minneapolis City Planning Commission

GENERAL PLAN SHOWING NEIGHBORHOODS

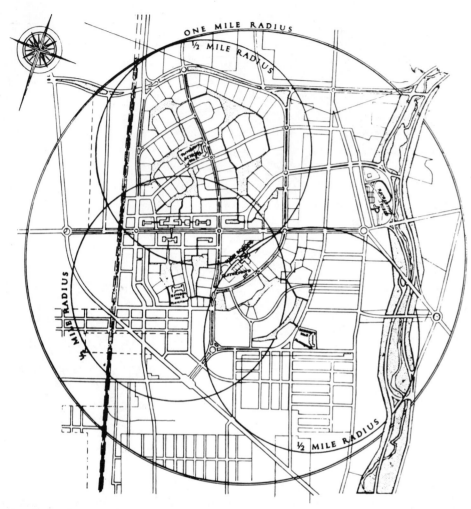

NORTHWEST NEIGHBORHOOD

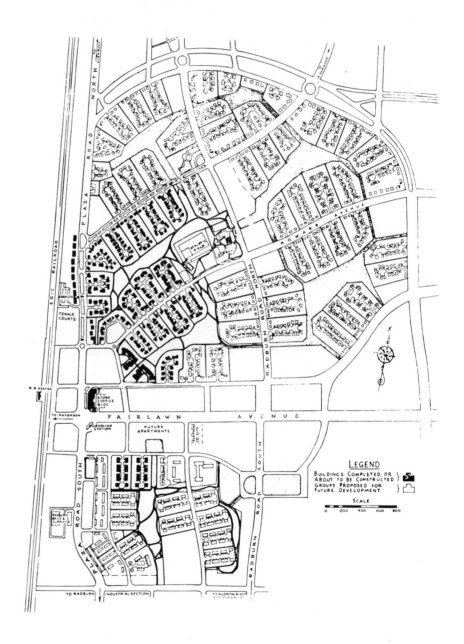

In their design of the suburb of Radburn in New Jersey, C. S. Stein and Henry Wright introduced a new approach to residential planning. They originated the superblock idea the main feature of which, is the separation of pedestrian and automobile traffic. At Radburn, houses are grouped around a series of culs-de-sac which are linked by walkways with the park, the school, and the shops, all of which are located in the interior of the superblock. The superblock is considered an ideal solution to the circulation problem since it provides a means of locating the houses off the main road.

SOURCE: Clarence Stein, Toward New Towns for America, Reinhold Publishing Corp., New York—1957

The illustration shows a typical cul-de-sac street employed at Radburn. Its characteristics may be summarized as follows: The short cul-de-sac acts as a service lane only; it provides vehicular access to houses and garages, permitting delivery and other services, and it also serves for most of the parking; footways located on the perimeter of each cul-de-sac house group serve as sidewalks. As opposed to established planning practices, houses have been "turned around," the living rooms, porches, and as many bed-rooms as possible facing the gardens at rear of dwellings, and kitchens and cellar storage, the service lane.

The dwellings are loosely disposed around the dead-end streets and, as a group, they show little of formal architectural discipline. The landscaping, judiciously planned, undoubtedly is the most important uniting element in the composition. Other uniting elements are the consistency in the use of building materials and the continuity in roof lines. Also, by joining houses by means of coupling their garages, the usual disorderly appearance of the free standing houses in relation to each other has been eliminated and sufficient space left on either side of the buildings. The architectural informality of the Radburn cul-de-sac distinguishes it from the British dead-end street in which a formal correlation of the houses predominates.

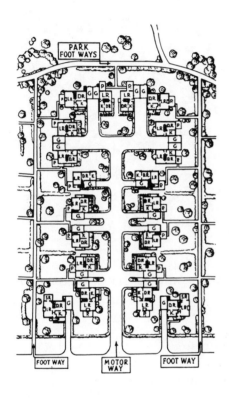

Plan of a typical "lane" at Radburn. The park in the center of the superblock is shown at the top; the motor ways to the houses are at right angles to the park.

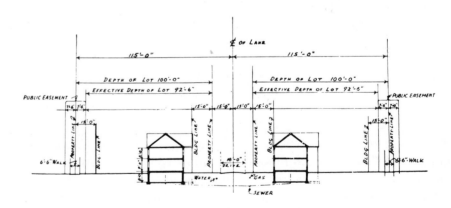

Typical transverse section of a "lane" in the first unit of Radburn.

SOURCE: Clarence Stein, Toward New Towns for America, Reinhold Publishing Corp., New York—1957

GARDEN CITIES OF TOMORROW

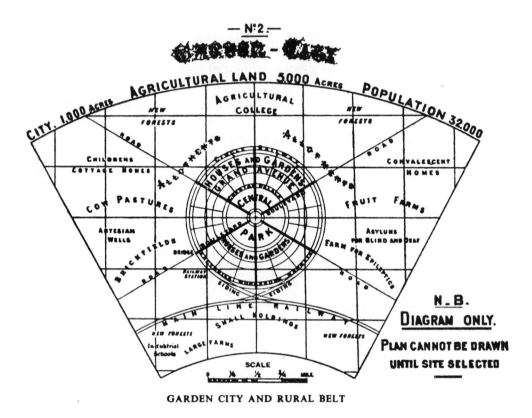

GARDEN CITY AND RURAL BELT

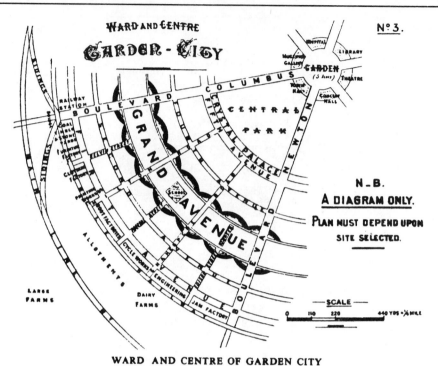

WARD AND CENTRE OF GARDEN CITY

Total area of city	—6000 acres
Built-up area	—1000 acres
Permanent green belt	—5000 acres
Total population	—32,000 people

City organization—

Center—	civic buildings
1st Ring—	central park
2nd Ring—	housing of various types bisected by Grand Avenue
3rd Ring—	crystal palace or covered promenades
4th Ring—	factories and warehouses
Green belt—	permanent open space

Ebenezer Howard put forth his concept of a garden city in a book entitled **Tomorrow: A Peaceful Path to Real Reform** in 1898. The basic goal was to combine the advantages of town life with that of the country. He advocated the building of "towns designed for healthy living and industry; of a size that makes possible a full measure of social life, but not larger; surrounded by a rural belt; the whole of the land being in public ownership, or held in trust for the community."

SOURCE: Ebenezer Howard, Garden Cities of Tomorrow—1946, Faber & Faber—London

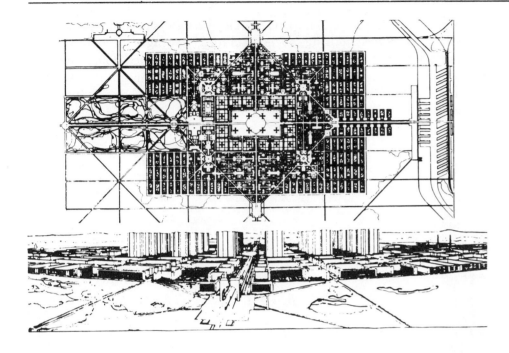

"LA VILLE CONTEMPORAINE" BY LE CORBUSIER

The City of Tomorrow for 3,000,000 people was proposed by Le Corbusier in 1922. Sixty-story office buildings with a density of 1,200 persons per acre and covering only 5 per cent of the ground area are set within landscaped open space. Eight-story apartment buildings with a density of 120 persons per acre surround the office skyscrapers and the cite jardins of single houses occupy the outskirts of the city. The hub of the plan is the transportation center for motor and rail lines, the roof of which is the airfield. Main highways are elevated.

After the introduction of "La Ville Contemporaine," Le Corbusier applied the same theories to a section of Paris. In this "Voisin Plan," the 60-story skyscraper office buildings are set in vast open space, main traffic highways are defined with complete separation of traffic, and parking space for vehicles is provided. The plan is a rectangular arrangement of streets, but local and through traffic are distinctly separated, and the large open spaces are treated with informal pedestrian circulation and landscaped. The difference in scale of open space and building coverage is indicated in the plan sketch.

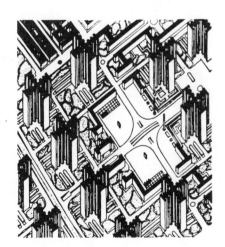

"PLAN VOISIN" by Le Corbusier, Paris, 1925

CONTRAST Between Old and New in "Plan Voisin"

SOURCE: From Gallion and Eisner The Urban Pattern, Copyright 1963 D. Van Nostrand Co., Inc., Princeton, N.J.

Essentially a "linear" city form, Frank Lloyd Wright's proposal distributes industry, commerce, housing, social facilities, and agriculture along the railroad artery and his access to highways. The unit which dominates this plan is the minimum of one acre of land for each family rather than the neighborhood unit, although the various neighborhood facilities are provided.

Area of Plan is
Two Square Miles

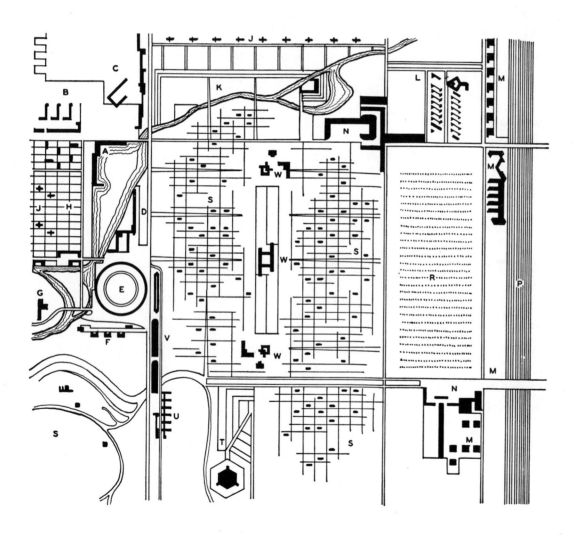

A	County Seat Administration	**M**	Industry
B	Airport	**N**	Merchandising
C	Sports	**P**	Railroad
D	Professional Offices	**R**	Orchards
E	Stadium	**S**	Homes and Apartments
F	Hotel	**T**	Temple and Cemetery
G	Sanitarium	**U**	Research
H	Small Industry	**V**	Zoo
J	Small Farms	**W**	Schools
K	Park		
L	Motor Inn		

SOURCE: From Gallion and Eisner The Urban Pattern, Copyright 1963 D. Van Nostrand Co., Inc., Princeton, N.J.

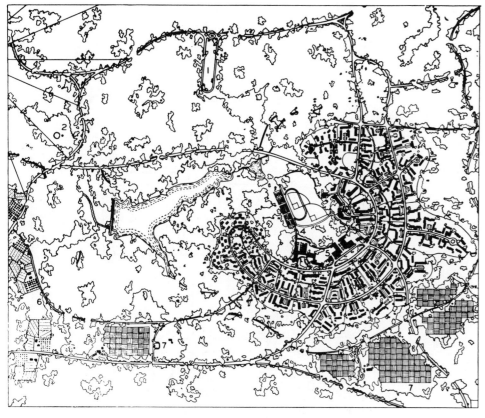

GREENBELT, Maryland

1 Water Tower

2 Disposal Plant and In-
   cinerator

3 Picnic Center and Lake

4 Community Center

5 Store Group

6 Rural Homesteads

7 Allotment Gardens

This development is on a 2,100-acre site about 25 minutes' drive by automobile from Washington, D.C., and includes 712 dwellings in group houses and 288 in apartments, a total of 1,000 units occupying an area of 250 acres. There are 500 garages. The sixteen-room elementary school is jointly used as a community center, and the shopping center includes space for a post office, food stores, a drug store, a dentist's and a doctor's offices, a 600-seat theater, and such service shops as shoe repair, laundry, tailor, barber, and beauty shops. There are a bus terminal, a garage and repair shop, a fire station, and a gas station. The recreation facilities include an athletic field, picnic grounds, and an artificial lake. The super-block is used, each block containing about 120 dwellings with interior play areas. Underpasses provide continuous pedestrian circulation without crossing main roads. The commercial and community center, in the approximate center of the plan, reduces to a minimum the walking distance from all dwellings.

As a component part of the Federal government's search for ways and means to cope with the modern city and its living environment, the Resettlement Administration planned four "greenbelt towns" beginning in 1935. They were satellite communities near large cities. The designs were inspired by Howard's Garden City idea, but they were not planned as self-contained towns; they were more like dormitory villages, the sources of employment for the residents being in the near-by cities. Each was surrounded by a belt of permanent open space, part of which could be farmed or gardened. A full complement of community facilities was included in each town— shopping, schools, and recreation space.

SOURCE: From Gallion and Eisner The Urban Pattern, Copyright 1963 D. Van Nostrand Co., Inc., Princeton, N.J.

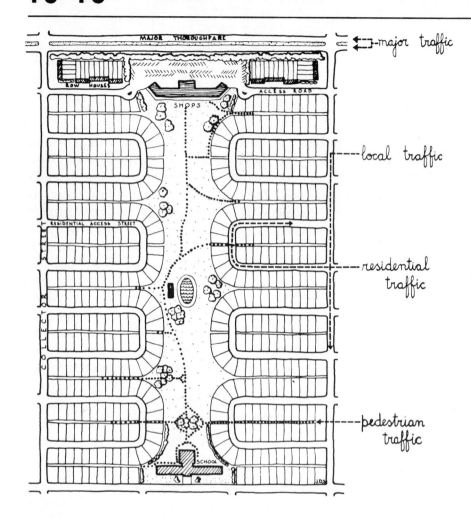

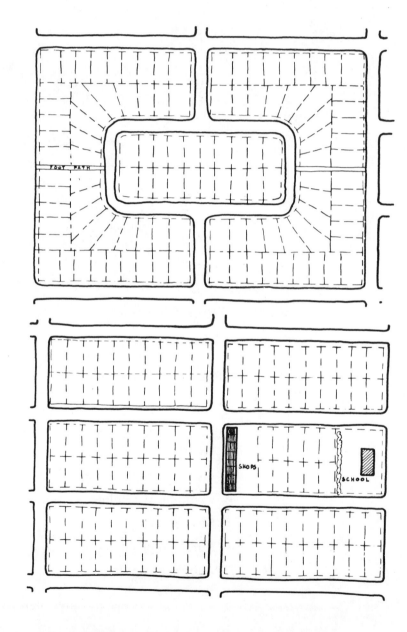

STANDARD GRID SYSTEM
—No separation of pedestrian
and vehicular traffic
—All roads used for all traffic purposes
—All lot sizes standard

OPEN PLAN
—Pedestrians and vehicles separated
—Roads planned for specific uses
STREET TYPES
      Major thoroughfares
      Collector Streets
      Access roads
      Minor residential roads

MODIFIED GRID PATTERN
—Some separation of pedestrians
and vehicles by provision of foot
paths
—Channelling of traffic—less road

SOURCE: Principles of Small House Grouping, Central Mortgage and Housing Corp., Ottawa, Canada

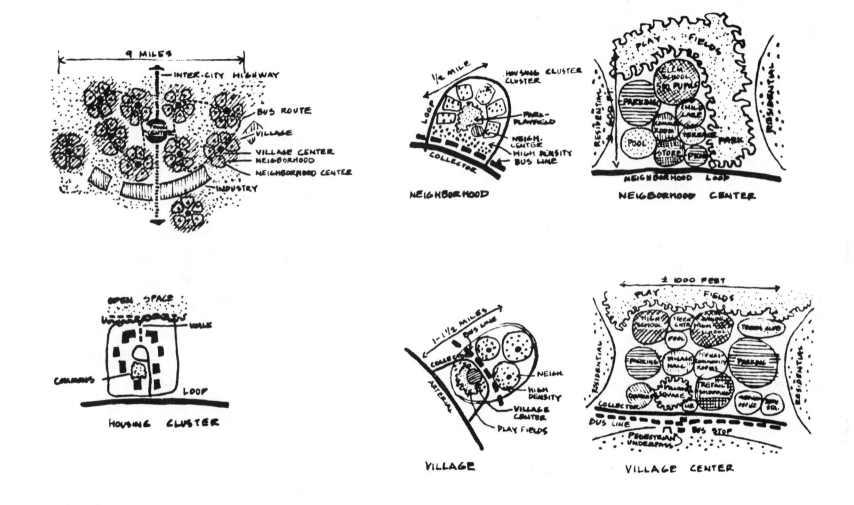

Columbia develops further the neighborhood principles of Perry, Stein and the new town of Harlow within the overall planning context of the entire new community. An orderly but also firm hierarchy of housing cluster, neighborhood, village and town is established. Whereas the planners of Columbia emphasize the system of overlapping communities, chiefly by means of village centers serving several adjacent neighborhoods and of a planned loop bus route, structure is hierarchical and rather rigid. The stated ambition of the planners is to establish patterns "as complex and overlapping as in every living city" by encouraging activity patterns which cut across service areas, but the forces of density and housing types and of self-contained sufficiency and physically hierarchical layout are structured so as to inhibit such complex and unpredictable overlapping.

SOURCE: *Morton Hoppenfeld, "A Sketch of the Planning Building Process for Columbia, Maryland," American Institute of Planners Journal, November 1967.

1. Area too small to be developed is landscaped to buffer the adjacent residential area from the noise and sight of interchange traffic.

2. Dashed line indicates closure of an old access point which would have impeded traffic and created unsafe conditions on the arterial.

3. Residential lots face on a frontage road or local street; landscaped buffer zones protect the residences from adverse effects of traffic.

4. Location of first arterial access point in relation to ramp terminals is based on distance required for safe and efficient merging and diverging of ramp traffic.

5. A minimum of 150 feet between intersections is needed to allow adequate storage of vehicles on access road.

6. Service stations, the most frequent road-user service destination, are located immediately adjacent to the access road.

7. Access and circulation pattern to all services within area is easily recognizable from cross route when approaching access point.

8. Buffer protects residential properties and screens other activities.

9. Restaurant is located convenient to motel patrons.

10. Major parking area intercepts patrons and eliminates unnecessary circulation through service area.

11. Residential and road-user service traffic is separated (i.e., the two activities front on different streets).

12. Motel units are set back from freeway and cross route to minimize traffic noise.

13. This area might be developed as a picnic and rest area for road-users.

14. Adequate building setbacks are provided along arterial.

15. Adequate off-street service and loading areas are provided to commercial and industrial activities.

16. Area might be developed for appropriate uses needing regional access and a location near the freeway.

17. Separate turning lanes and appropriate traffic control devices insure efficient intersection operation.

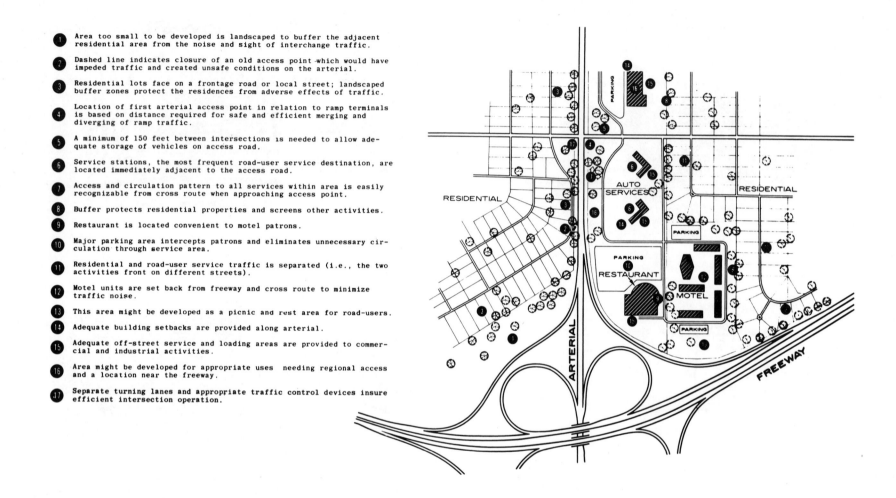

PLANNING PRINCIPLES
FOR INTERCHANGE AREA DEVELOPMENT

SOURCE: Guidelines for New Systems of Urban Transportation, *Volume 1: Urban Needs and Potentials. Barton-Aschman Associates, Inc. May, 1968.*

HIGH-DENSITY CENTER SYSTEMS

A great need is emerging for the development of transportation systems that can effectively handle the movement of large numbers of people and goods, within large, high-density complexes of multipurpose development.

As discussed below, such high-density multipurpose complexes exist today primarily in the form of central business districts, college, research, and medical campus areas, and major airports and entertainment centers. They also appear to be developing as office, hotel, and industrial districts around major freeway interchanges and outlying, regional shopping centers. In most instances, these complexes also will, or do, contain housing, educational, and other facilities secondary to their principal functions, but necessary if they are to develop the self-sufficiency, variety, and efficiency that would be desired.

Some new forms of transportation are required, both to serve existing multipurpose centers and to permit them to develop along improved lines. The lack of good systems for the movement of people within such areas is critical; it contributes to the decline of many existing centers, it forces very expensive, and sometimes inadequate, planning for others, and it prevents the sound and attractive development of new multipurpose complexes.

The usual image of a congested urban center is the traditional central business district. In actuality, most urban areas contain or are developing two, three, or even more "congested," multipurpose urban centers. Larger metropolitan areas may contain as many as 20 or 30 centers of this type. In Los Angeles, for example, the centers concept alternative is built around 30 major multipurpose centers, each with its own internal transit system.

Basically, a congested urban center may be any area in which a large number of people are frequently congregated for business, educational, entertainment, medical, or similar purposes. The exact number required to constitute "congestion" will vary depending on city size and the nature of the activities involved. For example, educational and shopping activities that generate substantial volumes of pedestrian interchange between facilities may become "congested" with much lower total "populations" than a large, single-purpose manufacturing or office activity.

Congestion is related to the number of persons assembled, the amount of interchange between activities or facilities within the area, the size of the area, and the modes of travel used within and to the area. Furthermore, congestion may be characterized by extensive conflicts between pedestrian and vehicular movements or between vehicular movements. These conflicts produce difficulty in gaining access to or in moving through or within an area, on foot or by other means. In extreme instances, congestion may involve the actual overloading of pedestrian facilities and result in conflicts between the pedestrian movements. It also may be reflected in conflicts between transportation and land-use.

Congestion, then, has a limiting effect upon movements between related activities and/or upon the functioning of the activities. Obviously, in these terms, congestion is found in many parts of urban areas; every strip or crossroads business center is the scene of some congestion. Most planning and much new development are directed to the elimination or reduction of congestion: vehicular and pedestrian movements are separated, related activities involving extensive interchange of persons are grouped close to each other in "campus-like" clusters, and improved highway and parking facilities are provided. Yet, with the application of all of these improvements, substantial congestion remains.

Figures 1, 2, and 3 illustrate how several important kinds of center systems might be planned and developed. Some desirable characteristics of high-density center systems are:

Service area: up to 10 square miles, most often one to four.

Maximum travel to connections with metropolitan or regional systems: up to 10 minutes.

Average population densities: not generally applicable, but should be capable of serving highest feasible densities.

Stop locations: major employment or educational facilities, hotels, airport gate positions, and transfers to metropolitan or regional systems up to 100 feet, or door-to-door and housing, parking, major recreational facilities, etc., up to 600 to 800 feet (highly dependent on environment).

Capacities: variable, very high to moderate.

Loading level: at or near principal level of pedestrian circulation.

Basic functions: (a) collection and distribution of persons traveling to and from the area by auto or by longer distance—community, metropolitan or regional —elements of the transportation system, (b) home or hotel to work, school, shopping or recreaton trips of many persons residing or visiting in the area, (c) terminal-to-terminal transfers (airline, bus or rail), (d) movement between functions and activities within the area: between convention facilities and hotels, classrooms and laboratories, retail facilities and place of employment, and the several stops on sightseeing tours, and (e) (possibly) the movement of baggage and goods.

Service periods: sustained high to very high volumes over much of each day. Moderate to low nighttime usage.

Connections: direct to community, metropolitan and regional systems and to parking.

SOURCE: Guidelines for New Systems of Urban Transportation, *Volume 1: Urban Needs and Potentials. Barton-Aschman Associates, 1968.* HUD, Washington, D.C.

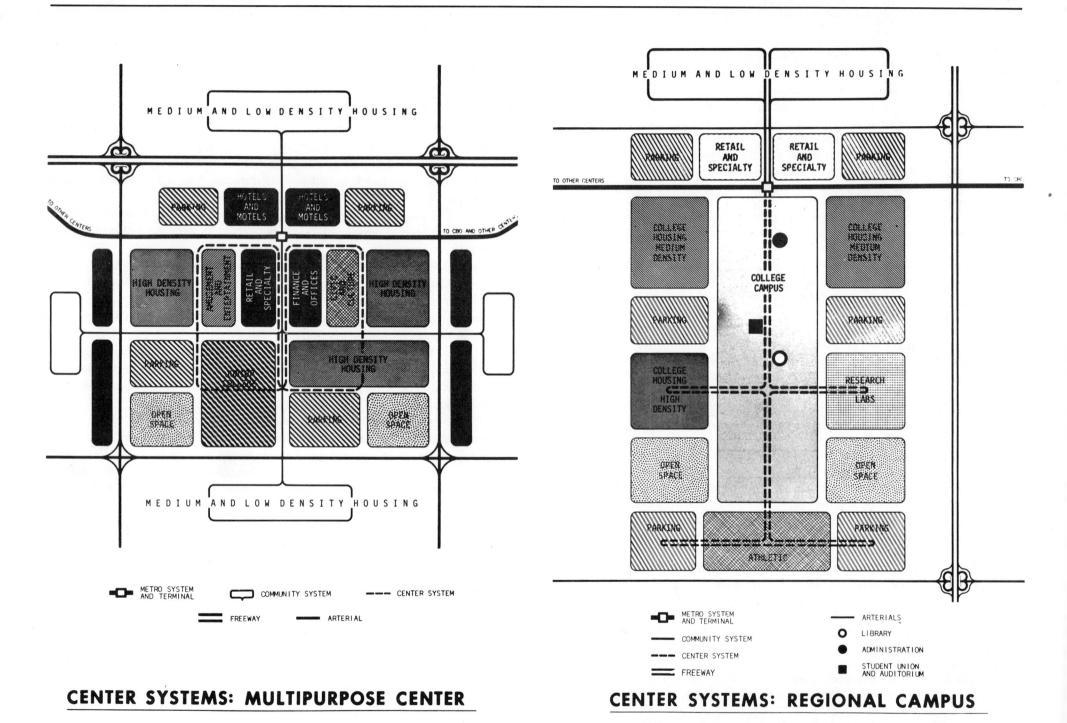

CENTER SYSTEMS: MULTIPURPOSE CENTER

CENTER SYSTEMS: REGIONAL CAMPUS

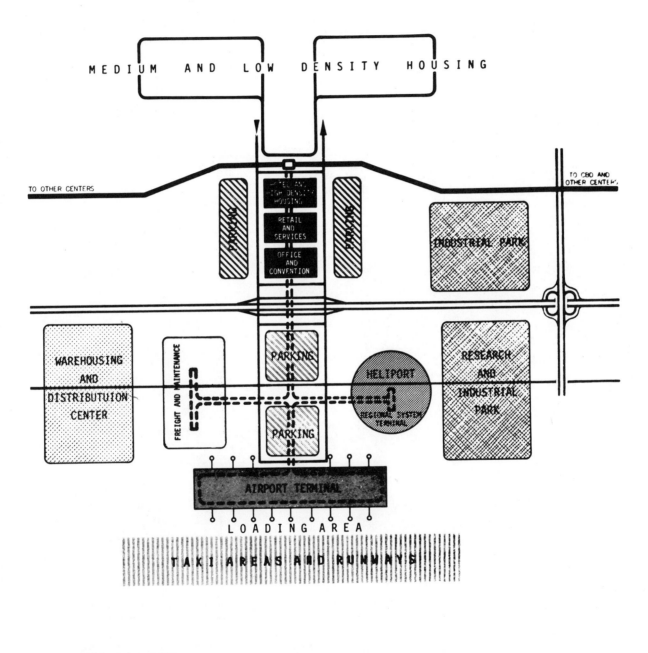

MEDIUM AND LOW DENSITY HOUSING

TO OTHER CENTERS

TO CBO AND
OTHER CENTERS

HOTEL AND
HIGH DENSITY
HOUSING

RETAIL
AND
SERVICES

OFFICE
AND
CONVENTION

PARKING

PARKING

INDUSTRIAL PARK

WAREHOUSING
AND
DISTRIBUTUION
CENTER

FREIGHT AND MAINTENANCE

PARKING

HELIPORT

RESEARCH
AND
INDUSTRIAL
PARK

REGIONAL SYSTEM
TERMINAL

PARKING

AIRPORT TERMINAL

LOADING AREA

TAXI AREAS AND RUNWAYS

⊏O⊐ METRO SYSTEM
AND TERMINAL

COMMUNITY SYSTEM

--- CENTER SYSTEM

═══ FREEWAY

ARTERIAL

Year	Proposed By	Area Involved	Proposal	Density Per Gross Acre	Optimum Population
1898	E. Howard	City	Book—Garden Cities	8–12 Dwelling Units	32,000 persons
1924	Le Corbusier	City	La Ville Contemporaine	1,200 persons	3,000,000 persons
1929	Clarence Perry	Neighborhood Unit	Neighborhood Unit Concept	5 dwelling units	5–9,000 persons
1932	Frank Lloyd Wright	City	Broadacre City	1 dwelling unit	no limit
1944	Jose L. Sert	Residential Unit	Book—Human Scale in City Planning	3–5 dwelling units	5–10,000 persons
1945	Walter Gropius & M. Wagner	Residential Unit	Book—A Program for City Reconstruction	4–10 dwelling units	5000 persons
1946	L. Justement	City	Book—New Cities for Old	10–35 dwelling units	1,000,000 persons
1947	P. Goodman P. Goodman	City	Book—Communitas	100 dwelling units	6–8 million persons

PUBLIC AND PRIVATE UTILITIES

WATER SUPPLY SYSTEMS

A water supply system consists of all of the necessary installations required to obtain, treat and distribute water to the eventual user. Principal features of water supply systems include:

1. Sources including rivers, lakes and wells and the facilities associated therewith.

2. Transmission mains, including aqueducts, canals, and pipelines used to transmit raw water to treatment facilities or direct to distribution systems if water is untreated.

3. Treatment facilities.

4. Distribution systems for conveying water to the near vicinity of customers premises. The distribution system ordinarily includes demand, balancing, and reserve reservoirs and pumping stations for maintenance of pressure.

5. Services to connect the distribution system to the customer's premises.

SYSTEM CHARACTERISTICS

Most water supply systems supply domestic, industrial and fire fighting requirements from a single distribution network. There are however many systems, particularly in high density districts, which have separate, high pressure fire main systems. These latter systems may use the same supply source as the domestic system and obtain the required pressure through pumps, or may use separate sources (sometimes of lower quality). In the latter case the systems are entirely separate in order to avoid contamination of the domestic system.

Water supply distribution networks in urban areas are of various types and combinations of types depending on the street plan, urban density, topography and other factors. The basic network patterns are branch and gridiron (or grid). Grid patterns are generally improved by the installation of loop header systems in high density urban districts to insure supply from at least two directions. A schematic diagram of the types of patterns is shown in Figure 1. Water distribution main systems are generally installed under street systems although in some cases they are installed at the rear of property in alleys or easements. In populated areas the previously described grid system is universally used and consists of either a single or dual main system as illustrated in Figure 3. Dual main systems are the most prevalent, particularly in the high density districts because of the cost of extra length of services for single main systems.

Customer services are provided through taps to mains for small demands and through valved connections for large. A typical tapped service connection is shown in Figure 2.

Materials used for mains for distribution systems include cast iron, ductile cast iron, wrought iron, asbestos-cement and steel for the smaller sizes and these plus reinforced concrete for the larger sizes. Plastic materials are also being used for

SOURCE: Feasibility of Utility Tunnels in Urban Areas. Special Report 39, American Public Works Association, Chicago, Ill., 1971.

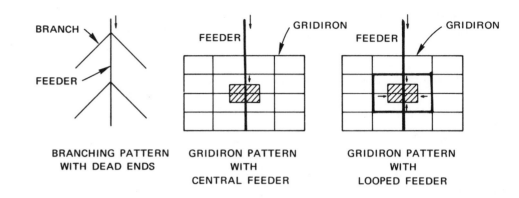

BRANCHING PATTERN WITH DEAD ENDS   GRIDIRON PATTERN WITH CENTRAL FEEDER   GRIDIRON PATTERN WITH LOOPED FEEDER

HIGH-VALUE DISTRICT IS CROSS-HATCHED

Figure 1. Water supply distribution system patterns.

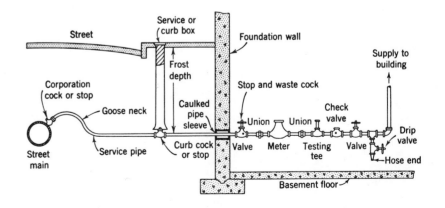

Figure 2. Typical water service connection.

the smaller sizes. A variety of interior and exterior coatings are employed to resist corrosion. Main sizes are generally dictated by fire protection requirements and minimums are specified as 6 inch for residential districts and 8 inch for high value districts.

Appurtenances and auxiliary requirements include valves, pressure control devices, surge protection devices, electrolytic corrosion control systems, air relief devices and pump stations.

Valves are provided so that no single break will affect more than about 500 feet of main. This generally requires valves on every branch connection and on at least two sides of every cross connection in a grid system. Fire hydrants are provided at a spacing ranging from 150 feet in high value central districts to 600 feet in suburban residential districts.

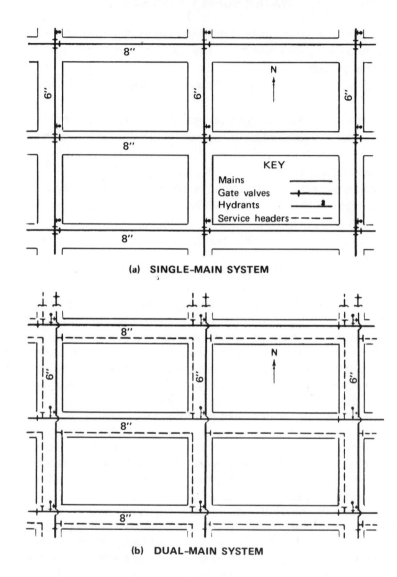

(a) SINGLE-MAIN SYSTEM

KEY
Mains ——————
Gate valves ——+——
Hydrants ——————•
Service headers ———————

(b) DUAL-MAIN SYSTEM

Figure 3. Single and dual main grid distribution systems.

SOURCE: *Feasibility of Utility Tunnels in Urban Areas, Special Report 39, American Public Works Association, Chicago, Ill.,* 1971.

SERVICE AREAS

A small number of community water utilities is preferable to a multiplicity of uncoordinated systems. Where practical, interconnection between distribution lines is recommended. A large number of relatively small water companies or municipal departments is often the result of a lack of a coordinated policy for community water resources. Widely different rate systems, insufficient capacity in some areas, and deficient fire protection service can often be traced to these conditions and illustrate the need for an area-wide coordinated plan for water service.

WATER MASTER PLAN

A master plan which shows future needs and facilities in relation to the area's growth and water resources is necessary for effective planning. Such a plan should be developed in connection with a sewerage master plan, and should encompass the long-range watershed needs, storage facilities, and, if appropriate, flood-control plans. Pipe networks, pumping facilities, treated water storage needs, and fire protection demands should also be considered.

Still another factor needed for a good community water program is a long-range financial plan. Both the master plan and capital budget should be related to other community needs.

CONNECTION REQUIREMENTS

Regulations calling for mandatory connection to public water supplies, where public water service is, or could be made available, are recommended for allowing better system planning and financing.

EXTENSION OF SERVICES

The community should have a definite policy for determining the method by which service extensions are made. Where water is provided by a private utility firm, extensions are largely dictated by economic factors. Where the system is publicly operated, there should be clear-cut processes by which service can be extended without undue "red tape."

Where vacant areas must be crossed, or where the pipe network calls for oversized lines, a policy should be firmly established describing any special financial arrangements for such cases.

WATER QUALITY

The treated water should meet State and Public Health Service quality standards. A recommended minimum standard suitable for States and local areas is given in Public Health Service Drinking Water Standards.

WATER QUANTITY

Capacity and storage should be such as to provide quantities adequate for maximum day demands, without significant loss of pressure. The system should also be capable of meeting fire flow demands. In most cities under 200,000 population, the water required for fire fighting purposes, plus the maximum day consumption, is the governing factor in design. Requirements for fire fighting needs are usually based on standards set by the National Board of Fire Underwriters.

RATE STRUCTURE

Although no emperical figure can be provided as a "reasonable" water rate, the cost of water should be fairly consistent throughout the study area and should be reasonable enough to encourage connection to the public supply. In some communities, water revenues are too low to allow sound fiscal planning for depreciation or anticipated expansion needs. In other areas, water rates are set high enough to give a surplus sometimes used for other purposes. A thorough study of the rate structure is desirable to avoid both of the above practices and to provide fiscally sound service rates.

AREAS SERVED

Public water supply service should be provided to those areas where service can be justified from health and economic standpoints. In making the following evaluation, the water service map should be compared with present and also future population density maps. The percentage of home served in each population density group can then be determined.

This chart is based on average cost of public vs. private water supplies compiled from various journals and reports. The policies of State utility commissions regarding capital investment-financial return were taken into account.

Local characteristics may indicate an adjustment to these criteria needed in some cases, but they are suitable for average conditions "rule-of-thumb" guide in determining economic justification of public service.

Population Density	Equivalent Lot Size	Service Economic Justification
Over 2,500 persons/sq. mi.	Less than 1 acre	Public water supply is justified
1,000 2,500 persons/sq. mi.	1 to 2 acres	Public water supply is normally justified.
500 1,000 persons/sq. mi.	2 to 4 acres	Public water supply is not normally justified.
Less than 500 persons/sq. mi	Over 4 acres	Public water supply is rarely justified.

SOURCE: Environmental Health Planning Guide, Public Health Service, U. S. Dept. of Health, Education, and Welfare—1962

1

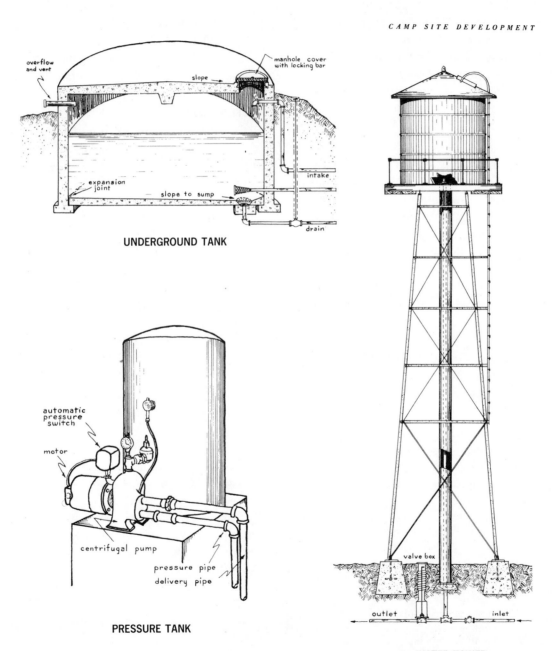

CAMP SITE DEVELOPMENT

overflow and vent

manhole cover with locking bar

slope

expansion joint

slope to sump

intake

drain

UNDERGROUND TANK

automatic pressure switch

motor

centrifugal pump

pressure pipe

delivery pipe

PRESSURE TANK

valve box

outlet

inlet

WATER TOWER

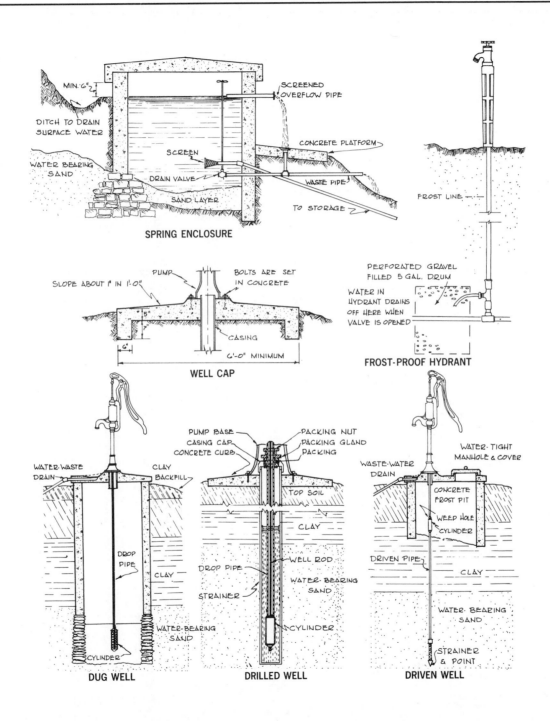

MIN. 6"

DITCH TO DRAIN
SURFACE WATER

WATER BEARING
SAND

SCREEN

DRAIN VALVE

SAND LAYER

SCREENED
OVERFLOW PIPE

CONCRETE PLATFORM

WASTE PIPE

TO STORAGE

SPRING ENCLOSURE

SLOPE ABOUT 1" IN 1'-0"

PUMP

BOLTS ARE SET
IN CONCRETE

5"

CASING

6"

6'-0" MINIMUM

WELL CAP

FROST LINE

PERFORATED GRAVEL
FILLED 5 GAL. DRUM

WATER IN
HYDRANT DRAINS
OFF HERE WHEN
VALVE IS OPENED

FROST-PROOF HYDRANT

WATER-WASTE
DRAIN

CLAY
BACKFILL

DROP
PIPE

CLAY

WATER-BEARING
SAND

CYLINDER

DUG WELL

PUMP BASE
CASING CAP
CONCRETE CURB

PACKING NUT
PACKING GLAND
PACKING

TOP SOIL

CLAY

DROP PIPE

STRAINER

WELL ROD

WATER-BEARING
SAND

CYLINDER

DRILLED WELL

WASTE-WATER
DRAIN

WATER-TIGHT
MANHOLE & COVER

CONCRETE
FROST PIT

WEEP HOLE

CYLINDER

DRIVEN PIPE

CLAY

WATER-BEARING
SAND

STRAINER
& POINT

DRIVEN WELL

Quantities of Water

Population Density[1]	Avg. Daily (gpcd)	Water Use Acre-Ft.[2] per 1000 Pop.	Max. Daily Water Use[3] (gpcd)	Acre-Ft. per 1000 Pop.	Total Daily Water Requirements Per 100 Acres of Residential Development				Total Yearly Requirements Per 100 Acres of Residential Development		Total Yearly Requirements Per 100 Pop. Acre Feet
					Avg. Day		Max. Day[3]		1,000,000 Gal.	Acre Feet	
					1000 Gal.	Ac. Ft.	1000 Gal.	Ac. Ft.			
1. Less than 1 d.u./acre	300	0.92	900	2.76	57	0.18	171	.54	21	64	335
2. 1–2.9 d.u./acre	225	0.69	675	2.07	171	0.53	513	1.59	62	190	252
3. 3–4.9 d.u./acre	190	0.58	570	1.74	253	0.78	759	2.34	92	282	212
4. 5–15 d.u./acre	150	0.46	450	1.38	455	1.40	1365	4.20	166	512	168
5. Over 15 d.u./acre	125	0.38	375	1.14	950	2.92	2850	8.76	346	1065	139

[1] Assumes 3.8 persons per dwelling unit.
[2] One acre-foot equals 325,830 gallons.
[3] Maximum daily consumption equals 3 times average daily consumption.

SOURCE: *George Nez, Standards for New Urban Development—The Denver Background.*
Reprinted by Permission of Urban Land, Vol 20, No 5 Urban Land Institute, 1200 18th Street N. W., Wash. D. C.

—PLANNING GUIDE FOR WATER USE

Types of establishments	Gallons per day
Airports (per passenger)	3–5
Apartments, multiple family (per resident)	60
Bathhouses (per bather)	10
Camps:	
Construction, semipermanent (per worker)	50
Day with no meals served (per camper)	15
Luxury (per camper)	100–150
Resorts, day and night, with limited plumbing (per camper)	50
Tourist with central bath and toilet facilities (per person)	35
Cottages with seasonal occupancy (per resident)	50
Courts, tourist with individual bath units (per person)	50
Clubs:	
Country (per resident member)	100
Country (per nonresident member present)	25
Dwellings:	
Boardinghouses (per boarder)	50
Additional kitchen requirements for nonresident boarders	10
Luxury (per person)	100–150
Multiple family apartments (per resident)	40
Rooming houses (per resident)	60
Single family (per resident)	50–75
Estates (per resident)	100–150
Hotels with private baths (2 persons per room)	60
Hotels without private baths (per person)	50
Institutions other than hospitals (per person)	75–125
Hospitals (per bed)	250–400
Laundries, self-serviced (gallons per washing; i.e., per customer)	50
Livestock (per animal):	
Cattle (drinking)	12
Dairy (drinking and servicing)	35
Goat (drinking)	2
Hog (drinking)	4
Horse (drinking)	12
Mule (drinking)	12
Sheep (drinking)	2
Steer (drinking)	12

Types of establishments	Gallons per day
Motels with bath, toilet, and kitchen facilities (per bed space)	50
With bed and toilet (per bed space)	40
Parks:	
Overnight with flush toilets (per camper)	25
Trailers with individual bath units (per camper)	50
Picnic:	
With bath houses, showers, and flush toilets (per picnicker)	20
With toilet facilities only (gallons per picnicker)	10
Poultry:	
Chickens (per 100)	5–10
Turkeys (per 100)	10–18
Restaurants with toilet facilities (per patron)	7–10
Without toilet facilities (per patron)	2½–3
With bars and cocktail lounge (additional quantity per patron)	2
Schools:	
Boarding (per pupil)	75–100
Day with cafeteria, gymnasiums, and showers (per pupil)	25
Day with cafeteria but no gymnasiums or showers (per pupil)	20
Day without cafeteria, gymnasiums, or showers (per pupil)	15
Service stations (per vehicle)	10
Stores (per toilet room)	400
Swimming pools (per swimmer)	10
Theaters:	
Drive-in (per car space)	5
Movie (per auditorium seat)	5
Workers:	
Construction (per person per shift)	50
Day (school or offices per person per shift)	15

SOURCE: Environmental Health Practice in Recreational Areas, Public Health Service, U. S. Dept. of Health, Education, & Welfare

TYPES OF WELLS

Wells may be classified with respect to construction methods as dug, bored, driven, drilled, and jetted.

Drilled wells may be drilled by either the rotary or percussion method.

Each type of well has distinguishing physical characteristics and is best adapted to meet particular water-development requirements.

The following factors should be considered when choosing the type of well to be constructed in a given situation.

1. Characteristics of the subsurface strata to be penetrated and their influence upon the method of construction.

2. Hydrology of the specific situation and hydraulic properties of the aquifer; seasonal fluctuations of water levels.

3. Degree of sanitary protection desired, particularly as this is affected by well depth.

4. Cost of construction work and materials.

Characteristics of various types of wells[1]

Characteristics	Type of Well					
	Dug	Bored	Driven	Drilled		Jetted
				Percussion	Rotary	
Range of practical depths (general order of magnitude)	0–50 feet	0–100 feet	0–50 feet	0–1000 feet	0–1000 feet	0–100 feet
Diameter	3–20 feet	2–30 inches	1¼–2 inches	4–18 inches	4–24 inches	4–12 inches
Type of geologic formation:						
Clay	Yes	Yes	Yes	Yes	Yes	Yes
Silt	Yes	Yes	Yes	Yes	Yes	Yes
Sand	Yes	Yes	Yes	Yes	Yes	Yes
Gravel	Yes	Yes	Fine	Yes	Yes	¼ " pea gravel
Cemented gravel	Yes	No	No	Yes	Yes	No
Boulders	Yes	Less than well diameter.	No	(In firm bedding)	(Difficult)	No
Sandstone	Soft	Soft	Thin layers	Yes	Yes	No
Limestone	Soft, fractured	Soft, fractured	No	Yes	Yes	No
Dense igneous rock	No	No	No	Yes	Yes	No

[1] The ranges of values in this table are based upon general conditions which may be exceeded for specific areas or conditions.

SOURCE: Individual Water Supply Systems, Public Health Service, U. S. Dept. of Health, Education & Welfare

DUG WELLS

A dug well like a spring is susceptible to surface pollution and needs to be amply protected against it. It should be located on ground higher than, and at least one hundred feet from, any nearby cesspool, septic tank, shower or drain. For a distance of at least ten feet below the surface the well should be cased with watertight concrete. This may rest on a dry laid stone or brick wall which allows the water to enter. A tight concrete cover on which the pump may be mounted should be provided as shown in the drawing.

If a hand pump is to be used, it should be of the self-priming variety. It should have a solid base which may be set on the cover with anchor bolts. The pump cylinder should be set below the lowest water level in the well so that priming will not be required. The "pitcher pump" or any other pump with an open top is not safe because the priming water may be polluted and the open top makes it possible for filth and insects to get into the water. These pumps are also subject to freezing.

DRIVEN WELLS

Where soil formations are porous, as in parts of the Great Lakes Region and on the coastal plain, it is sometimes possible to obtain a relatively large quantity of water by the use of driven wells. Such a well is made by fastening a "point," which is a perforated galvanized pipe covered with brass wire cloth and a perforated brass jacket, on short sections of wrought iron pipe and driving them into the sandy soil until ground water is encountered. Water is forced through the pipe and point as they are driven to prevent the strainer from becoming clogged and to facilitate driving. The depth of driven wells is limited to about thirty feet. This type of well needs the same type of base and general protection as does a dug well. As it can be easily polluted, water from it should be chlorinated and frequently tested.

DRILLED WELLS

Drilled wells perhaps offer the safest and best source of water supply. A drilled well essentially is an iron or steel pipe forced into a hole drilled through rock or clay and to a water bearing stratum where satisfactory quantities of water, free from contamination, may be obtained. The wrought steel pipe casing is generally five, six, or eight inches in diameter. Wrought iron casing, though it costs nearly twice as much as wrought steel, is recommended as it will last much longer. At its top and also at the point where it enters the rock, the casing should be tightly sealed to prevent the entrance of surface water. Brass strainers are attached to the casing when the well penetrates sand or gravel. Drilled wells which penetrate and draw water from limestone formations are often dangerous so the water should not be used until satisfactory results from tests have been obtained. Water from such a well should be chlorinated and tested regularly but water from drilled wells ordinarily does not require treatment.

The iron casing of a drilled well prevents the entrance of surface water provided it is properly sealed and a watertight concrete platform or pump room floor is provided at the top. The well casing should extend above this floor or platform, and if the pump is to be mounted on it, the extended casing should be long enough to permit the construction of a twelve-inch concrete pedestal.

Unless the pump is of the submersible type, it should be protected by installation in a pump house which, in freezing climates, should be insulated and heated if the equipment is to be used in winter. Frost proof hydrants may also be attached to the delivery pipe as winter supply points. This arrangement is preferable to the use of frost pits which are not recommended by some state health departments because the pits are often the cause of well pollution. When it is imperative to install a pump in a pit or cellar, it is necessary to provide for proper ventilation and drainage. Well pits should be of reinforced concrete construction and covered with a tight fitting platform.

SURFACE SUPPLIES

In some places where satisfactory ground water supplies do not exist or the cost of developing them is too great, the source of the water supply may be a lake, stream, or spring. This may be true in limestone country where drilled wells may produce polluted water or water of doubtful quality. Surface supplies will be satisfactory if they are properly treated. A complete sanitary survey of the drainage area should be made. In the case of a small lake or pond or wherever possible, the area may be fenced and sources of possible pollution removed. Without chlorination, surface supplies can never be considered safe.

LOCATION FROM SOURCES OF POLLUTION

Protective Horizontal Distances—Micimum horizontal protective distances between the well and common sources of pollution shall not be less than those specified in Table I. For wells terminating in creviced formations, or where the overlaying soil formation is highly permeable, greater distances may be required by the FHA.

Protective Depths—The well shall be watertight to the depth necessary to seal off waterbearing formations that are or may be polluted or have undesirable characteristics.

1. Any distances specified above shall be increased if necessary to meet the minimum requirements of the Health Authority.

2. The minimum safe distance from a lagoon shall be specified depending upon the nature of the waste, geological surface and subsurface conditions, and the recommendations of the FHA and Health Authority.

3. Radial water collectors, springs, and infiltration galleries shall comply with the minimum distances specified for dug wells.

MINIMUM DISTANCES
Type of Well

Distance From	Dug	Bored	Driven	Drilled
Property line	100'	50'	50'	20'
Improperly abandoned well or sinkhole		Unacceptable		200'
Seepage pit	200'	200'	200'	100'
Disposal field or bed	200'	200'	200'	100'
Industrial lagoon		Unacceptable		(2)
Watertight sewer lines	50'	50'	50'	10'
Other sewer lines	100'	100'	100'	50'

SOURCE: Minimum Design Standards for Community Water Supply Systems, *U.S. Dept. of Housing & Urban Development, 1968.*

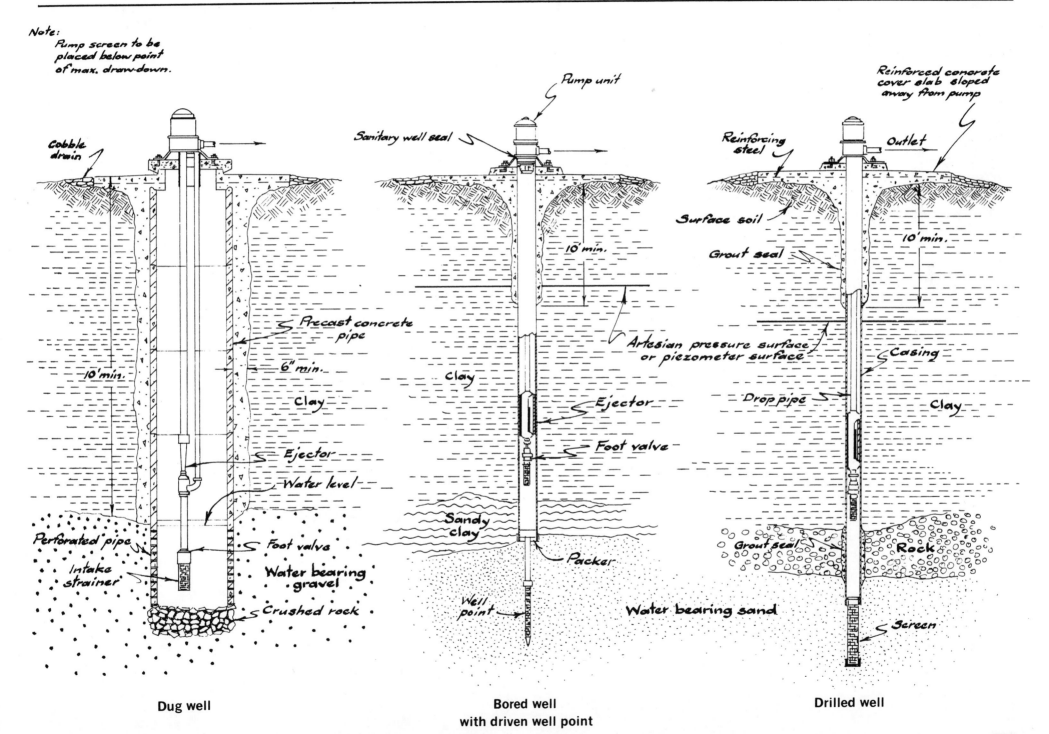

Note:
Pump screen to be placed below point of max. draw-down.

Cobble drain

Precast concrete pipe

6" min.

Clay

10' min.

Ejector

Water level

Perforated pipe

Intake strainer

Foot valve

Water bearing gravel

Crushed rock

Dug well

Sanitary well seal

Pump unit

10' min.

Clay

Ejector

Foot valve

Sandy clay

Packer

Well point

Artesian pressure surface or piezometer surface

Water bearing sand

**Bored well
with driven well point**

Reinforced concrete cover slab sloped away from pump

Reinforcing steel

Outlet

Surface soil

Grout seal

10' min.

Casing

Drop pipe

Clay

Grout seal

Rock

Screen

Drilled well

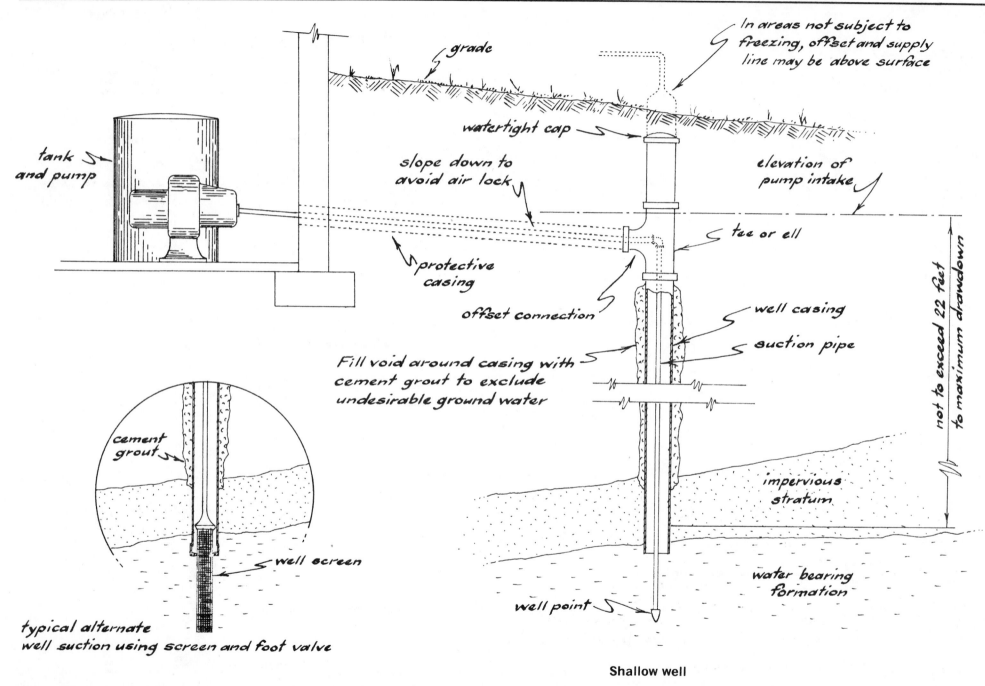

grade

In areas not subject to freezing, offset and supply line may be above surface

watertight cap

tank and pump

slope down to avoid air lock

elevation of pump intake

tee or ell

protective casing

offset connection

well casing

suction pipe

Fill void around casing with cement grout to exclude undesirable ground water

not to exceed 22 feet to maximum drawdown

cement grout

impervious stratum

well screen

water bearing formation

typical alternate well suction using screen and foot valve

well point

Shallow well

SOURCE: Minimum Property Standards for 1 & 2 Family Houses, Federal Housing Administration, HUD, Washington, D. C.

Deep well

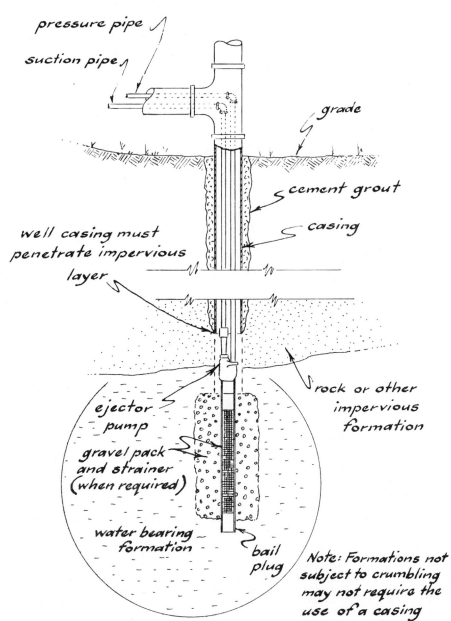

Alternate ejector type pump

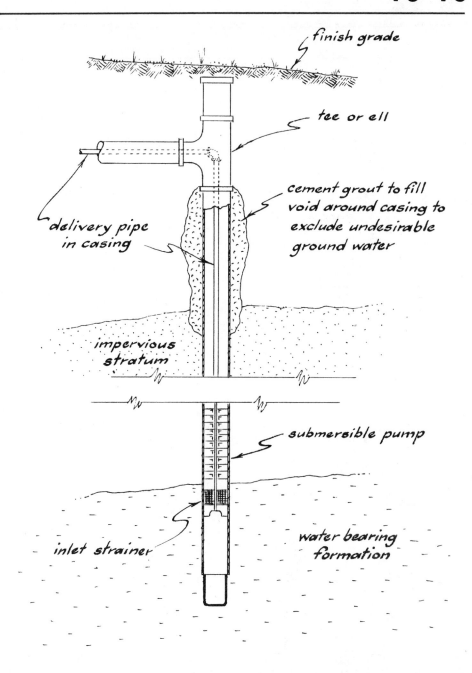

Submersible type

SOURCE: *Minimum Property Standards for 1 & 2 Family Houses. Federal Housing Administration, HUD,* *Washington, D. C.*

531

Type of pump	Practical suction lift[1]	Usual well-pumping depth	Usual pressure heads	Advantages	Disadvantages	Remarks
Reciprocating: 1. Shallow well ...... 2. Deep well	22–25 ft. 22–25 ft.	22–25 ft. Up to 600 ft.	100–200 ft. Up to 600 ft. above cylinder.	1. Positive action. 2. Discharge against variable heads. 3. Pumps water containing sand and silt. 4. Especially adapted to low capacity and high lifts.	1. Pulsating discharge. 2. Subject to vibration and noise. 3. Maintenance cost may be high. 4. May cause destructive pressure if operated against closed valve.	1. Best suited for capacities of 5–25 gpm against moderate to high heads. 2. Adaptable to hand operation. 3. Can be installed in very small diameter wells (2" casing). 4. Pump must be set directly over well (deep well only).
Centrifugal: 1. Shallow well a. straight centrifugal (single stage)	20 ft. max.	10–20 ft.	100–150 ft.	1. Smooth, even flow. 2. Pumps water containing sand and silt. 3. Pressure on system is even and free from shock. 4. Low-starting torque. 5. Usually reliable and good service life.	1. Loses prime easily. 2. Efficiency depends on operating under design heads and speed.	1. Very efficient pump for capacities above 50 gpm and heads up to about 150 ft.
b. Regenerative vane turbine type (single impeller)	28 ft. max.	28 ft.	100–200 ft.	1. Same as straight centrifugal except not suitable for pumping water containing sand or silt. 2. They are self-priming.	1. Same as straight centrifugal except maintains priming easily.	1. Reduction in pressure with increased capacity not as severe as straight centrifugal.
2. Deep well a. Vertical line shaft turbine (multistage)	Impellers submerged.	50–300 ft.	100–800 ft.	1. Same as shallow well turbine.	1. Efficiency depends on operating under design head and speed. 2. Requires straight well large enough for turbine bowls and housing. 3. Lubrication and alignment of shaft critical. 4. Abrasion from sand.	
b. Submersible turbine (multistage)	Pump and motor submerged.	50–400 ft.	50–400 ft.	1. Same as shallow well turbine. 2. Easy to frost-proof installation. 3. Short pump shaft to motor.	1. Repair to motor or pump requires pulling from well. 2. Sealing of electrical equipment from water vapor critical. 3. Abrasion from sand.	1. Difficulty with sealing has caused uncertainty as to service life to date.
Jet: 1. Shallow well	15–20 ft. below ejector.	Up to 15–20 ft. below ejector.	80–150 ft.	1. High capacity at low heads. 2. Simple in operation. 3. Does not have to be installed over the well. 4. No moving parts in the well.	1. Capacity reduces as lift increases. 2. Air in suction or return line will stop pumping.	
2. Deep well	15–20 ft. below ejector.	25–120 ft. 200 ft. max.	80–150 ft.	1. Same as shallow well jet.	1. Same as shallow well jet.	1. The amount of water returned to ejector increases with increased lift—50% of total water pumped at 50 ft. lift and 75% at 100 ft. lift.
Rotary: 1. Shallow well ...... (gear type)	22 ft.	22 ft.	50–250 ft.	1. Positive action. 2. Discharge constant under varible heads. 3. Efficient operation.	1. Subject to rapid wear if water contains sand or silt. 2. Wear of gears reduces efficiency.	
2. Deep well .... (helical rotary type).	Usually submerged.	50–500 ft.	100–500 ft.	1. Same as shallow well rotary. 2. Only one moving pump device in well.	1. Same as shallow well rotary except no gear wear.	1. A cutless rubber stator increases life of pump. Flexible drive coupling has been weak point in pump. Best adapted for low capacity and high heads.

[1] Practical suction lift at sea level. Reduce lift 1 foot for each 1,000 ft. above sea level.

SEWERAGE SYSTEMS

A sewerage system, more recently termed "wastewater systems," includes collection, treatment, and disposal elements. Collection may be of the separate "sanitary" and "storm" water type or may be a "combined" type which carries both sewage and stormwater. Combined sewerage systems are common in the older cities.

The collection system is of interest to this study although outfall or disposal sewers may be considered for inclusion in utility tunnels where their location is coincident with other systems.

SYSTEM CHARACTERISTICS

Sewerage collection systems in urban areas are arranged in networks permitting, for the most part, gravity flow to treatment or disposal points. Grades of sewers are kept constant depending on size and capacity and are sufficient to provide velocities (minimum of about 2.5 feet per second) to transport solid materials. Velocities are held to a maximum of about 10 feet per second. Grades required to accomplish solids transport vary generally between 0.5 and 2.0 percent. Where topographic conditions require, sharp vertical changes are introduced by drop manholes or pumped lift stations. Where pumping is required over considerable horizontal distances the conduit is termed a "force main."

Collection networks are dictated by topographical conditions, however, as in water supply systems, a grid pattern is associated with the street layout. A typical combined sewerage network is illustrated in Figure 1.

Collection networks are characterized by rather large variances in depth which are dictated by the grade requirements and by requirements to have a depth greater than adjacent building foundations or basements. This generally results in the sewer being the lowest structure under the street. Large interceptor sewers are frequently constructed by tunneling at great depths.

Sewer mains are generally installed singly in the center of the street although there may be one on each side in high density districts. Connections to buildings also must be on a grade although pumped services are found in special situations. A typical service connection is illustrated in Figure 2. The inlets for storm water for separate or combined systems are generally located at the curb line and lead to a catch basin designed to trap debris. The storm water is channeled to the main sewer by short laterals.

Sizes of sewers vary from a modern minimum of 8 inches for laterals to many feet in diameter for large interceptors and storm sewers. Materials used for sewer conduits include:

1. Vitrified clay is used widely for both sanitary and combined sewers because of its resistance to the corrosive action of sewage. Diameters are manufactured to 42 inches and lengths from 2 to 7 feet.

2. Concrete pipe is used primarily for storm water service. Linings are available for sanitary sewage service; however, unlined concrete pipe is used in climates where hydrogen sulphide corrosion is not a problem. Sizes range to 24 inches for plain concrete and to 144 inches for reinforced. Lengths are generally 3 to 8 feet for the smaller sizes and up to 24 feet for the larger reinforced sizes.

3. Asbestos-cement pipe is used for sanitary, combined or storm service and is also available with linings to resist corrosion in sanitary or combined service. Sizes vary from 4 to 36 inches. Lengths are generally 5, 10, or 13 feet.

4. Cast iron pipe is used primarily for force mains and is similar to water supply service pipe, previously described.

5. Corrugated metal pipe is used primarily for storm sewer service but is also available with coatings for sanitary and combined service.

6. Plastic pipe in sizes to 12 inches is being introduced for sanitary, combined or storm service.

7. A newly-developed lightweight fiberglass reinforced mortar plastic pipe in diameters to 48 inches and lengths to 20 feet is being used.

SOURCE: *Feasibility of Utility Tunnels in Urban Areas, Special Report 39, American Public Works Association, Chicago, Ill., 1971.*

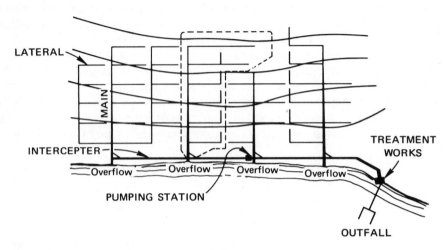

Figure 1. Typical combined sewerage system network.

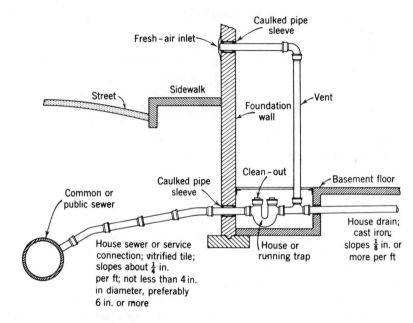

Figure 2. Typical sewer service connection.

SOURCE: Feasibility of Utility Tunnels in Urban Areas. Special Report 39, American Public Works Association, Chicago, Ill., 1971.

SERVICE AREA

Service areas should be based on population density and topography. A multiplicity of small sewage treatment plants indicates a lack of coordinated area planning. The practice of constructing many small plants, each designed to serve only its immediate area, is less desirable and often more expensive than a few large plants designed to serve entire drainage areas. A comparison of the service area map with the map previously prepared for drainage and soil conditions will be helpful in determining (a) most logical locations of treatment facilities and service areas, and (b) areas where public sewerage is most needed due to soil conditions which preclude the proper operations of private septic tank systems.

JURISDICTIONAL AREA

Jurisdictional areas should be related to drainage areas and should reflect anticipated growth patterns.

SEWERAGE MASTER PLAN

A sewerage master plan showing future needs and facilities is necessary in attacking the problem of urban growth. In areas currently without serious problems, such a plan will assist greatly in preventing future problems. Along with the master plan, a capital budget (long-range financial plan) is needed, in which expenditures are allocated for periods of several years. Both the master plan and the capital budget should be related to other community needs.

EXPANSION NEEDS

A sewerage system which allows flexibility to meet changing conditions is desirable. This can be accomplished by designing sewer sizes to handle both present and future needs, and by a treatment plant which will allow expansion at minimum expense. Where economics do not justify large sewer main construction in all areas, temporary pumping stations have been used until population densities warrant permanent trunk line installations.

SEWER CONNECTION REQUIREMENTS

When public facilities are available, connection to such a system should be required, since this allows better system planning. A determination is needed for availability, and a definite distance should be set. Some areas also use a time factor, allowing one to two years before connection is required. Still another system is that of requiring payment of a front foot benefit charge where a line is available regardless of whether connection is made.

SEWER LINE EXTENSIONS

The community should have a definite policy for determining the method by which service extensions are made. Whatever method is used, it should allow extensions to be made where economic and health factors make this desirable.

The policy should include provision for extension of lines across vacant lots. This requires a decision as to the method of payment or cost sharing. For over-sized lines designed to serve a large drainage area, a common method is for the government agency to pay the difference in cost between a sewer sized only for the immediate development area and the larger size which will be needed ultimately for the total drainage area.

ADEQUACY OF TREATMENT

The community should provide treatment for all sewage. In urban areas, the discharge of untreated sewage into the environment constitutes a definite health hazard. If such conditions exist, or if the present facilities do not provide treatment of all sewage, steps should be taken toward corrective measures for the community.

RATE STRUCTURE

A determination of total sewerage service costs is useful to compare local system costs with each other and with costs in adjacent areas. Average monthly residential sewerage cost is a convenient basis for this comparison. In some communities sewerage costs are paid from a general fund supported by ad valorem taxes and in this case, an estimate of average monthly residential cost should be made.

In other areas sewerage costs are based on water usage. If this is the case, a standard water consumption figure must be assumed and used throughout the study area for comparison purposes. One thousand cubic feet per residence per month (about 75 gallons per person per day) is suggested for this purpose.

SOURCE: *Environmental Health Planning Guide, Public Health Service, U. S. Dept. of Health, Education, and Welfare—1962*

Combined

Separate

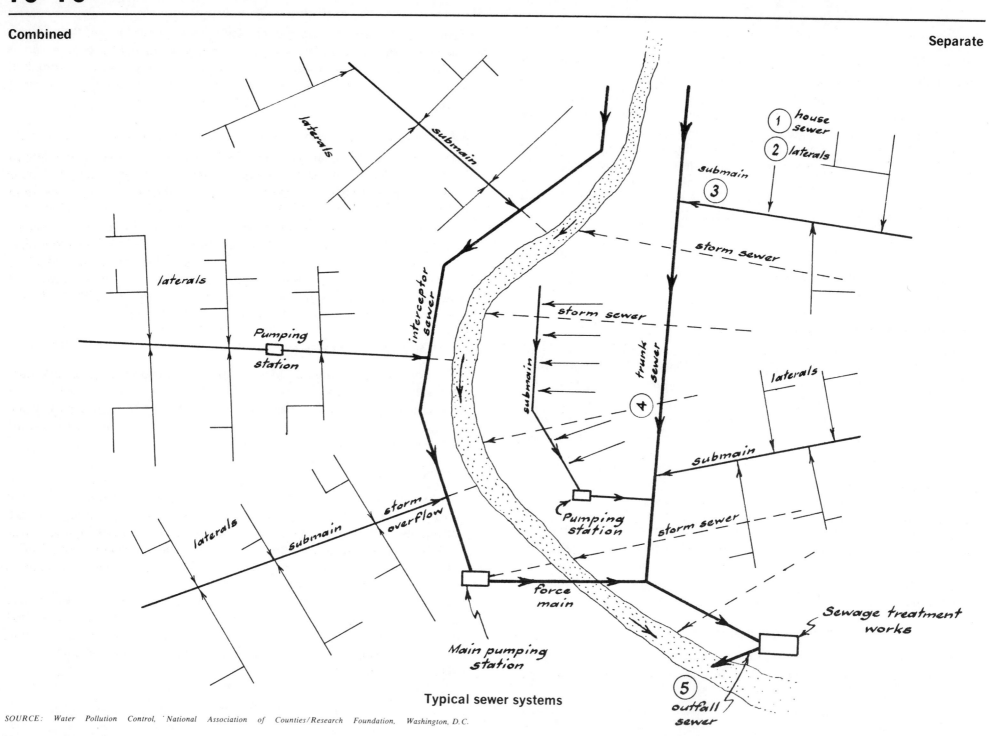

Typical sewer systems

SOURCE: *Water Pollution Control, National Association of Counties/Research Foundation, Washington, D.C.*

Sewerage System:—The collection of waste waters from occupied areas and conveying them to some point of disposal. The liquid wastes may or may not be treated before discharging into a body of water.

Sewage—is the liquid conveyed by a sewer.

Sanitary Sewage—That which originates from a dwelling unit, office building, factory, or institution. Sometimes refer to domestic sewage.

Industrial Waste—Liquid waste from an industrial process, such as papermaking, brewing, or chemicals.

Sewerage System:—The collection of waste waters from occupied areas and conveying them to some point of disposal. The liquid wastes may or may not be treated before discharging into a body of water.

SEWAGE—is the liquid conveyed by a sewer.

SANITARY SEWAGE—That which originates from a dwelling unit, office building, factory, or institution. Sometimes refer to domestic sewage.

INDUSTRIAL WASTE—Liquid waste from an industrial process, such as papermaking, brewing, or chemicals.

STORM SEWAGE—Liquid entering into sewers resulting during or after a period of rainfall.

INFILTRATION—Water that has leaked into a sewer from the surrounding ground.

SEWER—A closed pipe which carries sewage.

SANITARY SEWER—is one that carries only sanitary sewage. The size of sewer is not adequate to carry storm sewage or surface water. Sometimes called a separate sewer.

STORM SEWER—is one that carries storm sewage, surface runoff, and street wash.

COMBINED SEWER—carries sanitary sewage industrial waste, and storm sewage. Diameter is much larger than either a sanitary or storm sewer.

SEWERAGE WORKS—Refers to the complete system of collecting, treating, and disposing of sewage.

PUBLIC SEWER—is one that is municipally-owned and in which all abutting properties have equal rights to use.

PRIVATE SEWER—one that is owned by property owners or developer. Use by other parties will normally be limited or involve some form of payment.

HOUSE SEWER—Pipe carrying sewage from the plumbing system of a single building to a sanitary sewer or other disposal system.

LATERAL SEWER—Has no other common sewer discharging into it.

SUB MAIN SEWER—One that receives the discharge of a number of lateral sewers.

MAIN SEWER (TRUNK SEWER)—Receives the discharge from one or more sub-main sewers.

OUTFALL SEWER—Receives the discharge from the collecting system and conducts it to a treatment plant.

INTERCEPTING SEWER—One that cuts transversely a number of other sewers to intercept dry-weather flow.

RELIEF SEWER—One that has been built to relieve an existing sewer of inadequate capacity.

SEWAGE TREATMENT—Refers to any artificial process to which sewage is subjected in order to remove or alter its objectionable constituents and make it less dangerous or offensive.

AREAS SERVED

To make the following evaluations the sewerage service map is compared with (1) the present population density map, to determine current service needs and (2) the future population density map, to determine these areas which the future will find most in need of sewerage service. In this connection, there is considerable evidence that, within limits, the construction of new sewer systems to serve anticipated growth areas is often "self-insuring"; that is, the presence of adequate public sewerage facilities attracts home builders and home owners alike to the areas so served and in this way stimulates population growth in these areas. By computing the area provided with sewerage service as a percentage of the total area in each density grouping, the percentage of homes served for each of the population groupings may be determined.

Example:

49.6 sq. mi.—total in study area

7.9 sq. mi.—total area in "over 5,000 persons per sq. mi." density group

6.8 sq. mi.—of this 7.9 sq. mi. served by public sewerage service

Therefore: $100 \times \dfrac{6.8}{7.9} = 86$ per cent of this density group is served

Example:

The following chart relates the economic justification of public sewerage service with various population densities. The chart does not necessarily reflect the justification of public sewerage service from a health standpoint, since this cannot be determined except as a judgment factor.

With this limitation, the chart should serve as a "rule-of-thumb" guide for planning purposes. Local characteristics such as topography and subsoil conditions may alter the criteria, which are based on research results for average soil and topographic conditions.

Population Density	Equivalent Lot Size	Service Economic Justification
Over 5,000 persons/sq. mi.	Less than ½ acre	Public sewerage is justified
2,500–5,000 persons/sq. mi.	½ to 1 acre	Public sewerage is normally justified
1,000–2,500 persons/sq. mi.	1 to 2 acres	Public sewerage is not normally justified
Less than 1,000 persons/sq. mi.	Over 2 acres	Public sewerage is rarely justified

SOURCE: *Environmental Health Planning Guide, Public Health Service, U. S. Dept. of Health, Education, and Welfare—1962*

1. Cheaper
2. Larger pipes
3. Difficulty of treatment

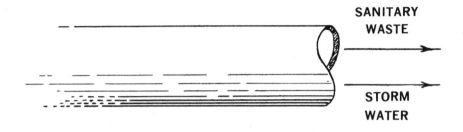

Combined—Storm water and sanitary waste are carried in the same line

1. Better in areas of large rainfall
2. Small pipes
3. Easier to maintain
4. Treatment plant smaller

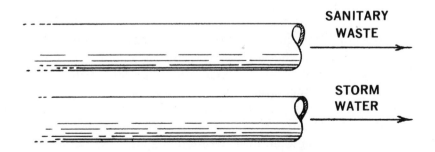

Separate—Two separate lines are used for storm water drainage and sanitary waste disposal

SOURCE: Ernest W. Steel, Water Supply and Sewerage, 3rd Edition, McGraw Hill Book Co., Inc.

Combined vs. Separate Sewers. Present-day construction of sewers is largely confined to the separate system except in those cities where combined systems were constructed many years ago. In newly developing urban areas the first need is for collection of sanitary sewage, and, since the sanitary sewers are relatively small and inexpensive, they can usually be constructed without long delay. For years the storm water will be cared for by the street gutters and the natural watercourses. As the city grows, however, underground conveyance of storm-water runoff may be needed, and a storm sewer system will be built. Many of the cities having combined systems were highly developed before the establishment of water-carried sewerage and already had storm sewer systems. It is interesting to note that a century ago in some cities the discharge of household wastes into the sewers was actually forbidden, but later the storm sewers received all liquid wastes and became combined sewers. Further extensions of such systems were then specially designed as combined sewers, often with provision for separating the dry-weather flow, which is largely sanitary sewage, from the large wet-weather flow.

Separate sewers are favored under the following conditions: where there is an immediate necessity for collection of sanitary sewage but not for the larger conduits required for the storm flow; where conditions are favorable for carrying storm sewage long distances over the ground surface; where disposal of the combined flow would necessitate pumping but where the separated storm flow need not be pumped; where mixture of storm and sanitary sewage would necessitate treatment of both while separation will allow disposal of storm flow without treatment; where an existing system of storm or combined sewers is inadequate in capacity and can be used for sanitary sewage alone, supplemented by another system for the storm waters.

Combined sewers are favored under the following conditions: where both types of sewage must be carried underground and it is necessary to keep the cost as low as possible; where the combined flow can be disposed of near by without objectionable conditions; where the storm flow, because of organic matter in street wash, is itself objectionable and requires treatment; where, as in crowded city streets, it is inadvisable to have more than one sewer.

It should also be pointed out that a system of sanitary sewers needs careful supervision to prevent unauthorized connection of roof gutters and other drains which will overload the sewers with rainwater during storms. Such supervision and danger are not a factor with combined sewers.

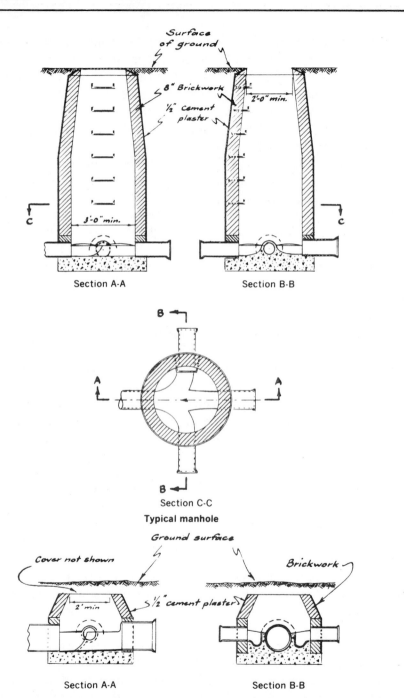

Section A-A   Section B-B

Section C-C

Typical manhole

Section A-A   Section B-B

SOURCE: Design and Construction of Sanitary and Storm Sewers, Joint Committee of American Society of Civil Engineers and the Water Pollution Control Federation—1960

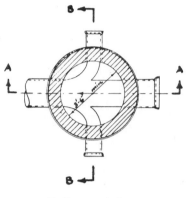

Shallow manhole

Manholes are among the most common appurtenances found in sewerage systems. Their principal purpose is to permit the inspection and cleaning of the sewers and the removal of obstructions.

Most manholes are circular in shape, with the inside dimension sufficient to perform inspecting and cleaning operations without difficulty. A minimum inside diameter of 4 ft for circular manholes has been widely adopted. However, 3 ft 6 in. is used in some localities, and where used solely for access into large sewers a diameter of 3 ft has been successful.

When the width of the sewer does not exceed the width of the manhole, the manhole is usually constructed directly over the center line of the sewer. For larger sewers the manhole is preferably constructed tangent to the side of the sewer for better accessibility. The manhole, for very large sewers, may be centered over the sewer, with a landing platform offset from an opening into the sewer itself. Consideration must be given to the need for introduction of cleaning equipment into the sewer.

The opening into the manhole must enable a man to gain access to the interior without difficulty. A minimum clear opening of 21 in. is recommended; it may be centered over the manhole, or, as is frequently done, it may be constructed off center in such a way as to provide a vertical side for the entire depth.

Typical manholes of the types used by many engineers and municipalities are shown.

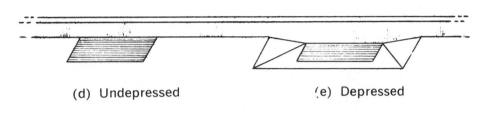

(d) Undepressed

(e) Depressed

Gutter inlets

(f) Grate placed directly in front
of curb open depressed

Combination inlet

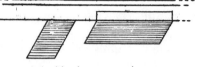

(g) Undepressed

Multiple inlet

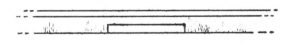

(a) Undepressed

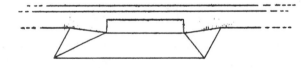

(b) Depressed

Curb inlets

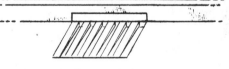

(c) Deflector inlet

SOURCE: Design and Construction of Sanitary and Storm Sewers, Joint Committee of American Society of Civil Engineers and the Water Pollution Control Federation—1960

A wastewater treatment plant speeds up natural processes of stabilization. A reduction of the pollutants in water which might take weeks or days in the receiving water is accomplished in hours in a treatment plant.

Wastewater treatment is of two general types, primary and secondary. In primary treatment solids are allowed to settle out. This reduces pollution by about 25-40%. Secondary treatment, a further step in purifying, uses biological processes in addition to settling. This reduces the pollution 85-95%.

PRIMARY TREATMENT

Primary treatment may be suitable when the receiving waters are large and swift enough to handle pollutants by natural processes without endangering health or causing odors.

As the wastewater enters the plant, it flows through a bar screen to remove large pieces of material which might clog or damage machinery. A comminutor or barminutor may take the place of the bar screen. These units shred or cut the solid material and it remains in the liquid.

In the grit chamber, sand, grit, cinders, and stones are allowed to settle out. Next, a coarse screen may be used to protect equipment and processes. At this point, a pumping station may be necessary to lift the wastewater into the sedimentation tank. In this tank, remaining solids settle to the bottom or float on top as scum. These solids, called sludge, are removed from the tank by skimming the scum from the top and by pumping the sludge from the bottom of the tank to the sludge digestion tank. In the digester, the sludge is reduced in volume and stabilized by bacterial action which results in material that can be disposed of safely.

While the sludge is digesting, a large volume of gas is produced. This gas contains 60-70% methane and has a net heat value of 540-675 B.T.U.'s per cubic foot.

Sludge gas produced by digestion is used in many treatment plants as a source of energy for operating parts of the plant.

Stabilized sludge is periodically drawn off and dried by being spread on drying beds, by centrifuging or by vacuum filters. Dried sludge can then be burned or used as land-fill.

However, there are some problems in disposal and use of dried sludge. The demand for it as fertilizer is limited. When used by homeowners, sludge should be sterilized to protect the public health.

As a final step in primary treatment, the settled wastewater may be passed through a chlorine contact tank where chlorine is added for disinfection. The effluent is then discharged to receiving waters through an outfall sewer.

SECONDARY TREATMENT

In secondary treatment, certain units are added to the primary treatment plant to treat the settled wastewater from primary sedimentation. These additional units are needed when the receiving waters are small or slow-flowing or wastes come from a large population. Secondary treatment involves biological processes which oxidize dissolved and finely suspended materials. The basic methods of providing this biological treatment are:

Trickling filers. Settled wastewater from the sedimentation tank is distributed over beds of gravel or crushed stone, usually by a rotary distributor. As the wastewater trickles through the stones, it contacts the biological slime which grows on the stones. The organisms in the slime oxidize most of the remaining impurities in the liquid, reducing the pollutional load.

Activated sludge or aeration. Settled wastewater from the sedimentation tanks is mixed with compressed air and biologically active sludges. This method also oxidizes the organic materials and reduces impurities.

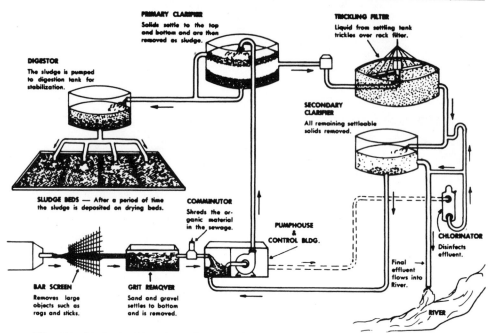

After this biological treatment, secondary sedimentation removes the remaining solids. A portion of the settled solids is returned to the aeration tank to provide the necessary biologically active material. The remainder is pumped to the digestor with the sludge from the primary sedimentation tank for treatment. The final effluent may be chlorinated before discharge.

Since the activated sludge process is more complex, it is more difficult to operate than a trickling filter. The trickling filter, however, is less efficient and requires a larger land area. There are many modifications of these basic processes available for use with particular types of wastes.

OTHER METHODS OF TREATMENT

There are several other processes in addition to these basic methods of treatment.

The Imhoff tank combines sedimentation and sludge digestion in a two-story tank. This is a common method of primary treatment in small communities because it is cheaper and requires less skilled operation than a standard primary treatment plant with separate digestion tanks. However, it is low in efficiency and provides less reliable sludge digestion, particularly in northern latitudes.

The Zimmerman Process is a patented method of treating sludge under high pressure and high temperature in a small area. If there is high sludge concentration the process is self-supporting in heat and power. For this method to be practical, an equivalent population of 30,000 is necessary.

Another patented method of sludge digestion involves the centrifuging of raw sludge followed by incineration under low pressure and high temperature. There are still other patented processes. Their applicability in a given situation must be evaluated by competent sanitary engineers.

Automation is an important new factor in wastewater treatment plant operation. Much progress has been made in the automation of recording and control equipment.

SOURCE: Water Pollution Control, National Association of Counties/Research Foundation, Washington, D. C.

GAS SYSTEMS

Gas systems include those installations and functions required to convey gas from source to customer. Although older systems obtained gas through the destructive distillation of coal or oil, essentially all modern North American systems utilize natural gas piped at considerable distances from well fields. The primary elements of gas systems include:

1. Gathering system facilities, including processing and compression stations.

2. Transmission lines installed for the purpose of transmitting gas to one or more distribution centers. Transmission pressures range from 100 to 500 psi and over.

3. Distribution systems which carry and control the gas supply from distribution centers to the customer's meters. Distribution systems may be further defined as:

a. High or medium pressure which operate at pressures higher than the standard service pressure delivered to customers. Typical pressures are in the range of 10 to 100 psi.

b. Low pressure in which pressures are substantially the same as those required by customers' appliances, thus not requiring pressure regulation at customers' premises. Typical pressures are in the range of 6 to 12 inches of water column.

System Characteristics

Gas systems networks are similar to water supply systems in layout including branching and looped patterns. As in water systems, loops provide alternate directions of supply in case of failures. In areas where gas is the primary source of fuel, the street layout dictates a grid pattern. Gas mains are laid by direct burial under streets, sidewalks or parking strips, with a line on both sides in the higher density districts to offset the cost of long service runs.

Service connections are provided by taps for small customers and valved branches to large. Taps are made in the same manner as water pipe taps for the large pipe sizes and by welded connections, clamps, or self-tapping devices for the smaller sizes. Pressure reduction and metering are generally accomplished on customer premises. A typical service connection is illustrated in Figure 1.

Modern pipe materials are primarily of welded steel, although there are large quantities of cast iron with bell and spigot, flanged and mechanical joints in service, since cast iron was the first material used in the gas industry.

A primary problem associated with the use of steel is prevention of corrosion in a direct burial environment. A variety of asphalt, coal, tar and extruded and taped plastic compounds are used for corrosion control purposes. Gas main sizes depend on use, pressure and volume to be carried. Typical size ranges for the various uses are:

1. Transmission—12 to 36 inches

2. High and Medium Pressure Distribution—1¼ to 20 inches

3. Low Pressure Distribution—4 to 24 inches

Auxiliary equipment required for the operation of distribution systems includes valves, pressure regulating stations, flow meters and in some cases compressor stations.

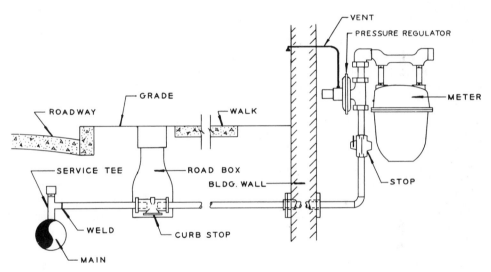

Figure 1. Typical gas service connection.

SOURCE: *Feasibility of Utility Tunnels in Urban Areas, Special Report 39, American Public Works Association, Chicago, Ill., 1971.*

ELECTRIC POWER SYSTEMS

Electric power systems have an extensive history of underground locations. The first installation planned by Thomas Edison for New York City was located underground. Over the years underground systems have progressed markedly in their extent and capacity.

Electric power systems include all of the installations and functions required to deliver electric power from source to customer. The principal features include:

1. *Generation Systems*—The source of electric energy produced by hydroelectric, thermal or nuclear generating plants.

2. *Transmission Systems*—The circuits carrying bulk electric power from source to one or more centers of distribution. Delivery points may be distribution substations or transmission switching and substations where further delivery is made to subtransmission systems.

3. *Subtransmission Systems*—The circuits carrying bulk power from transmission switching and substations to the distribution system substations.

4. *Distribution System*—Those elements of an electric power system between the transmission or subtransmission system and the customer's meter. Components of the distribution system include the following:

a. *Distribution Substation*—A facility where bulk power is reduced in voltage for distribution to a specific service area.

b. *Primary Distribution System*—A system of conductors serving distribution transformers from distribution substations.

c. *Distribution Transformers*—Systems of transformers for the purpose of reducing primary distribution voltages to those acceptable for customers services.

d. *Secondary Distribution System*—A system of conductors serving customers premises from distribution transformers.

SYSTEM CHARACTERISTICS

Although there is no defined standard of voltages for the various elements of electric power systems, general practice and the requirement to interconnect systems have resulted in "Preferred Voltages" which have been adopted generally for underground service by both electric utilities and manufacturers. Representative voltage ranges include:

1. Transmission—69 to 345 kv
2. Sub-Transmission—13.8 to 69 kv
3. Primary Distribution—2.4 to 46 kv
4. Secondary Distribution—120/240 v, single phase or 120/208—265/460 three phase.

Conventional underground primary distribution systems have a variety of patterns including branch, radial and loop. Loop patterns provide service from more than one direction in case of failure of part of the system. The loop is sectionalized by switches or circuit breakers, manual or automatic in order to attain flexibility and dependability.

In high density areas the common pattern for underground distribution is a grid network based essentially on the street pattern. The grid system provides dependability, flexibility and economy. A schematic diagram of an underground distribution network is illustrated in Figure 1.

Circuits for underground power systems are composed of various kinds of cables installed in duct systems in high density areas and directly buried in suburban and rural areas. Choice of cable and insulation type depends on voltage, installation conditions, load and other factors. Cable covering or sheath material is primarily lead for the higher capacities and rubber or plastic for lower. Insulation materials include rubber, plastic, varnished cambric, and oil impregnated paper. A variety of cable pressure systems are employed with the paper insulated types in high voltage service to preclude ionization of occluded gas. Table 6 illustrates the types of cables and insulations in general use.

Materials for duct systems include clay, steel, asbestos-cement, plastic and fiber pipe, all of which are generally encased in concrete. Multiple duct precast concrete and multiple duct clay tile are also used.

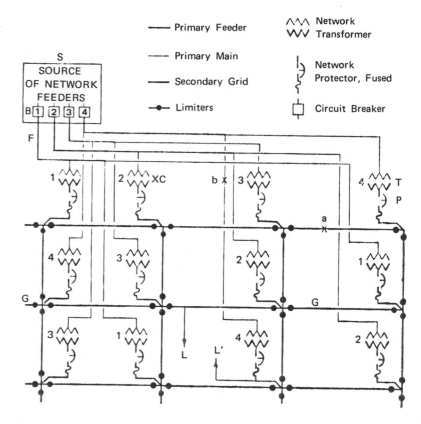

Figure 1. Underground electrical distribution grid network.

SOURCE: Feasibility of Utility Tunnels in Urban Areas. Special Report 39. American Public Works Association, Chicago, Ill., 1971.

Auxiliary equipment in underground distribution systems include transformers and switch and protection gear.

TELEPHONE AND OTHER WIRE COMMUNICATIONS SYSTEMS

Telephone and other wire communications systems, including telegraph, fire, traffic signal control, security service, are sufficiently similar to be considered collectively. The telephone system is by far the largest to be considered and will serve as the basis for discussion.

The continuity of service in telephone systems is an especially important consideration in that they are relied upon in a critical way in emergency and disaster situations.

A telephone system is an assemblage of telephone stations, lines, channels and switching arrangements for their interconnection, together with all accessories for providing telephone communication. The major features of the telephone system in an urban area include:

1. Central plant consisting of switching gear located at central offices.
2. Outside plant consisting of:
   a. Interstate long distance circuits connecting major long distance switching centers.
   b. Intercity trunk circuits connecting central offices to central offices in other cities.
   c. Interoffice local trunk circuits connecting central offices within a city or group of cities in an urban area.
   d. Local customer loop circuits connecting each customer to a local central office.

SYSTEM CHARACTERISTICS

Intercity and local interoffice trunk circuits have a defined pattern, seeking primarily the shortest distance between central offices.

Local customer loop circuits are essentially of the branch pattern, extending from a group of feeder cables, although they will of necessity take the general pattern of the street system in order to serve customers located thereon.

Essentially all modern telephone and other communications circuitry in urban areas is in the form of multi-pair cable in pole-supported (overhead) or underground locations. There is a general trend toward placing all telephone cable underground.

Telephone cable consists of assemblages of two or more circuit pairs encased in lead, rubber or plastic sheaths. Insulation is provided for the individual wires in the form of paper, fabric, rubber or plastic coatings. Cable is produced in sizes of up to 3 inches in diameter, containing as many as 2,700 pairs. The 3 inch size is the current limit for ready handling. The large cable sizes are pressurized from either central office or intermediate stations to prevent the entry of moisture.

The requirements for auxiliary equipment for telephone systems are loading coils, capacitors and electronic amplification equipment which is required at intervals of about one mile. Modern carrier systems require electronic repeater equipment, also located at intervals of about one mile. Terminal distribution frame space is required at various intervals. As technology charges, it is likely that satellite switching mechanisms may be required at various locations along the customer loop and trunk plant.

OTHER EXISTING SYSTEMS

Cable Antenna Television (CATV)

CATV is enjoying increased popularity in urban situations lacking conventional TV broadcast facilities, or where building heights, topographical features, mineral deposits and other conditions make conventional reception unsatisfactory.

CATV is also becoming of increasing importance in higher density urban situations where it is able to provide a variety of services not possible by conventional TV broadcast systems. Among the services possible are:
1. A much larger variety of TV channels (up to 80) compared with conventional TV broadcasting.
2. Comprehensive educational television services direct to homes.
3. Business and weather information services.
4. Centralized security surveillance services.
5. Centralized traffic surveillance systems.

A CATV system consists of a central station where signals are received on a community antenna and retransmitted over a network of coaxial cable. The central station may also originate and transmit signals over the cable, or it may be devoted solely to original program preparation and transmittal. In communities where comprehensive systems are located, the coaxial cable network will be associated with the street pattern. The cable is generally attached to above ground electric power, telephone or joint-use poles or is directly buried along with electric and telephone systems, sometimes in the same trench.

Potential New Systems

Although many new types of utility services are speculated as being on the horizon, most (such as home computer services and automatic meter reading) would use existing types of utility systems. A few, however, show some promise of being adopted in urban areas where they might affect utility tunnel installations. These include:

Pneumatic Mail Handling Systems—Mail has been handled by pneumatic tube in European cities for many years. London has a network of about 85 miles of such tubes radiating from the central post office which dates back over a hundred years. The system in Paris is also well known. Such systems have not enjoyed general use in the United States. With the proliferation of mail volume in the United States such systems might well be considered, particularly for interoffice transfer and collections from high density business districts. Installation problems in tunnels would be similar to those of other pipe systems except that sharp bends and branches must be avoided. The latter might result in space problems at branches. Vacuum power stations would have to be exterior to the tunnel. Pipe sizes would probably be in the 6-inch to one foot range.

Solid Waste Collection Systems—Central vacuum solid waste collection systems are in use in European cities and are being planned in the United States. It seems reasonable to assume that these systems will see future usage in the United States to serve large building complexes and possibly in high density urban districts to avoid congestion caused by collection vehicles. Solid waste materials may be shredded before introduction into the system to avoid large pipe sizes. Pipe size ranges would be in the 8- to 24-inch range. As in the pneumatic mail system sharp turns and branches would have to be avoided.

Solid Waste Slurry Systems—Experiments and studies are underway in connection with the bulk transportation of solid wastes to disposal sites in water mixed, slurry form. There appear to be no technical problems, however, the economics have not been established. It seems likely that if such systems are adopted they would be of limited application to utility tunnels because of the few such lines required. Pipe sizes would likely be of the 8- to 24-inch range.

Secondary Quality Water Systems—Increasing use of secondary quality water systems for fire fighting, certain industrial uses, and possibly sanitary sewage carriage, appears likely because of the deterioration of available water supply sources in the United States, both in quantity and quality. Problems associated with inclusion of such systems in utility tunnels are similar to those for conventional water supply systems.

SOURCE: Feasibility of Utility Tunnels in Urban Areas. Special Report 39, American Public Works Association. Chicago, Ill., 1971.

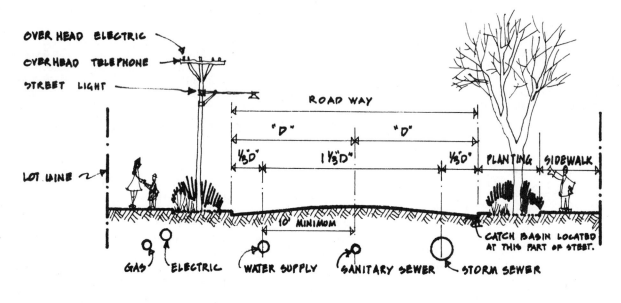

The street cross section is ideal and actual conditions can have all or some of the elements indicated.

STREET CROSS SECTION   no scale

DEFINITIONS OF UTILITY LOCATION

SANITARY SEWER

Generally located on center line of road. The line is a clay tile pipe. If it was located in the planting strip the roots of the trees might cause breaks in the pipes. This center line location also locates the pipe equidistant from building lines on both sides of the street.

STORM SEWER

Generally located the distance from curb line to center line of street. It is always located on the opposite side of the street from the water line.

WATER SUPPLY

May be located under sidewalk, in planting strip, or under street. Minimum design requirements will locate it at least 10 feet from nearest sewer or gas main and above highest sewer or gas main.

GAS

Generally located under sidewalk or in planting strip.

ELECTRICITY AND TELEPHONE

Best located in underground conduit. Sometimes located in overhead lines over planting strips. This causes interference with trees, danger of falling wires, and unsightly appearance.

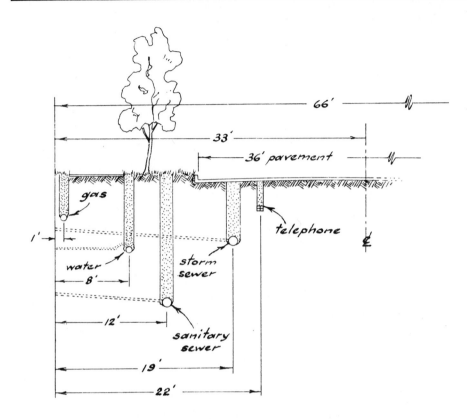

Location of underground utilities in soils of
uncertain characteristics

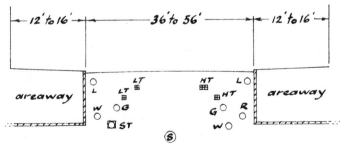

(a) Most common arrangement no original plan

SOURCE: *Committee of the City Planning Division on Location of Underground Utilities, American Society of Civil Engineers—1937*

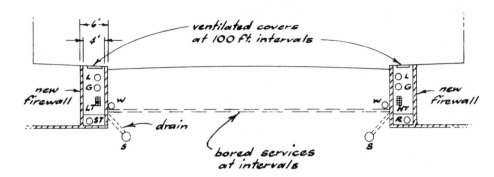

(b) Desirable plan when part of areaways can be recovered

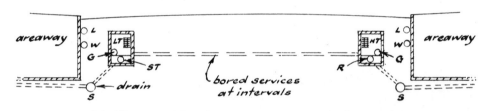

(c) Pipe tunnels where areaways cannot be used

Fig. a, b, and c, typical sections, central business section of Cincinnati, Ohio

Legend

L—Lighting circuit	LT—Telephone, telegraph fire alarm
W—Water	HT—Electric light and power
G—Gas	R—Refrigeration
ST—Steam	S—Sewer

UTILITY LINE LOCATIONS-GENERAL

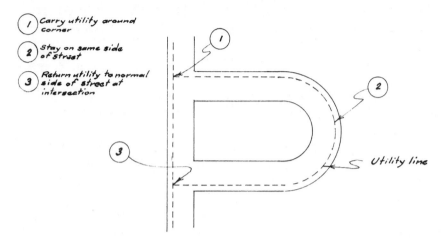

1. Carry utility around corner
2. Stay on same side of street
3. Return utility to normal side of street at intersection

Utility line

Example of a utility relocation
to a normal position at an intersection

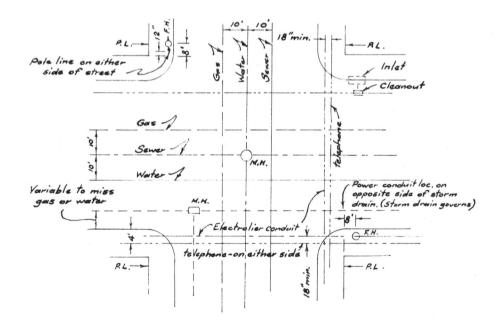

UTILITY LINE LOCATIONS-FRONTAGE ROADS

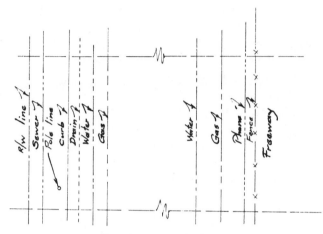

Frontage road plan

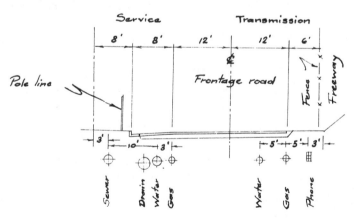

Frontage road section

SOURCE: Street and Urban Road Maintenance, Street Maintenance Committee, American Public Works Association, Public Administration Service, Chicago, Ill.

Septic-tank sewage disposal systems have been in use for several decades in both rural areas and suburban communities. In recent years, however, their number has greatly increased because of rapid expansion in the suburbs.

If you do not have access to a public sewage disposal system, which provides the best method of sewage disposal, doubtless you want a system that can give years of trouble-free service. The most satisfactory system probably is one in which the sewer line leads to an underground septic tank in the yard and the overflow from the tank disperses over a fairly large area through draintile or perforated pipe. The tile or pipe is laid in trenches or in a seepage bed and covered with soil; the soil is planted to grass, and no part of the system is visible.

Such a system should function well for many years if it is properly installed and maintained and if the soil in the disposal area is satisfactory. If the soil is not satisfactory, the sewage disposal system will not work properly regardless of how well it was constructed and installed.

SOIL ABSORPTION CAPACITY

In planning a septic-tank sewage disposal system, first find out if the soil can absorb the liquid sewage, the effluent, that flows from the septic tank. Some soils absorb effluent rapidly, others slowly.

How long and how well your sewage disposal system works depends largely on the absorption capacity of the soil. The effluent must be absorbed and filtered by the soil, otherwise unfiltered sewage may reach the surface or may contaminate ground water. Unfiltered sewage that reaches the surface smells bad and attracts flies and insects. These fly-breeding areas can be the source of disease.

Knowing the absorption capacity of the soil also helps you determine the size of absorption field you need. The slower the rate of absorption, the larger the field you need. If the soil has a slow rate of absorption, you may need an absorption field larger than your lot. Local ordinances may prohibit you from installing a sewage system and thus prevent you from building a house. And some soils, regardless of the size of the lot, are not suitable for use as septic-tank absorption fields.

WHY ABSORPTION FIELDS FAIL

Inspections by sanitary engineers have shown that sewage absorption fields fail to work properly mostly because the soils either are poorly drained or are so compact that the absorption rate is very slow.

Poorly drained soils are saturated with water during wet weather and in some places for long periods after heavy rains; there is no space left for septic tank effluent. Absorption fields on such soils may function well in dry weather and fail to function in wet weather.

If a soil has a very slow absorption rate, the effluent may rise to the surface even in dry weather. And in wet weather the absorption field usually is a boggy mess.

Absorption fields fail also because the land is too steep, there is a seasonal high water table, there is only a shallow layer of soil over bedrock, there is a cemented layer of soil just below the trench bottom, or the area is flooded periodically.

SEEPAGE PITS

Instead of being dispersed through subsurface tile in an absorption field, effluent can be disposed of by having it flow from the septic tank into a seepage pit. A seepage pit is a covered pit with a porous lining through which the effluent seeps into the surrounding soil.

Ordinarily, seepage pits are not permitted by local health inspectors except where a subsurface tile system is prohibited. If you should use a seepage pit, keep in mind that the effluent must be absorbed by the surrounding soil. Hence, the absorption capacity of the soil and other soil properties are fully as important in planning for a seepage pit as for a subsurface tile system, and soil depth is more important because of the greater depth required for a seepage pit.

SOURCE: Soils and Septic Tanks, by William H. Bender, Soil Scientist, Soil Conservation Service, U.S. Dept. of Agriculture, Washington, D.C., 1971.

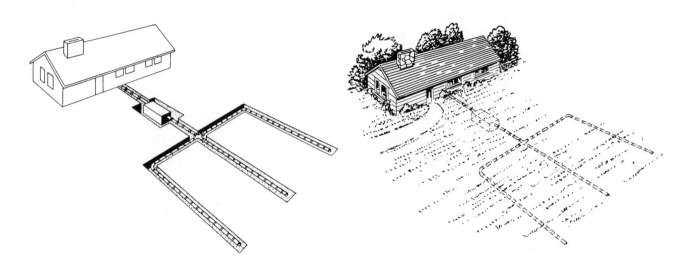

In a conventional septic-tank absorption field, draintile is laid in trenches (above, left). The tank and tile are covered with soil, and the area is planted to grass (above, right). The effluent from the tank is carried through the draintile to all points of the field where it is absorbed and filtered by the surrounding soil (right).

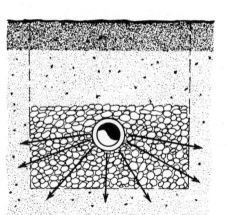

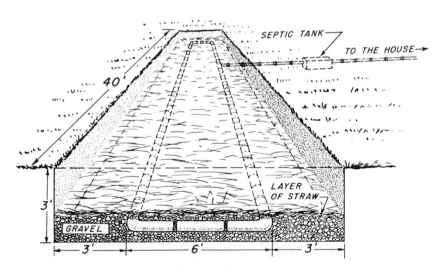

A seepage bed can be a satisfactory substitute for conventional trenches in some places. It operates on the same principle as trenches, but effluent is not dispersed over so large an area.

How well a septic-tank sewage disposal system works depends largely on the rate at which effluent moves into and through the soil—soil permeability. But several other soil characteristics may affect performance. Ground-water level, soil depth, underlying material, slope, and proximity to streams or lakes are among the characteristics to be considered in determining the location and size of an absorption field.

SOIL PERMEABILITY

Soil permeability is that quality of the soil that enables water and air to move through it. It is influenced by the amount of gravel, sand, silt, and clay in the soil, the kind of clay, and other factors. Water moves faster through sandy and gravelly soils than through clayey soils.

Some kinds of clay expand very little when wet; other kinds are very plastic and expand so much when wet that the pores of the soil swell shut. This slows water movement and reduces the capacity of the soil to absorb septic-tank effluent. The latest soil surveys give the shrink-swell potential of a soil.

Soils can be rated on the basis of permeability for use as septic-tank absorption fields. Some soil surveys give the permeability or percolation rate in inches per hour. Other surveys give a rating of *very rapid, rapid, moderate, slow,* or *very slow*. Some of the older surveys do not give the permeability or percolation rate, but it can be estimated from the soil descriptions.

GROUND-WATER LEVEL

In some soils the ground-water level is a foot or a few feet below the surface the year round. In other soils the ground-water level is high only in winter and early in spring. In still others the water level is high during periods of prolonged rainfall. A sewage absorption field under any of these conditions will not function properly.

If the ground-water level rises to the subsurface tile or pipe, the saturated soil cannot absorb effluent. The effluent remains near the surface or rises to the surface and the absorption field becomes a foul-smelling, unhealthy bog.

Soil surveys usually include information about soil drainage and ground-water level, especially those surveys of areas where the ground-water level is near the surface most of the time. Some surveys give the depth, in feet or inches, of the ground-water level. Others point out that a soil is well drained, poorly drained, or very poorly drained. Well-drained soils usually are suitable for use as septic-tank absorption fields, poorly drained soils are not.

SOURCE: Soils and Septic Tanks, by William H. Bender, Soil Scientist, Soil Conservation Service. U.S. Dept. of Agriculture, Washington, D.C., 1971.

DEPTH TO ROCK, SAND, OR GRAVEL

At least 4 feet of soil material between the bottom of the trenches or seepage bed and any rock formations is necessary for absorption, filtration, and purification of septic-tank effluent. In areas where the water supply comes from wells and the underlying rock is limestone, more than 4 feet of soil may be needed to prevent unfiltered effluent from seeping through the cracks and crevices that are common in limestone.

Soil surveys give the depth to rock or coarse gravel if these are near the surface. And they give the kind of rock and the type of soil material over the rock or gravel.

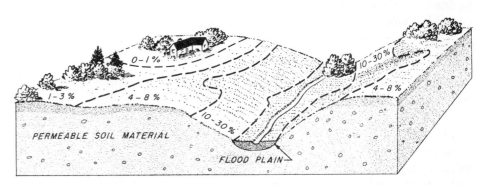

Septic-tank sewage disposal systems work very well in deep, permeable soils. Layout and construction problems may be encountered on slopes of more than 15 percent. Flood plains are not suitable for absorption fields.

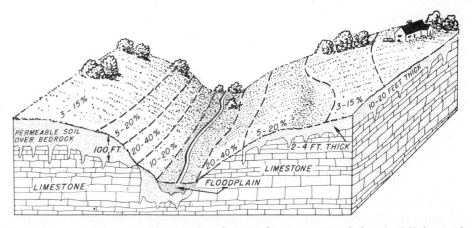

The deep soil over limestone, at the left, has moderate limitations for use as a septic-tank absorption field; layout and construction may be difficult on the steeper slopes. The soil that is 10 to 20 feet thick, at the extreme right, may not be suitable for absorption fields if the water supply is to come from a well. The shallow soil, 2 to 4 feet thick, has severe limitations. If absorption fields are placed there, the stream at the bottom of the hill may become polluted.

DIFFERENT KINDS OF SOIL

In some places the soil changes within a distance of a few feet. Having different kinds of soil in an absorption field is not significant if the different soils have about the same absorption capacity. But it may be significant if the soils differ greatly. Where this is so, serial distribution of effluent is recommended so that each kind of soil can absorb and filter effluent according to its capability.

On a soil map the lines, or boundaries, that separate one kind of soil from another are approximate. At the scale used most in published maps (1:20,000) these lines may not be accurate enough for selecting a suitable site for an absorption field without onsite inspection. This is especially true if some soils not suitable for use as absorption fields occur in the area. Hence, it is advisable to have a soil scientist examine the area, and it may be helpful to have a qualified person run percolation tests.

SLOPE

Slopes of less than 15 percent usually do not create serious problems in either construction or maintenance of an absorption field provided the soils are otherwise satisfactory.

On sloping soils the trenches must be dug on the contour so that the effluent flows slowly through the tile or pipe and disperses properly over the absorption field. Serial distribution is advised for a trench system on sloping ground.

On steeper slopes, trench absorption fields are more difficult to lay out and construct and seepage beds are not practical. Furthermore, controlling the downhill flow of the effluent may be a serious problem. Improperly filtered effluent may reach the surface at the base of the slope, and wet, contaminated seepage spots may result.

On a steep slope, if there is a layer of dense clay, rock, or other impervious material near the surface and especially if the soil above the clay or rock is sandy, the effluent will flow above the impervious layer to the surface of the slope and run unfiltered down the slope.

Soil surveys give information regarding slope, soil texture, clay and rock layers, and other conditions that affect sewage filtering.

NEARNESS TO STREAMS OR OTHER WATER BODIES

Local regulations generally do not allow absorption fields within at least 50 feet of a stream, open ditch, lake, or other watercourse into which unfiltered effluent could escape.

Never use the flood plain near a stream that is subject to flooding as an absorption field. Occasional flooding will impair the efficiency of the absorption field; frequent flooding will destroy its effectiveness.

Soil maps show the location of streams, open ditches, lakes, and ponds and of alluvial soils that are subject to flooding. Soil surveys usually give the probability of flooding for alluvial soils.

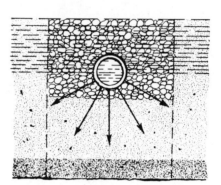

The high water table at tile level forces the effluent upward to the surface. This creates an unsanitary condition and health hazard.

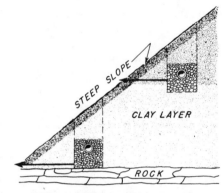

If an absorption field is placed on a steep slope where there is a layer of dense clay, rock, or other impervious material near the surface, the effluent will flow above the impervious layer to the surface and run unfiltered down the hillside.

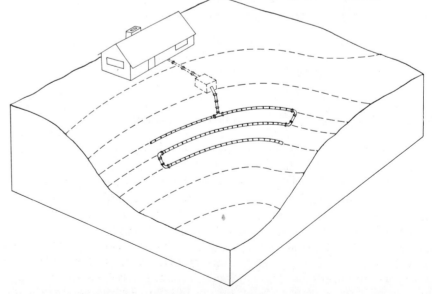

In constructing a septic-tank sewage disposal system on sloping land, the tile lines are laid on the contour. Serial distribution, as shown above, is necessary on most sloping fields or in fields where there is a change in soil type.

SOURCE: Soils and Septic Tanks, by William H. Bender. Soil Scientist, Soil Conservation Service, U.S. Dept. of Agriculture, Washington, D.C., 1971

CALCULATING THE SIZE OF ABSORPTION FIELD

The size of absorption field needed is determined mainly by the amount of sewage to be filtered and the absorption capacity of the soil. The amount of sewage depends largely on the number of people occupying a house. Most public health agencies set standards for the size of absorption fields on the basis of the number of bedrooms in a house, which probably gives the best estimate of the number of occupants.

Standard trenches. In calculating the size of absorption field needed where subsurface tile or perforated pipe is to be laid in trenches, first you need to know the percolation rate of the soil. Then look at the chart to get the square feet of absorption area needed per bedroom. Multiply this figure by the number of bedrooms and you have the total square feet of absorption area needed.

Count only the bottoms of the trenches as the effective absorption area. To find out how long the trenches should be and how much draintile or perforated pipe you will need, divide the square feet of absorption area needed by the width (in feet) of the trenches. This gives you total trench length.

The trenches should be spaced 6 to 8 feet apart; multiply the total trench length by the distance between the trench center lines to get the total area, in square feet, to be occupied by the absorption field.

Sample calculation for a two-bedroom house; trenches are to be 24 inches wide:

Soil percolation rate is 2 inches per hour. Chart at left shows that the required absorption area per bedroom is 250 square feet. Absorption area required for two bedrooms = 500 square feet. 500 square feet ÷ by 2 feet (trench width) = 250 feet — total length of trench and tile or pipe required.

For this system, the best layout would be four trenches, each about 62 feet long. But three trenches, each about 84 feet long, would also make a good layout. Trenches should not be longer than 100 feet.

Seepage beds. To calculate the size of seepage bed needed, first determine the size, in square feet, of the absorption field needed. This is determined the same way as for a trench system. Count the entire bottom of the bed as effective absorption area. For a two-bedroom house, if the soil percolation rate is 2 inches per hour, you need 500 square feet of seepage bed. A bed 10 feet wide and 50 feet long or a bed 12 feet wide and 42 feet long will meet the requirements.

Seepage pits. To calculate the size of seepage pit or pits needed, determine the size of absorption field needed (same method as for standard trenches and for seepage bed).

Count only the vertical walls below the inlet as the effective absorption area of a seepage pit. Do not count the area on the bottom of the pit. To find out the size of pit or pits needed divide the total square feet of absorption field needed by the effective depth (in feet) you can safely dig your pit. This will give you the circumference of the pit. Divide the circumference by 3.14 to get the diameter of the pit.

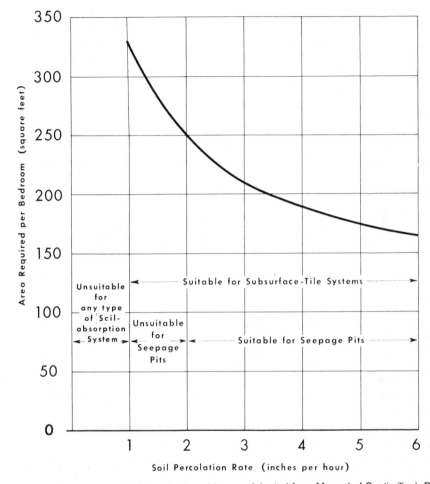

Size of absorption field needed for private residences. Adapted from Manual of Septic Tank Practice (1, p. 9)

SOURCE: Soils and Septic Tanks, *by William H. Bender. Soil Scientist, Soil Conservation Service. U.S. Dept. of Agriculture, Washington, D.C., 1971.*

Percolation tests can be helpful in determining the absorption capacity of the soil and in calculating the size of the absorption field. Most local regulations require that trained personnel, generally from local health departments, make percolation tests. These tests are often made under a wide range of soil moisture conditions. Results are reliable only if the soil moisture is at or near field capacity when the test is made. Excessive percolation rates are obtained when there are small cracks or crevices in the soil because of insufficient moisture. False rates are also obtained when percolation tests are made in naturally wet soils when they are dry during periods of low rainfall and are not thoroughly moistened before testing.

Percolation tests are made as follows:

1. Dig six or more test holes 4 to 12 inches in diameter and about as deep as you plan to make the trenches or seepage bed. Space the holes uniformly over the proposed absorption field. Move any smeared or slickened surface that could interfere with water entering the soil. Remove loose dirt from the bottom of the holes and add 2 inches of sand or fine gravel to prevent sealing.

2. Pour at least 12 inches of water in each hole. Add water, as needed, to keep the water level 12 inches above the gravel for at least 4 hours or preferably overnight during dry periods. *If percolation tests are made during a dry season, the soil must be thoroughly wetted to simulate its condition during the wettest season of the year.* The results, thus, should be the same regardless of the season.

3. If water is to remain in the test holes overnight, adjust the water level to about 6 inches above the gravel. Measure the drop in water level over a 30-minute period. Multiply that by two to get inches per hour. This is the percolation rate. After getting the percolation rate for all the test holes, figure the average and use that as the percolation rate.

4. If no water remains in the test holes overnight, add water to bring the depth to 6 inches. Measure the drop in water level every 30 minutes for 4 hours. Add water as often as needed to keep it at the 6-inch level. Use the drop in water level that occurs during the final 30 minutes to calculate the percolation rate.

5. In sandy soils, where water seeps rapidly, reduce the time interval between measurements to 10 minutes, and run the test for only 1 hour. Use the drop that occurs during the final 10 minutes to calculate the percolation rate.

6. Percolation tests for seepage pits are made in the same way except that each contrasting layer of soil needs to be tested. Use a weighted average of the results in figuring the size pit you need from the chart on page 553.

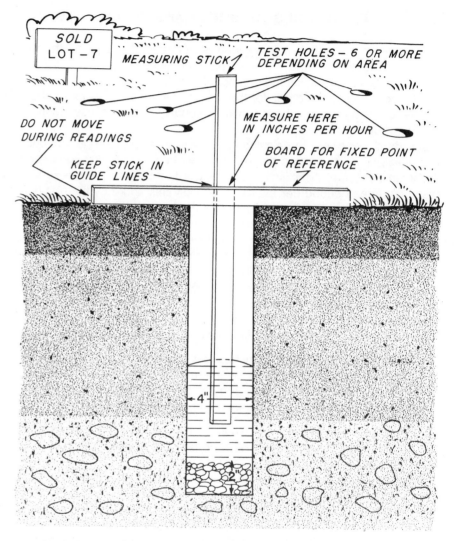

A percolation test hole with measuring stick is shown in the foreground; other test holes properly distributed over the field are in the background.

SOURCE: Soils and Septic Tanks, by William H. Bender, Soil Scientist, Soil Conservation Service. U.S. Dept. of Agriculture, Washington, D.C., 1971.

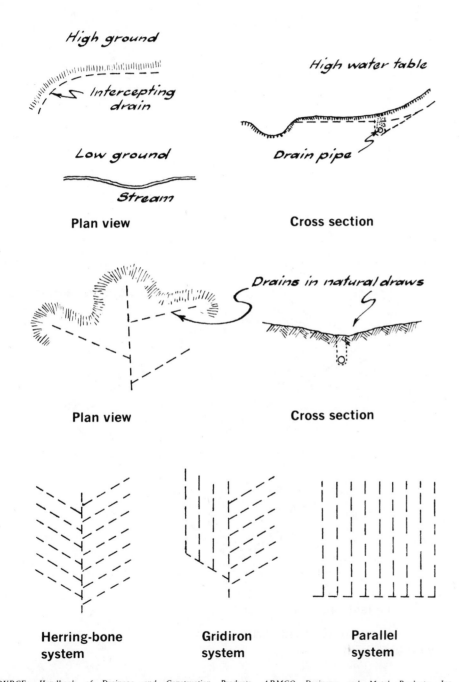

High ground

Intercepting drain

Low ground

Stream

Plan view

High water table

Drain pipe

Cross section

Drains in natural draws

Plan view

Cross section

Herring-bone system

Gridiron system

Parallel system

LOCATING THE SYSTEM; SPACING, DEPTH, SLOPE

The main should, so far as possible, follow the line of natural drainage. Drains should be in straight lines, or in long easy curves.

Submains should also follow the line of natural drainage. Laterals should be laid in the line of greatest slope. Intercepting drains are an exception, generally being placed across the slope.

DESIGN OF LATERAL SYSTEM

Three principal types of lateral subdrainage systems are in common use, the herring-bone, gridiron and parallel systems. The parallel system is the most economical type because it involves the least duplication of drainage by laterals and mains. The preferable arrangement is short mains and long laterals rather than the reverse.

The spacing of laterals depends on the physical composition and texture of the soils.

A minimum slope of 0.1 percent (1 ft in 100 ft) is recommended. Steeper slopes are better.

SOURCE: Handbook of Drainage and Construction Products, ARMCO Drainage and Metal Products, Inc., Middletown, Ohio

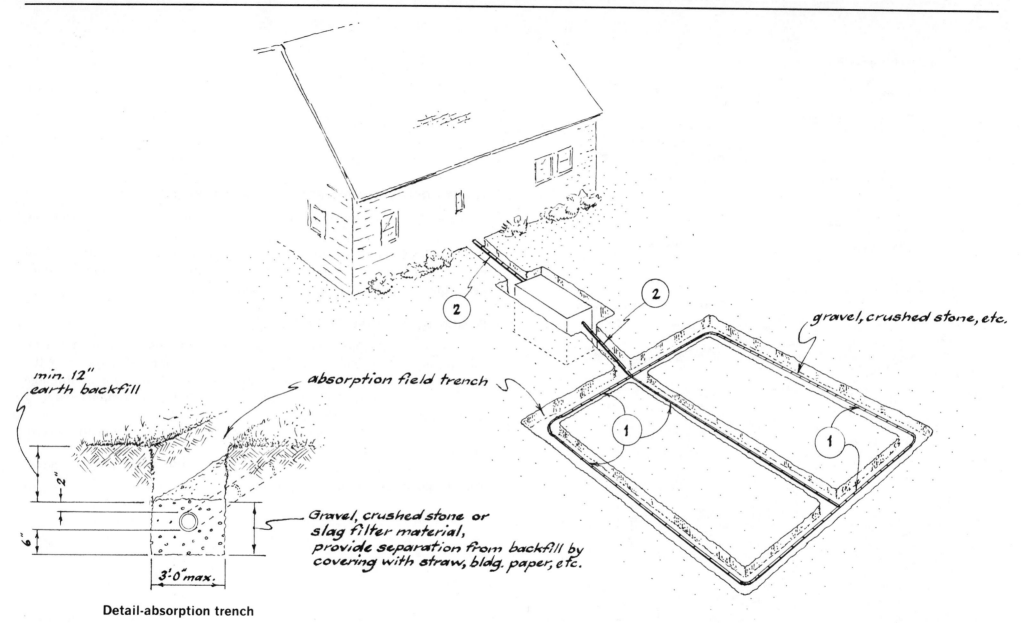

min. 12"
earth backfill

absorption field trench

gravel, crushed stone, etc.

2"

6"

3'-0" max.

Detail-absorption trench

Gravel, crushed stone or
slag filter material,
provide separation from backfill by
covering with straw, bldg. paper, etc.

1   Drain tile laid with open joints.

2   Pipe laid on undisturbed earth
    with tight joints.

SOURCE: *Minimum Property Standards for 1 & 2 Living Units, FHA No. 300, Washington, D. C.*

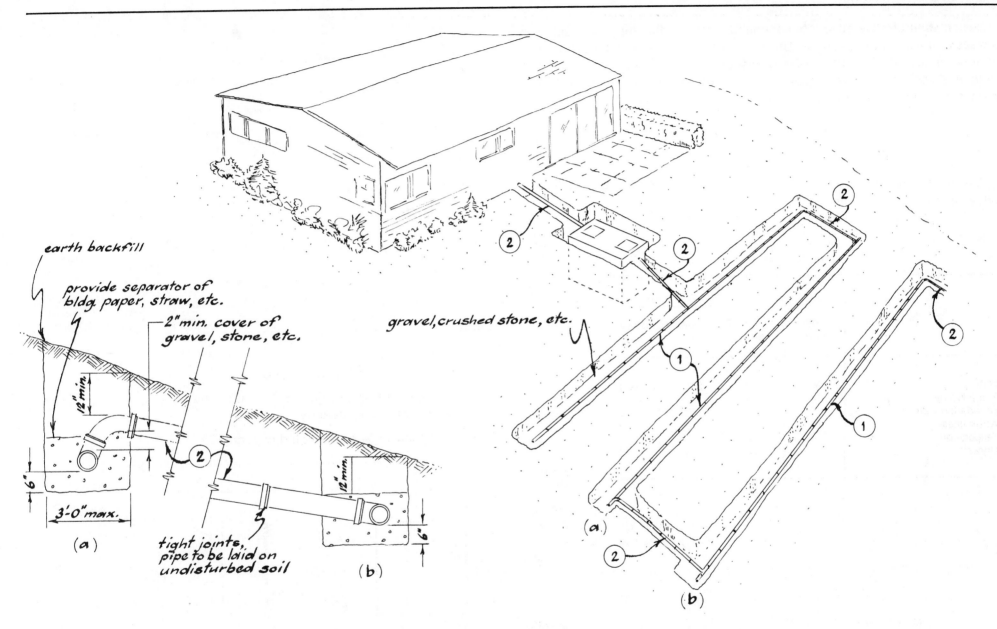

earth backfill

provide separator of
bldg. paper, straw, etc.

2" min. cover of
gravel, stone, etc.

12" min.

6"

3'-0" max.

(a)

tight joints,
pipe to be laid on
undisturbed soil

12" min.

6"

(b)

gravel, crushed stone, etc.

(a)

(b)

1 Drain tile laid with open joints

2 Pipe laid with tight joints

SOURCE: *Minimum Property Standards for 1 & 2 Living Units, FHA No. 300, Federal Housing Administration*

Design shall provide adequate volume for settling, for sludge and scum storage and access for cleaning. The structural design and materials used shall be in accordance with generally accepted good engineering practice providing a sound, durable tank which will safely sustain all dead and live loads and liquid and earth pressure involved in each case.

The location of the septic tank must be such that it will achieve the following minimum distances.

Minimum Distances

FROM	To			
	Septic tank	Absorption field	Seepage pit	Absorption bed
Well	50	100	100	100
Property line	10	5	10	10
Foundation wall	5	5	20	5
Water lines	10	10	10	10
Seepage pit	6	6		
Drywell	6	20	20	20

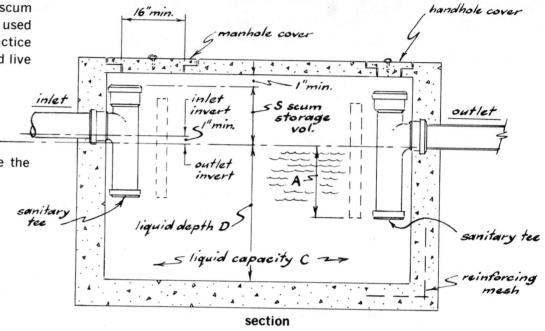

section

A approx. 40% of the liquid depth D

D not less than 30'' depth greater than 6 ft. shall not be considered in tank capacity.

S not less than 15% of the liquid capacity C.

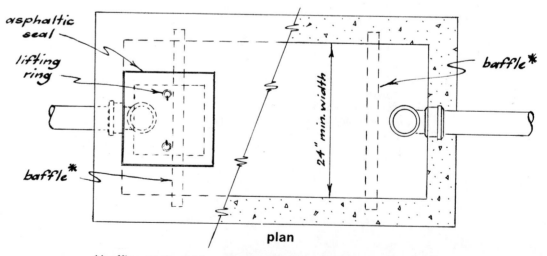

plan

*baffles optional to submerged inlet and outlet sanitary tee

SOURCE: *Minimum Property Standards for 1 & 2 Living Units. FHA No. 300, Federal Housing Administration*

Liquid capacity shall be based on the number of bedrooms proposed, or that can be reasonably anticipated in the dwelling and shall be at least as follows:

Minimum Capacities for Septic Tanks

Number of bedrooms	Minimum liquid capacity below outlet invert (gallons)
2 or less	750
3	900
4	1,000
Each additional bedroom, add	250

Note: These capacities provide for the plumbing fixtures and appliances commonly used in a single family residence (automatic sequence washer, mechanical garbage grinder and dishwasher included).

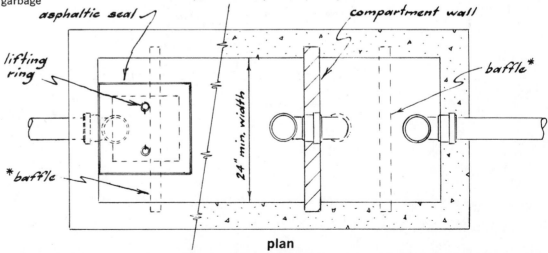

section

A approx. 40% of the liquid depth D

D not less than 30'' depth greater than 6 ft. shall not be considered in tank capacity.

S not less than 15% of the liquid capacity C.

plan

*baffles optional to submerged inlet and outlet sanitary tee

SOURCE: Minimum Property Standards for 1 & 2 Living Units, FHA No. 300, Federal Housing Administration

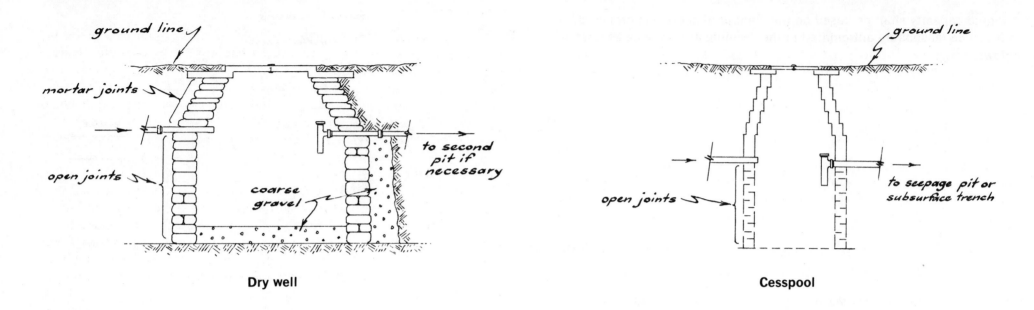

Dry well

Cesspool

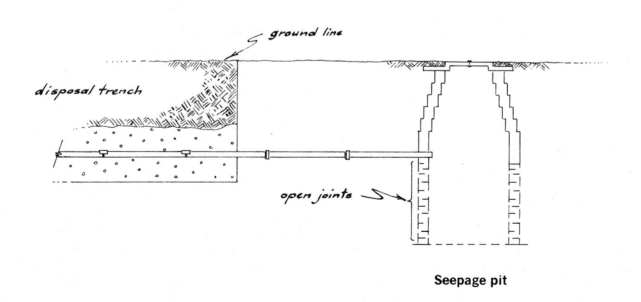

Seepage pit

SOURCE: Home Builders Manual for Land Development, National Association of Home Builders—1958

COLLECTION AGENCY

A governmentally regulated system of refuse collection is preferable to the practice of having individual competitive haulers deal directly with the homeowner. This regulation can be achieved by a governmentally operated system, by having private companies contract with the local government, or by having private companies franchised by the local government.

REFUSE MASTER PLAN

A master plan based on a thorough engineering analysis for the collection and disposal of refuse is vital in rapidly growing communities. The alternative is almost insurmountable future problems. Even the best planned refuse collection and disposal system will be one of the costliest services provided by a municipality. A poorly planned system is certain to place a continuous, undue burden on financial resources and create ill-will in the community.

Of prime economic importance is the proper location of disposal facilities in relation to future population concentrations. Sites for these facilities must be designated and acquired either through zoning, leasing, purchase, or condemnation to avoid future hostile public reaction as well as to avoid expensive future acquisition costs.

There must be close coordination of the refuse collection and disposal services (including any necessary transfer stations) and the community transportation plans to develop the most economic hauling system. Coordination with future recreational area plans may be mutually beneficial through improvement of low land by filling with refuse or incinerator residue.

EXTENSION OF SERVICE

A definite policy should be established for extending service areas. In contrast to water and sewerage services which require considerable long-range planning of physical needs, refuse collection lends itself to somewhat more flexible program planning.

Population Density	Equivalent Lot Size	Service Economic Justification
Over 2,500 persons/sq. mi.	Less than 1 acre	Service is justified
1,000 2,500 persons/sq. mi.	1 to 1 acres	Service is normally justified
500 1,000 persons/sq. mi.	2 to 4 acres	Service is not normally justified
Less than 500 persons/sq. mi	Over 4 acres	Service is rarely justified

SOURCE: Environmental Health Planning Guide, Public Health Service, U. S. Dept. of Health, Education, and Welfare—1962

COLLECTION

Collection should include both rubbish and garbage. Where only one type of refuse is collected routinely, experience has shown that the other type is often neglected. Closed body trucks are desirable for preventing material from scattering. Compaction trucks are advantageous under some circumstances because of larger capacity per unit volume. If garbage is collected, it should be done at least twice weekly during the warmer summer months. Weekly collection may suffice during winter months in many parts of the country.

Wrapping of garbage has been found to be an effective means of fly control during summer periods. A number of communities now require the installation of garbage grinders in newly constructed residences, and where sewage disposal facilities are capable of treating this load this practice is often desirable. Household incineration of combustible refuse should be carefully regulated to prevent insanitary conditions resulting from the possible introduction of non-combustible material, and to control air pollution. In those densely populated urban areas having adequate refuse collection, individual burning of refuse often creates serious air pollution problems and under these conditions communities may wish to restrict or prohibit this method of disposal.

DISPOSAL FACILITIES

Because of nuisance conditions and health hazards, open dumps are not acceptable. Other disposal methods such as the sanitary landfill or incinerator are satisfactory when properly operated. The disposal site should be as near as possible to the area it serves, preferably not more than 10 miles away.

AREAS SERVED

The refuse service area map should be compared with the population density maps to determine coverage in the various density groupings. The chart assumes average topography and reasonable length of haul, and is based on cost research using various numbers of collection stops per mile. As a "rule-of-thumb" guide, they can be used for determining the economic justifications of service under average conditions.

The table shown here presents the APWA* classification of refuse materials defining the character, nature and kinds of typical materials as well as their conventional point of origin.

APWA terminology and definitions are as follows:

1. Waste refers to the useless, unwanted, or discarded materials resulting from normal community activities, including solids, liquids, and gases.

2. Atmospheric wastes consist of particulate matter, such as dust and smoke, fumes, and gases.

3. Liquid wastes consist mainly of sewage and industrial wastewaters, including both dissolved and suspended matter.

4. Solid wastes are classed as refuse.

5. The physical state of wastes may change in their conveyance or treatment. Dewatered sludge from wastewater treatment plants may become solid wastes; garbage may be ground and discharged into sewers becoming waterborne wastes; and fly ash may be removed from stack discharges and disposed of as solid or as waterborne wastes.

6. Refuse comprises all of the solid wastes of the community, including semi-liquid or wet wastes with insufficient moisture and other liquid contents to be free-flowing.

7. The component materials of refuse can be classified by (a) point of origin, (b) the nature of the material itself, and (c) character of materials.

8. Special wastes are defined as (a) hazardous wastes by reason of their pathological, explosive, radioactive, or toxic nature, and (b) security wastes: confidential documents, negotiable papers, etc.

*American Public Works Administration

SOURCE: *Municipal Refuse Disposal. Public Administration Service, Chicago, Ill.*

CLASSIFICATION OF REFUSE MATERIALS

Kind or Character	Composition or Nature		Origin or Source
Garbage	Wastes from the preparation, cooking, and serving of food. Market refuse, waste from the handling, storage, and sale of produce and meats		From: households, institutions, and commercial concerns such as: hotels, stores, restaurants, markets, etc.
Rubbish or Mixed Refuse	Combustible (primarily organic)	Paper, cardboard, cartons Wood, boxes, excelsior Plastics Rags, cloth, bedding Leather, rubber Grass, leaves, yard trimmings	
	Noncombustible (primarily inorganic)	Metals, tin cans, metal foils Dirt Stones, bricks, ceramics, crockery Glass, bottles Other mineral refuse	
Ashes	Residue from fires used for cooking, heating buildings, incinerators, etc.		
Bulky Wastes	Large auto parts, tires Stoves, refrigerators, other large appliances Furniture, large crates Trees, branches, palm fronds, stumps, flotage		From: streets, sidewalks, alleys, vacant lots, etc.
Street refuse	Street sweepings, dirt Leaves Catch basin dirt Contents of litter receptacles		
Dead animals	Small animals: cats, dogs, poultry, etc. Large animals: horses, cows, etc.		
Abandoned vehicles	Automobiles, trucks		
Construction & Demolition wastes	Lumber, roofing, and sheathing scraps Rubble, broken concrete, plaster, etc. Conduit, pipe, wire, insulation, etc.		
Industrial refuse	Solid wastes resulting from industrial processes and manufacturing operations, such as: food-processing wastes, boiler house cinders, wood, plastic, and metal scraps and shavings, etc.		From: factories, power plants, etc.
Special wastes	Hazardous wastes: pathological wastes, explosives, radioactive materials Security wastes: confidential documents, negotiable papers, etc.		Households, hospitals, institutions, stores, industry, etc.
Animal and Agricultural wastes	Manures, crop residues		Farms, feed lots
Sewage treatment residues	Coarse screenings, grit, septic tank sludge, dewatered sludge		Sewage treatment plants, septic tanks

SOURCE: APWA – REFUSE COLLECTION PRACTICES

WASTE

The word waste refers to useless, unused, unwanted, or discarded materials. Waste includes solids, liquids, and gases. The gases are principally industrial fumes and smoke; the liquids consist mainly of sewage and the fluid part of industrial wastes; the solids are classed as refuse.

It is difficult to classify municipal wastes or to state absolutely the kinds of materials that constitute the part called refuse. Part of the solid refuse materials produced in a city, particularly particles of garbage and rubbish, finds its way into sewers and is disposed of with the liquid sewage wastes. And some semiliquid food wastes are accepted by private collectors of refuse as swill for hog feeding.

REFUSE

The term refuse refers to solid wastes. Its component materials can be classified in several different ways. The point of origin is important in solving some problems, so that classifying as domestic, institutional, commercial, industrial, street, demolition, or construction is useful. For other problems, the point of origin is not as important as the nature of the material and classification may be made on the basis of organic or inorganic character, combustibility or noncombustibility, putrescibility or nonputrescibility. One of the most useful classifications is based on the kinds of materials: garbage, rubbish, ashes, street refuse, dead animals, abandoned automobiles, industrial wastes, demolition wastes, construction wastes, sewage solids, and hazardous and special wastes. The table groups refuse materials by kind, composition, and indicates in a general way the source of the refuse.

GARBAGE

Garbage is the animal and vegetable waste resulting from the handling, preparation, cooking, and serving of foods. It is composed largely of putrescible organic matter and its natural moisture; it includes a minimum of free liquids. The term does not include food-processing wastes from canneries, slaughterhouses, packing plants, or similar industries; large quantities of condemned food products; or oyster or clam shells, which ordinarily are considered industrial wastes. Garbage originates primarily in home kitchens, stores, markets, restaurants, and other places where food is stored, prepared, or served.

Garbage decomposes rapidly, particularly in warm weather, and may quickly produce disagreeable odors. When carelessly stored, it is food for rats and other vermin and is a breeding place for flies.

There is some commercial value in garbage as animal food and as a base for commercial animal feeds. It may also have some value for its grease content or as a plant fertilizer after processing.

The terms "swill," "slops," and "offal," which are frequently found in city ordi-nances to define garbage, are not synonymous with garbage. "Swill" and "slops" connote semiliquid garbage and free liquids. Where cities do not collect and dispose of such materials, hog raisers operating as private collectors usually collect it from restaurants and institutions for use as hog feed. The word "offal" has had so many different meanings that its use is avoided except as it refers to discarded parts of slaughtered animals.

Market refuse is a special type of garbage that results from the handling, storage, and selling of foods at wholesale and retail stores and markets. It originates principally in meat, poultry, fish, vegetable, and fruit markets, and includes large quantities of putrescible food wastes along with some rubbish, such as wooden crates and cardboard boxes. It also includes some condemned foods but not large quantities of spoiled material.

As market refuse is usually highly putrescible, the protection of the fresh food supply and the appearance of the community make frequent collection of it necessary. In many cases official city agencies collect and dispose of it.

RUBBISH

Rubbish consists of a variety of both combustible and noncombustible solid wastes from homes, stores, and institutions. This waste is defined more specifically as "combustible rubbish" and "noncombustible rubbish," but whenever the term "rubbish" is used alone it means a mixture of combustible and noncombustible wastes. "Trash" is synonymous with "rubbish." If garbage is collected with rubbish it is necessary to have more frequent collections than if rubbish is collected separately.

Combustible rubbish is burnable material. In general, it is the organic component of refuse—paper, rags, cartons, boxes, wood, excelsior, furniture, bedding, rubber, plastics, leather, tree branches, lawntrimmings, and the like. Some cities use this term for only designated burnable materials that are accepted in regular collections. In such cases, some materials, such as food cans and bottles, are specifically included or excluded in the definitions of "rubbish" in the ordinance.

Combustible rubbish, though organic, is not highly putrescible, and therefore may be stored for relatively long periods without becoming a nuisance. It has high heat value and when dry it burns freely without forced draft and without added fuel. Often it is collected with wrapped garbage to provide the fuel necessary to burn garbage in an incinerator. Paper, rags, and cartons may have salvage value.

Noncombustible rubbish is material that is unburnable at ordinary incinerator temperatures (1,300° to 2,000° F). For the most part, it is the inorganic component of refuse, such as tin cans, heavy metal, mineral matter, glass, crockery, dust, metal furniture, ashes, and the like.

Although some of the metals undergo slow disintegration by oxidation, noncombustible rubbish is stable. When carelessly stored, however, it is aesthetically objectionable and it may harbor rodents and other vermin.

There has been a great deal of discussion among sanitary engineers and public

SOURCE: Municipal Refuse Disposal, Public Administration Service, Chicago, Ill.

health officials about the proper classification of tin cans that have been used as food containers and, when discarded, have particles of putrescible organic matter clinging to them. Because of this organic matter, some argue that cans should be included with garbage. It is now fairly generally accepted, however, that under ordinary conditions the organic matter desiccates rather than putrefies. For this reason, food cans and bottles may be included with noncombustible rubbish.

The metals, tin cans, bottles, and broken glass in noncombustible rubbish may have salvage value when prices are high.

Yard rubbish consists of tree branches, twigs, grass and shrub clippings, weeds, leaves, and other yard and garden waste materials. When collected, it often contains earth clinging to roots of grass, weeds, and discarded plants. Yard rubbish is usually a part of the combustible rubbish category rather than a category by itself. It is separately defined, however, because many cities make different arrangements for its collection and disposal from those for other combustible refuse and because some municipalities exclude it entirely from their collection service, leaving disposal up to the householder. Collection and disposal of palm fronds in some areas is a problem requiring special techniques.

A considerable part of yard rubbish is green vegetation, which, when kept moist or when stored in large amounts, decomposes fairly rapidly. It is not ordinarily objectionable but under some conditions it may be a breeding place for insects. This green material can be burned in an incinerator but normally it will not sustain a fire alone. Banana stalks are especially troublesome in this respect. Dried vegetation, dead leaves, and plants do not cause a sanitary nuisance and ordinarily will burn readily in an open fire. They can also be disposed of with other rubbish.

ASHES

Ashes are the residue from wood, coal, coke, and other combustible material burned in homes, stores, institutions, and small industrial establishments for heating, cooking, and disposing of combustible waste material. Residues produced in large quantities at steam generating plants are not included within the meaning of the term, since they are normally not the responsibility of a municipality.

Ashes are usually composed of a mixture of fine powdery residue, cinders, clinkers, and small portions of unburned or partially burned fuel or other material. Small pieces of metal, glass, and combustible materials are usually found in ashes when they are collected. Since the mixture is almost entirely inorganic, it is valuable for fills on low land, even in or near built-up communities, and it is acceptable some places for maintaining unpaved streets. Except for the dust that they can cause, ashes are not objectionable from a nuisance or aesthetic standpoint. In cities in which combustible and noncombustible refuse are separated for collection many cities ask that such noncombustibles as broken crockery, cans and bottles that are not food containers, and all metals be discarded with the ashes.

The residue in household refuse incinerators and yard rubbish burners is sometimes classed as ash, as are the remains from leaves and other yard rubbish

SOURCE: Municipal Refuse Disposal. Public Administration Service, Chicago, Ill.

burned in open fires. However, when garbage is only partly burned in low-temperature, inefficiently operated domestic incinerators, local authorities may require that the contents of incinerator pits be stored and collected as garbage or combustible refuse or they may refuse to collect them. In such cases, the incinerator or the operation of it should be modified so that garbage can be burned to ash, or attempts to incinerate garbage should be discontinued.

STREET REFUSE

Street refuse is material picked up by manual and mechanical sweeping of streets and sidewalks and litter from public litter receptacles. It includes paper, dirt, leaves, and the like. All or part of it is usually disposed of at a municipal disposal facility. Some cities assign the task of collection and disposal of street refuse to the regular refuse collection and disposal agency, while others assign it to the street department.

DEAD ANIMALS

As a category of refuse, dead animals are those that die naturally or from disease or are accidentally killed. Condemned animals or parts of animals from slaughterhouses or similar places are not included; they are regarded as industrial refuse.

Dead animals are ordinarily classified into one or two groups—"large" or "small." Large animals are horses, cows, goats, sheep, hogs, and the like. Small animals include dogs, cats, rabbits, squirrels, and rats. Some coastal cities frequently have problems with dead fish and dead aquatic mammals that float ashore at beaches. Collection of large animals usually requires special equipment.

Large animals have value because of the grease and tankage that can be produced from them in rendering plants. Their hides also have some value.

Dead animals are particularly offensive from sanitary and aesthetic points of view and usually must be collected promptly—often on an emergency basis. They putrefy rapidly, particularly in warm, moist atmosphere, and attract flies and other insects. Animal traffic victims are sometimes crushed by vehicles passing over them and therefore must be picked up promptly.

ABANDONED VEHICLES

Abandoned vehicles include passenger automobiles, trucks, and trailers that are no longer useful and have been left on city streets and in other public places. Usually they are found stripped of tires, wheels, lights, and other easily salvaged parts. While they must be removed from the streets by municipal authorities, the task is not usually considered a part of the work of the regular refuse collection agency, but a duty of the street cleaning, highway, or police forces.

INDUSTRIAL REFUSE

Industrial refuse consists of solid waste materials from factories, processing plants, and other manufacturing enterprises. The collection of such matter is rarely regarded as an obligation of the city or a governmental function, but as an obligation of industry. Refuse of this category includes putrescible garbage from food processing plants and slaughterhouses, condemned foods, building rubbish, cinders from power plants, and manufacturing refuse.

Because putrescible industrial refuse may cause serious nuisances and even endanger public health, its storage, hauling, and disposition are subject to municipal control, and many municipalities are now providing for disposal of this type of refuse.

DEMOLITION REFUSE

Demolition refuse is the waste material from razed buildings or other structures. It is found mostly in cities in which extensive areas of old or otherwise obsolete buildings are being torn down to make way for new structures. The federally-aided program or urban renewal has given impetus to these programs in recent years. The construction of new expressways in large cities also necessitates the destruction of many buildings and adds to the demolition refuse problem.

Demolition refuse is not usually collected by municipal agencies. Usually the company wrecking a building contracts to haul the debris away and dispose of it. In some cities, however, particularly if large landfill areas are available, the city allows wreckers to dump refuse at its disposal facility for a slight charge, or even free.

CONSTRUCTION REFUSE

Construction refuse is the waste material from the construction, remodeling, and repair of houses, commercial buildings, and other structures. It includes a great variety of matter, such as earth, stones, bricks, plaster, wallpaper, lumber, shingles and other roofing, concrete, plumbing parts, old heating systems, and worn out electrical parts.

A small amount of such refuse is usually accepted from households and stores but the bulk of it is considered industrial refuse that contractors and builders must remove. A municipality may agree to dispose of it but if it does, it creates problems.

SEWAGE

The disposal of some sewage solids is the responsibility of the municipal refuse disposal agency in many areas. Large, coarse solids, mostly organic, are screened from the influent at the sewage treatment plant, and if a municipal incinerator or sanitary landfill is convenient to the treatment plant these solids are disposed of by one method or the other. Solid inorganic matter from grit chambers may also be disposed of in a nearby sanitary landfill. This grit, however, even after going through a washing process, may contain substantial quantities of highly putrescible matter, and it is necessary, therefore, to bury it to effectively prevent an odor nuisance. Septic tank and cesspool pumpings are often disposed of in sanitary

SOURCE: Municipal Refuse Disposal, Public Administration Service, Chicago, Ill.

landfills in the absence of a sewage treatment plant, again under rigid controls to avoid nuisances.

HAZARDOUS OR SPECIAL REFUSE

Waste material that presents an unusual disposal problem or requires special handling comes within the definition of hazardous, or special, waste. Small quantities of such wastes are usually present in ordinary refuse. A small can of paint or paint thinner, a roll of photographic film, or a plastic household article is not hazardous and can be disposed of by incineration or landfill without special handling. On the other hand, large quantities of the same materials create problems that require special procedures to prevent explosions in an incinerator furnace or a dangerous fire at a sanitary landfill. Even under the strictest safety measures, such explosions occur.

On the other hand, some wastes from industry are hazardous under any conditions, and pathological wastes from hospitals and radioactive materials require special handling no matter the quantity.

CHARACTERISTICS OF METHODS

Sanitary Landfills Sanitary landfill operations are usually performed by depositing refuse in a natural or man-made depression or trench, or dumping it at ground level, compacting it to the smallest practical volume, and covering it with compacted earth or other material in a systematic and sanitary manner. Before operations begin, a site must be selected and surveyed; the site prepared; access roads, control grades, and drainage provided for; and equipment selected. Other steps may be required, depending on climate and the site. In some cases special provisions must be made for controlling blowing papers, odors, dust, and fire; and special equipment and personnel facilities may be needed.

Well planned and operated landfills have several advantages: they are economical; they require a relatively small capital investment; they may reclaim land that is otherwise useless; and they cause almost no air pollution. They do have disadvantages, however: they frequently require longer and more costly hauls than some other methods; they require more land than some other methods; and operational problems may be frequent in inclement weather.

Central Incineration A central incineration plant—either municipally or privately owned—is one in which combustible refuse is reduced to ash by high-temperature burning. Refuse from collection trucks is dumped on a charging floor or in a storage area or pit, the refuse is charged into furnaces, temperatures and drafts are carefully controlled to insure as complete combustion as possible, and ashes and noncombustible residues are disposed of in landfills or salvaged.

Incineration is advantageous because a relatively small site is required for the plant, the length and cost of the haul to the plant is usually less than for landfills and other methods; and the residue from the burning is usable fill material. On the other hand, the capital costs of an incineration plant are relatively high; operating costs, considered alone, are also usually relatively high; and it is not a complete disposal method—ashes and other residue from the furnaces must be hauled to a disposal site.

On-Site Incineration On-site incinerators are those used in and outside of houses, in apartment buildings, stores, small industries, hospitals, and other institutions to burn refuse produced on the premises. They are of many types and sizes for various uses. The advantages are that the amount of combustible refuse that must be collected and disposed of is reduced by the amount that is burned in such incinerators. Householders and others who use them often find them an advantage because refuse does not have to be stored on the premises; it can be disposed of almost as soon as it is produced, reducing nuisances and hazards from it. On-site incinerators do sometimes cause unpleasant odors, smoke, and fly ash, however.

Grinding Food Wastes Garbage can be disposed of by grinding it and flushing it into sewers. There are home grinders; grinders used in restaurants, produce terminals, and supermarkets; and grinders for centrally located stations operated by a municipality. The principle of operation is the same for all. Garbage is kept or collected separately from other refuse, it is ground or shredded in the grinder as water is added, and it is flushed into the sewers. Household grinders are considered the ultimate in convenience and sanitation because they almost eliminate garbage storage. Widespread use of household and commercial grinders reduces the amount of garbage that must be collected and disposed of; central grinder stations are especially advantageous to cities in which there is a great deal of wet garbage, which does not burn well and may not be suitable for feeding to hogs. Grinder stations are relatively simple to build and operate. However, grinding requires that other refuse, which is probably 85 to 90 per cent of the total volume, be collected separately.

Feeding Food Wastes to Swine Garbage can be disposed of by feeding it to swine. It is collected separately, the unedible refuse is separated from it, it is cooked to destroy disease organisms, and it is fed to hogs on farms, usually especially built for garbage feeding. Municipalities no longer operate such hog farms, but in some cases they contract with hog raisers to use the garbage for feed. In most places, garbage is collected by private haulers who make their own arrangements with restaurant owners and operators of institutions.

Because all states require that garbage be cooked before it is fed to hogs and because most farms are now far from cities, garbage feeding is not usually as attractive economically as it once was. Health and agriculture department regulations are necessary to prevent or control animal diseases and nuisances created by the disposal process. Furthermore, only edible food wastes are disposed of; other refuse must be collected and disposed of by other methods.

Composting Composting is sometimes defined as a rapid but partial decomposition of moist, solid, organic matter—primarily garbage—by the use of aerobic microorganisms under controlled conditions. The result is a sanitary, nuisance-free, humus-like material that can be used as a soil conditioner and fertilizer.

Salvage and Reclamation The term salvage and reclamation covers a number of "disposal" processes: sorting of refuse either manually or mechanically, for metals, tin cans, glass, paper, rags, and other materials that can be resold; rendering of animal waste for fats; dehydration of garbage to be used for hog feed; composting; and landfills that reclaim otherwise unusable land.

Dumping Open dumps are still common in some places, but since they are the source of a number of public health and safety problems—disease, air and water pollution, fires, mosquitoes, rodents, insects—they are not recommended. It usually requires little more cash outlay to turn them into sanitary landfills.

Sanitary landfill is a method of refuse disposal in which wastes are deposited, compacted and covered with earth at the end of each day. A sanitary landfill may be designed from its inception to be filled in with contours suitable for a community facility such as a park, golf course, playground or parking area.

A sanitary landfill is designed to eliminate the unsightliness, odor, insects and rats which contribute to the nuisances or health hazards of the open dump.

SOURCE: Municipal Refuse Disposal, Public Administration Service, Chicago, Ill.

	ADVANTAGES	DISADVANTAGES	CENTRAL LOCATION	AREA REQ.
DUMP Refuse is simply dumped in a designated area. Garbage & rubbish may or may not be separated. Refuse is periodically burned, separated and plowed under. Generally utilized by small communities with ample open land.	Provides fill for marginal areas. Inexpensive Simple operation and supervision.	Propogation of insects. Propogation of rodent population. Offensive odors produced.	Distance from residential areas. Located so winds blow odors away from developed areas. Industrial areas.	Approximately 2 acres per 10,000 population served
SANITARY FILL Process is similar to dumping, except that refuse is covered over with earth. Dump areas are well organized and specified. Garbage decomposes and fill. Generally utilized by medium or high-density urban areas.	Relatively inexpensive. Simple operation. Provides fill for marginal areas.	Requires constant supervision. May develop insects and rodents if poorly operated.	Marginal areas requiring fill.	Approximately 4 acres per 10,000 population served.
INCINERATOR Destruction by fire of all refuse in a furnace. The refuse is delivered to the incinerator plant and burned. There are different types of incinerators and each must be carefully engineered. Usually restricted to large, high density urban areas.	No insects. No rodents. Clean operation. Used in combination with sanitary fill. Process can be used to make steam.	Relatively expensive in initial cost and operation. Building adds to air pollution. Complicated operation.	In most industrial areas regardless of wind directions.	10-20 acres.

INTERMUNICIPAL COOPERATION

County or regional planning and management of solid wastes has a number of advantages. It can result in centralized sites with adequate personnel for supervision and the best modern equipment. Also, a larger area for site selection will result in more choices and a better chance of getting good sites.

Financial and management considerations are also important. With a broader tax base, a lower interest rate on bonds may be available with county or regional financing. Also, one or more centralized sites may be operated under the supervision of a permanent refuse agency, resulting in stronger supervision and continuity of management.

Larger landfill operations are also less expensive, on a $/ton basis, because of more efficient utilization of equipment and manpower.

Comprehensive planning for 15 or more years in the future and acquisition of sites at least 5 years prior to anticipated use is the recommended procedure.

Comprehensive planning must study all means of disposal, including incineration, composting, shredding, and other methods which may be applicable in special circumstances. Where landfill alone is the method of choice, the plan should include an engineering analysis of alternate sites and the volume and characteristics of wastes to be handled.

Other considerations in landfill planning are cost of land and site preparation, expected life of the site, haul distances from the sources of refuse to the site, cost of operation, possible value of the finished site, climate, prevailing winds, zoning ordinances, geology and topography, drainage to prevent surface and ground water pollution, access roads to major highways and the availability of earth fill for cover material.

Some sites will obviously be better than others; however, most any site can be used if properly designed and operated. Difficult sites, especially those requiring extensive drainage systems, will be very expensive to prepare and operate. These sites may prove to be the least expensive alternative, however, if better sites are not available at reasonable cost. Preferably, a professional engineer should be involved in site selection activities.

Once a site has been selected, and preliminary plans have been developed for use of the site when it is completed, the public should be informed. Public meetings, inspections of good sanitary landfill operations and publicity through the news media will help to gain public support and understanding.

The first step is a survey and a plan drawn to a scale of not more than 200 feet to the inch with contours at 2-foot intervals. The plan should show the boundaries of the property, location of structures within 1,000 feet, adjoining ownership, topography and drainage. In addition, the plan should show proposed year-round access roads, direction of operation, borrow areas, finished grade and drainage with allowance for settlement, proposed windrows and fences, and shelter for men and equipment. The latter requires a trailer or building with an office, locker room, showers and water supply and sewage disposal or privies.

Careful consideration should be given to the final use for the site and this information should be included in the engineering report. Plans prepared for final use become excellent selling points for the use of the site as a sanitary landfill.

Professional engineering services are necessary not only in site design, but also in directing the operation and maintenance of the site. The engineer should assure that the site is operated in accordance with the site plan.

The on-site supervisor of landfill operations should keep a daily record of the type and quantity of wastes received, sources of wastes, equipment use and repairs, personnel records, etc. He should be supplied with the equipment and personnel necessary to operate the site adequately.

LOCATION AND ACCESSIBILITY

If a site is remotely situated from the service area, the haul cost may be high and the total cost for disposal will rise. The normal economical hauling distance for collection vehicles is 10 to 15 miles, varying with the volume of refuse, road conditions, and other factors. If transfer stations or satellite container stations are used, with haul by large trucks, rail or barging, then haul distances totaling 30 or more miles are not unreasonable.

Another important consideration in site selection is accessibility. If possible, a disposal area should be located near major highways to facilitate use of existing arterial roads and lessen haul time. Highway wheel load and bridge capacity, as well as underpass and bridge clearances, must be investigated. Well maintained, all-season access roads to the site are a necessity.

Another consideration is minimizing the travel of collection vehicles through residential streets. Where the actual fill operation of a sanitary landfill is within 500 feet of residences, it is desirable to provide some type of screening. With proper design and operation, fill operations could be less than 50 feet from residences. This might be done to improve land adjacent to residential areas to create parks, playgrounds or for other recreational uses. In such cases, a temporary screen may be erected to conceal the operation and provide a more pleasing view to those living near the site.

SOURCE: Sanitary Landfill, N.Y. State Dept. of Environmental Conservation, 1971.

LAND AREA REQUIRED

The land area needed will depend on the amount of refuse generated in the service area, the depth to which refuse is to be placed, and period of time the site will be in operation. Normally, economics favor large capacity sites which will last 15 years or more; however, smaller sites may be easier to obtain and create less public resistance. A small site, with limited life, may be used to demonstrate to the public how a sanitary landfill should be operated. This should lessen the public resistance later when a larger site is contemplated.

Municipal refuse generation usually averages from 3½ to 5½ pounds per person each day. (See Figures 1. and 2. on p. 570.) Thus, a site should provide from 10 to 20 acre-feet (an acre-foot is one acre filled to a depth of one foot) each year per 10,000 population.

Industrial and agricultural waste generation must also be considered. In some areas these will more than double the amount of land required and may change the type of operation necessary. If it can be anticipated that industrial or agricultural wastes will become a significant portion of the total waste to be disposed, plans must be made accordingly.

PREVENTION OF WATER POLLUTION

To determine the depth at which filling operations can begin, the locations of bedrock and the ground water table must be established. This will usually require borings or test holes in the area under consideration. It is also necessary to determine the finished grade desired in order to calculate the usable volume of the site.

Refuse placed no deeper than 5 feet above the high ground water level should prevent underground water pollution, provided the surface water is drained off the site. A somewhat greater distance should be maintained between the refuse and bedrock. The lowest elevation for depositing refuse will be determined from the subsurface characteristics of the site.

If refuse is placed below the ground water table, leaching will result. Leachate is comparable to strong chemical waste and can cause severe degradation of water. Carbon dioxide formed in refuse stabilization may enter the ground water and increase hardness. In some cases, the ground water may be lowered or diverted using perforated underdrains.

All efforts should be made to prevent water from percolating down into the refuse. Once the refuse becomes saturated, any additional water entering the refuse will displace an equal volume of leachate. To minimize percolation, a fairly impermeable cover material should be used. The surface should be graded smooth, sloped slightly and planted to some cover crop.

The runoff from the drainage area tributary to the site must be determined to ensure that surface water is properly diverted to prevent flooding, erosion and leachate production. The topography and final contours of the soil cover should be carefully examined periodically to be sure that there will be no obstruction of natural drainage channels.

A new concept of leachate control is to allow it to develop, then collect and treat it before discharge. Although leachate is small in quantity, it is highly concentrated with pollutants and would require fairly sophisticated treatment. Special collection pipes and impermeable barriers would be required to intercept all of the leachate. Over a period of years the leachable materials in a landfill would be removed to the point where effluent from the landfill could be discharged without treatment.

OTHER REQUIREMENTS

Earth cover must be available to provide 6 inches of fill over the working face of the area each day, and 2 feet for the final surface. Cover material between lifts, which are usually 6 to 10 feet deep, should be at least 12 inches of compacted earth. A rough estimate of cover material needed is one cubic yard per capita of the population served each year. Another rough estimate is that the volume of cover required is one-quarter to one-third of the volume of compacted refuse.

The most suitable cover material is a sandy loam (about half sand and the rest equal parts of silt and clay). This material is easy to work during all times of the year,

SOURCE: Sanitary Landfill, *N.Y. State Dept. of Environmental Conservation, 1971.*

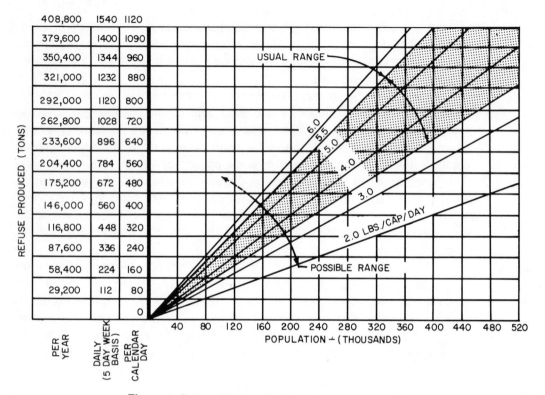

Figure 1. Refuse Produced: Varying Per Capita Figures.

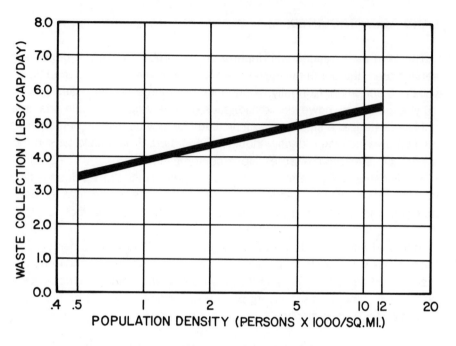

Figure 2. Unit Municipal Waste Collection vs. Population Density.

SOURCE: Sanitary Landfill, N.Y. State Dept. of Environmental Conservation, 1971.

CONVERSION OF A DUMP TO A SANITARY LANDFILL

Conversion of a suitable existing site from a dump to a landfill is desirable if the site can be operated as a sanitary landfill. This overcomes the problems of finding and acquiring a new site and provides an opportunity to demonstrate to the surrounding community the advantages of a properly-run landfill operation.

However, not all dumping sites are suitable for conversion. If the area available is limited, the best alternative, may be to grade, cover and abandon the dump. When terminating a dump, a rat poisoning program should be started about 4 weeks before the dump is covered to prevent migration of rats to other areas.

Possible water pollution can be prevented by constructing drainage ditches to intercept surface water and perhaps by constructing an earth dike between the refuse and the high water level of any adjacent streams.

The completed site should be covered with at least 2 feet of compacted earth, graded to a uniform slope and seeded.

Where there is adequate land and a suitable site, the conversion should begin with a rat poisoning program 4 weeks before covering. A plot layout should be drawn to scale showing the available land, source of available cover material and sequence construction. Operation, supervision and maintenance should be planned in advance, as described in other sections of this brochure.

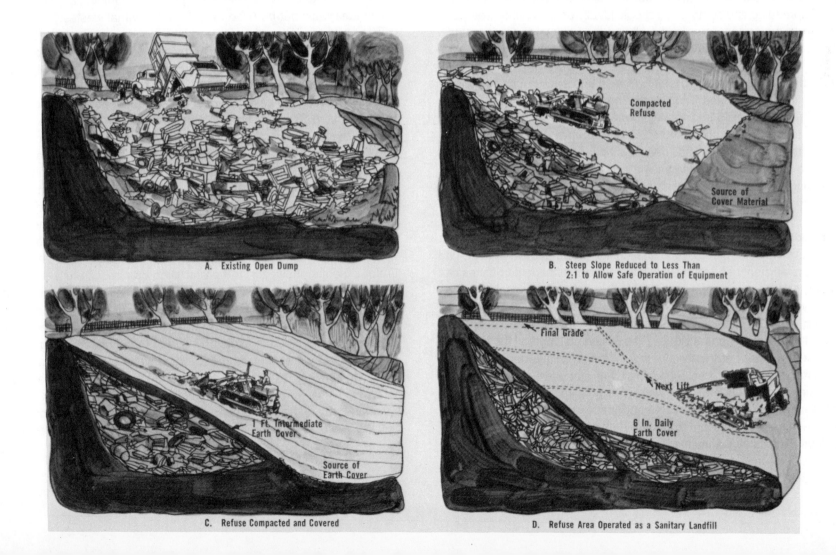

A. Existing Open Dump

B. Steep Slope Reduced to Less Than 2:1 to Allow Safe Operation of Equipment

C. Refuse Compacted and Covered

D. Refuse Area Operated as a Sanitary Landfill

SANITARY LANDFILL OPERATIONS

There are many methods of operating a sanitary landfill. The most common are the trench, area, ramp, valley and low area fill methods. The trench method has the advantage of providing more direct dumping control, which is not always possible with the area method. Since a definite place is designated for dumping, the scattering of refuse by wind is minimized and trucks can be more readily directed to the trench. The area method is suitable for level or rolling terrain. Here it is necessary to strip and stockpile sufficient cover material to meet the total anticipated need for earth cover. If this is not possible, earth must be hauled in from another source.

In all cases, refuse should be spread in 2-foot layers, as deposited, and promptly compacted. The spreading and compaction should ideally be on a 30-degree slope in order to minimize the surface area of the fill and the volume of cover material required. Additional 2-foot layers may be added until the design depth of the lift has been reached.

Trench Method   The trench method is used primarily on level ground, although it is also suitable for moderate slopes. The trench is constructed by making a shallow excavation maintaining at least 5 feet above ground water. Some excavated material may be used to form berms along the sides of the trench thus increasing the usable volume of the trench. Excess soil may be stockpiled for future use. Refuse is deposited in the excavated area, compacted and covered with earth each day. The cover material may be obtained from the area excavated for the next day's refuse, from soil stockpiled for the purpose, or from a trench dug parallel to the one being filled.

Trenches should be at least twice the width of the compaction equipment being used. The depth of fill is determined by the final design grade and depth to ground water or rock. More efficient use of the available land can be made if trenches can be made deeper, or, if cover material is available, by placing additional lifts using the area fill method.

Area or Ramp Method   On fairly flat and rolling terrain, the area method can best make use of the existing natural slopes. The width and length of the fill slopes are dependent on the nature of the terrain, the volume of refuse deposited daily, and the approximate number of trucks anticipated at any one time. Side slopes should be a maximum of 30 degrees. The width of fill strips and the surface grades are controlled during operation by line poles and grade stakes. The working face should be kept as small as practical to restrict dumping to a limited area, avoid scattering of debris and take maximum advantage of truck compaction. In the ramp method, earth cover is scraped from the base of the ramp. In the area method, cover material is hauled in from a nearby stockpile or from some other source.

Low Area Method   With approval from the Department of Environmental Conservation, the sanitary landfill can be used to improve marginal and submarginal lands such as lowlands, depressions, swamps and pits. The refuse fill must be designed and operated so that surface or ground waters are not polluted.

If it is proposed to use a low or wet area, surface water must be diverted and, if possible, the ground water table lowered. The low area should then be filled in to a height of at least 3 feet above the water level with non-putrescible wastes, such as demolition material, before depositing refuse containing any putrescible materials. A low area must not be used for soluble industrial wastes.

The basic area fill method is used, although cover may have to be brought in. In addition, some means must be provided to prevent the scattering of refuse throughout the area. Depending on the condition of the area, this can be done by diking or fencing.

In some wet areas, cover material may be obtained by using a dragline ahead of the active face. The dragline can stockpile wet soil in advance to let it drain. This soil will then be more stable and more easily handled by equipment for refuse cover. Soils with organic contents in excess of 20%, such as peat and muck, should not be used as cover because they are very difficult to work with.

Valley or Ravine Method   In valleys or ravines, the area method is usually best. Where the ravine is deep, the refuse should be placed in "lifts" of 6 to 10 feet deep. Cover material may be obtained from the sides of the ravine. It is not always desirable to extend the first lift the entire length of the ravine. To minimize differential settlement problems, it is desirable to allow the first lift to settle for a year. This is not essential, however, if the operation can be carefully controlled and good compaction is obtained. Succeeding lifts are constructed by trucking refuse over the first lift to the head of the ravine. When the final grade is reached, with allowance for settling, the lower lift can be extended and the process repeated.

Care must be taken to avoid pollution of both surface and ground waters. This can be done by intercepting and diverting water away from the fill area, by using diversion trenches, by directing its flow through pipes of suitable size, or by placing a layer of highly permeable soil beneath the refuse to intercept water before it can reach the refuse. As with other fill methods, it is important to grade during operations to avoid ponding on the surface of completed lifts or seepage into the lifts.

FIGURE 1. AREA METHOD. The bulldozer spreads and compacts solid wastes. The scraper (foreground) is used to haul the cover material at the end of the day's operations. Note the portable fence that catches any blowing debris. This is used with any landfill method.

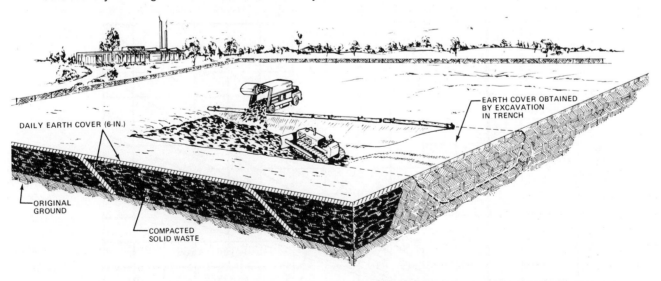

FIGURE 2. TRENCH METHOD. The waste collection truck deposits its load into the trench where the bulldozer spreads and compacts it. At the end of the day the dragline excavates soil from the future trench; this soil is used as the daily cover material. Trenches can also be excavated with a front-end loader, bulldozer, or scraper.

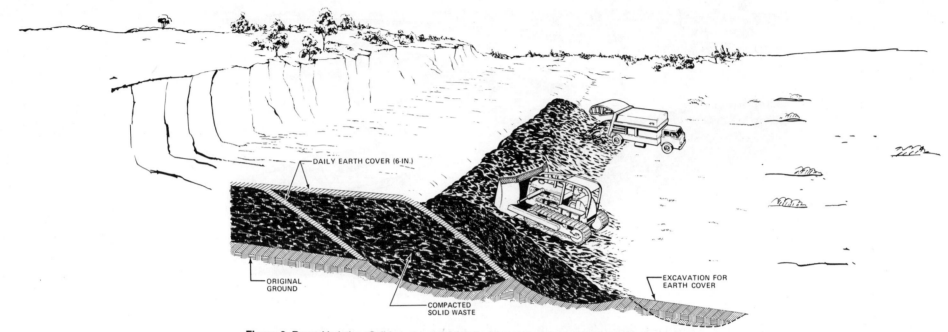

Figure 3. Ramp Variation. Solid wastes are spread and compacted on a slope. The daily cell may be covered with earth scraped from the base of the ramp. This variation is used with either the area or trench method.

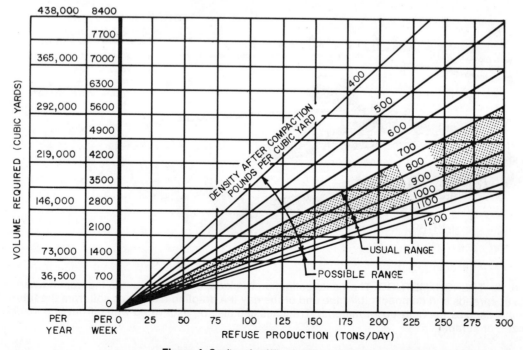

Figure 4. Sanitary landfill volume required.

EQUIPMENT

Proper equipment is important for effective site operation. One piece of refuse compaction and earth-moving equipment is needed for approximately each 250 tons of refuse received per day at the disposal site. The type of equipment selected must be suitable for the method of operation and the prevailing soil conditions. Additional stand-by equipment should be available for emergencies, breakdowns and equipment maintenance. (see page 31) The various equipment manufacturers can make recommendations based upon site characteristics.

TRACTORS

Tractor types include the crawler, rubbertired and steel-wheeled equipped with bulldozer blade, bullclam or front-end loader. The crawler tractor with a front-end bucket attachment is an all-purpose piece of equipment. It may be used to excavate trenches, place and compact refuse, transport cover material and level and compact the completed portion of the landfill. Some types can also be used to load cover material into trucks for transportation and deposit near the open face.

A bulldozer blade on a crawler tractor is good for landfills where hauling of cover material is not necessary. It is well-suited for the area method of landfill where cover material is taken from nearby hillsides. It can also be used for trench method operation with the proper blade adaptation to allow compaction to the sides of the trench. A bulldozer may be used with other earthmoving equipment, such as a scraper, where earth is hauled in from a nearby source.

USE OF A COMPLETED LANDFILL

The landfill plan should provide for a specific use of the area, when completed. Rather than requiring expensive excavation and regrading, the necessary contours should be established in advance. For example, a golf course can be constructed on rolling terrain while a parking lot would require a flat graded surface.

Permanent buildings should not be constructed over fill areas because of settling problems and underground gas production which could enter sewers or basements and develop explosive conditions. With special foundation structures and provisions to vent gas, it is possible to build on fill areas; however, it is much cheaper if an advance plan is drawn up leaving unfilled areas for building construction.

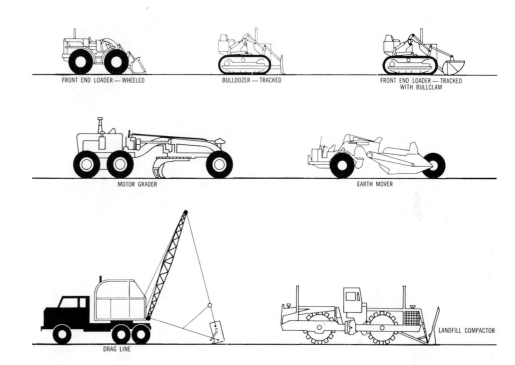

FRONT END LOADER — WHEELED   BULLDOZER — TRACKED   FRONT END LOADER — TRACKED WITH BULLCLAM

MOTOR GRADER   EARTH MOVER

DRAG LINE   LANDFILL COMPACTOR

It is recommended that large sites be planned to allow multiple use. For example, while waste is being landfilled in one portion of a site, other areas could continue to be used for farming. The entire site need not be filled before the planned final use is commenced. Portions of the site can be developed for final use as soon as filling is completed. The multiple use concept allows for maximum utilization of land and also builds good community relations.

With proper planning, airports, swimming pools, ski areas or practically any other type of facility can be made from a completed landfill. Advance planning is essential, however.

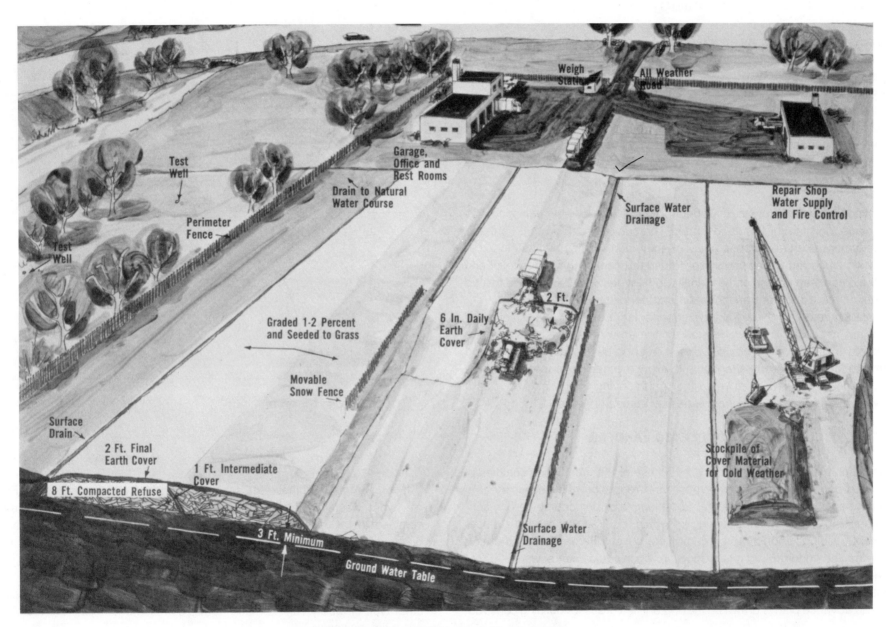

Test Well

Garage, Office and Rest Rooms

Weigh Station

All Weather Road

Drain to Natural Water Course

Perimeter Fence

Surface Water Drainage

Repair Shop Water Supply and Fire Control

Test Well

Graded 1-2 Percent and Seeded to Grass

6 In. Daily Earth Cover

2 Ft.

Movable Snow Fence

Surface Drain

2 Ft. Final Earth Cover

1 Ft. Intermediate Cover

Stockpile of Cover Material for Cold Weather

8 Ft. Compacted Refuse

3 Ft. Minimum

Surface Water Drainage

Ground Water Table

A SANITARY LANDFILL IN A FLAT AREA

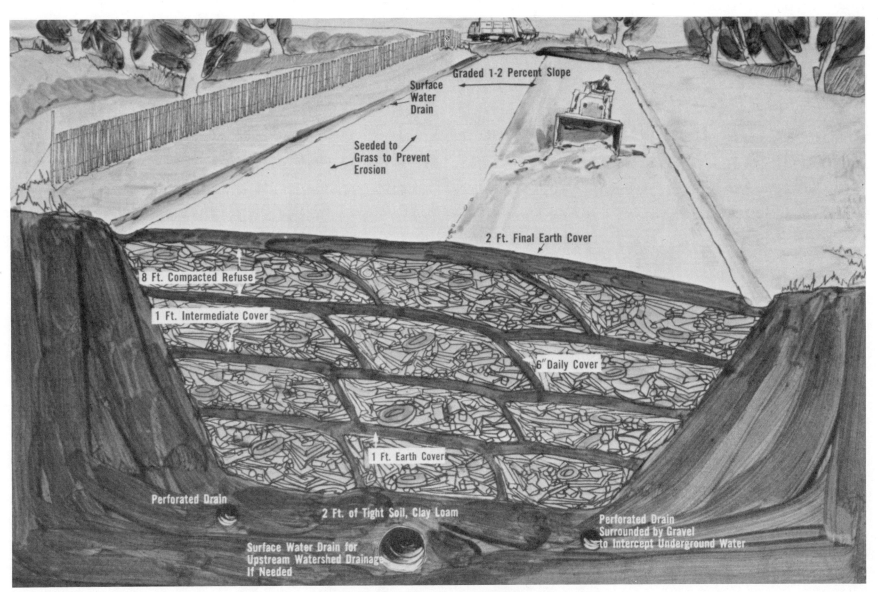

Graded 1-2 Percent Slope

Surface Water Drain

Seeded to Grass to Prevent Erosion

2 Ft. Final Earth Cover

8 Ft. Compacted Refuse

1 Ft. Intermediate Cover

6" Daily Cover

1 Ft. Earth Cover

Perforated Drain

2 Ft. of Tight Soil, Clay Loam

Perforated Drain Surrounded by Gravel to Intercept Underground Water

Surface Water Drain for Upstream Watershed Drainage If Needed

SANITARY LANDFILL IN RAVINE—
FILL STARTS AT UPPER END OF RAVINE BOTTOM

ZONING, CODES, AND REGULATORY CONTROLS

ORGANIZATION OF THE ORDINANCE

An analysis of any good zoning ordinance will show that it contains three basic divisions: (1) enactment and interpretation, (2) district regulations, and (3) administrative provisions.

The first of these relates to the purpose of the ordinance, its enactment into law, definitions of terms used, and similar items. The second includes the actual regulations pertaining to each of the districts and the additional provisions affecting all districts. The third part is composed of administrative details covering such matters as enforcement, the issuing of building permits, certificates of occupancy, and provisions for appeals and amendments.

The arrangement of the specific provisions within the three major divisions may vary. This is particularly so with regard to the regulations for the particular districts. Common practice has been to group these regulations in one of two ways. By one arrangement, the regulations are grouped according to type. For example, all the provisions dealing with use are given in order for each type of district. These are followed by the lot area requirements for each district, and in turn by height and density regulations, and so forth.

Although this method has certain advantages, such as showing the progressive restrictiveness of each district for each type of regulation, the alternative method of arrangement is probably the more useful. By this, the regulations relating to use, height, area, and density are grouped together for each district. This provides the reader with a complete picture of the provisions that must be met for his particular property. It has been held that zoning regulations should be arranged in such a way that the work of the building inspector or other administrative official is facilitated. It is argued that a building inspector has recourse to the ordinance many times while the private citizen may have to refer to the regulations but once. However, it would appear to be the best policy to have the regulations arranged so as to make the task of interpretation as easy as possible for the public user, as the purpose of a governmental agency is to serve the public. Thus, the private individual should be inconvenienced as little as possible and the zoning ordinance be prepared so that the groups or individuals affected can most readily understand them. The administrator, as an expert who uses the ordinance continuously, becomes familiar with all the requirements pertaining to each of the districts, as well as the many other provisions.

Illustrative Outline for an Ordinance

Article I. Purposes
   Section 1. Purposes

Article II. Definitions
   Section 2. Definitions

Article III. Establishment of Districts
   Section 3. Establishment of Districts
   Section 4. Zoning Map
   Section 5. Interpretation of District Boundaries

Article IV. Regulations
   Section 6. Application of Regulations
   Section 7. District Regulations
   (Alternate Section 7. Schedule of Regulations)
   Section 8. Standards for Special Permits
   Section 9. Supplementary Regulations
   Section 10. Nonconforming Uses

Article V. Administration
   Section 11. Enforcement
   Section 12. Board of Appeals
   Section 13. Violations

Article VI. Amendments
   Section 14. Procedure for Amendments

Article VII. Miscellaneous
   Section 15. Interpretation
   Section 16. Separability
   Section 17. Repealer
   Section 18. Short Title
   Section 19. When Effective

PORTION OF TYPICAL ZONING MAP
SHOWING DISTRICT DESIGNATIONS
BY PATTERN

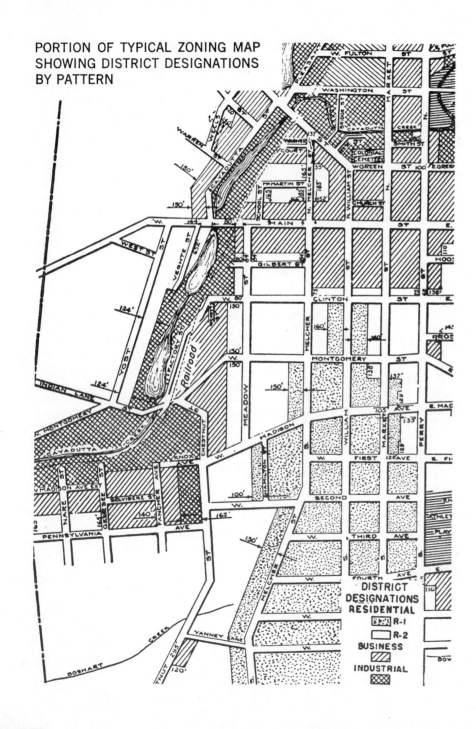

DISTRICT
DESIGNATIONS
RESIDENTIAL

R-1

R-2

BUSINESS

INDUSTRIAL

PORTION OF TYPICAL ZONING MAP
SHOWING DISTRICT DESIGNATIONS
BY LETTERS & NUMERALS

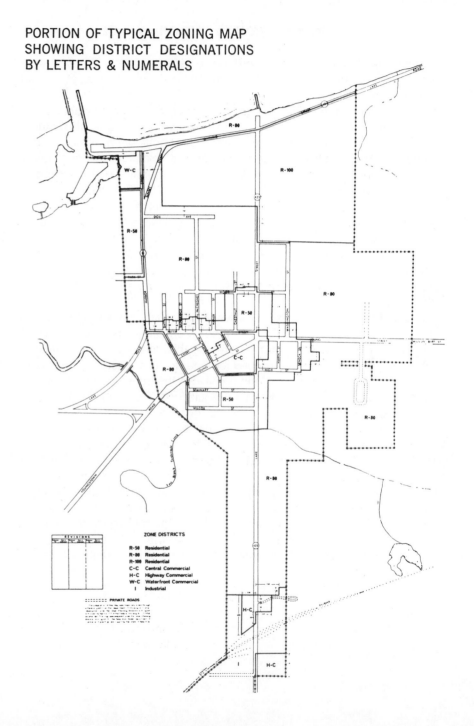

ZONE DISTRICTS

R-50   Residential
R-80   Residential
R-100   Residential
C-C   Central Commercial
H-C   Highway Commercial
W-C   Waterfront Commercial
I   Industrial

PRIVATE ROADS

DEFINITIONS

Words used in zoning ordinances may have meanings different from the usual dictionary definitions. It is necessary that terms having special meaning be defined. Definitions of words may be placed near the beginning of the ordinance in order to alert the reader to the fact that certain words and terms carry special meanings.

Local objectives will determine what words to define and the precise meaning to be given any particular term. It is unnecessary to define terms not included in the ordinance. The list which follows illustrates many of the definitions in common use today. In some instances more than one illustration is given for a term to show the different meanings that can be attached to it.

ESTABLISHMENT OF DISTRICTS

As the enabling laws specify, a municipality may be divided into districts and regulations prescribed for each type of district. The section of the ordinance formally establishing the districts lists the types of districts into which the community is to be divided, and describes their boundaries.

1. *R-1 Districts: One-Family Residential Districts*
2. *R-2 Districts: Two-Family Residential Districts*
3. *R-3 Districts: Multiple-Family Residential Districts*
4. *A Districts: Agricultural Districts*
5. *B-1 Districts: Retail Business Districts*
6. *B-2 Districts: General Business Districts*
7. *I-1 Districts: Light Industrial Districts*
8. *I-2 Districts: Heavy Industrial Districts*

Experience indicates that it is good practice to incorporate in the ordinance a map showing how the districts have been laid out. Examples of part of a zoning ordinance map showing both the differentiation of districts by pattern and by letter symbol are shown on page 590.

REGULATIONS

A specific provision must be included in the ordinance stating that the use of all land, buildings, or structures shall be in conformity with the regulations.

RESIDENTIAL DISTRICTS

The greatest percentage of the developed area of an urban community will be devoted to residential use. Even in rural areas, much of the land is now used for residence as a result of the continuing movement of people out of the built-up villages and cities into the more open areas in the towns. In determining how much of the community's area should be set aside for existing and future residential use, it is highly desirable to make a comprehensive community study. From this study, a plan should be developed showing how all the area in the municipality can be most advantageously used to meet existing needs and to make the best of all future opportunities. On this basis, the zoning ordinance and map, while not in itself any substitute for the community plan, puts into effect those land use controls felt to be most desirable in guiding development toward the goals set by the comprehensive plan.

The purpose of zoning areas for residence only is the protection of living areas from encroachment by other types of use not appropriate in such an area. A business use in a residence area can lead to loss of values due to a decrease in the desirable qualities of an area, such as its relative quiet and freedom from traffic. If such a mixture is widespread, deterioration, blight, and an eventual need for public assistance to remove or ameliorate the situation may occur.

However, only rarely would a zoning ordinance provide for no other uses than dwellings in a residence area. Every neighborhood will require schools, parks, playgrounds, churches, and other institutions. Also, in many cases it is feasible and desirable to permit a limited type of business use such as professional offices and home occupations. The important standard to be used in the regulation of these "non-residential" uses in such an area is the maintenance of the residential character. By so doing, the desirability and convenience which attract people to it will not be lost. Since residential areas usually represent the largest part of the local tax base, the maintenance of their value as places for persons to live is a vital municipal concern.

Many ordinances provide that non-residential uses in residential districts be permitted only after a review of the proposed development or use by the board of appeals or other local agency. This is a means of assuring that all the standards for such a use can be met.

In addition to the commonly accepted non-residential uses such as schools, parks and playgrounds, churches and other religious uses, public buildings, and philanthropic uses, it will be valuable to consider the need for, and type of, regulation applicable to museums, art galleries, public utility sub-stations, fraternal and social clubs, golf courses, swimming pools and tennis courts, nursery schools, greenhouses, plant nurseries, and agricultural uses.

In special cases it may be necessary to provide for the future development of boathouses and wharves, railroad stations, sewage disposal plants, incinerators, reservoirs, cemeteries, and similar uses. Uses needing careful consideration are sand and gravel mining, topsoil stripping, or some other exploitation of natural resources. The funeral home has sometimes been permitted in housing areas, but experience indicates that it is best located in business districts.

Certain non-housing uses are usually considered a normal part of residential development. The simplest use is the private garage, which is usually permitted in the rear or side yard with some additional regulation providing for a minimum setback from adjacent properties. The control of professional offices and home occupations is more complicated. Again, the objective to be kept in mind is maintenance of the desired residential character of the area.

Doctors and dentists are generally permitted to use part of their residence as an office, but if such a use becomes a clinic or needs more than one outside employee, it is better located in a business district where the automobiles of clients and employees will not be a disturbance to neighboring homes. Home occupations usually include dressmaking, millinery, or similar work, but would not include a tea room, barber shop, music school, or other use involving the frequent assembly of many persons. Signs used in connection with home occupations or professional offices need to be controlled and are normally limited to small announcement plates with no advertising.

Examples of residential district regulations are given below. These are illustrative only and are not intended to be applicable to a specific situation. These detailed regulations applying to each district can be presented as a part of the written text of the ordinance, starting with the most restricted district followed by each less restricted district in turn, or can be arranged in a table (usually called a "Schedule of Regulations"). The tabular form has the advantage of presenting the regulations in a manner permitting easy comparison of the requirements of the several districts, and is the form most widely used in recent ordinances. An example of such a tabular schedule is shown on page 588.

The residential districts presented as examples are chosen as applicable to the smaller residential community. The form, however, could be used for any residential district, even those in more urban areas, with appropriate changes in the specific requirements.

BUSINESS DISTRICTS

Perhaps the most common error in municipal zoning is setting aside too much land for business purposes. The belief that all lots on main thoroughfares and highways are actually potential business sites has often resulted in the over-zoning of frontage for business use. Economic waste has resulted from this because it encourages spotty, unplanned development, which in turn blights the land for the development of other valuable land uses.

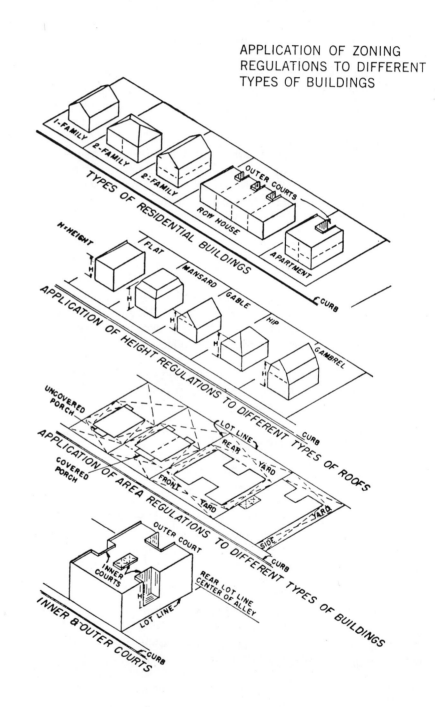

APPLICATION OF ZONING REGULATIONS TO DIFFERENT TYPES OF BUILDINGS

Scattered businesses also attract traffic into areas which cannot cope with it. This unwanted and unnecessary traffic can add to the deterioration of parts of a community, and can seriously depreciate an area for residential use. Land speculation, excessive public and expenditures for improvements, and rising tax delinquencies on unimproved parcels are among the conditions that may result from unwise business and commercial zoning. The fact that must eventually be faced is that the customer purchasing power of an area is a limiting factor on the number of commercial establishments which can be successfully supported. Again, the value of the community's comprehensive plan becomes evident, for the plan can forecast the pertinent factors and determine the need for business development, including the most desirable locations for the various activities.

Business districts may be of many types. They may range from neighborhood-retail centers devoted primarily to shops serving the day-to-day needs of the nearby residents, to the central business district containing a wide variety of business activities. In some communities there will be more than one area having the character of a central business district and in most there will be a need for more than one neighborhood shopping area. The trend is to use names which describe the principal use permitted in the area.

While older ordinances permitted in the business districts residences and all the uses permitted in residential districts, many recent ordinances restrict business and industry districts to these uses alone. This is done in order to avoid the problem of mixed uses in these areas. Hand laundries, shoe repair shops, candy stores, millinery and clothing stores, jewelers, and other similar uses may have some manufacturing or industrial character due to the production and repairing of goods incidental to the sale of goods or services. These uses usually are considered a necessary adjunct to the business district. However, heavy commercial uses not requiring much customer trade, such as contractor's yards, plumber's shops, and the like, are usually treated as industrial uses.

The techniques of zoning for commercial and business districts have changed considerably since 1916 when New York City adopted the country's first comprehensive zoning ordinance. The mapping of districts which created ribbon developments of business uses along major thoroughfares has now been succeeded by a trend toward creating more compact business development with requirements designed to meet the needs of each area as indicated in the community's comprehensive plan. The compact business district recognizes the change in retail business buildings, the best known style being the "shopping center."

Shopping centers have several important elements that need to be considered: an integrated architectural design, extensive off-street parking and loading space, and common or centrally supplied services. These centers can range from small neighborhood store groups to large so-called "regional" centers.

Planning to accommodate the traffic developed by automobile use is a primary feature of shopping center design, and must be an important consideration in zoning for them. Many zoning ordinances are requiring as much as four times the amount of off-street parking area as business floor area in the shopping center, while many successful shopping centers provide parking area ten times the amount of floor area. Off-street parking requirements are discussed further on page 96.

LOCAL RETAIL DISTRICTS

Local retail or neighborhood business districts should be mapped for those locations that will efficiently serve the adjoining residential districts and minimize the possibilities of traffic congestion. Permitted uses can include those that are needed to serve the daily needs of the neighborhood and thus help to encourage the pedestrian while discouraging heavy vehicle traffic, congestion, noise, and those other effects tending to be a disturbance to residential areas. Traffic generation can be kept at a minimum by controlling the density and type of use. Therefore, the permitted principal uses need to be carefully selected to exclude uses and enterprises that bear no relationship to retail businesses, but would merely add to traffic congestion. For example, warehouses, truck terminals, and the like should be excluded.

A frequently encountered zoning map situation is created by the zoning of opposite sides of a street for different types of use or the zoning of the corners at intersections. As a general rule both sides of the street and all four corners should be placed in similar zones. However, the new type of shopping center with buildings set back a considerable distance from the lot lines and roadway gives an opportunity for a "buffer" between the shopping area and adjacent property across the street or on the next lot. These buffer areas can, in many instances, be zoned for residential use. The community will want to decide what standard it wishes to require for these local retail centers. Then it can examine each local area to determine the best location for the local shopping center and how it can be best fitted into the pattern of land use in the vicinity.

BUSINESS IN RURAL AREAS

New commercial areas are needed in growing rural communities, but questions often arise as to what kind? and where? Strip commercial development usually results in a mixture of stores, filling stations, residences, and vacant lots. This increases road hazards, causes traffic congestion, and decreases the carrying capacity of highways. Widely scattered business areas can also add to the financial problems of the community and its taxpayers because the streets serving business units must usually be wider and costlier than residential streets, sewers must often be enlarged, and the cost of police protection and other needed public services can be increased.

The character of a neighborhood is usually determined by the presence of the business uses already established. In some communities, especially those that have not had zoning previously, it may only be a question of time before some of the present residential uses intermingled with commercial uses will be converted to commercial uses. This points to the need, especially in communities just establishing zoning, for a detailed study of existing commercial uses and possibilities for their expansion. The growing rural community will find it difficult to achieve a good pattern of business development and zoning unless it has taken the time to prepare a comprehensive plan for its future.

In general, it will be wise to plan for the concentration of commercial uses near stategic intersections of major roads with the buildings set back from the road so that traffic hazards are minimized. These intersections are natural locations for shopping and commerce, certain types of light industry, and transportation facilities such as warehouses and truck terminals. At these points the highway may need to have parallel service streets to provide safe access to the business area.

SETBACKS, YARDS, AND LOT COVERAGE

In neighborhood business districts buildings should be set back from the street line to maintain the openness of the area. As a general rule, it is impractical to require large front and side yards in the older central business districts. Rear yards are desirable in all business districts to permit control of fire hazards and space for motor vehicles.

The minimum requirement for such yards in central areas is usually 20 feet or the height of the main building. In some of the modern shopping centers it is difficult to determine which is the front and which the rear yard, as the buildings themselves are in the center of the plot with off-street parking on all sides. Some communities are handling these special requirements by establishing a special type of district called a designed shopping center district or by some similar term.

In the central business districts and in the existing built-up neighborhood business districts of many communities, the lot coverage may be 70 or 80 percent. In congested and built-up central business districts, the lot is often completely covered; the zoning regulations usually take this into account and allow 100 percent lot coverage. However, in newer commercial areas, especially in the shopping center developments, the percentage of lot coverage permitted should be very low. Many communities are finding it desirable to restrict lot coverage in new business districts to 20 percent to allow four times more parking area than floor area for one-story buildings.

PERMITTED USES IN BUSINESS DISTRICTS

In drafting business district regulations, two methods of indicating permitted uses can be employed. The first method is a list of permitted uses, similar to that in the illustrative residential district regulations given above. This procedure should be satisfactory for most communities. Some of the larger communities, however, have found it advantageous to resort to the alternative procedure of listing the uses that are excluded or prohibited.

To do this, a general statement is made that all uses not otherwise prohibited by law are permitted, after which the specifically prohibited uses are enumerated. This type of regulation may fail to encourage the development that the community desires for the area. Furthermore, no list ever covers all the possible undesirable uses. In some instances, a combination of these two methods has been found advantageous, i.e., first permitted uses are listed and then prohibited types.

In rural areas, a single type of business district may be sufficient. This may be designated as a "General Businsss" district or a "B-1" district, or as some special type of district with a descriptive term attached such as "Highway Service Business" district. A lot size should be required that is large enough to supply water and adequate land area for sewage disposal; yard requirements are generally equal to those that would be specified for residential districts so that the open character of the area can be maintained. Parking space should be set back from the highway to avoid the hazards created by parking movements in high-speed traffic lanes.

In the example below, the uses are those permitted in any residential district plus shops providing personal services, and the usual community services such as banks, theatres, offices, and restaurants. Garages and filling stations are allowed upon approval of a special permit by the board of appeals. (A discussion of special permit uses will be found on page 83 as well as in the section concerned with the board of appeals.) The illustration also shows an alternative regulation in which are enumerated the conditions under which garages and filling stations are permitted. Additional uses sometimes included in business areas are recreational activities such as bowling alleys, billiard parlors, and places of public assembly. Funeral parlors are sometimes allowed.

Wholesale businesses and storage warehouses for certain materials are often permitted in business districts. This may be particularly true in the case of a highway or service type of business district or in communities where one business district is sufficient. In some instances, zoning ordinances have restricted storage warehouses to industrial districts.

INDUSTRIAL DISTRICTS

The amount of land devoted to industrial purposes will vary considerably with the size, type, characteristics, and location of the community. Studies must be made to determine the total area and the places in each community which could be devoted to industrial use. It is extremely important that the best industrial sites be chosen and reserved for such use so that they will not be preempted by other types of development such as residences or other uses that could just as well have been located elsewhere.

Today, more ground space is required for new plants than in the past, since industries now look for a building with one or possibly two stories, a design which spreads the plant over a large lot area. Substantial setbacks, yards, and landscaping are being provided in many new industrial installations. This open space permits future expansion, promotes plant security, minimizes certain hazards to adjoining areas, obtains properly located off-street parking areas for employees and for the handling and storage of materials, helps capitalize on the advertising value of an attractive plant and grounds and assures more pleasant working conditions. Zoning ordinances have recognized these benefits by including regulations which require this type of industrial building. Good zoning can also help direct new industrial developments to those areas where heavy trucking through residential areas can be minimized.

Many types of uses are normally permitted in industrial areas. This has resulted from the practice of viewing the industrial district as the least restricted area in the community. Older ordinances, using this approach and not prohibiting residence use in such areas, have probably encouraged the blight caused by mixed land use typical of industrial slums. Modern zoning tries to encourage industry only in the places where it can be successfully developed and does not classify rundown areas as industrial districts simply because the land pattern is complex and the buildings obsolete. The community's comprehensive plan will indicate how obsolete areas need to be rebuilt. Industry might be the logical new use in some of these areas.

A frequent complaint by industrial location specialists has been that too many communities have zoned unusable land for industry. Again, as the result of a comprehensive local planning study, the industrial opportunities can be assessed and a zoning regulation drawn to obtain the best use of all the land in the community. Today, the industrial developer often looks for land as attractive as that sought by the homeseeker, and certainly never has seriously considered swampy, rocky, or otherwise expensive sites as possibilities.

INDUSTRY IN RURAL AREAS

Some rural communities will not wish to encourage industrial development because of a desire to maintain the existing open character of the area. Others may decide that some industrial use is appropriate in order to provide a source of local employment and a more complete community life, or to assist in meeting local public expense. For its part, industry may wish to consider a rural location if no suitable open land can be found elsewhere.

The open rural community can offer a real opportunity for substantial industrial development, particularly if it is close to a central city offering urban facilities. Where a suitably large tract of land is available, a planned industrial area or "industrial park" might be possible. This type of development would normally involve a single ownership of a tract with the developer providing the sites to industries on a sale or lease basis. The developer also provides the roads, utilities, and other services required, and public action would be limited to that degree of cooperation deemed desirable by the community. Part of this cooperation would be a modern zoning regulation, protecting both the planned industrial area from inappropriate intrusions and the public from poorly planned non-residential uses.

TYPES OF INDUSTRIAL DISTRICTS

As the municipality increases in size, or when the characteristics of the land-use pattern so indicate, two or more industrial districts may be desirable in order to sort out the various industrial uses into logical groups. The "heavy" industries, i.e., those liable to produce smoke, fumes, dust, or other objectionable effluents, will prosper best if located by themselves. When a single industrial district is established, it may be termed a "General Industrial" or simply an "Industrial" district. Where two districts are required, one is usually termed a "Light Industrial" district and the second a "Heavy Industrial" district.

In allocating industries to different classifications of industrial districts, the effect of the industry on its environment is more important as a basis for classification than is the material or product involved. Some slaughter houses, for example, are confined to enclosed buildings, largely air-conditioned, and not offensive to neighbors either by sight, sound, or odor, and might locate in a light industry section. Electric power and smokeless fuels have gone far toward eliminating smoke, steam, noise, and dirt. Smooth-running modern presses and other technology have already eliminated noise and vibration in some types of metal working operations. Thus, many plants formerly considered offensive have now become good neighbors.

THE ZONING SCHEDULE

Help in visualizing the many differing regulations and standards in the zoning ordinance can be provided by compiling a "Zoning Schedule," a summary in tabular form of the major requirements of each district set forth under appropriate headings.

One advantage of this device is the elimination of the vast amount of textual material that is used when all the requirements are written out in technical language in the text. The schedule is made a part of the ordinance in the same manner as the zoning map, and in the main body of the text reference is made to the zoning schedule together with such explanations and limitations as may be desirable.

ZONING SCHEDULE

DISTRICTS (Symbols as used on the zoning map)	PERMITTED PRINCIPAL USES or USES (If accessory uses are included)	PERMITTED ACCESSORY USES Exceptions and limitations	USES PERMITTED UPON ISSUANCE OF A SPECIAL PERMIT BY THE BOARD OF APPEALS Conditions and standards may be listed or placed in the text of the ordinance	MINIMUM LOT SIZE	
				Area in square feet	Width in feet
1	2	3	4	5	6
R-40 Residence					
R-20					
A Agriculture					
B-1 Business					
B-2					
I-1 Industry					
I-2					
Number of districts depends upon each community					

ZONING SCHEDULE EXPLANATION:

The Zoning Schedule, as illustrated, places the restrictions and regulations in numbered columns opposite the rows set up for the various zoning districts. The first column, at the extreme left, contains the districts and district designations (the symbols used should be the same as on the Zoning Map). To determine the regulations for any district, one need only look in the first column to find the correct district and then read across the schedule to determine the regulations for that district.

The second column, as illustrated, is for the Permitted Principal Uses. A variation of the title for this column may be just "Uses," which is appropriate if accessory uses are included with the principal uses. Another variation would be to make "Uses" the main heading for a group of three columns: Permitted, Permissible Upon Issuance of a Special Permit, and Prohibited.

Accessory Uses may be listed in a separate column as illustrated by column 3, or they may be included under column 2 "Uses." The regulation of accessory uses may be placed elsewhere or, if the community desires, they may be so simple or few as to be placed in the text or under the column "Other Provisions" or "Supplementary Regulations."

Many communities will want to list the special uses to be permitted by special permit from the Board of Appeals. As illustrated, these Special Permit Uses can be included in the schedule, as in column 4. They may also be embodied

MAXIMUM PERCENTAGE OF LOT TO BE OCCUPIED Total and/or		MINIMUM FLOOR AREA	MAXIMUM HEIGHT OF (PRINCIPAL) BUILDINGS		MINIMUM YARD DIMENSIONS in feet				ACCESSORY BUILDINGS				MINIMUM (MANDATORY) OFF-STREET PARKING SPACE	MINIMUM (MANDATORY) OFF-STREET LOADING SPACE	SIGNS PER-MITTED	OTHER PROVISIONS AND REQUIREMENTS Supplementary regula-tions, prohibitions, notes, etc.
						Each Side Yard			Maximum height in feet	Minimum Distance In Feet To						
Principal buildings	Accessory buildings		in stories	in feet	Front	One side yard	Two side yards	Rear		Principal building	Side lot line	Rear lot line	One unit for each			
7	8	9	10	11	12	13	14	15	16	17	18	19	20	21	22	23

in the text of the ordinance under Powers of the Board of Appeals or under Supplementary Regulations or General Provisions in either the text or the schedule.

Columns 5 and 6, as illustrated, have to do with minimum lot size. Column 5 shows the minimum area in square feet and column 6 the minimum width in feet (or, if preferred, "Frontage"). Another column that could be included here is "Lot Depth." Columns 7 and 8, as illustrated, deal with the maximum percentage of lot to be occupied or covered by buildings. This could be a single column with one figure showing percentage of occupancy of all buildings or it can be broken down to show percentage of occupancy allowed by principal buildings and accessory buildings, as shown here. A third method for this group would be three columns entitled "Total," "Principal Buildings," and "Accessory Buildings." A community with very small building lots has found it useful to do this, because it was found that many lots of the minimum size would hold a fairly large house but would not be desirable for a two-car garage. To allow some people to build a two-car garage the percentage under "Accessory Buildings" when added to the percentage under "Principal Buildings" came to more than that under "Total," which is the important figure. An owner, if he wanted a two-car garage, had to reduce the size of his house slightly.

A modern trend in zoning ordinances is the prohibition of dwellings below a certain size.

The most acceptable method for accomplishing this is by prescribing a minimum floor area. This type of requirement could be placed in a building code, although it is often placed in a zoning ordinance if the community has no building code. For purposes of illustration, it is column 9 in the outline schedule.

Height of buildings is covered in columns 10 and 11, as illustrated. Unless accessory buildings are allowed to be built as high as principal buildings or are included in this group, then this group heading should preferably read as "Maximum Height of Principal Building." It is still customary to specify height in stories as well as feet; thus, the two columns in this group. The next group of columns relate to the Yard Dimensions: Front, Side, and Rear. Many communities use the same dimensions for "each side yard" and thus they would only need one side yard column. The more popular trend is to specify a total for two side yards, with a minimum for the smallest side yard.

In this automobile age, communities are faced with traffic congestion and lack of parking space. Many communities have turned to zoning to help prevent further congestion, especially in newer business districts. The technique used is to require off-street parking and loading space for traffic generated. Columns 20 and 21 in the illustrated Schedule show how parking and loading space can be covered. The parking requirement usually is one unit for each dwelling unit and one unit (parking space) for a specified amount of floor area. The two items might

be combined into one column, combined with "Other Provisions and Requirements" or placed in the text.

Column 22 pertains to signs. This may be combined with the last column or omitted and included in the text. One advantage to including it as a separate column is to show that signs are considered important and have been controlled in each district.

The last column is for other provisions and requirements. Items included in this column are of the type usually found under "Supplementary Regulations or Provisions" in the text. This column may also contain notes referred to in other parts of the Schedule, when explanation or clarification beyond the space available in the column is needed.

If the requirements are to be carried over from one district to another, a notation such as "Same as (Symbol of District)"; or "Same as Specified for (Symbol or District)" can be inserted. It is not necessary to repeat all the regulations all the way down the columns for each new district.

The number and size of the columns as illustrated by the outline are not to be construed as being necessary for every community. The object of this illustration is to show what can be done by a tabular format to simplify and clarify the ordinance. Even if a Schedule is not used as part of the ordinance, it can be a valuable aid while the ordinance is being drafted.

FARM DISTRICTS

May be of the exclusive type or the cumulative type. Agriculture is the primary use. Other uses are secondary and accessory. Also permitted can be certain public and semi-public uses. Cumulative-type farm zoning districts can often serve as transition zones from agriculture to residential uses, including subdivisions. The transition may be facilitated by lowering lot size requirements. Usual minimum tract requirements for farm districts range from 10 to 80 acres.

FORESTRY DISTRICTS

Generally located in the Northwestern U. S. Developed from large acreage which is marginal for farming but valuable for forestry. Zoning is of the exclusive type. Such zones add to the recreational attraction of the area.

RECREATIONAL DISTRICTS

Primary use is for variety of recreational activities. This type of district can be used to protect and preserve mountainous, riverbank, lakeshore, or other areas that have natural or potential recreational features. Permitted uses can be agriculture, forestry, institutional uses, and limited commercial recreational uses.

FLOOD PLAIN DISTRICTS

Flood Plain Districts generally encompass all areas adjacent to rivers, streams, drainage channels, and ponds that are in danger of flooding. They can also include beds of water courses and of those portions of the adjoining flood plain that are required to carry and discharge the flood flow. Permitted uses usually include farming, forestry, and recreational activities.

WATERSHED DISTRICTS

Watershed districts reserve mountainous and hilly land for water production, forestry, wildlife, and recreation. Their purpose is to protect water sources and to avoid loss from improper use of land that has high water tables and is subject to periodic flooding. Forestry, agriculture, and grazing are deemed desirable principal uses. The types of recreation that need large acreages are suitable secondary uses.

OPEN-SPACE DISTRICTS

Open-space districts are used to reserve rural areas on the urban fringe for future generations, to provide permanent open space. Usually crop and tree farming may be allowed along with grazing and recreational activities.

LANDMARKS OR PRESERVATION DISTRICTS

Such districts are used to protect buildings and places that are of historical or cultural importance. Such districts help to safeguard our heritage and serve cultural educational, and recreational ends. The regulations pertain to buildings and structures of some significant architectural period. The concern is with exterior features only, mainly design, arrangement, texture, materials, and color. No changes can be made without approval from a review board.

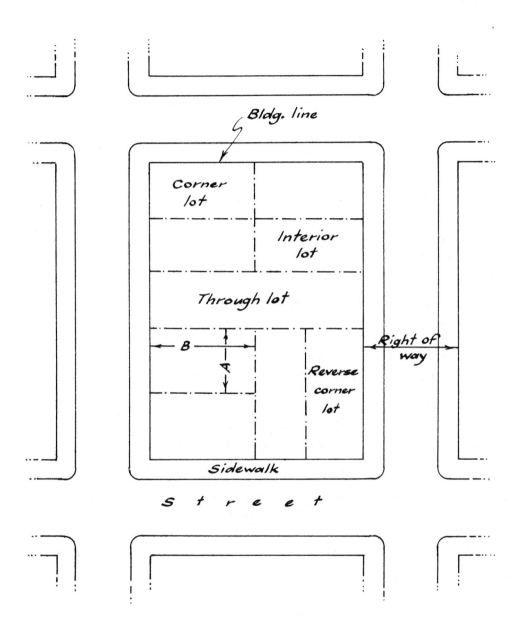

A—Width of lot

B—Length of lot

ZONING LOT

A "zoning lot" is either:

a. A lot of record existing on the effective date of the zoning ordinance or any applicable subsequent amendment thereto, or

b. A tract of land, either unsubdivided or consisting of two or more contiguous lots of record, located within a single block in single ownership.

LOT, INTERIOR

An "interior lot" is any zoning lot neither a corner lot nor a through lot.

LOT, CORNER

A "corner lot" is either a zoning lot bounded entirely by streets, or a zoning lot which adjoins the point of intersection of two or more streets and in which the interior angle formed by the extensions of the street lines in the directions which they take at their intersections with lot lines other than street lines, forms an angle of approximately 135 degrees or less.

LOT, THROUGH

A "through lot" is any zoning lot, not a corner lot, which adjoins two street lines opposite to each other and parallel or within 45 degrees of being parallel to each other. Any portion of a through lot which is not or could not be bounded by two such opposite street lines and two straight lines intersecting such street lines shall be subject to the regulations for an interior lot.

REVERSE CORNER LOT

A "reverse corner lot" is a corner lot which reverses the depth from the normal pattern of interior lots on a street. The front of the lot also changes from one street to the other.

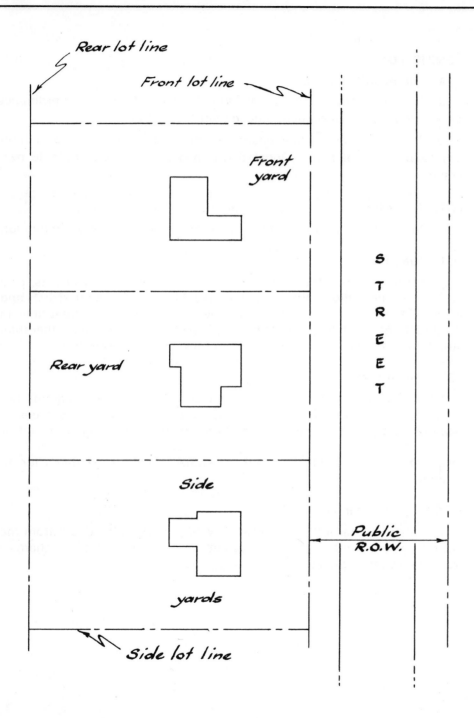

DEFINITIONS

YARD

A "yard" is that portion of a zoning lot extending open and unobstructed from the lowest level to the sky along the entire length of a lot line, and from the lot line for a depth or width set forth in the applicable district regulations.

YARD, FRONT

A "front yard" is a yard extending along the full length of a front lot line. In the case of a corner lot, any yard extending along the full length of a street line shall be considered a front yard.

YARD LINE, FRONT

A "front yard line" is a line drawn parallel to a front lot line at a distance therefrom equal to the depth of a required front yard.

YARD, REAR

A "rear yard" is a yard extending for the full length of a rear lot line.

YARD LINE, REAR

A "rear yard line" is a line drawn parallel to a rear lot line at a distance therefrom equal to the depth of a required rear yard.

YARD EQUIVALENT, REAR

A "rear yard equivalent" is an open area which may be required on a through lot as an alternative to a required rear yard.

YARD, SIDE

A "side yard" is a yard extending along a side lot line from the required front yard (or from the front lot line, if no front yard is required) to the required rear yard (or to the rear lot line, if no rear yard is required). In the case of a corner lot, any yard which is not a front yard shall be considered a side yard.

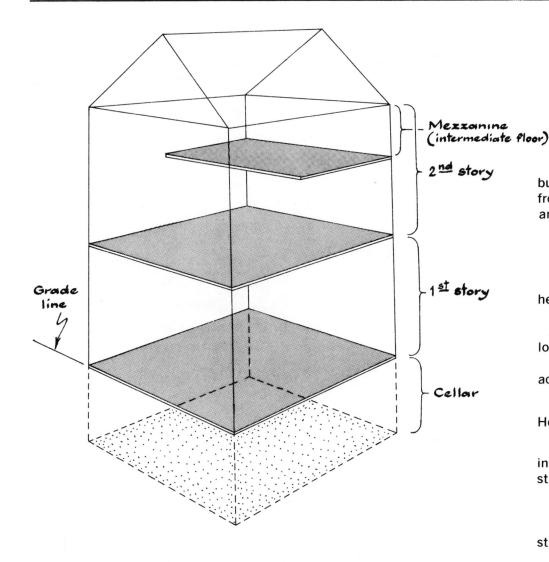

Floor area included

Floor area excluded

"Floor area" is the sum of the gross areas of the several floors of a building or buildings, measured from the exterior faces of exterior walls or from the center lines of walls separating two buildings. In particular, floor area generally includes:

a. Basement space, except as specifically excluded

b. Elevator shafts or stairwells at each floor

c. Floor space in penthouses

d. Attic space (whether or not a floor has been laid) providing structural headroom of eight feet or more

e. Floor space in interior balconies or mezzanines

g. Any other floor space used for dwelling purposes, no matter where located within a building

h. Floor space in accessory buildings, except for floor space used for accessory off-street parking

k. Any other floor space not specifically excluded.

However, the floor area of a building shall not include:

a. Cellar space, except that cellar space used for retailing shall be included for the purpose of calculating requirements for accessory off-street parking spaces and accessory off-street loading berths

b. Elevator or stair bulkheads, accessory water tanks, or cooling towers

c. Uncovered steps

d. Attic space (whether or not a floor actually has been laid) providing structural headroom of less than eight feet

h. Floor space used for mechanical equipment

Floor area ratio is the total floor area on a zoning lot, divided by the lot area of that zoning lot.

$$FAR = \frac{\text{total floor area}}{\text{total lot area}}$$

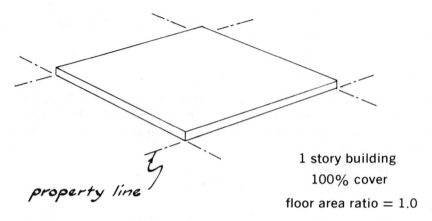

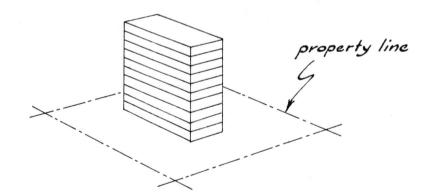

property line

1 story building

100% cover

floor area ratio = 1.0

property line

5 story building

20% cover

floor area ratio = 1.0

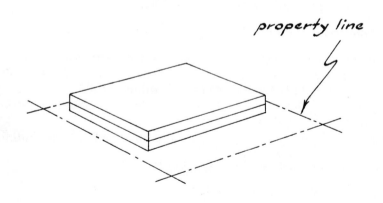

property line

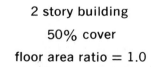

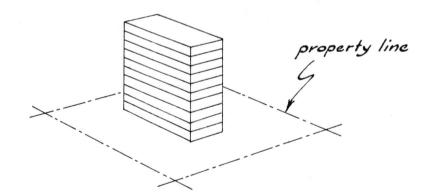

property line

2 story building

50% cover

floor area ratio = 1.0

10 story building

10% cover

floor area ratio = 1.0

A "Sky Exposure Plane" is an imaginary inclined plane beginning above the street line at a set height and rising over a zoning lot at a ratio of vertical distance to horizontal distance.

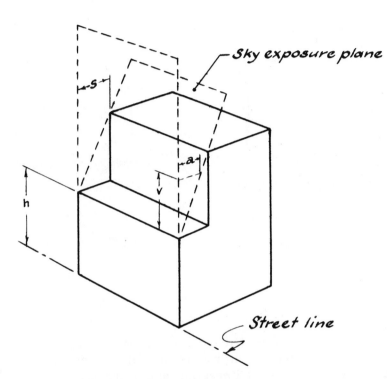

h is the height of
sky exposure plane
above **street line**

s is the **initial**
setback distance

v is the vertical distance

a is the horizontal distance

ILLUSTRATION OF SKY EXPOSURE PLANE

$$\text{Sky Exposure Plane} = \frac{\text{Vertical Distance}}{\text{Horizontal Distance}}$$

SOURCE: New York City Zoning Resolution—1961

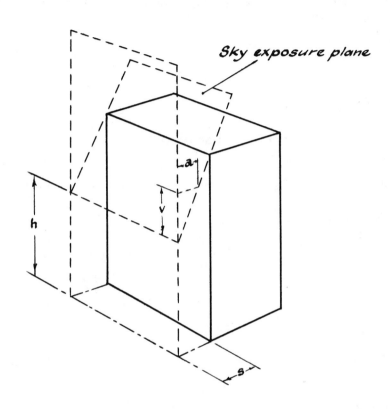

h is the height of
sky exposure plane
above **street line**

s is the depth of the
optional front open area

v is the vertical distance

a is the horizontal distance

ILLUSTRATION OF ALTERNATE SKY EXPOSURE PLANE

On narrow streets, the slope will be less than on wide streets.
The height (h) should relate to the general scale of the neighboring structures.

BUILDING HEIGHT

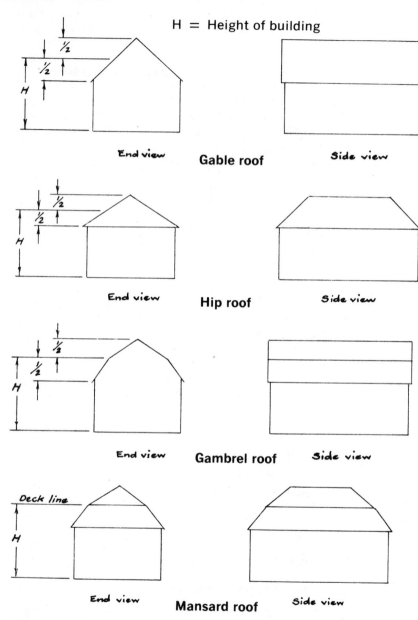

H = Height of building

End view — Gable roof — Side view

End view — Hip roof — Side view

End view — Gambrel roof — Side view

Deck line

End view — Mansard roof — Side view

Building Height: Is the vertical distance measured from the established grade to the highest point of the roof surface for flat roofs; to the deck line of mansard roofs; and to the average height between eaves and ridge for gable, hip, and gambrel roofs.

BASEMENT, CELLAR

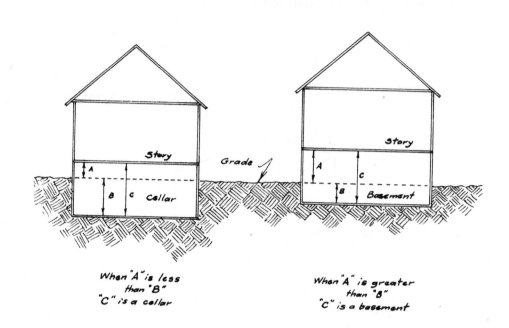

When "A" is less than "B" "C" is a cellar

When "A" is greater than "B" "C" is a basement

STORY

A "story" is that part of a building between the surface of a floor (whether or not counted for purposes of computing floor area ratio) and the ceiling immediately above. However, a cellar is not a story.

BASEMENT

A "basement" is a story (or portion of a story) partly below curb level, with at least one-half of its height (measured from floor to ceiling) above curb level. On through lots the curb level nearest to a story (or portion of a story) shall be used to determine whether such story (or portion of a story) is a basement.

CELLAR

A "cellar" is a space wholly or partly below curb level, with more than one-half its height (measured from floor to ceiling) below curb level. On through lots the curb level nearest to such space shall be used to determine whether such space is a cellar.

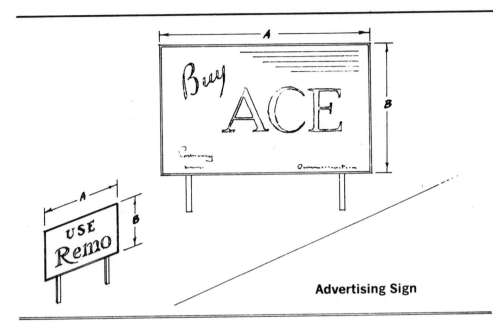

Advertising Sign

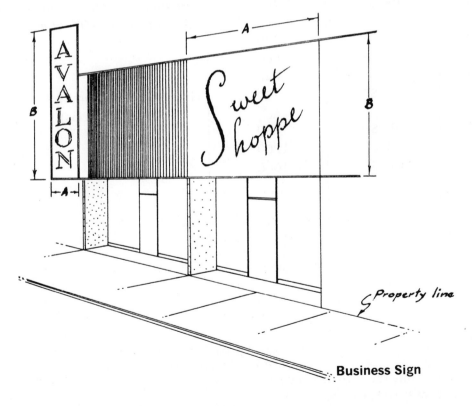

Business Sign

SIGN

A "sign" is any writing (including letter, word, or numeral); pictorial representation (including illustration or decoration); emblem (including device, symbol, or trademark); flag (including banner or pennant); or any other figure of similar character, which:

a. Is a structure or any part thereof, or is attached to, painted on, or in any other manner represented on a building or other structure, and

b. Is used to announce, direct attention to, or advertise, and

c. Is visible from outside a building. A sign shall include writing, representation, or other figure of similar character within a building only when illuminated and located in a window.

SIGN, ADVERTISING

An "advertising sign" is a sign which directs attention to a business, profession, commodity, service, or entertainment conducted, sold, or offered elsewhere than upon the same zoning lot.

SIGN, BUSINESS

A "business sign" is an accessory sign which directs attention to a profession, business, commodity, service, or entertainment conducted, sold, or offered upon the same zoning lot.

SIGN, FLASHING

A "flashing sign" is any illuminated sign, whether stationary, revolving, or rotating, which exhibits changing light or color effects, provided that revolving or rotating signs which exhibit no changing light or color effects other than those produced by revolution or rotation, shall be deemed flashing signs only if they exhibit sudden or marked changes in such light or color effects

SIGN, ILLUMINATED

An "illuminated sign" is a sign designed to give forth any artificial light or reflect such light from an artificial source.

SIGN, SURFACE AREA OF

Area of face of sign (A x B)

SIGN WITH INDIRECT ILLUMINATION

A "sign with indirect illumination" is any illuminated non-flashing sign whose illumination is derived entirely from an external artificial source and is so arranged that no direct rays of light are projected from such artificial source into residences or streets.

DENSITY (Families Per Acre)	GROSS AREA Per Family (Acre assumed to be 40,000 SF)	NO. OF PERSONS Per acre (4 Persons Per Family)	SUGGESTED Housing Type	DENSITY (Families Per Acre)	GROSS AREA Per Family (Acre Assumed to be 40,000)	NO. OF PERSONS Per Acre (4 Persons Per Family)	SUGGESTED Housing Type
1	40,000 SF	4	1 Family, Detached	50	800 SF	200	Low-Rise Multi-Family Apts. (6 Stories Max.)
2	20,000 SF	8	,, ,,	60	660 SF	240	,,
3	14,000 SF	12	,, ,,	70	580 SF	280	,,
4	10,000 SF	16	,, ,,	80	500 SF	320	,,
5	8,000 SF	20	,, ,,				
6	6,600 SF	24	,, ,,				
7	5,800 SF	28	,, ,,	100	400 SF	400	Medium-Rise Multi-Family Apartments (6-20 Stories)
8	5,000 SF	32	,, ,,				
10	4,000 SF	40	1 Family, Attchd. 2 Family, Detchd.	120	330 SF	480	,,
				140	280 SF	560	,,
12	3,300 SF	48	,, ,,	160	250 SF	640	,,
16	2,500 SF	64	,, ,,	180	220 SF	720	High-Rise Multi-Family Apts. (Over 20 Stories)
20	2,000 SF	80	Row Houses Or Garden Apts.				
				200	200 SF	800	,,
25	1,600 SF	100	,, ,,	300	150 SF	1200	,,
30	1,330 SF	120	,, ,,	400	100 SF	1600	,,
40	1,000 SF	160	,, ,,				

The height of building is limited by means of the Angle of Light Obstruction, so that adequate open air and light may reach the streets and rear yards. Each district is allotted a certain ALO. This is measured from the center line of the street and from the rear lot line. It is similar to many present regulations of height and setbacks, though expressed in angles instead of vertical and horizontal distances. However, to give more freedom of design and allow for more efficient building shapes, without sacrificing light and air, the ALO may be "averaged"; so that some sections of a building may rise above the allotted angle line, provided that an equally large or larger section drops below it. To avoid overlong stretches of high wall, this averaging is limited to a frontage length of not more than 1½ times the width of the street in residential districts and twice the width of the street in all other districts. To avoid too much height in any section on the street front, a minimum angle is set for calculating the low building sections, and buildings in residential districts may only exceed their allotted average angle for half the street frontage of the lot. And the overall bulk is still controlled by the Floor Area Ratio.

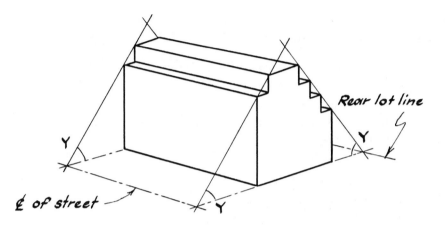

The Angle of Light Obstruction Y may be
kept constant along the whole street frontage,

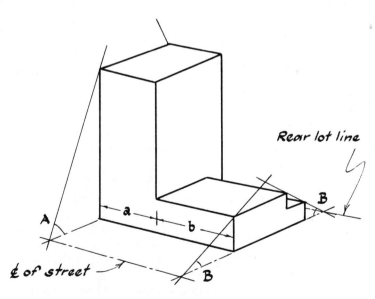

or averaged by the formula $Y = \dfrac{Aa + Bb}{a + b}$

SOURCE: Rezoning New York City Edited and Designed by Baker-Funaro New York Chapter, American Institute of Architects

All windows which are needed to satisfy the ventilation requirements of the Building Code and the Multiple Dwelling Law will have to give upon a certain minimum of open space known as the Area for Light Access. This can be easily and quickly measured with a graphic device marked off in a series of wedge-shaped sections.

The required ALA may be within the lot upon which the building is placed, or on the street, or on the required open yard of an adjoining lot.

The Area for Light Access is measured by a series of wedges marked out within the segments of a circle.

For residential buildings
the wedges are within the band between 40 and 60 ft. from the window.
Eight wedges (six of them contiguous) must be unobstructed.

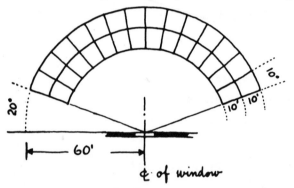

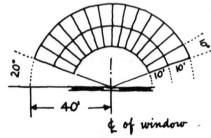

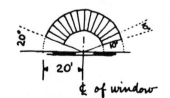

For low-bulk commercial buildings the wedges are within the band between 20 and 40 ft. from the window. Eight wedges (six of them contiguous) must be unobstructed.

For high-bulk commercial and manufacturing buildings the wedges are within the band between 10 and 20 ft. from the window. Eight wedges (all contiguous) must be unobstructed.

If an obstruction in front of the window is not higher (from the sill line) than two-thirds the distance from that window, it is not considered an obstruction when checking the window for Units of Light Access.

The window at **a** satisfies the requirements for residential buildings: a minimum of eight Units of Light Access, at least six of which are contiguous.

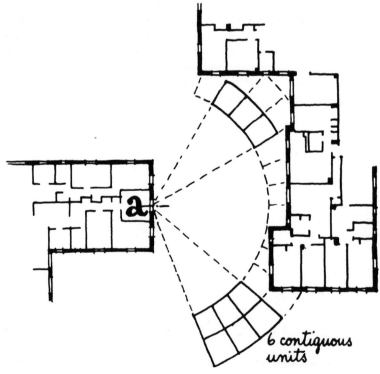

6 contiguous units

SOURCE: *Rezoning New York City Edited and Designed by Baker-Funaro New York Chapter, American Institute of Architects*

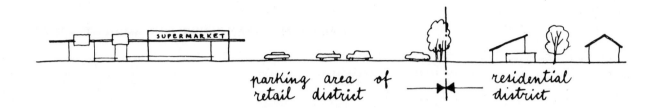

parking area of retail district — residential district

1. In retail and commercial districts parking areas which adjoin a residential zone must be shielded by walls, shrubs, or trees along the boundary line.

This is applied at the boundary between residential and non-residential districts to prevent this becoming a no-man's-land, undesirable for residences yet so zoned that it cannot be used for anything else. The Zoning Resolution should provide curbs upon business signs, show windows, and entrances to stores adjoining residential districts. Three examples are shown:

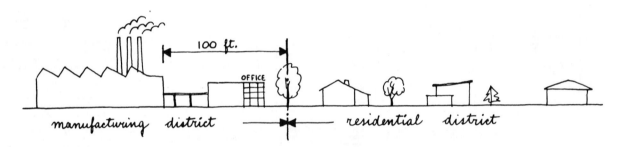

100 ft.

OFFICE

manufacturing district — residential district

2. In industrial districts adjoining a residential zone a 100 ft. wide strip along the boundary line cannot be used for actual manufacture but must be reserved for less objectionable uses, for example, an administration building or a parking lot.

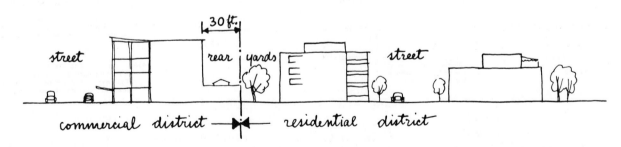

30 ft.

street — rear yards — street

commercial district — residential district

3. In non-residential lots which are back to back with residential, 30 ft. deep rear yards are prescribed, though a single story rising not more than 23 ft. above curb level may extend to the rear lot line.

SOURCE: Rezoning New York City Edited and Designed by Baker-Funaro New York Chapter, American Institute of Architects

CALIFORNIA STANDARDS FOR AMBIENT AIR QUALITY

POLLUTANT	"ADVERSE" LEVEL Level at which there will be sensory irritation, damage to vegetation, reduction in visibility or similar effects.	"SERIOUS" LEVEL Level at which there will be alteration of bodily function or which is likely to lead to chronic disease.	"EMERGENCY" LEVEL Level at which it is likely that acute sickness or death in sensitive groups of persons will occur.
Oxidant		Not applicable	Not applicable
Ozone	"Oxidant Index" 0.15 ppm for one hour by the potassium iodide method (eye irritation, plant damage and visibility reduction)	Footnote 1	Footnote 2
Nitrogen Dioxide		Footnote 3	Footnote 3
Hydrocarbons		Footnote 4	Footnote 4
Photochemical Aerosols		Not applicable	Not applicable
Carcinogens	Not applicable	Footnote 5	Not applicable
Sulfur Dioxide	1 ppm for 1 hour or 0.3 ppm for 8 hours (plant damage)	5 ppm for 1 hour (bronchoconstriction in human subjects)	10 ppm for 1 hour (severe distress in human subjects)
Sulfuric Acid	Footnote 6	Footnote 6	Footnote 7
Carbon Monoxide	Not applicable	30 ppm for 8 hours or 120 ppm for 1 hour (interference with oxygen transport by blood)	Footnote 8
Lead	Not applicable	Footnote 9	Footnote 9
Ethylene	Footnote 10	Not applicable	Not applicable
Particulates	Sufficient to reduce visibility to less than 3 miles when relative humidity is less than 70 percent	Not applicable	Not applicable

1. Ozone, at 1 ppm for eight hours daily for about a year, has produced bronchiolitis and fibrositis in rodents (Stokinger, H. E., Wagner, W. D., and Dobrogorski, O. J. A. M. A. Archives of Industrial Health, 16:514, (1957). Extrapolation of these data to man is difficult. Functional impairment data have been reported by Clamann and Bancroft (Clamann, H. G., and Bancroft, R. W. Advances in Chemistry. No. 21, pp. 352-359, 1959); at 1.25 ppm some effect is observed on residual volume and diffusing capacity. The variability of the tests was not reported. Additional data would be needed before a standard is set.

2. A value of 2.0 ppm of ozone for one hour may produce serious interference with function in healthy persons, and the assumption is made that this might cause acute illness in sensitive persons. (Clamann, H. G. op. cit.)

*3. Five ppm of nitrogen dioxide for eight hours will produce decreased pulmonary function in animals. Slightly more may produce pulmonary fibrosis (Stokinger, personal communication); nitrogen dioxide from air pollution exposures is usually combined with nitric oxide and ozone. More data on human exposures will be needed prior to setting a standard.

4. Hydrocarbons are a group of substances most of which, normally, are toxic only at concentrations in the order of several hundred parts per million. However, a number of hydrocarbons can react photochemically at very low concentrations to produce irritating and toxic substances. Because of the large number of hydrocarbons involved, the complexity of the photochemical reactions, and the reactivity of other compounds such as nitrogen dioxide and ozone, it is not yet possible to establish "serious" and "emergency" levels for hydrocarbons. From the public health standpoint, the concentration of those hydrocarbons which react photochemically should be maintained at or below the level associated with the oxidant index defined in the "adverse" standard.

5. Carcinogens include a few organic compounds such as some polycyclic hydrocarbons, and some metals such as arsenic and chromium. Studies on effects of such substances are currently under way, but there are not sufficient data, at present, to set standards. In the meantime, it is recommended that concentrations of carcinogens in air should be kept as low as possible.

6. A sulfuric acid mist level of 1 mg/M³ with an average particle size of one micron will produce a respiratory response in man. (Amdur, M. O., Silverman, L., and Drinker, P. Archives of Industrial Hygiene and Occupational Medicine, 6:305, 1952.) It is not possible to generalize from this for all air pollution conditions, because under natural conditions, particle size will vary. Only with large droplets would sensory irritation be produced without other physiological effects.

7. A level of 5 mg/M³ of sulfuric acid mist for a few minutes produces coughing and irritation in normal individuals (Amdur, M. O., Silverman, L., and Drinker, P. op. cit.). Presumably, it could cause acute illness in sensitive groups of persons in a period of one hour.

8. Given certain assumptions concerning ventilatory rates, acute sickness might result from a carbon monoxide level of 240 ppm for one hour in sensitive groups because of inactivation of ten per cent of the body's hemoglobin. In any event it is clear that when a population exposure limit has been set for carbon monoxide, because of exposures from other sources, community air pollution standards should be based on some fraction of this limit.

9. It is clear that lead levels should be set on the basis of average values for long periods. While data are abundant concerning human response to eight-hours-a-day, five-days-a-week exposures, data are insufficient for the effects of the continuous exposure inherent in community air pollution. While laboratory studies will be pursued with vigor, it becomes very important that local agencies collect data on existing lead levels. Since lead exposures are from multiple sources, community air pollution standards should be based on a portion of the total limit for population exposure.

10. Ethylene causes severe damage to vegetation. Ornamental plants are severely injured by exposures from 0.2 to 0.5 ppm. Tomatoes and fruit are adversely affected at similar levels. Current work is expected to permit a standard to be set within a year.

*Note: In regard to Footnote 3, Dr. Stokinger suggests changes in the first two sentences so that they would read: "Five ppm nitrogen dioxide for eight hours will produce temporarily decreased respiratory function in animals. High levels (150-200 ppm) in short exposures produce fibrotic changes in the lungs of man that may end fatally". However, this change has not yet been approved by the State Board of Public Health.

SOURCE: Air Pollution Control, Field Operations Manual, Public Health Service, U. S. Dept. of Health, Education & Welfare

Some of the well-known odor classification systems are indicated here. They are useful in training inspectors in making associations and analyzing the various component sensations which odors may produce. For field purposes, one system is as good as another. The advantage of all systems is that they yield a usable odor vocabulary.

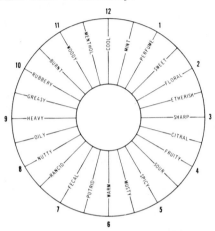

ODOR CHART. This chart attempts to present a complete range of odor terms which can be used to construct phrases of odor description. Each of these terms, moreover, can be numerically fixed from a "clock" chart for map notations, tabulations, or general reporting. Reported by Gruber, and attributed to Dean Foster, Head of the Psychophysical Laboratory at the Joseph E. Seagram Co., Louisville, Kentucky.

HENNING'S ODOR CLASSIFICATION
BASED ON SIX TYPES OF ODOR CLASSIFICATION

1. **Spicy:** Conspicuous in cloves, cinnamon, nutmeg, etc.
2. **Flowery:** Conspicuous in heliotrope, jasmine, etc.
3. **Fruity:** Conspicuous in apple, orange oil, vinegar, etc.
4. **Resinous:** Conspicuous in coniferous oils and turpentine.
5. **Foul:** Conspicuous in hydrogen sulfide and products of decay.
6. **Burnt:** Conspicuous in tarry and scorched substances.

CROCKER-HENDERSON CLASSIFICATION
A CONDENSATION OF THE HENNING ARRANGEMENT

1. Fragrant or sweet.
2. Acid or sour.
3. Burnt or empyreumatic.
4. Caprylic, goaty, or oenanthic.

SOURCE: Air Pollution Control, Field Operations Manual, Public Health Service, U. S. Dept. of Health, Education & Welfare

INTENSITY

Intensity is some numerical or verbal indication of the strength of an odor. Intensity may remain constant, vary or fluctuate depending on air/odorant dilution rates. A gradual increase in intensity is readily detected, although persons may have become fatigued by the odor. A sudden increase in odor intensity, however, such as might be encountered by suddenly opening a flask containing ammonia or chlorine in a room has an intensity which may be characterized by an impact. Thus, an intensity has shock value, particularly in relation to pungent or putrid odors.

Some general mathematical relationship exists between quantity of odorant (the stimulus) and odor intensity in any given situation. Equal degrees of subjective odor intensity are stimulated by quantities of odorant which have increased geometrically rather than arithmetically. This phenomenon is described by the well-known Weber-Fechner Psychophysical Law which states that the intensity of the sensation is proportional to the logarithm of the strength of the stimulus, for middling strengths of stimuli. Odorometers and other inanimate odor detection equipment appear to verify this principle both under field and laboratory conditions. According to Gruber, the Scentometer, devised by the Cincinnati Bureau of Air Pollution, provides 5 odorous inlets which permit dilution of 2, 4, 8, 16 and 32 parts total air to one part odorous air on the assumption that a trained observer can detect five levels of odor intensity.

Experimental findings on the discernment of odor intensity are still incomplete. It can be said, however, that the average observer or complainant can be expected to distinguish between three intensities, weak, medium and strong, whereas the expert should be able to distinguish between those five degrees of intensity shown below and at least 16 categories of odor quality in the following typical rating scheme:

The intensity of the odor may be noted as follows:

0. A concentration of an odorant which produces no sensation.
1. Concentration which is just detectable (the threshold dilution).
2. A distinct and definite odor whose unpleasant characteristics are revealed or foreshadowed (the recognition threshold).
3. An odor strong enough to cause a person to attempt to avoid it completely.
4. An odor so strong as to be overpowering and intolerable for any length of time.

This rating system is adapted especially for field work since it is made in terms of the behavior or response of a percipient that can be observed by an inspector. The response here is clearly one of avoidance. The fact that a person desperately attempts to avoid a strong and unpleasant odor clearly indicates the intensity of that odor.

NEW ENGLAND INTERSTATE WATER POLLUTION CONTROL COMMISSION CLASSIFICATION AND STANDARDS OF
QUALITY FOR COASTAL AND MARINE WATERS
(As Revised and Adopted December 12, 1969)

STANDARDS OF WATER QUALITY–INLAND WATERS

Water Use Classes	Description	Dissolved Oxygen	Sludge Deposits, Solid Refuse, Floating Solids, Oils, Grease and Scum	Color and Turbidity	Coliform Bacteria	Taste and Odor	pH	Allowable Temperature Increase
Class SA	Suitable for water supply with treatment by disinfection only, and all other water uses; character uniformly excellent. (See Notes 1 and 3.)	As naturally occurs.	None other than of natural origin.	None other than of natural origin	Total coliforms: not to exceed a monthly arthmetic mean of 100 per 100 ml. (See Note 4.)	None other than of natural origin.	As naturally occurs	None other than of natural origin.
Class SB	Suitable for bathing and other primary contact recreation. Acceptable for public water supply with appropriate treatment. (See Note 3.) Suitable for agricultural and certain industrial process cooling uses. Suitable as an excellent fish and wildlife habitat. Excellent aesthetic value.	Minimum 5 mg/l at any time. Normal seasonal and diurnal variations above 5 mg/l will be maintained.	None Allowable.	None in such concentrations that would impair any usages specifically assigned to this Class.	Total coliforms: not to exceed a monthly median of 1,000 per ml nor more than 2,400 per 100 ml in more than 20% of samples collected. (See Note 4.)	None in such concentrations that would impair any usages specifically assigned to this Class nor cause taste and odor in edible fish.	6.5 – 8.0	Only such increases that will not impair any usages specifically assigned to this Class. (See Note 5.)
Class SC	Suitable for fish and wildlife habitat, boating, fishing, and certain industrial process and cooling uses.	Minimum 5 mg/l any time. Normal seasonal and diurnal variations above 5 mg/l will be maintained. For sluggish, eutrophic waters, not less than 3 mg/l at any time. Normal seasonal and diurnal variations above 3 mg/l will be maintained.	None (See Note 2.)	None in such concentrations that would impair any usages specifically assigned to this Class.	(See Note 4.)	None in such concentrations that would impair any usages specifically assigned to this Class nor cause taste and odor in edible fish.	6.0 – 8.5	Only such increases that will not impair any usages specifically assigned to this Class. (See Note 5.)
Class SD	Suitable for navigation, power, certain industrial processes and cooling uses, and migration of fish. Good aesthetic value.	2 mg/l at any time. Normal seasonal and diurnal variations above 2 mg/l will be maintained.	None (See Note 2.)	None in such concentrations that would impair any usages specifically assigned to this Class.	None in such concentrations that would impair any usages specifically assigned to this Class.	None in such concentrations that would impair any usages specifically assigned to this Class.	6.0 – 9.0	Only such increases that will not impair any usages specifically assigned to this Class. (See Note 5.)

Notes: 1. Class A waters reserved for water supply may be subject to restricted use by state and local regulation.

2. Sludge deposits, floating solids, oils, grease, and scum shall not be allowed except in that amount that may result from the discharge of appropriately designed and operated sewage and/or industrial waste treatment plants.

[3]Waters shall be free from chemical and radiological constituents in concentrations or combinations that would be harmful to human, animal, or aquatic life for the most sensitive and governing water class use. In areas where fisheries are the governing considerations and approved limits have not been established, bioassays shall be performed as required by the appropriate agencies. For public drinking water supplies the raw water sources must be of such quality that the U.S. Public Health Service or higher appropriate state agency limits for finished water can be met after conventional water treatment.

[4]Water quality analyses on interstate waters should include tests for both total and fecal coliform supported by sanitary surveys for the development of background data and the establishment of base lines for these two parameters for the specific waters involved.

[5]The resultant temperature of a receiving water shall not exceed that for the most sensitive aspect of the most sensitive specie of aquatic life in that water. Normal seasonal and diurnal temperature variations that existed before the addition of heat of artificial origin shall be maintained. In addition: (a) For streams, the allowable total temperature rise shall not exceed 5°F above ambient unless it can be demonstrated to the satisfaction of the state regulatory agencies that greater rises at various times will not be harmful to fish, other aquatic life, or other uses. (b) For lakes, there shall be no discharge or withdrawal of cooling waters from the hypolimnion unless it can be demonstrated to the satisfaction of the state regulatory agencies that such discharges or withdrawals will not be harmful to fish, other aquatic life, or other uses. A heated discharge to a lake shall not raise the temperature more than 3°F at the surface immediately outside a designated mixing zone. (More restrictive requirements may be adopted by a state if deemed necessary to meet the Class use of the receiving waters.)

NEW ENGLAND INTERSTATE WATER POLLUTION CONTROL COMMISSION CLASSIFICATION AND STANDARDS OF
QUALITY FOR COASTAL AND MARINE WATERS
(As Revised and Adopted December 12, 1969)

STANDARDS OF WATER QUALITY MARINE WATERS*

Water Use Classes	Description	Dissolved Oxygen	Sludge Deposits, Solid Refuse, Floating Solids, Oils, Grease, and Scum	Color and Turbidity	Coliform Bacteria	Taste and Odor	pH	
Class A	Suitable for all seawater uses including shellfish harvesting for direct human consumption (approved shellfish areas), bathing, and other water contact sports; excellent aesthetic value.	Not less than 5.0 mg/l at any time. Normal seasonal and diurnal variations above 5 mg/l will be maintained.	None allowable	None in such concentrations that would impair any usages specifically assigned to this Class.	Not to exceed a median MPN of 70 and not more than 10% of the samples shall ordinarily exceed an MPN of 230 per 100 ml for a 5-tube decimal dilution or 330 per 100 ml for a 3-tube decimal dilution. (See Note S.1.)	None allowable	6.8 – 8.5	Allowable temperature increase. (See Note S.3.)
Class B								Chemical constituents. (See Note S.2.)
	Suitable for bathing, other recreational purposes, industrial cooling, and shellfish harvesting for human consumption after depuration; excellent fish and wildlife habitat; good aesthetic value.	Not less than 5.0 mg/l at any time. Normal seasonal and diurnal variations above 5 mg/l will be maintained.	None allowable	None in such concentrations that would impair any usages specifically assigned to this Class.	Not to exceed a median value of 700 per 100 ml and not more than 2,300 per 100 ml in more than 10% of the samples collected in a 30-day period. (See Note S.1.)	None in such concentrations that would impair any usages specifically assigned to this Class and none that would cause taste and odor in edible fish or shellfish.	6.8 – 8.5	
Class C								Radiological constituents. (See Note S.2.)
	Suitable fish, shellfish, and wildlife habitat; suitable for recreational boating and industrial cooling; good aesthetic value.	Not less than 5 mg/l during daylight hours nor less than 4 mg/l at any time. Normal seasonal and diurnal variations above 4 mg/l will be maintained.	None except that amount that may result from the discharge from a waste treatment facility providing appropriate treatment.	None in such concentrations that would impair any usages specifically assigned to this Class.	None in such concentrations that would impair any usages specifically assigned to this Class.	None in such concentrations that would impair any usages specifically assigned to this Class and none that would cause taste and odor in edible fish or shellfish.	6.8 – 8.5	
Class D	Suitable for navigation, power, certain industrial processes and cooling uses, and migration of fish; good aesthetic value.	A minimum of 2 mg/l at any time. Normal seasonal and diurnal variations above 2 mg/l will be maintained.	None except for such small amounts that may result from the discharge of appropriately treated sewage and/or industrial waste effluents.	None in such concentration that would impair any usages specifically assigned to this Class.	(See Note S.I.)	None in such concentrations that would impair any usages specifically assigned to this Class and none that would cause taste and odor in edible fish or shellfish.	6.0 – 9.0	

*Coastal and marine waters are those generally subject to the rise and fall of the tide.
Notes: S.1 Surveys to determine coliform concentrations shall include those areas most probably exposed to fecal contamination during the most unfavorable hydrographic and pollution conditions. Water quality analyses on interstate marine and coastal waters should include tests for both total and fecal coliform supported by sanitary surveys for the development of background data and the establishment of a base line for these two parameters for the specific waters involved.

S.2 Waters shall be free from chemical and radiological concentrations or combinations that would be harmful to human, animal, or aquatic life or that would make the waters unsafe or unsuitable for fish or shellfish or their propagation, impair the palatability of same, or impair the water for any other usage. In areas where fisheries are the governing considerations and approved limits have not been established, bioassays shall be performed as required

surface of coastal waters shall not be raised more than 4°F over the monthly means of maximum daily temperatures from October through June nor more than 1.5°F from July through September. (b) Estuaries or Portions of Estuaries. The water temperature at the surface of an estuary shall not be raised to more than 90°F at any point provided further, at least 50 percent of the cross-sectional area and/or volume of the flow of the estuary including a minimum of ⅓ of the surface as measured from water edge to water edge at any stage of tide, shall not be raised to more than 4°F over the temperature that existed before the addition of heat of artificial origin or a maximum of 83°F, whichever is less. However, during July through September, if the water temperature at the surface of an estuary before the addition of heat of artificial origin is more than 83°F, an increase in temperature not to exceed 1.5×F, at any point of the estuarine passageway as delineated above, may be permitted. (More restrictive requirements may be adopted by a state if deemed necessary for the protection of the mo???

AIR POLLUTION EMISSION TABLE

Type of Pollutant	Effect	Source	Possible Control Measures	Air Pollution Sampling Method
Fallout Particulate Matter	Soiling of property, nuisance	Industry, combustion processes, road mix plants, incinerators, etc.	Cyclones, bag filters, electrostatic precipitators, washers, etc.	Dustfall sampling
Suspended Particulate Matter, Smoke	Soiling of property, visibility reduction, nuisance	Industry, combustion processes, road mix plants, incinerators, etc.	Bag filters, electrostatic precipitators, better combustion	1. High Volume Sampling 2. AISI Smoke Sampling 3. Visibility Determinations
Hydrocarbons	Primary contributors to Los Angeles type smog (eye irritation, rubber cracking, visibility reduction, ozone formation).	Automotive vehicles, oil refineries, fuel handling, solvent handling.	Afterburner and other automotive devices (under development), automotive blowby devices, floating roof covers, vapor recovery systems.	Freezeout method
Oxides of Nitrogen		Automotive vehicles, combustion processes, industry	Automotive devices (under research), controlled combustion	Saltzman method
Oxidant (a measure of Los Angeles smog)		Photochemical reactions in the atmosphere	Controls for hydrocarbons and oxides of nitrogen	1. Potassium iodide method 2. Phenolphthalin method
Carbon Monoxide	Toxic pollutant	Automotive vehicles, industry	Afterburners for industry; automotive exhaust devices (under development)	A modification of the NBS colorimetric detector tube technique
Sulfur Dioxide	Corrosive, odorous plant damage, toxic	Combustion processes, industry, etc.	Absorption towers, control of sulfur content in fuel	West method
Pollen	Allergy, hay fever	Natural—trees, grasses, weeds, etc.	Farming methods, weed control	Collection on slides
Odors	Nuisance	Industry and miscellaneous	Good housekeeping, chemical control, masking, counteractant, etc.	Trained nose

AIR POLLUTION EMISSION TABLE

AIR POLLUTANT EMISSIONS: 1968 TO 1970

[Quantity in millions of tons per year. Estimates]

SOURCE CATEGORY	1968 total	1969 total	1970, total	POLLUTANT				
				Carbon monoxide	Sulfur oxides	Hydrocarbons	Particulates	Nitrogen oxides
Total quantity	264.4	272.6	263.9	147.0	33.9	34.7	25.6	22.7
Total controllable.	252.3	259.1	255.1	144.0	33.6	30.3	∠4.6	22.6
Transportation.........	145.7	144.8	143.8	111.0	1.0	19.5	0.7	11.7
Road vehicles......	126.3	124.3	123.1	96.6	0.3	16.7	0.4	9.1
Fuel combustion (stationary)	43.8	45.4	44.8	0.8	26.5	0.6	6.9	10.0
Steam and electric	25.1	26.5	28.1	0.2	19.4	0.1	3.7	4.7
Industrial processes	31.9	37.1	36.4	11.4	6.0	5.5	13.3	0.2
Agricultural burning.	19.4	19.3	19.2	13.8	—	2.8	2.4	0.3
Solid waste disposal	11.8	11.8	11.1	7.2	0.1	2.0	1.4	0.4
Percent of total, by source	100.0	100.0	100.0	100.0	100.0	100.0	100.0	100.0
Transportation.........	55.1	53.1	54.5	75.5	2.9	56.2	2.7	51.5
Road vehicles......	47.8	45.6	46.6	65.7	0.9	48.1	1.6	40.1
Fuel combustion (stationary)	16.6	16.7	17.0	0.5	78.2	1.7	27.0	44.1
Steam and electric.................	9.5	9.7	10.6	0.1	57.2	0.3	14.5	20.7
Industrial processes	12.1	13.6	13.8	7.8	17.7	15.9	52.0	0.9
Agricultural burning.	7.3	7.1	7.3	9.4	—	8.1	9.4	1.3
Solid waste disposal	4.5	4.3	4.2	4.9	0.3	5.8	5.5	1.8
Miscellaneous	4.5	5.1	3.3	2.0	0.9	12.7	3.9	0.4
Percent of total, by pollutant.	(x)	(x)	100.0	55.7	12.8	13.1	9.7	8.6
Transportation.........	(x)	(x)	100.0	77.2	0.7	13.6	0.5	8.1
Road vehicles......	(x)	(x)	100.0	78.5	0.2	13.6	0.3	7.4
Fuel combustion (stationary)	(x)	(x)	100.0	1.8	59.2	1.3	15.4	22.3
Steam and electric	(x)	(x)	100.0	0.7	69.0	0.4	13.2	16.7
Industrial processes	(x)	(x)	100.0	31.3	16.5	15.1	36.5	0.5
Agricultural burning.	(x)	(x)	100.0	71.9	—	14.6	12.5	1.6
Solid waste disposal	(x)	(x)	100.0	64.9	0.9	18.0	12.6	3.6
Miscellaneous	(x)	(x)	100.0	34.1	3.4	50.0	11.4	1.1
Miscellaneous, uncontrollable	12.0	13.9	8.8	3.0	0.3	4.4	1.0	0.1

— Represents zero.   x Not applicable.

SOURCE: *Environmental Health Planning Guide, Public Health Service, U. S. Dept. of Health, Education, and Welfare—1962*

DEFINITION AND CRITERIA

Historic preservation, as defined by the National Trust for Historic Preservation, is a well-rounded program of scientific research and study, protection, restoration, maintenance and the interpretation of sites, buildings and objects significant in American history and culture.

To be of historical and cultural significance, a structure or area should have outstanding historical and cultural significance in the nation or in the state, region, or community in which it exists. Such significance is found in

1. Historic structures or sites in which the broad cultural, political, economic, or social history of the nation, state or community is best exemplified, and from which the visitor may grasp in three-dimensional form one of the larger patterns of the American heritage.

2. Structures or areas that are identified with the lives of historic personages or with important events in the main currents of national, state or local history.

3. Structures or areas that embody the distinguishing characteristics of an architectural type-specimen, inherently valuable for a study of a period-style or method of construction; or a notable work of a master builder, designer or architect whose individual genius influenced his age. Mere antiquity is not sufficient basis for selection of a structure for permanent preservation, but can be a factor if other more significant examples have disappeared or if the building forms part of an especially characteristic section of a given community. Smaller structures, such as the first squared-log cabins or the sod houses of the pioneers, may be as important relatively as the mansions of the past.

4. Structures or sites of archaeological interest that contribute to the understanding of aboriginal man in America.

SUITABILITY

Preference should be given to those structures or sites where there is a preponderance of original material or other physical remains which have retained their integrity. (Integrity is a composite quality derived from original workmanship, original location, and intangible elements of feeling and association.) Repair or restoration of original elements or reconstruction of a building long destroyed demand high professional standards of historical and scientific techniques. Generally speaking, it is better to preserve than repair, better to repair than restore, better to restore than reconstruct.

Property boundaries adequate to protect the essential historical or cultural values of the project should be obtained at the outset if possible.

Other important practical considerations are accessibility to the public; encroachments by business, industry, housing, and traffic; availability of fire and police protection and of essential utilities.

The cost of restoration or reconstruction and of subsequent adequate maintenance and interpretation should not be beyond the means of the sponsors. A well-considered plan should contemplate that the project be fully endowed or potentially self-sustaining.

Since all historic structures significant enough to warrant preservation cannot support themselves as historic museums regularly open to the public, adaptation to other possible uses should be considered. It is essential, however, no matter what the proposed use, that every effort should be made to preserve those elements which account for the significance of a particular structure.

The primary purpose in preserving a structure as a historic museum is public use and enjoyment. Each project should have a place in the national, state or local programs for the preservation of historic sites or buildings and should be coordinated with all similar projects in its area to increase its usefulness as an educational force.

SOURCE: A Report by The Committee on Standards and Surveys National Trust for Historic Preservation Empire State Architect—September-October, 1967

BUILDING CLASSIFICATION ACCORDING TO TYPE OF CONSTRUCTION

Construction Classifications: A classification of buildings into types of construction which is based upon the fire properties of walls, floors, roofs, ceilings and other elements.

Type 1, Fire-resistive Construction: That type of construction in which the walls, partitions, columns, floors, roof, ceilings and other structural members are noncombustible with sufficient fire resistance to withstand the effects of a fire and prevent its spread from one story to another.

*Type 2, Noncombustible Construction: That type of construction in which the walls, partitions, columns, floors, roof, ceilings and other structural members are noncombustible but which does not qualify as Type 1, fire-resistive construction. Type 2 construction is further classified as Type 2a (1-hr. protected) and Type 2b, which does not require protection for certain members.

*Type 3, Exterior Protected Construction: That type of construction in which the exterior walls are of noncombustible construction having a fire resistance rating as specified and which are structurally stable under fire conditions and in which the interior structural members and roof are wholly or partly of combustible construction. Type 3 construction is divided into two subtypes as follows:

Type 3a: Exterior protected construction in which the interior exitways, columns, beams and bearing walls are noncombustible in combination with the floor system, roof construction and nonload bearing partitions of combustible construction.

Type 3b: Exterior protected construction in which the interior structural members are of protected combustible materials, or of heavy timber unprotected construction.

*Type 4, Wood Frame Construction: That type of construction in which the exterior walls, partitions, floors, roof and other structural members are wholly or partly of wood or other combustible materials.

BUILDING CLASSIFICATION ACCORDING TO OCCUPANCY

The classification of buildings according to occupancy, is as follows.

assembly occupancy means the occupancy or use of a building or structure or any portion thereof by a gathering of persons for civic, political, travel, religious, social, or recreational purposes.

business occupancy means the occupancy or use of a building or structure or any portion thereof for the transaction of business, or the rendering or receiving of professional services.

educational occupancy means the occupancy or use of a building or structure or any portion thereof by persons assembled for the purpose of learning or of receiving educational instruction.

high hazard occupancy means the occupancy or use of a building or structure or any portion thereof that involves highly combustible, highly flammable, or explosive material, or which has inherent characteristics that constitute a special fire hazard.

industrial occupancy means the occupancy or use of a building or structure or any portion thereof for assembling, fabricating, finishing, manufacturing, packaging, or processing operations.

institutional occupancy means the occupancy or use of a building or structure or any portion thereof by persons harbored or detained to receive medical, charitable, or other care or treatment, or by persons involuntarily detained.

residential occupancy means the occupancy or use of a building or structure or any portion thereof by persons for whom sleeping accommodations are provided but who are not harbored or detained to receive medical, charitable, or other care or treatment, or are not involuntarily detained.

storage occupancy means the occupancy or use of a building or structure or any portion thereof for the storage of goods, wares, merchandise, raw materials, agricultural or manufactured products, including parking garages, or the sheltering of livestock and other animals, except when classed as a high hazard.

SOURCE: Federal Housing Administration

SOURCE: National Building Code

PURPOSE OF FIRE LIMITS

The purpose of fire limits is the protection of closely built commercial districts of cities against the hazards of fire spreading from building to building, by supplementary restrictions on the construction permitted within such limits. This purpose can be served adequately by a single class of fire limits.

BRIEF STATEMENT OF WHAT FIRE LIMITS SHOULD INCLUDE

The fire limits should include all closely built districts of predominantly business or commercial occupancy, together with such blocks or portions of blocks surrounding these districts on all sides as constitute an exposure to these districts, including areas where a definite trend toward business or commercial development is manifested. The outer belt of blocks or part blocks surrounding the closely built districts ordinarily should be not less than 200 feet wide.

WHAT SHOULD BE INCLUDED IN COMMERCIAL OCCUPANCY

Commercial occupancies should include retail and wholesale mercantile and general business occupancies commonly found in closely-built and developing mercantile districts including banks, business and professional offices, show-rooms, restaurants, theaters, night-clubs, hotels, club buildings having restaurant and hotel accommodations, automobile service and filling stations, repair and storage garages, film exchanges, and shops of small tradesmen and artisans; also newspaper plants and other publishing houses, telephone and telegraph buildings, radio and television studios, freight and express offices and depots and railway and bus stations. Warehouse and storage buildings used for the storage of finished merchandise, goods or wares, except where located together with and forming a part of a manufacturing or industrial plant, shall also be classed as commercial as shall Federal, State or local government owned or leased buildings used for general business or commercial purposes such as business offices, garages or service buildings. Grade floor occupancies shall normally be regarded as governing.

WHAT DISTRICTS SHOULD BE CONSIDERED CLOSELY BUILT

A block or part block should be considered closely built if at least 50 per cent of the ground area is built upon and 50 per cent or more of the built-on area is devoted to commercial occupancy; except that where the average height of buildings is 2½ stories or more, a block or part block should be considered closely built if the ground area built upon is at least 40 per cent.

HOW LARGE SHOULD A DISTRICT BE TO WARRANT FIRE LIMITS PROTECTION

Any district consisting of two or more adjoining blocks or part blocks comprising an area of 100,000 square feet or more, exclusive of intervening streets, should be considered large enough to warrant fire limits protection.

THE OUTER BELT

The outer belt is included because of its location with respect to the closely built district not primarily because of what it contains. However the construction and occupancy existing in the outer belt may be a factor in determining the proper width of the belt for protection of the closely built district. The outer belt is for the purpose of protecting the closely built district against serious exposure fires starting outside the closely built district.

Full blocks should be taken for the outer belt wherever practicable. The outer belt should ordinarily have a width of at least 200 feet. Where closely built blocks of other than commercial occupancy constitute a serious exposure to the closely built commercial district, the width should be extended to include these areas. In certain cases for small closely built districts or for protection of narrow portions of closely built districts a width of 100 feet may be satisfactory.

Streets and other open spaces not subject to building construction, including rivers, streams, parks, parkways, plazas, railroads and other dedicated rights-of-way, having a width of at least 100 feet, may be appropriately included in the outer belt. Minor extensions of the fire limits to make use of such open spaces are generally desirable.

DEVELOPING COMMERCIAL AREAS

The areas where a definite trend toward commercial development is manifested should be included in anticipation of future growth likely to develop these areas into closely built districts.

A developing commercial area should be included if it consists of two or more adjoining blocks or part blocks comprising an area of 100,000 square feet, exclusive of intervening streets.

A block or part block should be considered as of developing commercial occupancy if at least 25 per cent of the ground area is built upon and 40 per cent or more of the built-on area is devoted to commercial occupancy.

Where appropriately located, developing commercial areas may be counted as part of the outer belt.

ROUNDING OUT THE LIMITS

The general outline of the fire limits should be fairly regular. Blocks or part blocks largely contained within adjacent commercial street frontages or extensions or lying between adjacent component areas should be carefully considered for inclusion on the basis of the general character of the neighborhood and recognized trend of development. In sections where rapid commercial development is manifested, moderate extension of the indicated limits may be warranted. Conversely, certain minor areas known to be of a static or declining nature may be excluded. Consideration should be given to known plans for new construction.

CORRELATION WITH ZONING

Where a land use or zoning ordinance has been adopted, it may be desirable to correlate the fire limits with the provision of the zoning ordinance regarding location of commercial occupancies. Some extension of the fire limits to include areas zoned for commercial occupancies may be appropriate, but it is seldom necessary or desirable to include all such areas within the fire limits.

OERIODIC REVIEW

Periodic review of the extent of the fire limits is desirable so that adjustment of the limits may be made in conformity with changes in the location or extent of commercial occupancies developing into closely built districts.

METHOD OF FIXING THE LIMITS

In the work of actually laying out the fire limits a map showing outlines of blocks and details of building construction is very useful. Up-to-date land use or Sanborn maps usually have sufficient data for the purpose. If tentative limits are drawn from a map, a site survey should be made of the area to check on the adequacy of the proposed limits.

Detailed analysis of individual blocks usually is not necessary as a visual examination of the map or of the area itself will usually permit a reasonably accurate determination of which are closely built and which are of developing commercial occupancy. In questionable cases a more detailed analysis may be made. The material given in the Appendix will be found useful in answering questions which may arise.

SOURCE: Recommended Method of Laying Out Fire Limits, National Board of Fire Underwriters—1956

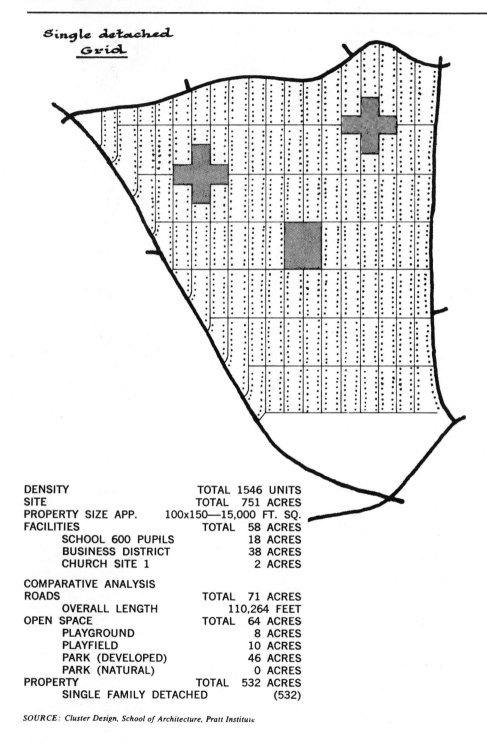

Single detached
Grid

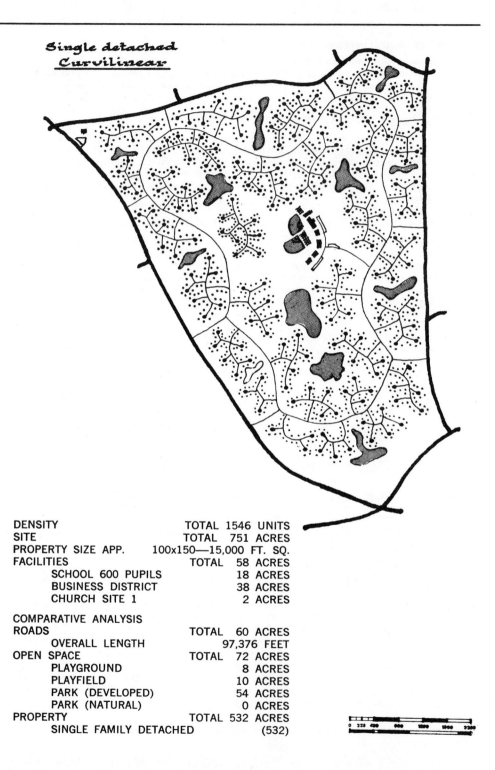

Single detached
Curvilinear

DENSITY	TOTAL 1546 UNITS	
SITE	TOTAL 751 ACRES	
PROPERTY SIZE APP.	100x150—15,000 FT. SQ.	
FACILITIES	TOTAL 58 ACRES	
SCHOOL 600 PUPILS	18 ACRES	
BUSINESS DISTRICT	38 ACRES	
CHURCH SITE 1	2 ACRES	

COMPARATIVE ANALYSIS

ROADS	TOTAL 71 ACRES
OVERALL LENGTH	110,264 FEET
OPEN SPACE	TOTAL 64 ACRES
PLAYGROUND	8 ACRES
PLAYFIELD	10 ACRES
PARK (DEVELOPED)	46 ACRES
PARK (NATURAL)	0 ACRES
PROPERTY	TOTAL 532 ACRES
SINGLE FAMILY DETACHED	(532)

SOURCE: Cluster Design, School of Architecture, Pratt Institute

DENSITY	TOTAL 1546 UNITS	
SITE	TOTAL 751 ACRES	
PROPERTY SIZE APP.	100x150—15,000 FT. SQ.	
FACILITIES	TOTAL 58 ACRES	
SCHOOL 600 PUPILS	18 ACRES	
BUSINESS DISTRICT	38 ACRES	
CHURCH SITE 1	2 ACRES	

COMPARATIVE ANALYSIS

ROADS	TOTAL 60 ACRES
OVERALL LENGTH	97,376 FEET
OPEN SPACE	TOTAL 72 ACRES
PLAYGROUND	8 ACRES
PLAYFIELD	10 ACRES
PARK (DEVELOPED)	54 ACRES
PARK (NATURAL)	0 ACRES
PROPERTY	TOTAL 532 ACRES
SINGLE FAMILY DETACHED	(532)

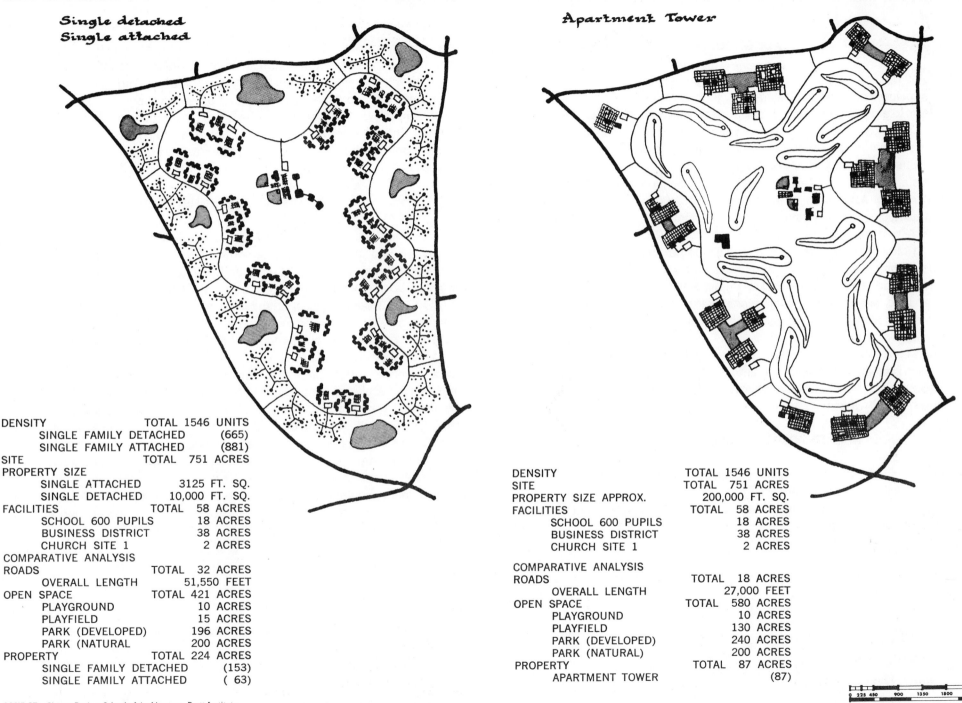

Single detached
Single attached

Apartment Tower

DENSITY   TOTAL 1546 UNITS
    SINGLE FAMILY DETACHED   (665)
    SINGLE FAMILY ATTACHED   (881)
SITE   TOTAL 751 ACRES
PROPERTY SIZE
    SINGLE ATTACHED   3125 FT. SQ.
    SINGLE DETACHED   10,000 FT. SQ.
FACILITIES   TOTAL 58 ACRES
    SCHOOL 600 PUPILS   18 ACRES
    BUSINESS DISTRICT   38 ACRES
    CHURCH SITE 1   2 ACRES
COMPARATIVE ANALYSIS
ROADS   TOTAL 32 ACRES
    OVERALL LENGTH   51,550 FEET
OPEN SPACE   TOTAL 421 ACRES
    PLAYGROUND   10 ACRES
    PLAYFIELD   15 ACRES
    PARK (DEVELOPED)   196 ACRES
    PARK (NATURAL   200 ACRES
PROPERTY   TOTAL 224 ACRES
    SINGLE FAMILY DETACHED (153)
    SINGLE FAMILY ATTACHED (63)

SOURCE: Cluster Design, School of Architecture, Pratt Institute

DENSITY   TOTAL 1546 UNITS
SITE   TOTAL 751 ACRES
PROPERTY SIZE APPROX.   200,000 FT. SQ.
FACILITIES   TOTAL 58 ACRES
    SCHOOL 600 PUPILS   18 ACRES
    BUSINESS DISTRICT   38 ACRES
    CHURCH SITE 1   2 ACRES

COMPARATIVE ANALYSIS
ROADS   TOTAL 18 ACRES
    OVERALL LENGTH   27,000 FEET
OPEN SPACE   TOTAL 580 ACRES
    PLAYGROUND   10 ACRES
    PLAYFIELD   130 ACRES
    PARK (DEVELOPED)   240 ACRES
    PARK (NATURAL)   200 ACRES
PROPERTY   TOTAL 87 ACRES
    APARTMENT TOWER   (87)

BACKGROUND

a. The purpose of airport hazard zoning is to prevent the creation or establishment of structures or objects of natural growth which would constitute hazards or obstructions to aircraft operating to, from, and in the vicinity of an airport. An airport zoning ordinance can be an effective means of controlling the height of structures and objects of natural growth and of generally attaining compatibility in the use of property in the immediate vicinity of the airport.

b. The standards established in FAR Part 77 make it possible to determine, for any location on or adjacent to an airport, the height above which any structure or growth would constitute an obstruction to air navigation.

c. The Airport and Airway Development Act of 1970, Public Law 91–258, enacted 21 May 1970, requires airport planning to be consistent with other plans for the development of the area in which the airport is located if Federal aid for the airport is involved. It also requires that appropriate action, including the adoption of zoning laws, be taken to the extent reasonable to restrict the use of land adjacent to or in the immediate vicinity of the airport to activities and purposes compatible with normal airport operations.

d. The Model Ordinance may be used as a guide in preparing a zoning ordinance which protects the airspace described in FAR Part 77, AC 150/5300-8, and AC 150/5390-1A. This Model is a revised version of the original Model Zoning Ordinance dated 7 November 1944.

USE OF MODEL ZONING ORDINANCE

a. An airport hazard zoning ordinance must conform to the prescribed authority of the particular airport zoning enabling act.

b. The Model Ordinance defines and provides for the establishment of various zones and prescribes height limitations for each zone as required to protect the airport from encroachment of obstructions or hazards to aircraft. The areas covered by these zones will vary from airport to airport depending upon the type, size, and layout of the airport, the type of aircraft using the airport, the elevation of the landing area above sea level, and the nature of the surrounding terrain. The Model Ordinance, therefore, leaves the specific zone measurements to be inserted by the political subdivisions adopting the Ordinance to suit the requirements of its particular airport.

AIRPORT HAZARD ZONING MAP

a. Attached to the airport hazard zoning ordinance and made a part thereof is an airport hazard zoning map. The airport hazard zoning map is similar for CTOL (Conventional Take Off Landing) airports, STOL (Short Take Off Landing) ports, and heliports and may be compiled from data in FAR Part 77, AC 150/5390-1A, and AC 150/5300-8. A typical example of the airport hazard zoning map was reduced in size for printing on the last page of this publication.

b. The airport hazard zoning map is of the area affected by the airport hazard zoning ordinance and shows the layout of the runways, the airport boundaries, the airport elevation, and the area topography. The map also sets forth the various zones with the applicable height limitations for each as described in the body of the ordinance. The zoning map should contain a method of land identification, as typical in different areas of the country, such as section, township and range, block and lot, or metes and bounds. This map also depicts other identifying geographic objects such as streams, rivers, railroads, roads, and streets. By using a map with this amount of detail, in conjunction with the text of an ordinance, a property owner should, without undue difficulty, be able to determine not only the location of his property but also the height limitations imposed thereon by the ordinance.

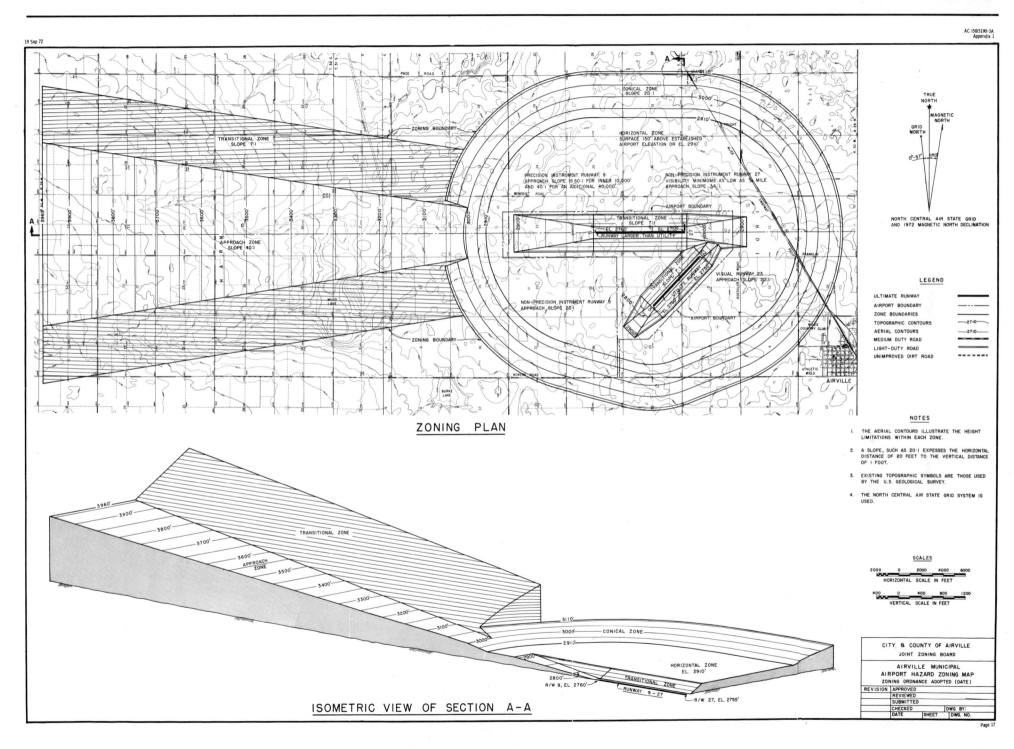

ZONING PLAN

ISOMETRIC VIEW OF SECTION A-A

BASIC DATA

FORMULATION OF THEORY

In systems analysis the theory is called the model of the problem, process, or system, and the setting up of the theory (or model) is known as simulation. The model may be the mathematical, or sometimes physical or analog, representation of the facts and behavior of whole systems—engineering, architectural, industrial, social, historical, economic, political, or otherwise. By manipulating the equations or values of the model, alternative means can be evaluated to test the effect of certain actions on results or goals. A general form of mathematical models may be expressed by the formula $E = f(X_i, Y_j)$ in which E, the effect of any system on the environment or performance, is a result of the interaction of X_i, the independent variables, and Y_j, the dependent variables. In practice, symbols in this model are replaced with numbers describing the actual system and its environment.

Figure 1 illustrates a block diagram of typical steps in the systems approach to a planning problem. Goals and objectives are frequently very difficult to state, and may in fact be multiple and conflicting in character. Constraints define the physical, financial, timing, risk, policy, and other considerations which the plan or design must satisfy. The search for alternatives encourages innovation and creativity and the avoidance of prejudgment, in a process popularly called "brainstorming." Feedback is the continual process of reviewing and modifying prior steps in the light of decisions reached at each stage of the progress. Optimization is the process of continual adjustment of a systems model until the best set of conditions is obtained.

Systems analysis has been termed a "horizontal approach" because it reaches out in contrast with the "vertical" or departmental approach, which reaches up or down.

While a departmental approach has certain acknowledged strengths it has also obvious shortcomings. To reach the problem solver, information and expert opinion must flow up or down the ladder of responsibility, each transfer subjecting the data or suggestion to review and often modification or veto. Creative suggestions are too often rejected or never reach the decision-maker; or expert opinion is modified on the basis of another point of view. Often within a given department there are men who could contribute essential knowledge or a fresh point of view to a problem under consideration; but for reasons inherent in any departmental organization, they are never heard from.

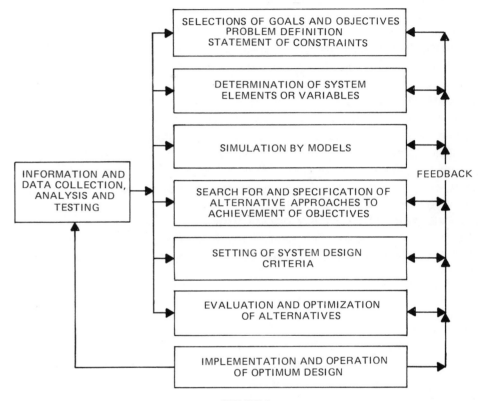

FIGURE 1

Systems analysis differs from the departmental approach in several significant respects. An essential feature of the systems approach is that it assembles a team of experts on the same level of authority who may discuss, and argue, all aspects of a problem freely in the presence of the person or persons who will make the decision. The decision-makers are thereby exposed to maximum intercommunication, and to an uninhibited exploration of the full range of factors bearing on the problem in question. Quantifiable data are presented as fact. Data which are nonquantifiable (in terms of present capabilities) such as social, historical, political, or esthetic values are discussed by men who are knowledgeable in these fields.

SOURCE: *The Freeway in the City, The Urban Advisors to the Federal Highway Administrators, Dept. of Transportation,* 1968.

Given the same body of experts, it is proposed that their effectiveness would be greater in the systems context and approach than if they were made to operate within and through a departmental structure.

In simplest terms the systems approach involves the following general steps:

1. PROBLEM DEFINITION. The specific problem to be studied is defined in detail by the project leader. It is described in its full and proper context and lists primary and secondary considerations.

2. TEAM ASSEMBLY. In light of the problem definition, a team of experts is assembled. Together, they should be knowledgeable in the various fields involved. They may serve the team full time, or appear as requested, during the period of study. It is important that the team members be advised from the start in whose hands the final decision-making will lie—in the full team, a subcommittee, the study director, or a separate group. It is also important that those responsible for the decision be present at all discussion conferences.

3. DEVELOPMENT OF STUDY PROCEDURES. Much thought is given to the best means of attacking the main problem and its subsidiary problems. This normally leads to the formulation of mathematical, graphic, physical, or analog mod-els. It is essential that means be devised by which, as the study progresses, information is gathered and processed and assumptions or conclusions tested and found to be correct or false—that there is constant feedback or readjustment of the models and input data.

4. INVESTIGATION AND ANALYSIS. The team must be provided with adequate means of investigation and analysis. Here on-site investigation, three-dimensional models, visual aids, comprehensive planning procedures, and the use of computer techniques are among the possibilities. The aim is to insure that the team and its decision unit become aware of all pertinent factors and information.

5. DECISION-MAKING. Once the decision unit has been exposed to all discussion and data that it feels to be necessary the team is dismissed, or perhaps left on call, and a judgment on the best feasible solution is then reached and reported.

6. IMPLEMENTATION. Often the team investigation and discussions include exploration not only of a proposed solution but also of the means by which it can be carried forward. Or it may fall to the decision-maker to plan and describe such measures. In either event it is clear that no proposals can be any better than the mechanism or means by which they are to be implemented.

REPRESENTATIVE FRACTION (RF)

The numerical scale of a map expresses the ratio of horizontal distance on the map to the corresponding horizontal distance on the ground. It usually is written as a fraction and is called the representative fraction (RF). The representative fraction is always written with the map distance as one (1). It is independent of any unit of measure. An RF of 1/50,000 or 1 : 50,000 means that one (1) unit of measure on the map is equal to 50,000 of the *same units* of measure on the ground.

The ground distance between two points is determined by measuring between the points on the map and multiplying the map measurement by the denominator of the RF.

EXAMPLE: $RF = 1:50,000$ or $\dfrac{1}{50,000}$

Map distance = 5 units

$5 \times 50,000 = 250,000$ units of ground distance

GRAPHIC (BAR) SCALES

On most maps there is another method of determining ground distance. It is by means of the graphic (bar) scales. A graphic scale is a ruler printed on the map on which distances on the map may be measured as actual ground distances. To the right of the zero (0) the scale is marked in full units of measure and is called the primary scale. The part to the left of zero (0) is divided into tenths of a unit and is called the extension scale. Most maps have three or more graphic scales, each of which measures distance in a different unit of measure.

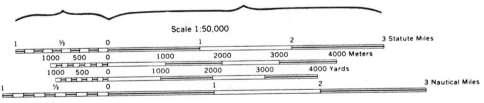

Graphic (bar) scale.

SCALE SELECTION

The selection of the proper scale for any particular map depends upon such considerations as:

a. What the map is attempting to show

b. The extent of the area covered

c. The degree and amount of detail on the map

d. Suitability for reproduction, at the same scale, or at reduced or enlarged scales

Base maps prepared by federal agencies are generally available in standardized scales. The various scales can be divided into five general groups.

SCALE A—STATE AND DISTRICT MAPS

1:10,000,000 or 1 inch = 160 miles (approximate)

1: 2,500,000 or 1 inch = 40 miles (approximate)

1: 500,000 or 1 inch = 8 miles (approximate)

1: 250,000 or 1 inch = 4 miles (approximate)

SCALE B—REGIONAL AND COUNTY MAPS

1:125,000 or 1 inch = 2 miles (approximate)

1: 62,500 or 1 inch = 1 mile (approximate)

1: 31,680 or 1 inch = ½ mile

SCALE C—DETAIL SECTION AND STUDY MAPS

1:24,000 or 1 inch = 2,000 feet

1:12,000 or 1 inch = 1,000 feet

SCALE D—CITY MAPS AND PLANS

1 inch = 800 feet

1 inch = 400 feet

SCALE E—MAPS FOR ACCURATE DESIGNING AND COST ESTIMATING

1 inch = 200 feet

1 inch = 100 feet

Ground Distance at Map Scale

Scale	1 inch equals	1 cm equals
1:5,000	416.67 ft 127.00 meters	164.0 ft 50 meters
1:10,000	833.33 ft 254.00 meters	328.1 ft 100 meters
1:12,500	1,041.66 ft 317.0 meters	410.1 ft 125 meters
1:20,000	1,666.7 ft 508.00 meters	656.2 ft 200 meters
1:25,000	2,083.3 ft 635.00 meters	820.2 ft 250 meters
1:50,000	4,166.7 ft 1,270.0 meters	1,640.4 ft 500 meters
1:63,360	5,280.0 ft (1 mile) 1,609.3 meters	2,078.7 ft 633.6 meters
1:100,000	8,333.3 ft 2,540.0 meters	3,280.8 ft 1,000 meters
1:250,000	20,833 ft 6,350.0 meters	8,202.0 ft 2,500 meters
1:500,000	41,667 ft 12,700 meters	16,404.0 ft 5,000 meters

A TRANSPARENT NOMOGRAPH FOR MEASURING THE AREA OF POLYGONAL FIGURES

AREAGRAPH

AREAS IN ACRES   **SCALE**

Instructions For Using The Areagraph

When the instrument is placed over any rectangle, as shown (Fig. 1), the number on the curve passing nearest the outer corner will give the area in units according to the scale of the areagraph. Where curves are omitted for clarity (as that between the 10 and 12 in fig. 1), the position must be estimated. For triangles, the reading must be doubled, or halved according to the method, as shown. Halved readings (Figs. 3, 4 & 8) are more accurate, but doubled readings are often more convenient. Any polygon may be reduced to a series of triangles, (see Figs. 7 & 8). In practice, short methods for figures with one or more right angles or with two sides parallel, will become apparent. Examples of these are given in Figs. 9 and 10.   Bryant Hall   May 1938

SOURCE: Land Use Inventory Manual, County of Santa Clara, California

(1) Rectangle (The basic figure) ● = Point of reading. Area = 11

(2) Right Triangle (By inscribed rectangle). Reading to be doubled. Area = 4·2 = 8

(3) Right Triangle (by circumscribed rectangle). Area = 8/ = 4. o = Reading to be halved

(4) Oblique Triangle (by circumscribed rectangle). Area = 10/2 = 5

(5) Oblique Triangle (Sum of 2 right triangles). Area = (2+1)·2 = 6

(6) Oblique Triangle (Difference of 2 right triangles). Area = (4−1)×2 = 6

(7) Quadrilateral (Sum of 4 right triangles) Two settings. Area = (1.5 + 2 + .75 + 1)×2 = 8.5

(8) Polygon, (N 2 sides) "n" settings "n" triangles, Area = ½ a b c

(9) Polygon, one 90° corner. Area = $\frac{6+1}{2} + 6 = 9\frac{1}{2}$

(10) Right Trapezoid. Parallelogram. Area = 3. Area = 4

File: 60.1-1A

1. Grade
2. Basement sash areaway
3. Siding
4. Building paper
5. Sheathing (diagonal)
6. Board and batten siding
7. Fascia
8. Rough window opening
9. Window header
10. Rafters
11. Collar beams
12. Ridge board
13. Chimney cap
14. Chimney flue
15. Flashing
16. Ceiling joists
17. Furring strips
18. Roof sheathing
19. Roof shingles
20. Gutter
21. Shutters
22. Wall studs
23. Entrance, frame and door
24. Downspout
25. Brick veneer
26. Concrete stoop
27. Interior doors and trim

28. Concrete block basement wall
29. Drain tile
30. Wall footing
31. Basement stair treads and risers
32. Gravel base
33. First floor joists
34. Heating unit
35. Beam
36. Concrete floor
37. Basement column
38. Plaster
39. Concrete basement wall
40. Waterproofing
41. Building paper
42. Sub-floor (diagonal)
43. Finish floor
44. Baseboard
45. Plaster or drywall
46. Insulation
47. Second floor joists
48. Bridging
49. Partition studs
50. Plaster base, gypsum lath
51. Double hung window
52. Insulation
53. Header joist

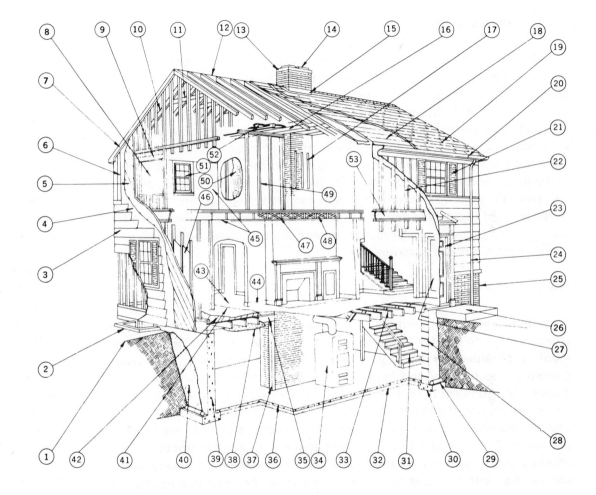

SOURCE: *Boeckh Building Valuation Manual, Boeckh Division, the American Appraisal Co., Milwaukee, Wis. 1967*

THE THREE APPROACHES TO VALUE

In appraising the market value of real property three basic approaches are recognized by appraisers:

The Market Data Approach

The market value of a given property is estimated by comparison with other similar properties in the same vicinity which have recently been sold or offered for sale in the open market.

The market data approach applies the principle of substitution since typical buyers will not purchase a property at a price higher than the prices of similar properties with comparable locations, characteristics, and future earning capabilities. Of all appraisal approaches the market data approach is the most direct, the most frequently used, the best understood, and the one generally preferred. It is the only approach to value that directly reflects the balance of supply and demand in actual trading in the market place and under ideal circumstances probably comes nearest to reducing an appraisal to the point of lease approximation.

The Cost Approach

In this approach the land is valued as if unimproved, on the basis of comparison with similar tracts of vacant land recently sold. The improvements are valued on the basis of their cost of replacement new, using current prices of labor and materials for construction of similar improvements. From this estimate of cost new is deducted the loss in value from depreciation, and the resulting amount is added to the land value. The cost approach in reality is another type of comparative or market data approach. The land is valued by comparison with similar tracts of land recently sold. The replacement cost of the improvements is developed by comparison with the cost of new improvements. Accrued depreciation is measured by comparison with known depreciation of similar improvements

The cost approach often develops the highest indication of value because the appraiser may not have recognized all the depreciation that has accrued to the property. Occasionally the cost approach develops a low indication of value because the estimate of depreciation is too high.

SUMMARY OF COST APPROACH

The cost approach has the distinct advantage of universal application to all types of real property. It is the principal and sometimes the sole approach for special purpose properties which rarely sell on the open market.

This manual provides reliable information for the preparation of a cost approach to all types of property. It sets forth proper procedures for making the inspection and recording the data, and contains numerous cost tables giving the unit-in-place, square-foot, and component costs for all kinds of structures. It also includes suggested depreciation schedules for various types of construction.

The Income Approach

The income approach is used in the valuation of investment properties such as stores, apartments, shopping centers, commercial buildings certain industrial buildings, and other real estate which is bought and sold primarily on the basis of the income produced. The value of such properties tends to be set by the quantity, quality, and durability of the net income generated by the property.

Capitalization of anticipated net income indicates the investment required to produce that income. Extreme care must be used both in estimating net income and in selecting the proper rate of capitalization.

One of the first steps is to secure a statement of the historical record of income and expenses for the past three to five years. An average of income and expenses is satisfactory if both income and expenses are relatively stable. If the historical record shows an upward or downward trend, more weight should be given to the latest years. Past income and expense information is used solely for an indication of the future as any prospective buyer would be purchasing future income.

The income approach, like the market data and cost approaches, is closely related to the market. The anticipated income, the operating expenses, the land value, the proper capitalization rate—all are developed and checked for reasonableness by comparisons with similar rental properties and investments.

DEPTH TABLES

The following are tables for apportioning the value of front lots that are longer or shorter than 25 x 100 feet. These rules are helpful guides, but actual value in each instance much depends on the use to which such lots or parts of lots can be profitably put, their marketability for such use, and the usual factors of value. The tables are not strictly applicable to rear or inside land when the frontage is in different ownership.

HOFFMAN RULE

The first recognized rule for appraising lots of varying depths is credited to Judge Murray Hoffman in 1866 and is generally known as the Hoffman Rule. In his opinion the front half (50 feet deep) of a 100-foot deep lot is worth two-thirds its whole value. It was assumed, therefore, that the first 25 feet was worth two-thirds of 50 feet, 12½ feet two-thirds of 25 feet, and so on.

4-3-2-1 RULE

This method gives the front 25 feet 40% of a full lot value, the next 25 feet 30% of the full value, the next 25 feet 20% and the last 25 feet 10% of a full lot value.

HOFFMAN-NEILL RULE

The following table revising and elaborating on the Hoffman Rule was published in the Evening Mail by its real estate editor, the late Henry Harmon Neill.

Standard appraisal methods:
The Hoffman Neill rule: "Two thirds of the value of a rectangular lot is in the front half."

Values of lot depth in percentage of 100 foot depth							
Depth	0/0	Depth	0/0	Depth	0/0	Depth	0/0
5	.17	55	.70.7	110	106.0	220	159.0
10	.26	60	.74.4	120	111.7	240	167.5
15	.33	65	.77.9	130	116.9	260	175.3
20	.39	70	.81.5	140	122.3	280	183.6
25	.44	75	.84.8	150	127.3	300	191.0
30	.49	80	.88.0	160	132.1	320	198.3
35	.54	85	.91.3	170	137.0	340	205.5
40	.58	90	.94.3	180	141.5	360	212.3
45	.62	95	.97.3	190	146.0	380	219.0
50	.66	100	1.00.0	200	150.0	400	225.0

SOURCE: *The Manual of the Real Estate Board of New York, Inc.*

Corner Lot Rules

Corner lots are usually considered as worth from 20% to 70% more than inside lots. The corner lot as worth the sum of an inside lot on both streets. Following is a table showing the percentage of side street lot value to be added to avenue lot value to find corner value and showing the degree of corner influence for every 10 feet from the corner, as given by John A. Zangerle in "Principles of Real Estate Appraising."

Feet	Zangerle Curve	Feet	Zangerle Curve
10	25%	60	68%
20	40	70	70
30	51	80	71
40	58	90	72
50	63	100	72

Ratio of Main St. to Side St. Value	Central Retail Districts Frontage on High Valued Street									Semi-Business Wholesale Suburban Retail	Residential†
	20'	30'	40'	50'	60'	70'	80'	90'	100'		
(1)	(2)	(3)	(4)	(5)	(6)	(7)	(8)	(9)	(10)	(11)	(12)
	%	%	%	%	%	%	%	%	%	%	%
10 to 10	125	98	85	74	65	60	54	47	43	50.0	10.0
10 to 9	108	85	75	64	57	51	47	41	36	43.6	9.1
10 to 8	92	74	65	55	50	44	41	35	31	38.2	8.3
10 to 7	79	63	55	47	43	37	35	30	27	33.3	7.6
10 to 6	68	53	47	40	36	31	29	26	23	28.9	7.0
10 to 5	57	45	39	33	29	27	23	22	19	25.0	6.5
10 to 4	48	37	33	27	25	22	20	18	16	21.2	6.1
10 to 3	40	31	26	23	20	18	16	15	13	18.5	5.8
10 to 2	33	25	22	19	17	14	13	12	11	16.4	5.6
10 to 1	25	20	17	15	13	12	10	9	8	15.0	—

* These rules are widely used throughout the Southwest. They are an outgrowth of an early corner rule devised by W. A. Somers, and first used in St. Paul in 1896, Camden, N.J., uses a similar rule. The table was compiled from percentages used by J. B. Stoner of San Antonio.

† In semi-business, wholesale, suburban retail and residential properties in a uniform percentage of base value is added for corner influence regardless of the frontage of the corner parcel on the high valued street.

Description of Rural Land. In the older portions of the United States, nearly all of the original land grants were of irregular shape, many of the boundaries following stream and ridge lines. Also, in the process of subdivision the units were taken without much regard for regularity, and it was thought sufficient if lands were specified as bounded by natural or artificial features of the terrain and if the names of adjacent property owners were given. Thus a description of a tract as recorded in a deed reads:

Bounded on the north by Bog Brook, bounded on the northeast by the irregular line formed by the southwesterly border of Cedar Swamp of land now or formerly belonging to Benjamin Clark, bounded on the east by a stone wall and land now or formerly belonging to Ezra Pennell, bounded on the south and southeast by the turnpike road from Brunswick to Bath, and bounded on the west by the irregular line formed by the easterly fringe of trees of the wood lot now or formerly belonging to Moses Puringt

1. **By Metes and Bounds.** As the country developed and land became more valuable, and as many boundaries such as those listed in the preceding description ceased to exist, land litigations became numerous. It then became the general practice to determine the lengths and directions of the boundaries of land by measurements with the link chain and surveyor's compass, and to fix the locations of corners permanently by monuments. The lengths were ordinarily given in rods or chains, and the directions were expressed as bearings usually referred to the magnetic meridian. Surveys of this character are now usually made with the transit and tape, distances being recorded in feet or chains, and directions being given in true bearings computed from angular measurements. In describing a tract surveyed in this manner the lengths and bearings of the several courses are given in order, and the objects marking the corners are described; if any boundary follows some prominent feature of the terrain, the fact is stated; and the calculated area of the tract is given. When the bearings and lengths of the sides are thus given, the tract is said to be described by **metes and bounds.**

2. **By Subdivisions of Public Land.** The type of description employed for lands which have been divided in accordance with the rectangular system of the Bureau of Land Management. The records and plats of the United States surveys are a part of the permanent public records and are accessible to anyone desiring to consult them. In conveying by deed a United States subdivision or fraction thereof, no doubt can at any time exist as to the tract involved if it is described by stating its sectional subdivision, section number, township, range, and name of the principal meridian on which the initial point is located. Following is an example of the legal description of a 40-acre tract comprising a full quarter-quarter section:

The north-east quarter of the south-west quarter of section ten (10), Township four (4) South, Range six (6) East, of the Initial Point of the Mount Diablo Meridian, containing forty (40) acres, more or less, according to the United States Survey.

3. **By Coordinates.** In some states, the locations of land corners are legally described by their coordinates with respect to the state-wide plane-coordinate system.

Description of Urban Land. The manner of legally describing the boundaries of a tract of land within the corporate limits of a city depends upon conditions attached to

the survey by which the boundaries of the tract were first established, as indicated by the following classification:

1. **By Lot and Block.** If the boundaries of the tract coincide exactly with a lot which is a part of a subdivision or addition for which there is recorded an official map, the tract may be legally described by a statement giving the lot and block numbers and the name and date of filing of the official map. Most city property is described in this way. Following is a description of this character occurring in a deed:

Lot 15 in Block 5 as said lots and blocks are delineated and so designated upon that certain map entitled **Map of Thousand Oaks, Alameda County, California,** filed August 23, 1909, in Liber 25 of Maps, page 2, in the office of the County Recorder of the said County of Alameda.

2. **By Metes, Bounds, and Lots.** If the boundaries of a given tract within a subdivision for which there is a recorded map do not conform exactly to boundaries shown on the official map, the tract is described by metes and bounds, with the point of beginning referred to a corner shown on the official map. Also, the numbers of lots of which the tract is composed are given. Following is an example of a description of this kind:

Beginning at the intersection of the Northern line of Escondido Avenue, with the Eastern boundary line of Lot 16, hereinafter referred to; running thence Northerly along said Eastern boundary line of Lot 16, and the Eastern boundary line of Lot 17, eighty-nine (89) feet; thence at right angles Westerly, fifty-one (51) feet; thence South 12°6' East, seventy-five (75) feet to the Northern line of Escondido Avenue; thence Easterly along said line of Escondido Avenue, fifty-three and $^{13}/_{100}$ (53.13) feet, more or less, to the point of beginning.

Being a portion of Lots 16 and 17, in Block 5, as said lots and blocks are delineated and so designated upon that certain map entitled **Map of Thousand Oaks, Alameda County, California,** filed August 23, 1909, in Liber 25 of Maps, page 2, in the office of the County Recorder of the said County of Alameda.

3. **By Metes and Bounds to City Monuments.** Some of the larger and older cities of the United States have, by precise surveys, established a system of reference monuments and have determined the coordinates of these monuments with respect to an arbitrarily selected initial point. If the tract cannot be defined by descriptions such as the preceding, the point of beginning may be definitely fixed by stating its direction and distance from an official reference monument and by describing the monument that marks the corner. The boundaries of the tract may then be described by metes and bounds.

The location of corners may also be defined by rectangular coordinates referred to the origin or initial point of the city system and/or the state system.

If the tract is within an area not so monumented, the point of beginning of the boundary description may be referred by direction and distance to the intersection of the center lines of streets. It is not good practice to refer to the intersection of sidewalk or curb lines, for these are apt to be changed from time to time. In sections of the country within the rectangular system of United States surveys, the point of beginning of a boundary description may properly be referred to section lines and corners.

SOURCE: Davis, Foote, Kelly, Surveying: Theory and Practice, McGraw-Hill Book Co. NY 5th Edition 1966

A topographic map shows by the use of suitable symbols (1) the configuration of the earth's surface, called the **relief,** which includes such features as hills and valleys; (2) other natural features such as trees and streams; and (3) the physical changes wrought upon the earth's surface by the works of man, such as houses, roads, canals, and cultivation. The distinguishing characteristic of a topographic map, as compared with other maps, is the representation of the terrestrial relief.

Topographic maps are used in many ways. They are a necessary aid in the design of any engineering project which required a consideration of land forms, elevations, or gradients, and they are used to supply the general information necessary to the studies of geologists, economists, and others interested in the broader aspects of the development of natural resources.

The preparation of general topographic maps is largely in the hands of governmental organizations. The principal example is the topographic map of the United States being constructed by the U.S. Geological Survey. This map is published in quadrangle sheets, which usually include territory 15' in latitude by 15' in longitude at a scale of 1:62,500 although they range from 7½' by 7½' at a scale of 1:24,000 to 4° by 12° at a scale of 1:1,000,000. A portion of a typical map the scale of which is 1:62,500 is shown. Altogether there are more than 30 Federal agencies engaged in surveying and mapping. The central source of information regarding all Federal maps and aerial photographs is the Map Information Office, U. S. Geological Survey, Washington, D. C. Likewise, many maps are available from state, county, and city agencies.

Land Survey. Land Surveying may consist of one or more of the following operations:

1. Rerunning old land lines to determine their length and direction.

2. Reestablishing obliterated land lines from recorded lengths and directions. This will require research into tax maps, building department files, subdivision maps, etc., to secure the required information.

3. Subdividing lands into parcels of predetermined shape and size.

4. Setting monuments to preserve the location of land lines.

5. Locating the position of such monuments with respect to permanent landmarks.

6. Calculating areas, distances and angles or directions.

7. Portraying the data of the survey on a land map.

8. Writing descriptions for deeds.

SOURCE: Davis, Foote, Kelly, Surveying: Theory and Practice, McGraw-Hill Book Co. NY 5th Edition 1966

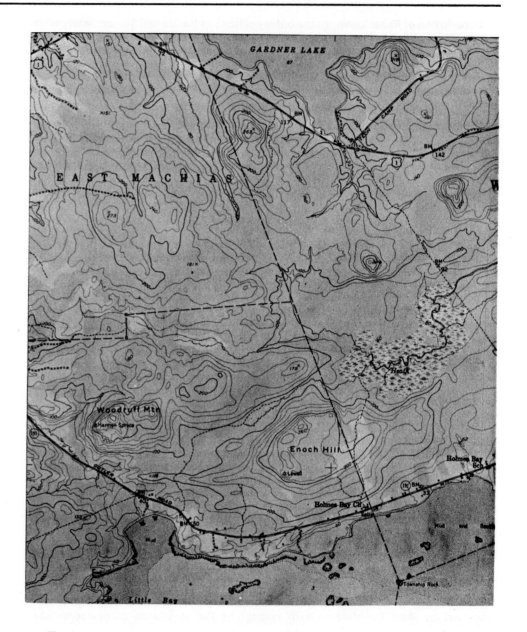

Typical contour map of U. S. Geological Survey. Scale approximately 1 in. = 1 mile (representative fraction 1/62,500). Contour interval 10 ft.

City Survey. The term city survey, has come to mean an extensive coordinated survey of the area in and near a city for the purposes of fixing reference monuments, locating property lines and improvements, and determining the configuration and physical features of the land. Such a survey is of value for a wide variety of purposes, particularly for planning city improvements. Briefly, the work consists in:

1. Establishing horizontal and vertical control, as described for topographic surveying. The primary horizontal control is usually by triangulation, supplemented as desired by precise traversing. Secondary horizontal control is by traversing of appropriate precision. Primary vertical control is by precise leveling.

2. Making a topographic survey and topographic map. Usually the scale of the topographic map is 1 in. = 200 ft. The map is divided into sheets which cover usually 5,000 ft. of longitude and 4,000 ft. of latitude. Points are plotted by rectangular plane coordinates.

3. Monumenting a system of selected points at suitable locations such as street corners, for reference in subsequent surveys. These monuments are referred to the plane-coordinate system and to the city datum.

4. Making a property map. The survey for the map consists in (a) collecting recorded information regarding property, (b) determining the location on the ground of street intersections, angle points, and curve points, (c) monumenting the points so located, and (d) traversing to determine the coordinates of the monuments. Usually the scale of the property map is 1 in. = 50 ft. The map is divided into sheets which cover usually 1,250 ft. of longitude and 1,000 ft. of latitude, thus bearing a convenient relation to the sheets of the topographic map. The property map shows the length and bearing of all street lines and boundaries of public property, coordinates of governing points, control, monuments, important structures, natural features of the terrain, etc., all with appropriate legends and notes

5. Making a wall map which shows essentially the same information as the topographic map but which is drawn to a smaller scale; the scale should be not less than 1 in. = 2,000 ft. The wall map is reproduced in the usual colors—culture in black, drainage in blue, wooded areas in green, and contours in brown.

6. Making an underground map. Usually the scale and the size of the map sheets are the same as those for the property map. The underground map shows street and casement lines, monuments, surface structures and natural features affecting underground construction, and underground structures and utilities (with dimensions), all with appropriate legends and notes

SOURCE: Davis, Foote, Kelly, Surveying: Theory and Practice, McGraw-Hill Book Co. NY 5th Edition 1966

Construction Survey. Construction surveys consist of the following operations:

1. Topographic survey of site, to be used in preparation of plans for the structure.

2. Establishment on ground of a system of stakes, or other markers, both in plan and in elevation, from which measurement of earthwork and structures can be conveniently taken by construction forces.

3. The giving of line and grade as needed.

4. The making of measurements necessary to verify the location of completed parts of structure and to determine volume of completed work, as a basis for payment to the contractor.

Route Survey. Route surveying is the operation necessary for the location and construction of lines of transportation and communication, such as highways, railroads, canals, transmission lines, pipe lines, etc. The preliminary work usually consists of a topographic survey. The location and construction surveys may further consist of the following:

1. Establishing the center line by setting stakes at intervals.
2. Running levels to determine the profile of the ground along the center line.
3. Plotting such profile, and fixing grades.
4. Taking cross sections.
5. Calculating volumes of earthwork.
6. Measuring drainage areas.
7. Laying out structures, such as culverts and bridges.
8. Locating right-of-way boundaries.

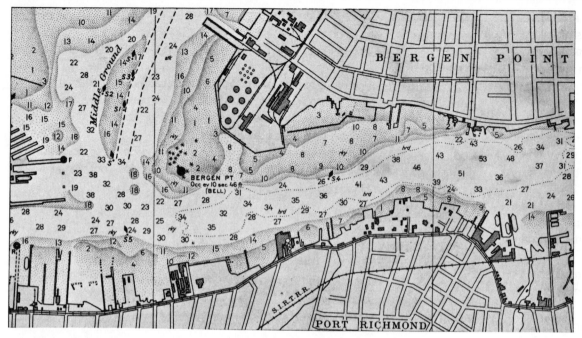

Typical hydrographic map of U.S. Coast and Geodetic Survey. Representative fraction, 1/80,000.

1.9 Hydrographic surveying refers to surveying bodies of water for purposes of navigation, water supply, or subaqueous construction. The operations of hydrographic surveying consist broadly in:

1. Making a topographic survey of shores and banks.
2. Taking soundings to determine the depth of water and the character of the bottom.
3. Locating such soundings by angular and linear measurements.
4. Plotting the hydrographic map showing the topography of the shores and banks, the depths of soundings, and other desirable details.
5. Observing the fluctuation of the ocean tide or of the change in level of lakes and rivers.
6. Measuring the discharge of streams.

In a sense, the surveys for drainage and for irrigation are hydrographic in character, but the principal work is essentially either topographic or route surveying.

a. Hydrographic Maps. A hydrographic map is similar to the ordinary topographic map but has its own particular symbols. These may be found in almost any book on topographic drawing or in the manual issued by the U. S. Coast and Geodetic Survey. The amount and kind of information shown on a hydrographic map vary with the use of the map. A harbor map should show enough shore-line topography to locate and plan wharves, docks, warehouses, roads, and streets along the water front. A navigation chart should show only shore details which are useful aids to navigation, such as church spires, smokestacks, towers, and similar landmarks. Maps of rivers should show both low-water and high-water marks and all topography within the zone between these marks. A hydrographic map should contain the following information:

1. Datum used for elevations.
2. High-water and low-water lines.
3. Soundings, usually in feet and tenths, with the decimal point occupying the exact plotted location of the point.
4. Lines of equal depth interpolated from soundings. On navigation charts for offshore areas, the lines of equal depth are usually shown in fathoms (1 fathom equals 6 ft.); for harbors, the lines of equal depth are shown in feet.
5. Conventional signs for land features as on topographic maps.
6. Lighthouses, navigation lights, buoys, etc., either shown by conventional signs or lettered on the map.

The illustration is a portion of a typical hydrographic map of the U. S. and Geodetic Survey. Soundings are shown in feet, referred to mean low water. Elevations of contours and high points on land are likewise shown in feet.

SOURCE: Davis, Foote, Kelly, Surveying: Theory and Practice, McGraw-Hill Book Co. NY 5th Edition 1966

A soil survey includes finding out which properties of soils are important, organizing the knowledge about the relations of soil properties and soil use, classifying soils into defined and described units, locating and plotting the boundaries of the units on maps, and preparing and publishing the maps and reports.

The soil survey report consists of a map that shows the distribution of soils in the area descriptions of the soils, some suggestions as to their use and management and general information about the area.

Reports usually are prepared on the soils of one county, although a single report may cover several small countries or only parts of countries.

Soil surveys are made cooperatively by the Soil Conservation Service of the Department of Agriculture, the agricultural experiment stations, and other Stations, and other State and Federal Agencies. Plans for the work in any area are developed jointly, and the reports are reviewed jointly before publication.

Soil maps have many uses, but generally they are made for one main purpose—to identify the soil as a basis for applying the results of research and experience to individual fields or parts of fields. Results from an experiment on a given soil can be applied directly to other areas of the same kind of soil with confidence. Two areas of the same kind of soil are no more identical than two oak trees, but they are so similar that (with comparable past management) they should respond to the same practices in a similar manner.

The soil map shows the distribution of specific kinds of soil and identifies them through the map legend. The legend is a list of the symbols used to identify the kinds of soil on the map.

The most common soil units shown on maps are the phases of soil types, but other kinds of units may be shown.

Soils are classified and named, just as plants and animals are. Soils are identified by such characteristics as the kinds and numbers of horizons, or layers, that have developed in them, the texture (the relative amounts of stones, gravel, sand, silt, and clay), the kind of minerals present and their amounts, and the presence of salts and alkali help distinguish the horizons.

Most of the characteristics that identify soils can be determined in the field.

The type is the smallest unit in the natural classification of soils. One or a few types constitute a soil series. These are the common classification units seen on soil maps and survey reports.

A soil series is a group of soils that have horizons that are essentially the same in the properties used to identify soils, with the exception of the

SOURCE: *The Use of Soil Maps, Soils—Yearbook of Agriculture—1957, U. S. Dept. of Agriculture*

Soil and capability map. The symbols refer to types of soil, steepness, and degree of erosion. Example: 2B1 refers to the kind of soil, the number 2 to the type of soil, B to steepness of slope, and 1 to degree of erosion. The Roman numerals, such as II, refer to the capability class in the areas that are suitable for cultivation. Capability class symbols are not shown on areas that are generally better suited for range or woodland than for cultivation. Heavy lines on map indicate the boundaries of a capability unit.

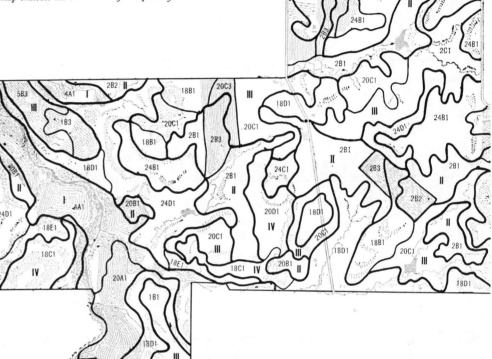

texture of the surface soil and the kinds of layers that lie below what is considered the true soil.

The names of soil series are taken from the towns or localities near the place where the soils were first defined.

The soil type, a subdivision of the soil series, is based on the texture of the surface soil. Stones, gravel, sand, silt, and clay have been defined as having the following diameters. Gravel, between 0.08 inch and 3 inches; sand, between 0.08 and 0.002 **inch**, silt, between 0.002 and 0.00003 inch, and clay, less than 0.00003 inch.

The full name of soil type includes the name of the soil series and the textural class of the surface soil equivalent to the plow layer, that is, the upper 6 or 7 inches. Thus, if the surface of an area of the Fayette series is a silt loam, the name of the soil type is "Fayette silt loam."

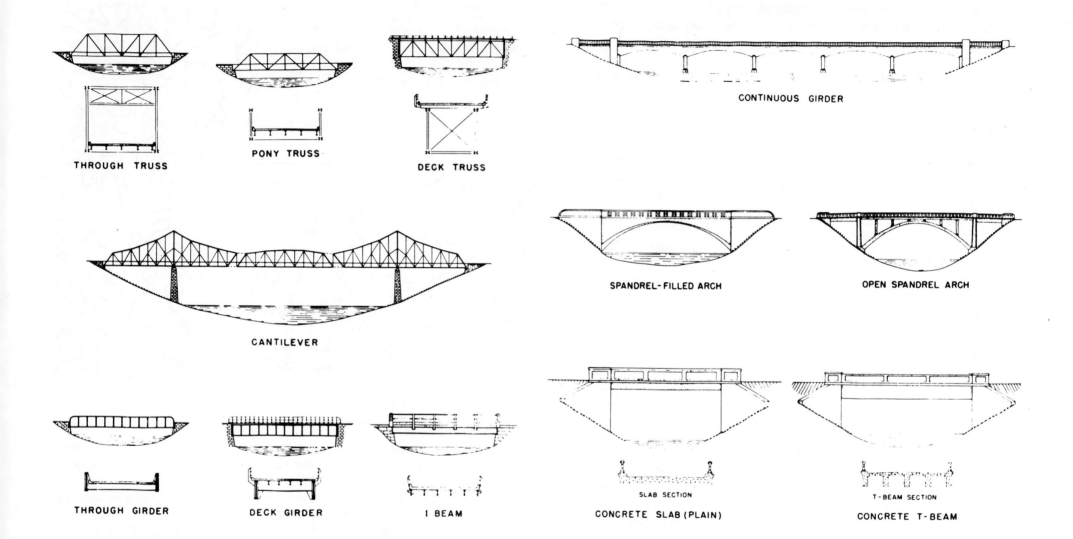

THROUGH TRUSS

PONY TRUSS

DECK TRUSS

CONTINUOUS GIRDER

CANTILEVER

SPANDREL-FILLED ARCH

OPEN SPANDREL ARCH

THROUGH GIRDER

DECK GIRDER

I BEAM

SLAB SECTION

CONCRETE SLAB (PLAIN)

T-BEAM SECTION

CONCRETE T-BEAM

SOURCE: *Guide for a Road Inventory-Manual of Instructions U. S. Dept. of Transportation, Federal Highway Administration Bureau of Public Roads, April 1967*

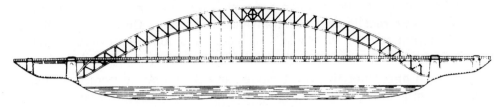

THROUGH-ARCH TRUSS

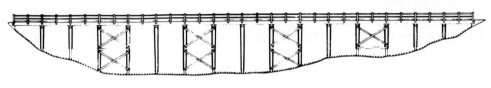

TIMBER TRESTLE

RIGID FRAME-STEEL

RIGID FRAME
(STEEL GIRDER ELEMENT)

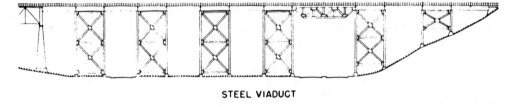

STEEL VIADUCT

RIGID FRAME-CONCRETE

SUSPENSION

AUTOPOSITIVE—A trade name for a direct contact positive intermediate translucent print on paper or film. Autopositives are made same size from positive translucent material or from opaque material by reflex printing. When working from a negative, the resulting print is an AUTONEGATIVE.

BLACK & WHITE PRINT—A trade name for a direct positive contact Diazo reproduction print. See DIAZO.

BLACK & WHITE TRANSPARENCY—A trade name for a translucent Diazo direct positive print (Sepia Intermediate). See DIAZO and SEPIA INTERMEDIATE.

BLUE LINE PRINT (Wet)—An opaque contact positive print having a blue line on a white background; made same size from translucent negative material. This type of Blue Line Print is superior to the Diazo type of print in permanency and durability, yet can be processed with speed and economy on either paper or cloth.

BLUE PRINT—An opaque contact print having white lines on a blue background. A Blue Print is made same size from positive translucent originals or intermediate material. This original Blue Print is still noted for its durability and strength plus speed and economy in production. It is available on paper and cloth.

BROWN LINE PRINT (Van Dyke Positive)—A translucent contact positive print having brown lines on a white background; this print is made on a high quality rag content paper stock and is readily used as an intermediate for printing. Made same size from translucent negative material, Brown Lines can be ordered enlarged or reduced from positive material if the proper intermediate negative is ordered reduced or enlarged.

C. B.—A trade name for a reproducible on paper or cloth.

CAMERA CONTRAST NEGATIVE—Made photographically. Depending on the copy photographed and the use intended, this translucent negative is available on paper, transloid or film. The positive material to be copied, opaque or translucent, can be photographed the same size, reduced or enlarged. The camera contrast process gives a reverse reading image which is one of the finest means available for direct contact printing particularly when film is used.

CAMERA CONTRAST POSITIVE—Made photographically, basically this translucent positive has all the qualities of the Camera Contrast Negative and can be made same size, reduced or enlarged from negative material.

CONTACT PHOTO—Print which has a photographic emulsion and is made same size by direct contact with translucent negatives. Offered in a variety of finishes from matte to hi-glossy ferrotyped, this opaque positive reproduction depends in quality upon the type of negative used.

DIAZO—A direct positive print made same size directly from translucent positive originals or intermediate material. Diazo Prints are available on opaque stock, translucent paper (Sepia Intermediates), cloth and film and are often preferred because they are quickly made and make excellent check prints. The image reproduced on Diazo Prints is available in a variety of colors, but black line on white paper is most widely used. Sepia Diazo prints are reproduced by two methods, an ammonia vapor development and a semi-dry (moist) developer. A variety of colors are available in both processes; in ammonia by changing stock and in semi-dry by changing developer.

DUPRO—A trade name for a reproducible on paper or cloth.

FILM NEGATIVE—A high quality Camera Contrast Negative.

GIANTSTAT—A giant Photoprint exceeding 18″ x 24″, enlarged from a film negative. As Photoprints are limited to 18″ x 24″ in one piece, prints exceeding maximum Photoprint size, which may not be joined, utilize this process. A Camera Contrast Film Negative is first made, usually 8″ x 10″, and the positive Giantstat on opaque or translucent stock is projected from it.

REPRODUCIBLE (On Cloth)—A positive reproduction on translucent reproducible waterproof cloth commonly referred to as a See Bee. Made from virtually any type of original material, this reproduction uses an extreme contrast translucent negative as an intermediate. It is available same size, reduced or enlarged and erases easily. Sections of the image can be blocked out or eliminated during the negative step before processing the final print. Available on a blue or white cloth

REPRODUCIBLE (On Vellum)—A positive reproduction on translucent waterproof vellum often referred to as a Vellum or Paper See Bee. These reproducibles are made essentially the same way as the Reproducibles on Cloth and in both cases the type of negative intermediate used is determined by the type and condition of the material to be reproduced and the final size of the Reproducible required. Reproducibles on Vellum have a very black image and make exceptionally fine 'second originals'.

SOURCE: Versatility in Reproduction Printing, Hudson Blue and Photo Print Co., Inc., New York—1959

LITHOGRAPHY—A type of printing. Defined under PHOTO OFFSET.

LITHOPRINT—A positive ink reproduction made by transferring an image from prepared gelatine onto a suitable material, translucent or opaque. Lithoprints can be obtained same size, reduced or enlarged from the material being reproduced.

MICROFILM—A reduced film negative used in copying original material to a smaller size for convenient storage. FLO-FILM, a trade name, is the 35mm microfilming of any length original in one continuous un-interrupted image.

MULTILITH PRINTS—Quantity reproductions made on a Multilith (trade name) press.

OZALID PRINT—A trade name for a DIAZO direct positive print made same size on an ammonia vapor machine.

PHOTO ENLARGEMENT—A photographic blow-up or enlargement made from a film negative by projection. Usually positive and opaque, these prints come in a variety of weights and finishes and can be mounted on cardboard or cloth for display or permanency.

PHOTO OFFSET PRINTS—As the name implies, the material to be reproduced is photographed, negatives are stripped onto flats, exposed to sensitized plates and run on a press. The image, positive and right reading, is transferred to a rubber blanket which actually makes the ink impression on the stock. This form of reproduction is highly recommended for 'quality in quantity'. Virtually any type of original material can be reproduced by the Photo Offset Process on a variety of stock including papers of various weights, colors and finishes, translucent vellum and cloth. Photo Offset prints, which utilize a camera process, can be had same size, reduced or enlarged

PHOTOPRINT—A photographic print on paper, sometimes referred to as a PHOTOSTAT.

PHOTOPRINT NEGATIVES—Right reading negatives on paper, which can be made same size, reduced or enlarged in one piece up to 18" x 24". These negatives are available in a variety of weights and finishes and are economical reproductions from opaque material. A black background with white lines.

PHOTOPRINT POSITIVES—Right reading paper positives which are available in the same weights and finishes as the Photoprint Negatives, from which they are usually made. They may be made larger by joining. A black image on a white background.

PHOTOSTAT PRINT—A trade name for a Photoprint on paper.

SEE BEE—A reproducible on waterproof cloth or vellum. Further information is available under REPRODUCIBLE (On Cloth) and REPRODUCIBLE (On Vellum).

SEPIA INTERMEDIATE—A same size contact DIAZO positive print having a sepia image. Frequently used as a 'second original', these transparencies can be made reverse reading for sharper contact reproductions.

VAN DYKE PRINT—A trade name for a translucent contact brown print. See BROWN LINE PRINT (Van Dyke Positive) and VAN DYKE NEGATIVE.

VAN DYKE NEGATIVE—Translucent negatives having a white image on a deep brown background on high quality, strong and durable rag content paper. Van Dyke Negatives are used instead of original tracings for reproductions, i.e., Brown Line Prints and Blue Line Prints. When made by contact from translucent positive material, these prints are the same size and are available reverse reading for sharper contact reproductions.

VIEW FILM—Contact reproductions on a clear transparent film base with line images available in a variety of colors. This Diazo type film is popular principally because it can be made direct from fairly clean positive translucent material. The availability of View Film as a direct positive in color makes it very advantageous for color overlays, presentations and visual instruction.

WHITE PRINT—A direct positive same size contact print made by the Diazo Process.

XEROGRAPHY—A trade name for a reproduction process.

ZINC-O-STAT—The same as PHOTO OFFSET PRINTS.

English System of Linear Measure

12 inches	=1 foot
36 inches	=1 yard
3 feet	=1 yard
1,760 yards	=1 mile statute
2,026.8 yards	=1 mile nautical
5,280 feet	=1 mile statute
6,080.4 feet	=1 mile nautical
63,360 inches	=1 mile statute
72,963 inches	=1 mile nautical

Metric System of Linear Measure

1 millimeter	=0.1 centimeter	=0.0393 inch
10 millimeters	=1.0 centimeter	= 0.3937 inch
10 centimeters	=1.0 decimeter	= 3.937 inches
10 decimeters	=1.0 meter	= 39.37 inches
10 meters	=1.0 decameter	= 32.81 feet
10 decameters	=1.0 hectometer	=328.1 feet
10 hectometers	=1.0 kilometer	= 0.62 mile
10 kilometers	=1.0 myriameter	= 6.21 miles

Equivalent Units of Angular Measure

1 mil ( )	=1/6400 circle	=0.05625°	=0.0625 grad
1 grad	=1/400 circle	=16.0 mils	=0°54'=0.9°
1 degree	=1/360 circle	=approx 17.8 mils	=approx 1.1 grad

UNITS OF MEASURE AND CONVERSION FACTORS

U.S.	to	Metric	Metric	to	U.S.
Inches	× 25.4	= millimeters	Millimeters	× 0.039	= inches
Feet	× 0.305	= meters	Meters	× 3.281	= feet
Yards	× 0.914	= meters	Meters	× 1.094	= yards
Miles	× 1.609	= kilometers	Kilometers	× 0.621	= miles
Square inches	× 6.452	= sq centimeters	Sq centimeters	× 0.155	= sq inches
Square feet	× 0.093	= sq meters	Square meters	× 10.764	= sq feet
Square yards	× 0.836	= sq meters	Square meters	× 1.196	= sq yards
Acres	× 0.405	= hectares	Hectares	× 2.471	= acres
Cubic inches	× 16.387	= cu centimeters	Cu centimeters	× 0.061	= cu inches
Cubic feet	× 0.028	= cu meters	Cu meters	× 35.315	= cu feet
Cubic yards	× 0.765	= cu meters	Cu meters	× 1.308	= cu yards
Quarts (1q)	× 0.946	= liters	Liters	× 1.057	= quarts (1q)
Gallons	× 0.004	= cu meters	Cu meters	× 264.172	= gallons
Ounces (avdp)	× 28.350	= grams	Grams	× 0.035	= ounces (avdp)
Pounds (avdp)	× 0.454	= kilograms	Kilograms	× 2.205	= pounds (avdp)
Horsepower	× 0.746	= kilowatts	Kilowatts	× 1.341	= horsepower

SOURCE: U.S. National Bureau of Standards

Conversion Factors

One	Inches	Feet	Yards	Statute miles	Nautical miles	mm
Inch	1	0.0833	0.0277			25.40
Foot	12	1	0.333			304.8
Yard	36	3	1	0.00056		914.4
Statute Mile	63,360	5,280	1,760	1	0.8684	
Nautical Mile	72,963	6,080	2,026	1.1516	1	
Millimeter	0.0394	0.0033	0.0011			1
Centimeter	0.3937	0.0328	0.0109			10
Decimeter	3.937	0.328	0.1093			100
Meter	39.37	3.2808	1.0936	0.0006	0.0005	1,000
Decameter	393.7	32.81	10.94	0.0062	0.0054	10,000
Hectometer	3,937	328.1	109.4	0.0621	0.0539	100,000
Kilometer	39,370	3,281	1,094	0.6214	0.5396	1,000,000
Myriameter	393,700	32,808	10,936	6.2137	5.3959	10,000,000

One	cm	dm	m	dkm	hm	km	mym
Inch	2.540	0.2540	0.0254	0.0025	0.0003		
Foot	30.48	3.048	0.3048	0.0305	0.0030	0.0003	
Yard	91.44	9.144	0.9144	0.0914	0.0091	0.0009	
Statute Mile	160,930	16,093	1,609	160.9	16.09	1.6093	0.1609
Nautical Mile	185,325	18,532	1,853	185.3	18.53	1.8532	0.1853
Millimeter	0.1	0.01	0.001	0.0001			
Centimeter	1	0.1	0.01	0.001	0.0001		
Decimeter	10	1	0.1	0.01	0.001	0.0001	
Meter	100	10	1	0.1	0.01	0.001	0.0001
Decameter	1,000	100	10	1	0.1	0.01	0.001
Hectometer	10,000	1,000	100	10	1	0.1	0.01
Kilometer	100,000	10,000	1,000	100	10	1	0.1
Myriameter	1,000,000	100,000	10,000	1,000	100	10	1

Example I

Problem: Reduce 76 centimeters to (?) inches
76 cm × 0.3937 = 29 inches.
Answer: There are 29 inches in 76 centimeters.

Example II

Problem: How many feet are there in 2.74 meters?

$$\frac{2.74}{.3048} = 9 \text{ feet}$$

Answer: There are approximately 9 feet in 2.74 meters.

	Square Inch	Square Link	Square Foot	Square Vara (Calif.)	Square Vara (Texas)	Square Yard	Square Meter	Sq. Rod, Pole, or Perch	Square Chain	Rood	Acre	Square Kilometer	Square Mile (Statute)
Square Inch	1	0.01594	0.00694										
Square Link	62.7264	1	0.4356	0.0576	0.05645	0.0484	0.04047	0.0016					
Square Foot	144	2.29568	1	0.13223	0.1296	0.11111	0.0929	0.00367					
Square Vara (Calif.)	1089	17.3611	7.5625	1	0.9801	0.84028	0.70258	0.02778	0.00174				
Square Vara (Texas)	1111.11	17.7136	7.71605	1.0203	1	0.85734	0.71685	0.02834	0.00177				
Square Yard	1296	20.6612	9	1.19008	1.1664	1	0.83613	0.03306	0.00207				
Square Meter	1549.80	24.7104	10.7639	1.42332	1.395	1.19599	1	0.03954	0.00247				
Sq. Rod, Pole, or Perch		625	272.25	36	35.2836	30.25	25.2930	1	0.0625	0.025	0.00625		
Square Chain		10000	4356	576	564.538	484	404.687	16	1	0.4	0.1		
Rood		25000	10890	1440	1411.34	1210	1011.72	40	2.5	1	0.25	0.00101	
Acre		100000	43560	5760	5645.38	4840	4046.87	160	10	4	1	0.00405	0.00156
Square Kilometer							1000000	39536.7	2471.044	988.418	247.104	1	0.3861
Square Mile (Statute)								102400	6400	2560	640	2.59	1

SOURCE: Boeckh Building Valuation Manual, Boeckh Division, the American Appraisal Co., Milwaukee, Wis. 1967

UNITS OF AREA

U.S. Measure		to Metric	Metric Measure	to U.S.
Sq inch (sq in.)		= 6.452 cm²		
Sq foot (sq ft)	= 144 sq in.	= 0.093 m²	Sq millimeter (mm²) = .000001m²	= 0.002 sq in.
Sq yard (sq yd)	= 1,296 sq in.	= 0.836 m²	Sq centimeter (cm²) = .0001 m²	= 0.155 sq in.
	or 9 sq ft		Sq decimeter (dm²) = .01 m²	= 15.5 sq in.
Sq rod (sq rd)	= 272¼ sq ft	= 25.293 m²	Sq meter (m²)	
	or 30¼ sq yd		or centare (ca)	= 10.764 sq ft
Acre	= 43,560 sq ft	= 0.405 ha	Sq dekameter (dkm²)	
	or 4,840 sq yd		or acre (a) = 100 m²	= 3,954 sq rd
	or 160 sq rd		Sq hectometer (hm²)	
Sq mile (Sq mi)	= 27,878,400 sq ft	= 2.59 km²	or hectare (ha) = 10,000 m²	= 2.471 acres
	or 3,097,600 sq yd			
	or 102,400 sq rd		Sq kilometer (km²) = 1,000,000 m²	= 0.386 sq mi
	or 640 acres			

UNITS OF LENGTH

U.S. Measure			to	Metric	Metric Measure			to	U.S.
Inch (in.)			=	25.4 millimeters	Millimeter (mm)	=	.001 meter	=	0.039 inch
Foot (ft)	=	12 in.	=	0.305 meter					
Yard (yd)	=	36 in. or 3 ft.	=	0.914 meter	Centimeter (cm)	=	.01 meter	=	0.394 inch
Rod (rd)	=	16½ ft or 5½ yd	=	5.029 meters	Decimeter (dm)	=	.1 meter	=	3.937 inches
Furlong (fur.)	=	660 ft or 220 yd. or 40 rd	=	201.168 meters	Meter (m)[1]			=	3.281 feet
Mile (mi)	=	5.280 ft or 1,760 yd. or 320 rd or 8 fur	=	1.609 kilometers	Dekameter (dkm)	=	10 meters	=	32.808 feet
					Hectometer (hm)	=	100 meters	=	328.083 feet
					Kilometer (km)	=	1,000 meters	=	0.621 mile

[1] Defined as 1,553, 164.13 wave lengths of the red light from cadmium.

	Inch	Link	Foot	Vara (Calif.)	Vara (Texas)	Yard	Meter	Rod, Pole, or Perch	Chain	Furlong	Kilo-meter	Mile (Statute)
Inch	1	0.12626	0.08333	0.03030	0.03	0.02778	0.02540	0.00505	0.00126			
Link	7.92	1	0.66	0.24	0.2376	0.22	0.20117	0.04	0.01	0.001		
Foot	12	1.51515	1	0.36364	0.36	0.33333	0.30480	0.06061	0.01515	0.00152		
Vara (Calif.)	33	4.16667	2.75	1	0.99	0.91667	0.8382	0.16667	0.04167	0.00417		
Vara (Texas)	33.333	4.20875	2.77778	1.01010	1	0.92583	0.84667	0.16835	0.04209	0.0042		
Yard	36	4.54545	3	1.09091	1.08	1	0.9144	0.18182	0.04545	0.00455		
Meter	39.37	4.97096	3.28083	1.19303	1.1811	1.09361	1	0.19884	0.04971	0.00497	0.001	
Rod, Pole, or Perch	198	25	16.5	6	5.94	5.5	5.02921	1	0.25	0.025	0.00503	0.00313
Chain	792	100	66	24	23.76	22	20.11684	4	1	0.1	0.02012	0.0125
Furlong	7920	1000	660	240	237.6	220	201.168	40	10	1	0.20117	0.125
Kilometer	39370	4970.96	3280.83	1193.03	1181.1	1093.61	1000	198.838	49.7096	4.97096	1	0.62137
Mile (Statute)	63360	8000	5280	1920	1900.8	1760	1609.35	320	80	8	1.60935	1

SOURCE: *Boeckh Building Valuation Manual, Boeckh Division, the American Appraisal Co., Milwaukee, Wis. 1967*

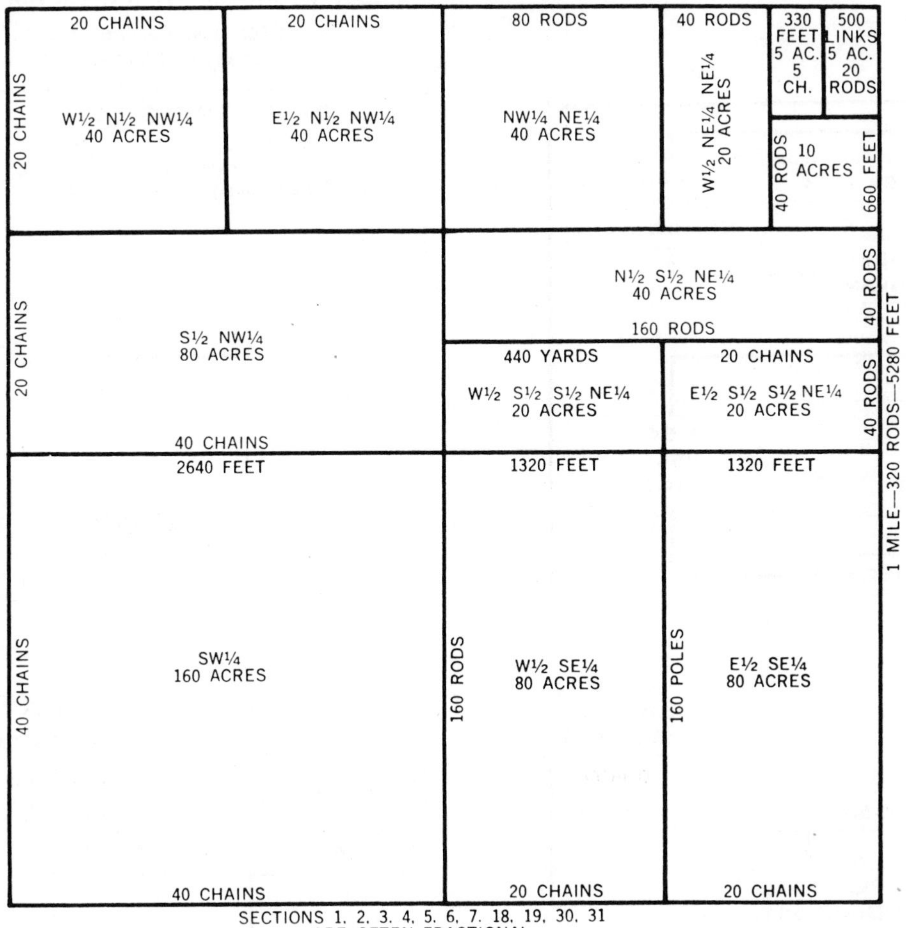

Diagram labels:

- 20 CHAINS — W½ N½ NW¼ 40 ACRES
- 20 CHAINS — E½ N½ NW¼ 40 ACRES
- 80 RODS — NW¼ NE¼ 40 ACRES
- 40 RODS — W½ NE¼ NE¼ 20 ACRES
- 330 FEET 5 AC. 5 CH.
- 500 LINKS 5 AC. 20 RODS
- E½ NE¼ NE¼ — 40 RODS — 10 ACRES — 660 FEET
- 20 CHAINS (left side)
- S½ NW¼ 80 ACRES — 40 CHAINS
- N½ S½ NE¼ 40 ACRES — 160 RODS
- 440 YARDS — W½ S½ S½ NE¼ 20 ACRES
- 20 CHAINS — E½ S½ S½ NE¼ 20 ACRES
- 40 RODS — 40 RODS (right)
- 20 CHAINS (left)
- 2640 FEET
- 1320 FEET
- 1320 FEET
- 40 CHAINS (left side)
- SW¼ 160 ACRES
- 160 RODS — W½ SE¼ 80 ACRES
- 160 POLES — E½ SE¼ 80 ACRES
- 1 MILE—320 RODS—5280 FEET (right side)
- 40 CHAINS
- 20 CHAINS
- 20 CHAINS

SECTIONS 1, 2, 3, 4, 5, 6, 7, 18, 19, 30, 31
ARE OFTEN FRACTIONAL

LAND MEASURE

1 mile	=	5,280	feet
	=	1,760	yards
	=	320	rods
	=	80	chains
1 chain	=	66	feet
	=	100	links
	=	4	rods
1 rod	=	25	links
	=	16.5	feet
	=	1	perch
	=	1	pole
1 link	=	7.92	inches

1 township	=	36	sections
1 full section	=	640	acres
1 sq. mile	=	640	acres
	=	1	full section
1 acre	=	43,560	sq. feet
	=	4,840	sq. yards
	=	160	sq. rods
	=	10	sq. chains
1 sq. chain	=	10,000	sq. links
1 sq. rod	=	30.25	sq. yards
1 sq. yard	=	9	sq. feet
1 sq. foot	=	144	sq. inches

SOURCE: Boeckh Building Valuation Manual, Boeckh Division, the American Appraisal Company, Milwaukee, Wis. 1967

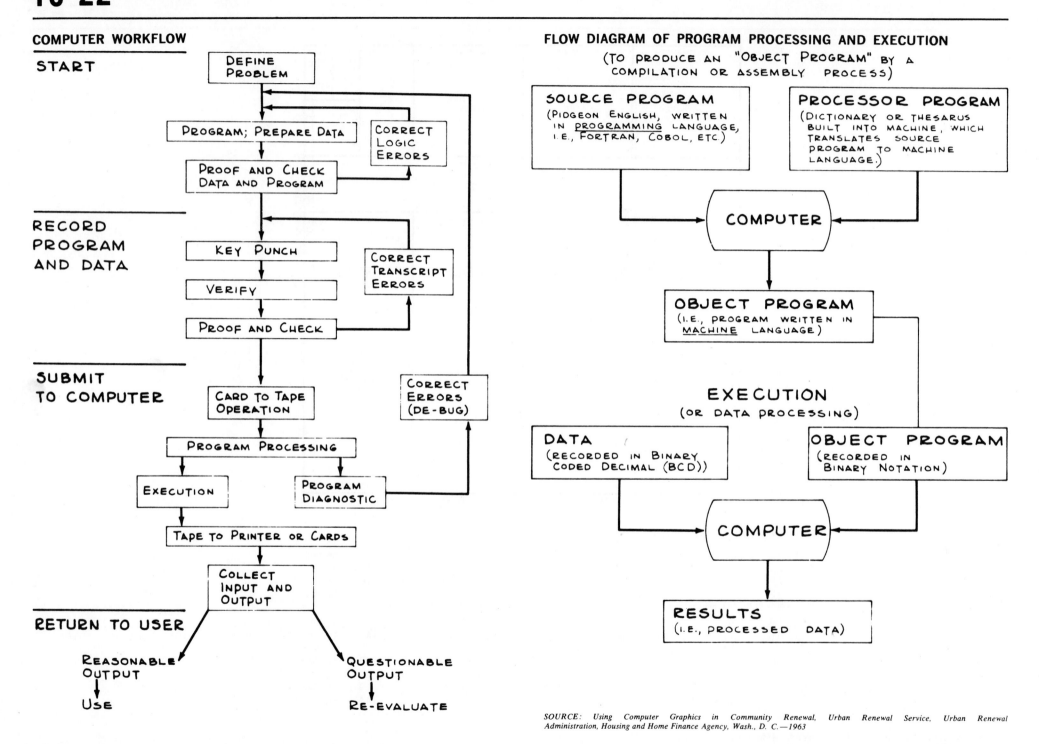

COMPUTER WORKFLOW

START

DEFINE PROBLEM

PROGRAM; PREPARE DATA

CORRECT LOGIC ERRORS

PROOF AND CHECK DATA AND PROGRAM

RECORD PROGRAM AND DATA

KEY PUNCH

CORRECT TRANSCRIPT ERRORS

VERIFY

PROOF AND CHECK

SUBMIT TO COMPUTER

CARD TO TAPE OPERATION

CORRECT ERRORS (DE-BUG)

PROGRAM PROCESSING

EXECUTION

PROGRAM DIAGNOSTIC

TAPE TO PRINTER OR CARDS

COLLECT INPUT AND OUTPUT

RETURN TO USER

REASONABLE OUTPUT

QUESTIONABLE OUTPUT

USE

RE-EVALUATE

FLOW DIAGRAM OF PROGRAM PROCESSING AND EXECUTION

(TO PRODUCE AN "OBJECT PROGRAM" BY A COMPILATION OR ASSEMBLY PROCESS)

SOURCE PROGRAM
(PIDGEON ENGLISH, WRITTEN IN PROGRAMMING LANGUAGE, I.E., FORTRAN, COBOL, ETC.)

PROCESSOR PROGRAM
(DICTIONARY OR THESARUS BUILT INTO MACHINE, WHICH TRANSLATES SOURCE PROGRAM TO MACHINE LANGUAGE.)

COMPUTER

OBJECT PROGRAM
(I.E., PROGRAM WRITTEN IN MACHINE LANGUAGE)

EXECUTION
(OR DATA PROCESSING)

DATA
(RECORDED IN BINARY CODED DECIMAL (BCD))

OBJECT PROGRAM
(RECORDED IN BINARY NOTATION)

COMPUTER

RESULTS
(I.E., PROCESSED DATA)

SOURCE: Using Computer Graphics in Community Renewal, Urban Renewal Service, Urban Renewal Administration, Housing and Home Finance Agency, Wash., D. C.—1963

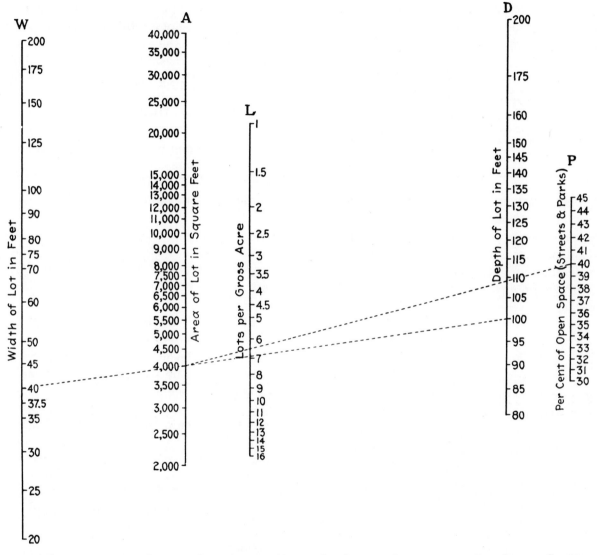

DIAGRAM FOR DETERMINING LOTS PER GROSS ACRE FOR VARYING LOT SIZES AND PERCENTAGES OF OPEN SPACE IN STREETS AND PARKS

Method of using diagram: Start with values on W and D scales; lay straight-edge between them and read area of lot on A scale; choose value on P scale; lay straight-edge between this value and determined value on A scale; read required answer on L scale.

In example shown, W = 40 feet and D = 100 feet; hence A = 4,000 square feet. With P = 40 per cent, L = 6.5 lots per gross acre.

SOURCE: NY Regional Survey of New York and Its Environs—1929

Land value is a local product. It arises from demand in the market where the property is located and bears only coincidental relation to the value of similar land in other localities. The valuation of land must therefore be based on analysis of its local market.

For valuation, land can be classified into five broad categories based on its potential use: natural resource, agricultural, residential, commercial, or industrial. Although the following basic valuation principles apply to each category, the forces which create value in the individual markets cause variations.

BASIC PRINCIPLES

Land, whether vacant or improved, is valued as if available for development to its highest and best use; that most likely legal use which will yield the highest present worth. That use must be acceptable to the market and it must conform to existing zoning and land use ordinances. Occasionally land value is reduced by the cost of demolition of an existing building which cannot generate a return sufficient to support the land.

Four methods are available to determine the value of land:

COMPARISON METHOD

This method is preferred whenever sufficient data exists to permit its use. Because comparison of the properties available for sale is the measure which investors use in choosing properties for purchase, this method of valuation most closely reflects the market. It therefore provides the most accurate measure of land value.

No two pieces of land are alike though they may be similar in many respects. Consequently, adjustments to sale prices are required to indicate the value of a specific parcel: adjustment for date of purchase, for location, for all the ways in which the sale property differs from the land being valued.

RESIDUAL METHOD

In heavily built-up areas where sales of vacant land cannot be found, an indication of land value can be developed by capitalizing net income which be produced by a proper new building improvement on the site, after deduction of the expenses required for the building.

To select a hypothetical improvement, highest and best use of the land must be determined, often obvious from the development of surrounding land. Whatever the improvement selected, it must be used with care, as variations in the capitalization rate or changes in the projected improvement may cause wide variation in the value indicated.

ALLOCATION METHOD

When the only sales available are those of improved property, a measure of land value can be gained by allocating from the total selling price that portion reasonably attributable to the building. The remainder is assumed to be land value. The building value can be estimated from study of sales of similar properties in other locations where land values also can be determined.

Allocation between land and building is sometimes derived from application of the reported ratio between assessed value and market value. The fairness of a value obtained in this way depends upon the skill and proficiency of the assessor.

DEVELOPMENT METHOD

Land with a potential use for residential or industrial subdivision is often valued by the development method. Since many estimates are required, the method should be used only when sales of comparable acreage are not available or as a check of the results indicated by the comparison method.

To indicate present value, the development method requires estimates of the selling price of the lots; of the costs required for the development, financing, carrying, and sales; of the period necessary to sell the developed lots; and of the amount by which the net sale price must be discounted.

This method has validity only if a ready and present market exists for the developed lots. To achieve reasonable results a thorough and comprehensive investigation of all variables is required.

SUMMARY

The comparison method of valuation is applicable to all classes of land, whether residential, agricultural, commercial, or industrial. If based on sufficient factual data properly processed, the comparison method provides the most accurate measure of land value. The residual, allocation, and development methods are helpful as alternates when market sales do not exist, or as checks on the comparison method.

SOURCE: Boeckh Building Valuation Manual, Boeckh Division, the American Appraisal Co., Milwaukee, Wis. 1967

INDEX

INDEX

INDEX